Advertising and Promotions: An Integrated Brand Approach

Sixth Edition

Richard J. Semenik

Professor of Marketing
Montana State University

Chris T. Allen

Arthur Beerman Professor of Marketing
University of Cincinnati

Thomas C. O'Guinn

Professor of Marketing
Executive Director, Center for Brand and Product Management
University of Wisconsin—Madison

Hans Rüdiger Kaufmann, Ph.D.

Diplom-Betriebswirt (FH)
School of Business
Associate Professor of Management
University of Nicosia

Australia • Brazil • Japan • Korea • Mexico • Singapore • Spain • United Kingdom • United States

Advertising and Promotions: An Integrated Brand Approach, Sixth Edition

Richard J. Semenik, Chris T. Allen, Thomas C. O'Guinn, and Hans Rüdiger Kaufmann

Executive Vice President, Academic Solutions—Business, Computers & Social Sciences: Jonathan Hulbert

Vice President of Editorial, Business: Jack W. Calhoun

Executive Editor: Mike Roche

Developmental Editor: Julie Klooster

Editorial Assistant: Kayti Purkiss

Marketing Manager: Gretchen Swann

Marketing Coordinator: Leigh T. Smith

Sr. Content Project Manager: Holly Henjum

Media Editor: John Rich

Print Buyer: Miranda Klapper

Sr. Marketing Communications Manager: Jim Overly

Production Service: Integra Software Services, Inc.

Sr. Art Director: Stacy Jenkins Shirley

Cover Design: Patti Hudepohl

Internal Designer: Joe Devine, Red Hangar Design

Photo Credits:

B/W Image: Getty Images/Hisham Ibrahim

Cover Image: Shutterstock Images/big

Sr. Rights Specialist: Deanna Ettinger

Photo Researcher: Susan Van Etten Lawson

Library of Congress Control Number: 2011920095

International Edition:

ISBN-13: 978-0-538-47986-8

ISBN-10: 0-538-47986-8

Cengage Learning International Offices

Asia
www.cengageasia.com
tel: (65) 6410 1200

Australia/New Zealand
www.cengage.com.au
tel: (61) 3 9685 4111

Brazil
www.cengage.com.br
tel: (55) 11 3665 9900

India
www.cengage.co.in
tel: (91) 11 4364 1111

Latin America
www.cengage.com.mx
tel: (52) 55 1500 6000

UK/Europe/Middle East/Africa
www.cengage.co.uk
tel: (44) 0 1264 332 424

Represented in Canada by Nelson Education, Ltd.
tel: (416) 752 9100/(800) 668 0671
www.nelson.com

Cengage Learning is a leading provider of customized learning solutions with office locations around the globe, including Singapore, the United Kingdom, Australia, Mexico, Brazil, and Japan. Locate your local office at: **www.cengage.com/global**

For product information: **www.cengage.com/international**

Visit your local office: **www.cengage.com/global**

Visit our corporate website: **www.cengage.com**

Printed in China by China Translation & Printing Services Limited
1 2 3 4 5 6 7 14 13 12 11

To Molly, the best partner I could ever hope to have. To Andi, you have done so much, so well, so quickly—you inspire me.

Rich Semenik

To Linda, Gillian, and Maddy, my three reasons for being.

Chris Allen

To Marilyn

Thomas O'Guinn

About the Authors

Richard J. Semenik is Professor of Marketing and former Dean of the College of Business at Montana State University-Bozeman, as well as founder and Executive Director of the College's Center for Entrepreneurship for the New West. Before coming to Montana State, Rich served as head of the Marketing Department at the Eccles School of Business at the University of Utah and Associate Dean for Research. He also has co-founded two companies. With expertise in marketing strategy, advertising, and branding, he has given numerous speeches and seminars across the United States, as well as in Ireland, Italy, the Netherlands, Finland, Mexico, Germany, France, Belgium, and Scotland. He also has been a visiting research scholar at the Vrije Universiteit in Amsterdam, the Netherlands, and a visiting scholar at Anahuac Universidad in Mexico City, Mexico. His research has appeared in the *Journal of Advertising, Journal of Consumer Research*, and *Journal of International Advertising*, as well as the proceedings of the American Marketing Association and Association for Consumer Research conferences. He has consulted with major corporations, advertising agencies, and early stage start-up companies including IBM, Premier Resorts International, SFX Entertainment, the Van Gogh Museum (Netherlands), American Investment Bank, Printingforless.com, InfoGears, Scientific Materials, and LigoCyte Pharmaceuticals. Professor Semenik also served on the National Board of Directors of the American Advertising Museum and the Industry Relations Board of the American Academy of Advertising. He received his undergraduate degree from the University of Michigan, an MBA from Michigan State University, and a Ph.D. from The Ohio State University.

Chris Allen is the Arthur Beerman Professor of Marketing at the University of Cincinnati. He has also held faculty positions at Northwestern University and the University of Massachusetts at Amherst. His research has investigated the influence of affect and emotion in decision-making and persuasive communication. Other published work has examined consumption issues in diverse domains such as determinants of household spending, motives for blood donation, fostering energy conservation, and the effects of news reporting on consumers' attitudes. It has appeared in numerous journals and compilations, including *JCR, JMR, JM, JPP&M, JBR, Journalism Quarterly, Journal of Advertising, Harvard Business Review, Advances in Nonprofit Marketing*, and *Handbook of Consumer Psychology*. Chris has served on the editorial review boards for *JCR, JCP, JM* and *JA*, and has been a frequent reviewer for programs such as the Ferber Award, and the AMA/Howard, ACR/Sheth, and MSI Dissertation Competitions. He has also served as program administrator for P&G's Marketing Innovation Research Fund--a funding source for dissertation research. He received his Ph.D. in Marketing and Consumer Psychology from Ohio State University.

Thomas C. O'Guinn is Professor of Marketing at The University Of Wisconsin-Madison. He is also Research Fellow in the Center for Brand and Product Management, also at U.W.-Madison. Thomas has published widely. He has served on many editorial and advisory boards, and his research has won several awards. He has assisted several major marketers with their advertising and marketing. He is currently involved with UW-Madison's Design for Business Thinking initiative. He has never owned a mini-van.

Hans Rüdiger Kaufmann completed his sponsored Ph.D. in 1997 and was a research assistant and part-time lecturer at Manchester Metropolitan University after having had extensive experience in German bank management. Later, he worked in Budapest—first as Course Director of Marketing for the Chartered Institute of Marketing and then as Assistant Professor in Marketing at the International Management Center in Budapest as well as a contractual consultant. At the University of Applied Sciences Liechtenstein, he was Academic Director of Private Banking and later Head of the Competence Centre in International Management. Since October 2006, he has been an associate professor at the University of Nicosia. He was a launching member and president (2007–2009) of the international research network on consumer behaviour, CIRCLE. He is currently Vice President of the EuroMed Research Business Institute (EMRBI). He is a member of the editorial board of various journals and an associate editor of the *World Review of Entrepreneurship, Management and Sustainable Development.*

Preface

You spoke. We listened. Throughout the first five editions of the book, we have sought and received extensive feedback from faculty, students and practitioners. As we began to prepare this 6th edition of *Advertising and Promotions: An Integrated Brand Approach*, the feedback was particularly informative and meaningful. You wanted a shorter book with more direct discussion. You wanted extensive coverage social networking and digital interactive media applications in both advertising and promotion. You wanted to us to keep the highly visual presentation of material so prominent in prior editions. And, you wanted us to retain the issue focused, contemporary topics from prior editions. We have addressed all of your desires and requests. This new edition is now reduced to 18 chapters from 20 chapters. The book is full of social networking and digital media content both in the main discussions and in special boxes which address current applications. The book is shorter and more direct.

One point we want to make emphatically. *Advertising and Promotions: An Integrated Brand Approach*, 6e remains the most current and forward thinking book on the market. Since the launch of the first edition in 1998, we have alerted students to leading-edge issues and challenges facing the advertising and promotion industries. We were the first to devote an entire chapter to the Internet as an advertising medium (1998); the first to alert students to the "dot-com" agency incursion on traditional advertising structure (2000); the first to raise the issue of consumers seeking and seizing control of their personal communications environment (2003); the first to highlight blogs and DVRs and the role they play in disseminating (or blocking) information about brands (2006). And, we were the first to alert students to the emergence and growing potential of the early social networking sites, MySpace and YouTube, that began showing up on the Web (2009). This 6th edition follows the legacy of the prior editions of the book by highlighting the most contemporary and significant changes being experienced in the advertising and promotion industries—particularly the application of social networking and digital media in the advertising and promotion process.

An Effective Student Resource.

There is a deep and lasting commitment among the authors to seek out both the best traditional and the newest contemporary thinking about advertising from a wide array of both academic and trade publications. You will see this commitment manifest in the breadth, depth, and currency of the references in each chapter. Within this context, let's consider the "personality" features of this new edition. We are confident you will find the content and perspective of this new edition a worthy addition to students' classroom experience.

First, we shortened the book to eighteen chapters. Based on user feedback, we discovered that faculty and students wanted more direct treatment of certain topics (more on this later) and we were able to accommodate that desire without sacrificing coverage. Second, we have retained all of the content and chapter features that students and instructors liked in our previous editions. Third, we have strengthened even further the integration of advertising and the full complement of promotional tools for brand building: sales promotion, point-of-purchase advertising, event sponsorship, branded entertainment and influencer marketing receive extensive coverage receives even greater emphasis in the sixth edition. In addition, the vast array of new opportunities facing advertisers in the peer-to-peer and digital communications environment are considered within both advertising and the promotional tools. Once again, we have committed to informative, entertaining ads, illustrations, photos, and graphics (over 400!)—printed on the highest quality paper available—to highlight the features of each visual. Every chapter has new content and new visuals—they need to as the world of advertising continues to evolve in a dynamic way. But even in these cases, there is still a lot of familiar, foundation material. We think you will find some examples of the changes to the sixth edition exciting and compelling.

Chapter 1: The World of Advertising and Integrated Brand Promotion. The first chapter received a *significant* revision to reflect the latest realities of industry practices, technological change, and the new challenges in using promotional techniques. From the very outset, this chapter signals the fact that companies are trying to keep up with how and where consumers want to receive information about brands. Mass media are not dead, but they are being supplemented and supported by all sorts of new ways to reach consumers. Consumers are turning to their smartphones and iPad tablet devices to stay connected to friends, family and the world at large. Advertisers want to be a part of that routine, and this chapter reveals the early strategies being used by firms to use Facebook, Twitter and other social networking sites.

Chapter 2: The Global Structure of the Advertising and Promotion Industry: Advertisers, Agencies, Media, and Support Organizations. A continuing emphasis in Chapter 2 is the more explicit coverage of media companies. Users of prior editions wanted more complete and explicit coverage of media options earlier in the book—so we delivered. Chapter 2 provides the essential perspective that consumers, who have been the target of advertising and promotion for decades, are discovering technologies and media options that give them more and more control over the communications they see and hear. Social media networks are more than just ways consumers communicate with peers. Consumers are using these networks and mobile technology to shape their information environments where *they* control their exposure to information, rather than an advertiser or media company being in control. Social media, mobile devices and blogs receive particular attention here, early in the text. In addition, the advent of "crowdsourcing" is considered as a way to get consumers more directly involved a firm's promotional efforts. The impact of social and technological change on the advertising and promotion process is dramatic, and Chapter 2 covers the changes.

Chapter 3: Regulatory, Social, and Ethical Aspects of Advertising and Promotion in the Global Market. Chapter 3 retains discussion of the fundament social, ethical and regulatory issues in advertising and promotion, but goes on to include the newest considerations. As an example, the ethics of "anonymous" bloggers, paid celebrity "tweeters" and privacy issues in social media, particularly Facebook, receive special attention. Of course, the plague of spam including "phishing" is highlighted as well. Discussions of new restrictions on the advertising and promotion process, such as the Children's Food and Beverage Advertising Initiative (i.e., advertising makes kids fat) the movement to regulate Internet promotions and new FTC regulations on disclosure of "incentivized" bloggers are discussed. We retain our coverage of the full spectrum of government regulatory bodies and policies but the discussions are now more focused.

Chapter 4: The History of Advertising and Brand Promotion. The book continues to distinguish itself with the most comprehensive coverage of the historical antecedents and economic forces that shaped today's modern advertising and promotional practices. Here we offer extended coverage of the recent changes in advertising and IBP set in historical context. This allows students to see what is truly new, and what is recycled from the past. We also show how significant events and social change has been leveraged as advertising strategy.

Chapter 5: Advertising, Consumer Behavior, and Integrated Brand Promotion. This chapter dedicates greater attention to the social (peer-to-peer brand communities) and cultural perspectives of advertising and consumer behavior. These social and cultural perspectives are shown in contrast to the psychological perspective offered in the first half of the chapter. No other book offers these dual and complementary perspectives. In addition, the chapter addresses the willingness of firms to allow brand communities to participate in the development of brand communications and, indeed, brand features.

Chapter 8: Planning for Advertising and Integrated Brand Promotion. Based on reviewer and user comments, we made a significant change in the book at this point. There is no longer a full chapter on the international advertising and promotion (Chapter 9 in prior editions). Instead, we integrate the discussion of the cultural context for advertising and promotion into this chapter and otherwise cover international and global advertising and promotional issues throughout each chapter. The globalization of communications media and information access has made the planning process for advertising and integrated brand promotion global as well and this chapter now reflects that important consideration.

Chapter 9: Managing Creativity in Advertising and Integrated Brand Promotion. This chapter has always been a distinguishing feature of the book. This topic is also a distinguishing feature of our philosophy about advertising and IBP—we know it is the soul and magic of the process. And while it is a huge challenge to articulate the nature of creativity, we are willing to take on the creative process directly and discuss the complexities and vagaries of this all-powerful aspect of advertising and IBP. The material here highlights why creativity is so important to the advertising and IBP effort. In addition, the chapter goes well beyond the simple perspective of account management versus the creative effort and provides extensive discussion of creativity across domains; conflict and tension in the creative/management interface; and the all-important team effort in coordination, collaboration, and creativity. This is the most comprehensive coverage of the creative effort you will find—anywhere.

Chapter 10: Creative Message Strategy. This chapter has always been a strength of this book. For this addition, we expanded the list of strategies and added examples and more discussion.

Chapter 11: Executing the Creative. This chapter represents the most dramatic change in this sixth edition. We sought the advice and insights of several distinguished academics and practitioners regarding how to treat the creative effort within the text. We followed their recommendations. This chapter now emphasizes the creative brief as the guiding force in advertising and promotion effort. We were also told to integrate the copywriting and art production processes more seamlessly with the creative. We did so by eliminating a separate chapter on these topics and folding the discussions in this single chapter on the overall process of executing the creative.

Chapter 13: Media Planning: Newspapers, Magazines, Television, and Radio. This chapter was revised significantly to reflect the massive changes being experienced within the traditional mass media environment. The newspapers, magazine, television and radio media industries have experienced declining revenues as advertisers turn to digital and interactive media. We cover the shift in advertiser emphasis as well as the attempts by these traditional media to adapt to and take advantage of (where possible) digital/interactive technologies.

Chapter 14: Media Planning: Advertising and IBP in Digital/Interactive Media. For each new edition of the book, we feel that much of the discussion of the role and application of the Internet to advertising and IBP basically must be rewritten from scratch. This edition was an extreme instance in that regard as reflected in a change to the title. This chapter in prior editions was titled Media Planning: Advertising and IBP on the Internet. The Internet is no longer the fundamental issue. Rather, the Internet is a gateway mechanism for a variety of new communication opportunities. We still provide students with the basics of the Web and statistics on Internet use and surfing behavior. But this edition, following through on the issues raised in Chapters 1 and 2, highlights the impact of peer-to-peer communication through **social networks**, **blogs** and **personal websites**—particularly the use of mobile devices to do so. **Paid search** gets a complete update, as do the current status of technological advances like **WiFi**, **WiMax**, **MiFi,** and **Ultra Broadband**. The chapter provides direct discussion of the use of digital and interactive media in advertising and IBP. Finally, the communications potential of virtual environments like **Second Life** has received updated treatment.

Chapter 15: Sales Promotion, Point-of-Purchase Advertising, and Support Media. This chapter is also updated to reflect the effect of technology on advertising and IBP opportunities. Most significantly, many sales promotions are now implement through the Web and point-of-purchase can now be targeted to shoppers though **location marketing** tactics made possible by mobile devices. While we have added these new issues, we retain the traditional coverage of the application of sales promotion in consumer, trade, and business markets as well as the risks of sales promotion to brand image and positioning.

Chapter 16: Event Sponsorship, Product Placements, and Branded Entertainment. As contemporary as we have tried to keep the entire book, this chapter is, in many ways the most contemporary of all. As firms have moved budgets from traditional mass media to other IBP options, the investment in **event sponsorship**, **product placement**, and **branded entertainment** has soared. This chapter offers the best contemporary examples and applications of these three powerful IBP tools.

Chapter 18: Public Relations, Influencer Marketing, and Corporate Advertising. We are pleased to present students with new content related to "**influencer marketing**," highlighting the role of mavens and connectors in creating social "epidemics" fostered by social media networks. This is all part of the discussion of the new role of public relations in the digital era. **Professional influencers**, **peer-to-peer communications**, **buzz**, **and viral marketing** are given extensive coverage.

These examples really do just scratch the surface of what is new with respect to topical coverage and the discussions of contemporary issues that reflect the leading-edge coverage that *Advertising and Promotions: An Integrated Brand Approach*, 6e provides students. As with past editions, we continue the practice of extensive use of written and visual examples to demonstrate points throughout each chapter.

Why We Write This Book.

When we introduced the first edition of *Advertising and Promotions: An Integrated Brand Approach*, we summed up our attitude and passion about advertising in this way:

> *Advertising is a lot of things. It's democratic pop culture, capitalist tool, oppressor, liberator, art, and theater, all rolled into one. It's free speech, it's creative flow, it's information, and it helps businesses get things sold. Above all, it's fun.*

We still feel the same way. Advertising and promotion are fun, and this book reflects it. Advertising and promotion are also important businesses, and this edition carries forward a perspective that clearly conveys that message as well. Like other aspects of business, advertising and integrated brand promotion are the result of hard work and careful planning. Creating good advertising is an enormous challenge . . . and we understand that and give homage and great respect to the creative process. We understand advertising and promotion in its business, marketing, and creative context. But we also felt, and still feel, that other books on the market do emphasize enough the focus on the *brand* in the advertising and promotional effort. While most books of this type have IMC in the title, we choose to emphasize the brand in the title and throughout the topics in the book.

This book was written by four people with lots of experience in both academic and professional settings. We have collectively been consultants for many firms and their agencies. Thus, this book is grounded in real-world experience. It is not, however, a book that seeks to sell you a "show-and-tell coffee-table book" version of the advertising and promotion industries. Rather, we highlight the challenges facing advertisers and offer complete treatment of the tools they use to meet those challenges.

Much has happened since we released the first edition that has strengthened our resolve to write and deliver the best advertising and promotions book on the market. First, we learned from our adopters (over 500 of you) and from our students that the book's (sometimes brutally) honest discussion of advertising practice was welcomed and applauded. We are not here to be cheerleaders for advertising, or to tell you we know what and where the magic bullets are—particularly in the current era where everybody—academics and practitioners alike—are struggling to understand the role social networks may ultimately play. We truly love advertising and the whole promotional effort, but we also know that it is not always wonderful. It can be frustrating to work with, particularly when you first learn there is no magic bullet. Advertising can also have a dark side. We understand that, and try to put it in a realistic context. We treat students like adults. When the best answer is "no one knows," we tell you that.

As much as we respected our academic and practitioner colleagues the first five times around, we respect them even more now. This book is completely real-world, but the real world is also explained in terms of some really smart academic scholarship. This book copies no one, yet pays homage to many. More than anything, this book seeks to be honest, thoughtful, and imaginative. It acknowledges the complexity of human communication and consumer behavior.

Students like this book—they tell us so over and over. You liked the last five editions, and you'll like this one even more. We've spent considerable time reviewing student and instructor likes and dislikes of other advertising textbooks, in addition to examining their reactions to our own book. With this feedback, we've devoted pages and pictures, ideas and intelligence, to creating a place for student and teacher to meet and discuss one of the most important and intrinsically interesting phenomena of contemporary times: advertising and promotion in the service of brands.

From Chapter 1 to Chapter 18.

As we said at the outset, *Advertising and Promotions: An Integrated Brand Approach*, 6e is different in that it explicitly acknowledges that advertising and promotion are all about brands. Brands can be goods or services, things or people (for example, political candidates, performers), and advertising and promotion are about marketers projecting brands into the consciousness of consumers.

This sixth edition is also about taking a wider view of advertising and promotion. The truth these days is that any boundary between advertising and other forms of promotion is a pretty porous border. We acknowledge that point without making a big deal of it *and* without ignoring the fundamentals of the advertising and promotional processes. In fact, we have made it very easy for instructors to cover what they want. We think that advertising and promotion should be discussed between the covers of the same book, just as their coordinated integration should occur in practice.

Relevant, Intelligent Organization.

We offer an organization we adamantly believe is superior. The organizational structure of this book is unique and highly valued by users. Rather than have a section with 1 or 2 chapters followed by a section with 9 or 10 chapters, we offer a patterned and well-paced, five-part organization. Instructors and students alike find this approach relevant, intelligent, and easy to follow. The organization of the text is so popular because it lays out the advertising and IBP process the same way it unfolds in practice and application:

Part One: Advertising and Integrated Brand Promotion in Business and Society. Part One recognizes that students really need to understand just what advertising and IBP are all about, and have a good perspective on how the process works. This section contains the core fundamentals (more about this in a minute). It describes the entire landscape of advertising and promotion, and provides a look at the structure of the industry and a historical perspective on the evolution of the process. But, we have infused the section with extensive coverage of the challenges and opportunities being presented by social networks and the mobile devices (smartphones and tablet readers primarily) that are changing the landscape for advertising and promotion.

Part Two: Analyzing the Environment for Advertising and Integrated Brand Promotion. Part Two provides all the essential perspectives to understand how to carry out effective advertising and IBP. Key strategic concepts of the process, including consumer behavior analysis, market segmentation, brand differentiation, and brand positioning, are considered. Then, this section proceeds to a discussion of the types of research advertising and promotion planners rely on to develop effective advertising and IBP. Additionally, there is special emphasis on "consuming in the real world" and how advertising and IBP need to adapt to consumer lifestyles and consumer adoption of new technologies to facilitate those lifestyles.

Whether you are teaching/studying advertising and promotion in a business school curriculum or an advertising/journalism curriculum, the first two parts of the book provide the background and perspective that show how advertising and IBP have become the powerful business and society forces they are in the 21st century.

Part Three: The Creative Process. Part Three is all about creativity: creativity in general, as a managerial issue, and as a part of art direction, copywriting, and message strategy. Most adopters in advertising and communication programs use this section and put particular focus on Chapter 10, in which the tensions between the creative and management processes are highlighted. Some business school adopters (particularly those on 6- and 10-week modules or classes) skip some of the creative chapters in Part Three. We believe everyone will find the new Chapter 11, which offers a highly integrated discussion of the overall creative effort, a useful and realistic perspective on the process.

Part Four: Placing the Message in Conventional and "New" Media. Part Four focuses on the use and application of all media—including digital and interactive media—to reach target audiences. These chapters are key to understanding many of the execution aspects of good advertising and integrated brand promotion strategies. It is in this section that you will learn not just about the traditional mass media, but also about the array of new media options and consumers' new-found power in managing their information environments through these options. Of particular note is the recognition of the opportunities now offered by mobile devices as another way to reach consumers.

Part Five: Integrated Brand Promotion. Part Five covers the many tools of integrated brand promotion. We bundled these four chapters together, since our business school adopters often use them. We think they are good for everyone. Here you will find the best coverage of sales promotion, event sponsorship, product placement, direct marketing, personal selling, branded entertainment, and influencer marketing. Nearly twenty percent of the book's pages are devoted to integrated brand promotional tools beyond advertising.

Compelling Fundamentals.

We fully expect our book to continue to set the standard for coverage of new topics and issues. It is loaded with features, insights, and common sense advertising perspectives about the ever-changing nature of the advertising and promotion industry. And, we continue to incorporated coverage of new issues in *every* chapter.

That said, we feel a truly distinguishing strength of this book is that we do not abandon complete and high-level treatment of the fundamentals of advertising and promotion. You simply *cannot* appreciate the role of the new media or new technologies without a solid understanding of the fundamentals. If you doubt our commitment to the fundamentals, take a good look at Chapters 2 through 8. This is where we, once again, part company with other books on the market. *Advertising and Promotions: An Integrated Brand Approach,* 6e, is the only book on the market that insures the deep economic roots of advertising and promotion are fully understood. And, we take the time to be certain that not just the business but also the social context of advertising are clear. Check out just how completely the foundational aspects are covered—you'll be surprised and impressed.

Also, notice that we don't wait until the end of the book to bring the legal, ethical, social issues (Chapter 3) into mainstream thinking about advertising and IBP. While most books put these issues as one of the last chapters—as if they are an afterthought—we feel strongly that they are mainstream to the development of high quality and responsible advertising and promotional efforts.

Extensive New Media Coverage.

In-depth consideration of new media vehicles is provided throughout Part One but is truly highlighted in Part Four of the book,"Placing the Message in Conventional and 'New' Media." Chapter 14 is all about advertising and marketing in the digital and interactive media, and it reviews many technical considerations for working with this—now not-so-new, but still challenging and evolving—method for reaching and affecting consumers. Chapter 15 highlights all the new ways advertising and promotion can provide an "experiential" encounter with the brand. But, these sections are not the only place new media coverage is prominent. Chapters 1 and 2 highlight how consumers use new social media options as a way to control their information flow. And Chapter 5 considers the effects of new media on consumer decision making.

Student Engagement and Learning.

You will find that this book provides a clear and sophisticated examination of advertising fundamentals and contemporary issues in lively, concise language. We don't beat around the bush; we don't avoid controversies; and we're not shy about challenging conventions. In addition, the book features a stylish internal design (worthy of an advertising book!) and hundreds of illustrations. Reading this book is an engaging experience.

The markers of our commitment to student learning are easily identified throughout the book. Every chapter begins with a statement of the *learning objectives* for that chapter. (For a quick appreciation of the coverage provided by this book, take a pass through it and read the learning objectives on the first page of each chapter.) Chapters are organized to deliver content that responds to each learning objective, and the *chapter summaries* are written to reflect what the chapter has offered with respect to each learning objective.

We also believe that students must be challenged to go beyond their reading to think about the issues raised in the book. Thus, you will note that the *Questions* at the end of each chapter demand thoughtful analysis rather than mere regurgitation, and the *Experiential Exercises* will help students put their learning to use in ways that will help them take more away from the course than just textbook learning. New *Project-Based Activities* for Parts One through Five are designed to have students think critically about Advertising and IBP in the business world. Complete use of this text and its ancillary materials will yield a dramatic and engaging learning experience for students of all ages who are studying advertising for the first time.

A Closer Look at Some Sixth Edition Features.

How the Text Is Organized.

As we discussed earlier, *Advertising and Promotions: An Integrated Brand Approach,* 6e is divided into five major parts reflecting the process of advertising and IBP as it unfolds in practice and application:

Part One: Advertising and Integrated Brand Promotion in Business and Society.

Chapter 1: The World of Advertising and Integrated Brand Promotion. Chapter 1 quickly sets the stage for what's to come. It begins with recognition of the changing consumer information environment. And, this edition quickly highlights consumers' use of social networking as part of controlling their information flow. Then, departing from decades-old communication models, the chapter presents a different model of advertising, which highlights the advertiser's sensitivity to target audiences' expectations and motivations. With this opening perspective, we recognize renewed industry emphasis on the integration of the account planning process and creative processes. Students learn that advertising is both a communications process and a business process, and they're shown why this is so. The book's seamless IBP coverage begins right here, with the students being introduced to the terminology and concept of coordinating and integrating promotional efforts to achieve advertising synergy and to speaking to consumers *in a single voice*. It's a great beginning.

This chapter has extensive discussions of the concepts of the brand, brand extensions, and brand equity. The concepts of advertising and brand management, types of advertising and promotion, and the role they play in marketing strategy are introduced here as the foundations for fully integrated brand promotion.

Chapter 2: The Global Structure of the Advertising and Promotion Industry: Advertisers, Agencies, Media, and Support Organizations. In Chapter 2, you'll read about trends that are transforming the structure of the advertising industry today. The chapter begins with recognition of the "great digital divide" in which consumers, who have been the target of advertising and promotion for decades, are discovering digital technologies and media options that give them more control over the communications they see and hear. From Facebook, to Twitter to millions of individual blogs and specialty websites, consumers are seeking out information environments, digital information access, where *they* control their exposure to information rather than an advertiser or media company being in control—thus permanently affecting the structure of the industry and the role of industry players.

The result of this digital divide is that advertisers are rethinking the way they try to communicate with consumers. Fundamentally, there is a greater focus on integrating more promotional tools with the overall advertising effort. Advertisers are looking to the full complement of promotional opportunities, including sales promotions, event sponsorships, new social media options, mobile/location marketing and public relations, as means to support and enhance the primary advertising effort for brands. The chapter concludes with coverage of the types of advertising and promotional agencies (and their structure) followed by the types of media organizations available and the structure of the media industry.

Chapter 3: Regulatory, Social, and Ethical Aspects of Advertising and Promotion in the Global Market. Advertising and promotion are dynamic and controversial. In Chapter 3, students will examine a variety of issues concerning advertising's effects on societal well being. Is advertising and promotion intrusive, manipulative, and deceptive? Does it waste resources, promote materialism, perpetuate stereotypes, invade privacy? Or does it inform, give exposure to important issues, raise the standard of living, and alert consumers to buying opportunities? After debating the social merits of advertising and promotion, students will explore the ethical considerations that underlie the development of campaigns and learn about the regulatory agencies that set guidelines for advertisers. Lastly, students are introduced to the concept of self-regulation and why advertisers must practice it.

Chapter 4: The History of Advertising and Brand Promotion. Chapter 4 puts advertising in a historical context. But before the history lesson begins, students are given the straight scoop about advertising as a product of fundamental economic and social conditions—capitalism, the Industrial Revolution, manufacturers' pursuit of power, and modern mass communication—without which there would be no advertising process. Students then study the history of advertising through ten interesting and entertaining eras, seeing how advertising has changed and evolved, and how it is forged out of its social setting. This chapter is rich with interesting ads representing advertising as a faithful documentation of social life in America. Definitely an entertaining and provocative chapter, it also gives students a necessary and important perspective on advertising before launching into advertising planning concepts and issues. Most strategies were created decades ago, and if you can learn how advertisers took advantage of various social conditions and trends yesterday, you can learn a lot about how to do it today—and tomorrow.

There are a couple of important and extensive changes in the sixth edition. First, the issue of privacy is discussed extensively as both a social and ethical issue, given new technologies that can track and profile consumers through the communication process and the risks (being tracked through location marketing) new technologies present. New material was also added on regulatory issues in e-commerce (anti-spam legislation), in sales promotion (privacy issues), and in public relations (regulating anonymous bloggers).

Part Two: Analyzing the Environment for Advertising and Integrated Brand Promotion.

Chapter 5: Advertising, Consumer Behavior, and Integrated Brand Promotion. Chapter 5, which describes consumer behavior from two different perspectives, begins Part Two of the text. The first perspective portrays consumers as systematic "decision makers" who seek to maximize the benefits they derive from their purchases. The second portrays consumers as active interpreters of advertising (consumers as social beings), whose membership in various cultures, subcultures, societies, and communities significantly affects their interpretations of and responses to advertising. Students, shown the validity of both perspectives, learn that, like all human behavior, the behavior of consumers is complex, multifaceted, and often symbolic. Understanding buyer behavior is a tremendous challenge to advertisers, who should not settle for easy answers if they want good relationships with their customers. The chapter also includes information about advertising and brands transmit meaning in a culturally constituted world.

Chapter 6: Market Segmentation, Positioning, and the Value Proposition. Chapter 6 opens with a look at how the Folgers brand team used segmentation, position, and targeting in a creative way to reach just-graduated 20-somethings. Students are introduced to the sequence of activities often referred to as STP marketing—**s**egmenting, **t**argeting, and **p**ositioning—and how advertising both affects and is affected by these basic marketing strategies. The remainder of the chapter is devoted to detailed analysis of how organizations develop market segmentation, positioning, and product differentiation strategies. The critical role of ad campaigns in successfully executing these strategies is emphasized over and over. Numerous examples of real-world campaigns that contrast different segmentation and positioning strategies keep the narrative fresh and fast moving. The chapter concludes by demonstrating that effective STP marketing strategies result in creating a perception of value in the marketplace.

Chapter 7: Research in Advertising and Promotion. Chapter 7, which contains a lot of new content, covers the methods used in developmental research, the procedures used for pre-testing messages prior to the launch of a campaign, the methods used to track the effectiveness of ads during and after a launch, and the many sources of secondary data that can aid the ad-planning effort. This chapter also provides coverage of the agency's new emphasis on account planning as a distinct part of the planning process.

Chapter 8: Planning for Advertising and Integrated Brand Promotion. Chapter 8 begins by recounting the sequence of events and strategies behind the exciting launch of Apple's iPad. Through this opening vignette, students see the importance of constructing a sound ad plan before launching any campaign. In addition, the introductory campaign for the iPad highlights the teamwork between client and agency to show an extraordinary example of IBP at work. After reading this chapter, students will be familiar with the basic components of an ad plan as it is placed with the overall marketing context including paying close attention to the cultural considerations for international advertising. The chapter goes on to emphasize two fundamental approaches for setting advertising objectives—communications versus sales. A complete assessment of the budgeting process and the role of the ad agency in formulating an advertising and IBP plan conclude this chapter.

Part Three: The Creative Process.

Chapter 9: Managing Creativity in Advertising and Integrated Brand Promotion. Chapter 9 takes on the seemingly awkward task of "talking" about creativity. All you creatives out there know, this is a nearly impossible task. But what we have tried to do for students in this chapter is completely different from what is done in all other texts. Rather than just describing the creative execution process (we do that in Chapter 11), we have tried to discuss the essence of what creativity is. The chapter starts by recounting how the Crispin Porter + Bogusky agency turned creative risk taking into huge advertising and IBP successes for Burger King in particular, but also Domino's and The Gap. Next, we highlight the commentary and achievements of creative geniuses—both within the advertising industry and completely removed from it. We've also revised and refocused the material on the organizational and managerial tensions of the creative/suit (read MBA) interface. The result is a thought-provoking and enriching treatment like no other that students will find.

Chapter 10: Creative Message Strategy. Building on Chapter 9, Chapter 10 explores the role of creativity in message strategy from a refreshingly honest perspective: No one knows exactly how advertising creativity works. Ten message strategy objectives are presented, along with the creative methods used to accomplish the objectives, including humor, slice-of-life, anxiety, sexual-appeal, slogan, and repetition ads. This chapter makes excellent use of visuals to dramatize the concepts presented.

Chapter 11: Executing the Creative. Recall that this chapter has gone through complete revision and is now a combination of two chapters from prior editions. This chapter begins with emphasis on the creative team and the creative brief as the "structure" in a process that does not lend itself readily to structure. Next, the role of copywriters and art directors is described as they plan the execution of the brief. At this point, students learn about the copywriting process and the importance of good, hard-hitting copy in the development of print, radio, and television advertising. Guidelines for writing headlines, subheads, and body copy for print ads are given, as well as guidelines for writing radio and television ad copy. We also include a new section on copywriting for digital/interactive media. At this point, the chapter turns to art direction and production. Here students learn about the strategic and creative impact of illustration, design, and layout, and the production steps required to get to the final ad. Numerous engaging full-color ads are included that illustrate important design, illustration, and layout concepts and principles. Again, we address digital and interactive media in this section on art direction.

At this point, the chapter turns to issues associated with radio and television production. Students learn about the role of the creative team and the many agency and production company participants involved in the direction and production processes. Students are given six creative guidelines for television ads, with examples of each. Radio is not treated as a second-class citizen in this chapter but is given full treatment, including six guidelines for the production of creative and effective radio ads. This chapter is comprehensive and informative without getting bogged down in production details.

Part Four: Placing the Message in Conventional and "New" Media.

Chapter 12: Media Planning Essentials. In Chapter 12, which begins Part Four, students see that a well-planned and creatively prepared campaign needs to be placed in media (and not just any media!) to reach a target audience and to stimulate demand. This chapter drives home the point that advertising placed in media that does not reach the target audience—whether new digital media or traditional media—will be much like the proverbial tree that falls in the forest with no one around: Does it make a sound? Students will read about the major media options available to advertisers today, the media-planning process, computer modeling in media planning, and the challenges that complicate the media-planning process. The chapter uses the "real-deal" headings to explain not how things should be done, but how they are done, and why.

Chapter 13: Media Planning: Newspapers, Magazines, Television, and Radio. The opening vignette for Chapter 13 highlights the challenges traditional mass media face from the rising prominence and importance of digital and interactive media—and their attempt to adapt with their own digital presence. The chapter then focuses on evaluating the unique capabilities of different traditional media as an important means for advertisers to reach audiences. The chapter details the advantages and disadvantages of newspapers, magazines, radio, and television as media classes and describes the buying and audience measurement techniques for each. New topics covered in this chapter highlight controversy caused by digital video recorders (DVRs) on television advertising audience measurement, the struggle of newspapers and magazines to survive in the digital era of e-readers, as well as the changes in listening behavior caused by satellite and Internet radio on the radio medium.

Chapter 14: Media Planning: Advertising and IBP in Digital/Interactive Media. The first edition of *Advertising* was the first introductory advertising book to devote an entire chapter to advertising on the Internet, and this edition continues to set the standard for coverage. But as stated earlier, the issue is no longer the "Internet" per se. Rather, the important consideration is the Internet as a gateway for advertisers to reach consumers through mobile marketing strategies. The emphasis at the outset of the chapter is how firms are trying to take advantage of consumers' positive disposition toward digital and interactive media. You will read about highly successful digital campaigns by Ford (The Ford Fiesta Movement), Pepsi (Refresh Everything), and Starbucks (MyStarbucks). The chapter also addresses the challenges inherent in measuring the cost effectiveness of various digital and interactive media versus other advertising media.

What has been added to this chapter is an in-depth discussion of how firms—large and small—are integrating Web-based, digital media communications into the advertising and promotion plan. In addition, the merging of website communication with sales promotion and sales transaction and fulfillment makes this a very powerful communications environment indeed. Finally, possible new communications venues like virtual worlds (e.g., Second Life) are considered for their potential as communications environments.

Part Five: Integrated Brand Promotion.

Chapter 15: Sales Promotion, Point-of-Purchase Advertising, and Support Media. Sales promotion is and has been a multibillion-dollar business in the United States. Chapter 15 explains the rationale for different types of sales promotions. It goes on to differentiate between consumer, trade, and business sales promotions and highlights the risks and coordination issues associated with sales promotions—a consideration overlooked by other texts. All the techniques of sales promotion are discussed: coupons, price-off deals, premiums, contests, sweepstakes, sampling, trial offers, product (brand) placements, refunds, rebates, frequency programs, point-of-purchase displays, incentives, allowances, trade shows, and cooperative advertising. This chapter has a comprehensive section on point-of-purchase. Point-of-purchase advertising is using new and powerful techniques at that precious moment when the consumer is making the final choice—mobile technologies have made this possible. Finally, the chapter retains its extensive treatment of the wide array of support media available to advertisers, including billboards, transit advertising, aerial advertising, cinema, and good old directory advertising. Packaging is also covered for its role in communicating brand values and creating a brand image.

Chapter 16: Event Sponsorship, Product Placements, and Branded Entertainment. This chapter begins with the great story of how Healthy Choice introduced Fresh Mixers to its product portfolio. Healthy Choice and its agencies created a high profile Web series (branded entertainment) to give energy to the introduction of the new product. From there, the chapter offers a thought-provoking discussion of the convergence of Madison & Vine—that is the phenomenon of advertising, branding, and entertainment converging to provide consumers a wider array of "touch points" with brands. The chapter continues from here to review the growing allure of event sponsorships and then takes a deep dive into the provocative subject of branded entertainment. We've come a long way from E.T. eating Reese's Pieces! If students didn't already appreciate the power of integrated brand promotion when they hit this chapter, they certainly will afterward…

Chapter 17: Integrating Direct Marketing and Personal Selling. In the excitement and, indeed, drama of digital and social media options, we sometimes forget the powerful role direct marketing and personal selling have across many integrated brand promotion strategies. This chapter opens with a fable about direct marketing guru Les Wunderman and the magic of his little gold box, and then moves quickly on to a historical perspective on direct marketing featuring the well-known L.L. Bean mail-order catalog. Students quickly learn about L.L. Bean's emphasis on building an extensive mailing list, which serves as a great segue to database marketing. Students will learn why direct marketing continues to grow in popularity, what media are used by direct marketers to deliver their messages, and how direct marketing creates special challenges for achieving integrated brand promotion. The chapter then turns to personal selling and the key role this tool plays with respect to face-to-face communications across a variety of product categories.

Chapter 18: Public Relations, Influencer Marketing, and Corporate Advertising. Chapter 18 is another chapter that has highly contemporary and exciting material with full coverage of "influencer" marketing. We give due respect to the traditional role of public relations with a discussion of how public relations fits into the overall integrated branding effort including proactive and reactive public relations and the strategies associated with each. The new coverage of influencer marketing is the best and most contemporary you will find anywhere. Professional influencer programs, peer-to-peer programs, buzz, viral marketing, and cultivating "connectors"—it's all here and fully covered. In addition, activating social media, engaging mainstream media, selecting celebrity spokespersons, staging a branded experience, and orchestrating skillful teamwork among client, PR firm, digital, design, and talent agencies rounds out the strategic perspective. This chapter concludes with a wide-ranging and complete discussion of corporate advertising. Various forms of corporate advertising are identified, and the way each can be used as a means for building the reputation of an organization in the eyes of key constituents is discussed.

Inside Every Chapter.

Inside every chapter of *Advertising and Promotions: An Integrated Brand Approach*, 6e you will find features that make this new book eminently teachable and academically solid, while at the same time fun to read. As we said earlier, this text was written and the examples were chosen to facilitate an effective meeting place for student and instructor. Who said learning has to be drudgery? It doesn't have to be and it shouldn't be.

Dynamic Graphics and Over 400 Ads and Exhibits. Ask any student and almost any instructor what an advertising book absolutely *must* have, and the top response will be—lots of ads! As you will see by quickly paging through *Advertising and Promotions: An Integrated Brand Approach*, 6e, this book sets the standard for ads and other instructional visuals. Over 400 ads, exhibits, illustrations and photos are used to highlight important points made in the chapters. Each exhibit is referenced in the text narrative, tying the visual to the concept being discussed.

As you can see, the book's clean, classic, graphic layout invites you to read it; it dares you to put it down without reading just one more caption or peeking at the next chapter. And, our commitment (and the publisher's) to the power of illustration is clear in the use of the highest quality (read really expensive) paper to make sure the ads "pop" off the pages.

Opening Vignettes. The majority of chapters include a classic or current real-world advertising or promotion story to draw students into the chapter and to stimulate classroom discussions. Each vignette illustrates important concepts that will be discussed in the chapter. These types of lively introductions ensure that students get off to a good start with every chapter.

In-Chapter Features. Every chapter contains two to three boxed features that highlight interesting, unusual, or just plain entertaining information as it relates to the chapter. The boxes are not diversions unrelated to the text nor are they rambling, page consuming, burdensome tomes. Rather, they provide concise, highly relevant examples that can be fully integrated into classroom lectures. The boxes are for teaching, learning, and reinforcing chapter content. Three different types of boxes are included in the text: *Ethics, Globalization,* and *Social Media.* Let's take a look at each.

Ethics: It is important that business decisions be guided by ethical practices. Advertising and integrated brand promotion practices are particularly prone to questions by lay people relating to ethics. Because of the importance of ethics, proper business practice, and its appeal to students' interests, special Ethics boxes appear throughout this edition. Students will gain insights into ethical business practices that will be useful not only in their advertising course, but in future business courses and their careers.

Globalization: The Globalization boxes provide an insightful, real-world look at the numerous challenges advertisers face internationally. Many issues are discussed in these timely boxes, including the development of more standardized advertising across cultures with satellite-based television programming, how U.S.-based media companies such as MTV and Disney/ABC are pursuing the vast potential in global media, obstacles to advertising in emerging markets, and cross-cultural global research.

Social Media: While we integrate social media issues and applications within main chapter content, there are so many facets to this emerging phenomenon that featuring social media examples in box treatments seemed useful and informative for students. These Social Media boxes highlight both the nature of the phenomenon and applications by firms of Facebook, Twitter, YouTube and other social media and networking sites.

Also in Each Chapter:

1

Learning Objectives and a Built-In Integrated Learning System. The text and test bank are organized around the learning objectives that appear at the beginning of each chapter, to provide you and your students with an easy-to-use, integrated learning system. A numbered icon like the one shown here identifies each chapter objective and appears next to its related material throughout the chapter. This integrated learning system can provide you with a structure for creating lesson plans as well as tests.

The integrated system also gives structure to students as they prepare for tests. The icons identify all the material in the text that fulfills each objective. Students can easily check their grasp of each objective by reading the text sections and reviewing the corresponding summary sections. They can also return to appropriate text sections for further review if they have difficulty with end-of-chapter questions.

Concise Chapter Summaries. Each chapter ends with a summary that distills the main points of the chapter. Chapter summaries are organized around the learning objectives so that students can use them as a quick check on their achievement of learning goals.

Key Terms. Each chapter ends with a listing of the key terms found in the chapter. Key terms also appear in boldface in the text. Students can prepare for exams by scanning these lists to be sure they can define or explain each term.

Critical Thinking Questions. End-of-chapter questions are designed to challenge students' thinking and to go beyond the "read, memorize, and regurgitate" learning process. The *Questions* sections require students to think analytically and to interpret data and information provided for them in the text. Detailed responses to these questions are provided in the Instructor's Manual.

Below is a sampling of the types of critical thinking questions found in *Advertising and Promotions: An Integrated Brand Approach*, 6e:

- As consumers exercise ever greater individual control over when and how they receive information, how are advertisers adapting their messages? What is the role, if any, for traditional media options in this new environment? Will mobile marketing efforts, including directing advertising to smartphones be accepted by consumers?
- If a firm developed a new line of athletic shoes, priced them competitively, and distributed them in appropriate retail shops, would there be any need for advertising? Is advertising really needed for a good product that is priced right?
- The 1950s were marked by great suspicion about advertisers and their potential persuasive powers. Do you see any lingering effects of this era of paranoia in attitudes about advertising today?
- Some contend that self-regulation is the best way to ensure fair and truthful advertising practices. Why would it be in the best interest of the advertising community to aggressively pursue self-regulation?

- Visit some of the corporate home pages described in this chapter, or think about corporate home pages you visited previously. Of those you have encountered, which would you single out as being most effective in giving the visitor a reason to come back? What conclusions would you draw regarding the best ways to motivate repeat visits to a website?
- There's a paradox here, right? On the one hand, it is common to talk about building relationships and loyalty with the tools of direct marketing. On the other hand, direct-marketing tools such as junk email and telephone interruptions at home during dinner are constant irritants. How does one build relationships by using irritants? In your opinion, when is it realistic to think that the tools of direct marketing could be used to build long-term relationships with customers?
- Imagine yourself as a connector. In that role, what kind of inside information would you find interesting enough to tell your friends about a new movie or TV show? What would it take for you to start that conversation?

Experiential Exercises. The chapters now have four of these illuminating exercises. Written by B. J. Parker and Gail Gibson, these exercises require students to apply the material they have just read by researching well-known brands and issues, writing short papers, or preparing brief presentations. Some exercises require students to get out of the classroom to seek information not provided in the text, while others are especially designed for teamwork both in and outside class.

Project-Based Activities. Written by Aubrey Fowler at Valdosta State University, the project-based activities provide practical experience working in groups. Your students can expand their advertising knowledge with challenging, new project-based group activities for each part (located at the end of the text). Students work together in teams to complete work that emphasizes many of today's well-known, actual companies.

A Full Array of Teaching/Learning Supplementary Materials.

Supplements:

Advertising Age: The Principles of Advertising and Marketing Communication at Work by Esther Thorson and Margaret Duffy, both of the University of Missouri—Columbia.

David Ogilvy, named one of the "100 most influential advertising people of the century" by *Advertising Age*, said this: "It takes a big idea to attract the attention of consumers and get them to buy your product. Unless your advertising contains a big idea, it will pass like a ship in the night." *Advertising Age* itself exemplifies a big idea. It's a journal that for 80 years has chronicled the day-to-day triumphs and heartbreaks of this dynamic profession. Its talented editors and reporters create compelling, informative stories that aren't only important—they're sharp, literate and fun to read. Taking a cue from *Advertising Age*, this book seeks to showcase the lessons and the fun of the business for students.

Instructor's Manual. The instructor's manual was prepared by one of the main text authors, Rich Semenik. We feel that key in-class resources like lecture outlines and PowerPoint® slides simply cannot be properly prepared by a non-author. The manual has been thoroughly revised to update all previous content, including comprehensive lecture outlines that provide suggestions for using other ancillary products associated with the text and suggested answers for all exercises found within the text. The Instructor's Manual is available on the companion website, www.cengage.com/international.

PowerPoint®. This edition's PowerPoint® presentation is of the highest quality possible and was also prepared by one of the main text authors, Rich Semenik. There are many improvements, including additional ads with accompanying discussion questions (answers provided in instructor's manual). All ads are accompanied with commentary on how they illustrate theories and concepts presented in the text and include at least one inductive question to generate classroom discussion. The Power Point® presentation is available on the companion website, www.cengage.com/international.

Test Bank. This comprehensive test bank is organized around the main text's learning objectives. Each question is labeled according to the learning objective that is covered, the page number on which the answer can be found, and the difficulty level of question (easy, moderate or difficult). Grouping the questions according to type allows for maximum flexibility in creating tests that are customized to individual classroom needs and preferences. The test bank includes true/false, multiple-choice, scenario application, and essay questions. There are approximately 1,800 questions. All questions have been carefully reviewed for clarity and accuracy. The test bank Word files are available on the companion website, www.cengage.com/international.

ExamView ® Testing Software. ExamView Computerized Testing Software, located on the companion website (www.cengage.com/international), contains all of the questions in the test bank. This program is an easy-to-use test creation software compatible with Microsoft ® Windows ®. Instructors can add or edit questions, instructions, and answers and select questions by previewing them on the screen, selecting them randomly, or selecting them by number. Instructors can also create and administer quizzes online, whether over the Internet, a local area network (LAN), or a wide-area network (WAN).

Product Support Site (http://www.cengage.com/international). The product support site features "Instructor Resources" that include the instructor's manual, test bank, PowerPoint®, and videos. For students, we include the following for each chapter: learning objectives, crossword puzzles using key terms, and interactive quizzes. Students will also find a section on Careers in Marketing Communications, IBP, and Advertising, in which we profile four professions in the industry.

On the product support website you will find a Healthy Choice Working Lunch video that will work in conjunction with the Chapter 16 introductory scenario. In addition, for the Chapter 18 introductory scenario there is a video about the Charmin Times square campaign. Students can answer questions about these videos and email their answers directly to the professor.

Online Video and Industry Content:

Ad Age on Campus Online Access

Students can access a wealth of resources through the Ad Age on Campus page of AdAge.com. This website provides access to a variety of resources including:

Daily News AdAge.com is the premier industry source of breaking news in the marketing, advertising and media world, and includes trend stories, features and analysis on the most important matters of the day.

Commentary Leading executives contribute every day to AdAge.com blogs and viewpoint columns, giving students critical insight into what the thought leaders are saying and advocating for the future of marketing.

The Work Each week, Ad Age publishes the best work of the week, as selected by the editors of Creativity, the Ad Age Group's source for advertising professionals in creative departments. Students have a window into the ideas, trends, and breakthrough work that has the industry sitting up and taking notice.

Research Ad Age on Campus subscribers have access to a select group of white papers published by the Ad Age Insights division, including demographic studies of female consumers, "Rise of the Real Mom" and "The Reality of the Working Woman", as well as a deep dive into "Building Brands Online" and a look at digital adopters, "Shiny New Things".

DataCenter Students also have access to AdAge.com's premium content in the DataCenter, the industry's source of key information about the industry's most important companies. Comprehensive and thorough reports rank by spending, revenue and income the 100 Leading National Advertisers; the top Global Marketers; 100 Leading Media Companies; Interactive ventures of top media and agency companies and Creativity's Awards Winners List, the definitive online tally of the best agencies, brands, creatives, production companies and directors, according to a weighted tabulation of the major advertising awards shows.

To ensure that your students receive access to Ad Age on Campus, contact your Cengage Learning sales representative to ensure that your bookstores receive copies of Semenik, Allen, O'Guinn, and Kaufmann's *Advertising and Promotions: An Integrated Brand Approach*, with an access code that provides an online subscription to Ad Age on Campus.

Acknowledgements

The most pleasant task in writing a textbook is the expression of gratitude to people and institutions that have helped the authors. We appreciate the support and encouragement we received from many individuals, including the following:

- We want to offer our deepest, sincerest, and everlasting thanks to Susan Van Etten Lawson, our photo and ad researcher. Remember, this book has approximately 400 ads and illustrations—and every one of them needs documented permission to be used. Some of the ads have needed 2, 3, or even 4 different permissions! Susan patiently and carefully dealt with our requests (and our tardiness) with utmost professionalism. Thank you Susan—we owe you a huge debt.
- Thank you also to Executive Editor, Mike Roche, Content Project Manager, Holly Henjum, and Developmental Editor, Julie Klooster, at Cengage Learning / South-Western for their dedicated efforts on this project.
- David Moore, Vice President/Executive Producer at Leo Burnett, who gave us invaluable insights on the broadcast production process and helped us secure key materials for the text.
- B.J. Parker for his professional writing assistance with the revision of the experiential exercises.
- Matt Smith of Arnold, Finnegan & Martin, for providing us with the Watermark ad and sketches in Chapter 11.
- Connie M. Johnson, for years and years of great and loving observations about the human condition. Connie is connected to the Universe in some very special way.
- Patrick Gavin Quinlan, for years of great advice and best friendship.
- Marilyn A. Boland, for her love, creativity, smart suggestions, great questions, support, and wonderful images.
- David Bryan Teets, University of Illinois, for help with the TV-commercial director- becomes-movie-director lists and references. Dave knows film.
- Professor John Murphy II, Joe C. Thompson Centennial Professor in Advertising at the University at Austin, who has given us great feedback and continued support. John went well beyond the call with effort and creativity with the author interview film. John also keeps our feet on the ground. Thanks, John.
- Steve Hall, who supports, critiques, and gives his all to his students at The University of Illinois. Steve is a creative and gifted teacher, whose continued feedback helps us write better books for real students. Like John Murphy, Steve goes well beyond the call and helped the team produce some really cool video projects. Steve, thanks.
- Rance Crain and Allison Arden of Ad Age for their help in bringing a rich set of video content to students.

We are also grateful to the following individuals from the business/advertising community:

Dick Antoine
President of the National Academy of Human Resources and the President of AOConsulting

Nate Carney
Bridge Worldwide

Jack Cassidy
Cincinnati Bell

Lauren Dickson
Saatchi & Saatchi

Patricia Dimichele
Procter & Gamble

Dixon Douglas
GMR Marketing

Denise Garcia
Conill Advertising Inc.

Mike Gold
Flying Horse Communications—
Bozeman, Montana

Jacques Hagopian
Procter & Gamble

Lisa Hillenbrand
Procter & Gamble

Karen Klei
Procter & Gamble

Dave Knox
Rockfish Interactive

Fred Krupp
Environmental Defense

Greg Lechner
Luxottica Retail

Liv Lewis
devries-pr

Marsha Lindsay
Lindsay, Stone & Briggs

Dave Linne
ConAgra

Brian Lipman
ConAgra

Mike Loyson
Procter & Gamble

James Moorhead
Procter & Gamble

Emily Morrison
GMR Marketing

Emily Neidhardt
Grey

Jim Neupert
IsthmusPartners

Bill Ogle
Motorola

Mason Page
imc^2

Kavya Peerbhoy
strawberryfrog

Jackie Reau
Game Day Communications

Kathy Selker
Northlich

Jim Stengel
The Jim Stengel Company

John Stichweh
Bridge Worldwide

Meghan Sturges
Saatchi & Saatchi

Candace Thomas
Jack Morton Worldwide

Mauricio Troncoso
Procter & Gamble

Ted Woehrle
Newell-Rubbermaid

We are particularly indebted to our reviewers—past and present—and the following individuals whose thoughtful comments, suggestions, and specific feedback shaped the content of *Advertising and Promotions: An Integrated Brand Approach*. Our thanks go to:

Robert B. Affe
Indiana University

Ron Bernthal
Sullivan County Community College

Jeff W. Bruns
Bacone College

Claudia M. Bridges
California State University, Sacramento

Trini Callava
Miami Dade College

Joshua Coplen
Santa Monica College

Anne Cunningham
University of Tennessee

John Davies
University of North Florida

Raj Devasagayam
Siena College

Jon Freiden
Florida State University

Cynthia Frisby
University of Missouri–Columbia

Gary E. Golden
Muskingum College

Corliss L. Green
Georgia State University

Thomas Groth
University of West Florida

Scott Hamula
Keuka College

Wayne Hilinski
Penn State University

E. Lincoln James
Washington State University

Karen James
Louisiana State University–Shreveport

Donald Jugenheimer
Southern Illinois University

Patricia Kennedy
University of Nebraska–Lincoln

Robert Kent
University of Delaware

Priscilla LaBarbera
New York University

Barbara Lafferty
University of South Florida

William LaFief
Frostburg State University

Debbie Laverie
Texas Tech

Gail Love
California State University, Fullerton

Tina M. Lowrey
University of Texas at San Antonio

Nancy Mitchell
University of Nebraska–Lincoln

Elizabeth Moore
University of Notre Dame

Cynthia R. Morton
University of Florida

Darrel Muehling
Washington State University

Andrew T. Norman
Iowa State

Marcella M. Norwood
University of Houston

James Pokrywczynski
Marquette University

John Purcell
Castleton State College

Ann H. Rodriguez
Texas Tech University

Jim Rose
Bauder College

Dana K. Saewitz
Temple University

Debra Scammon
University of Utah

Carol Schibi
State Fair Community College

Trina Sego
Boise State University

Andrea Semenik
Simon Fraser University

Kim Sheehan
University of Oregon

Alan Shields
Suffolk County Community College

Sloane Signal
University of Nebraska, Lincoln

Jan Slater
Syracuse University

Barry Solomon
Florida State University

Marla Royne Stafford
University of Memphis

Patricia Stout
University of Texas–Austin

Lynn Walters
Texas A&M

Brian Wansink
Cornell University

Jon P. Wardrip
University of South Carolina

Robert O. Watson
Quinnipiac University

Marc Weinberger
University of Massachusetts–Amherst

Professor Joan R. Weiss
Bucks County Community College

Gary B. Wilcox
University of Texas–Austin

Kurt Wildermuth
University of Missouri–Columbia

Christine Wright-Isak
Florida Gulf Coast University

Molly Ziske
Michigan State University

Lara Zwarun
UT Arlington

Thank you to the reviewers of the *Advertising and Promotions: An Integrated Brand Approach* 5th edition, whose feedback helped shape the 6th edition:

Dr. Edward E. Ackerley
University of Arizona

Dr. Janice Bukovac-Phelps
Michigan State University

Deborah S. David
Fashion Institute of Technology

Dr. De'Arno De'Armond
West Texas A&M University

Federico deGregorio
University of Akron

Jeffrey F. Durgee
Rensselaer Polytechnic Institute

Mary Edrington
Drake University

Brendan P. Ferrara
Savannah Technical College

Dr. Aubrey R. Fowler III
Valdosta State University

Cynthia Grether
Delta College

Michael Hanley
Ball State University

Joseph P. Helgert, Ph.D.
Grand Valley State University

David C. Houghton, Ph.D.
Charleston Southern University

Michelle Jasso
New Mexico State University

Ed Johnson, Ph.D
Campbell University

George Kelley
Erie Community College - City Campus

Kirk D. Kern
Bowling Green State University

Marshall R. Kohr, II
Northwestern University

Mary Alice LoCicero
Oakland Community College

Deanna Mader
Marshall University

Mike Marn
University of Nebraska at Kearney

Marty Matthews
University of Washington

John A. McCarty
The College of New Jersey

Norman D. McElvany
Johnston State College

Deborah Morrison
University of Oregon

John H. Murphy, II
University of Texas–Austin

William E. Rice
CSU Fresno

Maria del Pilar Rivera
University of Texas at Austin

Allen D. Schaefer
Missouri State University

Daniel A. Sheinin
University of Rhode Island

Lewis F. Small
York College of Pennsylvania

Melissa St. James
CSU Dominguez Hills

Dr. Janice K. Williams
University of Central Oklahoma

Patti Williams
Wharton

Dr. Amy Wojciechowski
West Shore Community College

Doreen (DW) Wood
Rogue Community College

Brief Contents

Contents

LIMITED TIME OFFER
BOLD TASTE BOLD SOUNDS
FREE MUSIC DOWNLOAD
DETAILS INSIDE
GOOD EARTH
All Natural
CAFFEINE FREE
ORIGINAL
A Natural Source of Antioxidants
Sweet & Spicy Herbal Tea
18 WRAPPED TEA BAGS

NOT EVEN THE IRISH RELY ON LUCK.
DON'T DRIVE DRUNK.
DESIGNATE A DRIVER THIS ST. PATRICK'S DAY.

UGG

GOOD MORNING

Part 3 The Creative Process 310

Chapter 9 Managing Creativity in Advertising and Integrated Brand Promotion 312

Chapter 10 Creative Message Strategy 340

Chapter 13 Media Planning: Newspapers, Magazines, Television, and Radio 458

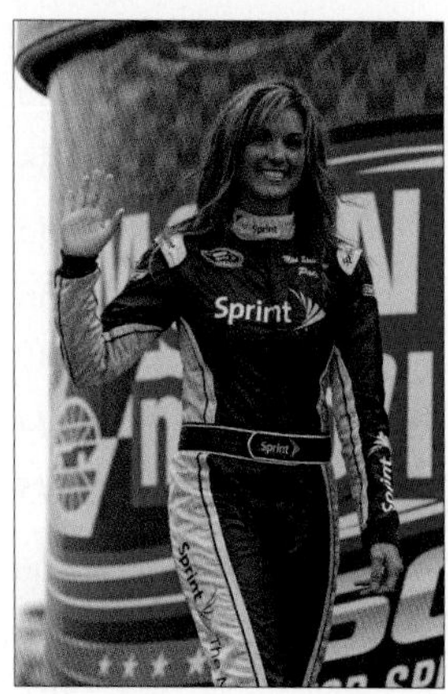

Chapter 14 Media Planning: Advertising and IBP in Digital/Interactive Media 496

Part 5 Integrated Brand Promotion 532

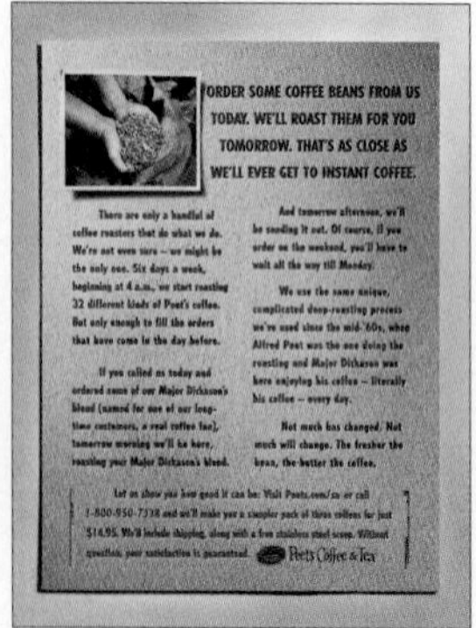

Chapter 15 Sales Promotion, Point-of-Purchase Advertising, and Support Media 534

Old Spice

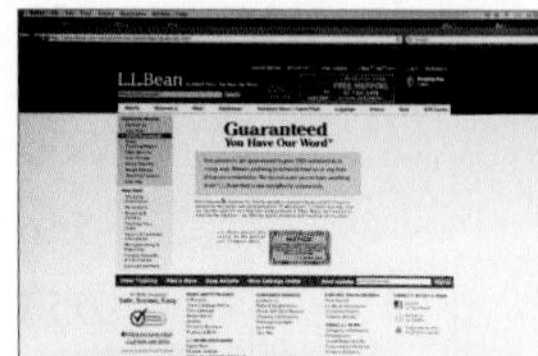

Chapter 18 Public Relations, Influencer Marketing, and Corporate Advertising 626

Advertising and Promotions: An Integrated Brand Approach

Sixth Edition

Part 1

Advertising and Integrated Brand Promotion in Business and Society

This first part of the book, “Advertising and Integrated Brand Promotion in Business and Society,” sets the tone for our study of advertising. The chapters in this part emphasize that advertising is much more than the old-style mass media messages of the past. Mass media are still, no doubt, a huge part of the advertising effort. But advertising is now much more diverse and dynamic and is part of a process you will learn about called integrated brand promotion (IBP). IBP is the process of using all sorts of different promotional techniques and tools—from television ads to iPad broadcasts—that send messages about brands to consumers. Now, the rapid assent of digital media—particularly social networking sites like Facebook, MySpace and Twitter, have radically changed the landscape for advertising and IBP. And advertising and IBP communications are not just marketing messages. They are also part of a social communication process that has evolved over time with changes in culture, technology, and business strategies. This is where the “brand” plays a leading role in communications. We all know brands because we hear about them and use them every day—Apple, Nike, Pantene, Starbucks, and literally hundreds of others. We know (and learn) about brands because companies use advertising and integrated brand promotion to tell us about them. But we also learn about brands by using them and by seeing them being used in society. This first part of the book lays out the broad landscape of the advertising and IBP processes that expose us to brands and what they have to offer.

Chapter 1

The World of Advertising and Integrated Brand Promotion introduces and defines advertising and integrated brand promotion and the roles they play within a firm's overall marketing program. We introduce the concept of IBP, which shows that firms communicate to consumers using a broad range of communications that often go far beyond advertising and traditional mass media. Sales promotion, event sponsorship, direct marketing, brand placements in movies and television programs, point-of-purchase displays, the Internet, podcasting, influencer marketing (social networks) personal selling, and public relations—the tools of IBP—are available to help a firm compete effectively, develop customer brand loyalty, and generate greater profits.

Chapter 2

The Global Structure of the Advertising and Promotion Industry: Advertisers, Agencies, Media, and Support Organizations highlights the powerful market and technology trends that are shaping the advertising industry and process. This chapter demonstrates that effective advertising requires the participation of a variety of organizations and especially skilled people, not just the companies who make and sell brands. Advertising agencies, research firms, production facilitators, designers, media companies, Web developers, public relations firms, and Internet portals all play a role. This chapter also highlights that the structure of the industry is in flux. New media options, like streaming video, blogs and social networking sites, and new organizations, like talent agencies, product placement firms, and software companies are forcing change. This chapter looks at the basic structure of the industry and how it is evolving with the market and consumer preferences. Special attention is given to the rising prominence of promotion agencies and networking facilitators as counterparts to advertising agencies.

Chapter 3

Regulatory, Social, and Ethical Aspects of Advertising and Promotion in the Global Market examines the broad societal aspects of advertising and IBP. From a social standpoint, we must understand that advertising and promotion can have positive effects on standard of living, address consumer lifestyle needs, support communications media, and are contemporary art forms. Critics argue that advertising and other promotions waste resources, promote materialism, are offensive and intrusive, perpetuate stereotypes, or can make people do things they don't want to do. Ethical issues focus on truthful communication, invasion of privacy, advertising and promoting to children, and advertising and promoting controversial products. Regulatory aspects highlight that while government organizations play a key role is shaping the way advertising and IBP are carried out, consumer groups and societal values also put pressure on advertising and IBP to change and evolve with cultural values.

Chapter 4

The History of Advertising and Brand Promotion puts the processes of advertising and integrated brand promotion into both a historical and a contemporary context. This chapter identifies the prominent eras of advertising—from the pre-1880s to present day—and the unique communications emphasis that has distinguished each era. Special recognition is given to the fact that advertising and IBP have evolved and proliferated because of fundamental market and cultural influences related to free enterprise, economic development, and tradition. Change has also occurred as a reflection of contemporary social values and the advent of new technologies.

Chapter 1

The World of Advertising and Integrated Brand Promotion

After reading and thinking about this chapter, you will be able to do the following:

1. Know what advertising and integrated brand promotion (IBP) are and what they can do.
2. Discuss a basic model of communication.
3. Describe the different ways of classifying audiences for advertising and IBP.
4. Explain the key role of advertising and IBP business processes.
5. Understand the concept of integrated brand promotion (IBP) and the role advertising plays in the process.

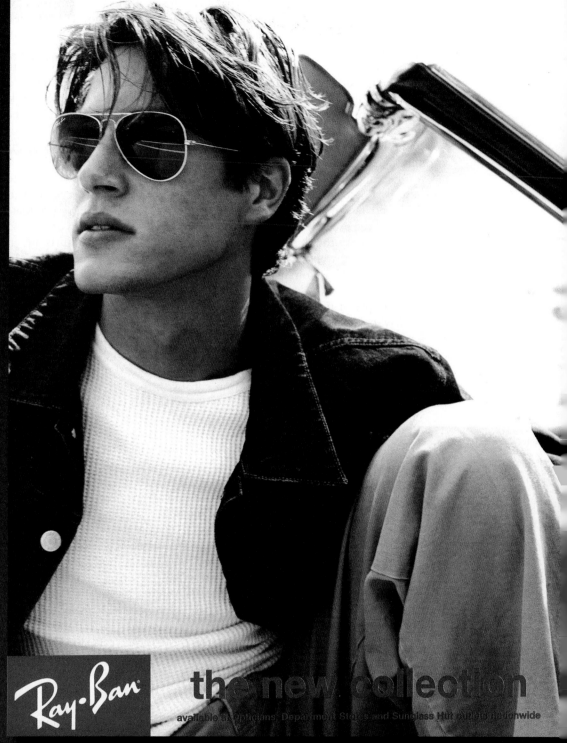

LUXOTTICA GROUP

Ray-Ban

the new collection

available at Opticians, Department Stores and Sunglass Hut outlets nationwide

Courtesy, Advertising Archives

Introductory Scenario: So Just What *Is* Going On?

The simple answer is—a lot. The more complete answer is that you likely spend more time in a week on MySpace, Facebook, Twitter, and reading blogs than you do reading magazines and newspapers. This is a big problem for advertisers trying to reach you with messages about their brands. You see, for decades, advertisers have been living in a comfortable mass media world where all they had to do was produce an ad or plan a promotional program and you, as a typical consumer, would run across these ads and encounter these programs as you used the mass media for your main sources for information and entertainment. Now, new technologies and a shift in consumers' desire to have more control over their information environment have radically changed the role of mass media in consumers' lives.

Does this sound familiar? It's a Friday night and you just battled your way through an online quiz in Anthropology on your iPad that had to be submitted by 11 p.m. and you beat the deadline by a couple of hours. Feeling pretty good about the quiz (and actually leaving a couple hours of a Friday night free), you check your friends' Facebook entries and Twitter tweets to see what they're up to. You notice that some friends you haven't seen for awhile are having a party, so you text two of your buddies on your BlackBerry to ask if they want to hit the party. Then you hurry up and get on the Ticketmaster website (http://www.ticketmaster.com) because Redeye Empire from Vancouver B.C. is coming to the big arena on campus (you signed up for the Ticketmaster "performer alert" service and got an email this afternoon) and you want to snag a couple of tickets as soon as possible. You message your buddies with the Redeye MySpace link (http://www.myspace.com/redeye29records) so that they can check out the band and decide if they want tickets too. Your buddies message back and say they are up for the party and do want tickets for the concert and will be at your place in half an hour to make plans. Before they get there, you have just enough time to buy the new Redeye Empire CD from cdbaby (http://www.cdbaby.com) and set your Slingbox (http://www.slingmedia.com) so that you can check the NBA scores on SportsCenter on your Blackberry while you're at the party.

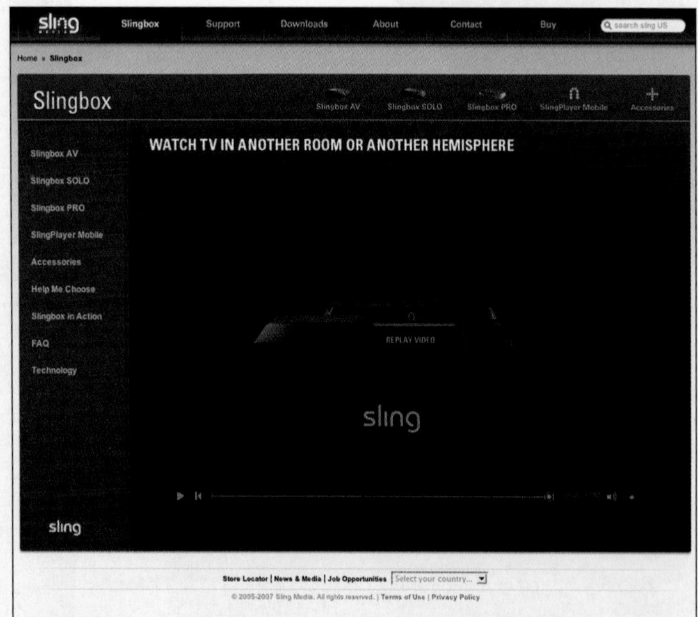

Exhibit 1.1 Along with blogs, emails, and instant messaging, devices like Slingbox allow consumers to control their information environment in a way that creates huge challenges for companies trying to get their brand messages to consumers.

Courtesy, SlingMedia.com

Does this sound familiar? If you're into being wired and keeping track of things that are important to you, then this scenario probably does sound pretty familiar (except maybe the Slingbox), which is still pretty new and expensive. If you haven't seen a Slingbox, it's a device that lets you access your television or DVR from your computer or your smartphone (See Exhibit 1.1). And you and your friends represent a huge challenge for companies that want to reach you with their advertising and promotion messages. As indicated at the outset, for the last 50 years, firms have primarily been using television, radio, newspapers, magazines, and other traditional media to send messages to consumers about their brands. Well, in this scenario about your (maybe typical) Friday night, you encountered little if *any* mass media advertising, even though you bought concert tickets and a CD and accessed television programming from your phone! Instead, you had a whole series of individually controlled information encounters that let you access all the information *you* wanted to see rather than information some company wanted you to see or hear.[1]

So, what are companies going to do to reach you with their advertising and brand messages? They are still going to try to reach you and every other consumer around the globe that, just like you, is turning to new ways of acquiring information. And these companies are going to use a blend of mass media and other, newer forms of communication to try to get their brand messages across. But, rather than the old style of mass media advertising, companies are turning to a wide range of new digital advertising and promotional techniques that complement their mass media advertising.[2]

You'll still see advertising during your favorite television show or in your favorite magazine—a lot of advertising, in fact. But if you haven't encountered some of the new "smart ads" from companies, you will before too long. If you are a smartphone user, advertising will work its way into a variety of your apps. If you're a video-game player, your favorite games are already full of ads in the cyberscenery—about $1 billion worth of advertising, actually.[3] The next time you go to the grocery store, you just might find an electronic video tablet attached to the shopping cart that asks you to swipe your store loyalty card before you start touring the aisles. That way the store's computers can prepare a shopping list of items you've purchased before for your convenience. And when you pass a product in the store that a marketer wants to feature, the screen might flash a coupon you can redeem electronically at checkout. When you've finished your shopping and are heading home, your smartphone might alert you to a special on oil changes just as you're approaching a lube shop.[4] Welcome to the new world of advertising and integrated brand promotion.

The New World of Advertising and Integrated Brand Promotion.

As the introductory scenario highlights, the world of advertising and integrated brand promotion is going through enormous change. What you will learn in this book and in your class discussions is that companies are trying to keep up with how and where consumers want to receive information about brands. Mass media are not dead, but they are being supplemented and supported by all sorts of new ways to reach consumers. Consumer preferences and new technologies are reshaping the communication environment. You'll also learn that the lines between information, entertainment, networking, and commercial messages are blurring. As one analyst put it, "The line of demarcation was obliterated years ago, when they started naming ballparks after brands."[5] Companies are turning to branded entertainment, the Internet, influencer marketing (i.e., social networks), and other communication techniques to reach consumers and get their brand messages across. You'll also read about how the world of advertising is being referred to as "Madison & Vine," as Madison Avenue advertising agencies attempt to use Hollywood entertainment-industry techniques to communicate about their brands to consumers.[6] You can go

1. Matthew Creamer and Rupal Parekh, "Ideas of the Decade," *Advertising Age*, December 14, 2009, 8.

2. Rita Chang, "Mobile Marketing Beyond the Mobile Phone," *Advertising Age*, November 30, 2009, 10.

3. Jake Gaskill, "In-Game Advertising Spending to Hit $1 Billion in 2014," G4TV, May 26, 2009, http://g4tv.com/thefeed/blog/post/695860/in-game-advertising-spending-to-hit-1-billion-in-2014.html

4. David H. Freedman, "The Future of Advertising," *Inc. Magazine*, August 2005, 70–77.

5. Question of the Week, Ad Infinitum, *BusinessWeek*, November 20, 2006, 18.

6. Burt Helm, "Hollywood's Ad Auteur," *Bloomberg Businessweek*, January 18, 2010, 50-52. To see current "Madison and Vine" campaign strategies, go to http://www.adage.com/madisonandvine

to http://www.adage.com/madisonandvine and read about how new agencies like Madison Road Entertainment are producing brand-filled reality shows like *Treasure Hunters* that expose consumers to dozens of brands, but not in the old "stop the program, show a 30-second ad" kind of way but rather with "product integration" into the show's storyline. As the vice president of marketing for Audi America described this new process of integrating brands into consumers' lifestyles, he believes in "acupuncture marketing" where you go "narrow and deep" with your messages.[7]

Analysts speculate that advertising, integrated brand promotion, and marketing overall will be more digital, more interactive, and more social. Their reasoning goes like this. Firms have not fully exploited all the opportunities presented by mobile marketing. **Mobile marketing** is communicating with target markets through mobile devices like smartphones or iPad tablet-like devices. As an example, spending on Internet advertising, including mobile marketing, is only about 12 percent of all advertising spending, but consumers are spending about 34 percent of their media time on the Internet relative to the traditional media of television, radio, newspapers, or magazines.[8] In addition, digital and interactive techniques can "funnel" consumers to retail site visits and online shopping and purchasing. But for now, the "new world of advertising" is still in transition and still has some fundamentals that will not change, as the next section describes.

Old Media/New Digital Media—It's All About the Brand.

We need to remain clear about one thing. No matter how much technology changes or how many new media options and opportunities are available for delivering messages—it's still all about the brand! Just because an advertiser offers consumers the opportunity to "follow them" on Twitter or visit the brand's Facebook page, these new communications options do not change the fundamental challenge and opportunity—communicating effectively about the brand. As consumers, we know what we like and want, and advertising—regardless of the method—can help expose us to brands that can meet our needs. And there is a simple truth—a brand that does *not* meet our needs will not succeed—no matter how much advertising there is or whether that advertising is delivered through old traditional media or new digital media and mobile marketing. Consider the case of Cadillac. In the early 1950s, Cadillac held a stunning 75 percent share of the luxury car market and was a leading advertiser in the market year after year. But by 2007, that market share had fallen to about 9 percent—an unprecedented loss in the history of the automobile industry or most other industries for that matter. What happened to the Cadillac brand? It wasn't the advertising. A series of product missteps confused the market's perception of the brand: the 1986 Cimarron, for example, used a Chevy chassis and looked cheap, and the 1987 Allante sports car was slow and leaked like a sieve. Formidable competitors like Lexus and Infiniti entered the market with powerful and stylish alternatives that were effectively advertised. Does it seem like social networking the brand on Twitter or Facebook could have changed Cadillac's fate during this period of decline? Not likely—even though there are nearly 10 million monthly users of Facebook over 55 years old[9] (see the *Social Media* box). Now, GM has reinvested in the Cadillac brand and committed $4.3 billion to redesign, advertise, and promote the brand to change consumers' perceptions (see Exhibit 1.2). It seems to be working as Motor Trend evaluators said, "With this bold, savvy, uncompromising showpiece

7. Jean Halliday, "Audi Taps Ad Whiz to Direct Branding," *Advertising Age*, May 8, 2006, 4, 88.

8. Josh Bernoff, "Why Marketing Will Be More Digital, More Interactive and More Social," *Marketing News*, October 30, 2009, 18.

9. Peter Corbett, Facebook Demographics and Statistics Report 2010 – 145% Growth in 1 Year, posted January 4, 2010, at http://www.istrategylabs.com/2010/01/facebook-demographics-and-statistics-report-2010-145-growth-in-1-year/

Exhibit 1.2 GM is trying to reinvent the Cadillac brand with new body and interior designs and new "brand story" advertising featuring music by artists like the Teddybears, Explosions in the Sky, and Melikka.

Courtesy, General Motors

Social Media

It's Big. It's Getting Bigger. But Can You Advertise?

Online social networks are big. And, they're getting bigger. Facebook has more than 350 million users worldwide with 103 million in the United States alone. Users of Facebook spend from 6 to 8 hours every month posting 55 million updates a day on the site and providing more than 350 *billion* pieces of content every week to share with friends and family. Beyond Facebook, a host of other online networks cater to specific interests and demographics: MySpace concentrates on music and entertainment, ResearchGATE connects scientists and researchers, LinkedIn targets career-oriented professionals, and Twitter lets members send out 140 word "tweets" about their daily whereabouts and activities. Everybody from your kid sister to venerable, conservative organizations like TIAA-CREF (the multi-billion dollar investment service) are members of one or more social networks. Social networks are not just a phenomenon in the United States—China has QQ, France has Skyrock, and Russia has VKontakte with millions of monthly visitors.

As big as these networks are and as much traffic as they attract, you can imagine that advertisers are delirious over the possibility of reaching users with all sorts of highly customized, persuasive, relatively low-cost messages. Everything about a social networking site is ideally suited for reaching audiences and touting the values of brands: identifiable users, easily accessed, heavily trafficked—an advertiser's dreams come true. Well, not exactly. Facebook's foray into advertising with its Beacon advertising tool for advertisers did not go well. Beacon was set up to track what people on Facebook purchased on other sites, then it would tell your Facebook friends in the hopes that they would want to buy similar products—all of this without Facebook users' consent. Facebook users went ballistic, called it an invasion of privacy, and filed a class action law suit. Ultimately, Facebook ended the Beacon program altogether.

Now advertisers are left on the outside looking in at all those millions of users. Sure, there is still the opportunity to create a Facebook page and promote its existence at a company website or in traditional media advertising. But that is not the same as being *on* Facebook users' sites as they spend all those hours a month networking. And, you can post banner ads at sites like LinkedIn, but that's just like any other Web ad. So, for now, it seems the answer is "no," you really can't advertise on the biggest thing going in Web user activity—at least not in the most powerful ways.

Sources: "A World of Connections," *The Economist,* January 30, 2010, 3-4; Peter Corbett, *Facebook Demographics and Statistics Report 2010 – 145% Growth in 1 Year*, posted January, 4, 2010, at http://www.istrategylabs.com/2010/01/facebook-demographics-and-statistics-report-2010-145-growth-in-1-year//; Jordon McCollum, "Facebook Bows Out," www.marketingpilgram.com, posted September 21, 2009.

of a sedan... GM has leapt straight from the rabble's side of the velvet rope into that coveted, highly selective inner sanctum marked 'World's Finest Cars.'"[10]

So, as you work your way through the class and the chapters in the book, you'll learn how advertising works and how it is changing. You'll also learn about all the new methods of communicating to consumers as firms are trying to successfully create effective integrated brand promotion.

1 What Are Advertising and Integrated Brand Promotion?

Now that we've set the new and dynamic context for communication, let's consider the tools companies are going to be using: advertising and integrated brand promotion. We'll start with advertising. You have your own ideas about advertising because you see some advertising every day—even if you try to avoid most of it, like the situation in the introductory scenario. You need to know that advertising means different things to different people, though. It's a business, an art form, an institution, and a cultural phenomenon. To the CEO of a multinational corporation, like Pepsi, advertising is an essential marketing tool that helps create brand awareness and brand loyalty. To the owner of a small retail shop, advertising is a way to bring people into the store. To the art director in an advertising agency, advertising is the creative expression of a concept. To a media planner, advertising is the way a firm uses the media to communicate to current and potential customers. To a website manager, it's a way to drive traffic to the URL. To scholars and museum curators, advertising is an important cultural artifact, text, and historical record. Advertising means something different to all these people. In fact, sometimes determining just what is and what is not advertising is a difficult task!

Even though companies believe in and rely heavily on advertising, it is not a process that the average person clearly understands or values. Most people have some significant misperceptions about advertising and what it's supposed to do, what it can do, and what it can't do. Many people think advertising deceives others but rarely themselves. Most think it's a semi-glamorous profession but one in which people are either morally bankrupt con artists or pathological liars. At worst, advertising is seen as hype, unfair capitalistic manipulation, banal commercial noise, mind control, postmodern voodoo, or outright deception. At best, the average person sees advertising as amusing, informative, helpful, and occasionally hip.

The truth about advertising lies somewhere between the extremes. Sometimes advertising is hard-hitting and powerful; at other times, it's boring and ineffective. Advertising can be enormously creative and entertaining, and it can be simply annoying. One thing is for sure: Advertising is anything but unimportant. Advertising plays a pivotal role in world commerce and in the way we experience and live our lives. It is part of our language and our culture. It reflects the way we think about things and the way we see ourselves. Now, advertising is integrating itself more seamlessly into our social interactions. A firm called Infegy tracks more than 20 million Web pages and creates a "Social Radar Sentiment Index." The index tracks brand comment volume. In 2009, the index identified tens of millions of brand comments led by Apple and Microsoft with 1.4 million combined mentions.[11] It is a complex communication process, a dynamic business process, and now a part of the social interaction process.

10. David Welch and Gerry Khermouch, "Can GM Save an Icon?" *BusinessWeek*, April 8, 2002, 60–67; David Welch, "The Second Coming of Cadillac," *BusinessWeek*, November 24, 2003, 79–80; Arthur St. Antoine, "One Giant Leap: Cadillac Aims for the Stars. And Builds One," *Motor Trend*, November, 2007.

11. Jack Neff, "Apple, Microsoft Top Social Media Kingpins," *Advertising Age*, October 5, 2009, 10.

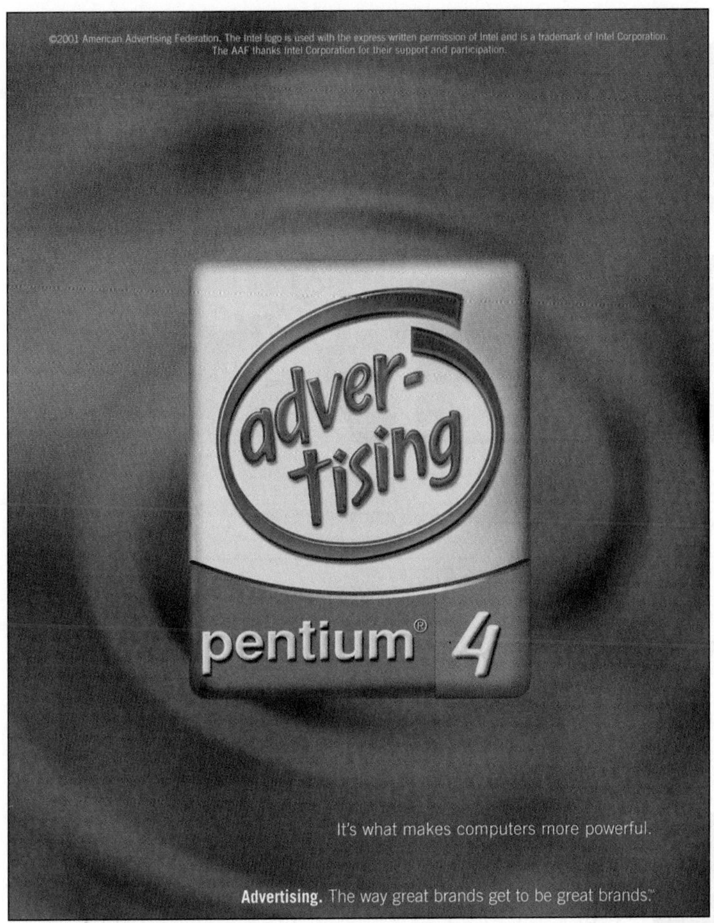

adver-tising
pentium® 4
It's what makes computers more powerful.
Advertising. The way great brands get to be great brands.

Exhibit 1.3 The American Advertising Federation (AAF) ran this ad touting the power of advertising's effect on brand building. The AAF used the Intel logo and brand "look" for this message because Intel is regarded as one of the most successful firms in using adverting to build brand name awareness and recognition. http://www.aaf.org

Courtesy, AAF

And, as a business process, advertising is relied on by companies big and small to build their brands—this is the central theme of this book. Advertising and integrated brand promotions are key to organizations' strategies to build awareness and preference for brands (see Exhibit 1.3).

Advertising Defined.

Keeping in mind that different people in different contexts see advertising so differently and that advertising suffers from some pretty complex controversies, we offer this straightforward definition:

Advertising *is a paid, mass-mediated attempt to persuade.*

As direct and simple as this definition seems, it is loaded with distinctions. First, advertising is *paid* communication by a company or organization that wants its information disseminated. In advertising language, the company or organization that pays for advertising is called the **client** or **sponsor**. If a communication is *not paid for*, it's not advertising. For example, a form of public relations promotion called *publicity* is not advertising because it is not paid for. Let's say Will Smith appears on the *Late Show with David Letterman* to promote his newest movie. Is this advertising? No, because the producer or film studio did not pay the *Late Show with David Letterman* for airtime. In this example, the show gets an interesting and popular guest, the guest star gets exposure, and the film gets plugged. Everyone is happy, but no advertising took place—it might be public relations, but it is not advertising. But when the film studio produces and runs ads on television and in newspapers across the country for the newest Will Smith movie, this communication is paid for by the studio, it is placed in media to reach consumers, and therefore is most definitely advertising.

For the same reason, public service announcements (PSAs) are not advertising either. True, they look like ads and sound like ads, but they are not ads. They are not commercial in the way an ad is because they are not paid for like an ad. They are offered as information in the public (noncommercial) interest. When you hear a message on the radio that implores you to "Just Say No" to drugs, this sounds very much like an ad, but it is a PSA. Simply put, PSAs are excluded from the definition of advertising because they are unpaid communication.

Consider the two messages in Exhibits 1.4 and 1.5. These two messages have similar copy and offer similar advice. Exhibit 1.4 has persuasive intent, is paid-for communication, and appears in the mass media. It is an advertisement. Exhibit 1.5 also has persuasive intent and appears in mass media outlets, but it is not advertising because it is not paid-for communication. PSAs are important and often strongly imitate their commercial cousins.

Second, advertising is *mass mediated*. This means it is delivered through a communication medium designed to reach more than one person, typically a large number—or mass—of people. Advertising is widely disseminated through

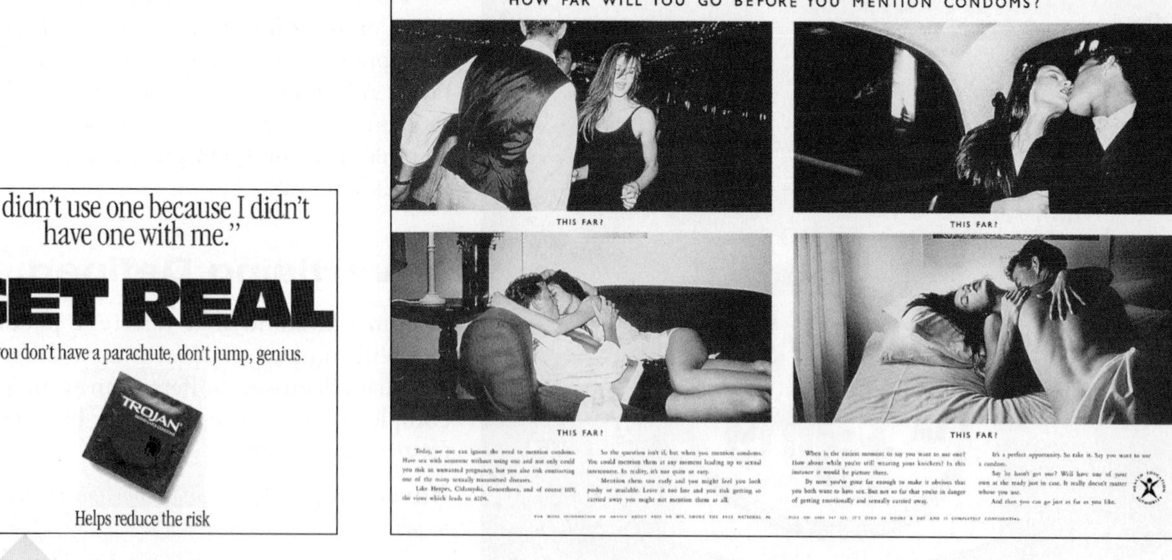

Exhibits 1.4 and 1.5 The messages in Exhibits 1.4 and 1.5 communicate nearly identical information to the audience, but one is an advertisement and one is not. The message in Exhibit 1.4 sponsored by Trojan is an advertisement because it is paid-for communication. The message in Exhibit 1.5, sponsored by the U.K.'s Health Education Authority, has a persuasive intent similar to the Trojan ad, but it is not advertising—Exhibit 1.5 is a PSA. Why isn't the Health Education Authority PSA message an ad? http://www.trojancondoms.com

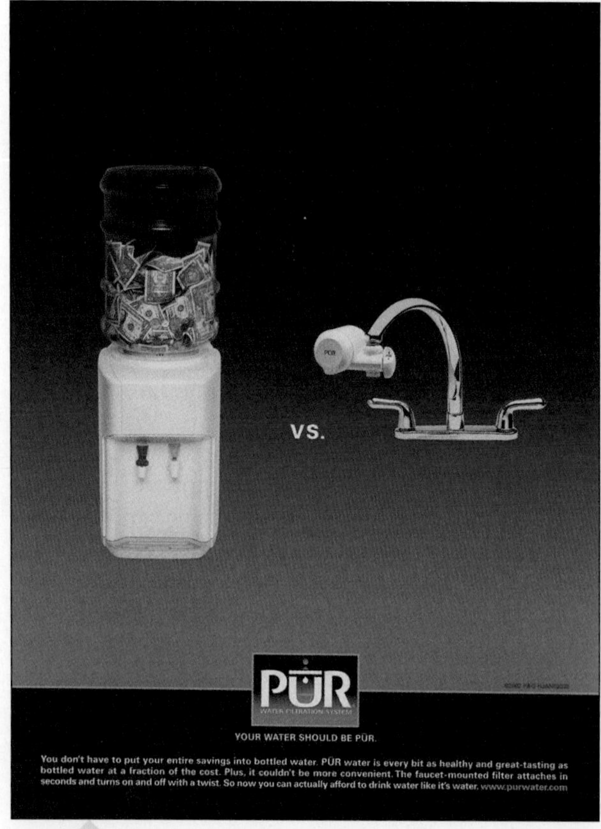

Exhibit 1.6 In order for a communication to be advertising, it has to have a persuasive intent. Even though this PUR water filter ad is not overtly persuasive, the fact that it is interesting creates a positive reaction in the audience, which can persuade people to try the brand. http://www.purwater.com

familiar means—television, radio, newspapers, and magazines—and other media such as direct mail, billboards, video games, the Internet, iPods, and smartphones. The mass-mediated nature of advertising creates a communication environment where the message is not delivered in a face-to-face manner. This distinguishes advertising from personal selling as a form of communication.

Third, all advertising includes an *attempt to persuade*. To put it bluntly, ads are communications designed to get someone to do something. Even an advertisement with a stated objective of being purely informational still has persuasion at its core. The ad informs the consumer for some purpose, and that purpose is to get the consumer to like the brand, and because of that liking, to eventually buy the brand. An "ad" can be extremely subtle, like a Sprite bottle and logo appearing in the "Green Eyed World" video series on YouTube. Or, it can be loud and blatant like a Saturday morning infomercial. Consider the PUR water filter ad in Exhibit 1.6. It doesn't carry a lot of explicit product information. But it's interesting, and most of us would say, "Yeah, I like that ad." With that reaction, this ad is persuasive. In the absence of a persuasive intent, a communication might be news, but it would not be advertising.

At this point, we can say that for a communication to be classified as advertising, three essential criteria must be met:

1. The communication must be *paid for.*
2. The communication must be delivered to an audience via *mass media.*
3. The communication must be *attempting persuasion.*

It is important to note here that advertising can be persuasive communication not only about a product or service but also about an idea, a person, or an entire organization. When Colgate and Honda use advertising, this is product advertising and meets all three criteria. When TD Ameritrade, Delta Air Lines, Terminix, or your dentist run advertisements, these service advertisements meet all three criteria.

Integrated Brand Promotion Defined.

Now that we have defined advertising, let's consider the other important context for the book—the process of integrated brand promotion, or IBP. As we discussed earlier, communication is all about the brand and, as such, promotion is all about the brand as well. To fully understand integrated brand promotion, let's first define IBP and describe all the tools used for IBP. Then we can talk about how it is related to and yet distinct from advertising. First the definition:

integrated brand promotion (IBP) *is the process of using a wide range of promotional tools working together to create widespread brand exposure.*

Just as the definition of advertising was loaded with meaning, so too is the definition of integrated brand promotion. First, IBP is a process. It has to be. It is complicated and needs to be managed in an integrated fashion. Second, IBP uses a wide range of promotional tools that have to be evaluated and scheduled. IBP creates exposure for the *brand.* It can be a branded product or an overall corporate brand, but the IBP process is squarely focused on brand exposure. Here is a list of the most prominent tools marketers use for IBP:

- Advertising in mass media (television, radio, newspapers, magazines, billboards)
- Sales promotions (coupons, premiums, discounts, gift cards, contests, samples, trial offers, rebates, frequent user-affinity programs, trade shows)
- Point-of-purchase (in-store) advertising
- Direct marketing (catalogs, telemarketing, email offers, infomercials)
- Personal selling
- Internet advertising (banners, pop-ups/pop-unders, websites)
- Social networks/Blogs
- Podcasting
- Event sponsorships
- Branded entertainment (product placement/insertion in television programming, Webcasts, video games, and films), also referred to as "advertainment"
- Outdoor signage
- Billboard, transit, and aerial advertising
- Public relations
- Influencer marketing (peer-to-peer persuasion)
- Corporate advertising

Notice that this long list of IBP tools includes various types of advertising but goes well beyond traditional advertising forms. From mass media of advertising to influencer marketing and social networks, the tools of IBP are varied and wide ranging. All of these tools allow a marketer to reach target customers in different ways with different kinds of messages to achieve broad exposure for a brand.

Third, the definition of IBP highlights that all of these tools need to work together. That is, they need to be integrated to create a consistent and compelling impression of the brand. Having mass media advertising send one message and create one image and then have Webcasts or personal selling deliver another message will confuse consumers about the meaning and relevance of the brand—this is a very bad thing!

Finally, the definition of IBP emphasizes that all of the advertising and promotional effort undertaken by a firm is designed to create widespread exposure for a brand. Unless consumers are reached by these various forms of messages, they will have a difficult time understanding the brand and deciding whether to use it regularly.

Advertisements, Advertising Campaigns, and Integrated Brand Promotion.

Now that we have working definitions of advertising and IBP, we can turn our attention to some other important distinctions and definitions. Let's start with the basics. An **advertisement** refers to a specific message that an organization has created to persuade an audience. An **advertising campaign** is a series of coordinated advertisements that communicate a reasonably cohesive and integrated theme about a brand. The theme may be made up of several claims or points but should advance an essentially singular theme. Successful advertising campaigns can be developed around a single advertisement placed in multiple media, or they can be made up of several different advertisements with a similar look, feel, and message. You are probably familiar with the "Got Milk?" campaign as an example. Another example is represented by the Altoids ads in Exhibits 1.7 through 1.10. Notice the excellent use of similar look and feel in this advertising campaign. Advertising campaigns can run for a few weeks or for many years. The advertising campaign requires a keen sense of the complex environments within which a company must communicate to different audiences.

And think about this important aspect of advertising campaigns. Most *individual* ads would make little sense without the knowledge that audience members have accumulated from previous ads for a particular brand. Ads are interpreted by each consumer through their personal experiences with a brand and having viewed previous ads for the brand. When you see a new Nike ad, you make sense of the ad through your personal history with Nike and its previous advertising. Even ads for a new brand or a new product are situated within each audience member's broader knowledge of products, brands, and advertising. After years of viewing ads and buying brands, people bring a rich history and knowledge base to every communications encounter.

How does IBP fit in with advertisements and advertising campaigns? As we discussed earlier, IBP is the use of many promotional tools, including advertising, in a coordinated manner to build and then maintain brand awareness, identity, and preference. When marketers combine contests, a website, event sponsorship, and point-of-purchase displays with advertisements and advertising campaigns, they create an integrated brand promotion. BMW did just that when the firm (re)introduced the Mini Cooper auto to the U.S. market. The IBP campaign used billboards, print ads, an interactive website, and "guerrilla" marketing (a Mini was mounted on top of a Chevy Suburban and driven around New York City). Each part of the campaign elements was coordinated with all the others.[12] Note that the word *coordinated* is central to the IBP effort. Without coordination among these various promotional efforts, there is not an integrated brand promotion. Rather, the consumer will merely encounter a series of individual, unrelated (and therefore confusing) communications about a brand.

12. John Gaffney, "Most Innovative Campaign," *Business 2.0*, May 2002, 98–99.

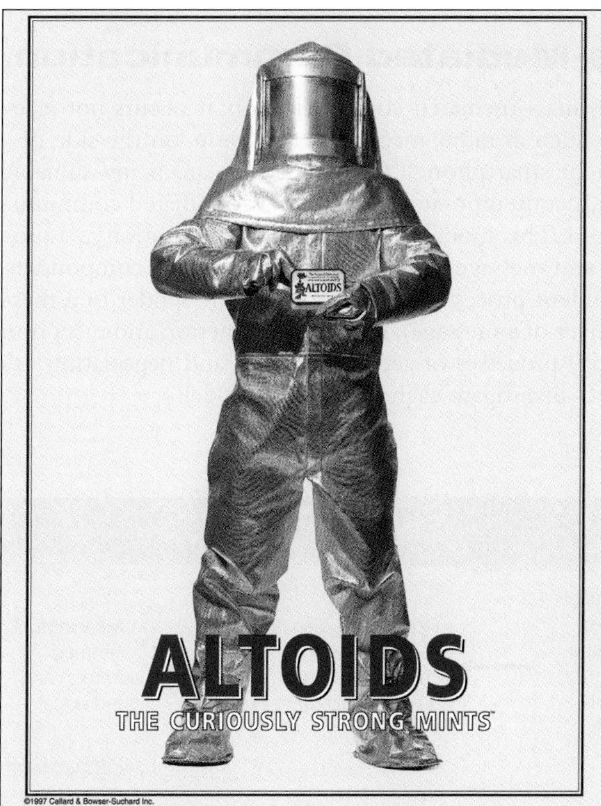

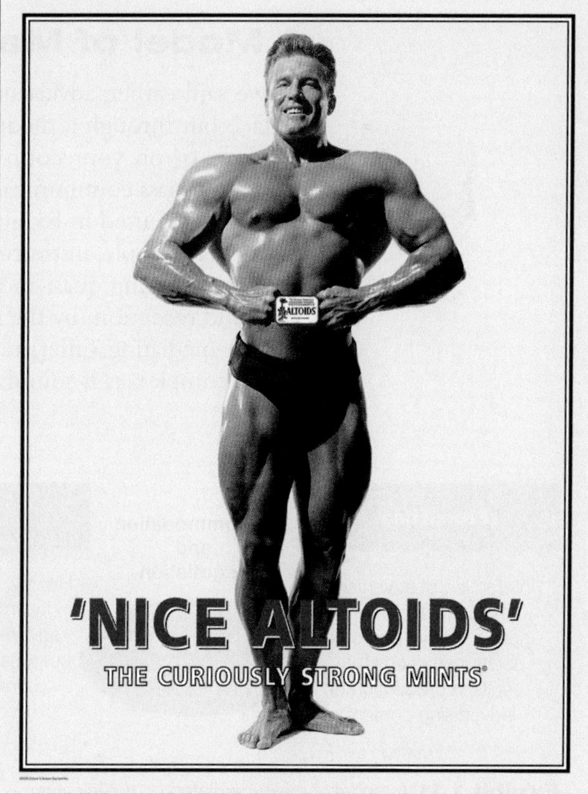

Exhibits 1.7 through 1.10 A well-conceived and well-executed adverting campaign offers consumers a series of messages with a similar look and feel. The series of ads for Altoids is an excellent example of a campaign that communicates with similar images to create a unified look and feel. http://www.altoids.com

A Focus on Advertising.

Integrated brand promotion will be a key concept throughout our discussion of advertising. The fact that this phrase is included in the title of the book signals its importance to the contemporary marketing effort. As consumers encounter a daily blitz of commercial messages and appeals, brands and brand identity offer them a way to cope with the overload of information. Brands and the images they project allow consumers to quickly identify and evaluate the relevance of a brand to their lives and value systems. The marketer who does not use advertising and IBP as a way to build brand exposure and meaning for consumers will, frankly, be ignored.

We will develop the concept and describe the execution of IBP throughout the text and demonstrate how advertising is central to the process. The encounters between consumers and advertising, advertisements, and advertising campaigns, specifically, are the focus of our next discussion. Elaboration on the features and application of other IBP tools will be covered extensively in Part 5 of the text.

2 Advertising as a Communication Process.

Communication is a fundamental aspect of human existence, and advertising is one of those communications. To understand advertising at all, you must understand something about communication in general and about mass communication in particular. At the outset, it's important to understand the basics of how advertising works as a means of communication. To help with gaining this understanding, let's consider a contemporary model of mass communication. We'll apply this basic model of communication as a first step toward understanding advertising.

A Model of Mass-Mediated Communication.

As we said earlier, advertising is mass-mediated communication; it occurs not face-to-face but through a medium (such as radio, magazines, television, on the side of a building, or on your computer or smartphone). Although there are many valuable models of mass communication, a contemporary model of mass-mediated communication is presented in Exhibit 1.11. This model shows mass communication as a process where people, institutions, and messages interact. It has two major components, each representing quasi-independent processes: production (by the sender of a message) and reception (by the receiver of a message). Between production and reception are the mediating (interpretation) processes of accommodation and negotiation. It's not as complex as it sounds. Let's investigate each part of the model.

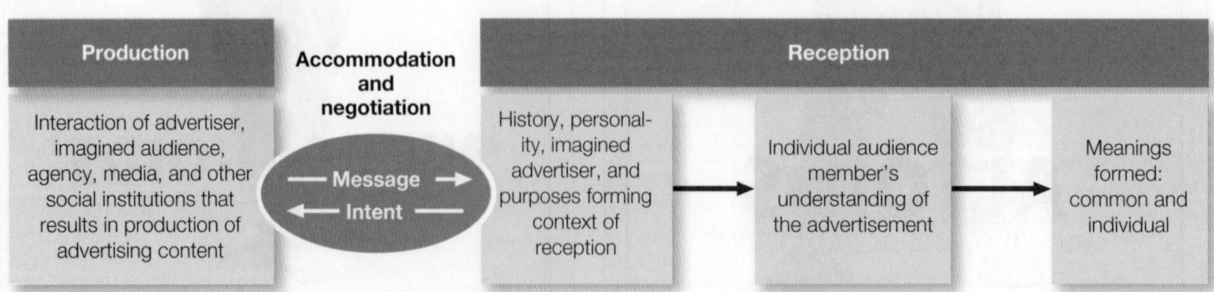

Exhibit 1.11 A model of mass-mediated communication.

Moving from left to right in the model, we first see the process of communication production, where the content of any mass communication is created. An advertisement, like other forms of mass communication, is the product of institutions (such as corporations, organizations, advertising agencies, and governments) interacting to produce content (what is created for a print ad, television ad, radio ad, podcast, or on a computer screen at a company's website). The creation of the advertisement is a complex interaction of the company's brand message; the company's expectations about the target audience's desire for information; the company's assumptions about how members of an audience will interpret the words and images in an ad; and the rules and regulations of the medium that transmits the message.

Continuing on to the right, we see that the mediating processes of accommodation and negotiation lie between the production and reception phases. Accommodation and negotiation are the ways in which consumers interpret ads. Individual audience members have some ideas about how the company wants them to interpret the ad (we all know the rules of advertising—somebody is trying to persuade us to buy something or like their brand or idea). And each consumer has needs, agendas, and preferred interpretations based on history, experience, and individual value systems. Given all this, every consumer who sees an ad arrives at an interpretation of the ad that makes sense to them, serves their needs, and fits their personal history with a product category and a set of brands. You'll learn more about wide range of influences on each consumer in Chapter 5—"Advertising, Consumer Behavior, and Integrated Brand Promotion."

What's interesting about the whole progression of consumer receipt and then interpretation of a communication is that it is often wholly *incompatible* with the way the company wants consumers to see an ad! In other words, the receivers of the communication must *accommodate* their perceived multiple meanings and personal agendas and then *negotiate* a meaning, that is an interpretation, of the ad according to their individual life experiences and value systems. That's why we say that communication is inherently a *social* process: What a message means to any given consumer is a function not of an isolated solitary thinker but of an inherently social being responding to what he or she knows about the producers of the message (the companies), other receivers of it (peer groups, for example), and the social world in which the brand and the message about it resides. Now, admittedly, all this interpretation happens very fast and without much contemplation. Still, it happens. The level of conscious interpretation by each receiver might be minimal (mere recognition) or it might be extensive (thoughtful, elaborate processing of an ad), but there is *always* interpretation.

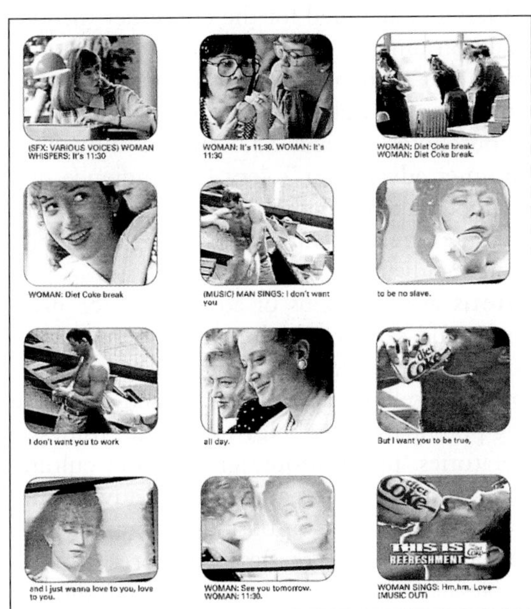

Exhibit 1.12 This ad is a good example of how the meaning of an ad can vary for different people. How would you interpret the meaning of this ad? Think of someone very different from you. What meaning might that person give this ad? http://www.cocacola.com

Courtesy of the Coca-Cola Company

The communication model in Exhibit 1.11 underscores a critical point: No ad contains a single meaning for all audience members. An ad for a pair of women's shoes means something different for women than it does for men. An ad that achieved widespread popularity (and controversy) is the ad for Diet Coke shown in Exhibit 1.12, which may be interpreted differently by men and women. For example, does the ad suggest that men drink Diet Coke so that they can be the object of intense daily admiration by a group of female office workers? Or does the ad suggest that Diet Coke is a part of a modern woman's lifestyle, granting her "permission" to freely admire attractive men in the same way women have been eyed by male construction workers (or executives) for years? Each audience member decides what meaning to take away from a communication.

3 The Audiences for Advertising.

We've been referring to audiences, so now it's time to define them. In the language of advertising, an **audience** is a group of individuals who receive and interpret messages sent from companies or organizations. The audience could be made up of household consumers, college students, or business people. Any large group of people can be an audience. A **target audience** is a particular group of consumers singled out by an organization for an advertising or IBP campaign. These target audiences are singled out because the firm has discovered that audience members like the product category and might prefer their particular brand within that product category. Target audiences are always *potential* audiences because a company can never be sure that the message will actually get through to them as intended. By the way, there is nothing sinister about the targeting process. Targeting audiences simply means that a company wants to reach you with a message. Do you feel like something bad happens to you when the Gap targets you with an ad and you see it on TV? Of course not! Somewhere along the line, the word *targeting* and the phrase *target audience* have picked up some negative connotations—ignore them.

Even though companies can identify dozens of different target audiences, five broad audience categories are commonly described: household consumers, members of business organizations, members of a trade channel, professionals, and government officials and employees.

Audience Categories.

Household consumers are the most conspicuous audience in that most mass media advertising is directed at them. McDonald's, Nissan, Miller Brewing, the Gap, and State Farm Insurance have products and services designed for the consumer market, and so their advertising targets household consumers.

The most recent information indicates that there are about 116 million households in the United States and approximately 307 million household consumers.[13] Total yearly retail spending by these households exceeds $5.0 trillion annually.[14] Under the very broad heading of "consumer advertising," very fine audience distinctions can be made by advertisers. A target audience definition such as men, 25 to 45, living in metropolitan areas, with incomes greater than $50,000 per year would be the kind of target audience description an advertiser might develop.

Members of business organizations are the focus of advertising for firms that produce business and industrial goods and services, such as office equipment, production machinery, supplies, and software. Although products and services targeted to this audience often require personal selling, advertising is used to create awareness and a favorable attitude among potential buyers. Not-for-profit businesses such as universities, some research laboratories, philanthropic groups, and cultural organizations represent an important and separate business audience for advertising. Exhibit 1.13 is an example of an ad directed at members of business organizations.

Members of a trade channel include retailers (like Best Buy for consumer electronics), wholesalers (like Castle Wholesalers for construction tools), and distributors (like Sysco Food Services for restaurant supplies). They are a target audience for producers of both household and business goods and services. So, for example, if Microsoft cannot gain adequate retail and wholesale distribution through trade channels for the Xbox, the brand will not reach target customers. That being the case, it's important to direct advertising at the trade level of the market. Various forms of advertising can be used to develop demand among members of a trade channel.

13. U.S. Census Bureau FactFinder, Population of the United States 2009, http://factfinder.census.gov, accessed online February 10, 2010.

14. "2009 Survey of Buying Power," *Sales and Marketing Management*, 2009, 18.

lose money
lose customers
WHEN SERVING YOUR CUSTOMERS,
WHATEVER CHOICE YOU MAKE, YOU'RE TOAST.
You know that the only way to succeed is by serving your customers better. But what organization can afford to throw endless dollars at improving the customer experience? With RightNow, you don't have to make a deal with the devil.
RightNow provides a breakthrough solution that lets you enhance your customer experience while reducing costs. By delivering knowledge at every customer touchpoint, RightNow helps you grow your business, one customer experience at a time. We've enabled more than a billion successful customer interactions for our clients in every major industry. Chances are, we can help you, too.
Find out why RightNow leads in client satisfaction. Download your free executive summary of CRMGuru's Solutions Guide at www.rightnow.com/toast or call us toll-free at 1.877.363.5678.
RIGHT NOW
TECHNOLOGIES

Exhibit 1.13 RightNow Technologies sells systems used by companies to cut sales costs and improve customer relationship management. When members of business organizations use advertising to communicate, the ads often emphasize creating awareness of the company's brand name. RightNow Technologies is combining high visual appeal with detailed ad copy to accomplish brand name recognition. http://www.rightnow.com

The promotional tool used most often to communicate with this group is personal selling. This is because this target audience represents a relatively small, easily identifiable group that can be reached with personal selling. When advertising is also directed at this target audience, it can serve an extremely useful purpose, as we will see later in the section on advertising as a business process.

Professionals form a special target audience and are defined as doctors, lawyers, accountants, teachers, or any other professional group that has special training or certification. This audience warrants a separate classification because its members have specialized needs and interests. Advertising directed to professionals typically highlights products and services uniquely designed to serve their more narrowly defined needs. The language and images used in advertising to this target audience often rely on esoteric terminology and unique circumstances that members of professions readily recognize. Advertising to professionals is predominantly carried out through trade publications. **Trade journals** are magazines published specifically for members of a trade and carry highly technical articles.

Government officials and employees constitute an audience in themselves due to the large dollar volume of buying that federal, state, and local governments do. Government organizations from universities to road maintenance operations buy huge amounts of various types of products. Producers of items such as office furniture, construction materials and equipment, vehicles, fertilizers, computers, and business services all target government organizations with advertising. Advertising to this target audience is dominated by direct mail, catalogs, and Web advertising.

Audience Geography.

Audiences can also be broken down by geographic location. Because of cultural differences that often accompany geographic location, very few ads can be effective for all consumers worldwide. If an ad is used worldwide with only minor changes it is called **global advertising**. Very few ads can use global advertising. These are typically brands that are considered "citizens of the world" and whose manner of use does not vary tremendously by culture. Using a Sony television or taking a trip

Globalization

Try This One On for Size

Here's a challenge of global proportions. Imagine that it is your job to develop the advertising for a retail store that sells women's lingerie. This shouldn't be too hard. After all, Victoria's Secret has done a great job with bold television advertising featuring Tyra Banks and Gisele Bündchen, not to mention those direct mail catalogs. It's a product category that's showing strong growth and the media are loosening up on restrictions for visuals.

Well, there is one other little detail that might make this a bit more difficult. The retail lingerie store's name is Al Mashat and it is located in Saudi Arabia. So, you ask? Lingerie is lingerie and women are women. That may be true, but Saudi Arabia is also Saudi Arabia and in Saudi Arabia, the detail that is most problematic was well articulated by Margo Chase, founder and executive director of Chase Design Group consulting firm: "The really huge problem is how to market lingerie in a country where you can't show photographs of women." Not being able to show women in lingerie is a somewhat important detail that would make this just a bit more difficult.

So, what *would* you do in a situation like this? One thing is for sure, there is no way that the religious culture of Saudi Arabia and the media restrictions it creates are going to change just because some retail store wants to more effectively advertise. But here are some details that might help you out: Saudi Arabia has an extremely young population, with 42.4 percent being under the age of 15. Additionally, shopping is one of the few recreations available to Saudi women.

Have you figured out an advertising strategy yet? Well, let's take a look at what the U.S. consulting firm Chase Design Group came up with for advertising for Al Mashat. First, the design firm decided that if they could not use the images of women, then the advertising campaign would be carried by "language that was rich, textured, layered, and sensual." An example of the language was a poem featured both in advertising and store banners: "Wrap this beautiful robe of words around you and dream." Second, to carry through on the force of the language, a special font and characters were developed. Finally, advertising was launched using print ads, radio ads, and a direct mail piece featuring bags imprinted with the store logo and filled with potpourri and an invitation card printed on iridescent pearl-colored paper. As a follow-up, another direct mail campaign mailed out gift vouchers worth 50 riyals (about $13) to prospective customers. How did it all work out? In the first year of the store's operations, more than $3.2 million in revenue was generated. The owner expects revenue to grow to $5 million in the store's second full year.

The lesson here is that in global markets, any number of unique circumstances can restrict the way we might use advertising. But the other lesson is that even though there may be what seem to be huge barriers (like not showing women in ads for a product designed exclusively for women), the breadth and creativity of advertising can be used to overcome such barriers.

Source: Arundhati Parmar, "Out from Under," *Marketing News*, July 21, 2003.

on Singapore Airlines doesn't change much from culture to culture and geographic location to geographic location. Exhibits 1.14 and 1.15 show extremely similar appeals in two different ads for Rolex watches—another product category where product use across cultures is the same. Firms that market brands with global appeal, like Singapore Airlines, IBM, Sony, and Pirelli Tires, try to develop and place advertisements with a common theme and presentation in all markets around the world where the firm's brands are sold. Global placement is possible only when a brand and the messages about that brand have a common appeal across diverse cultures. The *Globalization* box highlights a situation where a product category widely advertised in the U.S. market, lingerie, is somewhat more complicated to advertise in a different culture—Saudi Arabia.

International advertising occurs when firms prepare and place different advertising in different national markets outside their home market. Each international market may require unique advertising due to product adaptations or message appeals tailored specifically for that market. Unilever prepares different versions of ads for its laundry products for nearly every international market because consumers

Exhibits 1.14 and 1.15 Global advertising can be used for brands where there is little difference in use across cultures or geographic location. The only real difference in these two ads is language (German versus Italian), while other aspects—Rolex's appeal to an affluent elite who likely follow tennis and the Rolex brand imagery—remain the same. An interesting twist with Rolex is that it uses a website to describe, but not sell, its products (http://www.rolex.com). Instead the website directs surfers to the retailers who carry the brand. Is the Web likely to be Rolex's best advertising channel, anyway?

in different cultures approach the laundry task differently. Consumers in the United States use large and powerful washers and dryers and a lot of hot water. Households in Brazil use very little hot water and hang clothes out to dry. Few firms enjoy the luxury of having a brand with truly cross-cultural appeal and global recognition, as is necessary for global advertising as described in the previous section. International advertising differs from global advertising in that different ads are tailored for each market.

National advertising reaches all geographic areas of a single nation. National advertising is the term typically used to describe the kind of advertising we see most often in the mass media in the domestic U.S. market. Does international advertising use many different national advertising efforts? Yes, that is exactly the relationship between international advertising and national advertising.

Regional advertising is carried out by producers, wholesalers, distributors, and retailers that concentrate their efforts in a relatively large, but not national, geographic region. Albertson's, a regional grocery chain, has stores in 31 western, northwestern, midwestern, and southern states. Because of the nature of the firm's markets, it places advertising only in regions where it has stores.

Local advertising is much the same as regional advertising. **Local advertising** is directed at an audience in a single trading area, either a city or state. Exhibit 1.16

Exhibit 1.16 Daffy's (http://www.daffys.com) is a clothing retailer with several shops in the New York/New Jersey metropolitan area. It services a local geographic market. Retailers that serve a small geographic area use local advertising to reach their customers and typically rely on newspaper and radio ads to reach their local target market.

Courtesy of Rolex Watch U.S.A., Inc.; Courtesy of Daffy's

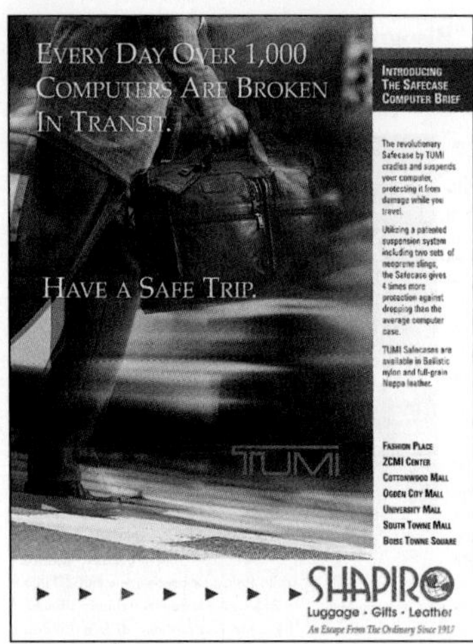

Exhibit 1.17 National companies will often share advertising expenses with local retail merchants if the retailer features the company's brand in local advertising. This sharing of expenses is called co-op advertising. Here a local retailer, Shapiro Luggage, is featuring TUMI brand luggage in this co-op ad.
http://wwww.tumi.com

Courtesy of Shapiro Luggage, Gifts, Leather

shows an example of this type of advertising. Daffy's is a discount clothing retailer with stores in the New York/New Jersey metropolitan area. Retailers with local markets like Daffy's use all types of local media to reach customers. Under special circumstances, national companies will share advertising expenses in a market with local dealers to achieve specific advertising objectives. This sharing of advertising expenses between national companies and local merchants is called **cooperative advertising** (or **co-op advertising**). Exhibit 1.17 illustrates a co-op advertisement run by TUMI luggage and one of its retailers, Shapiro. In a key strategy move several years ago, General Motors redesigned its co-op advertising program with dealers in an attempt to create a more fully coordinated integrated brand promotion.[15]

4 Advertising as a Business Process.

So far we have talked about advertising as a communication process and as a way companies reach diverse audiences with persuasive brand information. But we need to appreciate another dimension: Advertising is very much a business process as well as a communication process. For multinational organizations like Microsoft and Boeing, as well as for small local retailers, advertising is a basic business tool that is essential to retaining current customers and attracting new customers. We need to understand that advertising functions as a business process in three ways. First, we'll consider the role advertising plays in the overall marketing and brand development programs in firms. Second, we will look at the types of advertising used by firms. Finally, we will take a broader look at advertising by identifying the economic effects of the process.

The Role of Advertising in Marketing.

To truly appreciate advertising as a business process, we have to understand the role advertising plays in a firm's marketing effort. To begin with, realize that every organization *must* make marketing decisions. There simply is no escaping the need to develop brands, price them, distribute them, and advertise and promote them to a target audience. The role of advertising relates to four important aspects of the marketing process: (1) contributing to the marketing mix; (2) developing and managing the brand; (3) achieving effective market segmentation, differentiation, and positioning; and (4) contributing to revenue and profit generation.

The Role of Advertising in the Marketing Mix. A formal definition of marketing reveals that advertising (as a part of overall promotion) is one of the primary marketing tools available to any organization:

> **Marketing** *is the process of planning and executing the conception, pricing, promotion, and distribution of ideas, goods, and services to create exchanges that satisfy individual and organizational objectives.*[16]

Marketing people assume a wide range of responsibilities in an organization related to conceiving, pricing, promoting, and distributing goods, services, and even

15. Joe Miller, "Dealers Regain Ad Input as GM Revives Program," *Advertising Age*, October 16, 2000, 80.

16. This definition of marketing was approved in 1995 by the American Marketing Association (http://www.marketingpower.com) and remains the official definition offered by the organization.

ideas. Many of you know that these four areas of responsibility and decision making in marketing are referred to as the **marketing mix**. The word *mix* is used to describe the blend of strategic emphasis on the product versus its price versus its promotion (including advertising) versus its distribution when a brand is marketed to consumers. This blend, or mix, results in the overall marketing program for a brand. Advertising is important, but it is only *one* of the major areas of marketing responsibility *and* it is only one of many different IBP tools relied on in the marketing mix. Under Armour unleashed "an audacious $25 million campaign" with the slogan "The future is ours!" to introduce its non-cleated shoe line. Under Armour sales in that category did not grow the following year—competition from Nike, Adidas, and Reebok proved too formidable—advertising alone, no matter how "audacious" could not overcome competitors' product features and distribution.[17]

Generally speaking, the role of advertising in the marketing mix is to focus on communicating to a target audience the value a brand has to offer. Value consists of more than simply the tangible aspects of the brand itself. Indeed, consumers look for value in the brand's features, but they also demand such things as convenient location, credit terms, warranties and guarantees, and delivery. In addition, a wide range of emotional values such as security, belonging, affiliation, excitement, and prestige can also be pursued in the brand choice process. If you have any doubts that emotion plays a role, think about the fact that a $16,000 Ford Focus can get you from one place to another in pretty much the same way as a $120,000 BMW M5. Well, maybe without the same thrill and style—but that's the point. People look for more than function in a brand; they often buy the emotional kick that a brand and its features provide. We talk more about this in Chapter 5.

Because consumers search for such diverse values, marketers must determine which marketing mix ingredients to emphasize and how to blend the mix elements in just the right way to attract customers. These marketing mix decisions play a significant role in determining the message content and media placement of advertising.

Exhibit 1.18 lists factors typically considered in each area of the marketing mix. You can see that decisions under each of the marketing mix areas can directly affect the advertising message. The important point is that a firm's advertising effort must be consistent with and complement the overall marketing mix strategy being used by a firm.

The Role of Advertising in Brand Management. One of the key issues to understand about the role of advertising is that it plays a critical role in brand development and management. We have been referring to the brand and integrated brand promotion throughout our discussion of the process of advertising so far. All of us have our own understanding of what a brand is. After all, we buy brands every day. A formal definition of a **brand** is a name, term, sign, symbol, or any other feature that identifies one seller's good or service as distinct from those of other sellers.[18] Advertising plays a significant role in brand development and management. A brand is in many ways the most precious business asset owned by a firm. It allows a firm to communicate consistently and efficiently with the market.

BusinessWeek magazine, in conjunction with Interbrand, a marketing analysis and consulting firm, has attached a dollar value to brand names based on a combination of sales, earnings, future sales potential, and intangibles other than the brand that drive sales. The 20 most valuable brands in the world in 2009 are shown in Exhibit 1.19. Often, the brand name is worth much more than the annual sales of the brand. Coca-Cola, the most valuable brand in the world, is estimated to be worth almost $70 billion even though sales of branded Coca-Cola products are only about $31 billion a year.

17. Jeremy Mullman, "Under Armour Can't Live Up to Own Hype," *Advertising Age*, November 2, 2009, 3, 51.

18. Peter D. Bennett, *Dictionary of Marketing Terms*, 2nd ed. (Chicago: American Marketing Association, 1995), 4.

Exhibit 1.18 These are the factors that an organization needs to consider in creating a marketing mix. Advertising message, media placement, and IBP techniques must be consistent with and complement strategies in all the other areas of the marketing mix.

Product	Promotion
Functional features	Amount and type of advertising
Aesthetic design	Number and qualifications of salespeople
Accompanying services	Extent and type of personal selling program
Instructions for use	Sales promotion—coupons, contests, sweepstakes
Warranty	Trade shows
Product differentiation	Public relations activities
Product positioning	Direct mail or telemarketing
	Event sponsorships
	Internet communications/mobile marketing
Price	**Distribution**
Level:	Number of retail outlets
Top of the line	Location of retail outlets
Competitive, average prices	Types of retail outlets
Low-price policy	Catalog sales
Terms offered:	Other nonstore retail methods—Internet
Cash only	Number and type of wholesalers
Credit:	Inventories—extent and location
Extended	Services provided by distribution:
Restricted	Credit
Interest charges	Delivery
Lease/rental	Installation
	Training

A brand can be put at a serious competitive disadvantage without effective communication provided by advertising. Staples, the office supply retailer, was struggling with an outdated advertising campaign featuring the tagline "Yeah, we've got that." Customers were complaining that items were out of stock and sales staff didn't care. So the company's vice president of marketing, Shira Goodman, determined that shoppers wanted an "easier" shopping experience with well-stocked shelves and helpful staff. Once those operational changes were made, Staples introduced the "Staples: That Was Easy" campaign, featuring big red "Easy" buttons that were also available for sale at the stores. Now, with clear, straightforward ads and customers spreading the word (called "viral" marketing) by having their "Easy" push-buttons in offices all across the country, Staples is the runaway leader in office retail.[19]

For every organization, advertising affects brand development and management in five important ways.

Information and Persuasion. Target audiences learn about a brand's features and benefits through the message content of advertising and, to a lesser extent, other

19. Michael Myser, "Marketing Made Easy," *Business 2.0,* June 2006, 43–45.

2009 Rank	2008 Rank	Brand	Country of Origin	Sector	2009 Brand Value ($m)	Change in Brand Value
1	1	Coca-Cola	United States	Beverages	68,734	3%
2	2	IBM	United States	Computer Services	60,211	2%
3	3	Microsoft	United States	Computer Software	56,647	-4%
4	4	GE	United States	Diversified	47,777	-10%
5	5	NOKIA	Finland	Consumer Electronics	34,864	-3%
6	8	McDonald's	United States	Restaurants	32,275	4%
7	10	Google	United States	Internet Services	31,980	25%
8	6	Toyota	Japan	Automotive	31,330	-8%
9	7	Intel	United States	Computer Hardware	30,636	-2%
10	9	Disney	United States	Media	28,447	-3%
11	12	HP	United States	Computer Hardware	24,096	2%
12	11	Mercedes Benz	Germany	Automotive	23,867	-7%
13	14	Gillette	United States	Personal Care	22,841	4%
14	17	Cisco	United States	Computer Services	22,030	3%
15	13	BMW	Germany	Automotive	21,671	-7%
16	16	Louis Vuitton	France	Luxury	21,120	-2%
17	18	Marlboro	United States	Tobacco	19,010	-11%
18	20	Honda	Japan	Automotive	17,803	-7%
19	21	Samsung	Republic of Korea	Consumer Electronics	17,518	-1%
20	24	Apple	United States	Computer Hardware	15,433	12%

Source: InterBrand (http://www.interbrand.com/best_global_brands.aspx?langid=1000)

Exhibit 1.19 The World's 20 Most Valuable Brands in 2009

promotional tools (most other promotional tools, except the Web, are not heavy on content) that are used in the IBP effort. But advertising has the best capability to inform or persuade target audiences about the values a brand has to offer. No other variable in the marketing mix is designed to accomplish this communication. Analysts agree that branding is crucially important in the multibillion-dollar cell phone market as Verizon, Sprint Nextel, T-Mobile, and AT&T compete for 250 million wireless subscribers.[20] In many ways, marketing and advertising a cellular service brand is much like marketing and advertising brands of bottled water. One cell phone works just like another and there are plenty of alternatives, just like one brand of bottled water is pretty much the same as the next brand.

Introduction of New Brand or Brand Extensions (Variants). Advertising is absolutely critical when organizations introduce a new brand or extensions of existing brands to the market. New brands are often critically dependent on advertising. Consider the case of the new brand Snuggie—that somewhat funny-looking blanket with sleeves. The president of Snuggie used low-budget direct response ads on low ratings cable programs to introduce the brand and now has distribution in

20. Alice Z. Cuneo, "Cell Giants Plot $1.5B Ad Bonanza," *Advertising Age*, October 6, 2003, 1, 44.

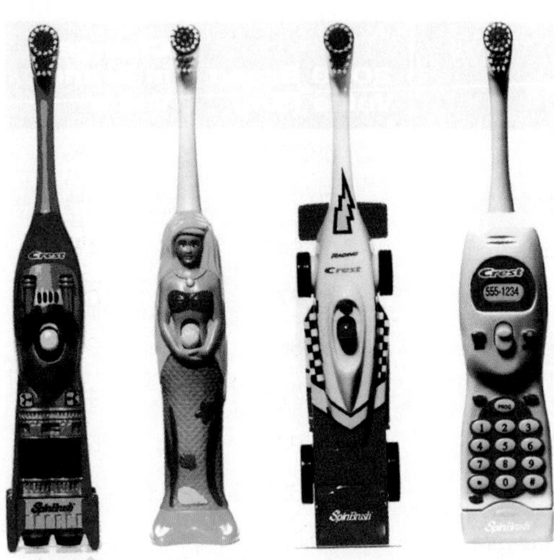

Exhibit 1.20 Advertising helps companies with brand extension strategies. Here, the famous Crest name is being used as the company extends the brand name into toothbrushes. What value does the widely recognized nature of a good brand name lend to the brand extension process?

Lord & Taylor, college book stores, and pet stores.[21] A **brand extension** (also referred to as a brand **variant**) is an adaptation of an existing brand to a new product area. For example, the Snickers Ice Cream Bar is a brand extension of the original Snickers candy bar, and Ivory Shampoo is a brand extension of Ivory Dishwashing Liquid. When brand extensions are brought to market, advertising and IBP play a key role in attracting attention to the brand—so much so that researchers now suggest that "managers should favor the brand extension with a greater allocation of the ad budget.[22] This is often accomplished with advertising working in conjunction with other promotional activities such as sales promotions and point-of-purchase displays. Mars (famous for candy) invested heavily in advertising when it extended the Uncle Ben's Rice brand into ready-to-eat microwave Rice Bowls of all varieties, including Italian, Mexican, and Chinese.[23] Exhibit 1.20 shows another example of advertising being used to extend a famous brand name into a totally different product category.

Building and Maintaining Brand Loyalty among Consumers. Loyalty to a brand is one of the most important assets a firm can have. **Brand loyalty** occurs when a consumer repeatedly purchases the same brand to the exclusion of competitors' brands. This loyalty can result because of habit, because brand names are prominent in the consumer's memory, because of barely conscious associations with brand images, or because consumers have attached some fairly deep meanings to the brands they buy.

Even though brand features are the most important influence on building and maintaining brand loyalty, advertising plays a key role in the process as well. Advertising reminds consumers of the values—tangible and intangible—of the brand. Advertising and integrated brand promotions often provide an extra incentive to consumers to remain brand loyal. Direct marketing can tailor communications to existing customers. Other promotional tools can offer similarly valuable communications that will help build and strengthen lasting and positive associations with a brand—such as a frequent-flyer or frequent-buyer program. The importance of brand loyalty cannot be overstated. When a firm creates and maintains positive associations with the brand in the mind of consumers and builds brand loyalty, then the firm goes on to develop brand equity. **Brand equity** is the set of brand assets linked to a brand, its name and symbol.[24] Even though brand equity occurs over long periods of time, short-term advertising activities are key to long-term success.[25] And, recent research has affirmed that integrated communications is a "critical component of brand equity strategy."[26] This advertising fact of life became clear to strategists at food giant Kraft as it devised a strategy to defend its Kraft Miracle Whip brand against a new campaign by com-

21. Jack Neff, "Snuggie," *Advertising Age*, November 16, 2009, 25.

22. Douglas W. Vorhies, "Brand Extension Helps Parent Gain Influence," *Marketing News*, January 20, 2003, 25. This concept was verified in academic research as well. See Franziska Volckner and Henrik Sattler, "Drivers of Brand Extension Success," *Journal of Marketing*, vol. 70 (April 2006), 18–34.

23. Stephanie Thompson, "The Bowl Is Where It's At for New Frozen Meal Lines," *Advertising Age*, August 14, 2000, 4.

24. David A. Aaker, *Managing Brand Equity* (New York: The Free Press, 1991), 15.

25. Kevin L. Keller, "Conceptualizing, Measuring, and Managing Customer-Based Brand Equity," *Journal of Marketing*, vol. 57 (January 1993), 4.

26. Streedhar Madhavaram, Vishag Badrinarayanan, and Robert E. McDonald, "Intergrated Marketing Communication (IMC) and Brand Identity as Critical Components of Brand Equity Strategy, *Journal of Advertising*, vol. 34, no. 4 (Winter 2005), 69–80.

petitor Unilever for Imperial Whip. In order to protect Miracle Whip's $229 million in sales and brand equity with consumers, Kraft invested heavily in television advertising just before Unilever lowered prices on the Imperial Whip brand.[27]

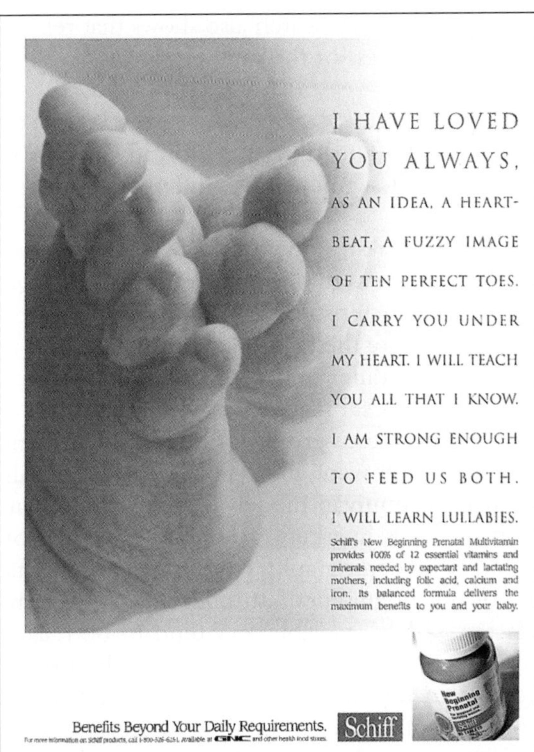

I HAVE LOVED
YOU ALWAYS,
AS AN IDEA, A HEART-
BEAT, A FUZZY IMAGE
OF TEN PERFECT TOES.
I CARRY YOU UNDER
MY HEART. I WILL TEACH
YOU ALL THAT I KNOW.
I AM STRONG ENOUGH
TO FEED US BOTH.
I WILL LEARN LULLABIES.
Schiff's New Beginning Prenatal Multivitamin provides 100% of 12 essential vitamins and minerals needed by expectant and lactating mothers, including folic acid, calcium and iron. Its balanced formula delivers the maximum benefits to you and your baby.
New Beginning Prenatal
Benefits Beyond Your Daily Requirements.
Schiff

Exhibit 1.21 The message in this Schiff ad creates meaning for vitamins that goes beyond the daily nutrition role vitamins can play. What are the many meanings in this message offered to consumers? http://www.schiffvitamins.com

Creating an Image and Meaning for a Brand. As we discussed in the marketing mix section, advertising can communicate how a brand can fulfill needs and desires and therefore plays an important role in attracting customers to brands that appear to be useful and satisfying. But advertising can go further. It can help link a brand's image and meaning to a consumer's social environment and to the larger culture, and in this way, it can actually deliver a sense of personal connection for the consumer.

The Schiff ad for prenatal vitamins in Exhibit 1.21 is a clear example of how advertising can create an image and deeper meaning. The message in this ad is not just about the health advantages of using a nutritional supplement during pregnancy. The message mines associations related to love and caring for an unborn or recently born child. Even the slogan for the brand, "Benefits Beyond Your Daily Requirements," plays on the notion that a vitamin is more than a vehicle for dosing up on folic acid. Other promotional tools in the IBP process, such as personal selling, sales promotions, event sponsorship, or the Internet, simply cannot achieve such creative power or communicate all the potential symbolic meanings a brand can have to a consumer as we will see later in the text (Chapter 11).

Building and Maintaining Brand Loyalty within the Trade. It might not seem as if wholesalers, retailers, distributors, and brokers would be brand loyal, but they will favor one brand over others given the proper support from a manufacturer. Advertising and particularly advertising integrated with other brand promotions is an area where support can be given. Marketers can provide the trade with sales training programs, collateral advertising materials (e.g., brochures, banners, posters), point-of-purchase advertising displays, premiums (giveaways like key chains or caps), Web-traffic building advertising, and foot traffic-building special events. Exide, the battery company, spends several million dollars a year to be the official battery of NASCAR racing. Mike Dever, Exide's vice president of marketing and product management, explains: "Both our distributors and our distributors' customers, for the most part, are race fans, so it's the place we want to be."[28]

Also, remember that trade buyers (retailers, wholesalers, distributors, brokers) can be key to the success of new brands or brand extensions, as we pointed out earlier in the discussion of the trade market as a target audience. Marketers have little hope of successfully introducing a brand if there is no cooperation in the trade channel among wholesalers and retailers. This is where IBP as a factor in advertising becomes prominent. This is because the trade is less responsive to advertising messages than they are to other forms of promotion. Direct support to the trade in terms of displays, contests, increased margins, and personal selling combined with advertising in

27. Stephanie Thompson, "Kraft Counters Unilever Launch," *Advertising Age*, August 25, 2003, 4.

28. Beth Snyder Bulik, "The Company You Keep," *Sales & Marketing Management*, November 2003, 14.

an IBP program helps ensure the success of a brand. Research also shows that retailer acceptance of a brand extension is key to the success of the new product.[29]

The Role of Advertising in Market Segmentation, Differentiation, and Positioning. The third role for advertising in marketing is helping the firm implement market segmentation, differentiation, and positioning.

Market segmentation is the process of breaking down a large, widely varied *(heterogeneous)* market into submarkets, or segments, that are more similar *(homogeneous)* than dissimilar in terms of consumer characteristics that consumers look for. Underlying the strategy of market segmentation are the facts that consumers differ in their wants and that the wants of one person can differ under various circumstances. The market for automobiles can be divided into submarkets for different types of automobiles based on the needs and desires of various groups of buyers. Identifying those groups, or segments, of the population who want and will buy large or small, luxury, economy or hybrid, sport or sedan, or minivan models is an important part of basic marketing strategy. In addition to needs, markets are often segmented on characteristics of consumers both in terms of demographics (such as age, marital status, education, gender, and income) or psychographics (attitudes, beliefs, personality, lifestyle, and values). These data are widely available and tend to be related to product preference and use. Advertising's role in the market segmentation process is to develop messages that appeal to the wants and desires of different segments and then to transmit those messages via appropriate media. For example, Bayer has four different versions of its basic aspirin brand. There is regular Bayer for headache relief; Bayer Enteric Safety Coated 81 mg aspirin for people with cholesterol and heart concerns; Women's Bayer, which includes a calcium supplement; and Children's Bayer, which is lower dose and chewable. Each of these versions of the Bayer brand of aspirin addresses both the needs and characteristics of consumers in the market (see Exhibit 1.22).

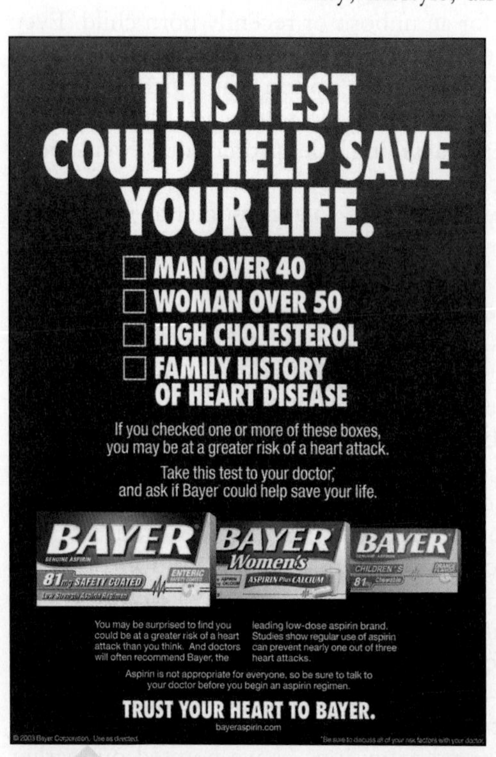

Exhibit 1.22 Advertising plays an important role in helping a firm segment the market based on needs and characteristics of consumers. Along with Bayer's regular aspirin for headache relief, Bayer offers these three additional versions of the brand that address both consumer needs (calcium-fortified aspirin for women) and consumer characteristics (a children's lower-dose aspirin). http://www.bayeraspirin.com

Courtesy of Bayer Health Care LLC, Consumer Care Division

Differentiation is the process of creating a perceived difference, in the mind of the consumer, between an organization's brand and the competition's. Notice that this definition emphasizes that brand differentiation is based on *consumer perception*. The perceived differences can be tangible differences, or they may be based on image or style factors. Consider the Fendi watch ad in Exhibit 1.23. A $20 Timex and a $12,000 Fendi keep time in exactly the same way. But the two brands are differentiated on perceptions of style and the deeper meaning brands can have, as discussed earlier. The critical issue in differentiation is that consumers *perceive* a difference between brands. If consumers do not perceive a difference, then whether real differences exist or not does not matter. Differentiation is one of the most critical of all marketing strategies. If a firm's brand is not perceived as distinctive and attractive by consumers, then consumers will have no reason to choose that brand over one from the competition or to pay higher prices for the "better" or "more meaningful" brand. Think about bottled water (Evian), bananas (Chiquita), or meat (Niman Ranch) where marketers have been able to differentiate their brands with excellent advertising and branding strategies.[30]

29. Franziska Volckner and Henrik Sattler, "Drivers of Brand Extension Success," *Journal of Marketing*, vol. 70 (April 2006), 18–34.

30. Paul Kaihla, "Sexing Up a Piece of Meat," *Business 2.0,* April 2006, 72–76.

Exhibit 1.23 Advertising is key to the marketing strategy of differentiation—creating a perceived difference between the company's brand and competitors' brands. This very expensive Fendi watch keeps time just like a $20 Timex. But you won't see an ad like this for a Timex. What is it about this ad that helps differentiate the Fendi brand from the Timex brand? http://www.fendi.it

Exhibit 1.24 An important role for advertising is to help a firm differentiate its brand from the competition with a distinctive message and presentation. This Hunter Fan ad focuses on the function features of its air purifier line as the basis for differentiation. http://wwww.hunterfan.com

In order for advertising to help create a difference in the mind of the consumer between an organization's brand and its competitors' brands, the ad may emphasize performance features, or it may create a distinctive image for the brand. The essential task for advertising is to develop a message that is different and unmistakably linked to the organization's brand. The ad in Exhibit 1.24 is distinctive and pursues product differentiation in a product category where differentiation is hard to come by.

Positioning is the process of designing a brand so that it can occupy a distinct and valued place in the target consumer's mind relative to other brands and then this distinctiveness is communicated through advertising. Positioning, like differentiation, depends on a perceived image of tangible or intangible features. The importance of positioning can be understood by recognizing that consumers create a *perceptual space* in their minds for all the brands they might consider purchasing. A perceptual space is how one brand is seen on any number of dimensions—such as quality, taste, price, or social display value—in relation to those same dimensions in other brands. Firms are turning to a wider variety of advertising and IBP combinations to achieve effective position.

There are really two positioning decisions. A firm must decide on the **external position** for a brand—that is, the niche the brand will pursue relative to all the competitive brands on the market. Additionally, an **internal position** must be achieved with regard to the other similar brands the firm itself markets. With the external-positioning decision, a firm tries to create a distinctive *competitive* position based on design features, pricing, distribution, or promotion or advertising strategy.

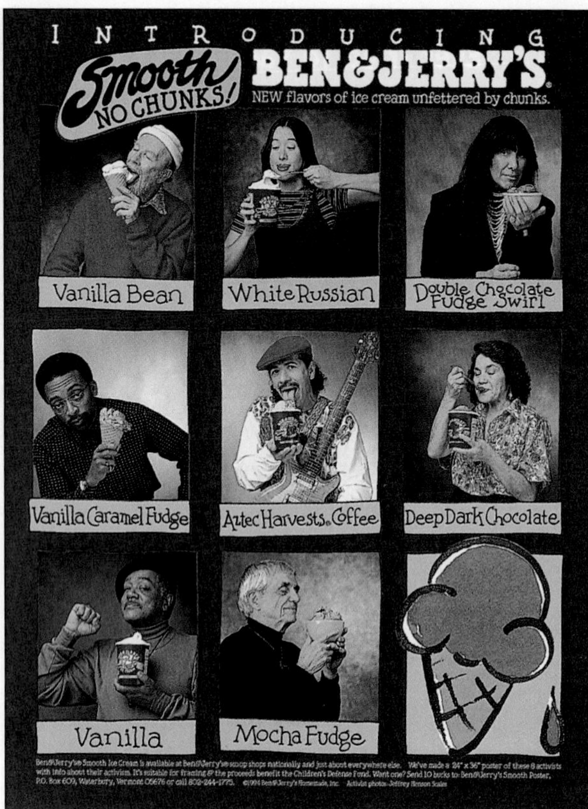

Exhibit 1.25 Firms with multiple brands in a single product category have to internally position these brands to differentiate them from each other in the minds of consumers. Ben & Jerry's achieves its product positioning by emphasizing the distinctly different flower of each of its ice creams. http://www.benjerry.com

Some brands are positioned at the very top of their competitive product category, such as BMW's 550i, priced around $100,000. Other brands seek a position at the low end of all market offerings, such as the Chevrolet Cobalt, with a base price of about $15,000.

Effective internal positioning is accomplished by either developing vastly different products *within* the firm's own product line (Ben & Jerry's ice cream, for example, offers plenty of distinctive flavors, as shown in Exhibit 1.25) or creating advertising messages that appeal to different consumer needs and desires. Procter & Gamble successfully positions its many laundry detergent brands both internally and externally using a combination of product design and effective advertising. Although some of these brands assume different positions within P&G's line due to substantive differences (a liquid soap versus a powder soap, for example), others with minor differences achieve distinctive positioning through advertising. One P&G brand is advertised as being effective on kids' dirty clothes, whereas another brand is portrayed as effective for preventing colors from running. In this way, advertising helps create a distinctive position, both internally and externally.

The methods and strategic options available to an organization with respect to market segmentation, product differentiation, and positioning will be fully discussed in Chapter 6. For now, realize that advertising plays an important role in helping an organization put these most basic marketing strategies into operation.

The Role of Advertising in Contributing to Revenue and Profit Generation. There are many who believe that the fundamental purpose of marketing (and the advertising that is used in marketing) can be stated quite simply: to generate revenue. Marketing is the only part of an organization that has revenue generation as its primary purpose. In the words of highly regarded management consultant and scholar Peter Drucker, "Marketing and innovation produce results: all the rest are 'costs.'"[31] The "results" Drucker refers to are revenues. The marketing process is designed to generate sales and therefore revenues for the firm.

Helping create sales as part of the revenue-generating process is where advertising plays a significant role. As we have seen, advertising communicates persuasive information to audiences based on the values created in the marketing mix related to the product, its price, or its distribution. This advertising communication then highlights brand features—price, emotion, or availability—and then attracts a target market. In this way, advertising makes a direct contribution to the marketing goal of revenue generation. Notice that advertising *contributes* to the process of creating sales and revenue. It cannot be solely responsible for creating sales and revenue—it's not that powerful. Some organizations mistakenly see advertising as a panacea—the salvation for an ambiguous or ineffective overall marketing mix strategy. Advertising alone cannot be held responsible for sales—period. Sales occur when a brand has a well-conceived and complete marketing mix—including good advertising.

31. Peter F. Drucker, *People and Performance: The Best of Peter Drucker* (New York: HarperCollins, 1997), 90.

The effect of advertising on profits is a bit more involved and complicated. Its effect on profits comes about when advertising gives an organization greater flexibility in the price it charges for a product or service. Advertising can help create pricing flexibility by (1) contributing to economies of scale and (2) helping create inelasticity (insensitivity) of demand to price changes. When an organization creates large-scale demand for its brand, the quantity of product produced is increased, and **economies of scale** lead to lower unit production costs. Cost of production decreases because fixed costs (such as rent and equipment costs) are spread over a greater number of units produced.

How does advertising play a role in helping create economies of scale? When Colgate manufactures hundreds of thousands of tubes of its Colgate Total toothpaste and ships them in large quantities to warehouses, the fixed costs of production and shipping per unit are greatly reduced. With lower fixed costs per unit, Colgate can realize greater profits on each tube of toothpaste sold. Advertising contributes to demand stimulation by communicating to the market about the features and availability of a brand. By contributing to demand stimulation, advertising then contributes to the process of creating these economies of scale, which ultimately translates into higher profits per unit for the organization.

Remember the concept of brand loyalty we discussed earlier? Well, brand loyalty and advertising work together to create another important economic effect related to pricing flexibility and profits. When consumers are brand loyal, they are generally less sensitive to price increases for the brand. In economic terms, this is known as **inelasticity of demand**. When consumers are less price sensitive, firms have the flexibility to maintain higher prices and increase profit margins. Advertising contributes directly to brand loyalty, and thus to inelasticity of demand, by persuading and reminding consumers of the satisfactions and values related to a brand.

These arguments related to the positive business effects of advertising were recently supported by a large research study. The study found that companies who build strong brands and raise prices are more profitable than companies who cut costs as a way to increase profits—by nearly twice the profit percentage. This research is supported by such real-world examples as Louis Vuitton. The maker of luxury handbags ($1,000 per bag or more) and other luxury items enjoys an operating margin of 45 percent.[32]

Types of Advertising.

So far, we've discussed advertising in a lot of different ways, from its most basic definition through how it can help an organization stimulate demand and generate profits. But to truly understand advertising, we need to go back to some very basic typologies that categorize advertising according to fundamental approaches to communication. Until you understand these aspects of advertising, you really don't understand advertising at all.

Primary versus Selective Demand Stimulation. In **primary demand stimulation**, a company would be trying to create demand for an entire *product category*. Primary demand stimulation is challenging and costly, and research evidence suggests that it is likely to have an impact only for totally new products on the market—not brand extensions or product categories that have been around a long time (known as mature products). An example of effective primary demand stimulation was the introduction of the VCR to the consumer market in the 1970s. With a product that is totally new to the market, consumers need to be convinced that the product category itself is valuable and that it is, indeed, available for sale.

32. The research study is reported in Robert G. Docters, Michael R. Reopel, Jeanne-Mey Sun, and Stephen M. Tanney, *Winning the Profit Game: Smarter Pricing, Smarter Branding* (New York: McGraw-Hill, 2004); Information on Louis Vuitton was taken from Carol Matlack et al., "The Vuitton Machine," *BusinessWeek*, March 22, 2004, 98–102.

Exhibit 1.26 When new, innovative products are first introduced to the market, a type of advertising called primary demand stimulation is often used. Primary demand stimulation attempts to stimulate demand for the entire product category by educating consumers about the values of the product itself, rather than the values of a brand within the product category. This ad from the early days of the VHS video cassette recorder is a classic example of primary demand stimulation in a new, innovative product category.

Exhibit 1.27 Advertising that attempts to stimulate primary demand is often tried by industry associations and advocacy groups, such as the National Fluid Milk Processor Promotion Board, rather than by specific manufacturers. Trouble is, it doesn't work. Primary demand stimulation has been shown to be ineffective in mature product categories, such as milk, but rather is appropriate for products totally new to the market like PDAs or MP3 players. http://www.gotmilk.com and http://www.elsie.com

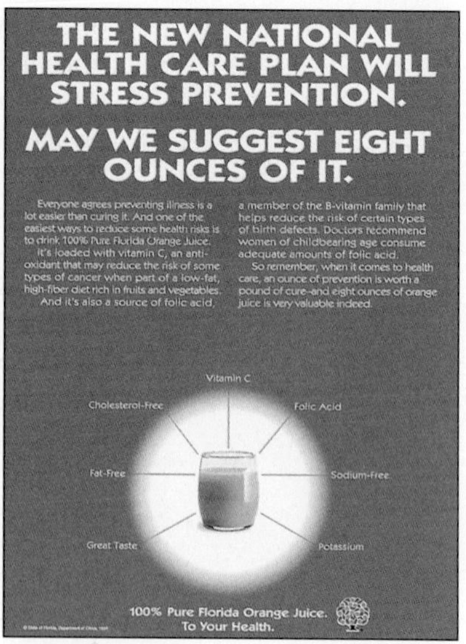

Exhibit 1.28 This ad promoting orange juice also attempts to stimulate primary demand, or demand for a product category rather than demand for a particular brand. Decades of literature demonstrate no relationship between aggregate levels of advertising in an industry and overall demand in an industry. It appears that advertising is indeed suited only to selective (brand) demand stimulation. http://www.floridajuice.com

When the VCR was first introduced in the United States, RCA, Panasonic, and Quasar (see Exhibit 1.26) ran primary demand stimulation advertising to explain to household consumers the value and convenience of taping television programs with this new product called a VHS video recorder—something no one had ever done before at home.

For organizations that have tried to stimulate primary demand in mature product categories, typically trade associations, the results have been dismal. Both the National Fluid Milk Processor Promotion Board and the Florida Department of Citrus have tried to use advertising to stimulate primary demand for the entire product categories of milk and orange juice. Examples of these campaigns are shown in Exhibits 1.27 and 1.28. Even though the "mustache" campaign is popular and wins awards, milk consumption has *declined* every year during the time of this campaign.[33] This is despite the fact that more than $1.1 billion dollars in advertising have been invested in the campaign. Even if it is argued that the attempts at primary demand stimulation have reduced the overall decline in milk consumption (which can't be determined), this is still not a very impressive result. This should come as no surprise, though. Research over decades has clearly indicated that attempts at primary demand stimulation in mature product categories (orange juice, beef, pork, and almonds have also been tried) *have never* been successful.[34]

33. "Got Results?" *Marketing News*, March 2, 1998, 1; Current data obtained from ProCon.org, http://milk.procon.org/viewresource.asp?resourceID=660#Introduction, accessed on February 15, 2010.

34. For excellent summaries of decades of research on the topic of primary demand stimulation, see Mark S. Abion and Paul W. Farris, *The Advertising Controversy: Evidence of the Economic Effects of Advertising* (Boston: Auburn House, 1981); and J. C. Luik and M. S. Waterson, *Advertising and Markets* (Oxfordshire, England: NTC Publications, 1996).

Exhibit 1.29 Selective demand stimulation advertising highlights a brand's superiority in providing satisfaction. In this ad, Tropicana touts its superiority as a brand of orange juice with very specific brand features. Compare this ad to the primary demand ad in Exhibit 1.28. http://www.tropicana.com

Although some corporations have tried primary demand stimulation, the true power of advertising is realized when it functions to stimulate demand for a particular company's brand—which is what has been described throughout this chapter. This is known as selective demand stimulation. The purpose of **selective demand stimulation** advertising is to point out a brand's unique benefits compared to the competition. For example, compare the Tropicana ad in Exhibit 1.29 touting the brand's superiority with the primary demand stimulation ad for orange juice in Exhibit 1.28.

Direct versus Delayed Response Advertising. Another important type of advertising involves how quickly we want consumers to respond. **Direct response advertising** asks consumers to act immediately. All those ads you see that suggests you "call this toll-free number" or "mail your $19.95 before midnight tonight" are examples of direct response advertising. In many cases, direct response advertising is used for products that consumers are familiar with, that do not require inspection at the point of purchase, and that are relatively low-cost. However, the proliferation of toll-free numbers, websites that provide detailed information, and the widespread use of credit cards have been a boon to direct response for higher priced products as well, as Exhibit 1.30 demonstrates.

Delayed response advertising relies on imagery and message themes that emphasize the benefits and satisfying characteristics of a brand. Rather than trying to stimulate an immediate action from an audience, delayed response advertising attempts to develop awareness and preference for a brand over time. In general, delayed response advertising attempts to create brand awareness, reinforce the benefits of using a brand (i.e., brand loyalty), develop a general liking for the brand, and create an image for a brand. When a consumer enters the purchase process, the information from delayed response advertising comes into play. Most advertisements we see on television and in magazines are of the delayed response type. Exhibit 1.31, an ad for hypoallergenic detergent, provides an example of this common form of advertising. In this ad, the message has as much to do with being a good parent (an image and delayed response-type message) as with the actual performance features of the brand.

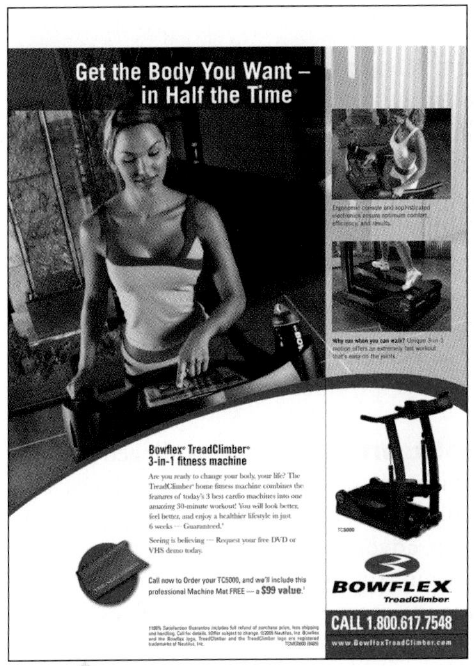

Exhibit 1.30 Direct response advertising asks consumers to take some immediate action. Notice in this ad for Bowflex that advertising copy implores consumers to call the toll-free number or visit the website for a free DVD or to place an order—calling for a direct response by consumers.

Corporate versus Brand Advertising. Corporate advertising is not designed to promote a specific brand but is meant to create a favorable attitude toward a company as a whole. Prominent users of corporate advertising include Apple, BP, and General Electric ("Imagination at Work"). As an example, Philips, the Dutch electronics and medical device conglomerate, turned to corporate advertising to unify the image of its brand name across a wide range of superior vtechnologies.[35] **Brand advertising**, as we have seen throughout this chapter, communicates the specific features, values, and benefits of a particular brand offered for sale by a particular organization. By contrast, the firms that have long-established corporate campaigns have designed them to generate favorable public opinion toward the corporation as a whole. This type of advertising can also have an effect on the shareholders of a firm. When shareholders see good corporate

35. Kerry Capell, "How Philips Got Brand Buzz," BusinessWeek.com, July 31, 2006, accessed at http://yahoo.businessweek.com on August 1, 2006.

all
YOU'LL FEEL IS THE CLEAN.
HYPO-ALLERGENIC.
NO IRRITATION.
"all" free clear's dermatologist-tested formula has none of the perfumes or dyes that can irritate your family's sensitive skin. And with the stain-lifting power of "all," you don't have to compromise on a bit of clean.
It's all the clean sensitive skin needs.
all
free clear

Exhibit 1.31 Delayed response advertising attempts to reinforce the benefits of using a brand and create a general liking for the brand. This ad for ALL detergent is an example of delayed response advertising. It builds an image for the brand rather than asking consumers to take action, like the Bowflex ad in Exhibit 1.30.

advertising, it instills confidence and, ultimately, long-term commitment to the firm and its stock. We'll consider this type of advertising in great detail in Chapter 18.

Another form of corporate advertising is carried out by members of a trade channel, mostly retailers. When corporate advertising takes place in a trade channel, it is referred to as **institutional advertising**. Retailers such as Nordstrom, The Home Depot, and Walmart advertise to persuade consumers to shop at their stores. Although these retailers may occasionally feature a particular manufacturer's brand in the advertising (Nordstrom features Clinique cosmetics), the main purpose of the advertising is to get the audience to shop at their store. Federated Department Stores, for example, invested $387 million to promote its national brand stores, Macy's and Bloomingdale's. The thrust of Federated's brand strategy comes from marketing research findings that show their target audience "considers shopping an enjoyable activity."[36]

The Economic Effects of Advertising.

Our discussion of advertising as a business process so far has focused strictly on the use of advertising by individual business organizations. But you cannot *truly* understand advertising unless you know something about how advertising has effects across the entire economic system of a country—the macro effects. (This isn't the most fun you'll have reading this book, but it is one of the most important topics.)

Advertising's Effect on Gross Domestic Product. Gross domestic product (GDP) is the measure of the total value of goods and services produced within an economic system. Earlier, we discussed advertising's role in the marketing mix. Recall that as advertising contributes to marketing mix strategy, it can contribute to sales along with the right product, the right price, and the right distribution. Because of this role, advertising is related to GDP in that it can contribute to levels of overall consumer demand when it helps introduce new products, such as DVRs, smartphones, or alternative energy sources. As demand for these new products grows, the resultant consumer spending fuels retail sales, housing starts, and corporate investment in finished goods and capital equipment. Consequently, GDP is affected by sales of products in new, innovative product categories.[37]

Advertising's Effect on Competition. Advertising is alleged to stimulate competition and therefore motivate firms to strive for better products, better production methods, and other competitive advantages that ultimately benefit the economy as a whole. Additionally, when advertising serves as a way to enter new markets, competition across the economic system is fostered. For example, Exhibit 1.32 shows an ad in which plastics manufacturers present themselves as competitors to manufacturers of other packaging materials.

Advertising is not universally hailed as a stimulant to competition. Critics point out that the amount of advertising dollars needed to compete effectively in many industries is often prohibitive. As such, advertising can act as a barrier to entry into an industry; that is, a firm may have the capability to compete in an industry in

36. Mercedes M. Cardona, "Federated Focuses Campaign on Macy's," *Advertising Age*, December 8, 2003, 6.

37. There are several highly sophisticated historical treatments of how advertising is related to demand and overall GDP. See, for example, Neil H. Borden, *The Economic Effects of Advertising* (Chicago: Richard D. Irwin, 1942), 187–189; and John Kenneth Galbraith, *The New Industrial State* (Boston: Houghton Mifflin, 1967), 203–207.

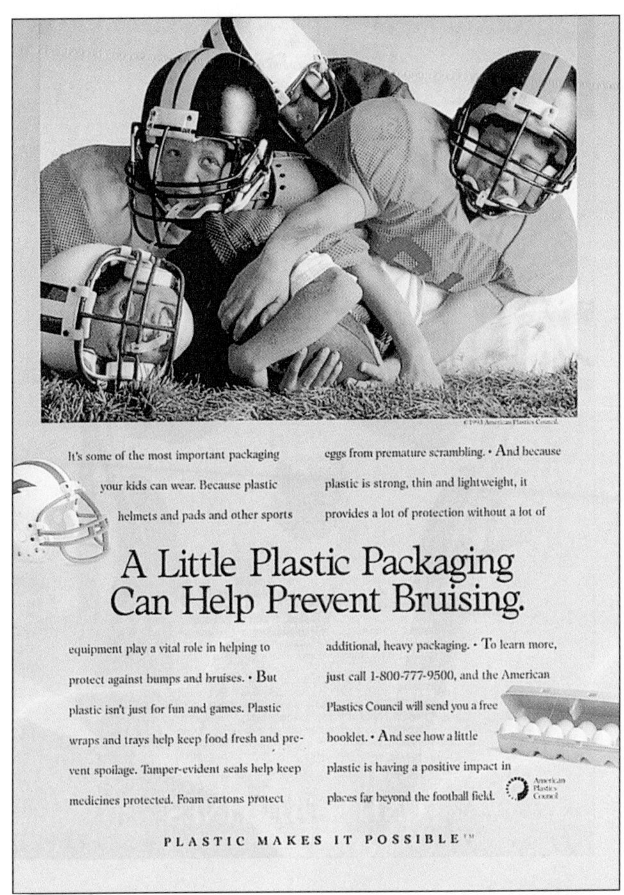

Exhibit 1.32
Advertising affects the competitive environment in an economy. This ad by a plastics manufacturers' council is fostering competition with manufacturers of other packaging materials. http://www.americanchemistry.com/plastics

every way *except* that the advertising dollars needed to compete are so great that the firm cannot afford to get into the business. In this way, advertising is argued to decrease the overall amount of competition in an economy.[38]

Advertising's Effect on Prices. One of the widely debated effects of advertising has to do with its effect on the prices consumers pay for products and services. Since we have seen that firms spend millions or even billions of dollars on advertising, products and services would cost much less if firms did no advertising. Right? Wrong!

First, across all industries, advertising costs incurred by firms range from about 2 percent of sales in the automobile and retail industries up to 30 percent of sales in the personal care and luxury products businesses. One important fact to realize is there is no consistent and predictable relationship between advertising spending and sales—it all depends on the product category—competition, size of market, and complexity of the message. In 2009, Honda spent about $1.2 billion in advertising to generate about $90 billion in sales or about 1.3 percent of sales; L'Oréal spent more than Honda on advertising ($1.6 billion) but generated only about $6 billion in sales, making ad spending about 26 percent of sales; and Walmart also spent $1.6 billion on advertising but generated a whopping $404 billion in sales making ad spending a puny three-tenths of 1 percent of sales![39] Different products and different market conditions demand that firms spend different amounts of money on advertising. These same conditions make it difficult to identify a predictable relationship between advertising and sales.

It is true that the cost of advertising is built into product costs, which may be ultimately passed on to consumers. But this effect on price must be judged against a couple of cost savings that lower the price. First, there is the reduced time and effort a consumer has to spend in searching for a product or service. Second, economies of scale, discussed earlier, have a direct impact on cost and then on prices. Recall that economies of scale serve to lower the cost of production by spreading fixed costs over a large number of units produced. This lower cost can be passed on to consumers in terms of lower prices, as firms search for competitive advantage with lower prices. Nowhere is this effect more dramatic than the price and performance of personal computers. In the early 1980s, an Apple IIe computer that ran at about 1 MHz and had 64K of total memory cost more than $3,000. Today, a Dell computer that has multiple times more power, speed, and memory costs about $800.

Advertising's Effect on Value. *Value* is the password for successful marketing. **Value**, in modern marketing and advertising, refers to a perception by consumers that a brand provides satisfaction beyond the cost incurred to obtain that brand. The value perspective of the modern consumer is based on wanting every purchase to be a "good deal." Value can be added to the consumption experience

38. This fundamental argument about the effect of advertising on competition was identified and well articulated many years ago by Colston E. Warn, "Advertising: A Critic's View," *Journal of Marketing*, vol. 26, no. 4 (October 1962), 12.

39. "100 Leading National Advertisers," *Advertising Age*, June 22, 2009, 5–14.

Exhibit 1.33 Advertising contributes to the symbolic value that brands have for consumers. What is it about this ad for Ray-Ban sunglasses that contributes to the symbolic value of this brand? http://www.ray-ban.com

Exhibit 1.34 Ads communicate social meaning to consumers, as a product or service carries meaning in a societal context beyond its use or purpose. This ad for United Airlines puts the company's service into such a context. http://www.ual.com

by advertising. Consider the effect of branding on bottled water. Advertising helps create enough value in the minds of consumers that they (we) will *pay* for water that comes free out of the tap.

Advertising also affects a consumer's perception of value by contributing to the symbolic value and the social meaning of a brand. **Symbolic value** refers to what a product or service means to consumers in a nonliteral way. For example, branded clothing such as Guess? jeans or Doc Martens shoes can symbolize self-concept for some consumers. Exhibit 1.33 shows an ad that seeks to create symbolic value for Ray-Ban sunglasses. In reality, all branded products rely to some extent on symbolic value; otherwise they would not be brands but just unmarked commodities (like potatoes).

Social meaning refers to what a product or service means in a societal context. For example, social class is marked by any number of products, such as cars, beverages, and clothes that are used and displayed to signify class membership. Exhibit 1.34 shows an ad for a service with clear social-class connections—note the references to wealth, leisure, and expensive vacation options. Often, the brand's connection to a social class values addresses a need within consumers to move up in class.

Researchers from various disciplines have long argued that objects (brands included) are never just objects. They take on meaning from culture, society, and consumers.[40] It is important to remember that these meanings often become just as

40. For a historical perspective on culture, consumers, and the meaning of goods, see Ernest Ditcher, *Handbook of Consumer Motivations* (New York: McGraw-Hill, 1964), 6. For a contemporary view, see David Glen Mick and Claus Buhl, "A Meaning-Based Model of Advertising Experiences," *Journal of Consumer Research*, vol. 19 (December 1992), 312–338.

Exhibits 1.35 and 1.36 Waterford crystal and Gucci watches are two advertised products that consumers will pay premium prices to own. Both products have value in that they epitomize the highest levels of quality craftsmanship. Such craftsmanship, in itself, may not be enough to command premium prices in the marketplace. Advertising that creates an image of exclusivity may also be needed. In what way does the Gucci site (http://www.gucci.com) contribute directly to consumers' perceptions of a brand's value? Compare this site with Waterford's site (http://www.waterford.com) and determine which communicates its brand's social meaning more effectively.

much a part of the brand as the physical features. Because advertising is an essential way in which the image of a brand is developed, it contributes directly to consumers' perception of the value of the brand. The more value consumers see in a brand, the more they are willing to pay to acquire the brand. If the image of a Gucci watch, a Nissan coupe, or a Four Seasons hotel is valued by consumers, then consumers will pay a premium to acquire that value. Waterford crystal and Gucci watches, shown in Exhibits 1.35 and 1.36, are examples of brands that consumers pay a premium to own and signal meaning about who they are.

5 From Advertising to Integrated Marketing Communications to Integrated Brand Promotion.

As we discussed at the beginning of your introduction to the world of advertising and IBP, it is important to recognize that advertising is only one of many promotional tools available to impress and persuade consumers. There is another distinction that is important for you to recognize as you embark on learning about advertising and IBP.

Beginning in about 1990, the concept of mixing various promotional tools was referred to as **integrated marketing communications (IMC)**. But as the discussions throughout this chapter have highlighted, the reality of promotional strategies in the 21st century demands that the emphasis on *communication* give way to an emphasis on the *brand.* Organizations of all types are not interested in merely communicating with potential and existing customers through advertising and promotion. They want to build brand awareness, identity, and preference through advertising and promotion.

Recall from the definition earlier in the chapter that integrated brand promotion (IBP) is the use of various communication tools, including advertising, in a coordinated manner to build and maintain brand awareness, identity, and preference. The distinction between IBP and IMC is pretty obvious. IMC emphasizes the communication effort, per se, and the need for coordinated and synergistic messages. IBP retains the emphasis on coordination and synergy of communication but goes beyond the parameters of IMC. In IBP, the emphasis is on the brand and not just the communication. With a focus on building brand awareness, identity, and ultimately preference, the IBP perspective recognizes that coordinated promotional messages need to have brand-building effects in addition to the communication effects. Recent research and publications on IMC are now quickly recognizing the central role of the brand in communications.[41]

Summary

1 Know what advertising and integrated brand promotion (IBP) are and what they can do.

Since advertising has become so pervasive, it would be reasonable to expect that you might have your own working definition for this critical term. But an informed perspective on advertising goes beyond what is obvious and can be seen on a daily basis. Advertising is distinctive and recognizable as a form of communication by its three essential elements: its paid sponsorship, its use of mass media, and its intent to persuade. An advertisement is a specific message that a company has placed to persuade an audience. An advertising campaign is a series of ads and other promotional efforts with a common theme also placed to persuade an audience over a specified period of time. Integrated brand promotion (IBP) is the use of many promotional tools, including advertising, in a coordinated manner to build and maintain brand awareness, identity, and preference.

2 Discuss a basic model of communication.

Advertising cannot be effective unless some form of communication takes place between the company and the audience. But advertising is about mass communication. There are many models that might be used to help explain how advertising works or does not work as a communication platform. The model introduced in this chapter features basic considerations such as the message-production process versus the message-reception process, and this model says that consumers create their own meanings when they interpret advertisements .

3 Describe the different ways of classifying audiences for advertising and IBP.

Although it is possible to provide a simple and clear definition of what advertising is, it is also true that

41. A special issue of the *Journal of Advertising* (vol. 34, no. 4, Winter 2005) featuring research and perspectives on IMC contains several articles that focus on the brand promotion aspects of IMC.

advertising takes many forms and serves different purposes from one application to another. One way to appreciate the complexity and diversity of advertising is to classify it by audience category or by geographic focus. For example, advertising might be directed at households or government officials. Using another perspective, it can be global or local in its focus.

4 Explain the key role of advertising and IBP business processes.

Many different types of organizations use advertising to achieve their business purposes. For major multinational corporations, such as Procter & Gamble, and for smaller, more localized businesses, such as the San Diego Zoo, advertising is one part of a critical business process known as marketing. Advertising is one element of the marketing mix; the other key elements are the firm's products, their prices, and the distribution network. Advertising must work in conjunction with these other marketing mix elements if the organization's marketing objectives are to be achieved. It is important to recognize that of all the roles played by advertising in the marketing process, none is more important than contributing to building brand awareness and brand equity.

Similarly, firms have turned to more diverse methods of communication beyond advertising that we have referred to as integrated brand promotion. That is, firms are using communication tools such as public relations, sponsorship, direct marketing, and sales promotion along with advertising to achieve communication goals.

Understand the concept of integrated brand promotion (IBP) and the role advertising plays in the process.

Integrated brand promotion (IBP) is the use of various promotional tools like event sponsorship, the Internet, public relations, and personal selling, along with advertising, in a coordinated manner to build and maintain brand awareness, identity, and preference. When marketers use advertising in conjunction with other promotional tools, they create an integrated brand promotion that highlights brand features and value. Note that the word *coordinated* is central to this definition. During the past 30 years, the advertising industry has evolved to recognize that integration and coordination of promotional elements is key to effective communication and lasting brand identity.

Key Terms

mobile marketing
advertising
client, or sponsor
integrated brand promotion (IBP)
advertisement
advertising campaign
audience
target audience
household consumers
members of business organizations
members of a trade channel
professionals
trade journals
government officials and employees
global advertising
international advertising
national advertising
regional advertising
local advertising
cooperative advertising, or co-op advertising
marketing
marketing mix
brand
brand extension (variant)
brand loyalty
brand equity
market segmentation
differentiation
positioning
external position
internal position
economies of scale
inelasticity of demand
primary demand stimulation
selective demand stimulation
direct response advertising
delayed response advertising
corporate advertising
brand advertising
institutional advertising
gross domestic product (GDP)
value
symbolic value
social meaning
integrated marketing communications (IMC)

Questions

1. As consumers exercise greater individual control over when and how they receive information, how are advertisers adapting their messages? What is the role, if any, for traditional media options in this new environment? Will mobile marketing efforts, including directing advertising to smartphones, be accepted by consumers?

2. What does it mean when we say that advertising is intended to persuade? How do different ads persuade in different ways?

3. Explain the differences between regional advertising, local advertising, and cooperative advertising. What would you look for in an ad to identify it as a cooperative ad?

4. How do the goals of direct response and delayed response advertising differ? How would you explain marketers' growing interest in direct response advertising?

5. Differentiate between global advertising and international advertising. Do you think consumers in foreign markets will react favorably to GM's new pop band-fueled Cadillac commercials, as do American consumers? Why or why not?

6. How does advertising affect brand management and development? If building brand loyalty is one goal, can you identify several examples of businesses that have successfully used advertising campaigns to create strong brand equity?

7. If a firm developed a new line of athletic shoes, priced them competitively, and distributed them in appropriate retail shops, would there be any need for advertising? Is advertising really needed for a good product that is priced right?

8. Many companies now spend millions of dollars to sponsor and associate their names with events such as NASCAR races or rock concerts. Do these event sponsorships fit the definition for advertising and IBP given in this chapter?

9. How does the process of market segmentation lead an organization to spend its advertising dollars more efficiently and more effectively?

10. What is the concept of integrated brand promotion (IBP)? How are IBP and advertising related? And how is IBP distinct from the advertising industry's prior emphasis on integrated marketing communications, or IMC?

Experiential Exercises

1. Box-office sensations like *Avatar, Harry Potter and the Deathly Hallows,* and *Spider-Man 3* don't happen by accident. To achieve big screen success, movie advertisers develop integrated brand promotion (IBP) campaigns that communicate unified messages to target audiences using diverse media. Select a film now showing in theaters and identify the various ways the movie is being promoted. What types of advertising and promotion are employed in the campaign? Do the different advertisements have a consistent look, feel, and message? Do the different media vehicles target different demographic groups? Suggest one additional media option that marketers might use to reach the film's target audience.

2. After perfecting the pizza delivery model in the 1980s, Domino's lost touch with its customers to the point that the brand was ridiculed as little more than cardboard and ketchup. To fix the brand, executives commissioned a reinvention of the Domino's pizza and launched a "Pizza Turnaround" campaign to renew customer loyalties. Using the Internet for research, write a brief report on the Domino's "Pizza Turnaround." Describe the campaign's role in managing the Domino's brand. What was the message strategy of the campaign? Do you think the ads were effective at restoring the brand's image? How might company leaders use the tools of advertising and promotion to keep consumers buying the new and improved Domino's pizza?

3. Cell phones and wireless computing products are nearly ubiquitous now in American life. In some ways, any one phone or service provider is seen not so much as a brand but as an unmarked commodity. But there are important exceptions. Consider the intense media attention and consumer interest that surrounded the release of Apple's iPhone. Providing examples from current ad campaigns, describe how advertising has affected *value* related to cellular services or products. Contrast that with the latest iPhone release. How did advertising and integrated brand promotion influence *symbolic value* and *social meaning* related to the new product?

4. Working in small groups, imagine that you have been hired to create an advertising strategy for the release of a new line of running shoes produced by the athletic apparel maker Under Armour. The Maryland-based company has seen rapid growth in recent years and is a globally recognized rival to Nike and Adidas. Beyond the central advertising campaign for the new shoe line, what tools would your team employ to achieve integrated brand promotion? Explain how you would coordinate your efforts to ensure maximum effectiveness.

Chapter 2

The Global Structure of the Advertising and Promotion Industry: Advertisers, Agencies, Media, and Support Organizations

After reading and thinking about this chapter, you will be able to do the following:

1. Discuss important trends transforming the advertising and promotion industry.
2. Describe the advertising and promotion industry's size, structure, and participants; analyze the differences between the advertising industries in Europe and the United States; and analyze the idiosyncratic conditions in Central and Eastern Europe.
3. Discuss the role that advertising and promotion agencies play, the services these agencies provide, and the way the agencies are compensated. Explain why advertisers and media agencies may need a high level of cultural competence and how the advertising industry can contribute to the development of a region. Also assess the benefits of newly developing agencies that focus on ethnic groups.
4. Identify key external facilitators who assist in planning and executing advertising and integrated brand promotion campaigns.
5. Discuss the role played by media organizations in executing effective advertising and integrated brand promotion campaigns.

BOLD TASTE BOLD SOUNDS

LIMITED TIME OFFER

FREE MUSIC DOWNLOAD

DETAILS INSIDE

GOOD EARTH®

CAFFEINE FREE

ORIGINAL™

A Natural
Source of Antioxidants

Sweet & Spicy™ Herbal Tea

18 WRAPPED TEA BAGS

NET WT. 1.43 OZ (41g)

PR NewsFoto/Good Earth

Introductory Scenario: The Great Digital Divide.

There have always been power struggles in the advertising and promotion industry: brand versus brand; one agency against another agency; agency versus media company; big advertiser with a lot of money versus big retailer with a lot of money. But those old-style power struggles were child's play compared with the 21st-century power struggle going on now. Estimates put the number of ads the average consumer encounters in a single day at somewhere between 1,000 and 5,000![1] Guess what? Consumers are tired of the barrage of ads and are looking for ways to avoid most of them. So, the big power struggle now is about how the advertising industry can successfully adapt to the new technologies that consumers are willing and, in many cases, eager to use as they seek more control over their information environment.

Stated more directly, how can the ad industry overcome the fact that no one is eager to have a 30-second television ad interrupt a television program he or she is enjoying? The solution, in part, seems to be that advertisers will start the "digital divide." That is, advertisers will divide their total spending into more digital media—Web advertising, social media, and mobile marketing—and away from traditional mass media like television, newspapers, magazines, and radio.

The reason for the digital divide is that consumers, who have been the target of advertising and promotion for decades, are discovering digital technologies and media options that give them more control over the communications they see and hear. From Facebook to Twitter to millions of individual blogs and specialty websites, consumers are seeking out information environments, digital information access, where *they* control their exposure to information rather than an advertiser or a media company being in control. The effects are widespread. Advertising in traditional media plunged by nearly 15 percent in 2009, with 77 percent of advertisers surveyed saying they would shift more than 70 percent of their savings from traditional media to digital alternatives—social network media and online advertising.[2]

We are all living the new technology reality—but how did it use to work? The old system worked like this: An advertiser, like Nike or Hewlett-Packard, would work with an advertising agency, like Leo Burnett and Omnicom, and think of really creative television, radio, newspaper, magazine, or billboard ads. Then, the advertiser and its agency would work with a media company, like NBC television or Hearst newspapers, and buy time or space to place the ad so that you, as the consumer, would see it when you watched television or read your morning newspaper.

Don't get us wrong, this still happens—a lot. Major media like television, radio, and magazines still rake in about $450 billion worldwide a year, and individual media companies like Hearst Corp. generate several billion dollars annually in revenue.[3] But much has changed about the way advertisers, agencies, and media companies are trying to reach control-seeking consumers. And some very smart people think that we are heading into a totally new age with the industry on the cusp of even more dramatic changes.[4] As Michael Mendenhall, chief marketing officer at Hewlett-Packard put it, "Marketers want to move from interruptive to engagement. They can do that more effectively in the digital space."[5]

1. Matthew Creamer, "Caught in the Clutter Crossfire: Your Brand," *Advertising Age,* April 2, 2007, 1, 35.

2. "Ad Spending Heads into Tepid Recovery," *Advertising Age,* Annual 2010, December 28, 2009, 8; Brian Steinberg, "Marketers Say TV Spending Will Drop. Nets Stay Bullish. Let the Deals Begin," *Advertising Age,* February 8, 2010, 3.

3. "Worldwide Ad Spending by Region 2008" Advertising Age Data Center, http://adage.com/globalmarketers09/#302

4. Bob Garfield, "The Chaos Scenario 2.0: The Post Advertising Age," *Advertising Age,* March 26, 2007, 1, 12–14. "Media 2015: The Future of Media," The Futures Company, Special Report 2010.

5. Tim Bradshaw, "Adverts Mark A Seismic Shift to Digital," FT.com (Financial Times), June 29, 2009, accessed at www.ft.com/cms73320_03_ch02_p042-077.indd 44 11/19/10 8:38 PM Chapter 2: The Structure of the Advertising and Promotion Industry: Advertisers, Agencies, Media, and Support Organizations 45.

Let's explore in greater detail what's going on in the structure of the industry. From the consumer side: With the large number of digital media options available for news, information, and entertainment, "media fragmentation" is a boon to consumers and a huge headache for advertisers and their agencies. The new "control-seeking" generation of consumers is behaving very differently from the cable-TV generation that preceded it. Today's consumers are insisting on the convenience and appeal (and control) of their PCs, smartphones, iPads, and TiVos or Slingboxes (as we saw in Chapter 1). There is some degree of irony in the control that consumers are starting to exert, however. Even though the traditional structure of the advertising and media industry may be changed forever, the *goal* of that traditional structure has not changed—the brand needs to be highlighted. In fact, the change in consumer orientation will make product branding even *more* important as consumers choose what persuasive messages they want to be exposed to and where they want to see them.

To that point, the importance of the brand in advertising and promotion was a key theme in Chapter 1. And advertising and promotion agencies and their media partners are struggling with how to insert themselves and their clients' brands into this new environment controlled by the consumer. Some think "going with the flow" is the answer by having agencies and media companies allow consumers to contribute to content (à la the Super Bowl ad competitions).[6] Many, as mentioned earlier, will invest more in digital media. But digital media is not the only "non-intrusive" option open to advertisers. Coca-Cola, for example, understands full well that consumers are losing their tolerance for passive television and magazine ads. So, Coke and other marketers are trying to insert their brands into consumers' daily lives in more subtle and seemingly natural ways. Part of Coke's approach is to pay $20 million to display Coke cups on the desks of the judges during Fox Network's *American Idol*, the U.S.-based spin-off of *Britain's Got Talent*[7] (see Exhibit 2.1). Another example is Kimberly-Clark dropping TV ads for Huggies diapers from its marketing plan to emphasize the digital media its "new mom" target market uses the most.[8]

Exhibit 2.1 Big advertisers like Coca-Cola (which still spends nearly $300 million a year on television advertising) realize that consumers are seeking more control over the commercial information to which they are exposed. Devices like TiVo DVRs and consumer-controlled content options like Facebook and blogs are allowing consumers to choose how and when they view information. In response, big advertisers are looking for more and varied subtle ways to reach consumers and have their brands become more a part of consumers' lifestyles—such as using promotional techniques like placing their brands with television shows. Notice the highly visible Coke cups in front of the *American Idol* judges.

While big advertisers like Coca-Cola and Kimberly-Clark recognize change and are trying to deal with it, so are big media companies. NBC Universal is often referenced as the "classic" big media company with the deepest roots in the old media structure. But now NBC is wooing advertisers by offering to help prepare advertising with the network's vast digital studio resources.[9] Other media companies like Viacom are trying similar experiments in their media-owned programming venues like Nick at Nite. Similarly, MTV Networks is offering new media distribution like broadband channel MotherLoad, which is associated with Comedy Central programming.[10]

6. Erick Schonfeld, "Tuning Up Big Media," *Business 2.0*, April 6, 2006, 61–63.
7. Dean Foust and Brian Grow, "Coke: Wooing the TiVo Generation," *BusinessWeek*, March 1, 2004, 77–78.
8. Jack Neff, "New Huggies, Old Spice Launches to Go TV-Free," *Advertising Age*, May 4, 2009, 8.
9. Jon Fine, "Now, an Ad from Our Network," *BusinessWeek*, November 27, 2006, 26.
10. Tom Lowry, "The Dilemma Vexing Big Media," *BusinessWeek*, July 3, 2006, 94–98.

Change in the advertising industry is nothing new, as the following section highlights. But the pace of change and the complexity of the change are more challenging than any the industry has faced. We'll spend our time in this chapter considering the structure in the industry and all the "players" that are creating and being affected by change.

The Advertising Industry in Constant Transition.

The introductory scenario gives examples of the deep and complex changes that are affecting the advertising industry. To say that the advertising industry is in *constant* transition might seem like an exaggeration, but it's not. If you consider changes in technology, economic conditions, culture, lifestyles, and business philosophies, one or more of these broad business and societal forces is always affecting the advertising and promotion effort.

This chapter highlights how the industry and its structure is changing now and has changed over time. While we consider the change and its effects, we need to keep in mind that the fundamental *process* of advertising and the role it plays in organizations remains steadfastly the same: persuasive communications directed at target audiences—no matter what is happening with technology, economic conditions, society, or business philosophies. The underlying role and purpose of advertising and promotion have not changed and will not change.

To appreciate the way the advertising industry is in a state of constant transition and the level of complexity this transition has reached, it is necessary to understand that advertising is an industry with great breadth and intricacy. The section that follows highlights trends affecting change. Then, we will turn our attention to understanding how advertising and other promotional tools are managed in the communications industry. Along the way, we'll consider all the different participants in the process, particularly the advertisers and their advertising and promotion agencies.

1 Trends Affecting the Advertising and Promotion Industry.

The following trends affect the advertising and promotion industry. Many of them have to do with new technologies and the way their application has changed the structure and very nature of the way communications occur. Other trends have to do with consumer culture and the sort of communication that makes sense to the modern consumer. But in the end, what is important is the critical need to focus on the brand, its image, and a persuasive and integrated presentation of that brand to the target market.

To understand the change that is affecting the advertising and promotion industry and the use of promotional tools, let's consider five broad trends in the marketplace.

Consumer Control: From Social Media to Blogs to TiVo.

Yep, top of the list. As we have highlighted so far, consumer control is at the top of the list of trends affecting the advertising and promotion industry. As featured in the introductory scenario, consumers are now in greater control of the information they receive about product categories and the brands within those categories. Collectively, individuals' sharing and creating content through blogs, social media, wikis, and video sites like YouTube are referred to as Web 2.0—the second generation of Web-based use

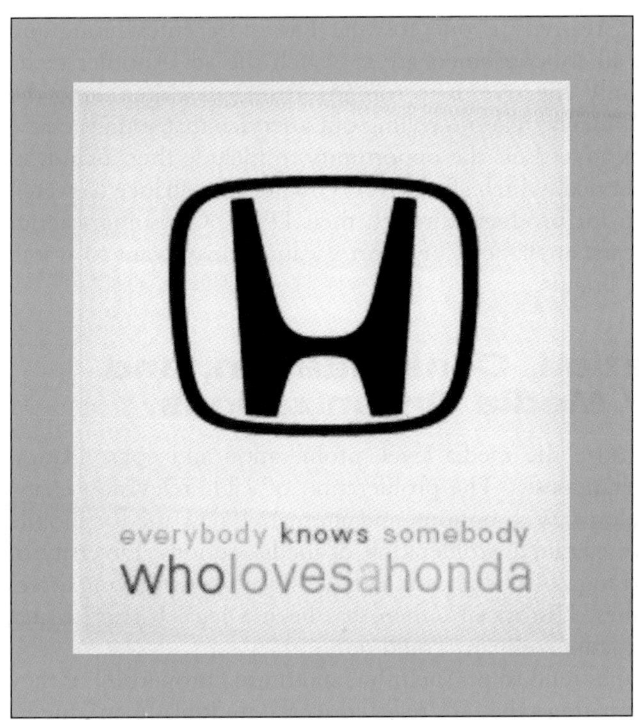
everybody knows somebody
wholovesahonda

Exhibit 2.2 Firms of all types are trying to tap social media as a way to communicate with target audiences. Honda launched a Facebook page in 2009 and within three months had 2 million "friends" on the site.

Photo Courtesy of Omniterra Images

and services that emphasize online collaboration and sharing among users. The simplest and most obvious example is when consumers log on to the Internet and visit sites *they* choose to visit for gathering information or for shopping. But it gets more complicated from there. **Social media,** highly accessible Web-based media that allow the sharing of information between individuals and between individuals and groups, have emerged as the most significant form of consumer control over information creation and communication. Facebook has more than 350 million users worldwide sharing 3.5 billion pieces of content with each other every week.[11] Twitter has more than 50 million users who post 8 billion tweets a year.[12] Honda launched a Facebook page in August 2009 and three months later had 2 million friends on the site (see Exhibit 2.2).[13] Firms are already spending nearly $1 billion on social media, and that number is expected to rise to more than $3 billion by 2014, surpassing email marketing, search marketing, and display ads.[14]

Another way consumers control their information is through blogs. **Blogs,** websites frequented by individuals with common interests where they can post facts, opinions, and personal experiences, have emerged as sophisticated (although typically not very objective) sources of product and brand information. Once criticized as the "ephemeral scribble" of 13-year-old girls and the babble of techno-geeks, blogs are gaining greater recognition and organization, with two-thirds of U.S. Internet users reading blogs on a regular basis. Web-based service firms like Blogdrive and Blogger are making blogs easier to create and use and more accessible to the masses. Estimates now put the number of active blogs at 133 million, with 346 million people globally visiting those blog sites.[15] Advertisers should pay attention not only to the popularity of social media sites and blogs but also to the power of their communications. Research has shown that such "word-of-mouth" communication between consumers results in longer-lasting impressions and greater new customer acquisition effects than traditional marketing efforts.[16]

As discussed earlier, another dramatic example of consumer control is the growth in use of digital video recorders (DVRs) like TiVo and controllers like Slingbox. Analysts expect the use of DVRs to reduce ad viewership by as much as 30 percent. That translates into taking approximately $20 billion out of U.S. advertising industry revenue. And advertisers and their agencies expected that by 2010, approximately 39 percent of all U.S. television households would have "ad-skipping" capability.[17]

Obviously, advertisers and their agencies are trying to adapt to the concept that consumers are gaining greater control over the information they choose to receive.

11. "A World of Connections," *The Economist,* January 10, 2010, 3.

12. Spencer E. Ante, "The Real Value of Tweets," *Bloomberg Businessweek,* January 18, 2010, 31.

13. Jean Halliday, "Honda Feels the Love on Facebook," *Advertising Age,* October 26, 2009, 53.

14. "U.S. Interactive Marketing Forecast, 2009 to 2014," Forrester Research, Inc., July 30, 2009, 7.

15. Adam Singer, "Social Media, Web 2.0 and Internet Stats," thefuturebuzz.com, January 12, 2009, www.futurebuzz.com

16. Michael Trusov, Randolph E. Bucklin, and Koen Pauwels, "Effects of Word-of-Mouth versus Traditional Marketing: Findings from an Internet Social Networking Site," *Journal of Marketing,* vol. 73 (September 2009), 90–102.

17. David Kiley, "Learning to Love the Dreaded TiVo," *BusinessWeek,* April 17, 2006, 88.

How will advertisers adapt? Creativity is one answer. The more entertaining and informative an ad, the more likely consumers are to watch the ad. Another technique, less creative but certainly effective, is to run advertising messages along the bottom of the programming. Finally, TiVo is rolling out a service that sounds crazy: ads on demand.[18] TiVo offers advertisers the opportunity to include their brands in the company's "Showcase" service, which allows TiVo owners the chance to watch promotional videos and shop for products through their DVR. Consumers about to buy expensive items like cars, appliances, or resort vacations may want to watch information about alternative brands.

Media Proliferation, Consolidation, and "Multiplatform" Media Organizations.

At another level of the industry, the media level, proliferation and consolidation have been taking place simultaneously. The proliferation of cable television channels, direct marketing technology, Web options, and alternative new media (mobile marketing, for example) have caused a proliferation of media options. Diversity of media options and the advertising dollars they attract have always been driving forces behind many media companies. Historically, there has been a legal barrier to just how much control any one media company could seize.

Media companies of all types tend to pursue more and more "properties" if they are allowed to legally, thus creating what are referred to as "multiplatform" media organizations.[19] Consider the evolution of media giant News Corp. and its holdings, which include television networks (Fox), newspapers (more than 20 worldwide), magazines (Gemstar-TV Guide International), satellite operations, and cable systems (Fox News). News Corp.'s worldwide media holdings generate more than $30 billion in revenue and reach every corner of the world. Now the firm is the proud new owner of MySpace in the social network media world and holds an interest in Hulu, the online video service. As big as News Corp. is, the ultimate multiplatform may be Disney, which owns the ABC broadcasting network and the ESPN cable network group in addition to other cable stations, 15 radio stations, a couple dozen websites, eight podcasting operations, video on demand, books, and magazines—you name it, Disney uses it to reach audiences.

Not to be outdone, the Web has its own media conglomerates. InterActiveCorp (IAC) has amassed a media empire of Internet sites that are as diverse as they are successful. IAC is an Internet conglomerate with a grab bag of online offerings, including search engine Ask.com; online dating service Match.com; ServiceMagic, a site that connects consumers to home-service professionals; and various Internet start-ups and smaller properties. Together, these sites generate about $1 billion in revenue. Other Internet merchants like Google are bigger, at about $7 billion in revenue, but not as diversified. In turn, the evolution of media options has spawned new specialized agencies to sell, manage, and consult for these new media options (see Exhibit 2.3).

The point is that media companies, in an effort to effectively "cover all the bases" in reaching audiences, have been wheeling and dealing during the last decade to engage consumers in as many ways as possible—from traditional media (broadcast television, newspapers, radio, and magazines) to cable and satellite broadcast and all forms of Internet-based communication.

18. Ibid.

19. Nat Ives, "Special Report: More Than Magazines," *Advertising Age,* March 12, 2007, s1–s6.

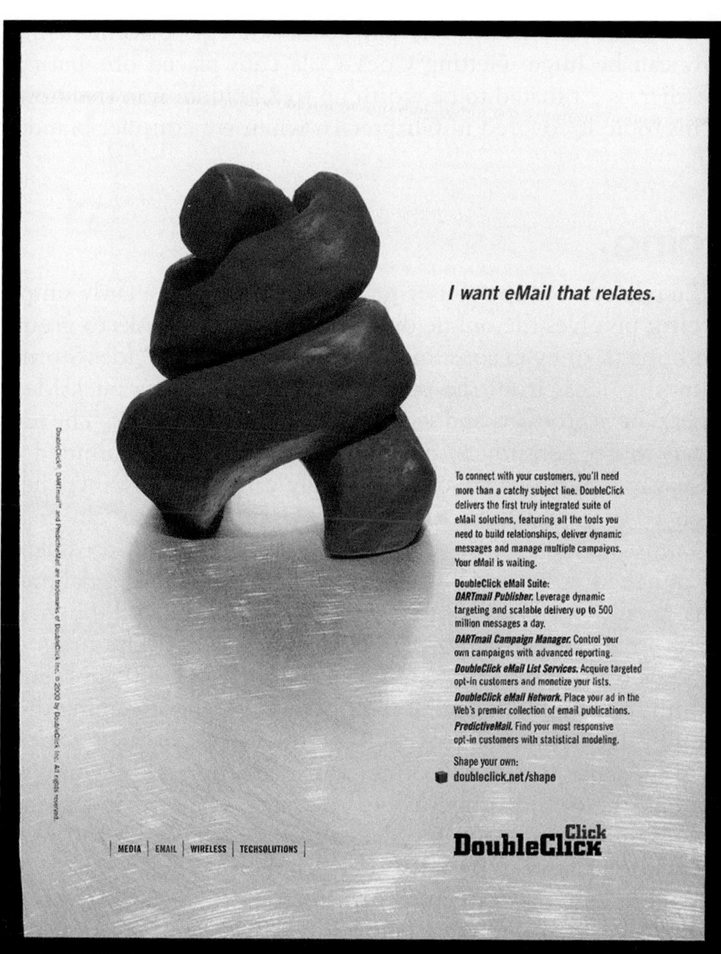

I want eMail that relates.
To connect with your customers, you'll need more than a catchy subject line. DoubleClick delivers the first truly integrated suite of eMail solutions, featuring all the tools you need to build relationships, deliver dynamic messages and manage multiple campaigns. Your eMail is waiting.
DoubleClick eMail Suite:
DARTmail Publisher. Leverage dynamic targeting and scalable delivery up to 500 million messages a day.
DARTmail Campaign Manager. Control your own campaigns with advanced reporting.
DoubleClick eMail List Services. Acquire targeted opt-in customers and monetize your lists.
DoubleClick eMail Network. Place your ad in the Web's premier collection of email publications.
PredictiveMail. Find your most responsive opt-in customers with statistical modeling.
Shape your own:
doubleclick.net/shape
MEDIA | EMAIL | WIRELESS | TECHSOLUTIONS
DoubleClick Click

Exhibit 2.3 Media proliferation and fragmentation has given rise to specialized media organizations. DoubleClick, now part of the Google organization, specializes in digital marketing and advertising solutions.

Courtesy of DoubleClick

Media Clutter and Fragmentation Means More IBP.

Even though the media and agency levels of the industry may be consolidating into fewer and fewer large firms, that does not mean there are fewer media options. Quite the contrary is true. There are more ways to *try* to reach consumers than ever before. In 1994, the consumer had access to about 27 television channels. Today, the average U.S. household has access to more than 100 channels. In 1995, it took three well-placed TV spots to reach 80 percent of women television viewers. By 2003, it took 97 spots to reach them![20] From television ads to virtual billboards to banner ads on the Internet to podcasts of advertising messages, new and increased media options have resulted in so much clutter that the probability of any one advertisement breaking through and making a real difference continues to diminish. Advertisers are developing a lack of faith in advertising alone, so promotion options such as online communication, brand placement in film and television, point-of-purchase displays, and sponsorships are more attractive to advertisers. For example, advertisers on the Super Bowl, notorious for its clutter and outrageous ad prices (about $2.5 million to $3 million for a 30-second spot), have turned instead to promotional tie-ins to enhance the effect of the advertising. To combat the clutter and expense at one Super Bowl, Miller Brewing distributed thousands of inflatable Miller Lite chairs by game day. The chairs were a tie-in with a national advertising campaign that began during the regular season before the Super Bowl.

Given the backlash against advertising that clutter can cause, advertisers and their agencies are rethinking the way they try to communicate with consumers. Fundamentally, there is a greater focus on integrating more tools in the overall promotional effort in an attempt to reach more consumers in more different ways. This approach by advertisers is wreaking havoc on traditional media expenditures. Consider the decision by Johnson & Johnson. In 2007, Johnson & Johnson announced that it had shifted $250 million in spending from traditional media—television, magazines, newspapers—to "digital media," including the Internet and blogs.[21]

Advertisers are shifting spending out of traditional media and are looking to the full complement of promotional opportunities in sales promotions (like the Miller chairs), event sponsorships, new media options, and public relations as means to support and enhance the primary advertising effort for brands. In fact, some advertisers are enlisting the help of Hollywood talent agencies in an effort to get their brands

20. Matthew Boyle, "Brand Killers," *Fortune,* April 11, 2003, 89–100.

21. Jack Neff, "J&J Jolts 'Old Media' with $250M Spend Shift," *Advertising Age,* March 19, 2007, 1, 29; Jean Halliday, "GM Cuts $600M off Ad Spend—Yes, Really," *Advertising Age,* February 21, 2007, 1, 25.

featured in television programs and films. The payoff for strategic placement in a film or television show can be huge. Getting Coca-Cola cups placed on *American Idol,* as was discussed earlier, is estimated to be worth up to $20 million in traditional media advertising.[22] This topic is covered in Chapter 16 when we consider branded entertainment in detail.

Crowdsourcing.

Crowdsourcing (and the related concept of user-generated content) is a fairly simple concept. **Crowdsourcing** involves the online distribution of certain tasks to groups (crowds) of experts, enthusiasts, or even consumers.[23] Dell launched the "Idea Storm" website to solicit computing ideas from the public. Starbucks' "MyStarbucksIdea" asks its fans to recommend new products and services for Starbucks' outlets. The idea behind crowdsourcing is to get consumers more involved with and committed to a brand in a way that passive, intrusive advertising simply cannot. Consumers help "build the brand" with recommendations for features. Consumers also can communicate about the brand to audiences in ways that seems natural and credible—something corporate-launched advertising struggles with. Consider the elaborate crowdsourcing effort conceived by Ford Motor Company. Ford initiated the Fiesta Movement as a way to attract attention to its Fiesta compact car. The program consists of 100 Fiesta "agents" (chosen from a pool of more than 4,000 applicants) who will spend six months behind the wheel of their own Fiesta, lifestreaming their experiences. Each month, agents post videos and commentaries on their experiences related to themed missions: travel, adventure, social activism, and technology (www.fiestamovement.com). Not surprisingly, Ford encourages you to view agents' videos and "follow everything across the social network sites you already use." Crowdsourcing is not without its risks for advertisers, though. When Kraft Foods put out the call for people to help the firm come up with a more spreadable version of the Australian favorite Vegemite, 48,000 people did come up with suggestions for a name for the product.[24] But, the project resulted in a global backlash against the name—iSnack2.0, as the *Social Media* box describes.

Mobile Marketing/Mobile Media.

Of all the trends affecting the advertising and promotion industry, mobile media may turn out to the biggest—or at least the most relevant. Whether that happens depends on consumer reaction. Technology has given advertisers many opportunities to reach consumers with messages directed to consumers' mobile devices—primarily smartphones, tablets like Apple's iPad, and e-readers like Amazon's Kindle—but personal navigation devices (known as PNDs and GPS systems) can also accommodate messages in the wireless world. But, doing so flies directly in the face of consumer control. The process of mobile marketing and mobile media is relatively simple.

Because all these mobile devices have wireless capability, advertisers can negotiate ways of including brand messages that show up on the devices. The obvious opportunity is to send ads directly to the devices—likely to meet with harsh reaction from consumers. But other, more subtle opportunities exist. One is to sponsor

22. Betsy Streisand, "Why Great American Brands Are Doing Lunch," *Business 2.0,* September 2003, 146–150.

23. Garrik Schmitt, "Can Creativity Be Crowdsourced?" *Advertising Age,* Digital Next, posted at ad.age.com/digitalnext on April 16, 2009.

24. Matthew Creamer, "Crowdsourcing Done Wrong," *Advertising Age,* Global News, posted at ad-age.com/globalnews on September 29, 2009.

Social Media

Crowdsourcing Gone Bad

Crowdsourcing is a fairly good idea. Get consumers involved in helping your firm develop integrated brand promotion ideas and then give them a lot of visibility for the effort and maybe even an award. Ford is doing it with its Fiesta Movement campaign. Starbucks is having customers submit ideas for new products and services at its MyStarbucksIdea site, and Dell is having computer users suggest new features and applications. You get consumers involved with your brand in a way that old-style, passive intrusive advertising could never hope to accomplish. So, Kraft thought it would be a *great* idea to have people suggest names for a new variation of its popular Australian product Vegemite. The new product would be a combination of cream cheese and Vegemite. Consumers jumped at the chance—48,000 submitted their ideas for a new name. The winner? iSnack2.0. The reaction in the market? A global backlash. For the most part, people thought the name had nothing to do with the product and was a mere exploitation of clichés in digital product nomenclature. Dozens of mainstream media articles have lambasted the name, and harsh criticism has shown up on hundreds of posts on Facebook and Twitter. There is even a website called "Names That Are Better Than iSnack 2.0." Advertising and marketing professionals argue that "iSnack2.0 is totally irrelevant to the iPod/Web 2.0 generation." Kraft executives, not surprisingly, don't see it that way. They claim that the name was chosen "based on a personal call to action, relevance to snacking and clear identification of a new and different Vegemite to the original." Well, the executive commentary sounds about right. Trouble is, people think it's a bad name.

Sources: Garrik Schmitt, "Can Creativity Be Crowdsourced?" *Advertising Age*, Digital Next, posted at ad.age.com/digitalnext on April 16, 2009; Matthew Creamer, "Crowdsourcing Done Wrong," *Advertising Age*, Global News, posted at adage.com/globalnews on September 29, 2009.

content and apps on e-readers. Another is to embed brand visuals in the rich multimedia content that tablets are capable of receiving.[25] But, analysts offer the, perhaps obvious, caution to advertisers: "But it's not, 'What's the available media I can buy?' It's thinking about how consumers are behaving and what role do devices play in the way they behave."[26] So far, consumers don't seem too put off. AdMob, the firm that serves up graphical banner and text link ads for mobile devices, is seeing 10 *billion* ad requests a month! And, within two months of Google's launch of its Android operating system, more than 1 billion ad requests were being received each month.[27] Advertisers seem eager to jump on board. Spending on mobile marketing is expected to grow to more than $1.2 billion annually by 2014—second only to spending on social media in the interactive marketing category.[28]

For decades to come, these trends and the changes they bring about will force advertisers to think differently about advertising and IBP. Similarly, advertising agencies will need to think about the way they serve their clients and the way communications are delivered to audiences. As you have read, big spenders such as Procter & Gamble, Starbucks, Miller Brewing, and Ford Motor Company are already demanding new and innovative programs to enhance the impact of their advertising and promotional dollars. The goal of creating persuasive communication remains intact—attract attention and develop preference for a brand—and so the dynamics of the communications environment just discussed all directly impact that overall goal.

25. Rita Chang, "Mobile Marketing Beyond the Mobile Phone," *Advertising Age,* November 30, 2009, 10.

26. Ibid.

27. AdMob Mobile Metrics Report, October 2009, www.metrics.admob.com; Brian White, "Google's Mobile Ad Requests Double in Just Two Months," January 6, 2010, www.bloggingstocks.com

28. U.S. Interactive Marketing Forecast, 2009–2014, op. cit., 7.

2 The Scope and Structure of the Advertising Industry and Promotion.

To fully appreciate the structure of the advertising and promotion industry, let's first consider the absolute size. Remember from Chapter 1 that the advertising industry is huge: more than $300 billion spent in the United States alone on various categories of advertising, with nearly $600 billion spent worldwide. Spending on other forms of integrated brand promotion is no less impressive. Spending on all forms of integrated brand promotion, including advertising, exceeds a trillion dollars a year.

Differentiation of the Advertising Industry Structure: Europe, Asia, and Latin America. International advertisers face the dichotomy between polycentrically designing advertising strategies and pursuing more standardized global approaches in cases of products and services with global appeal. International markets are a mosaic of a very complex and colorful mix of languages, cultures, and ethnicities. Serious decision-making problems for advertisers involve knowing which brands are locally preferred and which ads will resonate with the local people's culture or will travel well across countries.

Important strategic questions in this context refer to the dilemma of **standardization** and/or **adaptation**.[29] Often reflecting a cultural product in itself, international advertising must account for idiosyncratic local macro environmental factors to stimulate local consumers' purchase intentions, which are often influenced by local values, attitudes, and social roles.[30] Different degrees of standardization or adaptation have a bearing on the media choice and on the cultural competence of the media agency. The more a culture requires adaptation, the more culturally competent the media agency must be. A few current research activities are provided next to demonstrate the high relevance of this topic.

Based on a case in the fast-food industry, an international survey conceptualizes the role of cultural distance, learning, and memory on standardization versus adaptation strategies and the marketing mix. The results of the survey imply that cultural distance activates the standardization-differentiation continuum and degrees of marketing mix adaptation.[31]

On the other hand, a current trend in niche tourism is for consumers to gain momentum in experiencing local cultural heritage authentically. This requires the message to be targeted on local cultural values that might have implications on the media chosen. Having researched the setting of Chalkidiki, Greece, the study points to a newly emerging consumer interest in "the other's culture." The author suggests that current tourism marketing, for example, does not reflect the newly arising customer motive to experience the authentic local culture and heritage.[32]

A more recent multidisciplinary phenomenon is the interaction between brands and consumer groups paralleling social relationships leading to communities nestling around the brand (Kaufmann et al., 2010).[33] Additionally, in transition settings

29. Zou Shaoming, S. Tamer, and T. Cavusgil, "The GMS: A Broad Conceptualization of Global Marketing Strategy and Its Effect on Firm Performance," *Journal of Marketing*, vol. 66, no. 4, 2000, 40–46.

30. Lynne M. Ciochetto, "Advertising and Globalization, Presented at the 18th European Conference on Modern South Asian, NZ Wellington, 2004.

31. Elena Horska, Ludmila Nagyova, Olaf Loebel, Patrik Rovny, "Learning Process and Memory: Cultural Identity versus Homogenization of Values, Attitudes and Habits," 2011 in : Hans Ruediger Kaufmann, *International Consumer Behavior: A Mosaic of Eclectic Perspectives*, 44–55 (Darwen/UK: Access Press, UK, 2011) ISBN: 978-0-9562471-31.

32. Eugenia Wickens, "The Importance of Culture and Heritage in the Promotion of Chaldiki, Greece as a Tourist Destination", 2011, in Hans Ruediger Kaufmann, *International Consumer Behavior: A Mosaic of Eclectic Perspectives*, 35-43, (Darwen/UK: Access Press, UK, 2011 ISBN: 978-0-9562471-31.

33. Rohit Agraval, "Standardization or Adaptation—An Endless Debate," Enzine Articles, accessed at http://ezinearticles.com/?Standardization-Or-Adaptation---An-Endless-Debate&id=4471968 on October 10, 2010; and Albert Muniz Jr., and Thomas C. O'Guinn, 2001 in Hans Ruediger Kaufmann, Sandra, M.C. Loureiro, Gianpaolo Basile, and Demetris Vrontis, 3rd EMRBI Conference Proceedings (Cyprus: EuroMed Press, 2010) 537-549. ISBN: 978-9963-643-83-5.

such as Central and Eastern Europe and China, where consumption behavior must be relearned, advertising can play an active role in bringing about cultural change. Advertising, as an economic motor and revitalizer of cities and regions, can be regarded as a strategic location indicator that reflects a certain level of creativity and open-mindedness of the setting.[34]

Against this backdrop, this section aims to explain the diverse international advertising industry structures with a special focus on Europe, Asia, and Latin America. This analysis may serve as an informative knowledge pool for designing international advertising strategies and tactics. As discussed in more detail later, the three regions have shown vast growth in terms of advertising expenditure, participants, and supporting industries. The growth rates are impressive as they outnumber even those of the United States in recent years.

The first part of this section provides a general description of the structure of the global advertising industry. Thereafter, a detailed account of the respective advertising industry in terms of the most prominent advertisers and media agencies in the three aforementioned regions is provided. Reference is made to new trends in consumer behavior and legal aspects to be taken into consideration. The chapter closes with synthesized conclusions and recommendations derived from the investigation.

Global Advertising Industry Structure: A Trend Toward Integration.

This section illuminates the structure of the global advertising industry, especially in terms of size, participants, and media spending differentiated by global regions. Different types of marketing agencies comprising full-service agencies, specialized agencies, or in-house agencies are required for a variety of purposes. As the name implies, the full-service agencies provide a holistic marketing service embracing all the steps of the advertising function: planning, creating, producing, and placing advertisements, PR, and events. Specialized agencies focus on a precise aspect of the creative process, whereas in-house agencies are created inside the corporation with the advertising director deciding which services should be externally acquired or internally performed.[35]

Currently, advertising agencies are developing from individually acting agencies toward more integrated global holding companies. Such concentration was not only created from mergers of agencies but also derived from horizontal integration of several specialist-marketing services (for example, public relations, market research, design, and event management).[36] Each of these holdings is responsible for a large number of different agency brands allocated around the world. According to *Advertising Age*, four major international groups represent these holdings: WPP,

34. Lynn M.Ciochetto,"Advertising and Globalization, Presented at the 18th European Conference on Modern South Asian, NZ Wellington, 2004; Hans Ruediger Kaufmann, Zorica Zagorac, and Dolores Sanchez Bengoa, "The Influence of Identity on International Consumer Behavior in Transitional Settings: A Case Study of the Bosnian-Herzegovinian Banking Market," *Journal for International Business and Entrepreneurship Development*, vol. 3, no. 3-4, 2008, 412-432; and Christoph Glauner, "Locational Structure of Advertising Agencies in Germany: Creative Clusters in Global Cities," Conference Paper, RESER Conference, September 25, 2008, accessed at http://www.reser.net on October 10, 2010.

35. Michael Solomon, Lisa Duke Cornell, and Amit Nizan, *Launch! Advertising and Promotion in Real Time"* (Nizan Publisher, Flat World Knowledge, Inc., 2009) ISBN/ASIN: 0982043023.

36. Christoph Glauner, "Locational Structure of Advertising Agencies in Germany: Creative Clusters in Global Cities," Conference Paper, RESER Conference, September 25, 2008, accessed at http://www.reser.net on October 10, 2010.

Exhibit 2.4 Agencies Listed by Networks

Rank	Holding and Partners	2009 Revenues (billion US$)
1	WPP	13.6
2	Omnicom (BBDO, DDB, TBWA)	11.7
3	Publicis Group (Saatchi & Saatchi, Leo Burnett)	6.3
4	Interpublic (Draft BCF)	6.0
5	Dentsu	3.1
6	Aegis (Carat, Isobar, Synovate, Vizeum)	2.1
7	Havas (RSCG, Havas Media MPG, Arnold Worldwide)	2.0
8	Hakuhodo (Daiko, Yomiko)	1.5
9	Acxiom	0.750
10	MDC Partners (Crispin Porter & Bogusky and Kirshenbaum Bond)	0.546

Source: Based on *Advertising Age*, 2010.

Exhibit 2.5 Top 10 Global Advertising Agencies in 2009

Rank	Advertising Agency	Worldwide Revenue (billion US$)
1	Dentsu	Just over 3
2	McCann WorldGroup	2.67
3	Young and Rubicam Brands	2.65
4	DDB Worldwide Communications Group	2.22
5	Ogilvy & Mather	1.75
6	BBDO Worldwide	1.67
7	TWBA Worldwide	1.51
8	Euro RSCG Worldwide	1.20
9	DRAFTFCB	1.17
10	JWT	1.12

Source: Based on Top Ten Global Advertising Agencies by Scott Christ, eHow contributor, January 11, 2011.

Omnicom, Publicis, and Interpublic (see Exhibit 2.4).[37] The top 10 global advertising agencies are listed in Exhibit 2.5.[38]

The Nominal Winner: The Asia-Pacific Region. The size of the industry is measured by the level of media spending in each region (see Exhibit 2.6). Regarding the participants, the largest industry clients (in terms of worldwide revenue) consisting of agency companies, advertising agencies, direct marketing agencies, media agencies, and public relations agencies are provided.

37. *Advertising Age*, 2010, accessed at http://adage.com/datacenter/agencyfamilytrees2010.php on March 8, 2011.

38. Scott Christ, 2011, accessed at http://www.ehow.com/info_7749807_top-ten-advertising-agencies.html on March 8, 2011.

Region	Measured Media Spending (billion)			Percent of Total	
	2008	2007	% Change	2008	2007
Africa	3,111	2,689	15.7	0.7	0.6
Asia-Pacific	116,866	109,982	6.3	26.5	25.4
Europe	124,643	124,299	–0.3	28.3	28.7
Latin America	18,769	16,858	11.3	4.3	3.9
Middle East	9,922	8,105	22.4	2.3	1.9
Canada	9,934	9,290	6.9	2.3	2.1
Subtotal spending outside the United States	283,245	271,223	4.4	64.3	62.7
United States	157,559	161,693	–2.6	35.7	37.3
Worldwide	440,804	432,916	1.8	100.0	100.0

Source: Worldwide Advertising Spending by Regions. *Advertising Age*, Copyrighted 2011 Crain Communications.

Exhibit 2.6 Worldwide Advertising Spending by Regions

As can be seen from the data on global advertising spending in Exhibit 2.6, the advertising spending pattern changed throughout the regions in the world. The highest percentage increases in 2008 occurred in the Middle East (+22.4%), Africa (+15.7%), and Latin America (+11.3%), albeit from comparatively low levels. Of particular interest is the fact that the highest nominal growth of advertising spending appeared in the Asia-Pacific region. Considerable increases in these regions might reflect an alternating global perspective on "where to advertise" despite the lion share of advertising still being spent in the United States and Europe, although with slightly decreasing rates (–2.6%; –0.3%). These growth rates may have been due in part to the appreciation of foreign currencies against the downtrodden dollar (for example, the euro). In summary, U.S. institutions had the largest proportion of advertising expenditure in the world (35.7%), followed by Europe (28.3%) and the Asia-Pacific region (26.5%). In total, worldwide advertising spending experienced a moderate growth of 1.8 percent, from $432,916 billion to $440,804 billion. In the last two years, media advertising plummeted due to the global economic conjuncture. Although, estimates must be treated with caution, a forecast of ZenithOptimedia (in *WA Today*, 2010) sees that this downturn will be compensated for in the forthcoming years. Whereas the company anticipated an increase of global ad spending in 2010 (by 4.8%), this level is still 6.3 percent lower compared to that of 2008, when the decline started. For 2011, the company forecasted an increase of 4.6 percent in global spending. Reflecting a change in people's media habits, media expenditure around the world realized a significant shift from newspapers to TV and the Internet. Regarding differentiated regional growth rates, Latin America, mainly due to Brazil's advertising boom, is expected to grow by 16.8 percent and Western Europe by 3 percent (*WA Today*, 2010). Developing markets in Latin America and the Asia-Pacific region are seen to achieve differentiated growth rates. Those countries that are economically more advanced will face slower growth rates, and the economically less advanced countries will face higher growth rates. Concordantly, India, Indonesia, Brazil, and Costa Rica are envisioned to see double-digit growth rates, whereas for China, 9 percent is forecasted in 2009, 15 percent in 2010, and 9 percent in 2011.[39]

39. Heidi Dawley, "For Europe, a not so Harsh Slowdown," 2008, accessed at http://www.medialifemagazine.com on September13, 2010.

Nestlé and Kraft Foods: The Rising Stars. Exhibit 2.7 presents an excerpt of the top 10 global marketers in 2009. Regarding the country of origin, the United States accounted for 8 out of 10 groups in this list, followed by France (1) and Switzerland (1). The most prominent groups in this list were Procter & Gamble and Unilever, U.S.-based groups in first and second position, respectively, as well as L'Oréal, a French group, in third position. Compared to 2008 (*Advertising Age*, 2009), the leading trio remained unchanged, but the leader, P&G, significantly reduced its media spending by US $1.05 billion, whereas Unilever and L'Oréal increased spending by US $0.31 billion and US $0.52 billion, respectively. Of particular interest is the rise of Nestlé from tenth to fifth position and Kraft Foods from eighteenth to tenth position. Toyota Motors dropped two places, and Johnson & Johnson dropped one place.

The 100 global advertisers spend more outside than inside the United States (Europe having the highest nominal increase).

The top 100 global advertisers spent $117,925 million on advertising in 2008, signifying an increase of 3.1 percent from 2007 (see Exhibit 2.8). In 2008, advertising spending of the 100 global advertisers amounted to 26.75 percent, an increase of 0.35 percent of the total worldwide advertising spending.

Exhibit 2.7 Top 10 Marketers by Worldwide Media Spending in 2009

Rank	Agency Company	Country of Origin	Worldwide Revenue (billion US$)
1	Procter & Gamble	United States	8.68
2	Unilever	United States	6.03
3	L'Oréal	France	4.56
4	General Motors Co.	United States	3.27
5	Nestlé	Switzerland	2.62
6	Coca-Cola	United States	2.44
7	Toyota Motor Co.	United States	2.31
8	Johnson & Johnson	United States	2.25
9	Reckitt Benckiser	United States	2.24
10	Kraft Foods	United States	2.12

Source: Based on *Advertising Age*, 2010.

Exhibit 2.8 Top 100 Global Advertisers' Spending by Region

	Measured Media Spending (millions US$)			Percent of Total	
Region	2008	2007	% Change	2008	2007
Africa	780	864	–9.8	0.7	0.8
Asia-Pacific	17,590	16,636	5.7	14.9	14.5
Europe	46,260	42,747	8.2	39.2	37.4
Latin America	4,819	4,011	20.1	4.1	3.5
Middle East	1,992	1,777	12.1	1.7	1.6
Canada	2,037	2,173	–6.3	1.7	1.9
Subtotal spending outside the United States	73,478	68,210	7.7	62.3	59.7
United States	44,447	46,132	–3.7	37.7	40.3
Worldwide	117,925	114,342	3.1	100.0	100.0

Source: Based on *Advertising Age*, (2009).

In line with the global trend (–3.1%), U.S. spending of the 100 global advertisers was down 3.7 percent, to $44,447 million, whereas outside U.S. spending was up 7.7 percent, to $68,210 million. The highest percentage increases were registered in Latin America, and the Middle East. Here, Europe is the third largest in terms of percentage increase but the highest in terms of nominal increase. Also, the Asia-Pacific, Latin America, and Middle East regions experienced a moderate nominal increase. On the contrary, the highest percentage decreases materialized in Africa (9.8%), followed by Canada (6.3%) and the United States. In summary, in 2008, these top global advertisers no longer allocated most of their budget to the United States, instead investing it in the three regions discussed. Europe got the highest proportion of advertising budget (39.2%) compared to the United States (37.7%) in 2008. Europe was followed by Asia-Pacific (14.9%) and Latin America (4.1%).

Automotive and Personal Care—The Top Advertised Product Categories. Interestingly, Exhibit 2.9 depicts which product categories are most advertised by those global players: automotive ($25,613 billion), personal care ($25,480 billion), food ($11,914 billion), drugs ($10,323 billion), and entertainment and media ($9.608 billion). This means that five product categories constitute, quite stagnating, 70.33 percent of total media spending. Besides the monetary terms, the automotive category had the highest number of advertisers (18 companies) but faced the most challenges in the economic downturn. The highest percentage increases included other categories, such as electronics (20.7%), retail (17.8%), toys (12.8%), and cleaners (10.7%), while decreases occurred in the technology (11.5%) and financial (9.0%) categories.

Exhibit 2.9 Top 100 Global Advertisers' Spending by Category

	Measured Media Spending (billion US$)			Advertiser
Category	**2008**	**2007**	**% Change**	**Count**
Automotive	25,613	25,597	0.1	18
Personal care	25,480	24,630	3.4	11
Food	11,914	11,356	4.9	9
Drugs	10,323	10,143	1.8	11
Entertainment/media	9,608	9,787	–1.8	7
Retail	5,969	5,069	17.8	8
Restaurants	4,289	3,912	9.6	4
Soft drinks	4,064	3,861	5.3	2
Telephone	3,974	3,868	2.7	4
Cleaners	3,829	3,459	10.7	3
Beer, wine, and liquor	2,681	2,626	2.1	5
Financial	2,595	2,852	-9.0	6
Electronics and imaging	2,100	1,928	8.9	3
Technology	2,035	2,299	–11.5	4
Electronics	1,846	1,529	20.7	2
Toys	1,607	1,425	12.8	3

Source: Worldwide Advertising Spending by Regions. *Advertising Age*, Copyrighted 2011 Crain Communications.

In summary, the aforementioned tables and trends imply that global advertisers and agencies do indeed have an increased appetite to advertise in Europe, the Asia-Pacific region, and Latin America. This validates the need to analyze and discuss the three regions in more detail.

3 Advertising and Promotion Agencies.

Advertisers are fortunate to have a full complement of agencies that specialize in literally every detail of advertising and promotion. Let's take a closer look at the types of agencies advertisers can rely on to help create their advertising and IBP campaigns.

Advertising Industry in Europe.

In the context of the structure of the advertising industry, the media industry is of particular interest, as that industry player ultimately delivers any given advertising to the local target markets or end consumers.[40]

The European publishing industry, as one of the message delivery components, is estimated to account for some 0.5 percent of the gross domestic product across the European Union's 27 member states and employs around 750,000 jobs in more than 64,000 companies across today's European Union (BIS, 2010). Exemplifying the UK market, the publishing sector as a whole is the largest creative industry. It has a combined turnover of at least £20 billion with approximately 8,500 companies directly employing around 167,000 people (BIS, 2010). Exhibit 2.10 summarizes the top 10 European media company groups in 2007. It shows that the top three faced a decrease in revenue.

In line with the aforementioned global developments, European media companies suffered (and still suffer) from the global economic recession and were intensively engaged in cost management policies. Fortunately, some bright signs seemed

Exhibit 2.10 European Media Company Groups

Company	Country	Revenue 2007 (million euro)	Change 2007 versus 2006 (%)
Thomson Reuters	Great Britain	8,438	–7.1
WPP Group	Great Britain	8,422	–3.9
Reed Elsevier	Netherlands	7,791	–1.8
British Sky Broadcasting	Great Britain	6,761	12.7
RTL Group	Luxembourg	5,707	1.2
Pearson	Great Britain	5,667	-7.7
Thomson	France	5,630	–3.8
Publicis Groupe	France	4,671	6.5
Mediaset	Italy	4,033	8.7
Prisa	Spain	3,620	32.7

Source: Based on Handelsblatt.com.

40. Colin Blackman, "Paying the Price: The Future for Europe's Media Sector," Foresight, vol. 6, no. 5, 2004, 292–301.

to appear on the horizon—that revenues in 2010 did increase on a year-to-year basis and that the company groups became profitable again in the fourth quarter of 2009. However, these optimistic data cannot yet be interpreted as a general and sustainable change in the ad market.[41]

Accordingly, the leading German media group ProSiebenSat1 increased its results mainly due to higher advertising revenues in its German heartland. Regarding the first four months of 2010, the forecasts of ITV, the United Kingdom's biggest private television company, were very optimistic, ranging from 15–20 percent sales increases in April. Dawley also referred to a ZenithOptimedia forecast implying a divergent trend apparent for the Central European Media Enterprises, which had to report a decrease of net revenues by 30 percent, to US $714 million, on a year-to-year basis in 2009.[42]

This forecast is contradictory to last year's expectations, anticipating less of a downturn for Central and Eastern European (CEE) countries compared to their Western pendants. This suggests differentiating countries, which are more advanced in the free market arena and have slower growth rates, such as Turkey, Greece, and Hungary, from smaller markets such as Belarus, Bosnia, and Romania, which will experience double-digit growth rates in the next few years. In the context of systemic implications of the global economic crisis, dwindling advertising income, and the necessity to provide external democratic pluralism in Central and Eastern Europe, a discussion on media development as an alternative to that of the U.S. and Western European model is initiated by Peters (2010, 273): "Less trust in the market and support for a variety of models to fund journalism-advertising, sales, donations, paid services, public money, low-interest loans etc. seems to be the way forward and Europe and the United States can learn from the experiences in building independent media in the developing world."[43]

Internet: The Change Protagonist. In spite of the severe economic impact in 2009, the spending on online advertising continued to increase by 2 percent, to $55.2 billion, and is anticipated to grow to $61.8 billion globally in 2010.[44]

Media channel related ad expenditure forecasts in Western Europe for 2009 envisage a continuous double-digit growth rate of the Internet (11.9% compared to 17.2% in 2008) and an even stronger decline compared to 2008 for the TV (1.6% versus 1.3%) and newspapers (4.1% versus 3.8%). Exhibit 2.11 reflects the increasing level of replacement of the newspaper medium, especially in Scandinavian countries, by the Internet, referring to the degree of reading or downloading of newspapers/news magazines over the Internet.

Whereas magazines and outdoor channels are forecasted to decrease at the same level as they did in 2008 (4% and 1.5%, respectively), radio and cinema can slightly reverse the negative trend (0.4% versus 1.1% and 1.4% versus 2.3%, respectively) (Dawley, 2008). ZenithOptimedia reversed its pessimistic forecast for magazines from −1 to +2 percent for 2010.[45]

In 2009, a total of euro 14.7 billion was spent on digital advertising in 23 European countries. This signifies an increase of 4.5 percent compared to what was

41. Dataxis, 2010, accessed at http://openpr.com on October 29, 2010.

42. Heidi Dawley, "For Europe, a not so Harsh Slowdown," 2008, accessed at http://www.medialifemagazine.com on September 13, 2010; and Dataxis, 2010, accessed at http://openpr.com on October 29, 2010.

43. Bettina Peters, "The Future of Journalism and Challenges for Media Development. Are We Exporting a Model that No Longer Works at Home?" *Journalism Practice*, vol. 4, issue 3, 2010, 268-273.

44. ReportLinker, "Worldwide Ad Spending," accessed at www.repoterlinker.com/p0265745/worldwide-Ad-Spending.pdf on November 22, 2010.

45. "Global Advertising Growth Expected," *WA Today*, 2010, accessed at http://www.watoday.com.au/breaking-news-business on October 20, 2010.

Exhibit 2.11 Proportion of Individual Reading/Downloading Newspapers/News Magazines over the Internet for Private Purposes in 2008

Country	Percentage
Norway	73
Denmark	52
United Kingdom	37
Slovak Republic	34
Czech Republic	33
Austria	30
Spain	27
Germany	21
Poland	19
Italy	17

Source: Based on OECD ICT database, Korea, Japan, and New Cronos, Eurostat.

spent in 2008. Three big markets dominate the picture: the United Kingdom (euro 3.32 billion), Germany (euro 3.1 billion), and France (euro 1.8 billion).[46] In her report on Western European online ad spending, Karin von Abrams refers to eMarketer forecasting the Western European online advertising spending to be $17.1 billion in 2010 and $24.3 billion in 2014.[47]

In summary, a shifting trend in the media spending structure becomes apparent: the continuous decline of newspapers (to approximately a 20 percent share in 2011) will be compensated by the corresponding increase of the Internet (approximately a 15 percent share in media spending in 2011). Consequently, classic media consumption is changing to Internet-connected media (that is, PCs, smartphones, and game consoles).

Similar to what is seen in the United States and the rest of the world, the number of Internet users in Europe continues to grow. In 2009, already 50 percent of European households had Internet access (IAB, 2010). The usage time also increased drastically in the last few years. While in 2009 Europeans spent an average of nine hours per week online, it was predicted that by the middle of 2010, they would be spending more time on the Internet than in front of their TVs. Finally, whereas the traditional media have their peak times (for example, 7–9 a.m. for radio and 8–10 p.m. for TV), the Internet reaches audiences at different times of the day. Today, seventy percent of Europeans use the Internet and TV simultaneously (IAB, 2010). Some audience groups are less likely to use traditional media (TV and radio) and are accustomed to and more inclined to use online media. That is, the 14- to 19-year-old segment consists of particularly heavy users of the Web and social media. Today, more consumers have convenient Internet access through high-speed connections and a range of connected devices, thereby altering their media consumption habits even more (IAB, 2010).[48]

46. Catherine Borrel, "Europe Achieves Growth in Digital Ad Spend Despite Global Recession," 2010, accessed at http://www.nma.co.uk/opinion/industry/analyst-speak-europe-achieves-growth-in-digital-ad-despite-global-recesion/3014734.article on February 25, 2011.

47. Karin von Abrams, "Western Europe Online Ad Spending: Leading the Recovery," 2010, accessed at www.emarketer.com/Report.aspx?code=emarketer_2000724 on October 18, 2010.

48. IAB Europe AdEx 2009 Report, "European Internet Advertising Expenditure in 2009," accessed at http://www.scribd.com/doc/45741857/AdEx-2009-European-online-advertising-expenditure on October 20, 2010.

Country	Total (billion pounds)	Internet %	Newspaper %	TV %	Magazine %	Outdoor %	Radio %	Cinema %
United Kingdom	13.1	27	25	28	9	6	4	1
France	10.3	16	21	30	15	11	7	-
Germany	15.4	18	36	23	14	5	4	-
Italy	7.4	10	18	52	12	2	5	1
Spain	4.9	12	23	43	7	5	9	1
Netherlands	3.3	22	31	21	15	4	6	1
Sweden	1.8	25	35	22	9	5	3	1
Ireland	1.1	8	45	25	2	9	10	1

Source: Based on Warc Data, 2010.

Exhibit 2.12 2009 Advertising Expenditure Analysis

Exhibit 2.12 ranks the Western European countries in terms of overall advertising expenditure and provides the respective market shares of the different media. The table reflects the high level of cultural diversity across the Western European countries, leading to diverse priorities of media usage among the countries.

The leading Western European countries in advertising expenditures are Germany (UK£15.5 billion), followed by France (UK£10.3 billion) and the United Kingdom (UK£13.1 billion). Referring to the different types of media utilized, the United Kingdom (27%) invests more on the Internet than does any other Western European country, followed by Sweden (25%) and the Netherlands (22%). The countries scoring high in using newspapers as advertising media are Ireland (45%), followed by Germany (36%) and Sweden (35%). Mediterranean countries like Italy (52%) and Spain (43%), on the other hand, rely heavily on TV advertising. Related to magazine advertising, France (15%), the Netherlands (15%), and Germany (14%) lead in expenditures. Outdoor advertising is used mainly by France (11%), followed by Ireland (9%). Advertising on radio programs is used largely by the Irish (10%), followed by the Spanish (9%). Finally, expenditures on cinema media seem to be very low or even insignificant for all of the countries.

Exemplarily for the diverse and crisis-hit Western European advertising industry, the idiosyncratic French market conditions are referenced. Although the advertising industry in France has had a sharp decline in revenues of about 12 percent during the last couple of years, it still secures second place on the European advertising chart. The total advertising revenues for 2009 were approximately €10.3 billion as opposed to €11.8 billion in 2008.

This drop in advertising media revenues equals a net loss of nearly €1.5 billion for 2009 and, as anyone can expect, was directly impacted by the global economic crisis.

According to the Association of Consulting Agencies in Communication (*Association des Agences-Conseils en Communication*), the total communication expenses for advertisements in 2009 were estimated at euro 29.7 billion, with most being spent in direct marketing (30.3%) followed by promotion (15.7%), TV (12.3%), and the press (11.9%). The French situation confirms the general global trend of the press losing swift ground (–17.2%). Also, TV suffered a media share decline by 11 percent. However, compared to global development, with only 4 percent, the Internet still has a low market share (see Exhibit 2.13).

Exhibit 2.13 Communication Expenses Advertisers

Media	Amount (billion euro)	Evolution 2009/2008	Market Shares
TV	3.660	–11%	12.3%
Movies	0.117	0%	0.4%
Radio	0.839	–8.9%	2.8%
Internet	1.179	–1.5%	4.0%
Press	3.547	–17.2%	11.9%
Display	1.290	–11.3%	4.3%
Directories	1.259	–2.0%	4.2%
Direct marketing	9.027	–5.6%	30.3%
Promotion	4.683	–8.3%	15.7%
Exhibitions and fairs	1.439	–6.5%	4.8%
Sponsorship	0.768	–7.8%	2.6%
Philanthropy	0.332	–6.2%	1.1%
Public relations	1.659	–9.5%	5.6%
TOTAL	29.799	–8.6%	100.0%

Source: Based on IREP.

At the same time, in France, most of the advertising revenues for 2009 (see Exhibit 2.14) were generated from the press (36.3%) and television (30.0%). These two media covered more than two-thirds of all advertising revenues generated in the advertising industry of France.

Exhibit 2.15 shows the positive signs of recovery of the French advertising industry in the first half of 2010. Most of the media reflect a single-digit growth rate, with movies and TV enjoying a double-digit growth rate. However, the table also confirms the decreasing trend with regard to newspapers (–18.9%).

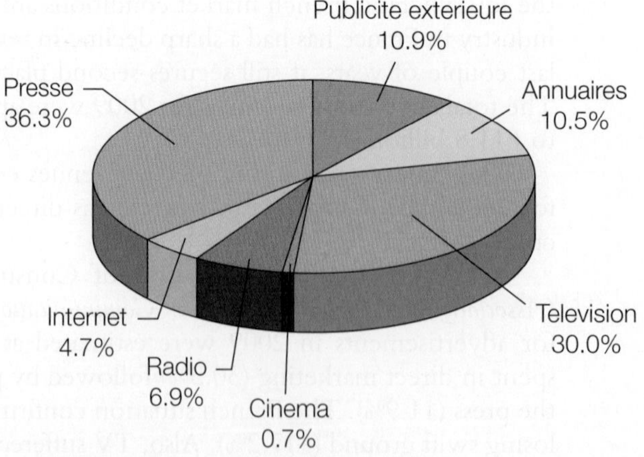

Source: Based on IREP—The French Advertising Market.

Exhibit 2.14 Market Share of Advertising Revenue by Media in 2009

Exhibit 2.15 Media Summary 2010 versus 2009

Media	H1. 2010 (M. €)	H1. 2010/1st half. 2009%	H1. 2009/1st half. 2008%
TV (screen and sponsorship)	1,655	+12	–19.4
Movies	29	+14.7	–24.2
Radio (national advertising)	290	+7.6	–14.7
Internet (display)	264	+9	–7
PQN (ad + ACC)	137	+2.4	–24.8
PQR (ad + ACC)	467	–4.3	–11.8
Magazine (advertising)	577	+2.6	–18.4
Press (advertising + PA)	206	–4.8	n
Free newspaper ad	277	–18.9	–32.2
Free press Information	60	+5.7	+3
PHR (ad + ACC)	64	+0.8	n
Outdoor advertising	600	+7.3	–14.7
Total	4,626	+4.6	–18.1

Source: Based on IREP.

Exhibit 2.16 presents the leading advertisers in four major Western European countries: Italy, the United Kingdom, France, and Germany.

Internet and Media Consumer Trends in Europe. To analyze and review the different trends with regard to consumer behavior in Western Europe, Bruner conducted a survey focusing on how French, British, and German consumers see the role of digital media in their purchase decisions.[49]

Exhibit 2.16 European Leading Advertisers in 2009 by Advertising Expenditure

Country	Leading Advertisers
Italy: Estimated US $11.9 bio in 2010	1. Telecom Italia 2. Wind 3. Ferrero
UK: Estimated US $18.3 bio in 2010	1. COI 2. Procter & Gamble 3. Unilever
France: Estimated US $13.3 bio in 2010	1. Vivendi 2. PSA 3. L'Oréal
Germany: Estimated US $22.1 bio in 2010	1. Media Markt/Saturn (Metro) 2. Procter & Gamble 3. Aldi

Source: Based on GroupM, 2009.

49. Rick E. Bruner, "How French, British, and German Consumers See the Role of Digital Media in Their Purchase Decision," DoubleClick Touchpoints IV—Europe, 2006, accessed at www.odgintelligence.com on November 10, 2010, 48.

This research involved online surveying of respondents from major Western European countries such as France, Germany, and the United Kingdom. The goal of the research was to determine the attitudes and factors of behavior influencing consumers' purchasing decisions when utilizing the Internet. The sample consisted of 1,245 adult consumers in the United Kingdom, 1,173 in France, and 1,166 in Germany and was contrasted with the results of a previous sample of 2,988 respondents from the United States. Some of the findings related to discovering new products, finding information about products, and identifying influential factors that affect customer behavior by utilizing the Internet are introduced.

Intending to determine how consumers in the particular countries find out about products of interest, the survey asked how the people first heard about the products they bought most recently.

The survey showed that consumers in the United Kingdom and the United States were using websites as a way to find particular new products, followed by word of mouth.

French consumers found out about recently purchased products mostly from salespeople, followed by word of mouth and websites. At the same time, similar results were shown in Germany, with word of mouth being at the top of the list, followed by salespeople, Web ads, and category influencers (experts). Similar to their French counterparts, German consumers chose word of mouth and the salesperson for their preferred information media. Consequently, the study's aim was to differentiate the role of the Internet for new product information as to different countries: U.S. and UK consumers predominantly used the Internet, whereas the Western European countries of France and Germany preferred personal face-to-face media. Interestingly, in France and Germany, the salesperson had a significantly stronger influence on new product information than he or she did in the United States. When consumers were searching for more information about products, the results from the survey showed similar trends among all market segments, with websites being the most influential factor for all consumers and the United States and the United Kingdom exhibiting the highest levels, followed by France and Germany. The survey showed that the salesperson had the strongest influence in the United States.

Beyond these findings, the survey tried to find the influential factors that largely affected consumers' behavior and their decision to purchase a product.

For French consumers, salespeople seemed to be very influential in decision making, with over 23 percent of the respondents showing trust in the salespeople and about 17 percent relying on word of mouth when deciding whether to purchase a product, closely followed by German consumers.

In Germany, word of mouth seemed to be the decisive factor influencing consumers' decisions, narrowly followed by salespeople and Web advertisements.

Finally, as expected, British and U.S. consumers cited websites as the most influential factor in deciding whether to purchase a product, follow by word of mouth in the United Kingdom and stores in the United States.

Comparing the different factors among the three consumer markets, word of mouth proved to be most consistent for consumers deciding on whether to purchase a particular product.

A further example of the necessity to differentiate international consumers with regard to their media selection process was provided by Bozbay's explanatory research study. She investigated the role of gender on website attribute perceptions and consumers' intentions to visit websites in Turkey. Conclusively, significant gender differences existed regarding perceptions of ease of use, personality, and fun attributes. The study implied a stronger focus on female consumers and gender-orientated and differentiated marketing strategies.[50]

50. Zehra Bozbay "The Role of Gender on Retailing: Gender Differences in Perceptions of Web-Site Attributes and Intention to Visit," 2011 in Hans Ruediger Kaufmann, *International Consumer Behavior: A Mosaic of Eclectic Perspectives*, 101-110, (Darwen/UK: Access Press, UK, 2011) ISBN: 978-0-9562471-31.

Rashid referred to preconditions for using the Internet as a means for relationship building. Having conducted a case study on students' perceptions of the Leeds Metropolitan University website, relational drivers were identified for relationship building. The research concluded that relational drivers such as customer orientation, service quality, experience, trust, shared values, communication, student satisfaction, commitment, and loyalty are reflected by newsgroups, chat forums, bulletin board systems, and voice and conferencing facilities.[51]

Similar to Rashid, Pantano proposed to use advanced technology for designing relationship strategies. She presented a new stimulating store concept based on virtual or augmented reality. Advanced media applications were seen to act as product knowledge communicators. In particular, augmented reality, mainly due to the presence of new, enjoyable elements, contributed to higher perception levels of "shopping as fun" due to the immersive and exciting experience provided in the store.[52]

Advertising Industry in European Transitional Economies.

In the discussion of global advertising structures in general and European aspects in particular, politics is one of the determinant macro environmental factors creating a new landscape of the advertising industry. As a historical political incidence, the collapse of Soviet communism gave birth to the so-called transitional economies in Central and Eastern European countries. Currently, the consequences are still being felt.

During Soviet times, in CEE countries, the practice of centrally allocating products was used and advertising was almost nonexistent. Not until 1991 was consumer advertising freed from state censorship. Previously, media were state-owned, and their main purpose was to inform consumers about product availability and to promote cultural and sport activities.[53] The impact of this time can be seen, for example, in Polish consumers who were reluctant to buy products that were overadvertised because this behavior reminded them of the communist propaganda techniques that led to brand damage.

In the initial stage, the Czech Republic was eager to embrace consumer trends imported from the West. Today, due to the changing conditions in the world's economy, attitudes of Czech consumers toward advertising can be considered middle of the road—being neither too enthusiastic nor too negative.[54] They do not seem to be easily impressed by the promises of smart TV ads because they are now more suspicious and aware of competition.

In 2005, the total advertising expenditure in the Czech Republic amounted to € 1,447 million. The lion's share of this expenditure was spent on advertising home/office equipment (€ 323.8 million), food and drink (€ 306.8 million), and pharmaceutical products (€ 272.6 million). The media market shares were split into TV (46.1%), magazines (20.1%), newspapers (16.5%), Internet and cinema (6.8%), radio (5.3%), and outdoor (5.2%) (Western Europe Market & MediaFact 2008, CIA Factbook 2009 accessed at http://www.business-process.org/members/Czech_republic/index.html on February 18, 2011).

51. Tahir Rashid, "Strategic Orientations for Customer Oriented Website Design," 2011 in Hans Ruediger Kaufmann, *International Consumer Behavior: A Mosaic of Eclectic Perspectives*, 310-319, (Darwen/UK:Access Press, 2011) ISBN: 978-0-9562471-31.

52. Eleonora Pantano, "New Advances in Retailing," 2011, in Hans Ruediger Kaufmann, *International Consumer Behavior: A Mosaic of Eclectic Perspectives*, 320-333 (Darwen/UK: Access Press, 2011) ISBN: 978-0-9562471-31.

53. Elena Millan and Banwari Mittal, "Advertising New Audiences, Consumer Response in the New Free Market Economies of Central and Eastern Europe—The Case of the Czech Republic," *Journal of Advertising*, vol. 39, no. 3, 2010, 81-87.

54. Shintaro Okazaki and Radoslav Skapa, "Global Web Site Standardization in the New EU Member States—Initial Observations from Poland and the Czech Republic," *European Journal of Marketing*, vol. 43, no. 11/12, 2008, 1124-1245.

Exhibit 2.17 Eastern European and Russian Advertising Expenditures

Advertising Expenditure as a % of GDP in 2010		TV Expenditures (million US$)
Bulgaria	1.94	$550
Croatia	2.37	960
Czech Republic	1.42	1,451
Estonia	0.72	51
Hungary	2.12	2,238
Poland	0.55	1,791
Romania	0.59	723
Russia	1.04	8,630

Source: ZenithOptimedia, 2008.

Exhibit 2.17 underlines the dominance of TV used for media spending across a variety of Eastern European countries, followed by magazines.

Current new consumer trends already having a significant influence refer to the presence of social networks (for example, Facebook, Twitter, and You Tube) in Central and Eastern Europe. Consistent with global development, Internet advertising budgets are gaining ground against more traditional means of advertising—for example, newspaper and print ads are already showing signs of decline.[55]

Exhibit 2.18 delineates the development of Eastern European Internet usage. The highest percentage of the population using the Internet can be found in the Baltic states of Estonia (75.1%) and Latvia (67.8%), followed by the Czech Republic (65.5%). In terms of absolute users, the highest level of Internet users is found in Poland, followed by Romania and the Czech Republic.

Relating to Internet acceptance in Central and Eastern European transition countries, Brčić-Stipčević, Guszak, and Sopta stress that transition countries embrace contemporary trends and strategies more slowly.[56] The authors investigated how Internet as an additional channel affects total sales of the two market leaders and how

Exhibit 2.18 Eastern Europe in Internet Usage

Country	Year	Users	% Population
Poland	2000 2010	3,700,000 22,450,600	9.7 58.4
Czech Republic	2000 2010	1,000,000 6,680,000	9.7 65.5
Estonia	2000 2010	366,000 969,700	28.2 75.1
Romania	2000 2010	800,000 7,786,700	3.6 35.5
Lithuania	2000 2010	225,000 2,103,000	15.5 59.3
Croatia	2000 2010	200,000 2,244,400	4.6 50.0
Latvia	2000 2010	150,000 1,503,400	6.5 67.8

Source: Based on Internet World Stats, 2010.

55. The Warsaw Voice, 2010, accessed at http://www.warsawvoice.pl on November 12, 2010.

56. Hans Ruediger Kaufmann, *International Consumer Behavior: A Mosaic of Eclectic Perspectives,* 44-55 (Darwin/UK: Access Press, 2011) ISBN: 978-0-9562471-31.

Exhibit 2.19 Leading Advertisers in Eastern Europe and Russia

Country	Three Leading Advertisers in 2009	Estimated Ad Expenditure in 2010 per Country (billion US$)
Czech Republic	1. Unilever 2. Procter & Gamble 3. Henkel	0.861
Russia	1. Procter & Gamble 2. L'Oréal 3. Unilever	7.8
Poland	1. Unilever 2. Nestlé 3. Polkomtel	2.5

Source: Based on GroupM, 2010.

consumers react to FMCG Web stores in Croatia. The results indicate that additional channel introduction did not result in high Internet sales. Rather, the Internet was and still is used to enhance promotion of the store network and to attract customers from competitors. Interestingly, the authors concluded that it is more likely that in the near future, customers will choose physical stores to satisfy their emotional needs while using the Internet for secondary shopping trips.

Exhibit 2.19 highlights the fact that some of the most successful global advertisers have embarked on entering Eastern Europe and Russia.

Advertising Industry in Asia.

Over the last three decades, East Asia, including Japan, China, Taiwan, and South Korea, as well as Asia Pacific (especially India) belonged to the fastest-growing regions of the world. Along with Brazil (Latin America) and Russia, India and China are commonly grouped as prospective growth nations under the acronym BRIC. Because the focus of global business is focused firmly on the BRIC countries, marketers and advertisers face a growing need to understand the idiosyncratic marketing environment in these countries. Japanese consumers, for example, are among the most demanding in the world; thus, international brands commonly need to modify their business strategies, products, and communications approaches to survive and thrive in the Japanese market.[57]

Asia, with over three-fifths of the world's population, presents many challenges and opportunities for global businesses, particularly in the advertising industry.[58] The people and stages of economic development of the Asian countries are quite diverse, yet many cultural factors (for example, Western culture and globalization) transcend the different societies.

While Japan is an industrialized nation, the Chinese Economic Area (including Taiwan) and Korea are among the 10 big emerging markets promising tremendous opportunities for trade.[59] In addition, these countries are key trading partners with each other as well as with the United States (South Korea, 1999). Therefore, it is critical to understand the complexities when advertising in these markets.[60]

57. See Lynne Ciochetto, "Advertising and Globalization in India," Emerging Markets Economy, 2004, accessed at www.sasnet.lu.se/EASASpapers/7LynneCiochetto.pdf on November 25, 2010; Katherine Toland Frith, "Advertising in Asia: Communication, Culture and Consumption, Ames," Iowa State University Press, 1996; and Warren J. Keegan and Mark C. Green, *Global Marketing* 5th Edition (New Jersey: Pearson Prentice Hall, 2008).

58. Charles C. Taylor and Mary Anne Raymond, "An Analysis of Product Category Restrictions in Advertising in Four Major East Asian Markets," *International Marketing Review*, vol. 17, no. 3, 2000, 287–304.

59. Lynne Ciochetto, "Advertising and Globalization in India," Emerging Markets Economy, 2004, accessed at www.sasnet.lu.se/EASASpapers/7LynneCiochetto.pdf on November 25, 2010.

60. Charles R. Taylor and Mary Anne Raymond, "An Analysis of Product Category Restrictions in Advertising in Four Major East Asian Markets," *International Marketing Review*, vol. 17, no. 3, 2000, 287–304.

Particularly in Asia, the development of advertising industries is subject to each country's unique regulatory environment and social structure.[61] As an example, the advertising industry in South Korea is different from that in China due to South Korea's economic atmosphere of increasing deregulation. On the other hand, China still emphasizes a heavily regulated environment.

Media discovered that the advertising demand in Asia was quite constant, yet one of the key challenges for any agency in this region was to help prioritize its clients' needs. Especially in China, the clients were hunting for ideas and breaking alignments and historic patterns, looking for new partnerships.[62] Besides, along with the intense pressure on results, there was also an increasing demand for ROI, both from international and regional clients. Business savvy is still the most critical competency as clients are expecting the agencies to help them with more upstream strategic thinking.[63]

Exhibit 2.20 shows that the Internet achieved its highest market penetration in Japan (78.2%), followed by Taiwan (70.1%), with a great deal of potential to be exploited in China (31.6%) and, especially, India (6.9%). The table also shows that social media are in the introduction stage of the product life cycle.

Advertising Industry in Japan. Japan represents the world's second-largest advertising market compared to the United States.[64] The proportion of advertising budget spent in various media is similar to what is spent in media in the United States, with TV being the most preferred medium although it is very expensive and there is huge competition for time slots. After TV, newspaper is very popular given the long travel distance and high literacy rate. A trend in Japan is to spend more of the promotion budget on sales promotion, event sponsorship, and direct marketing as they present more opportunities for advertising controversial products that might be hindered by various restrictions.[65] In addition, corporate branding is more important

Country	Year	Population	Internet Users	Market Penetration	Facebook Users	Market Penetration
Japan	2010	126,804,433	99,143,700	78.2%	1,348,860	0.6%
India	2010	1,173,108,018	81,000,000 (Nov. 2008)	6.9%	13,188,580	1.1%
China	2010	1,330,141,295	420,000,000	31.6%	24,060	0%
Taiwan	2010	23,024,956	16,130,000	70.1%	5,024,400 (June 2009)	Broadband subscriber
South Korea	2010	48,636,068	39,440,000	81.1%	15,474,900	Broadband subscriber

Source: Based on World Stats, 2010.

Exhibit 2.20 Internet and New Trends for Advertising in Asia

61. In-Bok Song, "The Next Frontier: Business Services in Asia," Asia Insight, 2010, accessed at http://mathews-funds.com on October 15, 2010.

62. *Advertising Age*, "Media Report: Agency Report Card," 2006, accessed at http://adage.com/datacenter/ on December 2, 2010.

63. Charles R.Taylor and Mary Anne Raymond, "An Analysis of Product Category Restrictions in Advertising in Four Major East Asian Markets," *International Marketing Review*, vol. 17, no. 3, 2000, 287–304.

64. Charles R.Taylor and Mary Anne Raymond, "An Analysis of Product Category Restrictions in Advertising in Four Major East Asian Markets," *International Marketing Review*, vol. 17, no. 3, 2000, 287–304.

65. Charles R.Taylor and Mary Anne Raymond, "An Analysis of Product Category Restrictions in Advertising in Four Major East Asian Markets," *International Marketing Review*, vol. 17, no. 3, 2000, 287–304.

Exhibit 2.21 Advertising Expenditures Classified by Medium

Media	Fluctuation
Newspapers	−18.6%
Magazines	−25.6%
Radio	−11.6%
TV	−10.2%
Satellite media-related	+4.9%
Internet	+1.2%
Promotional media	−11.8%

Source: Based on DENTSU INC., 2010.

than product branding, reflecting an emphasis on relationships in the high-context Japanese culture.[66]

Sharing the lot of many other countries, Japan's advertisement industry experienced the detrimental implications of the economic recession. The total amount of advertisement expenditures for 2009 amounted to yen 5,922.2 billion, plummeting by 11.5 percent for the second year in a row.[67] Whereas only the Internet and satellite media-related classifications slightly increased their market share, the market shares of all other media saw a double-digit decrease, especially magazines and newspapers (see Exhibit 2.21). The detailed structure of advertising expenditure by media and the structural changes provided in Exhibit 2.22 shows that the 1.5 percent structural decline of traditional media was compensated by the Internet (+1.5%), whereas promotional media stagnated at a share of approximately 39 percent.

Advertising Industry in China. In recent years, advertising in China has grown at a breathtaking rate: By 1996, the total advertising spending had already been estimated at $3.9 billion, making China the world's eighth-largest advertising market.[68] However, while traditional media (TV, radio, print, and outdoor advertising) were in use, the advertising industry was not yet fully fledged.[69] With a population of over 1.2 billion, China was predicted to have substantial growth potential.[70] In 12 years, China had grown its advertising spending to $20.7 billion, making it the fifth-largest market globally in 2008.[71] Moreover, taking the size and growth of the market into account, the advertising expenditure per person is extremely low, making China an ever-attractive opportunity for many advertisers.

66. Anthony Pecotich and Juliette C. Shultz, "*Marketing and Consumer Behavior in East and South-East Asia*," (Australia: McGraw-Hill, 1998).

67. Dentsu, 2010, "Advertising Expenditures in Japan 2009," accessed at http://wwwdentsu.com/marketing/pdf/expenditures_2009.pdf on November 10, 2010.

68. D. Cushman, J. Mayfield, and G. Wong, "Market Research Reports: China Advertising," National Trade Data Bank, Washington: U.S. Department of Commerce, 1997, in Charles R.Taylor and Mary Anne Raymond, "An Analysis of Product Category Restrictions in Advertising in Four Major East Asian Markets," *International Marketing Review*, vol. 17, no. 3, 2000, 287-304.

69. Ritu Lohtia, Wesley Johnston, and Linda Aab, "Creation of an Effective Print Advertisement for the China Market: An Analysis and Advice," *Journal of Global Marketing*, vol. 8, no. 2, 1994, 729-736; and Yong Zhang and Betsy Gelb, "Matching Advertising Appeals to Culture: The Influence of Products' Use Conditions," *Journal of Advertising*, vol. 25, no. 3, 1996, 29-46.

70. Hong Cheng and John C. Schweitzer, "Cultural Values Reflected in China and US Advertising," *Journal of Advertising Research*, vol. 36, no. 3, 1996, 27-41.

71. In-Bok Song, "The Next Frontier: Business Services in Asia," Asia Insight, 2010, accessed at http://mathewsfunds.com on October 15, 2010.

Exhibit 2.22 Japan Advertising Expenditures by Medium (2008–2009)

	Advertising Expenditures (billion)	
Media	**2008**	**2009**
Traditional Media		
Newspapers	827.6	673.9
Magazines	407.8	303.4
Radio	154.9	137.0
TV	1,909.2	1,713.9
Subtotal	3,299.5 (49.3%)	2,828.2 (47.76%) −1.54%
Satellite media-related	67.6	70.9
Internet		
Advertising placement	537.3	544.8
Advertising production	161.0	162.1
Subtotal	698.3 (10.43%)	706.9 (11.94%) +1.51%
Promotional Media		
Outdoor	370.9	321.8
Transit	249.5	204.5
Flyers	615.6	544.4
Direct mail	442.7	419.8
Free newspapers/magazines	354.5	288.1
POP	185.2	183.7
Telephone directories	89.2	76.4
Exhibitions/screen displays	319.6	277.5
Subtotal	2,627.2 (39.26%)	2,316.2 (39.11%)
Total	6,692.6	5,922.2

Source: Based on DENTSU INC., 2010.

Exhibit 2.23 illustrates an excerpt from the top 100 global advertisers' spending in China. Specifically, the data are drawn from 39 of those 100 advertisers that had measured media spending in China. The largest spenders in monetary terms are P&G (over $1 billion), Unilever (over $480 million), and L'Oréal (over $330 million). However, in terms of proportion to total worldwide advertising spending, P&G is only in fifth position (11.1%), Unilever is in seventh position (8.5%), and L'Oréal is in eighth position (8.3%). Here, Yum Brands is heading the list with 20.5 percent (over $280 million), followed by Pernod Ricard (14.9%, $50 million), and Avon Products (14.9%, $49 million). Thus, this trend somewhat portrays China's tremendous GDP growth, bulging trade surpluses, and huge flows of FDI.

However, even with immense industry growth, the vast pool of advertising agencies (69,000 advertising agencies in 2002), and its large market size, China's advertising industry is still hindered by strict regulations, the dominance of China Central TV (CCTV), financial difficulties of local TV stations, and the above-mentioned lack of transparency and business complexities (Song, 2010). Although this industry poses huge challenges for investors, it still remains an indispensable business as domestic consumption growth continues.

Further developments take place in the less regulated area, which is outdoor advertising (liquid crystal display panels; signage; and billboards in public venues, buildings, and vehicles). Additionally, the lack of transparency and the

Exhibit 2.23 Top 100 Global Advertisers' Spending in China

Rank	Advertiser	2008 Measured Media Spending in China (million US$)	China Spending as % of Worldwide Spending
1	Yum Brands	289.5	20.5
2	Pernod Ricard	50.2	14.9
3	Avon Products	49.6	14.9
4	Colgate-Palmolive Co.	145.2	13.8
5	Procter & Gamble Co.	1,079.1	11.1
6	Moet Hennessy Louis Vuitton	54.7	8.7
7	Unilever	487.0	8.5
8	L'Oréal	333.3	8.3
9	PepsiCo	105.3	7.6
10	Nokia Corp.	32.9	7.4

Source: Based on *Advertising Age*, 2009.

complexities in media buying practices (varying discounts, volume rebates, and bonus inventory deals) have also facilitated the development of companies that specialize in outdoor media. Recently, advertising business flourishes particularly in the field of digital communication.

International companies operating in the Chinese market find it indispensable to consider the market share of each medium and to use this knowledge for their communications mix strategies and tactics. The market shares of Chinese media are listed below. Also see Exhibit 2.24 as to the amount of media spending.

- Television has the largest market share at 41 percent.
- The second-highest market share is held by newspapers at 26 percent.
- The market size of China's outdoor media is approximately 14 percent.
- The Chinese online advertising and magazine market share is 7 percent.
- The lower market size is held by radio advertising, which is only 5 percent.[72]

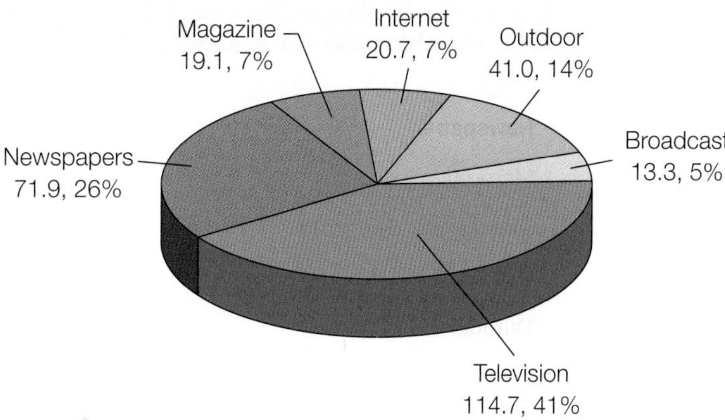

Exhibit 2.24 Total Amount of Media Spending—Media Preferences

Source: Research in China.

72. Researchinchina, 2010, accessed at http://www.researihchina.com/ on October 28, 2010.

Company	Country
McCann Worldgroup Asia Pacific	Hong Kong
BBDO/Proximity Asia	Singapore
TBWA	Korea
Diamond Ogilvy Group	Korea
Bates 141	India
M&C Saatchi	India

Source: Haymarket Media Ltd., a subsidiary company of Haymarket Publishing Ltd.

Exhibit 2.25 Top Advertising Companies in Asia

Company
Beijing Dentsu Advertising Co., Ltd.
Saatchi & Saatchi China
AVIC Culture Co., Ltd.
Leo Burnett Shanghai Advertising Co., Ltd.
Shanghai Advertising Co., Ltd.

Source: Based on IBISWorld, 2010.

Exhibit 2.26 Top Advertising Agencies in China

Exhibits 2.25 and 2.26 list the top advertising media companies and top advertising agencies in Asia and China, respectively.

Advertising Spending in Taiwan. Last year, Taiwan's overall media spending figure (see Exhibit 2.27) showed a decline by 13 percent to US $1.2 billion, affecting all forms of media except TV, which increased by 11 percent. From July 2008 to June 2009, the lion's share of expenditures (33.7%) flowed into pay TV, followed by newspapers (23.9%), magazines (13.6%), TV (12%), radio (9.2%), and the outdoor medium (7.5%).

Media Spending in South Korea. Reflecting the early effect of the economic downturn on South Korea's advertising sector, Exhibit 2.28 shows declines in all media activities, with the highest nominal decrease in the newspaper medium. All media forms suffered double-digit declining rates. Newspapers had the dominant market position (54.9%) in terms of share of the total media spending, followed by TV (35.4%), magazines (6%), and radio (3.5%).

Advertising Industry in India. In India, the advertising industry has experienced immense development since 1905, when the first agencies started to operate. In 1990, India's advertising industry was fueled due to the economical liberalization and media reform initiated in the 1980s by Prime Minister Rajiv Gandhi. This opened the market for foreign advertising companies as well as brands and products.[73]

Exhibit 2.27 Taiwan All Media Outlet Spending Trends

All Media Outlet Spending Trends (thousands US$)	July 2008/ June 2009	July 2007/ June 2008	% Change
TV	143,905	130,041	11
Newspaper	287,328	411,085	–30
Magazines	163,886	195,149	–16
Radio	110,986	121,955	–9
Pay TV	404,943	426,171	–5
Outdoor	89,749	100,352	–11
Total all media spending	1,200,795	1,384,754	–13

Source: Based on Advertising Trends of Asia Pacific 2008/2009. Compiled by The Nielsen Company.

73. Lynne M. Ciochetto, "Advertising and Globalization in India, Emerging Markets Economy, 2004, accessed at www.sasnet.lu.se/EASASpapers/7LynneCiochetto.pdf on November 25, 2010, and William Mazzarella, *"Shoveling Smoke: Advertising and Globalization in Contemporary India"* (London: Duke, 2003).

Exhibit 2.28 South Korea All Media Outlet Spending Trends

Media (thousands US$)	July 2008/ June 2009	July 2007/ June 2008	Change (%)
TV	1,990,435	2,276,802	–13
Newspaper	3,086,761	3,734,868	–17
Magazines	334,836	371,394	–10
Radio	196,082	262,942	–25
Total media spending	5,608,114	6,646,006	–16

Source: Based on Advertising Trends of Asia Pacific 2008/2009. Compiled by The Nielsen Company.

With a population of 1.2 billion, 22 official languages, and 35 states, the diverse attitudes toward and perceptions of advertising in this multinational country is a major challenge for marketers. The vibrant streets of New Delhi are characterized by this colorful picture of people, and an array of "visual, audible, emotional and scented stimuli swirl through all spheres of the city. Images and text provided on billboards, movie hoardings and posters are one of the main visual inputs. Advertising are [sic] part of most cities' canvasses and can be described as a key site that mirrors culture and society and simultaneously influences the same."[74] The potential problems culture can pose are reflected in Brown's research of thousands of ads in various markets across India.[75] He discovered that only one in seven advertisements achieves positive results. Cultural-related factors like using humor in advertising and using celebrities in Indian ads play a very important role. "A phenomenon peculiar to India is the presence of regional celebrities, particularly in the South. To leverage celebrities effectively, brands at times use a common advertising proposition but different celebrities in different regions. For instance, for its tariff ads, Vodafone uses Prakash Raj in the South and Irrfan Khan in other regions."[76]

To succeed, advertising strategies in India need to mirror Indian values together with cultural symbols. The product, traditional Indian values, Indian identity, and media are perceived as key success factors for sales and are used by foreign brands, international advertising agencies, and local businesses alike.[77]

Exhibit 2.29 summarizes India's leading advertisers and advertising agencies. Over the last decade, India's advertising industry experienced massive expansion and increased competition.

Regarding the media spending structure, Exhibit 2.30 shows media spending shortly before the occurrence of the global economic crisis in June 2009. Total media spending increased by 14 percent to US $7.37 billion. The highest market share was occupied by newspapers (46.6%), followed by TV (31.5%), radio (9.3%), magazines (5.8%), the outdoor medium (4.1%), other mediums (1.5%), and cinema (0.7%). Except for radio, which stagnated at the 2008 level, all media options enjoyed double-digit growth.

74. Mette Gabler, "The Good Life–Buy 1 Get 1 For Free," Südasien-Informationen, no. 17, 2010, accessed at www.suedasien.info/schriftenreihe/2869 on October 7, 2010.

75. Millward Brown, "The Advertiser's India: One Country or Many?" 2010, accessed at http://www.wpp.com/NR/rdonlyres/A2E22940-528-4632-8D4 on October 19, 2010.

76. Ibid.

77. Shailaja Bajpai and Namita Unnikrishnan, "The Impact of Television Advertising on Children" (New Delhi: Sage, 1996). ISBN: 81-7036-471-1; Lynne M. Ciochetto, "Advertising and Globalization in India, Emerging Markets Economy, 2004, accessed at www.sasnet.lu.se/EASASpapers/7LynneCiochetto.pdf on November 25, 2010; William Mazzarella, "Shoveling Smoke: Advertising and Globalization in Contemporary India" (London: Duke, 2003); Paolo Favero, "Indian Dreams. Cultural Identity among Young Middle Class Men in New Delhi" (Stockholm: Almqvist & Wiksell, International, 2005); and Leela Fernandes, "Nationalizing 'the Global': Media Images, Cultural Politics and the Middle Class of India," *Media Culture Society*, vol. 22, 611–628.

Exhibit 2.29 India's Leading Advertisers and Advertising Agencies

India's Leading Advertisers	Top Advertising Agencies in India
Unilever India	Ogilvy & Mather
Tata Group	J Walter Thompson India
Reckitt Benckiser	Mudra Communications Pvt. Ltd.
Procter & Gamble	FCB-Ulka Advertising Ltd.
Pantaloons	Rediffusion DY&R
Suzuki	Contract Advertising India Ltd.
ITC	Leo Burnett India Pvt. Ltd.
LG Group	Grey Worldwide (India) Pvt. Ltd.
Bharti Group	R.K. Swamy BBDO Pvt. Ltd.
Coca-Cola India Ltd.	McCann-Erickson India Pvt. Ltd.
Dabur India	
PepsiCo	
Nestlé India Ltd.	
Paras Pharmaceuticals	

Source: Based on AdEx India—a division of TAM India Research.

Exhibit 2.30 India All Media Outlet Spending Trends

Media (thousands US$)	July 2008/ June 2009	July 2007/ June 2008	Change (%)
TV	2,335,925	2,000,611	17
Newspapers	3,456,035	3,025,376	14
Magazines	426,161	350,554	22
Radio	685,695	687,559	0
Cinema	49,570	44,922	10
Outdoor	303,447	276,167	10
Other	112,929	74,589	51
Total media spending	7,369,762	6,459,778	14

Source: Based on AdEx India—a division of TAM India Research.

Advertising Industry in Latin America. As shown earlier, along with Europe and the Asia-Pacific region, the advertising industry in Latin America is developing rapidly. Advertising is the main source of revenue for the Latin American information and communication sector.[78]

Other communication activities also tend to be structured as a commercial global market, which is consistent with the North American market pattern. Along with

78. Guillermo Mastrini and Martin Becerra, "50 Years of Media Concentration in Latin America: From Artisanal Patriarchy to Large-Scale Groups," Cultural Industries and Dialogue between Civilizations in the Americas, Montreal: Panamerican Colloquium, 2002, accessed at http://www.er.uqam.ca/nobel/gricis/actes/panam/Mastrini.pdf on October 20, 2010.

other participants of cultural industries (for example, graphic arts, radio, and film-making), the advertising industry has a positive impact on the economy and employment in this region.[79]

In 2009, Publicis Groupe, the French-based global advertising player, received 4.8 percent of its worldwide revenue from Latin America (*Advertising Age*, 2010). In fourth position, Interpublic Group of Companies received 5.1 percent of its worldwide revenue. The globalization of markets has produced tremendous growth in specialized agencies, both inside and outside the United States (*Advertising Age*, 2006). One observable fact is the growth of Hispanic agencies in the United States to develop advertising and promotion for the fast-growing Spanish-speaking consumer market. These agencies have been experiencing huge growth for several years, with some agencies growing at 30–40 percent annually. Because Hispanic online spending has grown to over $150 million annually, more and more Hispanic agencies are starting a digital service.

Advertising Industry in Latin America. According to *Advertising Age*, the U.S. Hispanic market is slowly recovering and experienced a growth in 2010. "In the first quarter of 2010, spending on Spanish-language TV rose by 7.2%, and Spanish-language newspapers and magazines saw spending recover slightly by 4.5% and 1.5%, respectively, according to WPP's Kantar Media. The World Cup held this summer also helped to boost 2010 spending on Hispanic media. Data from the 2010 Census, due out early next year, will show major Hispanic population growth, a wakeup call for marketers. U.S. Hispanic measured media spending last year fell 8.6% to $6.3 bn., a rare decline in spending. Still, the Hispanic market continued to out-perform the general market; overall U.S. media spending fell 10.2%."[80]

As shown in Exhibit 2.31, Brazil is the Latin American country with the highest estimated revenue (US $14.6 billion) for 2010, followed by Mexico (US $4.3 billion), Colombia (US $3.8 billion), and Argentina (US $2.7 billion). Unilever belongs to the three leading advertisers in all countries except Mexico, whereas Procter & Gamble is in Argentina and Mexico only.

Exhibit 2.31 Leading Advertising Agencies in Latin America

Country	Leading Advertisers in 2009
Argentina: Estimated US $2.7 billion in 2010	1. Unilever 2. Procter & Gamble 3. Danone
Colombia: Estimated US $3.8 billion in 2010	1. Postobon 2. Unilever 3. Comcel
Brazil: Estimated US $14.6 billion in 2010	1. Casa Bahi 2. Unilever Brasil 3. AmBev
Mexico: Estimated US $4.3 billion in 2010	1. Genomma Lab 2. Procter & Gamble 3. Grupo Bimbo

Source: Based on GroupM, 2010.

79. Kenny Phillips, "Strategic Plan for the Entertainment Industry of Trinidad and Tobago," Final Report: The Music and Entertainment Industry Team of the Standing Committee on Business Development (SCBD), 2006, accessed at http://www.scribd.com/doc/44483493/Entertainment-Industry-Final-Report on October 30, 2010.

80. *Advertising Age*, 2010, accessed at http://www.adage.com/ on October 25, 2010.

Mobile Advertising Trends in Latin America. Internet advertising (wired and mobile) consists of advertisers spending on paid search, display, classified video, and other online formats and advertising delivered to mobile phones via formats designed for mobile handset screens.[81]

Mobile advertisement in Latin America has a great future. At the end of 2009, the Latin American region had exceeded 500 million mobile connections, with an average 86 percent market penetration. From this 500 million, one-third of mobile connections belong to Brazil (176 millions), followed by Mexico, Argentina, and Colombia. According to recent data from the Mobile Marketing Association, sixty-five percent of consumers in Mexico, Brazil, and Argentina have shown a moderate to high likelihood of adopting mobile marketing initiatives, with 30 percent appearing very likely to participate in mobile marketing campaigns in the future.[82]

4 External Facilitators.

Even though agencies offer clients many services and are adding more, advertisers often need to rely on specialized external facilitators in planning, preparing, and executing promotional campaigns. **External facilitators** are organizations or individuals who provide specialized services to advertisers and agencies. The most important external facilitators are discussed in the following sections.

Marketing and Advertising Research Firms. Many firms rely on outside assistance during the planning phase of advertising. Research firms such as Burke and Simmons can perform original research for advertisers using focus groups, surveys, and experiments to assist in understanding the potential market or consumer perceptions of a product or services. Other research firms, such as SRI International, routinely collect data (from grocery store scanners, for example) and have these data available for a fee.

Advertisers and their agencies also seek measures of promotional program effectiveness after a campaign has run. After an advertisement or promotion has been running for a reasonable amount of time, firms such as Starch INRA Hooper will run recognition tests on print advertisements. Other firms such as Burke offer day-after recall tests of broadcast advertisements. Some firms specialize in message testing to determine whether consumers find advertising messages appealing and understandable.

Consultants. A variety of **consultants** specialize in areas related to the promotional process. Advertisers can seek out marketing consultants for assistance in the planning stage. Creative and communications consultants provide insight on issues related to message strategy and message themes. Consultants in event planning and sponsorships offer their expertise to both advertisers and agencies. Public relations consultants often work with top management. Media experts can help an advertiser determine the proper media mix and efficient media placement.

Three new types of consultants have emerged in recent years. One is a database consultant, who works with both advertisers and agencies. Organizations such as Shepard Associates help firms identify and then manage databases that allow for the development of integrated marketing communications programs. Diverse databases from research sources discussed earlier can be merged or cross-referenced in developing effective communications programs. Another new type of consultant

81. PricewaterhouseCoopers, 2010, accessed at http://www.pwc.com/gx/en/about-pwc/index.jhtml on November 9, 2010.

82. Cathal O'Toole, "Mobile Advertisement Trends in Latin America," 2010, accessed at http://www.telecoms/markets/tel13008bu on November 15, 2010.

specializes in website development and management. These consultants typically have the creative skills to develop websites and corporate home pages and the technical skills to advise advertisers on managing the technical aspects of the user interface. The third type of consultant works with a firm to integrate information across a variety of customer contacts and to organize all this information to achieve customer relationship management (CRM).

In recent years, traditional management consultants—such as IBM, Accenture, and McKinsey—have started to work with agencies on structure and business strategy.[83] These sorts of consultants can also advise on image strategy, market research procedure, and process and account planning.

But the combination of traditional consulting and advertising has not always produced compelling results, and the typical role of consultants—focusing on marketing, creative, or technical issues—is the more likely role for consultants in the future.

Production Facilitators. External **production facilitators** offer essential services both during and after the production process. Production is the area in which advertisers and their agencies rely most heavily on external facilitators. All forms of media advertising require special expertise that even the largest full-service agency, much less an advertiser, typically does not retain on staff. In broadcast production, directors, production managers, songwriters, camera operators, audio and lighting technicians, and performers are all essential to preparing a professional, high-quality radio or television ad. Production houses can provide the physical facilities (including sets, stages, equipment, and crews) needed for broadcast production. Similarly, in preparing print advertising, brochures, and direct mail pieces, graphic artists, photographers, models, directors, and producers may be hired from outside the advertising agency or firm to provide the specialized skills and facilities needed in preparing advertisements. In-store promotions and trade show booths are other areas where designing and producing materials requires the skills of a specialty organization.

The specific activities performed by external facilitators and the techniques employed by the personnel in these firms will be covered in greater detail in Part 3 of the text. For now, it is sufficient to recognize the role these firms play in the advertising and promotions industry.

Software Firms. An interesting and complex new category of facilitator in advertising and promotion is that of software firms. The technology in the industry, particularly new media technology, has expanded so rapidly that a variety of software firms facilitate the process. Some of these firms are well established and well known, such as Microsoft, Novell, and Oracle. But others, such as Hyperion, are new to the scene.

These firms provide software ranging from gathering and analyzing Web surfer behavior to broadband streaming audio and video to managing relationships with trade partners. These firms provide the kind of expertise that is so esoteric that even the most advanced full-service or e-commerce agency would have to seek their assistance.

5 Media Organizations.

The next level in the industry structure, shown in Exhibit 2.32, comprises media available to advertisers. The media available for placing advertising, such as broadcast and print media, are well known to most people simply because they're exposed to the media daily. In addition, the Internet has created media organizations through which advertisers can direct and distribute their advertising and promotional messages.

83. Matthew Creamer, "March of the Management Consultants," *Advertising Age,* June 5, 2006, 1, 53.

Exhibit 2.32 Types of Media

Broadcast

Television
Major network
Independent station
Cable
Broadband

Radio
Network
Local

Satellite

Print

Magazines
By geographic coverage
By content

Direct Mail
Brochures
Catalogs
Videos

Newspapers
National
Statewide
Local

Specialty
Handbills
Programs

Banners

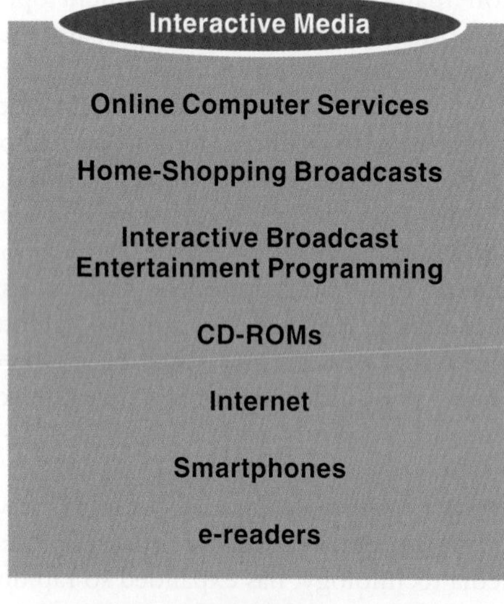

Interactive Media
Online Computer Services
Home-Shopping Broadcasts
Interactive Broadcast Entertainment Programming
CD-ROMs
Internet
Smartphones
e-readers

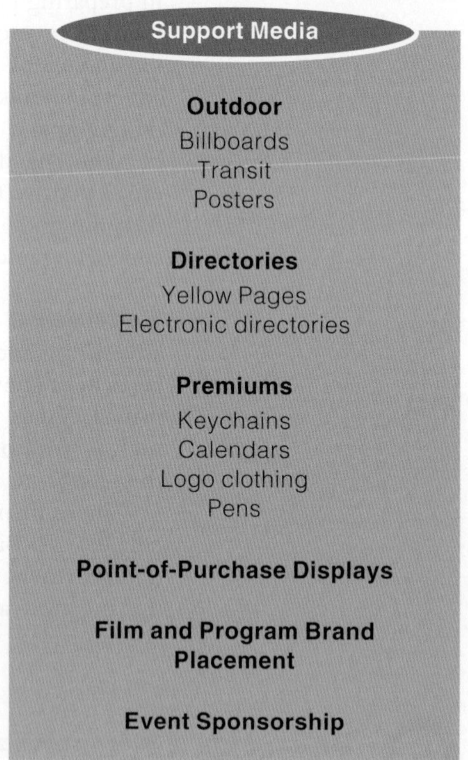

Support Media
Outdoor
Billboards
Transit
Posters
Directories
Yellow Pages
Electronic directories
Premiums
Keychains
Calendars
Logo clothing
Pens
Point-of-Purchase Displays
Film and Program Brand Placement
Event Sponsorship

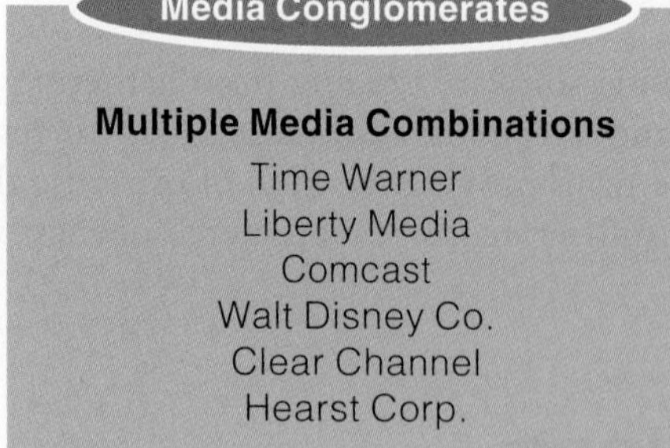

Media Conglomerates
Multiple Media Combinations
Time Warner
Liberty Media
Comcast
Walt Disney Co.
Clear Channel
Hearst Corp.

Advertisers and their agencies turn to media organizations that own and manage the media access to consumers. In traditional media, major television networks such as NBC and Fox, as well as national magazines such as *U.S. News & World Report* and *People,* provide advertisers with time and space for their messages at considerable cost.

Other media options are more useful for reaching narrowly defined target audiences. Specialty programming on cable television, tightly focused direct mail pieces, and a well-designed Internet campaign may be better ways to reach a specific audience. One of the new media options, broadband, offers advertisers the chance to target very specific audiences.

Broadband allows Internet users to basically customize their programming by calling on only specific broadcasts from various providers. For example, The FeedRoom (www.feedroom.com) is an interactive broadband television news network that allows Web users to customize the news broadcasts they receive. Advertisers can target different types of audiences using broadband for interactive broadcasts. The latest step in broadband communications is wireless broadband; firms are already developing technology and access for consumers.

Note the inclusion of media conglomerates in the list shown in Exhibit 2.32. This category is included because organizations such as Viacom and Comcast own and operate companies in broadcast, print, and interactive media. Viacom offers cable networks such as Nickelodeon, VH1, and TV Land. Time Warner and its sister company Time Warner Cable is one of the world's largest media conglomerates and provides broadcasting, cable, music, film, print publishing, and a dominant Internet presence. The support media organizations listed in Exhibit 2.32 include all those places that advertisers want to put their messages other than mainstream traditional or interactive media.

Often referred to as out-of-home media, these support media organizations include transit companies (bus and taxi boards), billboard organizations, specialized directory companies, and sports and performance arenas for sponsorships, display materials, and premium items.

Target Audiences.

The structure of the advertising and promotion industry and the flow of communication obviously would be incomplete without an audience: no audience, no communication. One interesting fact about the audiences for promotional communications is that, with the exception of household consumers, they are also the *advertisers* who use advertising and IBP communications. We are all familiar with the type of advertising directed at us in our role as consumers: toothpaste, window cleaner, sport-utility vehicles, soft drinks, insurance, and on and on.

But business and government audiences are key to the success of a large number of firms that sell only to business and government buyers. While many of these firms rely heavily on personal selling, many also use a variety of advertising and IBP tools. Accenture Consulting uses high-profile television and magazine advertising and sponsors events. Many business and trade sellers regularly need public relations, and most use direct mail to communicate with potential customers as a prelude to a personal selling call.

Summary

1 Discuss important trends transforming the advertising and promotion industry.

Recent years have proven to be a period of dramatic change for the advertising and promotion industry. The trend most affecting advertisers, agencies, and the media is that consumers are now in greater control of the information they receive about brands. Collectively, individuals are gravitating toward sharing and creating information through websites, blogs, social media, wikis, and video sites like YouTube.

The simplest example is when consumers log on to the Internet and visit sites to find information or to shop. Most recently, social media have emerged as the most significant form of consumer control over information creation and communication. Facebook has more than 350 million users worldwide sharing 3.5 billion pieces of content with each other every week. Twitter has more than 20 million users who post 8 billion tweets a year. As consumers search for more control over their information flow, advertisers, agencies, and media organizations are struggling to adapt to consumer desires. The proliferation of media from cable television to satellite radio to the Internet has created new advertising options, and giant media conglomerates are expected to control a majority of these television, radio, and Internet properties. Media proliferation has, in turn, led to increasing media clutter and fragmentation, reducing the effectiveness of advertisements; as a result, advertisers are using more IBP tools like sales promotions, event sponsorships, and public relations to supplement and enhance the primary advertising effort. Crowdsourcing is the next big trend affecting the industry. The idea behind crowdsourcing is to get consumers more involved with and committed to a brand in a way that passive, intrusive advertising simply cannot. Consumers help "build the brand" with recommendations for features, advertising, or events. They also can communicate about the brand to audiences in ways that seem natural and credible—something corporate-launched advertising struggles with. Finally, mobile marketing/mobile media may turn out to the biggest trend that affects the industry. Technology has resulted in significant opportunity for advertisers to reach consumers with messages directed to consumers' mobile devices—primarily smartphones, tablets like Apple's iPad, and e-readers like Amazon's Kindle—but personal navigation devices (PNDs) can also accommodate messages in the wireless world.

2 Describe the advertising and promotion industry's size, structure, and participants; analyze the differences between the advertising industries in Europe and the United States; and analyze the idiosyncratic conditions in Central and Eastern Europe.

Many different types of organizations make up the advertising industry. To appreciate what advertising is all about, you must understand who does what and in what order in the creation and delivery of an advertising or IBP campaign. The process begins with an organization that has a message it wants to communicate to a target audience. This is the advertiser. Next, advertising and promotion agencies are typically hired to launch and manage a campaign, but other external facilitators are often brought in to perform specialized functions, such as assisting in the production of promotional materials and managing databases for efficient direct marketing campaigns. New to the industry in recent years are digital/interactive agencies, which specialize in mobile marketing and social media campaigns. External facilitators also include consultants with whom advertisers and their agencies may confer regarding advertising and IBP strategy decisions. All advertising and promotional campaigns use some type of media to reach target markets. Therefore, advertisers and their agencies must work with companies that have media time or space.

In this section, the diverse advertising industry structures and underlying trends in Europe, the Asia-Pacific region, and Latin America were discussed. These three regions, now being back on the way to recovery after the global economic downturn, have shown vast growth in terms of advertising expenditure, participants, and supporting industries. Impressively, in most cases, these growth rates even outperformed those of the United States in recent years. First, the global advertising industry structure, especially in terms of size (media spending volume) and participants, was described. Regarding participants, the largest global companies—agency companies, advertising agencies, direct marketing agencies, media agencies, and public relations agencies (in terms of their worldwide revenue)—and clients (in terms of advertising spending) were highlighted. On a global scale, a high level of horizontal integration of specialist marketing agencies into holding groups took place. Apparently, the change in people's media habits is a global phenomenon, reflected in a significant shift from newspapers to TV and, mainly, the Internet. Although the other regions have shown considerable percentage increases of media expenditures, the Asia-Pacific region enjoys the highest nominal increase.

The high level of cultural heterogeneity in Europe leads to different preferences in media usage. In line with the global development, a quick absorption of the Internet and Internet-related media (including social media) can be observed with different levels of investment into this medium. Interestingly, current research implies that a different Internet usage pattern exists between the United States/United Kingdom and Western Europe/CEE. In certain instances (for example, in the search for new products or for emotional reasons), consumers in Western Europe and the CEE countries seem to favor contact with salespeople or the experience in the store. Those CEE countries with more advanced economies are predicted to have lower growth rates in advertising spending compared to those with less advanced or smaller economies.

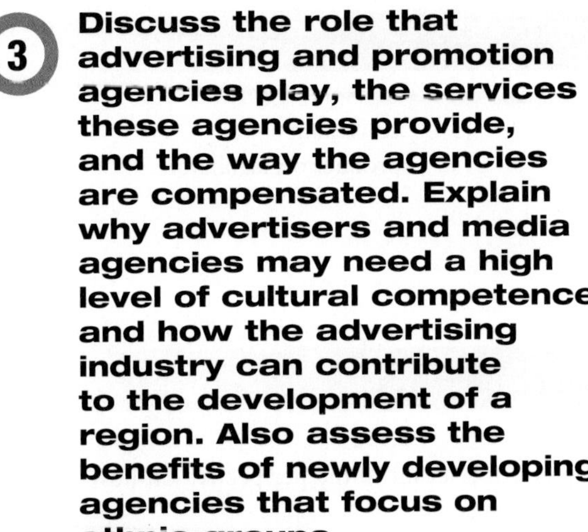

3 Discuss the role that advertising and promotion agencies play, the services these agencies provide, and the way the agencies are compensated. Explain why advertisers and media agencies may need a high level of cultural competence and how the advertising industry can contribute to the development of a region. Also assess the benefits of newly developing agencies that focus on ethnic groups.

Advertising and promotion agencies come in many varieties and offer diverse services to clients with respect to planning, preparing, and executing advertising and IBP campaigns. These services include market research and marketing planning, the actual creation and production of ad materials, the buying of media time or space for placement of ads, and traffic management to keep production on schedule. Some advertising agencies appeal to clients by offering a full array of services under one roof; other agencies, such as creative boutiques, develop a particular expertise and win clients with their specialized skills. Promotion agencies specialize in one or more of the other forms of promotion beyond advertising. Media agencies are proliferating to serve the Internet and other new media needs of advertisers. Compensation schemes in the industry vary. The four most prevalent ways to compensate an agency for services rendered are commissions, markups, fee systems, and the new pay-for-results programs.

In Asia, having an in-depth understanding of the complexities and idiosyncrasies of the markets is crucial. Such understanding is necessary as the development of advertising industries is subject to each country's unique culture, regulatory environment, and social structure. Some countries (for example, Japan, Taiwan, and India) are less strict in their advertising regulations, illustrated, for example, by Korea with its deregulation acts. China, on the other hand and despite its tremendous economic growth, is stricter in this context than the other countries. The latter led to the development of specialized niche agencies in media that are less strictly regulated. Several global trends, such as internationalization, concentration of major advertising agencies, and the Internet boom, also have occurred in this region.

Finally, regarding Latin America, advertising is still the main source of revenue for its information and communication sector. Here, the advertising market tends to reproduce the oligopoly pattern on a regional or local scale. The industry structure developed similarly to that in the United States. Along with the other participants of cultural industries, the advertising industry has actively contributed to the economic development of this region. Again, several global trends—internationalization, concentration of major advertising agencies, and the Internet boom—can be observed in this region as well. A new trend is the development of agencies focusing on the ethnic Hispanic market.

4 Identify key external facilitators who assist in planning and executing advertising and integrated brand promotion campaigns.

Marketing and advertising research firms assist advertisers and their agencies in understanding the market environment. Consultants of all sorts from marketing strategy through event planning and retail display are another form of external facilitators. Perhaps the most widely used facilitators are in the area of production of promotional materials. In advertising, a wide range of outside facilitators is used in the production of both broadcast and print advertising. In promotions, designers and planners are called on to assist in the creation and execution of promotional mix tools. Software firms fill a new role in the structure of the industry. These firms provide expertise in tracking and analyzing consumer usage of new media technology.

5 Discuss the role played by media organizations in executing effective advertising and integrated brand promotion campaigns.

Media organizations are the essential link in delivering advertising and IBP communications to target audiences. There are traditional media organizations such as television, radio, newspaper, and magazines. Interactive media options include not only the Internet and wireless access to consumers through smartphones and iPads but also CD-ROMs, electronic kiosks, and e-readers. Media conglomerates such as AT&T, Time Warner, and News Corp. control several different aspects of the communications system—from cable broadcast to Internet communications and emerging high-speed broadband communications technologies.

Key Terms

social media
blog
crowdsourcing
standardization
adaptation
external facilitator
consultant
production facilitator

Questions

1. Briefly describe the major trends affecting the advertising and promotion industry. Which of these trends do you think is most important and impactful? Why?

2. Do you think the increasing independence and the control consumers gain through new technologies like TiVo, iPads, and smartphones will make advertising and product branding more or less important? Explain.

3. In the structure of the advertising and promotion industry, what role do promotion agencies play?

4. The U.S. government spends millions of dollars each year trying to recruit young men and women into the armed services. What forms of advertising and IBP communication would be best suited to this recruiting effort?

5. Huge advertisers such as Procter & Gamble and Verizon spend billions of dollars on advertising every year. Put these billions of dollars into perspective. Is it really that much money? What information from Chapter 1 is relevant to the perspective on how much advertisers spend?

6. What is the advertiser's role in IBP?

7. As advertisers become more enamored with the idea of IBP, why would it make sense for an advertising agency to develop a reputation as a full-service provider?

8. Explain the viewpoint that a commission-based compensation system may give ad agencies an incentive to do the wrong things for their clients.

9. What makes the production of promotional materials the area in which advertisers and their agencies are most likely to call on external facilitators for expertise and assistance?

10. How might the skills of a public relations firm be employed to reinforce the message that a sponsor is trying to communicate through other forms of promotion?

Experiential Exercises

1. In response to the Haitian earthquake that brought devastation to more than 1 million people near Port-au-Prince, large corporations stepped up to provide medicine, shelter, food, and other forms of disaster relief. The primary coordinator of the effort was the Business Civic Leadership Center, a not-for-profit agency that partnered with Office Depot to create a National Disaster Help Desk. The sponsorship helped generate nearly $150 million in aid from Teva Pharmaceuticals, GE, and other well-known businesses. Choose a not-for-profit agency that champions a social cause and research the ways in which it uses advertising and promotion to accomplish humanitarian goals. How do ads by nonprofit organizations differ from those of profit-oriented businesses? How are the ads similar?

2. After two decades of advertising in Super Bowl matchups, PepsiCo opted out of the big game in 2010 and redirected funds into a social networking campaign called "Refresh Everything." The campaign, which harnessed the power of Facebook and blogs to offer financial grants for customer-led community projects, generated hundreds of thousands of Facebook friends and awarded millions to proposal winners. Devise an advertising campaign that uses interactive social media to attract audiences to a popular brand. Create a relevant crowdsourcing activity for the campaign. What award will your campaign offer to consumer participants? What types of agencies and support organizations will be involved in coordinating the campaign? In what ways might social media help your message break through media clutter?

3. This chapter highlights some of the challenges that advertisers and agencies face as consumers have gained greater control of information sources—blocking telemarketing calls, for instance, and carefully guarding the privacy of cell phone numbers and other contact information. Working in groups, brainstorm ways that advertisers could adapt to this reality and still reach out to consumers to invite them to learn more about products and brands. As your team develops ideas, explain how you would address these questions:

a. What ethical issues might arise in your approach to consumers?
b. How would you navigate privacy concerns?
c. Are there any legal risks or potential challenges to your approach? Explain.

4. Identify the four primary compensation methods discussed in this chapter and discuss which would best hold both clients and agencies to ethical and responsible business practices. What risks exist in each method? Apart from the threat of regulatory inquiries or criminal investigations, discuss why it is important for agency billing systems to be fully transparent and accountable.

Chapter 3

Regulatory, Social, and Ethical Aspects of Advertising and Promotion in the Global Market

After reading and thinking about this chapter, you will be able to do the following:

1. Identify the benefits and problems of advertising and promotion in a capitalistic society and debate a variety of issues concerning their effects on society's well-being.
2. Explain how ethical considerations affect the development of advertising and IBP campaigns.
3. Discuss the role of government agencies and consumers in the regulation of advertising and promotion.
4. Explain the meaning and importance of self-regulation for firms that develop and use advertising and promotion.
5. Discuss the regulation of the full range of techniques used in the IBP process.

MILLER BREWING Cº
SINCE 1855
MILWAUKEE, WIS. USA

NOT EVEN THE IRISH RELY ON LUCK.

DON'T DRIVE DRUNK.
DESIGNATE A DRIVER THIS ST. PATRICK'S DAY.

Miller Brewing Company and its distributors share a commitment to live responsibly.

Introductory Scenario: Who Do You Trust?

If you're like about 400 million other people in the world, you enjoy your Facebook account. You have the chance to share photos, places you've visited, movies you've seen, books you've read, and events you think are interesting and fun. You also may like using your Twitter account. You might tweet occasionally to let friends know what you are up to, and you might spend time following their Tweets to see what they are up to. Then there's the chance to follow the Tweets of your favorite singer or sports figure and even to get a peek at celebrity lifestyles. What about your favorite blogs and wikis? If you are into photography, snowboarding, hiking, travel, cooking, or whatever, blogs are a great way to get ideas about gear, recipes, or destinations. And then there is your smartphone. What a device—it's a cell phone, an Internet connection, and maybe even a GPS.

All of those things are wonderful and no doubt make your life more interesting, fun, and productive. But here comes the bubble burst. You came *this close* to having your Web searches and purchases on websites pop up on your Facebook page and then broadcast to all your connections: restaurants, hotels, music videos, books, blog posts—everything. That's what would have happened with Facebook's Project Beacon, where Facebook partner sites could have redirected your activities back to your Facebook site—and you would have had to opt out to make it stop. Massive protests from Facebook users and privacy advocates killed the project, but it had been implemented and would have continued without the widespread outcry.[1]

Now, about following those Tweets. What if you knew that your favorite celebrity was being paid $5,000 to $10,000 for every Tweet? Would it be as fun and interesting to follow him or her? Well, Greg Grunberg, the police officer on *Heroes* makes $7,000 to $10,000 per Tweet; Dr. Drew Pinsky from *Celebrity Rehab* (Exhibit 3.1) makes $10,000 and up per Tweet; and Samantha Ronson (SamRo) makes about $10,000 per Tweet.[2] Companies like Ad.ly in Beverly Hills set up deals with companies, and celebrities "just happen" to mention those companies' brands in their Tweets—look for a little name dropping the next time you follow the Tweets of your favorite celebrity. Now your favorite blog. Yes, people are being paid to post comments about brands on blog sites. At one point, a big global consumer goods company had tens of thousands of women and teens under contract to mention the company's brands in blogs they frequented. Now the Federal Trade Commission (FTC) has rules about making people reveal that they're being paid to voice their "opinions" about brands, but the disclosure may not be particularly prominent. And finally your beloved smartphone. You've probably become accustomed to all the ads that are being directed your way. After all, AdMob sends out billions of them every month. But consider this: you're standing in front of Gap, and suddenly its sale ad pops up on your phone. This can happen. It's called behavioral targeting based on the GPS capabilities of your phone's operating system. So far, firms are wary of going that far with their tracking of your behavior.[3] But companies still have contextual targeting to fall back on—a process where all your Web search behavior is tracked so they can determine which ads to post the next time you surf to a particular site. That probably makes you feel better.

1. Jordan McCollum, "Facebook Beacon Bows Out," Marketing Pilgrim, September 21, 2009, www.marketingpilgrim.com

2. Olivia Allin, "Prepare to Cry: What Celebrities Make for Twittvertizing," ABCNews.com, January 18, 2010, www.abcnews.go.com

3. Martini Giles, "Search Me," *The Economist, The World in 2010,* January 2010, 124–125.

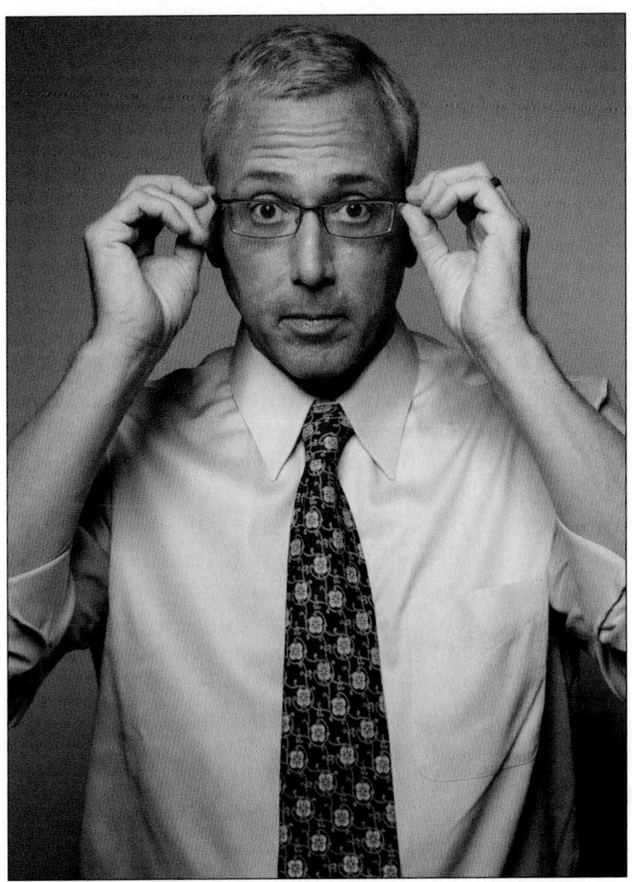

Exhibit 3.1 You may know "Dr. Drew" from his radio show or his role on the cable show *Celebrity Rehab*. What you probably don't know, though, is that Dr. Drew Pinsky gets about $10,000 (or more) every time he tweets on Twitter—or about $70 per word for a full 140-word Tweet! Does this make you want to follow Dr. Drew on Twitter?

All of that is true. The nature of these situations and the ways you are being followed and subtly(?) being targeted with communications highlights that the social, ethical, and regulatory aspects of advertising are as dynamic and controversial as any of the strategic or creative elements of the process. What is socially responsible or irresponsible, ethically acceptable, politically correct, or legal? As technology, cultural trends, and consumer behavior change, the answers are changing as well. As a society changes, so, too, do its perspectives. Like anything else with social roots and implications, advertising and promotion will affect and be affected by these changes.

The history of advertising and promotion includes all sorts of social, ethical, and legal issues and controversies. But advertising and promotion also have their triumphs, moral as well as financial. One important thing you will learn in this chapter is that many criticisms of advertising and promotion can be uninformed, naïve, and simplistic, often failing to consider the complex social and legal environment in which contemporary advertising and promotion operate. In some cases, the criticisms are justified because overzealous people in advertising and promotion do produce overzealous advertising and promotion programs. Other times, the criticism comes from intuition and emotion not supported by facts or reality.

In this chapter, we will consider a wide range of social, ethical, and legal issues related to advertising and the many tools of integrated brand promotion, and we will do so in an analytical and straightforward fashion. We will start with advertising—the promotional tool that tends to get the most scrutiny because of its global presence; then we will move on to the other promotional tools in IBP.

1 The Social Aspects of Advertising.

The social aspects of advertising are often volatile. For those who believe that advertising is intrusive, crass, and manipulative, the social aspects usually provide the most fuel for heated debate.

We can consider the social aspects of advertising in several broad areas that highlight both the positive and negative social aspects of advertising. On the positive side, we'll consider advertising's effect on consumers' knowledge, standard of living, and feelings of happiness and well-being and the potential positive effects of advertising on media. On the negative side, we'll examine a variety of social criticisms of advertising, ranging from the charge that advertising wastes resources and promotes materialism to the argument that advertising perpetuates stereotypes.

Our approach is to offer the pros and cons on several issues about which critics and advertisers commonly argue. Be forewarned—these are matters of opinion, with no clear right and wrong answers. You will have to draw your own conclusions. Above all, be analytical and thoughtful. These are important issues, and without understanding and contemplating these issues, you really haven't studied advertising and promotion.

Advertising Educates Consumers.

Does advertising provide valuable information to consumers, or does it seek only to confuse or entice them? Here's what the experts on both sides have to say.

Pro: Advertising Informs. Supporters of advertising argue that advertising educates consumers, equipping them with the information they need to make informed purchase decisions. By regularly assessing information and advertising claims, consumers become better educated about the features, benefits, functions, and value of products. Further, consumers can become more aware of their own tendencies toward being persuaded by certain types of product information. Historically, the very positive position has been offered that advertising is "clearly an immensely powerful instrument for the elimination of ignorance."[4] That may be a bit overstated, but according to this argument, better-educated consumers enhance their lifestyles and economic power through astute marketplace decision making—can't argue with that (see the following *Globalization* box).

A related argument is that advertising *reduces product search time*—that is, the amount of time an individual searches for desired products and services is reduced because of advertising and access to the Web. The large amount of information readily available through advertising and websites allows consumers to easily assess information about the potential value of brands without spending time and effort traveling from retail store to retail store trying to evaluate each one. The information contained in an advertisement "reduces drastically the cost of search."[5]

Another aspect of informing the public has to do with the role advertising can play in communicating about important social issues. Miller Brewing devotes millions of dollars a year to promoting responsible drinking with both television and print advertisements like the one shown in Exhibit 3.2.

Miller
MILLER BREWING CO
SINCE 1855
MILWAUKEE, WIS. USA
NOT EVEN THE IRISH RELY ON LUCK.
DON'T DRIVE DRUNK.
DESIGNATE A DRIVER THIS ST. PATRICK'S DAY.
Miller Brewing Company and its distributors share a commitment to live responsibly.
Live Responsibly Miller

Exhibit 3.2 Advertising can be used to inform the public about important social issues. Miller Brewing spends millions of dollars a year promoting responsible drinking behavior. www.millerbrewing.com

Courtesy, Miller Brewing Co.

Con: Advertising Is Superficial and Intrusive. Critics argue that advertising does not provide any good product information and that advertising is so pervasive and intrusive to daily life that it is impossible to escape. The basic criticism of advertising with respect to it being superficial focuses on the argument that many ads don't carry enough product information. What advertising does carry is said to be hollow ad-speak. Ads are rhetorical; there is no pure "information." All information in an ad is biased, limited, and inherently deceptive. Continuing, critics of advertising believe that ads should contain information on brands that relates strictly to functional features and performance results—things that can be measured and tested brand by brand (see Exhibit 3.3).

In response, advertisers argue that in many instances, consumers are interested in more than a physical product with performance features and a purely functional value.

4. George J. Stigler, "The Economics of Information," *Journal of Political Economy* (June 1961), 213–220.
5. Ibid., 220.

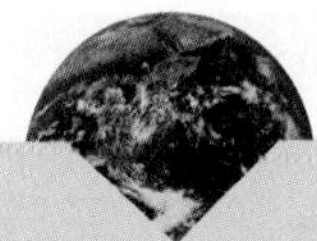

Globalization

A Giant Shoving Match: Google versus China

When it comes to heavyweights, few are bigger or heavier than Google and China. On the one hand, there is Google—the 900-pound gorilla of search engines: it handles 70 percent of all search traffic in the United States (nearly 90 percent in many parts of Europe); revenues are approaching $30 billion a year and growing at about 17 percent annually; and at any one time, the firm has about $25 billion cash in its coffers. On the other hand, there is China—the 900-pound gorilla of growth economies: a population of 1.4 billion people; a "middle class" that is expected to grow from about 200 million to 600 million by 2015; gross domestic product (GDP) growth from 9 to 11 percent annually (even though the rest of the world was muddling through the Great Recession of 2008–2009 with negative GDP); and about 400 million current Internet users (up from only 22 million in 2000), leaving a mere 800 million left to discover the Internet.

Google and China—seems like a match made in heaven for mutual growth and benefit. Not exactly. China is a highly controlled society, which means the government has restrictive and repressive rules about citizens' use of the Internet. (You can't access YouTube in China, for example.) From the beginning, Google has complied with Chinese laws requiring that some politically and socially sensitive issues be blocked from search results in China even though these same search results are available in other countries. But a tipping point came in early 2010 when Google discovered it had been hacked from within China. The hackers broke into computers of at least 20 major U.S. companies (mostly Gmail accounts) and tried to gather personal information on human rights activists who had been working to expose China's alleged human rights abuses. It appears that only two email accounts were actually accessed, though, and even then, only subject lines, not content, were viewed. Getting hacked is a bad thing. But even though managers at Google never said so directly, the Chinese government was suspected in the hacking—after all, who else would care about Chinese human rights activists operating in the United States? Google's immediate reaction to the hacking: stop censoring search results and threaten to pull out of the country altogether.

Some would say that if Google follows through and pulls the plug on China, the firm is not going to suffer all that much. Even though Google's search engine is the runaway leader worldwide, it's a distant second in China, where homegrown Baidu.com captures more than 60 percent of all search requests. And Google's Chinese operations account for "only" about $600 million of the firm's $30 billion in annual revenue. Other firms are joining Google's camp. Domain registrar GoDaddy has announced it is no longer signing up people for .cn (the China designation) domains in China due to onerous Chinese government requirements, which include photo IDs, identification numbers, and physical copies of all signed documents.

So what we have here is a giant social, ethical, and regulatory shoving match. Socially, citizens in China are having their freedom restricted. Ethically, social rights activists had their privacy invaded. From a regulatory standpoint, the Chinese government is exerting widespread control over the Internet. So, where do you stand on this social, ethical, and regulatory "mashup"?

Sources: "World Internet Users and Population Stats," Internetworldstats.com; Michael Liedtke, "Google to End China Censorship After Email Breach," *Associated Press*, January 13, 2010, at www.finance.yahoo.com/news; Normandy Madden, "Whether IT Stays or Goes, Google Wasn't Winning in China Anyway," *Advertising Age*, January 18, 2010; Robert X. Cringely, "China-Google: The Plot Thickens," *InfoWorld*, March 26, 2010, at www.pcworld.com.

The functional features of a brand may be secondary in importance to consumers in both the information search and the choice process. Emotional and lifestyle factors play an important role in consumers' choices (see Exhibit 3.4). The advertisers' position goes on to say that critics often dismiss as unimportant or ignore the totality of brand benefits that consumers seek, including emotional, hedonic (pleasure-seeking), or aesthetic aspects. The relevant information being used by a buyer may focus on criteria that are nonutilitarian or nonfunctional—but not irrelevant. Although the Toyota ad in Exhibit 3.3 carries the type of information critics would prefer, advertisers would argue that the information in the Honda ad in Exhibit 3.4 provides information that is just as relevant to consumers—emotional/lifestyle information.

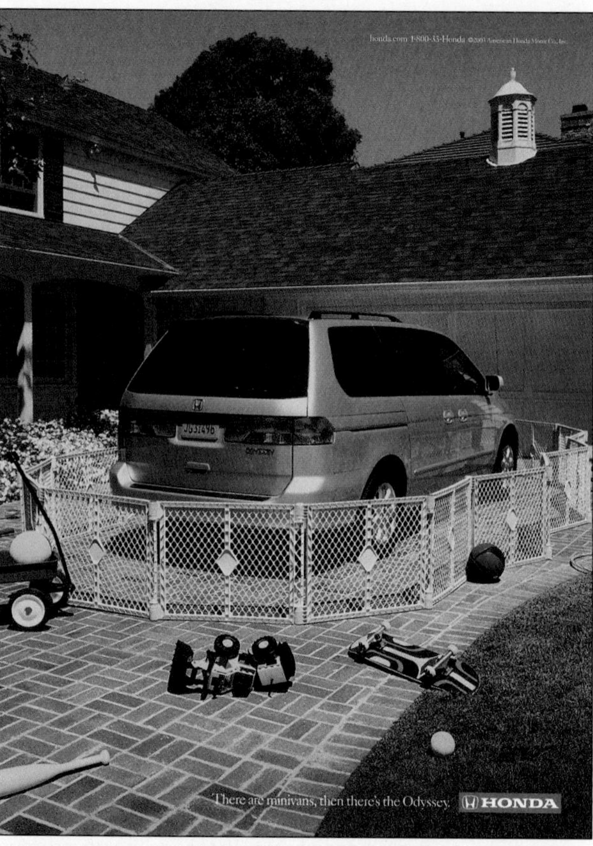

Exhibits 3.3 and 3.4 Critics of advertising complain that ads often carry little, if any, product information and would prefer that all advertising be rich in "information" like the Toyota ad in Exhibit 3.3. Do you think the Honda ad in Exhibit 3.4 is devoid of "information"?

With respect to the intrusive aspect of advertising, the argument is that advertising has become so widespread (in some critics' view, ubiquitous) that consumers are starting to revolt. In a Planetfeedback.com survey in which respondents expressed their annoyance with pop-up ads, the study found that more than 95 percent of consumers considered themselves "angry" or "furious" over email spam and website pop-up ads.[6] Similarly, consumers are getting increasingly concerned and frustrated with brands working their way into entertainment and information programming. The so-called commerce-content crossover—brand placement (like the American Idol Coke cups from Chapter 2) and paid bloggers who write about brands but don't reveal their affiliation with companies—was rated as allowing advertising to become too pervasive by 72 percent of consumers surveyed.[7] Despite widespread consumer aggravation, it would seem that advertisers aren't paying much attention. On the one hand, consumers seem to be saying loudly and clearly that advertising is becoming too widespread and is intruding on their lives and lifestyles. On the other hand, big advertisers like American Express are pushing to become more "relevant" to consumers than a mere 30-second advertising spot and to make their brands part of consumers' lifestyles. So much so that the chief marketing officer at American Express said in a keynote speech to a large advertising audience, "We need to adapt to the new landscape by thinking not in day-parts [referring to television advertising schedules] but to mindparts."[8] You can decide what you think of that comment.

6. Jack Neff, "Spam Research Reveals Disgust with Pop-Up Ads," *Advertising Age,* August 23, 2003, 1, 21.
7. Clair Atkinson, "Ad Intrusion Up, Say Consumers," *Advertising Age,* January 6, 2003, 1, 19.
8. Hank Kim, "Just Risk It," *Advertising Age,* February 9, 2004, 1, 51.

But the advertising industry should be paying attention to consumers' aggravation with the clutter and intrusiveness of advertising for one very important reason—clutter and intrusiveness reduce the effectiveness of advertising. According to one expert, "The ability of the average consumer to even remember advertising 24 hours later is at the lowest level in the history of our business."[9] Is the industry likely to work to reduce clutter? Probably not. Another industry expert suggests that "New media have more potential to deliver even more saturation, clutter, and intrusiveness than traditional media, in which case the new media will only worsen marketing resistance."[10]

Advertising Improves the Standard of Living.

Whether advertising raises or lowers the general standard of living is hotly debated. Opinions vary widely on this issue and go right to the heart of whether advertising is a good use of or a waste of energy and resources.

Pro: The Economic Effects of Advertising Lower the Cost of Products. Four aspects of the nature of advertising, supporters argue, help lower the cost of products:

- Due to the economies of scale (it costs less to produce products in large quantities), partly created by advertising's contribution to stimulating demand, products cost less than if there were no advertising at all. As stimulation of broad-based demand results in lower production and administrative costs per unit produced, lower prices are passed on to consumers.
- Consumers have a wider variety of choices in products and services because advertising increases the probability of success that new products will succeed. The more products that succeed, the fewer losses firms incur from failed product introductions. In the end, this should make products cost less.
- The pressures of competition and the desire to have fresh, marketable brands motivate firms to produce improved products and brands and to introduce lower-priced brands.
- The speed and reach of the advertising process aids in the diffusion of innovations. This means that new discoveries can be delivered to a large percentage of the marketplace very quickly. Innovations succeed when advertising communicates their benefits to the customer.

All four of these factors can contribute positively to the standard of living and quality of life in a society. Advertising may be instrumental in bringing about these effects because it serves an important role in stimulating demand and keeping customers informed.

Con: Advertising Wastes Resources and Raises the Standard of Living Only for Some. One of the traditional criticisms of advertising is that it represents an inefficient, wasteful process that does little more than "shuffling of existing total demand," rather than contributing to the expansion of total demand.[11] Advertising thus brings about economic stagnation and a lower, not higher, standard of living. Similarly, critics argue that brand differences are trivial and that the proliferation of brands does not offer a wider variety of choices, but rather a meaningless waste of resources and confusion and frustration for the

9. Matthew Creamer, "Caught in the Clutter Crossfire: Your Brand," *Advertising Age,* April 2, 2007, 1, 35.

10. Ibid., 35.

11. Richard Caves, *American Industry: Structure, Conduct, Performance* (Upper Saddle River, NJ: Prentice Hall, 1964), 102.

consumer. Finally, critics argue that advertising is a tool of capitalism that only helps widen the gap between rich and poor, creating strife between social classes.

Advertising Affects Happiness and General Well-Being.

Critics and supporters of advertising differ significantly in their views about how advertising affects consumers' happiness and general well-being. As you will see, this is a complex issue with multiple pros and cons.

Con: Advertising Creates Needs. A common cry among critics is that advertising creates needs and makes people buy things they don't really need or even want. The argument is that consumers are relatively easy to seduce into wanting the next shiny bauble offered by marketers. Critics would say, for example, that a quick examination of any issue of *Seventeen* magazine reveals a magazine intent on teaching young women of the world to covet slim bodies and a glamorous complexion. Cosmetics giants like Estée Lauder and Revlon typically spend from 15 to 30 cents of every dollar of sales to promote their brands as the ultimate solution for those in search of the ideal complexion.

Exhibit 3.5 This ad appeals to our physiological needs (protecting our health) in Maslow's hierarchy of needs.

CLOROX® Wipes, Courtesy of The Clorox Company; Advertising Agency: DDB SF; Photographer: Leigh Beisch

Pro: Advertising Addresses a Wide Variety of Basic Human Needs. A useful and informative place to start when discussing whether advertising can create needs is to consider the basic nature of human needs. Abraham Maslow, a pioneer in the study of human motivation (and someone you probably read about in a psychology or management class), conceived that human behavior progresses through the following hierarchy of needs:[12]

- ***Physiological needs:*** Biological needs that require the satisfaction of hunger, thirst, and basic bodily functions.
- ***Safety needs:*** The need to provide shelter and protection for the body and to maintain a comfortable existence.
- ***Love and belonging needs:*** The need for affiliation and affection. A person will strive for both the giving and receiving of love.
- ***Esteem needs:*** The need for recognition, status, and prestige. In addition to the respect of others, there is a need and desire for self-respect.
- ***Self-actualization needs:*** This is the highest of all the need states and is achieved by only a small percentage of people, according to Maslow. The individual strives for maximum fulfillment of individual capabilities.

Keep in mind that Maslow was describing *basic* human needs and motivations, not consumer needs and motivations. But in the context of an affluent society, individuals will turn to goods and services to satisfy needs. Many products are said to directly address the requirements of one or more of these need states. Food and healthcare products, for example, relate to physiological needs (see Exhibit 3.5). Home security systems and smoke

12. A. H. Maslow, *Motivation and Personality* (New York: Harper & Row, 1970).

Skin tells
the naked truth
All you need is Guinot, the
most complete and technically
advanced skin and body care system.
Found only in select salons
whose staffs have been expertly
trained. For Guinot products
call: 800-444-6621
GUINOT
PARIS
Lachman Imports, Inc.,
230 Fifth Avenue, Suite 900
New York, NY 10001. 212-532-1030

Exhibit 3.6 "All you need is Guinot." In what sense might a person need Guinot? Does the Guinot site (www.guinotusa.com) tie in to consumers' happiness and general well-being? Visit the site and identify message and design elements that target consumers' various need states.

Courtesy of Lachman Imports

detectors help address safety needs. Many personal care products, such as the skin care brand highlighted in Exhibit 3.6, promote feelings of self-esteem, confidence, glamour, and romance.

In the pursuit of esteem, many consumers buy products they perceive to have status and prestige: expensive jewelry, clothing, automobiles, and homes are examples. Although it may be difficult to buy self-actualization (the highest level of Maslow's hierarchy), educational pursuits and high-intensity leisure activities (for example, extreme sports and the gear it takes to pursue them) can foster feelings of pride and accomplishment that contribute to self-actualization. Supporters maintain that advertising may be directed at many different forms of need fulfillment, but it is in no way powerful enough to *create* basic human needs.

Con: Advertising Promotes Materialism. Another claim is that individuals' wants and aspirations may be distorted by advertising. The long-standing argument is that in societies characterized by heavy advertising, there is a tendency for conformity and status-seeking behavior, both of which are considered materialistic and superficial.[13] Material goods are placed ahead of spiritual and intellectual pursuits. Advertising, which portrays brands as symbols of status, success, and happiness, contributes to the materialism and superficiality in a society. It creates wants and aspirations that are artificial and self-centered. This, in turn, results in an overemphasis on the production of private goods, to the detriment of public goods (such as highways, parks, schools, and infrastructure).[14]

Pro: Advertising Only Reflects Society's Priorities. Although advertising is undeniably in the business of promoting the good life, defenders of advertising argue that it did not create the American emphasis on materialism. For example, in the United States, major holidays such as Christmas (gifts), Thanksgiving (food), and Easter (candy and clothing) have become festivals of consumption. This is the American way. Historian and social observer Stephen Fox concludes his treatise on the history of American advertising as follows:

> *One may build a compelling case that American culture is—beyond redemption—money-mad, hedonistic, superficial, rushing heedlessly down a railroad track called Progress. Tocqueville and other observers of the young republic described America in these terms in the early 1800s, decades before the development of national advertising. To blame advertising now for these most basic tendencies in American history is to miss the point.... The people who have created modern advertising are not hidden persuaders pushing our buttons in the service of some malevolent purpose. They are just producing an especially visible manifestation, good and bad, of the American way of life.*[15]

13. Vance Packard, *The Status Seekers* (New York: David McKay, 1959).

14. This argument was first offered by authors George Katona, *The Mass Consumption Society* (New York: McGraw-Hill, 1964), 54–61, and John Kenneth Galbraith, *The Affluent Society* (Boston: Houghton Mifflin, 1958).

15. Stephen Fox, *The Mirror Makers: A History of American Advertising and Its Creators* (New York: William Morrow, 1984), 330.

Although we clearly live in the age of consumption, all cultures throughout history have used goods and possessions to mark special events, to play significant roles in rituals, and to serve as vessels of special meaning long before there was modern advertising. Still, have we taken it too far? Is excess what we do best in consumer cultures?

Advertising: Demeaning and Deceitful or Liberating and Artful?

Without a doubt, advertisers are always on the lookout for creative and novel ways to grab and hold the attention of their audience. In addition, an advertiser has a very specific profile of the target customer in mind (more about this in Chapter 6) when an ad is being created. Both of these fundamental propositions about how ads get developed can spark controversy.

Con: Advertising Perpetuates Stereotypes. Advertisers often portray people in advertisements to look like members of their target audience with the hope that people who see the ad will be more prone to relate to the ad and attend to its message. Critics charge that this practice yields a negative effect—it perpetuates stereotypes. The portrayal of women, the elderly, and ethnic minorities is of particular concern. It is argued that women are still predominantly cast as homemakers or objects of desire (see Exhibit 3.7), despite the fact that women now hold top management positions and deftly head households. The elderly are often shown as helpless or ill, even though many active seniors enjoy a rich lifestyle. Critics contend that advertisers' propensity to feature African-American or Latin athletes in ads is simply a more contemporary form of stereotyping.

Pro: Advertisers Are Showing More Sensitivity. Much of the stereotyping described above is becoming part of the past. Advertisements from prior generations do show a vivid stereotyping problem. But in today's setting, the Dove ad in Exhibit 3.8 shows that women can be featured as strong and feminine in contemporary advertising. Dove launched its "Campaign for Real Beauty" in September 2004 with an ad campaign featuring real women whose appearances do not conform to the stereotypical and relatively narrow norms of beauty. The ads asked viewers to judge the women's looks (*Oversized? Outstanding?* or *Wrinkled? Wonderful?*) and invited them to cast their votes and join a discussion of beauty issues at www.campaignforrealbeauty.com. In addition, advertisers ranging from financial services to retirement communities to cruise lines now show seniors in fulfilling, active lifestyles—hardly a demeaning portrayal of that demographic group. Advertisers are realizing that a diverse world requires diversity in the social reality that ads represent and help construct. However, many remain dissatisfied with the pace of change; the Body Shop ad in Exhibit 3.9, promoting something other than the body of a supermodel as a valid point of reference for women, is still the exception, not the rule.

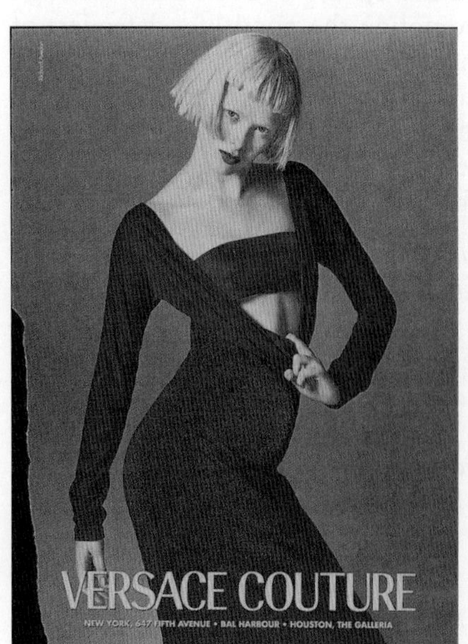

Exhibit 3.7 What is the advertiser claiming in this ad? How about—a Versace gown is the ultimate in chic. www.versace.com

Con: Advertising Is Often Offensive. A long-standing criticism of advertising is that it is often offensive and the appeals are in poor taste. We saw some of that in Chapter 3 from advertising eras gone by. Moreover, some would say that the trend in American advertising is to be rude, crude, and sometimes lewd, as advertisers struggle to grab the attention of consumers who have learned to tune out the avalanche

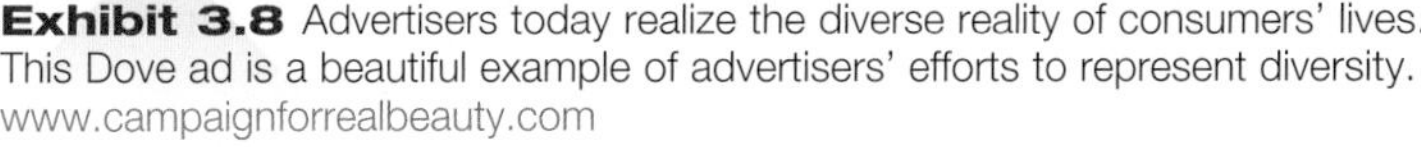

Exhibit 3.8 Advertisers today realize the diverse reality of consumers' lives. This Dove ad is a beautiful example of advertisers' efforts to represent diversity. www.campaignforrealbeauty.com

Exhibit 3.9 The Body Shop (www.bodyshop.com) is bucking trends by protesting the "supermodel" imagery often used in men's magazines such as *Playboy* and *Maxim*, which triumphantly display airbrushed "perfection."

of advertising messages they are confronted with each day. Of course, taste is just that, a personal and inherently subjective evaluation. What is offensive to one person is merely satiric to another. What should we call an ad prepared for the Australian market that shows the owner of an older Honda Accord admiring a newer model? The owner's admiration of the new car spurs the old version to lock its doors, rev its motor, and drive off a cliff—with the owner still inside. Critics decry the ad as trivializing suicide—an acute problem among young people, who are also the target market for this ad.[16]

But not all advertising deemed offensive has to be as extreme as these examples. Many times, advertisers get caught in a firestorm of controversy because certain, and sometimes relatively small, segments of the population are offended. The history of advertising is loaded with examples. An AIDS prevention campaign run by the Centers for Disease Control and Prevention (CDC), a highly respected government agency, has been criticized for being too explicit. A spokesperson for the Family Research Council said about the ads, "They're very offensive—I thought I was watching *NYPD Blue*."[17] A highly popular ad that some saw as controversial was the "People Taking Diet Coke Break" ad (featured in Exhibit 1.12 in Chapter 1). In this television spot, a group of female office workers is shown eyeing a construction worker as he takes off his T-shirt and enjoys a Diet Coke. Coca-Cola was criticized for using reverse sexism in this ad. Although

16. Normandy Madden, "Honda Pulls Suicide Car Ad from Australian TV Market," *Advertising Age,* September 22, 2003, 3.

17. Kevin Goldman, "From Witches to Anorexics, Critical Eyes Scrutinize Ads for Political Correctness," *The Wall Street Journal,* May 19, 1994, B1, B10.

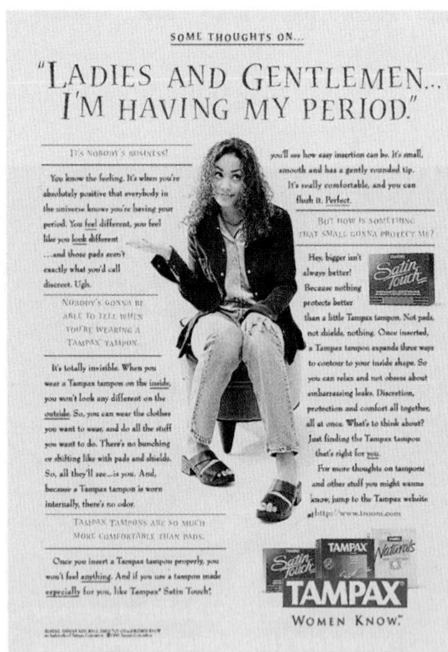

Exhibit 3.10 Oddly, frank talk about real-life issues is not all that common in advertising. Do you know anyone who would be put off by such frankness? www.tampax.com

Coca-Cola and the CDC may have ventured into delicate areas, consider the following advertisers that were caught by surprise when their ads were deemed offensive:

- In a public service spot developed by Aetna Life & Casualty insurance for a measles vaccine, a wicked witch with green skin and a wart was cause for a challenge to the firm's ad from a witches' rights group.
- A Nynex spot was criticized by animal rights activists because it showed a rabbit colored with blue dye.
- A commercial for Black Flag bug spray had to be altered after a war veterans' group objected to the playing of "Taps" over dead bugs.

Advertisers have long believed that they need to carefully consider the tastefulness of their ads. Expect the unexpected. An unpretentious ad like that in Exhibit 3.10, featuring frank copy about mundane realities of female life, could be expected to breach some consumers' sensibilities.

However, the marketer in this case was willing to take the risk in the hopes that the frank approach would get attention and ring true with the target customer.

On the other hand, maybe hypersensitivity to consumer reaction is not all that necessary. GoDaddy.com is making a nice living running risqué ads during the Super Bowl every year. In 2006, the Web firm had its first 13 ad submissions to Super Bowl–broadcaster ABC rejected as "tasteless." The still-racy ad that finally ran created a 15-fold spike in traffic to the firm's website.[18]

In the end, we have to consider whether advertising is offensive or whether society is merely pushing the limits of what is appropriate for freedom of speech and expression. The now infamous "wardrobe malfunction" that plagued Janet Jackson during a Super Bowl halftime show and incidents like shock radio DJs' profanity are drawing attention not only from fed-up consumers, but also from the U.S. Senate, which has approved a tenfold increase in fines for television and radio stations that violate rules on airing profanity and sexually explicit materials.[19] And even though government may move to provide a legal remedy to deter offensive broadcasts—whether advertising messages or programming—the fact is that what is acceptable and what is offensive changes over time in a culture.

Pro: Advertising Is a Source of Fulfillment and Liberation. On the other end of the spectrum, some argue that the consumption that advertising glorifies is good for society. Most people appreciate modern conveniences that liberate them from the more foul facets of everyday life, such as enduring body odor, coming in contact with dirty diapers, and washing clothes by hand. Some observers remind us that when the Berlin Wall came down, those in East Germany did not immediately run to libraries and churches—they ran to department stores and shops. Before the modern consumer age, the consumption of many goods was restricted by social class. Modern advertising has helped bring a "democratization" of goods. Observers argue that there is a liberating quality to advertising and consumption that should be appreciated and encouraged.

18. Georgia Flight, "Hits and Misses," *Business 2.0*, April 2006, 140.

19. Jeremy Pelofsky, "U.S. Senate Backs Ten Fold Hike in Indecency Fines," Reuters News Service, May 18, 2006, accessed at www.yahoo.reuters.com on May 19, 2006.

Ethics

Subliminal Advertising: A Really Bad Idea

Every few years, a story will surface claiming that an advertiser tried to sell a brand by putting subliminal (below the conscious threshold of awareness) messages or images in an ad. To set the record straight, subliminal advertising doesn't work—and you'll get in a lot of trouble if you try it.

This is how subliminal *communication* (not advertising) works. Research has shown that people can, indeed, process information that is transmitted to them below the level of conscious awareness, that is, subliminally. What is not proven is that you can send a *persuasive* message (like advertising) subliminally. Ever since a crackpot allegedly inserted the phrases *Eat Popcorn* and *Drink Coca-Cola* in a movie back in the 1950s, the world has been terrified that unscrupulous marketers will use the technique to sell products. Well, you can rest easy. Subliminal advertising doesn't work, but it does make for some interesting stories:

- In 2001, French TV network M6 and its production house Expand got in hot water with French regulators over the alleged insertion of 33 subliminal images of a Kodak disposable camera during the airing of an episode of a hit reality TV show called *Popstars*.
- Russian TV network ATN was pulled off the air in 2000 when Russian officials discovered that the broadcaster had been inserting the message *Sit and Watch Only ATN* into every 25th frame of its broadcasting during the summer of 2000. The station was off the air for nearly two years.
- During the 2000 presidential election campaigns in the United States, Democrats accused Republicans of using subliminal advertising in the so-called "Rats ad," which attacked Democratic candidate Al Gore's prescription drug plan. The allegation charged that during the ads, the word *bureaucrats* was reduced to *rats*, visible for a split second.

There is no evidence in any of these recent transgressions into subliminal messaging that the intended effects were achieved. Recently, the issue has resurfaced as a research topic among neural scientists, but what they seem to be "rediscovering" is that yes, you can communicate commercial messages to people below the conscious threshold of awareness. But the next effect has never been discovered: convincing people to buy something. Simply, you cannot get people to *act* on the information they may have received.

Whether or not subliminal advertising works, it does provide some great entertainment. And as long as people are suspicious of advertising, claims will surface that subliminal advertising is being used on unsuspecting consumers.

Sources: Timothy E. Moore, "Subliminal Advertising: What You See Is What You Get," *Journal of Marketing,* vol. 46 (Spring 1982), 38–47; Timothy E. Moore, "The Case Against Subliminal Manipulation," *Psychology and Marketing,* vol. 5, no. 4 (Winter 1988), 297–317; Lawrence J. Speer, "Off in a Flash," *Ad Age Global,* February 2002, 6; Bob Garfield, "Subliminal Seduction and Other Urban Myths," *Advertising Age,* September 18, 2000, 41; Don E. Schultz, "Subliminal Ad Notions Still Resonate Today," *Marketing News,* March 15, 2007, 5, 9.

Con: Advertisers Deceive via Subliminal Stimulation. Much controversy (and almost a complete lack of understanding) persists about the issue of subliminal (below the threshold of consciousness) communication and advertising.[20] Because there is so much confusion surrounding the issue of subliminal advertising, let us clarify: No one ever sold anything by putting images of breasts in ice cubes or the word *sex* in the background of an ad. Furthermore, no one at an advertising agency, except the very bored or the very eager to retire, has time to sit around dreaming up such things (see the *Ethics* box). It does make for a great story, but hiding pictures in other pictures doesn't get anyone to buy anything. Although there is some evidence for some types of unconscious ad processing, these effects are very short-lived and found only in laboratories. The Svengali-type hocus-pocus that

20. Don E. Schultz, "Subliminal Ad Notions Still Resonate Today," *Marketing News,* March 15, 2007, 5, 9.

Exhibit 3.11 Artist Andy Warhol demonstrated that the most accessible art was advertising. Both BMW (Z4 paintings) and Microsoft (butterflies) have used contemporary and fine art in their advertising.

has become advertising mythology simply does not exist.[21] If the rumors are true that some advertisers are trying to use subliminal messages in their ads, the best research on the topic would conclude that they're wasting their money.[22]

Pro: Advertising Is Democratic Art. Some argue that one of the best aspects of advertising is its artistic nature. The pop art movement of the late 1950s and 1960s, particularly in London and New York, was characterized by a fascination with commercial culture. Some of this art critiqued and simultaneously celebrated consumer culture. Above all, Andy Warhol (see Exhibit 3.11), himself a commercial illustrator, demonstrated that art was for the people and that the most accessible art was advertising. Art was not restricted to museum walls; it was on Campbell's soup cans, LifeSavers candy rolls, and Brillo pads. Advertising is anti-elitist, pro-democratic, widely accessible art. Warhol said this about America, democracy, and Coke:

> *What's great about this country is that America started the tradition where the richest consumers buy essentially the same things as the poorest. You can be watching TV and see Coca-Cola, and you can know that the President drinks Coke, Liz Taylor drinks Coke, and just think, you can drink Coke, too. A Coke is a Coke and no amount of money can get you a better Coke than the one the bum on the corner is drinking. All the Cokes are the same and all the Cokes are good. Liz Taylor knows it, the President knows it, the bum knows it, and you know it.*[23]

Advertising Has a Powerful Effect on the Mass Media.

One final issue that advertisers and their critics debate is the matter of advertising's influence on the mass media. Here again, we find a wide range of viewpoints.

Pro: Advertising Fosters a Diverse and Affordable Mass Media. Advertising fans argue that advertising is the best thing that can happen to an informed democracy. Magazines, newspapers, television, radio stations, and websites are supported by advertising expenditures. In 2009, measured mass media

21. Sheila Murphy, Jennifer Monahan, and Robert Zajonc, "Additivity of Nonconscious Affect: Combined Effects of Priming and Exposure," *Journal of Personality and Social Psychology,* vol. 69 (1995), 589–602.

22. Timothy E. Moore, "Subliminal Advertising: What You See Is What You Get," *Journal of Marketing,* vol. 46 (Spring 1982), 38–47; Timothy E. Moore, "The Case Against Subliminal Manipulation," *Psychology and Marketing,* vol. 5, no. 4 (Winter 1988), 297–317.

23. Andy Warhol, *The Philosophy of Andy Warhol: From A to B and Back Again* (New York: Harcourt Brace Jovanovich, 1975), 101.

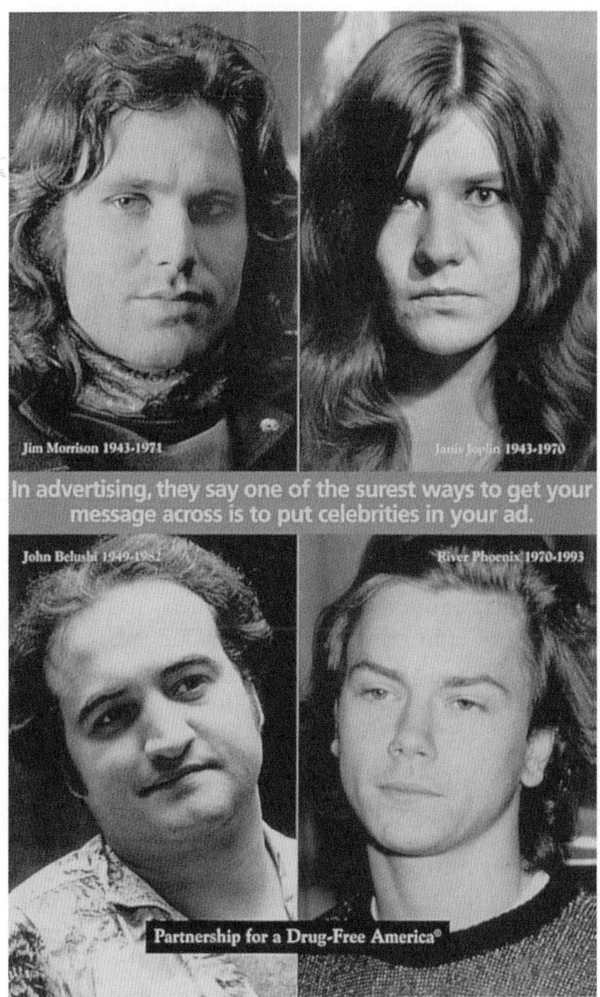

Jim Morrison 1943-1971
Janis Joplin 1943-1970
In advertising, they say one of the surest ways to get your message across is to put celebrities in your ad.
John Belushi 1949-1982
River Phoenix 1970-1993
Partnership for a Drug-Free America®

Exhibit 3.12 This ad both appeals to the viewer's fascination with celebrities and shocks the viewer with the realization that drug use can be fatal. At www.drugfreeamerica.org, the Partnership for a Drug-Free America hones its message that drug use is anything but glamorous.

advertising expenditures in the United States exceeded $140 billion.[24] Much of this spending went to support television, radio, magazines, and newspapers. If you include online advertising's support of websites, the number approaches $200 billion. With this sort of monetary support of the media, citizens have access to a variety of information and entertainment sources at a low cost. In the absence of advertising support, network television and radio broadcasts would not be free commodities and newspapers and magazines would likely cost two to four times more. Now as advertisers urgently try to access consumers through social media sites like Twitter and Facebook, social media are finding support from advertisers as well. Honda and Dell use Facebook and Twitter to connect to current and potential customers.[25]

Another argument in support of advertising is that it provides invaluable exposure to issues. When noncommercial organizations (like social service organizations) use advertising, members of society receive information on important social and political issues. A dramatic example of the noncommercial use of advertising was a multimedia campaign launched by the U.S. government, working in conjunction with the Partnership for a Drug-Free America, to remind the American public of the ruinous power of drugs such as heroin.[26] During five years, campaign spending approached $1 billion. A stockpile of nearly 400 ads was available for use in this comprehensive campaign. Some of the ads, like the one shown in Exhibit 3.12, involved powerful messages about the ultimate consequence of drug abuse.

Con: Advertising Affects Programming. Critics argue that advertisers that place ads in media have an unhealthy effect on shaping the content of information contained in the media. And there are some fairly dramatic examples. The CEO of a firm headed for prosecution was accused of hiring a public relations firm to turn out a series of newspaper articles sympathetic to the CEO's firm.[27] Similarly, there have been several instances of "stealth sponsorship" of newspaper opinion editorials where the journalists were being paid by corporations that were receiving favorable treatment in the editorials.[28]

24. "100 Leading National Advertisers," *Advertising Age,* June 22, 2009, S1.

25. Josh Bernoff, "How to Tweet Profitably," *Marketing News,* January 30, 2010, 12; Michael Learmonth, "Want 5000 More Facebook Friends? That'll Be $654.30," *Advertising Age,* September 2, 2009, 3.

26. B. G. Gregg, "Tax Funds Bankroll New Anti-Drug Ads," *Cincinnati Enquirer,* July 10, 1998, A1, A17.

27. Jay Reeves, "Scrushy Said to Pay for Positive Stories," *Associated Press,* January 19, 2006, accessed at www.news.yahoo.com on January 20, 2006.

28. Eamon Javers, "This Opinion Brought to You By…" *BusinessWeek,* January 30, 2006, 35.

Another charge leveled at advertisers is that they purchase air time only on programs that draw large audiences. Critics argue that these mass market programs lower the quality of television because cultural and educational programs, which draw smaller and more selective markets, are dropped in favor of mass market programs. After watching a few episodes of *Survivor* or *Bridezilla,* it's hard to argue against the proposition that shallow content is indeed winning out over culture and education.

In addition, television programmers have a difficult time attracting advertisers to shows that may be valuable, yet address controversial social issues. Programs that deal with abortion, sexual abuse, or AIDS may have trouble drawing advertisers that fear the consequences of being associated with controversial issues given the predictable public reaction that would come from the religious right.

2 The Ethical Aspects of Advertising.

Many of the ethical aspects of advertising border on and interact with both the social and legal considerations of the advertising process. **Ethics** are moral standards and principles against which behavior is judged. Honesty, integrity, fairness, and sensitivity are all included in a broad definition of ethics. Much of what is judged as ethical or unethical comes down to personal judgment. We will discuss the ethical aspects of advertising in three areas: truth in advertising, advertising to children, and advertising controversial products.

Truth in Advertising.

Although truth in advertising is a key legal issue, it has ethical dimensions as well. The most fundamental ethical issue has to do with **deception**—making false or misleading statements in an advertisement. The difficulty regarding this issue, of course, is in determining what is deceptive. A manufacturer that claims a laundry product can remove grass stains is exposed to legal sanctions if the product cannot perform the task. Another manufacturer that claims to have "The Best Laundry Detergent in the World," however, is perfectly within its rights to employ superlatives. The use of absolute superlatives such as *Number One* and *Best in the World* is called **puffery** and is considered legal. The courts have long held that superlatives are understood by consumers as simply the exaggerated commercial language of advertising and are interpreted by consumers as such.

We also need to be aware that various promotional tools are often challenged as being deceptive. The "small print" that accompanies many contests and sweepstakes is often challenged by consumers. Similarly, the appeal of a "free" gift for listening to a pitch on a resort time share often draws a harsh reaction from consumers. Now a consumer watchdog group is challenging brand placements in television shows as being deceptive. The group Commercial Alert argues that television networks are deceiving consumers by not disclosing that they are taking money for highlighting brands in shows and films.[29]

Another area of debate regarding truth in advertising relates to emotional appeals. It is likely impossible to legislate against emotional appeals such as those made about the beauty- or prestige-enhancing qualities of a brand because these claims are unquantifiable. (Take another look at Exhibits 3.6 and 3.7.) Because these types of appeals are legal, their ethics fall into a gray area. Beauty and prestige, it is argued, are in the eye of the beholder, and such appeals are neither illegal nor unethical.

29. Claire Atkinson, "Watchdog Group Hits TV Product Placement," *Advertising Age,* October 6, 2003, 12.

As you can see, there is nothing clear cut about the issue of ethics in advertising. Showing beautiful, slim, successful people in an ad is legal and puts a brand in a favorable setting—do you think that is unethical? When a newspaper or magazine features a brand in an editorial, do you think that is unethical? The challenge is to develop your own ethical standards and values against which you judge yourself and the actions of any organization for which you may work.

Advertising to Children.

Children are viewed as vulnerable consumers, and the desire to restrict advertising aimed at children is based on a wide range of concerns, not the least of which is that it is estimated that children between 2 and 11 years old see around 25,600 ads in a year.[30] One concern is that advertising promotes superficiality and creates values founded in material goods and consumption. Another concern is that children are inexperienced consumers and easy prey for the sophisticated persuasions of advertisers; as such, advertising influences children's demands for everything from toys to snack foods. These demands, in turn, create an environment of child-parent conflict. Parents find themselves having to say no over and over again to children whose desires are piqued by effective advertising. Add to that the historical view held by child psychologists who contend that advertising advocates violence, is responsible for child obesity, creates a breakdown in early learning skills, and results in a destruction of parental authority.[31]

Another concern is that many programs aimed at children constitute program length commercials. This movement began in 1990 when critics argued that 70 programs airing at the time were based on commercial products such as He-Man, the Smurfs, and the Muppets.[32] Special-interest groups have made several attempts to strictly regulate this type of programming aimed at children, but to date, the Federal Communications Commission permits such programming to continue.

There have been movements to restrict the amount of advertising children might see. One of the earliest restrictions was due to the efforts of the special interest group Action for Children's Television that helped get the Children's Television Act passed in 1990. This regulation restricts advertising on children's programming to 10.5 minutes per hour on weekends and 12 minutes per hour on weekdays.[33] Most recently, big food and beverage marketers—for example, McDonald's, Kraft, Pepsi, and General Mills—signed the Children's Food and Beverage Advertising Initiative. The initiative is a voluntary commitment by firms to address the issue of obesity in children. A key element of the agreement is that food and beverage marketers will devote half of their advertising dollars to ads directed at promoting healthier eating alternatives.[34]

On the other side of the issue of advertising to children, ethical debate is the argument that children grow up in a system where consumption is a part of everyday life. As such, they learn the rules of "commerce" early and understand full well that people are trying to sell them "stuff." Research would seem to support that proposition. Research has found that at a fairly young age, children understand what advertising is, gain a healthy skepticism for advertising, and clearly recognize its intent.[35]

30. "Children Not Seeing More Food Ads on Television," Federal Trade Commission Report, released June 1, 2007, www.ftc.gov

31. Richard Linnett, "Psychologists Protest Kids' Ads," *Advertising Age,* September 11, 2000, 4.

32. Patrick J. Sheridan, "FCC Sets Children's Ad Limits," *1990 Information Access Company,* vol. 119, no. 20 (1990), 33.

33. Laura Bird, "NBC Special Is One Long Prime-Time Ad," *The Wall Street Journal,* January 21, 1994, B1, B4.

34. Stephanie Thompson and Ira Teinowitz, "Big Food's Big Deal Not Such a Big Concession," *Advertising Age,* November 20, 2006, 1, 29.

35. J. Goldstein, "Children and Advertising—The Research," *Commercial Communications,* July 1998, 4–7; Tina Mangelburg and Terry Bristol, "Socialization and Adolescent's Skepticism Toward Advertising," *Journal of Advertising,* vol. 27, no. 3 (Fall 1998), 11–21.

Advertising Controversial Products.

Some people question the wisdom of allowing the advertising of controversial products and services such as tobacco, alcoholic beverages, gambling and lotteries, and firearms. Critics charge that tobacco and alcoholic beverage firms are targeting adolescents with advertising and with making dangerous and addictive products appealing.[36] This is, indeed, a complex issue. Many medical journals have published survey research claiming that advertising "caused" cigarette and alcohol consumption—particularly among teenagers.[37]

It is essential to note, however, that these recent studies completely contradict research conducted since the 1950s carried out by marketing, communications, psychology, and economics researchers—including assessments of all the available research by the FTC.[38] These early studies (as well as several Gallup polls during the 1990s) found that family, friends, and peers—not advertising—are the primary influence on teenagers' use of tobacco and alcohol. Studies published in the late 1990s and early in this decade have reaffirmed the findings of this earlier research.[39] Although children at a very early age recognize tobacco advertising characters like "Joe Camel," they also recognize as easily the Energizer Bunny (batteries), the Jolly Green Giant (canned vegetables), and Snoopy (life insurance)—all characters associated with adult products. Children are also aware that cigarettes cause disease and know that they are intended as an adult product. Research in Europe offers the same conclusion: "Every study on the subject [of advertising effects on the use of tobacco and alcohol] finds that children are more influenced by parents and playmates than by the mass media."[40]

Why doesn't advertising cause people to smoke and drink? The simple answer is that advertising isn't that powerful. Eight out of 10 new products fail, and if advertising was so powerful, no new products would fail. The more detailed answer is that advertising cannot create primary demand in mature product categories. **Primary demand** is demand for an entire product category. (Recall the discussion from Chapter 1.) With mature products—like milk, automobiles, toothpaste, cigarettes, and alcohol—advertising isn't powerful enough to have that effect. Research across several decades has demonstrated repeatedly that advertising does not create primary demand for tobacco or alcohol or any other product category.[41] Advertising

36. Kathleen Deveny, "Joe Camel Ads Reach Children, Research Finds," *The Wall Street Journal,* December 11, 1991, B1, B6.

37. See, for example, Joseph R. DiFranza et al., "RJR Nabisco's Cartoon Camel Promotes Camel Cigarettes to Children," *Journal of the American Medical Association,* vol. 266, no. 22 (1991), 3168–3153.

38. For a summary of more than 60 articles that address the issue of alcohol and cigarette advertising and the lack of a relationship between advertising and cigarette and alcohol industry demand, see Mark Frankena et al., "Alcohol, Consumption, and Abuse," Bureau of Economics, Federal Trade Commission, March 5, 1985. For a similar listing of research articles where the same conclusions were drawn during congressional hearings on the topic, see "Advertising of Tobacco Products," Hearings before the Subcommittee on Health and the Environment, Committee on Energy and Commerce, House of Representatives, 99th Congress, July 18 and August 1, 1986, No. 99–167.

39. For examples of the more recent studies that reaffirm peers and family rather than advertising as the basis for smoking initiation, see Charles R. Taylor and P. Greg Bonner, "Comment on 'American Media and the Smoking-Related Behaviors of Asian Adolescents,' " *Journal of Advertising Research* (December 2003), 419–430; Bruce Simons Morton, "Peer and Parent Influences on Smoking and Drinking Among Early Adolescents," *Journal of Health Education and Behavior* (February 2000); and Karen H. Smith and Mary Ann Stutz, "Factors that Influence Adolescents to Smoke," *Journal of Consumer Affairs,* vol. 33, no. 2 (Winter 1999), 321–357.

40. With regard to cartoon characters, see, for example, Lucy L. Henke, "Young Children's Perceptions of Cigarette Brand Advertising: Awareness, Affect and Target Market Identification," *Journal of Advertising,* vol. 24, no. 4 (Winter 1995), 13–27, and Richard Mizerski, "The Relationship between Cartoon Trade Character Recognition and Attitude toward the Product Category," *Journal of Marketing,* vol. 59 (October 1995), 58–70. The evidence in Europe is provided by Jeffrey Goldstein, "Children and Advertising—the Research," *Commercial Communications,* July 1998, 4–8.

41. For research on this topic across several decades, see Richard Schmalensee, *The Economics of Advertising* (Amsterdam and London: North-Holland, 1972); Mark S. Albion and Paul W. Farris, *The Advertising Controversy* (Boston: Auburn House, 1981); Michael J. Waterson, "Advertising and Tobacco Consumption: An Analysis of the Two Major Aspects of the Debate," *International Journal of Advertising,* 9 (1990), 59–72; Michael L. Capella, Charles R. Taylor and Cynthia Webster, "The Effect of Cigarette Advertising Bans on Consumption: A Meta-Analysis," *Journal of Advertising,* vol. 37, no. 2 (Summer 2008), 7–18.

is capable only of stimulating demand for a brand in a product category. Product category demand is the result of social and cultural trends, economic conditions, technological change, and other broad influences on consumers' needs and lifestyles.

No one has ever said that smoking or drinking is good for you (except perhaps that glass of wine with dinner). That's not what we're saying here either. The point is that these behaviors emerge in a complex social context, and the vast weight of research evidence throughout 50 years suggests that advertising is not a significant causal influence on initiation behavior (for example, smoking and drinking). Rather, advertising plays its most important role in consumers' choice of brands (for example, Camel and Coors) after consumers have decided to use a product category (for example, cigarettes and beer).

Gambling and state-run lotteries represent another controversial product area with respect to advertising. What is the purpose of this advertising? Is it meant to inform gamblers and lottery players of the choices of games and places to play? This would be selective (that is, brand) demand stimulation. Or is such advertising designed to stimulate demand for engaging in wagering behavior? This would be primary demand stimulation. What about compulsive gamblers? What is the state's obligation to protect "vulnerable" citizens by restricting the placement or content of lottery advertising?

When the term *vulnerable* is used, questions as to the basis for the claim of vulnerability can become complex and emotionally charged. Those on one side of the issue argue that gamblers as an audience are among the "information poor." That is, they are not prone to seeking out information from a wide range of sources. Those on the other side of the issue find such claims of "information poverty" demeaning, patronizing, and paternalistic. And a new era of gambling emerged when online gambling became widespread and proved to be a fast and easy way for people to lose their life savings. Stories of out-of-control online gambling were widespread.[42]

Then as online gaming revenues approached $1 billion, the U.S. government took the bold move of banning all online gambling in the United States in October 2006.[43]

The issue of advertising controversial products can be complex. One would not normally put food in the "controversial products" category. But as people began suing companies claiming that their advertising caused them to eat unhealthy food and made them fat—well, suddenly a controversy exists. McDonald's and other food companies had to defend themselves against lawsuits from people who claimed that food providers "made them fat." The food industry has countered with the proposition that children are fat because of unconcerned parents, underfunded school systems that have dropped physical activity programs, and sedentary entertainment like home video games.[44]

This issue is troublesome enough that the U.S. government had to pass legislation barring people from suing food companies for obesity. In March 2004, the U.S. House of Representatives overwhelmingly approved legislation nicknamed the "Cheeseburger Bill" that would block lawsuits blaming the food industry for making people fat. During the debate on the bill, one of the bill's sponsors said it was about "common sense and personal responsibility."[45] Many marketers are worried about the intense focus on this global health problem. The chief creative officer of Coca-Cola put it this way: "Our Achilles heel is the discussion about obesity. It dilutes our

42. Ira Singer et al., "The Underground Web," *Business Week,* September 2, 2002, 67–74.

43. Bloomberg News, "Frank Eyes Restoring Web Gaming," March 17, 2007, accessed at www.boston.com/news on May 30, 2007.

44. Mercedes M. Cardona, "Marketers Bite Back as Fat Fight Flares Up," *Advertising Age,* March 1, 2004, 3, 35.

45. Rep. Ric Keller (R-Florida), quoted in Joanne Kenen, "U.S. House Backs Ban on Obesity Lawsuits," Reuters, published on the Internet at biz.yahoo.com/rc/040310/congress_obesity_3.html on March 10, 2004; accessed on March 14, 2004.

marketing and works against us. It's a huge, huge issue."[46] And, as you read earlier, advertisers have entered into a voluntary agreement to devote 50 percent of their ad dollars to promoting healthy food alternatives to children.

Although we can group these ethical issues of advertising into some reasonable categories—truth in advertising, advertising to children, and advertising controversial products—it is not as easy to make definitive statements about the status of ethics in advertising. Ethics will always be a matter of personal values and personal interpretation. And as long as there are unethical people in the world, there will be ethics problems in advertising, as there are in every other phase of business and life.

3 The Regulatory Aspects of Advertising.

The term *regulation* immediately brings to mind government scrutiny and control of the advertising process. Indeed, various government bodies do regulate advertising. But consumers and several different industry organizations exert as much regulatory power over advertising as government agencies do. Three primary groups—consumers, industry organizations, and government bodies—regulate advertising in the truest sense: Together they shape and restrict the process. The government relies on legal restrictions, while consumers and industry groups use less formal controls. Like the other topics in this chapter, regulation of advertising can be controversial and opinions about what does and doesn't need to be regulated can vary greatly.

International Laws and Regulations Affecting Advertising.

Surveying international markets, the number of laws, regulations, and codes of practice affecting the advertising industry is increasing. This implies that marketers and businesspeople are well advised to stay current regarding the legal implications of international and national advertising. Although advertising makes a valuable contribution to a country's economic well-being, care has to be taken that it be done in a socially responsible manner, which is the reason it is governed by laws pertaining to "marketing" and "broadcasting."[47] Regulations are developed to protect citizens and should take into account the respective consumers' views. It must be noted that laws and regulations on advertising have to be differentiated by countries, as different cultures vary in their perceptions about ethical appropriateness. This is especially true for customer segments, mainly children, who may lack educational background or critical thinking, making them more vulnerable to unfair or deceptive advertising. In this context, Gao and Kim refer to a fundamental differentiated stance of countries based on a liberal individualist tradition and countries based on Confucian ethical values. As a consequence, societies based on Confucian philosophy might put more emphasis on regulating soft advertising issues reflecting their strong concern for morality.[48]

Whereas some countries may, to a smaller or larger extent, rely heavily on legislation, other countries may prefer higher levels of self-regulation, while still others may rely on a mixture of both.

46. Stephanie Thompson and Kate MacArthur, "Obesity Fear Frenzy Grips Food Industry," *Advertising Age,* April 23, 2007, 1, 46.

47. Debra Harker, "Regulating Online Advertising: The Benefit of Qualitative Insights," *Qualitative Market Research: An International Journal*, vol. 11, no. 3 (2008), 295–315.

48. Zhihong Gao and Joe H. Kim, "Regulation of Soft Issues in Advertising in Confucian Societies: A Comparative Examination," *Asia Pacific Journal of Marketing and Logistic*, vol. 21, no.1 (2009), 76–92.

The following information on European regulations on misleading and comparative advertising is based on www.europa.eu/legislation_summaries/consumers/consumer_information/l32010_en.htm.

Advertising Regulations in the European Union.

Misleading, Deceptive, and Comparative Advertising. Intending to protect public interest in general and consumer groups and the various commercial and professional players in particular, European legislation regulates misleading advertising as well as comparative advertising and its unfair social and competitive consequences (Directive of the European Parliament and of the Council of 12 December 2006). In recent years, consumers' growing disenchantment with these practices can be noted, which may seriously affect the trust in, functionality of, and survival of the marketplace and the well-being of all market constituents. For example, this legislation regulates issues on placement, timing, and content of advertising and, specifically as to controversial products, to food labeling, tobacco advertising, the protection of children, alcohol advertising, and product safety (Product Safety Directive) supervised by centralized EU and local authorities.

According to this directive, misleading advertising can be understood, potentially or in actual effect, as misleading or detrimentally affecting the judgment of the consumer or commercial partner as well as the competitive conditions of the competitors. This is similar to the notion of "deceptive advertising," which "misleads people, alters the reality and affects buying behavior."[49] When determining the level of misleading that occurs in the respective form of advertising, the factors in Table 3.1 are taken into account.

Deception and Unfairness. Agreement is widespread that deception in advertising is unacceptable. The problem, of course, is that it is as difficult to determine what is deceptive from a regulatory standpoint as it is from an ethical standpoint.

The FTC's policy statement on deception is the authoritative source with regard to defining deceptive advertising. It specifies the following three elements as essential in declaring that an ad is deceptive:[50]

1. There must be a representation, an omission, or a practice that is likely to mislead the consumer.
2. This representation, omission, or practice must be judged from the perspective of a consumer acting reasonably under the circumstance.
3. The representation, omission, or practice must be a "material" one. The basic question is whether the act or practice is likely to affect the consumer's conduct or decision with regard to the product or service. If so, the practice is material and consumer harm is likely because consumers would probably have chosen differently if not for the deception.

Table 3.1 Factors Determining the Level of Misleading Advertising

Factors
1. Characteristics of the goods or services
2. Price
3. Conditions governing the supply of goods or the provision of services
4. Nature, qualities, and rights of the advertiser

Source: Based on Directive 2006/114/EC of the European Parliament and of the Council of 12 December 2006 concerning misleading and comparative advertising, The European Commission.

49. Sheetal Kapoor, "Legal and Ethical Aspects of Advertising", 2010, accessed at www.exchange4media.com/e4m/media_matter/omnibus.asp; 2006/114/EC on January 7, 2011.

50. Gary T. Ford and John E. Calfee, "Recent Developments in FTC Policy on Deception," *Journal of Marketing*, vol. 50 (1986), 82–103.

Table 3.2 Criteria for Comparative Advantage

• It compares goods or services meeting the same needs or having the same purpose.
• It objectively compares material, relevant, verifiable, and representative features of those goods or services, which may include pricing.
• It does not cause confusion in the market place between the advertiser and a competitor.
• It does not discredit or mar the reputation of the trademarks, trade names, or other distinguishing signs of a competitor.
• For products with designation of origin, it relates to products with the same designation.
• It does not take unfair advantage of the trademark or other distinguishing sign of a competitor.
• It does not present goods or services as imitations or replicas of those bearing a protected trademark or trade name.

Source: Based on Federal Trade Commission.

Comparative advertising is understood as advertising that, explicitly or implicitly, identifies a competitor or its offered good or services.

However, comparative advertising, when it is not misleading, can be a legitimate means of informing consumers of what is in their interest. The criteria in Table 3.2 must apply.

Remedy. To protect their legitimate interest, people or organizations affected by misleading or comparative advertising may initiate court actions or involve relevant administrative bodies authorized by the Member States to exercise proper and reasonable powers. As a consequence, and irrespective of an actual loss or damage or intentional negligence of the advertiser, misleading or illicit comparative advertising might have to be omitted or withdrawn. The respective advertiser might be ruled to prove accuracy of the material used in the advertising and, eventually, publish the withdrawal or the notice of amendment. Under certain conditions, the Directive does not rule out voluntary control of misleading or comparative advertising exercised by self-regulatory bodies.

In case members of the advertising industry do not comply with the respective regulations, the Unfair Commercial Practices Directive (UCP), adopted on May 11, 2005, acts to remedy the situation. This directive regulates commercial practices from business to consumers (B2C).[51]

Social, Ethical, and Regulatory Aspects of Advertising.

Advertising to Children.

European Union. Special regulations apply in advertising to children. Some countries in the European Union (EU) (for example, the United Kingdom, Greece, Denmark, Belgium, Italy, and Spain) impose certain restrictions when advertising to children. In Sweden and Norway, advertising to children under the age of 12 is considered illegal.[52]

> *The European Union also has framework legislation in place, which sets down minimum provisions on advertising to children for its 27 member States. The EU Audiovisual Media Services Directive sets out several EU-wide rules on advertising*

51. European Union Legislation, 2011, accessed at www.europa.eu/legislation_summaries/consumers/consumer_information/l32010_en.htm on January 7, 2011.

52. Allmykids, "Media Literacy," 2011, accessed at www.allmykids.com/advertising_to_children/encyclopedia.htm#Media_Literacy on January 2, 2011. Greece, Denmark, Belgium.

and children: Advertising shall not cause moral or physical detriment to minors, and shall therefore comply with the following criteria for their protection:

- *It shall not directly exhort minors to buy a product or a service by exploiting their inexperience or credulity;*
- *It shall not directly encourage minors to persuade their parents or others to purchase the goods or services being advertised;*
- *It shall not exploit the special trust minors place in parents, teachers or other persons;*
- *It shall not unreasonably show minors in dangerous situations;*
- *Children's programs may only be interrupted if the scheduled duration is longer than 30 minutes*

http://ec.europa.eu/avpolicy/docs/library/studies/finalised/studpdf/minadv_int.pdf., p7.

An interesting new discipline for children as consumers is media literacy. The aim of media literacy is to teach children to understand and use media for their own advantage, preventing their becoming victims of consumerism. Institutions like the EU and the World Health Organization regard media literacy as a key tool for children to use in managing the complexity of the current media environment.[53]

Russia. In addition to the first four aforementioned protection criteria for children provided by EU regulation, in Russia, the following advertising practices are not allowed: Article 20

- "discrediting of the authority of parents and educators, or undermining of minors' trust in them;
- direct inducement of minors to convince parents or other persons to purchase the advertised goods;
- efforts to draw the attention of minors to the suggestion that possession of various goods gives them any advantages over other minors or that the absence of such goods has the opposite effect;
- understatement of the requisite level of skill in the use of the goods among minors. In the event, where the results of use of the goods are shown or described, the advertising must give information on what is actually attainable for minors of the age group for which the goods are intended;
- creation among minors of unrealistic (distorted) notion of the value (price) of the goods for minors, notably through the use of words like 'only' and 'no more than', and also by direct or indirect suggestion that the advertised goods are within the reach of any family budget"[54]

China. Regulations for children-targeted advertising are under the auspices of the Chinese government. The regulations state the following:

Children's advertising should not only accommodate children's limited cognitive capacity, but also teach children good behavior and ethics. It also stipulates that advertising for products not suitable for children's consumption should not employ child actors. The regulation has not been updated since 1993, so it contains no provisions on Internet advertising.[55]

53. Allmykids, "Media Literacy," 2011, accessed at www.allmykids.com/advertising_to_children/encyclopedia.htm#Media_Literacy on January 2, 2011.

54. Article 20, Protection of Minors in Production, Allocation and Circulation of Advertising, accessed at http://www.vii.org/monroe/issue 23/ad.html on January 28, 2011, p. 7.

55. Zhihong Gao and Hongxia Zhang, "A Comparative Study of Chinese and US Consumers' Attitudes toward Advertising Regulation," *Asia Pacific Journal of Marketing and Logistics*, vol. 23, no.1 (2011), 72–90.

Table 3.3 Regulations for Children's Television Programs in India

1. Programs on cable television should not denigrate children;
2. Programs meant for children should not contain any bad language or explicit scenes of violence;
3. Programs unsuitable for children must not be shown at times when the largest numbers of children are viewing;
4. Programs for adults should normally be aired after 11 p.m. and before 6 a.m.;
5. Unhealthy practice showing children begging or behaving in an undignified or indecent way are prohibited.[56]

India. In India, children's television programs must follow the codes established by the Cable Television Networks (Regulation) Act, 1995. Some of the regulations are shown in Table 3.3.

Responding to the global trend of increased social responsibility in general and to the popularity of the responsible advertising concept in India, seven leading food and beverage companies (Coca-Cola, PepsiCo, Nestlé, Kellogg's, Mars International, General Mills, and Hindustan Unilever) signed a self-regulatory pledge for the first time in India. This pledge pertaining to responsible marketing communication to children (especially in schools), which leans toward Indian and European laws, refers to omitting advertising for children under the age of 12 and aims to combat obesity. As a precondition for commercial communication in schools, the advertised products require scientific evidence to be nutritious.[57] In the same vein, Gray points to the beneficial impact of self-regulation in this field to reverse the trend toward childhood obesity.[58] Based on these views, this commendable initiative might have further global implications.

Advertising Controversial Products. The following sections discuss the diversity of international advertising regulations on the controversial alcohol industry.

Alcohol Advertising. Similar to tobacco advertising, a heated and controversial debate exists between the alcohol and advertising industries and political decision makers and consumer groups as to the contribution or damage created by alcohol advertising and to the appropriateness of banning the advertising of a legal product.

Alcohol advertising is seen by one camp as having detrimental individual and societal effects regarding "recruiting new drinkers and increasing sales among existing ones." The other camp foresees "adverse effects on the alcohol market and the media and rejects a causal link between advertising and the overall level of alcohol consumption or the amount of alcohol-related harm."[59]

Regulatory Agents on Alcohol Advertising. Exhibit 3.13 reflects each country's policy related to alcohol advertising restrictions and reflects significant differences between countries. Whereas statutory regulation is "imbedded in law and issued by the national government," the Combination column refers to the involvement of

56. Sharad Vadehra, "Advertising to Children in India," *Young Consumers*, vol. 11, Quarter 4 (2004), 75, accessed at www.gala-marketlaw.com/pdf/LegalIndia.pdf on January 28, 2011.

57. LIG, Law Is Greek, "Indian Law: Ready for Responsible Advertising," 2010, accessed at www.lawisgreek.com/india-law-ready-for-responsible-advertising on December 18, 2010.

58. Oliver Gray, "Responsible Advertising in Europe," *Young Consumers*, vol. 6, no. 4 (2005), 19–23.

59. Accessed at www.ias.org.uk/resources/factsheets/advertising.pdf on January 26, 2011.

Country	Self-Regulatory	Statuary Legislation	Combination	Banned	Some Control	No Control
China		X				
Hong Kong			X			
India		X				
Japan			X			
North Korea		X				
South Korea		X				
Taiwan		X				
Austria			X			
Croatia						X
Czech Republic			X			
France		X				
Germany	X					
Hungary		X				
Italy			X			
Latvia					X	
Belarus				X		
Spain			X			
Russia			X			
Ukraine				X		
Argentina	X					
Bolivia					X	
Brazil			X			
Chile	X					
Colombia		X				
Guatemala		X				
Puerto Rico			X			
Uruguay	X					

Source: Based on International Center for Alcohol Policies, ICAP Reports 9, January 2001.

Exhibit 3.13 Country's Policy on Alcohol Advertising Restrictions

industry in "only one or two" components of regulation (legislation, enforcement, and adjudication).[60]

Based on various national codes and regulations, the alcohol regulations of several countries are discussed in the following sections.

60. Peter Anderson, "The impact of Alcohol Advertisement: EIASA Project Report on the Evidence to Strengthen Regulation to Protect Young People," (Utrecht: National Foundation for Alcoholic Prevention, 2007), ISBN: 978-90-79070-05-3.

Czech Republic. Related to advertising and marketing alcoholic beverages, the Czech Republic has five regulatory mechanisms—three statutory and two non-statutory (self-regulations):[61]

1. Statutory Mechanisms:

   "Act No. 40/1995 Coll. on the Regulation of Advertisement

   Act No. 231/2001 Coll. on TV and Radio Broadcasting

   Act No. 37/1989 Coll. on the Protection against Alcoholism and Other Toxicomanias."

2. Non-Statutory Mechanisms:

   "Self-regulations: Code of Practice of the Association of Alcohol Producers

   Code of Advertising Practice of the Czech Advertising Standards Council"

Since 1989, the political transition of the Czech Republic from a centrally planned to free market economy caused a sea of change in alcohol advertising and alcohol consumption. The emergence of privately owned companies signified the birth of marketing, which was previously a system of centrally allocating products. In this wave, principally unrestricted advertising and promotional activities flourished and alcoholic consumption, especially among adolescents, increased (Eucam, 2011, p. 1).

"However, after the Czech Republic joined the European Union, they were harmonized with EU legislation. Nevertheless, provisions regulating advertisement and promotion of alcohol remain unsatisfactory."[62]

Poland. As mentioned, different national idiosyncrasies lead to different types of legal regulations. Although also being an Eastern European transition country, Poland and its alcohol marketing regulations differ from those of the Czech market. In Poland, two mayoral documents regulate issues related to marketing alcohol:

- Statutory: The Act of October 26th, 1982 on Upbringing in Sobriety and Counteracting Alcoholism (last version: 1.04.2005)
- Non-statutory: Polish Brewers Advertising Code of June 8th, 2005.

  Two articles of the first document (Art. 2 [1], Art. 13 [1]) contain regulations on the promoting, advertising, and sponsoring of alcoholic beverages.

According to the law, only beer may be advertised and promoted through media channels like TV, radio, and billboards. The exception is at the point of sale of the alcoholic beverages: in these places (a liquor store, a restaurant, a bar, a pub, a separate stall, a wholesale trade—all of them must have special permission to sell alcoholic beverages), any kind of alcoholic beverage may be promoted and advertised in any way.

The second document, Polish Brewers Advertising Code of June 8th, 2005, is a non-statutory one and refers only to beer advertising. Most of the rules from this regulation are reflected in the statutory document."[63]

61. European Union Legislation, 2011, accessed at http://ec.europa.eu/avpolicy/reg/avms/index_en.htm on January 27, 2011. EUCAM, European Centre for Monitoring Alcohol Marketing, 2007, accessed at www.eucam.info/eucam/czech_republic on January 15, 2011. EUCAM, European Centre for Monitoring Alcohol Marketing, 2007, accessed at www.eucam.info/eucam/poland on January 15, 2011. EUCAM, European Centre for Monitoring Alcohol Marketing, 2007, accessed at www.eucam.info/eucam/germany on January 15, 2011. EUCAM, European Centre for Monitoring Alcohol Marketing, 2007, accessed at www.eucam.info/eucam/spain on January 15, 2011, EUCAM, European Centre for Monitoring Alcohol Marketing, 2007, accessed at www.eucam.info/eucam/france on January 15, 2011.

62. Ibid.

63. Ibid.

Russia. Messages in alcohol advertisements in Russia must not associate alcohol consumption with achieving success in society and improving mental or physical heath and must not discredit abstention. Furthermore, the regulations are to protect minors from the exposure of alcohol advertising, and advertising time and positioning in the media are regulated. In detail, advertisements must not:

- "contain a demonstration of consumption of alcoholic drinks, or create the impression that consumption of alcohol is of great importance for the achievement of public, athletic or other success or for improvement of one's physical or mental state;
- discredit abstention from consumption of alcohol, contain information on the positive therapeutic properties of alcohol or present their high content in a product as an asset;
- address itself directly to minors or use images of natural persons under the age of 35 years, statements or participation by persons enjoying popularity among minors and persons under the age of 21 years;
- be circulated in radio and television programs from 7.00 hours to 22.00 hours local time;
- be circulated in any form in radio and television broadcasts, during cinema and video service or in printed publications for minors;
- be circulated on the first and last pages of newspapers, or on the first and last pages and covers of magazines and journals; and
- be circulated in children's educational, medical, sports or cultural organizations, or in the vicinity of less than 100 meters there from."[64]

China. In China, the *Methods on the Administration of Advertising for Alcohol* regulates alcohol advertising. Ads depicting scenes of "drink and driving behavior," showing and being targeted at minors, and associating drinking with success or stress relief are prohibited. At the most, two television commercials on high-volume liquor products may be aired during prime time (19:00 21:00), with a total of 12 per day as regulated by the *Methods on the Administration of Broadcast Advertising*, whereas two radio spots per hour can be transmitted.[65]

United Kingdom. The Committee of Advertising Practice (CAP) (UK) has designed the CAP Code for advertising products. According to CAP, "alcoholic drinks are defined as drinks containing at least 0.5% alcohol; for the purposes of this Code, low-alcohol drinks are defined as drinks containing between 0.5% and 1.2% alcohol."[66] The following principle aims to appeal to socially responsible behavior: "Marketing communications for alcoholic drinks should not be targeted at people under 18 and should not imply, condone or encourage immoderate, irresponsible or anti-social drinking."[67]

Germany. In Germany, three types of regulations exist concerning alcohol marketing and advertising. The first two regulations are of a statutory nature; the third, of a non-statutory nature:

1. The *Jugendschutzgesetz* (youth protection law—translated by the authors) regulates the broadcast time of commercials in movie performances only.

64. Accessed at www.vii.org/monroe/issue 23/ad.html on January 25, 2005.

65. Zhihong Gao and Hongxia Zhang, "A Comparative Study of Chinese and US Consumers' Attitudes toward Advertising Regulation," *Asia Pacific Journal of Marketing and Logistics*, vol. 23, no. 1 (2011), 72–90.

66. CAP, Committee of Advertising Practice, 2011, accessed at www.cap.org.uk/About-Us/BCAP-Broadcast.aspx on February 1, 2011.

67. Ibid.

2. *Jugendmedienschutz-Staatsvertrag* (youth media protection, state treaty—translated by the authors) is concerned with protecting the dignity of men, women, and youth in broadcasting and Telemedia.
3. Code of Conduct on Commercial Communication for Alcoholic Beverages represents the main regulation on alcohol marketing designed by the advertising and alcohol industry. "The German Advertising Council, a self-regulatory agency of the German Advertising Federation, is responsible for the complaint and sanctioning system."[68]

Spain. In Spain, a number of regional regulations on direct, indirect, and hidden advertising complement state legislation. Similar to other countries, the most common practices target media regulations on the protection of minors, often relating to timing and content of the advertisements.[69]

Switzerland. In Switzerland, the *Lebensmittelgesetz* (Federal Law of Foodstuffs) forbids alcohol advertising on TV and radio and to minors under the age of 18. In addition, "alcohol advertising is generally allowed if the advertising is socially responsible and does not encourage excessive drinking."[70]

France. France, a country with a long-standing tradition of producing and globally trading famous wines, banned alcohol advertising in February 2008. Currently, four different regulations (statutory and non-statutory codes) refer to alcohol advertising and marketing:[71]

"1. The Code de la Santé Publique (Code of Public Health)
2. The Code d'autodiscipline et de déontologie en matière de communication commercial (Self-Regulation Code on Communication and Sale of Alcoholic Beverages)
3. The Code d'éthique des Brasseurs (Brewers Code of Practice)
4. The Code de bonne conduite pour la retransmission télévisée d'événements sportifs regarding sports events (Code of practice in Sport Events Broadcast)"

The competent body on deceptive and misleading advertising is the Direction Générale de la Concurrence, de la Consommation et de la Répression des Fraudes (DGCCRF) (General Directorate on Competition, Consumption and Fraud Repression).[72]

Other State Regulations and International Regulatory Agents: Russia and China. In addition to the previous information, more detail follows for Russia and, especially, China, both generally accepted as future growth markets.

Russian Federation Advertising Law. Similar to the objectives of the European Union Directive (point 3.1.1), the Federal Law on Advertising dated March 13, 2006, No.38-FZ (the Advertising Law) of the Russian Federation (RF) aims to prevent harm to the interests, health, property, or reputation of consumers, citizens, legal entities, or society as a whole from misleading advertising.

68. European Union Legislation, 2011, accessed at http://www.eucam.info/eucam/germany on January 27, 2011.
69. Ibid.
70. Peter Hofer and Jeannette Bieri, "Advertising to Children in Switzerland," *Young Consumers*, quarter 2 (2005), 81.
71. European Union Legislation, 2011, accessed at http://www.eucam.info/eucam/france/ on January 27, 2011.
72. Accessed at www.aeforum.org/reg_env/france.html on February 1, 2011.

This is illustrated, for example, by Article 2:

- "improper advertising—unfair, unreliable, unethical, deliberately false and other advertising which allows breaches of requirements on its content, time, place and way of circulation, as established by RF legislation;
- counter-advertising—refutation of improper advertising circulated with the object of eliminating its consequences."[73]

China. Forty-nine laws and regulations in China for advertising affecting companies, advertising agencies, and publishers reflect China's transition policy.

The respective articles by Lehman and Chinagate define the terms and players involved and address the following examples (not an exhaustive list):[74]

- The protection of the rights of consumers, suppliers of commodities or services, and the social and economic order and the demand for a positive role advertising should play in the socialist market economy
- The required behavior of the various advertising agents (that is, fairness, honesty, creditworthiness, and no engagement in unfair competition)
- The required advertising content [that is, being true, being lawful, and "conforming to the requirements in the building of a socialist spiritual civilization"; being beneficial to the mental and physical health of the people (especially those who are underaged and handicapped); being compliant with the social, public, and professional ethics; and safeguarding the dignity and interest of the state]

Exhibit 3.14 summarizes elements that must not appear in advertisements.

- The products allowed to be advertised (not to be advertised include special purpose drugs such as anesthetics, psychotropic drugs, toxic drugs, and radioactive drugs and tobacco); tobacco is not allowed to be advertised through broadcast, films, TV, newspapers, and periodicals or to be posted in any waiting rooms, cinemas and theatres, meeting halls, sports sites, gyms, and other public places

Exhibit 3.14 China Advertising's Limitations

1. National flag, national emblem, and national anthem of the People's Republic of China
2. Names of government organizations and government functionaries
3. Words such as *state level, highest level,* and *the best*
4. Anything that would be injurious to social stability, safety of people and property, and social public interests
5. Anything that would jeopardize social and public order and violate good social conventions
6. Contents that are obscene, superstitious, terrorizing, violent, and evil
7. Contents that are discriminative against nationalities, races, religions, and sex
8. Contents that are harmful to the protection of the environment or natural resources
9. Other contents that are forbidden by laws and administrative decrees

Source: Based on Advertising Law of the People's Republic of China.

73. Accessed at http://www.vii.org/monroe/issue23/ad.html, p. 1, on February 1, 2011.

74. Lee Lehman, 1995, accessed at www.lehmanlaw.com/resource-centre/laws-and-regulations/advertising/advertisement-law-of-the-peoples-republic-of-China-1995.html on January 3, 2011; Chinagate,1995, accessed at http://chinagate.cn/english/434.htm#1 on January 19, 2011.

- Advertising activities to be based on written contracts defining the rights and obligations of the partners involved
- Aspects of legal responsibility

In case of violation of the provisions on publishing advertisements (Article 7, paragraph 2), advertising industry participants might face legal actions. This could mean that the publication has to be stopped and amendments openly to be made. The respective advertisers or publishers could be fined with up to five times the amount of the advertising expenses and the advertising business license could be terminated.[75]

According to Gao and Zhang, a number of government agencies underlining a strong administrative dimension are authorized to issue and enforce industry-wide regulations on advertising. "Challenges to unfair and deceptive advertising in China can be initiated by the government, competitors, and consumers through the administrative or judicial process, and the Chinese law does not require extrinsic evidence, literal falsehood, or materiality when interpreting deception."[76]

Some of these governmental institutions are as follows:

- State Administration for Industry & Commerce (SAIC), which is responsible for monitoring the advertising industry
- Administration for Industry and Commerce (AIC), which has strong local supervision of a particular advertising industry
- National Development and Reform Commission (NDRC)
- Ministry of Commerce, People's Republic of China (MOFCOM)[77]

4 Industry Self-Regulation.

Compared to statutory regulation issued by the government, the various players of the advertising industry consisting of advertisers, advertising agencies, media, or trade associations may commit to standards of advertising practice and a system to quickly correct or remove advertisements if they do not comply with those standards. In essence, the advertising industry regulates itself.[78]

Exhibit 3.15 compares self-regulations with governmental regulations and points out some advantages as well as criticisms; critical points can be perceived.

Europe. An umbrella organization, The European Advertising Standards Alliance (EASA), located in Brussels, was created with the mission of synthesizing and integrating the intentions of 33 national advertising self-regulatory organizations, 26 European and seven non-European bodies (SROs), and the organizations representing the advertising industry in Europe and beyond (some members are provided in Exhibit 3.16). The goal of this organization is to self-regulate high ethical standards in marketing communication, considering idiosyncratic cultural, legal, and commercial practice in the respective countries to the benefit of consumers and businesses.[79]

75. Lee Lehman, 1995, accessed at www.lehmanlaw.com/resource-centre/laws-and-regulations/advertising/advertisement-law-of-the-peoples-republic-of-China-1995.html on January 3, 2011.

76. Zhihong Gao, "An In-depth Examination of China's Advertising Regulation System," 2007, in Zhihong Gao and Hongxia Zhang, *Asia Pacific Journal of Markets and Logistics*, vol. 23, no. 1 (2011), 72–90.

77. Accessed at www.chinaknowledge.com/Marcom/Book-ChinaConsumer.aspx?subchap=4&content=12 on January 3, 2011.

78. Peter Anderson, "The Impact of Alcohol Advertisement: EIASA Project Report on the Evidence to Strengthen Regulation to Protect Young People" (Utrecht: National Foundation for Alcoholic Prevention, 2007), ISBN: 978-90-79070-05-3.

79. EASA, European Advertising Standards Alliance, 2010, accessed at www.easa-alliance.org on January 3, 2011.

Exhibit 3.15 Advantages and Criticism of Industry Self-Regulation

Self-Regulation	
Advantages	Criticism
There is improved efficiency, flexibility, and incentives for compliance and reduced costs.	It is difficult to balance industries' profits and the benefits of the public.
Industry participants have a deeper knowledge of the subject to be regulated.	It could subvert regulatory goals to one's own business goals.
The process to modify rules for a trade association is easy and quick.	Self-regulatory entities could experience higher industry pressure than could government agencies.
Self-regulation offers the possibility of tailoring a law to a particular industry.	In its private nature, self-regulation might overlook the needs that affect parties outside the industry.
Higher levels of commitment exist to apply the law developed by industry.	Resources need to be invested for the enforcement of self-regulatory regimes.
Being impartial: The cases are assessed in an impartial procedure by a jury composed of lay experts only eventually accompanied by professionals, thereby avoiding conflicts of interest while maintaining the trust of consumers.	
Diagnostic effect: Advice is provided to the campaigns of the advertising industry upon request before they are run to make sure they comply with the code.	

Source: Based on European Advertising Standards Alliance.

As already mentioned, besides the EASA, which is the authorized and centralized European voice on self-regulation, individual countries have localized self-regulation bodies. These are exemplified by the United Kingdom and France in the next sections. In particular, the UK provisions are regarded as role models for many other European countries.

Exhibit 3.16 European and Global Advertising Self-Regulatory Institutions

Organization	Web Address
Association of Commercial Television in Europe (ACT)	www.acte.be
European Newspaper Publishers' Association (ENPA)	www.enpa.be
European Advertising Standards Alliance (EASA)	www.easa-alliance.org
European Publishers Council (EPC)	www.epceurope.org
European Association of Communications Agencies (EACA)	www.eaca.be
Interactive Advertising Bureau (IAB)	www.iab.net
World Federation of Advertisers	www.wfanet.org

Source: Based on European Advertising Standards Alliance.

Exhibit 3.17 CAP Members

CAP Members	
Advertising Association	Mobile Broadband Group
Cinema Advertising Association	Mobile Marketing Association
Data Publishers Association	Newspaper Society
Direct Marketing Association	Outdoor Advertising Association
Direct Selling Association	Periodical Publishers Association
Incorporated Society of British Advertisers	Proprietary Association of Great Britain Royal Mail
Institute of Practitioners in Advertising	Scottish Newspaper Society
Institute of Promotional Marketing	
Internet Advertising Bureau	Clearcast (formerly BACC)
Mail Order Traders Association	Radio Advertising Clearance Centre

Source: Based on Committee of Advertising Practice, 2011.

UK Self-Regulation Bodies. The Advertising Standards Authority (ASA) is a national self-regulation system based on the principles of independence and support and commitment of the advertising industry. The standards laid down in the Advertising Codes, designed to protect consumers and to create a level playing field for advertisers, are maintained by the Committee of Advertising Practice (CAP) (ASA, 2011).

The members of CAP (some members are depicted in Exhibit 3.17) constitute representatives of advertisers, agencies, media owners, and other industry groups (table 5).… "CAP writes and reviews the British Code of Advertising, Sales Promotion and Direct Marketing that all advertisers have to adhere to.…[T]he Code broadly covers misleadingness, harm and offence, and breaches of taste and decency."[80]

The success of CAP and the regulation of print ads led to the formation of the co-regulatory Broadcast Committee of Advertising Practice (BCAP) (some members of the committee are provided in Exhibit 3.18). BCAP writes and reviews the advertising codes for TV and radio ads.[81]

Exhibit 3.18 Broadcast Committee of Advertising Practice

BCAP Members	
Advertising Association	Institute of Practitioners in Advertising
British Sky Broadcasting Limited	ITV plc
Channel 4 Television Corporation	RadioCentre
Direct Marketing Association	S4C
Electronic Retailing Association UK **Five.TV**	Satellite & Cable Broadcasters' Group Teletext Ltd
GMTV Limited	
Incorporated Society of British Advertisers	Clearcast (formerly BACC) Radio Advertising Clearance Centre

Source: Based on Broadcast Committee of Advertising Practice, 2011.

80. CAP, Committee of Advertising Practice, 2011, accessed at www.cap.org.uk/About-Us/BCAP-Broadcast.aspx on January 5, 2011.

81. Ibid.

In addition to its regular members shown in the preceding tables, CAP and BCAP capitalize on the incalculable support of two industry panels on sales promotion, direct marketing, and general media: Sales Promotion and Direct Response Panel (SPDRP) and General Media Panel (GMP).[82]

France Self-Regulation Body. Bureau de Vérification de la Publicité (BVP) is funded by the advertising industry. Being a member of EASA, BVP was created to develop and apply code and rules regulating advertising content. Mainly playing a preventive and "diagnostic" role, it provides copy advice in any media for its members and pre-clears all TV spots. BVP also exerts a remedy function in case of an upheld complaint requesting an advertiser to withdraw or amend an advertisement.[83]

India Self-Regulation by the Advertising Industry. Pursuing similar objectives and activities as the EASA, the Advertising Standards Council of India (ASCI) has adopted a Code for Self-Regulation in Advertising.

The members (only firms are accepted), by sending nominees to the Board of Governors, are involved in further development of the Code and future appointments to the Consumer Complaints Council (CCC).[84] ASCI encourages public complaints and remedies the situation by promptly and objectively considering the complaints through the use of an impartial committee, the Consumer Complaints Council (CCC), which communicates balanced decisions to all parties involved.[85]

ASCI requires advertisements to be:

- "Truthful and fair to consumers and competitors
- Within the bounds of generally accepted standards of public decency and propriety
- Not used indiscriminately for the promotion of products, hazardous or harmful to society or to individuals particularly minors, to a degree unacceptable to society at large"

According to Kapoor, higher levels of self-regulation (see Exhibits 3.19 and 3.20) were triggered in India by a variety of factors:[86]

- Increased criticism of advertising
- Reduced capacity of the governments to influence media due to the resistance of media, which are financed by advertising, to accept governmental restrictions and the spread of new communication and information technologies
- The industry's growing conviction of the interdependence between acting responsibly and achieving long-term profitability

Exhibit 3.19 Indian Agencies Involved in Self-Regulation

Advertising Trade Associations	Advertising Standards Council of India (ASCI) Advertising Agencies Association of India (AAAI) Press Council of India Prasar Bharati
Individual Media and Media Groups	Code for Commercial Advertising on Doordarshan All India Radio Code for Commercial Advertising

Source: Based on Advertising Standards Council of India (ASCI).

82. Accessed at www.cap.org.uk/About-Us/BCAP-Broadcast.aspx on January 5, 2011.

83. Accessed at www.aeforum.org/reg_env/france.html on January 6, 2011.

84. Accessed at www.ascionline/goals/whyselfregulation.htm on January 6, 2011.

85. Accessed at www.ascionline/goals/mission.htm on January 6, 2011.

86. Sheetal Kapoor, 2010, "Legal and Ethical Aspects of Advertising," accessed at www.exchange4media.com/e4m/media_matter/omnibus.asp on January 8, 2011.

Exhibit 3.20 Example of ASCI Members

ASCI Member
Abbott Healthcare Ltd.
Agro Tech Foods Ltd.
Bayer Pharmaceuticals P. Ltd.
Colgate-Palmolive Ltd.
Ford India Ltd.
IndianOil Corporation Ltd.
L'Oréal India P. Ltd.
Nestle India P. Ltd.
Nokia India Ltd.
Bombay Dyeing & Manufacturing Co. Ltd.

Source: Based on Advertising Standards Council of India.

Despite existing statutory legislation and self-regulation, Kapoor stills sees a lot of needed changes: "The need of the hour is better laws in keeping with the times, better enforcement, corrective advertisements, better self-regulation by industry independent regulator to regulate health and children-related advertisements."[87]

Asia. The Asian Advertising Agency Associations (CAAAA) serves as a forum where representatives of advertising agency associations (see Exhibit 3.21) in the Asian region convene to discuss issues concerning the advertising agencies.

China. In line with Kapoor's view on Indian conditions, Gao and Zhang also do not perceive a sufficient influence of self-regulation organizations in China. Although supervised by the State Administration for Industry & Commerce China (SAIC), the Advertising Association (CAA) is regarded as being a self-regulatory entity. The main activities are to provide professional consultation and expert legal advice for

Exhibit 3.21 Example of CAAAA Members

CAAAA Member
Advertising Agencies Association of India, India
Association of Accredited Advertising Agencies Philippines, Philippines
Association of Accredited Advertising Agents Singapore, Singapore
China Advertising Association, China
Indonesian Association of Advertising Agencies, Indonesia
Japan Advertising Agencies Association, Japan
Korea Association of Advertising Agencies, Korea
The Association of Accredited Advertising Agents of Taipei, Chinese Taipei
The Advertising Association of Thailand, Thailand

Source: Based on Confederation of Asian Advertising Agency Associations.

87. Ibid.

Exhibit 3.22 JAAA Code of Ethics

- "Advertising must present the truth and live up to the trust of the society
- Advertising must comply with laws, regulations and ethical codes, pay respect to human rights and provide fair-minded expression
- Advertising must not work against sound social order or good customs of the society
- Advertising must esteem grace and dignity to contribute to the establishment of sound and healthy life of the people
- Advertising must provide information that puts primary emphasis on the benefit of the consumers
- Advertising must contribute to the optimum solution of the client's issues through effective and efficient communications"

Source: Based on The Japanese Advertising Agencies Association.

those advertising agencies responsible for vetting advertisements and commercials (Chinaknowledge, 2011). According to Gao and Zhang, CAA "functions to publicize government laws and policies to the advertising industry. It consists of *The Self-Discipline Code on Promoting Spiritual Civilization in Advertising* in 1997 and *The Self-Discipline Code on Fair Competition in Advertising* in 1999. However, it does not directly monitor advertising in the media or process complaints by consumers or competitors."[88]

Japan. The Japanese Advertising Agencies Association (JAAA) embraces its code of ethics outlined in Exhibit 3.22.

Latin America. In Brazil, the National Council of Advertising Self-Regulation was founded in the 1980s. Its primary aim is to guarantee that advertisers comply with the existing national regulations. The Brazilian Consumer Defense Code (CDC), created in 1990, puts more emphasis on control through legislators and the judiciary.[89]

Internet and Digital Media Self-Regulation in Europe and the United States.

Europe. European industry self-regulation on the Internet and digital media—including Internet service providers (ISPs) and their respective industry associations, which are reflected in Codes of Practice—are concerned with issues related to content, privacy, public decency, protection of minors, accuracy, the application of filtering software, electronic game industry, and mobile Internet services.[90]

A study and publications by Oxford University in 2004 reveal that most EU countries apply Internet self-regulation, albeit with considerable differences.[91] The study, according to Kleinsteuber, concludes that self-regulation (on the legality of the content) is more successful the more a respective legal basis and clear public policy objectives and consensus exist. Gaps seem to exist regarding the knowledge of Codes of Practice as well as the transparency and accountability in code production and application. In this context, a further gap is provided by Dahl, Eagle, and Baez having examined advergames versus the reality of their claimed effects on children. The authors found that the majority of the websites reviewed did not comply with

88. Zhihong Gao and Hongxia Zhang, "A Comparative Study of Chinese and US Consumers' Attitudes toward Advertising Regulation," *Asia Pacific Journal of Marketing and Logistics*, vol. 23, no.1 (2011), 72–90.

89. Rosangela Delgado and Paula Foschia, "Advertising to Children in Brazil," *International Journal of Advertising and Marketing to Children*, 4, 3 (2003), 65–68.

90. Hans, J. Kleinsteuber, "The Internet between Regulation and Governance," accessed at www.osce.org/fom/13844 on October 10, 2010.

91. Ibid.

the existing broadcast code of practice. Consequently, this leads to the need of a critical examination of the Web content by the competent authority and the claim of fair and ethical online behavior.[92]

Media Organizations in the United States. Individual media organizations evaluate the advertising they receive for broadcast and publication. The National Association of Broadcasters (NAB) has a policing arm known as the Code Authority, which implements and interprets separate radio and television codes. These codes deal with truth, fairness, and good taste in broadcast advertising. Newspapers have historically been rigorous in their screening of advertising. Many newspapers have internal departments to screen and censor ads believed to be in violation of the newspaper's advertising standards.

Although the magazine industry does not have a formal code, many publications have high standards. Direct mail may have a poor image among many consumers, but its industry association, the Direct Marketing Association (DMA), is active in promoting ethical behavior and standards among its members. It has published guidelines for ethical business practices. In 1971, the association established the Direct Mail Preference Service, which allows consumers to have their names removed from most direct mail lists.

A review of all aspects of industry self-regulation suggests that a variety of programs and organizations are designed to monitor advertising and that many of these

Table 3.4 Principles on U.S. Self-Regulation on Online Advertising

- "**The Education Principle** calls for organizations to participate in efforts to educate individuals and businesses about online behavioral advertising and the Principles.
- **The Transparency Principle** calls for clearer and easily accessible disclosures to consumers about data collection and use practices associated with online behavioral advertising. It will result in new, enhanced notice on the page where data is collected through links embedded in or around advertisements, or on the Web page itself.
- **The Consumer Control Principle** provides consumers with an expanded ability to choose whether data is collected and used for online behavioral advertising purposes. This choice will be available through a link from the notice provided on the Web page where data is collected.
- **The Consumer Control Principle** requires "service providers," a term that includes Internet access service providers and providers of desktop applications software such as Web browser "tool bars," to obtain the consent of users before engaging in online behavioral advertising, and take steps to de-identify the data used for such purposes.
- **The Data Security Principle** calls for organizations to provide appropriate security for, and limited retention of data, collected and used for online behavioral advertising purposes.
- **The Material Changes Principle** calls for obtaining consumer consent before a Material Change is made to an entity's Online Behavioral Advertising data collection and use policies unless that change will result in less collection or use of data.
- **The Sensitive Data Principle** recognizes that data collected from children and used for online behavioral advertising merits heightened protection, and requires parental consent for behavioral advertising to consumers known to be under 13 on child-directed Web sites. This Principle also provides heightened protections to certain health and financial data when attributable to a specific individual.
- **The Accountability Principle** calls for development of programs to further advance these Principles, including programs to monitor and report instances of uncorrected non-compliance with these Principles to appropriate government agencies."

Source: Based on Self-Regulatory Principles for Online Behavioral Advertising.

92. Stephan Dahl, Lynne Eagle, Carlos Baez, "Analyzing Advergames: Active Diversions or Actually Deception. An Exploratory Study of Online Advergames Content," *Young Consumers: Insight and Ideas for Responsible Marketing*, vol. 10, no.1 (2008), 46–59.

programs are effective. Those whose livelihoods depend on advertising are just as interested as consumers and legislators in maintaining high standards. If advertising is perceived by consumers as being an unethical and untrustworthy business activity, the economic vitality of many organizations will be compromised. Self-regulation can help prevent such a circumstance and is in the best interest of all the organizations discussed here.

Exemplifying Internet self-regulation, the consumer friendly standards of the cross-industry Self-Regulatory Program for Online Behavioral Advertising developed by leading U.S. industry associations are provided. Balancing between a concern for consumers and preservation of innovative and robust advertising, the program is based on the seven principles in Table 3.4.[93]

Consumers as Regulatory Agents. Consumers are motivated to act as regulatory agents based on a variety of interests, including product safety, reasonable choice, the right to information, and privacy. Advertising tends to be a focus of consumer regulatory activities because of its conspicuousness. Consumerism and consumer organizations have provided the primary vehicles for consumer regulatory efforts.

Consumerism, the actions of individual consumers or groups of consumers designed to exert power in the marketplace, is by no means a recent phenomenon. The earliest consumerism efforts can be traced to 17th-century England. In the United States, there have been recurring consumer movements throughout the 20th century. *Adbusters* magazine and its website is a recent example. The organization claims to be "a global network of culture jammers and creative working to change the way information flows, the way corporations wield power, and the way meaning is produced in our society." (Adbuster)

In the preceding text, the growing disbelief and skepticism of consumers toward advertising, especially misleading advertising, was mentioned repeatedly. In addition, new interactive technologies such as the Internet and mobile phones have provided consumers with significantly more influence in continuously adapting the regulatory frameworks.[94]

These developments caused reactions both in academia and the marketplace. Representative of an increasing number of colleagues, Thrassou and Vrontis conceptualized a relationship between consumers and businesses in developed countries that should be characterized by consumer protection in terms of both visible aspects (that is, overpricing and shoddy/unsafe products) and communicative aspects that avoid puting the consumer under "the spell" of branding and marketing communication.[95]

In an attempt to continuously improve the quality of relationships with clients and to better tailor products and services to their needs, academics and companies had and still have to explore the "very core" of the client to illuminate the last dark factors of consumer decision making and behavior. In doing so, marketing theory increasingly resorted to the micro sociological theory of identity. However, the expansion of the marketing paradigm by this micro sociological component implies that customers increasingly expect confirmation of their salient identities through other benefits (especially social) rather than exclusively economic benefits.[96] Conclusively, this interdisciplinary interplay between the concepts of marketing and identity implies a further paradigm shift heralding a new era and quality of a company's relationships to its consumers and/or consumer groups.

93. Accessed at www.aboutads.info/principles on November 15, 2011.

94. Adbusters, 2011, accessed at http://www.adbuster.org on November 16, 2011.

95. Zhihong Gao and Hongxia Zhang, *Asia Pacific Journal of Markets and Logistics*, vol. 23, no. 1 (2011), 72–90.

96. Alkis Thrassou and Demetris Vrontis, "The Dawn of a New Business-Consumer Relationship in Developed Countries," 2011, in Hans Ruediger Kaufmann, "International Consumer Behavior: A Mosaic of Eclectic Perspectives" (Darwin/UK: Access Press), 2011, 307-321, ISBN: 978-09562471-3-1.

As a reaction in the marketplace, as mentioned before, a global independent lobby of consumers, Consumers International (CI), was created, being the world federation of consumer groups. To exert its lobby function effectively, CI has official representations at global institutions such as the United Nations (UN), the World Health Organization (WHO), the International Organization for Standardization (ISO), and the Food and Agriculture Organization (FAO). With its identity of an authoritative global consumers' voice, it aims to represent, together with its 220 member organizations in 115 countries, consumers' interests worldwide, influence governments and bodies as mentioned previously, protect consumers against marketplace abuses, gain support for consumers' interests, provide consumers with higher levels of market power, and raise awareness about purchasing choices.[97]

An example of how consumer perspectives are integrated into self-regulation is the Advertising Advisory Committee (AAC) established by the aforementioned Broadcast Committee of Advertising Practice in the United Kingdom. The AAC is a Consumer Panel that is independent of the advertising industry. It provides consumer perspectives, for example, on drafting and interpreting the TV and Radio Codes of the co-regulatory body of BCAP.[98] Further examples of European Consumer Organizations are provided in Exhibit 3.23.

As a further reaction to risks with regard to consumer safety, the members of the European Union have developed an alert system called RAPEX to identify potentially dangerous consumer products excluding food, pharmaceuticals, and medical devices, which are protected by other security mechanisms. The main objective of RAPEX is to increase the rapid exchange of information related to the prevention or restriction on marketing or the use of certain products that entail a risk to the consumer's health and safety among the Member States and the Commission. This alert system consists of the following steps:

1. "When a product (e.g. a toy, a childcare article or a household appliance) is found to be dangerous, the competent national authority takes appropriate

Exhibit 3.23 European Consumer Organizations

ANEC (the European Consumer Voice in Standardization)	www.anec.eu
AUC (Asociación de Usuarios de la Comunicación) Consumers Association in Advertising and Communication, Spain	www.auc.es
Trans Atlantic Consumer Dialogue (TACD) (a forum for U.S. and EU consumer organizations)	www.tacd.org
Office of Competition and Consumer Protection (UOKIK), Poland	www.uokik.gov.pl
Verbraucherzentrale Bundesverband vzbv (Federation of German Consumer Organizations)	www.vzbv.de/go/linksorga
Wettbewerbszentrale e.V. (Association for the Prevention of Unfair Competition), Germany	www.wettbewerbszentrale.de

Source: Based on European Consumer Organizations.

97. Dennis B. Arnett, Steve D. German, and Shelby D. Hunt, "The Identity Salience Model of Relationship Marketing Success: The Case of Nonprofit Marketing," *Journal of Marketing*, vol. 67, (April 2003), 89–105; Hans Ruediger Kaufmann, Zoriza Zagorac, and Dolores Sanchez, "The Influence of Identity on International Consumer Behavior in Transitional Settings: A Case Study of the Bosnian Herzegovinian Banking Market," *Journal for International Business and Entrepreneurship Development*, vol. 3. no 3-4 (2008), 241–253.

98. CI, Consumers International, 2011, accessed at www.consumerinternational.org on January 21, 2011.

action to eliminate the risk. It can withdraw the product from the market, recall it from consumers or issue warnings. The National Contact Point then informs the European Commission (Directorate-General for Health and Consumer Protection) about the product, the risks it poses to consumers and the measures taken by the authority to prevent risks and accidents.

2. The European Commission disseminates the information that it receives to the National Contact Points of all other EU countries. It publishes weekly overviews of dangerous products and the measures taken to eliminate the risks on the internet.
3. The National Contact Points in each EU country ensure that the authorities responsible check whether the newly notified dangerous product is present on the market. If so, the authorities take measures to eliminate the risk, either by requiring that the product be withdrawn from the market, by recalling it from consumers or by issuing warnings."[99]

According to the General Product Safety Directive 2001/95/EC (GPSD), the European Commission acknowledged 189 notifications that were transmitted to all Member States. According to the levels of risk, article 12 covers serious risk (165 notifications); article 11, moderate risk (3 notifications); and information, (21 notifications).

Although the majority of products comply with the established law and regulations, some may involve risks that are not perceived at first glance. Exhibits 3.24, 3.25, 3.26, and 3.27 may help raise the risk awareness of advertising companies and consumers.

A further wave of change for the rules of advertising might be expected from the new segment of multi-screen consumers. Reflecting the trend of media convergence

Exhibit 3.24 The Five Countries That Notify Most Frequently

Country	Notifications	Percentages
Italy	21	13
Germany	20	12
Greece	16	10
Bulgaria	13	8
Hungary	13	8

Source: Based on European Union, 1995–2011. RAPEX report in November 2010.

Exhibit 3.25 The Five Most Frequently Notified Products

Products	Notifications	Percentages
Clothing, textiles, and fashion items	53	32
Toys	35	21
Electric appliances	20	12
Motor vehicles	16	10
Children's articles	9	5

Source: Based on European Union, 1995–2011. RAPEX report in November 2010.

99. Accessed at www.cap.org.uk/About-Us/BCAP-Broadcast.aspx on January 21, 2011.

Exhibit 3.26 The Five Risk Categories Notified Most Frequently

Risk categories	Notifications	Percentages
Injuries	45	23
Chemical	42	22
Choking	38	20
Strangulation	21	11
Electric shock	18	9

Source: Based on European Union, 1995–2011. RAPEX report in November 2010.

Exhibit 3.27 Country of Origin of the Notified Product

Country	Notifications	Percentages
China, including Hong Kong	84	51
European Member States	32	19
Other countries	23	14
No information on country of origin	26	16

Source: Based on European Union, 1995–2011. RAPEX report in November 2010.

of TV, mobile, and PC, these multi-screen users use their mobile media, in addition to making calls and sending text messages, for example, to play, build virtual relationships, and watch video through the TV.[100]

5 The Regulation of Other Promotional Tools.

International Self-Regulation of Sales Promotion. The International Chamber of Commerce (ICC), based in Paris, is generally recognized as a pioneer and referenced role model (for the EASA) for self-regulation with high ethical and socially responsible standards in marketing and e-commerce for professional associations as well as for national legislation. Representing world business (see Exhibit 3.28), the ICC

Exhibit 3.28 ICC and Sales Promotion

ICC Principles: General Provision on Advertising and Marketing Communication Practice	Application to Food and Beverage Marketing Communication
"ARTICLE 18 and ARTICLE A6 (Sales Promotions): Marketing communication should not exploit the inexperience or credulity of children and young people. Sales promotions should be presented in such a way that they are made aware, before making a purchase, of any conditions likely to affect their decision to purchase."	"Sales promotion offers addressed to children should provide the conditions of the premium offer, sweepstake or contest being advertised in terms that children can understand. Marketers should strive to be sure that young children have an understanding of the products to be purchased, if any, to receive the premium; and for sweepstakes and contests, the conditions of entry, types of prizes and the likelihood of winning."

Source: Based on International Chamber of Commerce.

100. Accessed at http://ec.europa.eu/consumer/safety/rapex/docs/stats_11-2010.pdf on January 19, 2011.

developed the International Code of Sales Promotion aiming to complement existing national and international law with international trade and consumer benefits.[101]

ICC Promoting Growth and Prosperity.

- Contributing to the success of the Doha trade round by providing recommendations to the World Trade Organization
- Representing world business on issues such as intellectual property rights, transport policy, trade law, and the environment
- Providing the ICC's stance on trade, investment, and other business topics in various media
- Providing world business input to the G8 summit
- Being the main business partner of the United Nations and its agencies

Exhibit 3.29 provides a list of ICC members.

Change of European Regulatory Issues in Sales Promotion. Currently, diverse national regulations on sales promotions in various European countries inhibit cross-border trade of goods and services. For this reason, EU Commissioners have endorsed a proposal for a common, more transparent, and directly applicable EU-wide law on sales promotion.

The main provisions of the regulation proposal are shown in Table 3.5.

Regulatory Issues in Direct Marketing and e-Commerce from a European Perspective—The European Pharmaceutics Case. Direct marketing is a promotional strategy used by businesses to interact directly with customers via personal selling, email, direct mail, telephone calls, social media, or touch-screen channels. As a means of direct communication soliciting immediate customer feedback, direct marketing can be an effective promotional strategy. The line between e-commerce and commerce is fading.[102] However, the flood of Internet-based mail from cell phones and other PDA communication devices, together with e-business email spam and still-existing illegal and unethical

Exhibit 3.29 List of Some ICC Members

Examples of Some ICC Members	
3M	Fiat
ABB	McDonald's
AT&T	Mitsubishi
British Telecom	Procter & Gamble
Cadbury Schweppes	Sony
Citigroup	Toshiba
Coca-Cola	Unilever
Daimler	Volvo
El Corte Inglés	Wing Lung Bank

Source: Based on International Chamber of Commerce.

101. Microsoft Advertising, "A New Whitepaper from Microsoft Advertising, What's on Their Screens, What's on Their Minds, Multi-Screen Consumer Research Reveals Media Multiplier Effect," 2010, accessed at http://advertising.microsoft.com/europe/multi-screen-consumer-research on January 19, 2011.

102. Oliver Gray, "Responsible Advertising in Europe," *Young Consumers*, vol. 6, no. 4 (2005), 19-23; and ICC, The International Chamber of Commerce, accessed at www.iccwbo.org/uploadedFiles/ICC/Policy_pages/332%20FINAL_Framework_Food_and_Beverage.pdf on January 20, 2011.

Table 3.5 Proposal on EU-Wide Sales Promotion Regulations

1. Prohibiting general bans and restrictions on the use of commercial communication of sales promotions, such as on premiums, the participation in promotional games, discounts, and free gifts
2. Providing for higher levels of consumer protection by changing information requirements to be made available to consumers on request (that is, on the discount, free gift or premium, price of the promoted goods, and promoter's identity)
3. Providing for increased protection for children and adolescents in terms of prior parental consent on the collection of personal data from a child, potential health dangers of free gifts to children, and a ban on free alcoholic gifts to minors under the age of 18
4. Implementing a cross-border complaint system that ensures equal protection of foreign customers by requiring the promoter to provide an address to which complaints can be directed and to verify, at the request of a national court, the accuracy of the information provided in sales promotions

Source: Based on European Sales Promotion Restrictions to be Harmonised, Swan Turton.

Internet marketing fraud, makes the creation of online trust in terms of security and privacy concerns the order of the day.[103]

In the United Kingdom, a series of legislations, regulations, and agencies have been developed to protect UK citizens from unacceptable online advertising; these include the Broadcasting Act 1996, the Competition Act 1998, E-Commerce Regulations 2002, Consumer Protection (Distance Selling), Control of Misleading Advertisements, and Standards of Telephone Information Service.[104] In addition to these statutory regulations, Warholic points to the heightened importance of self-regulation.[105]

For example, a global discussion and debates in the European parliament are ongoing as to the appropriateness of using direct-to-consumer (DTC) advertising in the pharmaceutical industry.[106] Furthermore, the topic has been extensively researched by about 160 studies in academic journals over the past 12 years.[107] This form of direct marketing is directed at patients, not healthcare professionals, which was one reason it was banned in Europe, whereas this practice is permitted in the United States and New Zealand. "There are ethical and regulatory concerns regarding DTC advertising, specifically the extent to which these ads may unduly influence the prescribing of the prescription medicines based on consumer demands when, in some cases, they may not be medically necessary."[108] On the other hand, there seems to be an increasing demand by European consumers to improve access to medical information in a fragmented European medical market and, hence, potentially improve their healthcare.[109] The last author concludes that "in Europe,

103. Bette Ann Stead and Jackie Gilbert, "Ethical Issues in Electronic Commerce," 2001, in Debra Harker, "Regulating Online Advertising: The Benefit of Qualitative Insights," *Qualitative Market Research: An International Journal*, vol. 11, no. 3 (2008), 295–315.

104. James A. Warholic, "Internet Marketing Ethics Web Issues," 2011, accessed at http://pwebs.net/marketing/ethics/articles/internetethics.htm on January 9, 2011.

105. Debra Harker, "Regulating Online Advertising: The Benefit of Qualitative Insights," *Qualitative Market Research: An International Journal*, vol. 11, no. 3 (2008), 295–315.

106. James A. Warholic, "Internet Marketing Ethics Web Issues," 2011, accessed at http://pwebs.net/marketing/ethics/articles/internetethics.htm on January 9, 2011.

107. Nathan Jessop, "Will DTC Advertising Appear in Europe?" accessed at http://pharmtech.findpharma.com/pharmtech/article/articleDetail.jsp?id+702161 on January 15, 2011.

108. Denise E. DeLorme, Jisu Huh, Leonard N. Reid, and Soontae An, "The State of Public Research on Over-the-Counter Drug Advertising," *International Journal of Pharmaceutical and Healthcare Marketing*, vol. 4, no. 3 (2010), 208–231.

109. Accessed at www.infibeam.com/Books/direct-consumer-advertising-frederic-p-miller/9786133863682.html on January 29, 2011.

patient demand for increased access to information on medicines looks likely to result in pharma companies being permitted to directly communicate with patients. However, it is difficult to see DTC evolving into the advertising style typified by the US market, particularly as the European pharma industry itself has been careful to distance itself from such an approach. The culture and market conditions in Europe remain very different to those in the US and so it is unlikely that DTC advertising would ever have a receptive audience."[110]

Regulatory Issues in Terms of Brand Sharing, Advertising, Promotion, and Sponsorship—The Tobacco Case in the United Kingdom. In several stages, the Tobacco Advertising and Promotion Act in the United Kingdom regulated and banned the advertising and promotion of tobacco products regarding ASH (the information is not exhaustive).[111]

The use of brand sharing

The sponsorship of cultural and sport events (such as Formula One motor racing)

The advertising of tobacco products on billboards, in newspapers, and in magazines

Point of sales (limited to A5-sized ad per outlet)

All forms of TV advertising and teleshopping

Program sponsorship by tobacco products and companies

In addition, on December 2, 2002, the European Council "reached an agreement on a proposed directive to ban tobacco advertising. The directive covers four areas of cross border advertising (printed publications, internet, radio and sponsorship), but does not include indirect advertising."[112]

Regulatory Issues in Product Placement—The European Approach. Varying regulations of product placement in Western Europe and the United States are due to a different historical evolution of this promotional mix element: "Unlike in the U.S., in Western Europe the evolution of the television industry took place under government auspices, and only later on were licenses awarded to commercial entities. Many European countries never allowed advertising on television at first, and in some, advertising and even commercial underwriting are forbidden in public broadcasting until this very day."[113] In England, "for 15 years, only TV and radio programs have been allowed to carry sponsorship, with Cadbury's long-running sponsorship of ITV's flagship soap 'Coronation Street' one of the first."[114]

Whereas Article 11 paragraph 2 of the Audiovisual Media Services Directives (AVMS) prohibits product placement in general, a number of exceptions to the rule allow product placement:[115]

110. Nathan Jessop, "Will DTC Advertising Appear in Europe?" accessed at http://pharmtech.findpharma.com/pharmtech/article/articleDetail.jsp?id+702161 on January 15, 2011.

111. http://www.ash.org.uk/information/law-guide#advertising_promotion_sponsorship; http://www.ash.org.uk/information/law-guide#smoking_cessation

112. ASA, 2011, accessed at www.ash.org.uk/information/law-guide#advertising_promotion_sponsorship on January 20, 2011; ASH, 2011, accessed at www.ash.org/information/law-guide#broadcasting_guidelines on January 29, 2011.

113. Christina Angeopoulos, "Product Placement in European Audiovisual Productions," 2011, accessed at www.obs.coe.int/oea_publ/iris/iris_plus/iplus3LA_2010.pdf.en on January 29, 2011.

114. Sam Matthews, "Ofcom to Allow TV Channel Sponsorship under Strict Criteria," 2006, accessed at www.brandrepublic.com/news/539769/Ofcom-allow-TV-channel-sponsorship-criteria on December 29, 2010.

115. Christina Angeopoulos, "Product Placement in European Audiovisual Productions," 2010, accessed at www.obs.coe.int/oea_publ/iris/iris_plus/iplus3LA_2010.pdf.en on January 29, 2011.

- "in cinematographic works, films and series made for audiovisual media services, sports programs and light entertainment programs provided these are not children's programs;
- where there is no payment, but only the provision of certain goods or services free of charge, such as production props and prizes, with a view to their inclusion in a program"

Member states, however, are free to impose stricter regulations or a full ban.[116]

Summary

1 Identify the benefits and problems of advertising and promotion in a capitalistic society and debate a variety of issues concerning their effects on society's well-being.

Advertisers have always had their proponents and critics. Proponents of advertising argue that it offers benefits for individual consumers and society at large. At the societal level, proponents claim that advertising helps promote a higher standard of living by allowing marketers to reap the rewards of product improvements and innovation. Advertising also "pays for" mass media in many countries and provides consumers with a constant flow of information about not only products and services, but also political and social issues. Throughout the years, critics have leveled many charges at advertising and advertising practitioners. Advertising expenditures in the multibillions are condemned as wasteful, offensive, and a source of frustration for many in society who see the lavish lifestyle portrayed in advertising, knowing they will never be able to afford such a lifestyle. Critics also contend that advertisements rarely furnish useful information, but instead perpetuate superficial stereotypes of many cultural subgroups. Some critics have been concerned for many years that advertisers are controlling people against their will using subliminal advertising messages. Most recently, issues of privacy have been debated as new technologies offer the possibility of "behavioral targeting" based on consumers' Web search behavior or even tracking of consumers' physical whereabouts by virtue of GPS-equipped smartphones.

2 Explain how ethical considerations affect the development of advertising and IBP campaigns.

Ethical considerations are a concern in the creation of advertising and promotion. Deception in advertising and promotion is never acceptable or defendable. The ethical considerations get more complex especially when advertising is targeted at children or involves controversial products such as firearms, gambling, alcohol, or cigarettes. Although ethical standards are a matter for personal reflection, unethical people can create unethical advertising. But there are many safeguards against such behavior, including the corporate and personal integrity of advertisers.

3 Discuss the role of government agencies and consumers in the regulation of advertising and promotion.

The two tasks of governments in regulating advertising have been discussed. On the one hand, a catalytic framework for the effective functioning of the marketplace and mechanisms to remedy shortcomings of the system, especially related to misleading and comparative advertising, must be provided. In this context, global corporate thinking needs to consider idiosyncratic local cultural and legal conditions, which may considerably limit the standardization of global advertising. These conditions are exemplified by focusing on the European Union (and selected individual European countries), Russian, and Asian conditions. On the other hand, the government should take a balanced

116. For more detailed information on the directive and the various exceptions, which must adhere to minimum protection principles, visit http://europa.eu.in/eurlex/en/consleg/pdf/1989/en_1989L0552_do_001.pdf and Christina Angelopoulos (Ibid).

view when laying the foundation for the social and economic well-being of the market players involved. The role of increasingly empowered consumers as regulatory change agents is highlighted, concentrating on children as an especially vulnerable segment, risk-related products, and health-related controversial advertising of products such as alcohol and various consumer associations. These factors have a strong bearing on the increasingly necessary new quality of relationships with consumers.

4 Explain the meaning and importance of self-regulation for firms that develop and use advertising and promotion.

As opposed to statutory governmental legislation, companies, often represented by associated membership organizations, may agree on standards of best practice or codes of ethics. These are the basis for identifying, diagnosing, preventing, and remedying practices that are inconsistent with the local system. The high level of international complexity and diversity of this topic became apparent. The advantages and potential drawbacks of self-regulation were juxtaposed. A number of international self-regulatory institutions in Europe (with an emphasis on the United Kingdom), Asia (Japan, China, and India), and Latin America have been provided. As developments, regulations, and consumer requirements are still in a state of flux, self-regulation as to the Internet and digital media has been emphasized, comparing U.S. and European perspectives.

5 Discuss the regulation of the full range of techniques used in the IBP process.

Statutory and self-regulatory aspects of sales promotions in Europe have been provided. The ongoing debate about direct-to-consumer advertising in the pharmaceutical market, comprehensive limitations on a variety of promotional tools in the tobacco industry, and European perspectives on direct marketing and e-commerce reflect limitations on the IBP process. Once more, divergent U.S. and European perspectives are exemplified by the varying regulations on product placement.

Key Terms

ethics
deception
puffery
primary demand
consumerism

Questions

1. Advertising has been a focal point of criticism for many decades. In your opinion, what are the benefits of advertising? Which key factors make advertising controversial? In this context, explain your understanding of misleading advertising.

2. What are a couple of controversial topics being aggravated by country differences?

3. Do you see global commonalities in terms of controversial topics? Explain.

4. Where do you see differences of advertising regulation in the United States, Europe, and Asia?

5. Regarding regulations for advertising to children, reflect on your country's regulations (eventually do some research) and compare your findings with the regulations of another country provided in the chapter. How could self-regulation help reduce the global problem of childhood obesity?

6. Assume that you work for a U.S. company that manufactures alcohol products; the company is planning to enter European markets. What legal factors can you elicit calling for an adaptation strategy?

7. As one of the BRIC countries, China is a future potential growth market. What advertising limitations would you need to take into account when designing your communication mix for this country?

8. Refer to current trends that call for increased self-regulation. Where do you see potential benefits for global companies to engage in self-regulation?

9. As an Internet and social media user, where do you see that demand needs to catch up in terms of regulations?

10. Consumer empowerment is gaining momentum worldwide. What corporate strategic moves do you suggest to take this increasing power of consumers into consideration?

Experiential Exercises

1. Although public service announcements (PSAs) exist to educate society and are not a form of paid advertising, a recent texting-while-driving warning from England's South Wales Police Department was so graphic that many television networks banned it. In the spot, three British teenage girls text-and-drive their way into a head-on collision. The gruesome real-life highway carnage staged by professional filmmaker Peter Watkins-Hughes left international viewers shocked and in tears. For an in-class discussion, watch this PSA or another controversial ad and discuss the conflict between advertising's ability to educate and its potential to be offensive. When do edgy ads cross the line? Who decides that the ads have gone too far?

2. General Motors continues to struggle, even after receiving an unpopular multibillion-dollar bailout from taxpayers. During an attempt to win back consumers in 2010, the American automaker hit a truth-in-advertising snag. In one television ad, CEO Ed Whitacre boasted that GM repaid a $5.8 billion taxpayer loan after emerging from bankruptcy, citing the payback as proof of GM's financial recovery. Media quickly denounced the ads as deceptive for omitting that GM did not repay the other $52 billion still owed to taxpayers. The ads also concealed that the "payback" didn't come from GM profits—it was a reshuffling of taxpayer bailout cash from the U.S. Troubled Assets Relief Program (TARP). For an in-class discussion, debate whether GM's ad was deception or mere puffery. Who is responsible for investigating deceptive advertising? Would an investigation of GM by government regulatory agencies involve a conflict of interest? What should GM do to correct the issue if the ads are deceptive?

3. List two product categories—other than cigarettes—that you think require some kind of advertising regulation. Explain why. Do you think they require government regulation, industry self-regulation, or consumer regulation? Explain. Based on your answer, list regulatory agents that might get involved in controlling the advertising process for these products. Finally, use the Internet to search for one or more agency or watchdog sites that are relevant to the regulatory process. How does the site encourage consumers to get involved? What resources does the site offer to empower consumers' participation in the process?

4. Working in small teams, imagine that you have been hired by a large pizza chain to develop an IBP campaign for a new product, the KidZa Meal, which will consist of a 4-inch diameter pizza, a small drink, and a doll that looks like a traditional Italian pizza chef. The chain is hoping that sales of KidZa Meals will drive more families to its dine-in restaurants and increase takeout orders. But the chain is concerned about perceptions that it is targeting children in its advertising or contributing to concerns about childhood obesity rates. What type of campaign would you suggest for this client? As you evaluate the components of the marketing mix, what recommendations would you make regarding the product?

Chapter 4

The History of Advertising and Brand Promotion

After reading and thinking about this chapter, you will be able to do the following:

1. Tell the story of advertising's birth.
2. Describe the past and current relationship between advertisers, retailers, and consumers.
3. Discuss several significant eras in the evolution of advertising in the United States, and relate important changes in advertising practice to fundamental changes in society and culture. How did successful advertising leverage the social and cultural forces of their day?
4. Tell the story of consumer empowerment and branded entertainment, and understand how it works.
5. Identify forces that will continue to affect the evolution of advertising and integrated brand promotion.

Perma·lift Stitched cup
bras, with "The Lift that
never lets you down,"
glorify your figure
"Perma·lift"* stylists have the knack of bra designing down to a fine art. Now you can enjoy the compact, youthful beauty of a Stitched Cup bra with the famous lasting uplift that only "Perma·lift" gives you. In this wonderful brassiere, the Magic Insets gently support from below—the uplift is guaranteed to last the life of the garment no matter how often you wash it or how long you wear it. For the only Stitched Cup bra with "The Lift that never lets you down," be fitted in a "Perma·lift" Bra today.
Crisp Cotton $3.00 White
Shimmering Satin $3.50 White or Pink
Misty Nylon $4.00 White or Pink
Perma·lift
GIRDLES
BRASSIERES
Pert and perky is this wispy
"Perma·lift" Pantie—
dainty, yet marvelously
So comfortable too, and
Bones About It—Stays
Without Stays—the Magic
eliminates annoying bones,
it can't roll over, wrinkle
bind. Get yours at your
corsetiere's today, or write
name of nearest
Power Net Pantie $6.95 White or
Sizes 24 to 30
Power Net Girdle $5.95 White or
Sizes 24 to 30

Exhibit 4.1 Even though this ad for Lux laundry powder may seem curious to us today, it reflected the anxiety of the 1930s, during the Great Depression. Just as today's advertising reflects the values of contemporary society, this ad emphasized some very real concerns of the time—the economic well-being and status of women.

Courtesy, Lever United States, Inc.

The 1935 Lux advertisement shown in Exhibit 4.1 is surely curious now, but it probably made perfect sense at the time. In the middle of the Great Depression, anxiety about losing one's husband—and thus one's economic well-being—was not unfounded. This ad and others like it were targeted to a new generation of housewives potentially insecure about their exclusion from the modern world of their husbands, geographically separated from their usually agrarian parents, anxious about just anything sexual, and living in a rapid and unsure urban environment. These ads went out to women at a time when losing one's source of income (husband) could mean poverty and shame. Ads like this were read by women in a society where daily bathing was hardly universal, but where the creation and maintenance of pervasive self-doubts about personal hygiene was the advertiser's daily duty. Such an ad pushed just the right buttons. If Lux can "remove perspiration odor from underthings," it might save more than colors and fabrics. It might save affection; it might save intimacy; it might save marriages. If Bob's romantic indifference continues, Sally may soon be back home with Mom or even worse. But with Lux on the scene, Bob goes home for dinner.

This ad is illustrative of a larger point that you will see throughout this chapter and others. Some of the greatest advertising of all time had something in common: they leverage existing anxieties; they seek to resolve cultural contradictions and disruptions in society and identity. In the Lux example, women of the period were already anxious about their status, their worldliness, and certainly anything having to do with feminine hygiene and its effect on their sexual desirability. These things were not discussed publically, so who would provide the intimate advice: the advertiser. Problem solved.

Some ads today use the same general strategy to sell deodorants, soaps, feminine-hygiene products, and all sorts of things today. The strategy is the same, only the specifics differ. Ads are part of their times. To really understand advertising and do well in the advertising business, you must understand that successful advertisements convey a particularly perceptive (self-serving and sometimes pointedly paranoid) understanding of the contemporary social scene. If you are in the advertising business, you are in the culture and society business. The makers of this 1935 ad understood, helped create, and used the pressures bearing down on the young women of that time. Society was changing, and these changes affected Sally and lots of young women like her. Probably many young women of that day felt anxious (thanks partially to ads like this) and uncertain. The social change and associated anxiety gave advertisers a chance to offer new products and services to address these very fears, and to leverage this upheaval to their branded benefit. There is a valuable lesson here from history: When the sands of culture and society shift beneath consumers' feet, marketing and advertising opportunities usually present themselves. Social disruption opens up consumer "needs" and advertising opportunities. Today, Sally would likely have a job and be far less economically vulnerable and socially isolated. So we see the 1930s in this ad in the same way that students of the future will view ads of our time: as interesting, revealing, but still somewhat distorted reflections of daily life in the early 21st century. Even in the 1930s, consumers knew that ads were ads; they knew that ads were a little exaggerated; they knew that ads tried to sell things; and they knew that ads didn't exactly mirror everyday life. But ads often look enough like life to work, sometimes. Good advertising is in touch with its time and smart (if not "good/ethical") advertisers seek to point to the problems created by these changes and offer a branded solution. Let's face it, advertisers have made a lot of money based on created and exacerbated consumer anxiety—more often women's anxiety. Think of current examples; it won't be hard.

This chapter is about advertising history—not just some disconnected names and dates—but practical lessons learned in the past that can be applied right now, today. Throughout the decades, advertisers have tried many different strategies and approaches, and you can learn from their successes and failures. Just about every strategy used today came about decades ago—only the specifics have changed. Studying them will allow you to know when a given advertising technique is really something new, and when and (most importantly) why it worked. You can see particular advertising strategies leveraged the social forces of their day—and how you can leverage the ones of your day. Besides being interesting, history is very practical. Hint: When you are interviewing for a job in an advertising or marketing position, explain how an advertiser's current ad campaigns works (or doesn't). That usually really impresses them.

1 The Rise of Advertising.

Advertising is sometimes said to have had its origins in ancient times. Well… not really the case… at least not in any meaningful sense. Advertising is a product of modern times and modern media.

Before we get into a brief history of advertising in the Western world, let's first consider some of the major factors that gave rise to advertising in the first place. Advertising came into being as a result of at least four major factors:

1. The rise of capitalism
2. The Industrial Revolution
3. Branding
4. The rise of modern mass media

The Rise of Capitalism.

The tenets of capitalism warrant that organizations compete for resources, called *capital,* in a free-market environment. Part of the competition for resources involves stimulating demand for the organization's goods or services. When an individual organization successfully stimulates demand, it attracts capital to the organization in the form of money (or other goods) as payment. One of the tools used to stimulate demand is advertising. So, as the Western world turned to capitalism as the foundation of economic systems, the foundation was laid for advertising to become a prominent part of the business environment.

The Industrial Revolution.

The **Industrial Revolution** was an economic force that yielded the need for advertising. Beginning about 1750 in England, the revolution spread to North America and progressed slowly until the early 1800s, when the War of 1812 in the United States boosted domestic production. The emergence of the principle of interchangeable parts and the perfection of the sewing machine, both in 1850, coupled with the American Civil War a decade later, set the scene for widespread industrialization. The Industrial Revolution took Western societies away from household self-sufficiency as a method of fulfilling material needs to dependency on a marketplace as a way of life. The Industrial Revolution was a basic force behind the rapid increase in mass-produced goods that required stimulation of demand; something that advertising can sometimes be good at. By providing a need for advertising, the Industrial Revolution was a basic influence in its emergence and growth in Western economies.

Part of the Industrial Revolution was a revolution in transportation, dramatically symbolized by the east–west connection of the United States in 1869 by the railroad. This connection represented the beginnings of the distribution network needed to move the mass quantities of goods for which advertising would help stimulate demand. In the 1840s, the **principle of limited liability**, which restricts an investor's risk in a business venture to only his or her shares in a corporation rather than all personal assets, gained acceptance and resulted in the accumulation of large amounts of capital to finance the Industrial Revolution. Finally, rapid population growth and urbanization began taking place in the 1800s. From 1830 to 1860, the population of the United States nearly tripled, from 12.8 million to 31.4 million. During the same period, the number of cities with more than 20,000 inhabitants grew to 43. Historically, there is a strong relationship between per capita outlays for advertising and an increase in the size of cities.[1] Modernity gave rise to both urbanism and advertising. Overall, the growth and concentration of population provided the marketplaces that were essential to the widespread use of advertising. As the potential grew for goods to be produced, delivered, and introduced to large numbers of people residing in concentrated areas, the stage was set for advertising to emerge and flourish.

The Emergence of Modern Branding.

Modern capitalism required **branding.** Manufacturers had to develop brand names so that consumers could focus their attention on a clearly identified item. Manufacturers began branding previously unmarked commodities, such as work clothes and package goods. In the late 1800s, Ivory (1882), Coca-Cola (1886), Budweiser (1891), and Maxwell House (1892) were among the first branded goods to show up on shopkeepers' shelves. Once a product had a brand mark and name that consumers could identify, marketers gained power. Brands command a higher price than a commodity (think Ivory vs. soap). Branding required advertising. It's no accident of history that modern branding and modern advertising agencies appear at exactly the same time in the late 19th century. Brand demand also gives marketers added power over retailers: if consumers demand Charmin, the retailer better stock Charmin.[2]

The Rise of Modern Mass Media.

Advertising is also tied to the rise of mass communication. With the invention of the telegraph in 1844, a communication revolution was set in motion. The telegraph not only allowed nations to benefit from the inherent efficiencies of rapid communication, but also did a great deal to engender a sense of national identity. People began to know and care about people and things going on thousands of miles away.

1. Julian Simon, *Issues in the Economics of Advertising* (Urbana: University of Illinois Press, 1970), 41–51.

2. Vincent P. Norris, "Advertising History—According to the Textbooks," *Journal of Advertising,* vol. 9, no. 3 (1980), 3–12.

This changed not only commerce, but society as well.[3] Also, during this period, many new magazines designed for larger and less socially privileged audiences made magazines a viable mass advertising medium.[4] Through advertising in these mass-circulation magazines, national brands could be projected into national consciousness. National magazines made national advertising possible; national advertising made national brands possible. Without the rise of mass media, there would be no national brands, and no advertising.

It is critical to realize that for the most part, mass media are supported by advertising. Television networks, radio stations, newspapers, magazines, and websites produce shows, articles, films, programs, and Web content not for the ultimate goal of entertaining or informing, but to make a healthy profit from selling brands through advertising and branded entertainment. Media vehicles sell audiences to make money.

3 The Eras of Advertising.

So far, our discussion of the evolution of advertising has identified the fundamental social and economic influences that fostered advertising's rise. Now we'll turn our focus to the evolution of advertising in practice. A few important periods can be identified and considered. In each are valuable lessons on how advertising really works.

The Preindustrialization Era (Pre-1800).

In the 17th century, printed advertisements appeared in newsbooks (the precursor to the newspaper).[5] The messages were informational in nature and appeared on the last pages of the tabloid. In America, the first newspaper advertisement is said to have appeared in 1704 in the *Boston News Letter*. Two notices were printed under the heading "Advertising" and offered rewards for the return of merchandise stolen from an apparel shop and a wharf.[6]

Advertising grew in popularity during the 18th century in both Britain and the American colonies. The *Pennsylvania Gazette* printed advertisements and was the first newspaper to separate ads with blank lines, which made the ads both easier to read and more prominent.[7] As far as we know, it was also the first newspaper to use illustrations in advertisements. But advertising changed little during the next 70 years. Even though the early 1800s saw the advent of the penny newspaper, which resulted in widespread distribution of the news media, advertisements in penny newspapers were dominated by simple announcements by skilled laborers. As one historian notes, "Advertising was closer to the classified notices in newspapers than to product promotions in our media today."[8] Advertising was about to change dramatically, however.

3. James W. Carey, *Communication as Culture: Essays on Media and Society* (Winchester, MA: Unwin Hyman, 1989).

4. Christopher P. Wilson, "The Rhetoric of Consumption: Mass-Market Magazines and the Demise of the Gentle Reader, 1880–1920," in Richard Weightman Fox and T. J. Jackson Lears (Eds.), *The Culture of Consumption: Critical Essays in American History, 1880–1980.* (New York: Pantheon, 1983), 39–65.

5. Frank Presbrey, *The History and Development of Advertising* (Garden City, NY: Doubleday, Doran & Co., 1929), 7.

6. Ibid., 11.

7. Ibid., 40.

8. James P. Wood, *The Story of Advertising* (New York: Ronald, 1958), 45–46.

The Era of Industrialization (1800 to 1875).

In practice, users of advertising in the mid to late 1800s were trying to cultivate markets for growing production in the context of an increasing urban population. A middle class, spawned by the rise of regular wages from factory jobs, was beginning to emerge. This newly developing population with the economic means to consume was concentrated geographically in cities.

Exhibit 4.2 The expansion of newspaper circulation fostered more widespread use of advertising. Unfortunately, some of this new advertising did not contribute positively to the image of the practice. Ads like this one for a patent medicine carried bold claims, such as claiming to cure all liver ailments, including cancer.

By 1850, circulation of the **dailies**, as newspapers were then called, was estimated at 1 million copies per day. The first advertising agent—thought to be Volney Palmer, who opened shop in Philadelphia—basically worked for the newspapers by soliciting orders for advertising and collecting payment from advertisers.[9] This new opportunity to reach consumers was embraced readily by merchants, and newspaper advertising volume soared.[10]

With the expansion of newspaper circulation fostered by the railroads and growing urban centers, a new era of opportunity emerged for advertising. Further, there were virtually no laws or regulations to restrict advertisers from saying or doing anything they cared to. Advertisers could outright lie, deceive, and otherwise cheat with little or no threat of being punished by government. Many advertisers took advantage of the situation and advertising was commonly considered an embarrassment (or worse) by many segments of society. At one point, firms even risked their credit ratings if they used advertising—banks considered the practice a sign of financial weakness. Advertising for patent medicines reinforced this tawdry reputation. These advertisements promised a cure for everything from rheumatism and arthritis to cancer. They were also the first large category of products advertised on a mass scale. Exhibit 4.2 shows a typical ad of this period.

The "P. T. Barnum Era" (1875 to 1918).

Shortly after the Civil War in the United States, modern advertising began. This is advertising that we would recognize as advertising. Even though advertising existed during the era of industrialization, it wasn't until America was well on its way to being an urban, industrialized nation that advertising became a vital and integral part of the social landscape. From about 1875 to 1918, advertising ushered in what has come to be known as **consumer culture,** or a way of life centered on consumption. True, consumer culture was advancing prior to this period, but during this age it took hold, and the rise of modern advertising had a lot to do with it. Advertising became a full-fledged industry in this period. It was the time of advertising legends: Albert Lasker, head of Lord and Thomas in Chicago, possibly the most influential agency of its day; Francis W. Ayer, founder of N. W. Ayer; John E. Powers, the most important copywriter of the period; Earnest Elmo Calkins, champion of advertising design; Claude Hopkins, influential in promoting ads as "dramatic salesmanship"; and John E. Kennedy, creator of

9. Daniel Pope, *The Making of Modern Advertising and Its Creators* (New York: William Morrow, 1984), 14.

10. Cited in Stephen Fox, *The Mirror Makers: A History of American Advertising and Its Creators* (New York: William Morrow, 1984), 14.

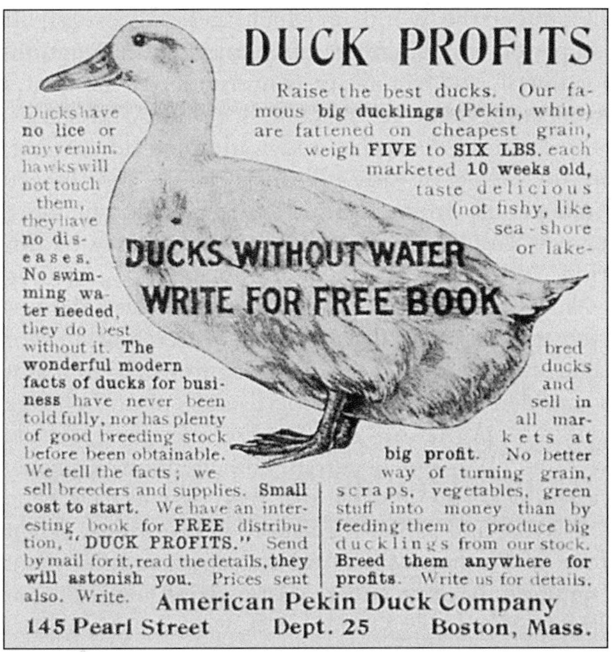

DUCK PROFITS
Raise the best ducks. Our famous big ducklings (Pekin, white) are fattened on cheapest grain, weigh FIVE to SIX LBS. each marketed 10 weeks old, taste delicious (not fishy, like sea-shore or lake-bred ducks and sell in all markets at big profit. No better way of turning grain, scraps, vegetables, green stuff into money than by feeding them to produce big ducklings from our stock. Breed them anywhere for profits. Write us for details.
Ducks have no lice or any vermin, hawks will not touch them, they have no diseases. No swimming water needed, they do best without it. The wonderful modern facts of ducks for business have never been told fully, nor has plenty of good breeding stock before been obtainable. We tell the facts; we sell breeders and supplies. Small cost to start. We have an interesting book for FREE distribution, "DUCK PROFITS." Send by mail for it, read the details, they will astonish you. Prices sent also. Write.
DUCKS WITHOUT WATER
WRITE FOR FREE BOOK
American Pekin Duck Company
145 Pearl Street Dept. 25 Boston, Mass.

Exhibit 4.3 Ads from the "P. T. Barnum era" were often densely packed with fantastic promises. This 1902 *Saturday Evening Post* advertisement featured many reasons why potential customers should get into the duck-raising business—even without water.

"reason why" advertising.[11] These were the founders, the visionaries, and the artists who played principal roles in the establishment of the advertising business. One interesting side note is that several of the founders of this industry had fathers who shared the very same occupation: minister. This very modern industry was founded in no small part by the sons of preachers. More that a coincidence, these young men would have been exposed to public speaking and the passionate selling of ideas, as well as to the need of 19th century clergy to adapt to modernity: city life, science, progress, and public consumption. Sons of preachers were the ideal apostles of advertising and consumer culture.

By 1900, total sales of patent medicines in the United States had reached $75 million—an early demonstration of the power of advertising.[12] During this period, the first advertising agencies were founded and the practice of branding became the norm. Advertising was motivated by the need to sell the vastly increased supply of goods brought on by mass production and by the demands of an increasingly urban population seeking social identity through (among other things) branded products. In earlier times, when shoppers went to the general store and bought soap sliced from a large, locally produced cake, advertising had no real place. But with advertising's ability to create meaningful differences between near-identical soaps, advertising suddenly became critical. Advertising made unmarked commodities into social symbols and identity markers, and it allowed marketers to charge far more money for them. Consumers are quite willing to pay more money for brands (for example, Ivory) than for unmarked commodities (generic soap wrapped in plain paper), even if they are otherwise identical. This is the power of brands; the power of advertising; helping bestow desired meanings on things for sale.

Advertising was completely unregulated in the United States until 1906. In that year, Congress passed the **Pure Food and Drug Act**, which required manufacturers to list the active ingredients of their products on their labels. You could still put some pretty amazing things in products; you just had to now tell the consumer. The direct effect of this federal act on advertising was minimal; advertisers could continue to say just about anything—and usually did. Many advertisements still took on the style of a "snake oil" sales pitch. The tone and spirit of advertising of this period owed more to P. T. Barnum—"There's a sucker born every minute"—than to any other influence. Of course, Barnum was the famous showman and circus entrepreneur (Barnum and Bailey Circus) of his day. So, it's no surprise that ads of this period were bold, carnivalesque, garish, and often full of dense copy that hurled incredible claims at prototype modern consumers. A fairly typical ad from this era is shown in Exhibit 4.3—raise ducks for profit and without water.

Several things are notable about these ads: lots of copy (words); the prominence of the product itself and the relative lack of real-world context (visuals) in which the advertised product was to be consumed; ads were usually small, had little color, few photographs, and plenty of hyperbole. During this period there was variation and steady evolution, but this is what ads were generally like up until around World War I.

11. Fox, *The Mirror Makers,* 14.

12. Presbrey, *The History and Development of Advertising,* 16.

Exhibit 4.4 A good example of advertisers joining the war effort.

Consider the world in which these ads existed. It was a period of rapid urbanization, massive immigration, labor unrest, and significant concerns about the abuses of capitalism. Some of capitalism's excesses and abuses, in the form of deceptive and misleading advertising, were the targets of early reformers. It was also the age of suffrage, the progressive movement, motion pictures, and mass culture. The world changed rapidly in this period, and it was no doubt disruptive and unsettling to many—but advertising was there to offer solutions to the stresses of modern life, no matter how real or imagined. Advertisers had something to solve just about any problem. Remember, social and cultural change opens up opportunities for advertisers. Further, had the first World War not occurred, and attention justifiably diverted, it is very possible that there would have been more severe and earlier regulation of advertising. Right before WWI there was a real and growing movement to significantly limit and regulate advertising, but that didn't happen.

The 1920s (1918 to 1929).

In many ways, the Roaring Twenties really began a couple of years early. After World War I, advertising found respectability, fame, and even glamour. Working in an advertising agency was the most modern of all professions; it was, short of being a movie star, the most fashionable. According to popular perception, it was where the young, smart, and sophisticated worked and played. During the 1920s, advertising was also a place where institutional freedom reigned. The prewar movement to reform and regulate advertising was pretty much dissipated by the distractions of the war and advertising's role in the war effort. During World War I the advertising industry learned a valuable lesson: Donating time and personnel to the common good is not only good civics but also smart business. Exhibit 4.4 is a World War I–era example. As a result of WWI, advertising became an often-used instrument of government policy and action.

The 1920s were generally prosperous times. Most (but not nearly all) enjoyed a previously unequaled standard of living. It was an age in which public pleasure was a lesser sin than in the Victorian era. A great social experiment in the joys of consumption was underway. Victorian repression and modesty gave way to a somewhat more open sexuality and a love affair with modernity. Advertising was made for this burgeoning sensuality; advertising gave people permission to enjoy. The 1920s and advertising were made for each other. Ads of the era exhorted consumers to have a good time and instructed them how to do it. Consumption and advertising were respectable. Being a consumer became synonymous with being a citizen... quite a change when you think about it.

During these relatively good economic times, advertising instructed consumers how to be thoroughly modern and how to avoid the pitfalls or side effects of this new age. Consumers learned of halitosis from Listerine advertising and about body odor from Lifebuoy advertising (see Exhibit 4.5, a Lifebuoy ad from 1926). Not too surprisingly, there just happened to be a product with a cure for just about any social anxiety and personal failing one could imagine, many of which had supposedly been brought on as side effects of modernity. This was perfect for the growth and entrenchment of advertising as an institution: Modern times bring on many wonderful new things,

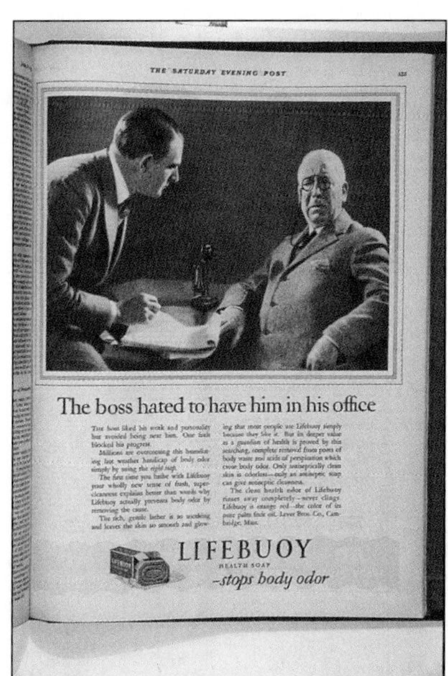

Exhibit 4.5 Many ads from the 1920s promised to relieve just about any social anxiety. Here, Lifebuoy offered a solution for people concerned that body odor could be standing in the way of career advancement.

Exhibit 4.6 This 1920s-era Gulf advertisement focuses on technological progress and the male prerogative in promoting its advancement. The work world is male space in this period's ads.

Exhibit 4.7 Ads from the 1920s often emphasized modernity themes, like the division between public and private workspace. This Fels-Naptha ad shows the private, "feminine" space of the home—where "her work" occurred.

but the new way of life has side effects that, in turn, have to be remedied by even more modern goods and services... and on and on. For example, modern canned food replaced fresh fruit and vegetables, thus "weakening the gums," causing dental problems—which could be cured by a modern toothbrush. But, the new toothbrush needed a new toothpaste... which then needed every better ingredients and additives. Thus, a seemingly endless consumption chain was created: Needs lead to products; new needs are created by new product side effects; newer products solve newer needs, and on and on. This chain of needs is essential to a capitalist economy, which must continue to expand in order to survive. This makes a necessity of advertising.

Other ads from the 1920s emphasized other modernity themes, such as the division between public workspace, the male domain of the office (see Exhibit 4.6), and the private, "feminine" space of the home (see Exhibit 4.7). Thus, two separate consumption domains were created, with women placed in charge of the latter; the one advertisers really cared about. Advertisers soon figured out that women were responsible for as much as 80 percent of household purchases. While 1920s men were out in the jungle of the work world, women made most purchase decisions. So, from this time forward, women became advertising's primary target.

Another very important aspect of advertising in the 1920s, and beyond, was the role that science and technology began to play. Science and technology were in many ways the new religions of the modern era. The modern way was the scientific way. So one saw ads appealing to the popularity of science in virtually all product categories of advertising during this period. Ads stressed the latest scientific offerings, whether in radio tubes or in "domestic science," as Exhibits 4.8 and 4.9 demonstrate.

The style of 1920s ads was more visual than in the past. Twenties ads showed slices of life, or carefully constructed "snapshots" of social life with the product. In these ads, the relative position, background, and dress of the people using or needing the advertised product were carefully crafted, as they are today. These visual lessons were generally about how to fit in with the "smart" crowd, how to be urbane and modern by using the newest conveniences, and how not to fall victim to the perils and pressure of the new fast-paced modern world. The social context of product

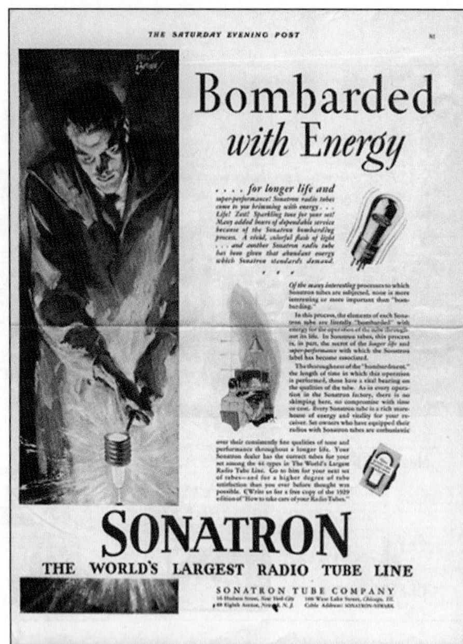

Exhibits 4.8 and 4.9 The cultural theme of modernity in the 1920s emphasized science and technology. These ads for Sonatron Radio Tubes and Pet Milk tout the science these brands brought to your home.

Courtesy of International Multifoods Corporation

use became critical, as one can see in Exhibits 4.10 through 4.12. This is when and where "slice-of-life" advertising came from. It remains one of advertising's most popular and successful message forms. Reasons for its power are its inherently social nature, and its ability to place brands in a carefully constructed social setting or moment in which on-going social tensions and cultural contradictions can be resolved by merely purchasing the advertised brand.

Sometime during the 1920s or just before, advertising began regularly constructing social-material relationships between people and products by depicting the social settings and circumstances into which people and things fit and what that fit yielded in terms of the consumer's life satisfaction. Consider Exhibit 4.11. Here is a major advertiser trying to sell plumbing. The ad doesn't say a word about the plumbing, its physical qualities, its price, or anything else. But look at the attention paid to the social setting into which plumbing fixtures were to fit. Is the ad really about plumbing? Yes, in a very important way it is. It's the 1920s, being a modern parent is very important. To be modern means to have a bathroom where there are few porous services, for example, tile replacing wood. The bathroom has to look almost as clean as an operating theater. Why? Well, in 1918 the Great Influenza epidemic killed millions of Americans, many of them children. Germ theory was new. People were being told that germs killed. Modern, scientific parents would be the first to protect their families from these things called germs. A baby is being weighed. Why did the advertising include this? Infant mortality was dropping rapidly due to the adoption of these very same sanitary practices, but was still a major concern. So, you should have this kind of bathroom with Standard Plumbing... and your new baby will have a better chance of reaching its second birthday. To this day the best way to know that your baby is doing well or "thriving" is to measure his weight. The father is in a suit: a modern professional man. The mother is in the style of the new modern 1920s woman. The ad is perfect and probably sold a lot of Standard Plumbing. The ad works because it demonstrates plumbing in a social context that works for both advertiser and consumer: it soothes anxieties, and resolves tensions and contradictions. It is great advertising.

Likewise, the ad in Exhibit 4.12 explains that soap isn't just soap, it is beauty weaponry. Advertising was becoming sophisticated and had discovered social context

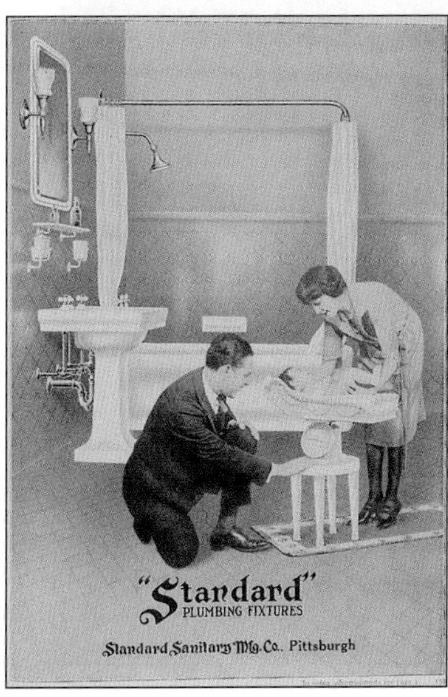

Exhibits 4.10 through 4.12 As the Kodak, Standard Sanitary, and Camay ads illustrate, ads from the 1920s often showed carefully constructed "snapshots" of social life with the products. The social setting and the product blur together within one image. Setting becomes brand; brand becomes setting. Take a minute and study what's going on in these ads.

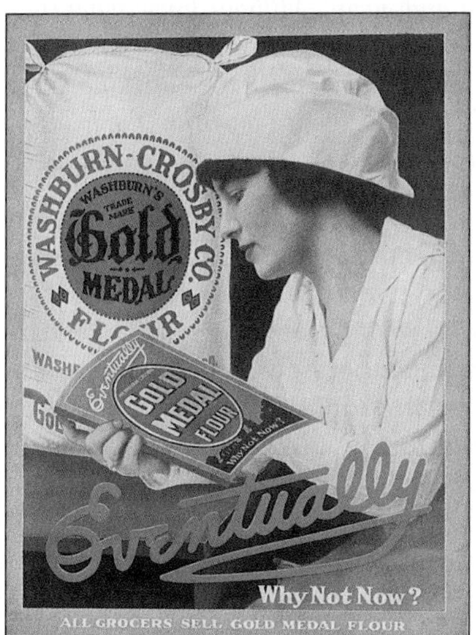

Exhibits 4.13 through 4.15 These three ads are more examples of the beautiful and stylish art direction of the 1920s. (Actually, the Gold Medal ad was produced in the early 1930s, but it is of the 1920s style.) Many believe this era was advertising's finest artistic moment. In an effort to make their advertising depict the technology and style of the era, advertisers in the 1920s enlisted the services of some of the best illustrators and artists of the time.

in a major way. In terms of pure art direction, the ads in Exhibits 4.13 through 4.15 are examples of the beauty of the period's ads.

The J. Walter Thompson advertising agency was the dominant agency of the period. Stanley Resor, Helen Resor, and James Webb Young brought this agency to a leadership position through intelligent management, vision, and great advertising. Helen Resor was the first prominent female advertising executive and was instrumental in J. Walter Thompson's success. Still, the most famous ad person of the era was a very interesting man named Bruce Barton. He was not only the leader of BBDO but also a best-selling author, most notably of a 1924 book called *The Man Nobody*

Exhibit 4.16 The very tough times of the Great Depression, depicted in this 1936 photo by Walker Evans, gave Americans reason to distrust big business and its tool, advertising.

Knows.[13] The book was about Jesus and portrayed him as the archetypal ad man. This blending of Christian and capitalist principles was apparently very attractive to a people struggling to reconcile traditional religious thought, which preached against excess, and the new consumer culture that embraced it. This was a best selling book, indicating the popularity of reconciling things people feel conflicted about—cultural contradictions. Remember, brands (including books) that can resolve cultural contradictions and social disruptions will generally be effective.

The Depression (1929 to 1941).

By 1932, a quarter of American workers were unemployed. But matters were worse than this suggests, for three quarters of those who had jobs were working part-time—either working short hours, or faced with chronic and repeated layoffs.... Perhaps half the working population at one time or another knew what it was like to lose a job. Millions actually went hungry, not once, but again and again. Millions knew what it was like to eat bread and water for supper, sometimes for days at a stretch. A million people were drifting around the country begging, among them thousands of children, including numbers of girls disguised as boys. People lived in shanty towns on the fields at edges of cities, their foods sometimes weeds plucked from the roadside.[14]

If you weren't there, you have no idea how bad it was. We don't, but your grandparents or great-grandparents did. The Great Depression was brutal, crushing, and mean. It killed people; it broke lives. Those who lived through it and kept their dignity are to be deeply admired. (See Exhibit 4.16.) Many of this greatest generation went on to fight in World War II. They gave of themselves for the common good; they may have been the last truly unselfish generation of Americans. The way people thought about work, money, and consumption would change forever after WWII. The change would be profitable for the advertising industry; whether or not it was good for society and its citizens is another question.

The **Great Depression** forever changed the way people thought about a great many things: their government, business, money, spending, saving, credit, and, not coincidentally, advertising. Just as sure as advertising was glamorous in the 1920s, it was suspect in the 1930s. Advertising was part of big business, and big business, big greed, and big lust had gotten America into the great economic depression beginning in 1929—or so the story goes. The public now saw advertising as something suspect, something that had tempted and seduced people into the excesses for which they were being punished. The advertising industry's collective response only made things worse.

Advertisers responded to the depression by adopting a tough, no-frills advertising style. The stylish ads of the 1920s gave way to harsher, more cluttered, inappropriately sexual, and often egregiously unethical advertising. As one historian said, "The new hard-boiled advertising mystique brought a proliferation of 'ugly,' attention-grabbing, picture-dominated copy in the style of the tabloid newspaper."[15] Clients wanted their money's worth, and agencies responded by cramming every bit of copy and image

13. Bruce Barton, *The Man Nobody Knows* (New York: Bobbs-Merrill, 1924).

14. James Lincoln Collier, *The Rise of Selfishness in America* (New York: Oxford University Press, 1991), 162.

15. Ibid., 303–304.

they could into their ads, or using obviously inappropriate sex appeals. Advertisers played on the anxieties and vulnerabilities of troubled people. In the short run, these ads may have worked more often than not because they leveraged the social disruptions and cultural contradictions of the times. But, their long-term effect was not positive. This type of advertising made the relationship between the public and the institution of advertising worse. It hurt advertising's public image; the public was getting wise to the opportunistic techniques and resented them, even when they worked. Regrettably, doing exactly the same thing is still an industry impulse in bad economic times today. The themes in advertisements traded on the anxieties of the day; losing one's job meant being a bad provider, spouse, or parent, unable to give the family what it needed (as seen in Exhibits 4.17 and 4.18), or when nothing else came to mind: sex. Have you seen these predictable responses in the **Great Recession** of your era?

Another notable event during these early years was the emergence of radio as a significant advertising medium. During the 1930s, the number of radio stations rose from a handful to 814 by the end of the decade, and the number of radio sets in use more than quadrupled to 51 million, slightly more than one radio set per household. Radio was in its heyday as a news and entertainment medium, and it would remain so until the 1950s when television emerged. An important aspect of radio was its ability to create a sense of community in which people thousands of miles apart listened to and became involved with their favorite radio soap opera, so named in reference to the soap sponsors of these shows. Radio's contribution to advertising history should not be underestimated, it not only ushered in the idea of broadcasting, but it also socialized consumers to depend on a connection to distant characters, programs, brands, and the idea that there were other people "out there" who shared this connection—a mass audience. Voices of radio friends from afar made good company particularly during hard times.

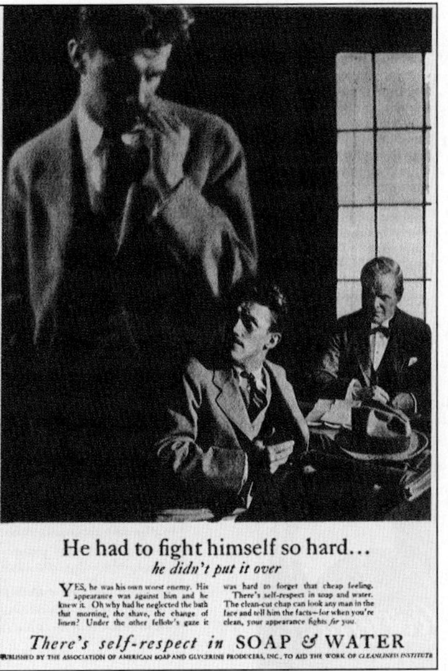

Exhibits 4.17 and 4.18 The themes in advertising during the 1930s traded on the anxieties of the day, as these ads for Paris Garters and the Association of American Soap and Glycerine Producers, Inc. illustrate.

The advertising industry, like the rest of the country, suffered during this period. Agencies cut salaries and forced staff to work four-day weeks without being paid for the mandatory extra day off. Clients demanded frequent review of work, and agencies were compelled to provide more and more free services to keep accounts. Advertising would emerge from this depression, just as the economy itself did, during World War II. However, the advertising industry would never again reach its pre-Depression cultural status. The U.S. Congress passed real advertising reform in this period. In 1938, the Wheeler-Lea Amendments to the Federal Trade Commission Act declared "decepti.ve acts of commerce" to be against the law; this was interpreted to include advertising. This changed the entire game: now individual advertisers could be held liable for deceptive practices. Between 1938 and 1940, the FTC issued 18 injunctions against advertisers, including "forcing Fleischmann's Yeast to stop claiming that it cured crooked teeth, bad skin, constipation and halitosis."[16] Believe it or not, eating yeast was successfully promoted by Fleishman's as a healthy practice. Government agencies soon used their new powers against a few large national advertisers, including Lifebuoy and Lux soaps. Advertisers would have to be at least a little more careful.

16. Fox, *The Mirror Makers,* 168.

World War II and the 1950s (1942 to 1960).

In the 1950s,

> *Almost one-half of all women married while they were still teenagers. Two out of three white women in college dropped out before they graduated. In 1955, 41 percent of women "thought the ideal number of children was four."*[17]

Many people mark the end of the Great Depression with the start of America's involvement in World War II in December 1941. During the war, advertising often made direct reference to the war effort, as the ad in Exhibit 4.19 shows, linking the advertised brand with patriotism, and helping to rehabilitate the tarnished image of advertising. During the war advertisers sold war bonds and encouraged conservation. Of all companies, Coca-Cola probably both contributed and benefited the most from their amazingly successful efforts to get Coca-Cola to the front lines. When the war was over, Coke had bottling plants all around the globe, and returning American G.I.s were super-loyal to Coke over competitors such as Pepsi by 4:1.[18] In addition, the war got women to join the workforce in what were nontraditional roles, as seen in the so-called Rosie the Riveter ads. The ad in Exhibit 4.20 for the Penn Railroad is a good example. During the war years, many women joined the workforce, and then left it (many involuntarily) after the war ended in 1945.

Exhibit 4.19 Advertisers often used America's involvement in World War II as a way to link their products with patriotism. This link provides advertising with a much-needed image boost after the dark period of the late 1930s. http://www.cocacola.com

Exhibit 4.20 During the war, advertisers encouraged women to join the workforce, as this ad for Penn Railroad illustrates.

17. Wini Breines, *Young, White and Miserable: Growing Up Female in the Fifties* (Boston: Beacon, 1992).
18. Mark Pendergrast, *For God, Country & Coca-Cola: The Definitive History of the Great American Soft Drink and the Company That Makes It* (New York: Basic Books, 2003).

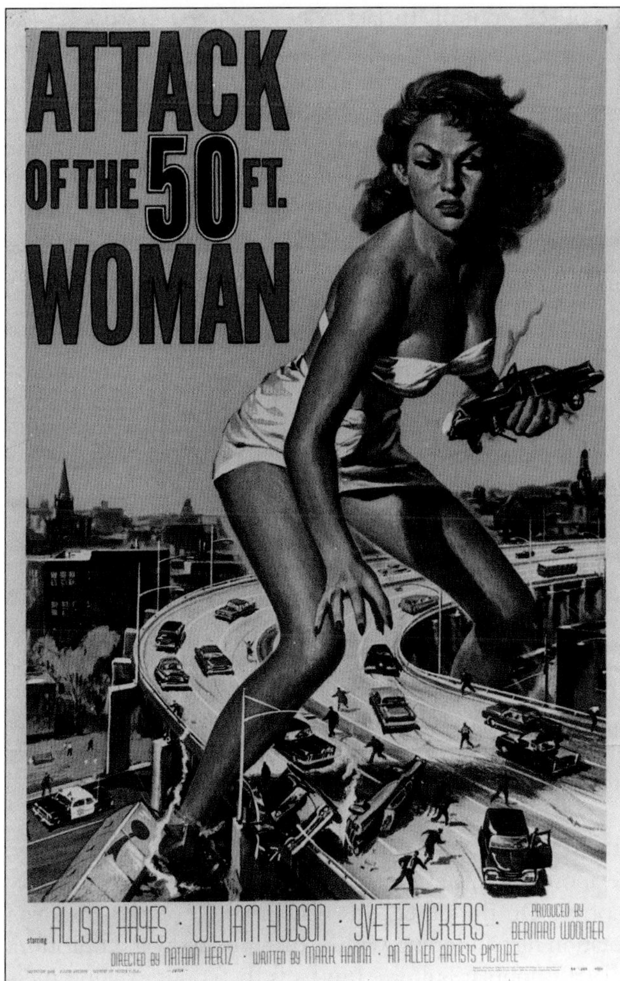

Exhibit 4.21 Irradiated 50s women were part of the 1950s culture of titillation and great ambivalence to modern science. This was the culture; and ads use the culture—no wonder 1950s ads were so thoroughly weird.

Exhibit 4.22 During the 1950s, with fears of communist mind control and a very real nuclear arms race, frightened people built bomb shelters in their backyards and became convinced of advertising's hidden powers.

Following World War II, the economy continued (with a few notable starts and stops) to improve, and the consumption spree was on again. The first shopping malls were built in the suburbs to follow affluent populations and to create a more "feminine" (and white) shopping environment. This time, however, public sentiment toward advertising itself was fundamentally different from what it had been in the 1920s, following WWI. It was more negative, more skeptical, and the public largely assumed that it was very powerful.

After WWII, there was widespread belief that America's successful propaganda experts at the War Department simply moved over to Madison Avenue and started manipulating consumer minds. At the same time, there was great concern about the rise of communism and its use of "mind control" in the Cold War. Perhaps it was only natural to believe that advertising was involved in the same type of pursuit. The United States was filled with suspicion related to McCarthyism, the bomb, repressed sexual thoughts (a resurgence of Freudian thought), and creatures from atomic science gonebad: *The Fifty-Foot Woman* (Exhibit 4.21), *Pods, Blob, The Un-Dead,* and *Body-Snatchers,* to name a few. One of the common themes of these films was that it was hard to know who was "one of them" and who was "one of us." This was often said to be allegory to not knowing who was a communist working to subvert American ideals while looking, acting, and sounding just like "us." Otherwise normal people were building bomb shelters in their backyards (see Exhibit 4.22), wondering whether listening to "jungle music" (a.k.a. rock 'n' roll) would make their daughters less virtuous. The 1950's were about fear, and advertisers again leveraged the accompanying disruption. Fearful people might be coaxed into anything that made them feel more secure. But at the same time, that fear of being manipulated by "modern science" and "mind control" made them very wary of advertising. Like other times, advertisers would turn these anxieties, contradictions, and social disruptions into advertising strategies.

In this environment of mass fear, stories began circulating in the 1950s that advertising agencies were doing motivation research and using the "psychological sell," which served only to fuel an underlying suspicion of advertising. It was also during this period that Americans began to fear they were being seduced by **subliminal advertising** (subconscious advertising) to buy all sorts of things they didn't really want or need. There had to be a reason that homes and garages were filling up with so much stuff; it must be all that powerful advertising—what a great excuse for lack

Exhibit 4.23 At first, advertisers didn't know what to do with television, the pre–World War II science experiment that reached 90 percent of U.S. households by 1960.

of self-control. In fact, a best-selling 1957 book, *The Hidden Persuaders,* offered the answer: Slick advertising worked on the subconscious.[19] This very popular book made a lot of sense to 1950s consumers, and suspicions about slick advertising's power persist to this day.

The most incredible story of the period involved a man named James Vicary. According to historian Stuart Rogers, in 1957, Vicary convinced the advertising world, and most of the U.S. population, that he had successfully demonstrated a technique to get consumers to do exactly what advertisers wanted. He claimed to have placed subliminal messages in a motion picture, brought in audiences, and recorded the results. He claimed that the embedded messages of "Eat Popcorn" and "Drink Coca-Cola" had increased sales of popcorn by 57.5 percent and Coca-Cola by 18.1 percent. He held press conferences and took retainer fees from advertising agencies. According to later research, he then skipped town, just ahead of reporters who had figured out that none of his claims had ever happened. He completely disappeared, leaving no bank accounts and no forwarding address. He left town with about $4.5 million (around $28 million in today's dollars) in advertising agency and client money.[20] The bigger problem is that a lot of people, including members of Congress, still believe in the hype Vicary was selling and that advertisers can actually do such things... and easily.

The 1950s were also about sex, and sex in a very paradoxical and conflicting way. On the one hand, the 1950s are about conformity, chastity, the nuclear family, and very strict gender roles and sexual norms. On the other, this was the time of neo-Freudian pop psychology and pre-sex-plotation films dripping with sexual innuendo and titillation. Sexual desire is everywhere in 1950s popular culture, but so is the countervailing message: chastity for women; a tempered "boys-will-be-boys" for young men. Double standards for adult sexual behavior were common—men couldn't help themselves—woman had to. In fact, it was during the latter part of this period that ad consultant Ernest Dichter actually advised one of the big three U.S. carmakers to remember: think of the family car (station wagon; big sedan) as a man's wife; the sports car his "mistress." Now, there is one large cultural contradiction to exploit—and they did.

What's more, the kids of the 1950s would be advertised to with a singular focus and force never seen before, becoming, as a result, the first TV- kid market, and then the first "teen" ad targets. Because of their sheer numbers, they would ultimately constitute an unstoppable youth culture, one that everyone else had to deal with and try to please—the baby boomers. They would, over their parents' objections, buy rock 'n' roll records in numbers large enough to revolutionize the music industry. Now they buy SUVs, mutual funds, and $10,000 bicycles... and will retire with you in the wake (and debt) of their consumption.

And then there was TV (Exhibit 4.23). Nothing like it had happened before. Its rise from pre–World War II science experiment to 90 percent penetration in U.S. households occurred during this period. At first, advertisers didn't know what to do with

19. Vance Packard, *The Hidden Persuaders* (New York: D. McKay, 1957). With respect to the effects of "subliminal advertising," researchers have shown that although subliminal *communication* is possible, subliminal *persuasion,* in the typical real-world environment, remains all but impossible. As it was discussed, as mind control, in the 1950s, it remains a joke. See Timothy E. Moore, "Subliminal Advertising: What You See Is What You Get," *Journal of Marketing,* vol. 46 (Spring 1982), 38–47.

20. Stuart Rogers, "How a Publicity Blitz Created the Myth of Subliminal Advertising," *Public Relations Quarterly* (Winter 1992–1993), 12–17.

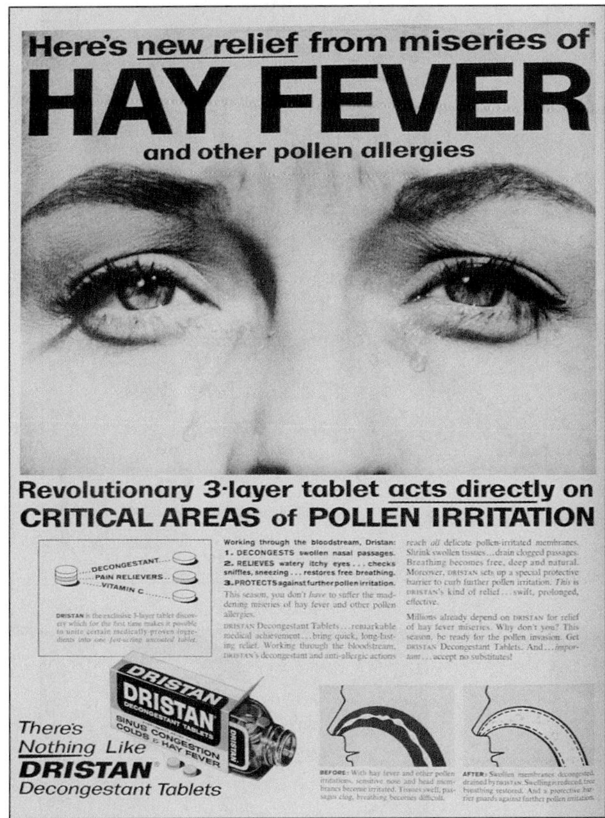

Exhibit 4.24 This is an ad from the famous Rosser Reeves at the Ted Bates agency. His style dominated the 1950s: harsh, abrasive, repetitive, and diagrammatic. He believed that selling the brand had virtually nothing to do with art or winning creative awards. His style of advertising is what the creative revolution revolted against.

it and produced two- and three-minute commercials, typically demonstrations. Of course, they soon began to learn TV's look and language.

This era also saw growth in the U.S. economy and in household incomes. The suburbs emerged, and along with them there was an explosion of consumption. Technological change was relentless and was a national obsession. The television, the telephone, and the automatic washer and dryer became common to the American lifestyle. Advertisements of this era were characterized by scenes of modern life, social promises, and reliance on science and technology.

Into all of this, 1950s advertising projected a confused, often harsh, while at other times sappy presence. It is rarely remembered as advertising's golden age. Two of the most significant advertising personalities of the period were Rosser Reeves of the Ted Bates agency, who is best remembered for his ultra-hard-sell style (see Exhibit 4.24), and consultant Ernest Dichter, best remembered for his motivational research, which focused on the subconscious and symbolic elements of consumer desire. *Mad Men* watchers, do you recognize these characters? Exhibits 4.25 through 4.28 are representative of the advertising from this contradictory and jumbled period in American advertising. Can you see why advertising (and the culture) needed a revolution?

These ads show mythic nuclear families, well-behaved children, our "buddy" the atom, an uneasy faith in science, and rigid (but about to break loose) gender roles, while the rumblings of the sexual revolution of the 1960s were just audible. In a few short years, the atom would no longer be our friend; we would question science; youth would rebel and become a hugely important market; women and African Americans would demand inclusion and fairness; and bullet bras would be replaced with no bras. Oral birth control's introduction in 1960 would change the culture's view of appropriate sexual behavior. A period of great social change would occur, which is usually a very good time for advertisers: new needs, new liberties, new anxieties, new goods and services, and new brands. Again, social disruption, cultural contradictions in need of resolution; it is in this space that great brands and great advertising emerge.

Peace, Love, and the Creative Revolution (1960 to 1972).

As you well know, there was a cultural revolution in the 1960s. It affected just about everything—including advertising. Ads started to take on the themes, the language, and the look of the 1960s. But as an institution, advertising during the 1960s was actually slow to respond to the massive social revolution going on all around it. While the world was struggling with civil rights, the Vietnam War, the sexual revolution, and the "youth" revolution, advertising was, for the most part, still portraying women and other minorities in subservient roles (Exhibits 4.29 and 4.30). As writer Thomas Frank has pointed out, advertising leveraged the trappings and the revolutionary impulse of the decade to sell things, yet it remained a fairly conservative capitalist institution. Advertising agencies stayed one of the whitest industries in

Courtesy, Wyeth Consumer Healthcard

Exhibits 4.25 through 4.28 These four ads show the 1950s as they were: contradictory (family values-dominated but titillating) and science obsessed. Exhibit 4.28 shows evidence of the 1950s' paradoxical view on sex: titillating but still "just an underwear ad."

America. Gays and lesbians, as far as advertising was concerned, didn't exist. And in ads, much of the sexual revolution wasn't exactly liberating for everyone.

The only thing really revolutionary about 1960s advertising was the **creative revolution.** This revolution was characterized by the "creatives" (art directors and copywriters) having a bigger say in the management of their agencies, and the look and feel of the ads. The emphasis in advertising turned "from ancillary services to the creative product; from science and research to art, inspiration, and intuition."[21] At first, the look of this revolutionary advertising was clean and minimalist, with simple copy and a sense of self-effacing humor. Later (around 1968 or so), it became something more. In the late 1960s, advertising had finally changed in meaningful ways. For one, it became fairly self-aware. Advertising admitted being advertising (and even poked fun at itself). Ads during the late 1960s and into the early 1970s conveyed the sentiment, "ok, here's an ad, you know it's an ad—and so do we." Advertising began to trade on insider status (we're all in on it)—making fun of the straight and now silly ads of the

21. Fox, *The Mirror Makers,* 218.

Exhibit 4.29 Well, there you have it. When I think of shoe polish, I think of....

Exhibit 4.30 Something special in the air.

Courtesy, Griffin Footwear Products; Photo courtesy, Susan Van Etten

1950s and by playing to a sense of irony. This insider ironic orientation made advertising occasionally hip. The 1960s was when advertising began to understand that it was all about hip, cool, youth, and rebellion. From that point on, defining and chasing cool was a prime advertising directive. The 60s Cultural Revolution soon became ad copy. Everything became rebellion; even an unhip brand like Dodge tried to cash in with the "Dodge Rebellion."[22] Once advertising learned that it could successfully attach itself to youth, hipness, and revolution, it never went back. Even hip anti-advertising sentiment could be used to help sell stuff through advertising. Now, that's ironic.

The creative revolution, and the look it produced, is most often associated with four famous advertising agencies: Leo Burnett in Chicago; Ogilvy & Mather in New York (a little less so); Doyle Dane Bernbach in New York (the most); and Wells Rich and Green in New York (deserving of more credit than they get). They were led in this revolution by agency heads Leo Burnett, David Ogilvy, Bill Bernbach, and Mary Wells. The Kellogg's Special K cereal, Rolls-Royce, Volkswagen, and Braniff ads pictured in Exhibits 4.31 through 4.34 are 1960s ads prepared by these four famous agencies, respectively. Recognize anyone in *Mad Men*?

22. Thomas Frank, *The Conquest of Cool: Business Culture, Counterculture, and the Rise of Hip Consumerism* (Chicago: University of Chicago Press, 1997).

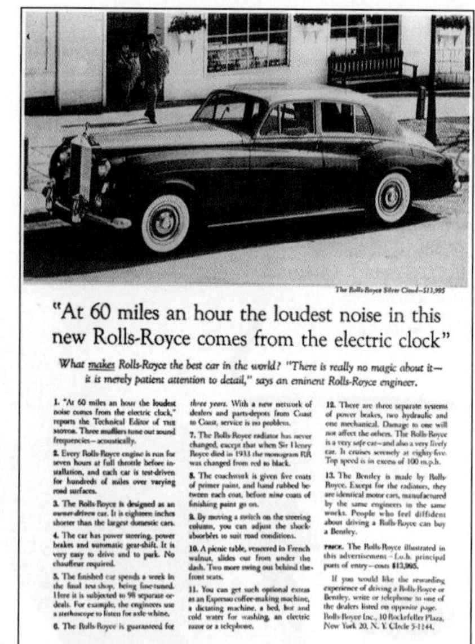

Exhibits 4.31 and 4.32 The new era of advertising in the 1960s was characterized by the creative revolution, during which the creative side of the advertising process rose to new prominence. Note the clean look and minimal copy in the Kellogg's ad in Exhibit 4.31, prepared by Leo Burnett in Chicago. The Rolls-Royce ad in Exhibit 4.32, from David Ogilvy of Ogilvy & Mather, was considered "revolutionary" for its copy (not its look), which took the consumer more seriously than the ads of the 1950s did. http://www.kelloggs .com and http://www.rolls-royce.com

Exhibit 4.33 Through innovative advertising, Volkswagen has, throughout the years, been able to refuel its original message that its cars aren't expensive luxuries but as much a household staple as broccoli and ground round (and, at $1.02 a pound, cheaper than either!). These ads from Doyle Dane Bernbach also acknowledged a sophisticated consumer. http://www.vw.com

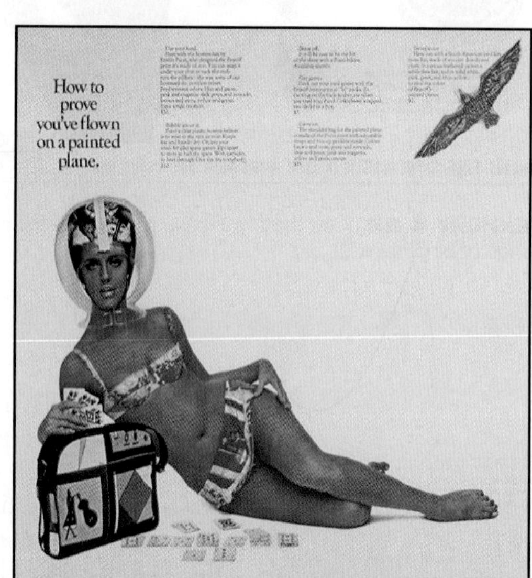

Exhibit 4.34 This is one of Mary Wells' famously futuristic (and fashionable) ads for Braniff Airlines.

Of course, not all 1960s ads were revolutionary. Plenty of ads in the 1960s still reflected traditional values and relied on relatively worn executions. Typical of many of the more traditional ads during the era is the Goodyear ad in Exhibit 4.35.

Pepsi may have taken better advantage of the disruptions of the 1960s than any other advertiser. As late as the mid 1950s, Coke had an enormous lead over Pepsi. Up until the 1960s, Pepsi kept trying to sell Pepsi as a product based on taste. It was only when they switched from trying to sell the product (a cola) to selling the consumers who drank it "those who think young," that they began to eat up Coke's lead. As noted by Thomas Frank and others, it was Pepsi's new strategy to "name and claim the youth revolution as their own." There was a growing generation gap/war; Pepsi leveraged that beautifully. Coke is for old un-hip people; Pepsi is for us cool kids (Exhibit 4.36), traded on youth and the idea of youth. Within a few short years, Pepsi had pulled almost even with Coke, erasing a 3 to 1 lead coming out of WWII. Again, they did it by leveraging the contractions, anxieties, and social dislocations of the day—cultural marketing at work.

A final point that needs to be made about the era from 1960 to 1972 is that this was a period when advertising as an institution became generally aware of its own role in consumer culture. While advertising played a role in encouraging consumption, it had become a symbol of consumption itself. Musicians (think Bob Dylan, The Who, The Rolling Stones), artists (think Warhol, Lichtenstein), film makers, poets, and authors are all very aware that advertising, consuming, youth, revolution, sex, satisfaction, and identity were all jumbled up together. The paradox of advertising/marketing/consuming had gone public. The love/hate relationship was now being celebrated in art (Warhol, Lichtenstein) and in movies and in songs. Bands like The Who simultaneously and smartly critiqued consumer culture and embraced it (see Exhibit 4.37). Advertisers learned that people (particularly youth) play out their

Exhibit 4.35 Not all the advertising in the 1960s was characterized by the spirit of the creative revolution. This Goodyear ad relies more on traditional styles and values. http://www.goodyear.com

Exhibit 4.36 Pepsi "created" a generation and traded on the discovery of the vast youth market. Pepsi claimed youth as its own. http://www.pepsiworld.com

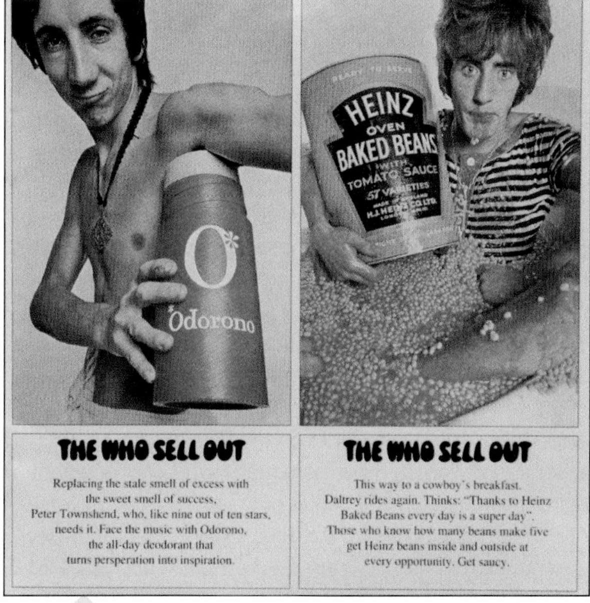

Exhibit 4.37 1960s counter-culture was known for its simultaneous critique and embrace of consumer culture. No one was more self aware on this front than The Who.

revolutionary impulse *through* consumption—even when it's an anti-consumption revolution, you've got to have the right look, the right clothes, the right revolutionary garb. In a very significant way, advertising learned how to forever dodge the harshest criticism of the very thing that advanced capitalism: Hide in plain sight. Paradox is good business.

Perhaps it's a bit too cynical, but Thomas Frank tells revolutionaries or us that since the 1960s nothing has been really new... just another branded faux-revolution. True?

> *Every few years, it seems, the cycles of the 60s repeat themselves on a smaller scale, with new rebel youth cultures bubbling their way to a happy replenishing of the various culture industries' depleted arsenal of cool. New generations obsolete the old, new celebrities render old ones ridiculous, and on and on in an ever-ascending spiral of hip upon hip. As ad-man Merle Steir wrote back in 1967, "Youth has won. Youth must always win. The new naturally replaces the old." And we will have new generations of youth rebellion as certainly as we will have generations of mufflers or toothpaste or footwear.*[23]

Ethics

Mother's Little Helper

Advertising targets women more than men, always has. One obvious reason is women buy more things than men, and make more purchasing decisions. They are thus, more powerful. Through the first half of the 20th century, women were also considered (seriously, actually said out loud) less rational, more foolish, more impulsive, and easier to persuade. They were often targeted with an especially effective, and especially nasty persuasive technique—induce social anxiety. Women were, due to all the social disruptions about them, thought to be more vulnerable to feeling bad about being a mother, a worker, a lover, a housekeeper... you name it.

This was noticed by two or three generations of women. Betty Friedan made a major point of it, as have other women advocates. In the 1970s and 1980s it was the role-conflict of motherhood and work. Isn't it still?

The advertising industry claims it has gotten much better. It says that it has moved women into senior management.... well, sort of, here and there. *An Advertising Age* White Paper on the *Rise of the Real Mom* asserts that women have more realistic role expectations, but remain the absolute center of the advertising universe. And while laudably trying to tell us (again) about the "new realities" of the "new (once again) mom," the industry is, after all, still first and foremost trying to push the right buttons, including role conflict or the denial of same, to sell things to women.

So, think about some of the ads shown in this chapter from the 1920s–1960s, and then consider ads from today. What do you think? Is the 1930s Lux ad any worse than the ones you can see right now, today? Have advertisers really quit trying to sell things by making women feel anxious about their bodies, their attractiveness, their competence, and their worth to men?

You tell us.

Sources: Susan Faludi (1991), "Beauty and the Backlash," *Backlash: The Undeclared War Against Women*, New York: Anchor, 200–226.

B. Friedan (1963). *The Feminine Mystique*, New York: W.W. Norton.

Roland Marchand (1985), *Advertising the American Dream,* Berkeley: University of California Press.

Marissa Miley and Ann Mack, "The Rise of the Real Mom," marissa.miley@mac.com, ann.mack@jwt.com, *Advertising Age,* White Paper, 2009, http://s3.amazonaws.com/ppt-download/aa-newfemale-whitepaper-091214091009-phpapp02.pdf?Signature=DEFQHCsxZ2CLg9%2B7QUSU9UGtGIQ%3D&Expires=1270572430&AWSAccessKeyId=AKIAJLJT267DEGKZDHEQ

23. Frank, *The Conquest of Cool,* 235.

The 1970s (1973 to 1980).

Mr. Blutarski, fat, drunk, and stupid is no way to go through life.

—Dean Vernon Wormer (John Vernon) in National Lampoon's *Animal House,* 1978

Dean Wormer's advice to John Belushi's character in *Animal House* captured essential aspects of the 1970s, a time of excess and self-induced numbness.

The reelection of Richard Nixon in 1972 marked the real start of the 1970s. The 1970s was the age of polyester, disco, blow, and driving 55. But more than anything else, it was America's age of self-doubt. America had just suffered through its first lost war, the memory of four student protesters shot and killed by the National Guard at Kent State University in the spring of 1970 was still vivid, Mideast nations appeared to be dictating the energy policy of the United States, and we were, as President Jimmy Carter suggested late in this period, in a national malaise. In this environment, advertising retreated a bit from the creative revolution, but not entirely. The ads of this period took sexual sell a bit further, seem a little less artistic, were a little more racially integrated, and used a bit more hard-sell.

The major social shifts of the decade were the second-wave of American feminism (see Exhibits 4.38 and 4.39), the self-doubt of Western democracies, and a significant mass identity/authenticity question "Who am I; What is real?" (See how the Coca-Cola company smartly answered the question, Exhibit 4.40.) "What can I believe in?" Part of this was the rise of the self-help-therapy industry; the philosophy and advice that seemed to sell the best was "it's ok to be selfish." "Me" became the biggest word in the 1970s; what a great environment for advertising. All of society was telling people that it was not only OK to be selfish, but it was the right thing to do. Selfishness was said to be natural and good. A refrain similar to "Hey babe, I can't be good to you if I'm not good to me?" became a 70s standard riff. Of course, being good to ones' self often meant self-indulgence, self-gifting, and buying stuff—always good for advertising. It's funny how that worked out.

Exhibit 4.38 Burn a bra, smoke a Virginia Slims for liberation.

Exhibit 4.39 This very successful campaign leveraged social disruption.

Exhibit 4.40 Claiming authenticity is tried and true, particularly when it is at the center of cultural conversations and social disruption. It was during the 1960s and 1970s. Is it now?

Still, all periods have counter-currents: the 70s saw added regulation for the protection of special audiences. First, there was growing concern over what effect $200 million a year in advertising had on children. A group of women in Boston formed **Action for Children's Television,** which lobbied the government to limit the amount and content of advertising directed at children. Established regulatory bodies, in particular the **Federal Trade Commission (FTC)** and the industry's **National Advertising Review Board,** demanded higher standards of honesty and disclosure from the advertising industry. A clever end-run around this was the advent what were essentially program-length commercials (PLCs), particularly in children's television. Product/show blends for toys like Strawberry Shortcake made regulation more difficult: If it's a show about a product, then it's not really an ad (and can't be regulated as an ad)—or is it? This drove regulators crazy, but program-length commercials were here to stay, at least in the United States.[24] They were generally treated by regulators as shows (with some degree of First Amendment protection) and opened the door for countless imitators. So in a real sense, what is now being called the "new" branded entertainment had its start in the 1970s.

Several firms were subjected to legislative mandates and fines because their advertising was judged to be misleading. Most notable among these firms were Warner-Lambert (for advertising that Listerine mouthwash could cure and prevent colds), Campbell's (for putting marbles in the bottom of a soup bowl to bolster its look), and Anacin (for advertising that its aspirin could help relieve tension).

Courtesy, Advertising Archives

24. Tom Engelhardt, "The Shortcake Strategy," in Todd Gitlin, (Ed.), *Watching Television* (New York: Pantheon, 1986), 68–110.

Exhibit 4.41 Although a bad economy and a national malaise caused a retreat to the tried-and-true styles of decades before, a bright spot of 1970s advertising was the portrayal of people of color. Thomas Burrell created ads that portrayed African Americans with "positive realism."

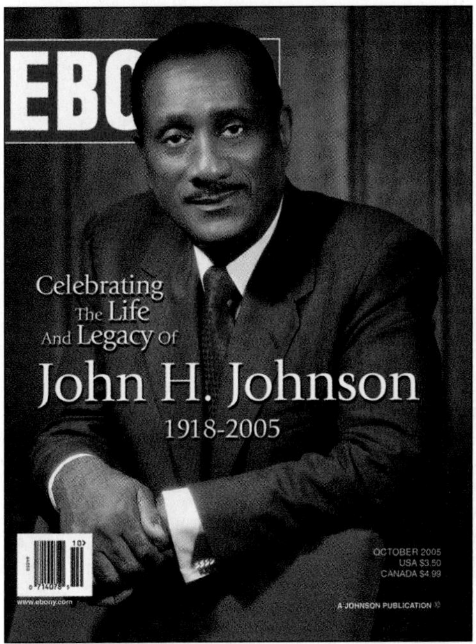

Exhibit 4.42 John H. Johnson made so much possible for black Americans in business.

During the 1970s, advertising agency hiring and promotion practices with respect to minorities were formally challenged in the courts. The industry remained very white. In what is to this day an odd segregation, "specialty" agencies emerged for serving various ethnic groups. Two important agencies owned and managed by African Americans thrived: Thomas J. Burrell founded Burrell Advertising, and Byron Lewis founded Uniworld. Burrell is perhaps best known for ads that rely on the principle of "positive realism." Positive realism is "people working productively; people engaging in family life... people being well-rounded... and thoughtful; people caring about other people; good neighbors, good parents... people with dreams and aspirations; people with ambition." Burrell once said "in 30 seconds you can build a brand and break a stereotype." He also believed that "whites are easier to reach through black advertising than vise versa."[25] "The idea was that we don't have to be the same as white people to be equal to white people; that we should celebrate our differences while not shying away from demanding our rights."[26]

One of Burrell's ads is shown in Exhibit 4.41. (Go to http://www.littleafrica.com/resources/advertising.htm for a current list of major African-American advertising agencies and resources.) Another very important person was John H. Johnson, founder of *Ebony* magazine, and in many ways the man who made the black American experience in publishing, marketing, and advertising possible (Exhibit 4.42). He opened up enormous opportunities for black entrepreneurs, advertisers, and artists. His funeral was attended by a former U.S. president, U.S. senators, celebrities, and a lot of people who simply adored him. He was very important in advertising and beyond.

The 1970s also signaled a period of growth in communications technology. Consumers began to surround themselves with devices related to communication. The VCR, cable television, and the laserdisc player were all developed during the 1970s. Cable TV claimed 20 million subscribers by the end of the decade. Similarly, cable programming grew in quality, with viewing options such as ESPN, CNN, TBS, and Nickelodeon. As cable subscribers and their viewing options increased, advertisers learned how to reach more specific audiences through the diversity of programming on cable systems.

There was, as always, a youth undercurrent of revolution (with a small "r") in the 1970s. This one was more cynical, and ambivalent about consumption and advertising than the one a decade earlier. Their anti-consumption rant was set to the music of most notably (and poetically) Patti Smith (see Exhibit 4.43), with a backing chorus of hundreds of British punk and American alternative bands. Although notably more ironic and cynical than their 1960s counter-parts, it was still about finding authenticity, identity, and meaning in a sea of consumption and ads.

The ads in Exhibits 4.44 and 4.45 are pretty typical of the period.

25. http://www.ciadvertising.org/studies/student/99_fall/theory/cal/aainadvertising/folder/burrell.html

26. http://blackmbamagazine.net/articles/docs/2005-2_an%20advertising%20legend%20leads%20with%20passion%20purpose%20and%20power.pdf

Exhibit 4.43 Patti's not cool with a lot of meaningless consumption.

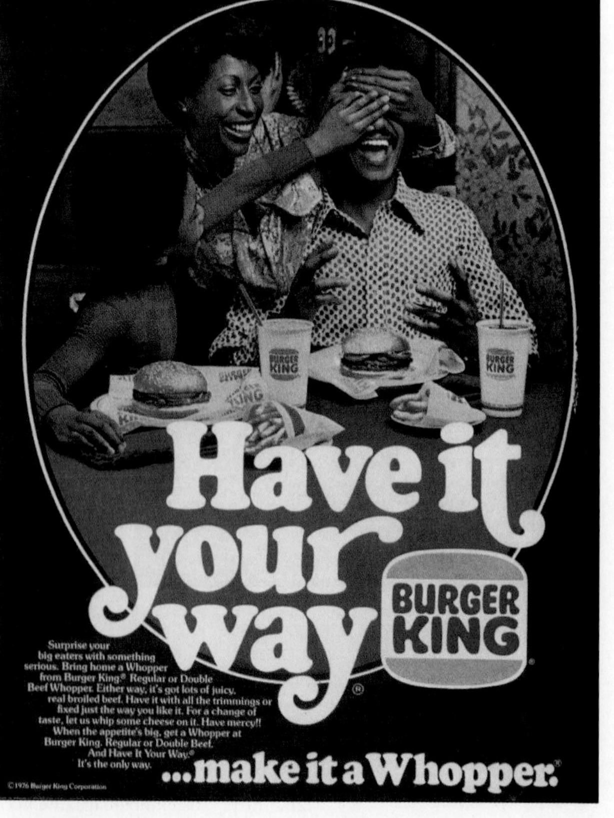

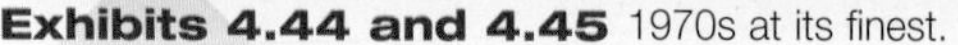

Exhibits 4.44 and 4.45 1970s at its finest.

Courtesy, Advertising Archives; Photo courtesy, Susan Van Etten; Courtesy, Advertising Archives

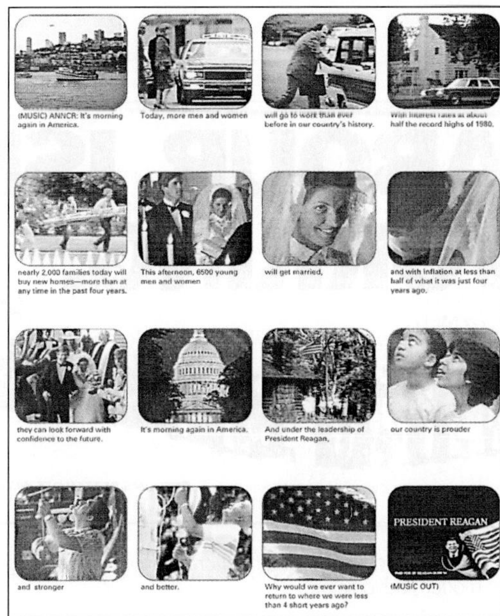

Exhibit 4.46 An ad that embodied the tone and style of 1980s advertising was Ronald Reagan's 1984 reelection campaign ad "Morning in America." The ad is soft in texture but firm in its affirmation of the conservative values of family and country.

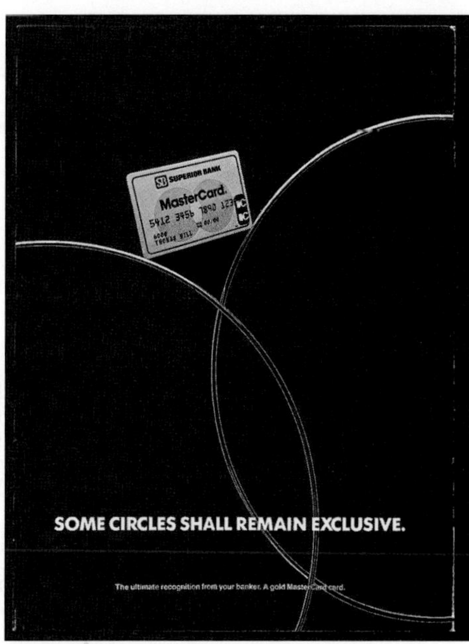

Exhibit 4.47 This MasterCard ad demonstrates the social-class and designer consciousness of the 1980s.

The Designer Era (1980 to 1992).

Greed, for a lack of a better word, is good.

—Gordon Gekko (Michael Douglas) in *Wall Street,* 1987

"In 1980, the average American had twice as much real income as his parents had had at the end of WWII."[27] The political, social, business, and advertising landscape changed in 1980 with the election of Ronald Reagan. The country made a right, and conservative politics were the order of the day. There was, of course, some backlash and many countercurrents, but the conservatives were in the mainstream. Greed was good, stuff was good, and advertising was good. American, Britain, and the West generally experienced a profound political and consumption shift. In the fall of 1989, the Berlin Wall fell and those in the East were now free to buy. Mass market capitalism and consumerism experienced some glory days.

In the 1980s we witnessed the label moving from inside the shirt to the outside. Although it had started in the 1970s, the 1980s saw the explosion of designer goods: everything became about public consumption status and their markers. Not surprisingly, many ads from the Designer era are particularly social-class conscious and values conscious. They openly promote consumption, but in a conservative way, wrapped up in "traditional American values." The quintessential 1980s ad may be the 1984 television ad for President Ronald Reagan's reelection campaign, "Morning in America." The storyboard for this ad is shown in Exhibit 4.46. This ad is soft in texture, but it is a firm reaffirmation of family and country—and capitalism. Other advertisers quickly followed with ads that looked similar to "Morning in America." The 1980s were also about designer labels, social-class consciousness, and having stuff, as the ad in Exhibit 4.47 demonstrates.

27 Collier, *The Rise of Selfishness in America*, 230.

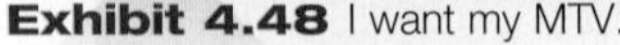

Exhibit 4.48 I want my MTV.

Exhibit 4.49 Saatchi and Saatchi, more than anyone, brought a political sensibility to modern advertising.

Television advertising of the 1980s period was influenced by the rapid-cut editing style of MTV. That's right: MTV changed advertising. George Lois, himself of the 1960s creative revolution, was hired by MTV to save the fledgling network after a dismal first year. After calling a lot of people who were unwilling to take the chance, he got Mick Jagger to proclaim, "I want my MTV" (see Exhibit 4.48). The network turned around and music television surged into popular consciousness. Most importantly for us, television ads in the 1980s started looking like MTV videos: rapid cuts with a very self-conscious character.

The advertising of the 1980s had a few other changes. One was the growth and creative impact of British agencies, particularly Saatchi and Saatchi (see Exhibit 4.49). One of the things Saatchi and Saatchi realized earlier than most was that politics, culture, and products all resonate together. The Saatchi and Saatchi ads of this period were often sophisticated and politically non-neutral. In the U.K., they more openly blended politics and advertising. They worked, and began to be copied (at least the sensibility) in other places, including the United States.

Exhibits 4.50 and 4.51 are pretty typical 1980s ads.

The E-Revolution Begins (1993 to 2000).

Some say that Internet advertising became truly viable around 1993. One can argue with the exact date, but somewhere near the mid 1990s is the point where it becomes clear that Internet adverting and other e- brand promotions were not only here to stay, but were going to change the entire advertising landscape. From that date until the dot.com meltdown in 2000, advertising was struggling with all sorts of new possibilities and challenges. Ads in traditional media were getting edgier while e-ads were still trying to define themselves: find their best form.

There were scary moments for those heavily vested in traditional advertising. In May 1994, Edwin L. Artzt, then chairman and CEO of Procter & Gamble, the then $40 billion-a-year marketer of consumer packaged goods, dropped a bomb on the advertising industry. During an address to participants at the American Association of Advertising Agencies (4As) annual conference, he warned that agencies must confront a "new media" future that won't be driven by traditional advertising. Although at that time P&G was spending about $1 billion a year on

Exhibit 4.50 Nothing comes between me and my Calvins.

Exhibit 4.51 Let's get drunk with designer gin.

television advertising, Artzt told the 4As audience, "From where we stand today, we can't be sure that ad-supported TV programming will have a future in the world being created—a world of video-on-demand, pay-per-view, and subscription TV. These are designed to carry no advertising at all."[28] This was not good news to those who preferred business as usual. Then, just when the industry had almost recovered from Artzt's dire proclamation, William T. Esrey, chairman and CEO of Sprint, gave it another jolt a year later at the same annual conference. Esrey's point was somewhat different but equally challenging to the industry. He said that clients are "going to hold ad agencies more closely accountable for results than ever before. That's not just because we're going to be more demanding in getting value for our advertising dollars. It's also because we know the technology is there to measure advertising impact more precisely than you have done in the past."[29] Esrey's point: new **interactive media** will allow direct measurement of ad exposure and impact, quickly revealing those ads that perform well and those that do not. Secondly, the agency will be held accountable for results. The saga continues. Still unsure of what could be delivered and what could be counted, in August 1998, Procter & Gamble hosted an Internet "summit," due to "what is widely perceived as the poky pace of efforts to eliminate the difficulties confronted by marketers using online media to pitch products."[30] Some of these problems were technological: incompatible standards, limited bandwidth, and disappointing measurement of both audience and return on investment. Others were the result of naïveté. Advertisers such as P&G want to know what they were getting and what it costs when they place an Internet ad. Does anyone notice these ads, or do people click right past them? What would "exposure" in this environment really mean? Is "exposure" really even a meaningful term in the new media ad world?

28. This quote and information from this section can be found in Steve Yahn, "Advertising's Grave New World," *Advertising Age,* May 16, 1994, 53.

29. Kevin Goodman, "Sprint Chief Lectures Agencies on Future," *The Wall Street Journal*, April 28, 1995, B6.

30. Stuart Elliot, "Procter & Gamble Calls Internet Marketing Executives to Cincinnati for a Summit Meeting," *The New York Times,* August 19, 1998, D3; available at http://www.nytimes.com, accessed February 20, 1999.

How do you use these new media to build brands? At the end of this summit, P&G reaffirmed its commitment to the Internet.

But history again showed that measurement of bang for buck (return on investment, ROI) in advertising (Internet or not) is very elusive. Although better than TV, the Internet was fundamentally unable to yield precise measurements of return on investment in advertisement, too many variables, too much noise in the system, too many delayed effects, and too many uncertainties about who is really online. But advertisers still became more demanding in terms of "results." This has been largely the case throughout advertising's history. Ad agencies are now operating with fewer staff and smaller margins than before. Clients are more tight-fisted these days and at least try to demand accountability. Things have certainly changed, particularly in print advertising, but not all old media are sick, much less dead.

Another change has come in the form of a significant challenge on New York's claim as the center of the advertising universe. In the United States, the center moved west, with the ascendancy of agencies in California, Minnesota, Oregon, and Washington, not to mention international hot spots such as London and Singapore. In the 1990s these agencies tended to be more creatively oriented and less interested in numbers-oriented research than those in New York. Other hot or nearly hot ad-shop markets include Minneapolis, Austin, Atlanta, Houston, and Dallas. Outside the United States, London emerged as the key player, with Singapore and Seoul as close seconds.

In terms of style and cultural connections, the 1990s was (like most eras) a mixed-bag. But one clear trend was what some have referred to as an abundance of irony and soft cynicism. In the '90s, self-parody of advertising was the inside joke, except everyone was "inside." Winks and nods to the media-savvy audience were pretty common. Ads said in a sense, "this is an ad… you know it, we know it, but we are still going to try to sell you something." This was said to be a product of the Generation-X mind-set. This was slacker cynicism: laid back cool; no ladder climbing… just hanging out… having heard it all before. These words from 1999's Fight Club say it well:

> *Advertising has us chasing cars and clothes, working jobs we hate so we can buy **** we don't need. We're the middle children of history, man. No purpose or place. We have no Great War. No Great Depression. Our Great War's a spiritual war … our Great Depression is our lives. We've all been raised on television to believe that one day we'd all be millionaires and movie gods and rock stars. But we won't. And we're slowly learning that fact. And we're, very p *** ed off.*

The Fight Club, Nirvana, et al. spirit was touchstone of cutting edge 1990s ads. Advertising was fast, and it was self-consciously hip. Exhibits 4.52 and 4.53 are good examples.

4 Consumer Empowerment, Branded Entertainment, and the Great Recession (2000–Present).

As you may be aware, the dot-com bubble burst in 2000. The economy slid for a while. Lots of Internet companies that burned cash like kindling never turned a profit and died. Part of the problem was the lack of a good Web advertising revenue model. Pop-ups and easy-to-avoid Internet ads had not generated enough advertising revenue. Online buying continued to grow, but online advertising couldn't catch up until companies became more sophisticated at using new media to general sales. The corner seems to have been turned around 2002. Phase II of the e-ad-revolution (tied to Web 2.0) has been much more

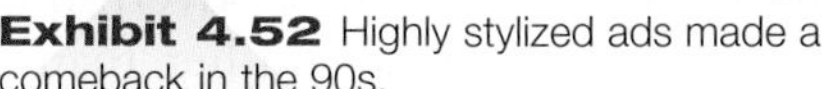

Exhibit 4.52 Highly stylized ads made a comeback in the 90s.

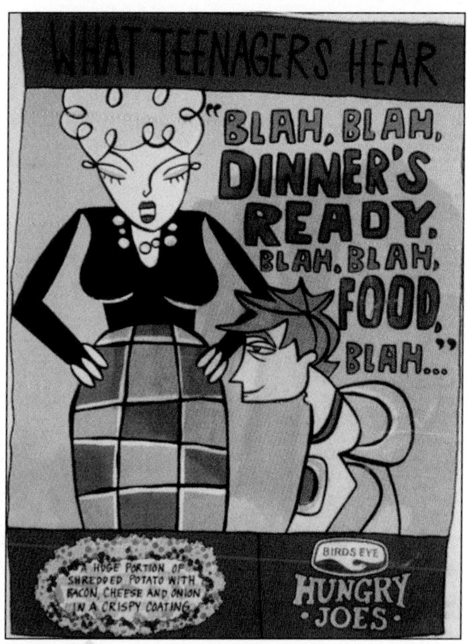

Exhibit 4.53 Does this ad look like anything in the frozen veggie category?

successful. One major difference between Web 2.0 and what came before is the basic consumer-advertising/brand promotion model—it is now much more about pull than push. Before Web 2.0, the model was still: find consumers through mass exposure, and push ads (and brands) at them. In Web 2.0 it is get consumers to seek you out, or bump into you on the Web, and then pull them to you. Of course, consumers still have to somehow hear about your brand in the first place, but that's where the integration of media comes in: one medium makes you aware, another pulls you, and another engages you (more in Chapter 15).

Although there are many social and cultural trends that could be leveraged, one thing is undeniable in this latest period: consumers are much more powerful than ever before. Consumers can now communicate with each other, actually talk back to the marketer with one voice or millions, and even make their own ads and distribute them on social media such as YouTube. The advertising industry has pretty much accepted the fact that consumers can now do many of the very same things that only big studios, agencies, and distributors could do a decade ago. Consumers now "co-create" brand messages and brands in a meaningful way. Consumers' reactions (particularly young people) are fused with agency "professional" creatives to make ads that are one step from homemade, or in some cases completely homemade. Doritos actually had consumers make Super-Bowl ads. This is typically called **consumer-generated content (CGC).** Because of this the industry bible, *Advertising Age,* has declared this era the "post-advertising age." Although that's a bit much, things really have changed a lot in the last few years, and consumer empowerment is a big part of it.

Think about this period. What do you think are the major cultural contradictions, social disruptions, and identity issues of this period? How have these been leveraged by smart advertisers? How have anxieties about security since 9/11 been used? How about the election of the first black U.S. President? What of growing Chinese power? What about the recent right-wing populism of the United States? What of the contradictions of the Great Recession? What about the rapidly growing gulf between the very rich in the United States and everyone else, the disappearance of U.S. middle class? What about shrinking populations in countries like Italy? What about a tough job market for college graduates... having to live with your parents until you are 30, but wanting (and almost expecting) the cool cribs seen on TV? How about a small gray cube instead of the corner office? Or maybe you will create the next Facebook or something equally cool and profitable.

See any reason to be nervous, anxious, conflicted, hopeful, independent/dependent, or resigned/determined?

Well, these all make for great leverage in advertising campaigns. Do you see any of these conditions being leveraged in these recent ads (Exhibits 4.54 through 4.57), or do you just see pretty traditional product-based pitches?

The Great Recession of 2008–2010 has had its impact on the advertising industry. Many advertisers cut their ad budgets during this period. Many used the economy as a reason to invest more in branded entertainment and nontraditional advertising and brand promotion. These changes have now been institutionalized. For example, media companies such as Nielsen now keep comprehensive data on product placements. Guerrilla marketing, Brand Hi-Jacks, and the building of brands like Red Bull and Pabst's Blue Ribbon through nontraditional means are now fairly commonplace.

And don't forget about business-to-business promotion on the Web, known as e-business. **E-business** is another form of e-advertising and promotion in which companies selling to business customers (rather than to household consumers) rely on the Internet to send messages and close sales (we'll cover this in detail in Chapter 16).

Because of advances in technology, firms like Procter & Gamble continue to invest heavily in newer means of connecting with consumers and potential consumers. Reaching target customers, P&G has developed and maintains dozens of websites for the company's approximately 300 brands to serve and interact with customers.[31] P&G also has gone beyond just product-oriented sites and has launched "relationship building" sites like Beinggirl, a teen community site (Exhibit 4.58). With such a site, the firm can gather data, test new product ideas, and experiment with interactivity. For example, if a website visitor wants to know what nail polish will match the lipstick she just saw in a commercial, she can get an immediate answer. Thus, target audiences do not have to be broadly defined by age or geographic groups—individual households can be targeted through direct interaction with audience members. Consumers come to the advertiser looking for things, rather than the advertisers merely shouting at millions hoping something sticks here and there. Also note that P&G can reach a global audience through Beinggirl.com without the cost and time-consuming effort of placing traditional media ads in dozens of markets. Furthermore, the consumer comes willingly to the advertiser, not the other way around as in the case of the more intrusive traditional media that seek consumers out, like it or not. Social networking sites such as Facebook have made brand communities and personal identity projects the stuff of e-commerce.

Exhibit 4.54 Seems intense to us. So is the idea to get you to associate one quality of the brand. And the image is for... what? See if you can explain.

Courtesy, The Clorox Company

31. Beth Snyder Bulik, "Procter & Gamble's Great Web Experiment," *Business 2.0,* November 28, 2000, 48–54.

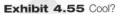

Exhibit 4.55 Cool?

Exhibit 4.56 Do you think this is the best positioning for Pepsi? What does this ad say about the brand?

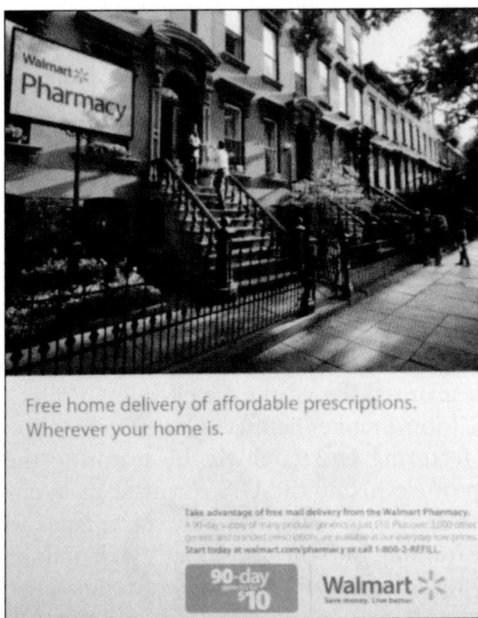

Exhibit 4.57 What about the NEW Walmart? Does this capture where they want to go?

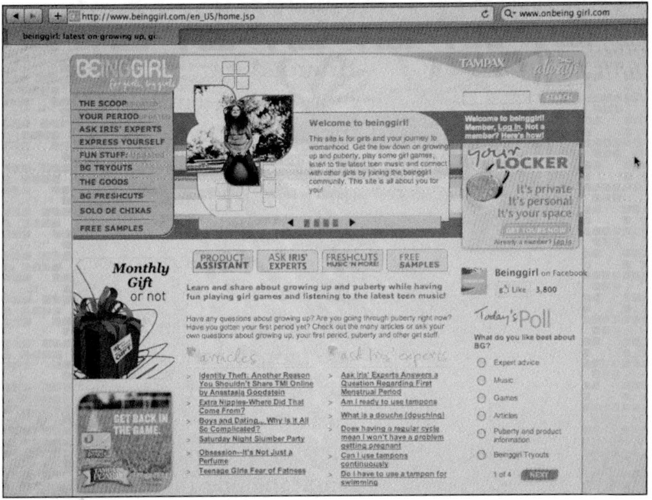

Exhibit 4.58 P&G's communal Beinggirl website is a good example of online brand community building with global reach. http://www.beinggirl.com

Photo courtesy, Susan Van Etten; PRNewFoto/MTV; Photo courtesy, Susan Van Etten; Photo courtesy, Susan Van Etten

Social Media

Love Child

Ok.... Lady Gaga is Andy Warhol and Madonna's Love Child. Has to be.

Simultaneous celebration and critique of branded products meets out-there pop-celebrity-performance art.

According to *Advertising Age*, *"the most-talked about aspect of Lady Gaga's Beyonce co-starring, Jonas Akerlund-directed music video for "Telephone"..., was not the singer's flagrant partial nudity, girl-on-girl kissing, or mass-murder sequence in a diner featuring Tyrese Gibson.*

It was the product placement.

At least nine different brands make appearances in the nine-minute music video, from Gaga's own Heartbeats headphones to a "Beats Limited Edition" laptop, from HP Envy to "telephone" partner Virgin Mobile, and from Miracle Whip and Wonder Bread to Diet Coke.

Troy Carter, CEO of Coalition Media Group, Gaga's management firm, said that if MJ's *Thriller* were shot today, that it would be chock full of placements.

Some of Gaga's placements were paid for, like Miracle Whip, but some were not... like Diet Coke. Apparently, she really does like to curl her hair with Diet Coke cans.

Plentyoffish.com, an online dating site paid for their placement and said they reaped a 15 percent bump in business almost immediately.

And, the cost of all this was way low compared to anything in traditional media...

So, pick a band/performer and figure out what you would do to promote the band/performer and use the promotion as an advertising/brand promotion vehicle.

How creative are you?

Source: *Advertising Age*, "How Miracle Whip, Plenty of Fish Tapped Lady Gaga's 'Telephone': Singer's Manager Dishes on All Those Product-Placement Deals (and Lack Thereof) in the Nine-Minute Video," by Andrew Hampp and Emily Bryson York, March 13, 2010.

Branded Entertainment.

Branded entertainment is the blending of advertising and integrated brand promotion with entertainment, primarily film, music, and television programming. A subset of branded entertainment is *product placement,* the significant placement of brands within films or television programs. When Tom Cruise wore Ray Bans in the film *Top Gun,* when James Bond switched to the BMW Z8 from his beloved Aston Martin (by the way, he has switched back), and when the cast of *Friends* drank Pepsi, audiences took notice. Well, branded entertainment takes product placement a quantum leap forward. With branded entertainment, a brand is not only a bit player; it also is the star of the program. An early participant in branded entertainment and still a leader in using the technique is BMW. BMW launched the BMW Web film series in 2001 and has featured the work of well-known directors, including Wong Kar-Wai, Ang Lee, John Frankenheimer, Guy Ritchie, and Alejandro González Iñárritu. Other sites featuring entertainment by featuring the brand include Lipton Tea (http://www.lipton.com) and the U.S. Army at its Web-based computer game (http://www.goarmy.com). There are many advantages to branded entertainment—among them, not running into the consumer's well-trained resistance mechanisms to ads and not having to go through all the ad regulations. In an ad BMW has to use a disclaimer ("closed track, professional driver") when it shows its cars tearing around, but in movies, like *The Italian Job,* no such disclaimer is required. Also, movies have been seen by the courts as artistic speech, not as the less protected "commercial speech." Branded entertainment, therefore, gets more First Amendment protection than ordinary advertising does. This is an important

Exhibit 4.59 Will this form of brand communication work?

Exhibit 4.60 Is this better than a traditional ad? Why?

Photo courtesy, Susan Van Etten; PRNewsFoto/Dr. Pepper

distinction, since regulation and legal fights surrounding ads represent a large cost of doing business. This merger of advertising with music, film, television, and other telecom arenas (such as cell phones) is often referred to as Madison & Vine, a nod to New York's Madison Avenue, the traditional home of the advertising industry, and the famous Hollywood intersection of Hollywood and Vine. We will talk more about this later. Suffice it to say for now, branded entertainment has opened up enormous real possibilities for what has become a much cluttered and a bit beat-up traditional advertising industry. See Exhibits 4.59 through 4.61 for examples.

As you can imagine, advertisers love the exposure that branded entertainment can provide. And entertainment venues are more fully protected (as artistic expression) by the First Amendment provisions for free speech in the United States and

Exhibit 4.61 Is this a good creative match for the medium?

PRNewsFoto/SKYY Vodka, Francine Fleischer

therefore skirt much of the regulation imposed on traditional advertising. But not all consumers are wildly enthusiastic about the blurring line between advertising and entertainment. One survey showed that 52 percent of respondents were worried about advertisers influencing entertainment content.

But in just exactly what real world is it that there are no real brands visible and being used? Personally, we don't think today's consumers find it particularly distracting at all, particularly if it's done well.

5 The Value of History.

As intriguing as new technology like Wi-Fi is, and as exciting as new communications options like Web films may be, we shouldn't jump to the conclusion that everything about advertising will change. So far, it hasn't. Advertising will still be a paid attempt to persuade. As a business process, advertising will still be one of the primary marketing mix tools that contribute to revenues and profits by stimulating demand and nurturing brand loyalty. Even though the executives at P&G believe there is a whole new world of communication and have developed dozens of websites to take advantage of this new world, the firm still spends about $3.5 billion a year on traditional advertising through traditional media.[32] It is also safe to argue that consumers will still be highly involved in some product decisions and not so involved in others, so that some messages will be particularly relevant and others will be completely irrelevant to forming and maintaining beliefs and feelings about brands. To this date, technology (particularly e-commerce) has changed the way people shop, gather information, and purchase. And although the advance in online advertising continues, net TV revenues are still attractive. Where else are you going to get such an enormous audience with sight and sound?

In this chapter, we have tried to offer a historical perspective on advertising, and a very practical one. As a lot of smart people know, history is very practical. You don't have to make the same mistakes over and over. Avoid Groundhog Day reality. Learn what works and doesn't work from the past.

32. "100 Leading National Advertisers," *Advertising Age,* June 8, 2004, S4.

Summary

1 Tell the story of advertising's birth.

Although some might contend that the practice of advertising began thousands of years ago, it is more meaningful to connect advertising as we know it today with the emergence of capitalistic economic systems. In such systems, business organizations must compete for survival in a free market setting. In this setting, it is natural that a firm would embrace a tool that assists it in persuading potential customers to choose its products over those offered by others. The explosion in production capacity that marked the Industrial Revolution gave demand-stimulation tools added importance. Mass moves of consumers to cities and modern times helped create, along with advertising, consumer culture.

2 Describe the past and current relationship between advertisers, retailers, and consumers.

Advertising and branding play a key role in the ongoing power struggle between manufacturers and their retailers. U.S. manufacturers began branding their products in the late 1800s. Advertising could thus be used to build awareness of and desire for the various offerings of a particular manufacturer. Retailers have power in the marketplace deriving from the fact that they are closer to the customer. When manufacturers can use advertising to build customer loyalty to their brands, they take part of that power back. Lately, big retailers have been reclaiming that power. Of course, in a capitalistic system, power and profitability are usually related.

3 Discuss several significant eras in the evolution of advertising in the United States, and relate important changes in advertising practice to fundamental changes in society and culture. How did successful advertising leverage the social and cultural forces of their day?

Social and economic trends, along with technological developments, are major determinants of the way advertising is practiced in any society. Before the Industrial Revolution, advertising's presence in the United States was barely noticeable. With an explosion in economic growth around the turn of the century, modern advertising was born: The "P. T. Barnum era" and the 1920s established advertising as a major force in the U.S. economic system. With the Great Depression and World War II, cynicism and paranoia regarding advertising began to grow. This concern led to refinements in practice and more careful regulation of advertising in the 1960s and 1970s. Consumption was once again in vogue during the designer era of the 1980s. The new communication technologies that emerged in the 1990s era seem certain to affect significant changes in future practice. Finally, the interactive, wireless, and broadband technologies that are leading advertising into the 21st century hold great promise but a hard-to-predict future.

4 Tell the story of consumer empowerment and branded entertainment, and understand how it works.

Integrated, interactive, and *wireless* have become the advertising buzzwords of the early 21st century. These words represent notable developments that are reshaping advertising practice. This is so because the technologies present advertisers with new options like Web films or feature films that highlight brands—a process known as advertainment. In addition, consumers can use Wi-Fi systems, limited-area wireless access systems, to provide more mobility in their use of computers. Integrated brand promotion may continue to grow in importance as advertisers work with more-varied media options to reach markets that are becoming even more fragmented. A variety of advertisers are using interactive media to reach consumers in the digital realm, while the use of services like TiVo demonstrates a consumer backlash against the ubiquity of advertising. Consumers are taking over many of the functions of traditional marketers and advertisers.

Identify forces that will continue to affect the evolution of advertising and integrated brand promotion.

History is practical. Consumers will always be affected by social and cultural change and thus represent advertising and IBP opportunity.

Key Terms

Industrial Revolution
principle of limited liability
branding
dailies
consumer culture
Pure Food and Drug Act
Great Depression
Great Recession
subliminal advertising
creative revolution
Action for Children's Television
Federal Trade Commission (FTC)
National Advertising Review Board
interactive media
consumer-generated content (CGC)
e-business
branded entertainment

Questions

1. Why does advertising that resolves cultural contradictions work?

2. Explain why there is a strong relationship between increasing urbanization and per capita spending.

3. How do manufacturers gain or lose power in the channel of distribution? What other parties are involved in this power struggle?

4. Describe the various factors that produced an explosion of advertising activity in the "P. T. Barnum era."

5. The 1950s were marked by great suspicion about advertisers and their potential persuasive powers. Do you see any lingering effects of this era in attitudes about advertising today?

6. The "creative revolution" that handed more authority to agency art directors and copywriters in the 1960s led to key shifts in the appearance and message of mainstream advertising. Describe these changes and how they continue to influence advertising today.

7. There were many important developments in the 1970s that set the stage for advertising in the Reagan era. Which of these developments are likely to have the most enduring effects on advertising practice in the future?

8. Why is branded entertainment important to the future of advertising and brand promotion?

9. Review the technological developments that have had the greatest impact on the advertising business. What new technologies are emerging that promise more profound changes for advertisers in the next decade?

10. What creative trends in ads have emerged in the period from 2001 to the present?

Experiential Exercises

1. What will be the next era in advertising? Some experts predict that smartphones will soon be more important to advertisers than the Internet was during the e-revolution. Identify today's most popular smartphone apps and suggest how advertisers might use them to advertise products and services to target audiences.

2. Branded entertainment has widespread acceptance in television and film, and now theme parks are getting in on the action. The *Harry Potter* book series may have reached its end, but Universal Orlando Resort is keeping the magic alive with the Wizarding World of Harry Potter, an enchanting amusement park exhibit where visitors become completely immersed in J. K. Rowling's fantasy world—complete with majestic replica of Hogwarts. Write a report on the 20-acre park and explain how Universal Studios, J. K. Rowling, and Warner Bros. use this branded entertainment to keep the Potter marketing franchise going.

3. The practice of advertising has evolved during the past century, adapting to the culture's social and economic changes. Following the directions below, analyze distinctions between key eras in advertising history using the online database adflip.com, which features advertisements from the 1940s to the present.

a. Browse Adflip's extensive database and select two ads from different decades of advertising history. Briefly describe the ads and explain how they fit the general characteristics of advertising during that era as defined in this chapter.

b. Select an ad from the Adflip site that does not seem to reflect general characteristics of its era. How does the ad differ from typical ads of this period? Do you think the difference is intentional? Explain.

4. As early as the 1920s, advertisers recognized that women had authority over as much as 80 percent of household purchases. From that point forward, women have been primary targets for the ad world—even in product categories that might traditionally be viewed as male oriented. To evaluate how that remains true today, locate a prominent advertisement for a product or service in each of these three categories: home improvement, automotive, and financial. For each ad, identify how the brand is appealing to women and why. Do you believe the campaign is likely to be successful in attracting female consumers? Why or why not?

Part 2

Analyzing the Environment for Advertising and Integrated Brand Promotion

Successful advertising and integrated brand promotion rely on a clear understanding of how and why consumers make their purchase decisions. Successful brand communication is rooted in sound marketing strategies and careful research about a brand's market environment. This understanding of the consumer and the market, sound strategy, and research are brought together in an advertising and IBP plan. Part 2, "Analyzing the Environment for Advertising and Integrated Brand Promotion," discusses the many important bases for the development of an advertising and IBP plan. Consumer behavior (Chapter 5) must be understood, segments must be analyzed, positioning the brand needs to be determined (Chapter 6), and research must be carried out in a systematic and analytical manner (Chapter 7). This section concludes with a complete chapter that lays out the process of planning advertising and integrated brand promotion, including the unique challenges of planning for international markets (Chapter 8).

Chapter 5

Advertising, Consumer Behavior, and Integrated Brand Promotion begins with an assessment of the way consumers make product and brand choices. These decisions depend on consumers' involvement and prior experiences with brands in a product category. This chapter also addresses consumer behavior, advertising, and IBP from both psychological and sociocultural points of view, considering individual and social/cultural influences on brand choice. This includes a discussion of ads as social text and how they transmit sociocultural meaning.

Chapter 6

Market Segmentation, Positioning, and the Value Proposition details how these three fundamental marketing planning efforts are developed by an organization. With a combination of audience and competitive information, including psychographics and lifestyle research, product and service brands are developed to provide benefits that are both valued by target customers and different from those of the competition. The process for segmenting business markets is also addressed. Finally, the way advertising contributes to communicating value to consumers is explained and modeled.

Chapter 7

Research in Advertising and Promotion is organized into three main parts that discuss the key types of research conducted by advertisers and their part in planning an advertising and IBP effort. These three parts are developmental advertising and IBP research, copy research, and results research. The methods used to track the effectiveness of ads during and after a launch are highlighted. Finally, account planning's role is also covered in this chapter.

Chapter 8

Planning for Advertising and Integrated Brand Promotion explains how formal advertising plans are developed. The chapter begins by putting the advertising and IBP planning process into the context of the overall marketing planning process. The inputs to the advertising and IBP plan are laid out in detail, and the process of setting advertising objectives—both communications and sales objectives—is described. The methods for setting budgets are presented, including the widely adopted and preferred objective-and-task approach. This chapter concludes with a discussion of planning for advertising and IBP in international markets. Overcoming cultural barriers to communication is considered. In the midst of a trend toward international trade, marketers are redefining the nature and scope of the markets for their goods and services while adjusting to the creative, media, and regulatory challenges of competing across national boundaries.

Chapter 5

Advertising, Consumer Behavior, and Integrated Brand Promotion

After reading and thinking about this chapter, you will be able to do the following:

1. Describe the four basic stages of consumer decision making.
2. Explain how consumers adapt their decision-making processes as a function of involvement and experience.
3. Discuss how advertising may influence consumer behavior through its effects on various psychological states.
4. Discuss the role of culture in creating effective ads.
5. Discuss the role of sociological factors in consumer behavior and advertising.
6. Discuss how effective advertising uses sociocultural meaning in order to sell things.

Introductory Scenario: Ay Caramba!

In the summer of 2007, 7-Eleven and *The Simpsons* teamed up for a very contemporary piece of branded entertainment, cross-promotion, and buzz advertising.[1] Literally overnight, 12 U.S. and Canadian 7–Elevens were remodeled into Kwik-E-Marts from *The Simpsons* show. (The new look lasted one month, and then the stores reverted to 7–Elevens.) The idea was to promote the release of *The Simpsons Movie* and, for 7–Eleven, to attract a crop of new customers: die-hard Simpson fans. The change was total: Professional set designers installed more than a thousand items, including KrustyO's and Buzz Cola (see Exhibit 5.1). Duff Beer was not included due to concerns of the rating of the movie (PG) and the age of some consumers… d'oh! Gracie Films, the production company for *The Simpsons*, fought hard but failed to get month-old stale hot dogs into the deal. The Squishee made it in. Some have called this "reverse product placement." Tim Stock, of Scenario DNA, said, "It's pop culture commenting on pop culture commenting on itself." So, what do you think? Good idea? Who wins—the Simpsons or 7-Eleven? Both? Neither? Welcome to 21st-century consumer culture and advertising. The agency was FreshWorks, an Omnicom Group virtual-agency network headed up by Tracy Locke of Dallas.

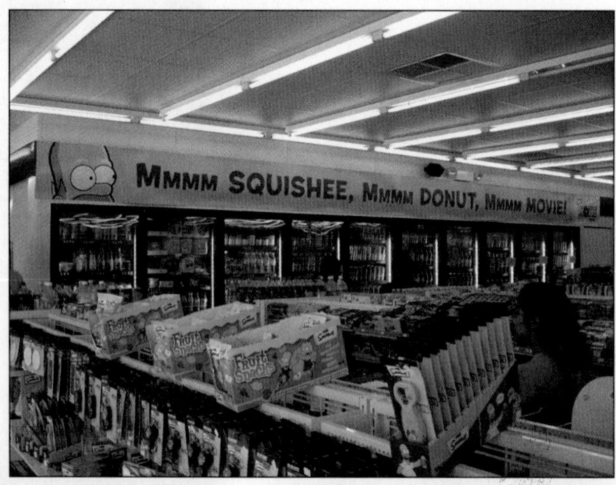

Exhibit 5.1 Buzz Cola wasn't the only buzz created by this partnership between the makers of The Simpsons Movie and 7-Eleven.

© Susan Sheldon

1. Kate MacArthur, "Marriage of Convenience: 7-Eleven, 'Simpsons'," *Advertising Age,* July 16, 2007.

Consumer behavior is defined as all things related to how humans operate as consumers. In other words, if it has anything to do with consuming, it's part of consumer behavior. Like all human behavior, the behavior of consumers is rich and varied. It is unarguably better for advertisers to understand consumer behavior than not, although we readily admit some companies sell lots of things with a pretty thin understanding of how their customers operate. Sometimes companies succeed despite their best efforts at maintaining ignorance, often due to factors such as being the first (pioneer effect), the biggest (round up the usual suspects), or the luckiest. But, if you would like to significantly improve your odds: understand your consumer.

This chapter summarizes the concepts and frameworks we believe are most helpful in trying to understand consumer behavior as it most closely related to advertising and integrated brand promotion. We will describe consumer behavior and attempt to explain it, in its incredible diversity, from two different perspectives. By "perspective" we literally mean a point-of-view or a focus. One is psychological: what happens in consumer's heads. It portrays consumers as systematic decision makers who process information, including information from advertisers. The second perspective views consumers as social beings who behave largely as a function of social circumstance and forces. These two perspectives are different ways of looking at the exact same people and many of the exact same behaviors. Although different in some assumptions, both of these perspectives offer something very valuable to the task of creating working advertising and brand promotion.

We discuss both perspectives because no one perspective can adequately explain consumer behavior. Consumers are psychological, social, cultural, and economic beings all at the same time. For example, suppose a sociologist and a psychologist both saw someone buying a car. The psychologist might explain this behavior in terms of attitudes, decision criteria, memory, and the like, whereas the sociologist would probably explain it in terms of the buyer's social circumstances (that is, income, housing conditions, social class, cultural capital of the brand, and so on), and forces acing upon him or her: social identity, resolution of cultural contradictions, and class considerations. Both explanations can be valid, but incomplete. Why you or any other consumer buys a movie ticket rather than a lottery ticket, or Pepsi rather than Coke, or KFC rather than Wendy's is a function of psychological, economic, sociological, anthropological, historical, and other forces. With this in mind, we offer two perspectives on consumer behavior and advertising.

1 Perspective One: The Consumer as Decision Maker.

One way to view consumer behavior is as a fairly predictable sequential process culminating with the individual's reaping a set of benefits from a product or service that satisfies that person's perceived needs. In this basic view, we can think of individuals as purposeful decision makers who either weigh and balance alternatives or resort, typically in times of complexity and too much information, to simple decision rules of thumb (heuristics) to make things easier. Often (but not always) this process occurs in a straightforward sequence and is a good way to think about consumer decision making generally. Many consumption episodes can be conceived as a sequence of four basic stages:

1. Need recognition
2. Information search and alternative evaluation
3. Purchase
4. Postpurchase use and evaluation

Exhibit 5.2 Every season has its holidays, and with those holidays come a particular array of consumption needs. Even lobsters.

PRNewsFoto/Red Lobster

The Consumer Decision-Making Process.

A brief discussion of what typically happens at each stage will give us a foundation for understanding consumers, and it can also illuminate opportunities for developing more powerful advertising.

Need Recognition. The consumption process begins when people perceive a need. A **need state** arises when one's desired state of affairs differs from one's actual state of affairs. Need states are accompanied by a mental discomfort or anxiety that motivates action; the severity of this discomfort can be widely variable depending on the genesis of the need. For example, the need state that arises when one runs out of toothpaste would involve very mild discomfort for most people, whereas the need state that accompanies the breakdown of one's automobile on a dark and deserted highway in North Dakota or Sweden in mid-February can approach true desperation.

One way advertising works is to point to and thereby activate needs that will motivate consumers to buy a product or service. For instance, in the fall, advertisers from product categories as diverse as autos, snowblowers, and footwear roll out predictions for another severe winter and encourage consumers to prepare themselves before it's too late. Every change of season brings new needs, large and small, and advertisers are always at the ready. The coming of the holidays is typically a cause for celebration and gifting. How about a lobster under that tree (Exhibit 5.2)? You can probably think of plenty of examples of an ad saying, "Hey, you need this because…"

Many factors can influence the need states of consumers. For instance, Maslow's hierarchy of needs suggests that a consumer's level of affluence can have a dramatic effect on what types of needs he or she perceives as relevant. The less fortunate are concerned with fundamental needs, such as food and shelter; more-affluent consumers may fret over which new piece of Williams-Sonoma kitchen gadgetry or other accoutrement to place in their uptown condo. The former's needs are predominantly for physiological survival and basic comfort, whereas the latter's may have more to do with seeking to validate personal accomplishments and derive status and recognition through consumption and social display. Even though income clearly matters in this regard, it would be a mistake to believe that the poor have no aesthetic concerns, or that the rich are always oblivious to the need for basic essentials. The central point is that a variety of needs can be fulfilled through consumption, and it is reasonable to suggest that consumers' needs are often sufficiently recognized and motivating to many consumers. Products and services should provide benefits that fulfill consumers' needs; hence, one of the advertiser's primary jobs is to make the connection between the two for the consumer. Benefits come in many forms. Some are more "functional"—that is, they derive from the more objective performance characteristics of a product or service. Convenience, reliability, nutrition, durability, and energy efficiency are descriptors that refer to **functional benefits.** Consumers may also choose products that provide **emotional benefits**; these are not typically found in some tangible feature or objective characteristic of a product. Emotional benefits are more subjective and may be perceived differently

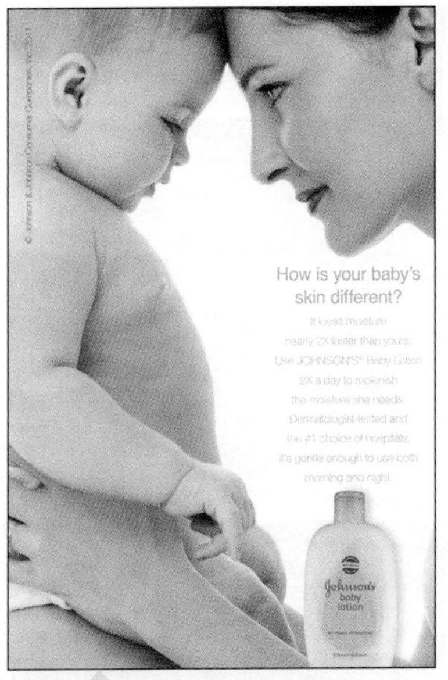

Exhibit 5.3 All parents want to be good to their child. This ad promises both functional benefits and emotional rewards for diligent parents. www.jnj.com

Exhibit 5.4 Functional benefits rule in this ad. It's all about precision and accuracy in time keeping.

Exhibit 5.5 This ad for a Dubey & Schaldenbrand watch is as much about feeling as it is about performance.

from one consumer to the next. Products and services help consumers feel pride, avoid guilt, relieve fear, and experience pleasure. These are powerful consumption motives that advertisers often try to activate. Can you find the emotional benefits promised in Exhibit 5.3?

Advertisers must develop a keen appreciation for the kinds of benefits that consumers derive from their brands. Even within the same product category, the benefits promised may vary widely. For instance, as shown in Exhibit 5.4, the makers of Ernst Benz timepieces present a simple, important promise. You buy an Ernst Benz watch and you will always know the precise time. Conversely, the ad for Dubey & Schaldenbrand watches, shown in Exhibit 5.5, is more about feelings than performance. Here, the implied benefit is the pride one feels from being recognized as the owner of a prestigious timepiece. These dramatically disparate ads illustrate that consumers will look for different kinds of benefits, even in a seemingly straightforward product category like watches. To create advertising that resonates with your consumers, you better have a good handle on the benefits they are looking for, or might look for, if only you suggested it.

Information Search and Alternative Evaluation. Given that a consumer has recognized a need, it is often not obvious what would be the best way to satisfy that need. For example, if you have a fear of being trapped in a blizzard in North Dakota, a condo on Miami Beach may be a much better solution than a Jeep or new snow tires. Need recognition simply sets in motion a process that may involve an extensive information search and careful evaluation of alternatives prior to purchase. Of course, during this search and evaluation, there are numerous opportunities for the advertiser to influence the final decision.

Once a need has been recognized, information for the decision is acquired through an internal or external search. The consumer's first option for information is to draw on personal experience and prior knowledge. This **internal search** for information may be all that is required. When a consumer has considerable prior experience with the products in question, attitudes about the alternatives may be well established and determine choice, as the Campbell's soup ad shown in Exhibit 5.6 suggests.

Exhibit 5.6 For a cultural icon such as Campbell's soup, an advertiser can assume that consumers have some prior knowledge. Here the advertiser seeks to enhance that knowledge to lead people to use more canned soup. www.campbellsoups.com

Courtesy, Campbell Soup Company

An internal search can also tap into information that has accumulated in one's memory as a result of repeated advertising exposures, such as "Tide's In, Dirt's Out," or stored judgments, for example, "Apple computers are best; that's what I've decided." Advertisers want the result of internal search to result in their brand being in the "evoked set," that is the set of brands (usually two to five) that come to mind when a category is mentioned. I say "laundry detergent, and you say "Tide, All, Wisk." Here, the evoked set consists of three brands, all stored internally, found through internal search, and probably the product of advertising, use, and habit. The evoked set is usually highly related to the **consideration set,** the set of the brands the consumer will consider for purchase. If your brand is the first mentioned, you have achieved something even better: "top of mind." Many people believe that top-of-mind awareness best predicts purchase of fairly inexpensive and low-risk consumer packaged goods. Affecting people's beliefs about a brand before their actual use of it, or merely establishing the existence of the brand in the consumer's consciousness, is a critical function of advertising and other integrated brand promotion. As noted in Chapter 1, the purpose of delayed response advertising is to generate recognition of and a favorable predisposition toward a brand so that when consumers enter into search mode, that brand will be one they immediately consider as a possible solution to their needs. If the consumer has not used a brand previously and has no recollection that it even exists, then that brand probably will not be the brand of choice. Good retailing (such as point-of-purchase displays) can help, but prior awareness is a very good thing, and something advertising can do.

It is certainly plausible that an internal search will not turn up enough information to yield a decision. The consumer then proceeds with an **external search.** An external search involves visiting retail stores to examine the alternatives, seeking input from friends and relatives about their experiences with the products in question, or perusing professional product evaluations furnished in various publications such as *Consumer Reports* or *Car and Driver.* In addition, when consumers are in an active information-gathering mode, they may be receptive to detailed, informative advertisements delivered through any of the print media, or they may deploy a

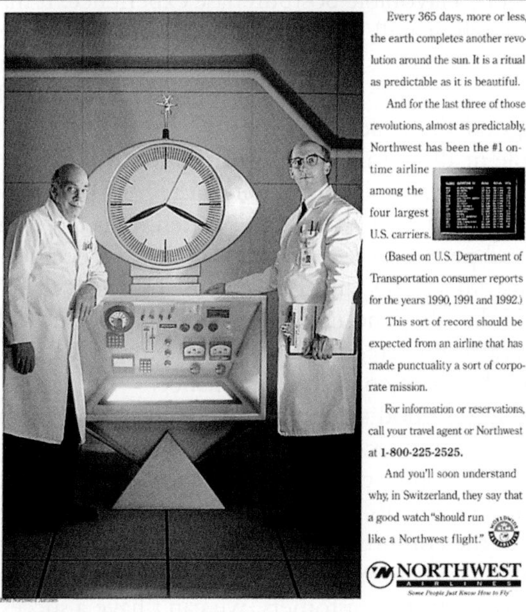

RECENTLY, SCIENTISTS IN BRAUNSCHWEIG, GERMANY, SET THE ATOMIC CLOCK BACK ONE FULL SECOND.
OUR FLIGHT SCHEDULES HAVE BEEN ADJUSTED ACCORDINGLY.
Every 365 days, more or less, the earth completes another revolution around the sun. It is a ritual as predictable as it is beautiful.
And for the last three of those revolutions, almost as predictably, Northwest has been the #1 on-time airline among the four largest U.S. carriers.
(Based on U.S. Department of Transportation consumer reports for the years 1990, 1991 and 1992.)
This sort of record should be expected from an airline that has made punctuality a sort of corporate mission.
For information or reservations, call your travel agent or Northwest at 1-800-225-2525.
And you'll soon understand why, in Switzerland, they say that a good watch "should run like a Northwest flight."
NORTHWEST
AIRLINES
Some People Just Know How to Fly

Exhibit 5.7 Advertisers must know the relevant evaluative criteria for their products. For an airline, on-time arrival is certainly an important matter. www.nwa.com

shopping agent or a search engine to scour the Internet for the best deal or for opinions of other users.

During an internal or external search, consumers are not merely gathering information for its own sake. They have some need that is propelling the process, and their goal is to make a decision that yields benefits for them. The consumer searches for and is simultaneously forming attitudes about possible alternatives. This is the alternative-evaluation component of the decision process, and it is another key phase for the advertiser to target.

Alternative evaluation will be structured by the consumer's consideration set and evaluative criteria. The consideration set is the subset of brands from a particular product category that becomes the focal point of the consumer's evaluation. Most product categories contain too many brands for all to be considered, so the consumer finds some way to focus the search and evaluation. For example, for autos, consumers may consider only cars priced less than $25,000, or only cars that have antilock brakes, or only foreign-made cars, or only cars sold at dealerships within a five-mile radius of their work or home. A critical function of advertising is to make consumers aware of the brand and keep them aware so that the brand has a chance to be part of the consideration set. A great many ads try to do just this.

As the search-and-evaluation process proceeds, consumers form evaluations based on the characteristics or attributes those brands in their consideration set have in common. These product attributes or performance characteristics are referred to as **evaluative criteria.** Evaluative criteria differ from one product category to the next and can include many factors, such as price, texture, warranty terms, service support, color, scent, or carb content. As Exhibit 5.7 suggests, one traditional evaluative criterion for judging airlines has been on-time arrivals.

It is critical for advertisers to have as complete an understanding as possible of the evaluative criteria that consumers use to make their buying decisions. They must also know how consumers rate their brand in comparison with others from the consideration set. Understanding consumers' evaluative criteria furnishes a powerful starting point for any advertising campaign and will be examined in more depth later in the chapter.

Purchase. At this third stage, purchase occurs. The consumer has made a decision, and a sale is made. Great, right? Well, to a point. As nice as it is to make a sale, things are far from over at the point of sale. In fact, it would be a big mistake to view purchase as the culmination of the decision-making process. No matter what the product or service category, the consumer is likely to buy from it again in the future. So, what happens after the sale is very important to advertisers. Advertisers want trial; they then want conversion (repeat purchase). They want brand loyalty. Some want to create brand ambassadors, users who will become apostles for the brand, spreading its gospel. At the same time, competitors will be working to convince consumers to give their brand a try.

Postpurchase Use and Evaluation. The goal for marketers and advertisers must not be simply to generate a sale; it must be to create satisfied and, ultimately, loyal customers. The data to support this position are quite astounding.

Research shows that about 65 percent of the average company's business comes from its present, satisfied customers, and that 91 percent of dissatisfied customers will never buy again from the company that disappointed them.[2] Thus, consumers' evaluations of products in use become a major determinant of which brands will be in the consideration set the next time around.

Customer satisfaction derives from a favorable postpurchase experience. It may develop after a single use, but more likely it will require sustained use. Advertising can play an important role in inducing customer satisfaction by creating appropriate expectations for a brand's performance, or by helping the consumer who has already bought the advertised brand to feel good about doing so.

Advertising plays an important role in alleviating the **cognitive dissonance** that can occur after a purchase. Cognitive dissonance is the anxiety or regret that lingers after a difficult decision, sometimes called "buyer's remorse." Often, rejected alternatives have attractive features that lead people to second-guess their own decisions. If the goal is to generate satisfied customers, this dissonance must be resolved in a way that leads consumers to conclude that they did make the right decision after all. Purchasing high-cost items or choosing from categories that include many desirable and comparable brands can yield high levels of cognitive dissonance.

When dissonance is expected, it makes good sense for the advertiser to reassure buyers with detailed information about its brands. Postpurchase reinforcement programs might involve direct mail, email, or other types of personalized contacts with the customer. This postpurchase period represents a great opportunity for the advertiser to have the undivided attention of the consumer and to provide information and advice about product use that will increase customer satisfaction. That's the name of the game: customer satisfaction. Without satisfied customers, we can't have a successful business. Nowadays, consumers often go to the Internet to find other purchasers of the product to tell them they did the right thing. Want to reduce your anxiety that you bought the right car? Go to a chat group or brand community for that brand, and the members will almost always tell you that you were really smart buying what you did. Some advertisers provide this type of post-purchase information to make you a satisfied customer.

2 Four Modes of Consumer Decision Making.

As you may be thinking, consumers aren't always deliberate and systematic; sometimes they are hasty, impulsive, or even irrational. Do they always go through these four stages in a slow and deliberate manner? No; not always. The search time that people put into their purchases can vary dramatically for different types of products. Would you give the purchase of a tube of toothpaste the same amount of effort as the purchase of a new backpack? Probably not, unless you've been chastised by your dentist recently: Buy a tartar control toothpaste! Why is that T-shirt you bought at Lollapalooza more important to you than the brand of orange juice you had for breakfast this morning? Does buying a Valentine's gift from Victoria's Secret create different feelings than buying a pack of gum? When you view a TV ad for car batteries, do you carefully memorize the information being presented so that you can draw on it the next time you're evaluating the brands in your consideration set, or will you wait to seek out that information when you really need it—like when your car won't start and the guy in the wrecker says your battery is dead?

Let's face it, some purchase decisions are just more engaging than others. In the following sections we will elaborate on the view of consumer as decision maker by explaining four decision-making modes that help advertisers appreciate the richness

2. Terry G. Vavra, *Aftermarketing: How to Keep Customers for Life through Relationship Marketing* (Homewood, IL: Business One Irwin, 1992), 13.

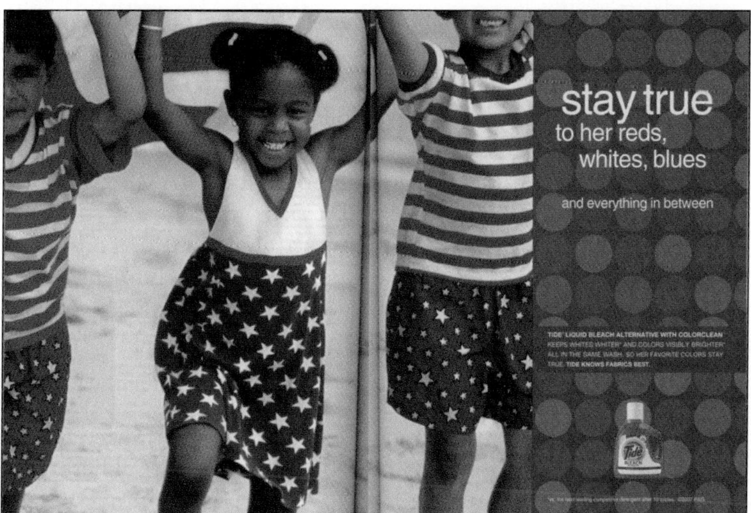

Exhibit 5.8 Sometimes feelings of patriotism can be aroused in a subtle, understated manner.

and complexity of consumer behavior. These four modes are determined by a consumer's involvement and prior experiences with the product or service in question.

Sources of Involvement. To accommodate the complexity of consumption decisions, those who study consumer behavior typically talk about the involvement level of any particular decision. **Involvement** is the degree of perceived relevance and personal importance accompanying the choice of a certain product or service within a particular context: how much it matters to you. Many things affect an individual's level of involvement with a consumption decision.[3] People can develop interests and avocations in many different areas, such as cooking, photography, pet ownership, and exercise and fitness. Such ongoing personal interests can enhance involvement levels in a variety of product categories. Also, any time a great deal of risk is associated with a purchase—perhaps as a result of the high price of the item, or because the consumer will have to live with the decision for a long period of time—one should also expect elevated involvement. So, cars are usually high involvement, things like gum are typically low involvement.

Consumers can also derive important symbolic meaning from products and brands. Ownership or use of some products can help people reinforce some aspect of their self-image or make a statement to other people who are important to them. If a purchase carries great symbolic and real consequences—such as choosing the right gift for a special someone on Valentine's Day—it will be highly involving.

Some purchases can also tap into deep emotional concerns or motives. For example, many marketers, from Walmart to Marathon Oil, have solicited consumers with an appeal to their patriotism. With Tide Bleach Alternative, as suggested in Exhibit 5.8, you don't have to be concerned with the red, white, and blue fading away. The ad for Casio watches (a Japanese product) in Exhibit 5.9 demonstrates that a product doesn't even have to be American to wrap itself in the stars and stripes. The passions of patriotism can significantly affect many things, including a person's level of involvement with a consumption decision.

Exhibit 5.9 The emotional appeal in this Casio ad is just one of the many involvement devices. The play on water resistance also increases involvement as the reader perceives the double meaning. Describe how these involvement devices work. How does Casio use involvement devices at its website, www.casio-usa.com, to encourage visitors to further explore its products on the site? Describe the involvement devices used by competitor Timex at its home page, www.timex.com.

3. Michael R. Solomon, *Consumer Behavior* (Upper Saddle River, NJ: Pearson/Prentice Hall, 2004), Ch. 4.

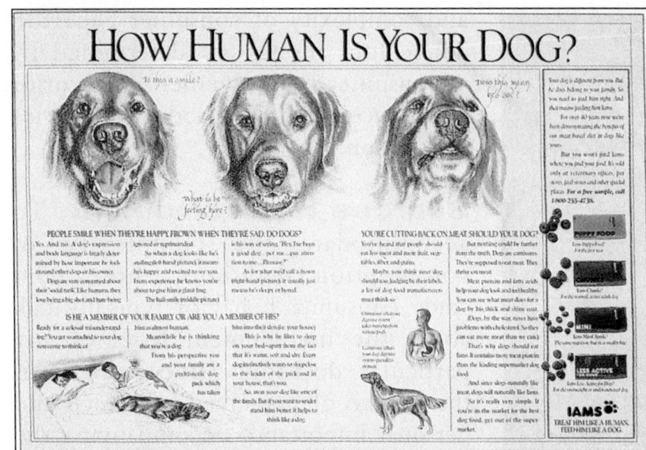

Exhibit 5.10 People who think of their pets as human take their selection of pet food very seriously. IAMS offers serious pet food for the serious dog owner. www.iams.com

Courtesy, The IAMS Company

Involvement levels vary not only among product categories for any given individual, but also among individuals for any given product category. For example, some pet owners will feed their pets only the expensive canned products that look and smell like people food. IAMS, whose ad is featured in Exhibit 5.10, understands this and made a special premium dog food for consumers who think of their pets as close-to-humans. Many other pet owners, however, are perfectly happy with feeding Rover from a 50-pound, economy-size bag of dry dog food.

Now we will use the ideas of involvement and prior experience to help conceive four different types of consumer decision making. These four modes are shown in Exhibit 5.11. Any specific consumption decision is based on a high or low level of prior experience with the product or service in question, and a high or low level of involvement. This yields the four modes of decision making: (1) extended problem solving; (2) limited problem solving; (3) habit or variety seeking; and (4) brand loyalty. Each is described in the following sections.

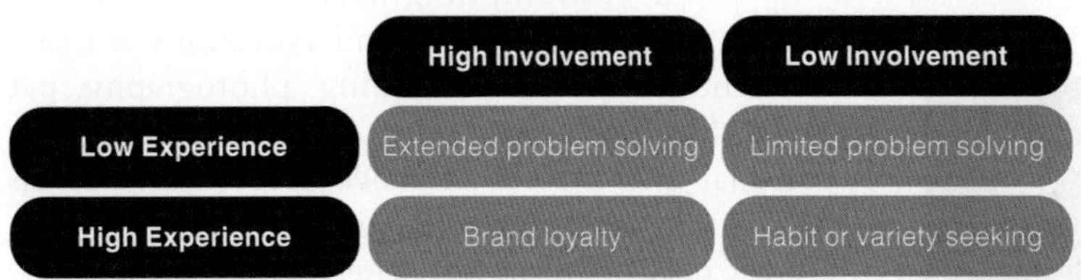

Exhibit 5.11 Four modes of consumer decision making.

Extended Problem Solving. When consumers are inexperienced in a particular consumption setting, yet find the setting highly involving, they are likely to engage in **extended problem solving.** In this mode, consumers go through a deliberate decision-making process that begins with explicit need recognition, proceeds with careful internal and external search, continues through alternative evaluation and purchase, and ends with a lengthy postpurchase evaluation.

Examples of extended problem solving come with decisions such as choosing a home or a diamond ring, as suggested by Exhibit 5.12.These products are expensive, are publicly evaluated, and can carry a considerable amount of risk in terms of making an uneducated decision. Buying one's first new automobile and choosing a college are two other consumption settings that may require extended problem solving. Extended problem solving is the exception, not the rule.

Limited Problem Solving. In this decision-making mode, experience and involvement are both low. **Limited problem solving** is a more common mode of decision making. In this mode, a consumer is less systematic in his or her decision making. The consumer has a new problem to solve, but it is not a problem that is interesting or engaging, so the information search is limited to simply trying the first brand encountered. For example, let's say a young couple has just brought home a new baby, and suddenly they perceive a very real need for disposable diapers. At the hospital they received complimentary trial packs of several products, including Pampers disposables. They try the Pampers, find them an acceptable solution to their messy new problem, and take the discount coupon that came with the sample to their local grocery, where they buy several packages. In the limited problem-solving mode, we often see consumers simply seeking adequate solutions to mundane problems. It is also a mode in which just trying a brand or two may be the most efficient way of collecting information about one's options. Of course, smart marketers realize that trial offers can be a

A MAN'S GUIDE *to buying* DIAMONDS

She's expecting DIAMONDS. *Don't* PANIC. We can help.

The way to a man's heart is through his stomach, but the way to a woman's usually involves a jeweler. Just think of golf clubs, or season tickets wrapped in a little black velvet box. That's how women feel about diamonds.

To know diamonds is to know her. Find out what she has her heart set on. Is it a pendant, anniversary band, or ear studs? You can find out by browsing with her, window shopping, watching her reactions to other women's jewelry. Go by body language, not just by what she says. Then, once you know the style, you can concentrate on the diamond.

Like people, no two diamonds are alike. Formed in the earth millions of years ago and found in the most remote corners of the world, rough diamonds are sorted by DeBeers' experts into over 5,000 grades before they go on to be cut and polished. So be aware of what you are buying. Two diamonds of the same size may vary widely in quality. And if a price looks too good to be true, it probably is.

Maybe a jeweler is a man's best friend. You want a diamond you can be proud of. So don't be attracted to a jeweler because of "bargain prices." Find someone you can trust. Ask questions. Ask friends who've gone through it. Ask the jeweler you choose why two diamonds that look the same are priced differently. You want someone who will help you determine quality and value using four characteristics called *The 4Cs.* They are: *Cut,* not the same as shape, but refers to the way the facets or flat surfaces are angled. A better cut offers more brilliance; *Color,* actually, close to no color is rarest; *Clarity,* the fewer natural marks or "inclusions" the better; *Carat weight,* the larger the diamond, usually the more rare. Remember, the more you know, the more confident you can be in buying a diamond you'll always be proud of. *Learn more.* For the booklet *"How to buy diamonds you'll be proud to give,"* call the American Gem Society, representing fine jewelers upholding gemological standards across the U.S., at 800-340-3028.

Compromise now? Where's your heart? Go for diamonds beyond her wildest dreams. Go for something that reflects how you really feel. You want nothing less than a diamond as unique as your love. Not to mention as beautiful as that totally perplexing creature who will wear it.

Diamond Information Center
Sponsored by De Beers Consolidated Mines, Ltd., Est. 1888.
A diamond is forever. DeBeers

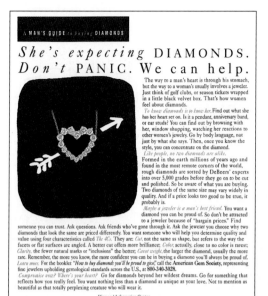

Exhibit 5.12 High involvement and low experience typically yield extended problem solving. Buying an engagement ring is a prefect example of this scenario. This ad offers lots of advice for the extended problem solver. De Beers is more than happy to be helpful here. www.adiamondisforever.com

preferred means of collecting information, and they facilitate trial of their brands through free samples, inexpensive "trial sizes," or discount coupons. It is in this mode that so much of consumer package goods (CPG) advertising and brand promotion occurs. Here, consumer memory is a huge factor.

Habit or Variety Seeking. Habit and variety seeking occur in settings where a decision isn't involving and a consumer repurchases from the category over and over again. In terms of sheer numbers, habitual purchases are probably the most common decision-making mode. Consumers find a brand of laundry detergent that suits their needs, they run out of the product, and they buy it again. The cycle repeats itself many times per year in an almost mindless fashion. Getting in the habit of buying only one brand can be a way to simplify life and minimize the time invested in "nuisance" purchases. When a consumer perceives little difference among the various competitive brands, it is easier to buy the same brand repeatedly. A lot of consumption decisions are boring but necessary. Habits help us minimize the inconvenience.

In some product categories where a buying habit would be expected, an interesting phenomenon called variety seeking may be observed instead. Remember, **habit** refers to buying a single brand repeatedly as a solution to a simple consumption problem. This can be very tedious, and some consumers fight the boredom through variety seeking; this of course happens in many life domains. **Variety seeking** refers to the tendency of consumers to switch their selection among various brands in a given category in a seemingly random pattern. This is not to say that a consumer will buy just any brand; he or she probably has two to five brands that all provide similar levels of satisfaction to a particular consumption problem. However, from one purchase occasion to the next, the individual will switch brands from within this set, just for the sake of variety.

Variety seeking is most likely to occur in frequently purchased categories where sensory experience, such as taste or smell, accompanies product use. In such categories, no amount of ad spending can overcome the consumer's basic desire for fresh sensory experience.[4] Satiation occurs after repeated use and leaves the consumer looking for a change of pace. Product categories such as soft drinks and alcoholic beverages, snack foods, breakfast cereals, and fast food are prone to variety seeking, so marketers in these categories must constantly be introducing new possibilities to consumers to feed their craving for variety. One day you open your lunch and your old, faithful bologna and cheese on white bread just doesn't cut it anymore—especially if a marketer has presented you with a fresh, new choice (see Exhibit 5.13).

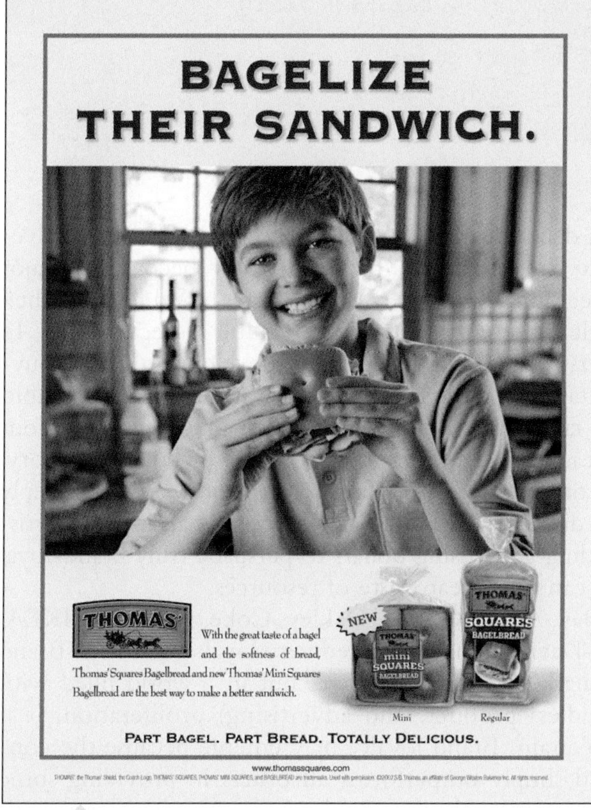

Exhibit 5.13 Bored with bread? Thomas offers you a chance for a little variety.

Courtesy, The Diamond Information Center; Courtesy, George Weston Bakeries

4. Shirley Leung, "Fast-Food Firms Big Budgets Don't Buy Consumer Loyalty," *The Wall Street Journal,* July 24, 2003, B4.

Ethics

Discovering Diversity, Courting Gay Consumers

With a simple ad about a couple shopping for a dining room table, Swedish home-furniture manufacturer IKEA in 1994 broke down a long-standing cultural barrier in advertising. What was so special about the no-frills television spot? The couple it featured debating furniture styles and finishing each other's sentences like an old married couple were two gay men.

The ad was one of the first gay-friendly commercials aired by a major corporation, and it generated controversy. But in the decade that followed, the ad became a touchstone for advertisers rethinking how to market to gay and lesbian consumers.

A steady stream of advertising aimed at the gay market followed. The car manufacturer Subaru reached out to lesbian women with tennis great Martina Navratilova, an openly gay athlete. More than 60 major marketers, including Anheuser-Busch, Dell, Sears, and Sony, have advertised on Logo, the fledgling gay cable channel from media giant Viacom. And IKEA in late 2006 prominently featured a gay couple in another mainstream ad, this time with a young child and a golden retriever, in an advertisement for living room furniture that closes with the line: "Why shouldn't sofas come in flavors, just like families?"

Much has changed since IKEA's breakthrough dining room ad in 1994, but minefields still exist. Some gay and lesbian advocates have bristled at the marketing assumption that all homosexual consumers are affluent and urbane, as portrayed in popular television programs such as *Will & Grace* or the Bravo Channel's makeover series *Queer Eye for the Straight Guy*. In late 2005, Ford Motor Co. dropped advertising for its Land Rover and Jaguar brands in gay-oriented publications after the threat of a boycott by the conservative American Family Association.

But the automaker reversed course swiftly. Less than two weeks after saying it would eliminate advertising in gay publications, the company said it actually would expand such advertising to include its core brands such as Ford, Mercury, Mazda, and Lincoln.

Sources: Aparna Kumar, "Commercials: Out of the Closet," http://www.wired.com, May 8, 2001; Stuart Elliott, "Hey, Gay Spender, Marketers Spending Time with You," *The New York Times*, June 26, 2006, C8; Jeremy W. Peters, "Ford, Reversing Decision, Will Run Ads in Gay Press," *The New York Times*, December 15, 2005, C4.

Brand Loyalty. The final decision-making mode is typified by high involvement and rich prior experience. In this mode, **brand loyalty** becomes a major consideration in the purchase decision. Consumers demonstrate brand loyalty when they repeatedly purchase a single brand as their choice to fulfill a specific need. In one sense, brand-loyal purchasers may look as if they have developed a simple buying habit; however, it is important to distinguish brand loyalty from simple habit. Brand loyalty is based on highly favorable attitudes toward the brand and a conscious commitment to find this brand each time the consumer purchases from this category. Conversely, habits are merely consumption simplifiers that are not based on deeply held convictions. Habits can be disrupted through a skillful combination of advertising and sales promotions. Spending advertising dollars to persuade truly brand-loyal consumers to try an alternative can be a great waste of resources.

Brands such as Starbucks, eBay, Apple, Gerber, Oakley, Coke, Heineken, IKEA, Calvin Klein, Tide, and Harley-Davidson have inspired very loyal consumers. Brand loyalty is something that any marketer aspires to have, but in a world filled with more-savvy consumers and endless product (and advertising) proliferation, it is becoming harder and harder to attain. Brand loyalty may emerge because the consumer perceives that one brand simply outperforms all others in providing some critical functional benefit. For example, the harried business executive may have grown loyal to FedEx's overnight delivery service as a result of repeated satisfactory experiences with FedEx—and as a result of FedEx's advertising that has repeatedly posed the question, "Why fool around with anyone else?"

Perhaps even more important, brand loyalty can be due to the emotional benefits that accompany certain brands. One of the strongest indicators for brand loyalty has to be the tendency on the part of some loyal consumers to tattoo their bodies with the insignia of their favorite brand. Although statistics are pretty new on this sort of thing, it is claimed that the worldwide leader in brand-name tattoos is Harley-Davidson. So, you are going to put something on your body for a lifetime, a brand name. What accounts for Harley's fervent following? Is Harley's brand loyalty simply a function of performing better than its many competitors? Or does a Harley rider derive some deep emotional benefit from taking that big bike out on the open road and leaving civilization far behind? To understand loyalty for a brand such as Harley, one must turn to the emotional benefits, such as feelings of pride, kinship, community with other Harley riders. Owning a Harley—and perhaps the tattoo—makes a person feel different and special. Harley ads are designed to reaffirm the deep emotional appeal of this product.

Strong emotional benefits might be expected from consumption decisions that we classify as highly involving, and they are major determinants of brand loyalty. Indeed, with so many brands in the marketplace, it is becoming harder and harder to create loyalty for one's brand through functional benefits alone. In fact, brand loyalty is usually much more about meaning and feelings than some often fictional "functional" benefit in the first place. There are a lot of product categories out there that could easily slip into being nothing more than interchangeable commodities (e.g., Wintel computers).To break free of this brand-parity problem and provide consumers with enduring reasons to become or stay loyal, advertisers are investing more and more effort in communicating the emotional benefits that might be derived from brands in categories as diverse as greeting cards (Hallmark—"When you care enough to send the very best") and vacation hot spots (Las Vegas—"What happens in Vegas, stays in Vegas"). You might go to YouTube and check out one of those Vegas spots, or some of the consumer-generated parodies. Many, probably most, companies are exploring ways to use the Internet to create dialogue and manage relations and even community with their customers. To do this, one must look for means to connect with customers at an emotional level.

3 Key Psychological Processes.

To complete our consideration of the consumer as a fairly thoughtful decision maker, one key issue remains. We need to examine the explicit psychological consequences of advertising. What does advertising leave in the minds of consumers that ultimately may influence their behavior? For those of you who have taken psychology courses, many of the topics in this section will sound familiar.

As we noted earlier in the chapter, a good deal of advertising is designed to ensure recognition and create favorable predispositions toward a brand so that as consumers search for solutions to their problems, they will think of the brand immediately. The goal of any delayed-response ad is to affect some psychological state that will subsequently influence a purchase.

Two ideas borrowed from social psychology are usually the center of attention when discussing the psychological aspects of advertising. First is attitude. **Attitude** is defined as an overall evaluation of any object, person, or issue that varies along a continuum, such as favorable to unfavorable or positive to negative. Attitudes are learned, and if they are based on substantial experience with the object or issue in question, they can be held with great conviction. Attitudes make our lives easier because they simplify decision making; that is, when faced with a choice among several alternatives, we do not need to process new information or analyze the merits of the alternatives. We merely select the alternative we think is the most favorable. We all possess attitudes on thousands of topics, ranging from political candidates to underage drinking. Marketers and advertisers, however, are most interested in one particular class of attitudes—brand attitudes.

Exhibit 5.14 An example of two consumers' beliefs about Caddies.

Consumer 1	Consumer 2
Cadillacs are clumsy to drive.	Cadillacs are luxurious.
Cadillacs are expensive.	Cadillacs have great resale value.
Cadillacs are gas guzzlers.	Cadillacs have OnStar.
Cadillacs are large.	Cadillac's TV ads rock!
Cadillacs are for senior citizens.	Cadillacs aren't what they used to be.

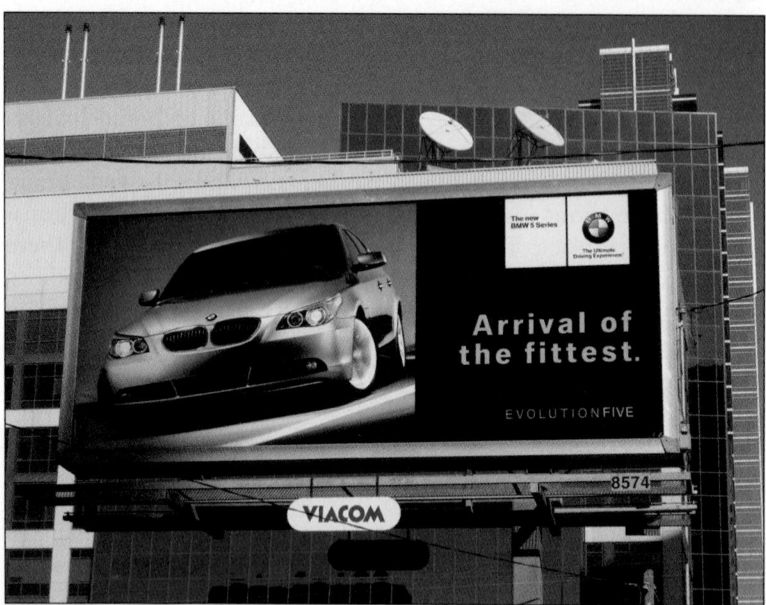

Exhibit 5.15 Changing consumers' beliefs is never an easy task. And the challenge is always made more complex by the fact that your best competition will only keep getting better. So for Cadillac the question becomes, even with a series of dramatic improvements, can they ever catch the Ultimate Driving Machine? It's the job of everyone who works for BMW to make sure that they don't....

Brand attitudes are summary evaluations that reflect preferences for various products and services. The next time you are waiting in a checkout line at the grocery, take a good look at the items in your cart. Those items are a direct reflection of your brand attitudes.

But what is the basis for these summary evaluations? Where do brand attitudes come from? Here we need a second idea from social psychology. To understand why people hold certain attitudes, we need to assess their specific beliefs. **Beliefs** represent the knowledge and feelings a person has accumulated about an object or issue. They can be logical and factual in nature, or biased and self-serving. A person might believe that the Mini Cooper is cute, that garlic consumption promotes weight loss, and that pet owners are lonely people. For that person, all these beliefs are valid and can serve as a basis for attitudes toward Minis, garlic, and pets.

If we know a person's beliefs, it is usually possible to infer attitude. Consider the two consumers' beliefs about Cadillac summarized in Exhibit 5.14. From their beliefs, we might suspect that one of these consumers is a prospective Cadillac owner, whereas the other will need a dramatic change in beliefs to ever make Cadillac part of his or her consideration set. It follows that the brand attitudes of the two individuals are at opposite ends of the favorableness continuum.

You may be aware that in recent years, General Motors has spent billions of dollars on its Cadillac brand in a determined effort to take on Japanese and German models like the exquisite BMW 5 Series, which is exalted on the Toronto billboard in Exhibit 5.15. Simply put, the folks at General Motors will need to change a lot of consumers' beliefs about Cadillac if they are to have success in regaining market share from the likes of Lexus and BMW. Among other things, our beliefs help determine the cars we drive (subject of course to the limitations of our pocketbooks).

People have many beliefs about various features and attributes of products and brands. Some beliefs are more important than others in determining a person's final evaluation of a brand. Typically, a small number of beliefs—on the order of five to nine—underlie brand attitudes.[5] These beliefs are the critical determinants of an attitude and are referred to as **salient beliefs**.

5. Icek Ajzen and Martin Fishbein, *Understanding Attitudes and Predicting Social Behavior* (Upper Saddle River, NJ: Prentice Hall, 1980), 63.

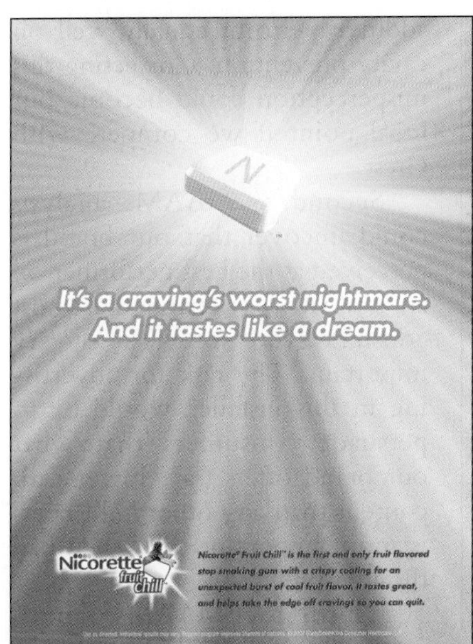

It's a craving's worst nightmare.
And it tastes like a dream.
Nicorette fruit chill
Nicorette® Fruit Chill™ is the first and only fruit flavored stop smoking gum with a crispy cooling for an unexpected burst of cool fruit flavor. It tastes great, and helps take the edge off cravings so you can quit.

Exhibit 5.16 Belief change is a common goal in advertising. Does this ad make you think differently about Nicorette?

Clearly, we would expect the number of salient beliefs to vary between product categories. The loyal Harley owner who proudly displays a tattoo will have many more salient beliefs about his bike than he has about his brand of shaving cream. Also, salient beliefs can be modified, replaced, or extinguished. For example, many people may have the belief that Nicorette Stop Smoking Gum doesn't taste very good. The ad for Nicorette Fruit Chill Gum in Exhibit 5.16 seeks to challenge that belief.

Since belief shaping and reinforcement can be one of the principal goals of advertising, it should come as no surprise that advertisers make belief assessment a focal point in their attempts to understand consumer behavior.

Multi-Attribute Attitude Models (MAAMs). **Multi-attribute attitude models (MAAMs)** provide a framework and a set of research procedures for collecting information from consumers to assess their salient beliefs and attitudes about competitive brands. Here we will highlight the basic components of a MAAMs analysis and illustrate how such an analysis can benefit the advertiser.

Any MAAMs analysis will feature four fundamental components:

- ***Evaluative criteria*** are the attributes or performance characteristics that consumers use in comparing competitive brands. In pursuing a MAAMs analysis, an advertiser must identify all evaluative criteria relevant to its product category.
- ***Importance weights*** reflect the priority that a particular evaluative criterion receives in the consumer's decision-making process. Importance weights can vary dramatically from one consumer to the next; for instance, some people will merely want good taste from their bowl of cereal, whereas others will be more concerned about fat and fiber content.
- The ***consideration set*** is that group of brands that represents the real focal point for the consumer's decision. For example, the potential buyer of a luxury sedan might be focusing on Acura, BMW, and Lexus. These and comparable brands would be featured in a MAAMs analysis. Cadillac could have a model, such as its reasonably new STS sedan, that aspired to be part of this consideration set, leading General Motors to conduct a MAAMs analysis featuring the STS and its foreign rivals. Conversely, it would be silly for GM to include the Chevy Malibu in a MAAMs analysis with this set of luxury/performance imports.
- ***Beliefs*** represent the knowledge and feelings that a consumer has about various brands. In a MAAMs analysis, beliefs about each brand's performance on all relevant evaluative criteria are assessed. Beliefs can be matters of fact—a 12-ounce Pepsi has 150 calories; a 12-ounce Coke Classic has 140—or highly subjective—the Cadillac XLR Roadster is the sleekest, sexiest car on the street. It is common for beliefs to vary widely among consumers.

In conducting a MAAMs analysis, we must specify the relevant evaluative criteria for our category, as well as our direct competitors. We then go to consumers and let them tell us what's important and how our brand fares against the competition on the various evaluative criteria. The information generated from this survey research will give us a better appreciation for the salient beliefs that underlie brand attitudes, and it may suggest important opportunities for changing our marketing or advertising to yield more favorable brand attitudes.

Three basic attitude-change strategies can be developed from the MAAMs framework. First, a MAAMs analysis may reveal that consumers do not have an accurate perception of the relative performance of our brand on an important evaluative criterion. For example, consumers may perceive that Crest is far and away the best brand of toothpaste for fighting cavities, when in fact all brands with a fluoride

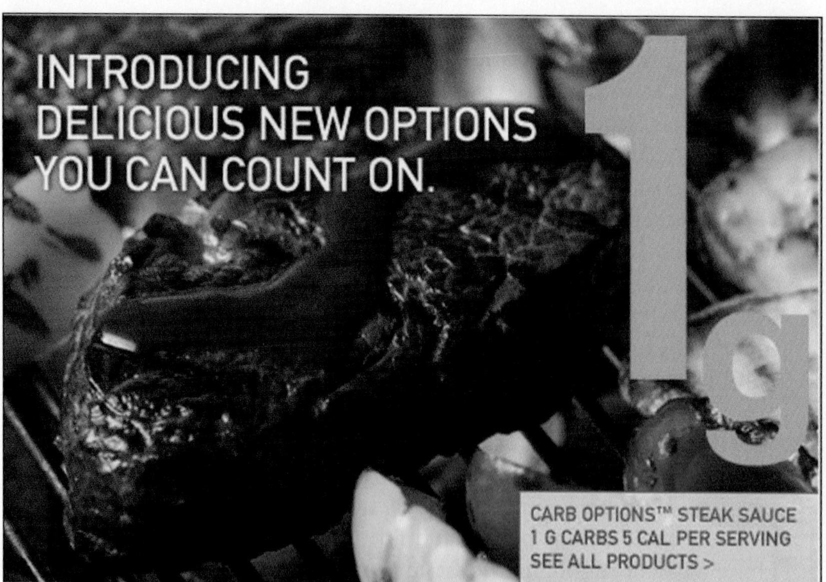

INTRODUCING
DELICIOUS NEW OPTIONS
YOU CAN COUNT ON.
1g
CARB OPTIONS™ STEAK SAUCE
1 G CARBS 5 CAL PER SERVING
SEE ALL PRODUCTS >

Exhibit 5.17 When fads emerge as major marketplace trends, marketers must respond or risk dramatic erosion in their customer base. Such has been the case in the food business, where carb-consciousness has affected the marketing of everything from peanut butter to steak sauce. Learn more at www.carboptions.com

additive perform equally well on cavity prevention. Correcting this misperception could become our focal point if we compete with Crest.

Second, a MAAMs analysis could uncover that our brand is perceived as the best performer on an evaluative criterion that most consumers do not view as very important. The task for advertising in this instance would be to persuade consumers that what our brand offers (say, lower carb content than any other light beer) is more important than they had thought previously.

Third, the MAAMs framework may lead to the conclusion that the only way to improve attitudes toward our brand would be through the introduction of a new attribute to be featured in our advertising. In some instances we could just add that attribute or feature (e.g., 10X, through the lens, optical zoom) to an existing product (e.g., our Olympus digital camera), and make that the centerpiece in our next ad campaign. Alternatively, if the attribute in question has emerged to be highly valued by 30 million Americans, we may want to reinvent an entire product line to feature this critical attribute. That's exactly what Unilever Bestfoods (makers of Ragu, Lipton, Skippy, and Wish-Bone) decided to do for carb-shy consumers when it introduced a line of products like the one in Exhibit 5.17.

When marketers use the MAAMs approach, good things can result in terms of more-favorable brand attitudes and improved market share. When marketers carefully isolate key evaluative criteria, bring products to the marketplace that perform well on the focal criteria, and develop ads that effectively shape salient beliefs about the brand, the results can be dramatic.

Information Processing and Perceptual Defense. At this point you may have the impression that creating effective advertising is really a straightforward exercise. We carefully analyze consumers' beliefs and attitudes, construct ads to address any problems that might be identified, and choose various media to get the word out to our target customers. Yes, it would be very easy if consumers would just pay close attention and believe everything we tell them, and if our competition would kindly stop all of its advertising so that ours would be the only message that consumers had to worry about. Of course, these things aren't going to happen.

Why would we expect to encounter resistance from consumers as we attempt to influence their beliefs and attitudes about our brand? One way to think about this problem is to portray the consumer as an information processor who must advance through a series of stages before our message can have its intended effect. If we are skillful in selecting appropriate media to reach our target, then the consumer must (1) pay attention to the message, (2) comprehend it correctly, (3) accept the message exactly as we intended, and (4) retain the message until it is needed for a purchase decision. Unfortunately, problems can and do occur at any or all of these four stages, completely negating the effect of our advertising campaign.

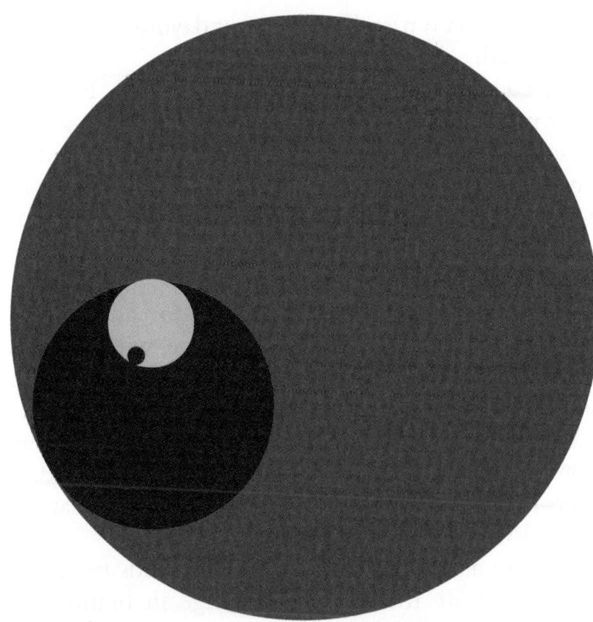

Exhibit 5.18 An ad in a sea of ads. So just how much can advertising really do anymore?

There are two major obstacles that we must overcome if our message is to have its intended effect. The first—the **cognitive consistency** impetus—stems from the individual consumer. Remember, a person develops and holds beliefs and attitudes for a reason: They help him or her make efficient decisions that yield pleasing outcomes. When a consumer is satisfied with these outcomes, there is really no reason to alter the belief system that generated them (e.g., why bother with a Cadillac if you love your BMW!). New information that challenges existing beliefs can be ignored or disparaged to prevent modification of the present cognitive system. The consumer's desire to maintain cognitive consistency can be a major roadblock for an advertiser that wants to change beliefs and attitudes.

The second obstacle—**advertising clutter**—derives from the context in which ads are processed. Even if a person wanted to, it would be impossible to process and integrate every advertising message that he or she is exposed to each day. Pick up today's newspaper and start reviewing every ad you come across. Will you have time today to read them all? The clutter problem is further magnified by competitive brands making very similar performance claims.[6] Was it Advil, Anacin, Aveda, Aleve, Avia, Aflexa, Aveya, Actonel, Motrin, Nuprin, or Tylenol Gelcaps that promised you 12 hours of relief from your headache? (Can you select the brands from this list that aren't headache remedies?) The simple fact is that each of us is exposed to hundreds, maybe thousands, of ads each day, and no one has the time or inclination to sort through them all (see Exhibit 5.18). Some industry experts and researchers believe that the simple mass of advertising, the enormous number of ads, is now working very hard against the institution of advertising itself.

Exhibit 5.18 is an excellent illustration of clutter: the outer green circle is the total amount of measured U.S. advertising in a recent year. The smaller and light green circle represents all automotive advertising (the largest category in the United States) that same year. The smaller blue circle represents estimated spending of a large automobile company, and the tiny black dot is the amount spent on one of its leading brands. When you do the math, only about one out of every 2,000 ads was for this typically advertised brand. So, what chance do you think that ad had to actually affect behavior in a sea of other ads? This is a very big question facing the industry right now.

Consumers employ perceptual defenses to simplify and control their own ad processing. It is important here to see that the consumer is in control, and the advertiser must find some way to engage the consumer if an ad is to have any impact. Of course, the best way to engage consumers is to offer them information about a product or service that will address an active need state. Simply stated, it is difficult to get people to process a message about your headache remedy when they don't have a headache. **Selective attention** is certainly the advertiser's greatest challenge and produces tremendous waste of advertising dollars. Most ads are simply ignored by consumers, again providing much of the reason for the growth of other forms of promotion such as branded entertainment. They turn the page, change the station,

6. Clutter creates a variety of problems that compromise the effectiveness of advertising. For instance, research has shown that clutter interferes with basic memory functions, inhibiting a person's ability to keep straight which brands are making what claims. For more details, see Anand Kumar and Shanker Krishnan, "Memory Interference in Advertising: A Replication and Extension," *Journal of Consumer Research,* vol. 30 (March 2004), 602–612.

mute the sound, head for the refrigerator, TiVo past the ad, or just daydream or doze off—rather than process the traditional ad.

Advertisers employ a variety of tactics to break through the clutter. Popular music, celebrity spokespersons, sexy models, rapid scene changes, and anything that is novel are devices for combating selective attention. Remember, as we discussed in Chapter 3, advertisers constantly walk that fine line between novel and obnoxious in their never-ending battle for the attention of the consumer. They really don't want to insult you or anyone else; they just want to be noticed. Of course, they often step over the annoyance line.

The battle for consumers' attention poses another dilemma for advertisers. Without attention, there is no chance that an advertiser's message will have its desired impact; however, the provocative, attention-attracting devices used to engage consumers often become the focal point of consumers' ad processing. They remember seeing an ad featuring 27 Elvis Presley impersonators, but they can't recall what brand was being advertised or what claims were being made about the brand. If advertisers must entertain consumers to win their attention, they must also be careful that the brand and message don't get lost in the shuffle.

Let's assume that an ad gets attention and the consumer comprehends its claims correctly. Will acceptance follow and create the enduring change in brand attitude that is desired, or will there be further resistance? If the message is asking the consumer to alter beliefs about the brand, expect more resistance. When the consumer is involved and attentive and comprehends a claim that challenges current beliefs, the cognitive consistency impetus kicks in, and cognitive responses can be expected. **Cognitive responses** are the thoughts that occur to individuals at that exact moment in time when their beliefs and attitudes are being challenged by some form of persuasive communication. Remember, most ads will not provoke enough mental engagement to yield any form of cognitive response, but when they occur, the valence of these responses is critical to the acceptance of one's message. It is also true that more contemporary models of human memory provide strong evidence that memory is a much more fluid and interpretive system than we have thought in the past.[7, 8]

Human memory is not a mental DVR; it's more likely to combine, delete, add, and rewrite things, etc., because memory is more fluid and intrepretive than previously thought. So, the long-standing idea of just counting up brand name mentions and correctly remembered copy points is still used, and is sometimes appropriate, but is increasingly being disputed by the science of memory research. But it does stand to reason that if a consumer can really remember most of your ad, that's a good thing. As we shall see in the next section, cognitive responses are one of the main components of an influential framework for understanding the impact of advertising labeled the **elaboration likelihood model (ELM).**

The Elaboration Likelihood Model (ELM). The ELM is another of those ideas that has been borrowed from social psychology and applied to advertising settings.[9] Like all models, it certainly has its limitations, but it is pretty easy to apply to many advertising situations. It is a model that has particular relevance in this chapter because it incorporates ideas such as involvement, information processing, cognitive responses, and attitude formation in a single, integrated framework. The basic premise of the ELM is that to understand how a persuasive communication

7. http://depts.washington.edu/uweek/archives/2001.07.JUL_05/_article5.html

8. Kathryn A. Braun-LaTour, Michael S. LaTour, Jacqueline E. Pickrell, and Elizabeth F. Loftus, "How and When Advertising Can Influence Memory for Consumer Experience," *Journal of Advertising,* vol. 33 (Winter 2004), 7–25.

9. For an expanded discussion of these issues, see Richard E. Petty, John T. Cacioppo, Alan J. Strathman, and Joseph R. Priester, "To Think or Not to Think: Exploring Two Routes to Persuasion," in Sharon Shavitt and Timothy C. Brock (Eds.), *Persuasion: Psychological Insights and Perspectives* (Boston: Allyn & Bacon, 1994), 113–147.

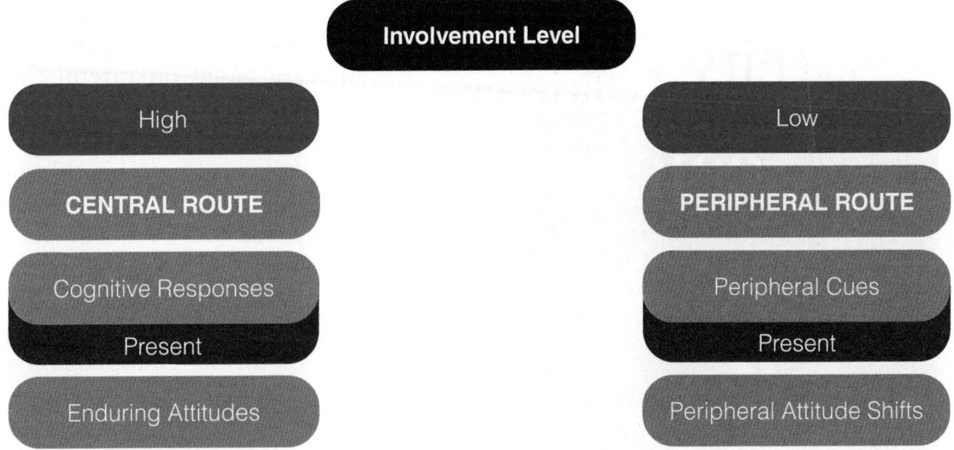

Exhibit 5.19 Two routes to attitude change.

may affect a person's attitudes, we must consider his or her motivation and ability to elaborate on the message during processing. For most advertising contexts, motivation and ability will be a function of how involved the person is with the consumption decision in question. Involving decisions will result in active, mental elaboration during ad processing, whereas uninvolving decisions will implicate passive ad processing.

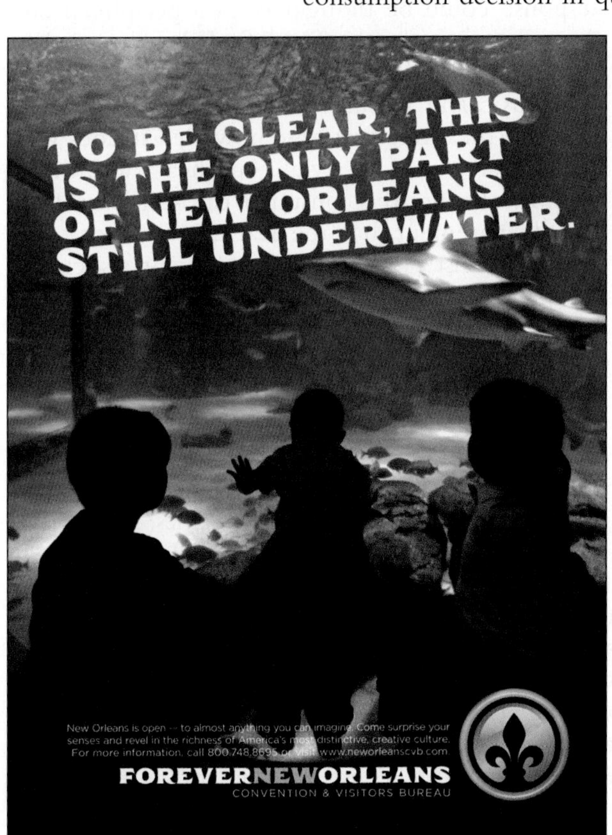

Exhibit 5.20 Cities can also engage in persuasive communications. Does this ad present an image of a post-Hurricane Katrina New Orleans that is compatible with your prior beliefs?

Courtesy, New Orleans Convention & Visitor Center

As indicated in Exhibit 5.19, the ELM uses the involvement dichotomy in spelling out two unique routes to attitude change. These are typically referred to as the central and peripheral routes to persuasion.

When involvement is high, we should expect the consumer to draw on prior knowledge and experience and scrutinize or elaborate on the message arguments that are central to the advertiser's case. The nature of the individual's effortful thinking about the issues at hand could be judged from the cognitive responses that the ad provokes. These cognitive responses may be positive or negative in tone, and can be reactions to specific claims or any executional element of the ad.

Messages designed to reinforce existing beliefs, or shape beliefs for a new brand that the consumer was unaware of previously, are more likely to win uncritical acceptance. Compare the ads in Exhibits 5.20 and 5.21. In this example, think of the cities of New Orleans and Singapore as two brands competing for a tourist's attention (and ultimately, dollars). Each of these ads tries to affect beliefs and attitudes about its focal city. The cognitive consistency impetus that manifests in cognitive responses (thoughts consumers have while viewing an ad) will work against the city that is better known, especially when the ad challenges existing beliefs. Which ad do you find more challenging to your beliefs?

If the cognitive responses provoked by an ad are primarily negative in tone, the ad has backfired: The consumer is maintaining cognitive consistency by disparaging your ad, and that person's negative thoughts are likely to foster negative evaluation of your brand. However, when positive

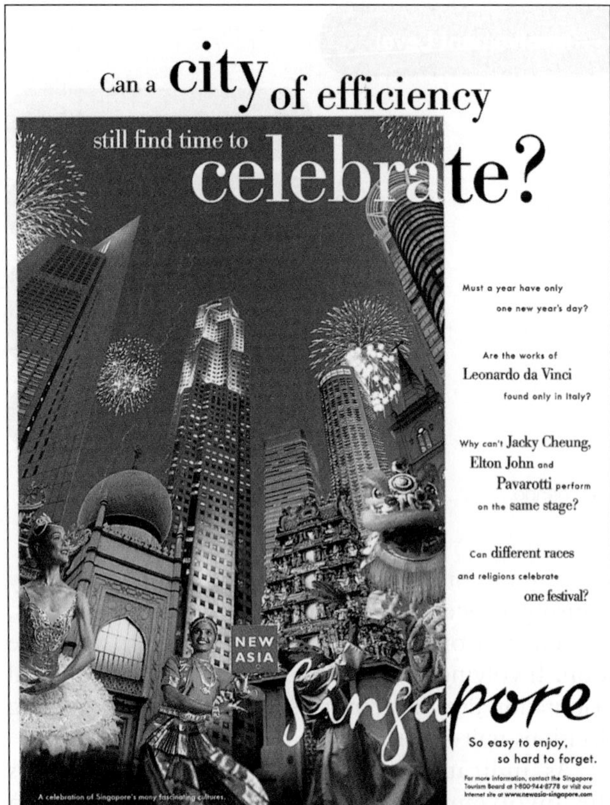

Exhibit 5.21 Singapore's Tourism Board uses this ad to educate readers about its broad cultural diversity, and to tickle their curiosity (www.newasia-singapore.com). Is Singapore an Asian city? Yes, but with influences from many cultures. The ad invites the reader to break out of a conceptual box, just as the Florida orange growers did with their "Orange Juice: It's Not Just for Breakfast Anymore" campaign.

attitudes can be affected through the central route, they have very appealing properties. Because they are based on careful thought, central-route attitudes will (1) come to mind quickly for use in product selection, (2) resist the change efforts of other advertisers, (3) persist in memory without repeated ad exposures, and (4) be excellent predictors of behavior. These properties cannot be expected of attitudes that are formed in the peripheral route.

For low-involvement products, such as batteries or tortilla chips, cognitive responses to advertising claims are not expected. In such situations, attitude formation will often follow a more peripheral route, and peripheral cues become the focal point for judging the ad's impact. **Peripheral cues** refer to features of the ad other than the actual arguments about the brand's performance. They include an attractive or comical spokesperson, novel imagery, humorous incidents, or a catchy jingle. Any feature of the ad that prompts a pleasant emotional response could be thought of as a peripheral cue. Actually, critics of the ELM find this the weakest part of the model: We can all think of ads where the music and pictures are anything but peripheral, but the ELM fans note how well it does with traditional (i.e., older style) copy-heavy ads. In the peripheral route the consumer can still learn from an advertisement, but the learning is passive and typically must be achieved by frequent association of the peripheral cue (for example, the Eveready Energizer Bunny) with the brand in question. It has even been suggested that classical conditioning principles might be employed by advertisers to facilitate and accelerate this associative learning process.[10] As consumers learn to associate pleasant feelings and attractive images with a brand, their attitude toward the brand should become more positive.

What do LeAnn Rimes, James Carville, Queen Latifah, Jerry Seinfeld, Mr. Peanut, Jay-Z, Shakira, Junji Takada, Michelin Man, LeBron (a.k.a. King) James, Paige Davis, the Geico Gecko, Missy Elliott, and the song "Instant Karma" by John Lennon have in common? They and hundreds of others like them have been used as peripheral cues in advertising campaigns. When all brands in a category offer similar benefits, the most fruitful avenue for advertising strategy is likely to be the peripheral route, where the advertiser merely tries to maintain positive or pleasant associations with the brand by constantly presenting it with appealing peripheral cues. Of course, peripheral cues can be more than merely cute, with the right ones adding an undeniable level of "hipness" to aging brands.[11] Selecting peripheral cues can be especially important for mature brands in low-involvement categories where the challenge is to keep the customer from

10. For additional discussion of this issue, see Frances K. McSweeney and Calvin Bierley, "Recent Developments in Classical Conditioning," *Journal of Consumer Research,* vol. 11 (September 1984), 619–631.

11. Associations like Jay-Z with Heineken, Missy Elliott with Gap, and Queen Latifah with Cover Girl illustrate the influence of Russell Simmons in bringing hip-hop into the advertising mainstream. (See "The CEO of Hip Hop," *BusinessWeek,* October 27, 2003, 91–98.) It is fair to say that Simmons found great success by lining up hip-hop icons as peripheral cues for all sorts of big-name advertisers.

getting bored;[12] however, this is an expensive tactic because any gains made along the peripheral route are short-lived. Television air time, lots of repetition, sponsorship fees, and a never-ending search for the freshest, most popular peripheral cues demand huge budgets. When you think of the peripheral route, think of the advertising campaigns for high-profile, mature brands such as Coke, Pepsi, Budweiser, Gap, McDonald's, Nike, and Doritos. They entertain in an effort to keep you interested. But again, remember that determining just exactly what is "peripheral" is not as easy as it may sound.

Perspective Two: The Consumer as Social Being.

The view of the consumer as decision maker and information processor has been a popular one. What goes on in consumers' minds is obviously important. But just as certainly it tells only part of the story of consumer behavior and advertising. Advertising and consumer behavior are so many things, and operate on so many levels, that a single-perspective approach is inadequate. So we offer a second perspective. Taken together, they work pretty well in understanding advertising and brand promotion.

In this section we present a second perspective on consumer behavior, a perspective concerned with social and cultural processes. It should be considered another part of the larger story of how advertising works. Remember, this is just another perspective. We are still talking about the same consumers discussed in the preceding section; we are just viewing their behavior from a different vantage point. When it comes to the complexities of consumer behavior and advertising, one perspective, one approach, is rarely enough.

The move away from purely psychological approaches (and towards social and cultural ones) has been going on in the advertising industry for quite some time, at least 40 years. It gathered significant momentum in the 1980s. At that time, U.S. West Coast agencies began adopting what they called "British Research," which was really just qualitative research as has been practiced by anthropologists, sociologists, and others for more than a century. The only thing really "British" about it at all is that some very hot London agencies had been doing research this way all along. (Actually, many had been, but these agencies used it as a point of differentiation.) At JWT-London, Judie Lannon's emphasis on meaning is a good example. She sums it up beautifully here:

> *And if advertising contributes to the meaning of inanimate goods, then the study of these values and meanings are of prime importance... the perspective of research must be what people use advertising for.*[13]
>
> —Judie Lannon, then creative research director, J. Walter Thompson, London

This industry trend toward qualitative research and naturalistic methods also resonated with a similar move in academic research toward more qualitative fieldwork in the study of human behavior, including consumer behavior, advertising, and brands. These researchers saw consumers as more than "information processors" and ads as more than socially isolated attempts at attitude manipulation. The truth is most major companies do almost no experimentation. But they do lots of qualitative research, often under the heading "consumer insights." In this approach, **meaning** becomes more important than attitudes. Consumers do "process" information, but they also do a whole lot more (see Exhibit 5.22). Advertising practice is not engineering or chemistry. The meaning-based approach centers on knowing how to connect with

12. The rationale for cultivating brand interest for mature brands is discussed more fully in Karen A. Machleit, Chris T. Allen, and Thomas J. Madden, "The Mature Brand and Brand Interest: An Alternative Consequence of Ad-Evoked Affect," *Journal of Marketing,* vol. 57 (October 1993), 72–82.

13. Martin Davidson, "Objects of Desire: How Advertising Works," in Martin Davidson, *The Consumerist Manifesto: Advertising in Postmodern Times* (London: Routledge, 1992), 23–60.

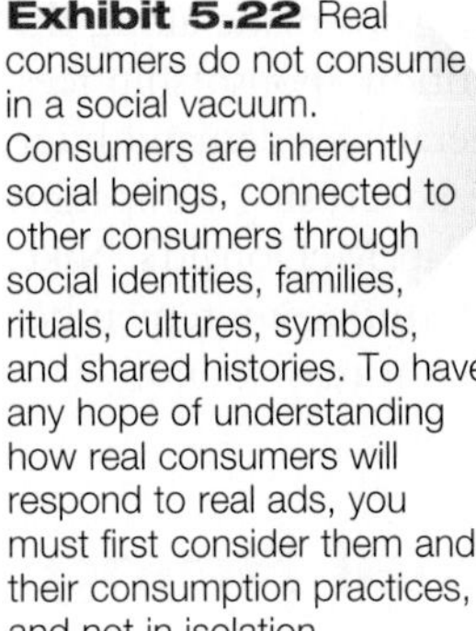

Exhibit 5.22 Real consumers do not consume in a social vacuum. Consumers are inherently social beings, connected to other consumers through social identities, families, rituals, cultures, symbols, and shared histories. To have any hope of understanding how real consumers will respond to real ads, you must first consider them and their consumption practices, and not in isolation.

human beings around their consumption practices with advertising and other brand promotion. That's why advertising agencies commonly hire people who know about material culture (anthropology), demography and social process (sociology), the history of brands and consumption practices (history), memory (psychology), communication, text (literature), and art (what a lot of ads are).

Generally speaking, the psychological perspective focuses on "information," whereas the sociocultural one focuses on meaning.

4 Consuming in the Real World.

Let's consider some major components of real consumers' lives:

Culture. If you are in the ad business, you are in the culture business.

Culture is what a people do, or "the total life ways of a people, the social legacy the individual acquires from his (her) group."[14] It is the way we eat, groom, celebrate, travel, play, get together, and express feelings. It is the way things are done. Cultures may be large and national, or they may be regional or local, or not geographic at all: *urban hipster culture, teen tech-nerd, Junior League*, and so on. It's usually easier to see and note culture when it's more distant and unfamiliar. For most people, this is when they travel to another place. For example, if you've traveled beyond your own country, you have no doubt noticed that people in other national cultures do things differently. Further, members of a culture often find the ways they do things to be perfectly natural and normal. Culture is also said to be nearly invisible to those who are immersed in it. If everyone around us behaves in a similar fashion, we do not easily think about the existence of some large and powerful force acting on us all. But it's there; this constant background force is the force of culture, and it's powerful. To really see the culture that is all around you, to really see what you take as ordinary, to see it like you were a visitor to a strange land is what the sociocultural perspective offers.

Culture surrounds the creation, transmission, reception, and interpretation of ads and brands, just as it touches every aspect of consumption. Culture is about as "real world" as it gets. How do you as an advertiser create or leverage cultural forces

14. Gordon Marshall, (Ed.), *The Concise Oxford Dictionary of Sociology* (New York: Oxford University Press, 1994), 104–105.

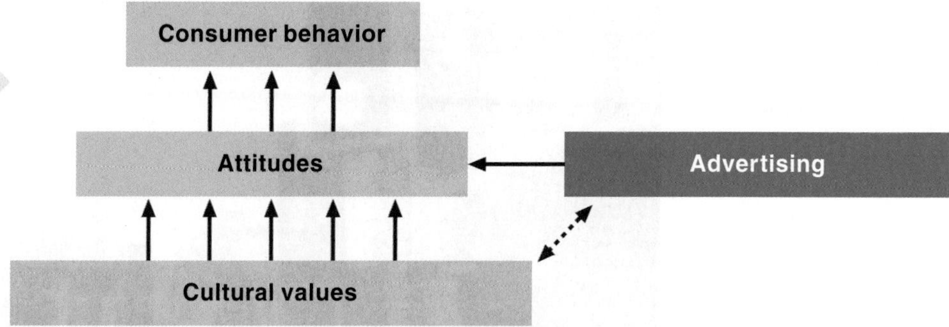

Exhibit 5.23 Cultural values, attitudes, and consumer behavior. Some believe that advertising can directly affect consumer behavior and, over time, cultural values as well.

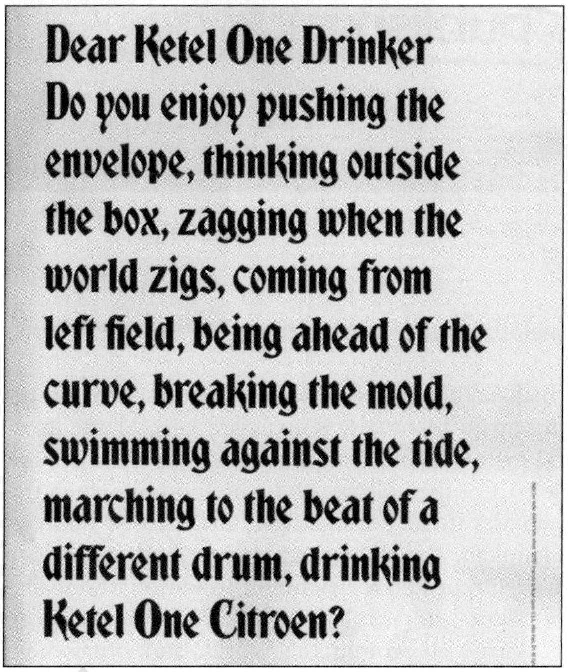

Dear Ketel One Drinker
Do you enjoy pushing the envelope, thinking outside the box, zagging when the world zigs, coming from left field, being ahead of the curve, breaking the mold, swimming against the tide, marching to the beat of a different drum, drinking Ketel One Citroen?

Exhibit 5.24 Ketel One recognizes that many consumers prefer to think of themselves as outside the mainstream mass market and celebrates their spirit.

to sell something? That's the idea. Why do we have the particular rituals we perform on certain days? Are there market opportunities in those rituals? Or who makes up the rules of gift giving? If you are Tiffany, Barnes & Noble, Hallmark, or De Beers, you have a very good reason to understand why people do things a certain way (for example, buy things for one holiday, but not for another).

Values are enduring expressions of culture. Values express in words and deeds what is important to a culture. For example, some value propriety and restrained behavior, whereas others value open expression. Values are cultural bedrock. Values are enduring. They cannot be changed quickly or easily. They are thus different from attitudes, which can be changed through a single advertising campaign or even a single ad. Think of cultural values as the very strong and rigid foundation on which much more mutable attitudes rest. Exhibit 5.23 illustrates this relationship. Values are the foundation of this structure. Attitudes are, in turn, influenced by values, as well as by many other sources. Advertising has to be consistent with, but cannot easily or quickly change, values. It is thus senseless for an advertiser to speak of using advertising to change values in any substantive way. Advertising influences values in the same way a persistent drip of water wears down a granite slab—very slowly and through cumulative impact, over years and years. It is also the case that cultural values change advertising.

Typically, advertisers try to either associate their product with a cultural value or criticize a competitor for being out of step with one. For example, in America, to say that a product "merely hides or masks odors" would be damning criticism, because it suggests that anyone who would use such a product doesn't really value cleanliness and thus isn't like the rest of us. Advertisements must be consistent with the values of a people. If they are not, they will likely be rejected. Look at the ad shown in Exhibit 5.24. What values does in rely on, affirm? Can you think of cultures where this ad would be a problem?

Globalization is a force that is said to be erasing local culture. Critics of globalism say it makes the world one big McDonald's. Everything starts to look the same, no matter where you are. The local is swamped by the global. Travel just about anywhere on this planet and you will be met by the *global brandscape* (see Exhibit 5.25). Global brands and a global culture of marketing, branding, advertising, and consuming is the reality, like it or not. Globalization values are commercial values. Some brands believe in being the same everywhere, others believe that the key to success is to

Exhibit 5.25 Global brandscape. From Tucson to Tucumcari, Madrid to Cork, the global brandscape is there.

add a touch of the local to ads for global brands so that they at least appear to be consistent with the local culture.

Rituals are "often-repeated formalized behaviors involving symbols."[15] Cultures participate in rituals; consumers participate in rituals. Rituals are core elements of culture. Cultures affirm, express, and maintain their values through rituals. They are a way in which individuals are made part of the culture, and a method by which the culture constantly renews and perpetuates itself. For example, ritual-laden holidays such as Thanksgiving, Christmas, Hanukah, and the Fourth of July help perpetuate aspects of American culture through their repeated reenactment (tradition). Globally, there are a myriad of very important cultural rituals, all involving consumption (e.g., feasts and gift giving). In fact, this is true all around the world, and rituals help intertwine culture and consumption practices in a very real way. For example, Jell-O may have attained the prominence of an "official" American holiday food because of its regular usage as part of the Thanksgiving dinner ritual.[16] In the American South, it is common to eat black-eyed peas on New Year's Day to ensure good luck. In one sense it is "just done," but in another it is just done because it is a ritual embedded in a culture. If you are a consumer packaged goods manufacturer, understanding these types of ritual is not a trivial concern at all (see Exhibits 5.26 and 5.27.)

Rituals also occur every day in millions of other contexts. For example, when someone buys a new car or a new home, they do all sorts of "unnecessary" things to make it theirs. They clean the carpets even if they were just cleaned, they trim trees that don't need trimming, they hang things from the mirror of the used car they just bought, they change oil that was just changed—all to make the new possession theirs and remove any trace of the former owner. These behaviors are not only important to anthropologists, they are also important to those making and trying to sell products such as paint, rug shampoos, household disinfectants, lawn and garden equipment, auto accessories, and on and on.

15. Gordon Marshall, (Ed.), *The Concise Oxford Dictionary of Sociology* (New York: Oxford University Press, 1994), 452.

16. Melanie Wallendorf and Eric J. Arnould, "We Gather Together: Consumption Rituals of Thanksgiving Day," *Journal of Consumer Research,* vol. 18, no. 1 (June 1991), 13–31.

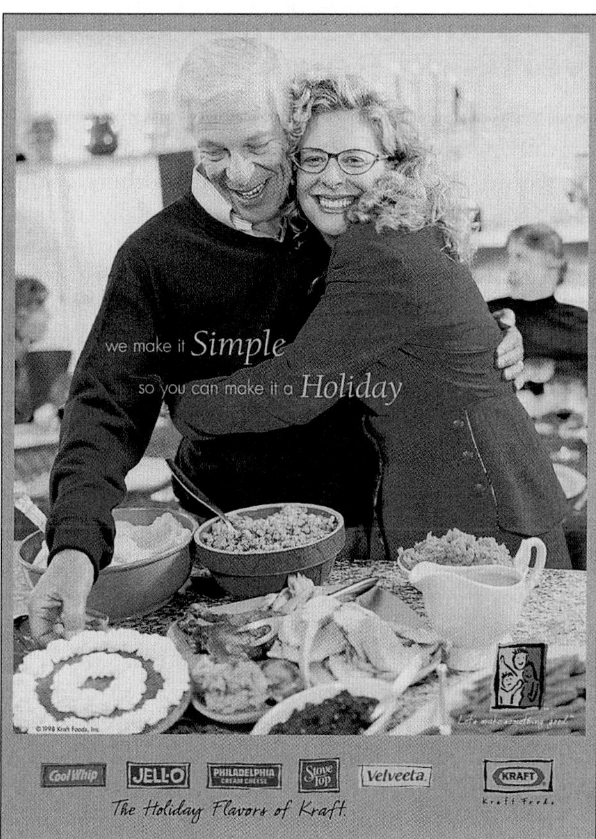

Exhibit 5.26 This ad promotes Kraft products as an integral part of family rituals and traditions. www.kraftfoods.com

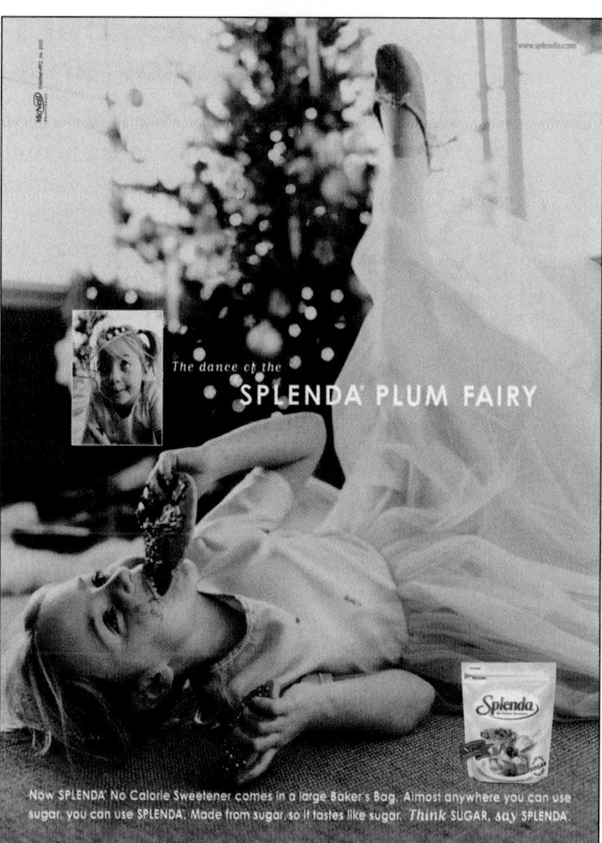

Exhibit 5.27 In this ad, Splenda is made part of holiday ritual.

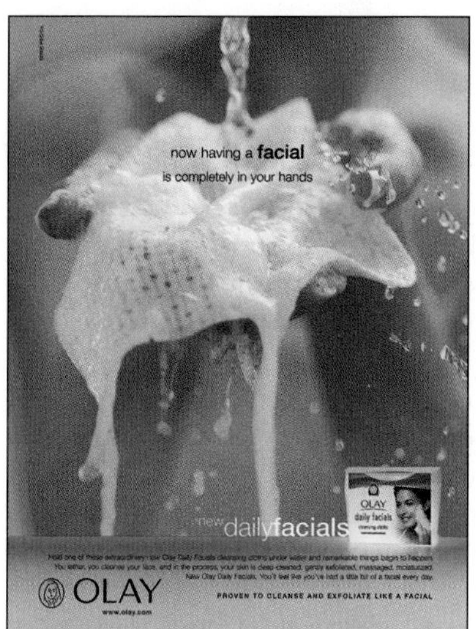

Exhibit 5.28 This ad helps Olay become part of an already existing ritual.

Rituals don't have to be the biggest events of the year. There are everyday rituals, such as the way we eat, clean ourselves, and groom. Think about all the habitual things you do from the time you get up in the morning until you crawl into bed at night. These things are done in a certain way; they are not random.[17] Members of a common culture tend to do them one way, and members of other cultures do them other ways. Again, if you've ever visited another country, you have no doubt noticed significant differences. An American dining in Paris might be surprised to have sorbet to begin the meal and a salad to end it.

Daily rituals seem inconsequential because they are habitual and routine, and thus "invisible." If, however, someone tried to get you to significantly alter the way you do these things, he or she would quickly learn just how important and resistant to change these rituals are. If a product or service cannot be incorporated into an already-existing ritual, it is very difficult and expensive for advertisers to effect a change. If, on the other hand, an advertiser can successfully incorporate the consumption of its good or service into an existing ritual, then success is much more likely. Imagine how important rituals are to the global beauty industry (Exhibit 5.28). Cleaning and beauty practices are highly ritualized.

Clearly, there are incredible opportunities for marketers who can successfully link their products to consumption rituals. In Exhibit 5.29, see an advertiser incorporating their brand into Easter rituals.

17. For a review, see Cele C. Otnes and Tina M. Lowrey, (Eds.), *Contemporary Consumption Rituals: A Research Anthology* (Mahwah, NJ: Lawrence Erlbraun, 2004).

5 Sociological Factors in Consumer Behavior and Advertising Response.

Exhibit 5.29 This ad incorporates an Easter ritual.

Stratification refers to systematic inequalities in things such as wealth, income, education, power, and status. For example, some members of society exist within a richer group (stratum), others within a less affluent stratum. Race and gender are also unequally distributed across income: For example, men generally have higher incomes than women. Thus a cross-section, or slice, of American society would reveal many different levels (or strata) of the population along these different dimensions. Some combination of these inequalities is what we think of when we say "social class." Social class is hard to pin down in some contemporary societies, easier in others. In America, a very large majority of folks with a huge range in income, wealth, and education call themselves "middle class."

"Social class" was typically thought most strongly determined by income: Higher-income Americans were generally seen as being in a higher social class, and lower-income Americans were considered to be in a lower class. But that was an imperfect relationship. For example, successful plumbers often had higher incomes than unsuccessful lawyers, but their occupation was (perhaps) less prestigious, and thus their social class designation was lower. So, the prestige of one's occupation also entered into what we called "social class." Education also has something to do with social class, but a person with a little college experience and a lot of inherited wealth would probably rank higher than an insurance agent with an MBA. Bill Gates left Harvard without a degree, and he has pretty high social standing, not to mention wealth. Thus income, education, and occupation are three important variables for indicating social class, but are still individually, or even collectively, inadequate at capturing its full meaning. Then there are rock stars, professional athletes, and successful actors, who have high incomes but are generally thought to be somewhat outside the social class system.

Important to marketers is the belief that members of the same social strata tend to live in similar ways, have similar views and philosophies, and, most critically, tend to consume in somewhat similar ways. You could supposedly tell "social class" from what people consume and how they consume; at least, that's what lots of marketers and advertisers believed. Social class and stratification was supposed to be reflected in a consumer's taste, and thus their consumption. The traditional view was that advertisers cared about social class and stratification because consumers used their choices to reflect their class-related. But this assumption has been challenged lately.

Some believe that traditional social class-consumption taste hierarchies have collapsed, or at least become much less stable. What do you think, can you tell someone's social standing by how they consume? Are tastes related to social stratification a thing of the past? Take a look at the photos in Exhibits 5.30 and 5.31: Does the woman in 5.31 get her hair done at the establishment shown in 5.30? How do you know? Why? Are social class markers a thing of the past?

What do you think? Put it to the test: Go to a mall, walk around, and check people out. Do you think you could guess their income, education, occupation, and whether they live downtown or in the 'burbs from the way they look, what they are wearing, and which stores they shop in? Most advertisers think you can, and that's why stratification matters.

This brings us to taste. **Taste** refers to a generalized set or orientation to consumer aesthetic preferences. If social class affects consumption through tastes, it also affects media preferences (e.g., *RV Life* versus *Wine Spectator.*) We think of tennis more than bowling as belonging to the upper classes, chess more than checkers, and brie

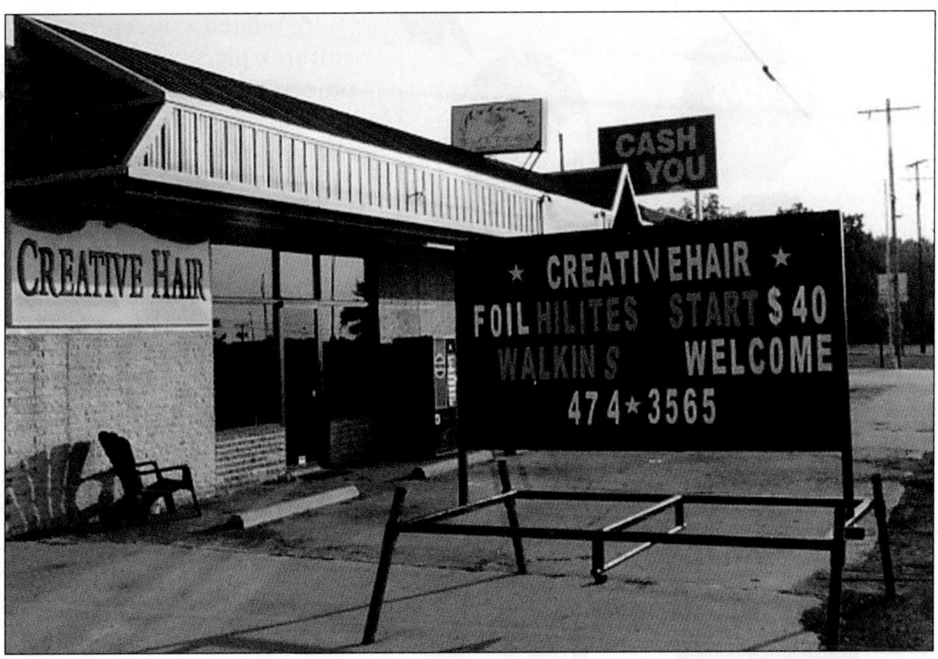

Exhibit 5.30 Does the woman in 5.31 use the services of the establishment shown here?

Exhibit 5.31 How do you know? What tells you?

more than Velveeta. Ordering wine instead of beer has social significance, as does wearing Tommy Hilfiger rather than Lee jeans, or driving a Volvo rather than a Chevy. We believe social stratification and taste are intertwined while acknowledging that preferences and strata are less dependable than in the past.

Fashion and taste cycle faster than they once did, and consumers may be more playful in their use of class markers than they once were, and they are less rigid boundaries than in the past. Some smart advertisers have successfully leveraged that change, and probably no one does it better than Target (see Exhibit 5.32). Target brought designers to the retail masses.

Exhibit 5.32 Throughout the years, Target has made the logo for its store mean more than the labels on many of its products. It is, in our view, the best branding communication of the past few years.

Photo courtesy of Target Stores, Minneapolis

A related concept is *cultural capital,* the value that cultures place on certain consumption practices and objects. For example, a certain consumption practice, say snowboarding, has a certain capital or value (like money) for some segment of the population. If you own a snowboard (a certain amount of cultural capital) and can actually use it (more cultural capital), and look good while using it (even more capital), then this activity is like cultural currency or cultural money in the bank. A pair of Prada boots has cultural capital. By buying and wearing them, the consumer gets a little cultural capital, points if you will, in the culture. Capital is by definition worth something. It gets you things you want. A Porsche has a certain cultural capital among some groups, as does wearing khakis, drinking PBR, ordering the right pinot noir, knowing how to hail a cab, flying first class, or knowing about the latest band or cool thing on YouTube. This capital may exist within a hipster culture, or a 40-something wine-snob culture, or a redneck culture—it's still cultural capital. In all of these cultures certain consumer practices are favored or valued. Advertisers try to figure out which ones are valued more, and why, and how to make their product sought after because it has higher cultural capital, and can be sold at a higher price. Does an iPhone have more cultural capital than a BlackBerry, or a really thin Motorola? To whom? To what cultural group? To what market segment? Maybe the coolest people don't have any of those things; they are free of their electronic leash. Having good "taste" helps you know which things have high cultural capital. These ads try to emphasize the cultural capital, style, and taste to be found in the product (see Exhibits 5.33 and 5.34), and then on to the consumer.

Stratification and cultural capital becomes apparent when a person moves from one stratum into another. Consider the following example: Bob and Jill move into a more expensive neighborhood. Both grew up in lower-middle-class surroundings and moved into high-paying jobs after graduate school. They have now moved into a fairly upscale neighborhood, composed mostly of "older money." On one of the first warm Sundays, Bob goes out to his driveway and begins to do something he has done all his life: change the oil in his car. One of Bob's neighbors comes over and chats, and ever so subtly suggests to Bob that people in this neighborhood have "someone else" do "that sort of thing." Bob gets the message: It's not cool to change your oil in your own driveway. This is not how the new neighbors behave. It doesn't matter whether you like to do it or not; it is simply not done. To Bob, paying someone else to do this simple job seems wasteful and uppity. He's a bit offended, and a little embarrassed. But, over time, he decides that it's better to go along with the other people in the neighborhood. Over time, Bob begins to see the error of his ways and changes his attitudes and his behavior.

This is an example of the effect of stratification and (negative) cultural capital on consumer behavior. Bob will no longer be a good target for Fram, Purolator, AutoZone, or any other product or service used to change oil at home. On the other hand, Bob is now a perfect candidate for quick-oil-change businesses such as Jiffy Lube.

Exhibits 5.33 and 5.34 These two ads point to the high cultural capital of the products.

Family. The consumer behavior of families is also of great interest to advertisers. Advertisers want not only to discern the needs of different kinds of families, but also to discover how decisions are made within families. The first is possible; the latter is much more difficult. For a while, consumer researchers tried to determine who in the traditional nuclear family (that is, Mom, Dad, and the kids) made various purchasing decisions. This was largely an exercise in futility. Due to errors in reporting and conflicting perceptions between partners, it became clear that the family purchasing process is anything but clear. Even though some types of purchases are handled by one family member, many decisions are actually diffuse nondecisions, arrived at through what consumer researcher C. W. Park aptly calls a "muddling-through" process.[18] These "decisions" just get made, and no one is really sure who made them, or even when. For an advertiser to influence such a diffuse and vague process is indeed a challenge. The consumer behavior of the family is a complex and often subtle type of social negotiation. One person handles this, one takes care of that. Sometimes specific purchases fall along gender lines, but sometimes they don't. Even though they may not be the buyer in many instances, children can play important roles as initiators, influencers, and users in many categories, such as cereals, clothing, vacation destinations, fast-food restaurants, and technology (like computers). Still, some advertisers capitalize on the flexibility of this social system by suggesting in their ads who *should* take charge of a given consumption task, and then arming that person with the appearance of expertise so that whoever wants the job can take it and defend his or her purchases.

We also know that families have a lasting influence on the consumer preferences of family members. One of the best predictors of the brands adults use is the ones their parents used. This is true for cars, toothpaste, household cleansers, and many more products. Say you go off to college. You eventually have to do laundry, so you go to the store, and you buy Tide. Why Tide? Well, you're not sure, but you saw it around your house when you lived with your parents, and things seemed to have worked out okay for them, so you buy it for yourself. The habit sticks, and you keep buying it. This is called an **intergenerational effect**.

Advertisers often focus on the major or gross differences in types of families, because different families have different needs, buy different things, and are reached by different media. Family roles often change when both parents (or a single parent)

18. C. Whan Park, "Joint Decisions in Home Purchasing: A Muddling-Through Process," *Journal of Consumer Research,* vol. 9 (September 1982), 151–162.

Exhibit 5.35 Who are the Cleavers? Demographically, they (working husband, stay-at-home mother, two children, upper-middle-class status) have become a pretty small minority, but maybe they still carry an important mythology about stability and the nuclear family. Remember ads and reality are not always the same thing. Do you think more people wish, down deep, that they had a family like this?

are employed outside the home. For instance, a teenage son or daughter may be given the role of initiator and buyer, while the parent or parents serve merely as influences. Furthermore, we should remember that Ward, June, Wally, and the Beaver (Exhibit 5.35) are not the norm. There are a lot of single parents and quite a few second and even third marriages. We know a few that have even surpassed three. *Family* is a very open concept. In addition to the "traditional" nuclear family and the single-parent household, there is the extended family (nuclear family plus grandparents, cousins, and others), including single parents and gay and lesbian households with and without children.

Beyond the basic configuration, advertisers are often interested in knowing things such as the age of the youngest child, the size of the family, and the family income. The age of the youngest child living at home tells an advertiser where the family is in terms of its needs and obligations (that is, toys, investment instruments for college savings, clothing, and vacations). When the youngest child leaves home, the consumption patterns of a family radically change. Advertisers like to track the age of the youngest child living at home and use it as a planning criterion. This is called a **life-stage** variable, and is used frequently in advertising and promotion planning.

Celebrity is a unique sociological concept, and it matters a great deal to advertisers. Twenty-first-century society is all about celebrity. Current thinking is that in a celebrity-based culture, celebrities help contemporary consumers with identity. Identity in a consumer culture becomes a "fashion accessory" prop for a day—head banger, corporate cube-slave in a *McJob*. The idea is that contemporary consumers are very good at putting on and taking off, trying on, switching, and trading various identities, in the same way that they have clicked through the channels since they could reach the remote. Somewhere in one's mid-to late 20s, (in the United States, at least) social identity stabilizes dramatically. Celebrity-inspired identities—the way they do their hair, the way they think about their bodies, their relationships, their aspirations, and certainly their styles. For this reason, the understanding of the celebrity is much more complex and vital than merely thinking in terms of similar attitudes and behaviors. Some sociologists believe that celebrities have become socialization agents, in the way that local communities and families used to function. For these reasons, they are powerful and important to advertisers (see Exhibits 5.36 through 5.38). Further, with social media sites like Facebook, the line between mass media and daily contemporary life blurs more all the time. Advertisers generally think this is a good thing because rapidly shifting social identities are just another way of saying marketing opportunity.

Race and Ethnicity. Race and ethnicity provide other ways to think about important social groups. Answering the question of how race figures into consumer behavior is very difficult. Our discomfort stems from having, on the one hand, the desire to say, "Race doesn't matter, we're all the same," and on the other hand not wanting (or not being able) to deny the significance of race in terms of reaching ethnic cultures and influencing a wide variety of behaviors, including consumer behavior. The truth is we are less and less sure what *race* is and what it means. Obviously, a person's pigmentation, in and of itself, has almost nothing to do with

Exhibits 5.36 through 5.38 These ads use celebrity in simple and sophisticated ways. Who do you want to be today?

preferences for one type of product over another. But because race has mattered in culture, it does still matter in consumer behavior. Exhibit 5.39 shows the trend of current and projected racial diversity in the United States. By the middle of the 21st century, whites will probably be very close to only 50 percent of the U.S. population. This demographic reality is very important to advertisers and marketers.

There probably isn't an area in consumer behavior where research is more inadequate. This is probably because everyone is terrified to discuss it, and because many of the findings we do have are suspect. What is attributed to race is often due to another factor that is itself associated with race. For example, you will sometimes hear advertisers say something to the effect that African Americans and Latinos are more brand loyal than their Anglo counterparts. Data on the frequency of brand switching is offered, and lo and behold, it does appear that white people switch brands more often. But why? Some ethnic minorities live in areas where there are fewer retail choices. When we statistically remove the effect of income disparities between white people and people of color, we see that the brand-switching effect often disappears. This suggests that brand loyalty is not a function of race, but of disposable income and shopping options.

But race does affect one's social identity to varying degrees. One is not blind to one's own ethnicity. African Americans, Latinos, and other ethnic groups have culturally related consumption preferences. Certain brands become associated with

Year	White	Black	Hispanic	Asian	American Indian
1996	194.4 (73.3%)	32.0 (12.1%)	27.8 (10.5%)	9.1 (3.4%)	2.0 (0.7%)
2000	197.1 (71.8%)	33.6 (12.2%)	31.4 (11.4%)	10.6 (3.9%)	2.1 (0.7%)
2010	202.4 (68.0%)	37.5 (12.6%)	41.1 (13.8%)	14.4 (4.8%)	2.3 (0.8%)
2020	207.4 (64.3%)	41.5 (12.9%)	52.7 (16.3%)	18.6 (5.7%)	2.6 (0.8%)
2030	210.0 (60.5%)	45.4 (13.1%)	65.6 (18.9%)	23.0 (6.6%)	2.9 (0.8%)
2040	209.6 (56.7%)	49.4 (13.3%)	80.2 (21.7%)	27.6 (7.5%)	3.2 (0.9%)
2050	207.9 (52.8%)	53.6 (13.6%)	96.5 (24.5%)	32.4 (8.2%)	3.5 (0.9%)

Source: U.S. Census Bureau.

Exhibit 5.39 Ethnic diversity in America: projected U.S. population by race in millions (and percentage of total population by race).

Exhibits 5.40 through 5.42 These ads are directed at Hispanic, Asian, and African-American consumers.

racial or ethnic groups. It is not enough, however, for advertisers to say one group is different from another group, or that they prefer one brand to another simply because they are members of a racial or ethnic category. If advertisers really want a good, long-term relationship with their customers, they must acquire, through good consumer research, a deeper understanding of who their customers are and how this identity is affected by culture, felt ethnicity, and race. In short, advertisers must ask why groups of consumers are different, or prefer different brands, and not settle for an easy answer. It wasn't until the mid to late 1980s that most American corporations made a concerted effort to court African-American consumers, or even to recognize their existence.[19] Efforts to serve the Latino consumer have been intermittent and inconsistent. Sample ads directed at diverse audiences are shown in Exhibits 5.40 through 5.42.

Politics. At first, it might seem odd to mention politics in the same breath as consumer behavior. It shouldn't. There are many places in the world where religious-ethnic-political strife is abundant and this strife is then played out in consumption contexts. This is done for many reasons, including a company's labor history (e.g. Coors, Walmart), its connection to a colonial power (think old British brands in Ireland and India), its perceived working class status (Pabst Blue Ribbon), or its degree of green-ness. Sometimes the associations are direct and hard to miss: Exhibit 5.43 shows Mecca Cola, a contemporary example. It kind of looks like Coca-Cola, right? But, Coca-Cola is an iconic America brand to much of the world. So, Mecca Cola is there to be the anti-brand. In many parts of the world, consumption and branding have a long political history, so brand-political associations are commonplace. That is happening more now in the United States as well. Think about the Great Recession and the recent rise of populism in the United States; how could brands leverage this social disruption? How about "green" politics (see Exhibit 5.44)? The politics of labor are leveraged in Exhibit 5.45.

19. Jannette L. Dates, "Advertising," in Jannette L. Dates and William Barlow (Eds.), *Split Image: African Americans in the Mass Media* (Washington, D.C.: Howard University Press, 1990), 421–454.

Exhibit 5.43 This is a brand with pretty clear politics.

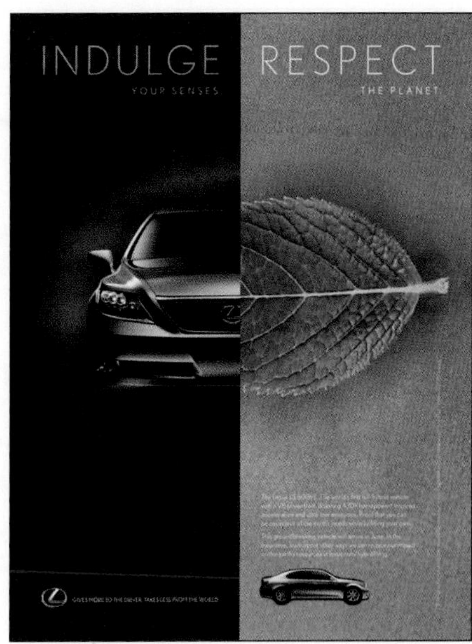

Exhibit 5.44 This ad for the hybrid Lexus LS 600h L ends with the promise "Gives more to the driver. Takes less from the world." Have you noticed an increase in the number of companies taking a "green" approach to their advertising message?

Gender. **Gender** is the sociocultural expression of sexual identity, sexual preference, or both. Obviously, gender matters in consumption. But are men and women really that different in any meaningful way in their consumption behavior, beyond the obvious? Again, to the extent that gender informs a "culture of gender," the answer is yes. As long as men and women are the products of differential socialization, then they will continue to be different in some significant ways. There is, however, no definitive list of gender differences in consumption, because the expression of gender, just like anything else social, depends on the situation and the social circumstances. In the 1920s, advertisers openly referred to women as less logical, more emotional, the cultural stewards of beauty.[20] (Some say that the same soft, irrational, emotional feminine persona is still invoked in advertising.) Advertising helps construct a social reality in which gender is a predominant feature. Not only is it a matter of conscience and social responsibility to be aware of this, but it is good business as well. Advertisers must keep in mind, though, that it's hard to keep the business of people you patronize, insult, or ignore.

Obviously, gender's impact on consumer behavior is not limited to heterosexual men and women. LGBT consumers comprise significant markets. Of late, these markets have been targeted by corporate titans such

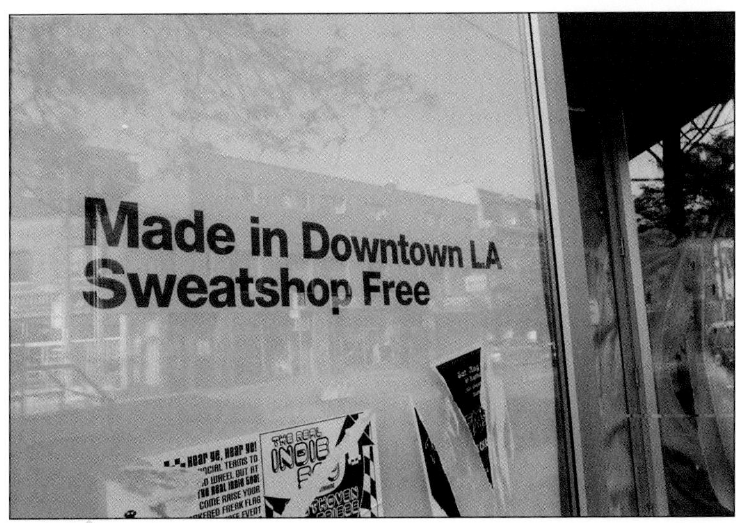

Exhibit 5.45 Having a social conscience isn't necessarily incompatible with smart marketing.

20. Roland Marchand, *Advertising: The American Dream* (Berkeley: University of California Press, 1984), 25.

Exhibit 5.46 Quite a few advertisers are beginning to recognize the advantages of marketing to gay and lesbian consumers. Here, American Express recognizes the special financial challenges faced by lesbian couples. www.americanexpress.com

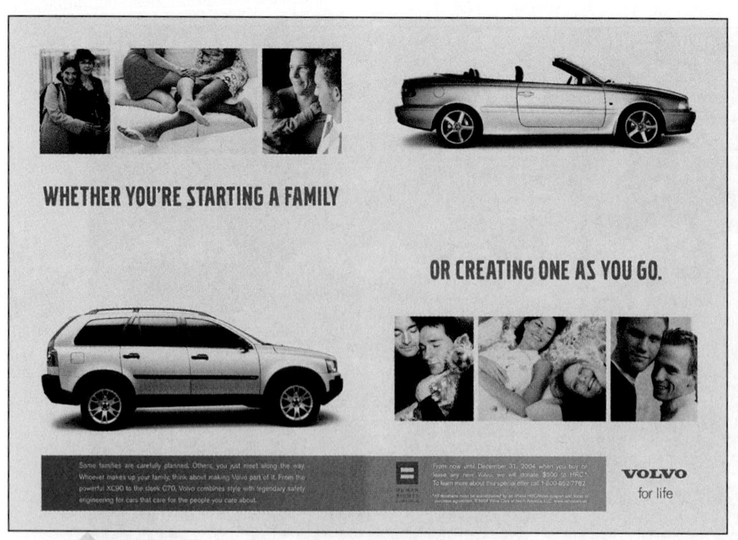

Exhibit 5.47 Here, Volvo attempts to appeal to gay consumers.

as IBM, United Airlines, and Citibank.[21] Again, these are markets that desire to be acknowledged and served, but not stereotyped and patronized. Exhibits 5.46 and 5.47 are ads directed at lesbian and gay audiences.

In the late 1970s, advertisers discovered "working women." In the 1980s, marketers discovered African-American consumers, about the same time they discovered Hispanic consumers. Later they discovered Asian Americans, and just lately they discovered gays and lesbians. Of course, these people weren't missing. They were there all along. These "discoveries" of forgotten and marginalized social groups create some interesting problems for advertisers. Members of these groups, quite reasonably, want to be served just like any other consumers. To serve these markets, consider what Wally Snyder of the American Advertising Federation said:

> *Advertising that addresses the realities of America's multicultural population must be created by qualified professionals who understand the nuances of the disparate cultures. Otherwise, agencies and marketers run the risk of losing or, worse, alienating millions of consumers eager to buy their products or services. Building a business that "looks like" the nation's increasingly multicultural population is no longer simply a moral choice, it is a business imperative.*[22]

Attention and representation without stereotyping from a medium and a genre that is known for stereotyping might be a lot to expect, but it's not that much. Websites such as Commercial Closet (Exhibit 5.48) offer reviews and opinions on LGBT representation in ads.

Community. **Community** is a powerful and traditional sociological concept. Its meaning extends well beyond the idea of a specific geographic place. Communities can be imagined or even virtual; they do not have to be face-to-face. Community members believe that they belong to a group of people who are similar to them in some important way, and different from those not in the community. Members of communities often share rituals and traditions, and feel some sort of responsibility to one another and the community.

21. Laura Koss-Feder, "Out and About: Firms Introduce Gay-Specific Ads for Mainstream Products, Services," *Marketing News,* May 25, 1998, 1, 20.

22. Wally Snyder, "Advertising's Ethical and Economic Imperative," *American Advertising* (Fall 1992), 28.

Exhibit 5.48
Commercial Closet reviews two ads here. What do you think?

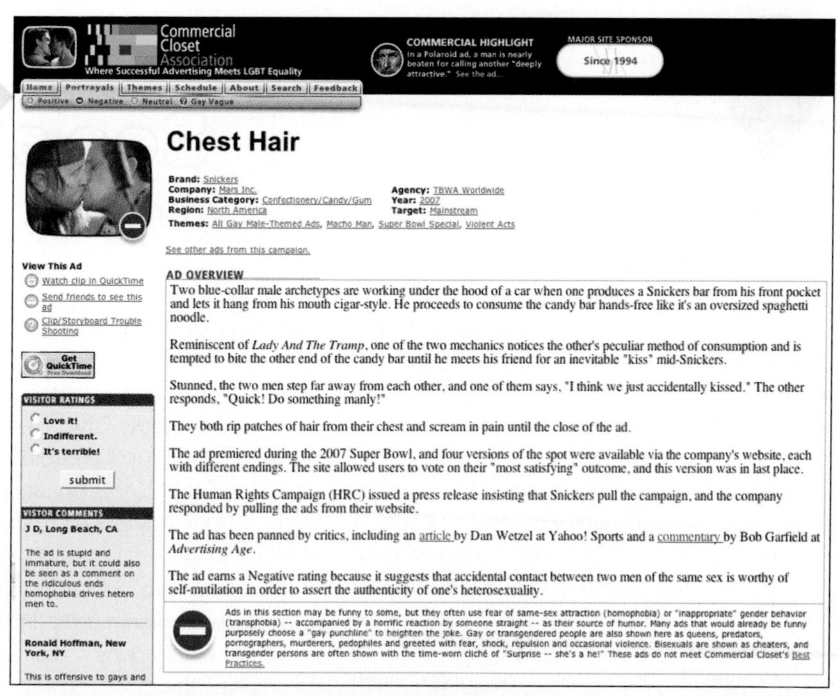

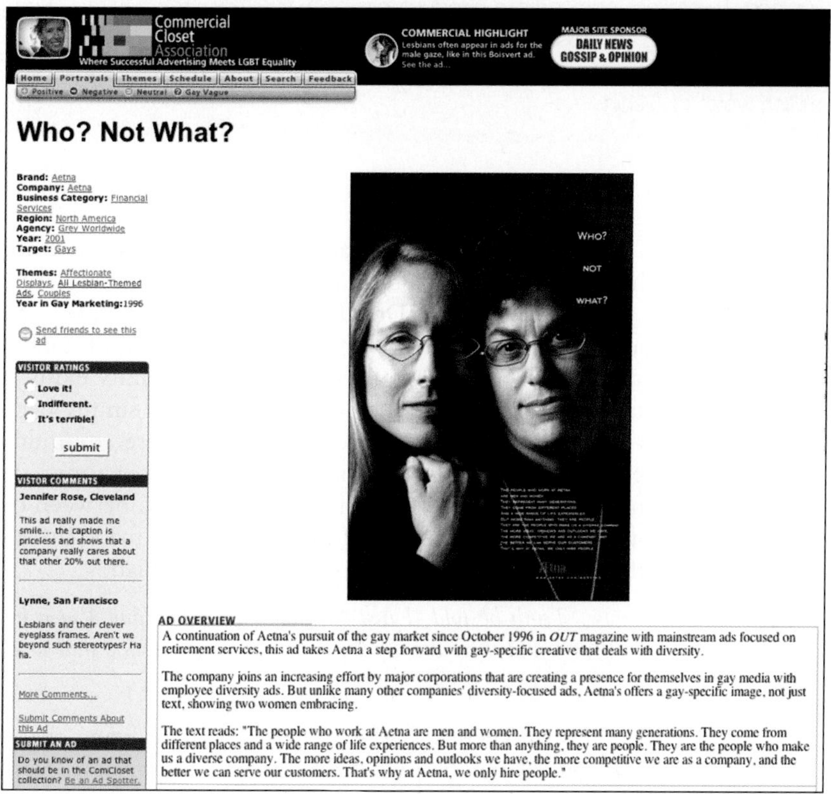

Courtesy, Commercial Closet Association

Advertisers are becoming increasingly aware of the power of community, particularly as it relates to social media. Products have social meanings, and community is the quintessential social domain, so consumption is inseparable from the notion of where we live (actually or virtually), and with whom we feel a kinship or a sense of belonging. Communities often exert a great deal of power. A community may be your neighborhood, or it may be people like you with whom you feel a kinship, such as members of social clubs, other consumers who collect the same things you do, or people who have, use, or admire the same brands you do.

Social Media

A Brand Community That Makes the Brand

Plenty of companies try to build communities around their brands. In Chicago, two young entrepreneurs took a more radical approach. When they launched the online T-shirt business Threadless in 2000, owners Jake Nickell and Jacob DeHart decided that all of the designs would come not from big-name stylists, but from the company's own customers.

Their business model is a simple one. The company accepts design ideas from anybody who wants to submit one, with about 125 new submissions coming in each day. The entries then are posted online, where visitors rate each design on a zero-to-five scale. Each week, the company picks six of the most popular designs to be printed on T-shirts. The winning designers each get $2,000, and Threadless.com gets a product pre-approved by its customers. The business has sold out of nearly every T-shirt it has offered; in 2006, the company sold $16 million worth of T-shirts.

Threadless.com also relies on its powerful online community to be the company's primary marketing tool. New visitors are encouraged to upload photos, leave comments, post blog entries, and refer friends. This powerful consumer audience even creates its own design stars. One 16-time winner, Ross Zietz, went to work for Threadless after graduating from Louisiana State University and has picked up freelance work designing shirts for musicians such as the Dave Matthews Band.

Threadless has gone well beyond merely cultivating a loyal customer community. In effect, its customers have become the company. "The bigger and more active the community, the more sales go up," said creative director Jeffrey Kalmikoff. "It's hard to argue with that formula."

Sources: Mark Weingarten, "Designed to Grow," *Business 2.0,* June 2007, p. 35; Rob Walker, "Consumed: Mass Appeal," *The New York Times Magazine,* July 8, 2007, p. 16.

Brand communities are groups of consumers who feel a commonality and a shared purpose attached to a consumer good or service.[23]

When owners of Doc Martens, Apple computers, Mountain Dew, Coca-Cola, or Threadless (Exhibit 5.49) experience a sense of connectedness by virtue of their common ownership or usage, a brand community exists. When two perfect strangers stand in a parking lot and act like old friends simply because they both own Volvos, a type of community is revealed. Most of these communities exist online, and some reveal a certain level of brand fanaticism. Other times, these communities reveal an important and more "mainstream" connection between owners, users, or admirers of brands, that with the rise of the Internet, has made these communities and this type of community conversation anything but trivial:

> *Truth be told, I just "found" this group and I'm a happy little person now that I've found there are other people out there like me that love their Miatas!*
>
> —From a Miata user-group post

This quote reveals the writer's joy at realizing that there are others out there who get it—who see what this "happy little person" sees in this material object, this car, and this brand: Miata. The promise of community—not to be alone, to share appreciation and admiration of something or someone, no matter how odd or inappropriate others feel it to be—is fulfilled in online communities. It is a rewarding and embracing social collective centered on a brand. This should not surprise us too much given how central consumption and branding have become in contemporary society. Brands matter socially, so brands matter.

23. Albert Muniz, Jr., and Thomas O'Guinn, "Brand Community," *Journal of Consumer Research,* vol. 27 (2001), 412–432.

Exhibit 5.49 More than a T-shirt... a community?

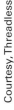

Courtesy, Threadless

Advertising, Social Rift, and "Revolution."

Thomas Frank, Doug Holt, Heath and Potter, and others have noted that consumers sometimes use their consumption choices to stake out a position in a "revolution" of sorts. Frank traces this to the 1960s cultural revolution (discussed in Chapter 4) and sees it as an opportunity, particularly for youth markets, to provide the costumes and consumable accessories for these "revolutions": certain "looks," such as dressing all in black, that say "I'm part of this political-social group." More generally, it must be remembered that anytime there is a great social movement, a time of rapid change, opportunities galore are opened up to the advertiser. When the earth moves under our feet, we feel off balance and in need of reassurance, and advertised products often promise that reassurance. Do you think you could buy some revolution, reassurance, tea, or sympathy at the Toronto establishments shown in Exhibit 5.50?

Some of these were mentioned in Chapter 4: how Pepsi used the youth revolution to tear into Coca-Cola's huge market share lead in the 1960s, how Virginia Slims used the feminist revolution of the 1970s to let women feel more rebellious (and liberated) by... smoking Virginia Slims..., or Apple giving those who chose not to see themselves as corporate a "computer for the rest of us." These were advertising's home runs—brands turned into cultural icons—by leveraging rifts or disruptions in the social sphere.

6 How Ads Transmit Meaning.

> *Start work in an ad agency and the first thing they teach you is the difference between a product and a brand. That is because it is advertising's job to turn one into another.*[24]
>
> —Martin Davidson

24. Martin Davidson, "Objects of Desire: How Advertising Works," in Martin Davidson, *The Consumerist Manifesto: Advertising in Postmodern Times* (London: Routledge, 1992), 23–60.

Exhibit 5.50 It may hurt, but it hurts so good.

Advertising can be thought of as a text. It is "read" and interpreted by consumers. You can think of it as being like other texts, books, movies, posters, paintings, and so on. It is a creative product. In order to "get" ads, you have to know something of the cultural code, or they would make no sense. In order to really understand a movie, to really get it, you have to know something about the culture that created it. Sometimes when you see a foreign film (even in your native tongue), you just don't quite get all the jokes and references, because you don't possess the cultural knowledge necessary to really effectively "read" the text. Ads try to turn already meaningful things into things with a very special meaning, a crafted meaning with the purpose of selling. Of course, consumers are free to accept, reject, or adjust that meaning to suit their taste. The advertisers say the thing they are selling is cool. The consumer might say, "No, it isn't," or "Yeah, it is," or "Well, yeah, but not in the way they think," or "Maybe for you, but not me." Even though advertisers try very hard to project just the right meaning, it is ultimately consumers who determine the meaning of ads and brands. Likewise, consumers determine what is or is not cool, what has cultural value (capital) to them, and how much. But advertisers are a big part of the conversation.

Yes, ads turn products into brands, and sometimes, successful ones. They do this, in large part, by trying to wrap material objects or marketed services with a certain meaning—a meaning that comes from culture. The link between culture and advertising is key. Anthropologist Grant McCracken has offered the model in Exhibit 5.51 to explain how advertising (along with other cultural agents) functions in the transmission of meaning. To understand advertising as a mechanism of cultural meaning transfer is to understand a great deal about advertising. In fact, one could legitimately say that advertisers are really in the meaning-transfer business. You take meaning that exists in the culture and massage it, shape it, and try to transfer it on to your brand.

Think about McCracken's model as you examine the ad for Ugg in Exhibit 5.52. The product—in this case, shoes—exists "out there" in the culturally constituted world (the real social world), but it needs advertising to link it to certain social scenes, certain slices of life. The advertiser places the advertised product and the

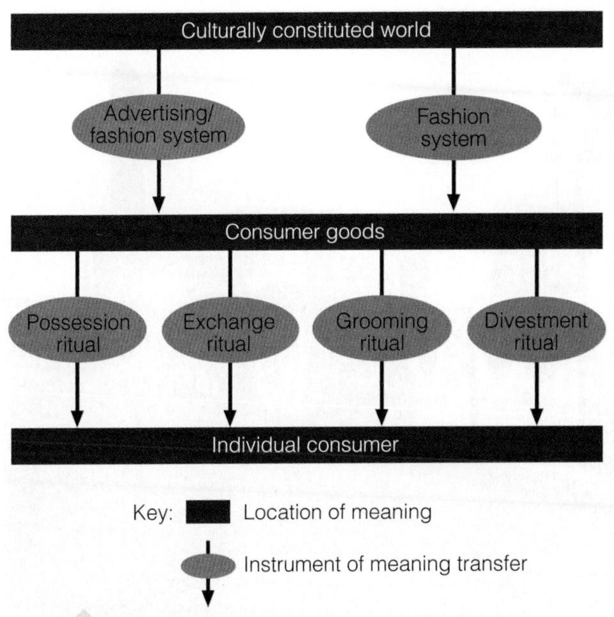

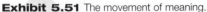

Exhibit 5.51 The movement of meaning.

Exhibit 5.52 Think about the social setting carefully constructed in this ad and how it gives the advertised brand its meaning.

Courtesy, Advertising Archives

slice of social life in an ad to get the two to rub off on each other, to intermingle, to become part of the same social scene. In other words, the product is given social meaning by being placed within an ad that represents an idealized context. This slice of life, of course, is the type of social setting in which potential customers might find, or desire to find, themselves. According to McCracken's model, meaning has moved from the world to the product (shoes) by virtue of its sharing space within the frame of the advertisement. When advertisers put things within the frame of an ad, they want the reader of the ad to put them together seamlessly, to take them together as part of each other. When a consumer purchases or otherwise incorporates that good or service into his or her own life, the meaning is transferred to the individual consumer. Meaning is thus moved from the world to the product (via advertising) to the individual. When the individual uses the product, that person conveys to others the meaning he or she and the advertisement have now given it. Their use incorporates various rituals that facilitate the movement of meaning from good to consumer. The rituals aren't central to this discussion, but they would be the kinds of things discussed above in the section on rituals. For example, one of the first things you probably do when you buy a home from someone is to make it more "yours" by vacuuming, scrubbing, and painting it, etc., even if you are completely happy with the paint and are convinced it is clean. You put your stuff on the walls partly to make it yours (possession rituals).

Ads also become part of consumers' everyday landscape, language, and everyday reality. Characters, lines, and references all become part of conversations, thoughts, and—coming full circle—the culture. Children, coworkers, family members, and talk-show hosts all pick up phrases, ideas, slogans, and agenda from ads, and then replay them, adapt them, and recirculate them just like things from movies, books, and other texts. Ads, in many ways, don't exist just within the sociocultural context; they *are* the sociocultural context of our time. (Exhibit 5.53 is a particularly poignant example: The Berlin Wall that once separated capitalism and consumer culture from Marxist-Socialist planned economy on state-produced goods is now a place to hang ads.) If you want to do well in the real ad world, it's a very good idea to understand that getting the contemporary culture and knowing how to move it into ads is worth its weight in gold.

Exhibit 5.53 The Berlin Wall is now a place for ads.

Summary

1 Describe the four basic stages of consumer decision making.

Advertisers need a keen understanding of their consumers as a basis for developing effective advertising. This understanding begins with a view of consumers as systematic decision makers who follow a predictable process in making their choices among products and brands. The process begins when consumers perceive a need, and it proceeds with a search for information that will help in making an informed choice. The search-and-evaluation stage is followed by purchase. Postpurchase use and evaluation then become critical as the stage in which customer satisfaction is ultimately determined.

2 Explain how consumers adapt their decision-making processes as a function of involvement and experience.

Some purchases are more important to people than others, and this fact adds complexity to any analysis of consumer behavior. To accommodate this complexity, advertisers often think about the level of involvement that attends any given purchase. Involvement and prior experience with a product or service category can lead to four diverse modes of consumer decision making. These modes are extended problem solving, limited problem solving, habit or variety seeking, and brand loyalty.

3 Discuss how advertising may influence consumer behavior through its effects on various psychological states.

Advertisements are developed to influence the way people think about products and brands. More specifically, advertising is designed to affect consumers' beliefs and brand attitudes. Advertisers use multi-attribute attitude models to help them ascertain the beliefs and attitudes of target consumers. However, consumers have perceptual defenses that allow them to ignore or distort most of the commercial messages to which they are exposed. When consumers are not motivated to thoughtfully process an advertiser's message, it may be in that advertiser's best interest to feature one or more peripheral cues as part of the message.

4 Discuss the role of culture in creating effective ads.

Advertisements are cultural products, and culture provides the context in which an ad will be interpreted. Advertisers who overlook the influence of culture are bound to struggle in their attempt to communicate with the target audience. Values are enduring beliefs that provide a foundation for more-transitory psychological states, such as brand attitudes. Rituals are patterns of behavior shared by individuals from a common culture. Violating cultural values and rituals is a sure way to squander advertising dollars. Advertising and integrated brand promotion help turn products into brands. They do this by wrapping brands with cultural meaning. Brands with high cultural capital are worth more. Brands are co-created by consumers and advertisers.

5 Discuss the role of sociological factors in consumer behavior and advertising.

Consumer behavior is an activity that each of us undertakes before a broad audience of other consumers. Advertising helps the transfer of meaning. Gender, ethnicity, and race are important influences on consumption. Who consumers are—their identity—is changeable; consumers can change aspects of who they are rapidly and frequently through what they buy and use. Celebrities are particularly important in this regard.

6 Discuss how effective advertising uses sociocultural meaning in order to sell things.

Advertising transfers a desired meaning to the brand by placing them within a carefully constructed social world represented in an ad, or "slice of life." The advertiser paints a picture of the ideal social world, with all the meanings they want to impart to their brand. Then, the brand is carefully placed in that picture, and the two (the constructed social world and the brand) rub off on each other, becoming a part of each other. Meaning is thus transferred from the carefully constructed social world within the ad to the brand.

Key Terms

consumer behavior
need state
functional benefits
emotional benefits
internal search
consideration set
external search
evaluative criteria
customer satisfaction
cognitive dissonance
involvement
extended problem solving
limited problem solving
habit
variety seeking
brand loyalty
attitude
brand attitudes
beliefs
salient beliefs
multi-attribute attitude models (MAAMs)
cognitive consistency
advertising clutter
selective attention
cognitive responses
elaboration likelihood model (ELM)
peripheral cues
meaning
culture
values
rituals
stratification (social class)
taste
intergenerational effect
life-stage
celebrity
gender
community
brand communities

Questions

1. When consumers have a well-defined consideration set and a list of evaluative criteria for assessing the brands in that set, they in effect possess a matrix of information about that category. Drawing on your experiences as a consumer, set up and fill in such a matrix for the category of fast-food restaurants.

2. Is cognitive dissonance a good thing or a bad thing from an advertiser's point of view? Explain how and why advertisers should try to take advantage of the cognitive dissonance their consumers may experience.

3. Most people quickly relate to the notion that some purchasing decisions are more involving than others. What kinds of products or services do you consider highly involving? What makes these products more involving from your point of view?

4. Explain the difference between brand-loyal and habitual purchasing. When a brand-loyal customer arrives at a store and finds her favorite brand out of stock, what would you expect to happen next?

5. Describe three attitude-change strategies that could be suggested by the results of a study of consumer behavior using multi-attribute attitude models. Provide examples of different advertising campaigns that have employed each of these strategies.

6. Watch an hour of prime-time television and for each commercial you see, make a note of the tactic the advertiser employed to capture and hold the audience's attention. How can the use of attention-attracting tactics backfire on an advertiser?

7. What does it mean to say that culture is invisible? Explain how this invisible force serves to restrict and control the activities of advertisers.

8. Give three examples of highly visible cultural rituals practiced annually in the United States. For each ritual you identify, assess the importance of buying and consuming for effective practice of the ritual.

9. Are you a believer in the intergenerational effect? Make a list of the brands in your cupboards, refrigerator, and medicine cabinet. Which of these brands would you also expect to find in your parents' cupboards, refrigerator, and medicine cabinet?

10. "In today's modern, highly educated society, there is simply no reason to separate men and women into different target segments. Gender just should not be an issue in the development of marketing and advertising strategies." Comment.

Experiential Exercises

1. How well do online advertisers understand your consumer behavior? Today's interactive ads are so personalized that Web users routinely encounter the products and messages most likely to appeal to their unique customer profile and preferences. As an out-of-class assignment, identify 20 ads that you see while browsing the Web on your computer or smartphone. For each, list whether or not the ad seemed relevant to your buying habits. Were the brands the ones you use or are likely to try? Did the messages address your social and cultural life context? Finally, judge whether online ads generally treated you as a "decision maker" or a "social being," and explain your answer.

2. Divide the class into teams and have each group create a campaign concept that directly addresses sociological factors of consumer behavior. Each group should create a campaign based on concepts of stratification, taste, and cultural capital. Once brands and campaigns are developed, each team should present its idea to the class and allow students to guess the income level, education, and occupational prestige of the campaign's target audience. (Team members should keep this information confidential until after the class makes its evaluation.) Finally, take a vote on which campaign is most effective at appealing to the sociological motivations and tastes of its intended audience.

3. A key issue in postpurchase evaluation is cognitive dissonance—the anxiety or "buyer's remorse" that can linger after high-involvement purchasing decisions. Research has shown that some consumers are more likely to read ads for a product they already have purchased than ads for competing brands. With this in mind, imagine that you have been hired by the luxury watchmaker Breitling to design an ad campaign specifically intended to ease potential cognitive dissonance. What steps could the company make to reach out to consumers after the purchase? What advertising messages and imagery could be most effective in reinforcing the consumer's decision to purchase the watch?

4. Working in small teams, brainstorm ideas for an advertising campaign that has as its primary target audience the community of consumers who are intensely loyal to Vans, the surf and skateboard brand best known for its quirky, slip-on canvas shoes. What steps would you take to tap into this brand community? As you develop ideas, explain how those approaches would connect to the rituals and values of that community. Also consider what sociocultural meaning the campaign would convey about the brand and its users.

Chapter 6

Market Segmentation, Positioning, and the Value Proposition

After reading and thinking about this chapter, you will be able to do the following:

1. Explain the process known as STP marketing.
2. Describe different bases that marketers use to identify target segments.
3. Discuss the criteria used for choosing a target segment.
4. Identify the essential elements of an effective positioning strategy.
5. Review the necessary ingredients for creating a brand's value proposition.

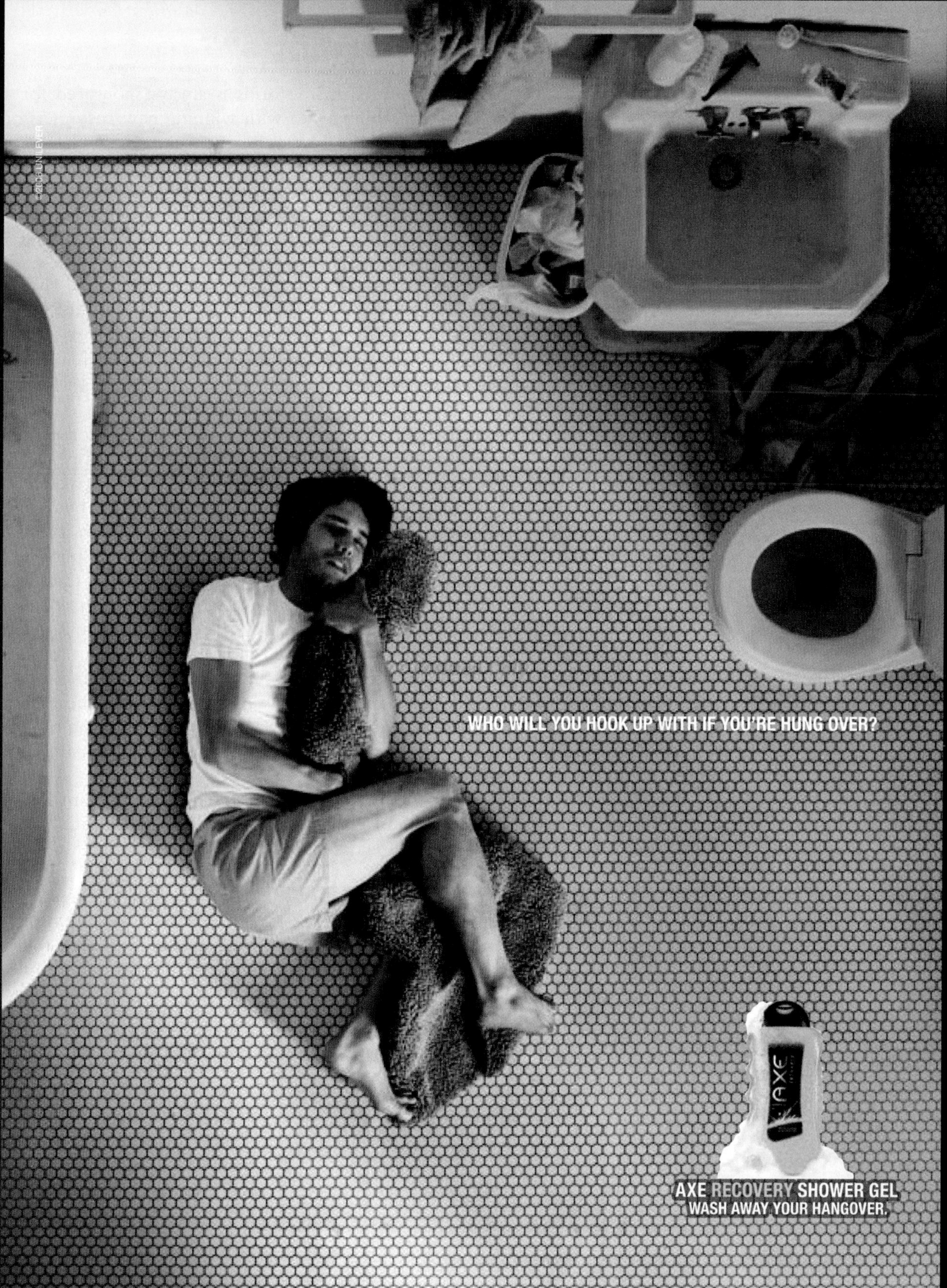

WHO WILL YOU HOOK UP WITH IF YOU'RE HUNG OVER?

AXE RECOVERY SHOWER GEL
WASH AWAY YOUR HANGOVER.

Courtesy, © Unilever USA

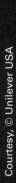

Introductory Scenario: How Well Do You "Tolerate Mornings"?

You know by now that advertising in its many forms is always sponsored for a reason. Generally that reason has something to do with winning new customers or reinforcing the habits of existing customers.[1] However, advertising has no chance of producing a desired result if we are unclear about who we want to reach. We need a target audience.

One special problem that most companies face is reaching potential customers just as they are experimenting in a product category for the first time. This is a pivotal time when one wants the consumer to have a great experience with your brand. So, for example, if we are Gillette and seek to market anything and everything associated with shaving, we will want one of our shavers in the hands of the consumer the first time he or she shaves. First-time users are not heavy users, but they represent the future. If we don't keep winning these beginners, eventually, we are out of business. Developing advertising campaigns to win with first-time users is often referred to as point-of-entry marketing. More on that later...

Folgers does a huge business in the coffee category but can take nothing for granted when it comes to new users. Thus, the marketers of Folgers must launch campaigns to appeal specifically to the next generation of coffee drinkers. These of course would be young people just learning the coffee habit. Attracted by coffee titans like Starbucks and Dunkin' Donuts, many people get to know coffee in their teens. But when it's time to start brewing coffee at home, Folgers sees its big chance to get in your cupboard.

To illustrate, the Folgers brand team launched an advertising initiative to attract just-graduated 20-somethings. When young adults move into the "real world" and take that first job with a new apartment in a strange city, they are primed to develop the coffee habit. Folgers aspires to be the brand of choice for this target as they potentially commit to a morning brew-it-yourself coffee ritual. We all know that mornings are tough, so Folgers just wants to make them tolerable. But how does Folgers, your grandparents' brand, make a connection with a new generation of coffee drinkers? Tried and true slogans ("The best part of waking up is Folgers in your cup") and 30-second TV spots just won't do.

Working with its ad agency Saatchi & Saatchi, the Folgers brand team found another way. It started with the premise that mornings are hard, filled with emails and bosses making demands and those darn "morning people" (who for some bizarre reason seem to love sunrises). Folgers exists to help a person tolerate mornings, and especially to tolerate those morning people. A short film, titled something like "Happy Mornings: The Revenge of the Yellow People," was produced to show Folgers as your first line of defense when the fanatical Yellow People try to invade your space first thing in the morning (that's them coming out of the sunrise and across the lake in Exhibit 6.1). The film was also designed to steer traffic to a website

Exhibit 6.1 The Yellow People glow like a sunrise and they want you!

1. Christie L. Nordhielm, *Marketing Management: The Big Picture* (Hoboken, NJ: John Wiley & Sons, Inc., 2006).

Exhibit 6.2 Your best defense when the Yellow People show up unannounced.

(per Exhibit 6.2) where other tools (boss-tracker, auto emails, wake-up calls, screen-saver) for making mornings go better were available. The campaign also included print ads code-named "Dreamscapes," reflecting that frightful moment just before dawn when the creepy Yellow People are planning their attack.

The provocative aspect of the Yellow People film is that zero dollars were spent on media. That's right, zero dollars. Rather, the spot was submitted to three websites (Adcritic, BestadsonTV.com, and Boards) where 20-somethings had their way with it. Chatter quickly spread across the blogosphere, website hits increased, and the film was soon posted on YouTube (receiving 4 out of 5 stars and more than 300,000 viewings). This little sample of YouTube comments suggests that the Folgers team was on the right track in their effort to engage new users:

> *"I now watch this every morning to wake up, cause it's just so damn funny and awesome that it wakes me right up. If I ever get rich I'm going to hire a bunch of people to dress like happy yellow people and come wake me up with that song every morning."*
>
> *"I am without speech at the sheer brilliance. If commercials were like this... I wouldn't skip them on the DVR."*
>
> *"I took one look at that video and went straight into the kitchen and made a cup of coffee at 9:30 pm, because after all, I can sleep when I am dead!"*

Many companies large and small share the problem we see embedded in the Folgers example. Simply stated, we must be clear on who we are trying to reach and then on what we can say that will resonate with them. Companies address this challenge through a process referred to as STP marketing. It is a critical process from our standpoint because it leads to decisions about *who* we need to advertise to, *what* value proposition we want to present to them, and *how* we plan to reach them with our message.

1 STP Marketing and the Evolution of Marketing Strategies.

The Folgers example illustrates the process that marketers use to decide who to advertise to and what to say. The Folgers brand team started with the diverse market of all possible coffee drinkers, and broke the market down by age segments. They then selected *just-graduated 20-somethings* as their target segment. The **target segment** is the subgroup (of the larger market) chosen as the focal point for the marketing program and advertising campaign.

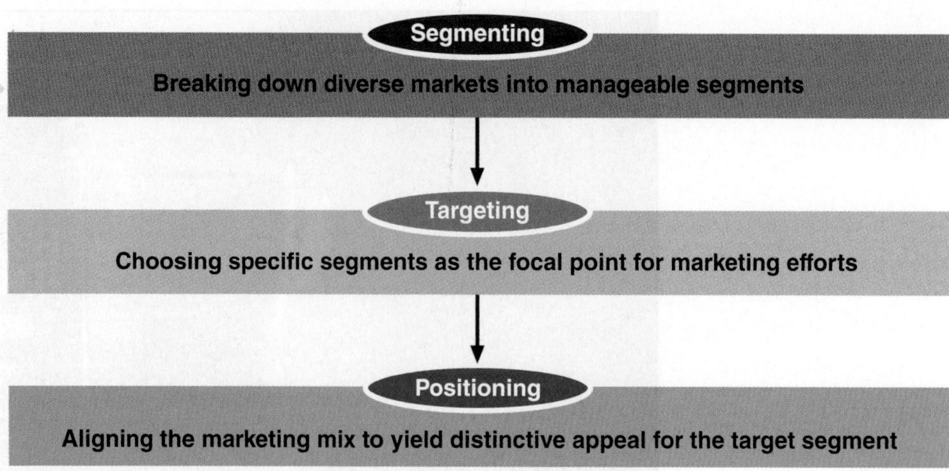

Exhibit 6.3 Laying the foundation for effective advertising campaigns through STP marketing.

Markets are segmented; products are positioned. To pursue the target segment, a firm organizes its marketing and advertising efforts around a coherent positioning strategy. **Positioning** is the process of designing and representing one's product or service so that it will occupy a distinct and valued place in the target consumer's mind. **Positioning strategy** involves the selection of key themes or concepts that the organization will feature when communicating this distinctiveness to the target segment. In Folgers's case, the positioning concept may not seem all that inspiring: it's all about "Tolerate Mornings." But the idea is to position Folgers in such a way that just-graduated 20-somethings can relate. Folks on the Folgers team assumed that they would not convert this segment with an old-fashioned slogan like "The best part of waking up is Folgers in your cup." And of course we see in this example a skillful, low-cost approach to getting the message in front of the target: Let YouTube do it!

Notice the specific sequence illustrated in Exhibit 6.3 that was played out in the Folgers example: The marketing strategy evolved as a result of *segmenting, targeting,* and *positioning*. This sequence of activities is often referred to as **STP marketing,** and it represents a sound basis for generating effective advertising.[2] Although no formulas or models guarantee success, the STP approach is strongly recommended for markets characterized by diversity in consumers' needs and preferences. In markets with any significant degree of diversity, it is impossible to design one product that will appeal to everyone, or one advertising campaign that will communicate with everyone. Organizations that lose sight of this simple premise run into trouble.

Indeed, in most product categories one finds that different consumers are looking for different things, and the only way for a company to take advantage of the sales potential represented by different customer segments is to develop and market a different brand for each segment. No company has done this better than cosmetics juggernaut Estée Lauder.[3] Lauder has more than a dozen cosmetic brands, each developed for a different target segment. For example, there is the original Estée Lauder brand, for women with conservative values and upscale tastes. Then there is Clinique, a no-nonsense brand that represents functional grooming for Middle America. Bobbi Brown is for the working mom who skillfully manages a career and her family and manages to look good in the process, just like the real Bobbi Brown.[4] M.A.C. is a brand for those who want to make a bolder statement: Its spokespersons have been

2. For more on STP marketing, see Philip Kotler, *Marketing Management* (Upper Saddle River, NJ: Prentice Hall, 2003), chs. 10, 11.

3. Nina Munk, "Why Women Find Lauder Mesmerizing," *Fortune,* May 25, 1998, 96–106.

4. Athena Schindelheim, "Bobbi Brown: How I Did It," *Inc. Magazine,* November 2007, 110–112.

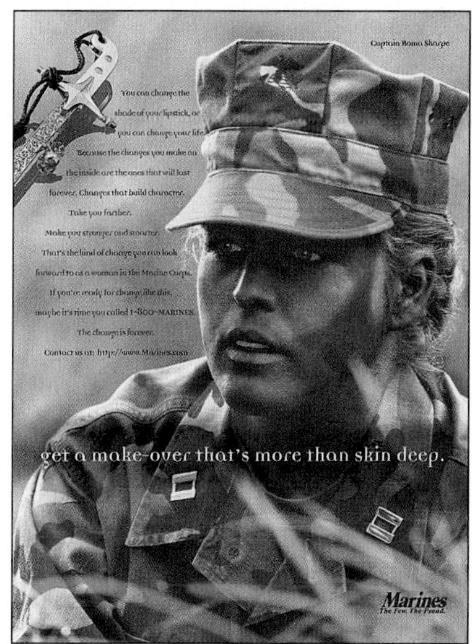

Exhibit 6.4 The U.S. Armed Forces, including the Marines, are very aggressive and sophisticated advertisers. Note how they position themselves with their advertising slogan: The Few, The Proud, The Marines (www.marines.com).

RuPaul, a 6-foot-7-inch drag queen; Boy George; Missy Elliot; Linda Evangelista; and a host of others. Prescriptives is marketed to a hip, urban, multiethnic target segment, and Origins, with its earthy packaging and natural ingredients, celebrates the connection between Mother Nature and human nature. These are just some of the cosmetics brands that Estée Lauder has marketed to appeal to diverse target segments. Check out the company's current brand lineup at www.elcompanies.com.

We offer the Estée Lauder example to make two key points before moving on. First, the Folgers case may have made things seem too simple: STP marketing is a lot more complicated than just deciding to target a particular age group. Age alone is rarely specific enough to serve as a complete identifier of a target segment. Second, the cosmetics' example shows that many factors beyond demographics can come into play when trying to identify valid target segments. For these diverse cosmetics' brands, we see that considerations such as attitudes, lifestyles, and basic values all may play a role in identifying and describing customer segments.

To reinforce these points, examine the two ads in Exhibits 6.4 and 6.5. Both ran in *Seventeen* magazine, so it is safe to say that in each case the advertiser was trying to reach adolescent females. But as you compare these exhibits, it should be pretty obvious that the advertisers were really trying to reach out to very different segments of adolescent females. To put it bluntly, it is hard to imagine a marine captain wearing Hard Candy lip gloss. These ads were designed to appeal to different target segments, even though the people in these segments would seem the same if we considered only their age and gender.

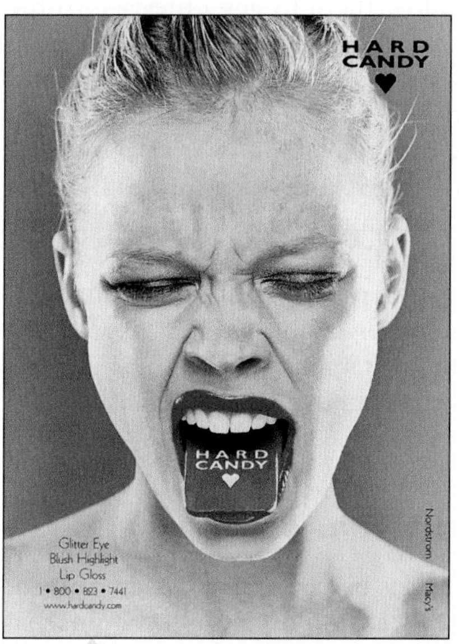

Exhibit 6.5 Hard Candy comes by its hip style perhaps in large part because of its uninhibitedly energetic founding by Gen-Xer Dineh Mohajer, who was unhappy with the choices traditional cosmetics firms offered her and her market demographic (www.hardcandy.com). There must be something in that California air. Internet technology company Cisco co-founder Sandy Lerner created Urban Decay (www.urbandecay.com)—another alternative for the fashion-mad—out of a similar dissatisfaction with the offerings of companies like Lancôme (www.lancome.com).

Beyond STP Marketing.

If an organization uses STP marketing as its framework for strategy development, at some point it will find the right strategy, develop the right advertising, make a lot of money, and live happily ever after. Right? As you might expect, it's not quite that simple. Even when STP marketing yields profitable outcomes, one must presume that success will not last indefinitely. Indeed, an important feature of marketing and advertising—a feature that can make these professions both terribly interesting and terribly frustrating—is their dynamic nature. To paraphrase a popular saying, shifts happen—consumer preferences shift. Competitors improve their marketing strategies, or technology changes and makes a popular product obsolete. Successful marketing strategies need to be modified or may even need to be reinvented as shifts occur in the organization's competitive environment.

To maintain the vitality and profitability of its products or services, an organization has two options. The first entails reassessment of the segmentation strategy. This may come through a more detailed examination of the current target segment to develop new and better ways of meeting its needs, or it may be necessary to adopt new targets and position new brands for them, as illustrated by the Estée Lauder example.

The second option is to pursue a product differentiation strategy. Product differentiation focuses the firm's efforts on emphasizing or even creating differences for its brands to distinguish them from competitors' offerings. Advertising plays a critical role as part of the product differentiation strategy because often the consumer will have to be convinced that the intended difference is meaningful. For example, Schick's response to Gillette's Mach3 Turbo was the Schick Quattro with four blades instead of three. But does that fourth blade really deliver a better shave? How could it be better than "The Best a Man Can Get"? Following a product differentiation strategy, the role for Schick's advertising is to convince men that that fourth blade is essential for a close shave. But next up is Gillette's Fusion, with five blades to shave you closer than close. And so it goes.

The message is that marketing strategies and the advertising that supports them are never really final. Successes realized through proper application of STP marketing can be short-lived in highly competitive markets where any successful innovation is almost sure to be copied or "one-upped" by competitors. Thus, the value creation process for marketers and advertisers is continuous; STP marketing must be pursued over and over again and may be supplemented with product differentiation strategies.

Virtually every organization must compete for the attention and business of some customer groups while de-emphasizing or ignoring others. In this chapter we will examine in detail the way organizations decide who to target and who to ignore in laying the foundation for their marketing programs and advertising campaigns. The critical role of advertising campaigns in executing these strategies is also highlighted.

2 Identifying Target Segments.

The first step in STP marketing involves breaking down large, heterogeneous markets into more manageable submarkets or customer segments. This activity is known as **market segmentation.** It can be accomplished in many ways, but keep in mind that advertisers need to identify a segment with common characteristics that will lead the members of that segment to respond distinctively to a marketing program. For a segment to be really useful, advertisers also must be able to reach that segment with information about the product. Typically this means that advertisers must be able to identify the media the segment uses that will allow them to get a message to the segment. For example, teenage males can be reached through product placements in video games and movies; selected rap, contemporary rock, or country radio stations; and all things Internet. The favorite syndicated TV show among highly affluent households (i.e., annual household income more than $100,000) is *Seinfeld,* making it a popular choice for advertisers looking to reach big spenders.

In this section we will review several ways that consumer markets are commonly segmented. Markets can be segmented on the basis of usage patterns and commitment levels, demographic and geographic information, psychographics and lifestyles, or benefits sought. Many times, segmentation schemes evolve in such a way that multiple variables are used to identify and describe the target segment. Such an outcome is desirable because more knowledge about the target will usually translate into better marketing and advertising programs.

Usage Patterns and Commitment Levels.

One of the most common ways to segment markets is by consumers' usage patterns or commitment levels. With respect to usage patterns, it is important to recognize that for most products and services, some users will purchase much more frequently than others. It is common to find that **heavy users** in a category account for the majority of a product's sales and thus become the preferred or primary target segment.[5]

For instance, Coffee-mate executives launched a program to get to know their customers better by returning calls to those who had left a complaint or suggestion using the toll-free number printed on the product packaging.[6] As a result they met Paula Baumgartner, a 44-year-old who consumes four jars of Coffee-mate's mocha-flavored

5. Don E. Schultz, "Pareto Pared," *Marketing News,* November 15, 2009, 24; Steve Hughes, "Small Segments, Big Payoff," *Advertising Age,* January 15, 2007, 17.

6. Deborah Ball, "Toll-Free Tips: Nestle Hotlines Yield Big Ideas," *The Wall Street Journal,* September 3, 2004, A7.

creamer every week. (Yes, that's more than 200 jars a year!) Now that's a heavy user. Conventional marketing thought holds that it is in Coffee-mate's best interest to get to know heavy users like Paula in great depth and make them a focal point of the company's marketing strategy. On a side note that the Folgers brand team would love, Baumgartner explained that she got her start as a regular coffee drinker at age 21 in her first full-time job (i.e., she was a *just-graduated 20-something.*) Don't know if she now brews Folgers...

Although being the standard wisdom, the heavy-user focus has some potential downsides. For one, devoted users may need no encouragement at all to keep consuming. In addition, a heavy-user focus takes attention and resources away from those who do need encouragement to purchase the marketer's brand. Perhaps most important, heavy users may differ significantly from average or infrequent users in terms of their motivations to consume, their approach to the brand, or their image of the brand.

Another segmentation option combines prior usage patterns with commitment levels to identify four fundamental segment types—brand-loyal customers, switchers (or variety seekers), nonusers, and emergent consumers.[7] Each segment represents a unique opportunity for the advertiser. **Nonusers** offer the lowest level of opportunity relative to the other three groups. **Brand-loyal users** are a tremendous asset if they are the advertiser's customers, but they are difficult to convert if they are loyal to a competitor.

Switchers or **variety seekers** often buy what is on sale or choose brands that offer discount-coupons or other price incentives. Whether they are pursued through price incentives, high-profile advertising campaigns, or both, switchers turn out to be a costly target segment. Much can be spent in getting their business merely to have it disappear just as quickly as it was won.

Emergent consumers offer the organization an important business opportunity. In most product categories there is a gradual but constant influx of first-time buyers. The reasons for this influx vary by product category and include purchase triggers such as puberty, college graduation, marriage, a new baby, divorce, a new job, a big raise, or retirement. Immigration can also be a source of numerous new customers in many product categories. Generation X attracted the attention of marketers and advertisers because it was a large group of emergent adult consumers. But inevitably, Generation X lost its emergent status and was replaced by a new age cohort—Generation Y—who took their turn as advertisers' darlings.[8]

Emergent consumers are motivated by many different factors, but they share one notable characteristic: Their brand preferences are still under development. Targeting emergents with messages that fit their age or social circumstances may produce modest effects in the short run, but it eventually may yield a brand loyalty that pays handsome rewards for the discerning organization. Developing advertising campaigns to win with first-time users is often referred to as **point-of-entry marketing.** Sound familiar? This was exactly Folgers' rationale in targeting *just-graduated 20-somethings.* As another case in point, banks actively recruit college students who have limited financial resources in the short term, but excellent potential as long-term customers. Exhibit 6.6 shows an ad from Wells Fargo Bank with an appeal to emergent consumers at the University of Arizona.

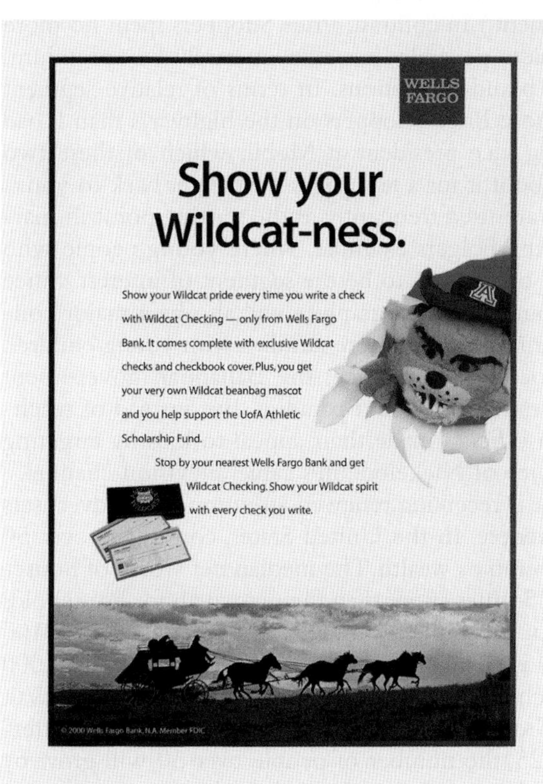

Exhibit 6.6 Emergent consumers represent an important source of long-term opportunity for many organizations. Have you ever thought of yourself as an emergent consumer? www.wellsfargo.com

7. This four-way scheme is detailed in David W. Stewart, "Advertising in Slow-Growth Economies," *American Demographics* (September 1994), 40–46.

8. Bonnie Tsui, "Generation Next," *Advertising Age,* January 15, 2001, 14, 16.

Demographic Segmentation.

Demographic segmentation is widely used in selecting target segments and includes basic descriptors such as age, gender, race, marital status, income, education, and occupation (see the array of possibilities at www.factfinder.census.gov). Demographic information has special value in market segmentation because if an advertiser knows the demographic characteristics of the target segment, choosing media to efficiently reach that segment is easier.

Demographic information has two specific applications. First, demographics are commonly used to describe or profile segments that have been identified with some other variable. If an organization had first segmented its market in terms of product usage rates, the next step would be to describe or profile its heavy users in terms of demographic characteristics such as age or income. In fact, one of the most common approaches for identifying target segments is to combine information about usage patterns with demographics.

Mobil Oil Corporation used such an approach in segmenting the market for gasoline buyers and identified five basic segments: Road Warriors, True Blues, Generation F3, Homebodies, and Price Shoppers.[9] Extensive research on more than 2,000 motorists revealed considerable insight about these five segments. At one extreme, Road Warriors spent at least $1,200 per year at gas stations; they bought premium gasoline and snacks and beverages and sometimes opted for a car wash. Road Warriors were generally more affluent, middle-aged males who drive 25,000 to 50,000 miles per year. (Note how Mobil combined information about usage patterns with demographics to provide a detailed picture of the segment.) In contrast, Price Shoppers spent no more than $700 annually at gas stations, were generally less affluent, rarely buy premium, and showed no loyalty to particular brands or stations. In terms of relative segment sizes, there were about 25 percent more Price Shoppers on the highways than Road Warriors. If you were the marketing vice president at Mobil, which of these two segments would you target? Think about it for a few pages—we'll get back to you.

Second, demographic categories are used frequently as the starting point in market segmentation. This was true in the Folgers example, where young people who had recently graduated from college turned out to be the segment of interest. Since families commonly plan vacations together, demographics will also be a major consideration for targeting by the tourism industry, where families with young children are often the marketer's primary focus. For instance, the Bahamian government launched a program to attract families to their island paradise. But instead of reaching out to mom and dad, Bahamian officials made their appeal to kids by targeting the 2-to-11-year-old viewing audience of Nickelodeon's cable television channel.[10]

Another demographic group that is receiving renewed attention from advertisers is the "woopies," or well-off older people. In the United States, consumers over 50 years old control two-thirds of the country's wealth. The median net worth of households headed by persons 55 to 64 is 15 times larger than the net worth for households headed by a person under age 35. Put in simple terms, for most people age 20, $100 is a lot of money. For woopies, $100 is change back from the purchase of a $10,000 home theatre system. Marketers such as Ford, Sony, Target, Anheuser-Busch, Walt Disney, and Virgin Entertainment Group have all reconsidered their product offerings with woopies in mind.[11] By 2025, the number of people over 50 will grow by 80 percent to become a third of the U.S. population. Growth in the woopie segment will also be dramatic in other countries, such as Japan and the nations of Western Europe. Still, like any other age segment, older consumers are a diverse group, and the temptation to stereotype must be resisted. Some marketers advocate partitioning

9. Allanna Sullivan, "Mobil Bets Drivers Pick Cappuccino over Low Prices," *The Wall Street Journal,* January 30, 1995, B1.
10. Sally Beatty, "Nickelodeon Sets $30 Million Ad Deal with the Bahamas," *The Wall Street Journal,* March 14, 2001, B6.
11. Kelly Greene, "Marketing Surprise: Older Consumers Buy Stuff, Too," *The Wall Street Journal,* April 6, 2004, A1, A12.

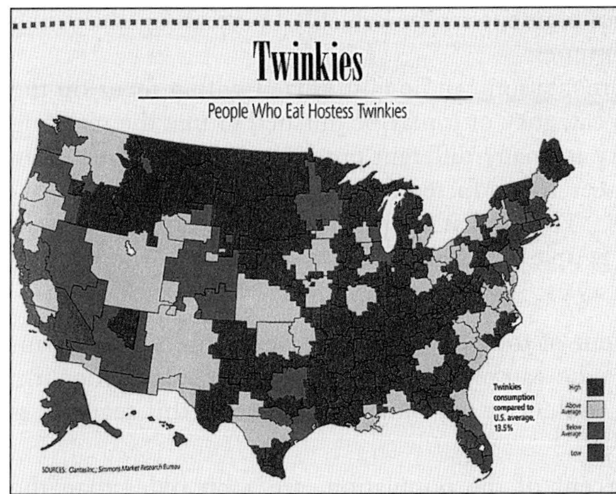

Exhibit 6.7 People who eat Hostess Twinkies (red marks the highest consumption).

Simmons Market Research Bureau

older consumers into groups aged 50–64, 65–74, 75–84, and 85 or older, as a means of reflecting important differences in needs. That's a good start, but again, age alone will not tell the whole story.

Geographic Segmentation.

Geographic segmentation needs little explanation other than to emphasize how useful geography is in segmenting markets. Geographic segmentation may be conducted within a country by region (for example, the Pacific Northwest versus New England in the United States), by state or province, by city, or even by neighborhood. Climate and topographical features yield dramatic differences in consumption by region for products such as snow tires and surfboards, but geography can also correlate with other differences that are not so obvious. Eating and food preparation habits, entertainment preferences, recreational activities, and other aspects of lifestyle have been shown to vary along geographic lines. As shown in Exhibit 6.7, even a brand like Hostess Twinkies has its red and blue states. In addition, recent research indicates that states and regions of the United States vary in meaningful ways regarding dominant personality traits. For example, Rhode Island residents are the most insecure, those in Georgia are conscientious and loyal, and the most extroverted—North Dakota, of course![12]

In recent years skillful marketers have merged information on where people live with the U.S. Census Bureau's demographic data to produce a form of market segmentation known as geodemographic segmentation. **Geodemographic segmentation** identifies neighborhoods (by zip codes) around the country that share common demographic characteristics. One such system, known as PRIZM (potential rating index by zip marketing), identifies 62 market segments that encompass all the zip codes in the United States. Each of these segments has similar lifestyle characteristics and can be found throughout the country.

For example, the American Dreams segment is found in many metropolitan neighborhoods and comprises upwardly mobile ethnic minorities, many of whom were foreign-born. This segment's brand preferences are different from those of people belonging to the Rural Industrial segment, who are young families with one or both parents working at low-wage jobs in small-town America. Systems such as PRIZM are very popular because of the depth of segment description they provide, along with their ability to precisely identify where the segment can be found (for more details, Google Claritas PRIZM).

Psychographics and Lifestyle Segmentation.

Psychographics is a term that advertisers created in the mid-1960s to refer to a form of research that emphasizes the understanding of consumers' activities, interests, and opinions (AIOs).[13] Many advertising agencies were using demographic variables for segmentation purposes, but they wanted insights into consumers' motivations, which demographic variables did not provide. Psychographics were created as a tool to supplement the use of demographic data. Because a focus on consumers' activities, interests, and opinions often produces insights into differences in the lifestyles of various segments, this approach usually results in **lifestyle segmentation**. Knowing

12. Beth Bulik, "How Would You Target the Stress Belt?" *Advertising Age,* September 29, 2008, 10.

13. Michael R. Solomon, *Consumer Behavior* (Upper Saddle River, NJ: Pearson/Prentice Hall, 2007), 215–219.

details about the lifestyle of a target segment can be valuable for creating advertising messages that ring true to the consumer.

Lifestyle or psychographic segmentation can be customized with a focus on the issues germane to a single product category, or it may be pursued so that the resulting segments have general applicability to many different product or service categories. An illustration of the former is research conducted for Pillsbury to segment the eating habits of American households.[14] This "What's Cookin'" study involved consumer interviews with more than 3,000 people and identified five segments of the population, based on their shared eating styles:

- ***Chase & Grabbits,*** at 26 percent of the population, are heavy users of all forms of fast food. These are people who can make a meal out of microwave popcorn; as long as the popcorn keeps hunger at bay and is convenient, this segment is happy with its meal.
- ***Functional Feeders,*** at 18 percent of the population, are a bit older than the Chase & Grabbits but no less convenience-oriented. Since they are more likely to have families, their preferences for convenient foods involve frozen products that are quickly prepared at home. They constantly seek faster ways to prepare the traditional foods they grew up with.
- ***Down-Home Stokers,*** at 21 percent of the population, involve blue-collar households with modest incomes. They are very loyal to their regional diets, such as meat and potatoes in the Midwest and clam chowder in New England. Fried chicken, biscuits and gravy, and bacon and eggs make this segment the champion of cholesterol.
- ***Careful Cooks,*** at 20 percent of the population, are more prevalent on the West Coast. They have replaced most of the red meat in their diet with pastas, fish, skinless chicken, and mounds of fresh fruit and vegetables. They believe they are knowledgeable about nutritional issues and are willing to experiment with foods that offer healthful options.
- ***Happy Cookers*** are the remaining 15 percent of the population but are a shrinking segment. These cooks are family-oriented and take substantial satisfaction from preparing a complete homemade meal for the family. Young mothers in this segment are aware of nutritional issues but will bend the rules with homemade meat dishes, casseroles, pies, cakes, and cookies.

Even these abbreviated descriptions of Pillsbury's five psychographic segments should make it clear that very different marketing and advertising programs are called for to appeal to each group. Exhibits 6.8 and 6.9 show ads from Pillsbury. Which segments are these ads targeting?

As noted, lifestyle segmentation studies can also be pursued with no particular product category as a focus, and the resulting segments could prove useful for many different marketers. A notable example of this approach is the VALS (for "values and lifestyles") system developed by SRI International and marketed by Strategic Business Insights (SBI) of Menlo Park, California.[15]

As shown in Exhibit 6.10, the VALS segments are organized in terms of resources (which include age, income, and education) and primary motivation. For instance, the Experiencer is relatively affluent and expressive. This enthusiastic and risk-taking group has yet to establish predictable behavioral patterns. Its members look to sports, recreation, exercise, and social activities as outlets for their abundant energies. SBI sells detailed information and marketing recommendations about the eight segments to a variety of marketing organizations.

14. Rebecca Piirto, *Beyond Mind Games: The Marketing Power of Psychographics* (Ithaca, NY: American Demographics Books, 1991), 222–223.

15. Ibid.; see chs. 3, 5, and 8 for an extensive discussion of the VALS system.

Exhibit 6.8 Which lifestyle segment is Pillsbury targeting with this ad? It looks like a toss-up between Chase & Grabbits and Functional Feeders. Does Pillsbury's site (www.pillsbury.com) target the same lifestyle segment as the ads? What features at the site are designed to build customer loyalty? Based on the site's message and design, what lifestyle choices does Pillsbury seem to assume that its target segment has made?

Exhibit 6.9 The convenience-oriented Functional Feeders seem the natural target for this novel ad. That Pillsbury Doughboy sure gets around! www.pillsbury.com

Exhibit 6.10 The eight VALS™ Segments. www.sric-bi.com

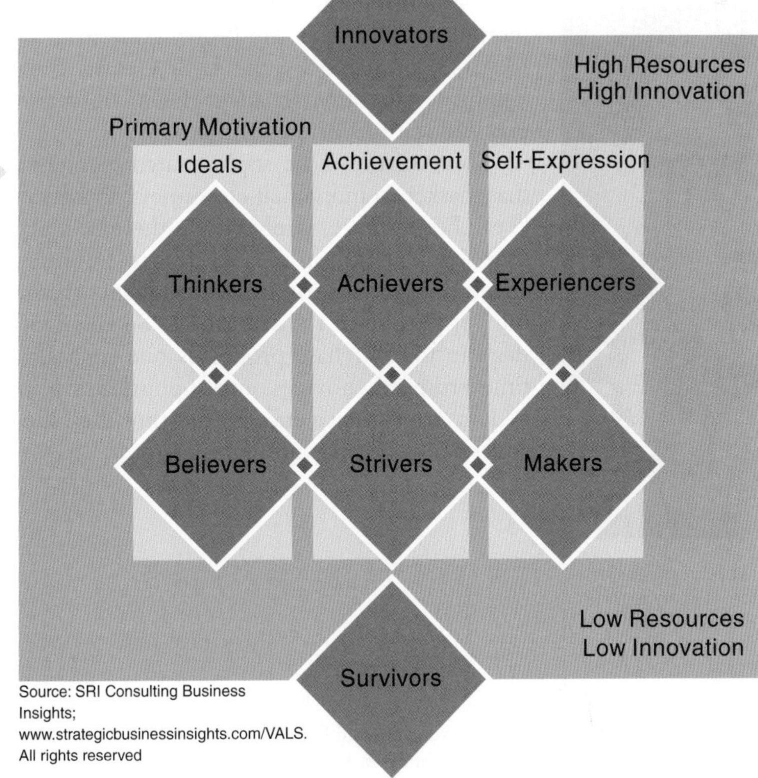

Source: SRI Consulting Business Insights; www.strategicbusinessinsights.com/VALS.

Courtesy, Pillsbury; Created by Foote, Cone & Belding, San Francisco; Courtesy, Pillsbury; Created by Leo Burnett, Chicago

Benefit Segmentation.

Another segmentation approach developed by advertising researchers is **benefit segmentation.** In benefit segmentation, target segments are delineated by the various benefit packages that different consumers want from competing products and brands. For instance, different people want different benefits from their automobiles. Some consumers want efficient and reliable transportation; others want speed, excitement, and glamour; and still others want luxury, comfort, and prestige. One product could not possibly serve such diverse benefit segments. Exhibits 6.11 and 6.12 feature two hair care products that promise different kinds of benefits to comparable consumers.

Exhibit 6.11 Benefit segmentation really comes to life in this ad for Bed Head. If that Superstar look is the benefit you desire, Think Thick!

Segmenting Business-to-Business Markets.

Thus far, our discussion of segmentation options has focused on ways to segment **consumer markets.** Consumer markets are the markets for products and services purchased by individuals or households to satisfy their specific needs. Consumer marketing is often compared and contrasted with business-to-business marketing. **Business markets** are the institutional buyers who purchase items to be used in other products and services or to be resold to other businesses or households. Although advertising is more prevalent in consumer markets, products and services such as smartphones, overnight delivery, Web hosting, consulting services, and a wide array of business machines and computer-support services are commonly promoted to business customers around the world. Hence, segmentation strategies are also valuable for business-to-business marketers.

Business markets can be segmented using several of the options already discussed.[16] For example, business customers differ in their usage rates and geographic locations, so these variables may be productive bases for segmenting business markets. In addition, one of the most common approaches uses the North American Industry Classification System (NAICS) prepared by the U.S. Census Bureau. NAICS information is helpful for identifying categories of businesses and then pinpointing the precise locations of these organizations.

Some of the more sophisticated segmentation methods used by firms that market to individual consumers do not translate well to business markets.[17] For instance, rarely would there be a place for psychographic or lifestyle segmentation in the business-to-business setting. In business markets, advertisers fall back on simpler strategies that are easier to work with from the perspective of the sales force. Segmentation by a potential customer's stage in the purchase process is one such strategy. It turns out that first-time prospects, novices, and sophisticates want very different packages of benefits from their vendors, and thus they should be targeted separately in advertising and sales programs.

Exhibit 6.12 Catwalk promises 3-D benefits: Defrizz—Define—Detangle. And the end result is unDeniable—Curls Rock!

Courtesy, TIGI Bed Head; Courtesy, TIGI Catwalk

16. Kotler, *Marketing Management,* 296–298.

17. Thomas S. Robertson and Howard Barich, "A Successful Approach to Segmenting Industrial Markets," *Planning Forum* (November/December 1992), 5–11.

3 Prioritizing Target Segments.

Whether it is done through usage patterns, demographic characteristics, geographic location, benefit packages, or any combination of options, segmenting markets typically yields a mix of segments that vary in their attractiveness to the advertiser. In pursuing STP marketing, the advertiser must get beyond this potentially confusing mixture of segments to a selected subset that will become the target for its marketing and advertising programs. Recall the example of Mobil Oil Corporation and the segments of gasoline buyers it identified via usage patterns and demographic descriptors. What criteria should Mobil use to help decide between Road Warriors and Price Shoppers as possible targets?

Perhaps the most fundamental criterion in segment selection revolves around what the members of the segment want versus the organization's ability to provide it. Every organization has distinctive strengths and weaknesses that must be acknowledged when choosing its target segment. The organization may be particularly strong in some aspect of manufacturing, like Gillette, which has particular expertise in mass production of intricate plastic and metal products. Or perhaps its strength lies in well-trained and loyal service personnel, like those at FedEx, who can effectively implement new service programs initiated for customers, such as next-day delivery "absolutely, positively by 10:30 AM." To serve a target segment, an organization may have to commit substantial resources to acquire or develop the capabilities to provide what that segment wants. If the price tag for these new capabilities is too high, the organization must find another segment.

Another major consideration in segment selection entails the size and growth potential of the segment. Segment size is a function of the number of people, households, or institutions in the segment, plus their willingness to spend in the product category. When assessing size, advertisers must keep in mind that the number of people in a segment of heavy users may be relatively small, but the extraordinary usage rates of these consumers can more than make up for their small numbers. In addition, it is not enough to simply assess a segment's size as of today. Segments are dynamic, and it is common to find marketers most interested in devoting resources to segments projected for dramatic growth. As we have already seen, the purchasing power and growth projections for people age 50 and older have made this a segment that many companies are targeting.

So does bigger always mean better when choosing target segments? The answer is a function of the third major criterion for segment selection. In choosing a target segment, an advertiser must also look at the **competitive field**—companies that compete for the segment's business—and then decide whether it has a particular expertise, or perhaps just a bigger budget, that would allow it to serve the segment more effectively.

Upon considering the competitive field, it often turns out that smaller is better when selecting target segments. Almost by definition, large segments are usually established segments that many companies have identified and targeted previously. Trying to enter the competitive field in a mature segment isn't easy because established competitors (with their many brands) can be expected to respond aggressively with advertising campaigns or price promotions in an effort to repel any newcomer.

Alternatively, large segments may simply be poorly defined segments; that is, a large segment may need to be broken down into smaller categories before a company can understand consumers' needs well enough to serve them effectively. Again, the segment of older consumers—age 50 and older—is huge, but in most instances it would simply be too big to be valuable as a target. Too much diversity exists in the needs and preferences of this age group, such that further segmentation based on other demographic or perhaps via psychographics variables is called for before an appropriate target can be located.

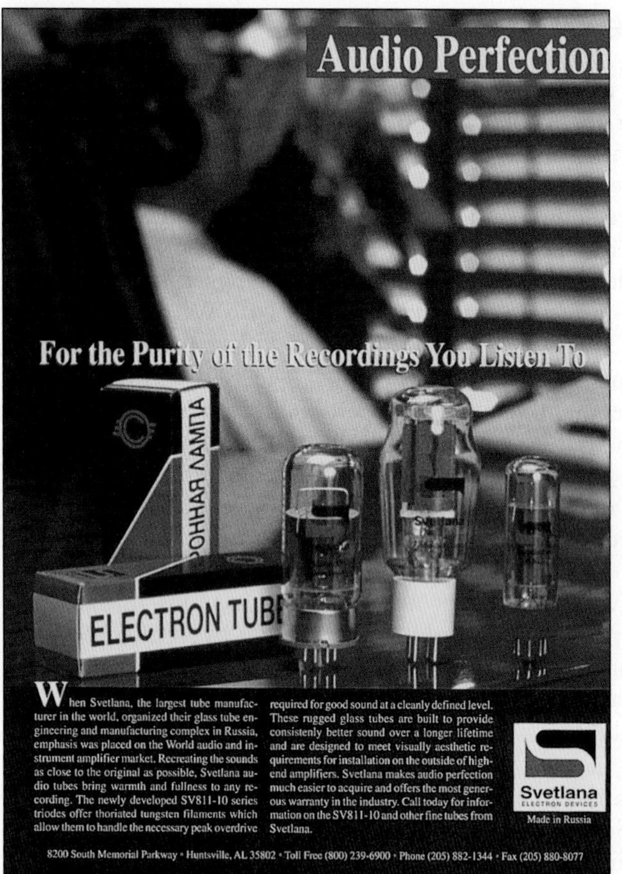

Audio Perfection
For the Purity of the Recordings You Listen To
ELECTRON TUB
When Svetlana, the largest tube manufacturer in the world, organized their glass tube engineering and manufacturing complex in Russia, emphasis was placed on the World audio and instrument amplifier market. Recreating the sounds as close to the original as possible, Svetlana audio tubes bring warmth and fullness to any recording. The newly developed SV811-10 series triodes offer thoriated tungsten filaments which allow them to handle the necessary peak overdrive required for good sound at a cleanly defined level. These rugged glass tubes are built to provide consistenly better sound over a longer lifetime and are designed to meet visually aesthetic requirements for installation on the outside of high-end amplifiers. Svetlana makes audio perfection much easier to acquire and offers the most generous warranty in the industry. Call today for information on the SV811-10 and other fine tubes from Svetlana.
Svetlana
ELECTRON DEVICES
Made in Russia
8200 South Memorial Parkway • Huntsville, AL 35802 • Toll Free (800) 239-6900 • Phone (205) 882-1344 • Fax (205) 880-8077

Exhibit 6.13 Niche marketers are usually able to charge a premium price for their distinctive products. If you decide to go with Svetlana the next time you are buying amplifier tubes, expect to pay a little extra.

The smaller-is-better principle has become so popular in choosing target segments that it is now referred to as niche marketing. A market niche is a relatively small group of consumers who have a unique set of needs and who typically are willing to pay a premium price to the firm that specializes in meeting those needs.[18] The small size of a **market niche** often means it would not be profitable for more than one organization to serve it. Thus, when a firm identifies and develops products for market niches, the threat of competitors developing imitative products to attack the niche is reduced. Exhibit 6.13 is an example of an ad directed toward a very small niche, those who prefer imported Russian tubes for their high-end tube stereo amplifiers.

Niche marketing will continue to grow in popularity as the mass media splinter into a more and more complex and narrowly defined array of specialized vehicles. Specialized cable programming—such as the Health & Fitness Channel, the History Channel, or the 24-hour Golf Channel—attracts small and very distinctive groups of consumers, providing advertisers with an efficient way to communicate with market niches.[19] In addition, perhaps the ideal application of the Internet as a marketing tool is in identifying and accessing market niches, as described in the *Social Media* box.

Now let's return to the question faced by Mobil Oil Corporation. Who should it target—Road Warriors or Price Shoppers? Hopefully you will see this as a straightforward decision. Road Warriors are a more attractive segment in terms of both segment size and growth potential. Although there are more Price Shoppers in terms of sheer numbers, Road Warriors spend more at the gas station, making them the larger segment from the standpoint of revenue generation. Road Warriors are also more prone to buy those little extras, such as a sandwich and a coffee, which could be extremely profitable sources of new business. It's just hard (impossible?) to win in gasoline retailing by competing on price.

Mobil selected Road Warriors as its target segment and developed a positioning strategy it referred to as "Friendly Serve." Gas prices went up at Mobil stations, but Mobil also committed new resources to improving all aspects of the gas-purchasing experience. Cleaner restrooms and better lighting alone yielded sales gains between 2 and 5 percent. Next, more attendants were hired to run between the pump and the snack bar to get Road Warriors in and out quickly—complete with their sandwich and beverage. Early results indicated that helpful attendants boosted station sales by another 15 to 20 percent. How can we really say that Mobil made the right choice in targeting Road Warriors? Just look at their competition (e.g., Exhibit 6.14). As suggested by BP's *Wild Bean Café,* coffee is king with the Road Warrior.

18. Kotler, *Marketing Management,* 280–281.

19. Timothy Aeppel, "For Parker Hannifin, Cable Is Best," *The Wall Street Journal,* August 7, 2003, B3.

Social Media

Finding Niches and Letting Niches Find You

Market segmentation is all about reaching groups of consumers that have common wants and needs. Usually the groups you want to reach are a small fraction of the overall market. In 1964 a market researcher by the name of Dik Twedt proposed that one group of consumers you definitely want to reach is your heavy users. He called it his theory of the "heavy half." That is, Twedt asserted that half of a brand's consumers will always account for the majority of the brand's sales. In a way he was saying, think niche, not mass.

Since 1964 markets have splintered and our ability to identify customer groups has been aided by all sorts of technological advancements. We now know that Twedt's heavy half theory doesn't go nearly far enough in encouraging an advertiser to think small. Today's marketing gurus like Don Schultz advocate the 4 percent rule. That is, data from the likes of Catalina Marketing Corp. indicate that it is just 4 percent of a brand's consumers who are critical to that brand's viability in the marketplace. The implication for many advertisers is clear. No need to chase a mass market with big budget ad campaigns; you'd be better off finding your 4 percent and engaging deeply with them.

Former mass advertisers like General Mills appear to be getting the message, and in today's marketplace the way one engages best with niche markets is to find them via social media. Celiac disease is an inherited autoimmune disease that inflicts about 2 percent of the population. People with this disease must avoid gluten in their diets or risk damage to their digestive system. The good news for General Mills is that consumers who require gluten-free foods are savvy social networkers. That's where General Mills found this market niche, creating a whole new line of products (more than 250 at last count) just for the 2 percent.

The 2 percent has proved easy to reach for General Mills because they are "hungry" (couldn't resist...) for news about gluten-free products, and they're looking for it online. Rumors that General Mills was developing gluten-free versions of its Betty Crocker baking mixes spread in a flash over Twitter. Entering 'celiac' or 'gluten-free' in a search engine takes you right to General Mills' complete list of gluten-free offerings. Dik Twedt would be amazed. No need to bother with a heavy half. Find your niches online. If you have a product they really need, they will eagerly engage with you there.

Sources: Beth Snyder, "Is Your Consumer Using Social Media?," *Advertising Age,* May 5, 2008, 12–13; Don E. Schultz, "Pareto Pared," *Marketing News,* November 15, 2009, 24; and Emily York, "Social Media Allows Giants to Exploit Niche Markets," *Advertising Age,* July 13, 2009, 3, 25.

Exhibit 6.14 When a major competitor like BP imitates our strategy, it's a pretty good sign that we got it right. Unfortunately, this may also mean that it's time for us to look for a new strategy to gain another advantage vis-à-vis our competitive field. This is that part of marketing and advertising that makes these fields both terribly interesting and terribly frustrating. Just when we get it right, it can be time to start over...

4 Formulating the Positioning Strategy.

Now that we have discussed the ways markets are segmented and the criteria used for selecting targets, we turn our attention to positioning strategy. If a firm has been careful in segmenting the market and selecting its targets, then a positioning strategy—such as Mobil's "Friendly Serve" or Gillette's "The Best a Man Can Get"—should occur naturally. In addition, as an aspect of positioning strategy, we entertain ideas about how a firm can best communicate to the target segment what it has to offer. This is where advertising plays its vital role. A positioning strategy will include particular ideas or themes that must be communicated effectively if the marketing program is to be successful.

Essentials for Effective Positioning Strategies.

Any sound positioning strategy includes several essential elements. Effective positioning strategies are based on meaningful commitments of organizational resources to produce substantive value for the target segment. They also are consistent internally and over time, and they feature simple and distinctive themes. Each of these essential elements is described below.

Deliver on the Promise. For a positioning strategy to be effective and remain effective over time, the organization must be committed to creating substantive value for the customer. Take the example of Mobil Oil Corporation and its target segment, the Road Warriors. Road Warriors are willing to pay a little more for gas if it comes with extras such as prompt service or fresh coffee. So Mobil must create an ad campaign that depicts its employees as the brightest, friendliest, most helpful people you'd ever want to meet. The company asks its ad agency to come up with a catchy jingle that will remind people about the great services they can expect at a Mobil station. It spends millions of dollars running these ads over and over and wins the enduring loyalty of the Road Warriors. Right? Well, maybe, and maybe not. Certainly, a new ad campaign will have to be created to make Road Warriors aware of the new Mobil, but it all falls apart if they drive in with great expectations and the company's people do not live up to them.

Effective positioning begins with substance. In the case of Mobil's "Friendly Serve" strategy, this means keeping restrooms attractive and clean, adding better lighting to all areas of the station, and upgrading the quality of the snacks and beverages available in each station's convenience store. It also means hiring more attendants and training and motivating them to anticipate and fulfill the needs of the harried Road Warrior. Effecting meaningful change in service levels at thousands of stations nationwide is an expensive and time-consuming process, but without some substantive change, there can be no hope of retaining the Road Warrior's lucrative business.

There's Magic in Consistency. A positioning strategy also must be consistent internally and consistent over time. Regarding internal consistency, everything must work in combination to reinforce a distinct perception in the consumer's eyes about what a brand stands for. If we have chosen to position our airline as the one that will be known for on-time reliability, then we certainly would invest in things like extensive preventive maintenance and state-of-the-art baggage-handling facilities. There would be no need for exclusive airport lounges as part of this strategy, nor would any special emphasis need to be placed on in-flight food and beverage services. If our target segment wants reliable transportation, then this should be our obsession. This particular obsession has made Southwest Airlines a

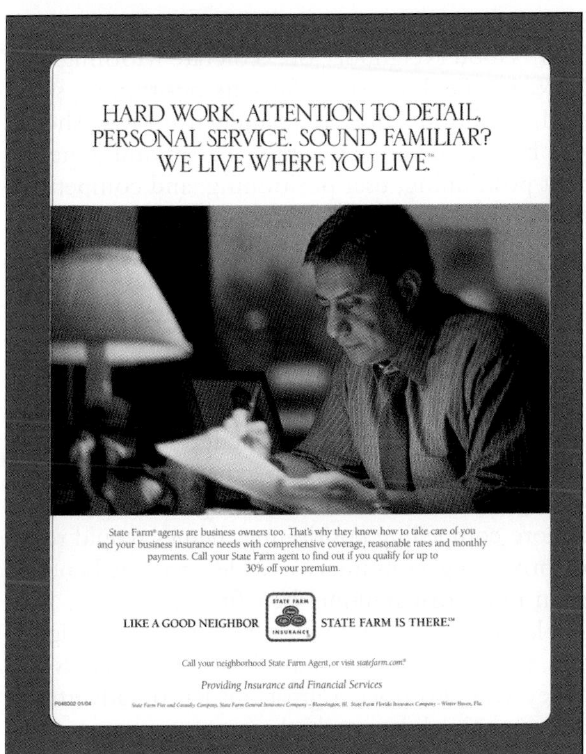

HARD WORK, ATTENTION TO DETAIL,
PERSONAL SERVICE. SOUND FAMILIAR?
WE LIVE WHERE YOU LIVE.℠
State Farm® agents are business owners too. That's why they know how to take care of you and your business insurance needs with comprehensive coverage, reasonable rates and monthly payments. Call your State Farm agent to find out if you qualify for up to 30% off your premium.
LIKE A GOOD NEIGHBOR
STATE FARM INSURANCE
STATE FARM IS THERE.℠
Call your neighborhood State Farm Agent, or visit statefarm.com®
Providing Insurance and Financial Services
P048002 01/04

Exhibit 6.15 Consistency is a definite virtue in choosing and executing a positioning strategy. State Farm's "Good Neighbor" theme has been a hallmark of its advertising for many years. Does State Farm's site (www.statefarm.com) produce substantive value for its target segment? How? What simple and distinctive themes can you find? Why are these elements essential to State Farm's positioning strategy?

very formidable competitor, even against much larger airlines, yielding 37 consecutive years of profitability, in a most challenging industry.[20] Doesn't it strike you as ironic that the only airline that can claim that kind of performance record is also one where Bags Fly Free?

A strategy also needs consistency over time. Consumers have perceptual defenses that allow them to screen or ignore most of the ad messages they are exposed to. Breaking through the clutter and establishing what a brand stands for is a tremendous challenge, but it is a challenge made easier by consistent positioning. If year in and year out an advertiser communicates the same basic themes, then the message may get through and shape the way consumers perceive the brand. An example of a consistent approach is the long-running "Good Neighbor" ads of State Farm Insurance. Even though the specific copy changes, the thematic core of the campaign does not change. Exhibit 6.15 shows an exemplar from this long-running campaign, including the "We Live Where You Live" extension to their "Good Neighbor" premise.

Make It Different Simply. Simplicity and distinctiveness are essential to the advertising task. No matter how much substance has been built into a product, it will fail in the marketplace if the consumer doesn't perceive what the product can do. In a world of harried consumers who can be expected to ignore, distort, or forget most of the ads they are exposed to, complicated, imitative messages simply have no chance of getting through. The basic premise of a positioning strategy must be simple and distinctive if it is to be communicated effectively to the target segment.

The value of simplicity and distinctiveness in positioning strategy is nicely illustrated in Jack Daniel's long-running campaign, with ads all around the world like the one in Exhibit 6.16. Jack Daniels began distilling whiskey in 1866 and would not be rushed. Patience was his secret ingredient for producing a smooth sippin' whiskey. It will be good and ready, when it's good and ready. Throughout the decades and around the world, Jack Daniel's advertising turned "can't be rushed" and made "the old-fashioned way" into an art form. The simplicity, consistency, and distinctiveness of their positioning strategy helped make Jack Daniel's a powerhouse global brand, from Lynchburg, Tennessee.

Fundamental Positioning Themes.

Positioning themes that are simple and distinctive help an organization make internal decisions that yield substantive value for customers, and they assist in the development of focused ad campaigns to break through the clutter of competitors' advertising. Thus, choosing a viable positioning theme is one of the most important decisions faced by advertisers. In many ways, the raison d'être for STP marketing is to generate viable positioning themes.

Positioning themes take many forms, and like any other aspect of marketing and advertising, they can benefit from creative breakthroughs. Yet although novelty and creativity are valued in developing positioning themes, some basic principles should be considered when selecting a theme. Whenever possible, it is helpful

20. Dan Reed, "Continental, Southwest Airlines Land Profits," *usatoday.com,* January 21, 2010.

飲酒は20歳を過ぎてから
洞穴に湧くこの水と樽を世話するリチャード・マッギー。
それは、テネシーの自然が育んでくれた2つの驚異だ。
ジャック・ダニエル蒸溜所の谷間では、ピュアで鉄分を含まない水が、洞穴の泉から
何百万年もの間、湧き続けている。ウイスキーづくりに理想的なその水を
すくっているのが、マッギー。洞穴の泉ほどではないが、誰よりも古くから、
誰よりも多く、樽をころがし、ウイスキーの世話を続けている名人だ。
まだ、味わっていない方は、ぜひ、ご一飲を。
テネシーの2つの驚異なしには生まれなかったジャック・ダニエルの
格別な滑らかさを、きっと確かめていただけるに違いない。
JACK DANIEL'S
TENNESSEE WHISKEY
テネシーウイスキー ジャック・ダニエル

Exhibit 6.16 You don't need to be able to read Japanese to get the point here, in part because this ad follows the same style as other Jack Daniel's ads around the world. If you want a smooth sippin' whiskey, it can't be rushed. And in the back hills of Tennessee, no one is rushing anything....

Courtesy, Jack Daniels Distillery

if the organization can settle on a single premise—such as "Good Neighbor" or "Tolerate Mornings" or "Relax, It's FedEx"—to reflect its positioning strategy.[21] In addition, three fundamental options should always be considered in selecting a positioning theme: benefit positioning, user positioning, and competitive positioning.[22]

"Friendly Serve" or "Relax, It's FedEx" are examples of **benefit positioning.** Notice in these premises that a distinctive customer benefit is featured. This single-benefit focus is the first option that should be considered when formulating a positioning strategy. Consumers purchase products to derive functional, emotional, or self-expressive benefits, so an emphasis on the primary benefit they can expect to receive from a brand is fundamental. Even though it might seem that more compelling positioning themes would result from promising consumers a wide array of benefits, keep in mind that multiple-benefit strategies are hard to implement. Not only will they send mixed signals within an organization about what a brand stands for, but they will also place a great burden on advertising to deliver and validate multiple messages.

Functional benefits are the place to start in selecting a positioning theme, but in many mature product categories, the functional benefits provided by the various brands in the competitive field are essentially the same. In these instances the organization may turn to emotion in an effort to distinguish its brand.[23] Emotional benefit positioning may involve a promise of exhilaration, like "Exciting Armpits" (see Exhibit 6.17), or may feature a way to avoid negative feelings—such as the embarrassment felt in social settings due to bad breath, dandruff, or coffee-stained teeth.

Another way to add an emotional benefit in one's positioning is by linking a brand with important causes that provoke intense feelings. Avon Products' former CEO, James E. Preston, insisted that tie-ins with high-profile social issues can cut through the clutter of rivals' marketing messages.[24] Not surprising then that Avon has been a regular sponsor of important causes, such as the Avon Walk for Breast Cancer. Likewise, Sears helped raise money for the homeless, Star-Kist has promoted dolphin-safe fishing practices, Coors Brewing has funded public literacy programs, and Visa in Germany supported the Friendship Card, featured in Exhibit 6.18. Microsponsorships, which feature smaller charities and require much smaller budgets, have become a popular way for a wide range of brands to help consumers feel better about what they buy.[25]

21. A more elaborate case for the importance of a single, consistent positioning premise is provided in Ries and Trout's classic, *Positioning: The Battle for Your Mind* (New York: Warner Books, 1982).

22. Other positioning options are discussed in Philip Kotler and Kevin Lane Keller, *A Framework for Marketing Management* (Upper Saddle River, NJ: Pearson / Prentice Hall, 2007), ch. 9.

23. David Aaker, "Beyond Functional Benefits," *Marketing News,* September 30, 2009, 23.

24. Geoffrey Smith and Ron Stodghill, "Are Good Causes Good Marketing?" *BusinessWeek,* March 21, 1994, 64–65.

25. Natalie Zmuda and Emily York, "Cause Effect: Brands Rush to Save the World One Deed at a Time," *Advertising Age,* March 1, 2010, 1, 22.

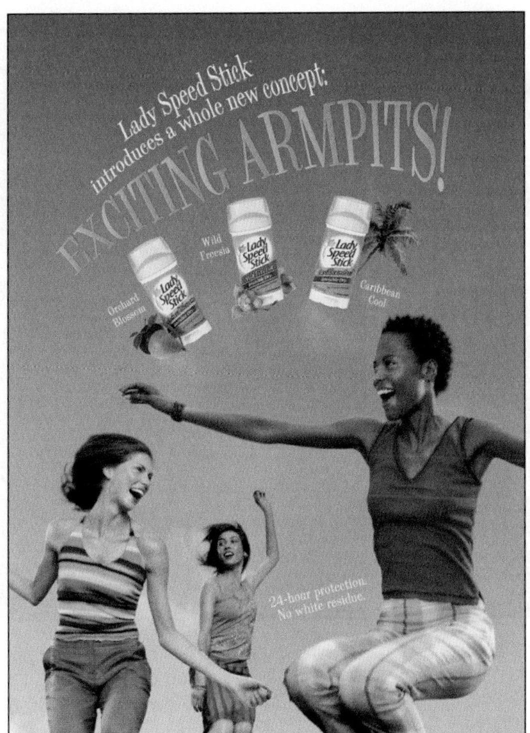

Exhibit 6.17 When the functional benefits of 24-hour protection and no white residue become old hat, then the advertiser may have no choice but to try to engage consumers through a promise of emotional benefits, as we see in this ad for Lady Speed Stick. www.mennen.com

Exhibit 6.18 Bonus points for children is the motto of Germany's first charitable credit card. Card users earn "payback" points on every transaction, which are then automatically credited to UNICEF. UNICEF, the United Nations Children's Fund, supports programs for children in 158 countries around the world, in an effort to bring more smiles.

Courtesy, Colgate-Palmolive Company; Courtesy of UNICEF; Ad Agency: Loyalty Partner GmbH München

Self-expressive benefits can also be the bases for effective positioning strategies. With this approach, the purpose of an advertising campaign is to create distinctive images or personalities for brands, and then invite consumers into brand communities.[26] These brand images or personalities can be of value to individuals as they use the brands to make statements about themselves to other people. For example, feelings of status, pride, and prestige might be derived from the imagery associated with brands such as BMW, Rolex, and Gucci. Brand imagery can also be valued in gift-giving contexts. The woman who gives Calvin Klein's Euphoria for men is expressing something very different than the woman who gives Avon's Wild Country. Advertisers help brands acquire meaning and self-expressive benefits to distinguish them beyond their functional forms.

Besides benefit positioning, another fundamental option is **user positioning.** Instead of featuring a benefit or attribute of the brand, this option takes a specific profile of the target user as the focal point of the positioning strategy. Ads like those shown in Exhibits 6.19 and 6.20 make unequivocal statements about who should consider the possibilities offered by Bigen Xpressive and Axe Recovery Shower Gel. Notice how these ads attempt to speak to clearly identifiable user segments.

The third option for a positioning theme is **competitive positioning.** This option is sometimes useful in well-established product categories with a crowded competitive field. Here, the goal is to use an explicit reference to an existing competitor to help define precisely what your brand can do. Many times this approach is used by smaller brands to carve out a position relative to the market share leader in

26. Albert M. Muniz, Jr., and Thomas C. O'Guinn, "Brand Community," *Journal of Consumer Research,* vol. 27 (2001), 412–432.

Exhibit 6.19 Even though this ad is busy with competing images and diverse product claims, it still communicates an unmistakable message about who should use this new line of coloring products from Bigen Xpressive.

Exhibit 6.20 A shower with Axe Recovery Shower Gel and a cup of Folgers are this fellow's best bet for fending off an attack of those creepy Yellow People.

their category. For instance, in the analgesics category, many competitors have used market leader Tylenol as an explicit point of reference in their positioning strategies. Excedrin, for one, has attempted to position itself as the best option to treat a simple headache, granting that Tylenol might be the better choice to treat the various symptoms of a cold or the flu. As shown in Exhibit 6.21, Excedrin's strategy must have been effective, because Tylenol came back with a very pointed reply.

Now that you've seen the three fundamental options for creating a positioning strategy, we need to make matters a bit messier. There is nothing that would prevent an advertiser from combining these various options to create a hybrid involving two or more of them working together. The combination of benefit and user is common in creating positioning strategies, and the Xootr ad in Exhibit 6.22 is a superb example of user and competitive positioning combined. Do keep in mind that we're looking for a strategy that reflects substance, consistency, simplicity, and distinctiveness. But the last thing we'd want to do is give you guidelines that would shackle your creativity. So don't be shy about looking for creative combinations.

Repositioning.

STP marketing is far from a precise science, so marketers do not always get it right the first time. Furthermore, markets are dynamic. Things change. Even when marketers do get it right, competitors can react, or consumers' preferences may shift for any number of reasons, and what once was a viable positioning strategy must be altered if the brand is to survive. One of the best ways to revive an ailing brand or to fix the lackluster performance of a new market entry is to redeploy the STP process to arrive at a revised positioning strategy. This type of effort is commonly referred to as **repositioning.**

Although repositioning efforts are a fact of life for marketers and advertisers, they present a tremendous challenge. When brands that have been around for decades are forced to reposition, perceptions of the brand that have evolved throughout the years must be changed through advertising. This problem is common for brands

Exhibit 6.21 In mature, saturated markets where the performance features of brands don't change much over time, it is common to see competitors making claims back and forth in an effort to steal market share from one another. Powerhouse brands such as Tylenol usually don't initiate these exchanges, because they have the most to lose. This ad is a reply from the makers of Tylenol, responding to a campaign of a smaller competitor. www.tylenol.com

Exhibit 6.22 The beauty of this ad for Xootr is its simple, unequivocal message. Ours versus Theirs equates to Joy versus Toy. www.xootr.com

that become popular with one generation but fade from the scene as that generation ages and emergent consumers come to view the brand as passé. So, for several years, the makers of Pontiac tried to breathe new life into the brand with catchy ad slogans such as "Luxury with Attitude," "Wider Is Better," and "Fuel for the Soul." Ultimately, none of these efforts were able to save a brand that had become passé.[27]

On the other hand, there are numerous examples of brands that have been able to get consumers to take a fresh look at them. Mazda found itself in a funk in the '90s when it tried to go head-to-head with Toyota and Honda around dependability and good value. So Mazda's new CEO decided to return the brand to its roots as a stylish and fun-to-drive vehicle, targeting the 25 percent of the car-buying market that consider themselves auto enthusiasts. The "Zoom Zoom" theme was the outcome of this application of STP marketing, and with it the Mazda brand got its groove back.[28]

5 Capturing Your Strategy in a Value Proposition.

In this chapter we have presented several important concepts for understanding how marketers develop strategies for their brands that then have major implications for the integrated advertising campaigns that are executed to build and maintain those brands. One needs to assess customer segments and target markets along with the

27. Jean Halliday, "Looking Back on 83 Years of Pontiac Advertising," *Advertising Age,* May 4, 2009, 14.

28. Jean Halliday, "Mazda Repositioning Begins to Show Results," *Advertising Age,* January 6, 2003, 4.

competitive field to make decisions about various kinds of positioning themes that might be appropriate in guiding the creation of a campaign.

Yes, it can get complicated. Furthermore, as time passes, new people from both the client and agency side will be brought in to work on the brand team. It can be easy for them to lose sight of what the brand used to stand for in the eyes of the target segment. Of course, if the people who create the advertising for a brand get confused about the brand's desired identity, then the consumer is bound to get confused as well. This is a recipe for disaster. Thus, we need a way to capture and keep a record of what our brand is supposed to stand for in the eyes of the target segment. Although there are many ways to capture one's strategy on paper, we recommend doing just that by articulating the brand's value proposition. If we are crystal clear on what value we believe our brand offers to consumers, and everyone on the brand team shares that clarity, the foundation is in place for creating effective advertising and integrated brand promotion.

At this point you should find the following definition of a **value proposition** a natural extension of concepts that are already familiar; it simply consolidates the emphasis on customer benefits that has been featured in this chapter:

> *A brand's value proposition is a statement of the functional, emotional, and self-expressive benefits delivered by the brand that provide value to customers in the target segment. A balanced value proposition is the basis for brand choice and customer loyalty, and is critical to the ongoing success of a firm.*[29]

Here are the value propositions for two global brands that are likely familiar to you.[30]

McDonald's

- ***Functional benefits:*** Good-tasting hamburgers, fries, and drinks served fast; extras such as playgrounds, prizes, premiums, and games.
- ***Emotional benefits:*** Kids—fun via excitement at birthday parties; relationship with Ronald McDonald and other characters; a feeling of special family times. Adults—warmth via time spent enjoying a meal with the kids; admiration of McDonald's social involvement such as McDonald's Charities and Ronald McDonald Houses.

Nike

- ***Functional benefits:*** High-technology shoe that will improve performance and provide comfort.
- ***Emotional benefits:*** The exhilaration of athletic performance excellence, feeling engaged, active, and healthy; exhilaration from admiring professional and college athletes as they perform wearing "your brand"—when they win, you win too.
- ***Self-expressive benefits:*** Using the brand endorsed by high-profile athletes lets your peers know your desire to compete and excel.

Notice from these two statements that over time many different aspects can be built into the value proposition for a brand. Brands like Nike may offer benefits in all three benefit categories; McDonald's from two of the three. Benefit complexity of this type is extremely valuable when the various benefits reinforce one another. In these examples, this cross-benefit reinforcement is especially strong for Nike, with all levels working together to deliver the desired state of performance excellence. The job of advertising is to carry the message to the target segment about the value that is offered by the brand. However, for brands with complex value propositions such as McDonald's and Nike, no single ad could be expected to reflect all aspects of the brand's value. However, if any given ad is not communicating some selected aspects of the brand's purported value, then we have to ask, why run that ad?

29. This definition is adapted from David Aaker, *Building Strong Brands* (New York: Free Press, 1996), ch. 3.
30. These examples are adapted from Aaker, *Building Strong Brands,* ch. 3.

Ethics

Mickey Mouse Tries the High Road

We've heard it over and over again. Many respected groups (including the American Psychological Association, the American Academy of Pediatrics, and the Rudd Policy Center at Yale University) are calling for restrictions on advertising targeted to children. One key concern is that advertising for junk food has played a role in America's obesity crisis. Internet games and websites promote products such as Lucky Charms, Cheetos, and Hershey's Syrup. Kids who visit branded sites like these are tantalized by sophisticated entertainment tactics that in the end are selling tactics devised by adults but targeted at kids. One tactic that has drawn special attention from food industry critics is the use of licensed characters, like Scooby-Doo, the Rugrats, or SpongeBob SquarePants, to do the selling. Based on its research into the link between marketing practices and childhood obesity, the U.S. Institute of Medicine recommended that food companies stop using licensed, animated characters to sell low-nutrient, high-calorie products.

There is an ethical dilemma here that is becoming impossible to ignore or rationalize away. Maybe, just maybe, we are beginning to see companies step up in an effort to do the right thing. Disney appears to be trying, given its announcement of a companywide initiative to phase out advertising of unhealthy foods to kids and eliminate the same from its theme-park menus and co-promotions with big corporate partners. But fear not. Mickey Mouse is not retiring. We will see Mickey and numerous other Disney characters (e.g., Buzz Lightyear and Woody, Winnie the Pooh and Tigger) on a new line of products branded *Disney Magic Selections.* Disney's goal with this new line of juices, pastas, soups, and snacks is to give parents healthy eating solutions for kids.

Yet who gets to say what is and isn't healthy? Can we trust Disney to set the right standard for itself and its partners? Only time will tell. But the new Disney guidelines do seem to have some teeth. For example, McDonald's Big Mac and Quarter Pounder with Cheese challenge the Disney standard because they are heavy on trans fats. And since there are numerous McDonald's restaurants within Disney theme parks, it will get interesting when Disney executives try to apply their standards to McDonald's. Similar issues loom for Disney and its long-time partner Kellogg. Co-promotions involving Disney films and Kellogg's sugary snacks have been common in the past. However, many Kellogg's products linked to recent Disney films don't meet the new Disney guidelines. As these corporate titans wrestle with the question of how to define a healthy snack, one can only hope that they don't set the bar too low or the scales too high.

Sources: Joseph Pereira and Audrey Warren, "Coming Up Next... ," *The Wall Street Journal*, March 15, 2004, B1, B3; Nanci Hellmich, "Food Websites Tempt Kids," *USA Today*, July 20, 2006, 6D; Merissa Marr and Janet Adamy, "Disney Pulls Characters from Junk Food," *The Wall Street Journal*, October 17, 2006, D1, D6.

So from now on, every time you see an ad, ask yourself, what kind of value or benefit is that ad promising the target customer? What is the value proposition underlying this ad? We expect you to carry forward an ability to assess target segments and isolate value propositions.

One gains tremendous leverage from the process of STP marketing because it is all about anticipating and servicing customers' wants and needs. But targeting groups for focused advertising and promotion has a controversial side, as do many things. The *Ethics* box features the ethical dilemma inherent in choosing children as your target.

Putting It All Together.

Before moving on it may be helpful to pull together the concepts presented in this chapter using a practical model. The strategic planning triangle proposed by advertising researchers Esther Thorson and Jeri Moore is perfect for this purpose.[31]

31. Esther Thorson and Jeri Moore, *Integrated Communication: Synergy of Persuasive Voices* (Mahwah, NJ: Erlbaum, 1996).

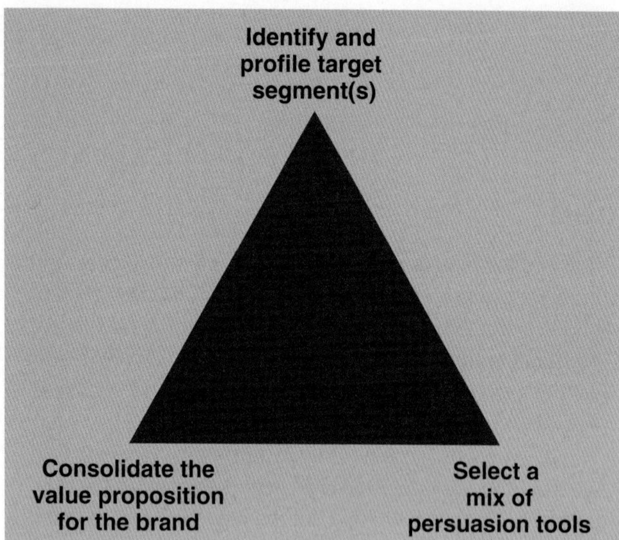

Exhibit 6.23 Thorson and Moore's strategic planning triangle.

Source: Based on Esther Thorson and Jeri Moore, *Integrated Communication: Synergy of Persuasive Voices* (Mahwah, N J: Erllbaum, 1996)

As reflected in Exhibit 6.23, the apexes of the planning triangle entail the segment(s) selected as targets for the campaign, the brand's value proposition, and the array of persuasion tools that will be deployed to achieve campaign goals.

As we have seen in this chapter, the starting point of STP marketing is identifying who the customers or prospects are and what they want. Hence, Thorson and Moore place identification and specification of the target segment as the paramount apex in their model. Building a consensus between the client and the agency about which segments will be targeted is essential to the campaign's effectiveness. Compelling advertising begins with insights about one's target segment that are both personal and precise.

The second important apex in the planning triangle entails specification of the brand's value proposition. A brand's value proposition is a statement of the functional, emotional, and/or self-expressive benefits delivered by the brand. In formulating the value proposition one should consider both what a brand has stood for or communicated to consumers in the past, and what new types of value or additional benefits one wants to claim for the brand going forward. For mature, successful brands, reaffirming the existing value proposition may be the primary objective for any campaign. When launching a new brand, there is an opportunity to start from scratch in establishing the value proposition.

The final apex of the planning triangle considers the various persuasion tools that may be deployed as part of the campaign. A description of these tools is yet to come. Chapters 12 and 13 emphasize traditional mass media tools; Chapter 14 looks at the dynamic digital options; Chapter 15 considers support media and sales promotions; Chapter 16 examines the exciting new arena of branded entertainment; Chapter 17 provides a comprehensive look at direct marketing; and Chapter 18 fills out the tool kit by discussing the public relations function. The mix of tools used will depend on campaign goals. The point here is simply to reinforce our mantra that advertising and integrated brand promotion always entails finding the right mix to do the job: Knowing the target segment and the value proposition are essential to doing the job right.

Summary

1 Explain the process known as STP marketing.

The term STP marketing refers to the process of segmenting, targeting, and positioning. Marketers pursue this set of activities in formulating marketing strategies for their brands. STP marketing also provides a strong foundation for the development of advertising campaigns. Although no single approach can guarantee success in marketing and advertising, STP marketing should always be considered when consumers in a category have heterogeneous wants and needs.

2 Describe different bases that marketers use to identify target segments.

In market segmentation, the goal is to break down a heterogeneous market into more manageable subgroups or segments. Many different bases can be used for this purpose. Markets can be segmented on the basis of usage patterns and commitment levels, demographics, geography, psychographics, lifestyles, benefits sought, SIC codes, or stages in the purchase process. Different bases are typically applied for segmenting consumer versus business-to-business markets.

Discuss the criteria used for choosing a target segment.

In pursuing STP marketing, an organization must get beyond the stage of segment identification and settle on one or more segments as a target for its marketing and advertising efforts. Several criteria are useful in establishing the organization's target segment. First, the organization must decide whether it has the proper skills to serve the segment in question. The size of the segment and its growth potential must also be taken into consideration. Another key criterion involves the intensity of the competition the firm is likely to face in the segment. Often, small segments known as market niches can be quite attractive because they will not be hotly contested by numerous competitors.

Identify the essential elements of an effective positioning strategy.

The "P" in STP marketing refers to the positioning strategy that must be developed as a guide for all marketing and advertising activities that will be undertaken in pursuit of the target segment. Effective positioning strategies should be linked to the substantive benefits offered by the brand. They are also consistent internally and over time, and they feature simple and distinctive themes. Benefit positioning, user positioning, and competitive positioning are options that should be considered when formulating a positioning strategy.

Review the necessary ingredients for creating a brand's value proposition.

Many complex considerations underlie marketing and advertising strategies, so some device is called for to summarize the essence of one's strategy. We advance the idea of the value proposition as a useful device for this purpose. A value proposition is a statement of the various benefits (functional, emotional, and self-expressive) offered by a brand that create value for the customer. These benefits as a set justify the price of the product or service. Clarity in expression of the value proposition is critical for development of advertising that sells.

Key Terms

target segment
positioning
positioning strategy
STP marketing
market segmentation
heavy users
nonusers
brand-loyal users
switchers, or variety seekers
emergent consumers
point-of-entry marketing
demographic segmentation
geodemographic segmentation
psychographics
lifestyle segmentation
benefit segmentation
consumer markets
business markets
competitive field
market niche
benefit positioning
user positioning
competitive positioning
repositioning
value proposition

Questions

1. Although STP marketing often produces successful outcomes, there is no guarantee that these successes will last. What factors can erode the successes produced by STP marketing, forcing a firm to reformulate its marketing strategy?

2. Why does the persuasion required with a product differentiation strategy present more of a challenge than the persuasion required with a market segmentation strategy?

3. Explain the appeal of emergent consumers as a target segment. Identify a current ad campaign (not Folgers!) targeting an emergent-consumer segment.

4. It is often said that psychographics were invented to overcome the weaknesses of demographic information for describing target segments. What unique information can psychographics provide that would be of special value to advertisers?

5. What criteria did Mobil Oil Corporation weigh most heavily in its selection of Road Warriors as a target segment? What do you think will be the biggest source of frustration for Mobil in trying to make this strategy work?

6. Explain why smaller can be better when selecting segments to target in marketing strategies.

7. What essential elements of a positioning strategy can help overcome the consumer's natural tendency to ignore, distort, or forget most of the advertisements he or she is exposed to?

8. Review the section *Essentials for Effective Positioning Strategies*. As you think about failed General Motors' brands like Pontiac and Oldsmobile, which essentials did they fail to meet?

9. Which of the market segmenting strategies discussed in this chapter are likely to be most effective for business-to-business marketing? Why would some techniques that are highly successful in targeting consumer markets, such as lifestyle segmentation, be less effective?

10. Carefully examine the two ads displayed in Exhibits 6.4 and 6.5. What positioning theme (benefit, user, or competitive) is the basis for these ads? If you say benefit positioning, what form of benefit promise (functional, emotional, or self-expressive) is being made in these ads? Write a statement of the value proposition that you believe is reflected by these two ads.

Experiential Exercises

1. Like other reality television programs, *Project Runway* entertains viewers by staging dramatic competitions between everyday people. A cable-TV hit for many years, *Runway* features supermodel host Heidi Klum, who follows amateur fashion designers as they make original clothing items with limited time and materials. Each week, contestants face professional judges, and a loser is sent home, leaving one final contestant to win the big money prize and a new career in fashion design. Identify the target viewing audience of *Project Runway,* and explain how segmenting, targeting, and positioning contribute to the show's success.

2. Electronic reading devices are hot, and Amazon's Kindle and Apple's iPad are in a heated battle to win over the bookworms of the world. Kindle focuses solely on reading, whereas iPad does reading, movies, music, office computing, and more. Some analysts predict that iPad will eclipse Kindle because it offers many powerful multimedia features; others think Kindle can hold its own. Make a case for how Amazon might use segmentation and a clever value proposition to dominate the growing e-books market with its Kindle stand-alone reader.

3. Compose value proposition statements for Starbucks Coffee and Levi Strauss jeans. Each value proposition should crystallize what the brand offers to consumers and serve as a clear mission statement for all subsequent STP marketing efforts.

4. The Folgers campaign featured in this chapter's introductory scenario was distinctive, in part, because the company spent no money on media, instead allowing the new ads to circulate for free through user sites such as YouTube. That strategic decision reflected an understanding that its young target market was more likely to be online than watching the evening news. What might be the most effective media to reach each of the following target segments?

a. Upper-income men, ages 45 to 60, for a financial services product.

b. Young homeowners, ages 30 to 40, for a new interior paint product.

c. Teenage boys who live in rural areas for a new basketball shoe.

d. Senior citizens for a new denture-paste product.

Chapter 7

Research in Advertising and Promotion

After reading and thinking about this chapter, you will be able to do the following:

1. Explain the methods used in developmental advertising research.
2. Identify sources of secondary data that can aid the IBP planning effort.
3. Discuss the methods used in copy research.
4. Discuss the basic research methods used after ads are in the marketplace.

GOOD MORNING

Courtesy, The Coca-Cola Company

Introductory Scenario: It's the Brand, Not the Product.

Coca-Cola discovered that consumers generally preferred Pepsi—in blind taste tests. Coke had apparently conducted thousands of taste tests, and knew it was true: When consumers didn't know which cola they were drinking, more preferred Pepsi for years. To make the point more painful, Coke had been losing market share to Pepsi. What to do?

The Coca-Cola Company's answer was a new formula. After conducting 190,000 or so blind taste tests, Coca-Cola discovered that consumers preferred New Coke over both Pepsi and Coke. So they announced the switch: New Coke replaced Coke. As you know, it was a disaster. Consumers were outraged and demanded their friend Coca-Cola back. They stayed away from New Coke in droves.

> *I do not drink alcoholic beverages, I don't smoke, and I don't chase other women, my only vice has been Coke. Now you have taken that pleasure from me.*
>
> *Would it be right to rewrite the Constitution? The Bible? To me, changing the Coke formula is of such a serious nature.*
>
> —From letters sent to The Coca-Cola Company in 1985 following the introduction of New Coke, which announced the end of Coke.[1]

"It was the only thing to do after the mule died."
Three years back, the Hinsleys of Dora, Missouri, had a tough decision to make.
To buy a new mule.
Or invest in a used bug.
They weighed the two possibilities.
First there was the problem of the bitter Ozark winters. Tough on a warm-blooded mule. Not so tough on an air-cooled VW.
Then, what about the eating habits of the two contenders? Hay vs. gasoline.
As Mr. Hinsley puts it: "I get over eighty miles out of a dollar's worth of gas and I get where I want to go a lot quicker."
Then there's the road leading to their cabin. Many a mule pulling a wagon and many a conventional automobile has spent many an hour stuck in the mud.
As for shelter, a mule needs a barn. A bug doesn't. "It just sets out there all day and the paint job looks near as good as the day we got it."
Finally, there was maintenance to think about. When a mule breaks down, there's only one thing to do: Shoot it.
But if and when their bug breaks down, the Hinsleys have a Volkswagen dealer only two gallons away.

Exhibit 7.1 Bill Bernbach created some of the best advertising of all time and he did it without research. In fact, he thought research got in the way of good advertising.

Courtesy of Volkswagen of America, Inc.

Why? Didn't the scientific research lead to the right decision? No, it didn't. Didn't the psychologists provide all the rights answers? No, they didn't. Maybe that's why The Coca-Cola Company and many other great companies have turned to more sociocultural approaches. This was a stark reminder that cultural meaning, not socially isolated and sterile product attitudes matter.

What went wrong with the research? For one, the right question was never asked, or no one paid attention to the answer: consumers didn't understand that their beloved Coke was being taken away, replaced by New Coke. Secondly, no one considered the cultural side of the equation. Coke was more than a sweet brown liquid. Coca-Cola confused the objective taste tests of a product with the cultural reality of a brand.

As others have noted, never, ever, ever confuse a brand and a product. The blind taste tests were about products; the market reaction of real consumers was about a brand—a brand that had enormous cultural meaning. Products are mere things. Brands hold meaning. Advertising helps turn products into brands.

Never forget: Meaning makes brands out of products. Advertising helps create brand meaning.

Tons of psychological research, and the Coca-Cola Company still made a huge mistake. So, never think that just throwing research, no matter how "scientific" it is, at a problem does anything good.[2]

1. See Mark Pendergrast, "The Marketing Blunder of the Century," in *For God, Country and Coca-Cola: The Definitive History of the Great American Soft-Drink and the Company That Makes It* (New York: Basic Books, 2000), 356.

2. Thomas Frank, *The Conquest of Cool: Business Culture, Counterculture, and the Rise of Hip Consumerism* (Chicago, IL: University of Chicago Press, 1997).

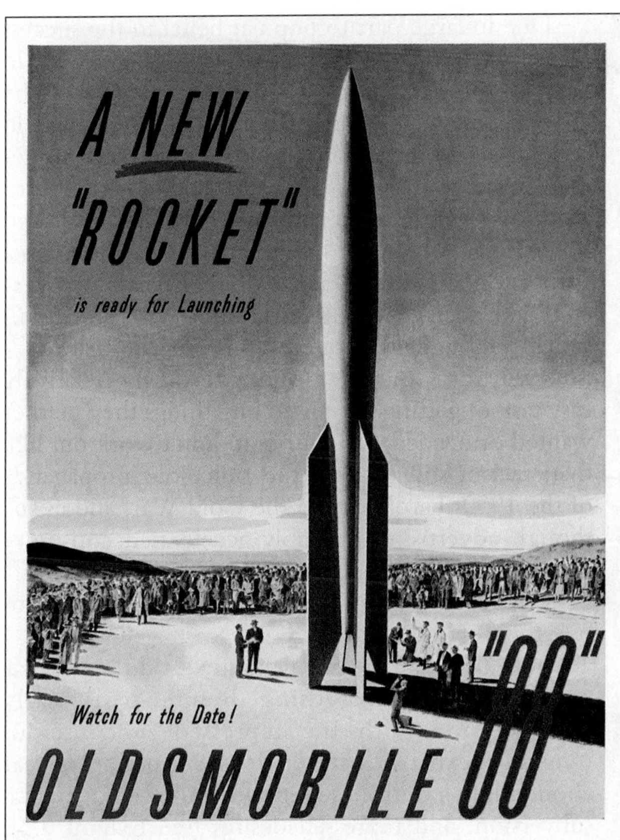

A NEW
"ROCKET"
is ready for Launching
Watch for the Date!
OLDSMOBILE "88"

Exhibit 7.2 Advertising research came to us from the 1950s, a period in which science was popularized to ridiculous heights and was commonly misapplied. Unfortunately, that legacy influenced the advertising industry for decades to come.

Courtesy, Oldsmobile Division of General Motors, Inc.

Ad luminaries such as Bill Bernbach (responsible for, among many other things, the amazing creative for brands like Volkswagen in the 1960s; see Exhibit 7.1) thought advertising research was worse than a waste. Lately, with shrinking agency margins, research has been regarded as more and more expendable by the bean counters. Advertising agencies have been cutting back on research lately; it's considered a luxury. There are a lot of reasons for this, but it actually goes well beyond economic conditions. It goes back a long way, and involves a basic confusion about what advertising and brand promotion research is, if it does any good at all. We won't end the research controversy, but we hope to make things a little clearer and provide perspective. Real-world bottom line: Research in general is threatened at most ad agencies, more and more is being farmed out to external suppliers or not practiced at all. In the growing list of nontraditional sources of advertising and brand promotion, it is even more rare. When there is research, it is dominated by qualitative methods, particularly on-scene, in-home, at usage site, types of fieldwork. That's how most real world advertising and integrated brand promotion research is done, if it is done at all.

First, to clarify our terms: Advertising and brand promotion research is any research that helps in the development, execution, or evaluation of advertising and promotion. Good advertising and promotion research can move one closer to producing effective advertising and promotion. Unfortunately, the wrong questions are often asked, the wrong methods are often applied, and people generalize way too much on limited data.

Although some advertising agencies have had research specialists or even departments for more than 100 years, their real growth occurred in the mid-20th century, with the 1950s being their real heyday. During this period, agencies adopted research departments for three basic reasons: (1) The popularity of, naiveté toward, and overconfidence in "social science" during this time legitimized anything called science or research, particularly psychological methods. (2) Other agencies had research departments. (3) There was a real need to better understand how ads worked... still is.

During the 1950s, advertising research established and legitimized itself in the industry. The popular adoration of science was at its height; the books, the plays, the movies, and the ads (see Exhibit 7.2) of this period are full of popular science. There was an economic boom in consumption; agencies could afford research departments—and indulge in the hope (maybe myth) of "scientific advertising." Of course, there was great ambivalence about science after World War II, about its use and misuse. It was a period of great faith in the power of science and technology, and great concern about its misuse for evil, for destructive and manipulative ends like getting people to buy things they really don't need or even really want, particularly by doing this through their subconscious, or subliminally. Watch some 1950s movies such as anything by Hitchcock or any of the great sci-fi B-movies. (Watch out for 50-foot women). They are all about this great ambivalence toward science. This ambivalence has waxed and waned throughout the years but has always remained. It exists today.

Exhibit 7.3 Advertising research had its biggest growth in the "mind control" fears and pop psychology of the 1950s. Unfortunately, this legacy lasted a long time.

Courtesy, Warner Brothers Entertainment, Inc.

Due in large part to popular belief in the success of propaganda and psychological warfare in World War II, there was a ready-made acceptance of the "science of persuasion." There was a widely held belief that sophisticated mind-control techniques used in the war effort were now being turned into Madison Avenue mind control through sophisticated advertising. A belief in hidden mass persuasion was a cornerstone of Cold War ideology. Amazingly overconfident social psychologists of the 1950s and 1960s actually thought they were going to eliminate racism, win the Cold War, and take on the relatively easy task of getting people to buy things they neither wanted or needed. Of course, it didn't work out like that: racism still existed, the ridiculous propaganda of the 1950s hardly ended the Cold War, and eventhough advertising probably accelerated consumer culture, individual marketers found out just how difficult it really was to get those pesky consumers to buy their brands.

Into this strange social context, add a popular renaissance in everything Freud, particularly his obsession with the repressed subconscious (typically sexual in nature). It was a period of fear about mind control, seduction, moral and mental subversion, and repressed desires (see Exhibit 7.3). In university environments, psychologists embraced science and experimentation as the only path to understanding persuasion, rather than the more popularized Freudian approach. This stream of work also had an impact on the industry and its mass importation of college-trained persuasion "experts." It was, not coincidently, the same time that many American universities decided they should spend resources on training advertising professionals; most of the advertising departments and courses were formed during this period. The reasons this class and book exist have to do with this period.

So into this social environment were born the advertising research departments. In the 1950s, advertising agencies and their clients clamored for more research, more science, and some for hidden messages. Agency research departments were justified by the sacred name of "science" and the reality of frightened consumers, scared by the Cold War, by the very real possibility of instant annihilation from a nuclear war, by a rapidly changing social system, and by the very idea that someone could control your mind (see *The Manchurian Candidate*). We tell you all this because this history still influences what we call advertising research today. This legacy is still with us; it's still in common beliefs about advertising, and even in the law.

But, there is change. In the early 1980s, advertising agencies began to openly voice their distrust for the sacred research methods established in 1950s America. These voices of dissent began in London, moved to the U.S. West Coast, and lately are heard just about everywhere. As we said before, in the past decade several advertising agencies have come to believe that stand-alone research departments are a luxury that they can no longer afford given increased demands for accountability, profit, and relevance. At least two things are being seen as replacements, when

Exhibit 7.4 Words to judge research by.

- **Reliability** means that the method generates generally consistent findings over time.
- **Validity** means that the information generated is relevant to the research questions being investigated. In other words, the research investigates what it seeks to investigate.
- **Trustworthiness** is a term usually applied to qualitative data, and it means exactly what it implies: Can one, knowing how the data were collected, trust them, and to what extent?
- **Meaningfulness** is the most difficult of all these terms. Just what does a piece of research really mean (if anything)? Meaningfulness is determined by asking what the methods and measures really have to do with determining a good ad. This simple question is not asked enough.

Good advertising and promotions research can actually help make better advertising and promotions.

there are replacements: (1) the account planning system, in which research is a more integral part of planning advertising and promotion strategy and execution, and (2) much greater research outsourcing, that is, going outside the agency for specific advertising research when and only when the need arises. Actual industry practice quickly showed 1950s-era research to be limited, and during the next half century advertising research morphed many times. As previously mentioned, it is now naturalistic and socio-cultural methods that are favored.

So, how do you know when research is good? On which dimensions can it be judged? Exhibit 7.4 gives you some terms and concepts that are very useful when talking about research.

Advertising and IBP Research.

A lot of things are called "advertising and brand promotion research." Not all of it, or even most of it, is done on the actual ads or promotions themselves. Most of this research is really done in preparation for making the ads and promotions. A lot is done on the client or brand side, at companies like P&G or Sony or Nokia. But the best way to divide the research world into three parts: (1) developmental advertising and promotion research (before ads are made); (2) copy research (as the ads are being finished or are finished); and (3) results-oriented research (after the ads are actually out there, running).

1 Stage One: Developmental Advertising and IBP Research.

Developmental advertising and promotion research is used to generate opportunities and messages. It helps the creatives (the people who dream up and actually make the ads) and the account team figure out the target audience's identity, what they perceive themselves as needing and wanting in a given good or service, and their usage expectations, history, and context, among others. It can provide critical information used by creatives in actually producing ads and promotions. It is conducted early in the process so that there is still an opportunity to influence the way the ads, branded

Exhibit 7.5 Design thinking is about process… it is about unleashing guided creativity.

entertainment, or other integrated brand promotions turn out. Because of this, many consider it the most valuable kind of research. It occurs when you can still do something about it, before you have spent a ton of money and made some really bad mistakes. It is sometimes called *consumer insight*.

Method: Design Thinking. Design thinking is a new way of looking at the integration of research and product development (see Exhibit 7.5). It is finding its way into advertising and brand promotion as well. The idea is to actually get marketers and advertisers to think like designers. Designers use a type of thought process that emphasizes getting rid of any preconceived notions of what a good or service is currently and replaces it with a process in which designers partner with users/potential users to actually create from scratch what the good or service should actually look like. Why should a wallet look like existing wallets? Why should a computer look like existing computers? Design thinking emphasizes data acquired from close work with consumers that reveals what they really need and want in a good or service, not what some engineer screwed together, or what they told you in a focus group. It then uses an on-going process of prototyping, use, feedback, prototyping to design (and then communicate) what the brand does for real consumers. The hotbeds of design thinking are Stanford, Silicon Valley, MIT, Chicago, and University of Wisconsin in Madison. Companies such as Apple, Intuit, P&G, Target, and The Coca-Cola Company are champions of the movement.

Exhibit 7.6 Hungry for more on the history of M&Ms? Check out www.mms.com

Concept Testing. A **concept test** seeks feedback designed to screen the quality of a new idea, using consumers as the judge and jury. Concept testing may be used to screen new ideas for specific advertisements or to assess new product concepts. Before a new product like the one in Exhibit 7.6 is launched, the advertiser should have a deep understanding of how the product fits current needs and how much consumers are willing to pay for the new product. Concept tests of many kinds are commonly included to get quick feedback on new product or advertising ideas. Sometimes an

Exhibit 7.7 This is probably the best ever example of creating new uses for a mature brand. Think about: Buy this; go home and put it down the drain; repeat. Brilliant.

ad agency is called on to invent new ways of presenting an advertised good or service to a target audience (Exhibit 7.7).

Further, just where does an advertiser get ideas for new and meaningful ways to portray a brand? Direct contact with the customer can be an excellent place to start. Qualitative research involving observation of customers and extended interviewing of customers can be great devices for fostering fresh thinking about a brand. Direct contact with and aggressive listening to the customer can fuel the creative process at the heart of a great advertising campaign. It can also be a great way to anticipate and shape marketplace trends.

Method: Audience Profiling. Perhaps the most important service provided by developmental advertising research is the profiling of target audiences for the creatives. Creatives need to know as much as they can about the people to whom their ads will speak. This research is done in many ways. One way is through lifestyle research. Lifestyle research, also known as AIO (activities, interests, and opinions) research, uses survey data from consumers who have answered questions about themselves. From the answers to a wide variety of such questions, advertisers can get a pretty good profile of the consumers they are most interested in talking to. Because the data also contain other product usage questions, advertisers can account for a consumption lifestyle as well. For example, it may turn out that the target for a brand of roach killer consists of male consumers, age 35 to 45, living in larger cities, who are more afraid of "unseen dirt" than most people and who think of themselves as extremely organized and bothered by messes. They also love watching *Cops*. Profiles like this present the creative staff with a finer-grained picture of the target audience and their needs, wants, and motivations. Of course, the answers to these questions are only as valuable as the questions are valid. In-depth interviews with individual consumers provide an excellent source of information to supplement the findings from AIO research, and vice versa. Sometimes a photo (from stock sources) of someone who seems to fit this "look" is provided to help the creative "picture" the "profile" (see Exhibit 7.8).

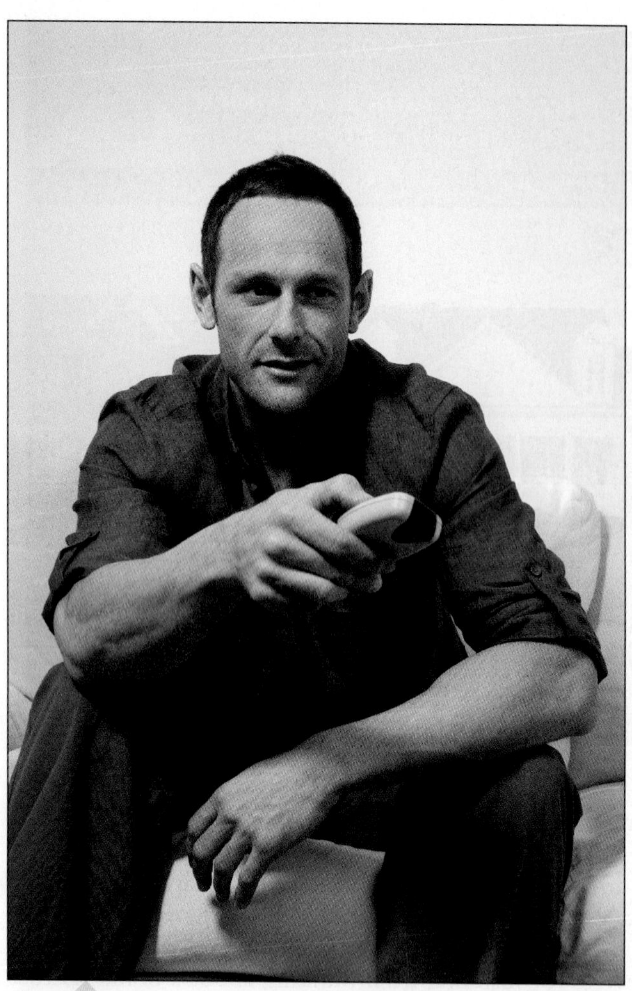

Exhibit 7.8 Sometimes creatives are provided with an image of the target profile. Does this person match the verbal description?

Method: Focus Groups. A **focus group** is a discussion session with (typically) six to 10 target customers who have been brought together to come up with new insights about the good or service. With a professional moderator guiding the discussion, the consumers are first asked some general questions; then, as the session progresses, the questioning becomes more focused and moves to detailed issues about the brand in question. Advertisers tend to like focus groups because they can understand them and observe the data being collected. Although focus groups provide an opportunity for in-depth discussion with consumers, they are not without limitations. Even multiple focus groups represent a very small sample of the target audience and are prone to all sorts of errors caused by group dynamics and pleasing the researcher. But remember that generalization is not the goal. The real goal is to get or test a new idea and gain depth of understanding. More than once in a while, what ends up being actual ad copy comes from the mouths of focus group members.

It takes skill to lead a focus group effectively. If the group does not have a well-trained and experienced moderator, some individuals will completely dominate the others. Focus group members also feel empowered and privileged; they have been made experts by their selection, and they will sometimes give the moderator all sorts of strange answers that may be more a function of trying to impress other group members than anything having to do with the product in question. Like most things, focus groups are good at what they do, but people feel compelled to push them in ways they were never meant to go. Again, focus groups are for understanding and insight, not scientific generalizations. They are very low in reliability, sometimes valid, but often produce meaningful insight. Their overall trustworthiness as a method is in the low to mid-range.

Method: Projective Techniques. **Projective techniques** are designed to allow consumers to "project" their thoughts, but mostly feelings (conscious or unconscious), onto a "blank" or neutral "surface," like an inkblot or benign painting or scene. It's like seeing zoo animals in clouds, or faces in ice cubes. Projective techniques share a history with Freudian psychology and depend on notions of unconscious or even repressed thoughts. Projective techniques often consist of offering consumers fragments of pictures or words and asking them to complete the fragment. The most common projective techniques are association tests, dialogue balloons, story construction, and sentence or picture completion.

Dialogue balloons offer consumers the chance to fill in the dialogue of cartoonlike stories. The story usually has to do with a product use situation. The idea is that the consumers will "project" appropriate thoughts into the balloons. Supposedly, their true feelings will emerge (see Exhibit 7.9).

Story construction is another projective technique. It asks consumers to tell a story about people depicted in a scene or picture. Respondents might be asked to

Exhibit 7.9 The idea is to let your real feelings emerge by projecting them into the space provided.

tell a story about the personalities of the people in the scene, what they are doing, what they were doing just before this scene, what type of car they drive, and what type of house they live in. Again, the idea is to use a less direct method to less obtrusively bring to the surface some often unconscious mapping of the brand and its associations.

Another method of projection is **sentence and picture completion.** Here a researcher presents consumers with part of a picture or a sentence with words deleted and then asks that the stimulus be completed. The picture or sentence relates to one or several brands of products in the category of interest. For example, a sentence completion task might be *Most American-made cars are* _____. The basic idea is to elicit honest and un-edited thoughts and feelings. Researchers can get some pretty good information from this method; other times they learn more about a particular individual than a meaningful group of consumers.

Another method that has enjoyed growing popularity in advertising and promotional developmental is the **Zaltman Metaphor Elicitation Technique (ZMET).**[3] It is also projective in nature. This technique claims to draw out people's buried thoughts and feelings about products and brands by encouraging participants to think in terms of metaphors. A metaphor simply involves defining one thing in terms of another. ZMET draws metaphors from consumers by asking them to spend time thinking about how they would visually represent their experiences with a particular product or service. Participants are asked to make a collection of photographs and pictures from magazines that reflect their experience. For example, in research conducted for DuPont, which supplies raw material for many pantyhose marketers, one person's picture of spilled ice cream

3. For three different viewpoints on ZMET, compare Kevin Lane Keller, *Strategic Brand Management* (Upper Saddle River, NJ: Prentice-Hall, 1988), 317–320; Ronald B. Liever, "Storytelling: A New Way to Get Close to Your Customer," *Fortune,* February 3, 1997, 102–108; and Gerald Zaltman, "Rethinking Market Research: Putting People Back In," *Journal of Marketing Research,* vol. 34 (November 1997), 424–437.

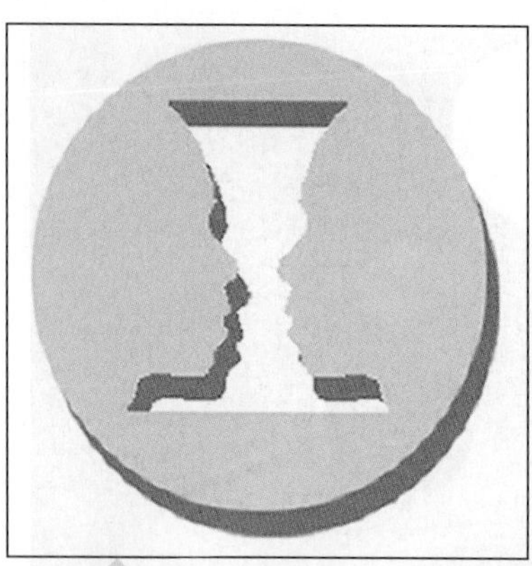

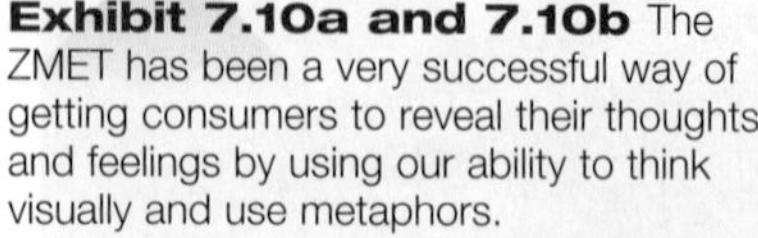

Exhibit 7.10a and 7.10b The ZMET has been a very successful way of getting consumers to reveal their thoughts and feelings by using our ability to think visually and use metaphors.

reflected her deep disappointment when she spots a run in her hose. In-depth interviews with several dozen of these metaphor-collecting consumers can often reveal new insights about consumers' consumption motives, which then may be useful in the creation of products and ad campaigns to appeal to those motives. Metaphors are believed by many to be one of the most powerful and useful organizing and expressive structures of the human mind and, if they can be tapped successfully, can provide advertisers (see Exhibit 7.10). with very useful information. The ZMET is now widely used by marketers and advertisers. It was notably used by P&G in the launch of Febreze.

Cookies aren't the only things
that can be dipped with milk.
Nothing keeps me going during a night out,
like the refreshing sensation of milk.
It tastes great and keeps my body limber
and my bones strong – necessities for
the twists and twirls of the tango!
got milk?

Exhibit 7.11 This campaign was largely inspired by qualitative research; Researchers actually went out into the "field" and found that there was nothing worse than having a cookie/brownie/etc. but no milk.

Method: Field Work. Field work is conducted outside the agency (i.e., in the "field"), usually in the home or site of consumption. Its purpose is to learn from the experiences of the consumer and from direct observation. Consumers live real lives, and their behavior as consumers is intertwined throughout these real lives. Their consumption practices are **embedded;** that is, they are tightly connected to their social context. More and more, researchers are attempting to caVWWpture more of the real embedded experiences of consumers. This research philosophy and related methods are very popular today. Campaigns such as the award-winning and successful "Got Milk?" campaign (see Exhibit 7.11) used field work to get at the real consumption opportunity for milk—a mouth full of cookies and an empty milk carton. This helped form, and then drive, the strategy and creative execution.

Consumers began to remember to be sure to have milk at home, to ask themselves when at the grocery store, "Got milk?" Other advertisers and their agencies make videorecordings, or have consumers themselves shoot home movies to get at the real usage opportunities and consumption practices of real consumers in real settings. Advertising researchers can make better messages if they understand the lives of their target audience, and understand it in its actual usage context. Field research uses observation and in-depth study of individuals or small groups of consumers in their own social environment.

Courtesy, Susan Van Etten; AP Topic Gallery

The advertising industry has long appreciated the value of qualitative data and is currently moving to even more strongly embrace extended types of fieldwork.

Method: Mining the Web.

It probably goes without saying for today's Web-savvy college student that the Internet can be an advertiser's best friend when looking for secondary data of almost any kind. The Internet has revolutionized developmental research, particularly for smaller agencies and advertisers. Common search engines allow the search of enormous amounts of data previously available only to the wealthiest agencies. Human search costs have been slashed. Of particular value are Web-based interest groups, or online communities. Google Groups (Exhibit 7.12) and Facebook (see Exhibit 7.13) are great resources. Without ever leaving your office, you can see the spread of

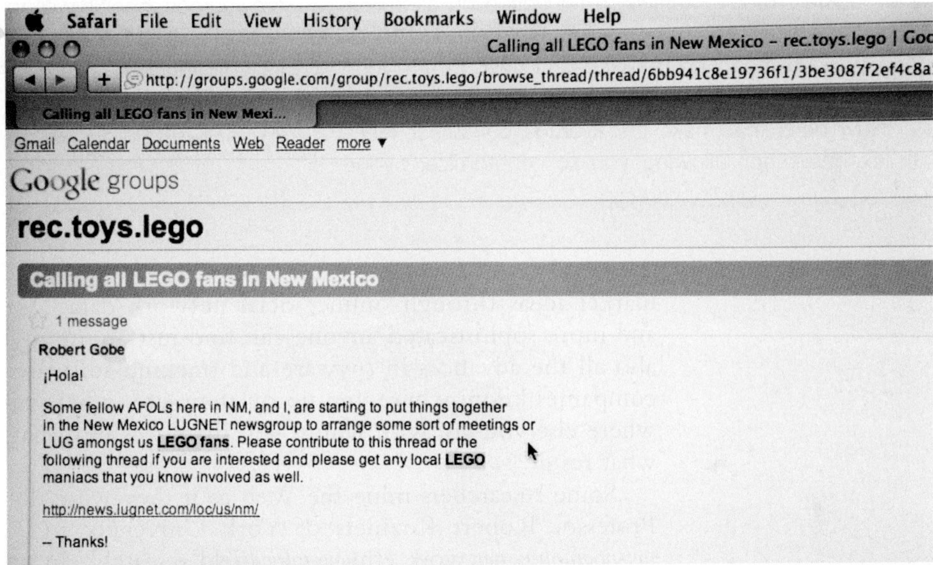

Exhibit 7.12 Google makes it easy and inexpensive to access brand communities.

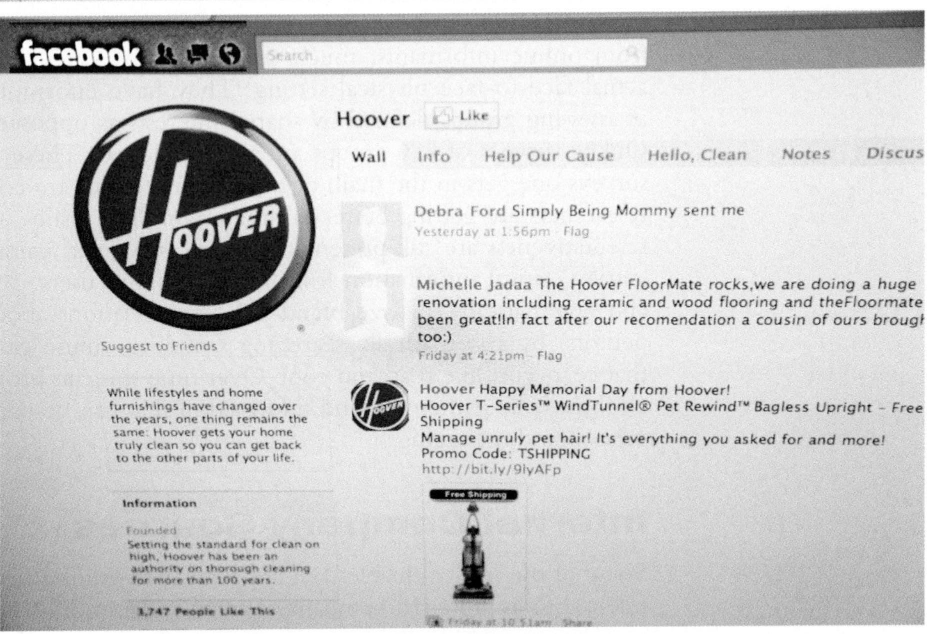

Exhibit 7.13 Brands have "friends."

Courtesy, Susan Van Etten; Courtesy, Susan Van Etten

Social Media

Facebook Creates a Research Tool: You

Facebook decided to automatically share YOUR data with a lot of marketers. And it is a LOT of data.

In early 2010, Facebook added the LIKE button. Facebook users go to other sites and stick a like button it and their page.... and the data goes to Facebook... where it can be sold ... to whomever they want. In the first 24 hours after launch, and estimated 1 billion stickers... and all that data. This is made possible by their OpenGraph platform.

Within hours, Sen. Charles Schumer, D-N.Y., asked the Federal Trade Commission for action on all social networking sites. According to Sen. Schumer and other privacy advocates, Facebook doesn't have to ask your permission for a thing.

How does that make the average consumer feel? In exchange for allowing you to "customize:" your preferences on their site, Facebook will collect and do whatever they please while? watching you... driven somewhat by consumer's belief that someone actually cares what THEY like or don't like. Maybe this is just the price of the user's narcissism.

So, Facebook has created a very important tool for advertisers wanting to gain knowledge of their customers. But, it depends on turning their customers into research tools.

Are you comfortable with that... are you, tool?

Sources: Sen. Schumer Questions Facebook on Privacy New Data-Sharing; Initiative AdAge.com, " Raises Questions for Regulators" by Kunur Patel , *published:* April 26, 2010; and With Universal 'Like' Button, Facebook Spreads Across Web; Announcement at F8 Developer Conference Reveals Platform Designed to Draw in Vast Data" by Kunur Patel *Published:* April 21, 2010.

market ideas through online social network data. As search engines get more and more sophisticated anyone can find just about anything. But then there are also all the advances in spyware and tracking software: software designed to let companies know where you go on their site, what you do when you are there, where else you go, with whom you share this information, and presumably with what result.

Some researchers mine the Web as if they were doing fieldwork, just online. Professor Robert Kozinets of York University in Toronto coined the term *net-nography: net* work eth*nography* (field research). In netnography, the researcher not only observes and collects data from the Web but also actively seeks answers from online informants, much the same way a field researcher would do in an actual face-to-face physical setting. They have enormous cost advantages as well as assessing groups defined by shared interests as opposed to shared physical space. Online surveys of key groups are also employed. These are similar to the kinds of surveys one gets in the mail, or on the phone, but are conducted online. Although researchers are getting better at online sampling, issues of generalizability and representativeness are still present. They are, however, gaining popularity as a way of getting critical information from targeted brand users. Some researchers download and systematically analyze brand-talk (conversations about their brands, and competitors) by systematically searching sampling online chatter and analyzing words that co-occur; like iPad and cool. Over time this can provide a very good source of unobtrusively gathered brand information that can be used to develop new ads and other brand messaging.

Internal Company Sources.

Some of the most valuable data are available within a firm itself and are, therefore, referred to as "internal company sources." Commonly available information within a company includes strategic marketing plans, research reports, customer service records, warranty registration cards, letters from customers, customer complaints, and various sales data (broken down by region, by customer type, by product line). All of these provide a wealth of information relating to the proficiency of the company's advertising programs and, more generally, changing consumer tastes and preferences. Sometimes really great data are right there under the client's or agency's nose. More and more of these data are gathered online.

Government Sources.

Various government organizations generate data on factors of interest to advertising planners; information on population and housing trends, transportation, consumer spending, and recreational activities in the United States is available through government documents.[4] Go to www.lib.umich.edu/govdocs/federal.html for a couple hundred or so pages of great links to data from federal, state, and international government sources. The Census of Population and Housing is conducted every 10 years in years ending in 0. The data (actually tables, not the data itself, unfortunately) are released at various times during the following handful of years after the census. The Census Bureau has a great website with access to numerous tables and papers (www.census.gov/).

A great source of data in the United States is the American Community Survey(ACS), which the Census Bureau actually hopes will replace many aspects of the 2010 census. It came online in 2003. The ACS is a new approach for collecting accurate, timely information. It is designed as an ongoing survey that will replace the so-called long form in the 2010 census. The ACS provides estimates of demographic, housing, social, and economic characteristics every year for states, cities, counties, metropolitan areas, and population groups of 65,000 people or more (www.factfinder.census.gov/home/en/acsdata.html). (See Exhibit 7.14a from the ACS.) Demographic changes are key to so many advertising and branding opportunities. Think of how many ads you see for retirement services and planning; do you think the enormous number of aging

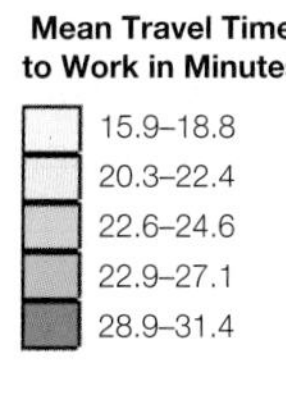

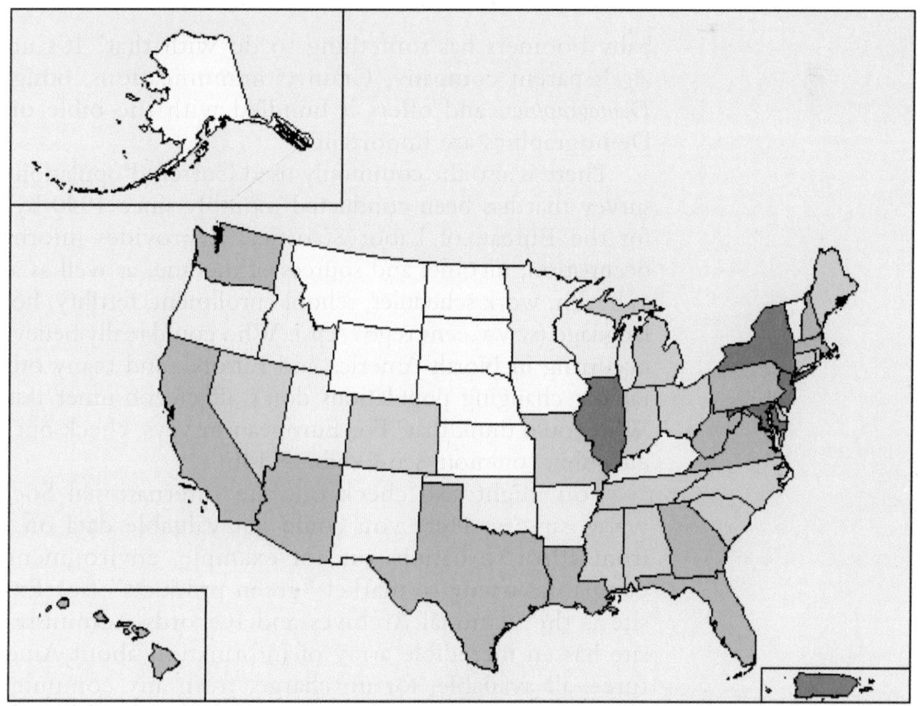

Exhibit 7.14a This map and the one in Exhibit 7.14b on the next page show commute times in the various states and where the most parents live. Advertisers need these kinds of data to know where the best potential customers are.

Courtesy, U.S. Census Bureau

4. We would like to thank Professor Gillian Stevens of the University of Alberta for her assistance with government data sources.

2008 Birth Rates per 1000 Women

- 43–44
- 47–52
- 53–58
- 59–66
- 69–79

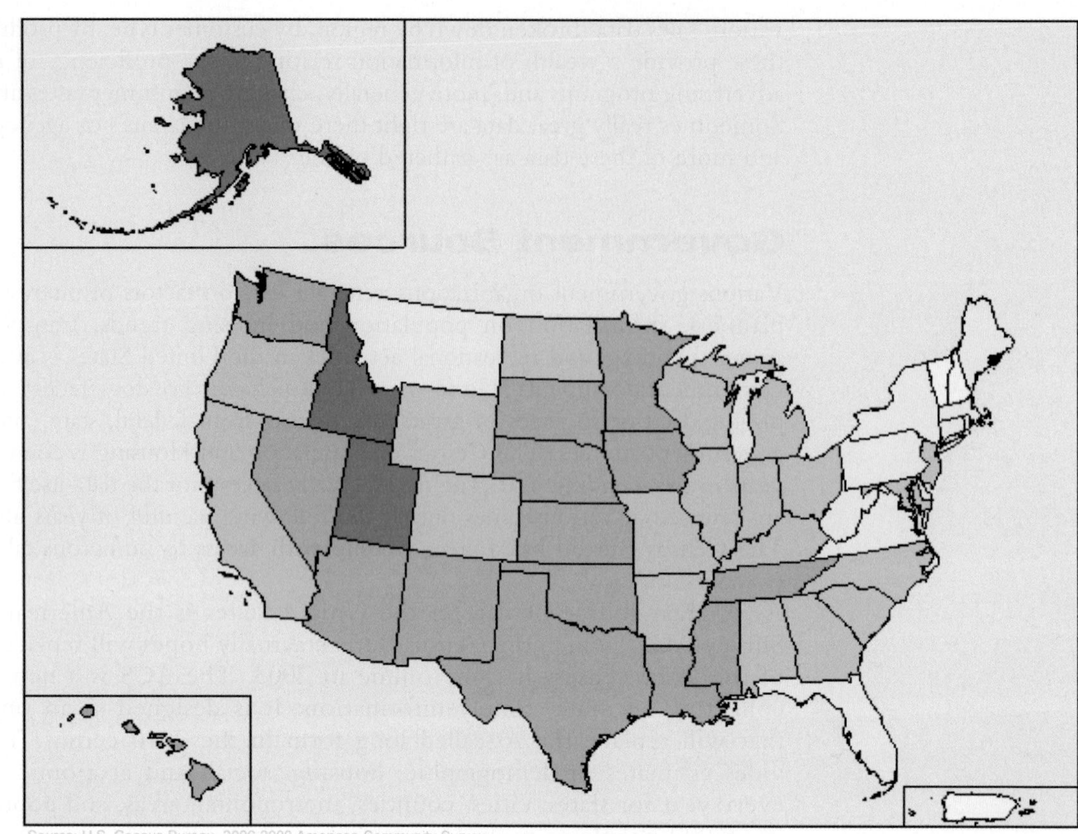

Exhibit 7.14b

baby boomers has something to do with that? It's no accident that *Advertising Age*'s parent company, Crain Communications, bought the magazine *American Demographics,* and offers it bundled with the bible of the advertising industry. Demographics are important.

There is also the commonly used Current Population Survey, which is a national survey that has been conducted monthly since 1940 by the Bureau of the Census for the Bureau of Labor Statistics. It provides information on unemployment, occupation, income, and sources of income, as well as a rotating set of topics such as health, work schedules, school enrollment, fertility, households, immigration, and language (www.census.gov/cps). Who could really believe, given all the immigration occurring in North America and Europe, and many other parts of the world, that rapidly changing populations don't affect consumer taste, needs, and preferences? Who could think that? For European surveys, check out Eurobarometer, ec.europa.eu/public_opinion (see Exhibit 7.14b).

You might also check out the International Social Survey Programme at www.issp.org. Here you could get valuable data on the feelings of consumers from 30 or so nations on, for example, environmental issues, quite a find for companies trying to market "green products" (see Exhibit 7.15). Another great site is the National Archives and Records Administration, www.nara.gov.This site has an incredible array of information about Americans and American culture—all available, for no charge, from any computer. The array of consumer data available from government sources is a wonderful resource in advertising and planning for businesses of all sizes. These publications/sites are reasonably

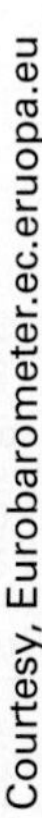

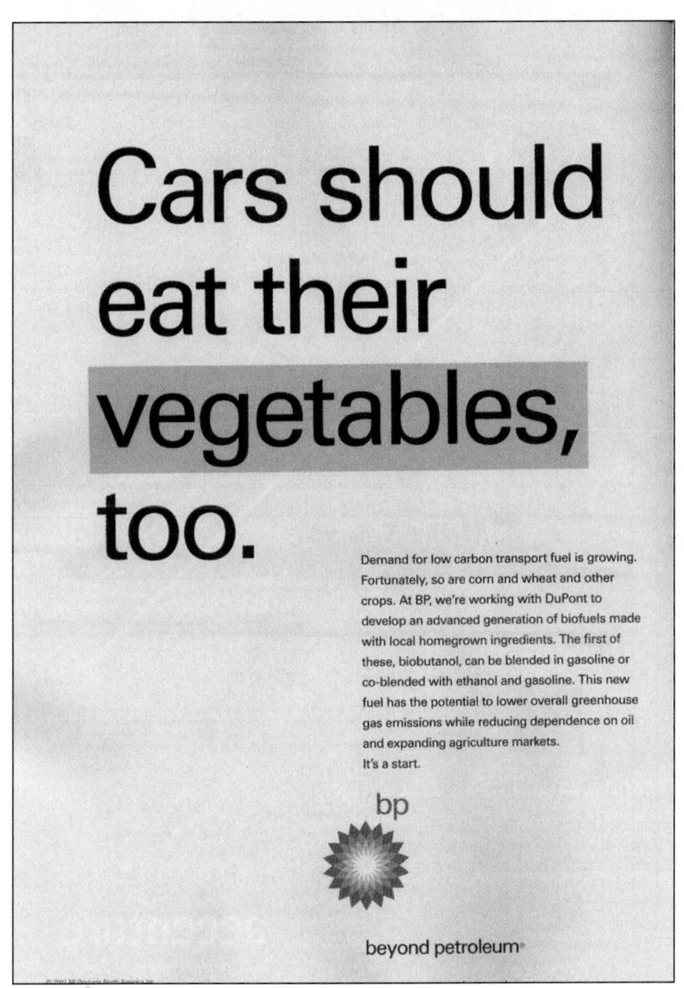

Cars should eat their vegetables, too.
Demand for low carbon transport fuel is growing. Fortunately, so are corn and wheat and other crops. At BP, we're working with DuPont to develop an advanced generation of biofuels made with local homegrown ingredients. The first of these, biobutanol, can be blended in gasoline or co-blended with ethanol and gasoline. This new fuel has the potential to lower overall greenhouse gas emissions while reducing dependence on oil and expanding agriculture markets.
It's a start.
bp
beyond petroleum

Exhibit 7.15
Recognition of the need for cleaner-burning fuels continues to grow across a long list of nations.

Courtesy, British Petroleum

current. Print versions are available at public libraries. This means that even a small-business owner can access large amounts of information for advertising planning purposes at little or no cost. Again, the Internet has changed the world and the practice of advertising and promotion. Small marketers and their agencies can now obtain data that would have simply either been unavailable or cost too much just a few years ago.

Method: Commercial Sources. First, let us be truthful: This is not a complete list. There are lots and lots of commercial research suppliers. We list a few but more important are the ideas that underlie most of them. Because information has become such a critical resource in marketing and advertising decision making, commercial data services have emerged to provide data of various types and to package existing data. So, while traditional advertising agencies are more and more getting out or downsizing the research business, innovative companies (some of them start-ups) see an opportunity opening up here, particularly for those who can collect, package, or repackage online data. Some firms specialize in data-gathering efforts at the household or neighborhood level. Prizm is a good example. Prizm's owner, Claritas, collects data at the ZIP code level on consumption. This way, a marketer can see a pretty interesting profile of who is most likely to consume a given good or service, and also *where* (see Exhibit 7.16). This is based on the assumption that most consumers within a given ZIP code are more alike than different in their consumption habits. However, this assumption is not accepted universally. Sometimes there are significant variations in consumer practices within a given geographic area. More often than not, people living in close proximity to one another are more like each other (in consumption practices) than people living in different geographic areas. That simple reality is what makes geographic clustering research methods work at all.

Information from commercial data vendors is reasonably comprehensive and is normally gathered using reasonably sound methods. Information from these sources costs more than information from government sources but is specifically designed to be of benefit to advertisers and marketers. Exhibit 7.17 lists a few of the major companies and their offerings. Many offer consumer surveys (one-shot attempts: one person answers the survey one time) and consumer panels (surveys in which the same members stay on the panel and are asked questions numerous times over months or years.)

Data from the Pew Center, a widely respected public opinion survey center, is also very valuable. It is particularly good at tracking general consumer attitudes. Given that advertising that is consistent with social trends and attitudes is often the best advertising, Pew data can be very valuable. Lately, much has been written about how little trust Americans have in institutions of all kinds, from government to banks (see Exhibit 7.18). Could a smart advertiser leverage this feeling to sell a brand? Sure they could.

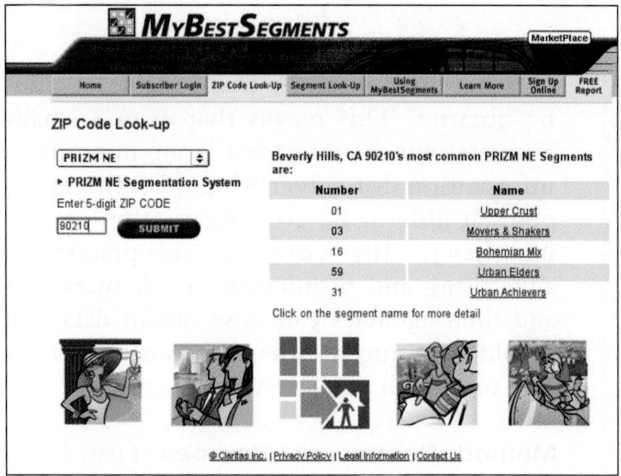

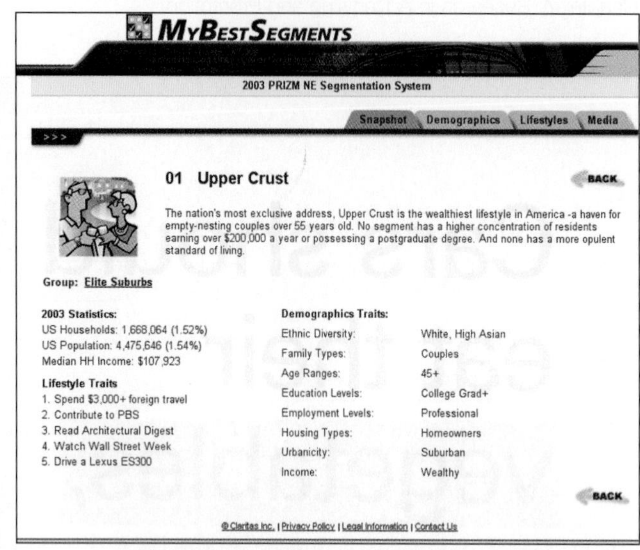

Exhibit 7.16 Here is ZIP code consumer data from Prizm. Nice zip code: 90210. Here are the menu and three of the "best" segments for Beverly Hills, California.

Claritas Inc. PRISM NE

Commercial Information Source	Type of Information
Dun & Bradstreet Market Identifiers (DMI)	DMI is a listing of 4.3 million businesses that is updated monthly. Information includes number of employees, relevant SIC codes that relate to the businesses' activities, location, and chief executive. Marketing and advertising managers can use the information to identify markets, build mailing lists, and specify media to reach an organization. www.dnb.com
Nielsen Retail Index	Nielsen auditors collect product inventory turnover data from 1,600 grocery stores, 750 drugstores, and 150 mass merchandise outlets. Information is also gathered on retail prices, in-store displays, and local advertising. Data from the index are available by store type and geographic location. www.nielsenmedia.com
National Purchase Diary (NPD) Panel	With more than 13,000 families participating, NPD is the largest diary panel in the United States. Families record on preprinted sheets their monthly purchases in 50 product categories. Information recorded includes brand, amount purchased, price paid, use of coupons, store, specific version of the product (flavor, scent, etc.), and intended use.
Consumer Mail Panel	This panel is operated by a firm called Market Facts. There are 45,000 active participants at any point in time. Samples are drawn in lots of 1,000. The overall panel is said to be representative of different geographic regions in the United States and Canada, then broken down by household income, urbanization, and age of the respondent. Data are provided on demographic and socioeconomic characteristics as well as type of dwelling and durable goods ownership. www.marketfacts .com

Exhibit 7.17 Examples of the commercial data sources available to advertisers.

The Pew Research Center for the People & the Press
Search people-press.org...
Search
Home
Survey Reports
Commentary
News Interest Index
Question Search
Datasets
Methodology
About the Center
Survey Reports
October 25, 2005
Public Sours on Government and Business
DeLay, Rove Viewed Unfavorably
Print
Email
Share
Summary of Findings
Americans express increasingly negative views of a wide range major institutions, reflecting strong discontent with national conditions. Over the past year, ratings have tumbled for the federal government and Congress. And it is not just Washington institutions that are being viewed less positively. Favorable opinions of business corporations are at their lowest point in two decades. In the face of high energy prices, just 20% express positive opinions of oil companies.
Favorable ratings for the federal government in Washington have taken the hardest hit, falling from 59% last year to 45% currently. The latest national
Favorability of Business Corporations
58
70
73
45
31
24
22
45
1985
1990
1995
2000
2005
Favorable
Unfavorable
REPORT MATERIALS
Complete Report
Topline Questionnaire
TABLE OF CONTENTS
Summary of Findings
About this Survey
Questionnaire
EMAIL UPDATES
Sign up to receive the Pew Research Center newsletter, a regular email update with new analysis on politics, the media and more. The newsletter also offers a round-up of recent releases from all seven projects of the Center.

Exhibit 7.18 Think about social disruption and how smart advertisers might leverage it.

Courtesy, Susan Van Etten

Method: Professional Publications. Another secondary data source is professional publications. Professional publications are periodicals in which marketing and advertising professionals report significant information related to industry trends or new research findings. Examples include be *Progressive Grocer* and *Beverage*.

3 Stage Two: Copy Research.

The second major type of advertising and promotion research is known as copy research, or *evaluative research*. It is the kind that people usually think of when one says "advertising research." It is research on the actual ads or promotional texts themselves, finished or unfinished. It is used to judge or *evaluate* ads and promotions. Even though most contemporary ads are more pictures than words, the name "copy" still reflects the time when it was the effect of advertising copy (words) that was supposed to be most important. These usually occur right before or after the ad is finalized.

In the best case, reliable, valid, trustworthy, and meaningful tests are appropriately applied. In the worst case, tests in which few still believe continue to survive because they represent "the way we have always done things." The pressure of history and the felt need for normative or historically comparative data significantly obscure questions of appropriateness and meaningfulness. This makes for an environment in which the best test is not always done, the wrong tests are more than occasionally done, and the right questions are not always asked. But such is life in the real world.

This brings us to motives and expectations of the agency and the client: Why are certain tests done? Aren't these smart people, trying to make money; why would they do these things? Well we all do things because of history and habit that we know don't make sense, some due to tradition. It may also be that we don't have anything much better with which to replace them. Maybe advertising is so complex that it defies simple measures, and even complex and involved (expensive) ones. Just what is it that advertising professionals want out of their copy research? The answer, of course, depends on who you ask. Generally speaking, the account team (AKA "suits") wants some assurance that the ad does essentially what it's supposed to do, or at least is defensible in terms of copy test scores. Many times, the team simply wants whatever the client wants. The client typically wants to see some numbers, generally meaning **normative test scores**—scores relative to the average for a category of ads. In other words, the client wants to see how well a particular ad scored against average commercials of its type that were tested previously. From a purely practical standpoint, having a good normative copy test score (above the average for the category) lowers the probability of getting fired later. You can point to the score and say it "tested well," and then assert that you (and/or your agency) should not be fired. There is a lot of cover in these scores, perhaps in reality their greatest value.

How about the people who actually make the ads, the creatives? What do they want out of this? Well, generally they hate copy testing and wish it would go away. They are generally uninterested in normative tests. The creatives who actually produced the ad typically believe there is no such thing as the average commercial, and they are quite sure that if there are average commercials, theirs are not among them. Besides benefiting the sales of the advertised product or service, the creatives wouldn't mind another striking ad on their reel or in their book, another Addy or Clio on their wall. But copy research scores are unlikely to predict awards, which are the official currency of creatives. So, creatives don't tend to be fans of copy tests. Creatives want awards. Copy tests often stand in the way and seem meaningless.

Copy tests generate a type of report card, and some people, particularly on the creative side of advertising, resent getting report cards from people in suits. Creatives also argue that these numbers are often misleading and misapplied. More often than not, they're right. Further, they argue that ads are artistic endeavors, not kitchen appliances to be rated by *Consumer Reports*. Advertising, they say, is art, not science. Again, they have a point. Because of these problems, and the often conflicting career agenda of creatives (awards, career as a filmmaker or writer) and account managers (keep your job, sell more stuff, maybe get to move to the brand side), copy research is often the center of agency tensions. Other than corner offices, copy tests have probably been at the center of more agency fights than just about anything.

Whenever people begin looking at the numbers, there is a danger that trivial differences can be made monumental. Other times, the mandatory measure is simply inappropriate. Still other times, creatives wishing to keep their jobs simply want to give the client what he or she wants, as suggested in Exhibit 7.19. If simple recall is what the client wants, then increasing the frequency of brand mentions might be the answer. It may not make for a better commercial, but it may make for a better score and, presumably, a happy client in the short run. A lot of games are played with copy tests.

Despite the politics involved, copy testing research is *probably* a good idea, at least some of the time. Properly conceived, correctly conducted, and appropriately applied, copy research can yield important data that management can then use to determine the suitability of an ad. Knowing when it is appropriate and when it is not, and sticking to your guns is, quite simply, very hard in the advertising and integrated

Exhibit 7.19 Creative pumps up DAR numbers.

Bob, a creative at a large agency, has learned from experience how to deal with lower-than-average day-after recall (DAR) scores. As he explains it, there are two basic strategies: (1) Do things that you know will pump up the DAR. For example, if you want high DARs, never simply super (superimpose) the brand name or tag at the end of the ad. Always voice it over as well, whether it fits or not. You can also work in a couple of additional mentions in dialogue; they may stand out like a sore thumb and make consumers think, "Man, is that a stupid commercial," because people don't talk that way. But it will raise your DARs. (2) Tell them (the account executive or brand manager and other suits) that this is not the kind of product situation that demands high DARs. In fact, high DARs would actually hurt them in the long run due to quick wearout and annoyance. Tell them, "You're too sophisticated for that ham-handed kind of treatment. It would never work with our customers." You can use the second strategy only occasionally, but it usually works. It's amazing.

brand promotion world—too many careers and too much money are on the line. Simple memory measures have lately found their way into product placement and branded entertainment. The following section will help you understand which test to use, and when to test at all.

Evaluative Criteria and Methods.

There are a few common ways ads are judged. Again, these "tests" are usually done right as the ad is being finished, or is finished. They are, more than anything else, traditional. Some make a great deal of sense and are very useful for brand advertising and integrated promotion; others are horribly overused and misapplied. Below we go through and discuss the major evaluative criteria and the major methods of assessing ads and promotions on these criteria. Of the three types of research, this is probably the least useful in actual industry practice. It is, however, alive (if not well) because of tradition.

Method: Communication Tests. A **communication test** simply seeks to discover whether a message is communicating something close to what the advertiser desired. Sometimes advertisers just want to know if audience members "get" the ad. Do they generally understand it, get the joke, see the connection, or get the main point? The reasoning behind this assessment is so obvious it hurts. It makes sense; it can be easily defended—even to copy-research-hating creatives. Brand managers understand this criterion; so do account executives. Do you get the ads in Exhibits 7.20 and 7.21?

Communication tests are usually done in a group setting, with data coming from a combination of pencil-and-paper questionnaires and group discussion. Members of the target audience are shown the ad, or some preliminary or rough version of it. They typically see it several times. Then a discussion is held. One reason communication tests are performed is to prevent a major disaster, to prevent communicating something completely wrong, something the creators of the ad are too close to see but that is entirely obvious to consumers. This could be an unintended double entendre, an inadvertent sexual allusion, or anything else "off the wall." With more transnational or global advertising, it could be an unexpected interpretation of the imagery that emerges as that ad is moved from country to country around the world. Remember, if the consumer sees things, it doesn't matter whether they're intended or not—to the consumer, they're there. However, advertisers should balance this against the fact that communication test

Exhibits 7.20 and 7.21 Do you get the message? Does the main message come across? Is the right image projected?

Courtesy, The Coca-Cola Company; Courtesy, Advertising Archives

members feel privileged and special, and thus they may try too hard to see things, and see things that no one else sees. This is another instance where well-trained and experienced researchers must be counted on to draw a proper conclusion from the testing. These tests are conducted both in-house (at advertising agency itself) or outsourced to a commercial testing service.

What Do They Remember? It is assumed that if the consumer was exposed to the ad, something of that ad remains in the consumer's mind: cognitive residue, pieces of the ads mixed with the consumer's own thoughts and reactions. It might be a memory of the headline, the brand name, the joke in a TV spot, a stray piece of copy, a vague memory trace of an executional element in the ad, or just about anything. So for decades advertisers have tried to score this cognitive residue, or the things left in consumer's minds from the ads. If "remembering stuff" from the ad matters, this makes sense at some basic level, yet we have known for at least 30 to 40 years that most memory measures of ads (not brands) don't tend to predict actual sales very well at all. Why is this? Well, for one thing, consumers may remember all sorts of things in ads, and not care for the advertised brand at all. Or they remember things that are completely irrelevant to the advertiser's intended message, or some of their thoughts actually interfere with associating the advertiser's brand name with the ad itself. Humorous ads are great example of this. The consumer remembers what is funny, but not the brand name—or worse yet, remembers the competitor's brand name. Now some companies are insisting on recall measures for branded entertainment.

It is also the case that these tests are premised on an increasingly out-of-fashion view of human memory. Not so very long ago, psychologists thought that whatever a human experienced made its way into memory pretty much like streaming video or an unedited movie of one's life. It is becoming clear that motivation is much more important in what is remembered than previously recognized. So the focus of lots of advertising research was on the accurate and faithful retrieval of an ad, or at least important pieces of the ad, as if it existed unaltered in memory. Lately, though, a new way of thinking about human memory has emerged. Inspired from research into false memories in child abuse cases, psychologists now believe memory to be fluid and highly subject to motivation: remembering things as we care to remember them, even things that never happened. Memory appears to be much more of an interpretive act than previously thought. Advertising researcher Kathryn Braun-LaTour has shown that one can actually be fairly easily made to remember brands that don't exist and consumption experiences that never happened.[5] This work tells us that to rely so strongly on memory as a measure of advertising effectiveness is a very bad idea. There are certainly times when such measures are appropriate, like memory of a brand name, or a key attribute, but nowhere near as much as they are used. There will be more on this in Chapter 9.

Common Methods for Assessing Cognitive Residue.

Method: Thought Listings. It is commonly assumed that advertising and promotions generate some thoughts during and following exposure. Wow, what an insight. Copy research that tries to identify specific thoughts that were generated by an ad is referred to as **thought listing,** or **cognitive response analysis**. These are tests of knowledge, cognitive residue, and to a lesser degree feelings and emotions. Thought-listing tests are either conducted in-house or obtained from a commercial testing service. They are most often used with television ads, although they can be applied to all ads. Here the researcher is interested in the thoughts that an ad or promotion generates in the mind of the audience. Typically, cognitive responses are collected by having individuals watch the commercial in groups and, as soon as it is over, asking them to write down all the thoughts that were in their minds while watching the commercial. They are then asked about these thoughts and asked to explain or amplify them. The hope is that this will capture what the potential audience members made of the ad and how they responded, or "talked back to it in their head."

These verbatim responses can then be analyzed in a number of ways. Usually, simple percentages or box scores of word counts are used. The ratio of favorable to unfavorable thoughts may be the primary interest of the researcher. Alternatively, the number of times the person made a self-relevant connection—that is, "That would be good for me" or "That looks like something I'd like"—could be tallied and compared for different ad executions. The idea itself is appealing: capturing people's stream of thoughts about an ad at time of exposure. But in its actual practice problems arise. These thoughts are in reality more retrospective than online; in other words, people are usually asked to write these down seconds to minutes after their thoughts actually occurred. They are also highly self-edited—some of your thoughts are not very likely to be shared. These thoughts are obtained in artificial environments and mental states typically unlike those in which real people are actually exposed to ads in real environments, such as sitting in their living room, talking, half-listening to the TV, and so on. But the researchers asked; you have to tell them something. Still, even with all these problems, there is something of value in these thoughts. The trick, of course, is to know what is valuable and what is just "noise." A lot has to do with how well matched the ad and the procedure are. Some ads, for example, are designed in such a way that the last thing the advertiser really wants is a lot of deep thought (more on this in Chapter 10). For other ads (those where certain conclusions and judgments are the desired goal), it can be a good test. Interestingly, research has shown that the single most common cognitive response to an ad, if there is one at all, is a counter-argument. The ad makes some claim, and the consumer says, "no it isn't; that's not true."[6] Do you think that's because it's being done in

5. Kathryn A. Braun, "Postexperience Advertising Effects on Consumer Memory," *Journal of Consumer Research*, vol. 25 (March 1999), 319–334.

6. Thomas J. Robertson, Joan Zielinski, and Scott Ward, *Consumer Behavior* (Glenview: Scott, Foresman and Company, 1984).

an artificial setting and the test consumer wants to look smart, or is that really most people's first and foremost reaction to ads? What do you think?

Method: Recall Tests. These are one of the most commonly employed tests in advertising, and the most controversial. They are used to get at the cognitive residue of ads. The basic idea is that if the ad is to work, it has to be remembered. Following on this premise is the further assumption that the ads best remembered are the ones most likely to work. Thus the objective of these tests is to see just how much, if anything, the viewer of an ad remembers of the message. Recall is used most in testing television advertising. In television **recall tests,** the big companies are Ipsos-ASI and Burke. In print, the major recall testing services are Gallup & Robinson and Mapes and Ross. In print, however, **recognition** is generally the industry standard. Recognition simply means that the audience members indicate that they have seen an ad before (i.e., recognize it), whereas recall requires more actual memory (recalling from memory) of an ad. Recall is more common for television, recognition for print. Cyber ads (such as banners) or social media sites, or branded video, tend to use both recall and recognition tests.

In television, the basic recall procedure is to recruit a group of individuals from the target market who will be watching a certain channel during a certain time on a test date. They are asked to participate ahead of time and are simply told to watch the show. A day after exposure, the testing company calls the individuals on the phone and determines, of those who actually saw the ad, how much they can recall. The day-after-recall (DAR) procedure generally starts with questions such as, "Do you remember seeing a commercial for any laundry detergents? If not, do you remember seeing a commercial for Tide?" If the respondent remembers, he or she is asked what the commercial said about the product: What did the commercial show? What did the commercial look like? The interview is recorded and transcribed. The verbatim interview is coded into various categories representing levels of recall, typically reported as a percentage. *Unaided recall* is when the respondent demonstrates that he or she saw the commercial and remembered the brand name without having the brand name mentioned. If the person had to be asked about a Tide commercial, it would be scored as *aided recall.* Industry leader Burke reports two specific measures: *claim-recall* (percent who claim seeing the ad), and *related-recall* (percent who accurately recall specific elements of the ad).[7] Ipsos-ASI uses a similar procedure but with one major difference. Like Burke, Ipsos-ASI recruits a sample but tells the participants that they are evaluating potential new television shows. What they are really evaluating are the ads. The shows are mailed to the sample audience members' home and they are given instructions. One day after viewing, the company contacts the viewers and asks them questions about the shows and the ads. From their responses, various measures are gathered, including recall. The advantage is the deception. If audience members think they are evaluating the shows, the researchers may get a more realistic assessment of the ads. It is not the same as a truly natural exposure environment, but it's probably an improvement over asking directly about the ad only.

Method: Recognition Tests. Recognition tests are the standard memory test for print ads and promotions. Rather than asking you if you recall something, they ask if you *recognize* an ad, or something in an ad. This type of testing attempts to get at little more than evidence of exposure residue. Recognition tests ask magazine readers and (sometimes television viewers) whether they remember having seen particular advertisements and whether they can name the company sponsoring the ad. For print advertising, the actual advertisement is shown to respondents,

7. Terence A. Shimp, *Advertising, Promotion and Supplemental Aspects of Integrated Marketing Communications* (Cincinnati, OH: South-Western, 2002).

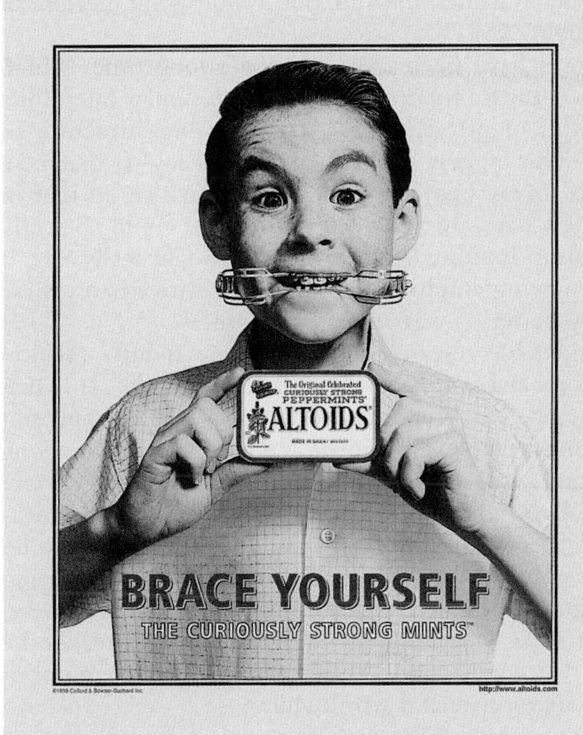

Exhibit 7.22 Recognition testing uses the ad itself to test whether consumers remember it and can associate it with its brand and message. This unusual, comically fanciful image would likely make this ad easy to recognize. But imagine this ad with the Altoids brand name blacked out. If consumers recognize the ad, will they also remember the Altoids brand name? Novel imagery sometimes actually distracts readers, enticing them to overlook brand names. Visit the Altoids site (www.altoids.com) and evaluate how it reinforces or dilutes recognition in the minds of consumers. Are the interactive features useful or distracting? Does the site achieve "cool," or is it too over-the-top to reinforce brand recognition?

and for television advertising, a script with accompanying photos is shown. For instance, a recognition test might ask, "Do you remember seeing [the ad in Exhibit 7.22]?" This is a much easier task than recall in that respondents are cued by the very stimulus they are supposed to remember, and they aren't asked to do anything more than say yes or no. Do you think any complications might arise in establishing recognition of the ad displayed in Exhibit 7.23?

Companies such as **Starch Readership Services** that do this kind of research follow some general procedures. Subscribers to a relevant magazine are contacted and asked if an interview can be set up in their home. The readers must have at least glanced at the issue to qualify. Then each target ad is shown, and the readers are asked if they remember seeing the ad (if they *noted* it), if they read or saw enough of the ad to notice the brand name (if they *associated* it), if they *read any* part of the ad copy, or if they claim to have read at least 50 percent of the copy *(read most)*. This testing is usually conducted just a few days after the current issue becomes available. The *noted, associated,* and *read most* scores are calculated (see Exhibit 7.24). With print ads, Starch is the major supplier of recognition (they also term them "readership") tests.

Bruzzone Research Company provides recognition scores for TV ads. Essentially, a sample of television viewers is selected. A photoboard (a board with still frames from the actual ad) of the TV commercial is sent out to a sample of viewers, but the brand name is obscured (both in picture and copy). Then recognition questions such as "Do you remember seeing this commercial on TV?" are asked. The respondent is asked to identify the brand and answer some attitude items. A recognition score is then presented to the client, along with attitude data. This method has advantages in that it is fairly inexpensive (and may be becoming less so through use of the Internet), and, due to its

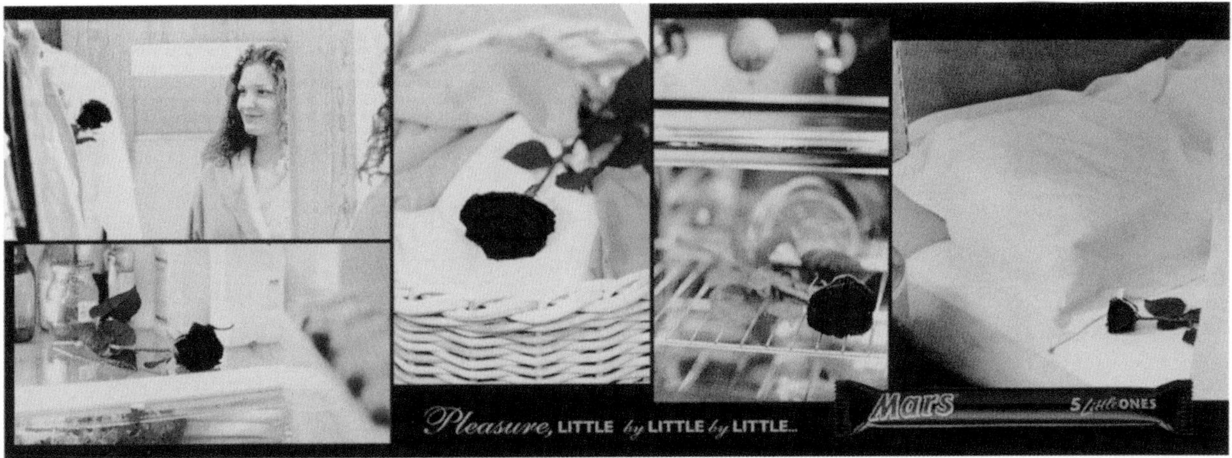

Exhibit 7.23 Even though the correlation between seduction and candy is not new, consumers might mistake this imagery for a valentine, not an advertisement. What is the advantage to the placement of the product in this ad?

STARCH™ AD-AS-A-WHOLE		
Noted %	Associated %	Read Most %
W 55	50	23-

Exhibit 7.24 55 % of Starch respondents said they noticed an ad, 50 % said they associated it with the advertised brand, and 23 % said they read more than half the body copy.

manner of blocking brand names, may provide a more valid measure of recognition (see Exhibit 7.25).

Recognition scores have been collected for a long time, which allows advertisers to compare their current ads with similar ones done last week, last month, or 50 years ago. This is a big attraction of recognition scores. The biggest problem with this test is that of a yea-saying bias. In other words, many people say they recognize an ad that in fact they haven't seen. After a few days, do you really think you could correctly remember which of the three ads in Exhibits 7.26 through 7.28 you really saw, if you saw the ads under natural viewing conditions? Still, on a relative basis, these tests may tell which ads are way better or way worse than others.

Now here's the rub: Considerable research indicates there is little relation between recall or recognition scores and actual sales.[8] But doesn't it make sense that the best ads are the ads best remembered? Well, the evidence for that is simply not there. This seeming contradiction has perplexed scholars and practitioners for a long time. And as ads become more and more visual, recall of words and claims is more and more irrelevant except, usually, simple brand names. The fact is that, as measured, the level of recall for an ad seems to have relatively little (if anything) to do with sales. This may be due to highly inflated and artificial recall scores. It may also be that ads that were never designed to elicit recall are being tested as if they were. By doing this, by applying this test so widely and so indiscriminately, it makes the test itself look bad. We believe that when, but only when, recall or recognition is the desired result, are these tests appropriate and worthwhile.

A recall measurement does make sense when simple memory goals are the aim of the commercial. For example, saying "Kibbles and Bits" 80 times or so in 30 seconds indicates an ad aimed at one simple goal: Remember "Kibbles and Bits." That's all. For an ad like that, recall is the perfect measure. But as advertising moves to fewer words and more pictures, recognition tests, good recognition tests, may become much more valuable than recall. And for most ads or branded entertainment that operate at a far more sophisticated and advanced level than either recall or recognition, these measures are very likely insufficient.

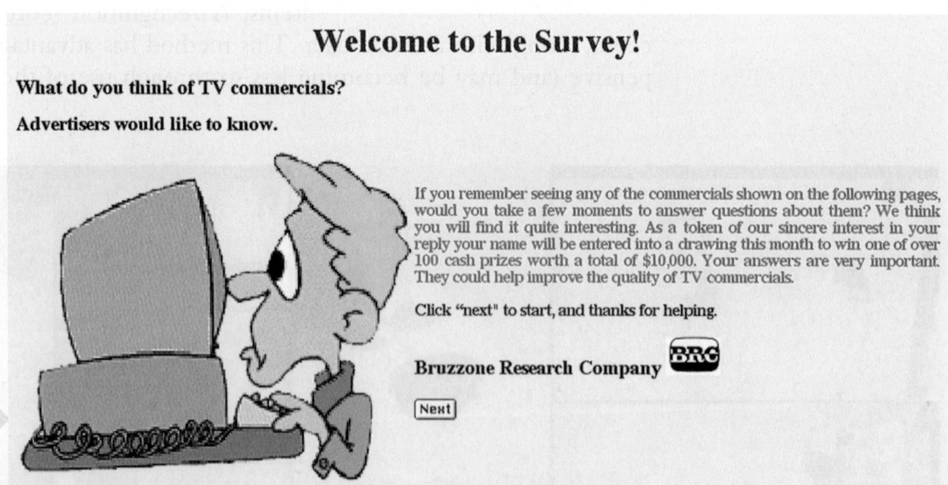

Exhibit 7.25 This company lets consumers test ads online.

8. Rajeev Batra, John G. Meyers, and David A. Aaker, *Advertising Management,* 5th ed. (Upper Saddle River, NJ: Prentice Hall, 1996), 469.

Courtesy, Bruzzone Research Company; Courtesy, Bruzzone Research Company

Exhibits 7.26 through 7.28 All of these ads, so strikingly similar, do little to (1) differentiate the product, (2) make it memorable for the consumer, or (3) promote the brand, although presumably GM and Ford had intended to do all three with these ads. Compare and contrast the new Cadillac models (www.cadillac.com) with the Ford luxury models (www.lincolnvehicles.com). Has either company broken any new ground in its approach to advertising these vehicles? Do you think in a few days you could distinguish between these models or remember the message of these websites?

Method: Implicit Memory Measures. What we have been discussing up to this point are explicit memory measures, measures and procedures that require the research subject to recall the actual exposure. As a contrast, **implicit memory measures** do not refer back to the ad or exposure but try to get at memory by using tasks like word fragments: say, part of a brand name, like S R N T for Sprint. Subjects are asked to complete the brand name (that is scored), along with other recollections. The idea is that this is a much more sensitive, less demanding (artificial), and perhaps a more meaningful measure of advertising. It is being used occasionally in actual practice, but its intensive procedure and instrumentation make it more of an academic pursuit than an applied one. Professor Julie Irwin at The University of Texas at Austin has produced some very promising research in this area showing that implicit attitude measures can be very meaningful indicators of closely held attitudes, rather than those reported to researchers.

Knowledge. Knowledge is a big step up from cognitive residue. To have knowledge about a brand that could have come only from an ad is a much more meaningful measure of advertising effectiveness. This knowledge may take several forms. It could be a brand claim, or a belief about the brand. For example, the advertisers may believe that Brand X cleans twice as well as Brand Y. If Brand X's advertising and promotion has been stressing this very fact, then we may generally assume that the consumer has learned something from the promotion and advertising, and that brand knowledge has been created. But with the explosion in available information for consumers, it's really getting hard to figure out just where some piece of knowledge came from.

Method: Surveys. In **surveys,** consumers are asked to answer questions about the advertised brand after the commercial. Sometimes this is immediately after, other times it is hours, days, or even weeks later. This is often done on-site, by phone, or on the Internet.

Attitude Change. Attitudes suggest where a brand stands in the consumer's mind. Attitudes can be influenced both by what people know and by what people feel about a brand. In this sense, attitude or preference is a summary evaluation that ties together the influences of many different factors.

Common sense tells us that sometimes attitudes would be worthwhile in assessing ads. Did the ads change the consumer's attitudes in the right direction? Even although the attitude concept itself has come under fire, attitude studies are still used, though more often at the results stage. One of the big problems is getting advertisers to run true scientific experiments with tight controls. They just don't seem to see the value in it, or the relevance of it. There just isn't much of this done other than on college campuses by professors generally pretending that stimulus material are the same as real ads. They are not. Industry rarely uses experiments. One cannot assume that a favorable attitude toward the ad will always lead to a favorable and meaningful attitude toward the brand. We can all think of ads we love for brands we don't. Further, attitude research is in decline generally. It turns out that attitudes are not very strong predictors of actual behavior, subject to all kinds of social desirability bias, and other measurement problems. Still, in the right circumstance, when the correct attitude dimensions are defined, assessing summary evaluations makes some sense. In practice, however, attitude research is all too rarely useful. There will more on this when we discuss specific methods and message strategies in Chapter 9.

Method: Attitude Studies. The typical industry **attitude study** measures consumer attitudes after exposure to an ad. Television ads are typically seen in a group setting; print ads are often shown one-on-one. The studies may also be administered by survey, including Internet surveys. Essentially, people from the target market are recruited, and their attitudes toward the advertised brand as well as toward competitors' brands are noted. Ideally, there would be pre- and post-exposure attitude measurement so that one could see the change related to seeing the ad in question. Unfortunately, industry practice and thinner agency profit margins have created a situation in which only post-exposure measures are now typically taken. True pre-post tests are becoming rare.

To the extent that attitudes reflect something meaningful, and something important, these tests may be very useful. Their validity is typically premised on a single ad exposure (sometimes two) in an unnatural viewing environment (such as a theater). Many advertisers believe that commercials don't register their impact until after three or four exposures in a real environment; others believe the number is much higher. Still, a significant swing in attitude scores with a single exposure suggests that something is going on, and that some of this effect might be expected when the ad reaches real consumers in the comfort of their homes. The hard cold bottom line is that attitude studies have not been very predictive of actual behavior under the best of conditions, conditions that almost never exist in commercial advertising research.

Feelings and Emotions. Advertisers have always had a special interest in feelings and emotions. Ever since the "atmospheric" ads of the 1920s, there has

Exhibit 7.29 This ad is supposed to work with both images and feelings.

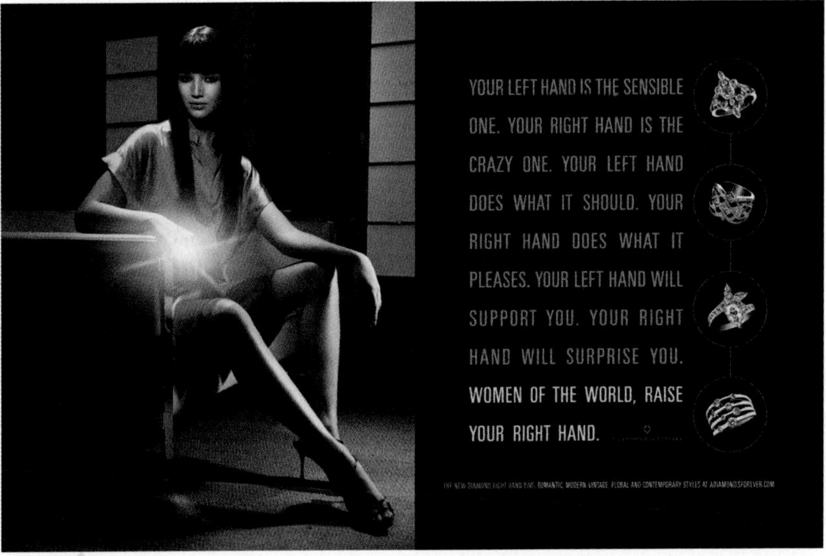

Exhibit 7.30 Words and arguments are not what makes this ad work.

Wisk tablets remove dirt like it never happened.
If only they could do the same for your daughter's new tattoo.
Introducing Wisk® Dual Action Tablets with blue stain-fighting enzymes. So powerful, it's as if dirt never happened at all.
Wisk
Tablets

Exhibit 7.31 Some ads are judged by their resonance, or how true they ring. www.wisk.com

been the belief that feelings may be more important than thoughts as a reaction to ads. Recent research by business professor Michel Pham and others[9] have shown that feelings have three distinct properties that makes them very powerful in reactions to advertisements and the advertised goods and services: (1) Consumers monitor and access feelings very quickly—consumers often know how they feel before they know what they think; (2) there is much more agreement in how consumers feel about ads and brands than in what they think about them; and (3) feelings are very good predictors of thoughts. This research adds a great deal of support to the argument that, in many ways, feelings are more important than thoughts when it comes to advertising. It also appears that ads that use feelings produce stronger and more lasting effects than those that try to persuade by thought alone. For example, the way a consumer feels about the imagery in the ads in Exhibits 7.29 and 7.30 may be far more important than what they say they think about them.

Method: Resonance Tests. In a **resonance test,** the goal is to determine to what extent the message resonates or rings true with target-audience members.[10] The question becomes: Does this ad match consumers' own experiences? Does it produce an affinity reaction? Do consumers who view it say, "Yeah, that's right; I feel just like that"? (Exhibit 7.31) Do consumers read the ad

9. Michel Tuan Pham, Joel B. Cohen, John W. Pracejus, and G. David Hughes, "Affect Monitoring and the Primacy of Feelings in Judgment," *Journal of Consumer Research,* vol. 28 (September 2001), 167–188.

10. David Glen Mick and Claus Buhl, "A Meaning-Based Model of Advertising Experiences," *Journal of Consumer Research,* vol. 19 (December 1992), 317–338.

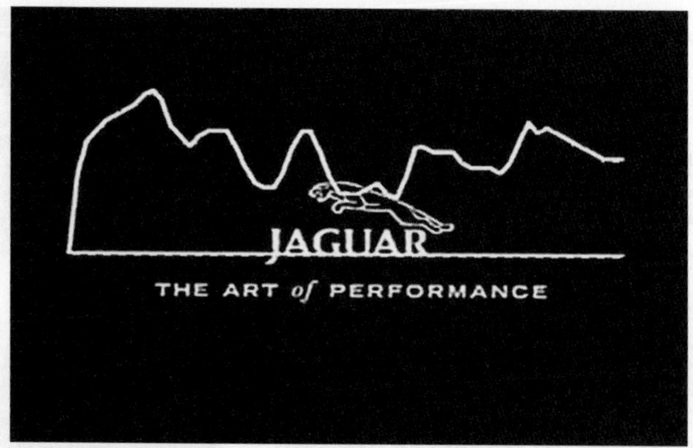

Exhibit 7.32 Here consumers' interest levels are measured while they watch an ad in real time.

and make it their own?[11] The method is pretty much the same as a communication test. Consumers see an ad in a group several times, and then discuss it. It can be conducted in-house by agency planners and researchers or "sent out" to a research supplier. How do you feel about this ad? How does it make you feel?

Method: Frame-by-Frame Tests. **Frame-by-frame tests** are usually employed for ads where the emotional component is seen as key, although they may also be used to obtain thought listing as well. These tests typically work by getting consumers to turn dials (like/dislike) while viewing television commercials in a theater setting. The data from these dials are then collected, averaged, and later superimposed over the commercial for the researchers in the form of a line graph. The height of the line reflects the level of interest in the ad. The high points in the line represent periods of higher interest in the ad, and the dips show where the audience had less interest in that particular point of the ad. Whereas some research companies do ask consumers what they were thinking or feeling at certain points along the trace, and sometimes these responses are diagnostic, others do not. In those cases (such as the one shown in Exhibit 7.32), what the trace line really does then is measure the levels of interest at each specific moment in the execution—it does not explain whether or why consumers' reactions were positive or negative. The downside of frame-by-frame tests is that they involve somewhat higher costs than other methods, and there are some validity concerns in that you are asking consumers to do something they do not normally do while watching television. On the other hand, the method has some fans. It is sexy; it impresses clients.

There is a lot of current interest in developing better measures of the feelings and emotions generated by advertising.[12] This has included better paper-and-pencil measures as well as dial-turning devices. Assessment of feelings evoked by ads is becoming a much more important goal of the advertising industry.

Physiological Changes. Every few years there is renewed interest in the technology of **physiological assessment** of advertising. Most recently, advances in brain imaging have raised hopes of understanding how the human mind actually processes advertisements. At this point most of the work involves Magnetic Resonance Imaging (MRI). The idea is to see which parts "light up" during exposure to various stimuli, or during certain tasks, and to understand what is

11. Stuart J. Agres, Julie A. Edell, and Tony M. Dubitsky, eds., *Emotion in Advertising* (Westport, CT: Quorum Books, 1990). See especially Chapters 7 and 8.

12. Ibid.

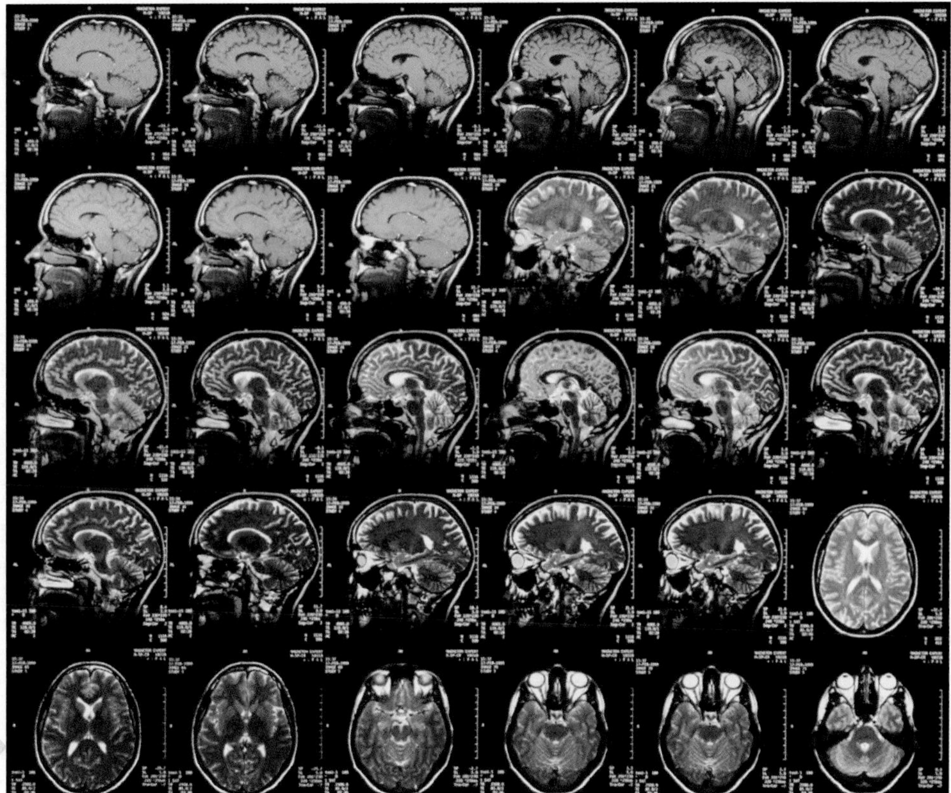

Exhibit 7.33 These are examples of MRIs. The tool is now being used for basic research on advertising. Its real-world application is unlikely.

happening when they light up. (Exhibit 7.33 shows MRI testing.) But at least at this point understanding of actual process—beyond isolating the activity in certain parts of the brain known to be involved in certain types of processing—has been promising. Practical applications to advertising appear at the level of a better basic understanding of the human mind, which is valuable in and of itself. Actual common use in copy research seems distant, and widespread use unlikely. The brightest hope is in the area of understanding emotional advertising. Stanford professor Baba Shiv and others have presented some very exciting findings on how emotion unconsciously affects decision making.

Method: Eye Tracking. **Eye-tracking systems** have been developed to monitor eye movements across print ads. With one such system, respondents wear a goggle-like device that records (on a computer system) pupil dilations, eye movements, and length of time each sector of an advertisement is viewed.

Behavioral Intent. This is essentially what consumers say they intend to do. If, after exposure to Brand X's advertising, consumers' stated intent to purchase Brand X goes up, there is some reason to believe that the tested advertising had something to do with it. Of course, we all know the problem with intended behavior: It's a poor substitute for actual behavior. Think about it: You really intended to call your mom, put the check in the mail, "I'll call you," and all those other things we say and maybe mean at the time. But it just didn't work out that way. The same thing is true when these are the criteria for testing consumer response to advertising. On a relative basis (say, percentage who intend to buy Pepsi versus percentage who intend to buy Coke, or at least who tell some researcher that), these measures can be meaningful and helpful, particularly if the changes are really large. Beyond that, don't take them to the bank.

Stage Three: Results.

At this stage, the ads are already out in the world, and the advertisers are trying to assess whether or not they are working.

Method: Tracking Studies. Tracking studies are one of the most commonly used advertising and promotion research methods. Basically, they "track" the apparent effect of advertising and branded entertainment over time. They typically assess attitude change, knowledge, behavioral intent, and self-reported behavior. They assess the performance of advertisements before, during, or after the launch of an advertising campaign or branded entertainment. This type of advertising research is almost always conducted as a survey. Members of the target market are surveyed on a fairly regular basis to detect any changes. Any change in awareness, belief, or attitude is usually attributed (rightly or wrongly) to the advertising effort. Even though the participants are susceptible to other influences (e.g., news stories about the brand or category), these are fairly valuable tests because they do occur over time and provide ongoing assessment, rather than the one-time, one-shot approach of so many other methods. The method has been extended to even things like advertising within gaming, which presents new ethical issues given that most gamers are young. Their weakness resides largely in the meaningfulness of the specific measures. Sometimes attitudes shift a bit but translate into no noticeable increase in sales and no return on investment (ROI).

Method: Direct Response. Direct response advertisements in print, the Internet, and broadcast media offer the audience the opportunity to place an inquiry or respond directly through a website, reply card, or toll-free phone number. These ads produce **inquiry/direct response measures.** An example is displayed in Exhibit 7.34. These measures are quite straightforward in the sense that advertisements that generate a high number of inquiries or direct responses, compared to historical benchmarks, are deemed effective. Additional analyses may compare the number of inquiries or responses to the number of sales generated. For example, some print ads will use different 800 numbers for different versions of the ad so that the agency can compute which ad is generating more inquiries. These measures are not relevant for all types of advertising, however. Ads designed to have long-term image building or brand identity effects should not be judged using such short-term response measures.

Internet response measures will be discussed in more detail in Chapter 14. With the Internet, various measures of drill-down, click-through, and actual purchase are employed. Again, there will be more on this in Chapter 14.

Method: Estimating Sales Derived from Advertising. Other advertisers really want to see evidence that the new ads will actually get people to do something: generally, to buy their product. It is, to some, the gold standard. But for reasons explained earlier, there are so many things that can affect sales that the use of actual sales as a measure of advertising effectiveness is considered inherently flawed, but not flawed enough not to be used. Here is a place where advertising and promotion are really different. In the case of the more easily and precisely tracked effects of promotions, some integrated brand promotions, and some sales data collected via the Internet, sales are the gold standard. That's because you can actually isolate the effect of the promotion, or come pretty close to isolating it. In the case of media advertising, statistical models are employed to try to isolate the effect of advertising on sales. Work by Dominique Hanssens, a marketing professor at the University of California at Los Angeles, has demonstrated that in some industries, such as automotive, very sophisticated and fairly time-intensive modeling can isolate advertising effects over time, but these powerful models are underemployed by industry and

Ethics

You Are a Really Rotten Mom

One thing advertising research has learned is that ads that leverage social anxiety tend to work pretty well. That means that ads work that make you feel anxious about how others see you. So, some methods of advertising research attempt to locate these individuals, plumb the depths and identify the specifics of their feared inadequacies, and then develop ads to exploit those. Sorry, it's true.

Advertisers defend themselves (and sleep at night) by saying that we are just finding out what people need most and then giving it to them. Critics say that years of this make vulnerable people more vulnerable. Women's groups say that it makes women feel fat, inadequate in just about every role they try to succeed in, and then offers them an advertised solution… that will be ultimately inadequate… and require a never-ending search for unattainable perfection. If you work in advertising research, you may (likely) have to find and push these buttons.

How do you feel about that?

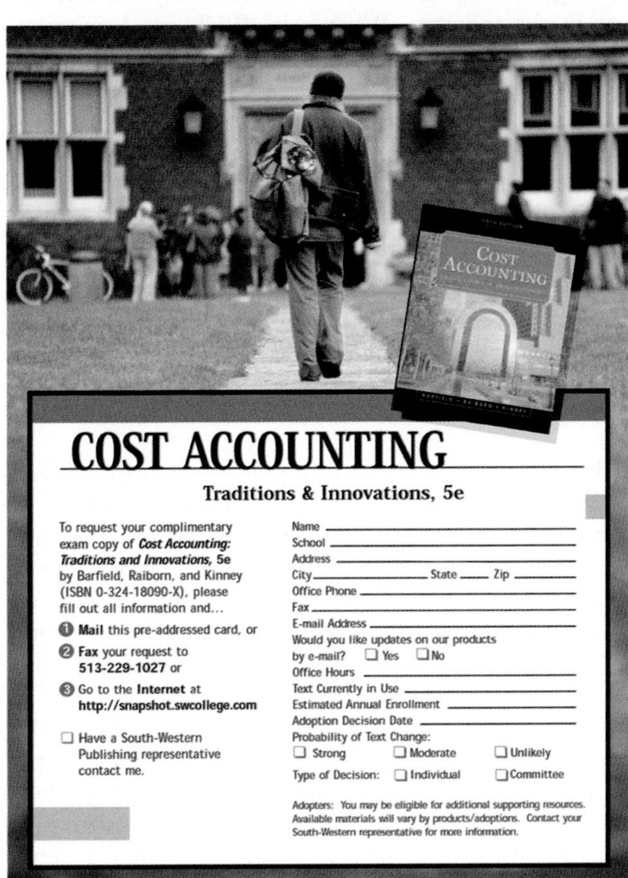

Exhibit 7.34 An ad like this allows for a very simple kind of advertising response management. When consumers call, click, or write, the advertiser knows.

require more time, data, and expertise than many companies have at their disposal. Results generally indicate that advertising has its greatest impact on sales early in the product life cycle, or when a new version or model or other innovation is made. After that, advertising loses steam. Sometimes a host of other variables that might also affect sales, from the weather (say you represent a theme park) to competing advertising, are factored into these mathematical models.

Another downside is that these models are constructed long after the fact, long after the ad campaign to be assessed has been in place, and sales data have come in. But if the model is strong (robust) enough, it will be applicable to many situations. Behavioral data are sometimes derived from test markets, situations where the advertising is tested in a few select geographic areas before its wider application. Although expensive, these tests can be very telling. Ideally, measures of actual behavior would come from tightly controlled field experiments. It's just that meaningfully controlled field experiments are incredibly difficult and expensive, and thus very rare in real advertising and IBP practice. The area of greatest hope for those who believe real behavior is the best test of advertising effectiveness is the use of the Internet for experiments, although that is still in its early stages; there have been some very promising and successful results (particularly in consumer electronics and software), but the jury is still out on a more widespread application.

Method: All-in-One Single-Source Data. With the advent of universal product codes (UPCs) on product packages and the proliferation of cable television, research firms are now able to engage in *single-source research* to document the behavior of individuals—or, more typically, households—in a respondent pool by tracking their behavior from the television set to the checkout counter. **Single-source data** provide information from individual households about brand purchases, coupon use, and television advertising exposure by combining grocery store scanner data with TV-viewing data from monitoring devices attached to the households' televisions. With these different types of data combined, a better assessment can be made of the real impact of advertising and promotion on consumers' actual purchases. This is not an inexpensive method of assessment, and it still remains difficult (if not impossible) to know exactly what specific aspects of advertising had what effects on consumers. The best-known supplier of this type of testing is **IRI BehaviorScan.**

Account Planning versus Advertising Research.

Jon Steel, director of account planning and vice chairman of Goodby, Silverstein and Partners—its clients include Anheuser-Busch, the California Milk Processors Board ("Got Milk?"), Nike, Porsche, and Hewlett-Packard—has called account planning "the biggest thing to hit American advertising since Doyle Dane Bernbach's Volkswagen campaign."[13] That is stretching it a bit, but account planning is a big story in the industry. What is it? Well, good question. (See Exhibit 7.35.)

You will hear a lot about **account planning**. It's quite the term, and has been for a decade or so. It is defined in contrast to traditional advertising research. We've mentioned this before, but it probably deserves repeating. It differs mostly in three ways. First, in terms of organization, agencies that use this system typically assign an "account planner" to work cooperatively with the account executive on a given client's business. Rather than depending on a separate research department's occasional involvement, the agency assigns the planner to a single client (just like an advertising executive) to stay with the projects on a continuous basis—even though, in this organizational scheme, there is typically an account planning department. In the more traditional system, the research department would get involved from time to time as needed, and members of the research department would work on several different clients' advertising. (There are several variations on this theme.)

Another difference is that this organizational structure puts research in a different, more prominent role. In this system, researchers (or "planners") seem to be more actively involved throughout the entire advertising process and seem to have a bigger impact on it as well. (Of course, some of the difference is more agency self-promotion than reality.) Agencies that practice "account planning" tend to do more developmental and less evaluative research. Third, "planning agencies" tend to do more qualitative and naturalistic research than their more traditional counterparts. But these differences, too, seem fairly exaggerated—even though Jay Chiat called planning "the best new business tool ever invented."[14] There is another, more cynical side to this story: Many advertising agencies have decided that they simply cannot afford the cost of a full-time research staff. It's cheaper and maybe even better to outsource the work. But a quieter and more devious way of downsizing (or eliminating these expensive departments) is to go to the "account planning" system, in which a researcher will always be a part of the team.

13. Jon Steel, *Truth, Lies & Advertising: The Art of Account Planning* (New York: John Wiley & Sons, 1998), jacket.
14. Ibid., p. 42.

Exhibit 7.35 Much ado is made about the account planner versus traditional advertising research.

American Association of Advertising Agency Magazine

One Last Thought on Message Testing.

None of these methods are perfect. There are challenges to reliability, validity, trustworthiness, and meaningfulness with all of them. Advertisers sometimes think that consumers watch new television commercials the way they watch new, eagerly awaited feature films, or that they listen to radio spots like they listen to a symphony, or read magazine ads like a Steinbeck novel. We watch TV while we work, talk, eat, and study; we use it as a night light, background noise, and babysitter. Likewise, we typically thumb through magazines very, very quickly. Even though these traditional methods of message testing have their strengths, more naturalistic methods are clearly recommended. Still, it would be a mistake to throw the baby out with the bathwater; good and appropriate behavioral science can produce better advertising.

What We Need.

Advertising and integrated brand promotion research could do with some change. The way we think about ads and advertising is certainly changing. The move to a visual advertising style has also put into question the appropriateness of a set of tests that focus on the acceptance of message claims, as well as verbatim remembrance of words (copy). Also, the Internet has significantly challenged and changed the whole concept of audience, response, and associated measures. It's a brave new world.

The account planning way of thinking merges the research and the brand management business. Good research can play an important role in this; it can be very helpful or an enormous hindrance, as advertisers are realizing more and more. Top-down delivered marketing is not considered realistic by many in the industry. With this new realization comes new terms. One is the idea of account planning as a substitute for the traditional research efforts of an agency. There has been a very recent but very significant turn in thinking about research and its role in advertising, promotion, and brand management.

As you can see, advertising and promotion research is used to judge advertising, but who judges advertising research, and how? First of all, not enough people, in our opinion, question and judge advertising research. Research is not magic or truth and it should never be confused with such. Issues of reliability, validity, trustworthiness, and meaningfulness should be seriously considered when research is used to make important decisions. Otherwise, you're just using research as a ritual that you know has limited meaning. Research can be a wonderful tool when applied correctly, but it is routinely poorly matched to the real-world situation.

Summary

1 Explain the methods used in developmental advertising research.

Advertising and promotion research can serve many purposes in the development of a campaign. There is no better way to generate fresh ideas for a campaign than to listen carefully to the customer. Qualitative research involving customers is essential for fostering fresh thinking about a brand. Audience definition and profiling are fundamental to effective campaign planning and rely on advertising research. In the developmental phase, advertisers use diverse methods for gathering information. Focus groups, projective techniques, the ZMET, and field work are trusted research methods that directly involve consumers and aid in idea generation and concept testing.

2 Identify sources of secondary data that can aid the IBP planning effort.

Because information is such a critical resource in the decision-making process, several sources of data are widely used. Internal company sources such as strategic marketing plans, research reports, customer service records, and sales data provide a wealth of information on consumer tastes and preferences. Government sources generate a wide range of census and labor statistics, providing key data on trends in population, consumer spending, employment, and immigration. Commercial data sources provide advertisers with a wealth of information on household consumers. Professional publications share insider information on industry trends and new research. Finally, the Internet is a revolutionary research tool that delivers rich data at virtually no cost. In particular, advertisers can obtain sophisticated research data at thousands of consumer- and brand-based online community sites.

3 Discuss the methods used in copy research.

Copy research (evaluative research) aims to judge the effectiveness of actual ads. Advertisers and clients try to determine if audiences "get" the joke of an ad or retain key knowledge concerning the brand. Tracking changes in audience attitudes, feelings and emotions, behavior, and physiological response is important in gauging the overall success of an ad, and various methods are employed before and after the launch of a campaign to assess the impact on audiences. Communication tests, recall testing, and the thought-listing technique are a few of the methods that try to measure the persuasiveness of a message. Some agencies, attempting to bypass the high cost and inconclusive results of research, substitute account planning for traditional advertising and promotion research. Advocates of this trend believe an account planning system merges the best in research and brand management.

Discuss the basic research methods used after ads are in the marketplace.

Once an ad campaign has reached the marketplace, agencies and firms turn to results-oriented research to try to determine whether the ad has succeeded—whether, quite simply, the ad prompted consumers to buy the product or service. One of the most commonly employed methods of results-oriented research is the use of tracking studies to measure the apparent effect of advertising over time. Another long-standing method is the use of reply cards or toll-free numbers, which can track the direct responses of consumers to a particular campaign. Technology also is producing new results-oriented techniques. The development of universal product codes, combined with television monitoring devices, allows advertisers in some instances to track household consumption patterns from the television to the checkout lane. Researchers also are evaluating sophisticated models to more accurately track estimated sales from advertising, what has been a painstaking and expensive endeavor.

Key Terms

concept test
focus group
projective techniques
dialogue balloons
story construction
sentence and picture completion
Zaltman Metaphor Elicitation Technique (ZMET)
field work
embedded
normative test scores
communication test
thought listing, or cognitive response analysis
recall tests
recognition
recognition tests
Starch Readership Services
implicit memory measures
surveys
attitude study
resonance test
frame-by-frame test
physiological assessment
eye-tracking systems
tracking studies
direct response
inquiry/direct response measures
single-source data
IRI BehaviorScan
account planning

Questions

1. Read the chapter opening and list two important lessons that can be learned from Coca-Cola's advertising and promotion research blunder with New Coke.

2. What historic factors led to the development and prominence of advertising and promotion research departments during the mid-1900s?

3. Focus groups are one of the advertising researcher's most versatile tools. Describe the basic features of focus group research that could lead to inappropriate generalizations about the preferences of the target audience.

4. ZMET is a technique that advertisers may use in place of focus groups. What aspects of ZMET and focus groups are similar? What particular features of ZMET could foster richer understanding of consumers' motives than is typically achieved with focus groups?

5. List the sources and uses of secondary data. What are the benefits of secondary data? What are the limitations?

6. Identify issues that could become sources of conflict between account managers and advertising creatives in the message-testing process. What could go wrong if people in an ad agency take the position that what the client wants, the client gets?

7. Criteria for judging ad effectiveness include "getting it," cognitive residue, knowledge, attitude change, feelings and emotions, physiological changes, and behavior. Identify specific evaluative advertising research methods that could be used to test an ad's impact on any of these dimensions.

8. How would you explain the finding that ads that achieve high recall scores don't always turn out to be ads that do a good job in generating sales? Are there some features of ads that make them memorable but could also turn off consumers and dissuade them from buying the brand? Give an example from your experience.

9. What is single-source research, and what is its connection to the universal product codes (UPCs) one finds on nearly every product in the grocery store?

10. Explain the industry trend of substituting account planning for traditional advertising and promotion research. Why do some agency directors claim that this trend is the biggest thing in advertising since the famous Bernbach Volkswagen campaign? Do you tend to believe the hype surrounding this trend, or are you cynical that forces of downsizing are driving it? Explain your reasoning.

Experiential Exercises

1. With millions of people interacting on sites like Facebook and Twitter, advertisers have turned to a new form of market research that measures "online buzz." Buzz-tracking companies sift consumer-generated content online and spot trends that advertisers can use to manage the reputation of brands. Use the Internet to research an online buzz-tracking company and answer the following questions: What information does the firm analyze for clients? How has the firm's research helped a client achieve its brand goals? Can buzz-tracking services really provide relevant data about brands, products, and media?

2. Is advertising more of an art than a science? As an out-of-class assignment, write a report on a current trend in advertising—such as viral videos or behavioral targeted advertising—and identify the role that research plays in that trend. Describe what research methods are used to support the advertising practice, and list how advertisers use research data in the creation of specific messages and campaign strategies. Do you think scientific testing methods are able to convey the true impact and effectiveness of advertising?

3. Advertisers increasingly are using metaphor associations in promotional development, tapping into the powerful organizing and expressive function that metaphor serves in the human brain. Test this method on yourself using each of these well-known brands or products discussed in the chapter: Coca-Cola, M&Ms, and milk. For each example, consider how you would visually represent your experiences with that brand or product, and then find photographs or graphics from magazines that best convey that experience.

4. The chapter identified several online sources that provide a variety of demographic information compiled by the government. This kind of widely available, no-cost information can be a boon to advertisers—particularly small businesses that might otherwise be unable to afford information compiled by commercial data vendors. Develop a demographic portrait of the city or metro area where your school is located using online government resources. What are your primary findings? How accurate do you think this demographic snapshot is? What brands or products do you think would find this community to be attractive? Why?

Chapter 8

Planning for Advertising and Integrated Brand Promotion

After reading and thinking about this chapter, you will be able to do the following:

1. Describe the basic components of an advertising plan.
2. Compare and contrast two fundamental approaches for setting advertising objectives.
3. Explain various methods for setting advertising budgets.
4. Discuss the role of the agency in formulating an advertising plan.

PR Newswire/Apple

Introductory Scenario: Polishing the Apple (Again and Again).

Advertising does not exist in a vacuum. Advertising and IBP are most often conceived to serve a business purpose, and the stakes are always high. Whether you are a small business investing $50,000 in a local ad campaign or a global marketer investing hundreds of millions of dollars around the world, you want your advertising to serve its purpose. All parties involved in the effort must be aware of things like goals, strategies, and timetables. There will need to be a plan.

When it comes to high-stakes and high-profile advertising campaigns, no one does it better than Apple. This time let's consider Apple's launch of the iPad. After a series of game-changing market successes like candy-colored iMacs (per Exhibit 8.1), the ubiquitous iPods + iTunes, and the hugely successful iPhone, it was time for another act in the remarkable evolution of Apple. The next big thing would be iPad + iBooks, which promised to revolutionize the publishing business, just as iPods + iTunes had revolutionized the music business.[1] But Steve Jobs faced many doubters on this one. Tablets (or slates) were not new at the time of the iPad launch, and they had never been a big hit. Some observers dismissed the iPad as an oversized version of the iPod Touch, and others wondered about the viability of another electronic gadget with a base price of $499 in an America with 15 percent real unemployment and eroding home prices and property values. And Apple had its own high standards to live up to with its latest gadget: first-year sales for iPhone came in at 6 million units.[2] Anything less than that for iPad could be considered a flop. The stakes were high. The Apple advertising juggernaut would need to rise to the occasion to carve out a market where none had existed before.

In Spring 2010, the iPad was scheduled to go on sale. But the launch campaign began months before and followed a plan much like previous Apple launches. Rumors circulated regarding the coming of iPad prior to Jobs finally providing a sneak preview on January 27, 2010. Naturally, he would claim that day that the iPad was perfectly positioned to be "so much more intimate than a laptop and so much more capable than a smart phone."[3] Sadly, consumers would have to wait at least another 60 days before they could actually buy an iPad. Of course, the 60-day waiting period was built into the plan to allow buzz to build about iPad and to do a bit more teaser advertising. The teaser TV advertising debuted during the Oscars on March 7 and was designed to address the question: What can you do with an iPad? With an iPad you can watch movies, play games, send email, read *The New York Times,* manage your calendar, view photos, and much more. "Meet iPad" went viral immediately and had a strong first week on YouTube with 2.4 million views.[4] As always with Apple, the buzz was building, exactly as planned.

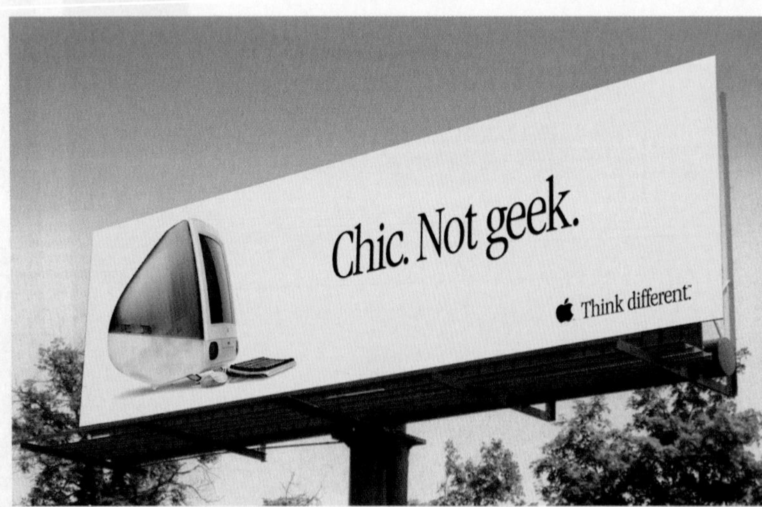

Exhibit 8.1 Apple's launch of the iMac in 1998 used billboards like this one to show off its chic new Internet appliances.

1. Daniel Lyons, "Think Really Different," *Newsweek,* April 5, 2010, 46–51.
2. Michael Copeland, "The iPad Changes Everything," *Fortune,* March 22, 2010, 150–153.
3. Yukari Kane, "Steve Jobs Takes Gamble on New iPad," *The Wall Street Journal,* January 28, 2010, B1.
4. Michael Learmonth, "Apple's iPad Ad? Yep, It Went Viral," adage.com, March 18, 2010.

As the weeks passed, Apple finally confirmed that iPads would go on sale April 3, 2010, and on March 31, they had another advertising coup ready to break.[5] ABC's comedy show—Modern Family—had just been announced as a Peabody Award winner and was riding high in the television ratings, even pitted against the always formidable American Idol. On Wednesday, March 31, the entire episode was built around a birthday celebration—Phil Dunphy, the bumbling dad on the show wanted just one thing for his birthday—a new iPad. Masterfully woven into the entire episode was his families' frustrating search for an iPad. Now of course it all worked out in the end and there was Phil on his couch surfing the net on his new toy. Not only is this a perfect example of integrated product placement, it also turns out that Apple paid nothing to make their product the star of this show. One writer in *Ad Age* concluded that the Modern Family love affair with the iPad on March 31, 2010, "was tantamount to a huge wet kiss of approval for a product that (had) yet to be tested by actual consumer use."[6] Once again, kudos and buzz for Apple.

So on Friday evening, April 2, long lines began to form outside Apple retail stores. Steve Wozniak, (a.k.a., the Woz), one of Apple's co-founders, proclaimed to *Newsweek* that he had placed an advance order for three iPads, and would be sure to be in line that Friday night to enjoy the hoopla. The lines were long in many places. You really would have had to be living in a cave to not be aware that the iPad went on sale for real on April 3, 2010. No doubt the advertising plan was working, and early signs suggested that the iPad would outperform the iPhone in its debut year.[7] But would the iPad become the game changer that Steve Jobs (and many media pundits) predicted? Changing everything from the publishing business to online retailing?[8] Time will tell.

As a CEO with rock-star status, Steve Jobs is constantly in the media limelight and is commonly praised for his marketing savvy.[9] But Steve Jobs knows that he's not in the thing alone, and he has always assigned credit elsewhere, especially when it comes to his advertising agency—TBWA/Chiat/Day of Venice, California. Said Jobs: "Creating great advertising, like creating great products, is a team effort. I am lucky to work with the best talent in the industry."[10] Indeed, it would be impossible to launch campaigns like those we have seen for devices like iPhones and iPads (compare Exhibits 8.2 and 8.3) without great teamwork between agency and client.

Exhibit 8.2 The elegant iPhone extended Apple's track record of high-profile product launches.

AP Topic Gallery/Apple Computers

We have merely scratched the surface in describing all that is involved in a campaign for a significant product introduction like iPad; however, we hope this example gives you a taste for the complexity that can be involved in executing a comprehensive advertising and IBP effort. You don't go out and spend millions of dollars promoting a new product that is vital to

5. Brian Steinberg, "Modern Family Featured an iPad, but ABC Didn't Collect," adage.com, April 1, 2010.
6. Ibid.
7. Anthony Carranza, "iPad Sales Projections Better Than Expected," examiner.com, April 9, 2010.
8. Natalie Zmuda, "iPad Poised to Revolutionize Retail Industry," adage.com, April 21, 2010.
9. Adam Lashinsky, "The Decade of Steve," *Fortune,* November 23, 2009, 93–100.
10. Bradley Johnson, "Jobs Orchestrates Ad Blitz for Apple's iMac PC," *Advertising Age,* August 10, 1998, 6.

Exhibit 8.3 Steve Jobs was confident that consumers would find many uses for his iPad.

PR Newswire/Apple

the success of a firm without giving the entire endeavor considerable forethought. Such an endeavor will call for a plan. As you will see in this chapter, Jobs and his team followed the process of building an advertising effort based on several key features of the advertising plan. An advertising plan is the culmination of the planning effort needed to deliver effective advertising and IBP.

1 The Advertising Plan and Its Marketing Context.

An ad plan should be a direct extension of a firm's marketing plan. As suggested in the closing section of Chapter 6, one device that can be used to explicitly connect the marketing plan with the advertising plan is the statement of a brand's value proposition. A statement of what the brand is supposed to stand for in the eyes of the target segment derives from the firm's marketing strategy, and will guide all ad-planning activities. The advertising plan, including all integrated brand promotion, is a subset of the larger marketing plan. The IBP component must be built into the plan in a seamless and synergistic way. Everything has to work together, whether the plan is for Apple or for a business with far fewer resources. And as Steve Jobs has said, there is no substitute for good teamwork between agency and client in the development of compelling marketing and advertising plans.

An **advertising plan** specifies the thinking, tasks, and timetable needed to conceive and implement an effective advertising effort. We particularly like Apple examples because they always illustrate the wide array of options that can be deployed in creating interest and communicating the value proposition for brands like iPad or iPhone. Jobs and his agency choreograph public relations activities, promotions and events, cooperative advertising, broadcast advertising, product placements, billboard advertising, digital media, and more, as part of their launches. Advertising planners should review all the options before selecting an integrated set to communicate with the target audience.

For a variety of reasons that will become increasingly clear to you, it is critical to think beyond traditional broadcast media when considering the best way to break through the clutter of the modern marketplace and get a message out to your customer. Miami's Crispin Porter + Bogusky (CP+B) is another agency that has built its

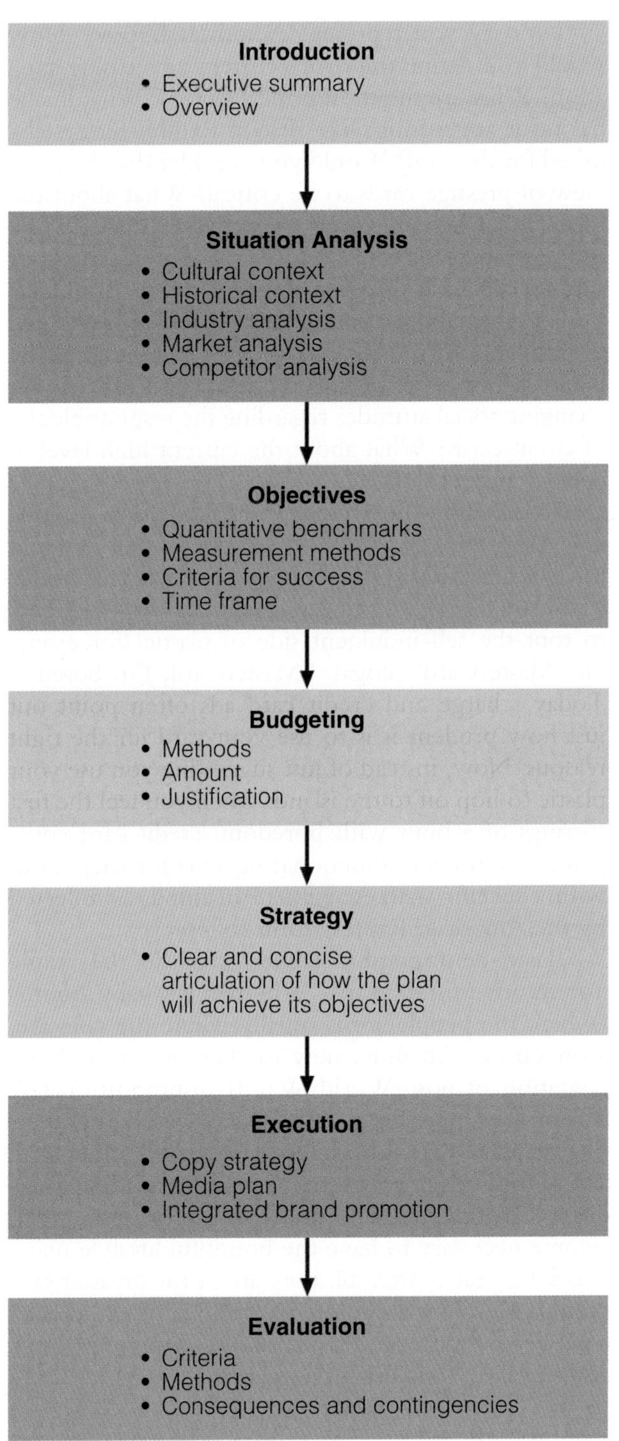
Introduction
• Executive summary
• Overview
Situation Analysis
• Cultural context
• Historical context
• Industry analysis
• Market analysis
• Competitor analysis
Objectives
• Quantitative benchmarks
• Measurement methods
• Criteria for success
• Time frame
Budgeting
• Methods
• Amount
• Justification
Strategy
• Clear and concise articulation of how the plan will achieve its objectives
Execution
• Copy strategy
• Media plan
• Integrated brand promotion
Evaluation
• Criteria
• Methods
• Consequences and contingencies

Exhibit 8.4
The advertising plan.

reputation on finding novel ways to register clients' messages with consumers. As you will learn in Chapter 9, one of CP+B's principles for success in campaign planning is to consider literally everything as media. When you adopt the philosophy that *everything* is media, it's much easier to surround the consumer with a message and make a deep connection on behalf of the brand.

Exhibit 8.4 shows the components of an advertising plan. It should be noted that there is a great deal of variation in advertising plans from advertiser to advertiser. Our discussion of the advertising plan will focus on the seven major components shown in Exhibit 8.4: the introduction, situation analysis, objectives, budgeting, strategy, execution, and evaluation. Each component is discussed in the following sections.

Introduction.

The introduction of an advertising plan consists of an executive summary and an overview. An executive summary, typically two paragraphs to a page in length, is offered to state the most important aspects of the plan. This is the take-away; that is, it is what the reader should remember from the plan. It is the essence of the plan.

As with many documents, an overview is also customary. An overview ranges in length from a paragraph to a few pages. It sets out what is to be covered, and it structures the context. All plans are different, and some require more setup than others. Don't underestimate the benefit of a good introduction. It's where you can make or lose a lot of points with your boss or client.

Situation Analysis.

When someone asks you to explain a decision you've made, you may say something like, "Well, here's the situation...." In what follows, you try to distill the situation down to the most important points and how they are connected in order to explain why you made the decision. An ad plan **situation analysis** is no different. It is where the client and agency lay out the most important factors that define the situation, and then explain the importance of each factor.

A lengthy list of potential factors (e.g., demographic, technology, social and cultural, economic, and political/regulatory) can define a situation analysis. Some books offer long but incomplete lists. We prefer to play it straight with you: There is no complete or perfect list of situational factors. The idea is not to be exhaustive or encyclopedic when writing a plan, but to be smart in choosing the few important factors that really describe the situation, and then explain how the factors relate to the advertising task at hand. Market segmentation and consumer research provide the organization with insights that can be used for a situation analysis, but ultimately you have to decide which of the many factors are really the most critical to address in your advertising. This is the essence of smart management.

COMEDIAN LOST
(MUSIC)
SEINFELD: Hot, hot, hot, hot, hot, hot. Pheu. (MUSIC)
(MUSIC) Um.
(MUSIC)
(MUSIC)
(MUSIC)
I was on a cruise ship, I slipped and --right overboard.
Hi, boys.
RENTAL CARS
2nd MAN: Ocean view?
SEINFELD: I don't think so.
I'm in a bit of a hurry.
(MUSIC/SFX)
That is so true.
So where was I?
ANNCR: The American Express Card, it's a life saver.
To apply look for this in your mailbox. (MUSIC/SFX OUT)

Exhibit 8.5 What is the image this ad establishes for the American Express card? How is this image a response to the company's situation analysis? Link your answer to a discussion of market segmentation and product positioning. Who is reached by this ad and how does reaching this segment fit into the overall strategy for American Express?

Let's say you represent American Express. How would you define the firm's current advertising situation? What are the most critical factors? What image has prior advertising, like that in Exhibit 8.5, established for the card? Would you consider the changing view of prestige cards to be critical? What about the problem of hanging onto an exclusive image while trying to increase your customer base by having your cards accepted at discount stores? Does the proliferation of gold and platinum cards by other banks rate as critical? Do the diverse interest rates offered by bank cards seem critical to the situation? What about changing social attitudes regarding the responsible use of credit cards? What about the current high level of consumer debt?

Think about how credit card marketing is influenced by the economic conditions of the day and the cultural beliefs about the proper way to display status. In the 1980s, it was acceptable for advertisers to tout the self-indulgent side of plastic (for example, MasterCard's slogan "MasterCard, I'm bored"). Today, charge and credit card ads often point out just how prudent it is to use your card for the right reasons. Now, instead of just suggesting you use your plastic to hop off to the islands when you feel the first stirrings of a bout with boredom, credit card companies often detail functional benefits for their cards with a specific market segment in mind, as reflected by the American Express ad in Exhibit 8.6.

Basic demographic trends may be the single most important situational factor in advertising plans. Whether it's baby boomers or Generation X, Y, or Z, where the people are is usually where the sales are. As the population age distribution varies with time, new markets are created and destroyed. The baby boom generation of post–World War II disproportionately dictates consumer offerings and demand simply because of its size. As the boomers age, companies that offer the things needed by tens of millions of aging boomers will have to devise new appeals. Think of the consumers of this generation needing long-term health care, geriatric products, and things to amuse themselves in retirement. Will they have the disposable income necessary to have the bountiful lifestyle many of them have had during their working years? After all, they aren't the greatest savers. And what of today's 20-somethings? When do you tend to model your parents? When do you look to put space between yourself and your parents? Knowing which generation(s) you are targeting is critical in your situation analysis.

Cultural Context. International advertising is advertising that reaches across national and cultural boundaries. Adopting an international perspective is often difficult for marketers and represents a major challenge in developing ad plans. The reason is that experience gained throughout a career and a lifetime creates a cultural "comfort zone." That is, one's own cultural values, experiences, and knowledge serve as a subconscious guide for decision making and behavior. Another name for "subconscious guide" is bias.

Managers must overcome two related biases to be successful in international markets. **Ethnocentrism** is the tendency to view and value things from the perspective of one's own culture. A **self-reference criterion (SRC)** is the unconscious reference to one's own cultural values, experiences, and knowledge as a basis for

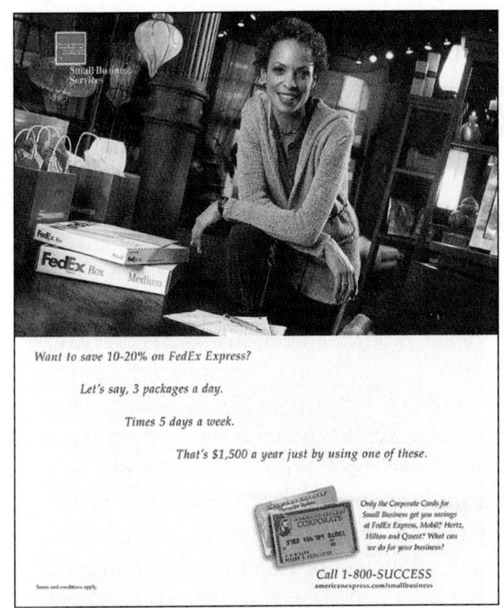

Exhibit 8.6 Here we see American Express offering a specific package of benefits to a well-defined target segment. Obviously, the folks at AMEX understand STP marketing (explained in Chapter 6).

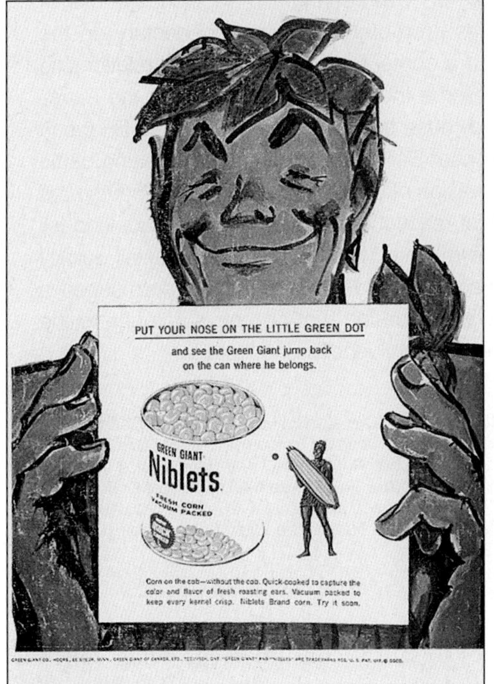

Exhibit 8.7 Knowing a brand's history can guide the development of future campaigns. Visit the Green Giant corporate site and read all about the history of the Green Giant character. He first appeared in advertising in 1928. How might this history determine future Green Giant ads? Is it time to ditch the Green Giant? Can you think of brands that made drastic changes in their popular icons? What might motivate a company to modernize or change an icon?

decisions. These two closely-related biases are primary obstacles to success when conducting marketing and advertising planning that demand a cross-cultural perspective.

A decision maker's SRC and ethnocentrism can inhibit his or her ability to sense important cultural distinctions between markets. This in turn can blind advertisers to their own culture's "fingerprints" on the ads they've created. Sometimes these are offensive or, at a minimum, markers of "outsider" influence. As suggested in the *Globalization* box, even the savviest of marketers can overlook cultural nuances in development of their advertising plans. It is the unanticipated or underappreciated elements that will get you in trouble every time, and many global marketers now subscribe to the theory that, to get the message right, you must get face time with consumers in any geographic market you are targeting.[11]

Historical Context. No situation is entirely new, but all situations are unique. Just how a firm arrived at the current situation is very important. Before trying to design Apple's iPad campaign, the agency should learn a lot about the history of all the principal players, the industry, the brand, the corporate culture, critical moments in the company's past, its big mistakes and big successes. Long relationships between client and agency, as between Apple and TWBA Chiat/Day, will obviously help with this, but most are not so fortunate. All new decisions are situated in a firm's history, and an agency should be diligent in studying that history. For example, would an agency pitch new business to Green Giant without knowing something of the brand's history and the rationale behind the Green Giant character? The history of the Green Giant dates back decades, as suggested in Exhibit 8.7. The fact is that no matter what advertising decisions are made in the present, the past has a significant impact.

Apart from history's intrinsic value, sometimes the real business goal is to convince the client that the agency knows the client's business, its major concerns, and its corporate culture. A brief history of the company and brand are included in ad plans to demonstrate the thoroughness of the agency's research, the depth of its knowledge, and the scope of its concern.

Industry Analysis. An **industry analysis** is just that; it focuses on developments and trends within an entire industry and on any other factors that may make a difference in how an advertiser proceeds with an advertising plan. An industry analysis should enumerate and discuss the most important aspects of a given industry, including the supply side of the supply-demand equation. When great advertising overstimulates demand that can't be matched by supply, one can end up with lots of unhappy customers.

No industry faces more dramatic trends and swings in consumers' tastes than the food business. In recent years, the low-carb craze has challenged industry giants from Nestlé to Hershey Foods to H.J. Heinz Co. to McDonald's to come up

11. Normandy Madden, "Unilever Puts in Face Time with Chinese Consumer," *Advertising Age,* March 22, 2010, 8.

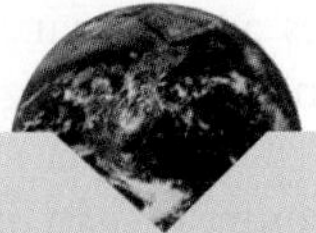

Globalization

Challenging China

With a population of more than a billion people, a robustly growing economy, new global status associated with hosting the Olympic games, and greater acceptance of capitalistic ways and means, it follows that many companies large and small have turned to China as a new source of business opportunity. It also follows that advertising spending in China is growing at unprecedented rates. Many experts are already predicting that in this decade, China will overtake Japan as the second largest advertising market in the world. Yet China presents many incredible challenges for advertisers from around the world. Some of these derive from the gargantuan nature of this country. China has 31 provinces, 656 cities, and 48,000 districts. There is no one Chinese language; rather, there are seven major tongues with 80 spoken dialects. The north of China is a frozen plateau and the south of China is tropical. There are huge income and lifestyle differences between city-dwellers and farmers, and between the prosperous east and the impoverished west. When you come right down to it, there really is no such thing as a single "China." And that's just the obvious stuff.

Matters get even more complex when one factors in the unique aspects of the Chinese culture, where the norms of a Confucian society often are in conflict with the drive toward economic reform and Western lifestyles. The Chinese are also keenly aware and proud of their rich history, which spans thousands of years. (Recall that Marco Polo set out to explore the mysteries of China in the 13th century.) For any outsider, China presents many mysteries that will need to be solved in the development of appropriate and effective advertising.

Toyota's launch of the Prado Land Cruiser in China provides a nice example of the challenges one must overcome in developing advertising to reach across national (and cultural) boundaries. Now keep in mind, this is Toyota, from just across the East China Sea in Toyota City, Japan, not some newcomer to the Asian continent. To launch its big SUV in China, Toyota's ad agency Saatchi & Saatchi created a print campaign showing a Prado driving past two large stone lions, which were saluting and bowing to the Prado. This seems to make sense because the stone lion is a traditional sign of power in the Chinese culture. As one Saatchi executive put it, "These ads were intended to reflect Prado's imposing presence when driving in the city: You cannot but respect the Prado."

Chinese consumers saw it differently. For starters, Chinese words often have multiple meanings, and Prado can be translated into Chinese as *badao*, which means "rule by force" or "overbearing." In addition, the use of the stone lions prompted scathing commentary on the Internet about a contentious time in China's relationship with Japan. Some thought the stone lions in the Prado ad resembled those that flank the Marco Polo Bridge in China, a site near Beijing that marked the opening battle of Japan's invasion of China in 1937. These of course are not the kind of reactions that an advertiser is looking for when launching a new product. The automaker quickly pulled 30 magazine and newspaper ads and issued a formal apology, illustrating that no one is immune to the subtle but powerful influences of culture.

Sources: Geoffrey Fowler, "China's Cultural Fabric Is a Challenge to Marketers," *The Wall Street Journal,* January 21, 2004, B7; Sameena Ahmad, "A Billion Three, But Not for Me," *The Economist,* March 20, 2004, 5, 6; Norihiko Shirouzu, "In Chinese Market, Toyota's Strategy Is Made in USA," *The Wall Street Journal,* May 26, 2006, A1, A8; Laurel Wentz, "China's Ad World: A New Crisis Every Day," *Advertising Age,* December 11, 2006, 6.

with new products and reposition old ones to satisfy consumers' growing concerns about sugar and white flour. When your industry research tells you that 30 million Americans describe themselves as being on a low-carb diet, and another 100 million are expected to join them in a matter of months, it's time to reposition and reformulate.[12] It is hard to imagine the marketing and advertising plans of any food maker not giving some consideration to the carb issue as part of an analysis of their industry. As suggested by Exhibit 8.8, no one is immune.

Market Analysis. A **market analysis** complements the industry analysis, emphasizing the demand side of the equation. In a market analysis, an advertiser

12. Stephanie Thompson, "Low-Carb Craze Blitzes Food Biz," *Advertising Age,* January 5, 2004, 1, 22.

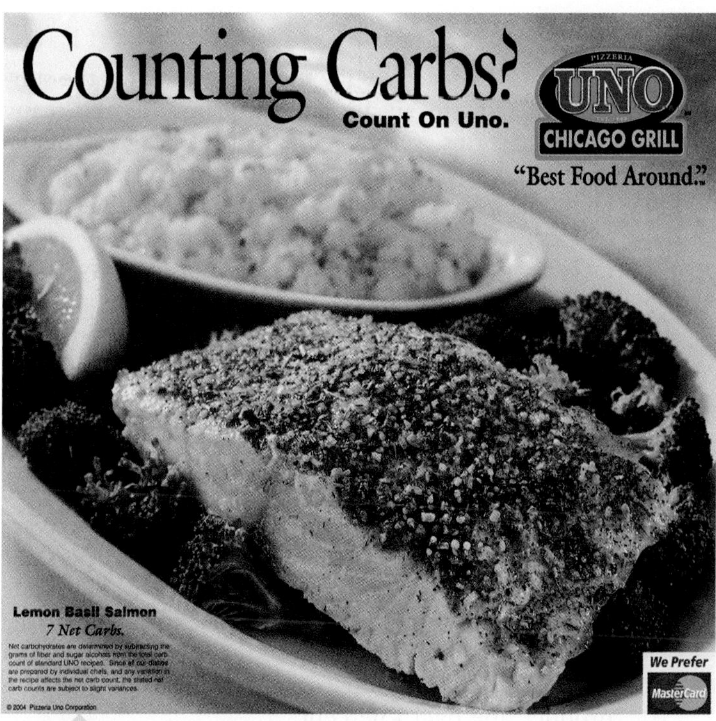

Exhibit 8.8 Pizzeria Uno built its business around the classic Chicago-style deep-dish pizza. But in a world gone mad with carb counting, the deep-dish pizza was bound to lose some appeal. Enter Uno Chicago Grill and Lemon Basil Salmon with just 7 net carbs. Can carb counters and deep-dish pizza lovers find a way to peacefully coexist? For Uno's sake, let's hope so.

examines the factors that drive and determine the market for the firm's product or service. First, the advertiser needs to decide just exactly what the market is for the product. Most often, the market for a given good or service is simply defined as current users. The idea here is that consumers figure out for themselves whether they want the product or not and thus define the market for themselves, and for the advertiser. This approach has some wisdom to it. It's simple, easy to defend, and very conservative. Few executives get fired for choosing this market definition. However, it completely ignores those consumers who might otherwise be persuaded to use the product.

A market analysis commonly begins by stating just who the current users are, and (hopefully) why they are current users. Consumers' motivations for using one product or service but not another may very well provide the advertiser with the means toward a significant expansion of the entire market. If the entire pie grows, the firm's slice usually does as well. The advertiser's job in a market analysis is to find out the most important market factors and why they are so important.

Competitor Analysis. Once the industry and market are studied and analyzed, attention turns to **competitor analysis.** Here an advertiser determines just exactly who the competitors are, discussing their strengths, weaknesses, tendencies, and any threats they pose. When planning the launch of its new smartphone in Fall of 2009, Motorola faced a formidable obstacle — Apple's iPhone. Fortunately for Motorola, they didn't have to go it alone versus Steve Jobs and company. The Motorola phone would run Google software and be supported on Verizon's nationwide network.[13] In addition, Verizon brought significant resources to the table for a bold launch of the Droid, taking aim at the iPhone.[14] With stark, futuristic, and robotic overtones (think Terminator), no way one could mistake a Droid ad for an iPhone ad. And with its tagline of "In a world of doesn't, Droid does," Motorola and Verizon definitely meant to suggest that their phone will outperform the iPhone. Good news for all players in this category — with surging primary demand for smartphones generally, it appears there is plenty of opportunity for both the cool and pretty versus the dark and daring phones to continue to grow their sales revenues well into the future.

When archrivals go head-to-head trying to win customers' loyalty, it is common to see their advertisements feature a competitive positioning strategy, as discussed in Chapter 6. Another excellent illustration is featured in Exhibit 8.9. Here we see a regional telecom provider (Cincinnati Bell) taking on its rival, Time Warner. In conjunction with its partner, DirecTV, Cincinnati Bell is seeking to win over Time Warner's core customer, the cable subscriber. There is nothing subtle in the approach here. And it's pretty hard to argue with the premise that "Cable bills bite."

13. Niraj Sheth and Yukari Kane, "Phone Makers Scramble to Stand Out," online.wsj.com, October 28, 2009.

14. Rita Chang, "With $100M Saturation Campaign, Droid Will Be Impossible to Avoid," *Advertising Age,* November 9, 2009, 3, 34.

Exhibit 8.9 Cincinnati Bell takes direct aim at the market share of a key competitor with a compelling visual element that works perfectly with its headline—Cable bills bite. The value proposition is based on packaging a bundle of services for one low monthly fee... perhaps the perfect antidote for cable bills that keep going up, up, and up.

Objectives.

Advertising objectives lay the framework for the subsequent tasks in an advertising plan and take many different forms. Objectives identify the goals of the advertiser in concrete terms. The advertiser, more often than not, has more than one objective for an ad campaign. An advertiser's objective may be (1) to increase consumer awareness of and curiosity about its brand, (2) to change consumers' beliefs or attitudes about its product, (3) to influence the purchase intent of its customers, (4) to stimulate trial use of its product or service, (5) to convert one-time product users into repeat purchasers, (6) to switch consumers from a competing brand to its brand, or (7) to increase sales. (Each of these objectives is discussed briefly in the following paragraphs.) The advertiser may have more than one objective at the same time. For example, a swimwear company may state its advertising objectives as follows: to maintain the company's brand image as the market leader in adult female swimwear and to increase revenue in this product line by 15 percent.

Creating or maintaining brand awareness is a fundamental advertising objective. **Brand awareness** is an indicator of consumer knowledge about the existence of the brand and how easily that knowledge can be retrieved from memory. For example, a market researcher might ask a consumer to name five insurance companies. **Top-of-the-mind awareness** is represented by the brand listed first. Ease of retrieval from memory is important because for many goods or services, ease of retrieval is predictive of market share.

This proved to be the case for Aflac (American Family Life Assurance Co.), an insurance company that used a determined duck quacking *aaa-flack* in its ad campaign as a means to building brand awareness. If you've seen these ads, we suspect that you'll never forget that duck. If you haven't seen them, you might be thinking that a duck as your primary spokesperson sounds pretty dopey. Maybe yes, maybe no, but that duck helped Aflac become a major player in the U.S. insurance market. Similarly, the Geico Gecko was so effective in winning attention for Geico Corporation that the chief marketing officer of rival Allstate Insurance has said, "I'd like to squash it."[15]

Creating, changing, or reinforcing attitudes is another important function of advertising, and thus makes for a common advertising objective. As we saw in Chapter 5, one way to go about changing people's attitudes is to give them information designed to alter their beliefs. There are many ways to approach this task. One way is exemplified by the Bose ad in Exhibit 8.10. Here we see an information-dense approach where a number of logical arguments are developed to shape beliefs regarding the QuietComfort 2 Noise-Cancelling Headphones. For the consumer willing to digest this complex, text-based ad, the arguments are likely to prove quite compelling. Conversely, one can let a picture tell the entire story, as in Exhibit 8.11. Here the approach depends on the visual imagery and the consumer's willingness to interpret the loudspeaker heads. Not a problem for anyone who has traveled coach class. The obvious serenity of the handsome young man

15. Suzanne Vranica, "How a Gecko Shook Up Insurance Ads," *The Wall Street Journal,* January 2, 2007, B1.

Exhibit 8.10 The makers of Bose audio equipment have the philosophy that sound reproduction is a matter of science, so it follows that the best way to impress a consumer is to simply lay out the facts. Learn more about Dr. Amar Bose and the philosophy behind his company at www.bose.com.

Exhibit 8.11 The approach taken by Sony plugs into any air traveler's nightmare scenario: a screaming baby on a flight to Paris!

wearing the Sony Noise-Canceling Headphones speaks for itself. One thus infers something about Sony without any text. Whether through direct, logical arguments, or thought-provoking visual imagery, advertisements are frequently designed to deliver their objective of belief formation and attitude change.

Purchase intent is another popular criterion in setting objectives. Purchase intent is determined by asking consumers whether they intend to buy a product or service in the near future. The appeal of influencing purchase intent is that intent is closer to actual behavior, and thus closer to the desired sale, than attitudes are. Even though this makes sense, it does presuppose that consumers can express their intentions with a reasonably high degree of reliability. Sometimes they can, sometimes they cannot. Purchase intent, however, is fairly reliable as an indicator of relative intention to buy, and it is, therefore, a worthwhile advertising objective.

Trial usage reflects actual behavior and is commonly used as an advertising objective. Many times, the best that we can ask of advertising is to encourage the consumer to try our brand. At that point, the product or service must live up to the expectations created by our advertising. In the case of new products, stimulating trial usage is critically important. In the marketing realm, the angels sing when the initial purchase rate of a new product or service is high.

The **repeat purchase,** or conversion, objective is aimed at the percentage of consumers who try a new product and then purchase it a second time. A second purchase is reason for great rejoicing. The odds of long-term product success go way up when this percentage is high.

Brand switching is the last of the advertising objectives mentioned here. In some product categories, switching is commonplace, even the norm. In others, it is rare. When setting a brand-switching objective, the advertiser must neither expect too much, nor rejoice too much, over a temporary gain. Persuading consumers to switch brands can be a long and expensive task.

2 Communications versus Sales Objectives.

Some analysts argue that as a single variable in a firm's overall marketing mix, it is not reasonable to set sales expectations for advertising when other variables in the mix might undermine the advertising effort or be responsible for sales in the first place. In fact, some advertising analysts argue that communications objectives are the *only* legitimate objectives for advertising. This perspective has its underpinnings in the proposition that advertising is but one variable in the marketing mix and cannot be held solely responsible for sales. Rather, advertising should be held responsible for creating awareness of a brand, communicating information about product features or availability, or developing a favorable attitude that can lead to consumer preference for a brand. All of these outcomes are long term and based on communications impact.

There are some major benefits to maintaining a strict communications perspective in setting advertising objectives. First, by viewing advertising as primarily a communications effort, marketers can consider a broader range of advertising strategies. Second, they can gain a greater appreciation for the complexity of the overall communications process. Designing an integrated communications program with sales as the sole objective neglects aspects of message design, media choice, public relations, or sales force deployment that should be effectively integrated across all phases of a firm's communication efforts. Using advertising messages to support the efforts of the sales force and/or drive people to your website is an example of integrating diverse communication tools to build synergy that then may ultimately produce a sale.

Yet there is always a voice reminding us that there is only one rule: *Advertising must sell.*[16] Nowhere is the tension between communication and sales objectives better exemplified than in the annual debate about what advertisers really get for the tremendous sums of money they spend on Super Bowl ads. Every year great fanfare accompanies the ads that appear during the Super Bowl, and numerous polls are taken after the game to assess the year's most memorable ads. But more often than not these polls turn out to be nothing more than popularity contests, with the usual suspects—like Budweiser, Doritos, and those brash E-Trade babies—having all the fun.[17] But the question remains—does likability translate to sales? If a Super Bowl ad introducing Sheryl Crow as the new spokesperson for a Revlon hair coloring product doesn't affect women's purchase intentions, can it be worth the millions of dollars it takes to produce and air it? And for that matter, who really believes that Sheryl Crow colors her hair herself out of a box?

Athough there is a natural tension between those who advocate sales objectives and those who push communications objectives, nothing precludes a marketer from using both types when developing an advertising plan. Indeed, combining sales objectives such as market share and household penetration with communication objectives such as awareness and attitude change can be an excellent means of motivating and evaluating an advertising campaign.

Objectives that enable a firm to make intelligent decisions about resource allocation must be stated in an advertising plan in terms specific to the organization. Articulating such well-stated objectives is easier when advertising planners do the following:

1. ***Establish a quantitative benchmark.*** Objectives for advertising are measurable only in the context of quantifiable variables. Advertising planners should begin with quantified measures of the current status of market share, awareness, attitude, or other factors that advertising is expected to influence. The measurement of effectiveness in quantitative terms requires a knowledge of the level of variables of interest before an advertising effort, and then afterward. For example, a statement of objectives in quantified terms might be, "Increase the market share of heavy users of the product category using our brand from 22 to 25 percent." In this case, a quantifiable and measurable market share objective is specified.
2. ***Specify measurement methods and criteria for success.*** It is important that the factors being measured be directly related to the objectives being pursued. It is of little use to try to increase the awareness of a brand with advertising and then judge the effects based on changes in sales. If changes in sales are expected, then measure sales. If increased awareness is the goal, then change in consumer awareness is the legitimate measure of success. This may seem obvious, but in a classic study of advertising objectives, it was found that claims of success for advertising were

16. Sergio Zyman, *The End of Advertising As We Know It* (Hoboken, NJ: Wiley, 2002).
17. "Top 10 Best-Liked, Most-Recalled TV Spots of 2009," adage.com, January 11, 2010.

unrelated to the original statements of objective in 69 percent of the cases.[18] In this research, firms cited increases in sales as proof of success of advertising when the original objectives were related to factors such as awareness, conviction to a brand, or product-use information. But maybe that just says when sales do go up, we forget about everything else.

3. ***Specify a time frame.*** Objectives for advertising should include a statement of the period of time allowed for the desired results to occur. In some cases, as with direct response advertising, the time frame may be related to a seasonal selling opportunity like the Christmas holiday period. For communications-based objectives, the measurement of results may not be undertaken until the end of an entire multi-week campaign. The point is that the time period for accomplishment of an objective and the related measurement period must be stated in advance in the ad plan.

These criteria for setting objectives help ensure that the planning process is organized and well directed. By relying on quantitative benchmarks, an advertiser has guidelines for making future decisions. Linking measurement criteria to objectives provides a basis for the equitable evaluation of the success or failure of advertising. Finally, the specification of a time frame for judging results keeps the planning process moving forward. As in all things, however, moderation is a good thing. A single-minded obsession with watching the numbers can be dangerous in that it minimizes or entirely misses the importance of qualitative and intuitive factors.

3 Budgeting.

One of the most agonizing tasks is budgeting the funds for an advertising effort. Normally, the responsibility for the advertising budget lies with the firm itself. Within a firm, budget recommendations come up through the ranks; e.g., from a brand manager to a category manager and ultimately to the executive in charge of marketing. The sequence then reverses itself for the allocation and spending of funds. In a small firm, such as an independent retailer, the sequence just described may include only one individual who plays all the roles.

In many cases, a firm will rely on its advertising agency to make recommendations regarding the size of the advertising budget. When this is done, it is typically the account executive in charge of the brand who will analyze the firm's objectives and its creative and media needs and then make a recommendation to the company. The account exec's budget planning will likely include working closely with brand and product-group managers to determine an appropriate spending level.

To be as judicious and accountable as possible in spending money on advertising and IBP, marketers rely on various methods for setting an advertising budget. To appreciate the benefits (and failings) of these methods, we will consider each of them in turn.

Percentage of Sales. A **percentage-of-sales approach** to advertising budgeting calculates the advertising budget based on a percentage of the prior year's sales or the projected year's sales. This technique is easy to understand and implement. The budget decision makers merely specify that a particular percentage of either last year's sales or the current year's estimated sales will be allocated to the advertising process. It is common to spend between 2 and 12 percent of sales on advertising.

18. Stewart Henderson Britt, "Are So-Called Successful Advertising Campaigns Really Successful?" *Journal of Advertising Research*, vol. 9 (1969), 5–15.

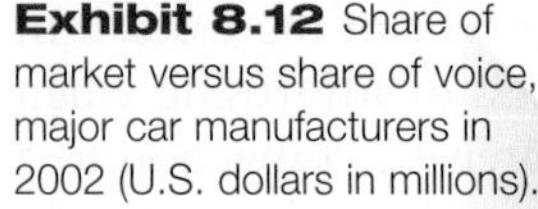

Exhibit 8.12 Share of market versus share of voice, major car manufacturers in 2002 (U.S. dollars in millions).

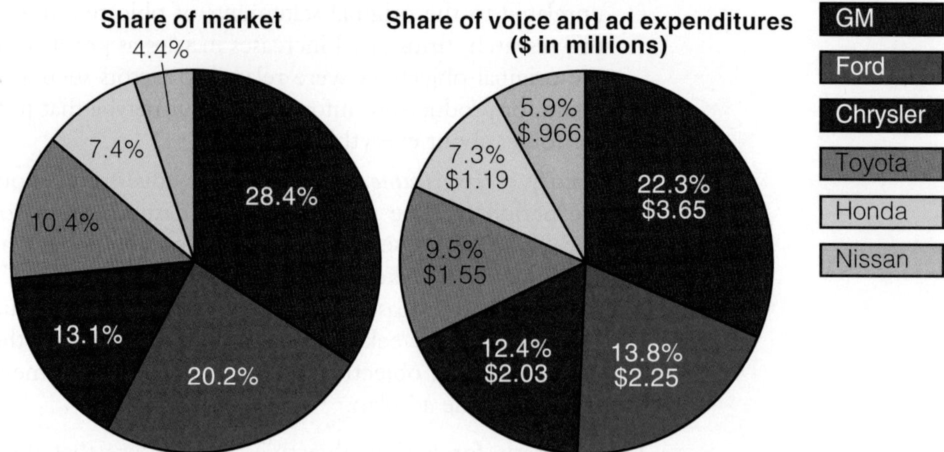

Source: Market share information taken from *Market Share Report, 2004, Los Angeles Times,* January 4, 2003, p. C1. Share of voice-ad expenditures calculated from *100 Leading National Advertisers, Ad Age, Special Report, 6.23.03* and *Domestic Advertising Spending by Company, Ad Age, 2002.*

Even though simplicity is certainly an advantage in decision making, the percentage-of-sales approach is fraught with problems. First, when a firm's sales are decreasing, the advertising budget will automatically decline. Periods of decreasing sales may be precisely the time when a firm needs to increase spending on advertising; if a percentage-of-sales budgeting method is being used, this won't happen. Second, this budgeting method can easily result in overspending on advertising. Once funds have been earmarked, the tendency is to find ways to spend the budgeted amount. Third, and the most serious drawback from a strategic standpoint, is that the percentage-of-sales approach does not relate advertising dollars to advertising objectives. Basing spending on past or future sales is devoid of analytical evaluation and implicitly presumes a direct cause-and-effect relationship between advertising and sales. But here, we have sales "causing" advertising. That's backward!

Share of Market/Share of Voice. With this method, a firm monitors the amount spent by various significant competitors on advertising and allocates an amount equal to the amount of money spent by competitors or an amount proportional to (or slightly greater than) the firm's market share relative to the competition.[19] This will provide the advertiser with a **share of voice,** or an advertising presence in the market, that is equal to or greater than the competitors' share of advertising voice. Exhibit 8.12 shows the share of market and share of voice for automakers in the United States.

This method is often used for advertising-budget allocations when a new product is introduced. Conventional wisdom suggests that some multiple of the desired first-year market share, often 2.5 to 4 times, should be spent in terms of share-of-voice advertising expenditures. For example, if an advertiser wants a 2 percent first-year share, it would need to spend up to 8 percent of the total dollar amount spent in the industry (for an 8 percent share of voice). The logic is that a new product will need a significant share of voice to gain notice among a group of existing, well-established brands.[20]

19. The classic treatment of this method was first offered by James O. Peckham, "Can We Relate Advertising Dollars to Market-Share Objectives?" in Malcolm A. McGiven (Ed.), *How Much to Spend for Advertising* (New York: Association of National Advertisers, 1969), 24.

20. James C. Shroer, "Ad Spending: Growing Market Share," *Harvard Business Review* (January–February 1990), 44–50.

Although the share-of-voice approach is sound in its emphasis on competitors' activities, there are important challenges to consider with this approach. First, it may be difficult to gain access to precise information on competitors' spending. Second, there is no reason to believe that competitors are spending their money wisely. Third, the flaw in logic with this method is the assumption that every advertising effort is of the same quality and will have the same effect from a creative-execution standpoint. Such an assumption is especially shaky when one tries to compare expenditure levels across today's diverse advertising forms. Take Dove's experience with Super Bowl advertising versus its short film placed on YouTube. The film, "Dove Evolution," generated the biggest traffic spike ever at CampaignForRealBeauty.com, three times more than Dove's Super Bowl ad.[21] The YouTube video aired for $0, versus $2 million or so for the Super Bowl ad. No doubt that "Dove Evolution" was a huge contributor to Dove's share-of-voice at the time, but predicting the effects of innovative executions such as this one will always challenge conventional models. Another example featuring Honda's 2 million Facebook friends is featured in the *Social Media* box.

Response Models. Using response models to aid the budgeting process has been a widespread practice among larger firms for many years.[22] The belief is that greater objectivity can be maintained with such models. Although this may or may not be the case, response models do provide useful information on what a given company's advertising response function looks like. An **advertising response function** is a mathematical relationship that associates dollars spent on advertising and sales generated. To the extent that past advertising predicts future sales, this method is valuable. Using marginal analysis, an advertiser would continue spending on advertising as long as its marginal spending was exceeded by marginal sales. Margin analysis answers the advertiser's question, "How much more will sales increase if we spend an additional dollar on advertising?" As the rate of return on advertising expenditures declines, the wisdom of additional spending is challenged.

Theoretically, this method leads to a point where an optimal advertising expenditure results in an optimal sales level and, in turn, an optimal profit. The relationship between sales, profit, and advertising spending is shown in the marginal analysis graph in Exhibit 8.13. Data on sales, prior advertising expenditures, and consumer awareness are typical of the numerical input to such quantitative models.

Exhibit 8.13
Sales, profit, and advertising curves used in marginal analysis.

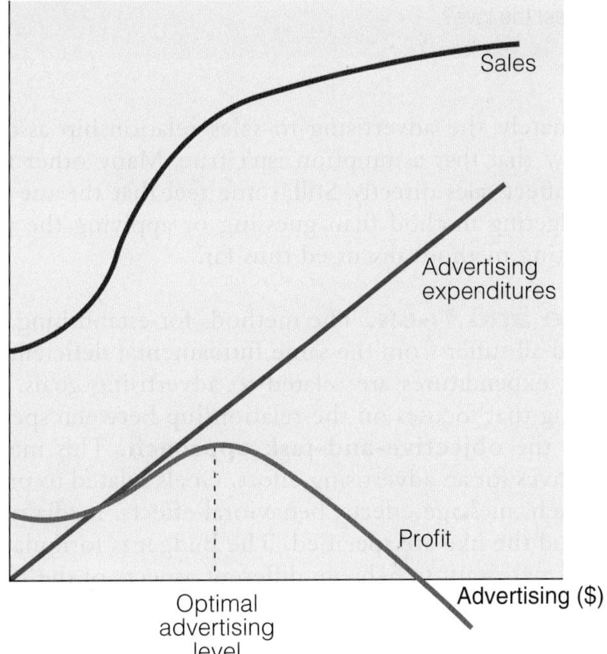

Source: David A. Aaker, Rajeev Batra, and John G. Meyers, *Advertising Management,* 4th ed. (Upper Saddle River, NJ: Prentice Hall, 1992). Reprinted by permission of the authors.

21. Jack Neff, "A Real Beauty: Dove's Viral Makes a Big Splash for No Cash," *Advertising Age,* October 10, 2006, 1, 45.

22. James E. Lynch and Graham J. Hooley, "Increasing Sophistication in Advertising Budget Setting," *Journal of Advertising Research* (February–March 1990), 72.

Social Media

Feel the Love?

As you already know firsthand, social media services like Twitter and Facebook have changed the way friends interact, and maybe even changed the definition for 'friend.' And where the consumer goes, marketers are sure to follow. Ford, Nike, Starbucks, Coca-Cola, Chevron, Levi Strauss, to name just a few, are also hanging out on Facebook, and want to be your friend.

And then there's Honda, who launched its Facebook page themed "Everybody Knows Somebody Who Loves a Honda" to recruit its own set of friends. Honda owners were encouraged to join as either overall fans or fans of a specific model. Uploading of photos of their favorite Hondas was of course encouraged, and lots of new connections among Honda owners were created. As part of its digital, social experiment, Honda tried many ways to get consumers to join the community. For example, a TV spot on MTV produced a few hundred new friends, but a spot run during an NFL football game produced 50,000. If we can recruit friends on TV, then maybe TV advertising still has a purpose. After just a few months, Honda had more than 2 million new cyber friends. Feel the love?

Real friends don't pester each other with lots of inane requests, and Honda tried to stay true by not collecting email addresses and not using their community as a forum to sell automobiles. But then, since Honda is in the business of selling automobiles, what objectives are being served by an online community of 2 million? Not clear, really, or as Tom Peyton from Honda said at the time, "We are learning, like everyone else, what we are permitted to do with these kinds of things." In the evolving digital media space, experimentation and learning are absolutely essential. But that nagging question about sales never goes away. At just about that time when Honda was celebrating its 2 million new Facebook friends, they were also confronted with a 24 percent drop in vehicles sales compared to the previous year. Twitter to Mr. Peyton—Better find a way to show that cyber friends are also loyal Honda **buyers.**

Sources: Jon Swartz, "More Marketers Sign on to Social Media," *USA TODAY,* August 28, 2009, 1B, 2B; Jean Halliday, "Honda Feels the Love on Facebook," *Advertising Age,* October 26, 2009, 53.

Unfortunately, the advertising-to-sales relationship assumes simple causality, and we know that that assumption isn't true. Many other factors, in addition to advertising, affect sales directly. Still, some feel that the use of response models is a better budgeting method than guessing or applying the percentage-of-sales or other budgeting methods discussed thus far.

Objective and Task. The methods for establishing an advertising budget just discussed all suffer from the same fundamental deficiency: a lack of specification of how expenditures are related to advertising goals. The only method of budget setting that focuses on the relationship between spending and advertising objectives is the **objective-and-task approach.** This method begins with the stated objectives for an advertising effort. Goals related to production costs, target audience reach, message effects, behavioral effects, media placement, duration of the effort, and the like are specified. The budget is formulated by identifying the specific tasks necessary to achieve different aspects of the objectives.

There is a lot to recommend this procedure for budgeting. A firm identifies any and all tasks it believes are related to achieving its objectives. Should the total dollar figure for the necessary tasks be beyond the firm's financial capability, reconciliation must be found. But even if reconciliation and a subsequent reduction of the budget result, the firm has at least identified what *should* have been budgeted to pursue its advertising objectives.

The objective-and-task approach is the most logical and defensible method for calculating and then allocating an advertising budget. It is the only budgeting method that specifically relates spending to the objectives being pursued. It is widely used

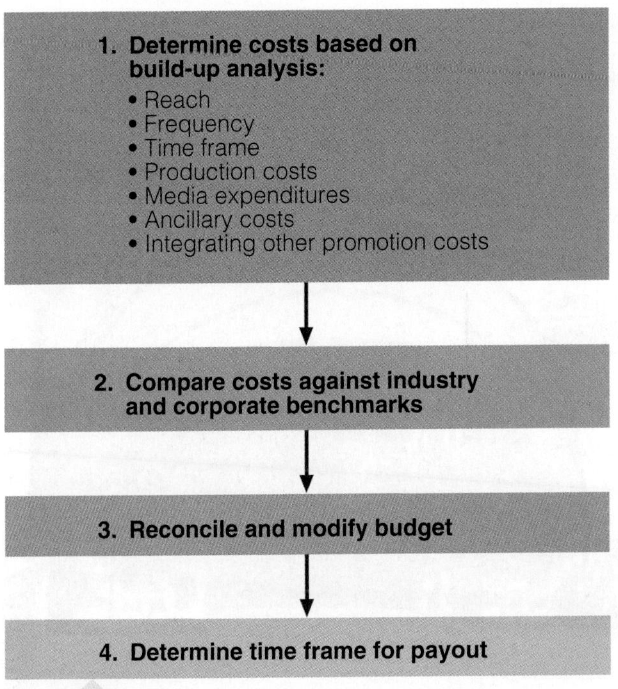
1. Determine costs based on build-up analysis:
• Reach
• Frequency
• Time frame
• Production costs
• Media expenditures
• Ancillary costs
• Integrating other promotion costs
2. Compare costs against industry and corporate benchmarks
3. Reconcile and modify budget
4. Determine time frame for payout

Exhibit 8.14 Steps in implementing the objective-and-task approach.

among major advertisers. For these reasons, we will consider the specific procedures for implementing the objective-and-task budgeting method.

Implementing the Objective-and-Task Budgeting Method. Proper implementation of the objective-and-task approach requires a data-based, systematic procedure. Because the approach ties spending levels to specific advertising goals, the process depends on proper execution of the objective-setting process described earlier. Once a firm and its agency are satisfied with the specificity and direction of stated objectives, a series of well-defined steps can be taken to implement the objective-and-task method. These steps are shown in Exhibit 8.14 and summarized in the following sections.

Determine Costs Based on Build-up Analysis. Having identified specific objectives, an advertiser can now begin determining what tasks are necessary for the accomplishment of those objectives. In using a **build-up analysis**—building up the expenditure levels for tasks—the following factors must be considered in terms of costs:

- ***Reach.*** The advertiser must identify the geographic and demographic exposure the advertising is to achieve.
- ***Frequency.*** The advertiser must determine the number of exposures required to accomplish desired objectives.
- ***Time frame.*** The advertiser must estimate when communications will occur and during what period of time.
- ***Production costs.*** The decision maker can rely on creative personnel and producers to estimate the costs associated with the planned execution of advertisements.
- ***Media expenditures.*** Given the preceding factors, the advertiser can now define the appropriate media, media mix, and frequency of insertions that will directly address objectives. Further, differences in geographic allocation, with special attention to regional or local media strategies, are considered at this point.
- ***Ancillary costs.*** There will be a variety of related costs not directly accounted for in the preceding factors. Prominent among these are costs associated with advertising to the trade and specialized research unique to the campaign.
- ***Integrating other promotional costs.*** In this era of advertising and integrated brand promotion, sometimes it is the novel promotion that delivers the best bang for the buck. New and improved forms of brand promotion, like the one illustrated in Exhibit 8.15, must also be considered as part of the planning and budgeting process.

Compare Costs Against Industry and Corporate Benchmarks. After compiling all the costs through a build-up analysis, an advertiser will want to make a quick reality check. This is accomplished by checking the percentage of sales that the estimated set of costs represents relative to industry standards for percentage of sales allocated to advertising. If most competitors are spending 4 to 6 percent of gross sales on advertising, how does the current budget compare to this percentage? Another recommended technique is to identify the share of industry advertising that the firm's budget represents. Another relevant reference point is to compare the current

Exhibit 8.15 What could be better on a warm summer day than a stroll down Chicago's Navy Pier? Smart marketers like Best Buy want to be part of your day, and thus they bring their high-tech playground right to where the action is. The idea here is to build deeper relationships with potential customers by contributing to their good times in a special venue. Concerts, sporting events, fairs, and carnivals are all great places to show off your brand.

budget with prior budgets. If the total dollar amount is extraordinarily high or low compared to previous years, this variance should be justified based on the objectives being pursued. The use of percentage of sales on both an industry and internal corporate basis provides a reference point only. The percentage-of-sales figures are not used for decision making per se but rather as a benchmark to judge whether the budgeted amount is so unusual as to need reevaluation.

Reconcile and Modify the Budget. It is always a fear that the proposed budget will not meet with approval. It may not be viewed as consistent with corporate policy related to advertising expense, or it may be considered beyond the financial capabilities of the organization. Modifications to a proposed budget are common, but having to make radical cuts in proposed spending is disruptive. The objective-and-task approach is designed to identify what a firm will need to spend in order to achieve a desired impact. To have the budget level compromised after such planning can result in an impotent advertising effort because necessary tasks cannot be funded.

Every precaution should be taken against having to radically modify a budget. Planners should be totally aware of corporate policy and financial circumstance *during* the objective-setting and subsequent task-planning phases. This will help reduce the extent of budget modification.

Determine a Time Frame for Payout. It is important that budget decision makers recognize when the budget will be available for funding the tasks associated with the proposed effort. Travel expenses, production expenses, and media time and space are tied to specific calendar dates. For example, media time and space are often acquired and paid for far in advance of the completion of finished advertisements. Knowing when and how much money is needed improves the odds of the plan being carried out smoothly.

If these procedures are followed for the objective-and-task approach, an advertiser will have a defendable budget with which to pursue key objectives. One point to be made, however, is that the budget should not be viewed as the final word in funding an advertising effort. The dynamic nature of the market and rapid developments in media require flexibility in budget execution. This can mean changes in expenditure levels, but it can also mean changes in payout allocation.

Like any other business activity, a marketer must take on an advertising effort with clearly specified intentions for what is to be accomplished. Intentions and expectations for advertising are embodied in the process of setting objectives. Armed with information from market planning and an assessment of the type of advertising needed to support marketing plans, advertising objectives can be set. These objectives should be in place before steps are taken to determine a budget for the advertising effort, and before the creative work begins. Again, this is not always the order of things, even though it should be. These objectives will also affect the plans for media placement.

Strategy.

Returning now to the other major components of the advertising plan (revisiting Exhibit 8.4 is a good idea at this point), next up is strategy. Strategy represents the mechanism by which something is to be done. It is an expression of the means to an end. All of the other factors are supposed to result in a strategy. Strategy is what you do, given the situation and objectives. There are numerous possibilities for advertising strategies. For example, if you are trying to get more top-of-the-mind awareness for your brand of chewing gum, a simple strategy would be to employ a high-frequency, name-repetition campaign (Double your pleasure with Doublemint, Doublemint, Doublemint gum). Exhibit 8.16 presents an ad from Danskin's campaign designed to address a more ambitious objective; that is, broadening the appeal of the brand beyond dance accessories to the much larger fitness-wear market. Danskin's advertising strategy thus features unique "fitness" celebrities as implicit endorsers of the brand.

More sophisticated goals call for more sophisticated strategies. You are limited only by your resources: financial, organizational, and creative. Ultimately, strategy formulation is a creative endeavor. It is best learned through the study of what others have done in similar situations and through a thorough analysis of the focal consumer. To assist in strategy formulation, a growing number of ad agencies have created a position called the account planner. This person's job is to synthesize all relevant consumer research and draw inferences from it that will help define a coherent advertising strategy. You will learn a great deal more about the connection between ad objectives and strategy options in Chapter 10.

Execution.

The actual "doing" is the execution of the plan. It is the making and placing of ads across all media. To quote a famous bit of advertising copy from a tire manufacturer, this is where "the rubber meets the road." There are two elements to the execution of an advertising plan: determining the copy strategy and devising a media plan.

Copy Strategy. A copy strategy consists of copy objectives and methods, or tactics. The objectives state what the advertiser intends to accomplish, while the methods describe how the objectives will be achieved. Chapter 11 will deal extensively with these executional issues.

Media Plan. The media plan specifies exactly where ads will be placed and what strategy is behind their placement. In an integrated communications environment, this is much more complicated than it might first appear. Back when there were just three broadcast television networks, there were already more than a million different combinations of placements that could be made. With the explosion of media and promotion options today, the permutations are almost infinite.

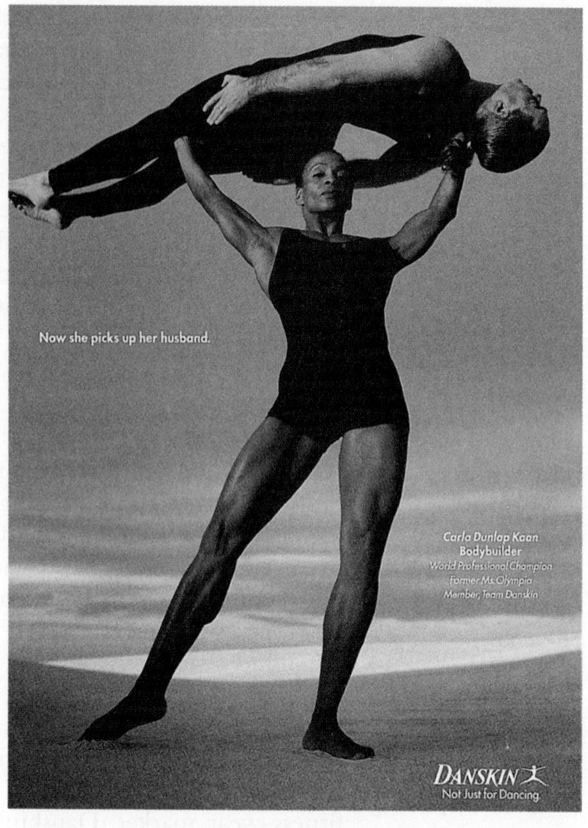

Exhibit 8.16 This ad provides an excellent example of repositioning. The slogan says it all: "Danskin—Not Just for Dancing."

Courtesy, Danskin, Inc.

It is at this point—devising a media plan—where all the money is spent, and so much could be saved. This is where the profitability of many agencies is really determined. Media placement strategy can make a huge difference in profits or losses and is considered in depth in Part 4. In addition, the dynamic influence on media planning of devices like iPad, Kindle, Droid, iPhone, HP Slate, and many more is another point of emphasis in Part 4. Mobile advertising systems developed specifically for the like's of iPad promise to cut media spend with precisely targeted messages delivered at precisely the right time.[23]

Integrated Brand Promotion. Many different forms of brand promotion may accompany the advertising effort in launching or maintaining a brand; these should be spelled out as part of the overall plan. There should be a complete integration of all communication tools in working up the plan. For example, in the launch of its Venus shaving system for women, Gillette had the usual multimillion-dollar budget allocation for traditional mass media. But along with its aggressive advertising effort, several other promotional tools were deployed.[24] At the Gillette Venus website, per Exhibit 8.17, women could sign up for an online sweepstakes to win vacations in Hawaii, New York City, and Tuscany, and provide friends' email addresses to increase their own chances of winning. Gillette also put a pair of 18-wheelers on the road (see Exhibit 8.18) to spread the word about Venus at beaches, concerts, college campuses, and store openings. So the launch of Venus integrated tools that ran the gamut from TV ads to the Web to Interstate 95. You'll learn much more about a variety of IBP tools in Part 5.

23. Niraj Chokshi, "Apple's iPad Advertising Aspirations," theatlantic.com/business, March 29, 2010.

24. Betsy Spethmann, "Venus Rising," *Promo Magazine,* April 2001, 52–61.

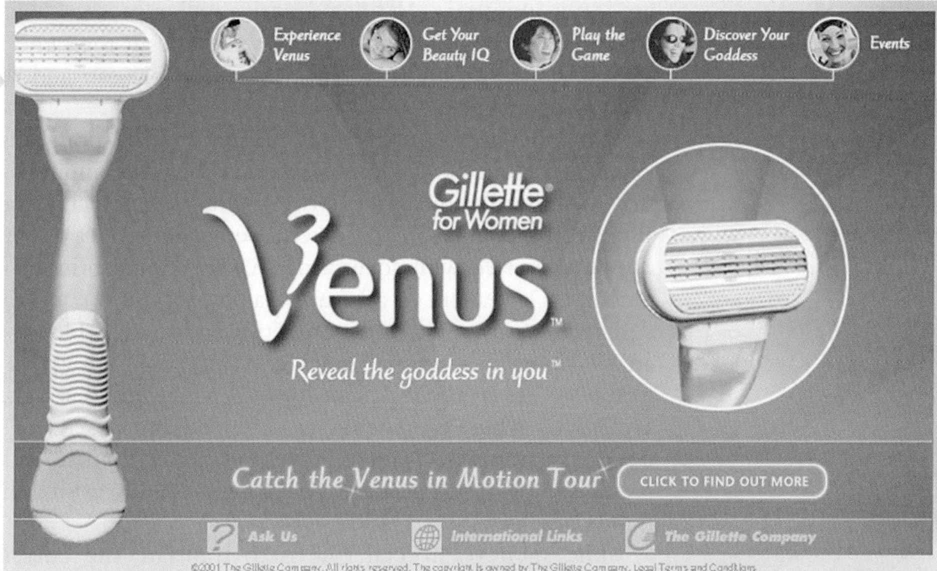

Exhibit 8.17 The Venus website has offered many possibilities, including the prospect of winning a great vacation, a beauty IQ test, and a way to "Reveal the goddess in you."

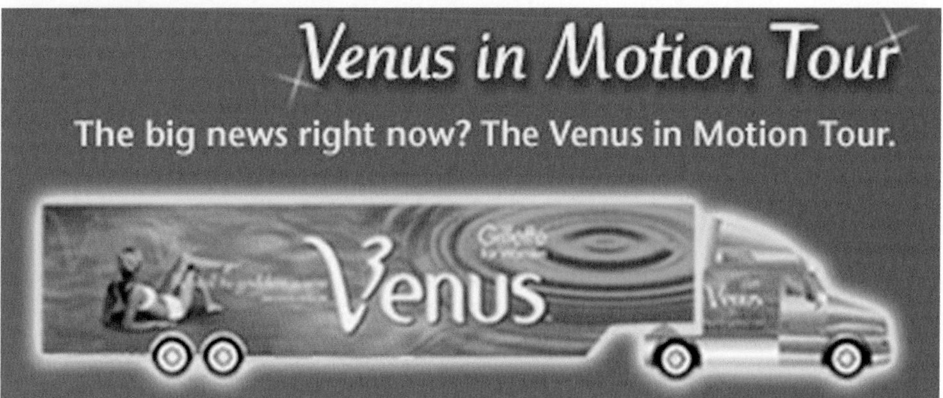

Exhibit 8.18 Hard to imagine a goddess going on the road in an 18-wheeler, but in today's world of integrated brand promotion, just about anything goes.

Courtesy, The Gillette Company; Courtesy, The Gillette Company

Evaluation.

Last but not least in an ad plan is the evaluation component. This is where an advertiser determines how the agency will be graded: what criteria will be applied and how long the agency will have to achieve the agreed-on objectives. It's critically important for the advertiser and agency to align around evaluation criteria up front. John Wanamaker's classic line still captures the challenge associated with evaluation; he said, "I know half my advertising is wasted, I just don't know which half." In a world where the pressures on companies to deliver short-term profitability continue to intensify, advertising agencies find themselves under increasing pressure to show quantifiable outcomes from all advertising and IBP activities.[25]

4 The Role of the Agency in Planning Advertising and IBP.

Now that we have covered key aspects of the advertising planning process, one other issue should be considered. Because most marketers rely heavily on the expertise of an advertising agency, understanding the role an agency plays in the advertising planning

25. Deborah Vence, "Proving Ground," *Marketing News*, May 15, 2007, 12–15.

process is important. Various agencies will approach their craft with different points of emphasis. Even though not everyone does it the same way, it is still important to ask: What contribution to the planning effort can and should an advertiser expect from its agency?

The discussion of advertising planning to this point has emphasized that the marketer is responsible for the marketing-planning inputs as a type of self-assessment that identifies the firm's basis for offering value to customers. This assessment should also clearly identify, in the external environment, the opportunities and threats that can be addressed with advertising. A firm should bring to the planning effort a well-articulated statement of a brand's value proposition and the marketing mix elements designed to gain and sustain competitive advantage. However, when client and agency are working in harmony, the agency may take an active role in helping the client formulate the marketing plan. Indeed, when things are going right, it can be hard to say exactly where the client's work ended and the agency's work began. This is the essence of teamwork, and as Steve Jobs noted about working with Apple's long-time partner, TBWA/Chiat/Day: "Creating great advertising, like creating great products, is a team effort."

The agency's crucial role is to translate the current market and marketing status of a firm and its advertising objectives into advertising strategy and, ultimately, finished advertisements and IBP materials. Here, message strategies and tactics for the advertising effort and for the efficient and effective placement of ads in media need to be hammered out. At this point, the firm (as a good client) should turn to its agency for the expertise and talent needed for planning and executing at the stage where design and creative execution bring marketing strategies to life.

In the final analysis, it's really no mystery what agencies and clients want from each other.[26] Marketers/clients know they need help in two key areas. The first involves integration. Clients have trouble keeping up with the dynamic media environment and expect their agency to be an expert on a wide array of options for getting the message out to the target consumer. So they need the various divisions and departments in an agency to be working as a team, coming up with communication solutions that build synergy between and among multiple channels. Simply stated, they want *integrated* brand promotion. Second, clients know they need new ideas and fresh approaches to break through the ever-increasing clutter in today's marketplace. Here again, the agency will be expected to ride to the rescue. Even though creativity can be an illusive aim, nonetheless, clients expect it.

In addition, an agency should never be shocked to learn that clients expect results from their investment in advertising. The relationship will unravel quickly if an agency is not sensitive to this issue. The best way for agencies to stay on top of this key issue is to spend lots of time and attention on the client's business during the ad planning process so that everyone is clear on the goals for a campaign and the metrics that will be used in judging success or failure. Most clients are reasonable people. They don't expect magic. They can live with an occasional failure. But if a campaign didn't work, the client will want to understand why, and will certainly expect better results the next time around.

Agencies also have a set of things that they want from every client. Here again the list starts with the need for collaboration and mutual respect. The agency wants to be treated as a partner, not a vendor. The agency also needs the time and resources so that it can do its best work. But of course, there is never enough time and the

26. Tim Williams and Ronald Baker, "New Value-Based Comp Model Needed," *Advertising Age,* June 11, 2007, 20, 21; Deborah Vence, "Proving Ground," *Marketing News,* May 15, 2007, 12–15.

budget is never large enough. There are two things clients must do to help everyone cope with resource issues. First, get the agency involved early in the planning process so that the agency is well informed about dates and deadlines. Second, the agency needs honest, upfront assessments regarding budget. Everyone is used to a world where one must do more with less. But it kills a relationship to find out at the last minute, "Oh no, we never had the funding for something like that."

Finally, because agencies know that clients are going to be results oriented, they are looking for clients that will set them up for success. Agencies love clients who can articulate clearly the outcomes they seek. Agencies love clients that provide constructive and timely feedback. Agencies love clients who respect and value their expertise and are ready to step aside and let the agency do its thing when the time is right. When you have that kind of trust in your expertise, you also have a partner.

Summary

1 Describe the basic components of an advertising plan.

An advertising plan is motivated by the marketing planning process and provides the direction that ensures proper implementation of an advertising campaign. An advertising plan incorporates decisions about the segments to be targeted, communications and/or sales objectives with respect to these segments, and salient message appeals. The plan should also specify the dollars budgeted for the campaign, the various communication tools that will be employed to deliver the messages, and the measures that will be relied on to assess the campaign's effectiveness.

2 Compare and contrast two fundamental approaches for setting advertising objectives.

Setting appropriate objectives is a crucial step in developing any advertising plan. These objectives are typically stated in terms of either communications or sales goals. Both types of goals have their proponents, and the appropriate types of objectives to emphasize will vary with the situation. Communication objectives feature goals such as building brand awareness or reinforcing consumers' beliefs about a brand's key benefits. Sales objectives are just that: They hold advertising directly responsible for increasing sales of a brand.

3 Explain various methods for setting advertising budgets.

Perhaps the most challenging aspect of any advertising campaign is arriving at a proper budget allocation. Companies and their advertising agencies work with several different methods to arrive at an advertising budget. A percentage-of-sales approach is a simple but naive way to deal with this issue. In the share-of-voice approach, the activities of key competitors are factored into the budget-setting process. A variety of quantitative models may also be used for budget determination. The objective-and-task approach is difficult to implement, but with practice it is likely to yield the best value for a client's advertising dollars.

4 Discuss the role of the agency in formulating an advertising plan.

An advertising plan will be a powerful tool when firms partner with their advertising agencies in its development. The firm can lead this process by doing its homework with respect to marketing strategy development and objective setting. The agency can then play a key role in managing the preparation and placement phases of campaign execution.

Key Terms

advertising plan
situation analysis
International advertising
ethnocentrism
self-reference criterion (SRC)
industry analysis
market analysis
competitor analysis
brand awareness
top-of-the-mind awareness
purchase intent
trial usage
repeat purchase
brand switching
percentage-of-sales approach
share of voice
advertising response function
objective-and-task approach
build-up analysis

Questions

1. Review the materials presented in this chapter (and anything else you may be able to find) about Apple's launch of the iPad. Based on the advertising utilized, what do you surmise must have been the value proposition for iPad at the time of its launch?

2. Now that some time has passed since the official launch of iPad, has this product lived up to its early hype? Has it become the next "big thing" for Steve Jobs and Apple?

3. Explain the connection between marketing strategies and advertising plans. What is the role of target segments in making this connection?

4. Describe the key elements in a situation analysis and provide an example of how each of these elements may ultimately influence the final form of an advertising campaign.

5. How would it ever be possible to justify anything other than sales growth as a proper objective for an advertising campaign? Is it possible that advertising could be effective yet not yield growth in sales?

6. What types of objectives would you expect to find in an ad plan that featured direct response advertising?

7. Write an example of a workable advertising objective that would be appropriate for a service like the Geek Squad.

8. In what situations would share of voice be an important consideration in setting an advertising budget? What are the drawbacks of trying to incorporate share of voice in budgeting decisions?

9. What is it about the objective-and-task method that makes it the preferred approach for the sophisticated advertiser? Describe how build-up analysis is used in implementing the objective-and-task method.

10. Briefly discuss the appropriate role to be played by advertising agencies and their clients in the formulation of marketing and advertising plans.

Experiential Exercises

1. Without energy companies, the world would lack health care, farm equipment, automobiles, indoor plumbing, and computers. Despite the many ways in which energy businesses improve the quality of life for the world's nearly 7 billion people, ad agencies face enormous challenges planning campaigns for energy firms. Analyze a current advertisement for a global energy company and explain how current and past events in the company's political, social, and competitive surroundings have shaped the campaign's message and visuals.

2. Form into teams and devise a campaign for a brand using one of the seven advertising objectives discussed in the chapter (increase awareness, change consumers' beliefs, influence purchase intent, stimulate trial use, create repeat purchasers, cause brand switching, increase sales). What messages and themes did you use to achieve your objective? How did the advertising objective guide the planning process for your group? Present your idea to the class and let others judge the ad's effectiveness as it relates to your chosen objective.

3. Working in small teams, prepare a situation analysis that could be included in an advertising plan for the online employment site Monster. The analysis should identify key factors that you consider most relevant to such a campaign and a brief assessment of each. Present your findings to the class in a 10- to 15-slide presentation.

4. Working in the same teams, identify potential placement and promotional opportunities that could be part of the media plan for a Monster campaign.

Part 3

The Creative Process

This section of the text marks an important transition in our study of advertising and IBP. The topics to this point have laid out the essential process and planning issues that make advertising and integrated brand promotion powerful business communication tools. Now we need to take the plunge into the actual preparation of advertising and IBP materials.

Creativity is the soul of advertising and IBP. Without the creative execution—no one will pay any attention. It's the one thing that communication cannot get by without. Yet most advertising and promotion books treat it as either a bunch of creative "rules" or dry lectures about the value of various fonts. We take a different approach. We first consider the idea of creativity itself: what is it, what distinguishes it, what is its beauty, when is it a beast? What makes creative people creative? We then present the creative/managerial interface—which doesn't always go smoothly but is a real and valuable part of the creative process. We discuss honestly what many textbooks don't mention at all: the problem of the competing reward systems of brand managers, account executives, and the creatives. We then offer a chapter like no other—Creative Message Strategy—in which we detail 10 message strategies and their strategic pluses and minuses. We then offer the best basic chapter on copywriting, art direction, and production available. These chapters have been developed and refined with constant input from industry professionals. If you read them carefully, you will know a lot about the process and execution of the creative effort.

Chapter 9

Managing Creativity in Advertising and Integrated Brand Promotion A famous dancer once said, "If I could describe dancing, I wouldn't have to do it." Well, we feel the same way about creativity in advertising—it really is impossible to describe fully. But in Chapter 9, "Managing Creativity in Advertising and Integrated Brand Promotion," we do our best to give you insights into the creative process by giving examples of how the creative process is worked out in an advertising context—how the "creatives" work with the "strategists." Here, special attention is paid to working through the tension that inevitably arises in the creative/management interface. Beyond strategy and management, though, we also try to provide insight into this wonderfully slippery thing called creativity. We do this by drawing on many sources and the examples of some of the most creative minds of the past century, from physics to painting. Although creativity is creativity, we move from the general to discussing the particular context of advertising creativity and its unique opportunities and problems. Creativity is the soul of advertising, and this chapter tries to reveal the magic of advertising that comes from the creativity.

Chapter 10

Creative Message Strategy Chapter 10, "Creative Message Strategy," is a chapter like no other anywhere. We take 10 key and primary message objectives and the multiple matching strategies of each and explore them in detail—including the newest strategic objective of tying a brand's appeal to social and cultural movements (think "green"). We give you a lot of specific real-world examples and walk you through each one. We discuss advantages and disadvantages of each and tell you when they should be used and when they should not.

Chapter 11

Executing the Creative Chapters 9–10 establish the process and context for the creative effort. Chapter 11 follows through on that context and describes the actual effort involved in bringing the "creative" to life through copywriting, art direction, and production. Executing the creative begins with the "creative brief": the details relating to how the creative effort can be manifest in the presentation of a brand to the target audiences. The entire creative team—copywriter, art director, account planner, and media planner—work together with the creative brief to build ads for any and all media. Copywriting explores the development of copy, including guidelines for writing effective copy and common mistakes in copywriting. A full discussion of print, broadcast, and digital/interactive copy formats are considered. A typical copy approval process used by advertisers and agencies is also presented. In Executing the Creative, you will first learn about creating effective print advertisements destined for magazines, newspapers, and direct-marketing promotions. The nature of the illustration, design, and layout components of print advertising are considered. Then the exciting and complex process of creating broadcast advertising is discussed. The emphasis in this chapter is on the creative team and how creative concepts are brought to life. This section follows a preproduction, production, and postproduction sequence. Once again, art direction and production for application in digital/interactive media, including mobile marketing applications, are considered.

Chapter 9

Managing Creativity in Advertising and Integrated Brand Promotion

After reading and thinking about this chapter, you will be able to do the following:

1. Describe the core characteristics of great creative minds.
2. Contrast the role of an agency's creative department with that of business managers/account executives and explain the tensions between them.
3. Assess the role of teams in managing tensions and promoting creativity in advertising and IBP applications.
4. Examine yourself and your own passion for creativity.

SPONSORED BY Charmin
SITORSQUAT
A place to find and record bathrooms anywhere in the world.
Version 2.01
Please email questions concerns or suggestions to support@sitorsquat.com

Introductory Scenario: Creativity Begets a Creepy King.

In 2004, Crispin Porter + Bogusky (CP+B) was the hot little underdog agency working on low-budget but high-buzz campaigns for clients like Mini, IKEA, and Molson. The business press had fallen in love with CP+B as the so-called prototype of ad agency fused with PR firm.[1] The agency's chief creative force, Alex Bogusky, was anointed as the ad industry guru who had figured out how to thrive in a world where 30-second TV ads appeared on everybody's death watch.[2] CP+B was thriving in its role as the underdog, but then along came the King—Burger King, that is—and nothing would ever be the same.

In 2004, Burger King was in pretty rough shape. Customer traffic was steadily declining and the product line was in need of some serious excitement. Poor results hadn't been good for Burger King's ad agencies either; four of them had been hired and fired in the previous four years. Given this track record, many agencies might have shied away from signing on with the King, but not feisty little CP+B. Skeptics, however, predicted doom and gloom. The sentiment was that CP+B had yet to prove itself with a major mass-market client. Doomsayers expected that CP+B's culture of creativity would be stifled by a company that expected to communicate with customers through 30-second TV spots.[3] Could the underdog survive?

It didn't take long for CP+B to give the King a new look. Right from the start, CP+B showed its dexterity with creative that befuddled the skeptics and maxed out the buzz factor. And confirming the basic thesis of Chapter 6, newfound success started with an unequivocal focus on the one target segment that everyone agreed Burger King had to win: 18- to 35-year-old males, who are among the heaviest users of fast foods of all kinds. With the target segment well defined, CP+B unleashed a series of offbeat characters to engage the segment. "Subservient Chicken" started it all with a viral, online campaign hyping the new TenderCrisp chicken sandwich. Next up was "Blingo," an over-the-top rapper who mocked diet-crazed consumers and pushed the Angus steak burger as the antidote to politically correct fast food.

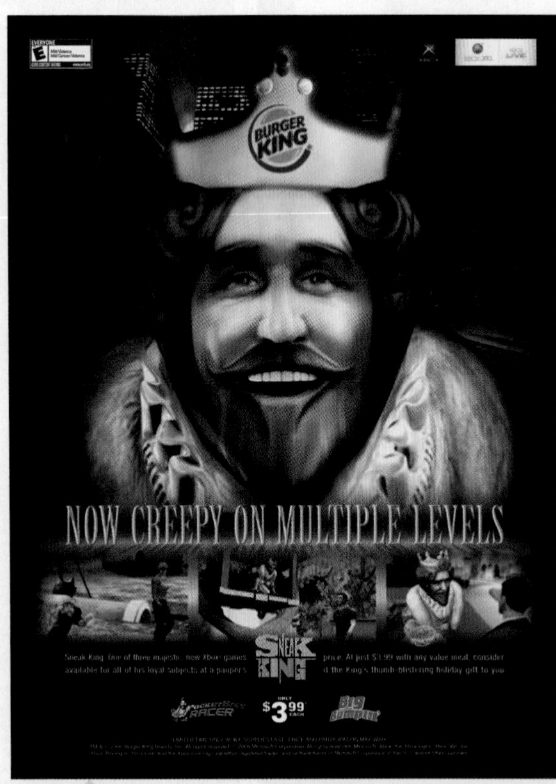

Exhibit 9.1 The King offered his loyal subjects a great deal with value meals; few could resist his creepy charm.

And of course, CP+B would resurrect The King, with a new and very strange persona. The King's first job would be to revive the breakfast menu, but ultimately he introduced us to a whole new dimension for evaluating corporate icons: No one does *creepy* better than The King. He also proved to be a selling machine. For example, a holiday promo with Xbox for the advergames Pocketbike Racer and Big Bumpin (see Exhibit 9.1) set sales records.[4] Not only did more than 2 million people pay $3.99 for a videogame, but they also took home with them a stealth advertisement for Burger King. Every time they played the game, it was one more subtle plug for Burger King. And it just so happens that purchasers were those young-adult males who don't watch much TV but instead spend some 20 hours per week playing video games. Gone are the concerns about CP+B's ability to survive a relationship with a hard-to-please, mass-market client.

1. Warren Berger, "Dare-Devils," *Business 2.0,* April 2004, 111–116.
2. Matthew Creamer, "Crispin Ups Ante," *Advertising Age,* January 10, 2005, S-1, S-2.
3. Ibid.
4. Kate MacArthur, "BK Sets High Score with its Adver-games," *Advertising Age,* January 8, 2007, 3, 31.

Ethics

CP+B's Not-So-Secret Recipe for "Hoopla"

Many have tried to decode the CP+B model to understand the agency's process for achieving creative breakthroughs. Now it turns out that the principals at CP+B have written a book (with Warren Berger) to give us the treasure map. If we can take them at their word (and keep in mind that these are folks who love a good practical joke) then the creatives at CP+B try to follow a few soft and loose principles to help them "rock the boat." They say it's just a matter of emulating P. T. Barnum and focusing on the Hoopla. In their own words, the seven key elements for manufacturing Hoopla are mutation, invention, candor, mischief, connection, pragmatism, and momentum. See if you believe...

Mutation: Make a decision that you will always do things differently. Give yourself an attitude adjustment. Start by looking for the established rules and then find a way to violate them. The folks at CP+B claim that "just about every major success we had came as a result of a conscious decision to reject a basic premise or fundamental principle of our industry or of our client's category."

Invention: Consumers constantly crave things that are new and different. As a result, invention is at the heart of Hoopla. CP+B likes to portray itself as an idea factory: constantly in the business of inventing new ideas. One business publication, *Fast Company,* even described CP+B as an agency where "ideas are an almost unhealthy obsession." What's the best way to get started in finding new ideas? Per Bogusky: "Do the opposite of what everybody else does."

Candor: Don't overlook your flaws and limitations. Don't be afraid to talk about them. "If you have a big wart on your face, you'd better make that your thing. Make people love the wart. Convince everyone that it's a beauty mark. Don't waste a second trying to hide it." CP+B claims that it is possible to generate a barrage of Hoopla around a product's "wart-like" limitations, and it is often the case that these limitations are the things that make the product unique and special.

Mischief: No surprise here. CP+B has always tended to "celebrate the troublemaker and pay attention to the rebel." Tricks, pranks, and playfully naughty behavior keep people interested and potentially more engaged with the ultimate message. For example, in the Whopper Freakout campaign, customers in a few restaurants were told the sandwich had been discontinued. No more Whoopers! The hoax was filmed via hidden cameras and the video piped back into TV ads showing the most outraged customers. Sales soared.

Connection: When you adopt the philosophy that *everything* is media, it's much easier to surround the consumer with your message and make a deep connection on behalf of the brand. This also makes it possible to build momentum at the grassroots level without spending huge sums of money. To really connect, stop shouting and get into a conversation. Remember, the good conversationalist "listens, answers questions, and engages the other party in a discussion." Social media make the conversation easy to do.

Pragmatism: People like stuff they can use. And fun stuff. Stuff they can pass around. There's no reason that advertising has to be useless stuff that people just ignore or dispose of as fast as possible. Alex Bogusky maintains that the most pragmatic way to promote a product is to just make the product experience better in some way, say by wrapping the product in better or reusable packaging, or by adding little gifts or perks for a repeat customer. Critical to Hoopla: Zero in on the product; find lots of little ways to make it more useful.

Momentum: Choose the right goal. Brand awareness is a simple goal. Momentum is what you really want. Brands have momentum when people are talking about them. News stories are being done about them. Bloggers are arguing about them. Celebrities are seen with them. Product enthusiasts are putting up YouTube videos showing their latest goofy antics. And so on. It's thus very easy to know whether or not your brand has momentum. This is what you're after. Momentum is about constant reinvention and doing tons of work. But it makes clients very happy.

Sources: "The Craziest Ad Guys in America," *BusinessWeek,* May 22, 2006, 73–80; Crispin Porter + Bogusky with Warren Berger, *Hoopla,* Brooklyn, NY: PowerHouse Books, 2006; Suzänne Vranica, "Hey, No Whopper on the Menu?!" *The Wall Street Journal*, February 8, 2008, B3.

It's not just the offbeat and out-of-the-box characters that make this story worth telling. Unlike its predecessors, CP+B did not get fired after one year. More importantly, it really did help turn around the fast food business for Burger King, and the success proved sustainable. Five years into the relationship, Burger King was celebrating 20 consecutive quarters of same-store sales growth, a key performance metric in the fast feeder business.[5] Burger King was relevant again and a part of the everyday conversations of men 18 to 35. For their work with Burger King and other clients like Domino's and The Gap, CP+B won lots of awards, including the title "Agency of the Decade" from *Advertising Age*.[6]

So in a matter of just a few years, CP+B went from Underdog to Big Dog. Yet it is noteworthy that Crispin remains an agency that the professional critics scold for edgy campaigns like Whopper Virgins and Sponge Bob SquareButt.[7] Hence, the agency's seven elements for creating "Hoopla," described in the *Ethics* box, will likely rile its disbelievers. But in a chapter on advertising creativity, this is exactly what we should expect. Creative people and creative organizations have to be risk takers. They shake things up. They step on some people's toes. They are commonly boastful, which of course irks their critics even more. They do things differently. So in a discussion of creativity, we should expect stories about great successes, and stories about great failures. But there can be absolutely no doubt that creativity is the secret ingredient in great advertising.[8] In this chapter we will attempt both to convince you of that and to help you understand how to get more of the secret ingredient into your recipe.

Why Does Advertising Need Creativity?

So what is it about creativity that makes it such a big deal in the advertising business? Why do big successful marketing firms like Procter & Gamble send their employees on expensive junkets to the Cannes Lions International Advertising Festival to make connections with the best creative minds in the ad business? Why is creativity the secret sauce that determines the winners and losers? What gives?

There are numerous ways that creativity contributes, but let's start with the pervasive problem of advertiser clutter. Everyone hates ad clutter. So to try to overcome it advertisers generate more ads, which typically just increase the clutter. Yes, clutter begets more clutter in a process that no one seems to be able to shut off.[9] If you want your message heard, you'll need a way to stand out from the crowd, and that will require good creative. Research shows that a primary benefit of award-winning, creative ads is that they break through the clutter and get remembered.[10] But as suggested by the cartoon in Exhibit 9.2, part of the challenge is always to make sure that the brand gets remembered as part of the process. Heed the warning...

So for starters we need to get the consumer's attention and be memorable. But that's hardly enough. Going back to Burger King's issues in 2004, the problem wasn't that consumers were unaware of Burger King or didn't know

5. Emily York, "Economy, Rivals, No Match for BK's Marketing," *Advertising Age,* May 5, 2008, 4, 58.

6. "Ad Age's Best of the Decade—Agencies," *Advertising Age,* December 14, 2009, 6.

7. Eloy Trevino and Scott Davis, "There's Nothing New in Desperate Marketing," *Advertising Age,* April 23, 2007, 22; Jeremy Mullman and Emily York, "What Crispin's Lauded BK Work Doesn't Do: Gain Ground on McD's," *Advertising Age,* June 22, 2009, 5, 31.

8. Sheila Sasser and Scott Koslow, "Desperately Seeking Advertising Creativity," *Journal of Advertising,* Winter 2008, 5–19.

9. Matthew Creamer, "Caught in the Clutter Crossfire: Your Brand," *Advertising Age,* April 2, 2007, 1, 35

10. Brian Till and Daniel Baack, "Recall and Persuasion: Does Creative Advertising Matter?" *Journal of Advertising,* Fall 2005, 47–57; Daniel Baack, Rick Wilson, and Brian Till, "Creativity and Memory Effects," *Journal of Advertising,* Winter 2008, 85–94.

Exhibit 9.2 Fox Trot reminds us of an all too common occurrence with "creative advertising."

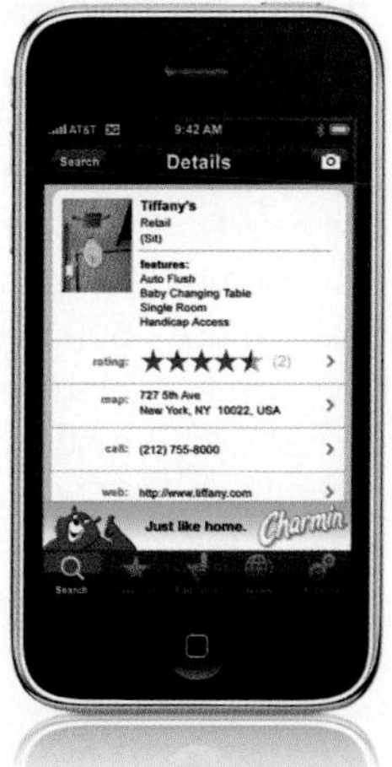

Exhibit 9.3 Gotta go? Charmin to the rescue!

Exhibit 9.4 Don't over-think it—it's an emotional appeal.

they served Whoppers. It was that Burger King was boring. Largely irrelevant. No momentum. A syndrome one could expect with many mature brands.[11] Burger King needed to become relevant again with its core customers. It needed to get back in their every-day conversations. That's what Subservient Chicken and the creepy King did for Burger King. All of a sudden, it's relevant, in play. This clearly called for a huge dose of creativity. Another brand that stays relevant with its core customers through big doses of creativity is featured in the *Social Media* box and Exhibit 9.3.

Another way of saying it is that great brands make emotional connections with consumers. You can advertise your tires through a lot of mundane details, or you can engage consumers emotionally, as in Exhibit 9.4. Brands make emotional connections when they engage consumers through complex sensory experiences and deep emotional episodes.[12] Advertising and IBP in its many forms helps create these experiences, but great creative execution brings it all to life. For instance, Apple's iPod wasn't the first MP3 player. Creative Technology Ltd. had a good one on the market almost two years before Apple.[13] But iPod

11. Karen Machleit, Chris Allen, and Thomas Madden, "The Mature Brand and Brand Interest," *Journal of Marketing,* October 1993, 72–82.

12. Marc Gobe, *Emotional Branding: The New Paradigm for Connecting Brands to People* (New York: Allworth, 2001); Hamish Pringle and Peter Field, "Why Emotional Messages Beat Rational Ones," *Advertising Age,* March 2, 2009, 13,

13. Cris Prystay, "When Being First Doesn't Make You No. 1," *The Wall Street Journal,* August 12, 2004, B1, B2.

Social Media

Creativity, Going Mobile... beep, beep!

Marketers have always embraced the idea that it is good to have consumers talking about their brands. But in a world where millions of the conversations have shifted to online, the stakes have been raised. Call it building the buzz ... maintaining momentum ... being part of the conversation of your target audience ... staying relevant. Whichever you call out, it is critically important. Not so hard to do if you market products like iPad or Starbucks—brand zealots in categories like these love to tweet about their latest encounters with the brand. But what about all those uninvolving products? Things like toothpaste and toilet paper. Building buzz and staying relevant in categories like these will require frequent and healthy doses of creativity.

Creative outcomes are also fostered when brand builders have aspirations for serving consumers that go beyond the basic benefits. Take Charmin bathroom tissue. For the last decade Charmin has embraced the challenge of helping consumers find safe and clean restrooms when they need them the most—away from home. So it made perfect sense for the Charmin brand to partner with SitOrSquat Inc. to help consumers find clean restrooms whenever and wherever. Or simply stated, there's an app for it—a Charmin sponsored app, that is.

The SitOrSquat iPhone app uses GPS technology to allow users to find public restrooms in any location, and then asks the user to provide a rating of the experience for potential future users. The 'Sit' rating is of course a good thing, while 'Squat' means undesirable. The Charmin brand shows up frequently as part of the interface. For example, those loveable Charmin bears show up in a desperate state as the application loads (see Exhibit 9.3), and a Charmin banner ad stays on screen throughout, with the tagline: *Gotta go? Relax ... we got your back.* According to Charmin's brand manager, Jacques Hagopian: "Our goal is to connect Charmin with innovative conversations and solutions as a brand that understands the importance of bringing the best bathroom experience to consumers, even when they're away from home." That's what the SitOrSquat app is all about.

But did it build buzz? Get Charmin in the conversation? Keep the brand relevant? After just 12 months more than 500,000 consumers had downloaded this Charmin-branded app where it would live permanently on their mobile phones. In that same period the program generated +500 million media impressions, numerous blogger posts, and coverage by +200 news outlets. All for a very modest ad spend. *The Wall Street Journal* designated SitOrSquat among the best marketing programs of the year. We call it just darn creative.

Sources: "Charmin Launches Global Sponsorship with SitOrSquat Website and Mobile Phone Application," prnewswire.com, March 24, 2009; Mickey Kham, "P&G's Charmin Brand Runs First Mobile Sponsorship," mobilemarketer.com, April 10, 2009; Suzanne Vranica, "Babies and Tigers: Best and Worst Ads of 2009," *The Wall Street Journal*, December 21, 2009, B1, B6.

was the first MP3 player to be brought to the market with great advertising; advertising that made iPod synonymous with hip and cool; advertising that made the brand relevant in a social context. And it all worked because of the simple creative genius of the iPod silhouettes. They were everywhere and we couldn't stop watching them. They showed us what we needed to do if we too wanted to become cool. Get that thing. So is creativity important to advertising? In today's world, there would be no advertising without it.

1 Creativity Across Domains.

The creative mind plays with the objects it loves.

—C. G. Jung[14]

14. Carl G. Jung, cited in Astrid Fitzgerald, *An Artist's Book of Inspiration: A Collection of Thoughts on Art, Artists, and Creativity* (New York: Lindisfarne, 1996), 58.

Before examining how the creative function plays out in the world of advertising and IBP, let's consider creativity as it manifests in other domains. Creativity, in its essence, is the same no matter what the domain. People who create, create, whether they write novels, take photographs, ponder the particle physics that drives the universe, craft poetry, write songs, play a musical instrument, dance, make films, design buildings, paint, or make ads. Great ads can be truly great creative accomplishments.

Creativity is the ability to consider and hold together seemingly inconsistent elements and forces, making a new connection. This ability to step outside of everyday logic, to free oneself of thinking in terms of "the way things are" or "the way things have to be," apparently allows creative people to put things together in a way that, once we see it, makes sense, is interesting, and is creative. To see love and hate as the same entity, to see "round squares," or to imagine time bending like molten steel is to have this ability. Ideas born of creativity reveal their own logic, and then we all say, "Oh, I see."

Creativity is sometimes seen as a gift; a special way of seeing the world. Throughout the ages, creative people have been seen as special, revered and reviled, loved and hated. They have served as powerful political instruments (for good and evil), and they have been ostracized, imprisoned, and killed for their art. For example, creativity has been associated with various forms of madness:

> *Madness, provided it comes as the gift of heaven, is the channel by which we receive the greatest blessings... [T]he men of old who gave their names saw no disgrace or reproach in madness; otherwise they would not have connected it with the name of the noblest of all arts, the art of discerning the future, and called by our ancestors, madness is a nobler thing than sober sense... [M]adness comes from God, whereas sober sense is merely human.*
>
> —Socrates[15]

Creativity reflects early childhood experiences, social circumstances, and cognitive styles. In one of the best books ever written on creativity, *Creating Minds,* Howard Gardner examines the lives and works of seven of the greatest creative minds of the 20th century: Sigmund Freud, Albert Einstein, Pablo Picasso (see Exhibit 9.5), Igor Stravinsky, T. S. Eliot, Martha Graham, and Mahatma Gandhi.[16] His work reveals fascinating similarities among great creators. All seven of these individuals, from physicist to modern dancer, were self-confident, alert, unconventional, hardworking, and committed obsessively to their work. Social life or hobbies are almost immaterial, representing at most a fringe on the creator's work time.[17]

Apparently, total commitment to one's craft is the rule. Although this commitment sounds positive, there is also a darker reflection:

> *[T]he self confidence merges with egotism, egocentrism, and narcissism: highly absorbed, not only wholly involved in his or her own projects, but likely to pursue them at costs of other individuals.*[18]

Let's be clear: One should not stand between a great creator and his or her work. It's not safe; you'll have tracks down your back. Or maybe the creator will just ignore you. Not coincidentally, these great creative minds had troubled personal lives and simply did not have time for ordinary people (such as their families). According to

15. Socrates, quoted in Plato, *Phaedrus and the Seventh and Eighth Letters,* Walter Hamilton, trans. (Middlesex, England: Penguin, 1970), 46–47, cited in Kay Redfield Jamison, *Touched with Fire: Manic-Depressive Illness and the Artistic Temperament* (New York: Free Press, 1993), 51.

16. Howard Gardner, *Creating Minds: An Anatomy of Creativity Seen through the Lives of Freud, Einstein, Picasso, Stravinsky, Eliot, Graham, and Gandhi* (New York: Basic Books, 1993).

17. Ibid., 364.

18. Ibid.

Exhibit 9.5 Pablo Picasso, seen here in a self-portrait, was one of the greatest creative minds of the 20th century. Read about the life of Pablo Picasso at Artcyclopedia (www.artcyclopedia.com), or visit the official Pablo Picasso website (www.picasso.fr).

1950-1-1 Picasso, Pablo, Self Portrait with Palette, 1906, Philadelphia Museum of Art: A.E. Gallatin Collection

Gardner, they were generally not very good to those around them. This was true even of Gandhi.

All seven of these great creative geniuses were also great self-promoters. Well-recognized creative people are not typically shy about seeking exposure for their work. Apparently, fame in the creative realm rarely comes to the self-effacing and timid. (A lesson we also see illustrated nicely by CP+B's self-promotional book *Hoopla.*)

All seven of these great creators were, very significantly, childlike in a critical way. All of them had the ability to see things as a child does. Einstein spent much of his career revolutionizing physics by pursuing in no small way an idea he produced as a child: What would it be like to move along with a strand of pure light? Picasso commented that it ultimately was his ability to paint like a child (along with amazingly superior technical skills) that explained much of his greatness. Freud's obsession with and interpretation of his childhood dreams had a significant role in what is one of his most significant works, *The Interpretation of Dreams.*[19] T. S. Eliot's poetry demonstrated imaginative abilities that typically disappear past childhood. The same is true of Martha Graham's modern dance. Even Gandhi's particular form of social action was formulated with a very simple and childlike logic at its base. These artists and creative thinkers never lost the ability to see the ordinary as extraordinary, to not have their particular form of imagination beaten out of them by the process of "growing up."

Of course, the problem with this childlike thinking is that these individuals also behaved as children throughout most of their lives. Their social behavior was egocentric and selfish. They expected those around them to be willing to sacrifice at the altar of their gift. Gardner put it this way: "[T]he carnage around a great creator is not a pretty sight, and this destructiveness occurs whether the individual is engaged in solitary pursuit or ostensibly working for the betterment of humankind."[20] They can, however, be extraordinarily charming when it suits their ambitions. They could be monsters at home, and darlings when performing.

Apparently, the creative mind also desires marginality.[21] They love being outsiders. This marginality seems to have been absolutely necessary to these people, and provided them with some requisite energy.

Emotional stability did not mark these creative lives either. All but Gandhi had a major mental breakdown at some point in their lives, and Gandhi suffered from at least two periods of severe depression. Extreme creativity, just as the popular myth suggests, seems to come at some psychological price.

Creative Genius in the Advertising Business.

Although perhaps not as influential as the Gandhis or the Freuds, it is common to see individuals from the ad business praised for remarkable careers that have

19. Ibid., 145; Sigmund Freud, The Interpretation of Dreams, in A. A. Brill (Ed.), *The Basic Writings of Sigmund Freud* (New York: Modern Library, 1900/1938).

20. Gardner, *Creating Minds,* 369.

21. Ibid.

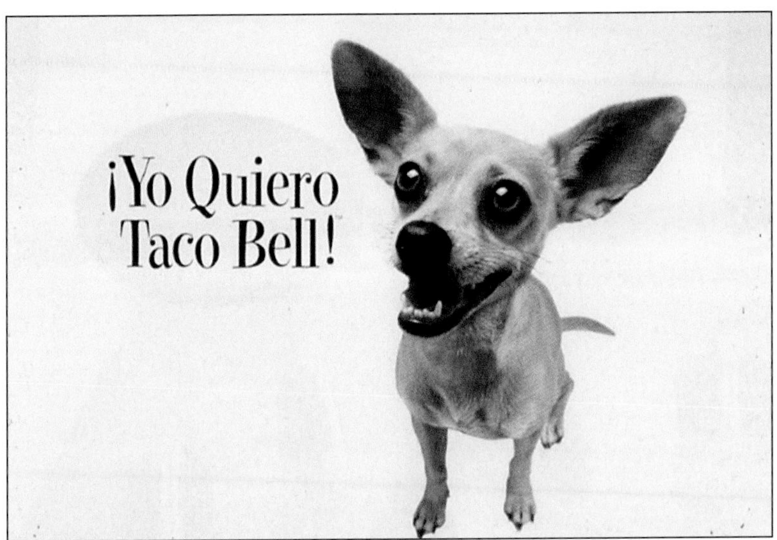

Exhibit 9.6 Chihuahuas want Taco Bell.

Exhibit 9.7 The ad that changed the music business forever.

AP Topic Gallery/Taco Bell; Courtesy, Apple Computers, Inc.; Ad Agency: TWBA Chiat Day, LA; Photographer: Matthew Welch; Model: Emory Livers/LA Models

clearly revealed sparks of creative genius. One example is Lee Clow, who at the time of this writing was 66 years old and still the main creative force with TBWA/Chiat/Day. You know his work. The Energizer Bunny, billboards for Nike, "Dogs Rule" for Pedigree, and the "1984" spot that launched Apple's Mac are from his portfolio. As are the ads featured in Exhibits 9.6 and 9.7.

Lee Clow is one of the great creative maestros of the modern advertising business. *Ad Age* referred to him simply as "The Dude Who Thought Different."[22] But those who have worked at his side say his real gift is as the synthesizer. Sorting through a wall full of creative ideas in the form of rough sketches, Lee is the guy who knows how to pick a winner. The one simplest marketing idea that is most likely to resonate with consumers, as in "Impossible is Nothing" for Adidas or "Shift" for Nissan. Some say he is fervent about great creativity; others say he is prone to fits of temper and can be mean to those who don't see things his way.[23] Now doesn't that sound a lot like the other great creators discussed above?

Creativity in the Business World.

The difficulty of determining who is creative and who is not or what is creative and what is not in the artistic world is paralleled in the business world. Certainly, no matter how this trait is defined, creativity is viewed in the business world as a positive quality for employees. It has been said that creative individuals assume almost mythical status in the corporate world. Everybody needs them, but no one is sure who or what they are. Furthermore, business types often expect that working with creative people will not be easy. Often, they are right.

Can One Become Creative?

This is an important question. The popular answer in a democratic society would be to say, "Yes, sure; you too can be a Picasso." But in the end the genius of a Picasso or an Einstein is a pretty high standard, one that most of us will not be able to achieve. And given some of the costs associated with intense creativity, maybe we don't want to be that anyway. But this question really depends on what one means by *creativity*. Is a person creative because he or she can produce a creative result? Or is a person

22. Alice Cuneo, "The Dude Who Thought Different," *Advertising Age*, July 31, 2006, 1, 25.

23. Ibid.

Exhibit 9.8 Artist David Ross' Swimming Suits, a view of corporate individuality and creative that is often shared by art directors and copywriters.

creative because of the way he or she thinks? Further, who gets to determine what is creative and what is not? When an elephant paints holding a brush with its trunk, and the paintings sell for thousands of dollars, does it mean that the elephant is creative?

Even though there are numerous elusive elements on the path to being creative, we need to keep coming back to the point that in the advertising business, we can't do without it. So we will take the point of view that although few of us are destined to become the next Pablo Picasso or even Lee Clow, that doesn't mean that we can't learn how to improve our own level of creativity. We all start from a different baseline, but we all can learn to be more creative and contribute to the creativity process in an advertising application. We'll revisit this later in the chapter.

Against Stereotype.

In concluding our discussion about the traits of extraordinarily creative people, a couple of notes of caution are in order. First, it should be understood that just because you are in a "creative" job, it doesn't follow that you are actually creative. Second, just because you are on the account or business side (a.k.a. "a suit") doesn't mean you are uninspired (as in Exhibit 9.8). As the folks at CP+B will tell you, good ideas can come from anyone, anywhere.[24] Sometimes even the client (gasp!) can have a good idea. Tension and conflict (a.k.a., suits versus the creatives) are regular occurrences in producing great advertising. It's normal. One needs to anticipate and manage this conflict in positive ways to get good outcomes. We take up the issues involved in this challenge in the section to follow.

2 Agencies, Clients, and the Creative Process.

As an employee in an agency creative department, you will spend most of your time with your feet up on a desk working on an ad. Across the desk, also with her feet up, will be your partner—in my case, an art director. And she will want to talk about movies.

> *In fact, if the truth be known, you will spend fully one-fourth of your career with your feet up talking about movies. The ad is due in two days. The media space has been bought and paid for. The pressure's building. And your muse is sleeping off a drunk behind a dumpster somewhere. Your pen lies useless. So you talk movies.*

24. Warren Berger, "Dare-Devils," *Business 2.0,* April 2004, 111–116.

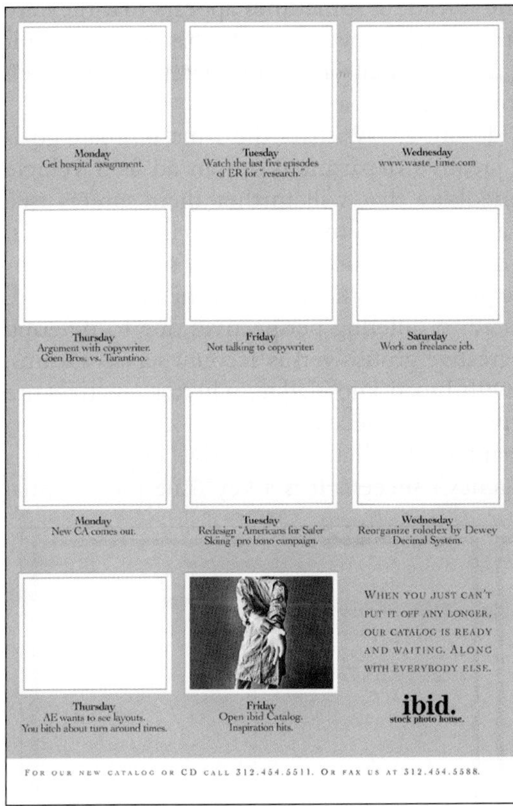

Exhibit 9.9 Companies like ibid (www.ibidphoto.com) cater to the creative: The ibid catalog offers images to jumpstart the imagination.

That's when the traffic person comes by. Traffic people stay on top of a job as it moves through the agency; which means they also stay on top of you. They'll come by to remind you of the horrid things that happen to snail-assed creative people who don't come through with the goods on time...

So you try to get your pen moving. And you begin to work; and working in this business means staring at your partner's shoes.

That's what I've been doing from 9 to 5 for almost 20 years. Staring at the bottom of the disgusting tennis shoes on the feet of my partner, parked on the desk across from my disgusting tennis shoes. This is the sum and substance of life at an agency.

—Luke Sullivan, copywriter and author[25]

Exhibit 9.9 is illustrative of many creative pursuits: lots of time trying to get an idea, or the right idea. You turn things over and over in your head, trying to see the light. You try to find that one way of seeing it that makes it all fall into place. Or it just comes to you, real easy, just like that. Magic. Every creative pursuit involves this sort of thing. However, advertising and IBP, like all creative pursuits, are unique in some respects. Ad people come into an office and try to solve a problem, always under time pressure, given to them by some businessperson. Often the problem is poorly defined, or there are competing agendas. They work for people who seem not to be creative at all, and who seem to be doing their best not to let them be creative. They are housed in the "creative department," which makes it seem as if it's some sort of warehouse where the executives keep all the creativity so that they can find it when they need it, and so that it won't get away. This implies that one can pick some up, like getting extra batteries at Target.

Oil and Water: Conflicts and Tensions in the Creative/Management Interface.

Here are some thoughts on management and creativity by two advertising greats:

> *The majority of businessmen are incapable of original thinking, because they are unable to escape from the tyranny of reason. Their imaginations are blocked.*
>
> —William Bernbach[26]

> *If you're not a bad boy, if you're not a big pain in the ass, then you are in some mush in this business.*
>
> —George Lois[27]

As you can see, this topic rarely yields tepid, diplomatic comments. Advertising is produced through a social process. As a social process, however, it's marked by the struggles for control and power that occur within departments, between departments, and between the agency and its clients on a daily basis.[28]

Most research concerning the contentious environment in advertising agencies places the creative department in a central position within these conflicts. One

25. Luke Sullivan, "Staring at Your Partner's Shoes," in *Hey Whipple, Squeeze This: A Guide to Creating Great Ads* (New York: Wiley, 1998), 20–22.

26. William Bernbach, quoted in Thomas Frank, *The Conquest of Cool: Business Culture, Consumer Culture, and the Rise of Hip Consumerism* (Chicago, IL: University of Chicago Press, 1997).

27. George Lois, quoted in Randall Rothenberg, *Where the Suckers Moon* (New York: Knopf, 1994), 135–172.

28. Christy Ashley and Jason Oliver, "Creative Leaders," *Journal of Advertising*, Spring 2010, 115–130.

explanation hinges on reactions to the uncertain nature of the product of the creative department. What do they do? From the outside it sometimes appears that they are having a lot of fun and just screwing around while everyone else has to wear a suit to the office and try to sell more stuff for the client. This creates tension between the creative department and the account services department.

In addition, these two departments do not always share the same ultimate goals for advertisements. Individuals in the creative department see an ad as a vehicle to communicate a personal creative ideology that will further their careers (see Exhibit 9.10). The account manager or account executive, serving as liaison between client and agency, sees the goal of the communication as achieving some predetermined objective in the marketplace, like growing market share for the client's brand.

Another source of conflict is attributed to differing perspectives due to differing background knowledge of members of creative groups versus account services teams. Account managers must be generalists with broad knowledge, whereas creatives are specialists who must possess great expertise in a single area.

Regardless of its role as a participant in conflict, the creative department is recognized as an essential part of any agency's success. It is a key issue for potential

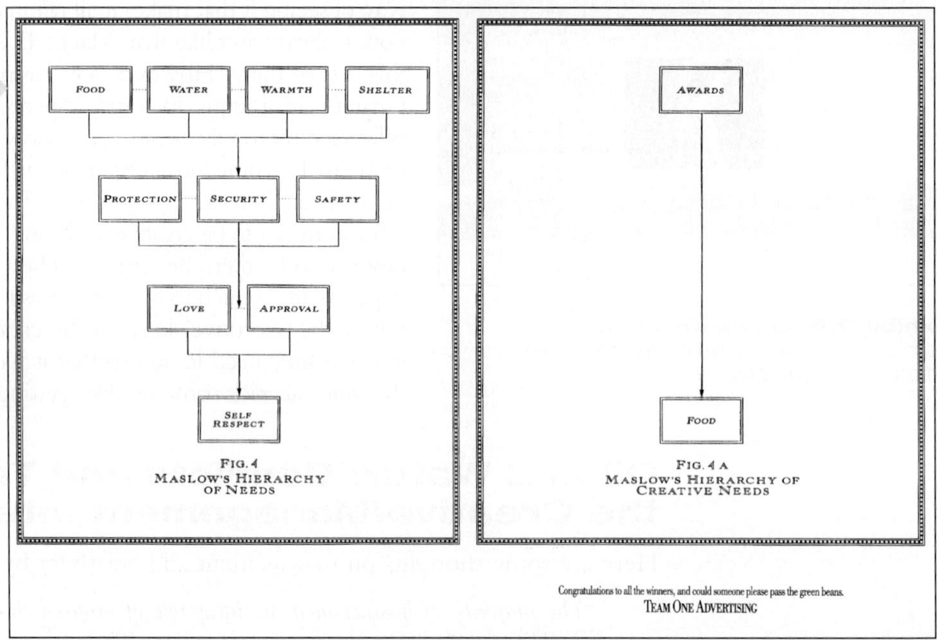

Exhibit 9.10 Team One Advertising has an interesting spin on what motivates agency creatives; here, it parodies Maslow's hierarchy to make its point.

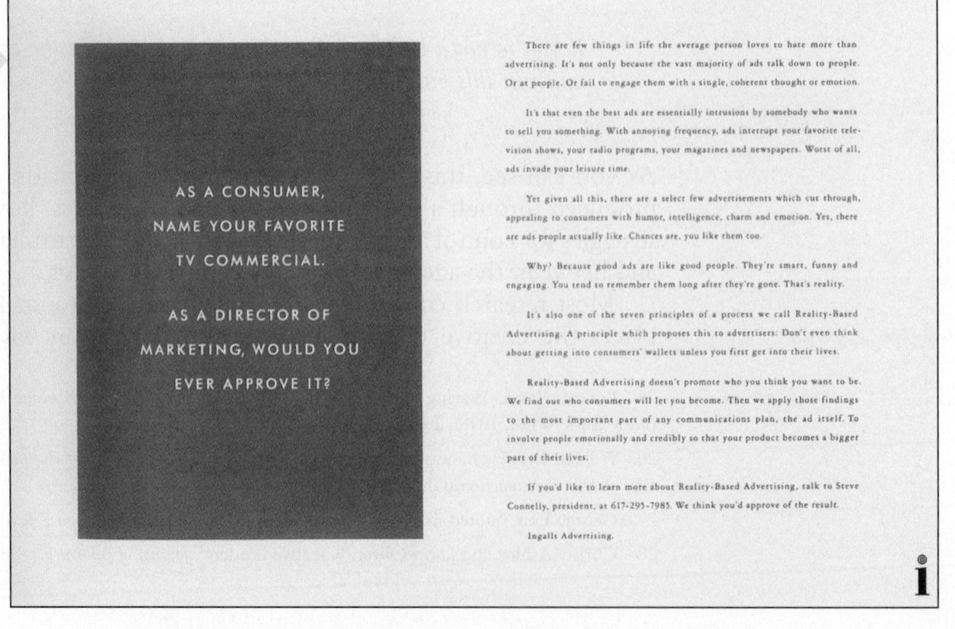

Exhibit 9.11 What clients like and what clients approve are often two very different things.

Courtesy, Team One Advertising; Ingalls Advertising

clients when they select advertising agencies. Creativity has been found to be crucial to a positive client/advertiser relationship.

However, many clients don't recognize their role in killing the very same breakthrough ideas that they claim to be looking for[29] (see also Exhibit 9.11). Anyone who has worked in the creative department of an advertising agency for any length of time has a full quiver of client stories—like the one about the client who wanted to produce a single 30-second spot for his ice cream novelty company. The creative team went to work and brought in a single spot that everyone agreed delivered the strategy perfectly, set up further possible spots in the same campaign, and, in the words of the copywriter, was just damn funny. It was the kind of commercial that you actually look forward to seeing on television. During the storyboard presentation, the client laughed in all the right places, and admitted the spot was on strategy. He then decided to move his money to a national coupon drop.

It's easy and sometimes fun to blame clients for all of the anxieties and frustrations of the creatives; especially if you've worked in a creative department. You can criticize the clients all you want and, since they aren't in the office next to you, they can't hear you. But, despite the obvious stake that creative departments have in generating superior advertising, it should be mentioned that no creative ever put $10 million of his or her own money behind a campaign.

Indeed, you can't always blame the client. Sometimes the conflicts and problems that preclude wonderful creative work occur within the walls of the advertising agency itself. To say there can be conflict between the creative department and other departments within an agency is a bit like saying there will be conflict when Jerry Springer walks into a TV studio. In advertising, the conflict often centers on the creative department versus account services. So why doesn't everybody pull together and love each other within an agency?

When a client is unhappy, it fires the agency. Billings and revenue drop. Budgets are cut. And pink slips fly. It's no wonder that conflict occurs. When someone is looking out for his or her job, it's tough not to get involved in struggles over control of the creative product. **Account executives** (AEs) are the liaison between the agency and the client. For AEs to rise in their career, they must excel in the care and feeding of clients. It's a job of negotiation, gentle prodding, and ambassadorship. For creatives to rise, their work must challenge. It must arrest attention. It must provoke. At times, it must shock. It must do all the things a wonderful piece of art must do. Yet, as we indicated earlier, this is all the stuff that makes for nervous clients. And that is an account executive's nightmare. As suggested in Exhibit 9.12, it is little wonder that it can be so hard to find AEs with just the right disposition.

This nightmare situation for the AEs produces the kind of ads that win awards for the creatives. People who win awards are recognized: Their work gets published in *The One Show* and *Communication Arts* and appears on the Clios. They are in demand and they are wined and dined by rival agencies (see Exhibit 9.13). They become famous and, yes, rich by advertising standards. Are they happier, better people? Some are. Some aren't.

So the trick is, how do you get creatives to want to pursue cool ads that also sell? The ideal AE finds a way to keep both clients and creatives happy. Not an easy thing, but in the end an essential thing. As ad agencies have downsized in recent years because of the economic slump, one of the first positions to be cut has been the AE. Given the critical role of AE's in bridging the gap between clients and creatives, cutting them out seems like a path that can only lead to more friction between agencies and clients. That's a path where nobody wins.[30]

The difficulty of assessing the effectiveness of an advertisement can also create antagonism between the creative department and the research department.[31]

29. Sheila Sasser and Scott Koslow, "Desperately Seeking Advertising Creativity," *Journal of Advertising*, Winter 2008, 5–19.

30. Jeremy Mullman, "Think Twice Before Axing Account Management," *Advertising Age*, April 26, 2010, 8.

31. A. J. Kover and S. M. Goldberg, "The Games Copywriters Play: Conflict, Quasi-Control, a New Proposal," *Journal of Advertising Research*, vol. 25, no. 4 (1995), 52–62.

Exhibit 9.12 How to identify a good AE.

For some 25 years, I was an advertising agency "AE," eventually rising through the crabgrass to become a founder, president, chairman, and now chairman emeritus of Borders, Perrin and Norrander, Inc.

During all those years, I pondered the eternal question: Why do some advertising agencies consistently turn out a superior creative product while others merely perpetuate mediocrity? Is the answer simply to hire great writers and art directors? Well, certainly that has a lot to do with it, but I would suggest that there is another vital component in the equation for creative success.

Outstanding creative work in an ad agency requires a ferocious commitment from all staffers, but especially from the account service person. The job title is irrelevant—account executive, account manager, account supervisor—but the job function is critical, particularly when it comes to client approvals. Yes, I am speaking of the oft-maligned AE, the "suit" who so frequently is the bane of the Creative Department.

So how in the wide world does one identify this rare species, this unusual human being who is sensitive to the creative process and defends the agency recommendations with conviction and vigor? As you might expect, it is not easy. But there are some signals, some semihypothetical tests that can be used as diagnostic tools:

To begin with, look for unflappability, a splendid trait to possess in the heat of battle. In Australia last year, I heard a chap tell about arriving home to "find a bit of a problem" under his bed. An eight-foot python had slithered in and coiled around the man's small dog. Hearing its cries, he yanked the snake out from under the mattress, pried it loose from the mutt, tossed it out the door, and "dispatched it with a garden hoe." Was he particularly frightened or distressed? Not at all. "I've seen bigger snakes," he said, helping himself to another Foster's Lager. Now, that's the kind of disposition that wears well in account service land.

Source: Wes Perrin, "How to Identify a Good AE," *Communication Arts Advertising Annual 1988* (Palo Alto, CA: Coyne and Blanchard, Inc., 1988), 210.

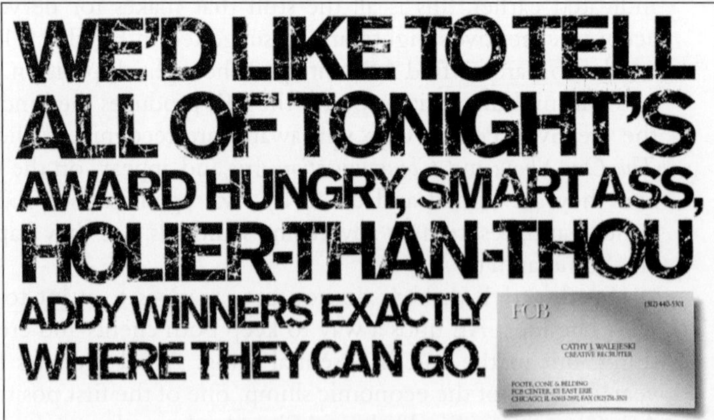

Exhibit 9.13 Foote, Cone & Belding used a bit of sassy, tongue-in-cheekiness to signal that résumés were wanted.

Courtesy, Foote, Cone & Belding

Vaughn states that the tumultuous social environment between creative departments and ad testers represents the "historical conflict between art and science... these polarities have been argued philosophically as the conflict between Idealism and Materialism or Rationalism and Empiricism."[32] In the world of advertising, people in research departments are put in the unenviable position of judging the creatives. So, again, "science" judges art. Creatives don't like this, particularly when it's bad science or not science at all. Of course, researchers are sometimes

32. R. L. Vaughn, "Point of View. Creatives versus Researchers—Must They Be Adversaries?" *Journal of Advertising Research,* vol. 22, no. 6 (1983), 45–48.

creative themselves, and they don't typically enjoy being an additional constraint on those in the creative department.

So is there any way around all the tension and conflict that is inherent in the very people-intensive business of creating advertising and integrated brand promotion? As detailed in Exhibit 9.14, the insights of John Sweeney—a true expert on advertising creativity—make it clear what *not* to do if creativity is the goal. Professor Sweeney also gives us the hint we need about what we should do. He notes that bad work is more a matter of structure than talent. So given a pool of talented people, we have to provide some structure that allows them to produce their best work. Creative types, AEs, marketing managers, and ad researchers have to find a way to make beautiful music together. Here's how they can.

One of the advantages of being a practitioner-turned-educator is the opportunity to interact with a large number of agencies. Much like Switzerland, an academic is viewed as a neutral in current affairs and not subject to the suspicions of a potential competitor.

The result of my neutral status has been the opportunity to watch different agencies produce both great and poor work. And, as a former associate creative director, I'd like to share the trends I've seen in the development of bad creative. The revelation: Bad work is more a matter of structure than talent. Here are 12 pieces of advice if you want to institutionalize bad creative work in your agency:

1. Treat your target audience like a statistic.

Substituting numbers for getting a feel for living, breathing people is a great way to make bad work inevitable. It allows you to use your gut instinct about "women 55 to 64" rather than the instinct that evolves from really understanding a group of folks. The beauty with staying on the statistical level is that you get to claim you did your homework when the creative turns out dreadful. After all, there were 47 pages of stats on the target.

2. Make your strategy a hodgepodge.

Good ads have one dominant message, just one. Most strategies that result in lousy work have lots more than one. They are political junkyards that defy a creative wunderkind to produce anything but mediocrity. So make everybody happy with the strategy and then tell your creatives to find a way to make it all work. You'll get bad work, for sure.

3. Have no philosophy.

William Bernbach believed in a certain kind of work. His people emulated his philosophy and produced a consistent kind of advertising that built a great agency. Now, to be controversial, I'll say the exact same thing about Rosser Reeves. Both men knew what they wanted, got it, and prospered.

The agency leaders who do hard sell one day, then new wave the next, create only confusion. More important, the work does not flow from a consistent vision of advertising and a code of behavior to achieve that advertising. Instead, there is the wild embrace of the latest fashion or the currently faddish bromide making the rounds at conventions. So beware of those who have a philosophy and really are true to it. They are historically at odds with lousy work.

4. Analyze your creative as you do a research report.

The cold, analytical mind does a wonderful job destroying uncomfortable, unexpected work. Demand that every detail be present in every piece of creative and say it is a matter of thoroughness. The creative work that survives your ice storm will be timid and compromised and will make no one proud.

5. Make the creative process professional.

"Creative types collect a paycheck every two weeks. They'd better produce and do it now. This is, after all, a business." The corporate performance approach is a highly recommended way of developing drab print and TV. Treating the unashamedly artistic process of making ads as if it were an offshoot of the local oil filter assembly plant promises to destroy risk taking and morale. Your work will become every bit as distinctive as a gray suit. More important, it will be on schedule. And both are fine qualities in business and we are a business, aren't we?

Continued

Exhibit 9.14 Assuring poor creative.

6. Say one thing and do another.

Every bad agency says all the right things about risk taking, loving great creative, and admiring strong creative people. It is mandatory to talk a good game and then do all the things that destroy great work. This will help keep spirits low and turnover high in the creatives who are actually talented. And then you'll feel better when they leave after a few months because you really do like strong creative people—if they just weren't so damn defensive.

7. Give your client a candy store.

To prove how hard you work, insist on showing numerous half-thought-out ideas to your client. The approved campaign will have lots of problems nobody thought about and that will make the final work a mess.

Campaigns with strong ideas are rare birds, and they need a great deal of thinking to make sure they're right. So insist on numerous campaigns and guarantee yourself a series of sparrows rather than a pair of eagles.

8. Mix and match your campaigns.

Bring three campaigns to your client, and then mix them up. Take a little bit of one and stick it on another. Even better, do it internally. It's like mixing blue, red, and green. All are fine colors, but red lacks the coolness of blue. Can't we add a little? The result of the mix will be a thick muddy clump. Just like so many commercials currently on the air.

9. Fix it in production.

Now that your procedure has created a half-baked campaign that is being mixed up with another, tell the creative to make it work by excellent production values. Then you can fire the incompetent hack when the jingle with 11 sales points is dull.

10. Blame the creative for bad creative.

After all, you told them what they should do. ("Make it totally unexpected, but use the company president and the old jingle.") The fault lies in the fact that you just can't find good talent anymore. Never mind that some creative departments have low turnover and pay smaller salaries than you do.

11. Let your people imitate.

"Chiat/Day won awards and sales for the Apple *1984* commercial, so let's do something like that for our stereo store account." This approach works wonders because your imitation appears lacking the original surprise that came from a totally expected piece of work. You can even avoid the controversy that surrounded Chiat/Day when half the industry said the ad was rotten. Your imitation can blend right in with all the other imitations and, even better, will have no strategic rationale for your bizarre execution.

12. Believe posttesting when you get a good score.

That way you can be slaughtered by your client when your sensitive, different commercial gets a score 20 points below norm. The nice things you said about posttesting when you got an excellent score with your "singing mop" commercial cannot be taken back. If you want to do good work, clients must somehow be made to use research as a tool. If you want to do bad creative, go ahead, and believe that posttesting rewards excellent work.

Naturally, a lot of bad creative results from egomania, laziness, incompetence, and client intractability—but a lot less than most believe. I have found that bad work usually comes from structures that make talented people ineffective and that demand hard work, human dedication, and tremendous financial investment to produce work that can be topped by your average high school senior.

John Sweeney, a former associate creative director at Foot, Cone & Belding, Chicago, teaches advertising at the University of North Carolina—Chapel Hill.

3 Making Beautiful Music Together: Coordination, Collaboration, and Creativity.

Metaphors help us understand, so let's use a metaphor to appreciate the challenge of executing sophisticated advertising and IBP campaigns. Executing an IBP campaign is very much like the performance of a symphony orchestra. To produce glorious music, many individuals must make their unique contributions to the performance, but it sounds right only if the maestro brings it all together at the critical moment. Make it a point to attend a symphony and get there early so that you can hear each individual musician warming up his or her instrument. Reflect on the many years of dedicated practice that this individual put in to master that instrument. Reflect on the many hours of practice that this individual put in to learn his or her specific part for tonight's performance. As you sit there listening to the warm-up, notice how the random collection of sounds becomes increasingly painful to the ears. With each musician doing his or her own thing, the sound is a collection of hoots and clangs that grows louder as the performance approaches. Mercifully, the maestro finally steps to the podium to quell the cacophony. All is quiet for a moment. The musicians focus on their sheet music for reassurance, even though by now they could play their individual parts in their sleep. Finally, the maestro calls the orchestra into action. As a group, as a collective, as a team, with each person executing a specific assignment as defined by the composer, under the direction of the maestro, they make beautiful music together.

So it goes in the world of advertising. Preparing and executing breakthrough IBP campaigns is a people-intensive business. Many different kinds of expertise will be needed to pull it off, and this means many different people must be enlisted to play a variety of roles. But some order must be imposed on the collection of players. Frequently, a maestro will need to step in to give the various players a common theme or direction for their work. Lee Clow of TBWA Worldwide quite naturally received a conductor's baton as a gift. About the role of maestro he has said: "I was a pretty good soloist when I joined the orchestra, but I think I'm a much better conductor than I was a soloist. If we can make beautiful music together, that makes me happy... And different people end up getting to do the solos and get the standing ovations."[33] Lee Clow gets it. Now you do too.

Coordination and collaboration will be required for executing any kind of advertising, which means simply that advertising is a team sport. Moreover, the creative essence of the campaign can be aided and elevated by skillful use of teams. Teams can generate a synergy that allows them to rise above the talents of their individual members on many kinds of tasks. (Yes, the whole can be greater than the sum of the individual parts.) So even without an Igor Stravinsky, Pablo Picasso, or Martha Graham in our midst, a group of diverse and motivated people can be expected to not only generate big ideas but also put them into action.

Great advertising and great teamwork go hand in hand, which of course means that we don't just want to hope for a good team, we need to make it happen. Great teamwork can't be left to chance. It must be planned for and facilitated if it is to occur with regularity. So next we will introduce several concepts and insights about teams to make you better at teamwork. In addition, you will come to appreciate how important teams can be in producing that one elusive thing that everyone wants: *creativity*.

What We Know about Teams.

No doubt you have taken a class where part of your grade was determined by teamwork. Get used to it. More and more instructors in all sorts of classes are incorporating teamwork as part of their courses because they know that interpersonal skills are highly valued

33. Alice Cuneo, "The Dude Who Thought Different," *Advertising Age*, July 31, 2006, 25.

in the real world of work. In fact, an impressive body of research indicates that teams have become essential to the effectiveness of modern organizations. In their book *The Wisdom of Teams,* consultants Jon Katzenbach and Douglas Smith review many valuable insights about the importance of teams. Here we summarize several of their key conclusions.[34]

Teams Rule! There can be little doubt that in a variety of organizations, teams have become the primary means for getting things done. The growing number of performance challenges faced by most businesses—as a result of factors such as more demanding customers, technological changes, government regulation, and intensifying competition—demand speed and quality in work products that are simply beyond the scope of what an individual can offer. Roger Martin, Dean of the Rotman School of Management at University of Toronto, asserts that the complexity of today's business problems can only be solved through collaboration.[35] In most instances, teams are the only valid option for getting things done. This is certainly the case for advertising.

It's All about Performance. Research shows that teams are effective in organizations where the leadership makes it perfectly clear that teams will be held accountable for performance. Teams are expected to produce results that satisfy the client and yield financial gains for the organization.

Synergy through Teams. Modern organizations require many kinds of expertise to get the work done. The only reliable way to mix people with different expertise to generate solutions where the whole is greater than the sum of the parts is through team discipline. Research shows that blending expertise from diverse disciplines often produces the most innovative solutions to many different types of business problems.[36] The "blending" must be done through teams.

The Demise of Individualism? Rugged individualism is the American way. Always look out for number one! Are we suggesting that a growing reliance on teams in the workplace must mean a devaluation of the individual and a greater emphasis on conforming to what the group thinks? Not at all. Left unchecked, of course, an "always look out for number one" mentality can destroy teams. But teams are not incompatible with individual excellence. Effective teams find ways to let each individual bring his or her unique contributions to the forefront. When an individual does not have his or her own contribution to make, then one can question that person's value to the team. As the old saying goes, "If you and I think alike, then one of us is unnecessary."

Teams Promote Personal Growth. An added benefit of teamwork is that it promotes learning for each individual team member. In a team, people learn about their own work styles and observe the work styles of others. This learning makes them more effective team players in their next assignment. Once team principles take hold in an organization, momentum builds.

Leadership in Teams. A critical element in the equation for successful teams is leadership. Leaders do many things for their teams to help them succeed.[37] Teams ultimately must reach a goal to justify their standing, and here is where the leader's job starts. The leader's first job is to help the team build consensus about the goals they hope

34. Jon R. Katzenbach and Douglas K. Smith, *The Wisdom of Teams: Creating the High-Performance Organization* (Boston, MA: Harvard Business School Press, 1993).

35. Roger Martin, *The Opposable Mind* (Boston, MA: Harvard Business School Press, 2009).

36. Dorothy Leonard and Susaan Straus, "Putting Your Company's Whole Brain to Work," *Harvard Business Review,* July–August 1997, 111–121.

37. Katzenbach and Smith, *The Wisdom of Teams,* Ch. 7.

to achieve and the approach they will take to reach those goals. Without a clear sense of purpose, the team is doomed. Once goals and purpose are agreed upon, then the leader plays a role in ensuring that the work of the team is consistent with the strategy or plan. This is a particularly important role in the context of creating IBP campaigns.

Finally, team leaders must help do the real work of the team. Here the team leader must be careful to contribute ideas without dominating the team. There are also two key things that team leaders should never do: *They should not blame or allow specific individuals to fail, and they should never excuse away shortfalls in team performance.*[38] Mutual accountability must be emphasized over individual performance.

Direct Applications to the Account Team. Think of an agency's **account team** as a bicycle wheel, with the team leader as the hub of a wheel. Spokes of the wheel then reach out to the diverse disciplinary expertise needed in today's world of advertising and IBP. The spokes will represent team members from direct marketing, public relations, broadcast media, graphic design, interactive, creative, accounting, and so on. The hub connects the spokes and ensures that all of them work in tandem to make the wheel roll smoothly. To illustrate the multilayered nature of the team approach to IBP, each account team member can also be thought of as a hub in his or her very own wheel. For example, the direct marketing member on the account team is team leader for her own set of specialists charged with preparing direct marketing materials. Through this type of multilevel "hub-and-spokes" design, the coordination and collaboration essential for effective IBP campaigns can be achieved.

Fostering Collaboration through the Creative Brief. The **creative brief** is a little document with a huge role in promoting good teamwork and fostering the creative process. It sets up the goal for any advertising effort in a way that gets everyone moving in the same direction but should never force or mandate a particular solution. It provides basic guidelines with plenty of room for the creatives to be creative. Preparation of the creative brief is a joint activity involving the client lead and the AE. When the creative brief is done right, a whole bunch of potential conflicts are prevented. An efficient template for the creative brief is featured in Exhibit 9.15.

Teams Liberate Decision Making. With the right combination of expertise assembled on the account team, a carefully crafted creative brief, and a leader that has the team working well as a unit, what appears to be casual or spur-of-the-moment decision making can turn out to be breakthrough decision making. This is one of the huge benefits of good teamwork. As they say at CP+B, a good idea can come from anywhere. Teams composed of members that trust one another are liberated to be more creative because no one is worried about having their best ideas stolen. No one is worried about trying to look good for the boss. It's the team that counts. This type of "safe" team environment allows everyone to contribute and lets the whole be greater than the sum of the parts.

When Sparks Fly: Igniting Creativity through Teams.

Whether account teams, sub-specialist teams, creative teams, or hybrid teams involving persons from both the client and agency side, all will play critical roles in preparing and executing integrated advertising campaigns. Moreover, impressive evidence shows that when managed in a proactive way, teams come up with better ideas; that is, ideas that are both creative and useful in the process of building

38. Katzenbach and Smith, *The Wisdom of Teams,* 144.

CLIENT: **DATE:** **JOB NO.:**
Prepared by:

WHAT IS THE PRODUCT OR SERVICE?
Simple description or name of product or service.

WHO/WHAT IS THE COMPETITION?
Provide a snapshot of the brand situation, including current position in the category, brand challenges, competitive threats, and future goals.

WHO ARE WE TALKING TO?
Clear definition of who the target is both demographically and psychographically. Be as specific as possible in defining the target so that the creative can connect target and brand in the most compelling way.

WHAT CONSUMER NEED OR PROBLEM DO WE ADDRESS?
Describe the unmet consumer need that this product or service fills or how this product addresses a need in a way that's unique.

WHAT DOES THE CONSUMER CURRENTLY THINK ABOUT US?
Uncover target insights to get at attitudes and behaviors related to broader context as well as specific category and brand. Determine whether insights currently exist or whether new research needs to be conducted.

WHAT ONE THING DO WE WANT THEM TO BELIEVE?
Be as single-minded as possible. Write in benefit (functional, emotional, or self-expressive) language. Should differentiate us... no other brand in the category can or is currently saying it.

WHAT CAN WE TELL THEM THAT WILL MAKE THEM BELIEVE THIS?
Not a laundry list of available support but the few things that clearly support the "one thing we want them to believe."

WHAT IS THE TONALITY OF THE ADVERTISING?
A few adjectives or phrase that captures the tonality and personality of the advertising.

Of particular note:
Write it in the consumer's language; not business-speak.

Make every word count; be simple and concise.

Make as evocative as possible. Think of the brief as the first "ad." The brief should make creatives jump up and down in their excitement to start executing it!

Exhibit 9.15 Template for a creative brief.

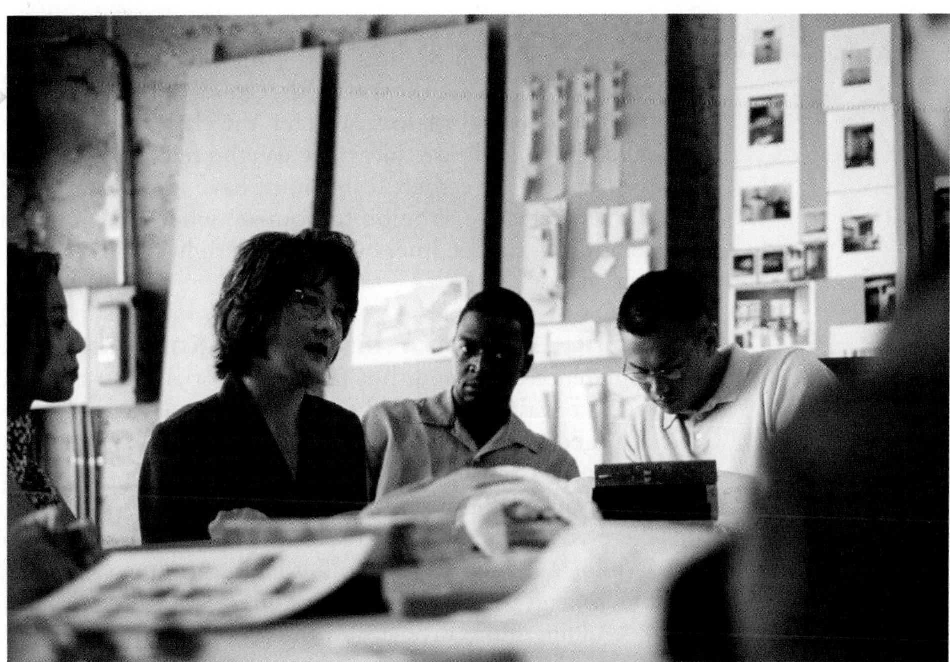

Exhibit 9.16 Teamwork really is both those things.

brands.[39] One can get pretty serious about the subject of managing creativity, and as reflected in Exhibit 9.16, good teamwork may be serious stuff. But it doesn't have to be complicated and it certainly will get rowdy at times. The key elements are building teams with the right expertise and diversity of thought, pushing individuals in those teams to challenge and build on each others' ideas, and creating just the right amount of tension to get the sparks flying.

Cognitive Styles. According to the stereotype, business types favor left-brain thinking and advertising types (especially the *creatives*) favor right-brain thinking. Business types like to talk about testing and data and return on investment, whereas advertising types like to talk about movies and the Cannes Film Festival.[40] Although such stereotypes misrepresent individual differences, the old left brain/right brain metaphor serves to remind us that people approach problem solving with different styles. That is, people prefer to think about things in their own style.

The unique preferences of each person for thinking about and solving a problem is a reflection of **cognitive style**. For instance, some people prefer logical and analytical thinking; others prefer intuitive and nonlinear thinking. Numerous categorization schemes have been developed for classifying people based on their cognitive styles. Psychologist Carl Jung was an early pioneer among cognitive stylists. He proposed essential differences among individuals along three dimensions of cognitive style: Sensing versus Intuiting; Thinking versus Feeling; and Extraverted versus Introverted. The important point for teams and creativity is that the more homogeneous a team is in terms of cognitive styles, the more limited will be the range of their solutions to a problem. Simply stated, diversity of thought nourishes creativity.

Creative Abrasion. Teamwork is not a picnic in the park. That's why it's called team*work*. Moreover, when teams bring together people with diverse cognitive styles, and they truly get engaged in the task, there will be friction. Friction

39. Jacob Goldenberg, Amnon Levav, David Mazursky, and Sorin Solomon, *Cracking the Ad Code* (Cambridge, UK: Cambridge University Press, 2009).

40. Dale Buss, "Bridging the Great Divide in Marketing Thinking," *Advertising Age,* March 26, 2007, 18, 19.

can be both good and bad.[41] On the one hand, we can have **creative abrasion**, which is the clash of ideas, and from which new ideas and breakthrough solutions can evolve. That's obviously the good thing. On the other hand, we can have **interpersonal abrasion**, which is the clash of people, from which communication shuts down and new ideas get slaughtered. That's obviously the bad thing. So as we pointed out earlier, teams must have leadership that creates a safe environment allowing creative abrasion to flourish, while always looking to defuse interpersonal abrasion. It's a fine line, but getting it right means the difference between creativity and chaos.

Using Brainstorming and Alien Visitors. Many of us have sat in a conference room and shot the breeze for an hour and when it was all over decided we just wasted another hour. Groups can waste a lot of time if not proactively managed, and one of the key means for getting groups or teams to generate novel solutions is through the use of a process called brainstorming. **Brainstorming** is an organized approach to idea generation in groups. As suggested by Exhibit 9.17, there is a right way and a wrong way to brainstorm. Follow the rules laid out in Exhibit 9.17, and you can call it brainstorming. Otherwise, you're just shooting the breeze, and most likely wasting time.

Adding more diversity to the group is always a way to foster creative abrasion; moreover, well-established teams can get stale and stuck in a rut. To ramp up the creative abrasion may require a visit from an alien. If you can get one from Pluto or Mars that's fine, but more likely this alien will just be a person or persons from

Exhibit 9.17 Don't waste time; do it right!

Eight Rules for Brilliant Brainstorming

#1—Build off each other. One proven path to creativity entails building on existing ideas; don't just generate ideas, build on each others'.
#2—Fear drives out creativity. If people believe they will be teased, demoted, or otherwise humiliated in the group, no need to even consider brainstorming. It won't work.
#3—Prime individuals before and after. Encourage individuals to learn about the problem before and after the group session; teams always benefit when individuals apply their unique expertise.
#4—Make it happen. Great organizations develop a brainstorming culture where everyone knows the rules and honors them; to achieve such a culture, it is essential that ideas developed in brainstorm sessions lead to actions. We can't just talk big ideas; we must also put them to work.
#5—It's a skill. Leading a productive brainstorming session is not a job for amateurs; facilitating a brainstorming session is a skill that takes months or years to master. Don't pretend to brainstorm without a skilled facilitator.
#6—Embrace creative abrasion. If your team has been formed appropriately, it will contain people with conflicting cognitive styles. Celebrate that diversity, welcome everybody into the group, and then let the sparks fly!
#7—Listen and learn. Good brainstorming sessions foster learning among people who have diverse expertise and divergent cognitive styles. Trust builds and suspicion fades.
#8—Follow the rules, or you're not brainstorming (and pretending just wastes everybody's time).

Source: Based on Robert I. Sutton, "The Truth about Brainstorming," *Inside Business Week*, September 25, 2006, 17–21.

41. Dorothy Leonard and Walter Swap, *When Sparks Fly: Igniting Creativity in Groups* (Boston, MA: Harvard Business School Press, 1999).

outside the normal network. They can be from elsewhere in your organization, or from outside the organization entirely. Perhaps the team will need to take a field trip together to visit some aliens. Teams that insulate themselves from outside influences run the risk over time of loosing their spark.[42] Tranquility and sameness can be enemies of creativity.

Final Thoughts on Teams and Creativity.

Creativity in the preparation of an IBP campaign can be fostered by the trust and open communication that are hallmarks of effective teams. But it is also true that the creativity required for breakthrough campaigns will evolve as personal work products generated by individuals laboring on their own. Both personal and team creativity are critical in the preparation of IBP campaigns. The daunting task of facilitating both often falls in the lap of an agency's creative director.

The position of creative director in any ad agency is very special because, much like the maestro of the symphony orchestra, the creative director must encourage personal excellence, but at the same time demand team accountability. We interviewed veteran creative directors to get more insights about the challenge of channeling the creative energies of their teams. All acknowledge that creativity has an intensely personal element, often motivated by the desire to satisfy one's own ego or sense of self. But despite this interpersonal element, team unity has to be a priority. In orchestrating creative teams, these are some good principles to follow:

- Take great care in assigning individuals to a team in the first place. Be sensitive to their existing workloads and the proper mix of expertise required to do the job for the client.
- Get to know the cognitive style of each individual. Listen carefully. Because creativity can be an intensely personal matter, one has to know when it is best to leave people alone, versus when one needs to support them in working through the inevitable rejection.
- Make teams responsible to the client. Individuals and teams are empowered when they have sole responsibility for performance outcomes.
- Beware of adversarial and competitive relationships between individuals and between teams. They can quickly lead to mistrust that destroys camaraderie and synergy.
- In situations where the same set of individuals will work on multiple teams over time, rotate team assignments to foster fresh thinking, or bring in some aliens!

Here we see once again that the fundamentals of effective teams—communication, trust, complementary expertise, and leadership—produce the desired performance outcome. There's simply no alternative. Advertising is a team sport.

4 Have *You* Decided to Become More Creative?

A great way to summarize the factors that foster creativity is via the **3P's creativity framework**.[43] People is the first P, and as we emphasized at the beginning of this chapter, the field of advertising has always embraced the concept of great creative minds, as in a Lee Clow, Alex Bogusky, or Bill Bernbach. But we also know that the Process used

42. Dorothy Leonard and Walter Swap, *When Sparks Fly: Igniting Creativity in Groups* (Boston, MA: Harvard Business School Press, 1999).

43. Sheila Sasser and Scott Koslow, "Desperately Seeking Advertising Creativity," *Journal of Advertising,* Winter 2008, 5–19.

in developing creative work, and the Place or environment wherein the work is done, are also big factors in generating creative outcomes. As one agency leader put it: "We sell ideas, and if your employees are unhappy, you are not going to get a lot of good ideas."[44] All that makes sense, but now, as promised, it's time to circle back to YOU.

Most of us are not going to model our lives after creative geniuses like Pablo Picasso or Martha Graham. Even though it's great to have role models to inspire us, we don't think it's realistic to aspire to be the next Gandhi or Einstein. But we all can take stock of our own special skills and abilities and should candidly assess our own strengths and weaknesses. This means YOU.

For example, referring to some of the terminology used earlier in this chapter, we all can complete assessments that reveal our own cognitive styles and then compare ourselves to others. And if you want to calibrate your level of creativity, just search the Internet for "creativity tests" or "creativity assessments" and a host of options will present themselves. It is a good thing to get to know your own self and start thinking about your unique skills and abilities. In addition, if you have any interest in a career in advertising, it would be a good thing to decide right now that you are going to make yourself more creative. Although we all may start in different places, it is a worthy goal to aspire to become more creative. Yale psychologist Robert Sternberg, who has devoted his professional career to the study of intelligence and creativity, advises his students as follows.

> *To make yourself more creative, decide now to:*
> *Redefine problems to see them differently from other people;*
> *Be the first to analyze and critique your own ideas, since we all have good ones and bad ones;*
> *Be prepared for opposition whenever you have a really creative idea;*
> *Recognize that it is impossible to be creative without adequate knowledge;*
> *Recognize that too much knowledge can stifle creativity;*
> *Find the standard, safe solution and then decide when you want to take a risk by defying it;*
> *Keep growing and experiencing, and challenging your own comfort zone;*
> *Believe in yourself, especially when surrounded by doubters;*
> *Learn to cherish ambiguity, because from it comes the new ideas;*
> *Remember that research has shown that people are most likely to be creative when doing something they love.*[45]

It's good advice.

44. Brooke Capps, "Playtime, Events, Perks Go Long Way in Team Building," *Advertising Age,* January 15, 2007, 30.

45. Robert J. Sternberg, "Creativity as a Decision," *American Psychologist,* May 2002, 376; and Robert J. Sternberg, "Identifying and Developing Creative Giftedness," *Roeper Review,* vol. 23, no. 2 (2000), 60–65.

Summary

1 Describe the core characteristics of great creative minds.

A look at the shared sensibilities of great creative minds provides a constructive starting point for assessing the role of creativity in the production of great advertising. What Picasso had in common with Gandhi, Freud, Eliot, Stravinsky, Graham, and Einstein—including a strikingly exuberant self-confidence, (childlike) alertness, unconventionality, and an obsessive commitment to the work—both charms and alarms us. Self-confidence, at some point, becomes crass self-promotion; an unconstrained childlike ability to see the world as forever new devolves, somewhere along the line, into childish self-indulgence. Without creativity, there can be no advertising. How we recognize and define creativity in advertising rests on our understanding of the achievements of acknowledged creative geniuses from the worlds of art, literature, music, science, and politics.

2 Contrast the role of an agency's creative department with that of business managers/account executives and explain the tensions between them.

What it takes to get the right idea (a lot of hard work), and the ease with which a client may dismiss that idea, underlies the contentiousness between an agency's creative staff and its AEs and clients. Creatives provoke. Managers restrain. Ads that win awards for creative excellence don't necessarily fulfill a client's business goals. All organizations deal with the competing agendas of one department versus another, but in advertising agencies, this competition plays out at an amplified level. The difficulty of assessing the effectiveness of any form of advertisement only adds to the problem. Advertising researchers are put in the unenviable position of judging the creatives, pitting "science" against art. None of these tensions changes the fact that creativity is essential to the vitality of brands. Creativity makes a brand, and it is creativity that reinvents established brands in new and desired ways.

3 Assess the role of teams in managing tensions and promoting creativity in advertising and IBP applications.

There are many sources of conflict and tension in the business of creating great advertising. It's the nature of the beast. One way that many organizations attempt to address this challenging issue is through systematic utilization of teams. Teams, when effectively managed, will produce outputs that are greater than the sum of their individual parts. Teams need to be managed proactively to promote creative abrasion but limit interpersonal abrasion if they are to produce "beautiful music together." Guidance from a maestro (like a Lee Clow or Alex Bogusky) will be required. Another important tool to get teams headed in the right direction and to pre-empt many forms of conflict in the advertising arena is the creative brief. It's a little document with a very big function.

4 Examine yourself and your own passion for creativity.

Self-assessment is an important part of learning and growing and now is the perfect time to be thinking about yourself and your passion for creativity. If advertising is a profession that interests you, then improving your own creative abilities should be a lifelong quest. Now is the time to decide to become more creative.

Key Terms

creativity
account executive
account team
creative brief
cognitive style
creative abrasion
interpersonal abrasion
brainstorming
3P's creativity framework

Questions

1. Throughout the years, creativity has been associated with various forms of madness and mental instability. In your opinion, what is it about creative people that prompts this kind of characterization?

2. Think about your favorite artist, musician, or writer. What is unique about the way he or she represents the world? What fascinates you about the vision he or she creates?

3. Much credence is given in this chapter to the idea that tension (of various sorts) is part of creative pursuits. Explain the connection between creativity and tension.

4. Which side of this debate do you have more affinity for: Are people creative because they can produce creative results, or are they creative because of the way they think? Explain.

5. What forces inside an advertising agency can potentially compromise its creative work? Is compromise always to be avoided? Imagine that you are an agency creative. Define "compromise." Now imagine that you are an account executive. How does your definition of compromise change?

6. Describe the conflict between the creative department and the research department. Do you think creatives are justified in their hesitancy to subject their work to advertising researchers? Is science capable of judging art any more than art is capable of judging science? Explain.

7. Examine Exhibit 9.14. Using this exhibit as your guide, generate a list of 10 principles to foster creativity in an ad agency.

8. The creative director in any agency has the daunting task of channeling the creative energies of dozens of individuals, while demanding team accountability. If the expression of creativity is personal and highly individualized, how can teamwork possibly foster creativity? What might a creative director do to "allow creativity to happen" in a team environment? Explain how the saying "The whole is greater than the sum of its parts" fits into a discussion of creativity and teamwork.

9. Advertising always has been a team sport, but the advent of advertising and IBP has made effective teamwork more important than ever. It also has made it more difficult to achieve. Explain how the growing emphasis on IBP makes effective teamwork more challenging.

10. Choose any ad from this book that represents exemplary creativity to you. Explain your choice.

Experiential Exercises

1. To be successful in the 21st century, advertisers must find creative ways to transform customers into life-long purchasers and diehard advocates. The lifetime value of a loyal customer far exceeds any short-term buzz generated by a one-time promotion gimmick.

Form into teams and think up a creative advertising concept that would help a client initiate and maintain relationships with new customers. Teams should brainstorm ways in which the client could establish regular, ongoing marketing interactions with individual customers. After the breakout session, each team should present its campaign idea to the class for evaluation.

2. Because great advertising and teamwork go together, test your teamwork skills with this gravity-defying team-building activity. Divide students into teams of eight and provide each team with a light wooden dowel rod approximately six to eight feet in length. Each team's objective is to lower the long dowel rod to the ground while the rod rests atop members' outstretched index fingers. To begin, team members should stand and form two lines facing each other, extending index fingers outward as if pointing to the opposite member. Next, have a facilitator lay the long dowel rod on top of the group's outstretched index fingers. The team must try to lower the rod slowly to the ground—no easy task.

3. This chapter emphasizes the importance of coordination and collaboration in the creative process for IBP campaigns. Break into small groups to conduct the following creative brainstorming exercises. When you are done, present your ideas to the class and explain how the "Eight Rules for Brilliant Brainstorming" listed in Exhibit 9.17 helped your team's collaborative effort. How did your ideas, in number and in substance, compare to others in the class?

- How many uses can you identify for baking soda?
- Put a ballpoint pen, a baseball cap, and a belt on a desk. How many alternative uses can you identify for those objects?
- What words do you associate with the following well-known brands? Taco Bell, Pampers, and John Deere.

Spend 10 minutes brainstorming each of these topics:

4. Working in the same small teams, develop a creative brief for one of the three brands listed above. The brief should establish the goal of any future advertising efforts and offer some basic guidance to the creative division. Your team should use the template in Exhibit 9.15 to develop the creative brief, but you may make adjustments as necessary to that model.

Chapter 10

Creative Message Strategy

After reading and thinking about this chapter, you will be able to do the following:

1. Identify ten objectives of creative message strategy.
2. Identify methods for achieving each creative message objective.
3. Discuss the strategic implications of various methods used to achieve each creative message objective.

THERE IS MORE TO WATCH IN HDTV.

SKY

Courtesy, Wright's Media

Message Strategy.

Now: actually creating messages. The first thing we need is an objective: what do you want to accomplish with your advertising and other brand messaging? How are you going to use advertising and brand promotion to achieve marketing goals?

The message strategy defines the goals of the advertiser. This chapter offers 10 essential message objectives, and then discusses and illustrates the methods most often used to achieve them. It covers the most important message strategies. Exhibit 10.1 summarizes the 10 message objectives presented here. Also, you must understand that you will certainly see ads that are not pure cases, and ads that are combinations of strategies.

When you see an ad you should ask: What is this ad trying to do, and how is it trying to accomplish that?

Exhibit 10.1 Message strategy objectives and methods.

Objective: What the Advertiser Hopes to Achieve	Method: How the Advertiser Plans to Achieve the Objective
Promote brand recall: To get consumers to recall its brand name(s) first; that is, before any of the competitors' brand names	Repetition Slogans and jingles
Link a key attribute to the brand name: To get consumers to associate a key attribute with a brand name and vice versa	Unique selling proposition (USP)
Persuade the consumer: To convince consumers to buy a product or service through high-engagement arguments	Reason-why ads Hard-sell ads Comparison ads Testimonials Demonstration Advertorials Infomercials
Instill brand preference: To get consumers to like or prefer its brand above all others	Feel-good ads Humor ads Sexual-appeal ads
Scare the consumer into action: To get consumers to buy a product or service by instilling fear	Fear-appeal ads
Change behavior by inducing anxiety: To get consumers to make a purchase decision by playing to their anxieties; often, the anxieties are social in nature	Anxiety ads Social anxiety ads
Transform consumption experiences: To create a feeling, image, or mood about a brand that is activated when the consumer uses the product or service	Transformational ads
Situate the brand socially: To give the brand meaning by placing it in a desirable social context	Slice-of-life ads Product placement/ short Internet films Light-fantasy ads
Define the brand image: To create an image for a brand by relying predominantly on visuals rather than words and argument	Image ads
Resolve Social Disruption and Cultural Contradictions: To leverage disruption and cultural contradictions in society to the brand's advantage. Get consumers to see the brand as a way to resolve these tensions and contradictions.	Tie Brand to Social/Cultural Movement

1 Essential Message Objectives and Strategies.

These 10 are presented from simplest to most sophisticated. For each one we will tell you about the logic behind the strategy, the basic mechanisms involved, how it works, how success or failure is typically determined, and a strategic summary of those methods.

Objective #1: Promote Brand Recall.

This is the simplest type of advertising there is. Since modern advertising's very beginning, getting consumers to remember the advertised brand's name has been a goal. The obvious idea behind this objective is that if consumers remember the brand name, and can easily recall it, they are more likely to buy it. It's a pretty simple and straightforward idea.

Although human memory is a very complex topic, the relationship between repetition and recall has been pretty well understood for a very long time. We know that repetition generally increases the odds of recall. So, by repeating a brand name over and over, the odds of recalling that brand name go up—pretty simple.

But advertisers typically don't just want consumers to remember their name; they want their name to be the *first* brand consumers remember, or what advertisers call *top of mind*. At a minimum, they want them to be in the *evoked set*, a small list of brand names (typically five or less) that come to mind when a product or service category (for example, airlines [United, American, Delta], soft drinks [Coke, Pepsi], or toothpaste [Crest, Colgate]) is mentioned. So, if someone says "soft drink," the folks in Atlanta (The Coca-Cola Company headquarters) want you to say "Coke."

Again, the odds of being either top of mind or in the evoked set increase with recall. In the case of parity products (those with few major objective differences between brands—for example, laundry soaps) and other "low-involvement" goods and services, the first brand remembered is often the most likely to be purchased. First-remembered brands are often the most popular brands. In fact, consumers may actually infer popularity, desirability, and even superiority from the ease with which they recall brands. The most easily recalled brand may be seen as the leading brand (most popular, highest market share), even when it isn't. Cognitive psychologists have shown that humans infer how common something is (frequency) by how easily they remember it. So, consumers will actually believe brand X's market share to be higher because it comes to mind so quickly. If people think a brand is the leading brand, it can actually become the leading brand. For things purchased routinely, you can't expect consumers to deliberate and engage in extensive consideration of product attributes. Instead, in the real world of advertising and brand promotion, you rely on recall of the brand name, recall of a previously made judgment (e.g., *I like Tide*) to get the advertised brand in the shopping cart. Sometimes, the simplest strategy is the best strategy.

Clearly, there is a very large advantage in simple brand recall in routinely purchased product categories, like consumer package goods.

So, how do advertisers promote easy recall?

There are two popular methods: repetition and memory aids: slogans, jingles, and point-of-purchase branding.

Method A: Repetition.

Repetition is a tried-and-true way of gaining easier retrieval of brand names from consumer's memory. Advertisers do this by buying a lot of ads and/or by frequently repeating the brand name within the ad itself. This is typically a strategy for television and radio but can be accomplished visually in print, with promotional placement in

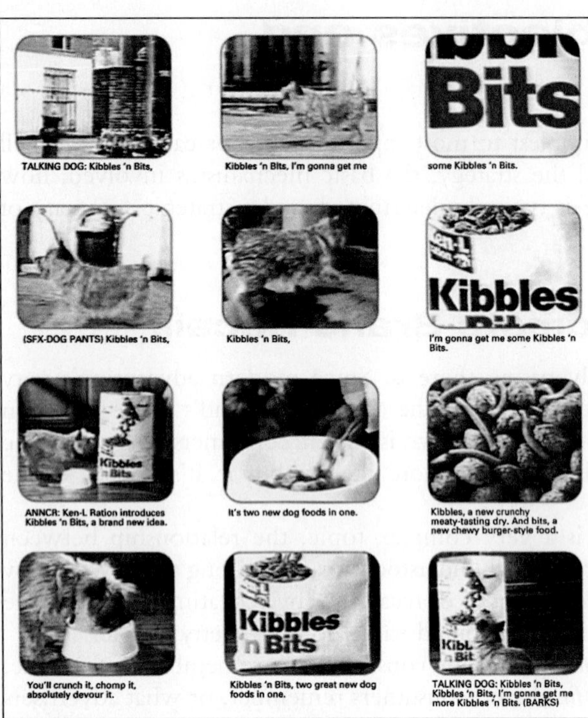

Exhibit 10.2 This ad may hold the all-time record for most brand mentions in a single 30-second ad. Kibbles and Bits, Kibbles and Bits . . . .

television shows and movies, and on the Web. The idea is that things said (or shown) more often will be remembered more easily than things said (or shown) less frequently. So the advertiser repeats the brand name over and over and over again. Then, when the consumer stands in front of, say, the laundry detergent, the advertised brand name is recalled from memory.

The more accessible (easier to remember) brand names are retrieved first and fastest from memory, making them (all else being equal) more likely to end up in the shopping cart. Getting into the consumer's evoked set gets you close to actual purchase, and achieving top of mind gets you even closer.

Does repetition always work? No, of course it doesn't. There are plenty of times when consumers remember one brand, and then buy another. Still, this type of advertising plays a probability game—being easily recalled tilts the odds of being purchased in favor of the advertisers willing to pay for the recall that repetition buys.

We think the all-time record for most brand mentions in a single ad might be a tie: either "Kibbles and Bits, Kibbles and Bits, I gotta get me some Kibbles and Bits" over and over and over (see Exhibit 10.2), or the endless "Meow, Meow, Meow, Meow" for Meow Mix. Can you think of one with more?

Visual repetition is also important. The very frequent image of the Geiko Gecko, paired with frequent use of the word makes this campaign one of the most successful of all time. It has repetition, verbal-visual pairing, and no doubt owns a big piece of the mind of American consumers.

Repetition strategies are being used on the Internet as well: Familiar names are placed so that consumers will see them again and again. In fact, many IBP efforts work in this way. Think sports arenas: Seeing a name over and over (and having it in a TV shot) is certainly one of the ideas behind named arenas such as Qualcomm Stadium, AT&T Park, and Minute Maid Park.

Method B: Slogans and Jingles. Slogans are one small step up from raw repetition in degree of complexity. Here, slogans and jingles are used to enhance the odds of recalling the brand name. The basic mechanism at work here is still memory, and the goal is still brand-name recall. Slogans are linguistic devices that link a brand name to something memorable by means of the slogan's simplicity, meter, rhyme, or some other factor. Jingles do the same thing, just set to a melody. Examples are numerous: "You Deserve a Break Today"; "You're in Good Hands with Allstate"; "Like a Good Neighbor, State Farm Is There"; "Two, Two, Two Mints in One"; "Get Met, It Pays"; and "It Keeps on Going and Going and Going." No doubt you've heard a few of these before. Slogans and jingles provide rehearsal, that is, encourage repetition because they are catchy, or prone to repeating, and the inherent properties of the slogan or jingle provide a retrieval cue for the brand name.

Also consider a practical application of the human need to complete or "close" a verse: For example, when you say, "Like a good neighbor," you pretty much are compelled to complete the phrase with "State Farm is there." As you know, slogans and jingles are hard to get out of your head. That's the idea.

Method C: Point-of-Purchase Branding. Part of remembering is being reminded. In the contemporary advertising IBP world, marketers often use point-of-purchase displays that help trigger, or cue, the brand name (and maybe an ad) from memory. That is the main idea behind point-of-purchase advertising—to provide a memory trigger. The in-store visual triggers retrieval of the brand name, and maybe memories of the actual ad itself... importantly, at the point-of-purchase decision—when it goes in the cart or stays on the shelf.

The aisle itself (its look, smells, etc.) or the packaging may cue the category. That is, on the shopper's highly repeated and routinized path down this aisle, the aisle or the packaging may prompt recollections about the category (say, detergent) and may make the heavily advertised brand (say, Tide) come right to mind.

Evaluation of repetition, slogans, and jingles is typically done through day-after-recall (DAR) tests and tracking studies emphasizing recall (e.g., "name three detergents"). In other words, these ads are evaluated with the most traditional ad copy research there is: simple recall measures. This is one time when the method of evaluation actually makes perfect sense: You are trying to get recall; you test for recall.

3 **Strategic Implications of Repetition, Slogans, and Jingles.**

- ***Extremely resistant to forgetting.*** These methods make it difficult to forget the brand. Once established, the residual amount of impact from the campaign is huge. If some advertisers stopped advertising today, you would remember their slogans, jingles, and names for a long, long time.
- ***Efficient for consumer.*** For routinely purchased items, consumers rely on a simple and easy decision "rule": Buy what you remember. So, this kind of advertising works well in repeat-purchase and low-involvement items.
- ***Long-term commitment/expense.*** To achieve an adequate level of recall, advertisers have to sign on for a lot of advertising. It takes lots and lots of repetition, particularly early on, or a very memorable slogan or jingle. Once advertisers have achieved a high recall level, they can fine-tune their spending so that they are spending just enough to stay where they want. But they have to get there first, and it can be a very expensive trip.
- ***Competitive interference.*** This is less a problem with repetition, but consumers may learn a slogan or jingle only to associate it with the wrong brand. This has happened more times than you might imagine. For example, "It keeps on going, and going, and going. . . ." It's Duracell, right? Wait, maybe it's Eveready? Not absolutely sure? Not good. This is why it is absolutely vital to firmly link brand name to slogan. You don't want to pay for your competitor's success.
- ***Creative resistance.*** Creatives generally hate this type of advertising. Can you imagine why? These ads are rarely called creative and don't usually win a lot of creative awards. So creatives are less likely to enjoy working on them. Thus, the client paying the bills is less likely to get the "hot" or even senior creative teams. A lot of rookies get these assignments.

Objective #2: Link Key Attribute(s) to the Brand Name.

Sometimes advertisers want consumers to remember the brand and associate it with one or two attributes. This type of advertising is most closely identified with the **unique selling proposition (USP)** style, a type of ad that strongly emphasizes a supposedly unique quality (or qualities) of the advertised brand. It is more complicated than simple brand recall, and a bit more challenging. It is one step up from Objective #1 in complexity. It requires more of the consumer, a little more thought, a little more learning. So, it requires more from those planning and making the ads. The ads provide a reason to buy, but don't require the consumer to think too much about that reason, just associate it with the brand name. In fact, many experts believe these ads work best if consumers don't think too much about the claim, just associate

Exhibit 10.3 Here we have a USP. Although a USP is often used with a consumer packaged good, here one is used to help brand a luxury car.

Courtesy, Lexus, a Division of Toyota Motor Sales, U.S.A., Inc.; Advertising: Team One; Photographer: Scott Downing

the two: the name and the claim. The primary mechanisms are memory and learning. The appeal may be through words (copy) or visuals (art direction).

Method: USP. The idea of emphasizing one and only one brand attribute is a very good idea—sometimes two are used if they are complementary, such as "strong but gentle." Ads that try to link several attributes to a brand while working to establish recall generally fail—they are too confusing and give too much information. Too much is attempted. Consider the Lexus ad in Exhibit 10.3. Clearly, the USP is that the car is built with headlights that turn in concert with the car. The headline delivers the single-minded message. The body copy explains it further. It's the headlights that make this car different. It's the headlights that make this car safer. That's all you have to know. Sometimes this type of advertising relies on a soft logic. The ad makes sense, but don't think too much about it: Listerine is strong, Ivory is pure. Evaluation of the USP method is typically done through recall tests, communication tests, and tracking studies. Did the consumer remember the USP? Sometimes price is the USP, but as you might imagine, a lot of advertisers use that as a claim, and it can be pretty crowded space.

Strategic Implications of the USP Method.

- ***Big carryover.*** USP advertising is very efficient. Once this link has been firmly established, it can last a very long time. An investment in this kind of advertising can carry you through some lean times.
- ***Very resistant.*** This type of advertising can be incredibly resistant to competitive challenge. Generations of consumers have been born, lived, and died remembering that Ivory is pure. Being the first to claim an attribute can be a huge advantage. Professionals will often say "Brand X owns that space" (meaning that attribute). For example, "Ivory owns the purity space," "Cheer owns the all-temperature space."
- ***Long-term commitment and expense.*** If advertisers are going to use the USP method, they have to be in it for the long haul. You can't keep switching strategies and expect good results. Pick an attribute and stay with it. If advertisers would just do this one thing, a lot more would be successful.
- ***Some creative resistance.*** Creatives tend not to hate this quite as much as simple repetition, but it does seem to get old with them pretty fast. Don't expect the best or most experienced creative teams.

Objective #3: Persuade the Consumer.

This style of advertising is about arguments. In this type of advertising, we move up from linking one (possibly two) attributes to a brand name using soft logic and simple learning to actually posing one or more (usually more) logical arguments to an engaged consumer. This is high-engagement advertising. That is, it assumes an actively engaged consumer, paying attention and considering the arguments. Its goal is to convince the consumer through arguments that the advertised brand is the right choice. The advertiser says, in effect, you should buy my brand because of *x*, *y*, and *z* reasons. These arguments have typically been verbal (copy) but have in the past few decades employed more visual arguments as well. As detailed below, there are several forms of this type of advertising.

For this general type of advertising to work as planned, the consumer has to think about what the advertiser is saying. The receiver must "get" the ad, understand the argument, and agree with it. In a pure persuasion ad, there is an assumed dialogue between the ad and the receiver, and some of the dialogue is the consumer disagreeing and counterarguing with the message. As mentioned in Chapter 7, some research has found counterarguments to be the single most common consumer response to these types of ads. This, its inherent wordiness, and its antiquated style are the reasons such advertising is becoming less popular. However, these ads are still found in the earliest phases of a technological innovation, where a new good or service has to be explained to consumers or in categories where the very nature of the product or service is complex, or the perceived risk of making a bad decision is very high.

Method A: Reason-Why Ads. In a reason-why ad, the advertiser reasons with the potential consumer. The ad points out to the consumer that there are good reasons why this brand will be satisfying and beneficial. Advertisers are usually relentless in their attempt to reason with consumers when using this method. They begin with some claim, like "Seven great reasons to buy Brand X," and then proceed to list all seven, finishing with the conclusion (implicit or explicit) that only a moron would, after such compelling evidence, do anything other than purchase Brand X (see Exhibit 10.4). Other times, the reason or reasons to use a product can be presented deftly. Psychologists have shown that humans value conclusions they have reached more than those made for them. So, really great reason-why ads will often give the reasons why, but let the consumer actually make the (obvious by then) conclusion that the advertised brand is best. Yet, the biggest trick to this method is making sure that the reasons make sense and that consumers actually care. Sometimes the reason why includes the reason why the choice actually matters. Price advertising can be a reason-why. There is a great deal of price advertising, and for that reason it is hard to make that claim unique. Wise advertisers have argued that value is a superior claim than price... someone may beat you on the objectively lower price, but you can always claim that your brand is a better value.

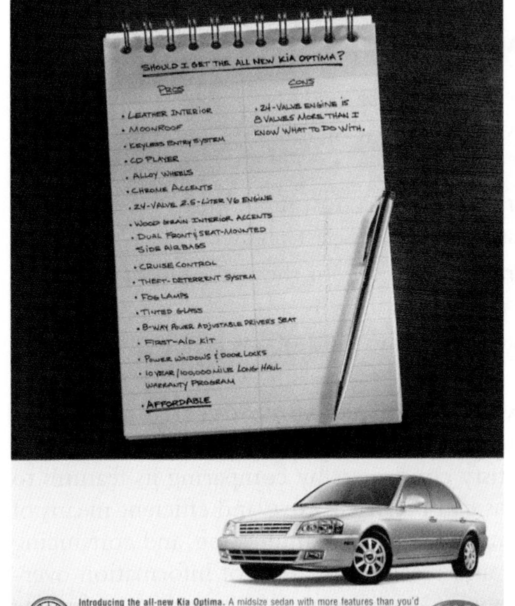

Exhibit 10.4 Kia uses reason-why.

Courtesy, Kia Motors America, Inc.

Strategic Implications of Reason-Why Ads.

- ***Permission to buy.*** Gives consumers reasons for purchasing the advertised brand.
- ***Socially acceptable def1ense.*** We all know that we sometimes have to defend our purchase decisions to friends and family. These types of ads are chock full of reasons why it was a smart idea.

JCPenney Catalog
Thank you
for your recent catalog order!
beds
49.99
Save 10%*
on your next order from
JCPenney Catalog or JCPenney.com
(See back for details.)
Hurry!
offer ends November 27th

Exhibit 10.5 Hurry! You better act fast to get the benefits of JCPenney. www.jcpenney.com

- ***High level of involvement.*** Consumers have to be paying attention for these ads to work. They have to engage with these ads. How much of the time do you think that actually happens? Sometimes consumers get swamped with too much information and just do something simple like buy what they did last time, or what a friend or *Consumer Reports* recommended.
- ***Potential for counterarguments.*** This type of advertising might actually convince consumers why *not* to buy the advertised brand. Remember, consumers love to argue with ads.
- ***Legal/regulatory challenges/exposure.*** The makers of these ads tend to get dragged into court or summoned by a regulatory body quite a bit. You'd better make sure that all your reasons why can stand up in court. Some haven't.
- ***Some creative resistance.*** Creatives are often ho-hum on these type of ads, but don't hate them.

Method B: Hard-Sell Ads. Hard-sell ads are a subcategory of reason-why ads: reason why with urgency. They are characteristically high pressure and urgent, thus "hard." Phrases such as "act now," "limited time offer," "your last chance to save," and "one-time-only sale" are representative of this method. The idea is to create a sense of urgency so that consumers will act quickly (see Exhibit 10.5). Sometimes these are done as IBP, and include "call or click *now*." Of course, many consumers have learned to ignore or otherwise discount these messages. We've all seen "Going Out of Business Sale" signs that remained up and the store open for months and even years. As one of our editors noted, this happens all the time. She lived in NYC; on the stretch of Fifth Avenue from 42nd to 48th she once (in four years of living and working in Midtown) saw only one electronics store that *didn't* have a "Going Out of Business" sign. Cry "*wolf*" too many times and no one believes any more.

Strategic Implications of Hard-Sell Approaches.

- ***"Permission to buy now."*** The sale was about to end.
- ***Socially acceptable defense.*** "I had to act"; "It was on sale that day only"; "It was such a good deal."
- ***Very bad reputation, low credibility.*** A lot of consumers know this is just a scam, and that "last chance" almost never means last chance.
- ***Legal/regulatory challenges/exposure.*** The makers of these ads tend to face the same legal and regulatory problems as the reason-why ads.
- ***Some creative resistance.*** Again, these are not the kind of ads creatives beg for.

Method C: Comparison Ads. **Comparison advertisements** are another form of advertising designed to persuade the consumer. Comparison ads try to demonstrate a brand's ability to satisfy consumers by comparing its features to those of competitive brands. Comparisons can be an effective and efficient means of communicating a large amount of information in a clear, interesting, and convincing way, or they can be extremely confusing and create a situation of information overload in which the market leader usually wins. Comparison advertising as a technique has traditionally been used by marketers of convenience goods, such as pain relievers, laundry detergents, and household cleaners. Advertisers in a wide range of product categories have tried comparison advertising from time to time. Every now and then, there are exceptions to this typically mundane class: two come immediately to mind: The classic: Avis "We're Number 2: We Try Harder," and the recent Mac vs. PC ads

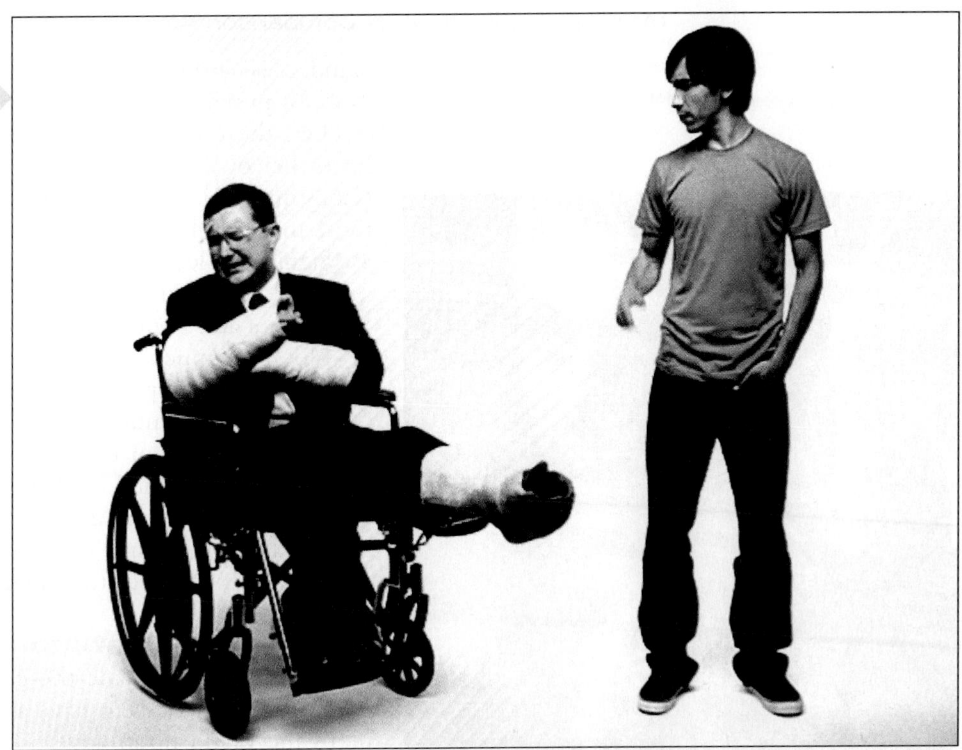

Exhibit 10.6 One of the best comparison ads of all time.

Courtesy, Susan Van Etten

(see Exhibit 10.6). This Apple campaign was brilliant in that it made all the right technical and performance comparisons (rarely more than one or two per ad) and did it in an amusing, interesting, and absolutely wonderful way. It drew on person-company stereotypes to contextualize the comparison. Once again, Apple was very smart.

Evaluation of comparison ads is typically done through tracking studies that measure attitudes, beliefs, and preferences over time.

Using comparison in an advertisement can be direct and name competitors' brands, or it can be indirect and refer only to the "leading brand" or "Brand X." Here are a few rules gleaned from consumer research.

- Direct comparison by a low-share brand (say Apple) to a high-share brand (say Windows) increases receivers' attention and increases their intent to purchase the low-share brand (Apple).
- Direct comparison by a high-share brand to a low-share brand does not attract additional attention to the high-share brand but actually helps the low-share brand. This is not good. Direct comparison is more effective if members of the target audience have not demonstrated clear brand preference in their product choices.[1]

For these reasons, established market leaders almost never use comparison ads. These ads are almost always used by the underdog brand, the brand that wishes to be seen in the company of the market leader.

1. Conclusions in this list are drawn from William R. Swinyard, "The Interaction between Comparative Advertising and Copy Claim Variation," *Journal of Marketing Research* 18 (May 1981), 175–186; Cornelia Pechmann and David Stewart, "The Effects of Comparative Advertising on Attention, Memory, and Purchase Intentions," *Journal of Consumer Research* (September 1990), 180–191; and Sanjay Petruvu and Kenneth R. Lord, "Comparative and Noncomparative Advertising: Attitudinal Effects under Cognitive and Affective Involvement Conditions," *Journal of Advertising* (June 1994), 77–90.

Strategic Implications of Comparison Ads.

- Can help a low-share brand.
- Provides social justification for purchase of the less popular brand.
- Gives permission to buy. Lets the consumer work through and then come to his or her own conclusion that it really is the best brand. (Consumer-generated conclusions are more powerful than those made on behalf of the advertiser.)
- Significant legal/regulatory exposure. Companies love to file complaints to agencies such as the NAD for these types of ads. Factor in legal costs.
- Not done much outside the United States; in much of the world, comparison advertising is either outlawed, not done by mutual agreement, or simply considered in such poor taste as to never be done.
- Not for established market leaders.
- These ads are sometimes evaluated as more offensive and less interesting than noncomparative ads. They have a tendency to turn some readers off.

Exhibit 10.7 Watches are a category in which celebrities have traditionally played a major role.

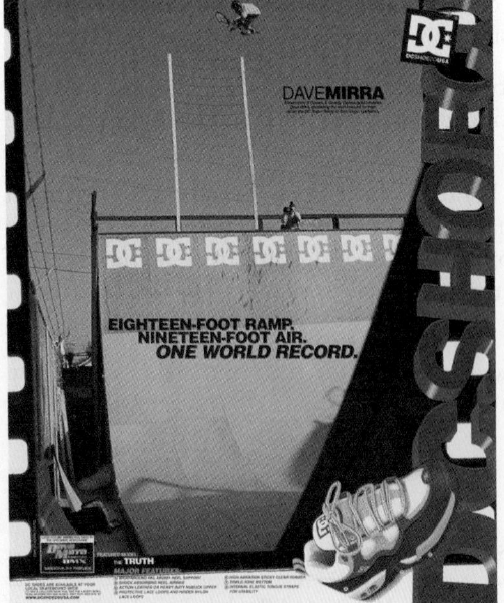

Exhibit 10.8 Dave Mirra is known as the Miracle Boy of freestyle BMX riding. What type of audience might find his testimonials persuasive?

Method D: Testimonials. Testimonials are another type of persuade-the-consumer ad. A frequently used message tactic is to have a spokesperson who champions the brand in an advertisement, rather than simply providing information. When an advocacy position is taken by a spokesperson in an advertisement, it is known as a **testimonial**. The value of the testimonial lies in the authoritative presentation of a brand's attributes and benefits by the spokesperson. There are three basic versions of the testimonial message tactic.

The most conspicuous version is the *celebrity testimonial* (see Exhibit 10.7). Sports stars and supermodels are widely used. The belief is that a celebrity testimonial will increase an ad's ability to attract attention and produce a desire in receivers to emulate or imitate the celebrities they admire.

Whether this is really true or not, the fact remains that celebrities remain pretty popular in contemporary advertising. Of course, there is the ever-present risk that a celebrity will fall from grace, as several have in recent years, and potentially damage the reputation of the brand for which he or she was once the champion.

Expert spokespeople for a brand are viewed by the target audience as having expert product knowledge. A spokesperson portrayed as a doctor, lawyer, scientist, gardener, or any other expert relevant to a brand is intended to increase the credibility of the message being transmitted. There are also real experts. Advertising for the Club, a steering-wheel locking device that deters auto theft, uses police officers from several cities to demonstrate the effectiveness of the product. Some experts can also be celebrities. This is the case when Michael Jordan gives a testimonial for Nike basketball shoes or Dave Mirra for BMX-riding shoes (see Exhibit 10.8).

There is also the *average-user testimonial*. Here, the spokesperson is not a celebrity or portrayed as an expert but rather as an average user speaking for the brand. The

Courtesy, Advertising Archives; Courtesy of D C Shoes, Inc.

philosophy is that the target market can relate to this person. Solid theoretical support for this testimonial approach comes from reference-group theory. An interpretation of reference-group theory in this context suggests that consumers may rely on opinions or testimonials from people they consider similar to themselves, rather than on objective product information. Simply put, the consumer's logic in this situation is, "That person is similar to me and likes that brand; therefore, I will also like that brand." In theory, this sort of logic frees the receiver from having to scrutinize detailed product information by simply substituting the reference-group information (see Exhibit 10.9). Of course, in practice, the execution of this strategy is rarely that easy. Consumers are very sophisticated at detecting this attempt at persuasion. Evaluation is usually through tracking studies and communications tests.

Exhibit 10.9 This testimonial is done with facial expression, body attitude, and "look." These days even testimonials don't have to have words.

Strategic Implications of Testimonial Advertising.

- 👍 Very popular people can generate popularity for the brand.
- 👍 People perceived to be very similar to the consumer, or an expert, can be powerful advocates for the brand.
- 👎 Consumers often forget who likes what, particularly when stars promote multiple goods and services.
- 👎 Can generate more popularity for the star than for the brand.

Celebrities, being human, are not as easy to manage as cartoon characters: think Tony the Tiger versus Tiger.

Method E: Demonstration. How close an electric razor shaves, how green a fertilizer makes a lawn, or how easy an exercise machine is to use are all product features that can be demonstrated by using a method known simply as demonstration. "Seeing is believing" is the motto of this school of advertising. When it's done well, the results are striking (see Exhibit 10.10). Evaluation of demonstration ads is typically done through tracking studies that measure attitudes, beliefs, and brand preferences over time.

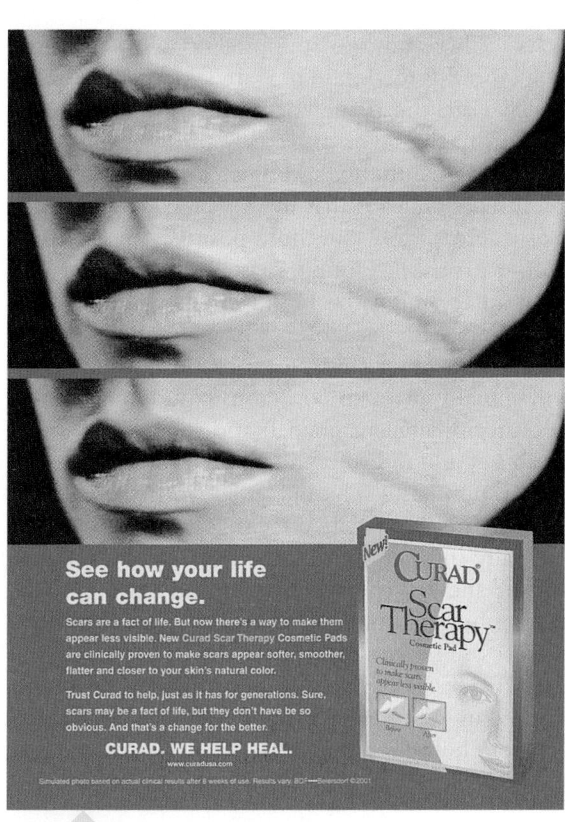

Exhibit 10.10 Straight demonstration of a product benefit by Curad. www.curadusa.com

Strategic Implications of Demonstration Ads.

- 👍 Inherent credibility of "seeing is believing."
- 👍 Can be used as social justification; helps the consumer defend his or her decision to buy.
- 👍 Provides clear permission to buy. ("I saw a test; it was the best.")
- 👎 Fairly heavy regulatory/legal exposure.

Method F: Infomercials. With the **infomercial**, an advertiser typically buys from five to 60 minutes of television time and runs an information/entertainment program that is really an extended advertisement. Real estate investment programs, weight-loss and fitness products, motivational programs, and cookware have dominated the infomercial format. The program usually has a host who provides information about a product and typically brings on guests to give testimonials about how successful they have been using the featured product. Most infomercials run on cable or satellite channels, although networks have sold early-morning and late-night time as well.

Strategic Implications of Infomercials.

- Long format gives advertisers plenty of time to make their case.
- As network ratings fall, day-parts (e.g., Sunday mornings 9–11) that were previously unaffordable have now opened up, making infomercials better deals for advertisers.
- Has the advantage of looking like an entertainment show, when it's really an ad.
- The genre of ads has a somewhat negative public image, which doesn't help build credibility or trust in the advertised brand.

There are other persuade-the-consumer formats, including ads posing as newspaper articles (advertorials), but all have the same basic mechanism at their core: Here's why you should buy this—providing supportive arguments for purchase.

Objective #4: Affective Association: Get the Consumer to Feel Good About the Brand.

Advertisers want consumers to like their brand. They believe that brand liking leads to purchase. But rather than provide the consumer with hard reasons to like the brand, these ads work more through feelings. Again, this is another pretty big step up in complexity.

There are several well-known approaches to getting the consumer to like one's brand. Let's look at some of the general approaches; most specific examples are merely finer distinctions within these more general categories.

Method A: Feel-Good Ads. These ads are supposed to work through affective (feeling) association or pre-decision distortion. They are supposed to either link the good feeling elicited by the ad with the brand, or by leveraging the propensity for humans to distort information in the favor of liked brands without even knowing they are doing so. Although the actual theory and mechanics of this seemingly simple association are complex, the basic idea is that by creating ads with positive feelings, advertisers will lead consumers to associate those positive feelings with the advertised brand, leading to a higher probability of purchase.

Of course, getting from liking the ad to liking the brand can be one big leap. Recent research by Stanford researcher Baba Shiv[2] and others have demonstrated an enrichment effect that occurs when the consumer thinks of a brand with attached positive emotions. The consumer will actually, prior to conscious consideration, bias information in the direction of the emotionally enriched brand. They don't even know they are doing this. So if you can get a brand to be liked, even just a little, and not even consciously, you can get more purchases. The evidence on how well this method works in practice is mixed. It may be that positive feelings are transferred to the brand, or it could be that they actually interfere with remembering the message or the brand name. From an advertising and IBP perspective, how do you get that to happen? Well, if you can create advertising that makes consumers connect positive emotions with the brand, you have success. The key is not to make the ad liked, but to make the brands liked. Liking the ad doesn't necessarily mean liking the brand. But message strategy development is a game of probability, and liking the ad may lead to a higher probability of purchase. There are many practitioners who believe

2 Baba Shiv and Antoine Bechara (2010), "Revisiting the Customer Value Proposition" in *Brands and Brand Management: Contemporary Research Perspectives,* Barbara Loken, Rohini Ahluwalia, and Michael J. Houston (Eds.), New York and London: Routledge, 189-206.

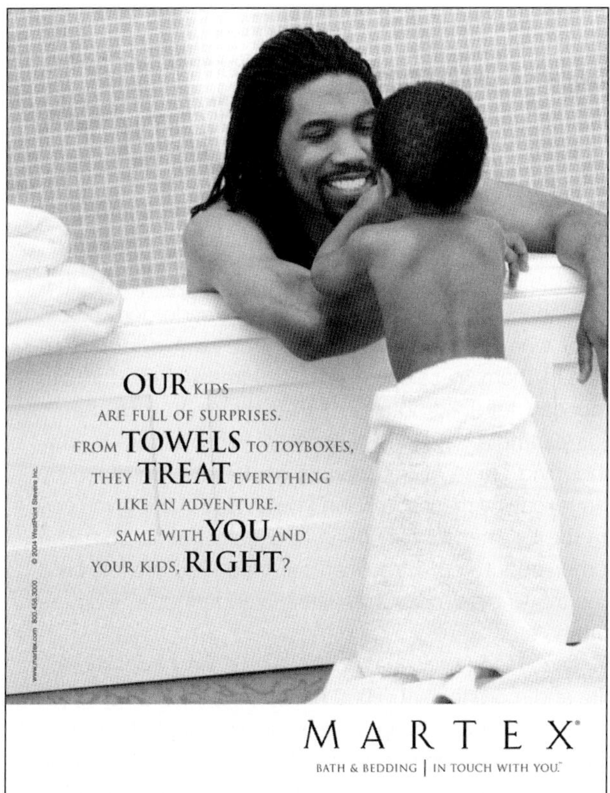

OUR KIDS
ARE FULL OF SURPRISES.
FROM TOWELS TO TOYBOXES,
THEY TREAT EVERYTHING
LIKE AN ADVENTURE.
SAME WITH YOU AND
YOUR KIDS, RIGHT?
MARTEX
BATH & BEDDING | IN TOUCH WITH YOU

Exhibit 10.11
A touching ad for Martex Bath & Bedding.
www.martex.com

in the method's intuitive appeal. We believe you must clearly associate the brand name and/or image with the feeling. Lots of ads don't do this—not even close. You may love ads for Miller Lite but be a Budweiser drinker. You may think, "Nice ads—wish they made a better beer."

Some feel-good advertising campaigns do work. Sometimes, feel-good ads try to get the consumer *not* to think about certain things. United Airlines could show how often its planes depart and arrive on schedule. Of course, why would they want to? Instead, it has shown successful business meetings and the happy reunion of family members, which create a much richer message, a wider field of shared meanings. And you don't have to think about being stuck at O'Hare or with a rude ticket agent. The emotions become the product attribute linked to the brand. Sometimes it works beautifully. Consider Kodak's highly successful print and television campaign that highlighted the "Memories of Our Lives" with powerful scenes: a son coming home from the military just in time for Christmas dinner, a father's reception dance with his newly married daughter. Here, Kodak makes it clear that it is in the memory business, and Kodak memories are good memories. Kodak has done this type of advertising, with occasional breaks, for about 100 years. It has worked. In Exhibit 10.11, Martex attempts to evoke warm feelings associated with the relationship between a father and son.

Recently, there has been progress in understanding the mechanisms involved in feel-good advertising.[3] It is becoming clearer that thought and feelings are, at some basic level, separate systems. Feelings are believed to be a more "primitive" system. That is, they emanate from a part of the brain that responds quickly to stimuli in the environment. The classic example is that a loud noise frightens us (feeling), before we know what we are frightened of (thought). So emotions are faster than thought, and sometimes even stronger. There is also evidence that as the media environment gets more cluttered, the affective (or feeling) ads may actually do better than thought-based ads that require a great deal of processing. Feeling ads may have a leg up in the contemporary media environment.

Evaluation of feel-good ads is typically done by measuring attitude change via pre- and post-exposure tests, tracking studies, theater dial-turning tests, and communication tests.

Strategic Implications of Feel-Good Advertising.

- Eager creatives. Creatives win awards and advance their careers with this style of advertising.
- May perform better in cluttered media environment.
- May generate competing thoughts and connections. An emotional ad about family and business travel may get the viewer to think about THEIR lives and their time on the road... but not really make any enduring connections to the brand. Your expensive emotional ad may make Joe or Mary consumer a better (or guilty) parent, but not a customer.

3 See Michel Tuan Pham, Joel B. Cohen, John W. Pracejus, and G. David Hughes, "Affect Monitoring and the Primacy of Feelings in Judgment," *Journal of Consumer Research*, vol. 28 (September 2001), 167–188.

Globalization

The Yogurt Rumor War in Argentina: I'm Dating a Supermodel Who Loves Yogurt

Argentina is a beautiful country with very sophisticated marketers. In early 2010, Actimel (DanActive in the United States) from Danone was the subject of a very serious viral slam campaign. In what appears to be a concerted and organized effort, emails were circulated widely to Argentines about the dangers of Actimel. According to *Ad Age Global*, they were then directed to a "web page that described supposed facts about Actimel, such as that the probiotic yogurt brand was addictive, destroyed the stomach's natural flora, and could harm childrens' health. Other blogs quickly picked up the story, and the damaging stories were soon the top ones returned in online searches for Actimel."

This was very bad. What to do?

First, the company did the usual: statements to the media and postings on their own website. But then, they got aggressive.

Accord to *Ad Age Global*, they then produced "a TV-spot in which Daniel Mainatti, a popular young investigative journalist, walks through a park surrounded by families playing with their children, and talks about the yogurt brand: 'You can trust Actimel. Anyone can have it. It's always good to have an Actimel.'"

Then, they really turned the tables. To show consumers just how easy it is to create ridiculous rumors, and how little you should trust them, they hired Buenos Aires-based Sinus, a digital agency. Sinus creates a campaign that gets consumers to go to a website (creadorderumores.com) where they can generate their own rumors and spread them to selected email addresses. On the site you can tell folks lots of untrue things from a menu. For example, "Argentine woman wins a free 10-day shopping spree at the world's best malls—followed by the takeaway message: 'Don't believe everything you see on the Internet. I'll show you how easy it is to spread a rumor about you.'" You can tell them you are off on a free trip to the World Cup, dating a supermodel, won the lottery, etc.

According to *Ad Age Global*, 40,000 people visited the site and more than 100,000 rumor emails were delivered.

"What we are trying to do is show people how easy it is to lie and deceive on the Web, and how careful we as consumers must be to get truths about brands," said Sebastian Garcia Padin, owner of Sinus. "What the Creador de Rumores is doing is telling people 'Be careful.'"

After all was said and done, Danone says that a valuable lesson was taught to consumers and no lasting harm to the brand occurred. Danone, however, would not release sales data to confirm.

Source: Based on *Advertising Age*, Danone Fights Damaging Viral Slurs in Argentina. In Response, Actimel Yogurt Creates Its Own Rumor Machine to Spread Playful Lies. Posted by Patricio Cavalli on 04.29.10 @ 02:16 PM.

Method B: Humor Ads. The goal of a humor ad is pretty much the same as that of other feel-good ads, but humor is a different animal. Generally, the goal of humor in advertising is to create in the receiver a pleasant and memorable association with the brand. Recent advertising campaigns as diverse as those for ESPN ("This Is SportsCenter"), California Milk Processor Board ("Got Milk?") and Las Vegas ("What Happens in Vegas, Stays in Vegas") have all successfully used humor as the primary message theme. But research suggests that the positive impact of humor is not as strong as the intuitive appeal of the approach. Quite simply, humorous versions of advertisements often do not prove to be more persuasive than nonhumorous versions of the same ad. Funny ads are usually great entertainment but may often be pretty bad business investments.

How many times have you been talking to friends about your favorite ads, and you say something like, "Remember the one where the guy knocks over the drink, and then says. . . ." Everybody laughs, and then maybe someone says something like, "I can't remember who it's for, but what a great ad." Wrong; this is not a great ad. You remember the gag, but not the brand. Not good. You and your friends didn't pay for the ad. How come with some funny ads you can recall the brand? The difference may be that in the ads you recall, the payoff for the humor is an integral part

Exhibit 10.12 *Here's Johnny.*

of the message strategy. Thus, it better ensures the memory link between humor and brand. If the ad is merely funny and doesn't link the joke (or the punch line) to the brand name, then the advertiser may have bought some very expensive laughs. Clients rarely consider this funny.

A great example of an explicitly linked payoff is the Bud Light "Give Me a Light" campaign of the early 1980s. "Miller Lite" was quickly becoming the generic term for light beer. To do something about this, Bud Light came up with the series of "Give Me a Light" ads to remind light beer drinkers that they had to be a little more specific in what they were ordering. The ads showed customers ordering "a light" and instead getting spotlights, landing lights, searchlights, lights in Wrigley Field, and all sorts of other types of lights. The customer in the ad would then say, "No, a Bud Light." The ads not only were funny but also made the point perfectly: Say "Bud Light," not just "a light," when ordering a beer. In addition, the message allowed thousands of customers and would-be comedians in bars and restaurants to repeat the line in person, which amounted to a lot of free advertising. The campaign, by Needham, Harper and Steers-Chicago (now DDB Chicago), was a huge success. Why? Because the punch line was firmly linked to the brand name, and the ad actually got consumers to repeat the tag line in actual consumer practice.

Evaluation of humorous ads is typically done through pre- and post-exposure tests; dial-turning attitude tests; and tracking studies that measure attitudes, beliefs, and preferences over time. The ad in Exhibit 10.12 is pretty funny. Have you seen *The Shining? "Here's Johnny"* in HD?

Strategic Implications of Humor Advertising.

- 👍 If the joke is integral to the copy platform, humor can be very effective. If it is not, it is just free entertainment.
- 👍 Very eager creatives. Creatives love to do funny ads. Funny ads tend to win awards and advance careers.
- 👎 Humorous messages may adversely affect comprehension. Humor can actually interfere with memory processes: The consumer doesn't remember what brand the ad was for.
- 👎 Very funny messages can wear out very quickly, leaving no one laughing, especially the advertiser.[4] It's like hearing the same joke over and over. Advertisers who use this technique have to keep changing the gag. Think "So Simple Even a Caveman Can Do It." They keep adding new gags to keep it interesting.

Because you have to keep the gag fresh, these can be very expensive ad campaigns.

Method C: Sex-Appeal Ads. Sex ads are a type of feelings-based advertising. Because they are directed toward humans, ads tend to focus on sex from time to time. Not a big surprise: Humans tend to think about sex from time to time. Sex ads are thought not to require much thought, just arousal and affect (feelings). But does sex sell?

In a literal sense, the answer is no, because nothing, not even sex, *makes* someone buy something. However, sexual appeals are attention-getting and occasionally

4. This claim is made by Video Storyboards Tests, based on its extensive research of humor ads, and cited in Kevin Goldman, "Ever Hear the One about the Funny Ad?" *The Wall Street Journal*, November 2, 1993, B11.

Courtesy, Wright's Media

arousing, which may affect how consumers feel about a product. The advertiser is trying to get attention and link some degree of sexual arousal and positive feelings to the brand. Sometimes this work, but the commonly held notion that "sex sells" is more over-simplification than reality.

Can you use sex to help create a brand image? Sure you can. Calvin Klein and many other advertisers have used sexual imagery successfully to mold brand image. But these are for products such as clothes and perfumes, which emphasize how one looks, feels, and smells. The context for the sex appeal is congruent, it fits, it makes sense. If you are trying to link a sexy image in an ad with a sexy brand image for lingerie, or perfume, or other relevant goods and services, it can work. Does the same appeal work as well for cars, telephones, computer peripherals, and file cabinets? How about breakfast cereals? In general, no. As recently noted by Professor Tom Reichert at the University of Georgia,[5] traditional wisdom in the ad business was that the use of sex is "amateurish and sophomoric, and a desperate—not to mention ineffective—attempt to rescue plummeting sales." The research on the topic generally confirms that sex-appeal ads can be effective when the context is appropriate, but a distraction or worse when it not. Think about it: a really hot ad comes on at night... you watch... what are you thinking about during the ad? The brand? You may remember the hot model in considerable detail and not remember a thing about the brand... unless that "heat" maps onto the meaning of the brand. Victoria's Secret wants to get you to link sex to their brand, and they have been very successful doing just that.

The four ads shown in Exhibit 10.13 use a sex-appeal message to one degree or another. How effective do you think these ads are in fulfilling the objective of instilling brand meaning and preference? Are they on target strategically? There is more discussion of sex in advertising than just about any other topic. So look at these ads and think about what is good, bad, effective, ineffective, OK, not OK, and why. Talk about which of these ads are good advertising, gratuitous advertising, demeaning, appropriate, and so on. You will be engaging in the same debate that advertising professionals do.

If you use a heavy dose of sex in an ad, you may have "issues" with some clients or advocacy groups. Although the fear of losing sales is an entirely reasonable concern, it is rarely a real one in practice. Just as consumers do not typically buy something (like a lawn mower) because of a poor-fitting sex appeal, they will rarely refrain from buying it either. After Nipple-Gate (Super Bowl with Janet Jackson), the advertising industry wondered publicly whether we were entering a new age of puritanical thought. We think the last few years have pretty much answered the question: no.

Evaluation of sex-appeal ads is typically done through communication tests, focus groups, pre- and post-exposure tests, and tracking studies that measure attitudes, beliefs, and preferences over time. When using sex appeal, clients sometimes order more focus groups and communication tests to make sure that they are not going over some invisible and always-moving line.

Strategic Implications of Sexual-Appeal Advertising.

- 👍 Higher attention levels.
- 👍 Higher arousal and affective (feeling). This can be good if it can be tied to brand meaning, bad if it can't.
- 👎 Possible poor memorability of brand due to interference at the time of exposure. In other words, the viewer is thinking about something else.
- 👎 Product-theme continuity excludes many goods and services.
- 👎 Legal, political, and regulatory exposure.

5. Tom Reichert, *The Erotic History of Advertising* (Amherst, NY: Prometheus, 2004).

Exhibit 10.13 Sex-appeal ads are among the most common and the most controversial in advertising. But often the issues of "what is appropriate" and "why" get completely mixed up and confused. Here, we provide a selection of current ads for your inspection and discussion. Which do you think are good, sound, on-strategy advertising? Which do you think use sex inappropriately? Which are in poor taste? Which may do the brand more harm than good? What might women think and feel about these ads and the companies that sponsor them? How about men? Should there be more regulations, or not? What do you think?

a) www.azzuredenim.com; b) Courtesy of Skyy Spirits, Importer of Cutty Sark Scots Whisky; c and d) Courtesy, Advertising Archives

Objective #5: Scare the Consumer into Action.

The strategy here is to scare the consumer into acting. Fear appeals are typically designed to illicit a specific feeling (fear) as well as a specific thought (buy x to prevent y). Fear is an extraordinarily powerful emotion and may be used to get consumers to take some very important action. But this fear must be coupled with some degree of thought in order for it to work. That's why we place this strategy a bit higher up the ladder in terms of its degree of complexity. It is generally considered hard to use effectively and is fairly limited in application. It is only used in few product and service categories.

Method: Fear-Appeal Ads. A fear appeal highlights the risk of harm or other negative consequences of not using the advertised brand or not taking some recommended action. Usually it's a little bit of fear designed to induce a little bit of thought, and then action. Getting the balance right is the tricky part. The intuitive belief about fear as a message tactic is that fear will motivate the receiver to buy a product that will reduce or eliminate the portrayed threat. For example, Radio Shack

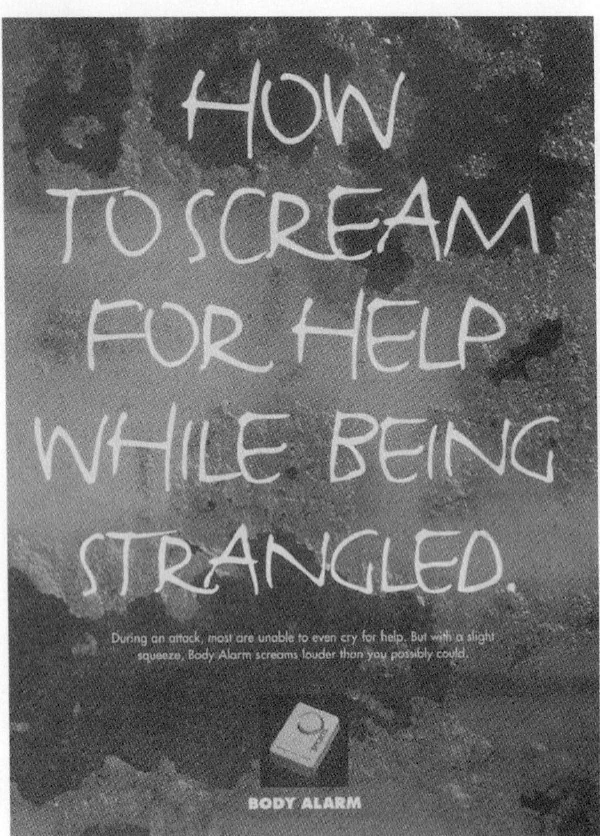

HOW TO SCREAM FOR HELP WHILE BEING STRANGLED.
During an attack, most are unable to even cry for help. But with a slight squeeze, Body Alarm screams louder than you possibly could.
BODY ALARM

Exhibit 10.14 Fairly scary. Get the point?

spent $6 million to run a series of ads showing a dimly lit unprotected house, including a peacefully sleeping child, as a way to raise concerns about the safety of the receiver's valuables as well as his or her family. The campaign used the theme "If Security Is the Question, We've Got the Answer." The ad closed with the Radio Shack logo and the National Crime Prevention Council slogan, "United Against Crime."[6] Similarly, the ad in Exhibit 10.14 for Body Alarm cuts right to the chase: It capitalizes on fears of not being able to cry for help during a bodily attack. ADT has had a long-running campaign showing a vulnerable woman (often single, sometimes with a child) being saved from sure victimization by the ADT security team.

The contemporary social environment has provided advertisers with an ideal context for using fear appeals. In an era of drive-by shootings, carjackings, gang violence, and terrorism, Americans fear for their personal safety. Manufacturers of security products such as alarm and lighting security systems leverage this fearful environment.[7] Other advertisers have recently tried fear as an appeal. One such advertiser, the Asthma Zero Mortality Coalition, urges people who have asthma to seek professional help and uses a fear appeal in its ad copy: "When those painful, strained breaths start coming, keep in mind that any one of them could easily be your last."[8] In Exhibit 10.15, Electrolux shows us the things that live in all our carpets, and how to get rid of them.

Research indicates that until a consumer gets to very high fear levels, more is better. So, moderate levels of fear appear to work better than low levels. However, the effect of truly intense levels of fear is either unknown or thought to be counterproductive. Traditional wisdom holds that intense fear appeals actually short-circuit persuasion and results in a negative attitude toward the advertised brand.[9] A few other researchers argue that the tactic is generally beneficial to the advertiser.[10] Our review of the science, plus our own professional experience, leads us to believe that moderate fear levels are the best, and to be successful, a fear-appeal ad must have a very clear benefit from acting now in a very specific way. Fear ads must offer a "way out" of harm's way. The ideal fear-appeal ad would thus be a moderate level of fear that is entirely believable[11] (one that people can't easily say doesn't apply to them or seems unlikely to be a real threat) and offers a very clear (completely obvious) and very easy way to avoid the bad thing threatened by the ad. Evaluation of fear-appeal ads is typically done through tracking studies that measure attitudes, beliefs, and preferences over time; pre- and post-exposure tests; and communication tests.

6. Jeffrey D. Zbar, "Fear!," *Advertising Age*, November 14, 1994, 18.

7. Ibid.

8. Emily DeNitto, "Healthcare Ads Employ Scare Tactics," *Advertising Age*, November 7, 1994, 12.

9. Irving L. Janis and Seymour Feshbach, "Effects of Fear Arousing Communication," *Journal of Abnormal Social Psychology* 48 (1953), 78–92.

10. Michael Ray and William Wilkie, "Fear: The Potential of an Appeal Neglected by Marketing," *Journal of Marketing*, vol. 34, no. 1 (January 1970), 54–62.

11. E. H. H. J. Das, J. B. F. de Wit, and W. Strobe, "Fear Appeals Motivate Acceptance of Action Recommendations: Evidence for a Positive Bias in the Processing of Persuasive Messages," *Personality and Social Psychology Bulletin*, vol. 29 (2003), 650–664.

Exhibit 10.15 Just to look at a dust mite close up is a little scary

Look who's been sleeping
with your daughter.
Electrolux
Surpreendendo você.

Courtesy of Electrolux

Strategic Implications of Fear-Appeal Advertising.

- Moderate levels of fear appear to work the best.
- You must have a plausible threat to motivate consumers.
- You must have a completely clear and easy-to-discern link between the alleviation of the threat and the use of the advertised brand.
- Too little or too much fear may do nothing.
- Legal, regulatory, and ethical problems.
- Some fear ads are simply ridiculous and have low impact.

Objective #6: Change Behavior by Inducing Anxiety.

Anxiety is fear's cousin. Anxiety is not quite outright fear, but it is uncomfortable and can last longer. Although it's hard to keep people in a state of outright fear, people can feel anxious for a bad long time. People try to avoid feeling anxious. They try to minimize, moderate, and alleviate anxiety. They use all sorts of mechanisms to avoid anxiety from thought to behavior. Often people will buy or consume things to help them in their continuing struggle with anxiety. They might watch television, smoke, exercise, eat, or take medication. They might also buy mouthwash, deodorant, condoms, a safer car, life insurance, or a retirement account, and advertisers know this. Advertisers pursue a change-behavior-by-inducing-anxiety objective by playing on consumer anxieties. The ads work through both thought and feelings. Regrettably, this is one of the most effective types of advertising around.

Method A: Anxiety Ads. There are many things to be anxious about. Advertisers realize this and use many settings to demonstrate why you should be anxious and what you can do to alleviate the anxiety. Social, medical, and personal-care products frequently use anxiety ads. The message conveyed in anxiety ads is that (1) there is a clear and present problem, and (2) the way to avoid this problem is to buy the advertised brand. Anxiety ads tout the likelihood of being stricken by gingivitis, athlete's foot, calcium deficiency, body odor, heart disease, and on and on. The idea is that these anxiety-producing conditions are

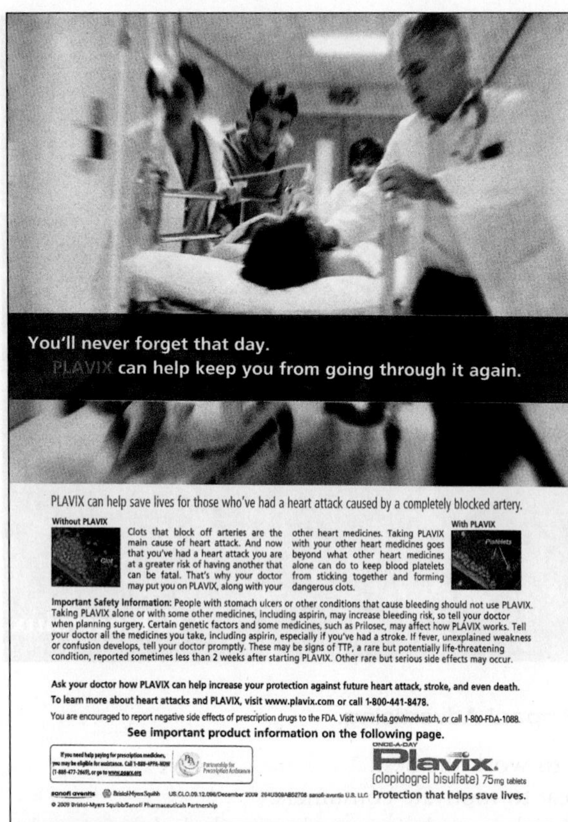

Exhibit 10.16 Feeling anxious about your heart, dads?

out there, and they may affect you unless you take the appropriate action. What anxieties might the ad in Exhibit 10.16 arouse?

Method B: Social Anxiety Ads. This is a subcategory of anxiety ads where the danger is negative social judgment, as opposed to a physical threat. Procter & Gamble has long relied on such presentations for its household and personal-care brands. In fact, Procter & Gamble has used this approach so consistently over the years that in some circles, the anxiety tactic is referred to as the P&G approach. When Head & Shoulders dandruff shampoo is advertised with the theme "You Never Get a Second Chance to Make a First Impression," the audience realizes that Head & Shoulders could spare them the embarrassment of having dandruff. One of the more memorable P&G social anxiety ads is the scene where husband and wife are busily cleaning the spots off the water glasses before dinner guests arrive because they didn't use P&G's Cascade dishwashing product, which, of course, would have prevented the glasses from spotting. Most personal-care products have used this type of appeal.

Anxiety ads are often used in the context of important social roles... and the consumer's perceived inadequacy in that role. Billions of dollars have been made selling products to make mothers feel a little less bad about their mothering skills, or father's about their ability to adequately provide for the family... and the list goes on and on (see Exhibits 10.17 and 10.18). Do you want consumer-generated content like Exhibit 10.18 out there? This type of ad works by pointing to anxieties that reside right on the surface of consumers in these roles, or are just slightly latent, or beneath the surface. We tend to worry about the things we care most about and the things where the standards of adequacy and excellence are unknowable. What makes a great husband, father, mother, worker, etc.? We are not quite sure. So, advertisers go to that anxiety and irritate it a bit, and then offer the consumer the way to feel better. It's really kind of a nasty thing to do, but it seems to work so well.

Fortunately, some degree of self-awareness comes to smart companies. Here Tampax spends its own money to lampoon the category it pretty much created (see Exhibit 10.19 on page 362).

Evaluation of anxiety ads is typically done by measuring attitudes and beliefs through tracking studies and communication tests.

Strategic Implications of Anxiety Advertising.

- Can generate perception of widespread (and thus personal) threat and motivate action (buying and using the advertised product). These ads have a pretty good track record of working.
- The brand can become the solution to the ever-present problem, and this results in long-term commitment to the brand. Once a solution (brand) is found, the consumer doesn't have to think about it again.
- Efficient: A little anxiety goes a long way.
- Too much anxiety, like fear, may overwhelm the consumer, and the ad and the brand may be avoided because it produces too much discomfort.
- If the anxiety-producing threat is not linked tightly enough to your brand, you may increase category demand and provide business for your competitors,

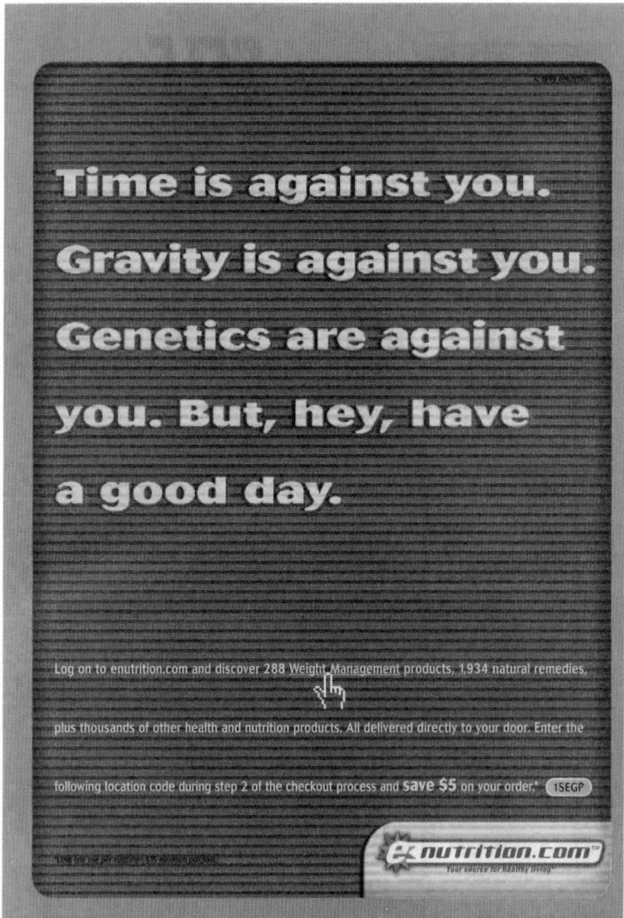

Exhibit 10.17 But, hey, have a good day.

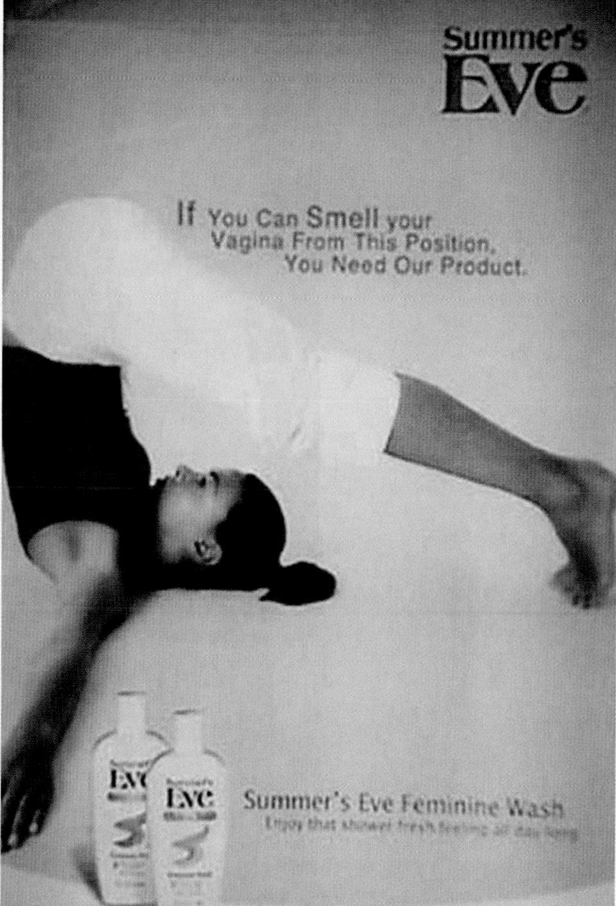

Exhibit 10.18 Feeling fresh? Given the ability of consumers to generate their own content, advertisers can be easy targets of lampoons. Social justice?

Courtesy, Susan Van Etten; Courtesy, Susan Van Etten

particularly the market leader. If total category share goes up, market leaders get most of it. Still, if the creative is good and the link to the specific brand is strong, it is a good method for any size player.

- Ethical issues: Some believe there is more than enough to feel anxious about without advertisers adding more.
- These ads have historically been disproportionately targeted at women. Critics note the inherent unfairness and sexism. They have a point.

Objective #7: Define the Brand Image.

The term "brand image" refers to the meaning of a brand, but at the level of impression, the quick take away of what the brand is all about. It is expressed in visual terms (image) because brand images typically rely on the visual impression a brand makes with only a glance. Truly iconic (another visual term) brands have the ability to convey their essential meaning with just the swoosh (Nike), or the red circle (Coke), or the stylized and familiar written brand name (Tide). Not surprisingly, defining brand image is typically achieved visually. Brand images are important for several reasons. For one, they allow for an enormously efficient form of communication in a crowded media environment. The McDonald's golden arches deliver a lot of meaning with just a glance. Second, once they are established (and properly maintained), they create clear differentiation of one brand from another. Finally, they are not very dependent on any one language and are this perfect for the transnational company.

MOTHER NATURE'S MONTHLY GIFT

Exhibit 10.19 Having a little fun with the average ad in this category.

Courtesy, Advertising Archives

Exhibit 10.20 Image.

Method: Image Ads. Image advertising attempts to distill the brand's essential meaning with a very sparse use of words and heavy reliance on visuals. Image ads don't tend to contain much hard product information. They may use images to point to a brand quality or attribute or evoke a certain set of feelings about the brand. But, whether feelings or thoughts, or both, the idea is to define brand meaning in an efficient visual manner.

Check out the three ads in Exhibits 10.20–10.22. Do they work? How well?

Evaluation of image ads is typically done through qualitative methods, and sometimes associative tests are used, along with attribute-related attitude tracking studies done over time. As we've said before, the evaluation of visual communication is still not where it should be. Further, these ads are often figurative rather than literal and require evaluation methods like the Zaltman (ZMET) metaphor-based techniques (discussed in Chapter 7). They are also heavily dependent upon the maker of the ad being completely in touch with the contemporary culture so that the audience "gets" the ad. It is the skillful use of this social and cultural knowledge that turns brands into very successful brands, or even brand icons.[12]

Brand managers must work closely with advertising professionals to make sure that (1) the desired brand identity is really understood by all parties, and (2) how that typically verbal description is translated in a visual. Think about the most successful brands in the world. They are almost all "iconic," meaning that their essential meaning is captured and efficiently transmitted visually. The *Marlboro Man* is said to be a perfect icon of what the brand means. Apple, Nike, McDonald's, and Coke come to mind. To get to that iconic status requires an enduring and very cultural connected creative effort. It requires management wise enough to either help in this effort or trust the creatives. From all reports, Philip Morris trusted Leo Burnet with Marlboro Man.

Exhibits 10.21 and 10.22 These are image ads. Even though some people think of these ads as light and fluffy, they are anything but that. They are carefully constructed to yield the right set of connections and the right images. Think about these. Do you get them?

Courtesy, Skyy Spirits; Image courtesy of Kohler Co.; Courtesy, DieselStyleLab

12. Douglas B. Holt, "What Becomes an Icon Most?" Harvard Business Review (March 2003).

Strategic Implications of Image Advertising.

- 👍 Generally, less counterarguments generated by consumers.
- 👍 Relatively little or no legal/regulatory exposure: hard to litigate the truth or falsity of a picture.
- 👍 Iconic potential.
- 👎 Very common in some categories (e.g. fashion, fragrance). Your image can get lost in the competitive cloud.
- 👎 Can be quickly rejected if advertised image rings untrue or poorly matches what the consumer currently thinks of the brand, particularly through direct experience.
- 👎 Don't tend to copy-test well. Why? Well, once again, existing copy-test procedures are designed predominately for words, not images.
- 👎 Managerial resistance: Client often argues for more words.
- 👍 Creatives tend to love them; you can get great people on your communication team.
- 👎 Poor understanding by brand management of the desired image. This is why the ZMET and other visual metaphor techniques are so helpful.

Objective #8: Give the Brand the Desired Social Meaning.

Maybe you haven't given it much thought, but if you're ever going to understand advertising, you have to get this: Objects have social meanings. Billions of dollars are spent annually in efforts to achieve very specific social meanings for advertised brands. As an advertising and brand messaging professional, you have to try to make material objects (and services like FedEx) that already carry some meaning, have the meaning you want them to have. How do you do it?

Advertisers have long known that when they place their brand in the right social setting, either in an ad, a branded promotion in a real environment, or a product placement in a television, show, movie, or video game, their brand takes on some of the characteristics of its surroundings. The social setting and the brand rub off on each other. That is what is meant by giving the brand social meaning.

All watches keep good time. But a Casio is different than a Tag Huer, a Rolex, and so on. They all do the same thing. They are, as far as keeping time, the same. So, a watch is not just a watch. A watch is a way of communicating social status, wealth, fashion, and a sense of self. For men, it is one of the most accepted statements of social identity. In the watch category, these kinds of ads are common because the brands so importantly rely on desired social meaning. Think of fashion ads, same thing. Many categories rely on this objective to sell.

Let us say it again: Objects have social meaning; they are not just things. Good social meaning advertising can let the advertiser shape that meaning. If done well, these can be very effective ads.

Method A: Slice-of-Life Ads. A brand placed in a social context gains social meaning by association. Slice-of-life advertisements depict an ideal usage situation for the brand. The social context surrounding the brand rubs off and gives the brand social meaning. Consumers may, of course, reject or significantly alter that meaning, but often they accept it. Think about it. You put the brand into a social setting and transfer meaning from that social setting to the brand. Look at Exhibit 10.23. Think about it, about how it works.

Evaluation of slice-of-life ads is typically done through tracking studies that measure attitudes, beliefs, and preferences over time; pre- and post-exposure tests; and communication tests.

Exhibit 10.23 By carefully constructing a social world within the frame of the ad into which the product is carefully placed, meaning is transferred to the product. "Background" and product meanings merge. This is the sophistication behind "slice-of-life" advertising. www.louisboston.com

Cheryl Heller Design; Art Direction, Copy Heller Communications

Strategic Implications of Slice-of-Life Ads.

- 👍 Generally, fewer counterarguments made by consumers.
- 👍 Legal/regulatory advantages. Advertisers' attorneys like pictures more than words because determining the truth or falsity of a picture is much tougher than words. Have you ever noticed how heavily regulated industries tend to use lots of pictures and little copy (other than mandated warning labels?)
- 👍 Iconic potential. To make their brands another Coca-Cola is many advertisers' dream. Socially embedding your brand in everyday life gives you this chance.
- 👍 Creation of brand-social-realities. You may be able to create the perfect social world for the brand, and its space in it.
- 👎 Fairly common. Unless the creative is outstanding (particularly visually) and you are generally willing to spend a reasonable amount for repetition, these ads can get lost in the clutter. In certain categories, such as fashion, a lot of ads are of this type.
- 👎 These ads don't tend to copy-test well. This is because so much of copy-testing is still designed around remembering words and verbal claims. Copy-testing has simply not caught up with the new reality of the prominence of visual forms of advertising and brand promotion.
- 👍 Creatives tend to love these ads (at least, art directors do); you will get some top-flight creative folks on the job.

Method B: Branded Entertainment: Product Placement. In the age of new media, we have gone well beyond a few product placements in movies and TV shows to a more and more broad-spectrum and integrated set of methods to bring brand messages to consumers. These methods are often gathered under one umbrella called Madison & Vine. It began as a conference to bring together Hollywood (the famous intersection of "Hollywood and Vine") and the advertising industry (traditionally based along New York's Madison Avenue, although agencies are now all over the place): thus "Madison & Vine." Madison & Vine then became a book, an *Ad Age* column, and now encompasses a wide array of nontraditional integrated brand promotions (IBP). Recording, gaming, and cell phone industries are involved as well now. The most important development is how many major advertisers are now involved in producing movies that are really brand promotions, TV

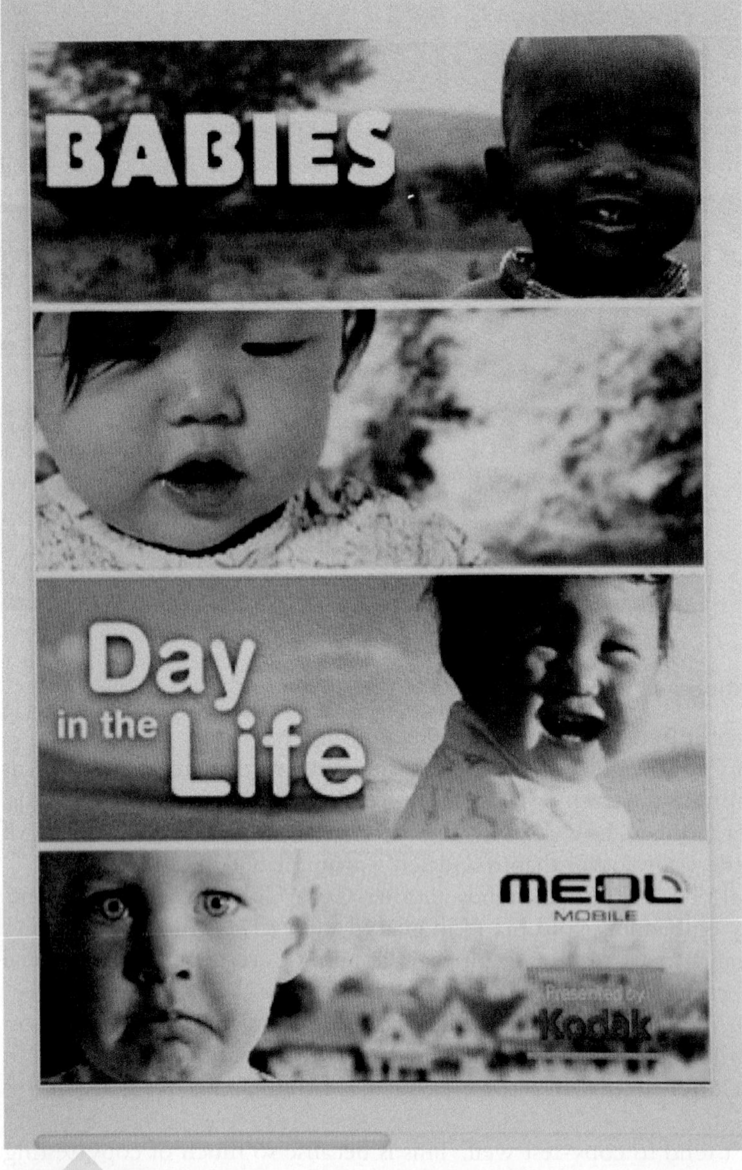

Exhibit 10.24 Documentary film is used effectively by several companies, including Johnson & Johnson.

shows that are really brand promotions, cell phone content that is really brand promotion, TV spots for new musical recordings that are also ads for product... and so on.) We will dig deeper into this topic in Chapter 16, but for now we'll focus on a common form and one that is in this strategic set: product placement and integration.

One way to integrate the product into a desired setting is to place the product in a television show or film (see Exhibits 10.24 and 10.25). An actor picks up a can of Coke, rather than just any soda, and hopefully the correct image association is made. Even more explicit are short films (usually less than 10 minutes) made for the Internet. A few years ago, BMW released six such films showing its cars in dramatic contexts. The most famous was a film starring Madonna and directed by her husband, British film director Guy Ritchie (*Lock, Stock, and Two Smoking Barrels; Snatch*). The films were all made by hot directors and had amazing story content, yet they were also a way of demonstrating the product by placing it in a deliberately and carefully created social world. BMW sales responded very nicely and executives believed it was a much better media buy than network television, where getting lost in the crowd is so easy. Ford alone spends nearly $2 billion a year on national advertising. What would BMW have to spend just to get noticed in that environment? BMW eventually pulled these films from their website, either because the models in the films were getting outdated as new

Exhibit 10.25 Oracle: Iron Man's personal choice in server software.

Courtesy, Susan Van Etten; Courtesy, Susan Van Etten

Social Media

Kraft Makes Mini-Movies

When you go to the movies, you occasionally see some ads mixed in with the previews. They are usually just re-cut versions of ads running on TV. But Kraft just changed all of that. With a big move into branded entertainment, Kraft is making and showing two to three minute mini-movies made specifically for movie theaters. Initial stars include: Oscar Meyer Lunchables, Ritz Crackers, and Cadbury's Stride Gum.

Cliff Marks, president of sales and marketing at National CineMedia, told *Ad Age* "Kraft really took the concept of creating two- to three-minute mini-movies and not only made history but did it in a very entertaining, compelling fashion that doesn't knock you over the head with a bat as a brand commercial."

Mark Stewart, Kraft's VP-global media services told *Ad Age,* "It's about layering the brand story in different channels and layering what each one does best. In most cases, people are seeing movies for the first time. We want to make sure our brand story is complimentary to what they're there to see."

Although many companies are engaged in branded entertainment, Kraft was the first to choose this specific form: mini-films shown in movie theaters... and then probably on the Internet as well. Kraft believes that the movies are entertaining, not too obvious, and polite in the sense that they are not straight TV commercials. After all, the audience paid to see the movie, not watch TV.

Source: *Advertising Age,* "Kraft Heads to Big Screen as Part of Cinema-Ad Deal; Food Giant Brings Branded Content, Not Re-purposed TV Spots, to Pre-show Programs" by Andrew Hampp, Published: April 29, 2010. adage.com/results?endeca=1&return=endeca&search_offset=0&search_order_by=score&search_phrase=04/29/2010

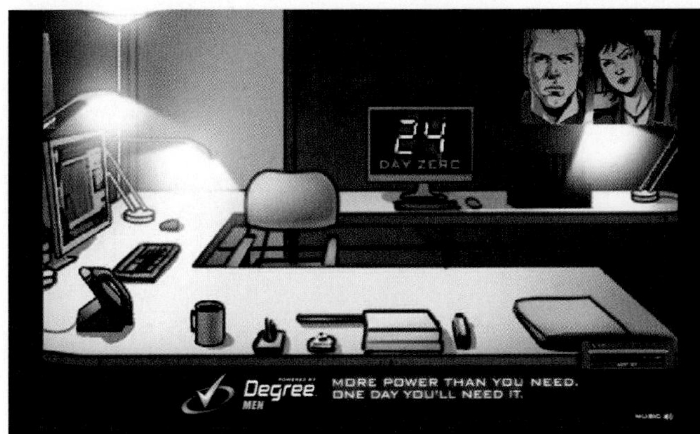

Exhibit 10.26 Product placement deals are becoming the norm.

Courtesy, Susan Van Etten

models were out, or for some other reason we simply don't know. However, since that time, the idea or similar ones has really caught on. Exhibit 10.24 shows how J&J used the documentary film to advance its brands, while Exhibit 10.25 shows the more traditional brand–movie cross-promotion. Both are forms of branded entertainment.

You can follow this evolving saga of this on adage.com/madisonandvine, so we will mention just a few other examples. Ford Motor Company has decided to be partners in the new motion picture studio Our Stories Films, a joint venture of Ford, entrepreneur and BET founder Robert L. Johnson, and movie moguls Bob and Harvey Weinstein to produce what Ford has called "the black Walt Disney." Their initial goal is to produce three to five "African-American family films." According to *Advertising Age*, Ford will have "script integration, sponsorships, and promotions." According to theory, everyone wins: Ford gets its cars into movies, the cost of producing the films is partially underwritten by the car company, and Robert L. Johnson serves an African-American audience.

The producers of *24* made a deal through their prequel *CTU Rookie* (Exhibit 10.26) and the animated *DayZero* with Unilever to promote Degree deodorant. In no time at all, Unilever had more than 1.5 million hits to its related website.

Exhibit 10.27 Placement activity report.

TOP 10 BRANDS WITH TV PRODUCT PLACEMENT
Jan. 18 to Feb. 14, 2010

Brand	Category	Total # Occurrences
Coca-Cola	Soft Drinks	43
Nike	Apparel	32
Apple	Computer Systems	22
Ford	Autos	22
24 Hours Fitness	Fitness Centers	21
Toyota	Autos	19
Disney Parks	Entertaiment Parks	18
Dell	Computer Systems	17
Microsoft	Computer Systems	16
Dolby	Business Services	15

TOP 10 SHOWS WITH TV PRODUCT PLACEMENT
Jan. 18 to Feb. 14, 2010

Program	Network	Total # Occurrences
The Jay Leno Show	NBC	315
American Idol	Fox	85
Extreme Makeover: Home Edition	ABC	70
The Biggest Loser	NBC	57
The Grammy Awards	CBS	49
Life Unexpected	CW	29
The Amazing race 16	CBS	25
Chuck	NBC	21
Undercover Boss	CBS	20
Mercy	NBC	19
Staturday Night Live Presents: Sports All-Stars	NBC	19
The Office	NBC	19

Surce: The Nielsen Company

Prime time entertaiment programming on 5 broadcast networks (ABC, CBS, CW, Fox and NBC); first-run episodes only included.

Note: Due to recent Place*Views coding enhencements, the total # of occurrences now reflect the number of show segments in which a brand placement appears Additionally, the above list is now Based only on first-run episodes, in order to profile those advertisers/programsthat are most active at the present time

Sales went up at least 20 percent in a category that is growing.13 At the same time, Degree was running more traditional TV spots.

There are thousands of these examples. To give you an idea of just how much branded content there is out there, check out Exhibit 10.27.

13. Jack Neff, "Case Study: Why Unilever Execs Are Loving '24.' Webisode Partnership with Fox Show Helps Degree Men Sales Climb 20%" adage.com, published June 21, 2007.

Exhibit 10.28 Placement activity report.

TOP 10 SHOWS WITH TV PRODUCT PLACEMENT Jan. 18 to Feb. 14, 2010				
1	7 UP	Soft drink brand awards cash and prizes to steve and allie for arriving in first place	The Amazing Race 16 (CBS, Mar 28)	147
2	Craftsman	Villains choose toll kit from Sears circular as Reward Challenge prize	Survivor Heroes vs. Villains (CBS, Mar 4)	134
3	Ride the Ducks	Joel Manby visits tour boat operation to see how staff performs	Undercover Boss (CBS, Mar 28	133
4	Coca-Cola	Cups sit on Judeges' table during contestant persormances	American Idol (Fox, Mar 24)	131
5	Coca-Cola	Soft drink's name appears onscreen and on couch as Siobhan is interviewed	American Idol (Fox, Mar 9)	129
6	Sears	Teams receive store's circular with items to select as prizes for Reward Challenge	Survivor Heroes vs. Villains (CBS, Mar 4)	126
7	Coca-Cola	Soft drink's name appears on-screen and on monitors as Casey is interviewed	American Idol (Fox, Mar 23)	125
8	Ford	Ryan Seacrest tells viewers to visit website to find out how to win a customized Fiesta	American Idol (Fox, Mar 17)	125
9	Coca-Cola	Cups sit on judges' table during contestant performances	American Idol (Fox, Mar 16)	124
10	Coca-Cola	Cups sit on judges' table during contestant performances	American Idol (Fox, Mar 23)	123

Source: Nielsen IAG In-Program Performance Data (www.nielseniag.com).

Exhibit 10.28 lists the most recalled in-product placements for a similar period. There is, however, debate about whether recall is even really desirable. Perhaps what advertisers really want is for their brand to become integral parts of a desired social reality, a media-created world where the brand is absolutely normal and expected, almost invisible. Some contemporary theories of memory suggest that this would indeed be best over time, as the source of the brand image becomes disassociated from the brand memory. In other words, consumers believe Degree is a very popular brand among the desired target market, part of their world. Recent research has, however, suggested that the effects of placement are strongest with so called "low-involvement" goods and services, lower priced, the result of fairly quick decision making. When consumers actually have to consider a major purchase, like a car, the effects of brand promotion appear to be much weaker and may even backfire.

Strategic Implications of Branded Entertainment.

- 👍 Low counterargument, if placement not too obvious.
- 👍 May reduce defensive measures by consumers, such as source discounting.
- 👍 May actually increase consumer's estimates about how many other people use the brand, thus making it appear more prevalent and popular than it actually is.
- 👍 A perceived cost advantage over the very expensive network TV.
- 👎 Nonstandardized rate structure; hard to price these; deals done in private.
- 👎 May not be very effective for high involvement categories.

Objective #9: Leverage Social Disruption and Cultural Contradictions.

We are now way up the sophistication scale. As mentioned in Chapter 4, some really great brands have used advertising to successfully leverage social disruption (youth revolution, second-wave of American feminism in the 1970s, the post-punk

Exhibit 10.29
Pabst Blue Ribbon... Heineken. An amazing job of leveraging the social dynamics of the times.

culture and energy, and now angry populism). The idea is to find a point where the social fabric is frayed (usually gender, race, age, politics, labor, economy, other opportunity inequities) and suggest that your brand gets it and is the unofficially sanctioned brand of the counter-culture. Among the brands that have been said to have achieved enormous success through this are: Marlboro (independence and reassertion of rigid gender/labor roles in the post-WWII period), Virginia Slims (2nd Wave of American Feminism), Mountain Dew (disaffected Gen-X slackers), Pepsi (60s youth revolution), etc.[14]

Method: Tie Brand to Social/Cultural Movement. Sometimes this is done very explicitly (Pepsi), other times very implicitly. Pabst Blue Ribbon (PBR) became the working-class hero beer of West Coast bike messenger culture (see Exhibit 10.29). PBR management was smart enough to notice and then capitalize on it through all sorts of promotional activities. Red Bull is said to have done something pretty similar. What do you think are the current social tensions that could be appropriated for selling brands through advertising and brand promotion?

This is a very sophisticated and typically difficult method. The reason it is difficult is not in the execution but being culturally attuned enough to know in the present what various target marketers are conflicted about... and how to offer a brand as a solution, even a partial one. This is different than merely chasing trends; it is seeing the cultural land beneath your feet shifting in significant ways, before it is obvious to everyone. What would you say are the ones going on these days, the bigger one: populist anger (see Exhibit 10.30), anger at the very rich, or the Wall Street crowd who are accused of betting against their fellow citizens (see Exhibit 10.31). Think about how you could leverage those (or others) to a brand's advantage.

Objective #10: Transform Consumption Experiences.

We view this as the most sophisticated strategies going. But, it is also very hard to do well.

You know how sometimes it's hard to explain to someone else just exactly why a certain experience was so special, why it was so good? It wasn't just this or that; the entire experience was somehow better than the sum of the individual parts. Sometimes that feeling is at least partly due to your expectations of what something will be like, your positive memories of previous experiences, or both.

Sometimes advertisers try to provide that anticipation and/or familiarity bundled up in a positive memory of an advertisement or other brand communication, to be activated during the consumption experience itself, and recalled positively after the experience. That's right: the advertiser is trying to help create positive memories of brand usage even before the consumer has used the brand, and (more commonly) weave those memories of actual use together with advertising supplied "memories" in a way that the advertising can effectively shape consumer memories of brand usage. The advertising or promotional experience is thus said to have *transformed* the actual consumption experience, both at the time of consumption and in the consumer's memory.

14 For a good discussion, see Thomas C. O'Guinn and Albert Muniz, Jr. (2010), "The Social Brand: Towards a Sociological Model of Brands," in *Brands and Brand Management: Contemporary Research Perspectives,* Barbara Loken, Rohini Ahluwalia, and Michael J. Houston (Eds.), New York and London: Routledge, 133–159.

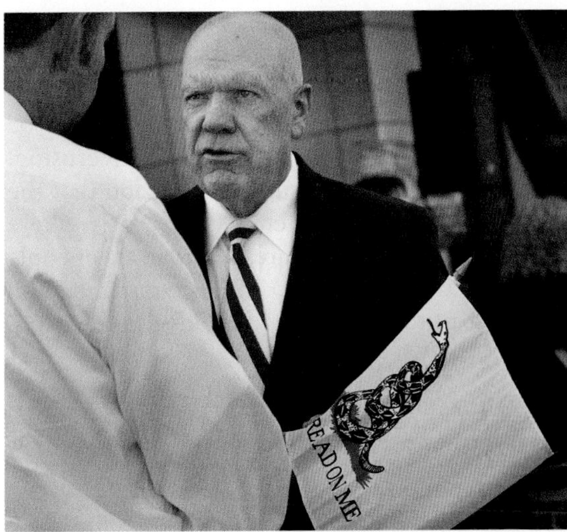

Exhibit 10.30 How could a brand leverage this expression of populist rage? Or not?

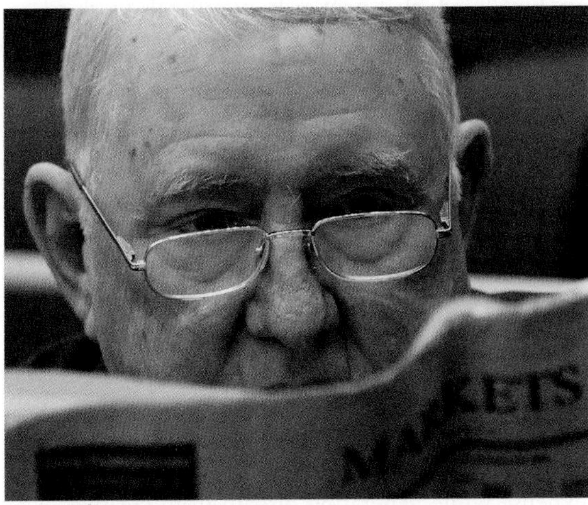

Exhibit 10.31 How could a smart advertiser use anger at Wall Street to their advantage?

Exhibit 10.32 Smart marketing.

Method: Transformational Ads. The idea behind transformational advertising is that it can actually make the consumption experience better. For example, after years of transformational advertising by McDonald's (an early user), the experience of actually eating at McDonald's may be "transformed" or made better by virtue of what you know and feel about McDonald's each time you walk in. Transformational advertising attempts to create a brand feeling, expectation, and mood that are activated when the consumer uses the product or service. Actual usage is thus transformed, made better. Transformational ads that are effective are said to connect the experience of the advertisement so closely with the brand experience that consumers cannot help but think of material from the ads (or in a more general sense, the memory of many things from many ads) when they think of the brand. Think about the transformational potential in Exhibit 10.32. What if you sign up for a trip to go to a theme park, take a cruise, or purchase anything that sells an experience? It could be a retail store, say Nordstrom or Tiffany. Prior to taking that cruise or going to that theme park, you saw an ad (or a received a video) that shows the ideal trip to that location, the perfect experience. What is seen becomes part of memory. Then, maybe after going, you get some type of similar one, but maybe this time it included photos or video of your trip there... great moments. Those also become part of long-term memory. If, as researchers have shown, it is possible to create false memories of brands that don't even exist, isn't it possible that over time commercial content and actual experience begin to merge in memory, and the consumer remembers things as they and the advertisers want them to? What if Disney mailed you a videotape of a perfect trip to the Magic Kingdom before you went, and one after you returned? Maybe in a year or two those memories would merge in a fashion that benefits Disney. Then, when you remember your time at the park, the hotel, the cruise, the store, you remember a blend of things: some from your actual experience, some from what was provided by the marketer. This has benefits for your feelings toward the brand, your recommendations to others, increases the likelihood to repurchase, and actually may shape, or transform, actual future consumption experiences. Product placements in movies and television shows, and other forms of branded entertainment, can accomplish the same thing. Traditional ads can do this as well.

Evaluation of transformational ads and other forms of IBP are typically done through field studies, tracking studies, ethnographic (on-site, qualitative) methods, and communication tests. On rare occasions, small-scale experiments are conducted.

Strategic Implications of Transformational Advertising.

- Can be extremely powerful due to a merging of ad and brand experience.
- Fosters long-term commitment.
- Can ring absolutely false and hurt the brand.
- Ethical issues: Some believe that this manipulation of experience is unethical.

In the End.

In the end, message development is where the advertising and branding battle is usually won or lost. It's where real creativity exists. It's where the agency has to be smart and figure out just how to turn the wishes of the client into effective advertising. It is where the creatives have to get into the minds of consumers, realizing that the advertisement will be received by different people in different ways. It is where advertisers merge culture, mind, and brand. Great messages are developed by people who can put themselves into the minds (and culture) of their audience members and anticipate their response, leading to the best outcome: selling the advertised brand.

Summary

Identify 10 objectives of message strategy.

Advertisers can choose from a wide array of message strategy objectives as well as methods for implementing these objectives. Three fundamental message objectives are promoting brand recall, linking key attributes to the brand name, and persuading the customer. The advertiser may also wish to create an affective association in consumers' minds by linking good feelings, humor, and sex appeal with the brand itself. Such positive feelings associated with the advertised brand can lead consumers to a higher probability of purchase. The advertiser may try to scare the consumer into action or change behavior by inducing anxiety, using negative emotional states as the means to motivate purchases. Transformational advertising aims to transform the nature of the consumption experience so that a consumer's experience of a brand becomes connected to the glorified experiences portrayed in ads. A message may also situate the brand in an important social context to heighten the brand's appeal. Finally, advertisers seek to define a brand's image by linking certain attributes to the brand, mostly using visual cues.

Identify methods for executing each message strategy objective.

Advertisers employ any number of methods to achieve their objectives. To get consumers to recall a brand name, advertisers use repetition, slogans, and jingles. When the advertiser's objective is to link a key attribute to a brand, USP ads emphasizing unique brand qualities are employed. If the goal is to persuade a consumer to make a purchase, reason-why ads, hard-sell ads, comparison ads, testimonials, demonstrations, and infomercials all do the trick. Feel-good ads, humorous ads, and sexual-appeal ads can raise a consumer's preferences for one brand over another through affective association. Fear-appeal ads, judiciously used, can motivate purchases, as can ads that play on other anxieties. Transformational ads attempt to enrich the consumption experience. With slice-of-life ads, product placement, and short Internet films, the goal is to situate a brand in a desirable social context. Finally, ads that primarily use visuals work to define brand image.

Discuss the strategic implications of various methods used to execute each message strategy objective.

Each method used to execute a message strategy objective has pros and cons. Methods that promote brand recall or link key attributes to a brand name can be extremely successful in training consumers to remember a brand name or its specific, beneficial attributes. However, these methods require long-term commitment and repetition to work properly, and advertisers can pay high expense while generating disdain from creatives. Methods used to persuade consumers generally aim to provide rhetorical arguments and demonstrations for why consumers should prefer a brand, resulting in strong, cognitive loyalty to products. However, these methods assume a high level of involvement and are vulnerable to counterarguments that neutralize their effectiveness—more-sophisticated audiences tune them out altogether, rejecting them as misleading, insipid, or dishonest. Methods used in creating affective association have short-term results and please creatives; however, the effect on audiences wears out quickly and high expense dissuades some advertisers from taking the risk. Methods designed to play on fear or anxiety are compelling, but legal and ethical issues arise, and most advertisers wish to avoid instigating consumer panic. Finally, methods that transform consumption experiences, situate the brand socially, or define brand image have powerful enduring qualities but often get lost in the clutter and can ring false to audiences.

Key Terms

unique selling proposition (USP)
comparison advertisements
testimonial
infomercial

Questions

1. What are the advantages of a simple repetition strategy? What kind of brands are most likely to use it?

2. Under what circumstances would it be relatively tough to successfully link one attribute to a brand name and thereby increase sales?

3. For reason–why ads to work, what has to happen?

4. Explain the difference between brand recall and affective association as message objectives.

5. Does sex sell? Explain.

6. Review the do's and don'ts of comparison advertising and then think about each of the brand pairs listed here. Comment on whether you think comparison ads would be a good choice for the product category in question, and if so, which brand in the pair would be in the more appropriate position to use comparisons: Coors Light versus Bud Light beer; Nuprin versus Tylenol pain reliever; Wendy's versus McDonald's hamburgers.

7. Is social anxiety advertising generally effective? Why?

8. Think about something that is disruptive in your society right now. How would you use it to make an effective brand advertising and brand promotion?

9. Do you think product placement and short Internet films are effective in executing the message strategy of situating the brand socially? What are the major advantages?

10. Think of a major purchase you have made recently. Which of the 10 message strategy objectives do you think were the most effective in influencing your purchase decision? Explain.

Experiential Exercises

1. Fear-based message strategies are powerful yet difficult to implement. In addition, ads that scare the consumer into action tend to have limited application, since few product categories are well suited to messages that invoke fear. Divide into teams and have each group plan a fear-based ad. The ads should include visual and written components, and each team must present its ad to the class for evaluation. Have a panel of student judges assess the effectiveness of ads using the guidelines for fear-based strategies discussed in the chapter.

2. Ford Motor Company is increasingly dedicated to message strategies that give social meaning to its brand. As an example, this chapter cites Ford's partnership to develop African-American family films with Ford models making cameo appearances. Ford's most popular venture into social situations is the Ford Music Video series—branded entertainment produced exclusively for *American Idol*. Research this multi-season music video campaign and answer the following questions: What desired social meaning does Ford want to convey to audiences? What are the benefits and risks to showing Ford music videos during the *American Idol* program?

3. For each of the 10 message strategies identified in the chapter, find one example of an advertisement, commercial, or specific product placement that demonstrates the strategy in action. For each example, also identify what method the advertising agency employed to achieve the objective and state briefly whether you think it was an appropriate and effective message strategy.

4. Humor can be effective as a method to help consumers feel good about a particular brand. But humorous ad messages can be difficult to pull off and are not always successful in building brand awareness. Identify three current ad campaigns where you think the creator has attempted to use humor to boost the brand's likeability factor, and then answer these questions: Does the joke work? Is the joke quickly and easily linked to the brand's name or identity? Could the same joke work over a long period of time?

Chapter 11

Executing the Creative

After reading and thinking about this chapter, you will be able to do the following:

1. Identify the main members of a creative team and how the creative brief guides their efforts.
2. Detail the elements of copywriting for print media, including the headline, subhead, and body copy.
3. Detail the elements of copywriting for radio and television.
4. Describe the copywriting approaches for digital/interactive ads.
5. Identify the components of art direction that are essential in creative execution of print ads.
6. Describe the production process in creating a television commercial.

©Yuri Arcurs/Shutterstock

Introductory Scenario: General Motors? Creative?

General Motors. These words do not conjure images of great creative execution, fine art direction, or memorable production value. Now, if we think about Apple or Nike or BMW, all sorts of interesting creative (www.expressionofjoy.com/) and memorable production *do* come to mind. General Motors? More anesthetic than inspiring. After all, this is the company that went from leading worldwide market share to bankruptcy in 35 years—obviously something went wrong, badly wrong. There are those (some insiders) who say that GM stifled the passion and creativity in its marketing ranks.[1] Others argue that it was the dour and gruff former CMO who led the firm into creative oblivion.[2] But, all that may be changing dramatically. GM has appointed a new advertising chief known as being a "champion of creative" who will keep her "hands off ads" and vigorously defends creative people. GM is headed out of bankruptcy with potentially the largest initial public offering (IPO) of stock in the history of the U.S. markets ($20 billion).

General Motor's long and painful market decline was obviously not caused solely by stodgy creative execution of advertising and IBP campaigns—but it didn't help. Certainly, vehicle design that missed the mark and pricing strategy that couldn't match Japanese and Korean competitors also contributed to the demise. But, with new product design and new energy behind creative execution, the firm may yet put it all together and become not just viable but competitive—and advertising and IBP programs will most certainly play a role in the would-be comeback. As the new ad chief at GM put it, we plan to "really push the envelope of art and science with new ad campaigns."[3]

Executing the Creative: Perspective.

"My job is to question the very definition of marketing and communications and corporate structure."

—Alex Bogusky, Chief Creative Insurgent, MDC Partners

There has been a lot of change in the advertising world... a lot of change.

One thing that hasn't change: there has always been a lot of skepticism on the brand management side about the creative function. This is especially true in hard economic times when brand managers are relying more on metrics to dictate how, when, and where messages appear.[4] A senior creative director at Leo Burnett in Chicago recently noted that there will be a lot less money and time for creative going forward, and you better get ready for it. It is the new reality. It's not only shrinking budgets and a lingering economic downturn but also a growing unwillingness of advertisers to pay for something that seems to have no rules, no explanations, but plenty of excuses. But, how does all this affect the creative task? Have all the rules fundamentally changed?

It turns out that experts give two, at first seemingly contradictory, answers to this question: (1) no, it is creative principles that matter, and they don't change... good creative is good creative, and (2) yes, the social world in which ads exist has changed as have the media that deliver them, thus impacting creative practice—some

1. Jean Halliday, "How GM Stifled 'Passion and Creativity' in Its Marketing Ranks," *Advertising Age*, June 12, 2009, 13.
2. Jean Halliday, "GM's Ad Chief Docherty Will Keep Her Hands Off Ads,' *Advertising Age*, December 7, 2009, 1, 20.
3. Laura Clark Geist, "Docherty: Cadillac to Return to 'Art and Science' of Brand," *Advertising Age*, March 22, 2010, 1.
4. Patrick Sarkissian, "Why Metrics Are Killing Creativity in Advertising," *Advertising Age*, March 4, 2010, 2.

Exhibit 11.1 Here is a creative.

practitioners even say "killing creativity."[5]

In reality there is no contradiction. The basic principles of creative communication, good writing, and effective visuals have not changed, but the media, economic, and social environments have. So, even though we continue with a principles-based approach to advertising creative, we also acknowledge and address the impact on the way contemporary creative is done. And practitioners adhere to the supremacy of creative. When asked what it takes for advertising to work effectively, practitioners responded emphatically, "It has to be creative."[6]

Chapter 9 (Managing Creativity in Advertising and Integrated Brand Promotion) and Chapter 10 (Creative Message Strategy) provided insights into the creative process itself and the way firms try to simulate and energize the creative effort in advertising and IBP. These chapters also highlighted specific message objectives and strategies and detailed the methods associated with each. Now, in this chapter, we'll turn our focus to how that all comes together in a creative concept—the roadmap for executing the creative effort. In addition, we will look at how all that creativity is executed through copywriting, art direction, and production.

1 The Creative Team and the Creative Brief.

When big ad agencies roamed the earth uncontested, a creative team usually meant an art director and a copywriter. These days, it can be a lot of folks. It often includes a **media planner** and/or an **account planner**. Media planners have joined the creative team because media are evolving so fast and are now so varied and so important to the shaping of the message that someone has to be driving that bus and informing the creative team of those realities on an on-going basis. This is particularly true as creatives struggle with the challenge of trying to use social media networks and new mobile marketing options as places to communicate. What sort of message fits in those media? Media planners can be a big help here. Account planners, usually armed with a lot of consumer research, get involved so that the consumer has a voice in the creative planning.

As you read in Chapter 9 (Managing Creativity in Advertising and Integrated Brand Promotion), creativity is the magic in advertising and IBP. At this stage in the process, executing the creative, the entire **creative team**—copywriters, art directors, media planners, and account planners—are driven by the creative brief. The **creative brief**, which can be thought of as the unique creative thought behind a campaign, has been described as the "ignition" for the creative team.[7] During this process,

5. Patrick Sarkissian, "Why Metrics Are Killing Creativity in Advertising," *Advertising Age,* March 4, 2010, 2.

6. Gergely Nyilasy and Leonard N. Reid, "Agency Practitioner Theories of How Advertising Works," *Journal of Advertising*, vol. 38, no. 3 (Fall 2009), 88.

7. Mario Pricken, *Creative Advertising* (London: Thames & Hudson, Ltd., 2008), 8.

copywriters, in addition to their role in creating the "language" of the messages, also sometimes suggest the idea for the visuals. Likewise, art directors sometimes come up with the headline or tagline. Media planners convey what is possible through the ever-expanding media choices, and account planners try to keep the profile of the target consumer in the team's mind. This is absolutely vital with social media and branded entertainment. When a company like American Girl creates retail **brandscapes** (the total environment within which the brand is presented and displayed) for their dolls to have tea-parties with customers, and they make full-length feature films around the brand, the creative team has to have exquisite coordination between all media and all strategic partners.

Copywriters and Art Directors.

So, let's consider the two most traditional job descriptions in the world of creative advertising, and discuss what they were and what they are becoming: copywriters and art directors.

Word vs. image purists have had a long running war. The advertising industry reflected this through artificial separation of the domains for decades. In reality, images and words overlap constantly. As you can see in Exhibits 11.2 and 11.3, some ads have no copy at all; some have no pictures. Even in those cases, both a copywriter and an art director are involved in creating the ad. This doesn't mean that copywriting and art directing are one and the same. There are special skill sets involved with each, but one must recognize that knowing how to do it all isn't bad.

Copywriting is the process of expressing the value and benefits a brand has to offer, via written or verbal descriptions. Copywriting requires far more than the ability to string product descriptions together in coherent sentences. One apt description of copywriting is that it is a never-ending search for ideas combined with a never-ending search for new and different ways to express those ideas. Copywriting has to be crafted to its medium or media, and in today's explosion of media, that could be anything from a fully stylized, copy-laden magazine ad to dialogue in a branded entertainment film, or even a brand "shout out" in social

Exhibit 11.2 Now apps are brand messaging.

Courtesy, Wright's Media

Exhibit 11.3
McDonald's uses a lot of different media, including this brand promotion.

Courtesy, Wright's Media

media. You can learn techniques, some of them principles, some of them hints and tips. But, even if you don't plan to be a copywriter, knowing something about the craft is essential to any working understanding of the creative execution in advertising.

Imagine you're a copywriter on the MasterCard account. You've sat through meeting after meeting in which your client, account executives, and researchers have presented a myriad of benefits one gets from using a MasterCard for online purchases. You've talked to customers about their experiences. You've even gone online to try the card out for yourself. All along, your boss has been reminding you that the work you come up with must be as inspiring as the work that focuses on building interest for the brand. Now your job is to take all the analytics—charts, numbers, and strategies—and turn them into a simple, emotionally involving, intellectually challenging campaign such as the one in Exhibits 11.4 and 11.5. Make MasterCard mean something... something that is consistent with the brand DNA, the essence of the brand. And do it in a way that is interesting and compelling to consumers. That's where creativity meets business reality.

Effective copywriters are well-informed, astute advertising decision makers with creative talent. Copywriters are able to comprehend and then incorporate the complexities of marketing strategies, consumer behavior, and advertising strategies into powerful communication. They must do this in such a way that the copy does not interfere with, but rather enhances, the visual aspects of the message.

An astute advertiser will go to great lengths to provide copywriters with as much information as possible about the objectives for a particular advertising effort. The responsibility for keeping copywriters informed lies with the client's brand managers, filtered through the account executives and creative directors in the ad agency, or brand communication firm. Without this information, copywriters are left without guidance and direction, and they must rely on intuition about what sorts of information are relevant and meaningful to a target audience. Effective brand communication relies on a good creative brief.

The creative brief serves as the guide used in the copywriting process to specify the message elements that must be coordinated during the preparation of copy (see Exhibit 11.6). These elements include main brand claims, creative devices, media that will be used, special creative needs a brand might have, and what we want the

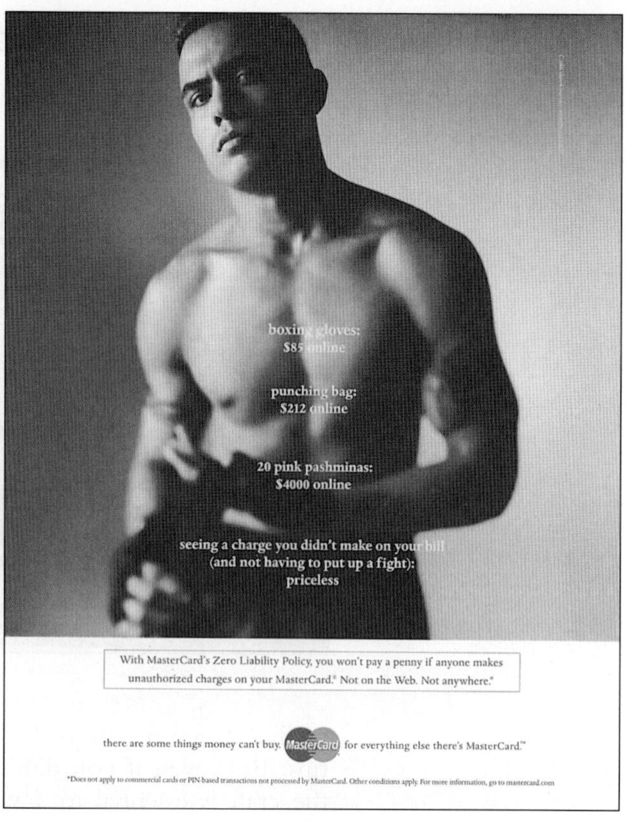

Exhibits 11.4 and 11.5 Take all the charts, numbers, and strategies and turn them into a simple, emotionally involving, intellectually challenging campaign.

Exhibit 11.6
A sample creative brief.

CREATIVE BRIEF	
Agency	Creative Stupor, Austin
Client	Jake's Fried Chicken
Brand	Jake's Fried Chicken Restaurants
Project	Best Fried Chicken Anywhere.
Date	June 12, 2012
Author	Blake N. Milton
Purpose	To Remind Fried Chicken Lovers of Jake's Chicken's USP: *High Fat and Proud of It.*
Creative opportunity	To leverage the under-served segment of don't care about my arteries give me the real thing.... Unapologetic comfort food.
Media mix	open
Message objective	Brand recall USP: real fried chicken; forget the guilt.
Tone	In your face, dripping down your chin.
Key consumer opportunity	Give consumer permission to indulge with Jack's Fried Chicken.
Message	You want it; go for it.
Reason to believe	You are already know it; know you have permission. Besides: Jake told you so.

Source: Courtesy, Tom O'Guinn

message recipients to think once they receive the message.[8] One of the main challenges faced by a copywriter is to make creative sense out of the tangled mass of product and market information, which is often technical. Part of the typical copywriting challenge is creating excitement around what can otherwise be dull product features. For example, the creative team responsible for the ad in Exhibit 11.7 turned a pretty ho-hum claim into an unexpected delight: a Venus flytrap might starve when this brand of insecticide is on the job... that's how good it is. The ad could have just said: "best insecticide on the market," but instead it engaged the audience by requiring them to think about what was being said and pictured, and by "getting it," created a memorable *ah-ha* moment.

Some of the key elements considered in devising a creative brief are the following:

1. The single most important thought you want a member of the target market to take away from the advertisement
2. The product features to be emphasized
3. The benefits a user receives from these features
4. The media chosen for transmitting the information and the length of time the advertisement will run (this one is getting tougher to know)
5. The suggested mood or tone for the ad or promotion
6. The production budget for the ad or brand promotion[9]

There are times, however, when these considerations can be modified or even disregarded. For example, sometimes a brilliant creative execution demands a different medium or a creative thought may require a completely different mood than the one specified in the creative brief. A creative brief is best thought of as a starting point. Once the creative brief is devised and adapted, the creative team can get on with the task of crafting the actual advertisement. Creative execution depends on both preparing the copy, the message language for an ad, and the visual components. We will first consider copywriting across different media and then turn our attention to the visual components executed through art direction and production.

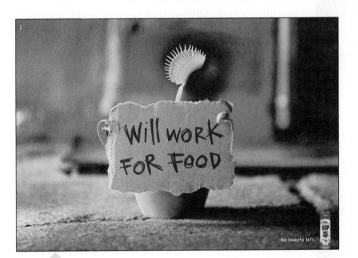

Exhibit 11.7 Expected product feature, unexpected creative delivery.

Executing the Creative: Copywriting.

Executing the creative with the copy varies from medium to medium. While the creative brief will always provide the emphasis for creative execution, regardless of the medium, the creative team needs to consider the opportunities and limitations different media present. But, regardless of medium, copy needs to be original and distinctive in order to engage the receiver. And, it has to be strategic in its execution of the objectives of the creative brief. We will consider executing copywriting for print advertising first and then move on to the interactive/digital media, and then consider broadcast advertising.

8. Tom Altsteil and Jean Grow, *Advertising Creative: Strategy, Copy and Design*, 2nd ed. (Los Angeles: Sage Publications, 2010), 53.

9. The last two points in this list were adapted from the classic perspectives of A. Jerome Jewler, *Creative Strategy in Advertising*, 3rd ed. (Belmont, CA: Wadsworth, 1989), 196.

Copywriting for Print Advertising.

In preparing copy for a print ad, the first step in the copy development process is deciding how to use (or not use) the three separate components of print copy: the headline, the subhead, and the body copy. (Slogans and taglines are also part of the copywriting process, but we consider that effort separately later in the chapter.) Be aware that the full range of components applies most directly to print ads that appear in magazines, newspapers, or direct mail pieces. These guidelines also apply to other "print" media such as billboards, transit advertising, and specialty advertising, but all media are in effect different animals.

The Headline. The **headline** in an advertisement is the leading sentence or sentences, usually at the top or bottom of the ad that attracts attention, communicates a key selling point, or achieves brand identification. Many headlines fail to attract attention, and the ad itself then becomes another bit of clutter in consumers' lives. Lifeless headlines do not compel the reader to examine other parts of the ad. Simply stated, a headline can either motivate a reader to move on to the rest of an ad or lose the reader for good. And be aware, there are certain ads where the creative execution depends completely on the headline and the entire ad is carried by the headline. Review the Altoids campaign featured in Chapter 1 as a great example of how a headline (and the visual) can carry the entire creative purpose of an ad.

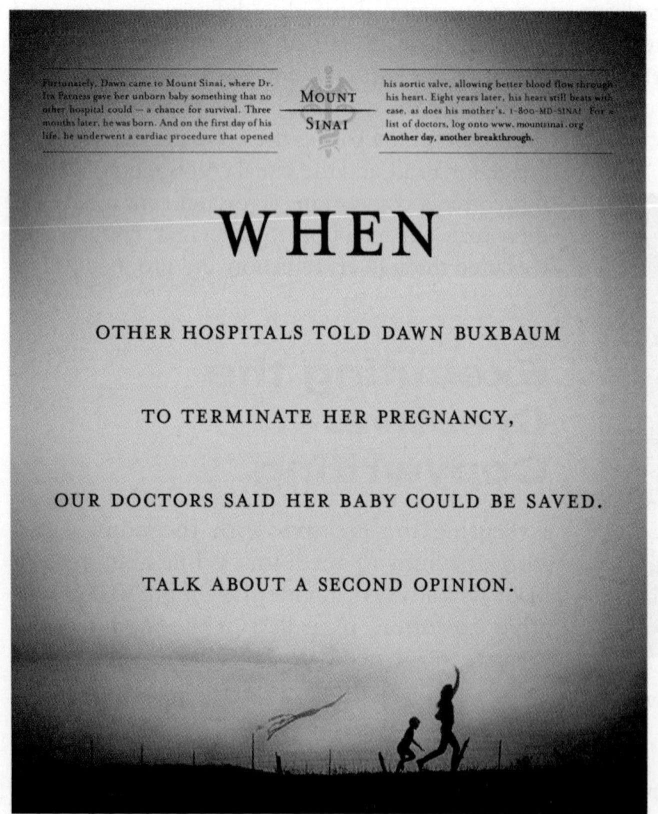

Exhibit 11.8 This ad gives important news about the brand.

Courtesy of Mt. Sinai Hospital; Ad Agency: Devito/Verdi, NY, NY

Purposes of a Headline. In preparing a headline, a copywriter begins by considering the variety of purposes a headline can serve in terms of executing the creative intent of the ad. In addition, gaining attention and encouraging the reader to examine the ad content more fully are key. In general, a headline is typically written to pursue one or more of the following purposes:[10]

- ***Get attention.*** First things first. If a headline does not get the reader's attention, then it hasn't done any good at all—regardless of the many purposes that follow.
- ***Give news about the brand.*** A headline can proclaim a newsworthy event focused on the brand. "Champion Wins Mt. Everest Run" and "25 of 40 Major Titles Won with Titleist" are examples of headlines that communicate newsworthy events about Champion spark plugs and Titleist golf balls. The Mount Sinai hospital ad in Exhibit 11.8 uses this approach in a gripping, emotional manner.
- ***Emphasize a brand claim.*** A primary and perhaps differentiating feature of the brand is a likely candidate for the headline theme. "30% More Mileage on Firestone Tires" highlights durability.
- ***Give advice to the reader.*** A headline can give the reader a recommendation that (usually) is supported by results provided in the body copy. "Increase Your Reading Skills" and "Save up to

10. There are several good copywriting books by practitioners that offer guidelines for headlines and body copy. Consider these: Robert W. Bly, *The Copywriter's Handbook* (New York: Henry Holt and Company, 2005), and Joseph Sugarman, *The Adweek Copywriting Handbook* (New Jersey: John Wiley & Sons, Inc., 2007).

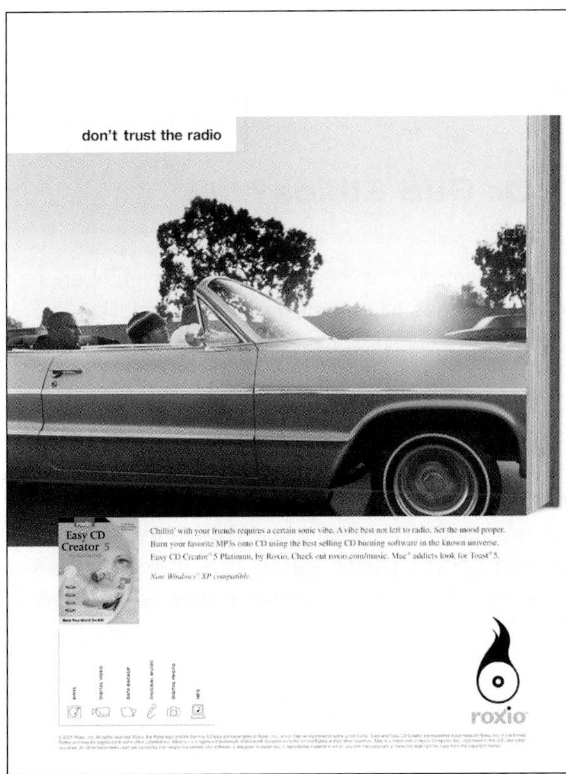

Exhibit 11.9 This headline offers advice.
www.roxio.com

90% on Commissions" both implore the reader to take the advice of the ad. The headline in Exhibit 11.9 advises readers to make sure that bad radio stations don't ever ruin a road trip.

- ***Select the audience.*** Headlines can attract the attention of the intended audience. "Good News for Arthritis Sufferers" and "Attention June Graduates" are examples of headlines designed to achieve prospect selection.
- ***Stimulate the reader's curiosity.*** Posing a riddle with a headline can serve to attract attention and stimulate readership. Curiosity can be stimulated with a clever play on words or a contradiction. Does the headline in the BMW ad shown in Exhibit 11.10 get your attention? It was written for that purpose.
- ***Set a tone or establish an emotion.*** Language can be used to establish a mood that the advertiser wants associated with its product. Teva sport sandals has an ad with the headline "When you die, they put you in a nice suit and shiny shoes. As if death didn't suck enough already." Even though there is no direct reference to the product being advertised, the reader has learned quite a bit about the company doing the advertising and the types of people expected to buy the product. The headline(s) in the ad shown in Exhibit 11.11 is far more about establishing the mood or tone of a Jamaican visit than it is about talking about its beaches and attractions.

According to our engineers,
tailpipe water can be quite delicious.

Exhibit 11.10 A headline that creates curiosity motivates readers to continue reading, perhaps after a slight disconcerting pause.

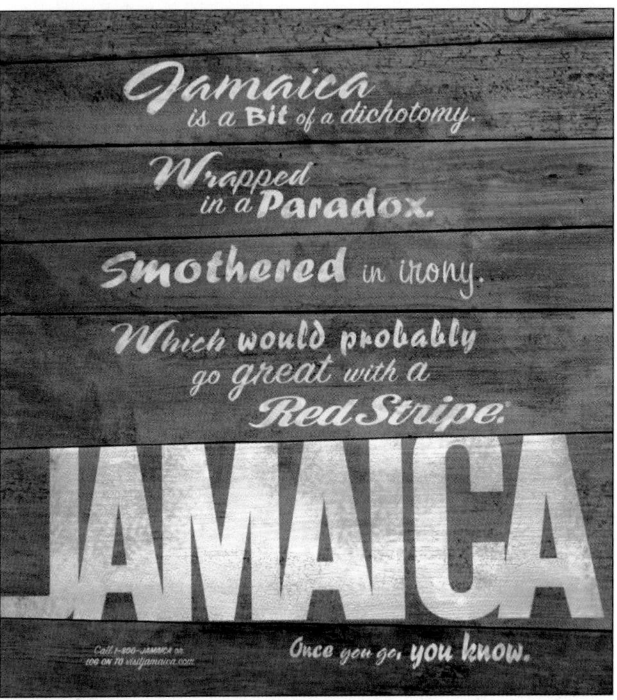

Exhibit 11.11 Even though there are no explicit product features being advertised, the reader has learned quite a bit about the island, its natives, and its tourists.

Ethics

Is This Good Creative Copywriting? Or Bad Ethics?

LONDON: An ad campaign for Glaceau Vitaminwater (from Coca-Cola) has caused a bit of controversy, and a lot of attention for the brand.

According to *Advertising Age*: A new promotional label on the bottle reads, "If you've had to use sick days because you've actually been sick, then you've been missing out." In a bid to promote the health-giving properties of Glaceau, it advises, "The trick is to stay perky and use sick days to just, not go in." The label goes on to suggest that coughing too much the day before your sick day is a "big giveaway" and concludes, "Just stick with the ever-elusive '24-hour bug'—no one can prove a thing."

This apparently didn't go over well with British bosses. In a statement from the Forum of Private Businesses, Coca-Cola was told that "it is unacceptable to encourage workers to throw 'sickies' in order to sell a soft drink. A company of the standing of Coca-Cola should know better."

Hmmm... sickies.

The ad campaign is designed to use a number of different messages to point to key brand benefits. This one pointed to Vitamin C. Drink Glaceau with C and say healthy... but take a day off anyway. Coca-Cola noted that part of the brand's personality is irreverence. In their statement, Coca-Cola said: This is clearly a tongue-in-cheek reference, very much in keeping with the humorous tone that Glaceau Vitaminwater has adopted with consumers right from its launch.... We are not seriously suggesting people should call in sick when they are not and on pack we state, 'taking a sickie is very, very naughty.'"

Naughty, indeed.

The ads are produced in-house by Coca-Cola.

Source: Coca-Cola Encourages Brits to Take Sick Days—Bosses Don't Find Glaceau Vitaminwater's Light-Hearted Labels Funny. Posted by Emma Hall on 04.14.10 @ 05:43 PM, *Advertising Age:* adage.com/globalnews/article?article_id=143306

- ***Identify the brand.*** This is the most straightforward of all headline purposes. The brand name or label is used as the headline, either alone or in conjunction with a word or two. The goal is to simply identify the brand and reinforce brand-name recognition. Advertising for Brut men's fragrance products often uses merely the brand name as the headline.

These purposes for a headline are meant only as a starting point. A headline may violate one or even all of these basic premises and still be effective. This list simply offers general opportunities to be considered. Remember, regardless of the traditional wisdom about what headlines might be able to accomplish, the creative team is going to focus on the creative brief in creating a headline. But, enthusiastic headlines can become a bit overzealous as the *Ethics* box describes. Here's some good creative advice about writing headlines.

> *"Certain headlines are currently checked out. You may use them when they are returned. Lines like "Contrary to popular belief. . ." or "Something is wrong when . . ." These are dead. Elvis is dead. John Lennon is dead. Deal with it. Remember, anything that you even think you've seen, forget about it. The stuff you've never seen? You'll know when you see it, too. It raises the hair on the back of your neck."*
>
> —Luke Sullivan[11]

The Subhead. A **subhead** consists of a few words or a short sentence and usually appears above or below the headline. It offers the opportunity to include important brand information not included in the headline. The subhead in the ad for Clorox in Exhibit 11.12 is an excellent example of a subhead conveying important

11. Luke Sullivan, *Hey Whipple, Squeeze This: A Guide to Creating Great Ads* (New York: Wiley, 1998), 78.

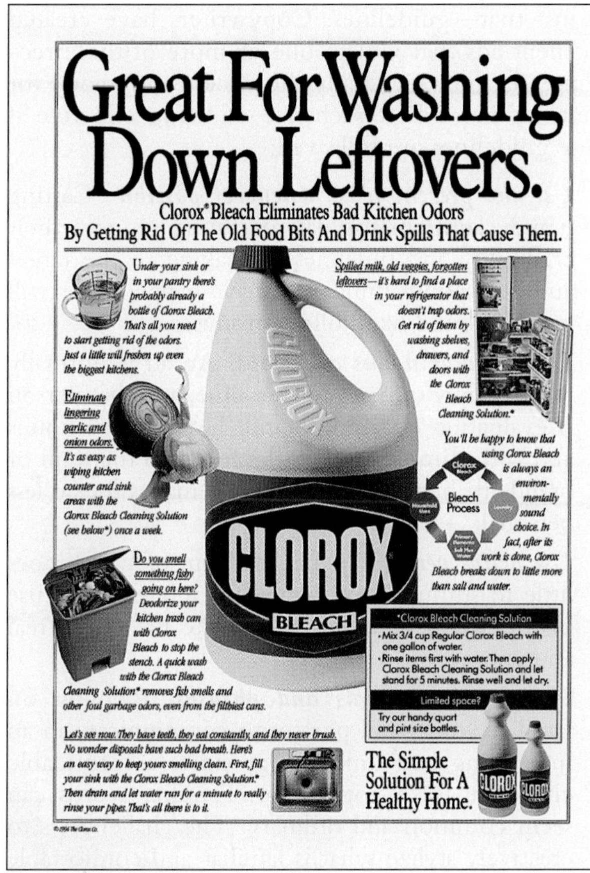

Exhibit 11.12 Subheads include important brand information not included in the headline. Where is the subhead in this Clorox ad? What does the subhead accomplish that the headline does not? www.clorox.com

brand information not communicated in the headline. A subhead serves basically the same purpose as a headline—to communicate key selling points or brand information quickly. A subhead is normally in print smaller than the headline but larger than the body copy. In most cases, the subhead is lengthier than the headline and can be used to communicate more complex selling points. The subhead should reinforce the headline and stimulate a more complete reading of the entire ad.

The Body Copy. Body copy is the textual component of an advertisement and tells a more complete story of a brand. Effective body copy is written in a fashion that takes advantage of and reinforces the headline and subhead, is compatible with and gains strength from the visual, and is interesting to the reader. Whether body copy is interesting is a function of how accurately the copywriter and other decision makers have assessed various components of message development, and how good the copywriter is. Even the most elaborate body copy will be ineffective if it is "off creative strategy." It will not matter if it's very clever but has little to do in advancing the strategy.

There are several standard techniques for preparing body copy. The **straight-line copy** approach explains in straightforward terms why a reader will benefit from use of a brand. This technique is used many times in conjunction with a benefits message strategy. Body copy that uses **dialogue** delivers the selling points of a message to the audience through a character or characters in the ad. Dialogue can also depict two people in the ad having a conversation, a technique often used in slice-of-life messages. A **testimonial** uses dialogue as if the spokesperson is having a one-sided conversation with the reader through the body copy. The Nicorette ad shown in Exhibit 11.13 is an example of the testimonial technique.

Narrative as a method for preparing body copy simply displays a series of statements about a brand. A person may or may not be portrayed as delivering the copy. It is difficult to make this technique lively for the reader, so the threat of writing a dull ad using this technique is ever present. **Direct response copy** is, in many ways, the least complex of copy techniques. In writing direct response copy, the copywriter is trying to highlight the urgency of acting immediately. Hence, the range of possibilities for direct response copy is more limited. In addition, many direct response advertisements rely on sales promotion devices, such as coupons, contests, and rebates, as a means of stimulating action. Giving deadlines to the reader is also a common approach in direct response advertising.

These techniques for copywriting establish a general set of styles that can be used as the format for body copy. Again, be aware that any message objective can be employed within any particular copy technique. There are a vast number of compatible combinations.

Guidelines for Writing Body Copy. Regardless of the specific technique used to develop body copy, the probability of writing effective body copy can be increased if certain guidelines are followed. However, guidelines are meant to

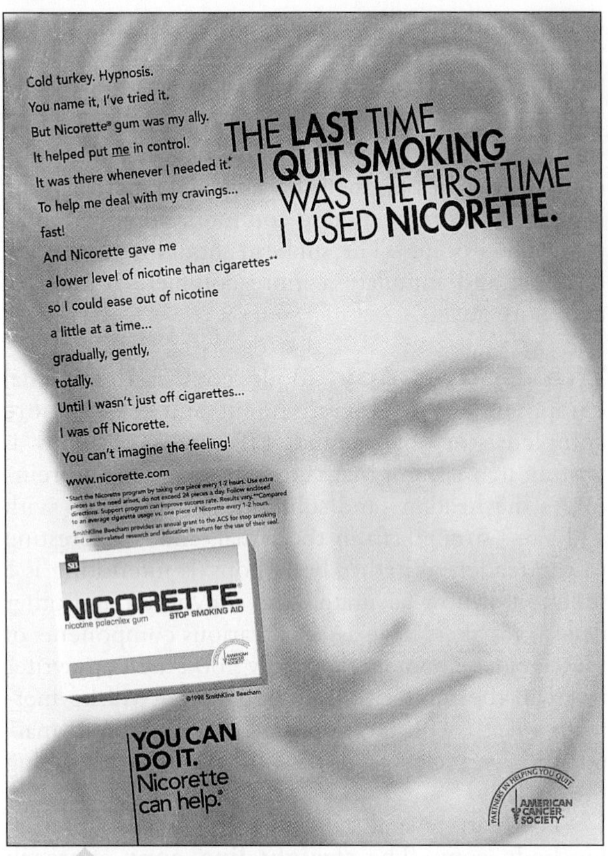

Cold turkey. Hypnosis.
You name it, I've tried it.
But Nicorette® gum was my ally.
It helped put me in control.
It was there whenever I needed it.*
To help me deal with my cravings...
fast!
And Nicorette gave me
a lower level of nicotine than cigarettes**
so I could ease out of nicotine
a little at a time...
gradually, gently,
totally.
Until I wasn't just off cigarettes...
I was off Nicorette.
You can't imagine the feeling!
www.nicorette.com
THE LAST TIME
I QUIT SMOKING
WAS THE FIRST TIME
I USED NICORETTE.
NICORETTE
STOP SMOKING AID
YOU CAN
DO IT.
Nicorette
can help.*
PARTNERS IN HELPING YOU QUIT
AMERICAN CANCER SOCIETY

Exhibit 11.13 In this testimonial ad from Nicorette, a spokesperson tells his story directly to the reader. Is this same copy technique used at the Nicorette site (www.nicorette.com)? What does Nicorette offer to its customers at the Committed Quitters resource site toward eliciting a direct response from consumers?

be just that—guidelines. Copywriters have created excellent ads that violate one or more of these recommendations. Generally, however, body copy for print ads has a better chance of being effective if these guidelines are followed:

- ***Use the present tense whenever possible.*** Casting brand claims in the past or future reduces their credibility and timeliness. Speaking to the target audience about things that have happened or will happen sound like hollow promises.
- ***Use singular nouns and verbs.*** An ad is normally read by only one person at a time, and that person is evaluating only one brand. Using plural nouns and verbs simply reduces the focus on the item or brand attribute being touted and makes the ad less personal.
- ***Use active verbs.*** The passive form of a verb does little to stimulate excitement or interest. The use of the active verb can help make the brand real and energetic.
- ***Use familiar words and phrases.*** Relying on familiar words and phrases to communicate in an interesting and unique way poses a formidable challenge for a copywriter. Familiar words can seem common and ordinary. The challenge is to creatively stylize what is familiar and comfortable to the reader so that interest and excitement result.
- ***Vary the length of sentences and paragraphs.*** Using sentences and paragraphs of varying lengths not only serves to increase interest but also has a visual impact that can make an ad more inviting and readable.
- ***Involve the reader.*** Talking at the receiver or creating a condescending mood with copy results in a short-circuited communication. Copy that impresses the reader as having been written specifically for him or her reduces the chances of the ad being perceived as a generalized, mass communication.
- ***Provide support for the unbelievable.*** A brand may have features or functions that the reader finds hard to believe. Where such claims are critical to the brand's positioning in the market and value to the consumer, it is necessary to document (through test results or testimonials) that the brand actually lives up to the claims. Without proper support of claims, the brand will lose credibility and therefore relevance to the consumer.
- ***Avoid clichés and superlatives.*** Clichés are rarely effective or attention-getting. The average consumer assumes that a brand touted through the use of clichés is old-fashioned and stale. Even though the foundation for puffery as a message method is the use of superlatives (best, superior, unbeatable), it is wise to avoid their use. These terms are worn out and can signal to the consumer that the brand has little new or different to offer.[12]

12. The last three points in this list were adapted from Kenneth Roman and Jan Maas, *The New How to Advertise* (New York: St. Martin's Press, 1992), 18–19.

Copywriting for Broadcast Advertising.

Relative to the print media, radio and television present totally different challenges for a copywriter. It is obvious that the audio and audiovisual capabilities of radio and television offer different opportunities for a copywriter. The use of sound effects, music, and voices on radio and the ability to combine copy with color and motion on television provide vast and exciting creative possibilities.

Compared to print media, however, broadcast media have inherent limitations for a copywriter. In print media, a copywriter can write longer and more involved copy to better communicate complex brand features. For consumer goods such as automobiles or home entertainment systems, a brand's basis for competitive differentiation and positioning may lie with complex, unique functional features. In this case, print media provide a copywriter the time and space to communicate these details, complete with illustrations. In addition, the printed page allows a reader to dwell on the copy and process the information at a personalized, comfortable rate.

These advantages do not exist in the broadcast media. Radio and television message are fleeting messages. In addition, introducing sound effects and visual stimuli can distract the listener or viewer from the copy of the advertisement. Despite the additional creative capabilities that radio and television offer, the essential challenge of copywriting remains—hold attention and communicate the brand value and image.

Writing Copy for Radio. Some writers consider radio the ultimate forum for copywriting creativity. Because the radio is restricted to an audio-only presentation, a copywriter is freed from some of the harsher realities of visual presentations. Yet it has been said that radio *is* actually visual. The copywriter must (inevitably) create images in the minds of listeners. The creative potential of radio rests in its ability to stimulate a "theater of the mind," which allows a copywriter to create images and moods for audiences that transcend those created in any other medium.

Despite these creative opportunities, the drawbacks of this medium should not be underestimated. Few radio listeners ever actively listen to radio programming (talk radio is an exception), much less the commercial interruptions. Radio may be viewed by some as the theater of the mind, but others have labeled it audio wallpaper—wallpaper in the sense that radio is used as filler or unobtrusive accompaniment to reading, driving, household chores, or homework. If it were absent, the average person would miss it, but the average person would be hard-pressed to recall the radio ads aired during dinner last evening.

The most reasonable view of copywriting for radio is to temper the enthusiasm of the theater-of-the-mind perspective and the pessimism of the audio-wallpaper view. (Of course, "reasonable" creative perspectives often are mind-numbingly dull.) A radio copywriter should recognize the unique character of radio and exploit the opportunities it offers. First, radio adds the dimension of sound to the basic copywriting effort, and sound (other than voices) can become a primary tool in creating copy. Second, radio can conjure images in the mind of the receiver that extend beyond the starkness of brand "information" actually being provided. Radio copywriting should, therefore, strive to stimulate each receiver's imagination.

Writing copy for radio begins the same way that writing copy for print begins. The copywriter reviews components of the creative brief to take advantage of and follow through on the marketing and advertising strategies integral to the brand's market potential. Let's consider formats for radio ads and guidelines for copy preparation the copywriter can turn to for direction.

Radio Advertising Formats. There are four basic formats for radio advertisements, and these formats provide the structure within which copy is prepared: the music format, the dialogue format, the announcement format, and the celebrity announcer format. Each of these formats is discussed here.

Music. Because radio provides audio opportunities, music is often used in radio ads. One use of music is to write a song or jingle in an attempt to communicate in an attention-getting and memorable fashion. Songs and jingles are generally written specifically to accommodate unique brand copy. On occasion, an existing tune can be used (with permission and for a fee), and the copy is fit to its meter and rhythm. This is done when the music is being used to capture the attention of a particular target segment. Tunes popular with certain target segments can be licensed for use by advertisers. Advertisements using popular tunes by Queen Bee and Barry Manilow would presumably attract two very different audiences. Singing and music can do much to attract the listener's attention and enhance recall. Singing can also create a mood and image with which the brand is associated. Modern scores can create a contemporary mood, while sultry music and lyrics create a totally different mood.

But what of jingles? Well, they have survived for more than a hundred years. One traditional view of jingles is that they can tie an entire campaign together as a unifying element.[13] Others warn that there are hazards to trying to use jingles. Few copywriters are trained lyricists or composers. The threat is ever present that a jingle will strike receivers as amateurish and silly. To avoid this, expert songwriters are often used. Further, ensuring that the copy information dominates the musical accompaniment takes great skill. The musical impact can easily overwhelm the persuasion and selling purposes of an ad. Still, just try to get a really good jingle out of your head. You may go to your grave with it on your mind.

Another use of music in radio commercials is to open the ad with a musical score and/or have music playing in the background while the copy is being read. The role of music here is generally to attract and hold attention. This application of music, as well as music used in a song or jingle, is subject to an ongoing debate. If a radio ad is scheduled for airing on music-format stations, should the music in the ad be the same type of music the station is noted for playing, or should it be different? One argument says that if the station format is rock, for example, then the ad should use rock music. The opposite argument, of course, is that using the same type of music as the station plays simply buries the ad in the regular programming and reduces its impact. There is no good evidence to suggest that music similar to or different from station programming is superior.

Dialogue. The dialogue technique, described in the section on print copywriting, is also used in radio. There are difficulties in making narrative copy work in the short time afforded by the radio medium (typically 15 to 60 seconds). The threat is that dialogue will result in a dull drone of two or more people having a conversation. (You hear enough of that, right?) To reduce the threat of boredom, many dialogues are written with humor, like the one in Exhibit 11.14.

Exhibit 11.14 This is GREAT radio.

Courtesy, Susan Van Etten

Announcement. Radio copy delivered by an announcer is similar to narrative copy in print advertising. The announcer reads important product information as it has been prepared by the copywriter. Announcement is the prevalent technique for live radio spots delivered by disc jockeys or news commentators. The live setting leaves little opportunity for much else. If the ad is prerecorded, sound effects or music may be added to enhance the transmission. One advantage of the announcement is that

13. Tom Altsteil and Jean Grow, *Advertising Creative: Strategy, Copy and Design*, 2nd ed. (Los Angeles: Sage Publications, 2010), 218.

any affinity the listener has for the DJ or commentator can carry over to the brand through a positive "halo effect."

Celebrity Announcer. Having a famous person deliver the copy is argued to increase the attention paid to a radio ad. Most radio ads that use celebrities do not fall into the testimonial category. The celebrity is not expressing his or her satisfaction with the product but merely acting as an announcer. Some celebrities (such as James Earl Jones) have distinctive voice qualities or are experts at the emphatic delivery of copy. These qualities, as well as listener recognition of the celebrity, increase attention to the ad.

Guidelines for Writing Radio Copy. The unique opportunities and challenges of the radio medium warrant a set of guidelines for the copywriter to increase the probability of effective communication. The following are a few suggestions for writing effective radio copy:

- ***Capture attention and get to the point early.*** The first five seconds can capture or lose the radio listener—grab attention. Then get to the main point and stick with it.
- ***Use common, familiar language.*** The use of words and language easily understood and recognized by the receiver is even more important in radio than in print copy preparation. Esoteric language or phrases will confuse and ultimately lose the listener.
- ***Use short words and sentences.*** The probability of communicating verbally increases if short, easily processed words and sentences are used. Long, involved, elaborate verbal descriptions make it difficult for the listener to follow the copy.
- ***Stimulate the imagination.*** Copy that can conjure up concrete and stimulating images in the receiver's mind can have a powerful impact on recall.
- ***Repeat the brand name.*** Because the impression made by a radio ad is fleeting, it may be necessary to repeat the brand name several times before it will register. The same is true for location if the ad is being used to promote a retail organization.
- ***Stress the main selling point or points.*** The premise of the advertising should always revolve around the creative brief. The urge to get "wild and crazy" with a radio ad to attract and hold attention needs to take a back seat to strategic goals. If the main selling points of a brand are mentioned only in passing, there is little reason for the listener to believe or remember them.
- ***Use sound and music with care.*** By all means, a copywriter should take advantage of all the creative audio capabilities afforded by the radio medium, including the use of sound effects and music. Although these devices can contribute greatly to attracting and holding the listener's attention, care must be taken to ensure that they do not overwhelm the copy and therefore the persuasive impact of the commercial.
- ***Tailor the copy to the time, place, and specific audience.*** Take advantage of any unique aspect of the advertising context. If the ad is created for a particular geographic region, use colloquialisms unique to that region as a way to tailor the message. The same is true with time-of-day factors or unique aspects of the audience.[14]

14. Tom Alsteil and Jean Grow, Advertising Creative: Strategy, Copy and Design, 2nd ed. (Los Angeles: Sage Publications, 2010), 218–219.

Writing Copy for Television (Video).

Great print can make you famous. Great TV can make you rich.

—Anonymous[15]

Television has always been a vastly creative forum for the copywriter and art director. In the current era of social media (YouTube and interactive websites) the addition of online video transmission offers the same opportunities as television. The comments in this section apply to ads that show up on social media sites or may even have been created for transmitted to mobile devices. The ability to create a mood or demonstrate brand values gives television and video wonderful capabilities; it also offers you the ability to really screw up in magnificent fashion for a very large and expensive audience (no pressure here!). Obviously, copy for television must be highly sensitive to the ad's visual aspects. Television is visual medium; you should try not to let the words get in the way.

The opportunities inherent to television as an advertising medium represent challenges for the copywriter as well. Certainly, their inherent capabilities do much to bring a copywriter's words to life. But the action qualities can create problems. First, the copywriter must remember that words do not stand alone. Visuals, special effects, and sound techniques may ultimately convey a message far better than the cleverest turn of phrase. Second, television commercials represent a difficult timing challenge for the copywriter. It is necessary for the copy to be precisely coordinated with the visuals. If the visual portion was one continuous illustration, the task would be difficult enough. Contemporary television ads, however, tend to be heavily edited (that is, lots of cuts), and the copywriting task can be a nightmare. The copywriter not only has to fulfill all the responsibilities of proper information inclusion (based on creative platform and strategy decisions) but also has to carefully fit all the information within, between, and around the visual display taking place. To make sure this coordination is precise, the copywriter, producer, and director assigned to a television advertisement work closely together to make sure the copy supports and enhances the video element. The road map for this coordination effort is known as a **storyboard**. A storyboard is an important shot-by-important-shot sketch depicting in sequence the visual scenes and copy that will be used in the advertisement. The procedures for coordinating audio and visual elements through the use of storyboards will be presented later in the chapter, when television production is discussed in more detail.

Guidelines for Writing Television Copy. Writing copy for television advertising has its own set of unique opportunities and challenges. The following are some general guidelines:

- ***Use the video.*** Allow the video portion of the commercial to enhance and embellish the audio portion. Given the strength and power of the visual presentation in television advertising, take advantage of its impact with copy.
- ***Support the video.*** Make sure that the copy doesn't simply hitchhike on the video. If all the copy does is verbally describe what the audience is watching, an opportunity to either communicate additional information or strengthen the video communication has been lost.
- ***Coordinate the audio with the video.*** In addition to strategically using the video, it is essential that the audio and video do not tell entirely different stories.
- ***Sell the brand as well as entertain the audience.*** Television ads can sometimes be more entertaining than television programming. A temptation for the copywriter and art director is to get caught up in the excitement of a good video

15. Cited in Luke Sullivan, *Hey Whipple, Squeeze This: A Guide to Creating Great Ads*, 103.

presentation and forget that the main purpose is to deliver persuasive communication. How many times have you seen a great, entertaining ad and then have no idea what brand the ad was promoting?

- ***Be flexible.*** Due to media-scheduling strategies, commercials are produced to run as 15-, 20-, 30-, or 60-second spots. The copywriter may need to ensure that the audio portion of an ad is complete and comprehensive within varying time lengths. Also, consider how the ad would play in the small formats of mobile devices.
- ***Use copy judiciously.*** If a television ad is too wordy, it can create information overload and interfere with the visual impact. Ensure that every word is a working word and contributes to the impact of the message.
- ***Reflect the brand personality and image.*** All aspects of an ad, copy and visuals, should be consistent with the personality and image the advertiser wants to build or maintain for the brand.
- ***Build campaigns.*** When copy for a particular advertisement is being written, evaluate its potential as a sustainable idea. Can the basic appeal in the advertisement be developed into multiple versions placed in other media that form a campaign?[16]

Copywriting for Digital/Interactive Media.

The challenge of copywriting for new digital/interactive media is really a hybrid of writing copy for print and broadcast media. Even though some take the position that writing is writing, we see enough evidence that the rapidly evolving media of cyberspace have their own styles, feel, writing, and demands for creativity.[17] Part of this is due to its history. Copy in digital/interactive media evolved from a very techno-speak community, with a twentysomething, Gen-X-meets-techno-nerd kind of voice. It has a style that has been influenced by this history. Some digital and interactive media have a structure that is closer to print than to television copy, but not really traditional print copy either. When an email communication is prepared, it is very much like a print ad that is heavy on copy and light on visual—usually lacking any visual. The same is true if a firm "seeds" blogs with brand appeals or preps paid bloggers with brand-appeal language. When someone visits a Web page, it looks a lot like a magazine ad or brochure. And consider the on-the fly copy generation that a corporate tweeter has to create (you'll read about Miss Sprint Cup tweeting from NASCAR races in Chapter 14).

In digital and interactive media, *audience* has a significantly different meaning than it does in traditional one-way (noninteractive) media. Audience members often seek out the ads or other online IBP material, rather than the other way around. And, they are doing it in much smaller formats like a computer screen or smartphone display. In addition, cyberads can pop up as one moves from Web page to Web page (more on this in Chapter 14). The media—computers and mobile devices—are fundamentally more user-directed than print, television, or radio. This means that consumers approach (and read) cyberads somewhat differently than other ads. Most have more incentive to read the copy than traditional print advertising. Further, much digital and interactive media copy is direct response, thus totally dictating copy style. There are those who argue that the copywriting in digital and interactive media is lower quality—particularly if you use the standards of traditional print and broadcast media as criteria. But, digital and interactive media copywriters are trying to meet the demands of vastly different audiences and often "real time" media creation

16. The last three points in this list were adapted from Roman and Maas, *The New How to Advertise*.

17. Megan McIlroy, "Nailing Just How Effective Online Creative Can Be," *Advertising Age*, October 10, 2007, 12; Advertising Age Editorial, "Online Advertising Needs a Different Kind of Creativity," *Advertising Age*, October 26, 2009, 11.

Exhibit 11.15 Cybercopy represents a new type of ad writing—closer to print than to television copy, but not really traditional print copy either.

(as in Tweets).[18] At this point, we believe that the basic principles of good print and broadcast copywriting just discussed generally apply. But the copy should assume a more active and engaged audience and has to adapt the creative brief objectives to the smaller format and potentially real-time challenges of the reception environment as the suggestions in the *Social Media* box suggest. Still, remember that odds are that receivers are not there for your ads. Consider the Johnsonville.com website in Exhibit 11.15. Does anything about the copy at this site remind you of traditional copywriting or is it cyberwriting?

Common Copywriting Approaches to Digital/Interactive Advertising.

> *"In this time of screaming technological advances, I find that what is considered old and near death is also what will never be replaced by technology. Mainly, that is good old fashioned creativity."*
>
> —Tracy Wong[19]

Digital/interactive ads are truly hybrids between print and broadcasting advertisements. On the one hand, the receiver encounters the message in a print format either at a website, in an email, at a blog, or from social media communication. On the other hand, the message is delivered electronically similar to television or radio. And, as the quote above highlights, just because this sort of copy delivery is made possible by technological advances, that does not mean that creativity is abandoned. The common approaches to copywriting are the following:[20]

- At a **long-copy landing page**, a website designed to sell a product directly, the copy might equal the equivalent of a four- to eight-page letter to a potential customer. The brand and its benefits are described in great detail with visuals included throughout.
- A **short-copy landing page** is simply a brand offer that may be accessed by a consumer through key word search and has the length and look of a magazine ad. Its components will resemble a magazine ad as well with headline, subhead, and body copy.
- **Long copy email** is designed to offer the receiver all sorts of incentives to buy the product and usually offers a link to a short-copy landing page.
- A **teaser email copy** is a short message designed to drive readers to a long-copy landing page where they can order the brand directly.
- A **pop-up/pop-under ad copy.** Pop-up and pop-under ads are discussed in Chapter 14 and are those sometimes annoying little ads that involuntarily show up while you are surfing. The "copy" in this sort of ad resembles a series of headlines and subheads without much or any body copy. Such an ad usually makes a special offer or drives the receiver to a website.
- **Social media copy** rarely has headlines or subheads but rather is more like pure copywriting. "Tweets" about a brand or brand "call outs" in a blog are subtle

18. Michael Learmonth, "Lowered Expectations: Web Redefines 'Quality,'" *Advertising Age*, February 22, 2010, 8.

19. Quoted in Christy Ashley and Jason D. Oliver, "Creative Leaders: Thirty Years of Big Ideas," *Journal of Advertising*, vol. 39, no. 1 (Spring 2010), 126.

20. Content in this section is drawn from Robert W. Bly, *The Copywriter's Handbook*, 3rd ed. (New York: Henry Holt and Company, 2006), 263–264.

Social Media

Can I Have Your Attention?

NEW YORK: Ashley Ringrose, co-founder of Soap Creative and curator of *Bannerblog*, has his six rules for making great Web ads. They were presented at Ad Age's Digital Conference. Ringrose is a pretty big deal in the digital ad world. His recommendations and commentary below suggest any ad destined for digital/interactive media should be:

1. Interactive: "Interactivity increases brand recall 63% more than non-interactive ads."
   - "Tell me and I'll forget;
   - Show me and I may remember;
   - **Involve me** and I'll understand."
2. Customizable: Allow the receiver to input personal information, alerts, and ideas
3. Contextual: Insert the brand into the ad
4. Entertaining: Make it visual or audio
5. Playable: Let the receiver engage the ad with graphics or gaming
6. Useful: Provide relevant information and benefits

So, what do you think? Do you still dislike banner ads? Do you find them annoying? Do you pay any attention to them? But, what if every advertiser followed these six rules? Then what would you think?

Source: Based on adage.com/digiconf10/article?article_id=143311. Accessed 4/27/10.

references to the brand that hope to build awareness and positive affinity (due to the association with the social media communication). The reality is that in many cases the advertiser is not in total control of the copy here. Even when a Tweet emanates from the firm, the tweeter is offering a free-form discussion of the brand—same with a blog entry.

Slogans/Taglines.

Copywriters are often asked to come up with a good slogan or tagline for a product or service. A **slogan** or **tagline** is a short phrase that is in part used to help establish an image, identity, or position for a brand or an organization, but it is most often used to increase memorability of the key benefit of a brand.[21] A slogan is established by repeating the phrase in a firm's advertising and other public communication as well as through salespeople and event promotions. Slogans are often used as a headline or subhead in print advertisements, or as the tagline at the conclusion of radio and television advertisements. Slogans typically appear directly below the brand or company name, on the brand website, or spoken in broadcast commercials as "You're in Good Hands" does in every Allstate insurance ad or digital application. Some classic and memorable ad slogans/taglines are listed in Exhibit 11.16.

A good slogan/tagline can serve several positive and important purposes for a brand or a firm. First, a slogan can be an integral part of a brand's image and personality. BMW's slogan, "The Ultimate Driving Machine," does much to establish and maintain the personality and image of the brand. Second, if a slogan is carefully and consistently developed over time, it can act as shorthand identification for the brand and provide information on important brand benefits. The long-standing slogan for De Beers Diamonds, "Diamonds Are Forever," communicates the benefits of the product and the brand. A good slogan also provides continuity across different media and between advertising campaigns. Nike's "Just Do It" slogan gave the firm an underlying theme for a wide range of campaigns and other promotions. In this

21. John R. Rossiter, "Defining the Necessary Components of Creative, Effective Ads," *Journal of Advertising*, vol. 37, no. 4 (Winter 2008), 141.

Exhibit 11.16 Classic and memorable slogans used for brands and organizations.

Brand/Company	Slogan
Allstate Insurance	You're in Good Hands with Allstate.
American Express	Don't Leave Home Without It.
AT&T (Consumer)	Reach Out and Touch Someone.
AT&T (Business)	AT&T. Your True Choice.
Beef Industry Council	Real Food for Real People.
Best Buy	Turn on the Fun.
BMW	The Ultimate Driving Machine.
Budweiser	This Bud's for You.
Chevrolet Trucks	Like a Rock.
Cotton Industry	The Fabric of Our Lives.
De Beers	Diamonds Are Forever.
Ford	Have You Driven a Ford Lately?
Goodyear	The Best Tires in the World Have Goodyear Written All Over Them.
Harley-Davidson	The Legend Rolls On.
Lincoln	What a Luxury Car Should Be.
Maybelline	Maybe She's Born with It. Maybe It's Maybelline.
Microsoft (Online)	Where Do You Want to Go Today?
Panasonic	Just Slightly Ahead of Our Time.
Prudential Insurance	Get a Piece of the Rock.
Rogaine	Stronger Than Heredity.
Saturn	A Different Kind of Company. A Different Kind of Car.
Sharp	From Sharp Minds Come Sharp Products.
Toshiba	In Touch with Tomorrow.
VH1	Music First.
Visa	It's Everywhere You Want to Be.
Volkswagen	Drivers Wanted.

sense, a slogan is a useful tool in helping to bring about thematic integrated brand promotion for a firm. Some argue that developing powerful slogans and taglines is a lost art that should be re-established as a key element in the copywriting effort.[22]

Common Mistakes in Copywriting.

The preceding discussions have shown that print, radio, television, and digital/interactive advertising present the copywriter with unique challenges and opportunities. Copy in each arena must be compatible with the various types of ads run in each medium and the particular capabilities and liabilities of each medium and format.

22. Steve Cone, "Help Taglines Regain Lost Glory," *Advertising Age*, April 14, 2008, 9.

Beyond the guidelines for effective copy in each area, some common mistakes made in copywriting can and should be avoided:

- ***Vagueness.*** Avoid generalizations and imprecise words. To say that a car is stylish is not nearly as meaningful as saying it has sleek, aerodynamic lines. And when being precise, always be justified. The *Ethics* box shows the penalty for a precise but misleading claim.
- ***Wordiness.*** Being economical with descriptions is paramount. Copy has to fit in a limited time frame (or space), and receivers bore easily. When boredom sets in, effective communication often ceases.
- ***Triteness.*** Using clichés and worn-out superlatives was mentioned as a threat to print copywriting. The same threat (to a lesser degree, due to audio and audio-visual capabilities) exists in radio and television advertising. Trite copy creates a boring, outdated image for a brand or firm.
- ***Bad taste.*** Sexist, racist, offensive, and vulgar language may seem like a good way to draw attention to your copy—but it's not. It's simple minded and not at all creative.
- ***Laundry lists.*** This happens when copy presents a group of features with no clear benefits communicated in the message. It is hard for the receiver to find the "big idea" behind the brand in this kind of message.
- ***Creativity for creativity's sake.*** Some copywriters get carried away with a clever idea. It's essential that the copy in an ad remain true to its primary responsibility: communicating the selling message. Copy that is extraordinarily funny or poses an intriguing riddle but fails to register the main selling theme will simply produce another amusing advertising failure.[23]

The Copy Approval Process.

> *"The client has some issues and concerns about your ads." This is how account executives announce the death of your labors: "issues and concerns." To understand the portent of this phrase, picture the men lying on the floor of that Chicago garage on St. Valentine's Day. Al Capone had issues and concerns with these men.*
>
> *I've had account executives beat around the bush for 15 minutes before they could tell me the bad news. "Well, we had a good meeting."*
>
> *"Yes," you say, "but are the ads dead?"*
>
> *"We learned a lot?"*
>
> *"But are they dead?"*
>
> *"Wellll, . . . They're really not dead. They are just in a new and better place."*
>
> —Luke Sullivan[24]

The final step in copywriting is getting the copy approved. For many copywriters, this is the most dreaded part of their existence—as the quote above reveals. During the approval process, the proposed copy is likely to pass through the hands of a wide range of client and agency people, many of whom are ill-prepared to judge the quality of the copy. And, there are those who argue convincingly that approval process stifles creativity as the creative team strives for approval rather than creative excellence.[25] The challenge at this stage is to keep the creative potency of the copy

23. Some considerations in this section drawn from Tom Altsteil and Jean Grow, *Advertising Creative: Strategy, Copy and Design*, 2nd ed. (Los Angeles: Sage Publications, 2010), 180–181.

24. Luke Sullivan, *Hey Whipple, Squeeze This: A Guide to Creating Great Ads*, 182.

25. Jean Halliday, "How GM Stifled 'Passion and Creativity' in Its Marketing Ranks," *Advertising Age*, June 12, 2009, 13.

intact. As David Ogilvy suggests in his commandments for advertising, "Committees can criticize advertisements, but they can't write them."[26]

The copy approval process usually begins within the creative department at the advertising agency. A copywriter submits draft copy to either a senior writer or creative director, or both. From there, the redrafted copy is forwarded to the account management team. The main concern at this level is to evaluate the copy on legal grounds. After the account management team has made recommendations, a meeting is likely held to present the copy, along with proposed visuals, to the client's product category manager, brand manager, and/or marketing staff. Inevitably, the client representatives feel compelled to make recommendations for altering the copy. In some cases, these recommendations realign the copy in accordance with important marketing strategy objectives. In other cases, the recommendations are amateurish and problematic. From the copywriter's point of view, they are rarely welcome, although the copywriter usually has to act as if they are.

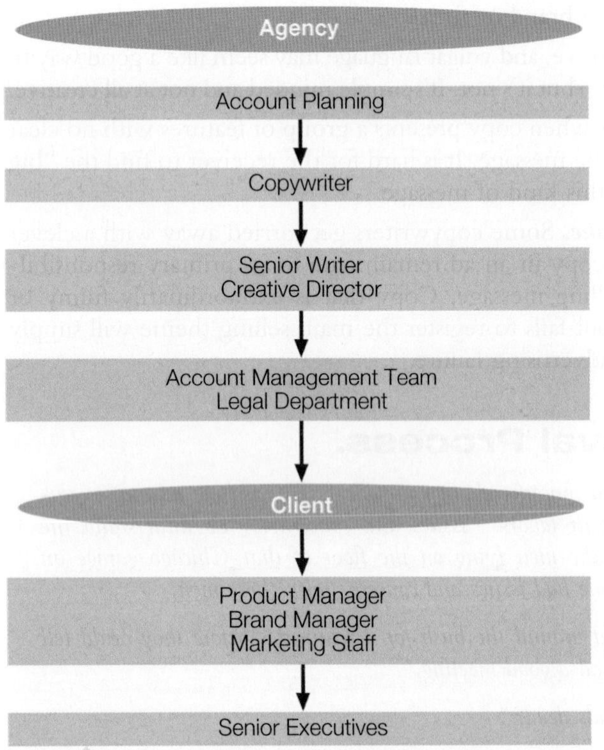

Exhibit 11.17 The copy approval process.

Depending on the assignment, the client, and the traditions of the agency, the creative team may also decide to turn to various forms of copy research to resolve any differences. Typically, copy research is either developmental or evaluative. **Developmental copy research** (see Chapter 7) can actually help copywriters at the early stages of copy development by providing audience interpretations and reactions to the proposed copy. **Evaluative copy research** (see Chapter 7) is used to judge copy after it has been produced. Here, the audience expresses its approval or disapproval of the copy used in an ad. Copywriters are not fond of these evaluative report cards. In our view, they are completely justified in their suspicion; for many reasons, state-of-the-art evaluative copy research just isn't very good.

Finally, copy should always be submitted for final approval to the advertiser's senior executives. Many times, these executives have little interest in evaluating advertising plans, and they leave this responsibility to middle managers. In some firms, however, top executives get very involved in the approval process. The various levels of approval for copy are summarized in Exhibit 11.17 and parodied in Exhibit 11.18. For the

Exhibit 11.18 Advertisers should allow copywriters to exercise their creative expertise, as suggested by this Dilbert cartoon.

26. David Ogilvy, *Ogilvy on Advertising* (New York: Vintage Books, 1985).

advertiser, it is best to recognize that copywriters, like other creative talent in an agency, should be allowed to exercise their creative expertise with guidance but not overbearing interference. Copywriters typically provide energy, originality, and distinctiveness to an often dry marketing strategy.

5 Executing the Creative: Art Direction.

At this point, we can turn our attention to the process of art direction. In the discussion of copywriting just completed, the issue of coordinating the copy with visuals was raised several times. Now, we want to focus on the process of how the visual elements of an advertisement and IBP materials are developed.

A hundred years ago advertisers largely relied on words to persuade consumers. They argued with consumers, attempted to reason with them, pleaded with them, and cajoled them. Then sometime in the early 20th century, particularly noticeable after about 1910, advertisers began to move away from all words and toward pictures. This trend would extend throughout the 20th century and into the 21st. Now, advertising has become mostly visual. There are several reasons for the rise of the visual in advertising. Among them are (1) improved technologies, which facilitate better and more affordable illustration and the opportunity to rotate visuals nearly instantaneously in digital media; (2) the inherent advantage of pictures to quickly demonstrate the values of a brand; (3) the ability to build brand "images" through visuals; (4) the legal advantage of pictures over words in that the truth or falsity of a picture is almost impossible to determine; (5) the widely held belief that pictures, although just as cultural as words, permit a certain type of global portability that words do not; and (6) pictures allow advertisers to place brands in desired social contexts, thus transferring important social meaning to them.

Illustration, Design, and Layout.

We'll begin with a discussion of three primary visual elements of a print or digital ad: illustration, design, and layout. We'll then identify aspects of each that should be specified, or at least considered, as a print or digital/interactive ad is being prepared. An advertiser must appreciate the technical aspects of coordinating the visual elements in an ad with the mechanics of the layout and ultimately with the procedures for print production or Web placement. Today, art directors and their designers are using Adobe's InDesign software to create highly illustrative print and digital ads suitable that are for presentation on new tablet devices or e-readers like the iPad.[27] This new software offers major improvements in the quality and speed of the illustration, layout, and design process (www.adobe.com/products/indesign/).

Initially, the art director, copywriter, and in the current era, a media planner and account planner (the contemporary creative team as identified at the outset of the chapter) decide on the general purpose and therefore content of an advertising visual. Then the art director, usually in conjunction with a graphic designer, takes this raw idea for the visual and develops it further. Art directors, with their specialized skills and training, coordinate the design and illustration components of the ad. The creative director oversees the entire process. The copywriter is still in the loop to achieve word/visual coordination.

Illustration. **Illustration**, in the context of print and digital advertising, is the actual drawing, painting, photography, or computer-generated art that forms the picture in an advertisement.

27. Nat Ives, "How to Make Over a Magazine for the iPad: Popular Science," *Advertising Age*, May 31, 2010, 6.

Illustration Purposes. There are several specific, strategic purposes for illustration, which can greatly increase the chances of effective communication. The basic purposes of an illustration are the following:

- To attract the attention of the target audience
- To make the brand heroic
- To communicate brand features or benefits
- To create a mood, feeling, or image
- To stimulate reading of the body copy
- To create the desired social context for the brand

Think about how each of these serves to execute the message strategies discussed in Chapter 10. For example, consider how creating the desired social context for a brand advances the slice-of-life method of socially situating. Consider how a USP (unique selling proposition) strategy would be advanced by communicating a certain brand feature visually.

Attract the Attention of the Target Audience. A primary role from illustration is to attract and hold attention along with the headline as discussed earlier. With all the advertising clutter, this is no easy task. In some advertising situations (for example, the very early stages of a new product launch or for very "low-involvement" repeat purchase items), just being noticed by consumers may be enough. In most cases, however, being noticed is a necessary, but not sufficient, goal. An illustration is made to communicate with a particular target audience and, generally, must support other components of the ad to achieve the intended communication impact. So, what do you think of the impact of the ad in Exhibit 11.19? Will it get noticed, will the brand be remembered?

Make the Brand Heroic. One traditional role of art direction is to make the brand "heroic." Visual techniques such as backlighting, low-angle shots, and dramatic use of color can communicate heroic proportions and qualities. Professionals even call this the "hero" or "beauty shot" (see Exhibit 11.20).

Communicate Product Features or Benefits. Perhaps the most straightforward illustration is one that simply displays brand features, benefits, or both (see Exhibit 11.21—and look carefully!). Even though a print ad is static, the product can be shown in use through an "action" scene or even through a series of illustrations.

Exhibit 11.19 Will this illustration get this ad noticed?

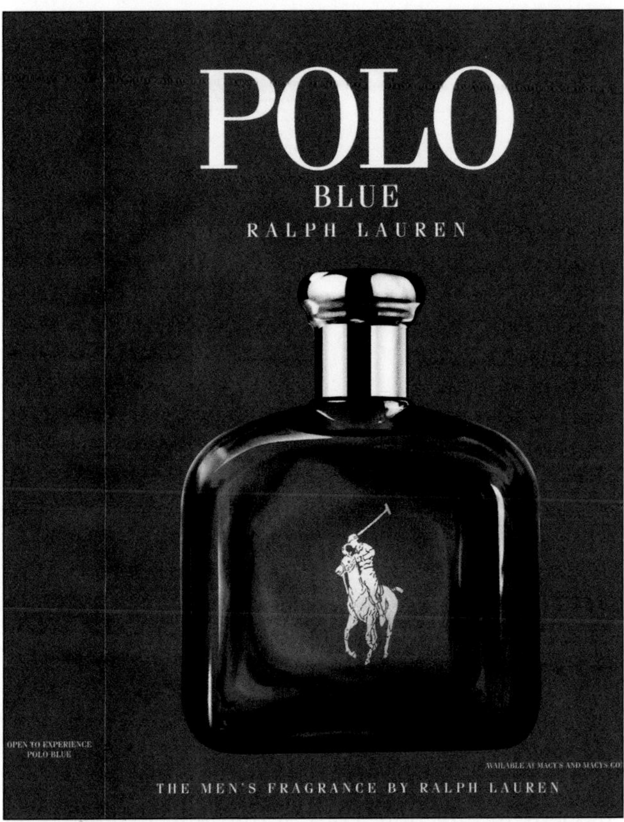

Exhibit 11.20 The art direction for this ad tries to make the brand "heroic."

The benefits of product use can be demonstrated with before-and-after shots or by demonstrating the result of having used the product.

Create a Mood, Feeling, or Image. Brand image is projected through illustration. The myriad of ways this is done is beyond enumeration, but the illustration interacts with the packaging, associated brand imagery (for example, the brand logo), and evoked feelings, which all contribute. The "mood" of an ad can help this along—created by color tones and highlighting. Whether these goals are achieved with an ad depends on the technical execution of the illustration. The lighting, color, tone, and texture of the illustration can have a huge impact. In Exhibit 11.22, the photograph used in this ad for a video rental store that specializes in horror movies captures an eerie, disconcerting feeling.

Stimulate Reading of the Body Copy. Just as a headline can stimulate examination of the illustration, the illustration can stimulate reading of the body copy. Because body copy generally carries essential selling messages, any tactic that encourages reading is useful (see Exhibit 11.23). Illustrations can create curiosity and interest. To satisfy that curiosity, readers may proceed to the body copy. Normally, an illustration and headline need to be fully coordinated and play off each other for this level of interest to occur. One caution is to avoid making the illustration too clever a stimulus for motivating copy reading. Putting cleverness ahead of clarity in choosing an illustration can confuse the receiver and cause the body copy to be

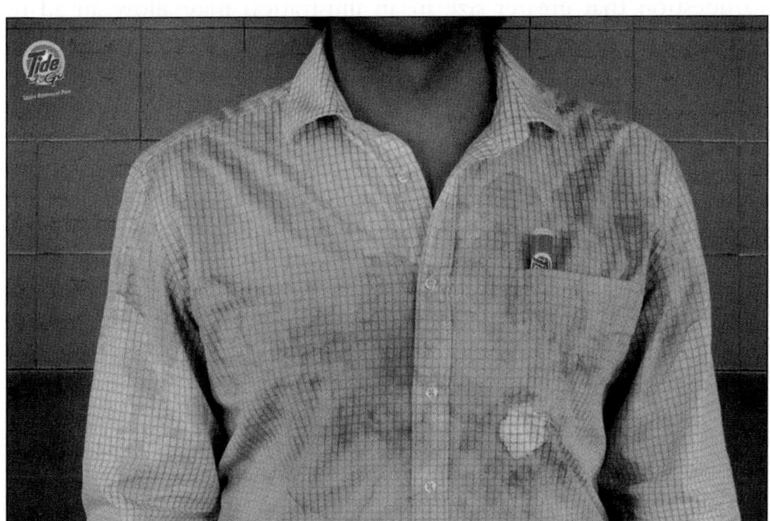

Exhibit 11.21 Sometimes a photograph of a product in use can present brand features or benefits in a simple, powerful manner.

Exhibit 11.22 Contrast and eerie lighting work here.

Exhibit 11.23 This ad tries to get you to read the body copy. Does it work?

Courtesy, Beck & Co.

ignored. As one expert puts it, such ads win awards but can camouflage the benefit offered by the product.[28]

Create the Desired Social Context for the Brand. As described earlier, advertisers often try to situate their brands within a type of social setting, thereby linking it with certain "types" of people and certain lifestyles. Establishing desired social contexts is a highly prized function of modern art direction. Look at the ad in Exhibit 11.24 and then think about what it would mean if the product were divorced from the social context. (See Exhibit 11.25.) See what we mean? Context can be everything.

Illustration Components. Various factors contribute to the overall visual presentation and impact of an illustration. Size, color, and medium affect viewers. Individual decisions regarding size, color, and medium are a matter of artistic discretion and creative execution. There is some evidence of the differing effects of various decisions made in each of these areas. But remember, the interpretation and meaning of any visual representation cannot be explained completely by a series of rules or prescriptive how-tos—but they do help.

Size. There is no question that greater size in an illustration may allow an ad to compete more successfully for the reader's attention, especially in a cluttered media environment. Consumers appear to infer brand importance from the relative size of an ad. Generally speaking, illustrations with a focal point immediately recognizable by the reader are more likely to be noticed and comprehended—often this is brand itself, the brand logo (think Nike) or the brand package. Conversely, illustrations that arouse curiosity or incorporate action are generally believed to score high in attracting attention, score low in inducing the reading of the total ad.

Color. Although not every execution of print advertising allows for the use of color (because of either expense or the medium being employed), color is a creative tool with important potential. Some product categories (such as furniture, floor coverings, or expensive clothing) may depend on color to accurately communicate a principal value. Color can also be used to emphasize a brand feature or attract the reader's attention to a particular part of an ad. But remember, color has no fixed meaning, so no hard rules can be offered. Color is cultural, situational, and contextual. To say that red always means this or blue always means that is to rely on

28. Tony Antin, *Great Print Advertising* (New York: Wiley, 1993), 38.

Exhibits 11.24 and 11.25 Context is (almost) everything. When you remove the advertised brand from the advertiser-created context, it isn't the same, is it?

a popular but unfounded myth. It's simply not true, but you will run into those who are absolutely sure that a certain shade of red is why Marlboro is the leading cigarette, or that a certain shade of green always means this or that. Sorry, these are just myths.

Medium. The choice of **medium** for an illustration is the decision regarding the use of drawing, photography, or computer graphics.[29] Drawing represents a wide range of creative presentations, from cartoons to pen-and-ink drawings to elaborate watercolor or oil paintings. Photos have an element of believability as representations of reality. Further, photos can often be prepared more quickly and at much less expense than other forms of art. And as we all know, photos can be greatly enhanced with software like PhotoShop to achieve desired creative effects. The American Society of Media Photographers is a trade association of thousands of photographers whose work is primarily used for publication. This society can help buyers find professional photographers. Buyers can also purchase photographs from various stock agencies, such as Corbis, Getty Images, or PhotoEdit. These photographs can usually be cropped to any size or shape, retouched, color-corrected, and doctored in a number of ways to create the user's desired effect.

With advancing technology, artists have discovered the application of computer graphics to advertising illustrations. Computer graphics specialists can create and manipulate images. As highlighted earlier, software like InDesign has greatly expanded

29. This section is adapted from Sandra E. Moriarty, *Creative Advertising: Theory and Practice*, 2nd ed. (Upper Saddle River, NJ: Prentice-Hall, 1991), 139–141.

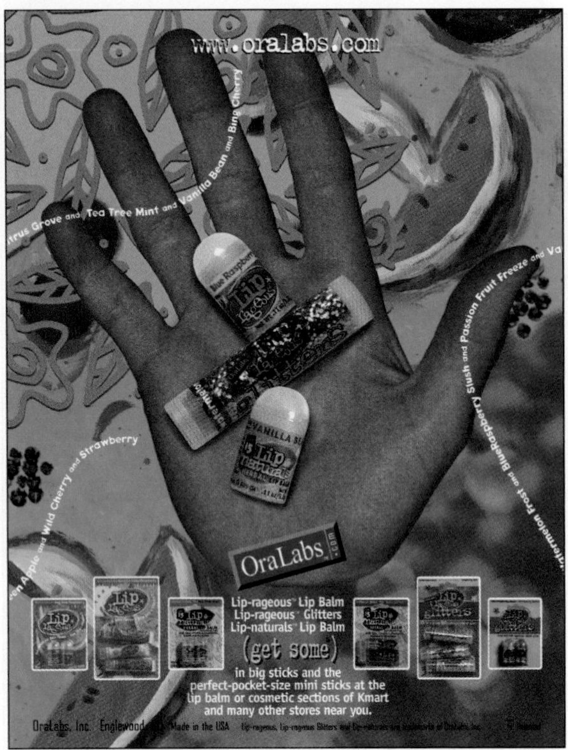

Exhibit 11.26 Computer graphics make this ad.

Exhibit 11.27 Color needed?

the options for visual management. With respect to illustrations for print advertising, the key development has been the ability to digitize images. With a digitized image, computer graphics specialists can break down an illustration and reassemble it or import other components into the original image. Age can be added to or taken away from a model's face, or the Eiffel Tower can magically appear on Madison Avenue. The creative possibilities are endless with computer graphics. Exhibit 11.26 is an example of an ad with multiple images imported through computer graphics. Some art directors are very fond of these software solutions.

The size, color, and media decisions regarding an illustration are difficult ones. It is likely that strategic and budgetary considerations will heavily influence choices in these areas. Once again, advertisers should not constrain the creative process more than is absolutely necessary. Great art directors know the language and syntax of visual persuasion (rhetoric) even if they can't always explain it in a way that brand managers and account executives understand.

Illustration Formats. The just-discussed components represent a series of decisions that must be made in conceiving an illustration. Another important decision is how a brand will appear as part of the illustration. **Illustration format** refers to the choices the advertiser has for displaying the brand. There are product shots of all sorts: Some emphasize the social context and meaning of the product (see Exhibit 11.27) or service; some are more abstract, some are minimal. Obviously, the illustration format must be consistent with the copy and creative strategy set for the ad. The creative department and the marketing planners must communicate with one another so that the illustration format selected helps pursue the specific objectives set for the total ad campaign.

Design.

Design is "the structure itself and the plan behind that structure" for the aesthetic and stylistic aspects of a print advertisement.[30] Design represents the effort on the part of the creative team to physically arrange all the components of a printed or digital/interactive advertisement in such a way that order and beauty are achieved—order in the sense that the illustration, headline, body copy, and special features of the ad are easy to read; beauty in the sense that the ad is visually pleasing to a reader. Even cyberspace ads (which we will consider specifically in a few pages) have to have visual appeal along with all the interactive options they present.

There are aspects of design that directly relate to the potential for an ad to communicate effectively based on its artistic form. As such, design factors are highly relevant to creating effective print advertising and we will consider those now.

30. This discussion is based on Roy Paul Nelson, *The Design of Advertising*, 7th ed. (Boston: McGraw-Hill 1996), 136.

Courtesy, OraLabs, Inc.; Courtesy, Advertising Archives

Principles of Design. Principles of design govern how a print advertisement should be prepared. The word *should* is carefully chosen in this context. It is used because, just as language has rules of grammar and syntax, visual presentation has rules of design. The **principles of design** relate to each element within an advertisement and to the arrangement of and relationship between elements as a whole.[31] Principles of design suggest the following:

- A design should be in balance.
- The proportion within an advertisement should be pleasing to the viewer.
- The components within an advertisement should have an ordered and directional pattern.
- There should be a unifying force within the ad.
- One element of the ad should be emphasized above all others.

We will consider each of these principles of design and how they relate to the development of an effective advertisement. Of course, as surely as there are rules, there are occasions when the rules need to be broken. An experienced designer knows the rules and follows them but is also prepared to break the rules to achieve a desired creative outcome. But first, you learn the rules.

Balance. **Balance** in an ad is an orderliness and compatibility of presentation. Balance can be either formal or informal. **Formal balance** emphasizes symmetrical presentation—components on one side of an imaginary vertical line through the ad are repeated in approximate size and shape on the other side of the imaginary line. Formal balance creates a mood of seriousness and directness and offers the viewer an orderly, easy-to-follow visual presentation (see Exhibit 11.28).

Informal Balance. **Informal balance** emphasizes asymmetry—the optical weighing of nonsimilar sizes and shapes. Exhibit 11.29 shows an advertisement using a

Exhibit 11.28 This ad achieves balance. www.miniusa.com

31. Based on Roy Paul Nelso, *The Design of Advertising,* 7th ed. (Boston: McGraw-Hill, 1996), 149.

Exhibit 11.29 This ad uses informal balance for creative effect.

Courtesy, First Base Imaging, London

range of type sizes, visuals, and colors to create a powerful visual effect that achieves informal balance. Informal balance in an ad should not be interpreted as imbalance. Rather, components of different sizes, shapes, and colors are arranged in a more complex relationship providing asymmetrical balance to an ad and a visually intriguing presentation to the viewer.

Proportion. **Proportion** has to do with the size and tonal relationships between different elements in an advertisement. Whenever two elements are placed in proximity, proportion results. Proportional considerations include the relationship of the width of an ad to its depth; the width of each element to the depth of each element; the size of one element relative to the size of every other; the space between two elements and the relationship of that space to a third element; and the amount of light area as opposed to the amount of dark area. Ideally, factors of proportion vary so as to avoid monotony in an ad. Further, the designer should pursue pleasing proportions, which means the viewer will not detect mathematical relationships between elements. In general, unequal dimensions and distances make for some of the liveliest designs in advertising (see Exhibit 11.30).

Order. **Order** in an advertisement is also referred to as sequence or, in terms of its effects on the reader, "gaze motion." The designer's goal is to establish a relationship among elements that leads the reader through the ad in some controlled fashion. A designer can create a logical path of visual components to control eye movement. The eye has a "natural" tendency to move from left to right, from up to down, from large elements to small elements, from light to dark, and from color to noncolor. Exhibit 11.31 is an example of an ad that takes advantage of many of these tendencies. The bright lights on top of the Land Rover and the white headlines against a dark background initially attract the gaze. The eye then moves down the shape of the car, and the headlights bring the gaze down to the body copy and logo. The natural tendency for the eye to move from top to bottom leads the eye to a final shot of the Land Rover. Order also includes inducing the reader to jump from one space in the ad to another, creating a sense of action. The essential contribution of this design component is to establish a visual format that results in a focus or several focuses.

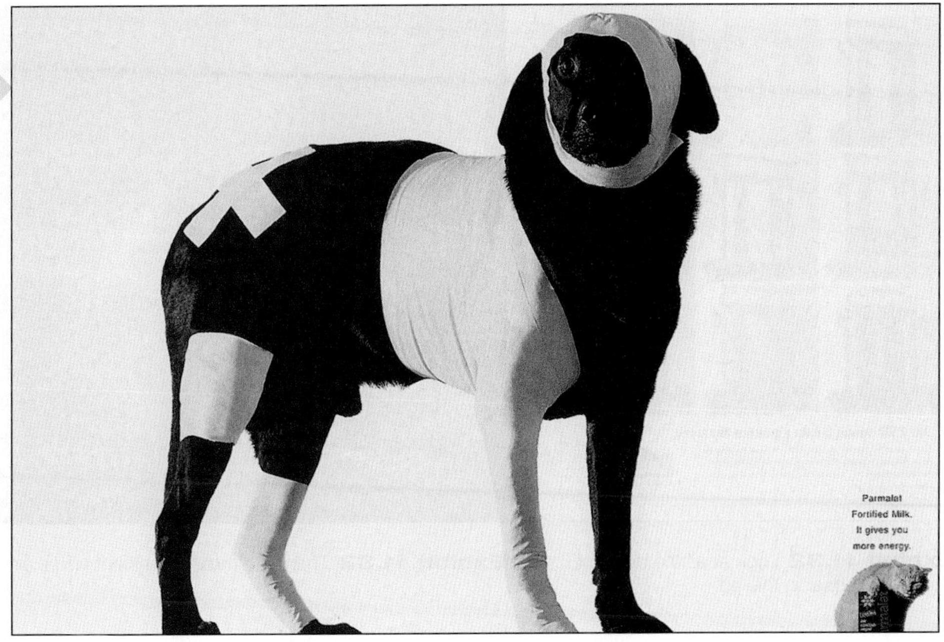

Exhibit 11.30
Proportion, when expertly controlled, can result in an inspired display of the oversized versus the undersized. www.parmalat.com

Exhibit 11.31 The order of elements in this ad for the Land Rover controls the reader's eye, moving it from the top of the ad through the body copy and logo, then down to the product shot at the bottom. www.landrover.com

Unity. Ensuring that the elements of an advertisement are tied together and appear to be related is the purpose of **unity**. Considered the most important of the design principles, unity results in harmony among the diverse components of an advertisement: headline, subhead, body copy, and illustration. Several design techniques contribute to unity. The border surrounding an ad keeps the ad elements from spilling over into other ads or into the printed matter next to the ad.

Another construct of unity is the axis. In every advertisement, an axis will naturally emerge. The **axis** is a line, real or imagined, that runs through an ad and from which the elements in the advertisement flare out. A single ad may have one, two, or even three axes running vertically and horizontally. An axis can be created by blocks of copy, by the placement of illustrations, or by the items within an illustration, such as the position and direction of a model's arm or leg. Elements in an ad may violate the axes, but when two or more elements use a common axis as a starting point, unity is enhanced. Note all the different axes that appear in Exhibit 11.32.

A design can be more forceful in creating unity by using either a three-point layout or a parallel layout. A **three-point layout structure** establishes three elements in the ad as dominant forces. The uneven number of prominent elements is critical for creating a gaze motion in the viewer (see Exhibit 11.33). **Parallel layout structure** employs art on the right-hand side of the page and repeats

Exhibit 11.32 Look at all the different axes that appear in this ad.

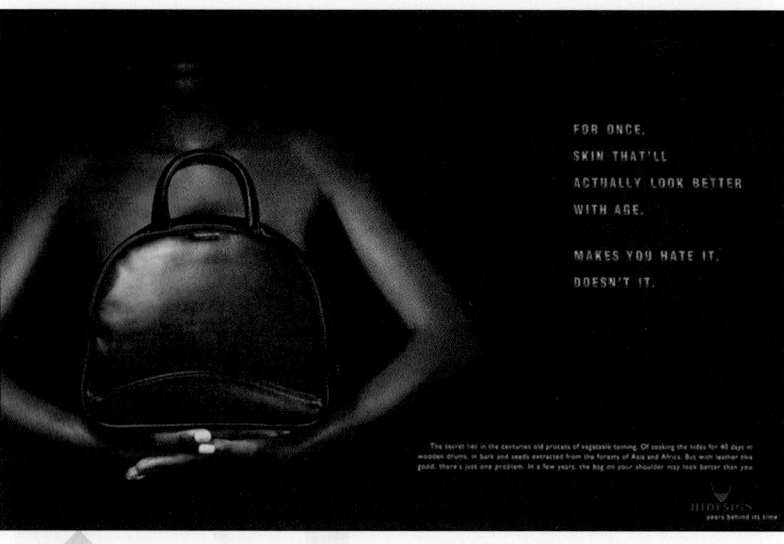

Exhibit 11.33 There are three prominent visual elements here.

Exhibit 11.34 Here, the visual layout on the left is repeated on the right.
www.epiphone.com

Courtesy, Lowe's; Reprinted with permission from Hidesign; Client: The Epiphone Company, a division of Gibson Guitar Corp.; Agency: CORE, St. Louis; Creative Director: Eric Tilford; Art Director: Eric Tilford; Copy Writer: Wade Paschall; Strategy: Jeff Graham; Photographer: James Schwartz.

the art on the left-hand side. This is an obvious and highly structured technique to achieve unity (see Exhibit 11.34).

Emphasis. At some point in the decision-making process, someone needs to decide which major component—the headline, subhead, body copy, or illustration—will be emphasized. The key to good design relative to emphasis is that one item is the primary but not the only focus in an ad. If one element is emphasized to the total exclusion of the others, then a poor design has been achieved, and ultimately a poor communication will result.

Balance, proportion, order, unity, and emphasis are the basic principles of design. As you can see, the designer's objectives go beyond the strategic and message-development elements associated with an advertisement. Design principles relate to the aesthetic impression an ad produces. Once a designer has been informed of the components that will make up the headline, subhead, body copy, and illustration to be included in the ad, then advertising and marketing decision makers *must* allow the designer to arrange those components according to the principles of creative design.

Layout. In contrast to design, which emphasizes the structural concept behind a print ad, layout is the mechanical aspect of design—the physical manifestation of design concepts. A **layout** is a drawing or digital rendering of a proposed print advertisement (digital interactive ads are digitized from the start, of course) showing where all the elements in the ad are positioned. An art director uses a layout to work through various alternatives for visual presentation and sequentially develop the print ad to its final stages. It is the part and parcel of the design process and inextricably linked to the development of an effective design.

An art director typically proceeds through various stages in the construction of a final design for an ad. The following are the different stages of layout development, in order of detail and completeness that an art director typically uses.

Thumbnails. Thumbnails are the first drafts of an advertising layout. The art director will produce several thumbnail sketches to work out the general presentation of the ad. Although the creative team refines the creative concept, thumbnails represent placement of elements—headline, images, body copy, and tagline. Headlines are often represented with zigzag lines and body copy with straight, parallel lines. An example of a thumbnail is shown in Exhibit 11.35. Typically, thumbnails are drawn at one-quarter the size of the finished ad.

Rough Layout. The next step in the layout process is the **rough layout**. Unlike a thumbnail sketch, a rough layout is done in the actual size of the proposed ad and is usually created with a computer layout program, such as InDesign. This allows the art director to experiment with different headline fonts and easily manipulate the placement and size of images to be used in the ad. Exhibit 11.36 features a rough layout.

Exhibit 11.35 A thumbnail showing the transition from idea to advertisement.

Exhibit 11.36 A rough layout.

Comprehensive. The comprehensive layout, or **comp**, is a polished version of the ad—but not the final version. Now for the most part computer-generated, a comp is a representation of what the final ad will look like. At this stage, the final headline font is used, the images to be used—photographs or illustrations—are digitized and placed in the ad, and the actual body copy is often included on the ad. Comps are generally printed in full color if the final ad is to be in color. Comps that are produced in this way make it very easy for the client to imagine (and approve) what the ad will look like when it is published. Exhibit 11.37 features a comp layout.

The client will make one last approval of the digital file before it is sent to the printer. Changes that a client requests, prior to the ad being sent to the printer, are still easily and quickly made. The stages of layout development discussed here provide the artistic blueprint for a print advertisement (see Exhibit 11.38). We now turn our attention to the matter of typography in print production.

Typography in Print Production. The issues associated with typography have to do with the typeface chosen for headlines, subheads, and body copy, as well as the various size components of the type (height, width, and running length). Designers agonize over the type to use in a print ad because decisions about type affect both the readability and the mood of the overall visual impression. For our purposes, some knowledge of the basic considerations of typography is useful for an appreciation of the choices that must be made.

Categories of Type. Typefaces have distinct personalities, and each can communicate a different mood and image. A **type font** is a basic set of typeface letters. For those of us who do word processing on computers, the choice of type font is a common decision. In choosing type for an advertisement, however, the art director has thousands of choices based on typeface alone.

There are six basic typeface groups: blackletter, roman, script, serif, sans serif, and miscellaneous. The families are divided by characteristics that reflect the personality and tone of the font. **Blackletter**, also called *gothic*, is characterized by the ornate design of the letters. This style is patterned after hand-drawn letters in monasteries

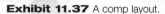

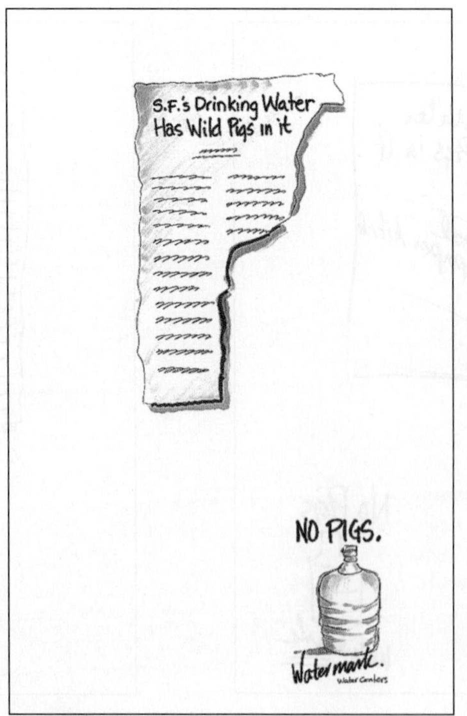

Exhibit 11.37 A comp layout.

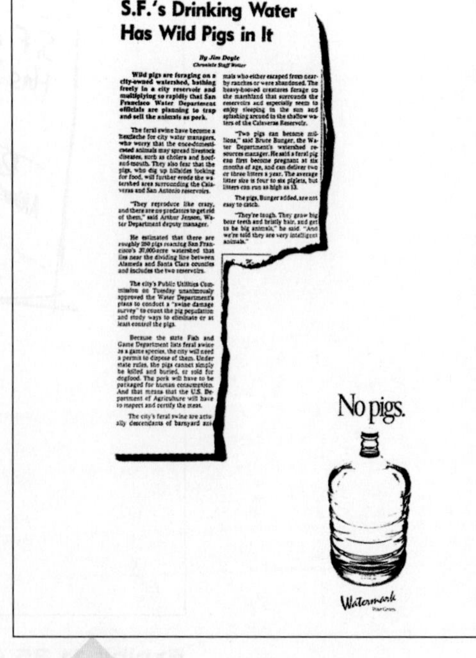

S.F.'s Drinking Water Has Wild Pigs in It

By Jim Doyle
Chronicle Staff Writer

Wild pigs are foraging on a city-owned watershed, bathing freely in a city reservoir and multiplying so rapidly that San Francisco Water Department officials are planning to trap and sell the animals as pork.

The feral swine have become a headache for city water managers, who worry that the once-domesticated animals may spread livestock diseases, such as cholera and hoof-and-mouth. They also fear that the pigs, who dig up hillsides looking for food, will further erode the watershed area surrounding the Calaveras and San Antonio reservoirs.

"They reproduce like crazy, and there are no predators to get rid of them," said Arthur Jensen, Water Department deputy manager.

He estimated that there are roughly 250 pigs roaming San Francisco's 37,000-acre watershed that lies near the dividing line between Alameda and Santa Clara counties and includes the two reservoirs.

The city's Public Utilities Commission on Tuesday unanimously approved the Water Department's plans to conduct a "swine damage survey" to count the pig population and study ways to eliminate or at least control the pigs.

Because the state Fish and Game Department lists feral swine as a game species, the city will need a permit to dispose of them. Under state rules, the pigs cannot simply be killed and buried, or sold for dogfood. The pork will have to be packaged for human consumption. And that means that the U.S. Department of Agriculture will have to inspect and certify the meat.

The city's feral swine are actually descendants of barnyard animals who either escaped from nearby ranches or were abandoned. The heavy-hooved creatures forage on the marshland that surrounds the reservoirs and especially seem to enjoy sleeping in the sun and splashing around in the shallow waters of the Calaveras Reservoir.

"Two pigs can become millions," said Bruce Bunger, the Water Department's watershed resources manager. He said a feral pig can first become pregnant at six months of age, and can deliver two or three litters a year. The average litter size is four to six piglets, but litters can run as high as 13.

The pigs, Bunger added, are not easy to catch.

"They're tough. They grow big boar teeth and bristly hair, and get to be big animals," he said. "And we're told they are very intelligent animals."

Exhibit 11.38 The finished ad.

Courtesy of Arnold, Finnegan & Martin; Courtesy of Arnold, Finnegan & Martin where illuminated manuscripts were created. You can see blackletter fonts used today in very formal documents, such as college diplomas. **Roman** is the most common group of fonts used for body copy because of its legibility. This family is characterized by the use of thick and thin strokes in the creation of the letterforms. **Script** is easy to distinguish by the linkage of the letters in the way that cursive handwriting is connected. Script is often found on wedding invitations and documents that are intended to look elegant or of high quality. **Serif** refers to the strokes or "feet" at the ends of the letterforms. Notice the serifs that are present in these letters as you read. Their presence helps move your eye across the page, allowing you to read for a long time without losing your place or tiring your eyes. **Sans serif** fonts, as the name suggests, do not have serifs, hence the use of the French word *sans*, meaning "without." Sans serif fonts are typically used for headlines and not for body copy. **Miscellaneous** includes typefaces that do not fit easily into the other categories. Novelty display, garage, and deconstructed fonts all fall into this group. These fonts were designed specifically to draw attention to themselves and not necessarily for their legibility. The following example displays serif and sans serif type:

This line is set in serif type.
This line is set in sans serif type.

Type Measurement. There are two elements of type size. **Point** refers to the size of type in height. In the printing industry, type sizes run from 6 to 120 points. Now, with computer layout programs such as QuarkXPress, the range is much larger, between 2 and 720 points. Exhibit 11.39 shows a range of type sizes for comparison purposes. **Picas** measure the width of lines. A pica is 12 points wide, and each pica measures about one-sixth of an inch. Layout programs make it very easy for the art director to fit copy into a designated space on an ad by reducing or enlarging a font with a few strokes on the keyboard.

Readability. It is critical in choosing type to consider readability. Type should facilitate the communication process. The following are some traditional recommendations when deciding what type to use (however, remember that these are only guidelines and should not necessarily be followed in every instance):

- Use capitals and lowercase, NOT ALL CAPITALS.
- Arrange letters from left to right, not up and down.
- Run lines of type horizontally, not vertically.
- Use even spacing between letters and words.

This is 8 point type
This is 12 point type
This is 18 point type
This is 36 point type
This is 60 point type

Exhibit 11.39 A range of type point sizes.

Different typefaces and styles also affect the mood conveyed by an ad. Depending on the choices made, typefaces can connote grace, power, beauty, modernity, simplicity, or any number of other qualities.

Art Direction and Production in Digital/Interactive Media.

We've referenced art direction and production in digital/interactive media in the previous sections. But, cyberspace has its own space qualities. It is its own medium, too. It's not television or radio, but ads produced for television or radio can certainly be transmitted over the Web. In that case, the considerations for radio and television production hold. But, when an ad is prepared primarily with the characteristics of headline, body copy, and illustration—like an email, banner, pop-up, or even a website, digital/interactive ads are closer to print than to anything. Even though the basic principles of art direction (design and concept) apply, the cyber media are fundamentally different in the way its audience comes to it, navigates it, and responds to it. This difference presents one of the real challenges of electronic advertising.

In most respects, cyber-production does not differ significantly from print production, but it does differ from print in how aspects of production are combined with programming language, such as HTML, and with each other. Advances in streaming audio and digital video keep art direction and production in cyberspace a fast-moving target. Still, many cyberads may be either produced in traditional ways and then digitized and combined with text or created entirely with computer design packages. Exhibits 11.40 through 11.42 are fairly representative of what's out there.

All media have to find their own way, their own voice. This is not just an aesthetic matter. It's figuring out what works, which has something to do with design. How the information is laid out matters. If you go back and look at the first few years of television advertising, you have to say that they really didn't fully understand the medium or the ways audiences would use this new technology. The ads went on forever and seemed to be written for radio. In fact, many of the early TV writers were radio writers. They tried to make television radio.

This same phenomenon seems to be happening with websites. At first, Web ads looked more like print ads than something truly cyber. Yet, unlike print ads, websites have the ability to change almost immediately. If a client wants to change a copy point, for example, it can happen many times in one afternoon. And Web consumers demand change. Although frequent changes may seem time-consuming and expensive, they ensure return visits from audiences. More importantly, digital/interactive ads offer the viewer direct interaction by clicking on the ad or a link in an email: an opportunity that can't be missed.

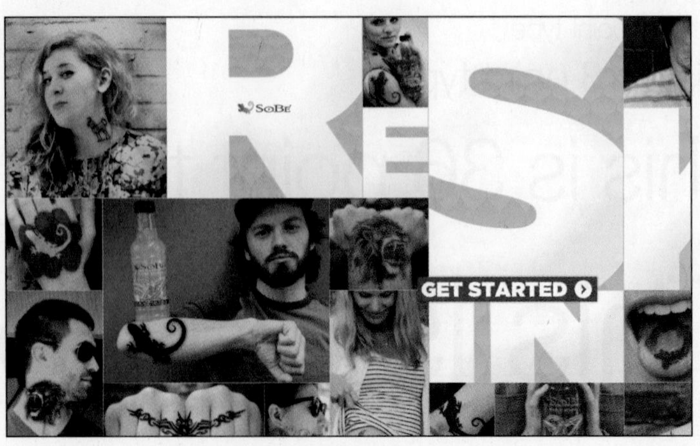

Courtesy, Wright's Media

Exhibits 11.40–11.41 Here are some examples of the current style of cyberads.

Exhibit 11.42
Go Fans!

Courtesy, Wright's Media

Web pages are often very busy, with lots of information crammed into small spaces. In short, the Web is not print *or* television: It is electronic and fluid and must be thought of in this way. In terms of design, this means trying to understand why people come to various sites, who they are, what they are looking for, what they expect to encounter, and what they expect in return for their very valuable click. One of the most valuable lessons out there right now is the case of **consumer generated content (CGC)**: where people are making their own ads for their favorite brands. Firms are starting to specifically encourage customers to offer suggestions (called "crowdsourcing") as a way to energize the creative process.[32] One Apple cyberad that was incredibly popular on the Web was not made by Apple's high-priced ad agency—a college kid did it. YouTube and other venues have allowed consumers to say, "Hey, it's my brand too... I get it more than you do... here's my ad."

Art Direction and Production in Radio.

Radio commercial production specifically highlights the role of the copywriter. Typically, other members of the creative team are not involved in the process (although an agency producer will be assigned). Further, the writer is relatively free to plan nearly all aspects of the radio production because of the significantly reduced costs of radio execution compared to television. In radio, there are far fewer expert/technical participants than in television. This more streamlined form of production does not mean, however, that the process is more casual. Successful achievement of the creative objectives still requires careful planning and execution.

Once the copy strategy and methods for the commercial are approved, the process begins with soliciting bids from production houses. The producer reviews bids and submits the best bid for advertiser approval. When the best bid (not always the lowest-priced bid) is identified, the agency submits an estimate to the advertiser for approval. The bid estimate includes both the production house bid and the agency's estimates of its own costs associated with production. When the agency and the advertiser agree, then the producer can award the job to a production house.

After awarding the job to a production house, the next step is to cast the ad. A radio ad may have only an announcer, in which case the casting job is relatively simple. If the dialogue technique is used, two or more actors and actresses may be needed. In addition, if music or a jingle are being used, then either the music

32. Garrick Schmitt, "Can Creativity Be Crowdsourced?" *Advertising Age*, April, 16, 2009, 14.

has to be recorded, which includes a search for musicians and possibly singers, or permission for prerecorded music has to be obtained. Securing permission for existing music, especially if it is currently popular, can be costly. Much music is in the public domain—that is, it is no longer rigidly protected by copyright laws and is available for far less cost. But, if contemporary, popular music is used, the cost for permission can easily exceed $100,000. Closely following the casting is the planning of special elements for the ad, which can include sound effects or special effects, such as time compression or stretching, to create distinct sounds.

Final preparation and production entails scheduling a sound studio and arranging for the actors and actresses to record their pieces in the ad. If an announcer is used in addition to acting talent, the announcer may or may not record with the full cast; her or his lines can be incorporated into the tape at some later time. Music is generally recorded separately and simply added to the commercial during the sound-mixing stage.

Radio and television production have some similarities. As in television production, the copywriter will have drawn on the copy platform plans approved in the message development stage to write copy for the radio spot. In addition, the script used in the production of a radio advertisement serves the same purpose that the storyboard does in television production. The copywriter must indicate the use of sound effects (SFX) on a separate line to specify the timing of these devices. Further, each player in the advertisement is listed by role, including the announcer if one is used.

One important element of writing radio copy not yet discussed is the number of words of copy to use given the length of the radio ad. As a general rule, word count relative to airtime is as follows:

10 seconds	20 to 25 words
20 seconds	40 to 45 words
30 seconds	60 to 65 words
60 seconds	120 to 125 words
90 seconds	85 to 190 words[33]

The inclusion of musical introductions, special effects, or local taglines (specific information for local markets) reduces the amount of copy in the advertisement. Special sound effects interspersed with copy also shorten copy length. The general rules for number of words relative to ad time change depending on the form and structure of the commercial.

After production, the ad goes through editing to create the best version of the production. Then, after advertiser approval, a sound mix is completed in which all music, special sound effects, and announcer copy are mixed together. The mixing process achieves proper timing between all audio elements in the ad and ensures that all sounds are at the desired levels. After mixing, the tape is duplicated and sent to radio stations for airing.

The most loosely structured production option essentially requires no production at all. It is called a fact sheet. A **fact sheet radio ad** is merely a listing of important selling points that a radio announcer can use to ad-lib a radio spot. This method works best with radio personalities who draw an audience because of their lively, entertaining monologues—like Howard Stern or Paul Harvey, Jr. The fact sheet provides a loose structure so that the announcer can work in the ad during these informal monologues. The risk, of course, is that the ad will get lost in the chatter and the selling points will not be convincingly delivered. On the positive side, radio personalities many times go beyond the scheduled 30 or 60 seconds allotted for the ad.

33. Sandra E. Moriarty, *Creative Advertising: Theory and Practice,* 2nd ed. (Upper Saddle River, NJ: Prentice Hall, 1991), 293.

Another loosely structured technique is the live script. The **live script radio ad** involves having an on-air radio personality, such as a DJ or talk-show host, read the detailed script of an advertisement. Normally there are no sound effects, because such effects would require special production. The live script ensures that all the selling points are included when the commercial is delivered by the announcer. These scripts are not rehearsed, however, and the emphasis, tone, and tempo in the delivery may not be ideal. The advantage of a live script is that it allows an advertiser to submit a relatively structured commercial for airing in a very short period of time. Most stations can work in a live script commercial in a matter of hours after it is received.

Art Direction and Production in Television Advertising.

In many ways, television was simply made for advertising. It is everywhere, serving as background to daily life. But as background, it tends to be ignored, or only half paid attention to. If you consider the 11 message strategies detailed in Chapter 10, use of the TV medium would dictate very different strategies. In some cases, you need high attention levels, which are difficult to get. In other strategies, you might actually prefer lower levels of attention and the counter-arguing that comes with it. Sometimes, it's just about leaving impressions, or setting moods, or getting you to notice; sometimes it tells stories. But in all of these cases, the visual is important—whether it's the main feature or plays a key supportive role.

The Creative Team in Television Advertising. Due to its complexity, television production involves a lot of people. These people have different but often overlapping expertise, responsibility, and authority. This makes for tremendous organizational skills. At some point, individuals who actually shoot the film or the tape are brought in to execute the copywriter's and art director's concepts. They are, more and more, also in contact with a media planner and/or account planner, making sure that what is being done for TV is consistent with, compatible with, or can do double duty with other media forms; such as longer TV ads on the Internet or visual captures that end up in print or on websites. The account planner is there to make sure that the consumer's values and interests continue to be represented.

At this point, the creative process becomes intensely collaborative: The film director applies his or her craft and is responsible for the actual production. The creative team (that is, the art director, copywriter, media director, and account planner) rarely relinquishes control of the project, even though the film director may prefer that. Getting the various players to perform their particular specialty at just the right time, while avoiding conflict with other team members, is an ongoing challenge in TV ad production. Someone has to be in charge on the set, and that is usually the chief creative on site.

Creative Guidelines for Television Advertising. Just as for print advertising, there are general creative principles for television advertising.[34] These principles are not foolproof or definitive, but they certainly represent good advice and provide organizational structure. Again, truly great creative work has at one time or another violated some or all of these conventions, but the decision to venture off guidelines was no doubt guided by the creative brief—so all is well.

34. Tom Altsteil and Jean Grow, *Advertising Creative: Strategy, Copy and Design*, 2nd ed. (Los Angeles: Sage Publications, 2010), 228–229.

- ***Use an attention-getting and relevant opening.*** The first few seconds of a television commercial are crucial. A receiver can make a split-second assessment of the relevance and interest a message holds. An ad can either turn a receiver off or grab his or her attention for the balance of the commercial with the opening. Remember, remote controls and DVRs are ubiquitous. It is incredibly easy to avoid commercials, so you, as an advertiser, must have a good hook to suck viewers in. Ads just don't get much time to develop. There is the belief that "slower" ads (ads that take time to develop) don't wear out as quickly as the hit-and-run ads. So, if you have a huge (almost inexhaustible) supply of money, an ad that "builds" might be best. If you don't, go for the quick hook. In Exhibit 11.43, the TV spot opens with a shot of "ManMom" sitting at a table with two young men and a bag of Combos. It's hard not to wonder what's going to come next.
- ***Emphasize the visual.*** The video capability of television should be highlighted in every production effort. To some degree, this emphasis is dependent on the creative concept, but the visual should carry the selling message even if the audio portion is ignored by the receiver. In Exhibit 11.44, Skittles tells its story with a minimum of words.

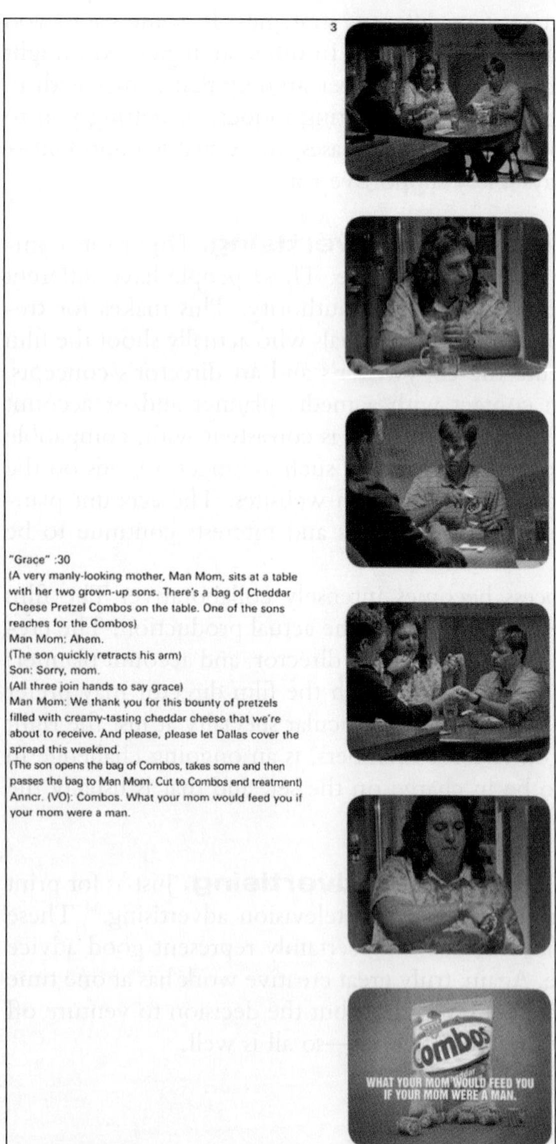

3
"Grace" :30
(A very manly-looking mother, Man Mom, sits at a table with her two grown-up sons. There's a bag of Cheddar Cheese Pretzel Combos on the table. One of the sons reaches for the Combos)
Man Mom: Ahem.
(The son quickly retracts his arm)
Son: Sorry, mom.
(All three join hands to say grace)
Man Mom: We thank you for this bounty of pretzels filled with creamy-tasting cheddar cheese that we're about to receive. And please, please let Dallas cover the spread this weekend.
(The son opens the bag of Combos, takes some and then passes the bag to Man Mom. Cut to Combos end treatment)
Anncr. (VO): Combos. What your mom would feed you if your mom were a man.
combos
WHAT YOUR MOM WOULD FEED YOU IF YOUR MOM WERE A MAN.

Exhibit 11.43 If the first seconds of this ad draw you in, there's a pretty good chance you'll stick around for the slogan at the end. "Combos. What your mom would feed you if your mom were a man."

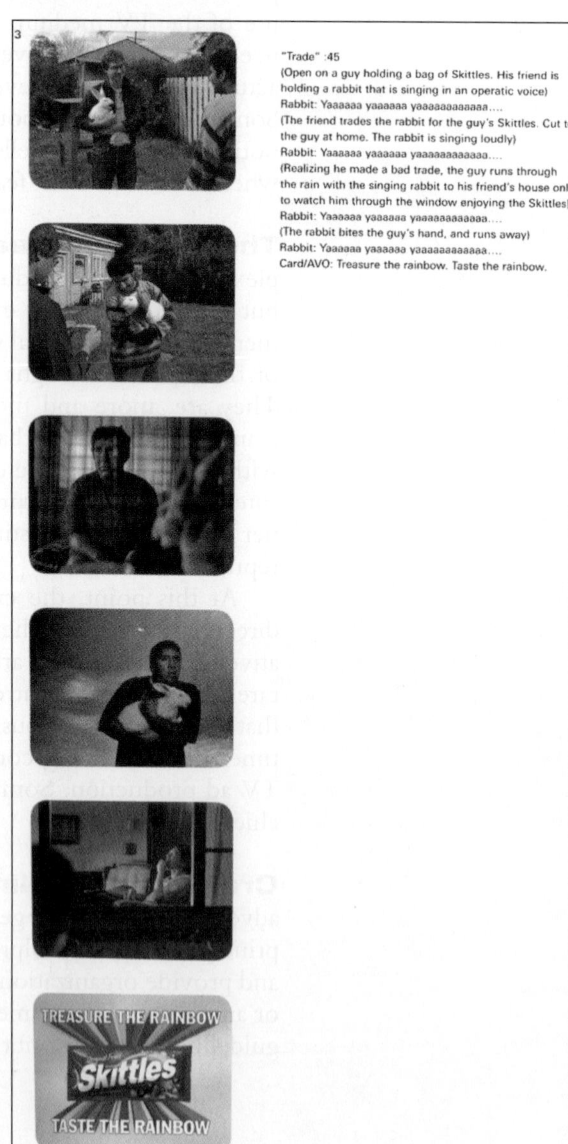

3
"Trade" :45
(Open on a guy holding a bag of Skittles. His friend is holding a rabbit that is singing in an operatic voice)
Rabbit: Yaaaaaa yaaaaaa yaaaaaaaaaaaa....
(The friend trades the rabbit for the guy's Skittles. Cut to the guy at home. The rabbit is singing loudly)
Rabbit: Yaaaaaa yaaaaaa yaaaaaaaaaaaa....
(Realizing he made a bad trade, the guy runs through the rain with the singing rabbit to his friend's house only to watch him through the window enjoying the Skittles)
Rabbit: Yaaaaaa yaaaaaa yaaaaaaaaaaaa....
(The rabbit bites the guy's hand, and runs away)
Rabbit: Yaaaaaa yaaaaaa yaaaaaaaaaaaa....
Card/AVO: Treasure the rainbow. Taste the rainbow.
TREASURE THE RAINBOW
Skittles
TASTE THE RAINBOW

Exhibit 11.44 Even the opera-singing rabbit doesn't need words in this spot for Skittles.

- ***Coordinate the audio with the visual.*** The images and copy of a television commercial must reinforce each other. Divergence between the audio and visual portions of an ad only serves to confuse and distract the viewer. In Exhibit 11.45, Miller High Life uses both words and visuals to create the world of a High Life man.
- ***Persuade as well as entertain.*** It is tempting to produce a beautifully creative television advertisement rather than a beautifully effective television advertisement. Creating an entertaining commercial is an inherently praiseworthy goal except when the entertainment value of the commercial completely overwhelms its persuasive impact. In Exhibit 11.46, Hewlett-Packard sells its photo-quality printers with a humorous yet persuasive demonstration of their reproductive powers.

Exhibit 11.45 Here's to the High Life!

(single and part of series)

"Donut" :30

(OPEN ON A CLOSE-UP OF BEER, DONUTS AND A MAN'S DIRTY HANDS ON TABLE. HE PICKS UP A DONUT)

ANNCR. (VO): Sometimes a man gets too hungry to clean his hands properly.

(CUT TO CLOSE-UP OF DONUTS)

ANNCR. (VO): The powdered sugar on this donut puts a semi-protective barrier between your fingerprint and your nutrition.

(CUT TO A MAN HOLDING BEER, EATING DONUTS)

ANNCR. (VO): But even if some grease does get on that donut, that's just flavor to a High Life man.

TITLE CARD: (FADE UP) Miller Time logo.

ART DIRECTOR: Jeff Williams
WRITER: Jeff Kling
CREATIVE DIRECTOR: Susan Hoffman
PRODUCER: Jeff Selis
DIRECTOR: Errol Morris
PRODUCTION COMPANY: @radical.media
AD AGENCY: Wieden & Kennedy (Portland, OR)
CLIENT: Miller Brewing Company

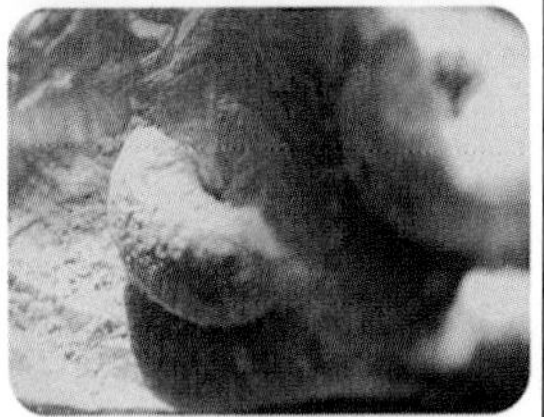

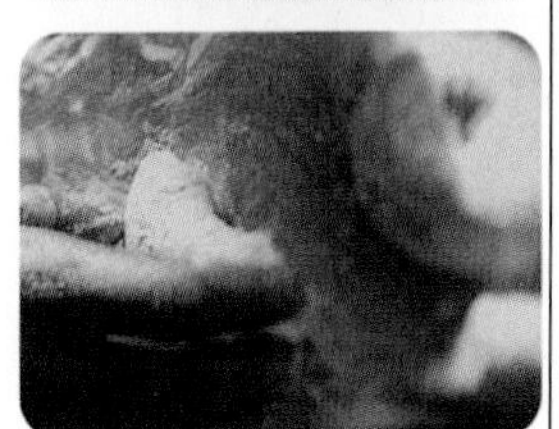

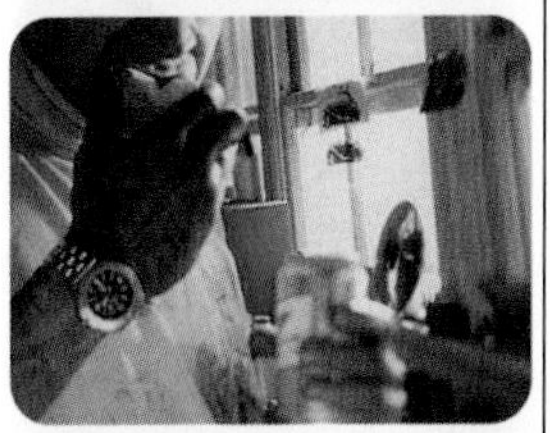

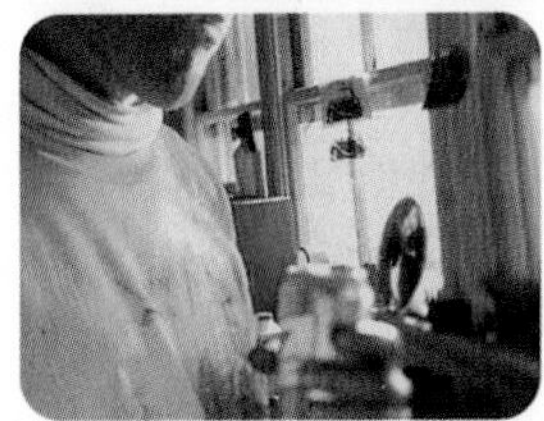

Exhibit 11.46 Humor meets demonstration.
www.hp.com

(SFX: QUIET TICKING OF CLOCK)
(SFX: WRESTLING ON TV)
GRANDPA: Ohhhhhh!
(SFX: THUD)
BABY: Wahhhhhhhhhhh!
GRANDPA: Don't worry, honey. Mom and Dad will be right back.
GRANDPA: Pretty baby!
BABY: Wahhhhhhhhhhh!
(SFX: SUDDEN QUIET)
(SFX: CLOCK TICKING)
ANNCR: HP photo-quality printers. Good enough to fool almost anyone.
SUPER: BUILT BY ENGINEERS. USED BY NORMAL PEOPLE.

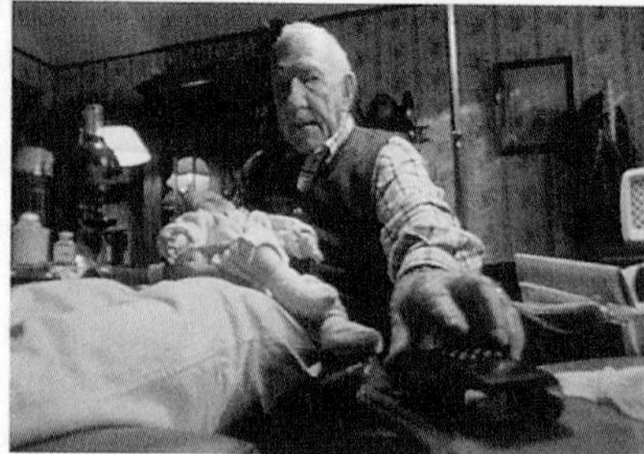

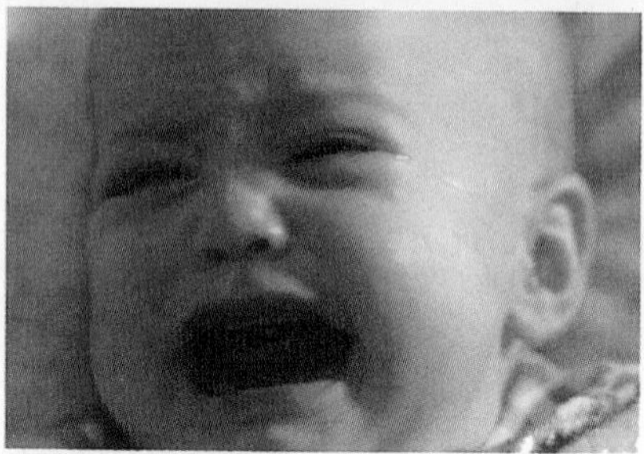

Courtesy of Hewlett Packard

- ***Show the brand.*** Unless a commercial is using intrigue and mystery surrounding the brand, the brand should be highlighted in the ad. Close-ups and shots of the brand in action help receivers recall the brand and its appearance. The client really likes this.

6 **The Production Process in Television Advertising.** The television production process can best be understood by identifying the activities that take place before, during, and after the actual production of an ad. These stages are referred to as preproduction, production, and postproduction. By breaking the process down into this sequence, we can appreciate both the technical and the strategic aspects of each stage.

Preproduction. The **preproduction** stage is that part of the television production process in which the advertiser and the advertising agency carefully work out the precise details of how the creative planning behind an ad can best be brought to life with the opportunities offered by television. Exhibit 11.47 shows the sequence of six events in the preproduction stage.

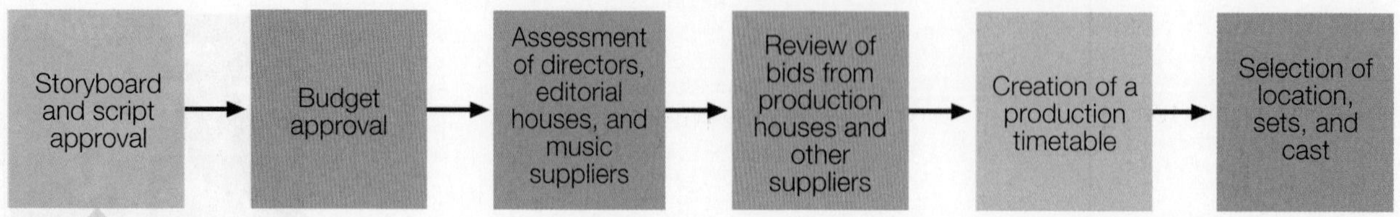

Exhibit 11.47 Sequence of events in the preproduction stage of television advertising.

Storyboard and Script Approval. As Exhibit 11.47 shows, the preproduction stage begins with storyboard and script approval. A storyboard is a shot-by-shot sketch depicting, in sequence, the visual scenes and copy that will be used in an advertisement. A **script** is the written version of an ad; it specifies the coordination of the copy elements with the video scenes. The script is used by the producer and director to set the location and content of scenes, by the casting department to choose actors and actresses, and by the producer in budgeting and scheduling the shoot. Exhibit 11.48 is part of a storyboard from the Miller Lite "Can Your Beer Do This?" campaign. This particular spot was entitled "Ski Jump" and involved rigging a dummy to a recliner and launching the chair and the dummy from a 60-meter ski jump. The storyboard gives the creative team and the client an overall idea of the look and feel of the ad.

The art director and copywriter are significantly involved at this stage of production. It is important that the producer has discussed the storyboard and script with the creative team and fully understands the creative concept and objectives for the advertisement before production begins. Because it is the producer's responsibility to solicit bids for the project from production houses, the producer must be able to fully explain to bidders the requirements of the job so that cost estimates are as accurate as possible.

Budget Approval. Once there is agreement on the scope and intent of the production as depicted in the storyboard and script, the advertiser must give budget approval. The producer needs to work carefully with the creative team and the advertiser to estimate the approximate cost of the shoot, including production staging, location costs, actors, technical requirements, staffing, and a multitude of other

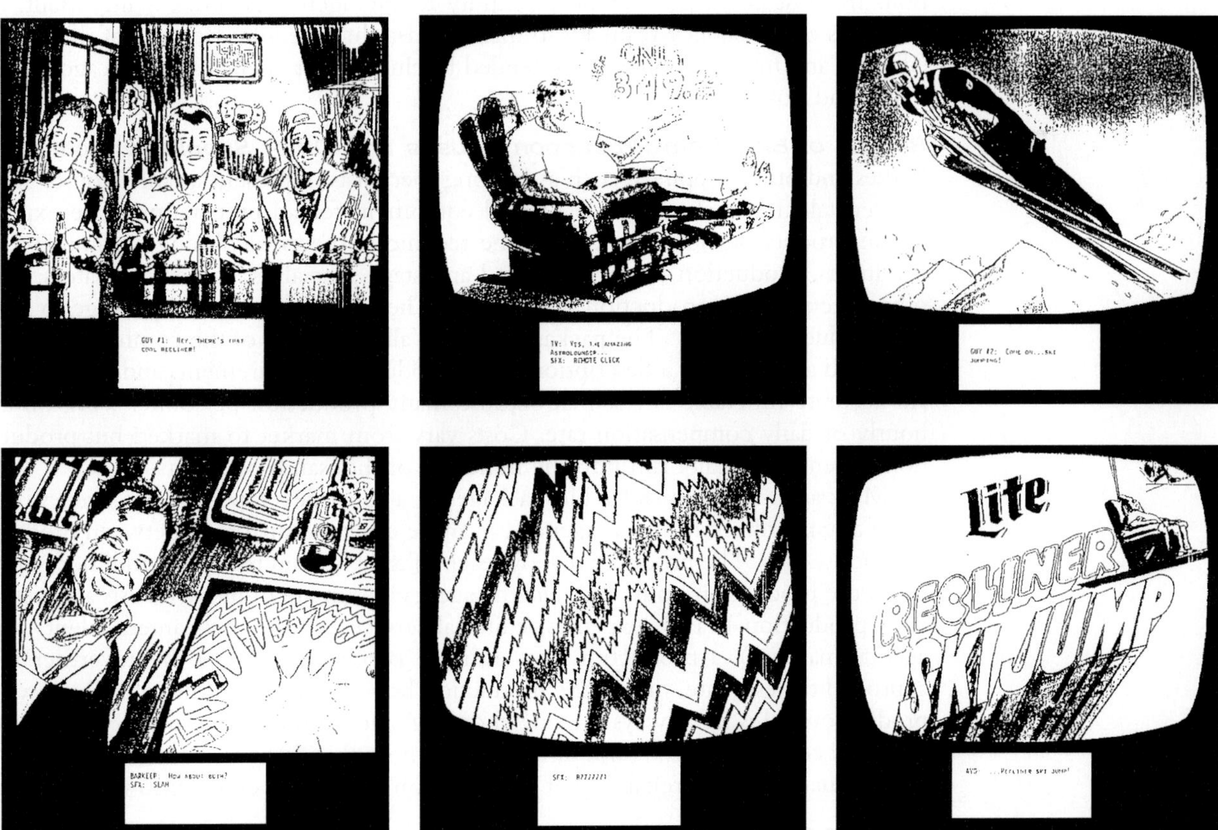

Exhibit 11.48 How does this storyboard for a Miller Lite Beer ad save the advertiser time and money during the television production process?

Courtesy, Miller Brewing Company

considerations. It is essential that these discussions be as detailed and comprehensive as possible, because it is from this budget discussion that the producer will evaluate candidates for the directing role and solicit bids from production houses to handle the job.

Assessment of Directors, Editorial Houses, Music Suppliers. A producer has dozens (if not hundreds) of directors, postproduction editorial houses, and music suppliers from which to choose. An assessment of those well suited to the task takes place early in the preproduction process. The combination of the creative talents of ad agencies and production houses can produce creative, eye-catching ads. Directors of television commercials, like directors of feature films, develop specializations and reputations. Some directors are known for their work with action or special effects. Others are more highly skilled in working with children, animals, outdoor settings, or shots of beverages flowing into a glass ("pour shots").

The director of an advertisement is responsible for interpreting the storyboard and script and managing the talent to bring the creative concept to life. A director specifies the precise nature of a scene, how it is lit, and how it is filmed. Choosing the proper director is crucial to the execution of a commercial. Aside from the fact that a good director commands a fee anywhere from $8,000 to $25,000 per day, the director can have a tremendous effect on the quality and impact of the presentation. An excellent creative concept can be undermined by poor direction. Among the now-famous feature film directors who have made television commercials are Ridley Scott (Apple), John Frankenheimer (AT&T), Woody Allen (Campari), Spike Lee (Levi's, Nike, the Gap, Barney's New York), and Federico Fellini (Coop Italia).

Similarly, editorial houses and music suppliers (and musicians) have particular expertise and reputations. The producer, the director, and the agency creative team actively review the work of suppliers that are particularly well suited to the production. In most cases, geographic proximity to the agency facilities is important, as members of the agency team try to maintain a tight schedule. Because of this need, editorial and music suppliers have tended to cluster near agencies in Chicago, New York, and Los Angeles.

Review of Bids from Production Houses and Other Suppliers. Production houses and other suppliers, such as lighting specialists, represent a collection of specialized talent and also provide needed equipment for ad preparation. The expertise in production houses relates to the technical aspects of filming a commercial. Producers, production managers, sound and stage specialists, camera operators, and others are part of a production house team. The agency sends a bid package to several production houses. The package contains all the details of the commercial to be produced and includes a description of the production requirements and a timetable. An accurate timetable is essential because many production personnel work on an hourly or daily compensation rate. Costs vary from market to market, but production expenses typically run into the hundreds of thousands of dollars.

Most agencies send out a bid package on a form developed by the agency. By using a standardized form, an agency can make direct comparisons between production house bids. The producer reviews each of the bids and revises them if necessary. From the production house bids *and* the agency's estimate of its own costs associated with production (travel, expenses, editorial services, music, on-camera talent, and agency markups), a production cost estimate is prepared. Once the advertiser has approved the estimate, one of the production houses is awarded the job. The lowest production bid is not always the one chosen. Aside from cost, there are creative and technical considerations. A hot director costs more than last year's model. The agency's evaluation of the reliability of a production house also enters into the decision.

Creation of a Production Timetable. In conjunction with the stages of preproduction just discussed, the producer will be working on a **production timetable**. This timetable projects a realistic schedule for all the preproduction, production, and

Exhibit 11.49 Example of a reasonable timetable for shooting a 30-second television advertisement.

Activity	Time
Assess directors/editorial houses/music suppliers	1 week
Solicit bids from production houses/other suppliers	1 week
Review bids, award jobs to suppliers, submit production estimate to advertiser	1 week
Begin preproduction (location, sets, casting)	1 to 2 weeks
Final preparation and shooting	1 to 2 weeks
Edit film	1 week
Agency/advertiser review of rough-cut film	1 week
Postproduction (final editing, voice mix, record music, special effects, etc.) and transfer of film to video; ship to media	2 weeks
Transfer film to videotape; ship to stations	1 week
Total	10 to 12 weeks

postproduction activities. To stay on budget and complete the production in time to ship the final advertisement to television stations for airing, an accurate and realistic timetable is essential. A timetable must allow a reasonable amount of time to complete all production tasks in a quality manner. Exhibit 11.49 is a typical timetable for a national 30-second spot, using location shooting.

Realize that a reasonable timetable is rarely achieved. Advertisers often request (or demand) that an agency provide a finished spot (or even several spots) in times as short as four or five weeks. Because of competitive pressures or corporate urgency for change, production timetables are compromised. Advertisers have to accept the reality that violating a reasonable timetable can dramatically increase costs and puts undue pressure on the creative process—no matter what the reason for the urgency. In fact, a creative director at one agency often told clients that they could pick any two selections from the following list for their television commercials: good, fast, and reasonably priced.[35]

Selection of Location, Sets, and Cast. Once a bid has been approved and accepted, both the production house and the agency production team begin to search for appropriate, affordable locations if the commercial is to be shot outside a studio setting.

A delicate stage in preproduction is casting. Although not every ad uses actors and actresses, when an ad calls for individuals to perform roles, casting is crucial. Every individual appearing in an ad is, in a very real sense, a representative of the advertiser and the brand (think about "Flo" the Progressive Insurance gal). This is another reason why the agency creative team stays involved. Actors and actresses help set the mood and tone for an ad and affect the image of the brand. The successful execution of various message strategies depends on proper casting. For instance, a slice-of-life message requires actors and actresses with whom the target audience can readily identify. Testimonial message tactics require a search for particular types of people, either celebrities or common folks, who will attract attention and be credible. The point to remember is that successfully casting a television commercial depends on much more than simply picking people with good acting abilities. Individuals must be matched to the personality of the brand, the nature of the audience, and the scene depicted in the ad.

35. Quote from Peter Sheldon, former creative director and head of creative sequences, University of Illinois Advertising Department.

Production. The **production stage** of the process, or the **shoot**, is where the storyboard and script come to life and are filmed. The actual production of the spot may also include some final preparations before the shoot begins. The most common final preparation activities are lighting checks and rehearsals. An entire day may be devoted to *prelight*, which involves setting up lighting or identifying times for the best natural lighting to ensure that the shooting day runs smoothly. Similarly, the director may want to work with the on-camera talent along with the camera operators to practice the positioning and movement planned for the ad. This work, known as *blocking*, can save a lot of time on a shoot day, when many more costly personnel are on the set.

Lighting, blocking, and other special factors are typically specified by the director in the script. Exhibit 11.50 is a list of common directorial specifications that show up in a script and are used by a director to manage the audio and visual components of a commercial shoot.

Script Specification	Meaning
CU	Close-up.
ECU	Extreme close-up.
MS	Medium shot.
LS	Long shot.
Zoom	Movement in or out on subject with camera fixed.
Dolly	Movement in or out on subject moving the camera (generally slower than a zoom).
Pan	Camera scanning right or left from stationary position.
Truck	Camera moving right or left, creating a different visual angle.
Tilt	Camera panning vertically.
Cut	Abrupt movement from one scene to another.
Dissolve	Smoother transition from one scene to another, compared to a cut.
Wipe	Horizontal or vertical removal of one image to replace it with a new image (inserted vertically or horizontally).
Split screen	Two or more independent video sources occupying the screen.
Skip frame	Replacement of one image with another through pulsating (frame insertion of) the second image into the first. Used for dramatic transitions.
Key insert, matte, chromakey	Insertion of one image onto another background. Often used to impose product over the scene taking place in the commercial.
Super title	Lettering superimposed over visual. Often used to emphasize a major selling point or to display disclaimers/product warnings.
SFX	Sound effects.
VO	Introducing a voice over the visual.
ANN	Announcer entering the commercial.
Music under	Music playing in the background.
Music down and out	Music fading out of commercial.
Music up and out	Music volume ascending and abruptly ending.

Exhibit 11.50 Instructions commonly appearing in television commercial scripts.

Shoot days are the culmination of an enormous amount of effort beginning all the way back at the development of the creative brief. They are the execution of all the well-laid plans by the advertiser and agency personnel. The set on a shoot day is a world all its own. For the uninformed, it can appear to be little more than high-energy chaos, or a lot of nothing going on between camera setups. For the professionals involved, however, a shoot has its own tempo and direction.

A successful shoot depends on the effective management of a large number of diverse individuals—creative performers, highly trained technicians, and skilled laborers. Logistical and technical problems always arise, not to mention the ever-present threat of a random event (a thunderstorm or intrusive noise) that disrupts filming and tries everyone's patience. There is a degree of tension and spontaneity on the set that is a necessary part of the creative process but must be kept at a manageable level. Much of the tension stems from trying to execute the various tasks of production correctly and at the proper time.

Another dimension to this tension, however, has to do with expense. As pointed out earlier, most directors, technicians, and talent are paid a daily rate plus overtime after 10 hours. Daily shooting expenses, including director's fees, can run $80,000 to $120,000 for just an average production, so the agency and advertiser, understandably, want the shoot to run as smoothly and quickly as possible.

There is the real problem of not rushing creativity, however, and advertisers often have to learn to accept the pace of production. For example, a well-known director made a Honda commercial in South Florida, where he shot film for only one hour per day—a half-hour in the morning and a half-hour at twilight. His explanation? "From experience you learn that cars look flat and unattractive in direct light, so you have to catch the shot when the angle [of the sun] is just right."[36] Despite the fact that the cameras were rolling only an hour a day, the $9,000-per-hour cost for the production crew was charged all day for each day of shooting. Advertisers have to accept, on occasion, that the television advertising production process is not like an assembly line production process.

The Cost of Television Production. Coordinating and taking advantage of the skills offered by creative talent is a big challenge for advertisers. As with most things, these costs have continued to rise, partly because of the escalating cost of creative talent, such as directors and editors. Other aspects of the cost have to do with more and better equipment being used at all stages of the production process, and longer shooting schedules to ensure advertiser satisfaction.

The average expense for a 30-second spot tends to be higher for commercials in highly competitive consumer markets, such as beer, soft drinks, autos, and banking, where image campaigns (which require high-quality production) are commonly used. Conversely, average production costs tend to be lower for advertisements in which functional features or shots of the product often dominate the spot, as with household cleansers and office equipment.

The high and rising cost of television production has created some tensions between advertisers and their ad agencies. Most agencies and production companies respond by saying that advertisers are demanding to stand out from the clutter, and to do so requires complex concepts and high-priced talent. Conversely, when an advertiser is not so image conscious, ways can be found to stand out without spending huge dollar amounts. There is little doubt that the cost factors in television production are responsible for millions of dollars being shifted to other forms of IBP and ventures into digital/interactive media. Aside from the many strategic advantages of other IBP tools and digital, the cost differences from television are significant as well.

Postproduction. Once shooting is completed, several postproduction activities are required before the commercial is ready for airing. At this point, a host of additional

36. Jeffrey A. Trachtenberg, "Where the Money Goes," *Forbes*, September 21, 1987, 180.

professional talent may enter the process. Editors, audio technicians, voice-over specialists, and musicians may be contracted.

Director's rough cut. Many directors prefer to do a preliminary video assembly before final editing. Generally, this will not include special effects or transitions between shots, and typically does not include audio.

Digital editing. Final assembly of the video in its finished form is done through computerized editing that includes all effects and transitions. If the spot was shot on film, it is transferred to digital format through a process that preserves the film look. It's important to understand that in a spot with on-camera talent the audio goes together first, then the video is timed to match.

Audio edit. A professional audio production studio does a final edit of the audio. Digital time code locks each millisecond of audio to its digital counterpart in the video. Final audio editing is typically done while simultaneously viewing the video. The audio producer will add required sound effects and music.

Master, dubs, and distribution. The production company makes a master digital copy of the spot, and usually a copy to be archived for safekeeping. The master is then used to produce enough copies of the spot for every TV station that is included in the media schedule.[37]

In all, it is easy to see why television commercials are so costly. Scores of people with specialized skills and a large number of separate tasks are included in the process. The procedures also reflect the complexity of the process. Aside from the mechanics of production, a constant vigil must be kept over the creative concept of the advertisement. Despite the complexities, the advertising industry continues to turn out high-quality television commercials on a timely basis.

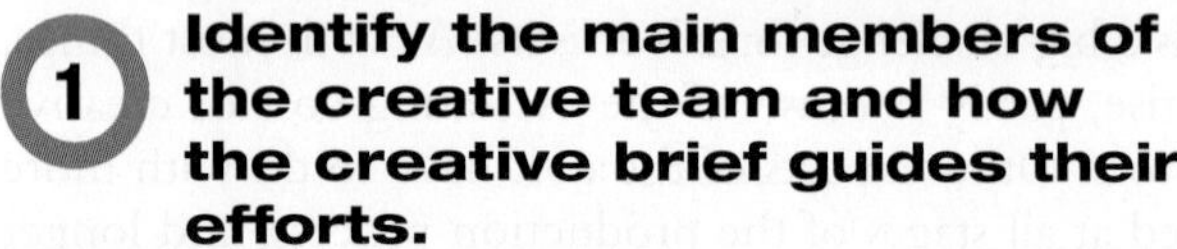

Summary

1 Identify the main members of the creative team and how the creative brief guides their efforts.

Effective creative execution depends on the input of the creative team: art director, copywriter, account planner, and media planner. The creative team will have access to a wide variety of inputs, including the client's and information sources, such as market research. A creative brief is used as a device to assist the creative team overall and the copywriter in particular in dealing with this challenge. Key elements in the creative brief include brand features and benefits that must be communicated to the audience, the mood or tone appropriate for the audience, and the intended media for the ad.

2 Detail the elements of copywriting for print media, including the headline, subhead, and body copy.

The three unique components of print copy are the headline, subhead, and body copy. Headlines need to motivate additional processing of the ad. Good headlines communicate information about the brand or make a promise about the benefits the consumer can expect from the brand. If the brand name is not featured in the headline, then that headline must entice the reader to examine the body copy or visual material. Subheads can also be valuable in helping lead the reader to and through the body copy. A subhead appears above or below the main headline and carries additional information beyond

37. Discussion in this section is taken from Scott Walker, "TV Commercial Production Primer," suite101.com, tv-advertising.suite101.com/, June 8, 2008.

the headline. In the body copy, the brand's complete story can be told. Effective body copy must be crafted carefully to engage the reader, furnish supportive evidence for claims made about the brand, and avoid clichés and exaggeration that the consumer will dismiss as hype.

Detail the elements of copywriting for radio and television broadcast media.

Four basic formats can be used to create radio copy. These are the music format, the dialogue format, the announcement format, and the celebrity announcer format. Guidelines for writing effective radio copy start with using simple sentence construction and language familiar to the intended audience. When the copy stimulates the listener's imagination, the advertiser can expect improved results as long as the brand name and the primary selling points don't get lost. When using music or humor to attract and hold the listener's attention, the copywriter must take care not to shortchange key selling points for the sake of simple entertainment.

Several formats can be considered in preparing television ad copy. These are demonstration, problem and solution, music and song, spokesperson, dialogue, vignette, and narrative. To achieve effective copy in the television medium, it is essential to coordinate the copy with the visual presentation, seeking a synergistic effect between audio and video. Entertaining to attract attention should again not be emphasized to the point that the brand name or selling points of the ad get lost. Developing copy consistent with the heritage and image of the brand is also essential. Finally, copy that can be adapted to various time lengths and modified to sustain audience interest over the life of a campaign is most desirable.

Describe the process and common copywriting approaches for digital/interactive ads.

Digital/interactive ads are hybrids between print and broadcasting advertisements. The receiver does encounter a message in a print format either at a website, in an email, at a blog, or from social media communication. But the message is delivered electronically similar to television or radio. Common approaches to copywriting include long-copy landing page, short-copy landing page, long copy email, teaser email copy, pop-up/pop-under ad copy, and social media copy. Copywriting in each of these digital/interactive formats may or may not employ the elements of headline and subhead or even body copy (in the case of pop-ups and pop-unders). But, there are "copy" elements in each case that communicates brand information.

Identify the components of art direction that are essential in creative execution of print ads.

In print ad design, all the verbal and visual components of an ad are arranged for maximum impact and appeal. Several principles can be followed as a basis for a compelling design. These principles feature issues such as balance, proportion, order, unity, and emphasis. The first component of an effective design is focus—drawing the reader's attention to specific areas of the ad. The second component is movement and direction—directing the reader's eye movement through the ad. The third component is clarity and simplicity—avoiding a complex and chaotic look that will deter most consumers.

The layout is the physical manifestation of all design planning for print ads. An art director uses various forms of layouts to bring a print ad to life. There are several predictable stages in the evolution of a layout. The art director starts with a hand-drawn thumbnail, proceeds to the digitized rough layout, and continues with a tight comprehensive layout that represents the look of the final ad. With each stage, the layout becomes more concrete and more like the final form of the advertisement. In the last stage, the digitized ad is sent out for placement in print media.

Describe the production process in creating a television commercial.

The intricate process of TV ad production can be broken into three major stages: preproduction, production, and postproduction. In the preproduction stage, scripts and storyboards are prepared, budgets are set, production houses are engaged, and a timetable is formulated. Production includes all those activities involved in the actual filming of the ad. The shoot is a high-stress activity that usually carries a high price tag. The raw materials from the shoot are mixed and refined in the postproduction stage. Today's editors work almost exclusively with computers to create the final product—a finished television ad. If all this sounds expensive, it is!

Key Terms

media planner
account planner
creative team
creative brief
brandscape
copywriting
headline
subhead
straight-line copy
dialogue
testimonial
narrative
direct response copy
storyboard
long-copy landing page
short-copy landing page
long copy email
teaser email copy
pop-up/pop-under ad copy
social media copy
slogan/tagline
developmental copy research
evaluative copy research
illustration
medium
illustration format
design
principles of design
balance
formal balance
informal balance
proportion
order
unity
axis
three-point layout structure
parallel layout structure
layout
thumbnails
rough layout
comp
type font
blackletter
roman
script
serif
sans serif
miscellaneous (type)
point
picas
consumer generated content (CGC)
fact sheet radio ad
live script radio ad
preproduction
script
production timetable
production stage/shoot

Questions

1. Who are the main participants in the "creative team" when it comes to copywriting, art direction, and production? What "roadmap" do they use to guide the creative effort?

2. Compare and contrast the dialogue and narrative formats for television ads. What common requirements must be met to construct convincing TV ads using these two formats?

3. Entertainment is both the blessing and the curse of a copywriter. Is it conceivable that ads that merely entertain could actually prove valuable in stimulating sales? If so, how so?

4. Describe the common mistakes that copywriters must avoid. From your personal experience with all types of ads, are there other common mistakes that you believe copywriters are prone to make on a regular basis?

5. Copywriters often are asked to develop slogans for a product or service. What role does an effective slogan play in promoting a brand's image and personality? Exhibit 11.16 provides a list of some of the most historically recognized slogans. Pick three of the listed brands and try to write a new slogan for each.

6. Identify the strategic roles that illustration plays in increasing the effectiveness of a print advertisement from a communications and marketing perspective.

7. This chapter reviewed five basic principles for print ad design: balance, proportion, order, unity, and emphasis. Give an example of how each of these principles might be employed to enhance the selling message of a print ad.

8. Digital/interactive media present a new and unique challenge for both the copywriting and art direction processes. When you visit a website, does it seem like there is "copy" or "design" at the site? What about when you use your favorite social networking sites? Do Twitter, Facebook, or YouTube show evidence of persuasive copy or design principles?

9. Identify the creative guidelines for developing television advertising. Think of an ad you have seen that does a particularly good job of employing items listed in the guidelines. Think of an ad that does not. Which one do you like better?

10. Identify the three main stages of the production process for television advertising. Describe the activities that take place within each stage.

Experiential Exercises

1. Although the elements of copywriting differ greatly for print and television ads, integrated brand promotion campaigns use both print and broadcast media alike to deliver consistent brand messages. Select a television ad and analyze its copy, visual aesthetics, tone, style, and persuasive strategy. Then write your own print version of the ad, attempting to provide a similar presentation of the brand's features and benefits. As you write your headline, subhead, and body copy, be sure to align your message and style with those seen in the television ad. Use the tips for writing print ads listed in the chapter.

2. Some ads are amateurish, poorly written, even downright annoying—especially cyberads created for the Web. Identify a digital ad that you consider to be ineffective or annoying, and offer a detailed critique on why the ad's copy and illustration left you with a negative impression and failed to stimulate you to action.

3. Working in small teams, write a script for a 15- to 60-second radio commercial for the campus bookstore that you will then present to the class. As you work on this project, clearly identify which of the radio advertising formats the script will follow. Also pay close attention to the radio copy guidelines and word count relative to airtime as you prepare the script.

4. Pull 10 print ads from a favorite magazine. Using the classifications outlined in the chapter, identify for each ad the headline, the subhead, and the body copy. For each ad, also offer a brief assessment of what you think was the copywriter's intended purpose and whether it was accomplished.

Part 4

Placing the Message in Conventional and "New" Media

Once again we transition to a new and totally different area of advertising and IBP, "Placing the Message in Conventional and 'New' Media." We are now at the point where reaching the target audience is the key issue.

Beyond the basic and formidable challenge of effectively choosing the right media to reach a target audience, contemporary advertisers and promotion professionals are demanding even more from the media placement decision: synergy and integration. Throughout the first three parts of the text, the issue of integrated brand promotion has been raised whenever the opportunity existed to create coordinated communications. But nowhere is IBP more critical than at the media placement stage. This challenge has been made more complex in the last five years as media beyond traditional mass media, new digital/interactive media—email, websites, blogs, social media networks—manifest themselves as opportunities to reach consumers. The challenge is to ensure that if diverse communications media options are chosen—traditional combined with new media—there is still a "one-voice" quality to the overall communication program.

Chapter 12

Media Planning Essentials Maintaining integration is indeed a challenge in the contemporary media environment. Chapter 12, "Media Planning Essentials," begins with a discussion of the major changes that have altered and now define the contemporary media landscape, particularly the role of social media and advertisers' use of social media networks. Next, the fundamentals of media planning are explained, followed by the details. We then tell it like it really is in the real world by discussing the "real deals" of media planning. Next, we discuss how the complex communications environment impacts the entire process of media strategy and planning, followed by particular attention to IBP's impact. We finish with a reminder of the value of traditional advertising and its continued prominence in the communications landscape despite the emergence of new communications options like social networks.

Chapter 13

Media Planning: Newspapers, Magazines, Television, and Radio Chapter 13, "Media Planning: Newspapers, Magazines, Television, and Radio," offers an analysis of the major traditional media options available to advertisers. Even in an environment where all sorts of new *media* options are available, the vast majority of the creative effort—and money—is still spent on print and broadcast advertising campaigns. Despite the many intriguing opportunities that new media options offer, print and broadcast media will likely form the foundation of most advertising campaigns. "New" media simply can't do what "old" media do. But we also raise the issue that these traditional media are turning to new, digital media opportunities as well. Both print and broadcast media have embraced digital options offering advertisers new opportunities to reach audiences. The chapter follows a sequence in which the advantages and disadvantages of each medium are discussed, followed by considerations of costs, buying procedures, and audience measurement techniques.

Chapter 14

Media Planning: Advertising and IBP in Digital/Interactive Media Advertisers are energized and somewhat mystified on just how to take full advantage of the digital/interactive options the Internet offers. Chapter 14, "Media Planning: Advertising and IBP in Digital/Interactive Media," describes the new Internet landscape and contemporary advertising and IBP environment it offers. Most of the discussion in this chapter focuses on two fundamental issues: the structure of the Internet as a digital and interactive communications environment and the potential of the Internet as an advertising and IBP media option. Through these discussions, we will come to a better understanding of how to use the Internet as part of an effective advertising and integrated brand promotion effort. And, a significant portion of the chapter is devoted to the prospect for social media networks to become effective communication networks.

After reading and thinking about this chapter, you will be able to do the following:

1. Describe the important changes that have altered the advertising and IBP media landscape, such as agency compensation, ROI demands, globalization, and multicultural media.
2. Describe the fundamentals of media planning.
3. Know the bottom line of IBP's impact on media planning.
4. Discuss the data quality problem in media planning.
5. Discuss the essentials of the contemporary media planning environment.
6. Discuss the value of traditional advertising.

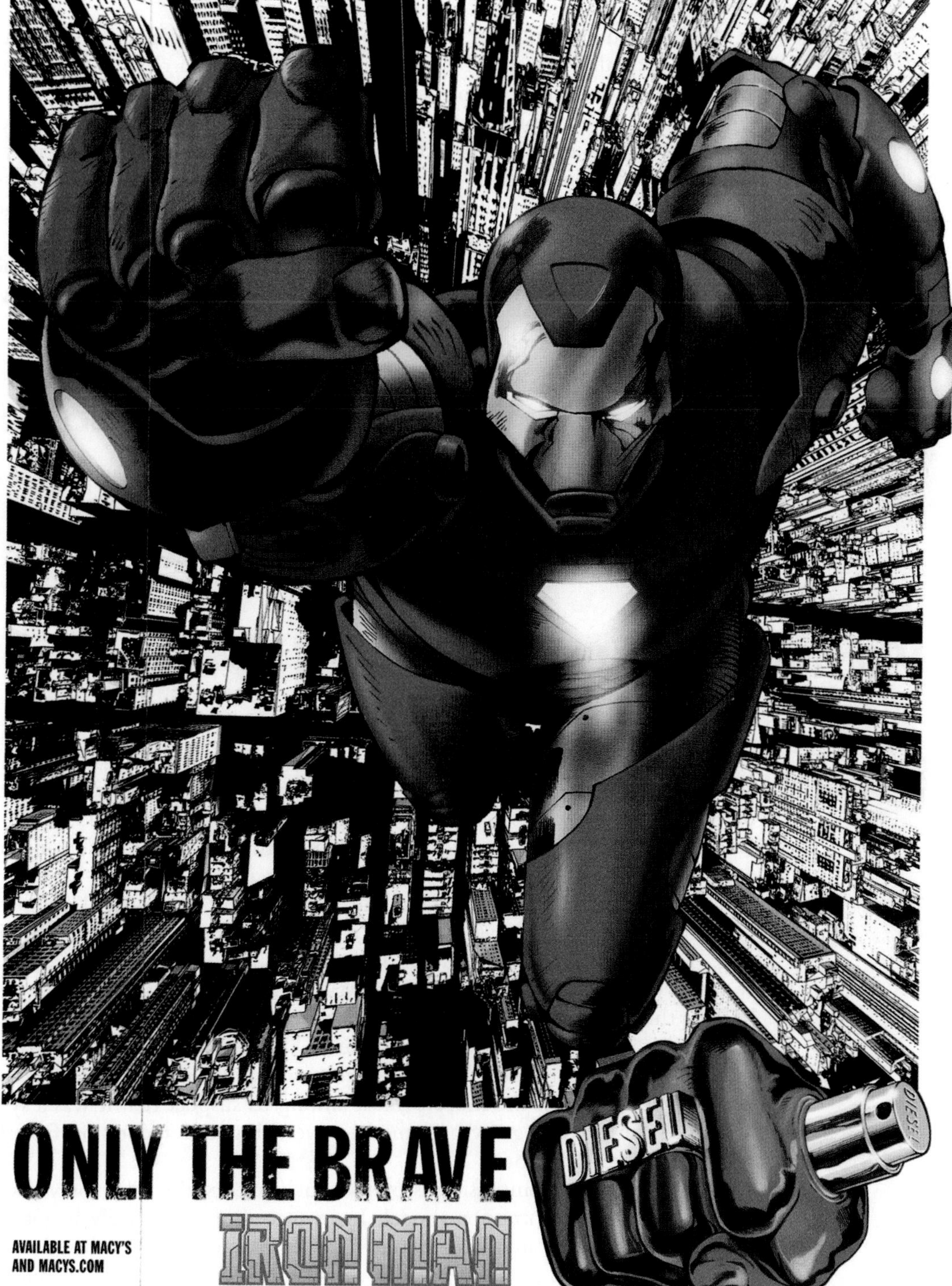
DIESEL
ONLY THE BRAVE
IRON MAN
LIMITED EDITION / EDITION LIMITEE
DIESEL
AVAILABLE AT MACY'S
AND MACYS.COM
LIFT HERE
www.facebook.com/DieselOnlyTheBrave

The medium is the message.

—Marshal McLuhan

A few years ago a few people were saying, "Advertising is dead." Advertising was not dead. It is not dead now. It is changing, thriving in some places, struggling in others. But it is alive.

It is absolutely true that advertising has merged, morphed, and meaningfully mingled with all manner of brand communications, both new and not-new. There are now more ways to promote brands than ever before. It is also true that advertising agencies are becoming more that just advertising agencies; many offer services in digital media and integrated brand promotion. There are all sorts of specialty agencies and shops that didn't exist 10 years ago. The lines of specialization are blurred. But, more people watch more hours of television than ever, and there is no shortage of ads on TV. What happens in China and India matters to everyone in the business. Agency revenues have been seriously squeezed, the traditional ad agency job market has contracted, and some media are in serious trouble (magazines and newspapers). So, different ad world, yes? Advertising dead, hardly.

The Very Wide World of Brand Media Vehicles.

The media arena (new or old) is vitally important, always has been, always will be. This is where the money is spent, invested wisely, or wasted. It is also a place where much has changed. We begin by noting the big changes, explaining some underlying reasons, and discussing their real-world implications.

1 Very Important Changes.

Agency Compensation.

Thirty years ago it was a pretty simple system: Around 80 percent of all advertising and promotional dollars went to media advertising (television, radio, newspapers, magazines, and outdoor). The advertising was created, produced, and placed by full-service advertising agencies—most everything was done under one roof. The agency purchased the media at a 15 percent discount, and that's how ad agencies made their money. Back in the day, ad agencies (say, J. Walter Thompson) got a 15 percent discount from the media (e.g., NBC), but they charged their clients (e.g., Ford) full price; the agencies kept the change, the 15 percent. Fifteen percent of a few million dollars (per account) was good money. The more ads a client bought through their ad agency, the more money the agencies made. Back then agencies would deny with their last breath that they ever encouraged clients to spend more just so that the agency would make more money. Yeah, right. It was very simple math and the more cynical among us suspect that it was a system that produced the massive growth in media advertising and agency profits. But those simple days are long gone.

The 15 percent commission is pretty much history. In 2009, only about 3% of agencies used the commission model. In its place are individually negotiated deals; not much is standard anymore. About 75% of agencies use a fee-based model; they pay for specific jobs, so much for this ad, so much for this study, so much for this campaign. Staff time is billed out to the client at an agreed upon rate. The new system most closely resembles a law firm's billing system. For all the noise (mostly from P&G) in the last few years about paying for results, like return on investment (ROI), only about 1 percent of total ad billings are from such a system. In reality, few have the muscle to force agencies to accept what are often bad deals.

Also, the people who actually create the ads may work at an entirely different agency from the people who actually buy the media. Quite a bit of media planning and buying is outsourced, or split off from the agency with the account management and/or creative function. The demise of the 15 percent flat commission is one factor that brought on the new media age. When the way agencies got paid changed, and it involved less financial reward for buying lots of mass media, there was less incentive to consider only the traditional forms.

More Media.

Even more fundamentally challenging to the old system is that "media" now include all sorts of new species: the Internet, cross-promotions, product placements, buzz and viral marketing, movies that are really feature-length commercials, and so on. The line between public relations and advertising has become a busy blur. Companies supply and push "news" stories about their brands or categories to media outlets as part of their overall integrated brand promotion effort. These "news" stories cost the companies nothing other than the salaries of the staff writers and placement specialists, so in a pure sense, no ads are actually purchased. But IBP is clearly being done. Obvious examples occur around holidays when food stories (let's say about cooking turkeys) show up on the local early news as a feature story. These "stories" are often written and produced by a poultry or seasoning marketer and sent out to the news media as news, not advertising. Some journalists are surprisingly willing to let marketers write and produce their stories for them. Newspapers, most struggling desperately for revenue just to survive, find a way to put aside ethical considerations and run the stories. Money rarely changes hands in a direct way, but having free stories allow newspapers to trim staff. We know of at least one major U.S. consumer package goods advertiser that has very quietly moved a small but significant percentage of its overall promotional budget into this type of news/media/advertising. A senior executive told us that the growth of ads as "news" is fast, strong, and significant, and suggests the model of the future. Other times, public relation firms are quick to write and disseminate a news story when their product is rated highly, say a car by *Consumer Reports*. This is sometimes called "earned media" as opposed to "paid media" (advertising). The same is true in entertainment, where movies can work as promotional vehicles for products while still entertaining. There is now IBP in video and computer games and on cell phones, just about everywhere. So, this large expansion of what we call "media" is another factor in bringing about this new media world. Social media is thought to be very important, but no one is sure how to price it, package it, or sell it. Social media is growing far faster as a branding and promotion method than the industry's ability to measure and price it.

Going Public.

Agencies have become much leaner operations since moving from being privately held to publicly traded companies. Now there is much more stockholder pressure for short-term profitability. In the ad world, the two quickest routes to greater short-term profit are (1) to fire staff and (2) to make more money on fees and media buys. As the ad world has moved away from flat media commissions, traditional media, and privately held companies, they have become much more like other traditional businesses and are constantly searching for ways to optimize short-term profits. This often pushes them in the direction of higher-return media buys and deals, often in the nonstandardized realm of "new media" where rate books and compensation formula either don't exist or are rarely made public. To understand media, and how it is bought and used to generate profit for the agency, is to understand a great deal about real-world advertising and marketing practice. So, these changes in agency profitability and stockholder pressure have also helped usher in the age of new media. Many agency creatives have noted that their production budgets for television ads are tiny compared to what they once were. Agency profit margins are razor thin; fewer people do more work, and for less money.

Globalization.

More and more, advertising and IBP media are truly worldwide. Contemporary media are not so contained by national borders, or even particularly concerned with them. Transnational corporations, particularly media, don't really care much about the borders of nation–states. From CNN to Al Jazeera, media exist in transnational space, and must be thought of that way. This is the new media reality. Even vehicles strongly associated with one particular country are more and more trying to soften that association. Have you noticed how CNN is looking less like a U.S. news agency and more like a global one? Watch CNN midday and it's pretty much CNN-Europe. The Internet is worldwide; search engines don't really care about nation–state boundaries. (Unless you are China and you try to force Google to help with state-mandated censorship.) Many of these global media organizations have large audiences outside of North America. BBC Worldwide TV, based in London, has several million viewers throughout Asia. As the European Union solidifies (if it does), the big media muscle of united Europe will be felt all across the globe. Then there are the BRIC countries, countries with huge emerging consumer markets: Brazil, Russia, India, and China, sometimes expanded to the BRICIT countries (adding Indonesia and Turkey). Companies must pay special attention to these four or six and are actively developing media platforms and vehicles just for these emerging mega-markets. For example, in 2011, India has 1.1 billion people, at least 25 percent of them under the age of 16. By 2050, it will have nearly 1.7 billion people. It is currently adding "an Australia" to its population every single year. It also has a growing middle class, although the size and definition of the "middle" is debatable. Then there is China and 1.3 billion people, and an economy growing at 8-9% per year. The Chinese want all the nice things the West has had, and then some (see Exhibit 12.1). That's why P&G, Coke, Pepsi, Microsoft, Motorola, Unilever, General Mills, J. Walter Thompson, and on and on all have operations there It is also significant that indigenous Indian brands like Kingfisher and Tatta are both huge and hugely successful. You cannot ignore numbers and signs of growth like these. Neither can you ignore the media challenge of reaching them. In India today, television remains the best media buy due largely to the high population density and the concentration of wealth in the even denser urban centers. But globalization is more than a marketplace phenomenon. It's a way of thinking, a mindset, a political agenda, a homogenized world of brand culture. Globalization is yet another factor in the rise of the "new media."

Exhibit 12.1 China matters.

Globalization presents media planners with new problems. The most serious one is lack of international standardized audience measurement and pricing, or even transparency. Pricing and buying media around the globe are very complicated, anything but standard, and sometimes involve

Globalization

IKEA and British Politics

The 2010 U.K. Election was a hard-fought battle of three candidates. Three candidates was an usual number. Also unusual was the first-time use of American-style televised debates. But perhaps most unusual was IKEA's entry into the fray.

With one week to go, IKEA launched an ad campaign that featured kitchen designs specifically created for the three candidates. A website allows consumers to check out the three designs, all interactive so that users can make changes.

The site is linked to one where you can design your own IKEA kitchen, just like the Prime Minister. This campaign by digital agency, Cake, has drawn lots of traffic to the site and created lots of buzz.

This is contemporary advertising and integrated brand promotion at work.

Source: AdAgeGlobal: adage.com/globalnews/article?article_,id=143574, IKEA Enters U.K. Election Campaign: Marketer Suggests Kitchens Designed for Each Prime Minister Candidate. Posted by Emma Hall <mailto:ehall@adage.com> on 04.28.10 <http://adage.com/results?endeca=1&return=endeca&search_offset=0&search_order_by=score&search_phrase=04/28/2010> @ 04:36 PM.

governments and local politics. Typically, foreign agencies partner with local ones or media buyers.

Free Content.

Maybe the single biggest change in the media world is the flood of "free" media content. Largely due to the Internet and other telecommunications changes, consumers are getting used to getting cool stuff for free, or next to free. So, why should they buy a magazine at a bookstore for $4.50 that's full of ads? They can go online and get much of the same, maybe better content without paying a dime, and can avoid the ads—if there are any ads at all. Younger people get their news online. This is making traditional ad-supported paid media vehicles an increasingly endangered species. Daily newspapers are fighting for their lives. So advertisers are putting more of their total promotional budget into nontraditional media, media environments that contemporary consumers clearly enjoy and use more. Some of this content is consumer-generated. That's right, consumers are making and distributing brand-related material and even ads on the Internet for their favorite brands. Some produce mock ads for disliked brands. These ads cost the marketer nothing, make the agency no money, and may or may not be on target.[1] Several major advertisers tell the story of getting lots of great feedback for an Internet ad, calling their agency to congratulate them, and finding out that their agency has no idea what they are talking about: the ad turns out to have been made by some 14-year-old kid in Ohio. This has become a worry for some advertisers; they really enjoy being in control.

Consumer in Charge.

It is now widely accepted that the days of the marketer as the sole creator of brand image is over. This admission has appeared on the cover of *Advertising Age,* been said by scores of major CEOs, and is now the accepted reality being practiced by most large advertisers. With the rise of the Internet, the rise of connected consumers capable

1. lbert M. and Hope Jensen Schau (2007), "Vigilante Marketing and Consumer-Created Communications," *Journal of Advertising*, vol. 36, no. 3 (Fall 2007), pp. 187–202.

and willing to talk back to marketers, and a changing consumer culture and consumer mind-set, there is a real battle for who owns the brand and who gets to say things about it. This is yet another big difference when describing the new media world. Brands and brand communication are now meaningfully co-created. Advertisers bring something to the table, and so do consumers.

E-commerce has been wildly successful. It has truly revolutionized the way consumers shop and consume. Its impact has been more than technological; it has been cultural and economic. It has given consumers considerably more power in the marketing channel: access to more and better information, access to millions of other consumers and their opinions of goods and services, and much higher expectations of finding good deals. In fact, two of the biggest changes the Internet has wrought are the rise of **deal-proneness** in consumers and **price/cost transparency**. It is now so incredibly easy to get a deal, to know what a good deal is, to operate with knowledge of what a good price would be, and even to know what the seller's cost is. A new-car buyer can very easily find out online what the local car dealer's invoice price was (how much it paid for the car) and what the breakeven point is for the dealer. Consumers can do the same for countless goods and services through the World Wide Web. It's now cool to talk about how little you paid for something; in the 1980's consumers bragged about how much they paid. Consumers have now become prone to seek deals more than ever before. E-commerce (shopping and consuming online), much more than e-advertising per se, has changed the ad and promotion world. Learning how to fit in and leverage that new world is now a key to success.

This gives the consumer unprecedented marketplace power. This is power that consumers are not going to easily give up. So this means that going forward consumers are going to want media that gives them this kind of information and power, often for free and without obtrusive and annoying ads. This has changed the media environment in a fundamental way.

Hyperclutter and Ad Avoidance.

While it has always been the case that consumers felt there were lots of ads in their environment, it has now become the stuff of serious industry concern. Before, consumers pretty much had no choice. Now they do. They can watch ad-free premium channels such as HBO or they can "TiVo" past the ads from network television shows. On the Internet, pop-up ad filters are some of the most popular software offerings available. People will pay to avoid ads. Too many ads have made traditional advertising less powerful. Ironically, traditional advertising is a victim of itself. To survive and prosper in the new media world, you have to figure out how not to be avoided.

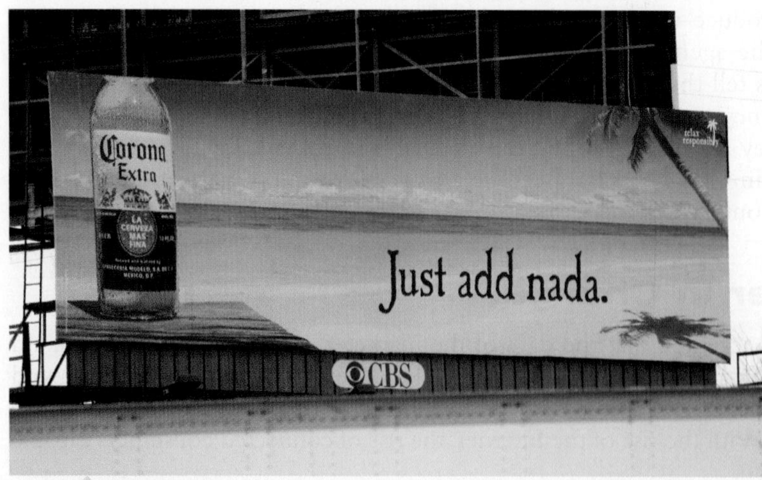

Exhibit 12.2 With a changing population, there is changing media.

Multicultural Media.

English is not the only language on the planet, or in the U.S. In the United States, the most attention is on the Hispanic/Latino market, due mostly to its size and growth rate. Most major advertisers are paying lots of attention to this (see Exhibit 12.2). There are at least 10 major cities in the United States now where English is the minority language, and this trend will continue. This is nothing compared to other parts of the world. In India, for example, there are 16 major dialects of Hindi as well as English, and a mix of world religions and their cultures. New media (and demography) allow (and demand) more diversity in ad languages.

2 The Fundamentals of Media Planning.

OK, so a lot has changed in media land, but not everything. There are still some ideas, names, concepts, and principles that are just as they always were. Traditional concepts still matter. Some basic tools remain the same. So now we are going to talk about what has stayed the same and what still matters. There are those things that endure, principles. One of them is the principle of good media planning.

No matter how new the media are, how great a marketing plan is, and how insightful or visionary advertising strategists are, poor message placement will undermine even the best-laid plans and the coolest media. Advertising placed in media that do not reach the target audience—whether via new media or traditional media—will be much like the proverbial tree that falls in the forest with no one around: Does it make a sound? From an advertising standpoint, no; it doesn't. Advertising placed in media that do not reach target audiences will not achieve the communications or sales impact an advertiser desires and is paying for.

Now, let's think about some fundamentals, and some hard, cold realities.

The Big Pie.

Think of all the money used to promote a brand as a big pie. The big pie (see Exhibit 12.3) includes advertising, direct mail, point-of-purchase promotion, coupons, promotional emails, buzz marketing, product placement, brand integration in computer games, everything spent to promote a good or service. Traditionally, companies would make the distinction between (1) **above-the-line promotion**, which meant traditional **measured media** advertising, and (2) **below-the-line promotion**, which is everything else. For consumer package goods companies, below-the-line promotion might be desirable retail shelving, in-store promotions, coupons, and events; for durable goods (say cars), it might be for dealer incentives and financing incentives. Below-the-line is also referred to as **unmeasured media**.

As defined by Competitive Media Reporting, the industry leader in the tracking of ad placement and spending, "measured media" include network TV, cable TV, spot TV, syndicated TV, network Spanish TV, the Internet (excluding broadband video and paid search), Net radio, spot radio, local radio (500 stations, top 28 markets), magazines (Sunday, consumer, business-to-business, and 30 local magazines), 250 local newspapers, Spanish newspapers, national newspapers (*The Wall Street Journal, USA Today*, *The New York Times*), and outdoor (200-plus markets). Unmeasured media is everything else: paid Internet search, coupons, product placement, events, and the like.

This is a very big pie. Let's call everything companies spend to promote the brand the Total Brand Promotions Pie. The most recent data reveal that measured media account for 56.5 percent and unmeasured account for 43.5 percent of total spending. Measured media is continuing a very slow decline, slow but real. The thing to remember is that unmeasured media slice has been growing at the expense of the measured. It is not, however, across the board. For example, in the latest figures available, The Coca-Cola Company actually increased its share of traditional

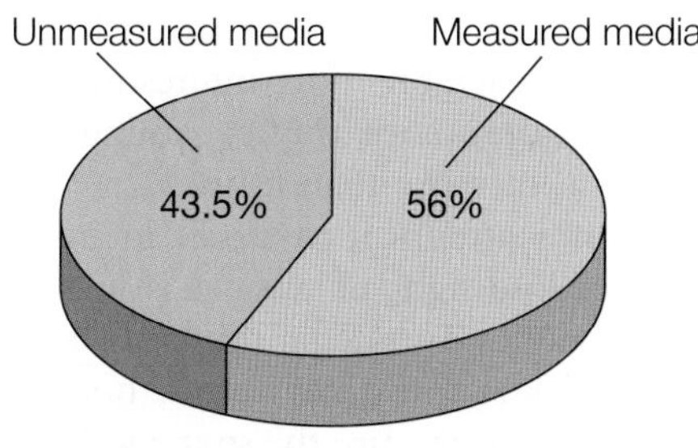

Exhibit 12.3 Measured media is in a very slow decline against unmeasured media.

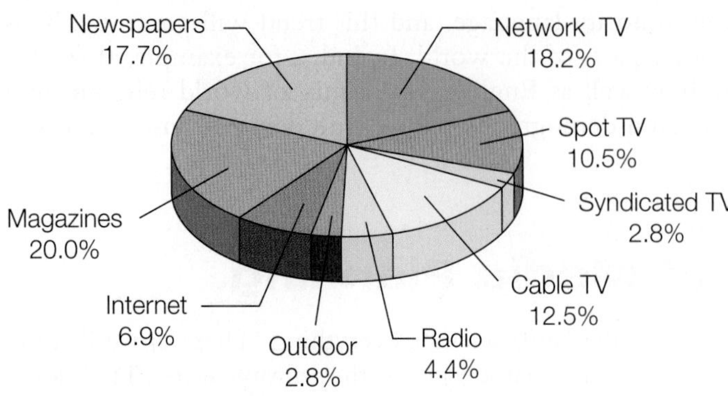

Note: Figures do not total 100 percent due to rounding.

Source: Advertising Age Data Center, 2010. adage.com/datacenter/datapopup.php?article_id=137427

Exhibit 12.4 This is how measured brand communication in the United States breaks down by medium.

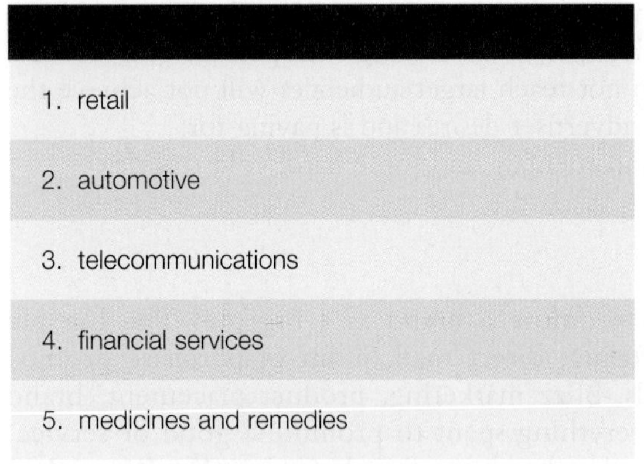

1. retail
2. automotive
3. telecommunications
4. financial services
5. medicines and remedies

Source: WPP's TNS Media Intelligence (www.tnsmi.com). Spending based on TNS's 18 measured media. Numbers rounded. Categories are aggregated from TNS classifications by Ad Age Data Center. See "Total U.S. Advertising Spending By Category" in AdAge.com/lna09

Exhibit 12.5 Top five categories of measured media spending.

measured media relative to unmeasured. So, even though some very big companies, like P&G, are moving in the direction of more non-traditional (mostly below the line) media at a fairly significant clip, this is far from universal. Again, it is the industry trend, but a slow one, a percentage point or two a year.

Why? Well, the simple answer is that these large companies believe these forms are more efficient than traditional mass media advertising. The belief is that some traditional forms are simply too expensive and too cluttered with competing ads. They are too easily avoided or ignored and that even though the Internet still represents less than 10% of advertising, unmeasured social media may hold the answer to consumer apathy. If you can make a brand a "friend" on Facebook and collect all kinds of data from users at a fraction of the cost of a 30-second TV ad, why not move more media money there?

If you break things down a bit more, you can see the relative standing of the different measured media (see Exhibit 12.4). Television in all its forms is still king by a long way. The Internet, which is growing rapidly, still amounts to only 8–9 percent of measured media spending, but that does not include paid search. It is more than double all outdoor advertising, on the heels of radio (which has been around since the 1920s), and climbing. That's big.

It is also interesting to see who spends where (see Exhibit 12.5). These data are from 2008, the latest available. They are reasonably stable year to year. These five categories account for approximately 44% of all measured media spending.

Marketers in some product categories spend more on media and rely more on certain types of media than others. For example, compare how the two industries shown in Exhibit 12.6 spread around their media money.

Media Planning.

Media planning is where money is spent. Hardly glamorous, it is, however, vital. A lot of people enter the ad industry through the media department. It has traditionally been a job of numbers, schedules, and deadlines, and relatively low salaries. But as the world of media has opened up, it has become considerably more interesting and desirable, if not better paying. Now, with the merger of movies, music, gaming, and other entertainment, media planning may become a lot more than it was.

True, the big matrix of media options demands attention to detail in media planning. But, at the same time, you should never lose sight of what it is you are really trying to do. Media planning requires creativity and strategic thinking. Sure, you need to know how to do the basic math, and know the key terms, but you should never let the raw numbers and techno-buzzwords obscure the strategy. What you need to understand is what you are trying to do with media, why you are doing it, and the key aspects of the various tools at your disposal.

Exhibit 12.6 Different categories spend advertising in different media. Think about the difference in these two categories and why they spend the media budgets the way they do.

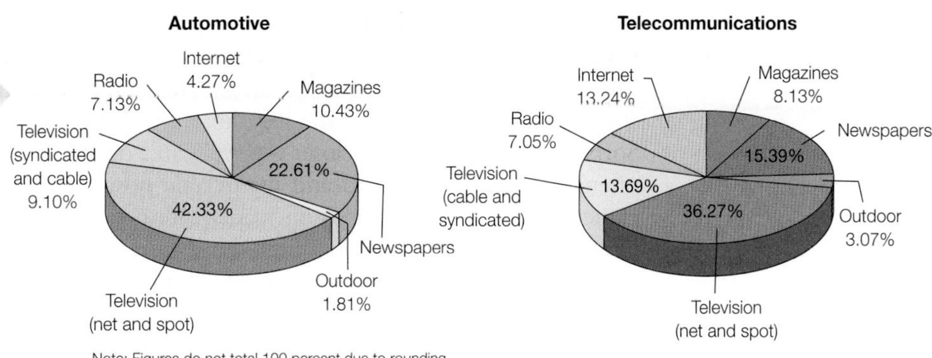

Source: Ad Age Data Center, 2010, adage.com/datacenter/datapopup.php?article_id=137426

Some important terms:

A **media plan** specifies the media in which advertising messages will be placed to reach the desired target audience. A **media class** is a broad category of media, such as television, radio, or newspapers. A **media vehicle** is a particular option for placement within a media class. For example, *Newsweek* is a media vehicle within the magazine-media class. The **media mix** is the blend of different media that will be used to effectively reach the target audience.

A media plan includes strategy, objectives, media choices, and a media schedule for placing a message. And remember: Everything must fit together. The advertising plan (Chapter 7) is developed during the planning stage of the advertising effort and is the driving force behind a media plan. Market and advertising research determines that certain media options hold the highest potential for shaping the consumer behavior (Chapter 5) of the target audience. The message strategy (Chapter 10) has enormous implications for where to place the messages, that is, in which media. Thus, in reality, the media-planning process takes place soon after the overall development of the advertising plan.

Media Strategies, Objectives, and Data.

The true power of a media plan rests in the media strategy. What are you trying to do with your media: buy simple awareness, counter a competitor's claims, reposition your brand, react to good or bad media publicity, or establish an image and good feel surrounding your brand? You have to know this before you start thinking about actual media buys. You need to match message objectives with media choices.

This strategy is then tactically executed in media terms of message weight, reach, frequency, continuity, audience duplication, and newer terms associated with branded entertainment and e-advertising; such as click-throughs. But don't miss the big picture; you should always know and pay close attention to the fundamental qualities of each medium and specific vehicle in terms of what your brand is trying to do. To be really good, you need to be able to see the media buys in the strategic context of brand communication and consumer behavior goals.

Perhaps the most obvious media objective is that the vehicle chosen *reaches the target audience*. Recall that a target audience can be defined by demographics, geography, lifestyle, attitude dimensions, or usage category. But this is actually where a lot of problems happen in the real advertising and IBP world.

Here's what happens too often. The people making the ads, the creatives, along with (maybe) account planners and/or folks from the research department (if there still is one), account executives, and brand managers, have determined a target market of something similar to this example: "housewives 18–49 who hate cooking, long for the day when their children are out of the house, and need a vacation from their husbands." Now, unfortunately, most media are bought and sold with much, much broader variables: age, income, geography, family size—in other words, very basic demographics associated with the total audience of a particular vehicle, say *Newsweek.* All that other stuff helps the creatives but doesn't do much for the media buyer. You really can't call a salesperson at *Newsweek* and say, "Give me just those women who meet this very specific profile." Sorry, can't do it; getting closer but still can't do it. So media planners are often (very often) put in the awkward and unenviable position of trying to deliver very specific audience characteristics based on inadequate data from media organizations. This is an industry-wide problem. Most of the time, there is simply no way to identify which television shows are watched by "women who believe their husbands are way too needy" *and* "regularly shop at Bed Bath & Beyond." Those data are not routinely collected in a single source and are not available. And no matter how many times you tell account executives and creatives this, they seem to still think these data exist. No, generally speaking, they don't, not yet. Media buyers have to use their creativity to figure out what the next best thing would be. A lot of the creativity involved in media planning is trying to find that next best thing. The Internet actually offers some behavioral targeting that can effectively get at this problem, but this is still in its beginning stages.

Sometimes, however, if advertisers are willing to spend the money, and you are reasonably lucky in terms of what you asked for, the data will be available from a media research organization. These organizations don't cover everything, but they sometimes cover what you are looking for. This information can greatly increase the precision and usefulness of media buys. The two most prominent providers of demographic information correlated with product usage data are Mediamark Research (MRI) (www.mediamark.com) and Simmons Market Research Bureau (SMRB) (www.smrb.com). An example of the type of information supplied is shown in Exhibit 12.7, where market statistics for four brands of men's aftershave and cologne are compared: Eternity for Men, Jovan Musk, Lagerfeld, and Obsession for Men. The most revealing data are contained in columns C and D. Column C shows each brand's strength relative to a demographic variable, such as age or income. Column D provides an index indicating that particular segments of the population are heavier users of a particular brand. Specifically, the number expresses each brand's share of volume as a percentage of its share of users. An index number above 100 shows particular strength for a brand. The strength of Eternity for Men as well as Obsession for Men is apparent in both the 18–24 and the 25–34 age cohorts. In magazines (their known specialty) and other print, Standard Rate and Data Service provides the exposure data (www.srds.com/portal/main?action=LinkHit&frameset=yes&link=ips).

Even more sophisticated data have become available. Research services such as A. C. Nielsen's Homescan and Information Resources' BehaviorScan are referred to as **single-source tracking services**, which offer information not only on demographics but also on brands, purchase size, purchase frequency, prices paid, and media exposure. BehaviorScan is the most comprehensive, in that exposure to particular television programs, magazines, and newspapers can be measured by the service. With demographic, behavioral, and media-exposure correlates provided by research services like these, advertising and media planners can address issues such as the following:

- How many members of the target audience have tried the advertiser's brand, and how many are repeat purchasers?
- What appears to affect brand sales more—increased amounts of advertising, or changes in advertising copy?
- What other products do buyers of the advertiser's brand purchase regularly?
- What television programs, magazines, and newspapers reach the largest number of the advertiser's audience?

Another critical element in setting advertising objectives is determining the **geographic scope** of media placement. Media planners need to identify media that cover the same geographic area as the advertiser's distribution system. Obviously,

Aftershave Lotion & Cologne for Men		Eternity for Men				Jovan Musk				Lagerfeld				Obsession for Men			
	TOTAL	A	B	C	D	A	B	C	D	A	B	C	D	A	B	C	D
BASE: MEN	U.S. '000	'000	% DOWN	% ACROSS	INDEX	'000	% DOWN	% ACROSS	INDEX	'000	% DOWN	% ACROSS	INDEX	'000	% DOWN	% ACROSS	INDEX
All Men	92674	2466	100.0	2.7	100	3194	100.0	3.4	100	1269	100.0	1.4	100	3925	100.0	4.2	100
Men	92674	2466	100.0	2.7	100	3194	100.0	3.4	100	1269	100.0	1.4	100	3925	100.0	4.2	100
Women	—	—	—	—	—	—	—	—	—	—	—	—	—	—	—	—	—
Household Heads	77421	1936	78.5	2.5	94	2567	80.4	3.3	96	1172	92.4	1.5	111	2856	72.7	3.7	87
Homemakers	31541	967	39.2	3.1	115	1158	36.3	3.7	107	451	35.5	1.4	104	1443	36.8	4.6	108
Graduated College	21727	583	23.7	2.7	101	503	15.8	2.3	67	348	27.4	1.6	117	901	23.0	4.1	98
Attended College	23842	814	33.0	3.4	128	933	29.2	3.9	113	*270	21.3	1.1	83	1283	32.7	5.4	127
Graduated High School	29730	688	27.9	2.3	87	1043	32.7	3.5	102	*460	36.3	1.5	113	1266	32.2	4.3	101
Did Not Graduate H.S.	17374	*380	15.4	2.2	82	*715	22.4	4.1	119	*191	15.0	1.1	80	*475	12.1	2.7	65
18–24	12276	754	30.6	6.1	231	*391	12.2	3.2	92	*7	0.5	0.1	4	747	19.0	6.1	144
25–34	20924	775	31.4	3.7	139	705	22.1	3.4	98	*234	18.5	1.1	82	1440	36.7	6.9	162
35–44	21237	586	23.8	2.8	104	1031	32.3	4.9	141	*311	24.5	1.5	107	838	21.3	3.9	93
45–54	14964	*202	8.2	1.4	51	*510	16.0	3.4	99	*305	24.0	2.0	149	481	12.3	3.2	76
55–64	10104	*112	4.6	1.1	42	*215	6.7	2.1	62	*214	16.9	2.1	155	*245	6.2	2.4	57
65 or over	13168	*37	1.5	0.3	10	*342	10.7	2.6	75	*198	15.6	1.5	110	*175	4.4	1.3	31
18–34	33200	1529	62.0	4.6	173	1096	34.3	3.3	96	*241	19.0	0.7	53	2187	55.7	6.6	156
18–49	62950	2228	90.4	3.5	133	2460	77.0	3.9	113	683	53.9	1.1	79	3315	84.5	5.3	124
25–54	57125	1563	63.4	2.7	103	2246	70.3	3.9	114	850	67.0	1.5	109	2758	70.3	4.8	114
Employed Full Time	62271	1955	79.3	3.1	118	2141	67.0	3.4	100	977	77.0	1.6	115	2981	76.0	4.8	113
Employed Part-time	5250	*227	9.2	4.3	163	*141	4.4	2.7	78	*10	0.8	0.2	14	*300	7.7	5.7	135
Sole Wage Earner	21027	554	22.5	2.6	99	794	24.9	3.8	110	332	26.2	1.6	115	894	22.8	4.3	100
Not Employed	25153	*284	11.5	1.1	42	912	28.6	3.6	105	*281	22.2	1.1	82	643	16.4	2.6	60
Professional	9010	*232	9.4	2.6	97	*168	5.3	1.9	54	*143	11.3	1.6	116	504	12.8	5.6	132
Executive/Admin./Mgr.	10114	*259	10.5	2.6	96	*305	9.6	3.0	88	*185	14.6	1.8	134	353	9.0	3.5	82
Clerical/Sales/Technical	13212	436	17.7	3.3	124	*420	13.2	3.2	92	*231	18.2	1.7	128	741	18.9	5.6	132
Precision/Crafts/Repair	12162	624	25.3	5.1	193	*317	9.9	2.6	76	*168	13.2	1.4	101	511	13.0	4.2	99
Other Employed	23022	631	25.6	2.7	103	1071	33.5	4.7	135	*261	20.6	1.1	83	1173	29.9	5.1	120
H/D Income																	
$75,000 or More	17969	481	19.5	2.7	101	*320	10.0	1.8	52	413	32.5	2.3	168	912	23.2	5.1	120
$60,000–74,999	10346	*368	14.9	3.6	134	*309	9.7	3.0	87	*142	11.2	1.4	100	495	12.6	4.8	113
$50,000–59,999	9175	*250	10.2	2.7	103	*424	13.3	4.6	134	*153	12.1	1.7	122	*371	9.4	4.0	95
$40,000–49,999	11384	*308	12.5	2.7	102	*387	12.1	3.4	99	*134	10.6	1.2	86	580	14.8	5.1	120
$30,000–39,999	12981	*360	14.6	2.8	104	542	17.0	4.2	121	*126	10.0	1.0	71	*416	10.6	3.2	76
$20,000–29,999	13422	*266	10.8	2.0	75	*528	16.5	3.9	114	*164	12.9	1.2	89	*475	12.1	3.5	84
$10,000–19,999	11867	*401	16.3	3.4	127	*394	12.3	3.3	96	*67	5.3	0.6	41	*481	12.3	4.1	96
Less than $10,000	5528	*31	1.3	0.6	21	*291	9.1	5.3	153	*69	5.4	1.2	91	*194	4.9	3.5	83

Source: 1. Based on "GfK MRI, GfK MRI Men's, Women's Personal Care Products Report," *GfK MRI*, Spring 1997, 16.

Exhibit 12.7 Commercial research firms can provide advertisers with an evaluation of a brand's relative strength within demographic segments. This typical data table from Mediamark Research shows how various men's aftershave and cologne brands perform in different demographic segments. www.mediamark.com

spending money on the placement of ads in media that cover geographic areas where the advertiser's brand is not distributed is wasteful.

Some analysts suggest that when certain geographic markets demonstrate unusually high purchasing tendencies by product category or by brand, then geo-targeting should be the basis for the media placement decision. **Geo-targeting** is the placement of ads in geographic regions where higher purchase tendencies for a brand are evident. For example, in one geographic area the average consumer purchases of Prego spaghetti sauce were 36 percent greater than the average consumer purchases nationwide. With this kind of information, media buys can be geo-targeted to reinforce high-volume users.[2]

Reach refers to the number of people or households in a target audience that will be exposed to a media vehicle or schedule at least one time during a given period of time. It is often expressed as a percentage. If an advertisement placed on the hit network television program *American Idol* is watched at least once by 10 percent of the advertiser's

2. This section and the example are drawn from Erwin Ephron, "The Organizing Principle of Media," *Inside Media*, November 2, 1992.

Exhibit 12.8 Reach is an important measure of a media vehicle's effectiveness. Who you reach is very important.

target audience, then the reach is said to be 10 percent. Media vehicles with broad reach are ideal for consumer convenience goods, such as toothpaste and cold remedies. These are products with fairly simple features, and they are frequently purchased by a broad cross-section of the market. Broadcast television, cable television, and national magazines have the largest and broadest reach of any of the media, due to their national and even global coverage. But their audiences have been shrinking. Now, vehicles like Telemundo (Exhibit 12.8) are claiming respectable reach among selected but prized "demos" (demographics).

Frequency is the average number of times an individual or household within a target audience is exposed to a media vehicle in a given period of time (typically a week or a month). For example, say an advertiser places an ad on a weekly television show with a 20 rating (20 percent of households) four weeks in a row. The show has an (unduplicated) reach of 43 (percent) during the four-week period. So, frequency is then equal to $(20 \times 4)/43$, or 1.9. This means that an audience member had the opportunity to see the ad an average of 1.9 times.

Advertisers often struggle with the dilemma of increasing reach at the expense of frequency, or vice versa. At the core in this struggle are the concepts of effective frequency and effective reach. **Effective frequency** is the number of times a target audience needs to be exposed to a message before the objectives of the advertiser are met—either communications objectives or sales impact. Many factors affect the level of effective frequency. New brands and brands laden with features may demand high frequency. Simple messages for well-known products may require less frequent exposure for consumers to be affected. Although most analysts agree that one exposure will typically not be enough, there is debate about how many exposures are enough. A common industry practice is to place effective frequency at three exposures, but analysts argue that as few as two or as many as nine exposures are needed to achieve effective frequency.

Effective reach is the number or percentage of consumers in the target audience that are exposed to an ad some minimum number of times. The minimum-number estimate for effective reach is based on a determination of effective frequency. If effective reach is set at four exposures, then a media schedule must be devised that achieves at least four exposures over a specified time period within the target audience. With all the advertising clutter (too many ads) that exists today, effective reach is likely a much higher number; some experts have advocated six as a minimum.

Message weight is another media measure; it is the total mass of advertising delivered. Message weight is the gross number of advertising messages or exposure opportunities delivered by the vehicles in a schedule. Media planners are interested in the message weight of a media plan because it provides a simple indication of the size of the advertising effort being placed against a specific market.

Message weight (at least in traditional media) is typically expressed in terms of gross impressions. **Gross impressions** represent the sum of exposures to the entire media placement in a media plan. Planners often distinguish between two types of exposure. *Potential ad impressions* or *opportunities* to be exposed to ads are the most common meanings and refer to exposures by the media vehicle carrying advertisements (for example, a program or publication). *Message impressions*, on the other hand, refers to exposures to the ads themselves. Information on ad exposure probabilities can be obtained from a number of companies, including Nielsen, Simmons, Roper-Starch, Gallup & Robinson, Harvey

Research, and Readex. This information can pertain to particular advertisements, campaigns, media vehicles, product categories, ad characteristics, and target groups.

For example, consider a media plan that, in a one-week period, places ads on three television programs and in two national newspapers. The sum of the exposures to the media placement might be as follows:

	Gross Impressions	
	Media Vehicle	**Advertisement**
Television		
Program A audience	16,250,000	5,037,500
Program B audience	4,500,000	1,395,000
Program C audience	7,350,000	2,278,500
Sum of TV exposures	28,100,000	8,711,000
Newspapers		
Newspaper 1	1,900,000	376,200
Newspaper 2	450,000	89,100
Sum of newspaper exposures	2,350,000	465,300
Total gross impressions	**30,450,000**	**9,176,300**

The total gross impressions figure is the media weight.

Of course, this does not mean that 30,450,000 separate people were exposed to the programs and newspapers or that 9,176,300 separate people were exposed to the advertisements. Some people who watched TV program A also saw program B and read newspaper 1, as well as all other possible combinations. This is called **between-vehicle duplication** (remember, "vehicles" are shows, newspapers, magazines—things that carry ads). It is also possible that someone who saw the ad in newspaper 1 on Monday saw it again in newspaper 1 on Tuesday. This is **within-vehicle duplication**. That's why we say that the total *gross* impressions number contains audience duplication. Data available from services such as SMRB report both types of duplication so that they may be removed from the gross impressions to produce the *unduplicated* estimate of audience, or *reach,* as discussed above. (You should know, however, that the math involved in such calculations is fairly complex.)

Another way of expressing media weight is in terms of gross rating points (GRP). GRP is the product of reach times frequency (GRP = $r \times f$). When media planners calculate the GRP for a media plan, they multiply the rating (reach) of each vehicle in a plan times the number of times an ad will be inserted in the media vehicle and sum these figures across all vehicles in the plan. Exhibit 12.9 shows the GRP for a combined magazine and television schedule. The GRP number is used as a relative measure of the intensity of one media plan versus another. Whether a media plan is appropriate is ultimately based on the judgment of the media planner.

Media Class/ Vehicle	Rating (reach)	Number of Ad Insertions (frequency)	GRP
Television			
American Idol	25	4	100
Law & Order	20	4	80
Good Morning America	12	4	48
Days of Our Lives	7	2	14
Magazines			
People	22	2	44
Travel & Leisure	11	2	22
News & World Report	9	6	54
Total			**362**

Exhibit 12.9 Gross rating points (GRP) for a media plan.

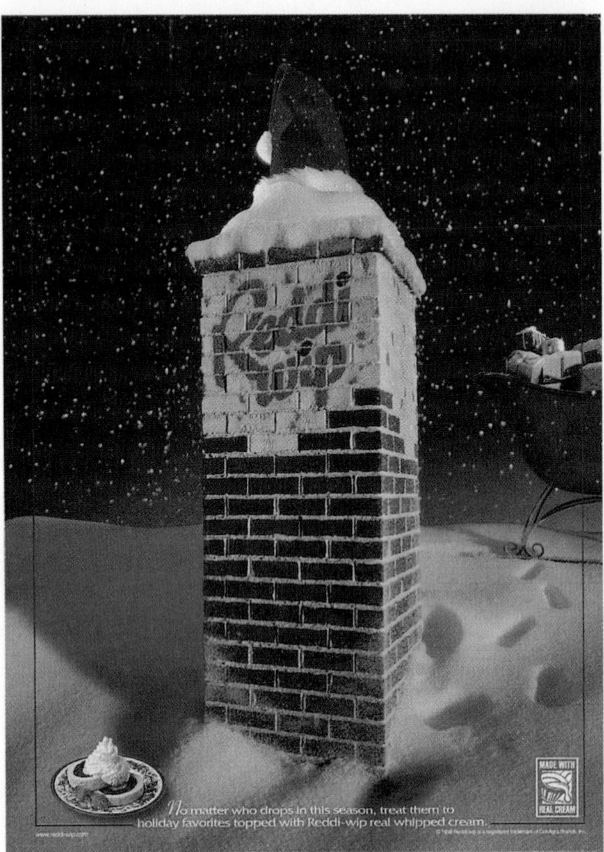

Exhibit 12.10 An example of a print ad that was flighted during December—a month in which whipped-cream dessert toppings figure prominently. www.reddi-wip.com

Courtesy, ConAgra Foods, Inc.

The message weight objective provides only a broad perspective for a media planner. What does it mean when we say that a media plan for a week produced more than 30 million gross impressions? It means only that a fairly large number of people were potentially exposed to the advertiser's message. It provides a general point of reference. When Toyota introduced the Avalon in the U.S. market, the $40 million introductory ad campaign featured 30-second television spots, newspaper and magazine print ads, and direct mail pieces. The highlight of the campaign was a nine-spot placement on a heavily watched Thursday evening TV show, costing more than $2 million. The message weight of this campaign in a single week was enormous—just the type of objective Toyota's media planners wanted for the brand introduction.[3]

Continuity is the pattern of placement of advertisements in a media schedule. There are three strategic scheduling alternatives: continuous, flighting, and pulsing. **Continuous scheduling** is a pattern of placing ads at a steady rate over a period of time. Running one ad each day for four weeks during the soap opera *General Hospital* would be a continuous pattern. Similarly, an ad that appeared in every issue of *Redbook* magazine for a year would also be continuous. **Flighting** is another media-scheduling strategy. Flighting is achieved by scheduling heavy advertising for a period of time, usually two weeks, then stopping advertising altogether for a period, only to come back with another heavy schedule.

Flighting is often used to support special seasonal merchandising efforts or new product introductions, or as a response to competitors' activities. The financial advantages of flighting are that discounts might be gained by concentrating media buys in larger blocks. Communication effectiveness may be enhanced because a heavy schedule can achieve the repeat exposures necessary to achieve consumer awareness. For example, the ad in Exhibit 12.10 was run heavily in December issues of magazines, to take advantage of seasonal dessert-consumption patterns.

Finally, **pulsing** is a media-scheduling strategy that combines elements from continuous and flighting techniques. Advertisements are scheduled continuously in media over a period of time, but with periods of much heavier scheduling (the flight). Pulsing is most appropriate for products that are sold fairly regularly all year long but have certain seasonal requirements, such as clothing.

Continuity and the Forgetting Function. Although many may not know it, industry media continuity practices were actually strongly influenced by academic research in the area of human memory. When people first started trying to understand how and when to place ads, the idea of forgetting soon came into play. It makes sense. Very early in advertising's history, this very useful piece of psychological research was recognized. It turns out that people's forgetting is fairly predictable; that is, all else being equal, we know at about what interval things fade from people's memory. It seems to obey a mathematical function pretty well; thus it is often called

3. Bradley Johnson, "Toyota's New Avalon Thinks Big, American," *Advertising Age,* November 14, 1994, 46.

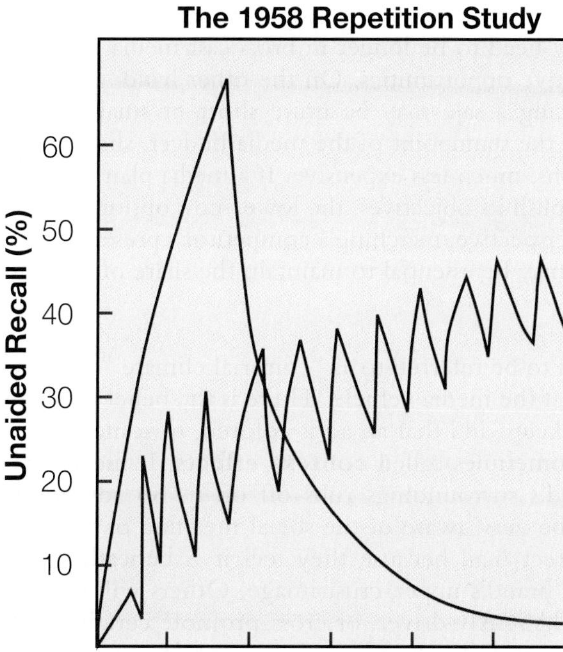

Source: Based on Hubert A. Zielske, "The Remembering and Forgetting of Advertising," *Journal of Marketing,* American Marketing Association, January 23, 1959, 239–243. Reprinted in R. Batra, J. Myers, and D. Aaker, *Advertising Management*, 4th ed. (Upper Saddle River, NJ: Prentice Hall, 1992).

Exhibit 12.11 Work your way through this graph of a very important and influential piece of media research. It links what we know about the manner in which humans forget things with the optional frequency of advertising.

the **forgetting function**. The original work for this was done more than a century ago by psychologist Hermann Ebbinghaus in the late 19th century and most notably in the advertising world by Hubert Zielske in 1958. In his very famous study, Zielske sent food ads to two randomly selected groups of women. One received the ad every four weeks for 52 weeks (13 total exposures), the other received the ad once every week for 13 straight weeks (13 total exposures). Exhibit 12.11 shows what happened. The group that received all 13 ads in the first 13 weeks (called a flighting schedule) scored much higher in terms of peak unaided recall, but the level of recall fell off very fast, and by halfway through the year was very low. The group that got the ads at an evenly spaced schedule (called a continuous schedule) never attained as high a level of recall as the other group, but finished much higher at the end of the year, and had an overall higher average recall.

This research has been very influential in terms of guiding industry media planners for several decades. The real-world implications are pretty clear. If you need rapid and very high levels of recall—say for the introduction of a new product, a strategic move to block the message of a competitor, or a political ad campaign, where there is only one day of actual shopping (election day)—use a flighting (sometimes called "heavy-up") schedule. A continuous schedule would be more broadly effective and would be used for established brands with an established message.

We do, however, offer a note of caution here. As you know, the idea of recall and its measurement have received considerable criticism from both industry managers and academic researchers. We agree with this criticism; simple memory measures are inadequate at best in most advertising situations. As discussed earlier, they are most appropriate when a simple outcome like brand name recall is sought. In that case, forgetting (or not forgetting) is an important factor in advertising success or failure.

Length or Size of Advertisements. Beyond whom to reach, how often to reach them, and in what pattern, media planners must make strategic decisions regarding the length of an ad in electronic media or the size of an ad in print media. Certainly, the advertiser, creative director, art director, and copywriter have made determinations in this regard as well. Television advertisements (excluding infomercials) can range from 10 seconds to 60 seconds, and sometimes even two minutes, in length. Is a 60-second television commercial always six times more effective than a 10-second spot? Of course, the answer is no. Is a full-page newspaper ad always more effective than a two-inch, one-column ad? Again, not necessarily. Some research shows an increase in recognition scores of print advertising with increasing image size. Some call this the **square root law**; that is, "the recognition of print ads increases with the square of the illustration."[4] So a full-page ad should be twice as memorable as a quarter-page ad. Such "laws" should not be considered laws but rather general guidelines; they show a general relationship but are not completely precise. Still, advertisers use full-page newspaper ads when a product claim, brand image, or market situation warrants it.

The decision about the length or size of an advertisement depends on the creative requirements for the ad, the media budget, and the competitive environment

4. John R. Rossiter, "Visual Imagery: Applications to Advertising," *Advances in Consumer Research* (Provo, UT: Association for Consumer Research, 1982), 101–106.

within which the ad is running. From a creative standpoint, ads attempting to develop an image for a brand may need to be longer in broadcast media or larger in print media to offer more creative opportunities. On the other hand, a simple, straightforward message announcing a sale may be quite short or small, but it may need heavy repetition. From the standpoint of the media budget, shorter and smaller ads are, with few exceptions, much less expensive. If a media plan includes some level of repetition to accomplish its objectives, the lower-cost option may be mandatory. From a competitive perspective, matching a competitor's presence with messages of similar size or length may be essential to maintain the share of mind in a target audience.

Media Context. This used to be referred to as "editorial climate." It refers to the feel, spirit, look, or image of the media vehicle. There is the belief that you are known by the company you keep, and that an ad is colored, to some extent, by where it appears. These are sometimes called **context effects**. It means that some of the meaning of your ad's surroundings rubs off on it. So advertisers and media professionals have to be very aware of the social meaning of context. Some advertisers will not do direct mail because they feel it is beneath them, that to do so would tarnish their brand's upper-crust image. Others will not use certain magazines, or sponsor a NASCAR driver, or cross-promote certain kinds of movies. Conversely, some purposefully choose exclusive magazines or other media, including sponsorships, precisely because they want to be elevated by their surroundings. Although there have been attempts to grade, quantify, and automate editorial climate in media selection models, it has proven to be a task best suited for knowledgeable human interpretation. You should always make media context a consideration in media strategy. Quantifiable or not, it counts. As branded entertainment and other forms of new media spread, context will become more critical.

Competitive Media Assessment.

Even though media planners normally do not base an overall media plan on how much competitors are spending or where competitors are placing their ads, a competitive media assessment can provide a useful perspective. A competitive media assessment is particularly important for product categories in which all the competitors are focused on a narrowly defined target audience. This condition exists in several product categories in which heavy-user segments dominate consumption—for example, snack foods, soft drinks, beer and wine, and chewing gum. Brands of luxury cars and financial services also compete for common-buyer segments.

When a target audience is narrow and attracts the attention of several major competitors, an advertiser must assess its competitors' spending and the relative share of voice its brand is getting. **Share of voice** is a calculation of any one advertiser's brand expenditures relative to the overall spending in a category:

$$\text{Share of voice} = \frac{\text{one brand's advertising expenditures in a medium}}{\text{total product category advertising expenditures in a medium}}$$

This calculation can be done for all advertising by a brand in relation to all advertising in a product category, or it can be done to determine a brand's share of product category spending on a particular advertising medium, such as network television or magazines. For example, athletic-footwear marketers spend approximately $310 million per year in measured advertising media. Nike and Reebok are the two top brands, with approximately $160 million and $55 million, respectively, in annual expenditures in measured advertising media. The share-of-voice calculations for both brands follow.

$$\text{Share of voice, Nike} = \frac{\$160\text{ million} \times 100}{\$310\text{ million}} = 51.6\%$$

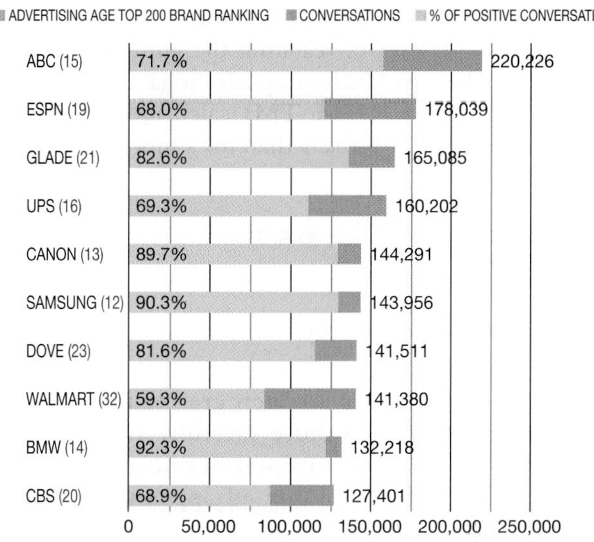

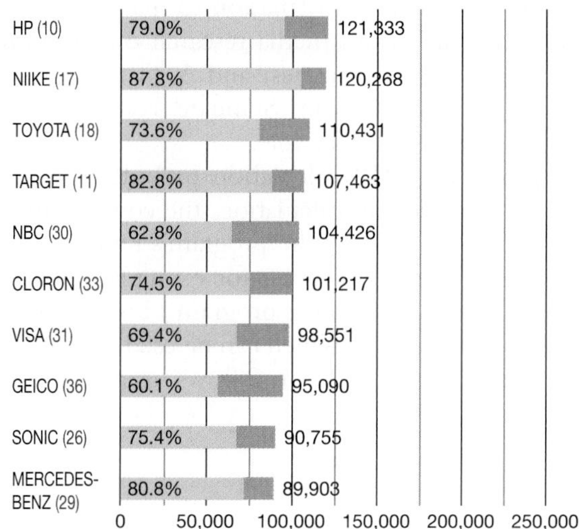

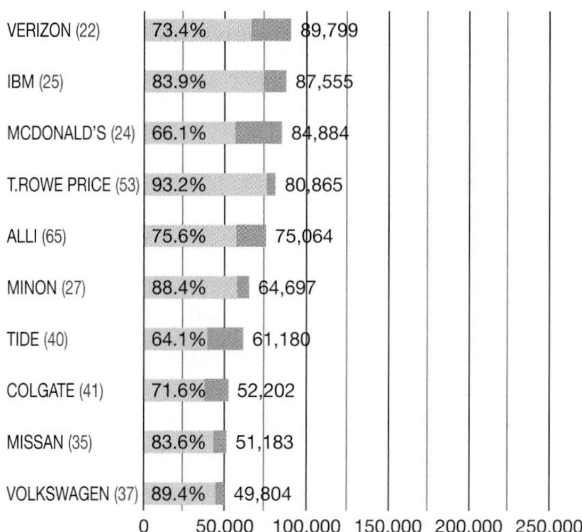

Source: "Apple, Microsoft Are Megabrand Kingpins in Social Radar Index" by Jack Neff, 10/05/2009.

Exhibit 12.12 An industry measure of brand talk volume.

$$\text{Share of voice, Reebok} = \frac{\$55 \text{ million} \times 100}{\$310 \text{ million}} = 17.7\%$$

Together, both brands dominate the product category advertising with a nearly 70 percent combined share of voice. Yet Nike's share of voice is nearly three times that of Reebok.

Research data, such as that provided by Competitive Media Reporting, can provide an assessment of share of voice in up to 10 media categories. A detailed report shows how much a brand was advertised in a particular media category versus the combined media category total for all other brands in the same product category. Knowing what competitors are spending in a medium and how dominant they might be allows an advertiser to strategically schedule within a medium. Some strategists believe that scheduling in and around a competitor's schedule can create a bigger presence for a small advertiser.[5]

Media Efficiency.

The advertiser and the agency team determine which media class is appropriate for the current effort, based on criteria similar to those listed in Exhibit 12.12. These criteria give a general orientation to major media and the inherent capabilities of each media class.

Each medium under consideration in a media plan must be scrutinized for the efficiency with which it performs. In other words, which media deliver the largest target audiences at the lowest cost? A common measure of media efficiency is **cost per thousand (CPM)**, which is the dollar cost of reaching 1,000 (the M in CPM comes from the Roman numeral for 1,000) members of an audience using a particular medium. The CPM calculation can be used to compare the relative efficiency of two media choices within a media class (magazine versus magazine) or between media classes (magazine versus radio). The basic measure of CPM is fairly straightforward; the dollar cost for placement of an ad in a medium is divided by the total audience and multiplied by 1,000. Let's calculate the CPM for a full-page black-and-white ad in the Friday edition of *USA Today*:

$$\text{CPM} = \frac{\text{cost of media buy} \times 1{,}000}{\text{total audience}}$$

$$\text{CPM for } \textit{USA Today} = \frac{\$72{,}000 \times 1{,}000}{5{,}206{,}000} = \$13.83$$

5. Andrea Rothman, "Timing Techniques Can Make Small Ad Budgets Seem Bigger," *The Wall Street Journal*, February 3, 1989, B4; see also Robert J. Kent and Chris T. Allen, "Competitive Interference Effects in Consumer Memory for Advertising: The Role of Brand Familiarity," *Journal of Marketing* (July 1994), 97–105.

These calculations show that *USA Today* has a CPM of $13.83 for a full-page black-and-white ad. But this calculation shows the cost of reaching the entire readership of *USA Today*. If the target audience is college graduates in professional occupations, then the **cost per thousand–target market (CPM–TM)** calculation might be much higher for a general publication such as *USA Today* than for a more specialized publication such as *Fortune* magazine:

$$\text{CPM–TM for } \textit{USA Today} = \frac{\$72{,}000 \times 1{,}0000}{840{,}000} = \$85.71$$

$$\text{CPM–TM for } \textit{Fortune} = \frac{\$54{,}800 \times 1{,}000}{940{,}000} = \$58.30$$

You can see that the relative efficiency of *Fortune* is much greater than that of *USA Today* when the target audience is specified more carefully and a CPM–TM calculation is made. An advertisement for business services appearing in *Fortune* will have a better CPM–TM than the same ad appearing in *USA Today*.

Information about ad cost, gross impressions, and target audience size is usually available from the medium itself. Detailed audience information to make a cost per thousand–target market analysis also is available from media research organizations, such as Simmons Market Research Bureau (for magazines) and A. C. Nielsen (for television). Cost information also can be obtained from Standard Rate and Data Service (SRDS) and Bacon's Media Directories, for example.

Like CPM, a **cost per rating point (CPRP)** calculation provides a relative efficiency comparison between media options. In this calculation, the cost of a media vehicle, such as a spot television program, is divided by the program's rating. (A rating point is equivalent to 1 percent of the target audience—for example, television households in the designated rating area tuned to a specific program.) Like the CPM calculation, the CPRP calculation gives a dollar figure, which can be used for comparing TV program efficiency. The calculation for CPRP is as follows, using television as an example.

$$\text{CPRP} = \frac{\text{dollar cost of ad placement on a program}}{\text{program rating}}$$

For example, an advertiser on WLTV (Univision 23) in the Miami–Ft. Lauderdale market may wish to compare household CPRP figures for 30-second announcements in various dayparts on the station. The calculations for early news and prime-time programs are as follows.

$$\text{CPRP for WLTV early news} = \frac{\$2{,}205}{9} = \$245$$

$$\text{CPRP for WLTV prime time} = \frac{\$5{,}100}{10} = \$510$$

Clearly an early news daypart program delivers households more efficiently at $245 CPRP, less than half that of prime time, with 90 percent of the typical prime-time rating.

It is important to remember that these efficiency assessments are based solely on costs and coverage. They say nothing about the quality of the advertising and thus should not be viewed as indicators of advertising effectiveness. When media efficiency measures such as CPM and CPM–TM are combined with an assessment of media objectives and media strategies, they can be quite useful. Taken alone and out of the broader campaign-planning context, such efficiency measures may lead to ineffective media buying.

Internet Media.

We cover the topic of Internet media in considerable detail in Chapter 14. We devote an entire chapter to it because Internet media has its own terms, its own unique calculation issues. Many Internet portals post their advertising rates. Other good resources include the Interactive Advertising Bureau (www.iab.net) and Iconocast (www.iconocast.com). The most important thing to remember is that these media are fundamentally different in one very major way: with a few exceptions, they are "pull" media. With pull media, the consumer goes looking for the advertiser or advertising and thus "pulls" the advertised brand toward them. This is just the opposite of the traditional "push" media (e.g., a 30-second television ad) in which the brand is "pushed" at the consumer.

Interactive Media.

The media environment has gotten considerably more challenging as interactive media have been refined. First, the term is, in our opinion, overused and imprecise. To be truly interactive, consumers, the media itself, marketers (and other consumers sometimes) have to actually deal with one another in a meaningful way. But for now the term is pretty broad and includes things from kiosks to Internet shopping environments to **RSS (Really Simple Syndication)**. RSS is simply a channel or feed from blogs, podcasts, or other content that the computer user has linked to. Often an aggregator is used to collect, assemble, and deliver the RSS content. Of course, these RSSs are often commercial in nature. Also included are interactive telephones, interactive CDs, online services, the Internet, computer gaming, and online versions of magazines. Absolut Vodka has developed a successful interactive Internet campaign. The confounding factor for media placement decisions is that if consumers truly do begin to spend time with interactive media, they will have less time to spend with traditional media such as television and newspapers. This will force advertisers to choose whether to participate in (or develop their own) interactive media. (Chapter 14 deals exclusively with the Internet, media buying on the Internet, and audience measurement problems.)

The biggest lessons here are (1) this type of advertising and IBP is growing rapidly, and (2) it works, for the most part, in a fundamentally different way: consumers seek out the advertiser/advertising (pull) and then interact (two-way, or multiway communication) with brand communication, rather than the traditional model where ads intrude in programming and seek consumers out. It's more the consumer's choice: The consumer chooses to go there and interact; it is not pushed at them.

Social Media.

Social Networking.

Facebook, MySpace, Twitter, and others have revolutionized the way we think about mediated communication. From the earliest work on brand communities, Muniz and O'Guinn noted that this new paradigm is represented by three nodes rather than the traditional two: marketer-consumer-consumer (see Exhibit 12.13). Consumers talk to other consumers and like to talk to other consumers, and like to talk to other consumers about stuff, consumer stuff. Now, through the Internet, they can, for almost no cost, instantaneously, and with the power of huge numbers. Marketers can use the services for fairly small sums relative to traditional media. Nielsen estimates that two-thirds of Internet users visit a social network or blog site, and that this collectively accounts for about 10% of total Internet traffic. So, clearly, it is important.

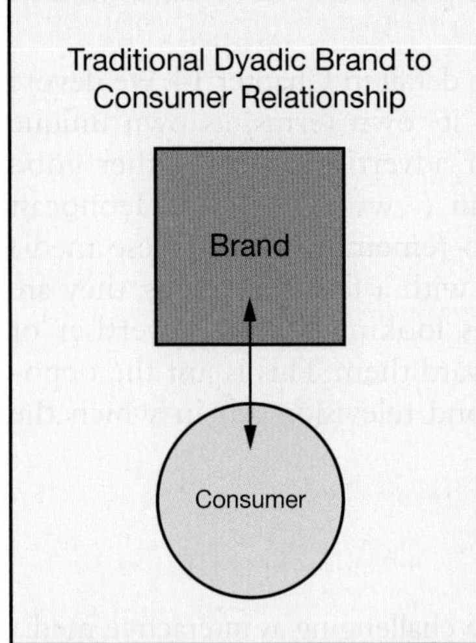

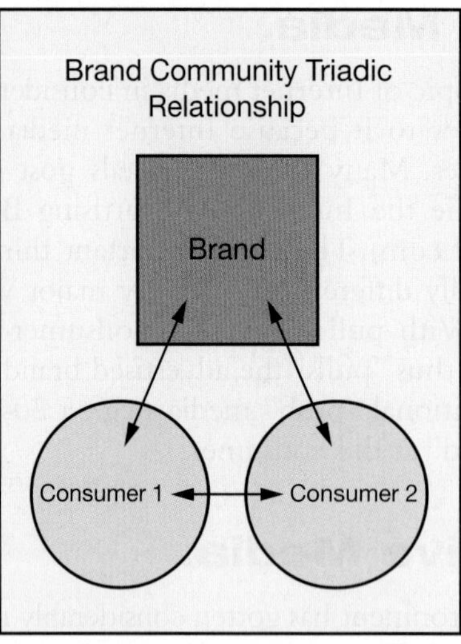

Exhibit 12.13 The World Wide Web has made us re-think the brand-consumer relationship.

So, we know social media are used to discuss brands, and we know that marketers use these media to create buzz and eventual sales for their brands. But, how social media are counted and then priced is still an emerging story. Several companies track conversations about brands on the Web, analyze the data and report various metrics, such as **net promoter scores** (essential good mentions-bad mentions), net volume (how much conversation about a brand in a given period), etc. Exhibit 12.14 shows brand-chat volume for a one-week period. It is fair to say that there will likely be a shake out pretty soon, and the industry will decide on an agreed-upon set of metrics. That has yet to happen. At the time of this writing, several of these metrics, by several companies, are being used. Razorfish (see Exhibit 12.15) does a great job of using social media to discover, design, and implement new media strategies for brands. This very telling quote comes from their website:

> *We hate advertising. But we love brands. Are we crazy? Of course not. We just think that most advertising is designed to shout at people until they pay attention. And we'd*

Exhibit 12.14 The top 15 mega brands, ranked by conversation volume.

Rank	Brand	Conversation Volume	Positive Conversations
1	Apple	921,267	74.6%
2	Microsoft	574,004	78.9%
3	Fox	496,865	61.4%
9	AT&T	476,450	62.1%
24	Dannon	415,751	65.2%
4	Disney	334,655	86.5%
6	Sony	306,763	85.9%
5	Nintendo	303,326	84.3%
7	BlackBerry	264,768	86.9%
8	Ford	237,433	87.6
15	ABC	220,226	71.7%
19	ESPN	178,039	68.0%
21	Glade	165,085	82.6%
16	UPS	160,202	69.3%
13	Canon	144,291	89.7%

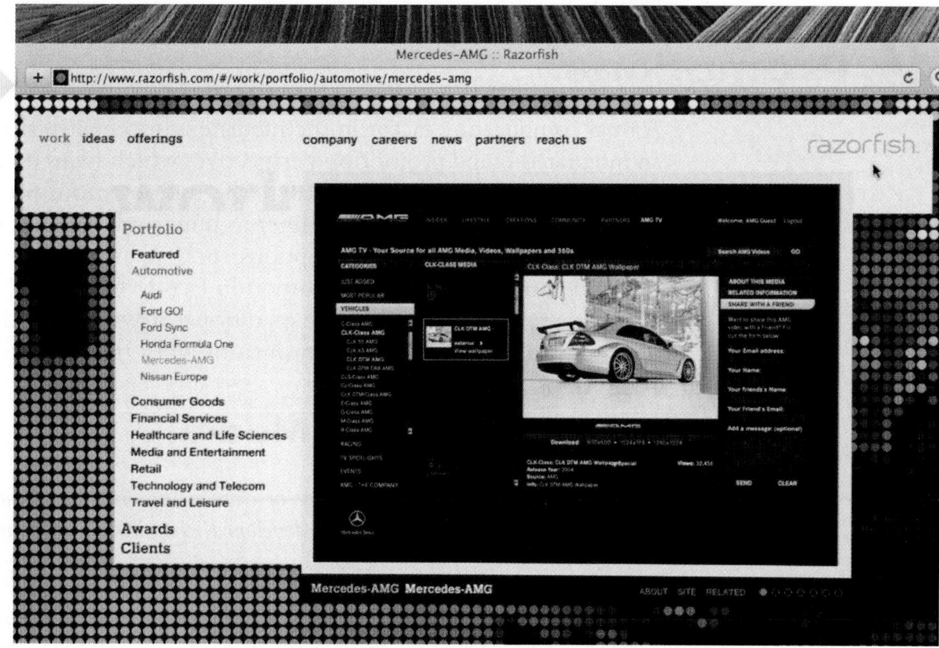

Exhibit 12.15 Razorfish supplies valuable social media metrics for advertisers.

rather not shout. We'd rather just start a compelling conversation between a brand and its customer. Engage customers on their terms, where they hang out. Encourage them to share. Then we'd like to measure whether that conversation made the brand, the publisher and the customer happy. And if it didn't, we'd like to do it better the next time. We think that's the future of advertising.

The Wikia folks (see Exhibit 12.16) also do a great job on mining and leveraging brand community data. Given that there is no agreed-upon exposure or impact measure, pricing is still very much an ad hoc and fairly opaque practice.

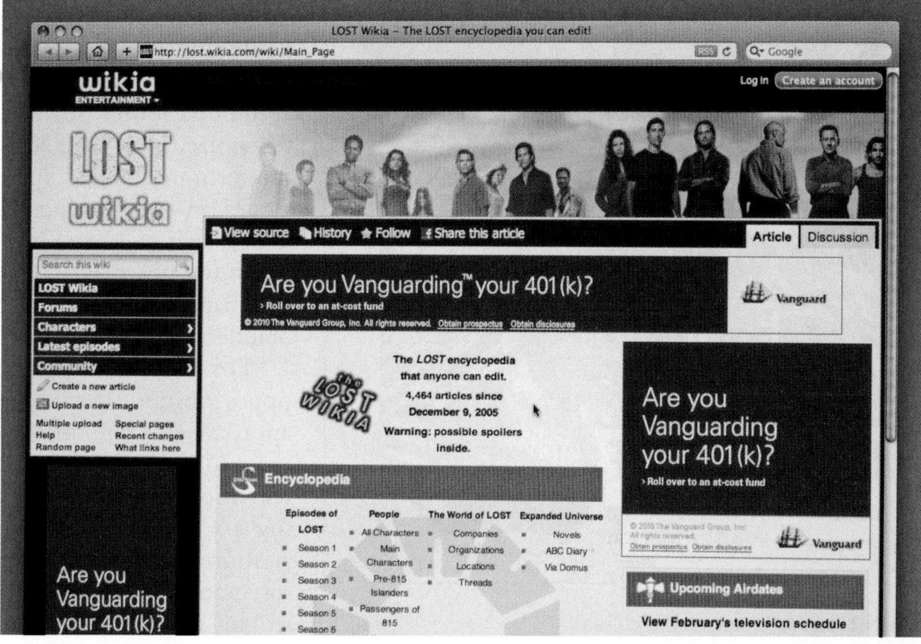

Exhibit 12.16 Wikia is valuable at leveraging brand community.

Courtesy, Omni-Terra Images; Courtesy, Omni-Terra Images

3 Media Choice and Integrated Brand Promotions.

A final complicating factor in the media environment is that more firms are adopting an integrated brand promotion perspective, which relies on a broader mix of communication tools. As you know, IBP is the use of various promotional tools, including advertising, in a coordinated manner to build and maintain brand awareness, identity, and preference. Promotional options such as event sponsorship, direct marketing, branded entertainment, sales promotion (see Exhibit 12.17), and public relations are drawing many firms away from traditional mass media advertising. But even these new approaches still require coordination with the advertising that remains.

Madison & Vine Media.

> *"It's a magnitude and urgency of change that isn't evolutionary—it's transformational.... If a new model isn't developed, the old one will simply collapse."*
>
> —Steven J. Heyer, President and COO, Coca-Cola Co.[6]

This is the chief operating officer of Coca-Cola saying in no uncertain terms that something has to change: 30-second spot advertising just isn't doing it anymore.

The credit for coining the enormously popular term *Madison & Vine* goes to Scott Donaton at *Advertising Age* and his very good book by the same title. The term refers to the combination and meaningful merger of entertainment media and advertising. Even though this is covered elsewhere as well as in the book, let us just say a few things about this very exciting turn of events. This concept is also referred to as branded entertainment. It began, actually long ago, with simple product placements in movies, radio, and then television shows. It actually goes back to the 1920s and 1930s, but it really began to escalate in the late 1980s. The basis for the idea was that traditional advertising was no longer cost effective and that the cost of making and promoting films and music was also out of control. Hollywood, the record industry, and advertising all had a stake in finding a better, less regulated, less expensive, accountable, and more effective means of marketing communications. So, Madison & Vine was born: a recognized, full-fledged attempt to merge media in the form of branded entertainment on television, in games, in retail settings called brandscapes (think of stores such as NikeTown), on mobile phones—all across the board. We discussed the basic mechanism in Chapter 10, but it also is important to consider branded entertainment from the media side of things.

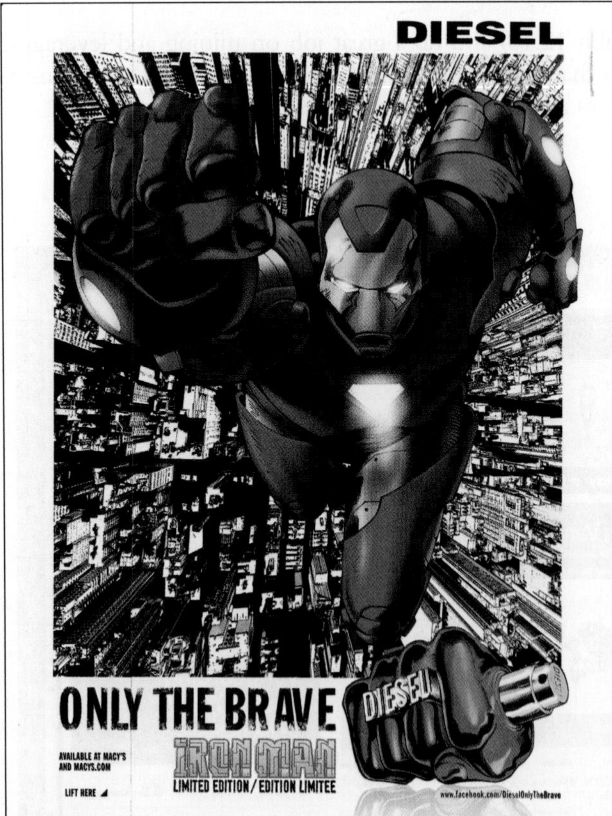

Exhibit 12.17 Iron Man 2 and Diesel.

Courtesy, Susan Van Etten

For clients seeking branded entertainment opportunities, there typically are three primary approaches. The most straightforward and least expensive is product placement. A character on television might be seen drinking Diet Pepsi, driving a Cadillac, or dropping off a FedEx package. A more sophisticated approach involves storyline integration, such as putting a UPS delivery truck in an EA Sports NASCAR game or sending

6. Steven J. Heyer (keynote address, Advertising Age Madison & Vine Conference, Beverly Hills, CA, February 5, 2003).

Ethics

A Mile Wide, an Inch Deep

Social media is bad for you. Social media is, as *The New York Times* recently suggested, really asocial.

According to the Pew Research Center, half of American teenagers "send 50 or more text messages a day and that one third send more than 100 a day." Only one in three said they actually talked face-to-face with a friend daily. Intimacy and "emotional give and take" may be the victims. If the medium is, as Marshal McLuhan famously said, the message, then maybe the staccato style of texting may lead to friendships and other social relationships that are equally quick, surface, and have no time to spare. It is, after all, in childhood that one learns to have relationships, and how to have them.

Advertisers have been blamed for more than their share of social evils. Social networking was not initially driven by branded interests, still isn't. But, as advertisers take more of an active role in social network space, will the supposedly shallow social nature of the medium be the perfect fit for conversations or "relationships" with brands? Maybe this is the kind of relationship we should have with brands... shallow, occasional, and after all, about something that is just a thing... not a person.

Maybe advertising and consumer culture have found their perfect intersection.

Source: Hilary Stout (2010), "Anti-Social Networking," *The New York Times*, May 2, 2010, pp. 1, 10.

the Geico caveman down the red carpet during the Oscars (see Exhibit 12.18). Original content, as when the cavemen graduated to their own primetime show or BMW produced short online film clips featuring their vehicles, is the most expensive, but potentially most compelling, form of branded entertainment. Yet, as Lawson notes, measuring the value of these various forms of branded entertainment is difficult. "We're trying to find meaningful ways to measure this sort of stuff," Lawson says. "Ultimately, the clients still want that, and as they spend more money in that area, they will want to feel more comfortable knowing that their message is getting out there in a meaningful way."[7]

In terms of media measurement: IAG gives scores to the most recalled brand placement.

Nielsen is also in the interactive game. The company measures, among other things, the number of placements in shows (see Chapter 7).

Data Quality.

A problem that gets way too little attention, at least in textbooks, is this: GIGO. This is an old, but still very appropriate, rule in computer data management: garbage in, garbage out. In other words, no matter how much you process data, if it was garbage coming in to the system, it is still garbage going out. In media planning, there is enormous reliance on very sophisticated mathematical models and computer programs to optimize media schedules. But throwing the calculus book at the problem isn't sufficient. We have a big cultural hang-up about numbers. In fact, let us say that again: We have a big cultural hang-up about numbers. When we put a number to something it makes it appear more precise, more scientific, and more certain. But that is often pure illusion. Yes, these optimization programs are good, they are valuable, they save clients billions of dollars—but they also distract attention from a more basic problem: Media exposure data are often just not very good. We are not saying that media data are complete trash, but we are saying that what it means to be exposed to an advertisement is not adequately addressed by most exposure data.

7. Brooke Capps, "The Man Who Brought UPS to NASCAR and Geico Cavemen to Hollywood," *Advertising Age*, May 3, 2007.

Exhibit 12.18 Cavemen and three levels of branded entertainment.

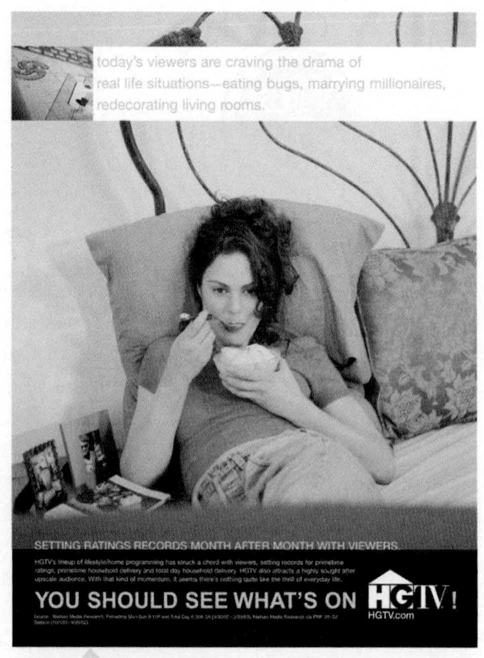

Exhibit 12.19 There are ads for advertising professionals, particularly media buyers. They tell why their particular vehicle is the best at reaching some desired audience.

This is a sad reality, and one that is well known but rarely acknowledged until fairly recently. With the radically changing media landscape, clients are less willing to pay for, or rely on, an even highly "optimized" media schedule when the data going into those calculations are highly suspect. There are now too many other games in town with better and more meaningful exposure estimates and ROIs to have to pay for poor data. This is now a common industry complaint. It is almost at crisis stage.

Think about it: Is being in the room when a TV is on sufficient to say you were exposed to the ad? Did you see it in any meaningful way? Shouldn't "exposure" be more, mean more than that? Well, sure it should. But the media measurement companies argue that (1) it's the best we have, (2) everyone is playing by the same rules, and if you use the measures simply to judge *relative* strengths, then they are OK, and (3) they are always working on better methods. They are right about the second point: If used only for relative measurement (one schedule against another), exposure data are probably reasonably good. Unfortunately, most exposure data in all mass media are a long way from capturing and delivering what it means to see or hear an ad. You need to keep this in mind when you see all those precise-looking numbers.

Another thing that is generally poorly covered: How do media vehicles sell themselves to advertisers and advertising agencies? What is the role of this business-to-business (B2B) advertising? Well, it's a big effort, and a big role. Media companies spend lots of money selling their time and space to advertisers through their ad agencies. Pick up any issue of *Ad Age* and count the ads. Who is spending the money? Exhibit 12.19 is a pretty creative ad for media vehicles placed in *Ad Age* to attract advertisers. This is an important part of the real world of advertising and IBP media.

5 Computer Media Planning Models.

The explosion of available data on markets and consumers has motivated media planners to rely heavily on electronic databases, computers, and software to assist with the various parts of the media planning effort.

Nearly all of the major syndicated research services offer electronic data to their subscribers, including advertisers, agencies, and media organizations. These databases contain information helpful in identifying target markets and audiences, estimating or projecting media vehicle audiences and costs, and analyzing competitive advertising activity, among many others. Companies that offer data electronically, such as Nielsen, Arbitron, MRI, SMRB, Scarborough, and the Audit Bureau of Circulations, also typically provide software designed to analyze their own data. Such software often produces summary reports, tabulations, ranking, reach-frequency analysis, optimization, simulation, scheduling, buying, flowcharts, and a variety of graphical presentations.

Advertisers that use a mix of media in their advertising campaigns often subscribe to a variety of electronic data services representing the media they use or consider using. However, the various syndicated services do not provide standardized data, reports, and analyses that are necessarily comparable across media categories. Also, individual syndicated service reports and analyses may not offer the content and depth that some users prefer. Nor do they typically analyze media categories that they do not measure. Consequently, media software houses such as Interactive Market Systems (IMS) and Telmar Information Services Corporation (Telmar) offer hundreds of specialized and standardized software products that help advertisers, agencies, and media organizations worldwide develop and evaluate markets, audiences, and multimedia plans. Exhibit 12.20 shows typical screens from one such computer

ADplus(TM) RESULTS: SPOT TV (30S)
Walt Disney World
Off-Season Promotion
Monthly
Target: 973,900
Jacksonville DMA Adults

Message/vehicle = 32.0%

Frequency (f) Distributions

f	VEHICLE % f+	% f+	MESSAGE % f	% f+
0	5.1	-	9.1	-
1	2.0	94.9	7.5	90.9
2	2.2	92.9	8.1	83.4
3	2.3	90.7	8.1	75.2
4	2.4	88.3	7.8	67.1
5	2.4	85.9	7.2	59.3
6	2.5	83.5	6.6	52.1
7	2.5	81.0	6.0	45.5
8	2.5	78.5	5.3	39.5
9	2.5	76.0	4.7	34.2
10+	73.5	73.5	29.5	29.5
20+	49.8	49.8	6.1	6.1

Summary Evaluation

	Vehicle	Message
Reach 1+ (%)	94.9%	90.9%
Reach 1+ (000s)	923.9	885.3
Reach 3+ (%)	90.7%	75.2%
Reach 3+ (000s)	882.9	732.8
Gross rating points (GRPs)	2,340.0	748.8
Average frequency (f)	24.7	8.2
Gross impressions (000s)	22,789.3	7,292.6
Cost-per-thousand (CPM)	6.10	19.06
Cost-per-rating point (CPP)	59	186

Vehicle List	RATING	AD COST	CPM-MSG	ADS	TOTAL COST	MIX %
WJKS-ABC-AM	6.00	234	12.51	30	7,020	5.1
WJXT-CBS-AM	6.00	234	12.51	30	7,020	5.1
WTLV-NBC-AM	6.00	234	12.51	30	7,020	5.1
WJKS-ABC-DAY	5.00	230	14.76	60	13,800	9.9
WJXT-CBS-DAY	5.00	230	14.76	60	13,800	9.9
WTLV-NBC-DAY	5.00	230	14.76	60	13,800	9.9
WJKS-ABC-PRIM	10.00	850	27.27	30	25,500	18.4
WJXT-CBS-PRIM	10.00	850	27.27	30	25,500	18.4
WTLV-NBC-PRIM	10.00	850	27.27	30	25,500	18.4
		Totals:	19.06	360	138,960	100.0

ADplus(TM) RESULTS: DAILY NEWSPAPERS (1/2 PAGE), SPOT TV (30S)
Walt Disney World
Off-Season Promotion
Monthly
Target: 973,900
Jacksonville DMA Adults

Message/vehicle = 28.1%

Frequency (f) Distributions

f	VEHICLE % f+	% f+	MESSAGE % f	% f+
0	1.2	-	4.0	-
1	0.8	98.8	4.9	96.0
2	0.9	98.0	5.9	91.1
3	0.9	97.2	6.5	85.2
4	1.0	96.2	6.7	78.7
5	1.1	95.2	6.8	72.0
6	1.1	94.2	6.6	65.2
7	1.2	93.0	6.3	58.6
8	1.3	91.8	5.9	52.4
9	1.3	90.6	5.5	46.5
10+	89.3	89.3	41.0	41.0
20+	73.3	73.3	9.6	9.6

Summary Evaluation

	Vehicle	Message
Reach 1+ (%)	98.8%	96.0%
Reach 1+ (000s)	962.6	934.6
Reach 3+ (%)	97.2%	85.2%
Reach 3+ (000s)	946.5	829.7
Gross rating points (GRPs)	3,372.0	948.0
Average frequency (f)	34.1	9.9
Gross impressions (000s)	32,839.9	9,232.3
Cost-per-thousand (CPM)	10.96	38.99
Cost-per-rating point (CPP)	107	380

Vehicle List	RATING	AD COST	CPM-MSG	ADS	TOTAL COST	MIX %
1 Daily Newspapers		Totals:	114.00	80	221,040	61.4
Times-Union	42.00	8,284	104.93	20	165,680	46.0
Record	4.00	866	115.18	20	17,320	4.8
News	3.20	926	153.95	20	18,520	5.1
Reporter	2.40	976	216.35	20	19,520	5.4
2 Spot TV (30s)		Totals:	19.00	360	138,960	38.6
WJKS-ABC-AM	6.00	234	12.51	30	7,020	2.0
WJXT-CBS-AM	6.00	234	12.51	30	7,020	2.0
WTLV-NBC-AM	6.00	234	12.51	30	7,020	2.0
WJKS-ABC-DAY	5.00	230	14.76	60	13,800	3.8
WJXT-CBS-DAY	5.00	230	14.76	60	13,800	3.8
WTLV-NBC-DAY	5.00	230	14.76	60	13,800	3.8
WJKS-ABC-PRIM	10.00	850	27.27	30	25,500	7.1
WJXT-CBS-PRIM	10.00	850	27.27	30	25,500	7.1
WTLV-NBC-PRIM	10.00	850	27.27	30	25,500	7.1
		Totals:	38.99	440	360,000	100.0

Exhibit 12.20 The explosion of data about markets and consumers has caused advertisers to rely more on computerized media planning tools.

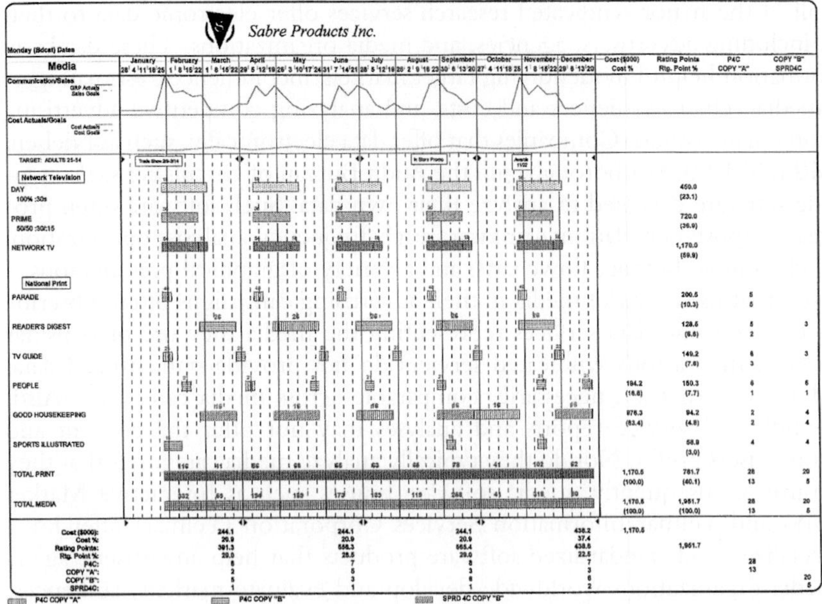

Source: Telmar Information Services Corp., FlowMaster for Windows™ New York, 1999. Reprinted with permission.

Exhibit 12.21 A media flowchart gives an advertiser a visual representation of the overall media plan.

program. The first screen is reach and cost data for spot TV ads, and the second screen is the combined reach and cost data for spot TV and newspaper ads.

Computerization and modeling can never substitute for planning and judgment by media strategists. Computer modeling does, however, allow for the assessment of a wide range of possibilities before making costly media buys. It can, and does, save advertisers a lot of money.

One of the most important aspects of the media-scheduling phase involves creating a visual representation of the media schedule. Exhibit 12.21 shows a media schedule flowchart that includes both print and electronic media placement. With this visual representation of the schedule, the advertiser has tangible documentation of the overall media plan.

Making the Buy.

Once an overall media plan and schedule are in place, the focus must turn to **media buying**. Media buying entails securing the electronic media time and print media space specified in the schedule. An important part of the media-buying process is the agency of record. The **agency of record** is the advertising agency chosen by the advertiser to purchase time and space. The agency of record coordinates media discounts and negotiates all contracts for time and space. Any other agencies involved in the advertising effort submit insertion orders for time and space within those contracts.

Each spring, television programming and ad execs participate in a ritual called the "**upfronts**." The upfronts is a period where the television networks reveal their fall line-ups and pre-sell advertising on them. About 75 percent of prime time television advertising is bought this way, in advance. Only the remaining 25 percent is really "in play" for the season. There are all sorts of unofficial rules in this ritual. Viewed from the outside, it's much like a typical American trying to understand cricket. Let's just say it's played a bit like poker—you can see some cards for free; others will cost you. Whatever the best game metaphor, it looks like the TV networks are not getting as much premium pricing as they use to. Why? It's the TV clutter, TiVo, branded entertainment, competition from computer-delivered entertainment, and its very high price. Several media soothsayers predict the end of the upfronts within the next decade. Personally, we think they will probably still be around.

Rather than using an agency of record, some advertisers use a **media-buying service**, which is an independent organization that specializes in buying large blocks of media time and space and reselling it to advertisers. Some agencies and companies have developed their own media-buying units (e.g., GM's GMplanworks) to control both the planning and the buying process. Regardless of the structure used to make the buys, media buyers evaluate the audience reach, CPM, and timing of each buy. The organization responsible for the buy also monitors the ads and estimates the actual audience reach delivered. If the expected audience is not delivered, then media organizations have to *make good* by repeating ad placements or offering a refund or price reduction on future ads. For example, making good to advertisers because of shortfalls in delivering the 1998 Winter Olympics prime-time cost CBS an estimated 400 additional 30-second spots.[8]

6 In Defense of Traditional Advertising.

Even though it is absolutely undeniable that the world of media advertising and promotion has changed a great deal, we would like to throw a bit of cold water (maybe more like a light mist) on the media revolution. Traditional advertising, even the "30 Net-TV" (30-second network television) ad, is not dead. They still perform a very valuable function. There are just some things you can't accomplish without them, like a Super Bowl or the Olympics: delivering to the truly mass audience. Sometimes their unique qualities get lost in the optimized promotional numbers. Brand building still needs traditional ads, at least for a while longer. Yet the traditional ad world has learned that it can never rest on its laurels, nor can the traditional media. But throwing around planning buzzwords doesn't work either.

Summary

1 Describe the important changes that have altered the advertising and IBP media landscape, such as agency compensation, ROI demands, globalization, and multicultural media.

The demise of the 15 percent commission means that there is less economic incentive for agencies to buy media advertising. With more media of all sorts of advertising and IBP out there, dollars get spread around a lot more than they used to. The consolidated media buying allows agencies to get better deals and exert more power on the media. Still, agencies now operate with fewer staff to do even bigger jobs, thus making the newer and more lucrative types of media more attractive than traditional media. Globalization of media is exerting considerable pressure on the industry to standardize media measurement across the globe. Consumers who are spoiled by free content are less and less interested in obtrusive advertising, thus favoring alternative pull communications forms going forward. The increasing deal-proneness and cost transparency provided by the Internet has made consumers considerably more powerful in their ability to get consumer information without having to rely on traditional media advertising. Add to this the incredibly ad-cluttered state of traditional media, and you can see why nothing in advertising media is sacred, nothing. Don't forget the growing influence of multicultural media available across the globe. It's a new world of media out there. Last, but far from least, advertisers are now demanding greater accountability and documented return on investment (ROI) from their media buys, traditional or new media.

2 Describe the fundamentals of media planning.

Although many important changes are taking place in the advertising industry, the components of the media-planning process remain essentially the same. A media plan specifies the media vehicles that will be used to deliver the advertiser's message. Developing a media plan entails setting objectives such as effective reach and frequency and determining strategies to achieve those objectives. Media planners use several quantitative indicators, such as CPM and CPRP, to help them judge the efficiency of prospective media choices. The media planning process culminates in the scheduling and purchase of a mix of media vehicles expected to deliver the advertiser's message to specific target audiences at precisely the right time to affect their consumption decisions. Although media planning is a methodical process, it cannot be reduced to computer decision-making models and statistical measurements; data quality and human and personal factors prohibit media planning from being an exact science.

3 Know the bottom line of IBP's impact on media planning.

There is a very real possibility of a continued decline in advertising's reliance on traditional media. IBP efforts that rely on database efforts are very attractive due to their highly selective targeting and measured response. It's also true that better and better measures of advertising

8. "CBS Faces Olympics Make-Goods," www.adage.com, February 19, 1998.

effectiveness will be required with more reliance on IBP. To work in the contemporary ad and IBP environment, you will have to know a lot about a much wider array of "media." Further, central control of these far-flung promotional efforts is a must. Things can really get away from you in this new environment.

4 Discuss the "data quality problem" in media planning.

In the real ad and IBP world, there is an illusion of precision because of all the numbers used. In reality there is a lot of slop in the media measurement system. Data quality is just not all that great. They are good enough for some purposes, but don't be fooled into thinking numbers equal truth. Not so. Bad measurement is still bad measurement no matter how many computers crunch the data. Also, a lot of real-world media planning comes from ads for advertisers. Media planners are the target market of lots of ads for lots of media outlets. And never forget the power of the media lunch: the "free lunch" or cocktail party hosted by your friendly media rep. That's how a lot of media get planned. That's the truth.

5 Discuss the essentials of the contemporary media planning environment.

You should know the particular measurement demands and essential terms of Internet media. You should also know the importance of share-of-voice calculations; they allow you to see, across all kinds of contemporary media, what percent your brand's spending is of the total category, and they provide quick and easy competitive comparisons. You should also understand that standard practice these days involves the uses of computer-media models that optimize media schedules for the most mathematically cost-efficient media buy. This should be used as a tool, but not a substitute for media strategy. You should also understand that the growing category of interactive media demands special attention from media planners and will probably make traditional media less important over time. You should also know that more and more media buys are made by a stand-alone media buying company.

6 Discuss the value of traditional advertising.

A lot of very smart, creative, and powerful people believe in traditional advertising, and don't see it going away... at all, ever.

Key Terms

deal-proneness
price/cost transparency
above-the-line promotion
measured media
below-the-line promotion
unmeasured media
media plan
media class
media vehicle
media mix
single-source tracking services
geographic scope
geo-targeting
reach
frequency
effective frequency
effective reach
message weight
gross impressions
between-vehicle duplication
within-vehicle duplication
continuity
continuous scheduling
flighting
pulsing
forgetting function
square root law
context effects
share of voice
cost per thousand (CPM)
cost per thousand–target market (CPM–TM)
cost per rating point (CPRP)
RSS (Really Simple Syndication)
net promoter scores
media buying
agency of record
upfronts
media-buying service

Questions

1. The opening section of this chapter describes radical changes that have taken place in the world of media planning. Compare and contrast the way things used to be and the way they are now. What factors contributed to this shift? Do you think the job of media planning has become more or less complicated? Explain.

2. Of all the changes taking place in the world of media planning, which do you think will continue to have the greatest impact on the future of the advertising industry?

3. The proliferation of media options has created increasing complexities for media planners, but useful distinctions can still be made concerning the relative standing of the different choices available to advertisers. What advertising and brand promotion options dominate the "big pie" of total promotion options? Who is doing the most ad spending?

4. Media plans should of course take a proactive stance with respect to customers. Explain how geo-targeting can be used in making a media plan more proactive with respect to customers.

5. Media strategy models allow planners to compare the impact of different media plans, using criteria such as reach, frequency, and gross impressions. What other kinds of criteria should a planner take into account before deciding on a final plan?

6. Review the mathematics of the CPM and CPRP calculations, and explain how these two indicators can be used to assess the efficiency and effectiveness of a media schedule.

7. Why is data quality becoming an increasingly important issue in real-world media planning?

8. In the real world, do media planners always make strategic decisions based on sophisticated data, or are there other influences that sway their media-buying decisions? Explain.

9. How has the increased emphasis on branded entertainment and the meteoric rise in popularity of social networking sites, such as Facebook, influenced media planning?

10. Discuss the issues raised in this chapter that represent challenges for those who champion integrated brand promotions. Why would central control be required for achieving IBP? If media planners wish to play the role of central controller, what must they do to qualify for the role?

Experiential Exercises

1. When BP needed to reach the public about oil gushing from the Deepwater Horizon rig in the Gulf of Mexico, the company developed an interesting media strategy. In addition to allocating $50 million for TV ads, BP spent an estimated $1 million per month to purchase search engine key words like "oil spill," "Gulf spill," and other related terms. When keyed in at popular search engines, the words directed audiences to BP's disaster-response website. Using the Internet, search for key words related to one or more of your favorite products. Identify sponsored links that appear among search results, and click to see where those links lead. Which brands are getting top spots in the paid search results? Where do the sponsored links take Web users, and for what purpose? Is this an effective form of advertising for these brands? Why or why not?

2. The proliferation of media options, in combination with the trend towards longer ads, is leading some analysts to predict the end of the traditional 30-second television spot. Using the Internet, identify and review two or three video ads that extend well beyond the length of the 30-second traditional spot. Do you think the longer ads are more compelling and engaging than a traditional television spot? What goals might advertisers have for the ads? In your view, did the length of the ads help advertisers achieve their goals? Explain.

3. Assume that you are advising a regional snack-food manufacturer whose brands have a low share of voice. Which pattern of continuity would you recommend for such an advertiser? Would you place your ads in television program that is also sponsored by competing national brands such as Pringles or Doritos? Why or why not?

4. As discussed in the chapter, context is a critical part of the media planning equation. To better understand context effects, obtain recent copies of *Sports Illustrated*, *InStyle*, and *The New Yorker*. For each magazine, what are the primary types of brands, products, and services advertised? What similarities do you find between brands and their ad messages within each magazine? What social meaning does the magazine itself lend to the advertisers? Also list five examples of brands, products, or services you would least expect to advertise in each magazine and explain why.

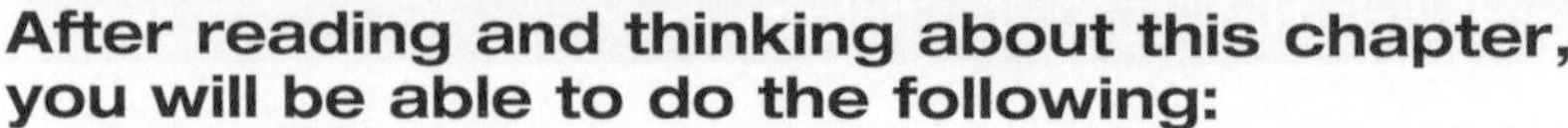

After reading and thinking about this chapter, you will be able to do the following:

1. Understand the changes taking place in the traditional "mass" media of newspapers, magazines, television, and radio relative to new digital media options.
2. Detail the pros and cons of newspapers as a media class, identify newspaper categories, and describe buying and audience measurement for newspapers.
3. Detail the pros and cons of magazines as a media class, identify magazine categories, and describe buying and audience measurement for magazines.
4. Detail the pros and cons of television as a media class, identify television categories, and describe buying and audience measurement for television.
5. Detail the pros and cons of radio as a media class, identify radio categories, and describe audience measurement for radio.

Courtesy, Susan Van Etten

1 Introductory Scenario: The Present and Future World of "Traditional" Mass Media.

In Chapters 1 and 2 we discussed that the advertising industry as a whole continues to evolve and change in very significant ways. No place is that change more tangible or dramatic than in the traditional media of newspapers, magazines, television, and radio. For 75 years, choosing media to deliver advertising messages has been a fairly simple and straightforward process. Advertisers would work with their advertising agencies to develop messages for their brands. Then the agencies would negotiate for airtime with television and radio networks or space with newspapers and magazines. Most of these media options were owned by a few big media companies.

Well, it just doesn't work like that anymore. The last decade has been one of unprecedented change in media options and applications. Consumers have turned to multiple new sources of information and entertainment and are more active in their media choice and patronage. User-generated content from blogs, wikis, and social media sites now offer "non-commercial" information about brands and brand experiences—and the future portends that change will continue. As a result, advertisers are turning more often to digital media that offer new, different, and cost-effective ways to reach target markets. In addition, digital media allow advertisers to make rapid changes in campaigns changes that might take months to accomplish with traditional media. And let's not forget that a digital campaign can be a global campaign if the advertiser chooses to make it so—a monumental task in traditional media.

The advantages of digital media are changing not only advertisers' perceptions of how to develop effective campaigns but also the way they are spending their money on media. Digital/interactive advertising is now a $30 billion industry, or about 14 percent of total U.S. spending on advertising and promotion, up from just 4 percent in 2004.[1] The other important change is that media companies are catching on to the fact that the old traditional way of delivering content through traditional mass media (and the ads that supported that content) are fading. One example is that total advertising dollars spent on newspapers by advertisers has dropped from 23 percent of all ad spending to just 16 percent—taking literally billions of dollars of revenue away from newspaper publishers.[2] Now, Google and Yahoo! offer precisely targeted local ads (the power of newspapers in the past), craigslist.com has free classified ads, and news information is free *everywhere* on the Web. In response, newspaper companies are making aggressive moves into interactive media to shore up flagging revenues.[3]

Even though newspapers have been particularly hard hit by digital media, television companies are feeling the pinch as well—and responding with their own makeovers. Consider the case of CBS, the 60-plus-year-old traditional media television network (you know, the folks that bring you all the *CSI* programs). CBS owns CBS.com, TV.com, Gamespot, and CNET—all interactive television programming sites. In addition, the network has other online media organizations like music-based social network Last.fm and financial video start-up Wallstrip. The reason for all these modern media maneuvers by an old-style media company: CBS wants ad revenue coming in from as many sources as possible related to the ways people are seeking information in this new media environment. So far, it seems to be working. Digital revenue is growing and now represents about 10 percent of CBS's overall revenue.[4]

1. Emily Steel, "Advertising's Brave New World," *The Wall Street Journal*, May 25, 2007, B1, B3; Forrester Research, Inc., "U.S. Interactive Marketing Forecast, 2009–2014," July 30, 2009, 7.

2. *Advertising Age*, "100 Leading National Advertisers," June 21, 2010, 22.

3. Abbey Klaassen, "How Scripps Turned into a Digital Darling," *Advertising Age*, January 22, 2007, 3, 23; Nat Ives, "Print Veterans Looking to Go Digital Learn It's Tough to Make the Switch," *Advertising Age*, March 22, 2010, 3, 22.

4. Jon Fine, "Not Bad, for a TV Network," *BusinessWeek*, June 25, 2007, 24; *Advertising Age*, "Media Family Trees 2009," October 5, 2009 available at www.adage.com, Data Center.

Big traditional media companies like CBS *have* to get into new media because of the way advertisers are setting their media strategies. Consider the way Delta Air Lines designed its advertising campaign for the firm's emergence from bankruptcy. First, the company enlisted the services of traditional ad agency SS&K and digital marketing company Publicis Modem. The two agencies worked out the message, images, and story line for the Delta campaign. Then SS&K developed a traditional media campaign (primarily print media—see Exhibit 13.1) and Publicis designed different ads for online media, including banner ads and emails to frequent fliers. The new digital media campaign also included a social networking site and the purchase of paid search terms so that Delta would list high on any Google or Yahoo! consumer searches.[5]

The media environment is by no means settled into any predictable structure, and media companies on all sides of the "digital divide" are scrambling to properly position themselves for the new ways consumers seek out brand information. One thing is for sure. Traditional media still command the majority of all ad dollars. So, no matter how exciting and attention-getting digital/interactive media are, they still take a back seat (in terms of advertiser dollars) to newspapers, magazines, television, and radio. The discussions that follow will give you an overview of these traditional mass media options so that you'll be aware of the options available to advertisers as they plan their brand advertising strategies. The next chapter, Chapter 14,"Media Planning: Advertising and IBP in Digital/Interactive Media," addresses the digital media options specifically and comprehensively.

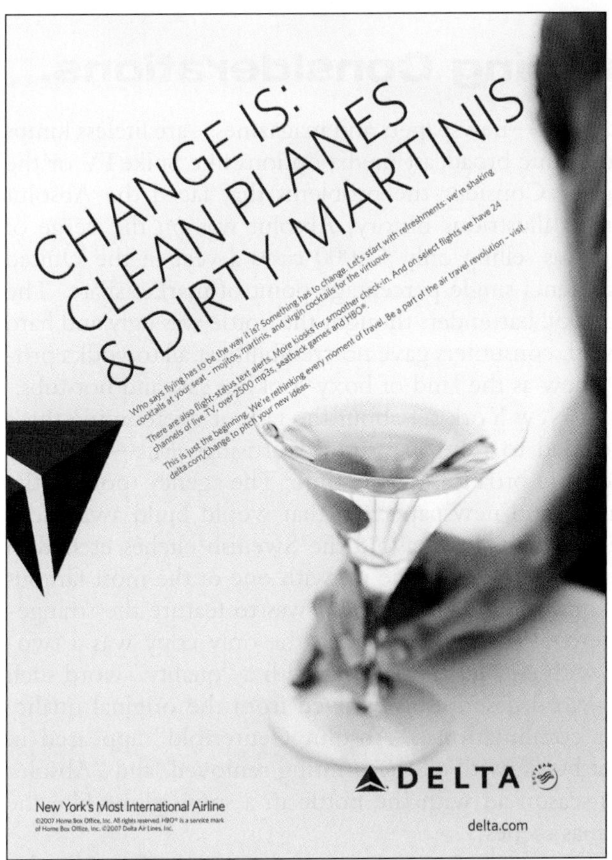

Exhibit 13.1 Delta used both the traditional medium of magazines and online digital media for the airline's advertising/IBP campaign as it emerged from bankruptcy.

Courtesy, Delta Airlines. Created by SS+K, a creatively-driven, strategic communications firm.

Which Media? Strategic Planning Considerations.

Media decisions made by advertisers are critically important for two reasons. First, advertisers need media to reach the audiences that are likely to buy their brands. Not much of a mystery there. Second, when advertisers choose their media, these choices ultimately determine which media companies earn the billions of dollars spent on newspaper, magazine, television/cable, and radio advertising slots.

In Chapter 12, "Media Planning Essentials," you gained an overall perspective on all classes of media. This chapter focuses on the challenge advertisers face in evaluating the major print and broadcast media options as key ways to reach audiences. As the discussion of media planning in the previous chapter emphasized, even great advertising can't achieve communications and sales objectives if the media placement misses the target audience.

Our discussion of print, television, and radio media will concentrate on several key aspects of using these major traditional mass media. With respect to the print media—newspapers and magazines—we'll first consider the advantages and disadvantages of the media themselves. Both newspapers and magazines have inherent capabilities and limitations that advertisers must take into consideration in building a media plan.

5. Steel, "Advertising's Brave New World." Ibid.

Next, we'll look at the types of newspapers and magazines from which advertisers can choose. Finally, we will identify buying procedures and audience measurement techniques.

After we look at the print media, we will consider television and radio in the same way. First, the types of television and radio options are described. Next, the advantages and disadvantages of television and radio are considered and the buying procedures and audience measurement techniques are identified. Finally, the future of television and radio in the context of new Internet, satellite, and broadband technology is considered.

Print, television, and radio media represent major traditional alternatives available to advertisers for reaching audiences. As the introductory scenario to this chapter points out, there is significant spending on new media—and huge energy and excitement around the prospects for new media. But, let's not lose perspective—over 80 percent of all advertising dollars in the United States still go to traditional print, radio, and television media![6] In addition, the vast majority of the creative effort—and money—is expended on print and broadcast advertising campaigns. Despite the many intriguing opportunities that new digital media might offer, print and broadcast media will likely form a significant foundation for most advertising campaigns. There are certain objectives advertising can achieve—particularly creative goals—only with these traditional mass media that digital media simply cannot match. The discussions in this chapter will demonstrate why these media represent such rich and necessary communication alternatives for advertisers.

Print Media—Strategic Planning Considerations.

You might think that the print media—newspapers and magazines—are lifeless lumps and lack impact compared to dynamic broadcast media options like SpikeTV or the Discovery Channel. Think again. Consider the problems that faced the Absolut Vodka brand. At one point in its illustrious history, Absolut was on the verge of extinction. The Swedish brand was selling only 12,000 cases a year in the United States—not enough to register even a single percentage point of market share. The name Absolut was seen as gimmicky; bartenders thought the bottle was ugly and hard to pour from; and to top things off, consumers gave no credibility at all to vodka produced in Sweden, which they knew as the land of boxy-looking cars and hot tubs.

TBWA advertising agency in New York set about the task of overcoming these liabilities of the brand and decided to rely on print advertising *alone*—primarily because spirits ads were banned from broadcast at the time. The agency took on the challenge of developing magazine and newspaper ads that would build awareness, communicate quality, achieve credibility, and avoid the Swedish clichés etched in the minds of American consumers. The firm came up with one of the most famous and successful print campaigns of all time. The concept was to feature the strange-shaped Absolut bottle as the hero of each ad, in which the only copy was a two-word tagline always beginning with *Absolut* and ending with a "quality" word such as *perfection* or *clarity*. The two-word description evolved from the original quality concept to a variety of clever combinations. "Absolut Centerfold" appeared in *Playboy* and featured an Absolut bottle with all the printing removed, and "Absolut Wonderland" was a Christmas-season ad with the bottle in a snow globe like the ones that feature snowy Christmas scenes.

In the end, the Absolut campaign was not only a creative masterpiece but also a resounding market success—using print media alone, without the flashier television or digital media. Absolut has become one of the leading imported vodkas in the United States. The vodka with no credibility and the ugly bottle became

6. *Advertising Age*, "100 Leading National Advertisers," June 21, 2010, 10.

sophisticated and fashionable with a well-conceived and well-placed print campaign.[7] To this day, the Absolut brand still relies heavily on magazine advertising in the IBP mix with continued success.

Newspapers.

The newspaper is the still a medium accessible to a wide range of advertisers. Advertisers big and small—even you and I when we want to sell that old bike or snowboard—can use newspaper advertising. In fact, annual investment in newspaper advertising now stands at about $21 billion—only behind network television and magazines—and about the same as spending on Internet display advertising.[8] Exhibit 13.2 shows the top 10 advertisers in newspapers. Several national newspapers reach primarily business audiences. Newspapers are, of course, ideally suited to reaching a narrow geographic area—precisely the type of audience retailers want to reach.

There are some sad truths, however, about the current status of newspapers as a medium. Since the 1980s, newspapers across the United States have been suffering circulation declines, and the trend has continued into the 21st century. Note that this decline in readership and circulation is reflected in the fact that 60 percent of the advertisers in Exhibit 13.2 have reduced their newspaper spending—significantly.

What may be worse is that the percentage of adults reading daily newspapers is also declining. Only about 30 percent of adults in the United States read a printed daily newspaper, compared with about 78 percent in 1970.[9] Much of the decline in both circulation and readership comes from the fact that newspapers have been losing patronage to television news programs and Internet news sites. Although shows such as *Good Morning America* and *CNN News* cannot provide the breadth of coverage that newspapers can, they still offer news, and they offer it in a lively multisensory format. On the Internet, news seekers can access news 24/7, not just when a newspaper is delivered. Newspapers' foray into digital media has been somewhat

Exhibit 13.2 Top 10 newspaper advertisers (U.S. dollars in millions).

2009 Rank	Marketer	2009	% Change from 2008
1	General Motors	632.0	110.6
2	Macy's	536.1	-8.1
3	Verizon Communications	475.5	-30.3
4	AT&T	257.9	-10.7
5	Fry's Electronics	206.9	0.9
6	News Corp.	201.0	2.2
7	Procter & Gamble	187.7	2.4
8	Sears Holdings Corp.	168.3	-12.0
9	Target Corp.	146.6	-8.9
10	Kohl's Corp.	136.5	-11.2

Source: *Advertising Age*, June 21, 2010, 14.

7. Historical information about the Absolut Vodka campaign was adapted from information in Nicholas Ind, "Absolut Vodka in the U.S.," in *Great Advertising Campaigns* (Lincolnwood, IL: NTC Business Books, 1993), 15–32.

8. Advertising Age, "100 Leading National Advertisers," June 21, 2010, 22.

9. Data on newspaper readership are available at the Newspaper Association of America and the Pew Research Center for the People & the Press: websites, www.nnn-naa.com and www.people-press.org. Data cited here were drawn from those sites on April 9, 2010.

successful. Web readers of newspapers has grown to 9 percent of the adult population. But, Web readership of newspapers has not been great enough to offset the overall decline in newspaper readership. But, recent moves by both newspapers and magazines into digital media do provide a broader, global audience as the *Globalization* box shows.

Advantages of Newspapers. Newspapers may have lost some of their luster during the past four decades, but they still do reach about a third of U.S. households, representing about 100 million adults. And, as mentioned earlier, the newspaper is still an excellent medium for retailers targeting local geographic markets. But broad reach isn't the only attractive feature of newspapers as a medium. Newspapers offer other advantages to advertisers:

Geographic Selectivity. Daily newspapers in cities and towns across the United States offer advertisers the opportunity to reach a geographically well-defined target audience—particularly densely populated urban markets. Some newspapers are beginning to run zoned editions, which target even more narrow geographic areas within a metropolitan market. Zoned editions are typically used by merchants doing business in the local area.

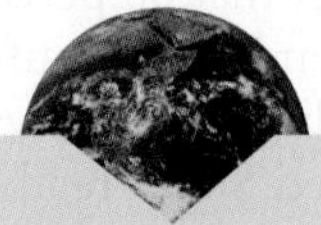

Globalization

All the News that Fit to Print—or Post

The fact that newspapers and magazines are struggling in the digital age is not a "news" flash. Newspaper advertising revenues declined by 20 percent during the three-year period from 2006 to 2009; magazine ad revenues fell nearly 10 percent in a single year from 2007 to 2008; *The New York Times*, which paid $1.1 for the *Boston Globe* in 1993, is entertaining bids for the newspaper in the range of $100 million; and *USA Today* has watched its circulation erode at a rate of about 7 percent annually during a three-year period. Can't get news much worse than that.

So, is this a hopeless situation? Are the print media organizations going to disappear completely? Well, newspapers and magazines have a few trends working in their favor. First, more than 70 percent of the population in developed countries starts each day by checking the news and more than 78 percent of those younger than 25 checks the news from time to time throughout the day. (Note this figure is much higher than the 30 percent of the population in the U.S. who read a newspaper every day). Further, newspapers and magazines attract a much higher demographic profile than broadcast media: 76 percent of readers have a college education and more than 70 percent have household incomes higher than $100,000. The main problem, of course, is that these news hungry patrons want something more convenient than a page printed on paper to access their news.

The challenge for the print media then is to provide the news in the format that will retain readers. A recent survey identified that the number of people accessing news on the Internet from mobile devices more than doubled from 2008 to 2009. The model for adapting to the new global, digital environment would seem to be *The Economist* news magazine. *The Economist* is by no means a new digital media upstart. The magazine first started publication in 1843 with the guiding principle to "take part in a severe contest between intelligence that presses forward and an unworthy, timid ignorance obstructing our progress." Probably not the guiding principle for reality TV shows like *Bridezilla* or *Joe Millionaire*. But, despite its historical and principled roots, *The Economist* is rapidly adapting to the new media environment. With a sturdy worldwide print circulation of 1.4 million weekly, the magazine has grown its online circulation from 1.8 million in 2006 to 2.6 million in 2010. Further, the 169,000 Facebook fans and 75,000 followers on Twitter access *The Economist* online as well.

Getting up in the morning and pouring over a newspaper with a good cup of coffee is a ritual that will no doubt persist for some time. But, as the world is more digital, so must the news providers be digital. Online, mobile and podcating versions of news information will help traditional print publishers, like *The Economist*, survive and maybe even flourish.

Sources: "U.S. Ad Spending Totals by Medium", *Advertising Age*, June 22, 2009; Nancy Coltun Webster, "Multiplatform News," *Advertising Age Integrated Media Guide*, November 16, 2009; Russell Adams, "Gannett Sees No Relief in Ad Turndown," *The Wall Street Journal*, April 17, 2009; Michael Kinsley, "All the News That Fit to Pay for," *The Economist: The World in 2010*, January 2010, 50.

Exhibit 13.3 The newspaper medium offers a large format for advertisers. This is important when an advertiser needs space to provide the target audience with extensive information.

Courtesy, Tire America

Timeliness. The newspaper is timely even in its printed form. Because of the short time needed for producing a typical newspaper ad and the regularity of daily publication, the newspaper allows advertisers to reach audiences in a timely way. This doesn't mean on just a daily basis. Newspaper ads can take advantage of special events or a unique occurrence in a community on a weekly or monthly basis as well.

Creative Opportunities. Even though the newspaper page does not offer the breadth of creative options available in the broadcast media, there are things advertisers can do in a newspaper that represent important creative opportunities. Since the newspaper page offers a large and relatively inexpensive format, advertisers can provide a lot of information to the target audience at relatively low cost. This is important for products or services with extensive or complex features that may need lengthy and detailed copy. The Tire America ad in Exhibit 13.3 needs just such a large format to provide detail about tire sizes and prices.

Credibility. Newspapers still benefit from the perception that "if it's in the paper it must be the truth." As an example, this credibility element played a key role in the decision by Glaxo Wellcome and SmithKline Beecham to announce their megamerger (creating the $73 billion GlaxoSmithKline Corporation) using newspapers.[10]

Audience Interest and Demographics. Regular newspaper readers are truly interested in the information they are reading. Even though overall readership may be down in the United States, there are those readers that remain are loyal and interested—and upscale. Newspapers reach a higher percentage of highly educated and affluent consumers in both the print and Web versions than do broadcast or cable television. In addition, many readers buy a newspaper specifically to see what's on sale at stores in the local area, making this an ideal environment for local merchants. And newspapers are a primary medium for local classified advertising despite Internet options like craigslist.com, which have cut into newspaper classified revenue.

Cost. In terms of both production and space, newspapers offer a low-cost alternative to advertisers. The cost per contact may be higher than with television and radio options, but the absolute cost for placing a black-and-white ad is still within reach of even a small advertising budget.

Disadvantages of Newspapers. Newspapers offer advertisers many good opportunities. Like every other media option, however, newspapers have some significant disadvantages.

10. David Goetzl, "GlaxoSmithKline Launches Print Ads," *Advertising Age*, January 8, 2001, 30.

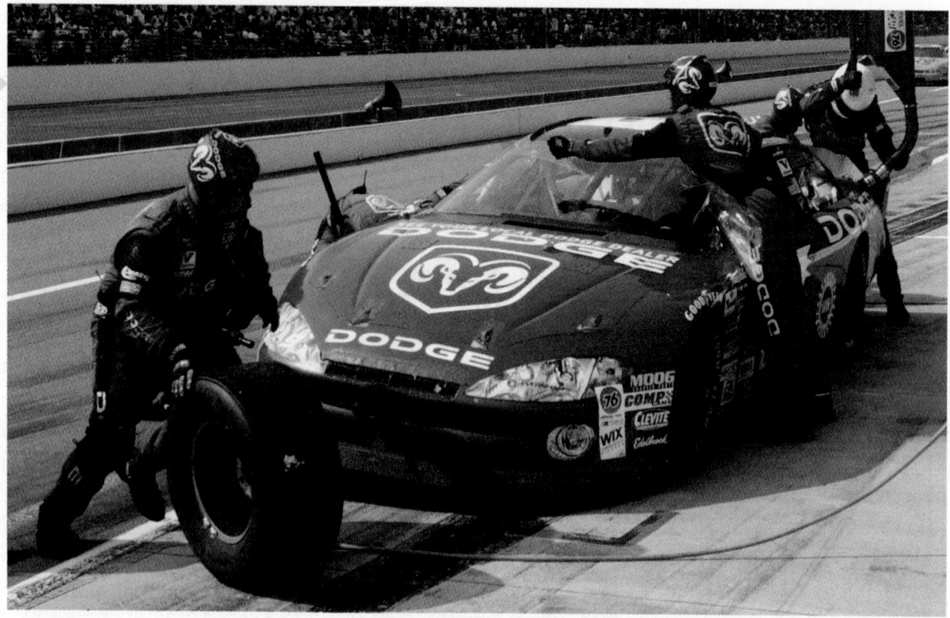

Exhibit 13.4 Many newspapers are trying to increase their target selectivity by developing special sections for advertisers, such as a NASCAR section for race fans.

© Robin Jerstad/Reuters/Landov

Limited Segmentation. Although newspapers can achieve good geographic selectivity and reach upscale consumers, the ability to target a specific audience with any precision is limited. Newspapers simply cut across too broad an economic, social, and demographic audience to allow for the isolation of specific targets. The placement of ads within certain sections can achieve minimal targeting by gender, but even this effort is somewhat fruitless. Some newspapers are developing special sections to enhance their segmentation capabilities (See Exhibit 13.4). Many papers are developing sections on e-business and e-film reviews to target specific audiences.[11] In addition, more and more newspapers are being published to serve specific ethnic groups, which is another form of segmentation. The industry feels it has made great progress in this regard and is approaching advertisers with the argument that newspaper advertising, if purchased strategically, can rival the targeting capability of many magazines.[12]

Creative Constraints. The opportunities for creative executions in printed newspapers are certainly outweighed by the creative constraints. First, newspapers have comparatively poor reproduction quality. Led by *USA Today,* most newspapers now print some pages in color. But even the color reproduction does not enhance the look of most products in advertisements. For advertisers whose brand images depend on accurate, high-quality reproduction (color or not), newspapers simply have severe limitations compared to other media options. Second, newspapers are a unidimensional medium—no sound, no action. For brands that demand a broad creative execution, this medium is often not the best choice.

Cluttered Environment. The average printed newspaper is filled with headlines, subheads, photos, and announcements—not to mention the news stories. This presents a terribly cluttered environment for an advertisement. To make things worse, most advertisers in a product category try to use the same sections to target audiences. For example, all the home equity loan and financial services ads are in the business section, and all the women's clothing ads are in the metro, or local, sections.

Short Life. In most U.S. households, printed newspapers are read quickly and then discarded (or, hopefully, stacked in the recycling pile). The only way advertisers can overcome this limitation is to buy several insertions in each daily issue, buy space

11. Jon Fine, "Tribune Seeks National Ads with 3 New Special Sections," *Advertising Age*, October 9, 2000, 42.

12. Jon Fine, "Papers' Ad Group Goes on Offensive," *Advertising Age*, February 9, 2004, 6.

several times during the week, or both. In this way, even if a reader doesn't spend much time with the newspaper, at least multiple exposures are a possibility.

The newspaper has creative limitations, but what the average newspaper does, it does well. If an advertiser wants to reach a local audience with a simple black-and-white ad in a timely manner, then the newspaper is an excellent choice.

Categories of Newspaper Advertising. Advertisers have several options when it comes to the types of ads that can be placed in newspaper: display advertising, inserts, and classified advertising.

Display Advertising. Advertisers of goods and services rely most on display advertising. **Display advertising** in newspapers includes the standard components of a print ad—headline, body copy, and often an illustration—to set it off from the news content of the paper. An important form of display advertising is co-op advertising sponsored by manufacturers. In **co-op advertising**, a manufacturer pays part of the media bill when a local merchant features the manufacturer's brand in advertising. Co-op advertising can be done on a national scale as well (See Exhibit 13.5). Intel invests heavily in co-op advertising with computer manufacturers who feature the "Intel Inside" logo in their print ads.

Inserts. There are two types of insert advertisements. Inserts do not appear on the printed newspaper page but rather are folded into the newspaper before distribution. An advertiser can use a **preprinted insert**, which is an advertisement delivered to the newspaper fully printed and ready for insertion into the newspaper.

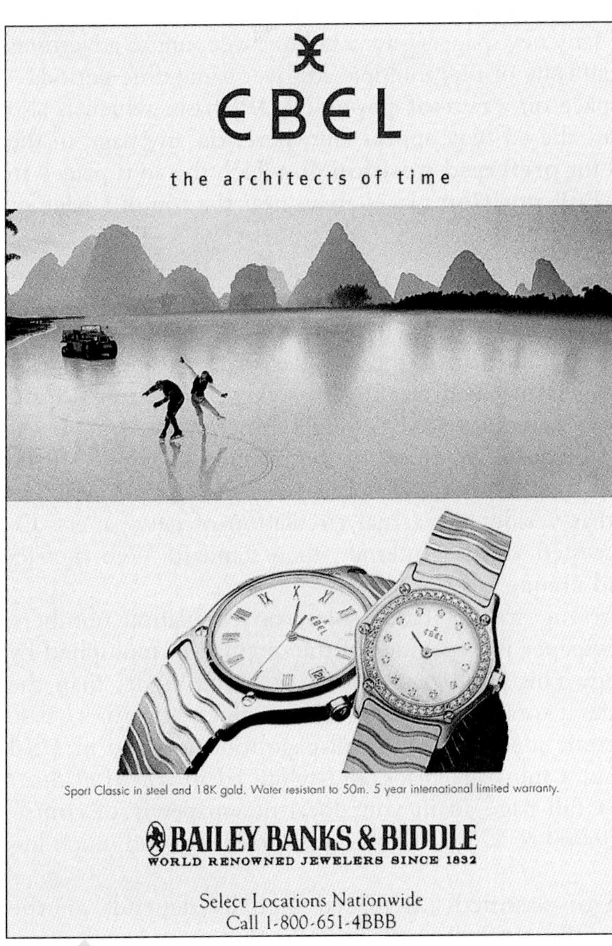

Exhibit 13.5 Retailers who feature a particular brand can receive co-op advertising money for media placement.

Exhibit 13.6 This example of a free-standing insert (FSI) from Pizza Hut shows how an ad can be delivered via a newspaper distribution system without having to become part of the paper itself. What are the production and attention-getting advantages that this insert provides? www.pizzahut.com

Courtesy, Zale Corporation; Photo courtesy of Pizza Hut

The second type of insert ad is a **free-standing insert (FSI)**, which contains cents-off coupons for a variety of products and is typically delivered with Sunday newspapers. The Pizza Hut ad in Exhibit 13.6 is part of a free-standing insert. Nearly $2 billion per year is spent by advertisers on free-standing inserts.

Classified Advertising. **Classified advertising** is newspaper advertising that appears as all-copy messages under categories such as sporting goods, employment, and automobiles. Many classified ads are, of course, taken out by individuals, but real estate firms, automobile dealers, and construction firms also buy classified advertising. In the past 10 years, literally billions of dollars in classified advertising has shifted from traditional newspaper posting to digital placement on sites like Craigslist.

Costs and Buying Procedures for Newspaper Advertising. When an advertiser wishes to place advertising in a newspaper, the first step is to obtain a rate card from the newspaper. A **rate card** contains information on costs, closing times (when ads have to be submitted), specifications for submitting an ad, and special pages or features available in the newspaper. The rate card also summarizes the circulation for the designated market area and any circulation outside the designated area.

The cost of a newspaper ad depends on how large the advertisement is, whether it is black-and-white or color, how large the total audience is, and whether the newspaper has local or national coverage. Advertising space is sold in newspapers by the **column inch**, which is a unit of space one inch deep by one column wide. Each column is 2 inches wide. Most newspapers have adopted the **standard advertising unit (SAU)** system for selling ad space, which defines unit sizes for advertisements. There are 57 defined SAU sizes for advertisements in the system so that advertisers can prepare ads to fit one of the sizes. Many newspapers offer a volume discount to advertisers who buy more than one ad in an issue or buy multiple ads over some time period.

When an advertiser buys space on a **run-of-paper (ROP)** basis, which is also referred to as a *run-of-press basis,* the ad may appear anywhere, on any page in the paper. A higher rate is charged for **preferred position**, in which the ad is placed in a specific section of the paper. **Full position** places an ad near the top of a page or in the middle of editorial material.

Measuring Newspaper Audiences. There are several different dimensions to measuring newspaper audiences. The reach of a newspaper is reported as the newspaper's circulation. **Circulation** is the number of newspapers distributed each day (for daily newspapers) or each week (for weekly publications). **Paid circulation** reports the number of copies sold through subscriptions and newsstand distribution. **Controlled circulation** refers to the number of copies of the newspaper that are given away free. The Audit Bureau of Circulations (ABC) is an independent organization that verifies the actual circulation of newspapers. Of course, if the newspaper is accessed via the Internet, then standard Web metrics apply, like hits, page views, and unique visitors.

Rates for newspaper advertising are not based solely on circulation numbers, however. **Readership** of a newspaper is a measure of the circulation multiplied by the number of readers of a copy. This number, of course, is much higher than the circulation number and provides a total audience figure on which advertisers base advertising rates. To give you some idea of costs, a full-page four-color ad in *USA Today* costs about $150,000, and a full-page black-and-white ad in *The Wall Street Journal* costs about $200,000. A full-page ad in your local newspaper is, of course, considerably less—probably $10,000 to $25,000 for a good-sized city and much less for small-town newspapers.

Measuring the readership of classified ads placed digitally depends on the websites' tracking service. Normally, a calculation of unique visitors and page views will be available. More about the measurement of digital/interactive advertising will be covered in Chapter 14.

The Future of Newspapers. Earlier in the chapter, we talked about the fact that newspaper circulation has been in a long, sustained downward trend, and that traditional print readership is following the same pattern. To survive as a viable advertising medium, newspapers will have to evolve with the demands of both audiences and advertisers, who provide them with the majority of their revenue. Primarily, newspapers will have to exploit their role as a source for local news—that some new media like the Web cannot do very effectively. Some analysts refer to this opportunity for newspapers as "**hyper-localism**" where people will get their global and national news from the Web but turn to local newspapers for sale on paint at the local hardware store.[13]

May analysts feel that another important transition for newspapers to make is to adopt a pay-for-inquiry advertising model.[14] A **pay-for-inquiry advertising model** is a payment scheme in which the medium, in this case newspapers, gets paid by advertisers based solely on the inquiries an advertiser receives in response to an ad. Radio, television and the Internet (pay-per-click) have been using pay-for-inquiry models of various types for several years. Some feel that newspaper publishers have little to lose by switching to such a model since they are losing advertising to the Internet anyway. To compete in the future as a viable advertising medium, newspapers will have to do the following:[15]

- Continue to provide in-depth coverage of issues that focus on the local community.
- Continue to provide some coverage of national and international news for readers who want both global and local news.
- Borrow from the Internet's approach to advertisers—be accountable to advertisers and offer local advertisers a pay-per-inquiry model for ad costs.
- Maintain and expand their role as the best local source for consumers to find specific information on advertised product features, availability, and prices (hyper-localism).
- Provide consumer–buyers the option of shopping through an online newspaper computer service not unlike eBay or craigslist.
- Use bloggers to cover events and take advantage of local social networking.
- Become more mainstream in integrated brand promotions particularly relating to new media (See Exhibit 13.7).

3 Magazines.

Like newspapers, magazines have been struggling in a changing media world as well. Spending on magazine advertising still commands about $24 billion annually, but that is down from around $34 billion in advertising revenue at the peak of magazines' popularity.[16] That loss of several billion dollars in annual revenue has created some casualties. Illustrious magazine titles like *Signature*, *Mode*, and even the *Gourmet Magazine*, founded in 1940, have ceased publication. But, big advertisers like Procter & Gamble still find that magazines "work hard" for the firm in reaching target customers effectively and efficiently (See Exhibit 13.8). P&G strategists have moved media spending from television to magazines, and magazines now capture about 20 percent of the consumer goods marketer's nearly $5 billion annual media spending.[17]

13. Michael Kinsley, "The World in 2010," *The Economist,* January 2010, 50.

14. Nat Ives, "Pay-for-Inquiry Ad Model Gains Modest Traction at Newspapers," *Advertising Age,* February 8, 2010, 2, 21; Rance Crain, "Newspapers ought to Embrace the Pay-per-Inquiry Ad Model," *Advertising Age,* February 12, 2010, 12.

15. Based in part on Jon Fine, "The Daily Paper of Tomorrow," *BusinessWeek*, January 9, 2006, 20.

16. Advertising Age, 100 Leading National Advertisers, June 21, 2010, 22.

17. Jeff Neff, "P&G Pumps Up Ring Spending, Trims TV," *Advertising Age*, November 6, 2006, 1, 78.

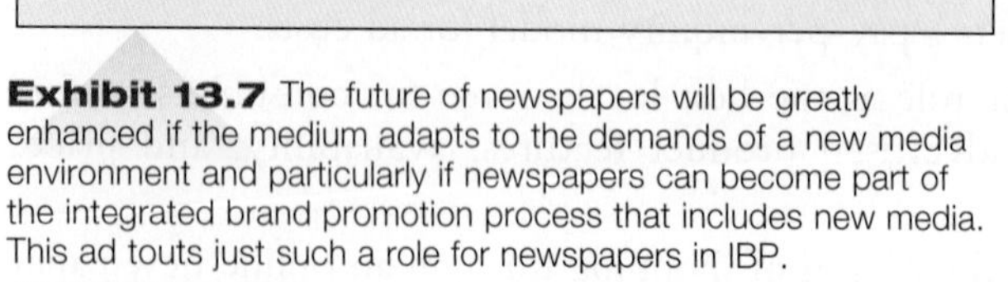

Nothing attracts online shoppers to your website like newspapers.
Newspapers can help your website achieve the critical mass it needs to drive your business. According to a recent study, daily newspapers reached over 59% of those who had made a purchase on the Internet within the previous 30 days.* No other medium delivers this amount of traffic with greater velocity. So if you're looking for shoppers you'll find them browsing through newspapers. For more information call the number below. Nobody delivers the paper like we do.
Newspaper Association of America
newspaper national network
Call Jack Grandcolas, VP of High Tech advertising, at 415-454-9168 or e-mail granj@nnn-naa.com

Exhibit 13.7 The future of newspapers will be greatly enhanced if the medium adapts to the demands of a new media environment and particularly if newspapers can become part of the integrated brand promotion process that includes new media. This ad touts just such a role for newspapers in IBP.

www.nnn-naa.com

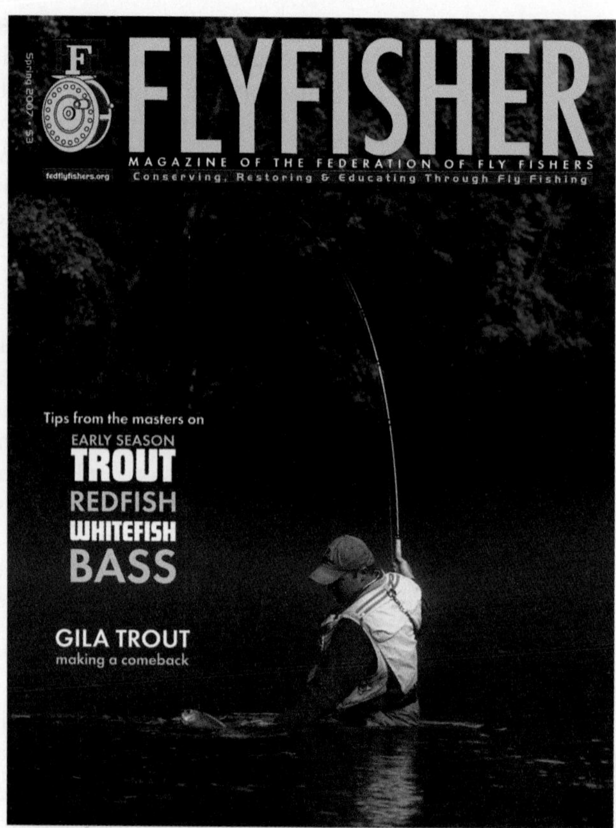

Exhibit 13.8 Specialty magazines like FlyFisher (www.fedflyfishers.org) help advertisers target highly specialized markets with efficiency and effectiveness.

No doubt, many of the most popular and successful magazines are ones you read yourself—*People, Sports Illustrated, Elle,* and *Car and Driver* make the annual list of leading magazines. The top 10 magazines in the United States, based on circulation, are listed in Exhibit 13.9. This list suggests the diversity of magazines as a media class. Exhibit 13.10 shows the top 10 advertisers in magazines. Note that circulation and revenue for magazines is down, reflecting the general decline in advertising placement in traditional media.

Exhibit 13.9 Top 10 magazines by circulation for 2009.

Rank	Magazine	2009	% Change from 2008
1	AARP The Magazine	24,371,637	0.1
2	Better Homes and Gardens	7,621,786	-0.5
3	Reader's Digest	7,099,558	-13.1
4	Good Housekeeping	4,652,904	-0.7
5	National Geographic	4,495,931	-11.2
6	Woman's Day	3,966,414	1.2
7	Ladies' Home Journal	3,858,773	0.5
8	Family Circle	3,853,253	-2.3
9	Game Informer Magazine	3,805,038	8.2
10	People	3,613,902	-2.1

Source: AdAge.com Data Center, Magazines by Circulation 2009, December 31, 2009.

Exhibit 13.10 Top 10 magazine advertisers for 2009 (U.S. dollars in millions).

Measured Ad Spending in Magazines-2009			
2009 Rank	**Marketer**	**2009**	**% Change from 2008**
1	Procter & Gamble Co.	$949.3	2.6
2	L'Oréal	387.9	16.2
3	Johnson & Johnson	323.3	–18.8
4	Pfizer	317.8	21.0
5	Kraft Foods	301.1	–25.5
6	Unilever	300.2	31.6
7	General Motors Co.	274.2	–37.0
8	Merck & Co.	247.0	28.7
9	Time Warner	242.4	5.7
10	Walmart Stores	231.7	–13.1

Source: *Advertising Age*, June 21, 2010, 14.

Exhibit 13.11 One distinct advantage of magazines over most other media options is the ability to attract and target a highly selective audience. Magazines such as Men's Journal attract an audience based on special interests and activities—in this case, readers interested in health issues.

Courtesy, Susan Van Etten

Like newspapers, magazines have advantages and disadvantages, offer various ad costs and buying procedures, and measure their audiences in specific ways. We will consider these issues now.

Advantages of Magazines. Magazines have many advantages relative to newspapers. These advantages make them more than just an ideal print medium—many analysts conclude that magazines are, in many ways, superior to even broadcast media alternatives.

Audience Selectivity. The overwhelming advantage of magazines relative to other media—print or broadcast—is the ability of magazines to attract and target a highly selective audience. This selectivity can be based on demographics (*Woman's Day*), lifestyle (*Muscle & Fitness*), or special interests (*Men's Journal*), as shown in Exhibit 13.11. The audience segment can be narrowly defined, as is the one that reads *Modern Bride,* or it may cut across a variety of interests, like *Time* readers. Magazines also offer geographic selectivity on a regional basis, as does *Southern Living,* or city magazines, such as *Atlanta,* which highlight happenings in major metropolitan areas.

Audience Interest. Perhaps more than any other medium, magazines attract an audience because of content. Although television programming can attract audiences through interest as well, magazines have the additional advantage of voluntary exposure to the advertising. Parents seek out publications that address the joys and challenges of parenting in a wide range of strong-circulation magazines like *American Baby* and *Cookie.*[18] When a magazine attracts a highly interested readership, advertisers, in turn, find a highly receptive audience for their brand messages (see Exhibit 13.12).

18. Joseph Weber, "The Boomlet in Baby News," *BusinessWeek*, May 15, 2006, 82.

Exhibit 13.12 The advantage of magazines: Specialized content attracts audiences with special interests, and those audiences attract advertisers. This ad by Escort Radar appeared in Car and Driver magazine.

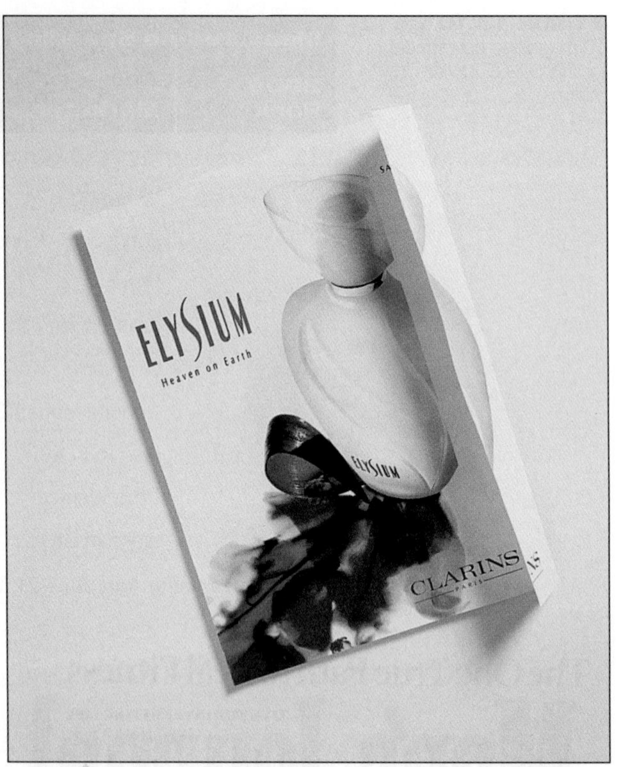

Exhibit 13.13 Magazines offer unique creative opportunities to advertisers. Perfume marketers such as Clarins include scent strips in the magazine ads for consumers to sample.

Creative Opportunities. Magazines offer a wide range of creative opportunities. Because of the ability to vary the size of an ad, use color, use white space, and play off the special interests of the audience, magazines represent a favorable creative environment. Also, because the paper quality of most magazines is quite high, color reproduction can be outstanding—another creative opportunity.

These factors are precisely why Infiniti invests nearly $60 million annually in magazine advertising. A case in point was when the firm introduced its full-size QX56 SUV, magazines offered the perfect combination of audience selectivity and high-quality visual presentation to effectively advertise the brand.[19] In an attempt to expand the creative environment even further, some advertisers have tried various other creative techniques: pop-up ads, scratch-and-sniff ads, ads with perfume scent strips, and even ads with small computer chips that flash lights and play music. The Clarins perfume ad in Exhibit 13.13 shows how an advertiser can take advantage of the creative opportunities offered by magazines.

Long Life. Many magazines are saved issue-to-issue by their subscribers. This means that, unlike newspapers, a magazine can be reexamined over a week or a month. Some magazines are saved for long periods for future reference, such as *Architectural Digest, National Geographic,* and *Travel & Leisure.* In addition to multiple subscriber exposure, this long life increases the chance of pass-along readership as people visit the subscriber's home (or professional offices) and look at magazines.

Disadvantages of Magazines. The disadvantages of magazines as a media choice have to do with the fact that although having selectivity is good, being too selective in their reach can be problematic and actually attract too many advertisers.

19. Jean Halliday, "Auto Industry Pushes Print's Creative Limits," *Advertising Age*, March 8, 2004, 4.

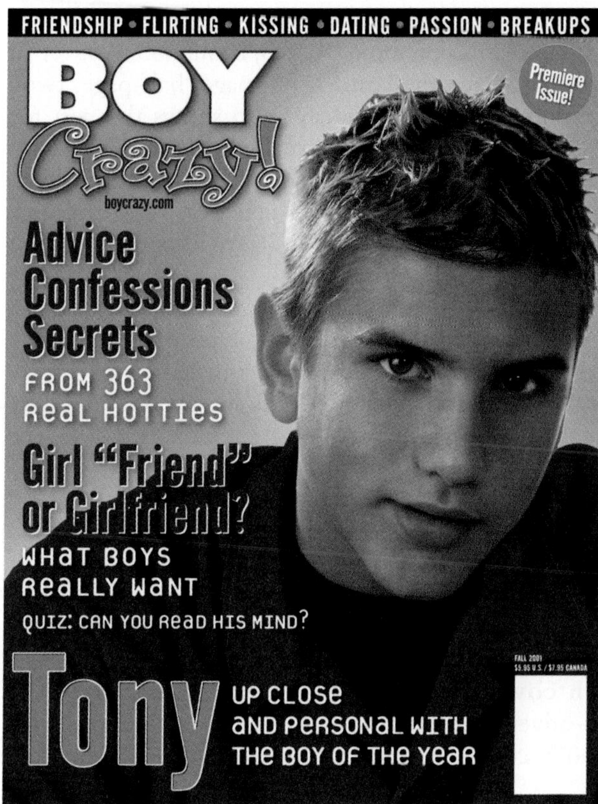

FRIENDSHIP • FLIRTING • KISSING • DATING • PASSION • BREAKUPS
BOY
Crazy!
Premiere Issue!
boycrazy.com
Advice
Confessions
Secrets
FROM 363
REAL HOTTIES
Girl "Friend" or Girlfriend?
WHAT BOYS REALLY WANT
QUIZ: CAN YOU READ HIS MIND?
Tony
UP CLOSE AND PERSONAL WITH THE BOY OF THE YEAR

Exhibit 13.14 In the consumer magazine category, publishers try to appeal to target audiences' special interests. Boy Crazy! is one of many titles targeted to teenagers.

AP/Topic Gallery

Limited Reach and Frequency. The tremendous advantage of selectivity discussed in the previous section actually creates a limitation for magazines. The more narrowly defined the interest group, the less overall reach a magazine will have. Since most magazines are published monthly or perhaps every two weeks, there is little chance for an advertiser to achieve frequent exposure using a single magazine. To overcome this limitation, advertisers often use several magazines targeted at the same audience. For example, many readers of *Better Homes and Gardens* may also be readers of *Architectural Digest*. By placing ads in both publications, an advertiser can increase both reach and frequency within a targeted audience.

Clutter. Magazines are not quite as cluttered as newspapers, but they still represent a fairly difficult context for message delivery. The average magazine is about half editorial and entertainment content and half advertising material, but some highly specialized magazines, like *Bride*, can have as much as 80 percent of their pages devoted to advertising. And given the narrowly defined audiences, this advertising tends to be for brands in direct competition with each other. In addition to this clutter, there is another sort of clutter that has recently begun to plague magazines. As soon as a new market segment is recognized, there is a flood of "me too" magazines. The teen magazine market suffered precisely this problem from 2000 to 2005. Traditional titles like *Seventeen* and *YM* suddenly found themselves amid a glut of teen girl magazines including *Teen, Teen People, Teen Vogue, Cosmo Girl, ElleGirl,* and *Boy Crazy!* (see Exhibit 13.14). This may be good in terms of coverage, but it may devalue individual ads, and the magazines in which they appear may reach fewer consumers than the advertiser expected (note that two of the newer teen girl magazines have already failed).

Long Lead Times. Advertisers are required to submit their ads as much as 90 days in advance of the date of publication. If the submission date is missed, there can be as much as a full month's delay in placing the next ad. And once an ad is submitted, it cannot be changed during that 90-day period, even if some significant event alters the communications environment.

Cost. Even though the cost per contact in magazines is not nearly as high as in some media (direct mail in particular), it is more expensive than most newspaper space and many times the cost per contact in the broadcast media. The absolute cost for a single insertion can be prohibitive. For magazines with large circulations, such as *AARP* (24 million) and *Good Housekeeping* (4.4 million), the cost for a one-time, full-page, four-color ad can run from $100,000 to about $250,000.

Costs and Buying Procedures for Magazine Advertising.

The cost for magazine space varies dramatically. As with newspapers, the size of an ad, its position in a publication, its creative execution (black and white or color, or any special techniques), and its placement in a regular or special edition of the magazine all affect costs. The main cost, of course, is based on the magazine's circulation. A full-page four-color ad in *Reader's Digest* costs about $200,000 (based on about 7 million readers); a full-page four-color ad in *People* costs about $150,000; a full-page ad in *Skiing* costs about $35,000; and a full-page ad in *UpHere,* the magazine about Canada's northern frontier with a circulation of about 30,000, is only $3,000.

Each magazine has a rate card that shows the cost for full-page, half-page, two-column, one-column, and half-column ads. The rate card also shows the cost for black-and-white, two-color, and four-color ads. Rate cards for magazines, as with newspapers, have been the standard pricing method for many years. In recent years, however, more and more publishers have been willing to negotiate rates and give deep discounts for volume purchases—discounts as large as 30 to 40 percent off the published card rate.

In addition to standard rates, there is an extra charge for a **bleed page**. On a bleed page, the background color of an ad runs to the edge of the page, replacing the standard white border. **Gatefold ads**, or ads that fold out of a magazine to display an extra-wide advertisement, also carry an extra charge. Gatefolds are often used by advertisers on the inside cover of upscale magazines. An example of a gatefold is the ad for dishes and flatware in Exhibit 13.15.

Placement. When buying space in a magazine, advertisers must decide among several placement options. A run-of-edition advertisement, as mentioned earlier, can appear anywhere in the magazine, at the discretion of the publisher. The advertiser may pay for a preferred position, however. **First cover page** is the front cover of a magazine; **second cover page** is the inside front cover; **third cover page** is the inside back cover; and **fourth cover page** is the back cover. When advertisers prepare **double-page spreads**—advertisements that bridge two facing pages—it is important that no headlines or body copy run through the *gutter,* which is the fold between the magazine pages.

Buying procedures for magazine advertising demand that an advertiser follow several guidelines and honor several key dates. A **space contract** establishes a rate for all advertising placed in a publication by an advertiser over a specified period. A **space order**, also referred to as an *insertion order,* is a commitment by an advertiser to advertising space in a particular issue. It is accompanied by production specifications for the ad or ads that will appear in the issue. The dates that an advertiser must be aware of are as follows:

- **Closing date:** The date when production-ready advertising materials must be delivered to a publisher for an ad to appear in an issue.

Exhibit 13.15 Gatefold ads display extra-wide advertisements, like this one for Lenox dishes. www.lenox.com

Company: Lenox Brands 1998; Agency: Grey Advertising, NY

- **On-sale date:** The date on which a magazine is issued to subscribers and for newsstand distribution. Most magazines put issues on sale far in advance of the cover date.
- **Cover date:** The date of publication that appears on a magazine.

Measuring Magazine Audiences. Most magazines base their published advertising rates on **guaranteed circulation**, which is a stated minimum number of copies of a particular issue that will be delivered to readers. This number guarantees for advertisers that they are achieving a certain minimum reach with an ad placement. In addition, publishers estimate **pass-along readership**, which is an additional number of people, other than the original readers, who may see a publication. Advertisers can verify circulation through the Audit Bureau of Circulations, which reports total and state-by-state circulation for magazines, as well as subscriber versus newsstand circulation. When an advertiser wants to go beyond basic circulation numbers, the syndicated magazine research services such as Simmons Market Research Bureau and Mediamark Research can provide additional information. Through personal interviews and respondent-kept diaries, these services provide advertisers with information on reader demographics, media use, and product usage.

The Future of Magazines. Magazines have had a roller-coaster history during the past 10 to 15 years. The most recent data show that readership is on an upward trend and that ad revenues are either up slightly or down slightly, depending on the year. Between 1994 and 2008, the number of adults who read magazines on a monthly basis has grown from 166 million to nearly 190 million. Additional good news for magazines and many advertisers is that the percentage of men and women in the key 18- to 24-year-old demographic who read a magazine on a monthly basis has grown to 90 percent.[20]

Three important factors need to be considered as influences on magazines as an advertising medium in the future. First, magazines will, like other traditional media, have to determine how to adapt to new media options. In the late 1990s, magazines rushed to publish online, with more than 250 magazines offering online versions. These electronic versions were touted as having several advantages to both the publisher and the subscriber, but the initial experience with "digizines" was less than successful. Consider the fact that when the paid circulation for the print version of *Reader's Digest* was 11 million copies, there were only about 100,000 subscribers online.[21] But, a new era is dawning for digital magazines and this time around it may be different. The introduction of tablet readers, like the Apple iPad (by the way, not the only tablet reader around), promise to offer a better and easier reader experience (see Exhibit 13.16). Many analysts believe that magazine publishers will be able to offer "stunning" versions of their publications with dynamic typography, video inserts, and social media overlays that may be very attractive to advertisers.[22] Big magazine publishers like the Conde Nast Media Group already have iPad editions of *GQ*, *Wired*, and *Vanity Fair* and have realized dramatic growth in paid subscriptions for the mobile access.[23] And, many of the interactive deals carry a combined print/digital media buy. Procter & Gamble secured sponsorship of digital issues of *Men's Health* by increasing its ad spending in the print version of the magazine.[24] Although tablet readers offer a new, dynamic environment for magazines to attract

20. "MRI Magazine Readership," *Advertising Age*, October 6, 2008.

21. Jon Fine, "Magazines Recorded Declines in Late 2003," *Advertising Age*, February 23, 2004, 39.

22. Ben Kunz, "Five Ways the 'iPad' May Change the World," *Bloomberg Businessweek*, January 18, 2010, 72.

23. Nat Ives, "App for That: Magazines Forge New Vision for Digital Future," *Advertising Age*, Digital Issue, February 22, 2010, 44.

24. Nat Ives, "Are iPad Editions 'Print Plus' or Something Else?," *Advertising Age*, April 2, 2010, 9.

Exhibit 13.16 The introduction of new and better tablet readers, like the Apple iPad, promises to provide magazine publishers the opportunity to expand circulation beyond print.

PRNewsFoto/Netflix

advertisers, there are some significant drawbacks. First, the magazine publisher has to share revenue with service provider. Amazon takes a 30 percent royalty on publisher revenues generated by providing a publication on its e-reader, the Kindle. In addition, magazine publishers have to worry about cannibalizing their print circulation, which would lower advertising revenue possibilities in that venue.[25]

The second factor affecting the future of magazines is that publishers are exploring other ways to take advantage of the interactive digital environment beyond digital versions publications. In an effort to generate additional revenue, some magazines are starting to make the products advertised in the publication available for sale online—thus earning a margin on the sales. *Maxim* opened Shop Maxim Online, which allowed readers direct access to products seen in the publication and *Maxim* received a cut of sales. The project met with marginal success, but the model seems to be viable for other publishers to try.[26]

Third, big advertisers are working their way into becoming media companies. Procter & Gamble has started a custom beauty magazine publication, *Rogue*, which quickly achieved a circulation of 11 million households—nearly double the combined paid circulation of *Allure*, *Glamour*, and *Cosmopolitan*. Other big marketers, like Kraft, Walmart, and Costco, also publish their own magazines and attract advertisers as well as touting the firm's own products. And, why not? The advertiser can reach a specific audience and save the cost of placement in traditional magazine outlets.[27]

Television and Radio: Strategic Planning Considerations.

When you say the word *advertising*, the average person thinks of television and radio advertising. It's easy to understand why. Television advertising can be advertising at its very best. With the benefit of sight and sound, color and music, action and special effects, television advertising can be the most powerful advertising of all. It has

25. Nat Ives, "Pubs Flirt with Kindle but Don't Carry a Torch," *Advertising Age*, January 25, 2010, 4.
26. Nat Ives, "Magazines Dabble in E-commerce," *Advertising Age*, December 11, 2006, 18.
27. Jack Neff, "Newest Print Media Owner: Procter & Gamble," *Advertising Age*, October 12, 2009, 3, 21.

some other advantages as well. In many parts of the world, particularly in the United States, television is the medium most widely used by consumers for entertainment and information. Radio advertising also has key advantages. The ability to reach consumers in multiple locations and the creative power of radio rank as important communications opportunities. Advertisers readily appreciate the power of television and radio advertising and invest billions of dollars a year in these media.

4 Television.

To many, television is the medium that defines what advertising is. With its multisensory stimulation, television offers the chance for advertising to be all that it can be. Television presents two extraordinary opportunities to advertisers. First, the diversity of communication possibilities allows for outstanding creative expression of a brand's value. Dramatic color, sweeping action, and spectacular sound effects can cast a brand in an exciting and unique light—especially in an era of widescreen and HDTV. Second, once this expressive presentation of a brand is prepared, it can be disseminated to millions of consumers through various broadcast, cable, satellite, and interactive means, often at a fraction of a penny per contact.

These opportunities have not been lost on advertisers. In the United States in 2010, advertisers invested about $65 billion in television advertising for media time alone—this does not include the many billions of dollars spent on production costs. And, global spending on television advertising is expected to reach $189 billion by 2015.[28] To fully appreciate all that television means to advertisers, we need to understand much more about this complex medium.

Television Categories. Without careful evaluation, the natural tendency is to classify television as a single type of broadcast medium. When we turn on the television, we simply decide what program we find interesting and then settle in for some entertainment. The reality is that during the past 20 years, several distinct versions of television have evolved, from which consumers can choose for entertainment and advertisers can choose for reaching those consumers. There are four categories of basic television: network, cable, syndicated, and local television (we'll get to Web and interactive TV shortly). Exhibit 13.17 shows the spending in these four television categories for 2008 and 2009. Notice, once again, spending has declined dramatically with about $7 billion less spent in 2009 than in 2008. Let's examine the nature of each of the four categories for television advertising and the then the growing satellite/closed-circuit option as well.

Network Television. Network television broadcasts programming over airwaves to affiliate stations across the United States under a contract agreement. "Broadcast" is a bit of a misnomer since programming from these networks can be delivered

Exhibit 13.17
Spending by advertisers on the four major television categories (U.S. dollars in billions).

	Total Measured Advertising Spending		
	2009	2008	% Change
Network TV	$23.6	$25.4	−7.2
Spot TV	13.1	17.1	−23.4
Syndicated TV	4.2	4.4	−4.9
Cable TV	19.3	19.6	−1.5

Source: *Advertising Age*, June 21, 2010, 22.

28. Brian Steinberg, "Marketers Say TV Spending Will Drop. Nets Stay Bullish. Let the Deals Begin." *Advertising Age*, February 10, 2010, 3; Michael Bush, "Magna Predicts Global Ad Spending Rise of 6% in 2010,' *Advertising Age*, December 8, 2009, 4.

Exhibit 13.18 Top 10 network TV advertisers (U.S. dollars in millions).

2008 Rank	Advertiser	2009	% CHG From 2008
1	AT&T	$726.7	2.8
2	Pfizer	605.2	30.7
3	General Motors Corp.	544.2	−13.7
4	Verizon Communications	510.1	1.1
5	Ford Motor Co.	509.5	16.5
6	Procter & Gamble	496.4	−38.9
7	Sprint Nextel Corp.	442.4	14.8
8	Time Warner	396.9	11.1
9	Toyota Motor Corp.	340.0	−1.5
10	Walmart Stores	329.6	85.0

Source: *Advertising Age*, June 21, 2010

on-air, over cable, through satellite transmission, or by mobile apps to smartphones. The method of delivery does not change the fact that advertisers can buy time within these "broadcast" programs to reach audiences in hundreds of markets. Estimates are that network television reaches more than 90 percent of U.S. households. Exhibit 13.18 shows the top 10 advertisers on network television.

Despite speculation throughout the last decade that alternative television options (discussed next) would ultimately undermine network television, the broadcast networks still continue to flourish—mostly due to innovative programming. For example, episodes of *American Idol* regularly draw audiences in the range of 50 million viewers and the Super Bowl now draws nearly 100 million viewers, with a 30-second spot costing about $3 million.[29] Regular programming costs are somewhat more reasonable. Thirty seconds on *Two and a Half Men* costs about $226,000 and on *CSI* costs $198,000; *Ugly Betty* seems like a bargain at $65,000.[30] No other television option gives advertisers the breadth of reach of network television. But the point is that broadcast networks are alive and well, delivering huge audiences, and attracting solid advertising revenues.

Cable Television. From its modest beginnings as community antenna television (CATV) in the 1940s, cable television has grown into a worldwide communications force. **Cable television** transmits a wide range of programming to subscribers through wires rather than over airwaves. In the United States, more than 60 million basic-cable subscribers (nearly 58 percent of all U.S. households) are wired for cable reception and receive dozens of channels of sports, entertainment, news, music video, and home-shopping programming.[31] Cable's power as an advertising option has grown enormously during the past decade as cable's share of the prime-time viewing audience has grown, and advertisers now invest about $20 billion for advertising time on cable.

Aside from more channels and hence more programming, three other aspects distinguish cable from network television. First is the willingness of cable networks to invest in original programming. With the success of programs such as USA network's *JAG*, cable networks are investing record dollar amounts in new programs to continue to attract well-defined audiences (see Exhibit 13.19). Second, because of cable's unique delivery technology, cable firms are now investing in software

29. Abby Klaassen, "How to Boost Your Super Bowl ROI," *Advertising Age*, December 7, 2009, 3.

30. Brian Steinberg, "'Sunday Night Football' Remains the Costliest TV Show, *Advertising Age*, October 26, 2009, 8.

31. Data drawn from the National Cable & Telecommunications Association, Industry Statistics, accessed at www.ncta.com on April 10, 2010.

Like car shows?
We've got 'em Monday thru Thursday. 8PM ET 11PM PT
Go to speedtv.com for programs and times. To get SPEED Channel call 1-888-22-SPEED today.
SPEED CHANNEL
FUEL YOUR PASSION

Exhibit 13.19 The power and success of cable comes from offering very specific programming through a wide range of cable networks. An example is the Speed Channel, which offers all forms of motor sports programming and commentary.

that can send different ads to different viewers. Time Warner is testing a system that tracks what channel each TV in any household is tuned to and what channels the household surfs. The software then can track the age, gender, and probable interests of the viewer.[32] This offers much more targeting efficiency for the advertiser and allows the cable company to increase ad placement prices. Finally, there is huge potential revenue from **video on demand (VOD)**. Data shows that video on demand will grow to be used by 66 million households by 2010.[33]

Syndicated Television. Television syndication is either original programming or programming that first appeared on network television. It is then rebroadcast on either network or cable stations with pending distribution on the Internet. Syndicated programs provide advertisers with proven programming that typically attracts a well-defined, if not enormous, audience. There are several types of television syndication. **Off-network syndication** refers to programs that were previously run in network prime time. The popular off-network syndicated shows *Home Improvement* and *Seinfeld* command significant ad dollars—in the range $150,000 to $200,000 for a 30-second ad. Less popular shows are more affordable, with prices set between about $25,000 and $60,000.[34] **First-run syndication** refers to programs developed specifically for sale to individual stations. The most famous first-run syndication show is *Star Trek: The Next Generation*. **Barter syndication** takes both off-network and first-run syndication shows and offers them free or at a reduced rate to local television stations, with some national advertising pre-sold within the programs. Local stations can then sell the remainder of the time to generate revenues. This option allows national advertisers to participate in the national syndication market conveniently. Two of the most widely recognized barter syndication shows are *Jeopardy* and *Wheel of Fortune*.

Local Television. Local television is the programming other than the network broadcast that independent stations and network affiliates offer local audiences. Completely independent stations air old movies, sitcoms, or children's programming. Network affiliates get about 90 hours of programming a week from the major networks, but they are free to air other programming beyond that provided by the network. News, movies, syndicated programs, and community-interest programs typically round out the local television fare. Local television commands significant advertising dollars—in the range of $4 billion annually.[35]

Satellite/Closed-Circuit. New technology offers another version of television available to advertisers. Programming can now be transmitted to audiences via **satellite and closed-circuit** transmission. The most widely accessed satellite programming is available from DirecTV and DISH Network. As stated earlier, satellite providers offer programming from major media companies. The distinction is the technology

32. David Kiley, "Cable's Big Bet on Hyper-Targeting," *BusinessWeek*, July 4, 2005, 58–59.

33. Andrew Hampp, "Cablers Chase Revenue from VOD, Online Video," *Advertising Age*, May 14, 2007, 14; Brian Steinberg, "The Future of TV," *Advertising Age*, November 30, 2010, 18.

34. Richard Linnett, "Host of TV Superstars Boost Bullish Syndication Market," *Advertising Age*, March 8, 2004, S-4.

35. Brian Steinberg, "Local TV Ad Spending Down 1.6% in First Quarter," *Advertising Age*, June 19, 2008, 6.

for delivery. The best known of the closed-circuit programming comes from the CNN Airport Network, which transmits news and weather programming directly to airport terminals around the world.

Web/iPod/Smartphone TV. Of course, the next evolution of television is transmitting programs over the Web, as iPod/iPad downloads, or through smartphone reception. Referred to as "TV everywhere," this capability is still emerging, and it may be premature to call this a television "category." But the capability has advertisers excited and we need to consider the potential here. Bear with us if by the time you read this, delivery of video through the Web and mobile devices has changed dramatically.

First, let's consider the distribution of video over the Web. Tracking data indicates that in 2009, more than 104 billion video streams of television programming occurred in 2009 with Hulu adding another half-billion streams through its video sharing cite.[36] Major media players like Fox, CBS, NBC, and ABC all have platforms to stream programming through the Web. And, advertisers are anxious to place ads on Web broadcasts. CBS sold $37 million in digital advertising in 2010 and estimates are that Web video attracted about $2 billion overall that year.[37]

Second, Apple's iPad, attracted media companies nearly instantaneously. ABC immediately offered free, advertising supported episodes from approximately 20 different series, including *Lost*, *Grey's Anatomy*, and *Desperate Housewives*. CBS followed suit but offers its full-length programs for purchase via iTunes.[38] The sorting out that needs to take place is whether iPad users will pay access fees or tolerate ads within the shows.

Finally, cell or smartphone TV seems to have huge potential. Verizon Wireless's V CAST Mobile TV started with distribution in 25 markets in 2007 and has been aggressively expanded. Broadcast shows need to be watched as scheduled—there is no on-demand viewing (yet). With a 2.2-inch display, 20 available channels, and a monthly fee of $15 dollars for the cell phone (in addition to voice and text fees), there seems to be good potential for generating ad revenue. Smartphone manufacturers have sold millions of iPhones with the capability of playing video and this allows advertisers to reach viewers "everywhere" further increasing advertisers' opportunities. In addition, integrating TV programming with social networking sites can further expand advertisers reach as the *Social Media* box explains.

Advantages of Television. Throughout the book, we have referred to the unique capability of television as an advertising medium. There must be some very good reasons why advertisers such as AT&T, Nike, and Procter & Gamble invest hundreds of millions of dollars annually in television advertising. The specific advantages of this medium are as follows.

Creative Opportunities. The overriding advantage of television compared to other media is, of course, the ability to send a message using both sight and sound. With recent advances in transmission and reception equipment, households now have brilliantly clear visuals and stereo-enhanced audio to further increase the impact of television advertising. Now, with HDTV capabilities becoming mainstream, all sorts of new creative opportunities present themselves.

36. Brian Steinberg, "The Future of TV," *Advertising Age*, November 30, 2009, 18.

37. Michael Learmonth, "CBS Scores $37M Beyond TV with Help of March Madness," *Advertising Age*, March 15, 2010, 2; Michael Learmonth, "This Is the Year TV Dollars Start Pouring into Web Video, Right? *Advertising Age*, Digital Issue, February 22, 2010, 60.

38. Ad Age Staff, "Media Brands on the iPad From Day One," *Advertising Age*, April 2, 2010, www.adage.com

Social Media

You Have Network. You Have Cable. Now You Might Have Social TV.

First, network television provided entertainment in the comfort of consumers' living rooms with the likes of *Gunsmoke*, the *Ed Sullivan Show* and the *Andy Griffith Show*. Then cable television burst on the scene and started offering highly specialized sports, news, and entertainment programming. Now, experts feel that television programming needs to move to having a built-in "social" component over the next decade. The belief is that consumers no longer want an "isolated" TV experience where they are passively taking in a broadcast. Rather, consumers want to be involved, like they are with the other forms of information they control like Web surfing or social networking communications.

The roots of social TV can arguably be found in programming like *American Idol* or *Dancing with the Stars* where viewers have a formative effect on next week's program by voting (along with judges) on which contestants will make it back for the next show. But, the emerging concept of social TV is much more elaborate. The next step will be for TV networks to connect consumers to programming through Twitter, Facebook, MySpace, and other networking sites that will somehow be linked into a new breed of television sets.

Currently, producers of television shows are trying to monitor when viewers talk about shows. The idea is to identify who and when people are texting and tweeting about the content of a show and integrate that with the show itself. One example is when Time Warner's TBS ran a scroll of selected Tweets from fans across the screen during the *Lopez Tonight Show*. Another example is a new feature on the ABC.com video player that allows users to read comments from the producers and writers of the show and then add their own comments to a running dialog that can be shared on Facebook. The feature launched during the première episode of the sci-fi "V."

Earlier attempts at integrating social media feeds with programming have been a bit clumsy and new formatting may need to be worked out. Some fans have complained that the scrolling content interfered with their ability to see the action on their TV screens. But, programmers and networks are convinced that they need to engage the viewer more and social networking media have proven to be engaging. The senior VP of media at Warner Bros. Digital believes that, "Extending the customer base to online is going to broaden out your demographic push." Similarly, the head of a discount luxury-goods marketer feels that in order to use social networking effectively "marketers need to get a lot more comfortable that (social networking) is a conversation. It's not something that you can *use* per se. It's something that you participate in."

So, what do you think? Do you want to be "engaged" with television programming? Or do you want to sit back and enjoy the show?

Sources: Brian Steinberg, "First Network, Then Cable, Now 'Social TV,'" *Advertising Age*, November 16, 2009, 3; Patricia Sellers, "How to Market in a Recession," CNNMoney.com, February 10, 2010, www.postcards.blogs.fortune.cnn.com

Coverage, Reach, and Repetition. Television, in one form or another, reaches more than 98 percent of all households in the United States—an estimated 300 million people. These households represent every demographic segment in the United States, which allows advertisers to achieve broad coverage. We have also seen that the cable and satellite television option provides reach to hundreds of millions of households throughout the world. With the new mobile TV options just discussed, coverage and reach capabilities are enhanced even more. Further, no other medium allows an advertiser to repeat a message as frequently as television.

Cost per Contact. For advertisers that sell to broadly defined mass markets, television offers a cost-effective way to reach millions of members of a target audience. The average prime-time television program reaches 11 million households, and top-rated shows can reach more than 60 million households. This brings an advertiser's cost-per-contact figure down to an amount unmatched by any other media option—literally fractions of a penny per contact.

Audience Selectivity. Television programmers are doing a better job of developing shows that attract well-defined target audiences. **Narrowcasting** is the development and delivery of specialized programming to well-defined audiences. Cable television is far and away the most selective television option. Cable provides not only well-defined programming but also entire networks—such as MTV and ESPN—built around the concept of attracting selective audiences.

Disadvantages of Television. Television has great capabilities as an advertising medium, but it is not without limitations. Some of these limitations are serious enough to significantly detract from the power of television advertising.

Fleeting Message. One problem with the sight and sound of a television advertisement is that it is gone in an instant. The fleeting nature of a television message, as opposed to a print ad (which a receiver can contemplate), makes message impact difficult. Some advertisers invest huge amounts of money in the production of television ads to overcome this disadvantage.

High Absolute Cost. Although the cost per contact of television advertising is the best of all traditional media, the absolute cost may be the worst. The average cost of air time for a single 30-second television spot during prime time is about $100,000, with the most popular shows, like *American Idol,* bringing in as much as $500,000 for a 30-second spot.[39] Remember this is prime-time pricing. Off-prime-time slots go for a more modest $20,000 to $50,000 for 30 seconds. In addition, the average cost of producing a quality 30-second television spot is around $300,000 to $400,000. These costs make television advertising prohibitively expensive for many advertisers. Of course, large, national consumer products companies—for which television advertising is best suited anyway—find the absolute cost acceptable for the coverage, reach, and repetition advantages discussed earlier.

Poor Geographic Selectivity. Although programming can be developed to attract specific audiences, program transmission cannot target small geographic areas nearly as well. This is especially true for satellite subscribers. For a national advertiser that wants to target a city market, the reach of a television broadcast is too broad. Similarly, for a local retailer that wants to use television for reaching local segments, the television transmission is likely to reach a several-hundred-mile radius—which will increase the advertiser's cost with little likelihood of drawing patrons.

Poor Audience Attitude and Attentiveness. Since the inception of television advertising, consumers have bemoaned the intrusive nature of the commercials. Just when a movie is reaching its thrilling conclusion—on come the ads. The involuntary and frequent intrusion of advertisements on television has made television advertising the most distrusted form of advertising among consumers. In one of the few surveys tracking consumer sentiment, only 17 percent of consumers surveyed felt that television advertising affected them in their purchase of a new car, compared with 48 percent who claimed that direct mail advertising was a factor in their decision.[40] But be aware that it is not fundamentally the job of television advertising to motivate an immediate purchase. Image building and awareness are the key achievements for television ads.

Along with—and perhaps as a result of—this generally bad attitude toward television advertising, consumers have developed ways of avoiding exposure. Making a trip to the refrigerator or conversing with fellow viewers are the preferred low-tech ways to avoid exposure. On the low-tech side, **channel grazing**, or using a remote control to monitor programming on other channels while an advertisement is being broadcast, is the favorite way to avoid commercials.

39. Piet Levy, "Touching that Dial," *Marketing News*, March 30, 2010, 17.

40. Jean Halliday, "Study Claims TV Advertising Doesn't Work on Car Buyers," *Advertising Age*, October 13, 2003, 8.

On the high-tech side, new technology has created yet another potential method for avoiding advertising—and this development has advertisers greatly concerned. The problems centers on the so-called "V-chip." The **V-chip** is a device that can block television programming based on the program rating system. It was developed as a way for parents to block programming that they do not want their children to see. Although that was the original and intended use for the V-chip, the technology can be easily adapted to block advertisements as well.

And, of course, the biggest news and highest-tech way to avoid television advertising is with digital video recorders (DVR) like TiVo. **Digital video recorders (DVRs)** use computer hard drives to store up to 140 hours of television programming. Consumers can use the devices to skip commercials and watch only the programming itself. Indeed, the overwhelming reason consumers use DVRs *is* to skip commercials. A survey of DVR users revealed that 81 percent of them invested in a DVR primarily to skip commercials, and they claim to fast-forward through 75 percent of the ads that appear in the programming that they watch. By 2009, about 27 percent of U.S. households had DVRs, and that percentage is expected to rise rapidly.[41] Obviously, widespread use of DVRs has advertisers looking for ways to get exposure for their brands on television. More brand placement within programming and those annoying little "runners" at the bottom of the screen during programs are ways to reach DVR users.

Clutter. All the advantages of television as an advertising medium have created one significant disadvantage: clutter. The major television networks run about 15 minutes of advertising during each hour of prime-time programming, and cable channels carry about 14 minutes of advertising per hour.[42] Research has found that 65 percent of a surveyed group of consumers felt that they were "constantly bombarded with too much" advertising.[43] Critics of television advertising have also raised an issue beyond clutter. There are those who feel that television advertising has a unique power over its viewers. As such, there is occasionally a call for banning certain types of advertising. Currently, groups in various parts of the world call for a ban on alcohol advertising on television as the *Ethics* box explains.

Buying Procedures for Television Advertising. Discussions in Chapter 12 as well as in this chapter have identified the costs associated with television advertising from both a production and a space standpoint. Here we will concentrate on the issue of buying time on television. Advertisers buy time for television advertising through sponsorship, participation, and spot advertising.

Sponsorship. In a **sponsorship** arrangement, an advertiser agrees to pay for the production of a television program and for most (and often all) of the advertising that appears in the program. Sponsorship is not nearly as popular today as it was in the early days of just network television. Contemporary sponsorship agreements have attracted big-name companies such as AT&T and IBM, who often sponsor sporting events, and Hallmark, known for its sponsorship of dramatic series.

Participation. The vast majority of advertising time is purchased on a participation basis. **Participation** means that several different advertisers buy commercial time during a specific television program. No single advertiser has a responsibility for the production of the program or a commitment to the program beyond the time contracted for.

41. Brian Steinberg, "The Future of TV," op.cit., 18.

42. Andrew Green, "Clutter Crisis Countdown," *Advertising Age*, April 21, 2003, 22.

43. 2004 Yankelovich Partners poll, cited in Gary Ruskin, "A 'Deal Spiral of Disrespect,'" *Advertising Age*, April 26, 2004, 18.

Ethics

Binge Drinking and Banning Television Ads

In the United States and Britain, it's called binge drinking, in Germany they call it "coma drinking," and in France when you drink to excess, you "se prendre une cuite." Whatever name it goes by, advertisers and advertising are being blamed for excessive alcohol consumption. In the U.K., the British Medical Association is recommending a complete ban on alcohol advertising. In France, there has been a long-time ban on alcohol advertising. Austria and Belgium have also banned spirits ads from television and Italy blocks alcohol advertising on television between 4 p.m. and 9 p.m. Similarly, German sellers of alcohol cannot show sports stars drinking and alcohol ads are strictly prohibited before 8 p.m.

The tendency to blame advertising for excess seems irresistible on a global scale. But, consider the realities of the restrictions, like those above, on alcohol consumption. Despite the long time advertising ban in France, binge drinking is just now beginning to spread through French culture. Ireland has some of the toughest laws on drinking in the European Union, yet binge drinking is as big a problem there as in other parts of Europe. Why aren't bans on alcohol advertising working—the reason is that advertising bans in mature product categories don't work—period (revisit the discussion in Chapter 3 on primary demand stimulation).

Not surprisingly, advertising practitioners in Europe have issued statements about the futility of advertising bans in the face of the current resurgence in the call for them. The director of the ad agency Chick Smith Trott in London has said "People who blame advertising for binge drinking have misunderstood the whole purpose of advertising—it's about stealing market share, not persuading people to drink." And, the director of Refresh Digital Communications in Dublin argues that "The realities are that it would be the view of a lot of informed people that advertising is not the root cause of the problem." Although advertising practitioners would obviously have a vested interest in deterring bans, advertising researchers, with no vested interest, have produced more than a dozen sophisticated research studies over 40 years demonstrating that advertising bans do not work. Research on the topic began in the 1970s and as recently as 2008 a comprehensive study on the effects of advertising in mature product categories, like alcohol concluded, once again, "Our results suggest that both full and partial advertising bans are equally ineffective in reducing consumption."

Considering the role of advertising in alcohol consumption, and particularly any role it might play in binge drinking is clearly an important ethical issue. And, it is somewhat understandable that a process as visible as advertising would become the popular scapegoat. But, when objective, conclusive research demonstrates that advertising does not affect consumption behavior, then all the energy put into blaming advertising is uniformed and misplaced. The real cause obviously lies elsewhere and energy should be put into identifying and addressing that cause.

Sources: Emma Hall, "Europe Faults Alcohol Marketers for Binge Drinking; UK Proposes $286 Million Ban," *Advertising Age*, October 12, 2009, 6; Gary Wilcox and B. Vacker, "Beer Brand Advertising and Market Share in the United States: 1977 to 1998," *International Journal of Advertising*, vol. 20, 149–168. Michael L. Capella, Charles R. Taylor, and Cynthia Webster, "The Effect of Cigarette Advertising Bans on Consumption," *Journal of Advertising*, vol. 37, no. 2 (Summer 2008), 1–18.

Spot Advertising. Spot advertising refers to all television advertising time purchased from and aired through local television stations. Spot advertising provides national advertisers the opportunity to either adjust advertising messages for different markets or intensify their media schedules in particularly competitive markets. Spot advertising is the primary manner in which local advertisers, such as car dealers, furniture stores, and restaurants, reach their target audiences with television. Recently, big national advertisers have been turning away from spot advertising in pursuit of digital media options. Revenues from spot advertising fell more than 23 percent from 2008 to 2009.[44]

A final issue with respect to buying television advertising has to do with the time periods and programs during which the advertising will run. Once an advertiser has

44. Ken Wheaton, "Showing Signs of Strength, Local TV Should Face the Future," *Advertising Age*, January 18, 2010, 12.

Exhibit 13.20
Television dayparts (in U.S. Eastern time zone segments).

Morning	7:00 a.m.	to	9:00 a.m.	Monday through Friday
Daytime	9:00 a.m.	to	4:30 p.m.	Monday through Friday
Early fringe	4:30 p.m.	to	7:30 p.m.	Monday through Friday
Prime-time access	7:30 p.m.	to	8:00 p.m.	Sunday through Saturday
Prime time	8:00 p.m. 7:00 p.m.	to	11:00 p.m. 11:00 p.m.	Monday through Saturday Sunday
Late news	11:00 p.m.	to	11:30 p.m.	Monday through Friday
Late fringe	11:30 p.m.	to	1:00 a.m.	Monday through Friday

determined that sponsorship, participation, or spot advertising meets its needs, the time periods and specific programs must be chosen. Exhibit 13.20 shows the way in which television programming times are broken into **dayparts**, which represent segments of time during a television broadcast day.

Measuring Television Audiences. Television audience measurements identify the size and composition of audiences for different television programming. Advertisers choose where to buy television time based on these factors. These measures also set the cost for television time. The larger the audience or the more attractive the composition, the more costly the time will be.

The following are brief summaries of the information used to measure television audiences.

Television Households. Television households is an estimate of the number of households that are in a market and own a television. Since more than 98 percent of all households in the United States own a television, the number of total households and the number of television households are virtually the same, about 110 million.

Households Using Television. Households using television (HUT), also referred to as sets in use, is a measure of the number of households tuned to a television program during a particular time period.

Program Rating. A **program rating** is the percentage of television households that are in a market and are tuned to a specific program during a specific time period. Expressed as a formula, program rating is:

$$\text{program rating} = \frac{\text{TV households tuned to a program}}{\text{total TV households in the market}}$$

A **ratings point** indicates that 1 percent of all the television households in an area were tuned to the program measured. If an episode of *CSI* is watched by 19.5 million households, then the program rating would be calculated as follows:

$$\textit{CSI}\ \text{rating} = \frac{19{,}500{,}000}{95{,}900{,}000} = 20\ \text{rating}$$

The program rating is the best-known measure of television audience, and it is the basis for the rates television stations charge for advertising on different programs. Recall that it is also the way advertisers develop their media plans from the standpoint of calculating reach and frequency estimates, such as gross rating points.

Share of Audience. Share of audience provides a measure of the proportion of households that are using television during a specific time period and are tuned to a particular program. If 65 million households are using their televisions during the *CSI* time slot, and *CSI* attracts 19.5 million viewers, then the share of audience is:

$$CSI \text{ share} = \frac{\text{TV households tuned to a program}}{\text{total TV households using TV}} = \frac{19{,}500{,}000}{65{,}000{,}000} = 30 \text{ share}$$

Controversy in Television Measurement. There has been some controversy in the area of measuring television audiences in that advertisers have been disputing Nielsen Media ratings (Nielsen is the premier provider of television audience data). The importance of this controversy is that advertisers rely on Nielsen ratings to determine the programs on which they will buy time and media companies rely on the same ratings as the basis for how much they will charge advertisers for the time.

There are two key aspects to this controversy surrounding the rating data. First, since Nielsen data report households "tuned" to a program, that measure does not really measure "commercial" viewership in the first place nor does it account for all of us who leave the room during commercial breaks. Second, there is the issue of technological change, like the digital video recorders discussed earlier, and their effect on actual television viewing behavior since DVR users can "skip" the ads all together.[45] Obviously, advertisers do not want to pay for mere "program" viewership but rather want to pay for "commercial" viewership—potentially a lower number at lower cost.[46] The first foray into "commercial" ratings took place in the spring of 2007 with great success as advertisers signed up for commercial airtime on the upcoming network season. One industry analyst said, "It was a truly transformational 'upfront' [buying season]," given the new commercial rating metric.[47]

The Future of Television. The future of television is exciting for several reasons. First, the emerging digital interactive era will undoubtedly affect television as an advertising medium. As discussed earlier, the prospects include greater viewer participation in programming as currently happens with *American Idol* and *Dancing with the Stars*. Equally as important, though, is that technology is creating the ability to transmit advertising to a wide range of new devices from smartphones, to PDAs, to tablets. And remember the "TV everywhere" concept raised earlier in the chapter. Estimates are that by the year 2014 global mobile advertising (not including social media, email, display, and search) through such devices could reach $1.3 billion in the United States alone.[48] And recall the discussion from Chapter 2 regarding the growth of broadband access. About 40 percent of all adult Americans (about 63 million people) have broadband connections and that figure is growing rapidly.[49] Broadband has made it possible to stream television programming and therefore television advertising via the Internet to either PCs or handheld devices. Advertisers are still considering the implications of this mode of communication and how well it serves as a way to send persuasive communications. Some analysts believe that while television works well on the Web, so far TV advertising does not. The issue relates to "ad loads" that consumers are willing to tolerate while watching television on their televisions (about 22 per hour) versus the much lighter ad load (about 6 per hour) for Web transmission. This lighter ad load is seen as unsustainable in order for Web TV to achieve profitability—but will heavy loads kill Web viewership?[50]

45. David Bauder, "Network Execs Question Nielsen Accuracy," Yahoo! News, November 16, 2003, accessed at www.news.yahoo.com on November 17, 2003.

46. Brian Steinberg and Andrew Hampp, "Commercial Ratings? Nets Talk TiVo Instead," *Advertising Age*, June 4, 2007, 3, 60.

47. Nat Worden, "Ratings Metric Boosts TV Ad Buys," TheStreet.com, June 26, 2007, accessed via the Web at www.thestreet.com on June 26, 2007.

48. Forrester Research, *U.S. Interactive Marketing Forecast 2009–2014,* 7.

49. Pamela Varley, "World Broadband Statistics," Point Topic LTD., September 2007, Table 1, 21.

50. Thomas Morgan, "TV Works on the Web, but TV Advertising Won't," *Advertising Age*, April 2, 2010, 14.

Another major change that is affecting the future of television is transmission technology. **Direct broadcast by satellite (DBS)** is a program delivery system whereby television and radio (like Sirius satellite) programs are being sent directly from a satellite to homes and cars equipped with small receiving dishes. This transmission has resulted in access to hundreds of different channels by households. Even though advertisers will still be able to insert advertising in programs, the role of networks and cable stations in the advertising process will likely be changing dramatically.

Finally, consolidation in the industry cannot be ignored. Comcast has acquired about $20 billion in cable companies.[51] Similarly, Rupert Murdock has been expanding the DirecTV empire of cable holdings and media holdings that generates $30 billion in revenue from literally every corner of the earth.[52] And let's not forget traditional media giants CBS, Time Warner, and Disney, all of which in their own right have great broadcast media power. The issue, of course, is the extent to which these big and powerful media companies can end up controlling programming content. It is not automatically the case that big media companies shape programming in a biased way, but that is the concern of media watchdogs.

Although it is hard to predict what the future will hold, one thing seems sure—television will hold its own as an entertainment and information medium for households. The convenience, low cost, and diversity of programming make television an ideal medium for consumers. With the addition of technologies that allow television programming to a variety of mobile devices, television would seem destined to reach a wider variety of markets. As a result, television, despite its limitations, will continue to be an important part of the integrated brand promotion mix for many advertisers.

5 Radio.

Radio may seem like the least glamorous and most inconspicuous of the major media. This perception does not jibe with reality. Radio plays an integral role in the media plans of some of the most astute advertisers. Because of the unique features of radio, advertisers invest about $7 billion annually in radio advertising to reach national and local audiences.[53] There are good reasons why advertisers of all sorts use radio to reach target audiences. Let's turn our attention to the different radio options available to advertisers.

Radio Categories. Radio offers an advertiser several options for reaching target audiences. The basic split of national and local radio broadcasts presents an obvious geographic choice. More specifically, though, advertisers can choose among the following categories, each with specific characteristics: networks, syndication, AM versus FM, satellite, and Internet/mobile.

Networks. Radio networks operate much like television networks in that they deliver programming via satellite to affiliate stations across the United States. Network radio programming concentrates on news, sports, business reports, and short features. Some of the more successful radio networks that draw large audiences are ABC, CNN, and AP News Network.

Syndication. Radio syndication provides complete programs to stations on a contract basis. Large syndicators offer stations complete 24-hour-a-day programming packages that totally relieve a station of any programming effort. Aside from full-day programming, they also supply individual programs, such as talk shows. Large

51. Tom Lowry, Amy Barrett, and Ronald Grover, "A New Cable Giant," *BusinessWeek*, November 18, 2002, 108–118.

52. Catherine Young, et al., "Rupert's World," *BusinessWeek*, January 19, 2004, 53–61.

53. *Advertising Age,* 100 Leading National Advertisers, June 21, 2010, 22.

syndication organizations such as Westwood One place advertising within programming, making syndication a good outlet for advertisers.

AM versus FM. AM radio stations send signals that use amplitude modulation (AM) and operate on the AM radio dial at signal designations 540 to 1600. AM was the foundation of radio until the 1970s. Today, AM radio broadcasts, even the new stereo AM transmissions, cannot match the sound quality of FM. Thus, most AM stations focus on local community broadcasting or news and talk formats that do not require high-quality audio. Talk radio has, in many ways, been the salvation of AM radio. FM radio stations transmit using frequency modulation (FM). FM radio transmission is of a much higher quality. Because of this, FM radio has attracted the wide range of music formats that most listeners prefer. AM/FM broadcast, of course, is now available via the Web and through smartphones providing mobile advertising opportunities to advertisers.

Satellite Radio. Of course one of the newest options in radio is satellite radio, which is transmitted from satellites circling the earth. Currently, satellite radio costs a consumer anywhere from $99 to $200 to set up and then about $10 per month for a subscription. The advantages of satellite radio have to do with variety of programming, more crisp and clear sound reproduction, access to radio in places where broadcast does not reach, and, of course, *no ads*. The two leading satellite radio providers, Sirius/XM Satellite Radio merged in 2008 to avoid joint bankruptcy. The new company Sirius/XM radio has about 19 million subscribers and provides 135 channels of news, sports, music, and entertainment programming in the United States and Canada (see Exhibit 13.21). Satellite radio is primarily installed in consumers' vehicles, although there is some in-home installation as well. It remains to be seen whether consumers like the variety and quality offered by satellite radio enough to pay the subscription fee or whether they will prefer to keep "free" radio and listen to ads.

Internet/Mobile Radio. Internet radio has a wide and enthusiastic following. Sites like Pandora (the runaway leader) and Rhapsody allow listeners to access radio stations or build their own radio "stations" that play listeners' preferred music genres. And, unlike satellite radio, there is no fee. Recently, Internet radio providers have adopted technology to allow access through all varieties of smartphones. Mobile access, of course, once again provides advertisers the opportunity to reach target audiences while they are at the gym, on the train, jogging, or taking a walk in the park. A recent court ruling could hurt Internet radio providers. Broadband providers such as Comcast, AT&T,

Sirius Satellite Radio. Creative by Crispin, Porter & Bogusky, Miami

Exhibit 13.21 Satellite radio provider Sirius is gaining wider acceptance among radio listeners. Subscription fees and a downturn in new car sales stalled the growth of satellite radio for several years.

and Verizon won a court ruling that will allow them to prevent certain applications from "hogging capacity" as Internet radio does. The ruling basically means that there may not be such a thing as "free Internet radio" because broadband providers will start charging for Internet radio access, which consumes so much transmission capacity.[54]

Types of Radio Advertising. Advertisers have three basic choices in radio advertising: local spot radio advertising, network radio advertising, or national spot radio advertising. Local spot radio advertising attracts 80 percent of all radio advertising dollars in a year. In **local spot radio advertising**, an advertiser places advertisements directly with individual stations rather than with a network or syndicate. Local spot radio dominates the three classes of radio advertising because there are more than 10,000 individual radio stations in the United States, giving advertisers a wide range of choices. And local spot radio reaches well-defined geographic audiences, making it the ideal choice for local retailers.

Network radio advertising is advertising placed within national network programs. Since there are few network radio programs being broadcast, only about $600 million a year is invested by advertisers in this format.

The last option, **national spot radio advertising**, offers an advertiser the opportunity to place advertising in nationally syndicated radio programming. An advertiser can reach millions of listeners nationwide on more than 5,000 radio stations by contracting with Clear Channel's Premiere Radio Networks.

Advantages of Radio. Even though radio may not be the most glamorous or sophisticated of the major media options, it has some distinct advantages over newspapers, magazines, and television.

Cost. On both a per-contact and absolute basis, radio is often the most cost-effective medium available to an advertiser. A full minute of network radio time can cost between $5,000 and $10,000—an amazing bargain compared with the other media we've discussed. In addition, production costs for preparing radio ads are quite low; an ad often costs nothing to prepare if the spot is read live during a local broadcast.

Reach and Frequency. Radio has the widest exposure of any medium with nearly 80 percent of adults over the age of 18 listening to broadcast radio on a daily basis. (Some perspective here—only 6 percent of adults listen to Internet radio daily).[55] It reaches consumers in their homes, cars, offices, and backyards and, now with mobile access, even while they exercise. The wireless and portable features of radio provide an opportunity to reach consumers that exceeds all other media. The low cost of radio time gives advertisers the opportunity to frequently repeat messages at low absolute cost and cost per contact.

Target Audience Selectivity. Radio can selectively target audiences on a geographic, demographic, and psychographic/lifestyle basis. The narrow transmission of local radio stations gives advertisers the best opportunity to reach well-defined geographic audiences. For a local merchant with one store, this is an ideal opportunity. Radio programming formats and different dayparts also allow target audience selectivity. CBS Radio made the decision several years ago to convert four of its 13 stations to a rock 'n' roll oldies format to target 35-to-49-year-olds—in other words, the baby boomers. Hard rock, new age, easy listening, country, classical, news, and talk radio formats all attract different audiences. Radio dayparts, shown in Exhibit 13.22, also attract different audiences. Morning and afternoon/evening drive times attract a male audience. Daytime attracts predominantly woman; nighttime, teens.

54. Brandon Matthews, "Court Ruling Could Hurt Pandora, Benefit Sirius," Satwaves, April 8, 2010, accessed via the Web at www.seekingalpha.com

55. A.C. Nielsen, "How U.S. Adults Use Radio and Other Forms of Audio, 2009."

Exhibit 13.22 Radio dayparts used for advertising scheduling.

Daypart			
Morning drive time	6:00 a.m.	to	10:00 a.m.
Daytime	10:00 a.m.	to	3:00 p.m.
Afternoon/evening drive time	3:00 p.m.	to	7:00 p.m.
Nighttime	7:00 p.m.	to	12:00 a.m.
Late night	12:00 a.m.	to	6:00 a.m.

Flexibility and Timeliness. Radio is the most flexible medium because of very short closing periods for submitting an ad. This means an advertiser can wait until close to an air date before submitting an ad. With this flexibility, advertisers can take advantage of special events or unique competitive opportunities in a timely fashion. And, on-air personalities can read altered copy the day of a scheduled ad.

Creative Opportunities. Even though radio may be unidimensional in sensory stimulation, it can still have powerful creative impact. Radio has been described as the "theater of the mind." Ads such as the folksy tales of Tom Bodett for Motel 6 or the eccentric humor of Stan Freberg are memorable and can have tremendous impact on the attitude toward a brand. In addition, the musical formats that attract audiences to radio stations can also attract attention to radio ads. Research has discovered that audiences who favor certain music may be more prone to listen to an ad that uses songs they recognize and like.

Disadvantages of Radio. As good as radio can be, it also suffers from some severe limitations as an advertising medium. Advertising strategists must recognize these disadvantages when deciding what role radio can play in an integrated marketing communications program.

Poor Audience Attentiveness. Just because radio reaches audiences almost everywhere doesn't mean that anyone is paying attention. Radio is often described as "verbal wallpaper." It provides a comfortable background distraction while a consumer does something else—hardly an ideal level of attentiveness for advertising communication. Consumers who are listening and traveling in a car often switch stations when an ad comes on and divide their attention between the radio and the road.

Creative Limitations. Although the theater of the mind may be a wonderful creative opportunity, taking advantage of that opportunity can be difficult indeed. The audio-only nature of radio communication is a tremendous creative compromise. An advertiser whose product depends on demonstration or visual impact is at a loss when it comes to radio. And like its television counterpart, a radio message creates a fleeting impression that is often gone in an instant.

Fragmented Audiences. The large number of stations that try to attract the same audience in a market has created tremendous fragmentation. Think about your own local radio market. There are probably four or five different stations that play the kind of music you like. Or consider that in the past few years, more than 1,000 radio stations in the United States have adopted the talk-radio format. This fragmentation means that the percentage of listeners tuned to any one station is likely very small.

Chaotic Buying Procedures. For an advertiser who wants to include radio as part of a national advertising program, the buying process can be sheer chaos. Since national networks and syndicated broadcasts do not reach every geographic market, an advertiser has to buy time in individual markets on a station-by-station basis. This could involve dozens of different negotiations and individual contracts.

Measuring Radio Audiences. There are two primary sources of information on radio audiences. Arbitron ratings cover several hundred local radio markets. The ratings are developed through the use of diaries maintained by listeners who record when they listened to the radio and to what station they were tuned. The *Arbitron Ratings/Radio* book gives audience estimates by time period and selected demographic characteristics. Several specific measures are compiled from the Arbitron diaries:

- **Average quarter-hour persons:** The average number of listeners tuned to a station during a specified 15-minute segment of a daypart.
- **Average quarter-hour share:** The percentage of the total radio audience that was listening to a radio station during a specified quarter-hour daypart.
- **Average quarter-hour rating:** The audience during a quarter-hour daypart expressed as a percentage of the population of the measurement area. This provides an estimate of the popularity of each station in an area.
- **Cume:** The cumulative audience, which is the total number of different people who listen to a station for at least five minutes in a quarter-hour period within a specified daypart. Cume is the best estimate of the reach of a station.

RADAR (Radio's All Dimension Audience Research): The other major measure of radio audiences. Sponsored by the major radio networks, RADAR collects audience data twice a year based on interviews with radio listeners. Designated listeners are called daily for a one-week period and asked about their listening behavior. Estimates include measures of the overall audience for different network stations and audience estimates by market area. The results of the studies are reported in an annual publication, Radio Usage and Network Radio Audiences. Media planners can refer to published measures such as Arbitron and RADAR to identify which stations will reach target audiences at what times across various markets.

Exhibit 13.23 The radio industry continues to be in a state of flux. Sirius/XM is providing satellite radio. Radio programming is now accessible on the Web through computers and mobile devices. But, despite this change, big communications firms like Clear Channel continue to own and operate hundreds of radio stations.

Courtesy, Clear Channel Worldwide

The Future of Radio. Three factors must be considered with respect to the future of radio. First, the prospects for subscription satellite radio should not be underestimated—especially with recent court ruling that may pave the way for broadband providers to start charging for Internet radio access. Satellite radio does away with radio advertising clutter and offers listeners multiple, detailed choices to match their listening preferences. This is a huge advantage along with the increased audio quality. The key issue, of course, is whether radio listeners will be willing to pay for an entertainment medium that has been free from its inception.

Second, radio will be affected by emerging technologies much in the same way that television will be affected. High-definition radio, HD radio, is becoming a reality and big firms like Clear Channel now offer dozens of digital channels.[56] There are no subscription fees, but an HD receiver will cost a radio fan about $200, which may present a barrier to adoption and use. Finally, there has been a large degree of consolidation going on in the traditional radio market. Led by Clear Channel Communications (see Exhibit 13.23), fewer big competitors are owning more and more radio stations. Through an aggressive period of acquisitions in

56. Tom Lowry, "From Vanilla to Full Metal Racket," *BusinessWeek*, May 1, 2006, 42.

the early 2000s, Clear Channel now owns approximately 900 radio stations in all regions of the United States and generates about $7 billion in revenue, nearly half of that from its radio operations.[57] Consolidation provides both opportunities and liabilities for both consumers and advertisers. Opportunities for consumers relate to the consistency of quality in the radio programming available and advertisers have an easier time buying and placing radio spots.

Summary

1 Understand the changes taking place in the traditional "mass" media of newspapers, magazines, television, and radio relative to new digital media options.

The changes in the advertising industry are tangible and dramatic with respect to advertisers' use of the traditional media of newspapers, magazines, television, and radio. For decades, advertisers would work with their advertising agencies to develop messages for their brands and then the agencies would negotiate for airtime with television and radio networks or for space in newspapers and magazines. Most of these media options were owned by a few big media companies. Now, advertisers are fast adopting the belief that digital and interactive media—primarily Internet ads and mobile device ads—offer a more cost-effective and timely way to reach target markets. In addition, digital media allow advertisers to rapidly make changes in campaigns that might take months to accomplish with traditional media. Also, if the advertiser chooses, an Internet campaign can easily be a global campaign—a monumental task in traditional media. Advertisers are shifting literally billions of dollars out of traditional media in preference for digital media.

2 Detail the pros and cons of newspapers as a media class, identify newspaper categories, and describe buying and audience measurement for newspapers.

Newspapers can be categorized by target audience, geographic coverage, and frequency of publication. As a media class, newspapers provide an excellent means for reaching local audiences with informative advertising messages. Precise timing of message delivery can be achieved at modest expenditure levels. But for products that demand creative and colorful executions, this medium simply cannot deliver. Newspaper costs are typically transmitted via rate cards and are primarily a function of a paper's readership levels. Newspapers are struggling to survive in the digital age and are looking for ways to adopt pay-for-inquiry advertising models to attract advertisers back to the medium. In addition, traditional newspapers are offering digital editions, which could be successful on e-readers and tablet devices.

3 Detail the pros and cons of magazines as a media class, identify magazine categories, and describe buying and audience measurement for magazines.

Three important magazine categories are consumer, business, and farm publications. Because of their specific editorial content, magazines can be effective in attracting distinctive groups of readers with common interests. Thus, magazines can be superb tools for reaching specific market segments. Also, magazines facilitate a wide range of creative executions. Of course, the selectivity advantage turns into a disadvantage for advertisers trying to achieve high-reach levels. Costs of magazine ad space can vary dramatically because of the wide range of circulation levels achieved by different types of magazines. Like newspapers, magazines are adapting to the digital/interactive era. Paid electronic subscriptions with access through a variety of mobile devices is just beginning to take hold as options for magazines.

4 Detail the pros and cons of television as a media class, identify television categories, and describe buying and audience measurement for television.

The four basic forms of television are network, cable, syndicated, and local television. Television's principal advantage is obvious: Because it allows for almost

57. Data obtained from Adage.com, *Media Family Trees 2009*, accessed via the Web on April 12, 2010 at www.adage.com/mediatrees09

limitless possibilities in creative execution, it can be an extraordinary tool for affecting consumers' perceptions of a brand. Also, it can be an efficient device for reaching huge audiences; however, the absolute costs for reaching these audiences can be staggering. Lack of audience interest and involvement certainly limit the effectiveness of commercials in this medium, and digital devices like DVRs that allow the viewer to skip commercials make TV advertising nonexistent for many. The three ways that advertisers can buy time are through sponsorship, participation, and spot advertising. As with any medium, advertising rates will vary as a function of the size and composition of the audience that is watching—yet audience measurement for television is not an exact science and its methods are often disputed. The spread of broadband access to more consumers both at home and through mobile devices is allowing transmission of television programming in new and different ways. Advertisers are taking advantage of this opportunity to reach target markets beyond just in-home television advertising.

Detail the pros and cons of radio as a media class, identify radio categories, and describe audience measurement for radio.

Advertisers can choose from three basic types of radio advertising: local spot, network radio, or national spot advertising. Radio can be a cost-effective medium, and because of the wide diversity in radio programming, it can be an excellent tool for reaching well-defined audiences. Poor listener attentiveness is a drawback to radio, and the audio-only format places obvious constraints on creative execution. Satellite radio, which is subscriber-based, does away with advertising entirely on its music stations. Radio ad rates are driven by considerations such as the average number of listeners tuned to a station at specific times throughout the day. Buying and placing ads for radio is becoming easier due to ever-increasing consolidation in the industry. Like the other traditional mass media, radio is taking advantage of mobile transmission through smartphones and tablet devices. And, again, advertisers find this new access attractive in reaching target markets.

Key Terms

display advertising
co-op advertising
preprinted insert
free-standing insert (FSI)
classified advertising
rate card
column inch
standard advertising unit (SAU)
run-of-paper (ROP), or run-of-press
preferred position
full position
circulation
paid circulation
controlled circulation
readership
hyper-localism
pay-for-inquiry advertising model
bleed page
gatefold ads
first cover page
second cover page
third cover page
fourth cover page
double-page spreads
space contract
space order
closing date
on-sale date
cover date
guaranteed circulation
pass-along readership
network television
cable television
video on demand (VOD)
off-network syndication
first-run syndication
barter syndication
local television
satellite and closed-circuit
narrowcasting
channel grazing
V-chip
digital video recorder (DVR)
sponsorship
participation
spot advertising
dayparts
television households
households using television (HUT)
program rating
ratings point
share of audience
direct broadcast by satellite (DBS)
radio networks
radio syndication
local spot radio advertising
network radio advertising
national spot radio advertising
average quarter-hour persons
average quarter-hour share
average quarter-hour rating
cume
RADAR (Radio's All Dimension Audience Research)

Questions

1. With reference to the chapter opener, why are advertisers shifting billions of dollars from the traditional media of newspapers, magazines, television, and radio to digital media? What is your preference for viewing brand messages—traditional media or on the Internet and mobile devices?

2. Why are newspapers losing circulation and what effect does that have on their advertising revenue?

3. Magazines certainly proved to be the right media class for selling Absolut Vodka. Why are magazines a natural choice for Vodka advertisements? What has Absolut done with its advertising to take full advantage of this medium?

4. Peruse several recent editions of your town's newspaper and select three examples of co-op advertising. What objectives do you believe the manufacturers and retailers are attempting to achieve in each of the three ads you've selected?

5. Place your local newspaper and an issue of your favorite magazine side-by-side and carefully review the content of each. From the standpoint of a prospective advertiser, which of the two publications has a more dramatic problem with clutter? Identify tactics being used by advertisers in each publication to break through the clutter and get their brands noticed.

6. The costs involved in preparing and placing ads in television programming such as the Super Bowl broadcast can be simply incredible. How is it that advertisers such as Pepsi and Nissan can justify the incredible costs that come with this media vehicle?

7. Think about the television viewing behavior you've observed in your household. Of the five ways people avoid TV ad exposure discussed in this chapter, which have you observed in your household? What other avoidance tactics do your friends and family use?

8. The choice between print and broadcast media is often portrayed as a choice between high- and low-involvement media. What makes one medium inherently more involving than another? How will the characteristics of an ad's message affect the decision to employ an involving versus an uninvolving medium?

9. Have you started to listen to radio over the Internet either at your computer or through your smartphone? What if you have to start paying a monthly subscription fee to listen to stations? Will you do so? Would you switch to satellite radio where you might also have to pay a subscription but won't have the ads?

10. What are the potential liabilities and risks to consumers and advertisers of the consolidation of radio station ownership by a few, large media companies?

Experiential Exercises

1. Since 1970, Mother Earth News has been the magazine of choice for environmental-minded consumers. The bimonthly lifestyle rag, which boasts national circulation of 470,000 readers, covers topics ranging from organic gardening and natural foods to green homemaking. Mother Earth News is not suitable for all advertisers, however; the magazine's diehard environmentalist readers loudly protest companies that don't meet high standards of sustainability. List pros and cons of placing ads in Mother Earth News, and identify two brands that should advertise in the magazine and two that should not.

2. Newspapers are struggling to survive as readers increasingly go online to get news and information. Nevertheless, newspapers continue to offer unique benefits to advertisers. Write a report about the state of newspapers and make an argument for what may happen to newspaper advertising during the next decade. Be sure to answer the following questions: Could newspapers go extinct? Do advertisers still need this medium? Can news organizations find a way to make newspapers a viable business again?

3. Program sponsorship is one way for advertisers to cut through the clutter of television advertising. Working in small teams, propose existing and potential television shows or specials that would present powerful sponsorship opportunities for the sports-drink maker Gatorade. Identify any additional marketing opportunities that could accompany such a sponsorship.

4. Draft a media plan for a new cosmetics line with a target segment of Hispanic women between the ages of 15 and 25. Identify examples within each of the traditional media groups—newspapers, magazines, television, and radio—that could be effective and then recommend which of the four areas is the best choice for the campaign.

Chapter 14

Media Planning: Advertising and IBP in Digital/Interactive Media

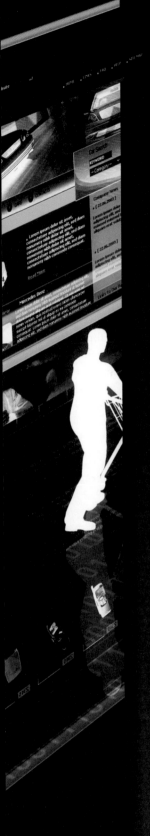

After reading and thinking about this chapter, you will be able to do the following:

1. Understand the current role of digital and interactive media in advertising and IBP.
2. Identify the advantages of digital/interactive media for implementing advertising and IBP campaigns.
3. Describe the different advertising options available through digital/interactive media on the Internet.
4. Discuss the ways different IBP tools can use digital/interactive media.
5. Discuss the future of advertising and IBP using digital and interactive media.

Sprint
Sprint
Sprint
Sprint
Sprint
Sprint
Sprint
Sprint

Introductory Scenario: Racing Through the Web.

Since 2007, Miss Sprint Cup (see Exhibit 14.1) has traveled weekly to NASCAR Sprint Cup Series races donning a Sprint-branded driver's suit and stirring up excitement at the races. She interviews drivers, hangs out in the pit area, attends victory celebrations, and interacts with fans. But the real power of Miss Sprint Cup as a brand icon for the racing series comes from her work on social networking sites, primarily Twitter and Facebook. Sprint introduced both Facebook and Twitter accounts in 2008 allowing Miss Sprint Cup to communicate real time with racing fans. When Sprint Series management first ventured into social media with Miss Sprint Cup (there are actually three Miss Sprint Cups now), the general manager of NASCAR Sprint Cup sponsorship thought "Here's a woman living a lifestyle that [NASCAR] fans would die to be part of—hanging out in the garage area, meeting drivers at pre-race festivities, and fans would love to get a real-time look at the inner-workings of a NASCAR race."[1] He was right. On race weekends while she is attending an event, she will update her Facebook (www.facebook.com/misssprintcup) and Twitter (www.twitter.com/misssprintcup) pages about 20 times. Every time she posts, she gets more than 100 responses from fans and 98 percent are positive. Now, she has more than 100,000 fans on Facebook and more than 10,000 followers on Twitter.

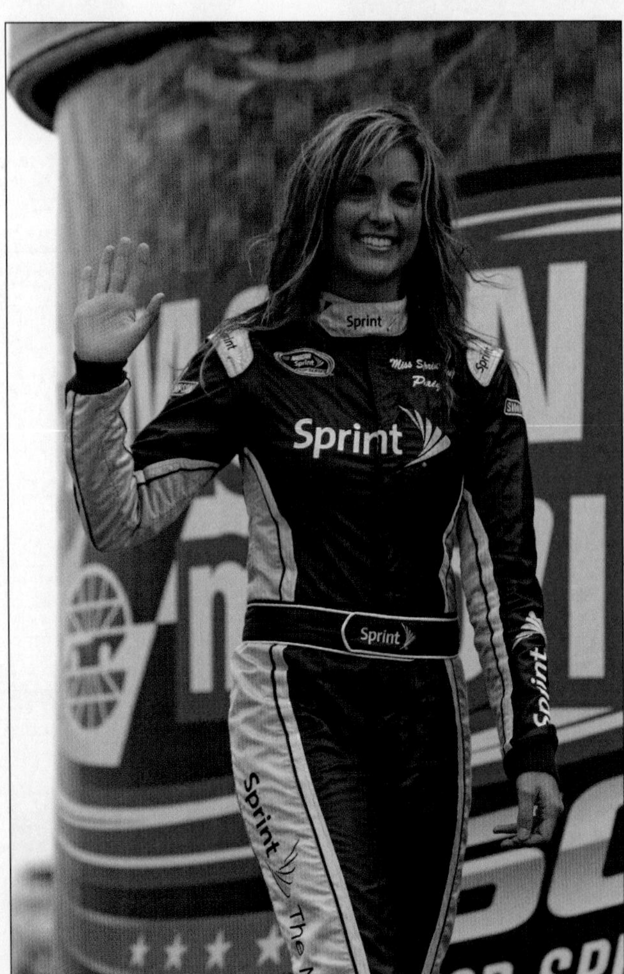

Exhibit 14.1 Sprint started using social media as part of its IBP program for the NASCAR Sprint Cup Series in 2008. Now "Miss Sprint Cup" has more than 100,000 fans on Facebook and more than 10,000 followers on Twitter.

© AP Photo/Brandon Wade

What's in it for Sprint as an advertiser using social media as a communications tool? Sprint does not have Miss Sprint Cup talk about the latest sales price on a new BlackBerry—that's not subtle enough. Rather, the marketing managers at Sprint explain, "... let's say Miss Sprint Cup takes a picture with her new BlackBerry Tour, uploads it to Facebook, and mentions the device in the photo caption. The handset gets mentioned in a very real way, and we've shown some of the device's capabilities without it feeling like a product pitch."[2] Well, there you have it. Precisely the way social media can be effectively worked into an IBP program. Potential customers encounter a social media site *voluntarily* based on a personal interest and a brand exposure/message just happens to show up on the site in a "natural" way in a very positive communication environment.

The whole idea behind combining Web content with traditional media is that the Web generation (of which you are a key part) will seek out messages on the Web and attend to those messages more readily than traditional media messages sent through magazines or television. Advertising messages or brand "shout outs" that find their way on to YouTube, Facebook, LinkedIn, or Twitter are argued to communicate in a more natural, "social" way. The managing director of NASCAR puts it this way, "When

1. Matthew Schwartz, "NASCAR: Driving Social Media," *Advertising Age Integrated Marketing Guide*, November 16, 2009, C3, C13.

2. Ibid, C3.

you couple TV with in-person marketing with an average of 110,000 fans [attending each race], you've got a powerful one-two punch. Social-media aspects help sew those two components together."[3] And, as discussed throughout the book, when a message shows up on a social networking site, it seems to be more part of "life" and less like big corporate, commercial-speak. In addition, as with the Miss Sprint Cup strategy, global target markets can be reached nearly instantaneously if the right message catches on and spreads through the networks.

Sprint is not, of course, the first firm to think of using strategies that unleash the power of the Web on a brand. Red Bull has done little traditional media advertising in the 100 countries where the energy drink is sold. Instead you'll find Web-based interactive contests where people create sculptures out of Red Bull cans and win a trip to Switzerland. Another example is DirecTV's organization of a championship video-gaming series with tournaments broadcast on satellite television. Firms around the world are discovering that working brand messages into media that will be "voluntarily" viewed is powerful stuff.

No Wires Means New Rules.

Digital and interactive media options are made possible because of the Internet. The Internet has been a wild ride for advertisers since 1999. First a boom. Then the dot. bomb. Now we are firmly into another boom—and it is permanent. Despite skepticism resulting from the large list of high-profile Internet sites that went from dot. darlings to dot.nots—including eToys, Garden.com, and Pets.com—the Internet is growing at an astounding rate. Networked business-to-business Internet transactions are now approaching $4 *trillion* annually. Consumer e-commerce is also spectacular exceeding $300 billion annual spending by consumers on goods and services.[4]

The Internet has also finally become the advertising option that everyone expected it to be. As we talked about in Chapter 2 and Chapter 13, marketers are discovering that they can incorporate Web advertising messages into their IBP programs and are, indeed, channeling money from traditional media over to the Web. Expenditures on digital and interactive advertising now exceed $30 billion annually with "paid search" (more on this later) leading the way at about $17 billion (expected to grow to more than $30 billion by 2012) followed by rich media/video at about $3 billion.[5]

But for all that the Internet is fundamentally—an information search, email, entertainment medium—it has become so much more in the last few years. Why? One word—wireless. No doubt, you are all regularly accessing the Web through WiFi on campus or at your favorite coffeeshop. **WiFi** first became widely popular in 2004 because it allowed Internet-access connections that reach out about 300 feet. So everyone from coffee drinkers at Starbucks to emergency workers at disaster sites could have wireless access to information through their laptops. But WiFi was just the beginning. Now, the new wireless revolution has the potential for making WiFi look like a landline telephone. During the next few years WiFi will likely yield to three innovative technologies that will push wireless networking into every facet of life from cars to homes to offices to the beach. These technologies are:

- **WiMax** (Worldwide Interoperability for Microwave Access), which like WiFi, creates "hot spots" around a central antenna within which people can wirelessly tap into the Net. But while WiFi creates a hot spot of perhaps 300 feet, WiMax has a potential range of 25–30 miles! Both Sprint and Clearwire are

3. Matthew Schwartz, "NASCAR: Driving Social Media," Advertising Age Integrated Marketing Guide, November 16, 2009, C3.

4. Data on e-commerce is available at http://www.census.gov/econ/estats/2008/2008reportfinal.pdf, May, 27, 2010.

5. Forrester Research, Inc., "U.S. Interactive Marketing Forecast, 2009–2014," July 30, 2009, 7; Advertising Age, "Digital Marketing Facts 2010," *Advertising Age,* February 22, 2010.

using WiMax technology branded as "4G" networks with Clearwire launching a WiMax networks across the United States and in Europe. The *Globalization* box shows that WiMax is ideal for rural environments.

- **Mi-Fi** (Mobile Fi) is similar to WiMax in that it has multi-mile access but adds the capability of accessing the Net while the user is moving in a car, on the beach—virtually anywhere. Described as a "private hot spot" the first Mi-Fi devices were introduced in 2009. Users access through any web-enabled device through 3/4G networks.[6]
- **Ultrabroadband** is the technology that allows people to move extremely large files quickly over short distances. On the road, a driver could download a large file from an on-board PC to a handheld computer. Or, at home, you could do a wireless upload of your favorite concert from your PC to your TV. Ultrabroadband is a boon to social network users who want to share photos and those who use tablet devices to download movies and books.

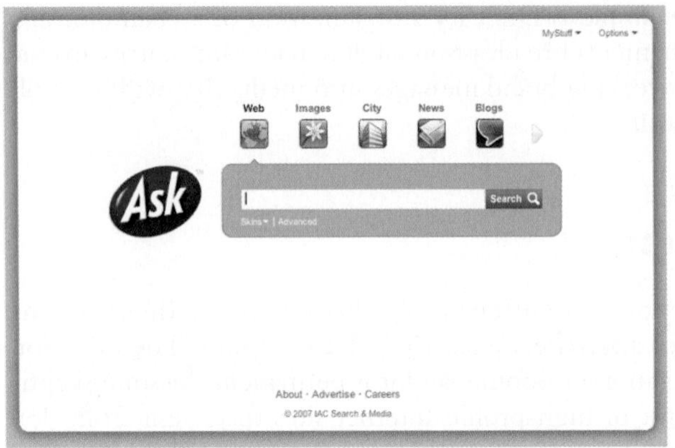

Exhibit 14.2 In the next decade, new technologies like WiMax will provide wireless access to the Internet that extends up to 30 miles. This will open up more ways for consumers to tap into their favorite information sources, like Ask.com, and more ways for advertisers to reach those surfers.

Scientists at Intel, Alcatel-Lucent, and Motorola are working on these technologies primarily as modes of communication for the high-speed transmission of data. But, in their practical application, these technologies will allow advertisers to communicate with audiences as Net surfers access the Internet through WiMax, WiFi, or Mi-Fi. These new technologies are going to make it that much easier for consumers using search services like Ask.com to find what they are searching for faster, from wherever they are! (See Exhibit 14.2.)

1 The Role of Digital/Interactive Media in the Advertising and IBP Process.

As the Internet has provided digital and interactive opportunities, many firms like Pepsi (www.pepsiworld.com) and BMW (www.bmw.com) have been highly successful in folding the Internet into their integrated brand promotion strategies. A trip to these sites shows that these firms funnel a lot of information and promotion through their websites and engage consumers through social programs or Web videos. But what about the Internet *overall* as a medium? What is and what will likely be the role of the Internet in a promotional effort? A few "truths" have made themselves evident to this point.

First, the Internet will *not* be replacing all other forms of advertising. Nor is it likely that the biggest spenders on advertising and promotion (you know those multibillion-dollar types) will use the Internet as the *main* method of communicating with target audiences. But, like Pepsi, Starbucks, and Ford, advertisers are discovering ways to use the Internet as a key component of integrated brand promotions. Second, yes, things are changing dramatically regarding all aspects of the Internet. Auction sites like eBay have provided huge opportunities for small businesses all around the world. And as we have pointed out throughout the book, Web 3.0 and its social networking emphasis provides a whole new way of delivering promotional messages.

In the current view of the Internet and advertising, we will spend most of our time in this chapter focusing on two fundamental issues: the structure of the Internet and the potential of the Internet as an advertising medium. Through these

6. David Pogue, "Wi-Fi to Go, No Café Needed," *The New York Times,* May 7, 2009.

Globalization

To Russia with WiMax

The Russian market is a mystery in many ways when it comes to advertising and promotion. Data on just how much money is spent in what media to send commercial messages is hard to come by. But when it comes to the technology that advertisers want and need to send messages over the Internet, the picture is getting much more clear. Alcatel-Lucent, developers of WiMax technology and hardware, just landed a deal to build a nationwide rural WiMax access network in Russia—the most rural country in the world. There are more than 160 cities and towns in Russia with 50,000 to 100,000 people and hundreds more with a population less than 50,000.

Alcatel-Lucent will work with Russian telecom company Synterra, the firm that holds the national license for the 2.5 GHz bands needed for WiMax communications, to build the WiMax infrastructure in towns with populations smaller than 100,000. The project will install "steered beams" that will provide greater range and coverage than any other form of transmission.

The project is enormous, providing Internet access to more than 40 million Russians who do not have DSL or cable modem connection to the Internet. This, in turn, will give advertisers and Internet service providers a vast new market of Russian consumers who, up to this point, had limited or no access to the Web. Most recently, Clearwire, known for WiMax networks across the United States, has launched a WiMax network in Spain that will reach 600,000 people. Which leaves one burning question: Do you think Russians and Spaniards will Tweet Miss Sprint Cup with their high-speed mobile networks?

Sources: Dan O'Shea, "Study: WiMax, MobileFi No Threat to DSL," *TelephonyOnline*, June 8, 2004; Kevin Fitchard, "Alcatel-Lucent to Build WiMax in Russia," *TelephonyOnline*, July 6, 2007; Stuart Corner, "Alcatel-Lucent to Build 1000 City Russian WiMAX Network" *ITWire*, July 9, 2007; "Clearwire Launches WiMax in Spain,' GoingWiMax.com, January 8, 2010.

discussions, we will gain a better understanding of how to use the Internet as part of an effective overall advertising and integrated brand promotion effort. First, we will consider a short history of the evolution of the Internet. Next, we'll consider the different types of advertising that can be used and some of the technical aspects of the process. Finally, we will look at the issues involved in establishing a website and developing a brand in the "e-community."

The (R)evolution of the Internet.

Technology changes everything—or at least it has the power and potential to change everything. When it's communications technology, such as the Internet, it can change something very fundamental about human existence and behavior. The Internet-connected consumer is connected to other consumers in real time, and with connection comes community, empowerment, even liberation. And, what can be truly revolutionary about the Internet is its ability to alter the basic nature of communication within a commercial channel.

In 1994, advertisers began working with Prodigy and CompuServe, which were the first Internet service providers. These advertisers had the idea that they would send standard television commercials online. Well, the technology was not in place back then for that to work and the mentality was still firmly anchored in traditional media rather than the vast capability of this new medium. That condition sent the advertisers and the ISPs back to the drawing board. With the emergence of more commercial ISPs such as America Online and EarthLink, the new Web browsers were worth exploring as a way to send commercial messages. The first true Web browser was Mosaic, the precursor to Netscape 1.0, and the first ads began appearing in *HotWired* magazine (the online version of *Wired* magazine) in October 1994. The magazine boasted 12 advertisers, including MCI, AT&T, Sprint, Volvo, and Club Med, and each one paid $30,000 for a 12-week run of online display/banner ads with no guarantee of the number or profile of the viewers.

Well, things have certainly changed since those early days. Now, the Internet is being accessed worldwide by slightly more than 1.7 billion users through portals like Yahoo! and Google with literally hundreds of ISPs providers.[7] In historical perspective, advertising spending on the Internet was estimated at about $12 billion in 2005 and is estimated to grow to more than $40 billion by 2012—about 17 percent of all ad spending.[8] The medium is used by all forms of companies, large, small, bricks and mortar, virtual, e-commerce, not-for-profit, you name it. Further, the medium is home to literally millions of websites, and the value of the Internet to individual consumers is growing daily. Let's turn our attention to some of the technical aspects of the Internet and then we'll explore the Internet as a strategic advertising and IBP option for advertisers. Exhibit 14.3 shows that Internet access around the world has continued its accelerated rate of increase with about 1.8 billion users estimated worldwide as of 2009—a 10-fold increase in just an 12-year period.[9] And, let's not jump to the conclusion that the Internet is a "young persons" medium or target market. More than 17.5 million "seniors" aged 65 and over use the Internet on a daily basis.[10]

Do not overlook the potential that still remains for digital and interactive communications, however. Note from Exhibit 14.3 that the 1.8 billion Internet users worldwide represent only about 26 percent of the world's population. Further, some large-population countries, such as Russia, China, and India, have only recently begun to provide widespread access to the Internet and represent billions more potential users, notwithstanding the restrictions China has placed on Internet access.

World Regions	Population (2009 Est.)	Internet Users Latest Data	Penetration (% Population)	Growth 2000-2009
Africa	991,002,342	86,217,900	8.7%	1,809.8%
Asia	3,808,070,503	764,435,900	20.1%	568.8%
Europe	803,850,858	425,773,571	53.0%	305.1%
Middle East	202,687,005	58,309,546	28.8%	1,675.1%
North America	340,831,831	259,561,000	76.2%	140.1%
United States	307,212,123	227,719,000	74.1%	138.8%
Canada	33,487,208	25,086,000	74.9%	97.5%
Latin America/Caribbean	586,662,468	186,922,050	31.9%	934.5%
Oceania / Australia	34,700,201	21,110,490	60.8%	177.0%
WORLD TOTAL	6,767,805,208	1,802,330,457	26.6%	399.3%

Source: Internet World Stats, www.internetworldstats.com/stats

Exhibit 14.3 Worldwide Internet usage as of 2009.

Using Internet Digital/Interactive Media: The Basics.

The two main digital/interactive media used by consumers are email (including electronic mailing lists) and the World Wide Web, which, in turn, make these media for advertisers. It may seem odd to refer to email and the Web as "media." After all, we use email and the Web for all sorts of personal use reasons. But remember, to

7. Global use of the Web statistics obtained from Internetworldstats.com, accessed June 15, 2010 at www.internetworldstats.com/stats

8. Forrester Research, Inc., "U.S. Interactive Marketing Forecast, 2009–2014," July 30, 2009.

9. Global use of the Web statistics obtained from Internetworldstats.com, accessed June 15, 2010 at www.internetworldstats.com/stats

10. Jack Marshall, "Study: More People 65 and Older Flock to the Web," ClickZ, December 22, 2009.

an advertiser, email and the Web are ways to reach you as a consumer—therefore, they are media.

Exhibit 14.4 Various firms help marketers place highly targeted email messages through the Web that serve as customized one-to-one advertising.

Email.

We all know that the email system is used by advertisers to reach potential and existing customers. We get emails solicitations every day. A variety of companies collect email addresses and profiles that allow advertisers to direct email to a specific group. Widespread, targeted email advertising is facilitated by organizations like Advertising.com (www.advertising.com) (see Exhibit 14.4). These organizations target, prepare, and deliver emails to highly specific audiences for advertisers.

Advertisers are addressing consumer resistance to email advertising through "opt-in email." **Opt-in email** is commercial email that is sent with the recipient's consent, such as when website visitors give their permission to receive commercial email about topics and products that interest them. If you have purchased a product online, it is likely you were asked to check a box acknowledging that you would like to receive future information about the company and its products. Service providers like Data Solutions, Inc. (www.datasolutionsinc.com) help firms like OfficeMax, American Express, and Exxon manage their opt-in email promotions. Other firms like L-Soft (www.lsoft.com) offer software for managing electronic mailing lists, providing advertisers with readily available target market access (see Exhibit 14.5).

As we discussed in Chapter 3 as an ethical/social issue, uninvited commercial messages sent to electronic mailing lists, Usenet groups, or some other compilation of email addresses is a notorious practice known as **spam**. Various estimates suggest 14.5 *billion* spam emails are being sent every day worldwide and represents up to 45 percent of all email traffic.[11] As we saw in Chapter 3, few promotional techniques have drawn as much wrath from consumers and regulators. But before we close the discussion on spam, here is an interesting note: As annoying as spam seems to be to Web users, it appears to be effective. Those mass emailings can get a 3 to 5 percent response compared with 1 to 3 percent for offline direct marketing efforts. So before we write off mass emails, we had better consider the results, not just the public reaction.

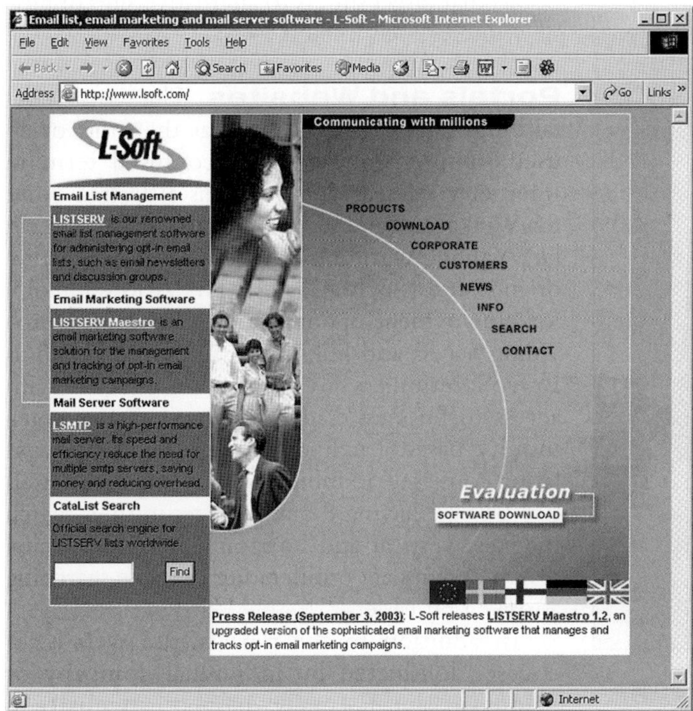

Exhibit 14.5 Similar to email messaging, firms can buy complete lists of email groups from companies like L-Soft to distribute electronic newsletters and opt-in email campaigns.

Courtesy of Advertising.com; L-Soft International, developers of LISTSERV®

The World Wide Web.

The **World Wide Web (WWW)** is a "web" of information available to most Internet users, and its graphical environment makes navigation simple and exciting. Of all the options

11. "Spam Statistics and Facts," Spamlaws.com, accessed at www.spamlaws.com/spam-stats on June 15, 2010.

available for Internet advertisers, the WWW provides the greatest breadth and depth of opportunity. It allows for detailed and full-color graphics, audio transmission, delivery of customized messages, mobile delivery of messages, 24-hour availability, and two-way information exchanges between the marketer and customer. For some people, spending time on the Web is replacing time spent viewing other media, such as print, radio, and television. There is one great difference between the Web and other cyber-advertising vehicles: The consumer actively searches for the marketer's home page or can receive messages via mobile marketing through cell phones, table readers, and other mobile devices. Firms are searching for ways to make their use of the Web more effective particularly by tapping into social media. Much has been learned about building the brand through social media networks as the *Social Media* box on p. 506 demonstrates.

Surfing the World Wide Web. About 75 percent of Americans use the World Wide Web. Of these users, 72 percent use email, 50 percent use the Web to access the latest news and special interest information sites, 34 percent have made a purchase online, and more than 30 percent use the Web to pay bills.[12]

This desire for information, entertainment, and personal services leads to **surfing**—gliding from page to page. Users can seek and find different sites in a variety of ways: through search engines, through direct links with other sites, and by word-of-mouth. Surfing is made fast and efficient by various search engine technology. A **search engine** allows an Internet user to surf by typing in a few key words, and the search engine then finds all sites that contain the key words. Search engines all have the same basic user interface but differ in how they perform the search and in the amount of the WWW accessed. The big Internet sites like Yahoo! and Google use search engine technology to optimize the search results that direct surfers to alternative sites of possible interest (see Exhibit 14.6).

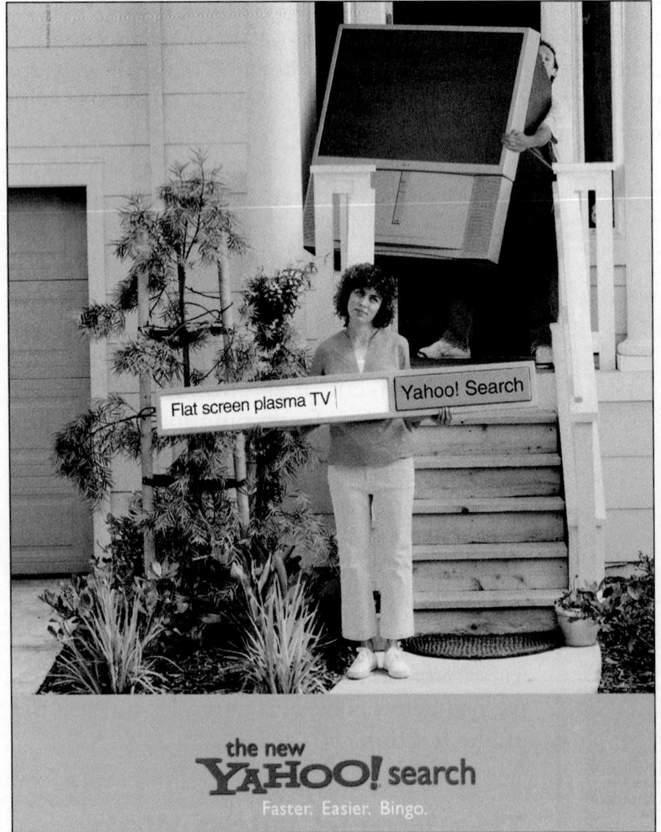

Exhibit 14.6 Big Internet sites like Yahoo! and Google offer Internet users quick and efficient searches through search engine technology for their information, entertainment, and service needs.

Portals and Websites. The word "portal" has assumed the position as the most overused, misused, abused, and confused term in Internet vocabulary. A **portal** is a starting point for Web access and search. Portals can be general, like Yahoo!; vertical (serving a specialized market or industries, such as Jobster, www.jobster.com, for employment opportunities); horizontal (providing access and links across industries, such as BravoSolution, www.bravosolution.com, with access to business trade communities); or community-based (such as Latina Online, www.latina.com; see Exhibit 14.7). With big portals like Google having 8 billion pages in their search indexes, vertical and horizontal subject-specific search engines are proliferating to make searching a topic a bit easier.[13]

In addition to the portals, the Web is, of course, dominated by individual company or brand website. Formally defined, a **website** is a collection of Web pages, images, videos, and

12. Digital Market Facts 2010, *Advertising Age,* February 22, 2010, insert.

13. Om Malik, "Growing in the Shadow of Google," *Business 2.0,* December 2006, 40.

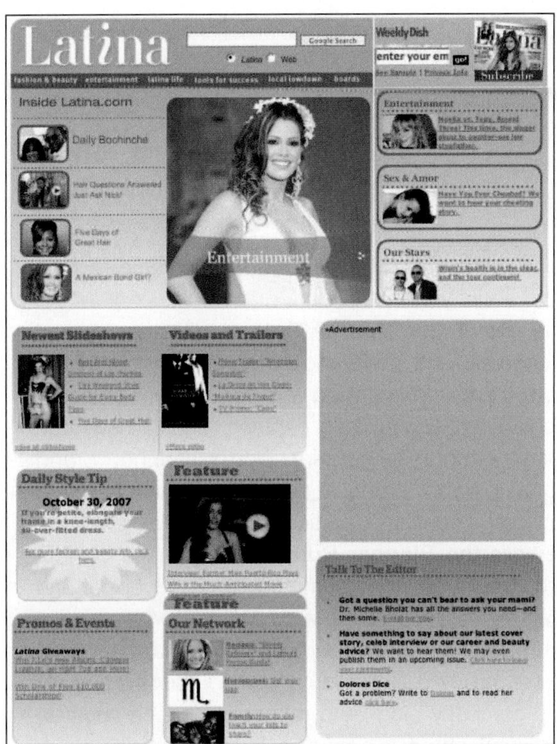

Exhibit 14.7 Community portals like Latina Online offer a site that matches surfers' interests for information on a variety of topics from politics to culture to entertainment. What is teen site Alloy (www.alloy.com) doing to make sure it wins the community portal war? Are Alloy's search functions and navigational features designed to direct surfers to particular sites?

other digital content that is hosted on a Web server. Think about your own surfing behavior. You probably start out at a portal and then navigate your way around a series of website. A variation of the standard website is the "mash-up." A **mash-up** is the combination of one or more websites into a single site. An example is Chicagocrime.org, where local crime statistics are overlaid on GoogleMaps so that you can see what crimes have been committed in your neighborhood. Large news agencies like *The New York Times* and *Reuters* allow users to "mash-up" their news content into what amounts to a personalized newspaper. Another example is Book Burro (see Exhibit 14.8), which shows the price for a book at several competing online booksellers.[14]

Personal Websites and Blogs. Many people have created their own Web pages that list their favorite sites. This is a fabulous way of finding new and interesting sites—as well as feeding a person's narcissism. For example, the website for this book www.cengage.com/international is a resource for information about advertising and IBP, including links to a wide range of industry resources.

Although most people find Web pages via Internet resources, sites can also be discovered through word-of-mouth communications—in-person, email, or social networks. Internet enthusiasts tend to share their experiences on the Web through discussions in coffeehouses, by reading and writing articles, and via other non-Web venues. There are also mega–search engines, like Dogpile (www.dogpile.com), which combine several search engines at once.

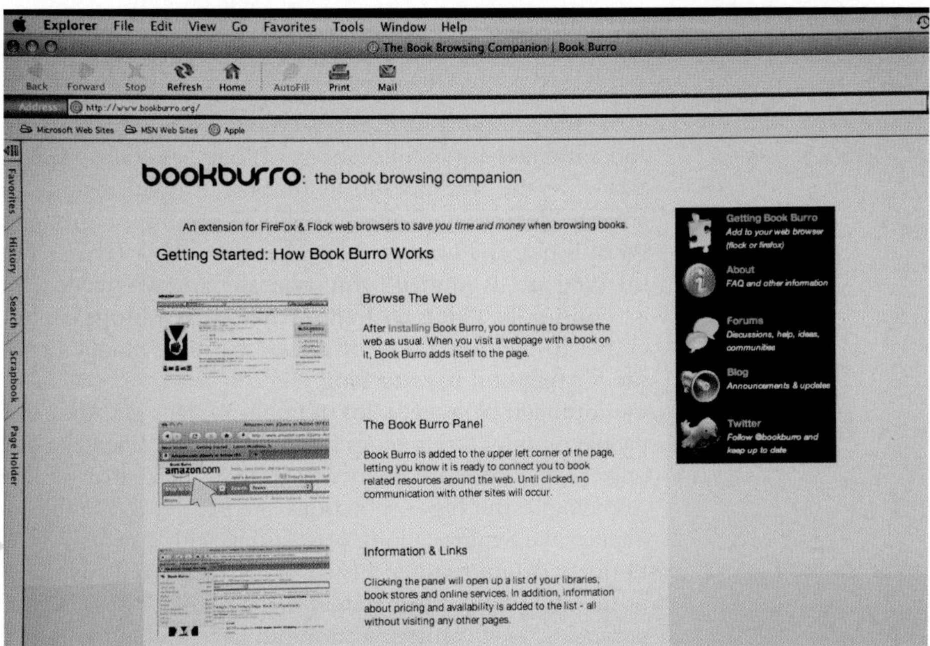

Exhibit 14.8
A "mash-up" is the combination of one or more websites into a single site. Book Burro allows users to combine several book-selling sites into one to search for the best prices.

14. Robert D. Hof, "Mix, Match, and Mutate," *BusinessWeek,* July 25, 2005, 72–74.

Social Media

8 Rules for Brands in Social Media

1. **The Small Is Big Rule:** A small portion of site visitors are responsible for site traffic. High volume users generate 40 to 50 percent of site traffic and are the ones who share their experiences. Identify who they are and recognize and reward them.
2. **The Conversion Rule:** Visitors driven to your site by peers are four times more likely to be converted to brand users than those who come from other sources like display ads or paid search. Encourage site visitors to share their experience or forward your link.
3. **Users Are More Powerful Rule:** If a company puts brand content on its own Facebook page, it is far less powerful than the word-of-mouth generated by an influential consumer who shares the very same content on his or her Facebook page. Consider ways to make your brand content "viral" from consumer to consumer.
4. **Throw Your Own Party Rule:** Try to create your own social site that attracts visitors—a branded social site, contest site, or customer forum—where you can control content and activities. Visit the Pepsi Refresh (www.refresheverything.com) site to see a great example of this technique.
5. **Keep the Email Rule:** Although new social media networks are highly visible, email and IM are still very popular ways for consumers to share information. Don't dump email campaigns as a way to spread the word about your brand.
6. **The Be Truly Social Rule:** Cultivating brand awareness and preference though social media is more than simply sticking ads and content on social media sites. Brands and content need to have true social attributes—content worth sharing, brand features worth talking about, and site features that encourage consumer participation and dialogue.
7. **Beware the Blogger Rule:** Seeding brand content through bloggers or a company blog are popular and relatively easy. But there are huge risks. Data shows that 90 percent of all seeding has no material effect. Worse, only 16 percent of consumers trust the content in a company blog. And, worst of all, one negative comment about a brand on a blog spreads much faster and more extensively than positive comments.
8. **The Be Useful Rule:** Social marketing programs need to provide a service to the consumer to be successful. Mere brand hype and posturing will not be effect. Provide consumers with content they can use to make their lives better, more fulfilling, or even simply more pleasant.

Sources: Taddy Hall, "10 Essential Rules for Brands in Social Media," *Advertising Age,* March 22, 2010, 6; Josh Bernoff, "Blogs, Marketing and Trust," *Marketing News,* February 15, 2009, 17.

A **blog**, a short form for Weblog, is a personal journal that is frequently updated and intended for public access. Blogs generally represent the personality of the author or the website and its purpose. Topics include brief philosophical musings, favorite hobbies and music, political leanings, commentary on Internet and other social issues, and links to other sites the author favors. The essential characteristics of the blog are its journal form, typically a new entry each day, and its informal style. The author of a blog is often referred to as a **blogger**. People who post new journal entries to their blog may often say that they blogged today, they blogged it to their site, or they still have to blog.

Although blogs get a lot of publicity, let's get some perspective. About 57 million people reported using blogs but only about 12 percent of those blog users visit a blog once a week or more frequently. And 88 percent of all Internet users seldom or never read blogs.[15] But big corporations like Procter & Gamble are finding that some of their brands, like Swiffer (a long plastic stick with a swatch of dust-attracting cloth attached to the end), are featured on customer blogs, and advertisers in general feel this aspect of the Web holds great potential for peer-to-peer communication and the power of persuasion such communication can have on brands. And, it's important to remember

15. Digital Marketing & Media Fact Pack, *Advertising Age,* April 23, 2007, 21.

that blogs do not necessarily engender a lot of trust among consumers. Consumers trust traditional media at a much higher rate: 46 percent for newspapers, 39 percent for magazines, and even 38 percent for television but only 16 percent for blogs.[16] Remember from Chapter 3 that the FTC had to pass new regulations that require that bloggers reveal any affiliations with companies whose brands they might feature in a blog post.

Advertising on Digital and Interactive Media.

With the basics in place, advertisers try to take advantage of the opportunities that digital and interactive media offer. As we have referenced before, the growth of advertising using digital and interactive media is growing dramatically but sporadically. In 1995, $54.7 million was spent advertising on the Internet, and the year 2000 logged in at slightly more than $8 billion. Then the boom turned to bust and the dot. bomb hit when literally dozens of Internet-based companies went out of business. In 2002, billions went out of the Internet ad market and revenues came in at slightly more than $6 billion. By 2003, a recovery was in process and revenues spiked back to $7.25 billion and are now estimated to be in the range of $23 billion in 2010.[17]

A variety of complex issues are associated with using the Internet for advertising purposes. This section begins by exploring the advantages of Internet advertising. Then we'll look at who is advertising on the Internet, the costs associated with Internet advertising, and the different types of Internet advertising.

2 The Advantages of Digital and Interactive Media Advertising.

Digital and interactive media available through the Web advertising has finally emerged as a legitimate advertising option—and it is not only because the Web represents a new and different technological option. Several unique characteristics of the Internet offer advantages for advertising over traditional media options.

Target Market Selectivity. The components of the Web offer advertisers a new and precise way to target market segments. Not only are the segments precisely defined—you can place an ad on the numismatist (coin collecting) society page, for example—but the Internet allows forms of targeting that truly enhance traditional segmentation schemes such as demographics, geographics, and psychographics. Advertisers can focus on specific interest areas, but they can also target based on geographic regions (including global), time of day, computer platform, or browser. With the newest GPS enabled mobile devices, advertisers can now target consumers as they enter shopping areas. Companies like Foursquare, which allows friends to check in with each other as they explore cities can help advertisers target consumers on the go at restaurants or shopping malls with coupons and discounts (see Exhibit 14.9). As example, Filipacchi Media U.S. shut down its print version of *ElleGirl* and instead created a website (www.ellegirl.elle.com). The publisher discovered that teen girls were forgoing print media altogether in preference for Web access to information.[18] When American Airlines enlisted the help of TM Advertising to track the Web behavior of the readers of *The Wall Street Journal* (www.wsj.com) online travel columns and then "follow" those surfers around with American Airlines ads at various other sections, response to the online advertising increased 115 percent.[19]

16. Josh Benoff, "Blogs, Marketing and Trust," *Marketing News,* February 16, 2007, 17.

17. "Digital Marketing Facts 2010," *Advertising Age,* February 22, 2010, insert.

18. Jon Fine, "Smells Like Teen Progress," *BusinessWeek,* May 8, 2006, 22.

19. Kris Oser, "Targeting Web Behavior Pays, America Airlines Study Finds," *Advertising Age,* May 17, 2004, 8.

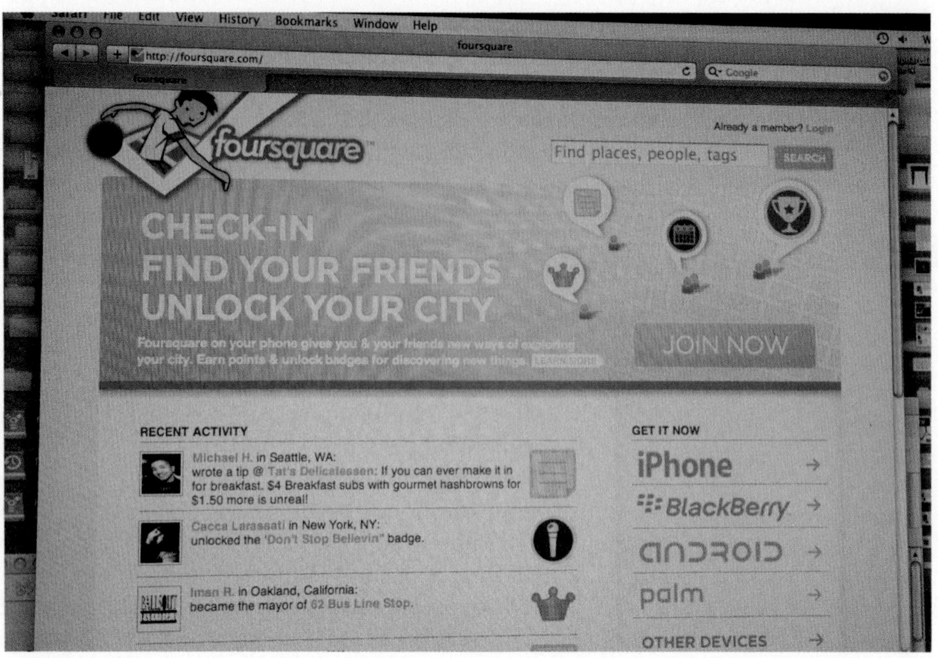

Exhibit 14.9
Companies like Foursquare help business and advertisers engage mobile customers with "Specials," which are discounts and prizes for loyal customers.

Courtesy, Susan Van Etten

Tracking. The Internet allows advertisers to track how users interact with their brands and learn what interests current and potential customers. Display/banner ads and websites also provide the opportunity to measure the response to an ad by means of hits, a measure that is unattainable in traditional media. We'll discuss tracking and measurement in more detail a bit later in the chapter.

Deliverability, Flexibility, and Reach. Online advertising, mobile messages, and website content are delivered 24 hours a day, seven days a week, at the convenience of the receiver. Whenever receivers are logged on and active, advertising is there and ready to greet them. For advertisers, a campaign can be tracked on a daily basis and updated, changed, or replaced almost immediately. This is a dramatic difference from traditional media, where changing a campaign might be delayed for weeks, given media schedules and the time needed for production of ads. The Maui Jim sunglasses website (www.mauijim.com) is a perfect example of this kind of deliverability and flexibility. The site allows consumers to visit the site at any time to dig for information and check out new products. And, as mentioned earlier, as Web delivery continues to have wireless options, for even more flexibility and deliverability for Web communications. Finally, behind television and radio, no medium has the reach (use of a medium by audiences) of the Internet. As we saw in Exhibit 14.3, nearly 75 percent of U.S. households have Internet access. And, the number of mobile Internet subscribers has now passed 100 million. Among these subscribers, portals, email, weather, news, and search were the top uses listed—all of which are accessible by advertisers.[20]

Interactivity. A lofty and often unattainable goal for a marketer is to engage a prospective customer with the brand and the firm. This can be done with Internet advertising in a way that just cannot be accomplished in traditional media. A consumer can go to a company website or click through from a display/banner ad and take a tour of the brand's features and values. A **click-through** is a measure of the number of page elements (hyperlinks) that have actually been requested (that

20. "Mobile Internet Usage Continues to Climb," Mobile Marketing Association, www.mmaglobal.com/research, January 6, 2010.

is, "clicked through" from the display/banner ad to the link). Software is a perfect example of this sort of advantage of the Web. Let's say you are looking for software to do your taxes. You can log on to H&R Block tax consulting (www.hrblock.com) and you will find all the software, tax forms, and online information you need to prepare your taxes. Then you can actually file your taxes with both the IRS and your state tax agency! And this sort of interactivity is not reserved for big national companies. Try this as an exercise. Find a signage company in your local area. It is likely that one will have a website where you can design your own sign, order it, and ask for it to be delivered. You have complete interaction with the firm and its product without ever leaving your computer.

The click-through is an important component of Web advertising for another very important reason. If advertisers can attract surfers to the company or brand website, then there is the opportunity to convert that surfer to a buyer if the site is set up for e-commerce (more on this in Chapter 17, Integrating Direct Marketing and Personal Selling). Researchers are discovering that design components of various Internet ad formats can have an important effect on click-through and therefore sales potential.[21]

Once again, social media provide new and important opportunity for advertisers with respect to interactivity. You can suggest new menu items at My Starbucks Idea (www.mystarbucks.com) for your favorite Starbucks location—and then Tweet your friends about your most recent experience. AARP, the organization for senior citizens, runs a trivia contest at its website to engage consumers with the brand and the organization (aarp.promo.eprize.com/trivia/). And, of course, the ultimate in interactivity is the Ford Fiesta Agent (www.fiestamovement2.com). If you had been chosen as one of the Ford Fiesta "agents," you would be driving a Ford Fiesta for free and blogging, Facebook-ing, Tweeting, and YouTube-ing about your experiences with the brand.

Integration. Web advertising is the most easily integrated and coordinated with other forms of promotion. In the most basic sense, all traditional media advertising being used by a marketer can carry the website URL (uniform resource locator; the website's address). Web display/banner ads can highlight themes and images from television or print campaigns. Special events or contests can be featured in display/banner ads and on general or special interest websites. Overall, the integration of Web activities with other components of the marketing mix is one of the easiest integration tasks in the IBP process. This is due to the flexibility and deliverability of Web advertising discussed earlier. A great example of integrating consumer Web behavior with another part of the promotional process, personal selling, is the strategy used by Mazda Corp. It used to be that the salespeople hated the Web because shoppers would come to the showrooms armed with "cost" data on every vehicle, obtained from various websites. Rather than battle consumers, Mazda embraced the fact that car shoppers surf the Web and search out pricing information. Now, visitors to Mazda showrooms can access Web data from onsite Internet kiosks. Rather than interfering with the personal selling process, one dealership owner claims that the Internet access right at the dealership "helps build trust and close sales faster."[22] Social media also provide a seamless interface with the most traditional of IBP tools—television. Television ratings for live events, such as the Grammys and the Oscars have spiked in recent years as viewers Tweet and Facebook post to alert friends to awards and their reactions to the proceedings.[23]

21. Kelli S. Burns and Richard J. Lutz, "The Function of Format," *Journal of Advertising,* vol. 35, no. 1 (Spring 2006), 53–63.

22. Bob Parks, "Let's Remake a Dealership," *Business 2.0,* June 2004, 65–67.

23. Andrew Hampp, "Live TV's Alive as Ever, Boosted by Social Media," *Advertising Age,* February 15, 2010, 1–2.

The Cost of Internet Digital/Interactive Advertising.

It used to be that you could prepare and buy banner ads for a few thousand dollars. But now, with the huge audiences that can now be reached on the Web and new technology that can track the number of people who "visit" a website and click on an ad, the cost has skyrocketed. A banner ad on a leading portal like Yahoo! or Internet Explorer can cost more than $100,000 per day depending on traffic—about the same as a 30-second television spot on a highly rated network television show. Granted, the ad runs all day versus one 30-second insertion, but costs are escalating dramatically.

On a cost-per-thousand (CPM) basis, the cost of Web ads for the most part compares favorably with ads placed in traditional media. Exhibit 14.10 shows the comparison of absolute cost and CPM for ads placed in traditional media and on the Web. The real attraction of the Internet is not found in raw numbers and CPMs but rather in terms of highly desirable, highly segmentable, and highly motivated audiences (see Exhibit 14.11). The Internet is ideally suited for niche marketing—that is, for reaching only those consumers most likely to buy what the marketer is selling. This aspect of the Internet as an advertising option has always been its great attraction: the ability to identify segments and deliver almost-customized (or in the case of email, actually customized) messages directly to them—one by one. With respect to banner ads specifically, most agencies (about 90 percent) price banner ads on a cost-per-thousand basis (CPM), whereas a smaller number (about 33 percent) use click-throughs (i.e., the number of times an ad visitor goes to the advertiser's site) as the basis for pricing.[24]

Exhibit 14.10 The cost per thousand (CPM) for display/banner ads has been falling steadily during the past several years. However, compared with television or radio broadcasts, display/banner ad CPM is still relatively high. Notice, however, that the absolute cost in dollars of placing display/banner ads and other Internet-based communications can be much lower than traditional media.

	Absolute Cost	Cost per Thousand (CPM)
Traditional Media		
Local TV (30-second spot)	$4,000 to 45,000	$12 to 15
National TV (30-second spot)	$80,000 to 600,000	$10 to 20
Cable TV (30-second spot)	$5,000 to 10,000	$3 to 8
Radio (30-second spot)	$200 to 1,000	$1 to 5
Newspaper (top-10 markets)	$40,000 to 80,000	$80 to 120
Magazines (regional coverage)	$40,000 to 100,000	$50 to 120
Direct mail (inserts)	$10,000 to 20,000	$15 to 40
Billboards	$5,000 to 25,000	—
Internet Media		
Banner ads	$1,000 to 5,000	$50 to 85
Rich media	$1,000 to 10,000	$40 to 50
Email newsletters	$1,000 to 5,000	$25 to 200
Sponsorship	Variable based on duration	$30 to 75
Pop-up/pop-under	$500 to 2,000	$2 to 50

24. Fuyuan Shen, "Banner Advertisement Pricing, Measurement, and Pretesting Practices: Perspectives from Interactive Agencies," *Journal of Advertising*, vol. 31, no. 3 (Fall 2002), 59–68.

3 Types of Digital/Interactive Internet Advertising.

There are several ways for advertisers to place advertising messages on the Web. "Paid search" is now the most prominent, even though display/banner ads are more widely known. And many more options exist, including sponsorship, pop-up and pop-under ads, email communication, rich media/video and audio, corporate websites, virtual malls, widgets, and virtual worlds, video games, and social media sites. We will consider the features and advantages of each of these types of Internet advertising options.

Paid Search. The biggest news in Internet advertising is "paid search." **Paid search** is the process by which advertisers pay websites and portals to place ads in or near relevant search results based on key words. For example, if you Google "running shoes," you will find links to Onlineshoes.com and Zappos.com next to the search results as sources for purchasing running shoes. Paid search has grown astronomically and advertisers now spend more than $15 billion a year.[25] The catalyst for growth in paid search is the success of Google, which pushed the concept from its beginning, although all sites can accommodate paid search. Paid-search technology can fine-tune a Web user's search to more relevant and specific websites. For example, if an astronomy buff enters the word "saturn" in a search, paid search results would be returned for the planet, not the (now defunct) car company.[26]

Paid search is extremely valued by firms as they try to improve the effectiveness and efficiency of their use of the Internet as a promotional tool. Artbeads.com buys terms like "how to make jewelry" and then links searchers who click on the term to YouTube company videos.[27] The top "key words" that lead Internet users to advertiser sites are health and medical, education, food and beverage, and government. Paid search is not particularly cheap—about 58 cents per verified click for second-tier search sites to about $1.61 on Google.[28] To get some perspective on paid search, in one month, Americans conduct more than 15 billion searches for key words or phrases and 65 percent of those are conducted on Google sites.[29]

Another term you should be familiar with related to paid search is **search engine optimization (SEO)**. SEO is a process whereby the volume and quality of traffic to a website from search engines is improved based on surfers' profiles. Basically, the goal is that the higher a site is presented in a surfer's search results, the more likely surfers are to visit that site—but the more it will cost as well.

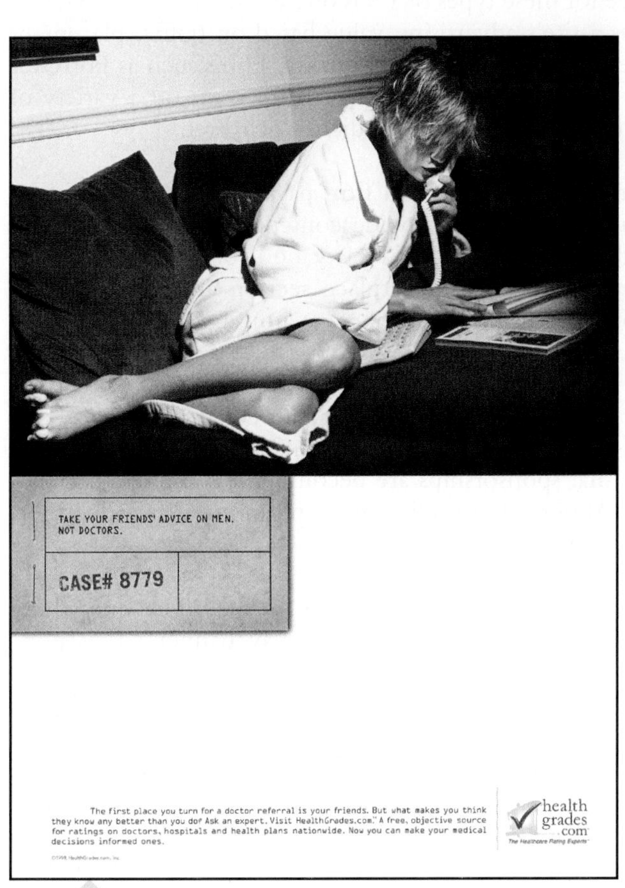

TAKE YOUR FRIENDS' ADVICE ON MEN.
NOT DOCTORS.
CASE# 8779
The first place you turn for a doctor referral is your friends. But what makes you think they know any better than you do? Ask an expert. Visit HealthGrades.com. A free, objective source for ratings on doctors, hospitals and health plans nationwide. Now you can make your medical decisions informed ones.
health grades .com
The Healthcare Rating Experts

Exhibit 14.11 One of the key advantages of the Internet is that websites can be targeted to the very specific information needs of narrowly defined segments. www.healthgrades.com

Display/Banner Ads. **Display/banner ads** are paid placements of advertising on websites that contain editorial material. One feature of a display/banner

25. Abbey Klaassen, "Search Marketing," *Advertising Age,* November 2, 2009, 16.

26. "comScore Releases April 2010 U.S. Search Engine Rankings," www.comscore.com, May, 11, 2010.

27. Michael Learmonth, "Can YouTube Rake in Google-size Revenue?," *Advertising Age,* February 1, 2010, 1, 19.

28. Search Marketing Fact Pack 2006, *Advertising Age,* November 6, 2006, 20.

29. "comScore Releases April 2010 U.S. Search Engine Rankings," www.comscore.com, May, 11, 2010.

ad is that consumers not only see the ad but also can make a quick trip to the marketer's home page by clicking on the ad (this is the "click-through" defined earlier). Thus, the challenge of creating and placing display/banner ads is not only to catch people's attention but also to entice them to visit the marketer's home page and stay for a while. Research indicates that the ability to create curiosity and provide the viewer resolution to that curiosity can have important impact on learning and brand attitude.[30] The downside to display and banner ads is the enormous clutter. Research has determined that Web users are bombarded by more than 1,800 Web ads daily and, consequently, click-through rates have fallen to 0.1percent (yes, one-tenth of 1 percent).[31]

A more targeted option is to place these ads on sites that attract specific market niches. For example, a display or banner ad for running shoes would be placed on a site that offers information related to running. This option is emerging as a way for advertisers to focus more closely on their target audiences. Currently, advertisers consider Web users to be a focused segment of their own. However, as the Web continues to blossom, advertisers will begin to realize that, even across the entire Web, there are sites that draw specific subgroups of Web users. These niche users have particular interests that may represent important opportunities for the right marketer with the right brand.

A pricing evaluation service for these types of ads is offered by Interactive Traffic. The I-Traffic Index computes a site's advertising value based on traffic, placement and size of ads, ad rates, and evaluations of the site's quality. Firms such as Forrester Research (see Exhibit 14.12) assess the costs of display/banner ads on a variety of sites and provide an estimate to advertisers of the audience delivered.

Sponsorship. **Sponsorship** occurs when a firm pays to maintain a section of a site. In some instances a firm may also provide content for a site along with sponsorship. If you go to Yahoo!'s home page (www.yahoo.com) you'll find that the Yahoo! Movies section and Yahoo! Marketplace section are almost always "sponsored by" a major movie studio and a brokerage house respectively. The Weather Channel website (www.weather.com) is also a site that attracts sponsors. Public service or not-for-profit websites often try to recruit local sponsors. In the context of more animated display/banner ads and paid search, it appears that sponsorships are becoming less and less popular. About $320 million is spent annually by advertisers on sponsorship.[32]

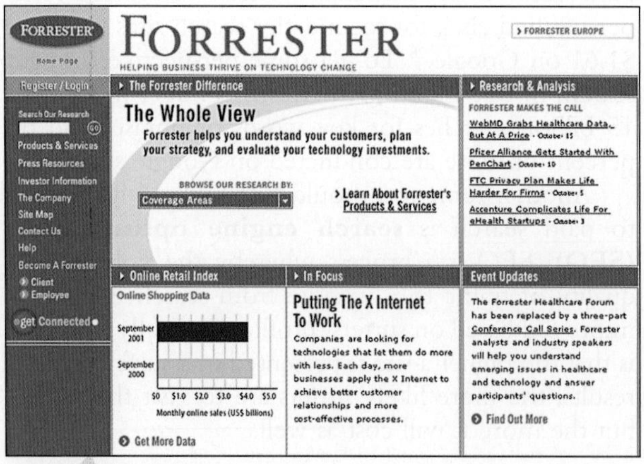

Exhibit 14.12 New service and research organizations can track advertising cost and audience delivered for various websites. www.forrester.com

Courtesy, Forrester.com

Pop-Up/Pop-Under Ads. The only thing surfers hate more than display/banner ads is pop-up Internet ads. The idea is borrowed from TV. A **pop-up ad** is an Internet advertisement that opens in a separate window while a Web page is loading. The more times people click on these ads, the more money can be charged for the privilege of advertising. The future of pop-ups must be considered—a recent study found that nearly 80 percent of surfers said that pop-ups were annoying and about 65 percent felt that display/banner ads were annoying.[33] But, like spam,

30. Satya Menon and Dilip Soman, "Managing the Power of Curiosity for Effective Web Advertising Strategies," *Journal of Advertising,* vol. 31, no. 3 (Fall 2002), 1–14.

31. Rita Chang, "Travelocity Offers Hope in Evolution of Display Advertising," *Advertising Age,* October 26, 2009, p. 14.

32. "Digital Marketing Facts 2010," *Advertising Age,* February 22, 2010, insert.

33. Stephen Baker, "Pop-Up Ads Had Better Start Pleasing," *BusinessWeek,* December 8, 2003, 40.

pop-ups are relatively effective, with 2 percent of Web visitors clicking on the pop-up—that's multiple times the click-through rate for display/banner ads.[34] But many service providers are offering "blockers" that greatly reduce an advertiser's ability to get a pop-up onto a user's screen.

A subcategory of pop-up ads is the *interstitial,* also called "**splash screen**." These appear on a site after a page has been requested but before it has loaded, and stay onscreen long enough for the message to be registered. So a surfer who wants to go to a certain site has to wade through an ad page first, just as a television viewer must watch a commercial before seeing a favorite show. It is often not merely a word from a sponsor but an invitation to link to another related site.

Pop-under ads are ads that are present "under" the Web user's active window and are visible only once the surfer closes that window. It is debatable as to whether pop-ups or pop-unders are the greater nuisance. Regardless, if the click-through rate is not identifiable or if paid search begins to completely dominate online advertising investment (as it appears it may), then the pop-up and pop-under ad may end up being a bit of curious Internet history (please!).

Rich Media/Video and Audio. **Rich media/video and audio** is the process in which a Web ad uses advanced technology like streaming video or audio that is launched when the user's mouse passes over the ad. For example, if you go to the Yahoo! main page, you may see an ad for a new movie about to be released. As you pass your mouse over the ad, it launches a video clip from the film. Firms such as RealNetworks, NetRadio, and MusicVision insert streaming video into ads for advertisers. The advantage, aside from being more interesting than a display/banner or a pop-up, is that streaming audio and video can realize click-through rates of 3.5 percent—hundreds of times greater than display/banner click-throughs. There is also academic literature that supports the proposition that adding animation to Internet ads increases click-through rates, recall, and favorable attitudes toward Web ads.[35] The widespread use of MP3 players (iPod) allows for podcasting of audio-content that can carry advertising and promotional messages. Now, the introduction of higher capability tablet devices (iPad and others) allows for more elaborate video communications and potentially more elaborate advertising and promotional messages.

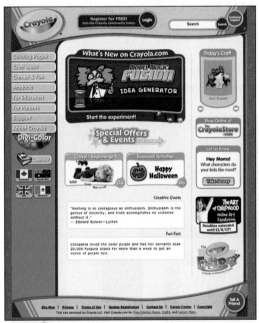

Exhibit 14.13 In contrast to purely information sites, other websites are more "lifestyle" oriented. The Crayola site (www.crayola.com) offers parents, educators, and kids all sorts of interesting, entertaining, and educational options. Compare the Crayola site to the Good Humor–Breyer's Popsicle site (www.popsicle.com), and evaluate which one does a better job of focusing on the needs of parents and children.

Corporate/Brand Home Pages. A **corporate/brand home page** is simply the website where a business provides current and potential customers with information about the firm and usually its brands in great detail. The best corporate home pages not only provide corporate and brand information but also offer other content of interest to site visitors. An example of such a site is the Crayola site (www.crayola.com) in Exhibit 14.13. Rather than focusing on its rather famous product, the company decided to focus on the needs of the parents and children who use Crayola crayons. Visitors can do such things as plan parties, look up family travel ideas, and, of course, create art with computerized Crayolas.

34. The statistics referenced here were from a Forrester Research survey cited in Digital Marketing & Media Fact Pack, *Advertising Age,* April 23, 2007, 45.

35. Heather Green and Ben Elgin, "Do E-Ads Have a Future?" *BusinessWeek e.biz,* January 22, 2001, 46–49; S. Shyam Sundar and Sriram Kalyanaraman, "Arousal, Memory, and Impression Formation Effects of Animation Speed in Web Advertising," *Journal of Advertising,* vol. 33, no.1 (Spring 2004), 7–17.

The biggest failing of many corporate/brand home pages is that they do not take advantage of the interactive capability of the Web and are little more than "video brochures" with little engaging information or interactive features.

Widgets. A relatively new piece of technology that has potential as an advertising option is a "widget." A **widget** is a module of software that people can drag and drop on to a desktop or mobile device. Widgets look like a website window but carry the power of a full website. Widgets allow users to customize the information they want to receive on an ongoing basis such as current weather, stock reports, or sports scores. Advertisers can create widgets that feature their brands or that direct the widget clicker to an e-commerce site. The advertiser will pay a fee each time a user installs the widget. Southwest Airlines created the "Ding" widget (so named for the sound it makes when there is a message) featuring the firm's logo. Consumers who download Ding to their smartphone or computer can be alerted to Southwest fare specials. Within a year, Southwest hit the 2 million mark in downloads.[36]

Second Life/Virtual Worlds. A potential new Internet option available to advertisers is within virtual worlds. Virtual worlds are interactive Internet "spaces" where "residents" can explore, meet and socialize with other residents (in avatar form), engage in individual and group activities, and create and trade virtual property and services, or simply visit "islands" throughout the world (which residents refer to as "the grid"). The most prominent of the virtual worlds is **Second Life**, an online virtual world launched in 2003. (See Exhibit 14.14.) Second Life is primarily a virtual world where Web enthusiasts create idyllic environments, interact with virtual acquaintances, or play games and accumulate "Linden dollars." Within a virtual world, advertisers can create "billboards" and branded product use (remember the discussion of brand placement), and avatars can wear branded apparel or use branded items. Several automobile firms have tried Second Life as a branding and IBP venue. Nissan and

Exhibit 14.14 Virtual worlds, like Second Life, offer opportunities for advertisers to insert advertising and IBP messages into virtual world spaces, like this one. It remains to be seen, however, whether virtual world residents will accept commercial messages in their spaces.

36. Bob Garfield, "Widgets Are Made for Marketing, So Why Aren't More Advertisers Using Them?" *Advertising Age*, December 1, 2008, 26.

Toyota established virtual dealerships for their most popular youth-oriented brands: the Toyota Scion and Nissan Sentra. Launched with great fanfare, Second Life immediately attracted about 2 million active participants. Today, there are estimated to be 800 million virtual world accounts with two-thirds belonging to under 16-year-olds.[37]

But despite all the intuitive excitement virtual worlds create in advertisers' minds, the ultimate potential of this venue as an advertising/IBP option is most certainly still in question. One analyst described Second Life as "so popular, no one goes there anymore."[38] Another noted that firms invested in brand assets called "virtual islands" that no one visited.[39] But, with the vast number of virtual world accounts and the attractive younger demographic, virtual worlds may yet emerge as an exciting and effective digital/interactive advertising and IBP option.

Video Games. Video games offer an attractive option for advertisers because they reach the elusive 18–34-year-old-male segment that has abandoned many traditional media for digital media. For example, the hot auto-racing game from Electronic Arts, *Need for Speed: Carbon,* is full of ads on billboards, store fronts, and the racing cars themselves. Advertising and brand placement within video games, primarily through embedded billboards and posters, has reached nearly $400 million and 68 percent of American households play video games, the average user is 35 years old (surprise), and 37 percent of players also play games on mobile wireless devices.[40] A question for advertisers to address, however, is the effectiveness of in-game placement. Although there is some evidence of a positive effect on brand recall, there is also evidence that repeated playing of the game can actually have a negative effect on players' attitudes toward embedded brands.[41]

4 Integrated Brand Promotion Tools and Digital/Interactive Media.

Even though advertising on the Internet is conspicuous and widely used, we can't forget the tools of integrated brand promotion and the opportunities that the Internet provides for using these other forms of promotion.

Sales Promotion on the Internet.

The digital/interactive options on the Internet are ideally suited to executing various aspects of sales promotion as part of the IBP effort. Coupon distribution and contests are the leading tools that are well suited to digital/interactive implementation, but sampling and trial offers can be promoted as well.

Coupons. Companies such as e-centives distribute coupons via the Internet and via the sites of other commercial online services. E-centives simply allows users to print coupons on their home printers and then take them to the store for redemption. The company charges clients anywhere from $3 to $15 per thousand coupons distributed. The average cost to manufacturers for coupons distributed via freestanding inserts or in magazines is $7 per thousand. However, only a small portion of those coupons are even clipped (2 to 3 percent redemption rate), whereas

37. Phil Jones, "Why Virtual Worlds Are Getting a Second Life," The Next Web, www.nextweb.com/uk/, May 6, 2010.

38. Frank Rose, "Lonely Planet," *Wired,* August 2007, 140–145.

39. Phil Jones, "Why Virtual Worlds Are Getting a Second Life," The Next Web, www.nextweb.com/uk/, May 6, 2010.

40. Industry Facts, Entertainment Software Association, www.theesa.com/facts, 2008, accessed June 18, 2010.

41. Verolien Cauberghe and Patrick De Pelsmacker, "Advergames: The Impact of Brand Prominence and Game Repetition on Brand Responses," *Journal of Advertising,* vol. 39, no. 1 (Spring 2010), 5–18.

with online coupons the manufacturer is paying only per thousand clipped, or in this case printed, by consumers. This makes digital distribution more effective in getting the coupons into the hands of consumers.

Contests and Sweepstakes. Sites like iwon.com and LuckySurf.com run ongoing contests to try to gain the loyalty of Web users. But, firms like Pepsi and Disney will partner with big portals like Yahoo! to run contests that draw attention to the brand over the Web along with similar promotions being run offline. Pepsi partnered with Yahoo! for an under-the-bottle-cap promotion called Stuff.com. The promotion allowed users to earn points or discounts from under-the-cap awards on bottles of brands across the Pepsi line. The contest was also launched on network TV and local spot radio. Drinkers of Pepsi brands were able to redeem points online and accumulate enough points to purchase goods or get discounts from merchants like Sony Music and Foot Locker.

To explain how these programs are put together, consider this example. MyFamily.com, an online community dedicated to connecting families on the Web, teamed up with Walt Disney Co. to promote Disney's animated feature film "The Tigger Movie." The partnership was arranged in this way: Disney and MyFamily.com entered into a barter arrangement whereby MyFamily featured The Tigger Movie in its advertising and all of Disney advertising for the film listed the URL for MyFamily and directed ad viewers to the Web community's home page. The campaign by both firms featured a sweepstakes with a grand prize of a 25-person family reunion at Walt Disney World in Orlando, Florida. Both partners benefited in that Disney got highly targeted exposure for the film and MyFamily.com got a boost from affiliating with a high-profile family-oriented entertainment conglomerate.

Sampling, Trial Offers, Price-off Deals. Firms can use their websites or email communications to offer consumers a wide range of sales promotion special deals. Samples, trial offers, and price-offs (discounts) can be offered over the Internet either with email campaigns, pop-up/banner ads or directly at the company website. Surfers merely need to click through on an interactive ad, respond to an email, or visit the website to explore and take advantage of the offer. One advantage of using the Internet for these sales promotion techniques is that the firm acquires the consumers email information for new prospects and achieves a de-facto "opt-in" contact. To see examples of these techniques in action, visit ProFlowers.com (www.proflowers.com) or Global Golf (www.globalgolf.com).

Public Relations and Publicity on the Internet.

Companies can use the Web to disseminate information about the firm in a classic public relations sense. Web organizations like Business Wire (www.businesswire.com) and PR Newsgirl (www.prnewswire.com) offer services where firms can request the dissemination of a press release over the Internet. These are often highly targeted press releases. Business Wire Connect Software gives its clients easy point-and-click access to its services and allows them to transmit news directly into the company's system at any modem speed up to 56k bps. Cost of the service varies by topic category–business, entertainment, news, or sports. Generally, a domestic national press release is $525 for 400 words and $135 for a 100-word release. Global distribution is $1,995. Business Wire is also able to provide targeted email distribution of the release for 50 cents per destination—a little pricey for most companies to consider. These press releases can be picked up by major news services like CNN, Reuters, or the Associated Press for dissemination over the Web through big portals like Yahoo! Take a quick trip to finance.yahoo.com/ to see a variety of corporate press releases that are disseminated on that site.

Direct Marketing/E-commerce on the Internet.

The Internet is extremely well suited to implementing a direct marketing IBP effort. Aside from the direct contact through email, mobile marketing, or virtual mall, direct marketing efforts can be coordinated with traditional media advertising campaigns through television, radio, newspapers, and magazines by directing consumers to either company websites or e-commerce sites that sell a variety of brands. The following describes the most widely used direct marketing techniques and e-commerce through the Internet.

Email Communication. As mentioned earlier, email communication is one of the Internet's most advantageous application. Through email, the Internet is the only mass medium capable of customizing a message for thousands or even millions of receivers. The message is delivered in a unique way, one at a time, which no other medium is capable of doing. There are about 200 million email users in the United States alone and advertisers are spending more than $1.6 billion annually on newsletters, direct messaging, and email list rental. Email from organizations is most effective when Web users have agreed to receive it; this is called opt-in email, as discussed earlier, or **permission marketing**. Some Web firms, such as InetGiant (see Exhibit 14.15), specialize in developing "opt-in" lists of Web users who have agreed to accept commercial emails.

Through email and electronic mailing lists, advertisers can encourage viral marketing. **Viral marketing** is the process of consumers marketing to consumers over the Internet through word-of-mouth transmitted through emails and electronic mailing lists. Hotmail (www.hotmail.com) is the king of viral marketing. The newest venue for viral campaigns is online videos of either television ads or follow-ons to television ads. Nike's three-minute "Write the Future" 2010 World Cup video attracted nearly 16 million views on YouTube within three weeks after it was placed.[42] Effective placement and delivery of these video campaigns is greatly aided by using firms that specialize in video campaign management (see Exhibit 14.16).

Exhibit 14.15 Email as an IBP alternative can meet with some heavy resistance from Web users. One way to avoid the resistance is to use a permission marketing firm. Firms like InetGiant have lists of consumers who "opt in," or agree to have email sent to them by commercial sources. www.inetgiant.com

Courtesy, InetGiant, Inc.

Mobile Marketing. Mobile marketing is the process of reaching consumers on Internet-enabled mobile devices like smartphones, iPods, and tablet e-readers. Even though mobile marketing is really a phenomenon brought about by mobile, wireless access through smartphones, MP3 players, laptops and tablet devices, it represents a form of direct marketing as well by virtue of wireless technology. As stated earlier, with more than 100 million Americans being mobile subscribers, marketers can initiate direct marketing campaigns to consumers through mobile devices. It is not only that email campaigns, text messaging, or sales promotions will reach mobile users directly on their devices, but also firms can sponsor mobile videos that are downloaded on video handsets. Even though only 10 percent of users of 3G handsets currently download videos, more than 60 percent of mobile

42. Michael Learmonth, "Nike Breaks Own Viral Record with World Cup Ad," AdAge.com, May 27, 2010.

subscribers have such devices making for significant potential. And, more than 80 million mobile users played a game on their handsets allowing exposure to advertising within the games. In addition, 20 million mobile users watch television as well, providing yet another opportunity for message exposure. IBP communications through mobile devices achieve surprisingly high recall. Thirty-nine percent of mobile phone users remembered advertising or promotion received on their phone.[43]

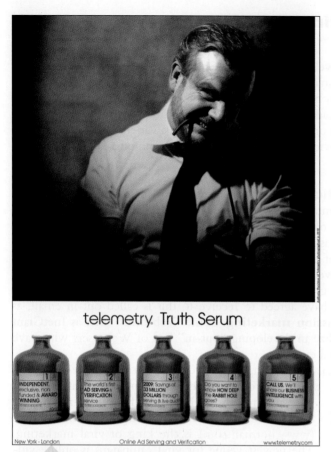

Exhibit 14.16 New, sophisticated firms like telemetry are helping firms both deliver and confirm delivery of online video campaigns as part of a direct marketing effort.

Courtesy, telemetry.com

Virtual Malls. A variation on the corporate website is a website placed within a website called a virtual mall. A **virtual mall** is a gateway to a group of Internet storefronts that provide access to mall sites by simply clicking on a category of store, as shown on the Mall Internet site (www.mall-internet.com). Notice that this site is set up to lead shoppers to product categories. Also notice that when a click is made to a product category, Mall Internet offers "featured store" click-throughs that lead to corporate websites and home pages. Having this additional presence gives stores such as Nordstrom and ESPRIT more exposure.

E-Commerce/Online Retailing. E-commerce and online retailing generates an enormous amount of revenue annually and could be considered a separate category of IBP on the Internet. For clarification, **e-commerce** includes all electronic transactions, including business-to-business (b-to-b) activities as well as online retailing directed at consumers. But, in every way, e-commerce is direct marketing—it's just that these types of merchants may sell many brands (industrial and consumer products and services) as opposed to a company website that focuses on only one brand or a firms' proprietary line of brands. E-commerce is conducted through highly interactive websites where surfers can find information and order products directly. Many high volume e-commerce sites like Amazon.com, auction site eBay, and travel site Orbitz are highly visible and well known. But other sites like globalgolf.com, shoes.com, or summitracing.com specialize in well-defined consumer product lines. Remember from your intro marketing class the concept of "category killer" retail stores and you have a good idea of how the best e-commerce sites appeal to consumers. Overall e-commerce, including b-to-b and online retailing transactions, total more than $5 trillion dollars a year with online retailing to consumers accounting for about $200 billion as Exhibit 14.17 shows.[44] This means, of course, that the b-to-b marketers account for the overwhelming majority of electronic transactions. With a focus on advertising and IBP, we tend to forget about the huge volume of business among manufacturers and merchant wholesalers. But, when it comes to the digital interactive process of e-commerce, this group of marketers uses the Web as a primary business tool.

43. Data in this section reported by the Mobile Marketing Association at www.mmaglobal.com/research, November 2008 and January 2009.

44. U.S. Census Bureau, E-Stats, www.census.gov/estats, May 27, 2010.

Exhibit 14.17 Online retail sales in the United States (U.S. dollars in billions).

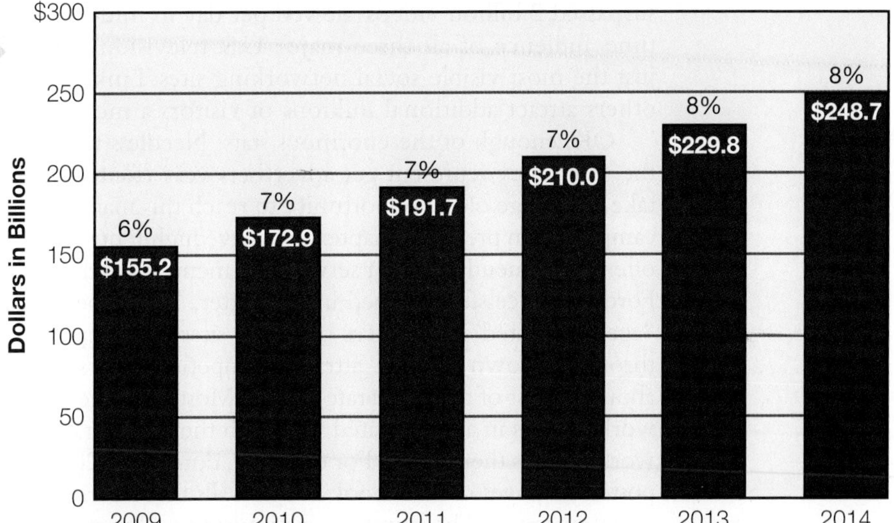

Source: Based on Erik Schonfeld, "Forrester Forecast: Online Retail Sales Will Grow to $250 Billion by 2014," TechCrunch, www.techcrunch.com, March 8, 2010

Personal Selling on the Internet.

Personal selling on the Internet is, of course, a term full of contradiction. Personal selling as an IBP technique is most effectively carried out face-to-face, in person as you will learn in Chapter 17. But, the Internet is a facilitating technology for the personal selling effort in a variety of ways. This is particularly true in the current environment where customers are demanding speedy response from marketers and the physical presence of a salesperson may take too much time to achieve. First, Internet advertising, through banner ads or website access, can be coordinated with sales force support. Firms can direct potential customers to salespeople through advertising by providing contact information. Second, salespeople can stay in touch with customers through email communication, text messaging, or Twitter-like communications now made more prevalent by the salesperson's ever present BlackBerry or smartphone. Finally, email and website inquiries that come directly to the company can be turned over to field sales staff that can use old-fashioned methods of communication like a phone call or sales call.

Using Social Media for Advertising and IBP.

Even though we have considered social media many times within several chapters in the text, it is time to assess the potential for such networks for advertising and IBP campaigns. In addition, it is also worth considering the way in which they are currently being used and the kind of success (or lack of) that marketers are having. To reiterate, social networks offer huge opportunity. There are currently more than 125 million Facebook users in the United States alone—the global user estimate is 400 million. And what might be surprising is that the largest demographic group using Facebook are 35- to 54-year-olds representing nearly 30 percent of all users. Further, the fastest-growing user group (a 35 percent increase in one year) is the 55+ age group.[45] Twitter is now processing 50 million Tweets a day (by the time you read this it could be 100 million)

45. Peter Corbett, "Facebook Demographics and Statistics Report June 2010—Privacy Concerns Don't Stop Growth," iStrategyLabs, istragegylabs.com, June 8, 2010; Jack Neff, "Once Skeptics, Brands Drink the Facebook Kool-Aid," *Advertising Age,* February 22, 2010, 40.

and about 1.5 billion Tweets a month.[46] And, finally, YouTube (owned by Google) surpassed 2 billion videos viewed per day in mid-2010—nearly double the prime-time audience of all three major U.S. television networks combined.[47] These are just the most visible social networking sites. LinkedIn, Plaxo, Classmates.com, and others attract additional millions of visitors a month.

OK, enough of the enormous stats. Needless to say, these kinds of numbers and the reach they represent get advertisers very excited. The question remains, how to take advantage of the opportunity to reach this many people with advertising and IBP campaigns. In previous chapters, we have highlighted how Starbucks asks customers to offer recommendations for service and menu items through MyStarbucks and Twitter. Ford has successfully tapped into Twitter, YouTube, and Facebook with Ford Fiesta "agents" posted experiences on those sites, and Pepsi's "Refresh Project" campaign through its own website attracts competitors for social impact projects. But what about the rest of the corporate world? Most firms are exploring ways to use social networking sites in an integrated way with their corporate home pages and between networking sites themselves. For example, during the 2010 Olympics, Procter & Gamble posted messages on Facebook brand walls that referred visitors to YouTube videos of ad campaigns.[48] The numbers are impressive. Procter & Gamble's Pringles brand has 3.7 million fans on Facebook. Similarly, Unilever has established a Facebook page for its popular Axe brand of personal care products and the brand has nearly 300,000 fans. YouTube has taken an active role in facilitating advertisers' use of the site for messaging purposes. The YouTube site (Exhibit 14.18) has a link for advertisers that provides access to a media kit for setting up an Advertising Brand Channel and guidelines on how to launch promoted videos on the site directly. Or, there is the simple, more direct route of simply posting a banner ad at a site when that opportunity is provided.

The point is that firms are finding ways to get exposure for brands on social networking sites. The other point, though, is whether using such sites is building brand awareness and affinity. You can Tweet, post, and blog all you want, but in the end the message has to have a positive impact on consumers' attitudes and desire to use the brand. Advertisers are not totally sure how effective the use of social networking sites really is as

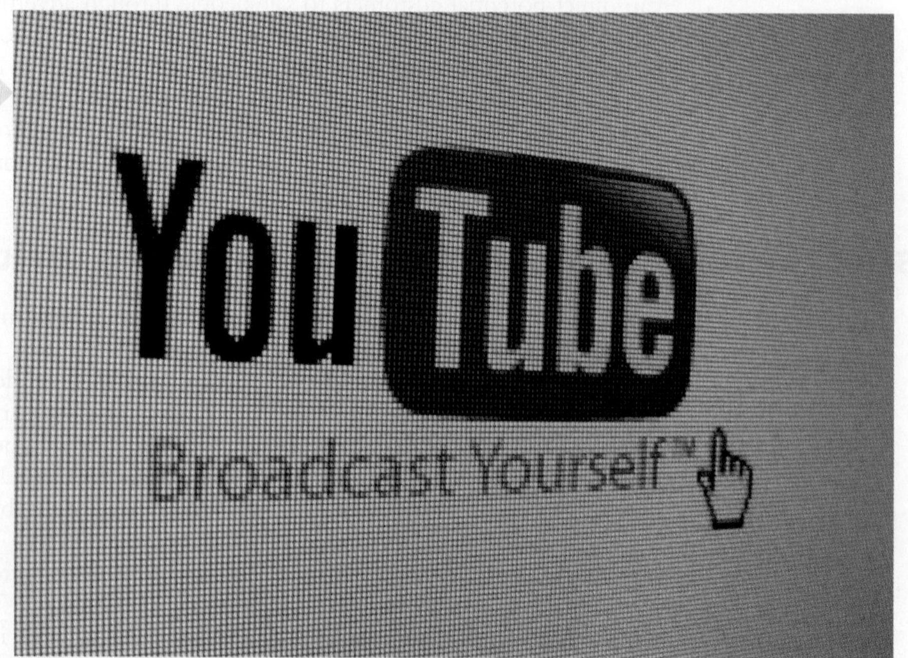

Exhibit 14.18
Advertisers are trying to tap into the enormous popularity of social networking sites. YouTube is facilitating advertisers' use of the video sharing site by providing Advertising Brand Channels and guidelines on how to post ad campaigns on the site directly (www.youtube.com).

46. Erick Schonfeld, "Twitter Hits 50 Million Tweets Per Day," TechCrunch, www.techcrunch.com, February 22, 2010.

47. Glenn Chapman, "YouTube Serving Up Two Billion Videos Daily," AFP, posted at www.google.com/hostednews, May 16, 2010.

48. Jack Neff, "Once Skeptics, Brands Drink the Facebook Kool-Aid, *Advertising Age,* February 22, 2010, 40.

reflected in the comment of P&G's Global Brand Building Officer who gave this assessment of Facebook, "What Facebook does is connect people into communities. It's also just a pretty good way to reach consumers through messages."[49] Well, "pretty good" is not wildly enthusiastic by any means, but as social networking sites continue to grow in popularity, you can be sure advertisers will continue to work to take strategic advantage of the opportunity of reaching millions (billions?) of consumers.

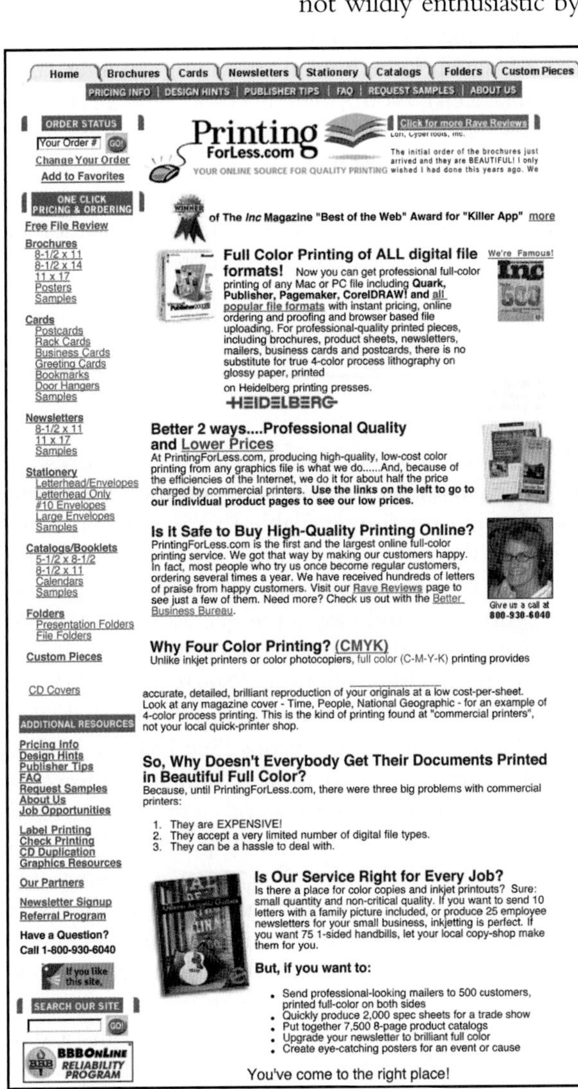

Exhibit 14.19 The Web is not only effective in serving household consumers. Business product and service firms of all sorts can use the Web to provide customer service and build brand awareness. From large multinational corporations like Caterpillar (www.cat.com) to smaller firms like PrintingForLess.com (www.printingforless.com), the Web is highly effective in providing customer contact, customer service, and brand building.

Developing a Website.

One fundamental task in having a digital/interactive presence on the Internet, beyond the types of internet advertising or social networking opportunities discussed, is the basic process of developing a website. Although setting up a website can be done fairly easily, setting up a commercially viable one is a lot harder and a lot more expensive. The top commercial sites can cost $1 million to develop, about $4.9 million for the initial launch, and about $500,000 to more than $1 million a year to maintain.[50] Setting up an attractive site costs so much because of the need for specialized designers to create the site and, most important, to constantly update the site. The basic hardware for a site can be a personal computer, and the software to run the site ranges from free to several thousand dollars, depending on the number of extras needed. A site anticipating considerable traffic will need to plan for higher-capacity connections—and hence, a bigger phone bill.

But what if you're not a big Internet firm with several millions to spend for the first year of operating of a website? Not to fear. There are actually some very inexpensive ways of setting up a site and finding hosts to maintain it if you are a small or medium-size business and want an Internet presence. Companies like 1&1 Internet (www.1and1.com) offer a wide range of services to the small business, including hosting at extremely low cost. These small-business service firms offer hosting that includes maintenance of domain names, website connectivity, email accounts, and some limited e-commerce applications for as little as $9.99 per month. One company that set up an inexpensive site (and still maintains a very simple structure) that is experiencing great success is Backcountry.com (www.backcountry.com). The two founders, former ski bums, started with $2,000 in the year 2000 and now run the second-largest online outdoor gear organization, behind REI.[51] So, although there are ways to spend millions to develop and maintain a site, it is not an absolute necessity. And, keep in mind,; if you are an e-commerce merchant, like Backcountry.com, you can defray the cost of site maintenance by attracting sponsorships and banner ads.

We also need to keep in mind that using the Web as a key component of a brand-building strategy is not only reserved for consumer brands. Business products advertisers—large firms like Caterpillar (www.cat.com) or small firms like PrintingForLess.

49. Ibid.

50. Lynn Ward, "Hidden Costs of Building an E-Commerce Site," available at www.ecommercetimes.com, accessed on April 28, 2003.

51. Duff McDonald, "A Website as Big (and Cheap) as the Great Outdoors," *Business 2.0,* October 2003, 70–71.

com (www.printingforless.com)—are discovering the power of the Web in providing both customer service and brand building (see Exhibit 14.19). Plus, there is no more efficient or speedy way to reach a global market.

One thing advertisers should know in building a site is that the interactivity of a site has important consequences for loyalty and intention to purchase items from a site. Research shows that when consumers engage in more human-messaging (an interactive message) or human-human interaction (like a chat room), there is a more positive attitude toward the site, which, in turn, relates to higher purchase intention.[52] For an excellent example of a highly interactive site visit the skinID.com (www.skinid.com) site developed by Neutrogena. This site allows you to enter a wide range of individual characteristics and the site produces a personalized skin evaluation. Then, you get a recommendation of which skin care products (Neutrogena, of course) to address any skin problems.

Measuring the Effectiveness of Digital/Interactive Advertising and IBP.

The information a website typically gets when a user connects is the IP address of the computer that is requesting the page, what page is requested, and the time of the request. This is the minimum amount of information available to a website. If a site is an opt-in site and requires registration, then additional information (for example, email address, zip code, gender, age, or household income) is typically requested directly from the user. Attempts at registration (and easy audience assessment) have been largely rejected by consumers because of the privacy concern, but plenty of service providers, like Nielsen//NetRatings (www.nielsen-netratings.com), are available to guide marketers through Web measurement options (See Exhibit 14.20).

WITH A LITTLE BAD INFORMATION YOU COULD ACTUALLY GO DOWN IN HISTORY.
Keep your Internet strategies afloat with high-quality Internet audience research from Nielsen//NetRatings.
Bad information. It can lead to bad decisions and big disasters. Especially when it comes to Internet e-commerce, content or advertising strategies. To help you make the right decisions, Nielsen//NetRatings is dedicated to Information Quality.
Our secret? We capture comprehensive Internet user activity in real time from our representative panel of more than 38,000 Internet users: sites visited, ads viewed, media players used, purchasing activity and user connection speeds. It's a great way to know what's really happening on the Internet. How do we do it? Proprietary Internet measurement technology from NetRatings coupled with 50 years of proven research methods from Nielsen Media Research.
iQ
What's more, because we collect data in real time from our entire panel, nobody can provide it to you faster. Even overnight analysis is not a problem.
Another Nielsen//NetRatings advantage: our unique in-depth analysis. Nielsen//NetRatings team of analysts pinpoint emerging Internet trends, hot sectors and companies in weekly, monthly and quarterly reports–based on our rich database of user behavior.
Whenever you need high quality information and analysis to keep your head above water, count on Nielsen//NetRatings. In fact, call 1-888-634-1222 now for a free copy of our latest E-commerce Trends Report.
Nielsen//NetRatings
Your decisions are only as good as your data.

Exhibit 14.20 Because of the technology of the Web, tracking the behavior of website visitors is relatively easy. Firms like Nielsen//NetRatings help marketers measure the behavior of Web visitors. www.nielsen-netratings.com

Courtesy, Nielsen Media Research

Several metrics are used in Web audience measurement. **Hits** represent the number of elements requested from a given page and consequently provide almost no indication of actual Web traffic. For instance, when a user requests a page with four graphical images, it counts as five hits. Thus by inflating the number of images, a site can quickly pull up its hit count. Consider what might happen at the Seventeen magazine site (www.seventeen.com). The Seventeen site may get 3 million hits a day, placing it among the top website. However, this total of 3 million hits translates into perhaps only 80,000 people daily. Thus, hits do not translate into the number of people visiting a site. But another measure of site effectiveness is the extent to which a site will motivate visitors to click through and request information from an ad, as we have discussed before. Most analysts feel that the click-through number (and percentage) is the best measure of the effectiveness of Web advertising. If an ad is good enough to motivate a visitor to click on it and follow the link to more information, then that is verification that the ad was viewed and was motivating (more on this later).

Page views are defined as the pages (actually the number of HTML files) sent to the requesting user's computer. However, if a downloaded page occupies several screens, there is no indication that the user examined the entire page. Also, the page-view count doesn't tell you

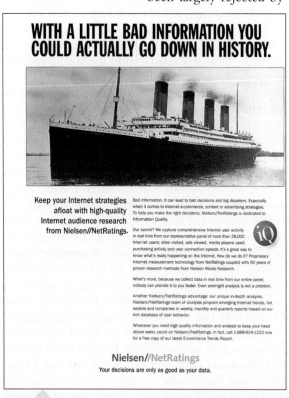

52. Hanjun Ko, Chang-Hoan Cho, and Marilyn S. Roberts, "Internet Uses and Gratifications," *Journal of Advertising*, vol. 34, no. 2 (Summer 2005), 57–70.

how many visitors the page actually has: 100,000 page views in a week could be 10 people reading 10,000 pages, or 100,000 people reading one page, or any variation in between.

Visits are the number of occasions in which a user X interacted with site Y after time Z has elapsed. Usually Z is set to some standard time such as 30 minutes. If the user interacts with a site and then interacts again more than 30 minutes later, the second interaction would be counted as a new visit.

Unique visitors are the number of different "people" visiting a site (a new user is determined from the user's registration with the site) during a specified period of time. Besides the address, page, and time, a website can find out the referring link address. This allows a website to discover what links are directing people to the site. This can be extremely helpful in Internet advertising planning. The problem is that what is really counted are unique IP numbers. Many Internet service providers use a dynamic IP number, which changes every time a given user logs in through the service, so you might show up as 30 different unique visitors to a site you visited daily for a month.

Web analytic software is measurement software that not only provides information on hits, pages, visits, and users but also lets a site track audience traffic within the site. A site could determine which pages are popular and expand on them. It is also possible to track the behavior of people as they go through the site, thus providing inferential information on what people find appealing and unappealing. This type of software allows marketers to track what information is viewed, when it is viewed, how often it is viewed, and where users go within a site. An advertiser can then modify the content and structure accordingly. It can also help marketers understand how buyers make purchase decisions in general. But although it is possible to know a lot about users' behavior at sites, it still isn't possible to know what people actually do with website information (see the discussion that follows).[53]

Plenty of companies offer measurement services for interactive media. Yet there is really no industry standard for measuring the effectiveness of one interactive ad placement over another. There also is no standard for comparing Internet with traditional media placements. Moreover, demographic information on who is using the Web is severely limited to consumers who have signed up for opt-in programs and, for example, allow targeted emails to be sent to them. Here is a list of just some of the companies providing measurement and evaluation services:

- **Arbitron** (www.arbitron.com)–One of the oldest advertising measurement firms and better known for its traditional media (especially radio and television) measures, Arbitron also specializes in providing data on Internet radio broadcasts including cell phone penetration of radio listening behavior.
- **Audit Bureau of Circulations** (www.accessabc.com)–The Audit Bureau has been for many years the main print circulation auditing organization. Recently, the firm has established ABC Interactive (ABCI), which offers independent measurement of online activity to ensure that website traffic and ad delivery metrics are accurately reported.
- **Lyris Inc.** (www.lyris.com) is a Web analytics program that makes it easy for marketers to compile website navigation patterns by users and then develops ROI stats for Web advertising.
- **eMarketer** (www.emarketer.com)–eMarketer accumulates data from various research sources and provides summary statistics on social media user profiles, blogging behavior, and a wide range of other digital/interactive general statistics.
- **Forrester Research** (www.forrester.com)–Similar to eMarketer, this firm provides a wide range of data analysis, research, and advice for firms using the Internet for both promotion and e-commerce.

53. Definitions in this section adapted from Brian Getting, "Web Analytics: Understanding Visitor Behavior," Practical eCommerce, January 2006, 8.

- **Nielsen//NetRatings** (www.nielsen-netratings.com)–Probably the highest profile of the data providers, Nielsen has ruled the ratings game for many years. Nielsen relies on its traditional method of finding consumers who are willing to have their media behavior (in this case Internet use) monitored by a device attached to the consumers' computers. In addition, Nielsen monitors and measures more than 90 percent of global Internet activity and provides data about online behavior—including audiences, advertising, video, e-commerce, and consumer behavior.
- **Ranking.com** (www.ranking.com)–Performs market research on a statistically, geographically, and demographically significant number of Internet surfers. By recording these surfers' website visits, the company calculates the ranking for the top 1 million (and growing every month) most visited website. This is one of the very few free Web-data-research sites.
- **Experian Simmons** (formerly Simmons Market Research Bureau–www.smrb.com)–Experian Simmons measures the media and purchase behaviors of consumers and offers data on more than 8,000 brands over more than 460 product categories. Included in these analyses is information on Web use and product purchase.

Measuring the traffic and demographics of users of individual social media sites is a new science. We have seen that firms like iStrategyLabs can provide total users and demographics for Facebook. Similarly, Google can provide data on paid search statistics. YouTube Insight is YouTube's external analytics program and reporting product that enables anyone with a YouTube account to view detailed statistics about the videos that they upload to the site. YouTube Insight then can provide advertisers with information that helps them better understand their audience: who they are, where they come from, what they watch, and when. Overall, the business of generating metrics for social media site visits and behavior is evolving rapidly to the benefit of advertisers.

Internet Data and Click Fraud.

No medium is able to provide detail on audiences like the Internet. With Internet tracking services, an advertiser used to just be able to know how many people see an ad and how many respond to it with a click. But new technologies now allow tracking of mouse movement on Web pages and grouping of shoppers by age, zip code, and reading habits. DoubleClick (now a Google service), through its DART for Advertisers (DFA), can provide 50 different types of metrics for an Internet campaign. With mouse tracking, advertisers can know which parts of a banner ad appear to be of interest to visitors and how long they spend on different parts of an ad. With new control monitors, referred to as "dashboards," advertising strategists can check the performance of their online ads in real time. There is so much data available that agencies are hiring teams of analytic people, including PhDs in statistics, to make sense of the data. And academics are deep into the evaluation process, researching such things as the effect of animation speed on attention, memory, and impression formation.[54]

One issue you need to be aware of with respect to digital/interactive metrics is **click fraud**—clicking on Internet advertising solely to generate illegitimate revenue for the website carrying the ad. Those doing the clicking typically also get paid.[55] Click fraud is a crime and occurs when an advertiser has a pay-per-click agreement with a website. Click fraud takes place when a person is paid to visit website, or when a computer program roams the Web and imitates a legitimate Web user by "clicking" on ads. Click fraud thus generates a charge per click without there having been actual interest in the ad's link. There have been arrests related to click fraud

54. Sundar and Kalyanaraman, "Arousal, Memory, and Impression Formation Effects of Animation Speed in Web Advertising." *Journal of Advertising,* vol. 33, no. 1 (Spring 2004), 7–17.

55. Brian Grow and Ben Elgin, "Click Fraud," *BusinessWeek,* October 2, 2006, 46–57.

Ethics

Click Fraud—A Nasty Business

Martin Fleischmann built his business with online advertising. MostChoice offers consumers rate quotes and information on insurance and mortgages. Fleischmann paid Yahoo! and Google a total of $2 million in advertising fees based on clicks (or click-throughs) from the sites to his MostChoice Web page.

But after a while, he noticed a growing number of clicks coming from places like Botswana, Mongolia, and Syria. This was odd since his customers primarily were U.S. based and seeking information on car insurance and mortgage rates in U.S. cities. Fleischmann found some specialized software to track the click patterns and found that his ads were being clicked not on the pages of Google or Yahoo! but on curious sites with names like insurance1472.com and insurance060.com. In the end, he calculated that he had paid more than $100,000 for bogus clicks during a three-year period.

MostChoice.com was the victim of "click fraud." Fleischmann paid for clicks on his ads that were made by people or computer programs that imitate legitimate Web users, thereby generating a charge per click without having actual interest in the ad's link. Scammers that perpetrate click fraud can use a "clickbot," a program that can be used to produce automatic clicks on ads. These are sophisticated programs that can hide the origin and timing of clicks to mimic the behavior of real Web surfers. So, Fleichmann had to pay for the clicks generated by the computer program when no "real" prospects were visiting his sites.

Click fraud is a big and growing problem. About half of all Internet advertising spending is tied to deals requiring advertisers to pay by the click. Expert estimates are that about 15 to 20 percent of all ad clicks are fake, meaning that click fraud costs about $1 billion a year. And it is pervasive. Forty-two percent of Internet advertisers report that they have been a victim of click fraud, although 78 percent of them have received credit for fake clicks from their paid search provider. Not all of the click fraud is promulgated by off-shore, shadowy crooks. Of the advertisers reporting being victimized, more than half report that the click fraud was initiated by competitors in an attempt to deplete advertising dollars.

An important question is what is being done about the problem. Yahoo! has named a senior executive to lead the company's effort to combat click fraud in its advertising business. The Internet media company also discards as invalid or inferior quality about 12 to 15 percent of clicks on advertisements; in the case of invalid clicks, it will not charge the advertiser. In a similar move, Google said its computers automatically reject up to 10 percent of potential advertising billings resulting from invalid clicks.

Use of a computer to commit this type of Internet fraud is a felony in many jurisdictions. It is covered by Penal Code 502 in California and the Computer Misuse Act 1990 in the United Kingdom. The Internet industry is doing what it can in a "self-regulation" way, but it may take harsh legal action, as in the case of spammers going to jail, to effectively deal with the issue.

Sources: Brian Grow and Ben Elgin, "Click Fraud," *BusinessWeek*, October 2, 2006, 46–57: Search Marketing Fact Pack, *Advertising Age*, November 6, 2006, 46: "Yahoo! Taps Click Fraud Watchdog," Reuters News Service, March 22, 2007, accessed at www.cnnmoney.com on March 22, 2007; "Click Fraud Report Q1 2010," Click Forensics, www.clickforensics.com, April 1010.

with regard to malicious clicking in order to deplete a competitor's advertising budget. And this is no small problem. Forty percent of Web advertisers claim they have been victims of click fraud. Google and Yahoo!, prime targets for click scammers, are working to stop click fraud by monitoring Web traffic for repeated clicks or unusual visit patterns from anonymous servers.[56] See the *Ethics* box for more on this issue.

Managing the Brand in an E-Community.

A final strategic issue to be considered is the concept of creating a brand community, or e-community, for a brand by using the Internet. The Internet, in addition to

56. Burt Helm, "How Do You Clock the Clicks?" *BusinessWeek,* March 13, 2006, 44.

providing a new means for advertisers to communicate to consumers, also provides consumers a new and efficient way to communicate with one another. In fact, the social aspect of the Internet is one of the most important reasons for its success. Via Usenet newsgroups, email, blogs, and social networking websites, consumers have a way to interact and form communities. Remember the comment earlier in the chapter from the P&G executive, whereas he was wary of the messaging power of social networks, he was more positive about the community-building impact of sites.

Sometimes communities are formed online among users of a particular brand. These online brand communities behave much like a community in the traditional sense, such as a small town or ethnic neighborhood. They have their own cultures, rituals, and traditions. Members create detailed Web pages devoted to the brand. Members even feel a sense of duty or moral responsibility to other members of the community. For example, among many Volkswagen drivers, it is a common courtesy to pull over to help another VW broken down on the side of the road. Harley-Davidson riders feel a similar sense of affinity and desire to help others who use the same brand when they are in trouble.

We have referenced social networking sites extensively throughout the chapter, but the affinity to these sites cannot be underestimated—or ignored. Sites like Facebook attract up to 100 million unique visitors per month![57] It seems clear that the credibility of these sites is appealing to consumers who are weary of the blatant promotional intent of both traditional media and e-commerce-oriented websites.

Since the Internet makes it easier for members of these communities to interact, brand communities are likely to continue to proliferate in coming years. Consequently, dealing effectively with these communities will be one of the challenges facing advertisers. Several sites, such as Collabrio Technologies' MyEvents (www.myevents.com), have emerged to facilitate the community interaction process by providing shared access to the site that promotes communication between members, which now total more than 600,000 (see Exhibit 14.21). Harley-Davidson is a company whose site tries to accomplish e-community interaction. Notice at the Harley website (www.harley-davidson.com) that the events around the country are a highlight for riders. Another technique is to create a community around the brand in a portal-like manner—that is, drawing consumers to a brand site with content and features that include lifestyle and entertainment information much like what the big portals provide. One firm that has always tried to develop community within its website is teen apparel seller Candie's. Visit www.candies.com to see how the Candie's site is as community-oriented as it is sales-oriented in that you can "join" the Candies community.

5 The Future of Digital/Interactive Advertising and IBP.

When it comes to digital and interactive media and the Internet, talking about the future is somewhat futile. The future seems to come with every new issue of *BusinessWeek, Fortune,* or *Wired.* But the future of the Internet and advertising and IBP seems unavoidably linked to technological advances and the emergence of location-based mobile marketing.

From a technological standpoint, two technologies—wireless communication (particularly mobile access) and Web-launched video and audio—will have the biggest impact (see Exhibit 14.22). Early on, the AOL/Time Warner merger in 2001 signaled the future direction for the Web and Web advertising. Then interactive media giant

57. Peter Corbett, "Facebook Demographics and Statistics Report June 2010—Privacy Concerns Don't Stop Growth," iStrategyLabs, istragegylabs.com, June 8, 2010.

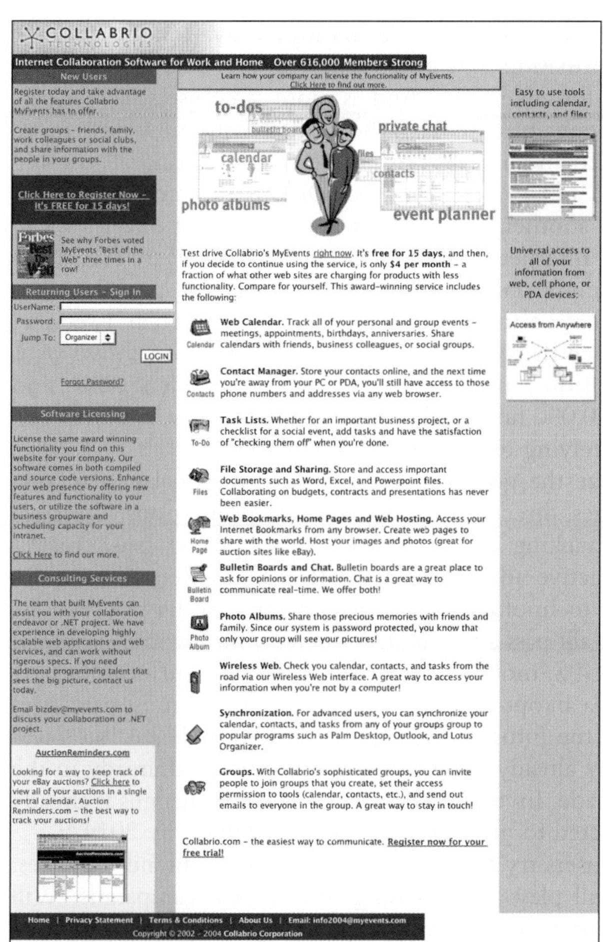

Exhibit 14.21 Building an e-community with great loyalty to a site is a tall task. Today's typical computer users have islands of disparate information located everywhere, from on their computer and home bulletin board to in their electronic organizer. Collabrio Technologies provides these users with a free, central place to manage and organize their lives and to share information with any group of people—their friends or family, their investment or book club, or even their co-workers.

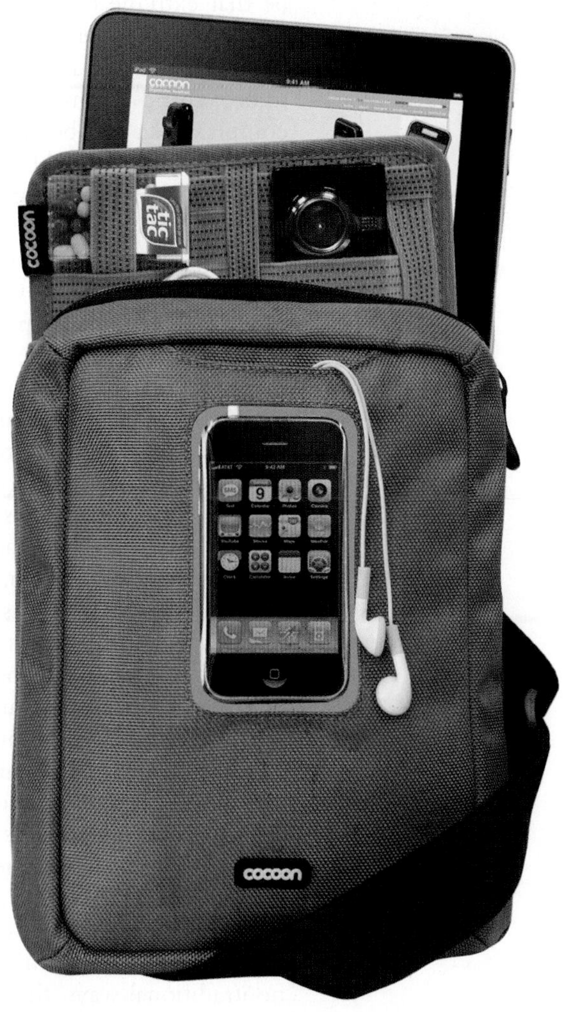

Exhibit 14.22 Whatever direction the dynamic nature of Web advertising and IBP takes, it will no doubt be influenced by wireless technology and location-based mobile marketing. As more consumers access the Web through their laptops, smartphones, or tablets, advertisers have more and more ways of sending messages and communicating about their brands—including right at the point-of-purchase.

IAC/InterActiveCorp put together a conglomerate of Internet companies that can promote and sell each other's products. Finally, a wave of acquisitions are occurring that are aimed at amassing better online data to help track consumer interests and intentions, thereby letting websites target audiences with more relevant ads—which they can charge more for. Google spent $3.1 billion to buy DoubleClick and Yahoo! paid $680 million to assume complete ownership of RightMedia Inc.[58]

Mergers and partnerships of broadcast and Internet firms are one side of the story. On the other side, advertisers and advertising agencies are preparing for new opportunities with "broadcast Web." Mobile Internet subscribers now total more than $100 million and spending on mobile advertising alone is approaching $1 billion per year, and podcast ad spending is nearly at $250 million per year.[59] Does this mean that in the near future every television ad is really a Web ad? Well, maybe it won't

58. Robert D. Hof and Catherine Holahan, *BusinessWeek,* May 21, 2007, 46.

59. "Mobile Internet Usage Continues to Climb," Mobile Marketing Association, www.mmaglobal.com, January 6, 2010; Forrester Research, U.S. Interactive Marketing Forecast, 2009–2014.

be that extreme (more on this follows), but the technology is available to provide direct links to websites for information and purchasing through television ads—a huge opportunity and potential for advertisers. And as more Web users have access to broadband—as more than 60 percent of users in the United States now do—more complex data can be streamed to them. The possibilities are attracting all the big players—Microsoft, ABC, CBS, and Warner Brothers Online, to name just a few. They all see video streaming as another piece of this Web broadcast puzzle.[60] The next evolution of this process is Internet television. Other big players are fast introducing services that blend streams from the Internet and broadcast programming on television screens—Google has partnered with Sony to provide such a service. Hulu has developed a paid service that will deliver broadcast television shows over the Internet to computers, televisions, smartphones, and tablet/e-readers. This is no minor trend either. By 2010, 800,000 households in the United States had cancelled cable television service and are relying exclusively on online services.[61]

Finally, we have to recognize the growing potential for location-based mobile marketing for advertising messages, direct marketing, and sales promotions. We covered this GPS-based consumer tracking issue in Chapter 3 as a privacy issue. But, it clearly represents a digital/interactive advertising and IBP issue as well. Companies like Foursquare already have the technology and services in place to allow advertisers to beam you a message as you walk pass a restaurant or enter your favorite shopping mall. Whether it's collected by GPS, mobile carrier, cell tower triangulation, or personally provided by customers via an opt-in interactive campaign, the most successful mobile marketing campaigns of the future will likely be those that deliver the message of a campaign to consumers already close to the point of sale or already in the store where a purchase can be made. Investment in these mobile campaigns is already $400 million annually and expected to grow to more than $1 billion by 2014.[62]

It seems likely that as advertisers try to "engage" consumers in brand messages, the digital/interactive media will play an increasing role in IBP campaigns. Will digital/interactive media advertising and promotion become the "lead" tool in most IBP campaigns? From a total spending standpoint, it is not likely. But expect that as technology advances and consumers become accustomed to accessing information in nontraditional ways, the digital and interactive media will be an increasingly valued tool in the IBP kit.

Summary

Understand the current role of digital and interactive media in advertising and IBP.

First, it is unlikely that digital and interactive media will replace all other forms of advertising and promotion through IBP. It is even unlikely that the biggest spenders on advertising and promotion will use the Internet as the *main* method of communicating with target audiences. But, given all the new and different opportunities that digital/interactive media offer, much effort and energy are being put into these new options.

Second, technologies are changing dramatically regarding all aspects of digital/interactive media. Auction sites like eBay have provided huge opportunities for small business all around the world. Social networking sites provide a whole new way of delivering promotional messages and IBP campaigns. New venues like Facebook, Twitter, and YouTube offer advertisers ways to reach consumers in a less "corporate" way.

Third, the structure of the Internet and as an advertising medium offer ways for advertisers to both create and deliver interactive messages and IBP programs that are significantly different from traditional mass media.

60. John Kuczala, "Online Video Ads Get Ready to Grab You," *Business 2.0,* May 2005, 25.

61. James Templeton, "Internet Products Ready to Challenge TV," SFGate, www.sfgate.com, July 4, 2010.

62. "Location Based Mobile Marketing Poised for Expansion," *Mobile Marketer,* www.mobilestorm.com, February 24, 2010.

Identify the advantages of digital/interactive media for implementing advertising and IBP campaigns.

Digital/interactive media have several advantages as a medium for communicating advertising and IBP messages: target market selectivity, tracking, deliverability, flexibility, reach, and integration.

Target Market Selectivity. Digital/interactive media offer advertisers a way to target market segments very precisely. This precision allows targeting that is more finely tuned than traditional segmentation schemes such as demographics, geographics, and psychographics. Advertisers can focus on specific interest areas of Internet users and can also target users based on geographic regions (including global), time of day, computer platform, or browser.

Tracking. Digital/interactive media allow advertisers to track how users interact with their brands and learn what interests current and potential customers.

Deliverability, Flexibility, and Reach. Online advertising, website content, and social media communicatioin is delivered 24 hours a day, seven days a week, at the convenience of the receiver. Whenever receivers are logged on and active, advertising is there and ready to greet them. A campaign can be tracked on a daily basis and updated, changed, or replaced almost immediately. In addition, the Internet is immediately a global medium unlike any traditional media option.

Interactivity. A marketer is able to engage a prospective customer with the brand and the firm's digital/interactive media in ways that just cannot be accomplished in traditional media. A consumer can go to a company website or click through from a display/banner ad and take a tour of the brand's features and values.

Integration. Digital/interactive advertising is the most easily integrated and coordinated with other forms of promotion. In the most basic sense, all traditional media advertising being used by a marketer can carry the website URL. Web display/banner ads can highlight themes and images from television or print campaigns. Special events or contests can be featured in display/banner ads and on websites. Overall, the integration of Web activities with other components of the marketing mix is one of the easiest integration tasks in the IBP process.

Describe the different advertising options available through digital/interactive media on the Internet.

Paid search is the process by which advertisers pay websites and portals to place ads in or near relevant search results based on key words.

Display/banner ads are paid placements of advertising on other sites that contain editorial material. These ads allow advertisers to have their brands associated with popular websites.

Sponsorship occurs when a firm pays to maintain a section of a site. In some instances a firm may also provide content for a site along with sponsorship.

A pop-up/pop-under ad is an Internet advertisement that appears as a website page is loading or after a page has loaded.

Rich media/video and audio is the process of inserting TV- and radio-like ads into music and video clips that advertisers send to Web users as they visit content networks.

A corporate or brand home page is a website where a marketer provides current and potential customers with information about the firm in great detail.

A widget is a module of software that people can drag and drop on to their personal Web page of their social network (e.g., Facebook) or on to a blog. Advertisers can create widgets that feature their brands or that direct the widget clicker to an e-commerce site.

Second Life is an online virtual world where participants log into a space, then use their mouse and keyboard to roam landscapes, chat, create virtual homes, or conduct real business. Participants "exist" in Second Life as avatars—on screen graphic characters. Advertisers can create "billboards" within the virtual world and avatars can wear branded apparel or use branded items.

Discuss the ways different IBP tools can use digital/interactive media.

Marketers have discovered ways to effectively use all forms of IBP in a digital and interactive way through the Internet. Sales promotions, including coupons, contests and sweepstakes, and samples can be distributed digitally. Public relations campaigns can use email or Web distribution through specialty PR sites. Direct marketing and e-commerce allow both brand evaluation and brand purchase. Some merchants sell multi-brands through venues like virtual malls or merchant sites, whereas other sites are company sponsored-brand specific. Be aware that the largest dollar amount of sales happens in the industrial sector through e-commerce. Finally, whereas personal selling can be facilitated through digital and interactive media, personal selling by definition is a face-to-face process.

Discuss the future of advertising and IBP using digital and interactive media.

The future of advertising and IBP on using digital and interactive media will be guided by the emergence of more wireless technology delivery systems, Web launched video and audio, and the emergence of location-based mobile marketing efforts. Mergers and acquisitions have created huge, multi-faced digital companies that can offer advertisers many new options—particularly with respect to digital video- and audio-enhanced messages. GPS-enabled mobile devices provide the opportunity to reach consumers with messages or promotional offers at locations near purchasing sites.

Key Terms

WiFi
WiMax
Mi-Fi (Mobile-Fi)
Ultrabroadband
opt-in email
spam
World Wide Web (WWW)
surfing
search engine
portal
website
mash-up
blog
blogger
click-through
paid search
search engine optimization (SEO)
display/banner ads
sponsorship
pop-up ad
splash screen
pop-under ad
rich media/video and audio
corporate/brand home page
widget
Second Life/virtual worlds
permission marketing
viral marketing
mobile marketing
virtual mall
e-commerce
hits
page views
visits
unique visitors
Web analytic software
click fraud

Questions

1. Despite its ups and downs during the past decade, the Internet and digital/interactive media are experiencing a strong recovery. Why is there reason to believe that the current Internet boom could be permanent?

2. What may have driven advertisers to embrace the Internet early on in its development despite considerable uncertainty about audience size, audience composition, and cost-effectiveness?

3. How effective do you think mobile advertising and IBP will be through delivery systems like the iPod, iPad, and smartphones?

4. What unique characteristics of digital/interactive advertising and IBP offer advantages over traditional forms?

5. Explain the two basic strategies for developing corporate home pages, exemplified in this chapter by the Crayola Web home page.

6. Niche marketing will certainly be facilitated by the Web. What is it about the Web that makes it such a powerful tool for niche marketing?

7. Visit some of the corporate home pages and websites described in this chapter, or think about websites you have visited previously. Of those you have encountered, which would you single out as being most effective in giving the visitor a reason to come back? What conclusions would you draw regarding the best ways to motivate repeat visits to a website?

8. The Internet was obviously not conceived or designed to be an advertising medium. Thus, some of its characteristics have proven perplexing to advertisers. If advertising professionals had the chance to redesign the Internet, what single change would you expect they would want to make to enhance its value from an advertising perspective?

9. What are the challenges that face advertisers when they try to measure the impact of advertising and IBP digital and interactive campaigns on the Internet? If you were a manager, which metric(s) would you rely on to judge success of a campaign?

10. How do you feel consumers will react to the use of location-based mobile marketing techniques for advertising messages and IBP programs?

Experiential Exercises

1. Now that everyone and their grandmothers are plugged into the social networking craze, brands are expanding digital campaigns to include Facebook, Twitter, and YouTube. Examine the digital campaigns of Old Spice, Aeropostale, Zappos, and Starbucks and give your view on which campaign does the best job of establishing sustained interaction with customers. What features do the campaigns use to hold consumers' interest? Propose an idea for how one of these brands might use social networking tools to develop long-lasting brand communities.

2. When skiing and skateboarding enthusiasts want the best deals on used and closeout model sports gear, they look to Evo. In addition to operating a flagship store in Seattle, Evo sells merchandise and promotes its brand internationally through two e-commerce sites, Evogear.com and Culture.evogear.com. Research Evo online and explain how the company uses websites to integrate its business with active skiing and skateboarding communities around the world.

3. Do shoppers really enjoy the online shopping experience? Compare and contrast the experience of shopping at your favorite retail store with the experience of shopping online. Make one list of things you enjoy about shopping in stores, and create a separate list of things you like about shopping online. How do your lists differ? What are the advantages and disadvantages of shopping in a physical store? What are advantages and disadvantages of shopping online? Can Internet-based businesses deliver the rich shopping experience that brick-and-mortar stores provide? How might smartphones and other handheld devices change the way people shop?

4. Much of traditional advertising now incorporates some form of online promotion or information, even if it is as simple as including a website URL on a magazine, newspaper, or television advertisement. Each of the Web addresses below leads to the online component of a traditional media ad campaign. Review each site and then answer these questions: What added value does the online component bring to the campaign? What other ways could the advertiser incorporate digital media in the campaign? Why would a consumer go the website, and why would he or she stay?

www.drinkarizona.com
www.schickhydro.com/
www.apple.com/ipad/
www.goarmy.com/

Part 5

Integrated Brand Promotion

Part Five of the text brings us to the end of our journey in the study of advertising and IBP. This part highlights the full range of communication tools a firm can use in creating an integrated brand promotion campaign. Throughout the text, we have been emphasizing that IBP is a key to effective brand development. You will find that the variety and breadth of communication options discussed here represent a tremendous opportunity for marketers to be creative and break through the clutter in today's marketplace. Each of the tools discussed in Part Five has the unique capability to influence the audience's perception of and desire to own a brand while insuring that consistency with advertising is maintained. And, this part of the text has gone through significant revision to bring you the latest emerging techniques in support media, product placement, branded entertainment, and influencer marketing and the role social media play across all the options.

Chapter 15

Sales Promotion, Point-of-Purchase Advertising, and Support Media All the techniques of both consumer and trade sales promotion are discussed. Coupons, price-off deals, premiums, contests, sweepstakes, sampling, trial offers, refunds, rebates, frequency programs, and point-of-purchase displays are highlighted for the consumer market, while incentives, allowances, trade shows, and cooperative advertising are presented in this chapter as they relate to trade promotion. Coverage of sales promotion and new media provides the most forward-thinking discussion of using new distribution and communication techniques for sales promotion as well as the use of mobile/location marketing for point-of-purchase promotions. The chapter concludes with extensive treatment of the wide array of out-of-home support media available to advertisers, including outdoor signage, billboards, transit advertising, aerial advertising, cinema advertising, packaging, and good old (and new media) directory advertising.

Chapter 16

Event Sponsorship, Product Placements, and Branded Entertainment This chapter highlights the thought-provoking issue of the convergence of Madison & Vine—that is the phenomenon of advertising, branding, and entertainment converging to provide consumers a wider array of "touch points" with brands. The chapter continues from here to review the growing allure of event sponsorships with emphasis on the experiential impact of events on consumers and the "leverage" events can have on communication to other important constituents like salespeople and employees. Product placements on television, in movies, and in video games are discussed as a way to embed brand images "authentically" in consumer lifestyle activities. The chapter then takes a deep dive into the provocative subject of branded entertainment. If you had any lingering doubts about the power of integrated brand promotion, the topics discussed in this chapter will dispel those.

Chapter 17

Integrating Direct Marketing and Personal Selling Consumers' persistent desire for greater convenience and marketers' never-ending search for competitive advantage continue to create an emphasis on direct marketing in IBP programs. With direct marketing, the opportunity exists not only to communicate to a target audience but also to seek an immediate response. You will learn why direct marketing continues to grow in popularity, what media are used by direct marketers to deliver their messages, and how direct marketing creates special challenges for achieving integrated brand promotion. In the excitement and, indeed, drama of digital media options, we sometimes forget the powerful role personal selling has across many integrated brand promotion strategies. The chapter provides a perspective on this important IBP process, including the basic types of personal selling and the role of personal selling in customer relationship management.

Chapter 18

Public Relations, Influencer Marketing, and Corporate Advertising Chapter 18 is another chapter that has new and exciting material with the addition of full coverage of "influencer" marketing and new issues in corporate advertising (fueled by corporate social responsibility). This chapter begins with a discussion of the key role public relations can play in the overall IBP effort and differentiates between proactive (creating "buzz" for a brand) and reactive (damage control) public relations strategies. You will learn that public relations is an important option in IBP, but rarely will it ever take the lead role. The new coverage of influencer marketing is the best and most contemporary you will find anywhere. Professional influencer programs, peer-to-peer programs, buzz and viral marketing, cultivating "connectors"—it's all here. This chapter concludes with a wide-ranging and complete discussion of corporate advertising. Various forms of corporate advertising are identified, and the way each can be used as a means for building the reputation of an organization in the eyes of key constituents is discussed. In the current era, corporate advertising is being used more frequently as a way to demonstrate a firm's social and environment responsibility.

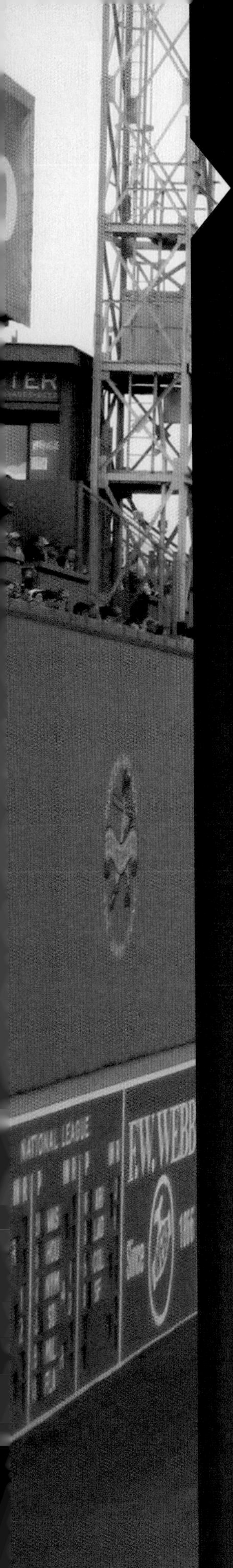

Chapter 15

Sales Promotion, Point-of-Purchase Advertising, and Support Media

After reading and thinking about this chapter, you will be able to do the following:

1. Explain the importance and growth of sales promotion.
2. Describe the main sales promotion techniques used in the consumer market.
3. Describe the main sales promotion techniques used in the trade channel and business markets.
4. Identify the risks to the brand of using sales promotion.
5. Understand the role and techniques of point-of-purchase advertising.
6. Describe the role of support media in a comprehensive IBP plan.

© Eric Broder Van Dyke/Shutterstock

ORDER SOME COFFEE BEANS FROM US TODAY. WE'LL ROAST THEM FOR YOU TOMORROW. THAT'S AS CLOSE AS WE'LL EVER GET TO INSTANT COFFEE.

There are only a handful of coffee roasters that do what we do. We're not even sure – we might be the only one. Six days a week, beginning at 4 a.m., we start roasting 32 different kinds of Peet's coffee. But only enough to fill the orders that have come in the day before.

If you called us today and ordered some of our Major Dickason's blend (named for one of our long-time customers, a real coffee fan), tomorrow morning we'll be here, roasting your Major Dickason's blend.

And tomorrow afternoon, we'll be sending it out. Of course, if you order on the weekend, you'll have to wait all the way till Monday.

We use the same unique, complicated deep-roasting process we've used since the mid-'60s, when Alfred Peet was the one doing the roasting and Major Dickason was here enjoying his coffee – literally his coffee – every day.

Not much has changed. Not much will change. The fresher the bean, the better the coffee.

Let us show you how good it can be: Visit Peets.com/sa or call 1-800-950-7338 and we'll make you a sampler pack of three coffees for just $14.95. We'll include shipping, along with a free stainless steel scoop. Without question, your satisfaction is guaranteed. Peet's Coffee & Tea

Introductory Scenario: OK. This is Getting a Little Weird.

You're reading the news in your home on your e-reader and an ad pops up on the screen for a $1 off coupon you can use at Starbucks which is only 2 blocks from your house—the e-reader knows this. Or, you walk into a hotel room and a sensor sets the lights and the room temperature, switches on the TV to ESPN at just the right volume—the loyalty program on your smartphone knows all this. You're on your way home from work and you get a text message that the local grocery store has a special on Diet Pepsi which you drink in huge quantities—the grocery store scanner knows this. Or, you drive by a billboard and it flashes, "Hi Lucy, you need an oil change in 312 miles." The billboard can talk to your car GPS and computer.

This is not futuristic, Orwellian speculation. All the technology is in place for these kinds of sales promotions and point—of—purchase IBP campaigns to take place right now. The potential for knowing when and where consumers are is blurring the lines between advertising and promotions. Google, for instance, knows that about one-third of all consumer mobile searches are local in nature making location-based sales promotions a timely and potent IBP tool.[1] Companies like Placecast "geo-fence" retail locations and once a consumer opts-in to the program, Placecast will send offers to mobile devices once a consumer is within a determined radius of a retail location. Initial tests of the system found that 79 percent of participating consumers said their likelihood of visiting a store or restaurant increased with geo-fencing.[2] There is an old saying in point-of-purchase that it is the "last three feet of marketing." With new technologies, that old saying may have to be changed to the "last 3 blocks or last 3 miles of marketing."

Sales Promotion Defined.

Sales promotion is often a key component within an integrated brand promotion campaign—particularly campaigns seeking short-term sales effects. Sales promotions like dealer incentives and consumer price discounts and free samples can attract attention and give new energy to the overall advertising and the IBP effort. While mass media advertising is designed to build a brand image over time, sales promotion is conspicuous and designed to make things happen in a hurry. Particularly with new mobile/location based techniques as the introductory scenario described. Used properly, sales promotion is capable of almost instant demand stimulation, like the kind that contests and sweepstakes can create. The "message" in a sales promotion features price reduction, free samples (see Exhibit 15.1), a prize, or some other incentive for consumers to try a brand or for a retailer to feature the brand in a store. Sales promotion has proven to be a popular complement to mass media advertising because it accomplishes things advertising cannot.

Formally defined, **sales promotion** is the use of incentive techniques that create a perception of greater brand value among consumers, the trade, and business buyers. The intent is to generate a short-term increase in sales by motivating trial use, encouraging larger purchases, or stimulating repeat purchases. **Consumer-market sales promotion** includes:

1. Kunar Patel, "Forget Foursquare: Why Location Marketing is the New Point-of-Purchase," *Advertising Age,* March 22, 2010, 1, 19.

2. Ibid., 19.

Exhibit 15.1 Advertisers have long used sampling, like this free offer from Glad, as a component in sales promotion IBP campaigns.

- coupons
- price-off deals
- premiums
- contests and sweepstakes
- sampling and trial offers
- rebates
- loyalty/frequency programs
- phone and gift cards

All these incentives are ways of inducing household consumers to purchase a firm's brand rather than a competitor's brand. Notice that some incentives reduce price, offer a reward, or encourage a trip to the retailer.

Trade-market sales promotion uses the following ways of motivating distributors, wholesalers, and retailers to stock and feature a firm's brand in their store merchandising programs:

- point-of-purchase displays
- incentives
- allowances
- cooperative advertising
- sales training

Business-market sales promotion is designed to cultivate buyers in large corporations who are making purchase decisions about a wide range of products, including computers, office supplies, and consulting services. Techniques used for business buyers are similar to the trade-market techniques and include:

- trade shows
- premiums
- incentives
- loyalty/frequency programs

1 The Importance and Growth of Sales Promotion.

Sales promotion is designed to affect demand differently than advertising does. As we have learned throughout the text, most advertising is designed to have awareness-, image-, and preference-building effects for a brand over the long run. The role of sales promotion, on the other hand, is primarily to elicit an immediate purchase from a customer group. Coupons, samples, rebates, contests and sweepstakes, and similar techniques offer household consumers, trade buyers, or business buyers an immediate incentive to choose one brand over another, as exemplified in Exhibit 15.2. Notice that Oreck is offering a free product (referred to as a premium offer) just for trying the Oreck vacuum cleaner.

Other sales promotions, such as frequency programs (for example, airline frequent-flyer programs), provide an affiliation value for a brand, which increases a consumer's ability and desire to identify with a particular brand. Sales promotions featuring price reductions, such as coupons, are effective in the convenience goods category, where frequent purchases, brand switching, and a perceived homogeneity (similarity) among brands characterize consumer behavior.

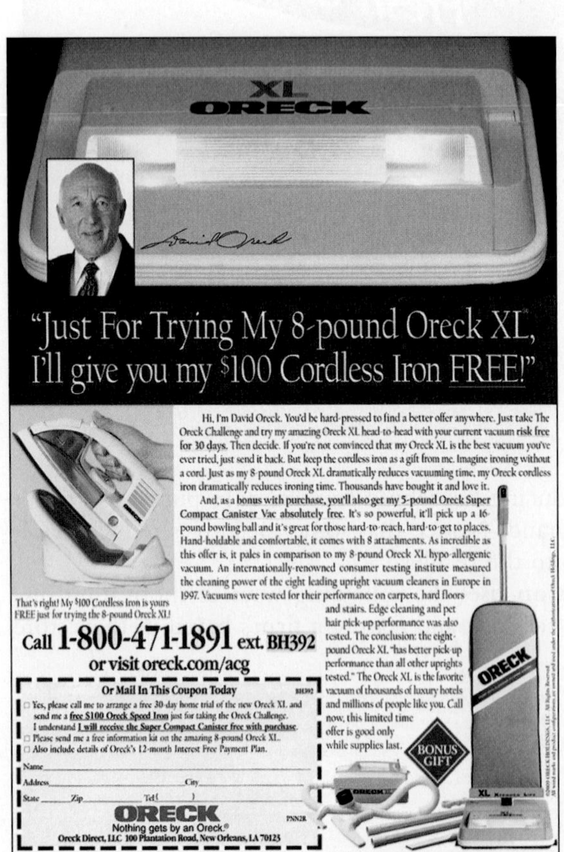

Exhibit 15.2 Marketers use a wide range of incentives to attract attention to a brand. Here, David Oreck offers new buyers a free iron for trying the Oreck lightweight vacuum.

Courtesy, Oreck Corporation

Sales promotions are used across all consumer goods categories and in the trade and business markets as well. When a firm determines that a more immediate response is called for—whether the target customer is a household, business buyer, distributor, or retailer—sales promotions are designed to provide that incentive. The goals for sales promotion versus those of advertising are compared in Exhibit 15.3. Notice the key differences in the goals for these different forms of promotion. Sales promotion encourages more immediate and short-term responses, whereas the purpose of advertising is to cultivate an image, loyalty, and repeat purchases over the long term.

The Importance of Sales Promotion.

The importance of sales promotion in the United States should not be underestimated. Sales promotion may not seem as stylish and sophisticated as mass media advertising, but expenditures on this tool are impressive. Big consumer products firms have shifted dollars out of media advertising and into promotions in recent years. The chairman and CEO of Procter & Gamble told analysts that the firm's advertising and IBP spending was shifting

Exhibit 15.3 Sales promotion and advertising serve very different purposes in the promotional mix. What would you describe as the key difference between the two based on the features listed here?

Purpose of Sales Promotion	Purpose of Advertising
Stimulate short-term demand	Cultivate long-term demand
Encourage brand switching	Encourage brand loyalty
Induce trial use	Encourage repeat purchases
Promote price orientation	Promote image/feature orientation
Obtain immediate, often measurable results	Obtain long-term effects, often difficult to measure

"and it's shifting from measured media to in-store, to the Internet, and to trial activity [i.e., product sampling]."[3]

It is important to realize that full-service advertising agencies specializing in advertising planning, creative preparation, and media placement typically do not prepare sales promotion materials for clients. These activities are normally assigned to sales promotion agencies that specialize in coupons, premiums, displays, or other forms of sales promotion and point-of-purchase techniques that require specific skills and creative preparation.

The development and management of an effective sales promotion program requires a major commitment by a firm. During any given year, it is typical that as much as 30 percent of brand management time is spent on designing, implementing, and overseeing sales promotions.

Growth in the Use of Sales Promotion.

Many marketers have shifted the emphasis of their promotional spending during the past decade. Much of the shift has been away from mass media advertising. Some has made its way to the Internet, as we saw in the last chapter, and more spending has found its way to consumer, trade, and business sales promotions. There are several reasons why many marketers have been shifting funds from mass media advertising to sales promotions, from the need for greater cost accountability to the problem of media clutter.

Demand for Greater Accountability. In an era of cost cutting and shareholder scrutiny, companies are demanding greater accountability across all functions, including marketing, advertising, and promotions. When activities are evaluated for their contribution to sales and profits, it is often difficult to draw specific conclusions regarding the effects of advertising. But the more immediate effects of sales promotions are typically easier to document. Various studies have shown that only 18 percent of TV advertising campaigns produced a short-term positive return on investment (ROI) on promotional dollars.[4] Conversely, point-of-purchase in-store displays have been shown to positively affect sales by as much as 35 percent in some product categories.[5]

Short-Term Orientation. Several factors have created a short-term orientation among managers. Pressures from stockholders to increase quarter-by-quarter revenue and profit per share are one factor. A bottom-line mentality is another factor. Many organizations are developing marketing plans—with rewards and punishments for manager performance—that are based on short-term revenue generation. This being the case, companies are seeking tactics that can have short-term effects. There is some sound reasoning behind the strategy, though. If a customer

3. Bradley Johnson, "Leading National Advertisers Report: Spending up $3.1% to $105 Billion," *Advertising Age*, June 25, 2007, S-2.

4. Jack Neff, "TV Doesn't Sell Packaged Goods," *Advertising Age*, May 24, 2004, 1, 30.

5. Cara Beardi, "Pop-Ups Sales Results," *Advertising Age*, July 23, 2001, 27.

stops in for free fries, he or she might also buy a burger and drink—an immediate effect on sales. And a free product also presents the chance to "convert the curious into loyalists." McDonald's, for example, claims that at least half the customers who come in for free coffee wind up buying something.[6]

Consumer Response to Promotions. The precision shopper in the contemporary marketplace is demanding greater value across all purchase situations, and that trend is battering overpriced brands. These precision shoppers search for extra value in every product purchase. Coupons, premiums, price-off deals, and other sales promotions increase the value of a brand in these shoppers' minds. The positive response to sales promotion goes beyond value-oriented consumers, though. Historically, consumers have reported that coupons, price, and good value for their money influence 75 to 85 percent of their brand choices.[7] (Be careful here—coupons, price reduction, and value seeking do not necessarily mean consumers are choosing the *lowest*-priced item. The analysis suggests that these sales promotion techniques act as an incentive to purchase the brand *using* a promotion, even if another brand has a lower basic price.)

Proliferation of Brands. Each year, thousands of new brands are introduced into the consumer market. The drive by marketers to design products for specific market segments to satisfy ever more narrowly defined needs has caused a proliferation of brands that creates a mind-dulling maze for consumers. Consider this case of brand proliferation—in one 12-month period, Coca-Cola's new head of marketing launched *1,000* (not a typo) new drinks or new variations of existing brands worldwide (has anybody tried Coca-Cola Blak?).[8] At any point in time, consumers are typically able to choose from about 60 spaghetti sauces, 100 snack chips, 50 laundry detergents, 90 cold remedies, and 60 disposable diaper varieties. As you can see in Exhibit 15.4, gaining attention in this blizzard of brands is no easy task. Because of this proliferation and "clutter" of brands, marketers turn to sales promotions—contests, coupons, premiums, loyalty programs, point-of-purchase displays—to gain some attention.

Exhibit 15.4 As you can see by this shelf of spaghetti sauces, getting the consumer to pay attention to any one brand is quite a challenge. This proliferation of brands in the marketplace has made marketers search for ways to attract attention to their brands, and sales promotion techniques often provide an answer. Notice the point-of-purchase promotion attached to the shelves.

6. Kate MacArthur, "Give It Away: Fast Feeders Favor Freebies," *Advertising Age,* June 18, 2007, 10.
7. Cox Direct 20th Annual Survey of Promotional Practices, Chart 22, 1998, 37.
8. Dean Foust, "Queen of Pop," *BusinessWeek,* August 7, 2006, 44–450.

Ethics

Big Brother Has New Toys—And You're Being Watched

In an attempt to understand every last aspect of how shoppers make their choices, packaged goods marketers are turning to new research methods to learn as much as they can. The newest research relies on what is basically "surveillance" technology in retail stores. Cameras could be monitoring the time it takes you to browse the aisle and put a box of Cheerios in your shopping cart. Or, a purchase itself might have been driven by your encounter with a little shelf message that Kraft calls "mom cues" designed to tug at your heart strings as you consider one brand of lunch meat versus another. Kraft might have been watching as you approached the shelf and the "mom cue." Once the surveillance takes place, then firms can examine purchase data (you know that loyalty card you use at check-out?) and match it up with economic models to see if the retail store is getting its fair share of the 10 percent of the packaged dinner dollar, for example.

All of this is called "shopper programs" and firms are trying to learn more about the psychology behind how and why consumers buy. They are enlisting teams of technologists and scientists who can sort through all sorts of data to uncover consumers' needs and emotional states at the point-of-purchase. ConAgra has doubled its integrated-customer-marketing team, which includes shopper marketing, shopper insights, and in-store marketing strategists. Given the conventional wisdom that 70 percent of purchase decisions are made in the store, the investment seems well placed.

But what about the ethics of watching people going about their everyday "business" when they don't know they are being watched? Companies that employ the surveillance and tracking technologies say it is used strictly to determine characteristics such as age, gender, product inspection, or store movement patterns. One firm widened the aisles of its stores after watching consumers struggle to navigate tight areas. However, privacy advocates fear that as the technology becomes more sophisticated, it will be used to identify individuals right down to name, address, and phone numbers. The founder of Consumers Against Supermarket Privacy Invasion and Numbering believes that such identification is "absolutely inevitable." So, the next time you're in the grocery store and feel like someone is watching you—they just might be.

Sources: Emily Bryson York, "They Learned It by Watching You," *Advertising Age*, March 15, 2010, 1, 19; Stephanie Rosenbloom, "Buyer Beware: You May Be on Tape," *The New York Times*, March 23, 1020, A1, A10.

Increased Power of Retailers. Big retailers like Target, Home Depot, Costco, and the most powerful of all, Walmart, now dominate retailing in the United States. These powerful retailers have responded quickly and accurately to the new environment for retailing, where consumers are demanding more and better products and services at lower prices. Because of these consumer demands, retailers are, in turn, demanding more deals from manufacturers. Many of the deals are delivered in terms of trade-oriented sales promotions: point-of-purchase displays, slotting fees (payment for shelf space), case allowances, and co-op advertising allowances. In the end, manufacturers use more and more sales promotions to gain and maintain good relations with the powerful retailers—a critical link to the consumer. And retailers use the tools of sales promotion as competitive strategies against each other. Manufacturers are coming up with clever ways to provide value to retailers and thus maintain the balance of power. But some of these tools may be just another intrusion on privacy, as the *Ethics* box highlights.

Media Clutter. A nagging and traditional problem in the advertising process is clutter. Many advertisers target the same customers because their research has led them to the same conclusion about whom to target. The result is that advertising media are cluttered with ads all seeking the attention of the same people. When consumers encounter a barrage of ads, they tune out (remember the discussion in Chapter 5). And clutter is getting worse, not better, across all media—including the Internet, where pop-ups, pop-unders, and banners "clutter" nearly every website.[9] One way to break through the clutter is to feature a sales promotion. In print ads, the featured deal is often a coupon. In television and radio advertising, sweepstakes, premium, and rebate offers can attract viewers' and listeners' attention. The combination of advertising and creative sales promotions has proven to be a good way to break through the clutter.

2 Sales Promotion Directed at Consumers.

It is clear that U.S. consumer-product firms have made a tremendous commitment to sales promotion in their overall marketing plans. During the 1970s, consumer goods marketers allocated only about 30 percent of their budgets to sales promotion, with about 70 percent allocated to mass media advertising. Now we see that for many consumer-goods firms, the percentages are just the opposite, with nearly 75 percent of promotional budgets being spent on various forms of promotion and point-of-purchase materials. With this sort of investment in sales promotion and point-of-purchase as part of the integrated brand promotion process, let's examine in detail the objectives for sales promotion in the consumer market and the wide range of techniques that can be used.

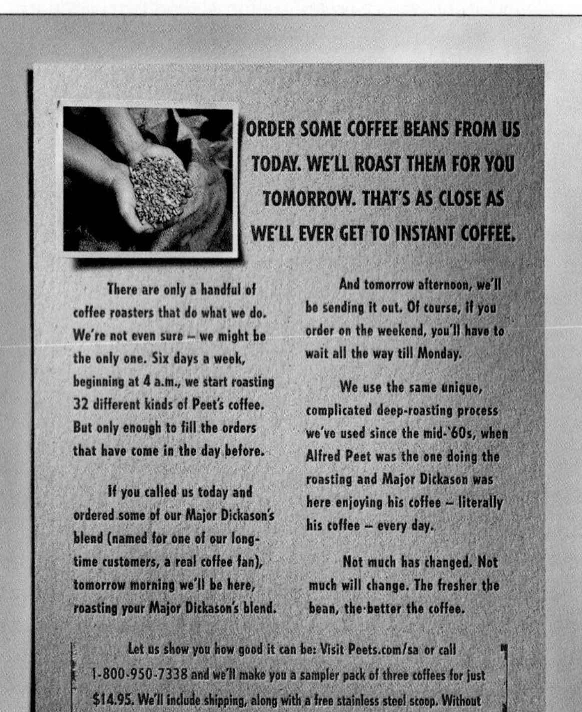

Exhibit 15.5 One objective for sales promotion in the consumer market is to stimulate trial use of a brand. Here, Peet's Coffee & Tea is offering consumers a sample pack they can request either online or by calling a toll-free number.

Courtesy, Vitro Robertson

Objectives for Consumer-Market Sales Promotion.

To help ensure the proper application of sales promotion, specific strategic objectives should be set. The following basic objectives can be pursued with sales promotion in the consumer market.

Stimulate Trial Purchase. When a firm wants to attract new users, sales promotion tools can reduce the consumer's risk of trying something new. A reduced price, offer of a rebate, or a free sample may stimulate trial purchase. Exhibit 15.5 illustrates an attempt to stimulate trial use. Note that this promotion is trying to get consumers to try a *brand* for the first time—not the product category. Recall the discussions in Chapters 2 and 3 (primary versus selective demand stimulation) highlighting the fact that advertising and promotion cannot *initiate* product category use in mature product categories, like coffee—but can only affect brand choice among people who already use the product category.

Stimulate Repeat Purchases. In-package coupons good for the next purchase, or the accumulation of points with repeated purchase, can keep consumers loyal to a particular brand. Loyalty or frequent purchase programs are the best techniques for pursuing this objective (more detail on these shortly). The most prominent frequency programs are found in the airline and hotel industries. Or how about that loyalty "punch card" at your favorite coffee shop—same idea. Firms try to retain their most loyal and lucrative customers by enrolling them in frequency programs.

9. Matthew Creamer, "Caught in the Clutter Crossfire: Your Brand," *Advertising Age,* April 2, 2007, 1, 35.

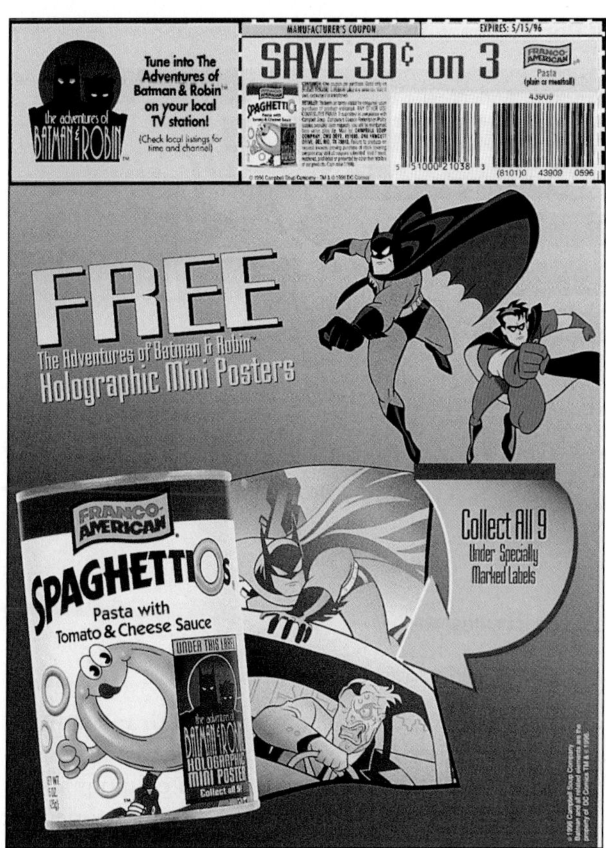

Exhibit 15.6 Sales promotions are often used to encourage larger purchases. This coupon for SpaghettiOs offers consumers the opportunity to stock up on three cans.

Courtesy of Campbell Soup Company

Stimulate Larger Purchases. Price reductions or two-for-one sales can motivate consumers to stock up on a brand, thus allowing firms to reduce inventory or increase cash flow. Shampoo is often double-packaged to offer a value to consumers. Exhibit 15.6 is a sales promotion aimed at stimulating a larger purchase ("Save 30 cents on 3").

Introduce a New Brand. Because sales promotion can attract attention and motivate trial purchase, it is commonly used for new brand introduction. One of the most successful uses of sales promotions to introduce a new brand was when the makers of Curad bandages introduced their new kid-size bandage by distributing 7.5 million sample packs in McDonald's Happy Meal sacks. The promotion was a huge success, with initial sales exceeding estimates by 30 percent.

Combat or Disrupt Competitors' Strategies. Because sales promotions often motivate consumers to buy in larger quantities or try new brands, they can be used to disrupt competitors' marketing strategies. If a firm knows that one of its competitors is launching a new brand or initiating a new advertising campaign, a well-timed sales promotion offering deep discounts or extra quantity can disrupt the competitors' strategy. Add to the original discount an in-package coupon for future purchases, and a marketer can severely compromise competitors' efforts. *TV Guide* magazine used a sweepstakes promotion to combat competition. In an effort to address increasing competition from newspaper TV supplements and cable-guide magazines, *TV Guide* ran a Shopping Spree Sweepstakes in several regional markets. Winners won $200 shopping sprees in grocery stores—precisely the location where 65 percent of *TV Guide* sales are realized.

Contribute to Integrated Brand Promotion. In conjunction with advertising, direct marketing, public relations, and other programs being carried out by a firm, sales promotion can add yet another type of communication to the mix. Sales promotions suggest an additional value, with price reductions, premiums, or the chance to win a prize. This is a different message within the overall communications effort a firm can use in its integrated brand promotion effort.

Consumer-Market Sales Promotion Techniques.

Several sales promotion techniques are used to stimulate demand and attract attention in the consumer market. Some of these are coupons, price-off deals, premiums, contests and sweepstakes, samples and trial offers, phone and gift cards, rebates, and frequency (continuity) programs.

Coupons. A **coupon** entitles a buyer to a designated reduction in price for a product or service. Coupons are the oldest and most widely used form of sales promotion. The first use of a coupon is traced to around 1895, when the C. W. Post Company used a penny-off coupon as a way to get people to try its Grape-Nuts cereal. Annually,

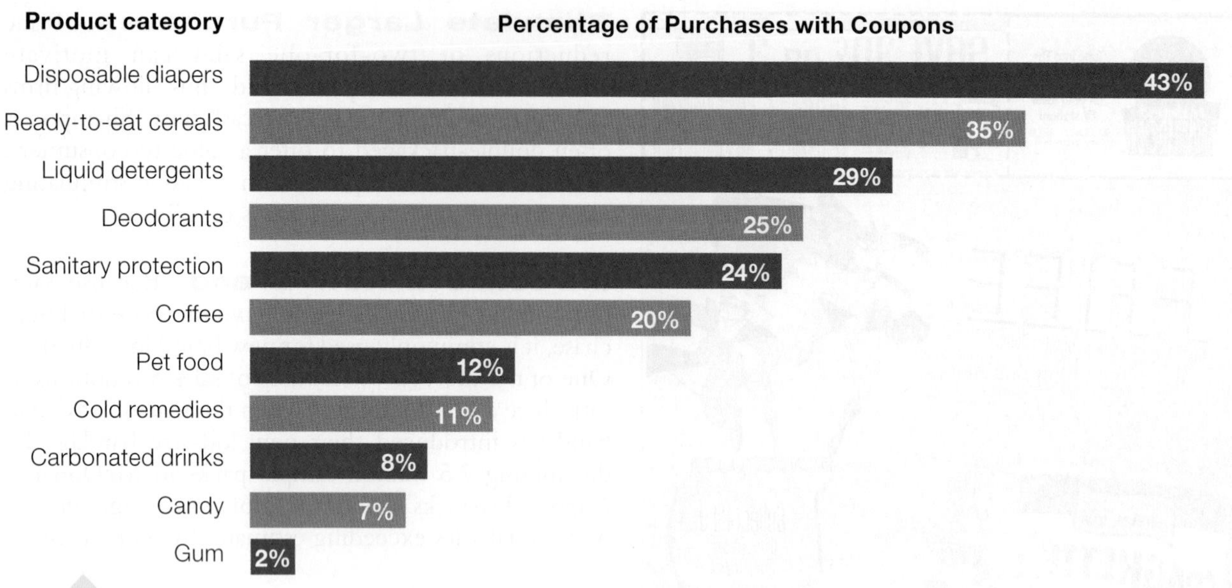

Exhibit 15.7 Percentage of purchases made with coupons in various product categories.

about 360 billion coupons are distributed to American consumers, with redemption rates ranging from 2 percent for gum purchases to nearly 45 percent for disposable diaper purchases. Overall, U.S. consumers redeem more than 3 billion coupons annually.[10] Exhibit 15.7 shows coupon-redemption rates for several product categories.

There are five advantages to the coupon as a sales promotion tool:

- The use of a coupon makes it possible to give a discount to a price-sensitive consumer while still selling the product at full price to other consumers.
- The coupon-redeeming customer may be a competitive-brand user, so the coupon can induce brand switching.
- A manufacturer can control the timing and distribution of coupons. This way a retailer is not implementing price discounts in a way that can damage brand image.
- A coupon is an excellent method of stimulating repeat purchases. Once a consumer has been attracted to a brand, with or without a coupon, an in-package coupon can induce repeat purchase.
- Coupons can get regular users to trade up within a brand array. For example, users of low-priced disposable diapers may be willing to try the premium version of a brand with a coupon.

The use of coupons is not without its problems. There are administrative burdens and risks with coupon use:

- Although coupon price incentives and the timing of distribution can be controlled by a marketer, the timing of redemption cannot. Some consumers redeem coupons immediately; others hold them for months.
- Heavy redemption by regular brand buyers merely reduces a firm's profitability.
- Couponing entails careful administration. Coupon programs include much more than the cost of the face value of the coupon. There are costs for production and distribution and for retailer and manufacturer handling. In fact, the cost for handling, processing, and distribution of coupons is typically equal to about

10. PromoMagazine Staff, "Coupon Use Skyrocketed in 2009," PromoMagazine.com, January 27, 2010.

two-thirds of the face value of the coupon. Marketers need to track these costs against the amount of product sold with and without coupon redemption.

- Fraud is a chronic and serious problem in the couponing process. The problem relates directly to misredemption practices. There are three types of misredemption that cost firms money: redemption of coupons by consumers who do not purchase the couponed brand; redemption of coupons by salesclerks and store managers without consumer purchases; and illegal collection or copying of coupons by individuals who sell them to unethical store merchants, who in turn redeem the coupons without the accompanying consumer purchases.

Price-Off Deals. The price-off deal is another straightforward technique. A **price-off deal** offers a consumer cents or even dollars off merchandise at the point-of-purchase through specially marked packages. The typical price-off deal is a 10 to 25 percent price reduction. The reduction is taken from the manufacturer's profit margin rather than the retailer's (another point of contention in the power struggle). Manufacturers like the price-off technique because it is controllable. Plus, the price off, judged at the point of purchase, can affect a positive price comparison against competitors. Consumers like a price-off deal because it is straightforward and automatically increases the value of a known brand. Regular users tend to stock up on an item during a price-off deal. Retailers are less enthusiastic about this technique. Price-off promotions can create inventory and pricing problems for retailers. Also, most price-off deals are snapped up by regular customers, so the retailer often doesn't benefit from new business.

Premiums and Advertising Specialties. **Premiums** are items offered free, or at a reduced price, with the purchase of another item. Many firms offer a related product free, such as a free granola bar packed inside a box of granola cereal. Service firms, such as a car wash or dry cleaner, may use a two-for-one offer to persuade consumers to try the service. Premiums represent a large investment in sales promotion, with over $15 billion spent on premiums during 2009.[11]

There are two options available for the use of premiums. A **free premium** provides consumers with an item at no cost. The item is can be included in the package of a purchased item, mailed to the consumer after proof of purchase is verified, or simply given away at the point-of-purchase or at an event. The most frequently used free premium is an additional package of the original item or a free related item placed in the package (e.g., free conditioner with shampoo purchase).

A **self-liquidating premium** requires a consumer to pay most of the cost of the item received as a premium. For example, Snapple can offer a "Snapple Cooler" with the purchase of six bottles of Snapple for $6.99—the cost of the cooler to Snapple. Self-liquidating premiums are particularly effective with loyal customers. However, these types of premiums must be used cautiously. Unless the premium is related to a value-building strategy for a brand, it can serve to focus consumer attention on the premium rather than on the benefits of the brand. Focusing on the premium rather than the brand erodes brand equity. For example, if consumers buy a brand just to get a really great looking T-shirt at $4.99, then they won't purchase the brand again until there is another great premium available at a low price.

Advertising specialties have three key elements: a message, placed on a useful item, given free to consumers, with no obligation to make a purchase. Popular advertising specialties are baseball caps, T-shirts, coffee mugs, computer mouse pads, pens, and calendars. Sales of specialty products in 2009 totaled about $16 billion.[12] Advertising specialties allow a firm to tout its company or brand name

11. Richard Alan Nelson and Rick Ebel, "2009 PPAI Sales Volume Study: The Only Direction To Go is Up," Promotional Products Business, July 2010, 8.

12. Ibid.

Exhibit 15.8 Advertising specialty items, like these pens and ball caps, allow a firm to regularly remind target customers of the brand name and logo. Even though a sales promotion item like this will never be the main strategic tool in an IBP campaign, it does serve to create a regular brand presence and conversation piece with consumers.

with a target customer in an ongoing fashion. Many of us have ball caps or coffee mugs that carry brand names (see Exhibit 15.8).

Contests and Sweepstakes. Contests and sweepstakes can draw attention to a brand like no other sales promotion technique. Technically, there are important differences between contests and sweepstakes. In a **contest**, consumers compete for prizes based on skill or ability. Winners in a contest are determined by a panel of judges or based on which contestant comes closest to a predetermined criterion for winning, such as picking the total points scored in the Super Bowl. Contests tend to be somewhat expensive to administer because each entry must be judged against winning criteria. Firms invest heavily in contests and sweepstakes as an IBP tool spending nearly $2 billion a year on the technique.[13]

A **sweepstakes** is a promotion in which winners are determined purely by chance. Consumers need only to enter their names in the sweepstakes as a criterion for winning. Sweepstakes often use official entry forms as a way for consumers to enter the sweepstakes. Other popular types of sweepstakes use scratch-off cards. Instant-winner scratch-off cards tend to attract customers. Gasoline retailers, grocery stores, and fast-food chains commonly use scratch-off-card sweepstakes as a way of building and maintaining store traffic. Sweepstakes can also be designed so that repeated trips to the retail outlet are necessary to gather a complete set of winning cards. In order for contests and sweepstakes to be effective, advertisers must design them in such a way that consumers perceive value in the prizes and find playing the games intrinsically interesting.

Contests and sweepstakes can span the globe. British Airways ran a contest with the theme "The World's Greatest Offer," in which it gave away thousands of free airline tickets to London and other European destinations. Although the contest increased awareness of the airline, there was definitely another benefit. Contests like these create a database of interested customers and potential customers. All the people who didn't win can be mailed information on future programs and other premium offers.

Contests and sweepstakes often create excitement and generate interest for a brand, but the problems of administering these promotions are substantial. Consider these challenges to effectively using contest and sweepstakes in the IBP effort.

- There will always be regulations and restrictions on contests and sweepstakes. Advertisers must be sure that the design and administration of a contest or sweepstakes complies with both federal and state laws. Each state may have slightly different regulations. The legal problems are complex enough that most firms hire agencies that specialize in contests and sweepstakes to administer the programs.
- The game itself may become the consumer's primary focus, while the brand becomes secondary. Like other sales promotion tools, this technique thus fails to build long-term consumer affinity for a brand.
- It is hard to get any meaningful message across in the context of a game. The consumer's interest is focused on the game, rather than on any feature of the brand.

13. Patricia O'Dell, "Spending Up by a Nose," PromoMagazine.com, December 1, 2009.

- Administration of a contest or sweepstakes is sufficiently complex that the risk of errors in administration is fairly high and can create negative publicity.
- If a firm is trying to develop a quality or prestige image for a brand, contests and sweepstakes may contradict this goal.

Sampling and Trial Offers. **Sampling** is a sales promotion technique designed to provide a consumer with an opportunity to use a brand on a trial basis with little or no risk. To say that sampling is a popular technique is an understatement. Most consumer-product companies use sampling in some manner, and invest approximately $2.2 billion a year on the technique. Surveys have shown that consumers are very favorable toward sampling, with 43 percent indicating that they would consider switching brands if they liked a free sample that was being offered.[14]

Sampling is particularly useful for new products but should not be reserved for new products alone. It can be used successfully for established brands with weak market share in specific geographic areas. Ben & Jerry's "Stop & Taste the Ice Cream" tour gave away more than a million scoops of ice cream in high-traffic urban areas in an attempt to reestablish a presence for the brand in weak markets.[15] Six techniques are used in sampling:

- **In-store sampling** is popular for food products (Costco) and cosmetics (Macy's). This is a preferred technique for many marketers because the consumer is at the point-of-purchase and may be swayed by a direct encounter with the brand. Increasingly, in-store demonstrators are handing out coupons as well as samples, as any trip to Costco will verify.
- **Door-to-door sampling** is extremely expensive because of labor costs, but it can be effective if the marketer has information that locates the target segment in a well-defined geographic area. Some firms enlist the services of newspaper delivery people, who package the sample with daily or Sunday newspapers as a way of reducing distribution costs.
- **Mail sampling** allows samples to be delivered through the postal service. Again, the value here is that certain zip-code markets can be targeted. A drawback is that the sample must be small enough to be economically feasible to mail. Specialty sampling firms provide targeted geo-demographic door-to-door distribution as an alternative to the postal service. Cox Target Media has developed a mailer that contains multiple samples related to a specific industry—like car-care products—and that can reach highly targeted market segments.[16]
- **Newspaper sampling** has become very popular in recent years, and 42 percent of consumers report having received samples of health and beauty products in this manner.[17] Much like mail sampling, newspaper samples allow very specific geographic and geo-demographic targeting. Big drug companies like Eli Lilly and Bristol-Myers Squibb have used newspaper distribution of coupons to target new users for antidepressant and diabetes drugs.[18]
- **On-package sampling,** a technique in which the sample item is attached to another product package, is useful for brands targeted to current customers. Attaching a small bottle of Ivory conditioner to a regular-sized container of Ivory shampoo is a logical sampling strategy.

14. Cox Direct 20th Annual Survey of Promotional Practices, 1998, 28; Patricia O'Dell, "Steady Growth," PromoMagazine.com, December 1, 2009.

15. Betsy Spethmann, "Branded Moments," *Promo Magazine,* September 2000, 84.

16. Cara Beardi, "Cox's Introz Mailer Bundles Samples in Industry," *Advertising Age,* November 2000, 88.

17. Cox Direct 20th Annual Survey of Promotional Practices, 1998, 27.

18. Susan Warner, "Drug Makers Print Coupons to Boost Sales," *Knight Ridder Newspapers,* June 4, 2001.

- **Mobile sampling** is carried out by logo-emblazoned vehicles that dispense samples, coupons, and premiums to consumers at malls, shopping centers, fairgrounds, and recreational areas.

Of course, sampling has its critics. Unless the brand has a clear value and benefit over the competition, a trial of the brand is unlikely to persuade a consumer to switch brands. This is especially true for convenience goods because consumers perceive a high degree of similarity among brands, even after trying them. The perception of benefit and superiority may have to be developed through advertising in combination with sampling. In addition, sampling is expensive. This is especially true in cases where a sufficient quantity of a product, such as shampoo or laundry detergent, must be given away for a consumer to truly appreciate a brand's value. Finally, sampling can be a very imprecise process. Despite the emergence of special agencies to handle sampling programs, a firm can never completely ensure that the product is reaching the targeted audience and not just consumers in general.

Trial offers have the same goal as sampling—to induce consumer trial use of a brand—but they are used for more expensive items. Exercise equipment, appliances, watches, hand tools, and consumer electronics are typical of items offered on a trial basis. Trial offers can be free for low-priced products, as we saw in Exhibit 15.5 with Peet's Coffee. Or trials can be offered for as little as a day to as long as 90 days for more expensive items like vacuum cleaners or computer software. The expense to the firm, of course, can be formidable. Segments chosen for this sales promotion technique must have high sales potential.

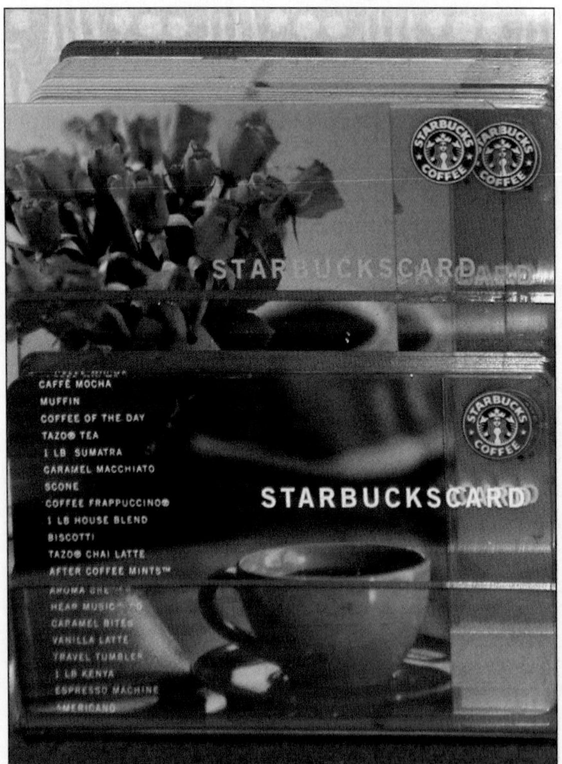

Exhibit 15.9 Firms use gift cards as a way to draw attention to the brand and as a way for loyal customers to introduce their friends and family to the brand.

Phone and Gift Cards. Phone and gift cards represent a new and increasingly popular form of sales promotion. The use of phone and gift cards is fairly straightforward. Manufacturers or retailers offer either free or for-purchase debit cards that provide the holder with a pre-set spending limit or perhaps minutes of phone time. The cards are designed to be colorful and memorable. A wide range of marketers, including luxury car manufacturers like Lexus and retailers like the Gap, have made effective use of phone and gift cards. The really good news about gift cards is that gift card holders tend to use them freely to pay the full retail price for items, which means retailers and brand marketers earn higher profit margins from gift card purchases.[19] Exhibit 15.9 shows a Starbucks gift card as a promotional tool.

Rebates. A **rebate** is a money-back offer requiring a buyer to mail in a form (although many are redeemed instantly at checkout) requesting the money back from the manufacturer, rather than from the retailer (as in couponing). The rebate technique has been refined throughout the years and is now used by a wide variety of marketers with more than 400 million rebates offered each year for products as diverse as computers (Dell) to mouthwash (Warner-Lambert).[20] Rebates are particularly well suited to increasing the quantity purchased by consumers, so rebates are commonly tied to multiple purchases.

19. Louise Lee, "What's Roiling the Selling Season," *BusinessWeek,* January 10, 2005, 38.

20. Brian Grow, "The Great Rebate Runaround," *BusinessWeek,* December 5, 2005, 34–38.

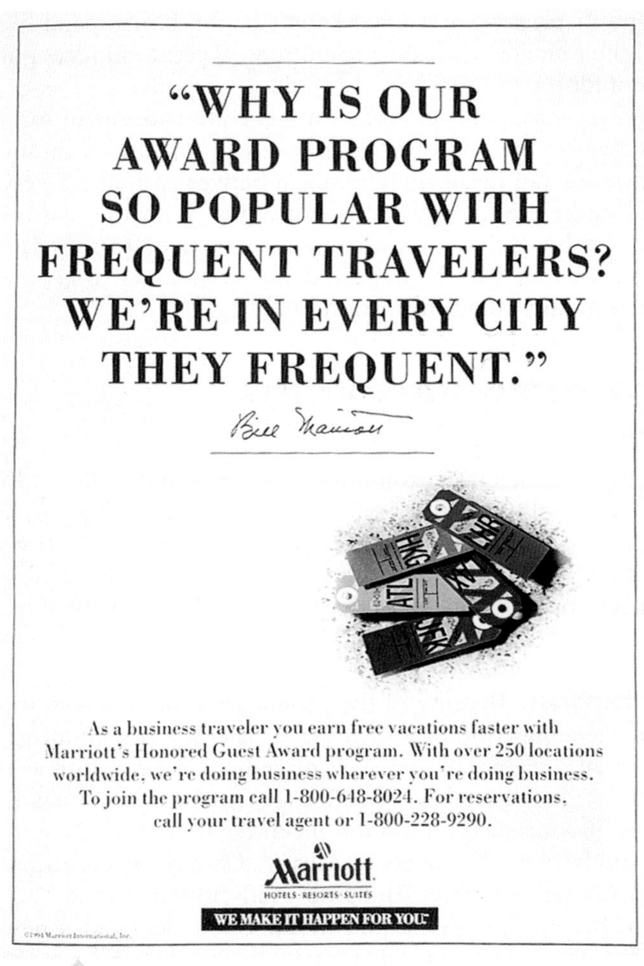

"WHY IS OUR AWARD PROGRAM SO POPULAR WITH FREQUENT TRAVELERS? WE'RE IN EVERY CITY THEY FREQUENT."
As a business traveler you earn free vacations faster with Marriott's Honored Guest Award program. With over 250 locations worldwide, we're doing business wherever you're doing business. To join the program call 1-800-648-8024. For reservations, call your travel agent or 1-800-228-9290.
Marriott
HOTELS · RESORTS · SUITES
WE MAKE IT HAPPEN FOR YOU

Exhibit 15.10 Frequency (continuity) programs build customer loyalty and offer opportunities for building a large, targeted database for other promotions.

Another reason for the popularity of rebates is that relatively few consumers actually take advantage of the rebate offer after buying a brand. The best estimate of consumer redemption of rebate offers is that only 60 percent of buyers ever bother to fill out and then mail in the rebate request—resulting in an extra $2 billion in revenue for manufacturers and retailers who offer rebates.[21]

Frequency (Continuity) Programs. In recent years, one of the most popular sales promotion techniques among consumers has been frequency programs. **Frequency programs**, also referred to as continuity programs or loyalty card programs, offer consumers discounts or free product rewards for repeat purchase or patronage of the same brand, company, or retailer. These programs were pioneered by airline companies. Frequent-flyer programs such as Delta Air Lines' SkyMiles, frequent-stay programs such as Marriott's Honored Guest Award program, and frequent-renter programs such as Hertz's #1 Club are examples of such loyalty-building activities. But frequency programs are not reserved for big national airline and auto-rental chains. Chart House Enterprises, a chain of 65 upscale restaurants, successfully launched a frequency program for diners, who earned points for every dollar spent. Frequent diners were issued "passports," which were stamped with each visit. Within two years, the program had more than 300,000 members. Firms spend more than $2 billion a year on frequency and loyalty programs.[22] From a new media standpoint, 73 percent of U.S. Internet users report using a loyalty card of some sort when shopping online.[23] Exhibit 15.10 features Marriott's frequency program.

3 Sales Promotion Directed at the Trade Channel and Business Markets.

Sales promotions can also be directed at members of the trade—wholesalers, distributors, and retailers—and business markets. For example, Hewlett-Packard designs sales promotion programs for its retailers, like Best Buy, in order to ensure that the HP line gets proper attention and display. But HP will also have sales promotion campaigns aimed at business buyers like Accenture or IHC HealthCare. The purpose of sales promotion as a tool does not change from the consumer market to the trade or business markets. It is still intended to stimulate demand in the short term and help *push* the product through the distribution channel or cause business buyers to

21. PromoMagazine Staff, "Coupon Use Skyrocketed in 2009," PromoMagazine.com, January 27, 2010, 34.
22. Patricia O'Dell, "Faithful Following," PromoMagazine.com, December 1, 2009.
23. Allison Enright and Elisabeth A. Sullivan, "Marketers, Come on Down," *Marketing News,* July 30, 2010, 14.

act more immediately and positively toward the marketer's brand. Firms spend big money to attract business to their brands with sales promotions. Recent estimates put business-to-business sales promotions at more than $44 billion annually.[24]

Effective trade- and business-market promotions can generate enthusiasm for a product and contribute positively to the loyalty distributor's show for a brand. In the business market, sales promotions can mean the difference between landing a very large order and missing out entirely on a revenue opportunity. With the massive proliferation of new brands and brand extensions, manufacturers need to stimulate enthusiasm and loyalty among members of the trade and also need a way to get the attention of business buyers suffering from information overload.

Objectives for Promotions in the Trade Channel.

As in the consumer market, trade-market sales promotions should be undertaken with specific objectives in mind. Generally speaking, when marketers devise incentives for the trade market they are executing a **push strategy**; that is, sales promotions directed at the trade help push a brand into the distribution channel until it ultimately reaches the consumer. Four primary objectives can be identified for these promotions.

Obtain Initial Distribution. Because of the proliferation of brands in the consumer market, there is fierce competition for shelf space. Sales promotion incentives can help a firm gain initial distribution and shelf placement. Like consumers, members of the trade need a reason to choose one brand over another when it comes to allocating shelf space. A well-conceived promotion incentive may sway them.

Bob's Candies, a small family-owned business in Albany, Georgia, is the largest candy cane manufacturer in the United States. But Bob's old-fashioned candy was having trouble keeping distributors. To reverse the trend, Bob's designed a new name, logo, and packaging for the candy canes. Then, each scheduled attendee at the All-Candy Expo trade show in Chicago was mailed three strategically timed postcards with the teaser question "Wanna Be Striped?" The mailing got a 25 percent response rate, and booth visitations at the trade show were a huge success.[25]

Increase Order Size. One of the struggles in the channel of distribution is over the location of inventory. Manufacturers prefer that members of the trade maintain large inventories so that the manufacturer can reduce inventory-carrying costs. Conversely, members of the trade would rather make frequent, small orders and carry little inventory. Sales promotion techniques can encourage wholesalers and retailers to order in larger quantities, thus shifting the inventory burden to the trade channel.

Encourage Cooperation with Consumer-Market Sales Promotions. It does a manufacturer little good to initiate a sales promotion in the consumer market if there is little cooperation in the channel. Wholesalers may need to maintain larger inventories, and retailers may need to provide special displays or handling during consumer-market sales promotions. To achieve synergy, marketers often run trade promotions simultaneously with consumer promotions. When Toys "R" Us ran a "scan and win" promotion, the retailer actually ran out of several very popular toy items during the critical holiday-buying season because distributors (and Toys "R" Us) were unprepared for the magnitude of the response to the promotion.

24. 2007 Marketing Fact Book, *Marketing News,* July 15, 2007, 32.

25. Lee Duffey, "Sweet Talk: Promotions Position Candy Company," *Marketing News,* March 30, 1998, 11.

Increase Store Traffic. Retailers can increase store traffic through special promotions or events. Door-prize drawings, parking-lot sales, or live radio broadcasts from the store are common sales promotion traffic builders. Burger King has become a leader in building traffic at its 6,500 outlets with special promotions tied to Disney movie debuts. Beginning with a *Beauty and the Beast* tie-in promotion, Burger King has set records for generating store traffic with premium giveaways. The *Pocahontas* campaign distributed 55 million toys and glasses. A promotion tie-in with Disney's enormously successful film *Toy Story* resulted in 50 million toys, based on the film's characters, being given away in $1.99 Kids Meals. Manufacturers, in addition to retailers, can also design sales promotions that increase store traffic for retailers. A promotion that generates a lot of interest within a target audience can drive consumers to retail outlets.

Trade-Market Sales Promotion Techniques.

The sales promotion techniques used within the trade market are incentives, allowances, trade shows, sales-training programs, and cooperative advertising.

Incentives. Incentives to members of the trade include a variety of tactics not unlike those used in the consumer market. Awards in the form of travel, gifts, or cash bonuses for reaching targeted sales levels can induce retailers and wholesalers to give a firm's brand added attention. Consider this incentive ploy: The Volvo national sales manager put together an incentive program for dealerships, in which the leading dealership in the nation won a trip to the Super Bowl, including dinner with Hall of Fame footballer Lynn Swann.[26] But the incentive does not have to be large or expensive to be effective. Weiser Lock offered its dealers a Swiss Army knife with every dozen cases of locks ordered. The program was a huge success. A follow-up promotion featuring a Swiss Army watch was an even bigger hit. And firms are finding that Web-based incentive programs can be highly effective as well. When the sales manager at Netopia, a manufacturer of broadband equipment, wanted to offer an incentive to dealers, he did *not* want to manage the whole process. The solution? Implement "innergE," an online incentive-management program that features a website where salespeople can track their sales progress and claim their rewards.[27]

Another form of trade incentive is referred to as push money. **Push money** is carried out through a program in which retail salespeople are offered a monetary reward for featuring a marketer's brand with shoppers. The program is quite simple. If a salesperson sells a particular brand of, say, a refrigerator for a manufacturer as opposed to a competitor's brand, the salesperson will be paid an extra $50 or $75 "bonus" as part of the push money program.

One risk with incentive programs for the trade is that salespeople can be so motivated to win an award or extra push money that they may try to sell the brand to every customer, whether it fits that customer's needs or not. Also, a firm must carefully manage such programs to minimize ethical dilemmas. An incentive technique can look like a bribe unless it is carried out in a highly structured and open fashion.

Allowances. Various forms of allowances are offered to retailers and wholesalers with the purpose of increasing the attention given to a firm's brands. Allowances are typically made available to wholesalers and retailers about every four weeks

26. Ron Donoho, "It's Up! It's Good!" *Sales and Marketing Management,* April 2003, 43–47.

27. Michelle Gillan, "E-Motivation," *Sales and Marketing Management,* April 2003, 50.

during a quarter. **Merchandise allowances**, in the form of free products packed with regular shipments, are payments to the trade for setting up and maintaining displays. The payments are typically far less than manufacturers would have to spend to maintain the displays themselves.

In recent years, shelf space has become so highly demanded, especially in supermarkets, that manufacturers are making direct cash payments, known as **slotting fees**, to induce food chains to stock an item. The slotting fee for a new brand is sometimes called a "product introduction fee." The proliferation of new products has made shelf space such a precious commodity that these fees now run in the hundreds of thousands of dollars per product. Another form of allowance is called a bill-back allowance. **Bill-back allowances** provide retailers a monetary incentive for featuring a marketer's brand in either advertising or in-store displays. If a retailer chooses to participate in either an advertising campaign or a display bill-back program, the marketer requires the retailer to verify the services performed and provide a bill for the services. A similar program is the **off-invoice allowance**, in which advertisers allow wholesalers and retailers to deduct a set amount from the invoice they receive for merchandise. This program is really just a price reduction offered to the trade on a particular marketer's brand. The incentive for the trade with this program is that the price reduction increases the margin (and profits) a wholesaler or retailer realizes on the off-invoiced brand.

One risk with allowances is monitoring the extent to which retailers actually use the allowance to either cover extra-effort to feature a brand or reduce prices to consumers. Procter & Gamble alone spends about $2 billion per year on trade promotions and has implemented controls to ensure that displays and other merchandising of the firm's brands are actually occurring.[28]

Sales-Training Programs. An increasingly popular trade promotion is to provide training for retail store personnel. This method is used for consumer durables and specialty goods, such as personal computers, home theater systems, heating and cooling systems, security systems, and exercise equipment. The increased complexity of these products has made it important for manufacturers to ensure that the proper factual information and persuasive themes are reaching consumers at the point of purchase. For personnel at large retail stores, manufacturers can hold special classes that feature product information, demonstrations, and training about sales techniques.

A popular and efficient method for getting sales-training information to retailers is the use of videotapes and brochures. Manufacturers can also send sales trainers into retail stores to work side-by-side with store personnel. This is a more costly approach, but it can be very effective because of the one-on-one attention it provides.

Cooperative (Co-op) Advertising. **Cooperative advertising** as a trade promotion technique is also referred to as vertical cooperative advertising and provides dollars directly to retailers for featuring company's brand in local advertising. (Such efforts are also called vendor co-op programs.) Manufacturers try to control the content of this co-op advertising in two ways. They may set strict specifications for the size and content of the ad and then ask for verification that such specifications have been met. Alternatively, manufacturers may send the template for an ad, into which retailers merely insert the names and locations of their stores. Just such an ad is featured in Exhibit 15.11. Notice that the Hublot watch ad elements are national (even international) with the co-op sponsorship of the California retailer highlighted in the lower left.

28. Jack Neff, "P&G Trims Fat off Its $2B Trade-Promotion System," *Advertising Age*, June 5, 2006, 8.

Exhibit 15.11 Here is a classic example of co-op advertising between manufacturer and retailer. Hublot is being featured by a California retailer in a magazine ad. Is there another form of sales promotion going on here as well?

Courtesy, Jean-Claude Biver, CEO of Hublot Geneve

Business-Market Sales Promotion Techniques.

Often the discussion of sales promotion focuses only on consumer and trade techniques. It is a major oversight to leave the business market out of the discussion. The Promotional Product Association estimates that several billion dollars a year in sales promotion is targeted to the business buyer.

Trade Shows. **Trade shows** are events where several related products from many manufacturers are displayed and demonstrated to members of a trade. Literally every industry has trade shows, from ones featuring gourmet products to the granddaddy of them all, Comdex. Comdex is the annual computer and electronics industry trade show held in Las Vegas that attracts more than a quarter of a million business buyers. Spending on trade shows continues to grow and now stands at about $11 billion dollars per year.[29] Advertisers are finding that a trade show is an efficient way to reach interested current and potential buyers with the brand right at hand for discussion and actual use. The Promotional Products Association reports that when trade show visitors receive a promotional item from a firm at a trade show booth, more than 70 percent of the visitors remember the name of the company that gave them the item.[30]

At a typical trade show, company representatives staff a booth that displays a company's products or service programs. The representatives are there to explain the products and services and perhaps make an important contact for the sales force. Trade shows can be critically important to a small firm that cannot afford advertising and has a sales staff too small to reach all its potential customers. Through the trade-show route, salespeople can make far more contacts than they could with direct sales calls.

Business Gifts. Estimates are that nearly half of corporate America gives business gifts. These gifts are given as part of building and maintaining a close working relationship with suppliers. Business gifts that are part of a promotional program may include small items like logo golf balls, jackets, or small items of jewelry. Extravagant gifts or expensive trips that might be construed as "buying business" are not included in this category of business-market sales promotion.

Premiums and Advertising Specialties. As mentioned earlier, the key chain, ball cap, T-shirt, mouse pad, or calendar that reminds a buyer of a brand name and slogan can be an inexpensive but useful form of sales promotion. A significant portion of the $15 billion premium and advertising specialty market is directed to business buyers. Although business buyers are professionals, they are not immune to the value perceptions that an advertising specialty can create. In other words, getting something for nothing appeals to business buyers as much as it does to household

29. 2004 Industry Trends Report, *Promo Magazine,* 31.

30. Data available at Promotional Products Association International website, www.ppa.org, accessed on August 5, 2007.

consumers. Will a business buyer choose one consulting firm over another to get a sleeve of golf balls? Probably not. But advertising specialties can create awareness and add to the satisfaction of a transaction nonetheless.

Trial Offers. Trial offers are particularly well suited to the business market. First, since many business products and services are high cost and often result in a significant time commitment to a brand (i.e., many business products and services have long life), trial offers provide a way for buyers to lower the risk of making a commitment to one brand over another. Second, a trial offer is a good way to attract new customers who need a good reason to try something new. The chance to try a new product for 30 days with no financial risk can be a compelling offer.

Frequency Programs. The high degree of travel associated with many business professions makes frequency programs an ideal form of sales promotion for the business market. Airline, hotel, and restaurant frequency programs are dominated by the business market traveler. But frequency programs for the business market are not restricted to travel-related purchases. Retailers of business products like Staples, OfficeMax, and Costco have programs designed to reward the loyalty of the business buyer. Costco has teamed with American Express to offer business buyers an exclusive Costco/American Express credit card. Among the many advantages of the card is a rebate at the end of the year based on the level of buying—the greater the dollar amount of purchases, the greater the percentage rebate.

4 The Risks of Sales Promotion.

The discussion so far has demonstrated that sales promotion techniques can be used to pursue important sales objectives. As we have seen, there are a wide range of sales promotion options for the consumer, trade, and business markets. But there are also significant risks associated with sales promotion, and these risks must be carefully considered.

Creating a Price Orientation.

Since most sales promotions rely on some sort of price incentive or giveaway, a firm runs the risk of having its brand perceived as cheap, with no real value or benefits beyond the low price. Creating this perception in the market contradicts the concept of integrated brand promotion. If advertising messages highlight the value and benefit of a brand only to be contradicted by a price emphasis in sales promotions, then a confusing signal is being sent to the market. Chrysler dealers challenged corporate management on just this point, arguing that escalating price incentives on various vehicles were "wrecking" the brand.[31]

Borrowing from Future Sales.

Management must admit that sales promotions are typically short-term tactics designed to reduce inventories, increase cash flow, or show periodic boosts in market share. The downside is that a firm may simply be borrowing from future sales. Consumers or trade buyers who would have purchased the brand anyway may be motivated to stock up at the lower price. This results in reduced sales during the next few time periods of measurement. This can play havoc with the measurement and evaluation of the effect of advertising campaigns or other image-building communications.

31. Jean Halliday, "Dealers: Chrysler Is Wrecking Brands," *Advertising Age,* June 12, 2006, 1, 39.

If consumers are responding to sales promotions, it may be impossible to tease out the effects of advertising.

Alienating Customers.

When a firm relies heavily on sweepstakes or frequency programs to build loyalty among customers, particularly their best customers, there is the risk of alienating these customers with any change in the program. Airlines suffered just such a fate when they tried to adjust the mileage levels needed for awards in their frequent-flyer programs. Ultimately, many of the airlines had to give concessions to their most frequent flyers as a conciliatory gesture.

Managerial Time and Expense.

Sales promotions are both costly and time-consuming. The process is time-consuming for the marketer and the retailer in terms of handling promotional materials and protecting against fraud and waste in the process. As we have seen in recent years, funds allocated to sales promotions are taking dollars away from advertising. Advertising is a long-term, franchise-building process that should not be compromised for short-term gains.

Legal Considerations.

With the increasing popularity of sales promotions, particularly contests and premiums, there has been an increase in legal scrutiny at both the federal and state levels. Legal experts recommend that before initiating promotions that use coupons, games, sweepstakes, and contests, a firm check into lottery laws, copyright laws, state and federal trademark laws, prize notification laws, right of privacy laws, tax laws, and FTC and FCC regulations. The best advice for staying out of legal trouble with sales promotions is to carefully and clearly state the rules and conditions related to the program so that consumers are fully informed.

5 Point-of-Purchase Advertising.

From 1981 to 2008, marketers' annual expenditures on point-of-purchase (P-O-P) advertising rose from $5.1 billion to more than $20 billion per year.[32] Why this dramatic growth? First, consider that P-O-P is the only medium that places advertising, brands, and a consumer together in the same place at the same time. Then, think about these results. Research conducted by the trade association Point-of-Purchase Advertising International (http://www.popai.com) indicates that 70 percent of all product selections involve some final deliberation by consumers at the point of purchase.[33] In addition, in an early study on the effects of P-O-P sponsored by K-Mart and Procter & Gamble, the research showed that P-O-P advertising boosted the sales of coffee, paper towels, and toothpaste by 567 percent, 773 percent, and 119 percent, respectively.[34] With results like these, it is plain to see why P-O-P advertising is one of the fastest-growing categories in today's marketplace. Even though point-of-purchase commands large investment in the United States and most parts of the world, P-O-P and other forms of sales promotion are less popular in some other parts of the world as the *Globalization* box highlights.

32. Patricia O'Dell, "Shopping Trip," PromoMagazine.com, December 1, 2009.

33. Data on point-of-purchase decision making cited in Patricia O'Dell, "Shopping Trip," PromoMagazine.com, December 1, 2009.

34. Data cited in Lisa Z. Eccles, "P-O-P Scores with Marketers," *Advertising Age,* September 26, 1994.

Globalization

Point-of-Purchase and Sales Promotion in China—A Tough Sell

You would think that in a market like China with a rapidly expanding middle-class that sales promotions and point-of-purchase advertising in particular would be easy IBP strategies to implement for U.S. and other foreign marketers of consumer goods—not so. The Chinese consumer has several unique characteristics and consumption values that make the implementation difficult and complex. First, Chinese consumers are developing a growing preference for homemade brands (partly fostered by the Chinese government's growing protectionist policies). On the surface, that fact would seem to make sales promotions for foreign brands even more important. But, a second attitude among Chinese consumers—the public display of upward mobility embodied in foreign brand ownership—runs counter to process of discounting the price of a brand.

Sony is struggling with this seeming contradiction. Even though ownership of a Sony television would most certainly be a brand that signals "success" and upward mobility, the leading appliance brands in China, without exception, are cheaply priced domestic brands like Haier, TCL, and Changhong. McDonald's too is struggling with how to counter a drop in sales. When McDonald's dropped prices to compete with local restaurants (which sell meals for as much as 40 percent below a burger and fries at McDonald's), the price cuts did little to boost sales. The firm quickly changed strategy and set out upgrading restaurants and launched an ad campaign emphasizing the "happiness" that comes from eating at McDonald's. The most complicated approach is being used by Unilever—the Dutch household products firm. Unilever's Chairman for Greater China has taken to the road and visits with Chinese consumers in stores as they go about their shopping. He asks about their daily lives, hygiene habits, fears, and dreams. One thing he learned was that "in-store promoters" (something like our in-store sampling process in the United States) can be a highly successful way to implement sales promotion to the Chinese consumer. Chinese consumers are still learning the "architecture" of brands (i.e., the many features and capabilities of even simple product categories like shampoo) and static point-of-purchase materials are just not good enough to get the job done.

Overall, the vast experience with sales promotions of all types—including point-of-purchase techniques—that global brand marketers have perfected in developed markets need to be adapted and actively managed in the Chinese market.

Sources: David Wolf, "Understanding New China," *Advertising Age*, June 9, 2010, 7; Tom Doctoroff, "3 Golden Rules of Brand Management in China," *Advertising Age*, November 4, 2009, 8; Normandy Madden, "Not Lovin' a Drop in China Sales, McDonald's Revamps Its Image," January 6, 2010, 3; Normandy Madden, "Unilever Puts in Face Time with the Chinese Consumer," *Advertising Age*, March 22, 2010, 8.

Point-of-Purchase Advertising Defined.

Point-of-purchase (P-O-P) advertising refers to materials used in the retail setting to attract shoppers' attention to a brand, convey primary brand benefits, or highlight pricing information. P-O-P displays may also feature price-off deals or other consumer sales promotions. A corrugated-cardboard dump bin and an attached header card featuring the brand logo or related brand information can be produced for pennies per unit. When the bin is filled with a brand and placed as a freestanding display at retail, sales gains usually follow.

Effective deployment of P-O-P advertising requires careful coordination with the marketer's sales force. Gillette found this out when it realized it was wasting money on lots of P-O-P materials and displays that retailers simply ignored.[35] Gillette sales reps visit about 20,000 stores per month and are in a position to know what retailers will and will not use. Gillette's marketing executives finally woke up to this fact when their sales reps told them, for example, that 50 percent of the shelf signs being shipped to retailers from three separate suppliers were going directly to retailers' garbage bins. Reps helped redesign new display cards that mega-retailers such as Walmart approved for their stores and immediately put into use. Now any time Gillette launches a new P-O-P program, it tracks its success carefully.[36] Having

35. Nicole Crawford, "Keeping P-O-P Sharp," *Promo Magazine,* January 1998, 52, 53.

36. Jack Neff, "P&G Trims Fat off Its $2B Trade-Promotion System," *Advertising Age,* June 5, 2006, 8.

a sales force that can work with retailers to develop and deliver effective P-O-P programs is a critical element for achieving integrated brand promotion.

Objectives for Point-of-Purchase Advertising.

The objectives of point-of-purchase advertising are similar to those for sales promotion in general. The goal is to create a short-term impact on sales while preserving the long-term image of the brand being developed and maintained by advertising for the brand. Specifically, the objectives for point-of-purchase advertising are as follows:

- Draw consumers' attention to a brand in the retail setting.
- Maintain purchase loyalty among brand-loyal users.
- Stimulate increased or varied usage of the brand.
- Stimulate trial use by users of competitive brands.

These objectives are self-explanatory and follow closely on the objectives of sales promotion. Key to the effective use of P-O-P is to maintain the brand image being developed by advertising.

Types of Point-of-Purchase Advertising and Displays.

A myriad of displays and presentations are available to marketers. P-O-P materials generally fall into two categories: **short-term promotional displays**, which are used for six months or less, and **permanent long-term displays**, which are intended to provide point-of-purchase presentation for more than six months. Within these two categories, marketers have a wide range of choices:[37]

- ***Window and door signage:*** Any sign that identifies and/or advertises a company or brand or gives directions to the consumer.
- ***Counter/shelf unit:*** A smaller display designed to fit on counters or shelves.
- ***Floor stand:*** Any P-O-P unit that stands independently on the floor.
- ***Shelf talker:*** A printed card or sign designed to mount on or under a shelf.
- ***Mobile/banner:*** An advertising sign suspended from the ceiling of a store or hung across a large wall area.
- ***Cash register:*** P-O-P signage or small display mounted near a cash register designed to sell impulse items such as gum, lip balm, or candy, as in Exhibit 15.12.
- ***Full line merchandiser:*** A unit that provides the only selling area for a manufacturer's line. Often located as an end-of-aisle display.
- ***End-of-aisle display/gondola:*** Usually a large display of products placed at the end of an aisle, as in Exhibit 15.13.
- ***Dump bin:*** A large bin with graphics or other signage attached.
- ***Illuminated sign:*** Lighted signage used outside or in-store to promote a brand or the store.
- ***Motion display:*** Any P-O-P unit that has moving elements to attract attention.
- ***Interactive unit:*** A computer-based kiosk where shoppers get information such as tips on recipes or how to use the brand. Can also be a unit that flashes and dispenses coupons.

37. This is a representative list of the most widely used types of displays from Marketing's Powerful Weapon: Point-of-Purchase Advertising (Washington, DC: Point-of-Purchase Advertising International, 2001), 177–180.

Exhibit 15.12 Displays at a cash register checkout lane are designed to sell impulse items such as candy, or easily forgotten items such as batteries.

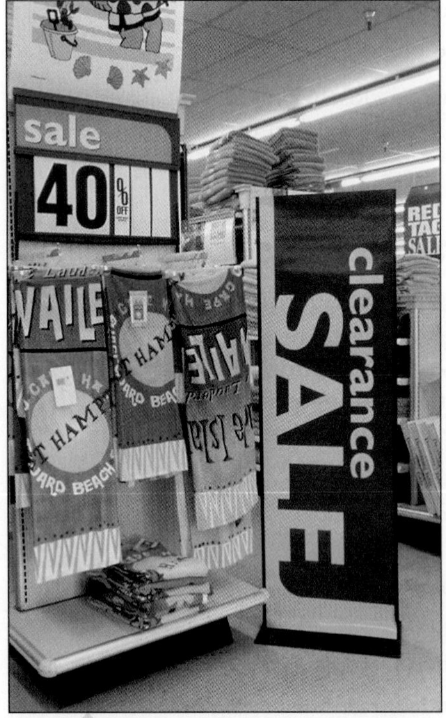

Exhibit 15.13 End-of-aisle displays provide space to draw attention to a large display of product.

Exhibit 15.14 A shopping-cart ad carries an immediate message to shoppers.

- ***Overhead merchandiser:*** A display rack that stocks product and is placed above the cash register. The cashier can reach the product for the consumer. The front of an overhead merchandiser usually carries signage.
- ***Cart advertising:*** Any advertising message adhered to a shopping cart, as in Exhibit 15.14.
- ***Aisle directory:*** Used to delineate contents of a store aisle; also provides space for an advertising message.
- ***Retail digital signage:*** The newest P-O-P device available is retail digital signage. These are video displays that have typically been ceiling- or wall-mounted and are now being moved to end-of-aisle caps or given strategic shelf placement to relay special pricing or new product introductions.[38]

This wide array of in-store options gives marketers the opportunity to attract shoppers' attention, induce purchase, and provide reinforcement for key messages that are being conveyed through other components of the IBP plan. Retailers are increasingly looking to P-O-P displays as ways to differentiate and provide ambience for their individual stores, which means that the kind of displays valued by Whole Foods versus Walgreens versus Albertson's versus Target (to name just a few) will often vary considerably. Once again, it is the marketer's field sales force that will be critical in developing the right P-O-P alternative for each retailer stocking that marketer's products. Without the retailers' cooperation, P-O-P advertising has virtually no chance to work its magic.

P-O-P and Mobile/Location Marketing.

We have considered mobile marketing in several contexts throughout the book, including highlighting the firm Foursquare in the last chapter. There are those who argue that the new point-of-purchase advertising *is* mobile marketing.[39] Mobile marketing through smartphones and other mobile devices adds another dimension to the retailers' in-store or near-store marketing. What a billboard used to do—alert the consumer to a nearby location—a smartphone can now do. And, when the consumer is in front of a store shelf, sensors can identify the location and let the marketer send one last message to try to convert the browsing into a purchase. The full breadth of potential for location marketing and point of purchase is still being explored—particularly consumers' attitude and reaction toward the practice. But, the technology offers compelling possibilities.

P-O-P Advertising and the Trade and Business Markets.

Although we have focused our discussion of the use of point-of-purchase advertising as a technique to attract consumers, this promotional tool is also strategically valuable to manufacturers as they

38. Dale Smith, "Coming Down to Eye Level," *Marketing at Retail,* June 2007, 28–31.

39. Kunur Patel, "Forget Foursquare: Why Location Marketing Is the New Point-of-Purchase," *Advertising Age,* March 22, 2010, 1, 19.

try to secure the cooperation in the trade and business markets. Product displays and information sheets offered to retailers often encourage retailers to support one distributor or manufacturer's brand over another. P-O-P promotions can help win precious shelf space and exposure in a retail setting. From a retailer's perspective, a P-O-P display can enhance the atmosphere of the store and make the shopping experience easier for customers. Brand manufacturers and distributors obviously share that interest. When a retailer is able to move a particular brand off the shelf, that in turn, positively affects both the manufacturer and distributor's sales.

In an attempt to combat the threat of losing business to online shopping, retailers are trying to enliven the retail environment, and point-of-purchase displays are part of the strategy. Distributors and retailers are trying to create a better and more satisfying shopping experience. The president of a large display company says, "We're trying to bring more of an entertainment factor to our P-O-P programs."[40]

6 Support Media.

This section discusses traditional support media: outdoor signage and billboard advertising, transit and aerial advertising, cinema advertising, directory advertising, and packaging. We placed this section in this chapter because these supportive IBP tools are more similar to sales promotion and point-of-purchase devices than they are to the major media covered in Chapters 12 to 13.

Support media are used to reinforce or supplement a message being delivered via some other media vehicle; hence the name *support media.* Exhibits 15.15 and 15.16 show a pair of ads for Adidas, with the outdoor signage supporting the print campaign. Support media are especially productive when used to deliver a message near the time or place where consumers are actually contemplating product

Exhibit 15.15 Brands like Adidas need to be in constant contact with the sports fan. In this case, Adidas delivers its "forever sport" mantra through a print ad that appeared in the college football preview issue of *Sports Illustrated*. Hence the first line of copy: "Leaves that let you know it's football season."

Exhibit 15.16 Here we see the Adidas logo providing the backdrop for everyday life in a building-side billboard. Note how this support media vehicle—the billboard—supports the print media message in Exhibit 15.15.

Photo by Susan Van Etten; © Chris T. Allen

40. 2004 Industry Trends Report, *Promo Magazine*.

Exhibit 15.17 Advertising in the United States began with posters and billboards. Circuses were the early pioneers in this medium.

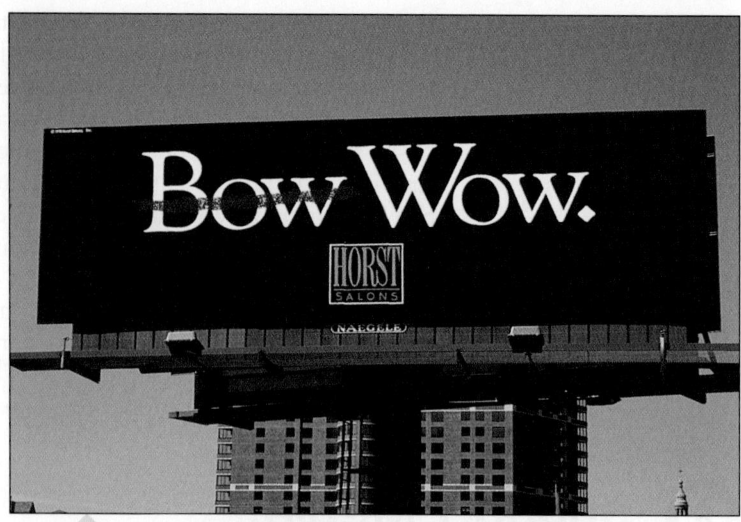

Exhibit 15.18 Minimal verbiage is one key to success with billboard advertising. This example easily satisfies the minimal-verbiage rule.

selections (e.g., imagine that building in Exhibit 15.16 as a Foot Locker store). Since these media can be tailored to local markets, they can have value to any organization that wants to reach consumers in a particular venue, neighborhood, or metropolitan area.

Outdoor Signage and Billboard Advertising.

Billboards, posters, and outdoor signs are perhaps the oldest advertising form. Posters first appeared in North America not as promotional pieces, but rather were used during the Revolutionary War to keep the civilian population informed about the war's status. In the 1800s, they became a promotional tool, with circuses and politicians among the first to adopt this new medium. Exhibit 15.17 shows a classic ad execution for the "Greatest Show on Earth."

Today, the creative challenge posed by outdoor advertising is as it has always been—to grab attention and communicate with minimal verbiage and striking imagery, as does the billboard in Exhibit 15.18.

In recent years, total spending on outdoor advertising in the United States has been holding fairly steady at about $6 billion per year.[41] Outdoor advertising offers several distinct advantages. This medium provides an excellent means to achieve wide exposure for a message and a brand in specific local markets. Size of the display is, of course, a powerful attraction of this medium, especially when combined with special lighting and moving features. Billboards can be captivating when clever creative is conceived for the board to highlight the brand or company name.[42] Billboards created for a retail store in Minneapolis have even wafted a mint scent throughout the city as part of a candy promotion for Valentine's Day. Billboards also offer around-the-clock exposure for an advertiser's message and are well suited to showing off a brand's distinctive packaging or logo.

41. Richard Alan Nelson and Rick Ebel, "2009 PPAI Sales Volume Study: The Only Direction to Go Is Up," *Promotional Products Business,* July 2010, 8.

42. Charles R. Taylor, George R. Franke, and Hae-Kyong Bang, "Use and Effectiveness of Billboards, *Journal of Advertising*, vol. 35, no. 4 (Winter 2006), 21–34.

Exhibit 15.19 Here is a clever example of how a billboard can deliver the right message at the right time.

Courtesy of David Auerbach Opticians

Billboards are especially effective when they reach viewers with a message that speaks to a need or desire that is immediately relevant. For instance, billboards are commonly deployed by fast-food restaurants along major freeways to help hungry travelers know where to exit to enjoy a Whopper or Big Mac. Exhibit 15.19 features a clever example of putting outdoor signage in the right place at the right time to maximize its appeal. The product categories that rely most heavily on outdoor advertising are local services (like gas stations), real estate and insurance companies, hotels, financial institutions, and automobile dealers and services.[43]

Billboards have obvious drawbacks. Long and complex messages simply make no sense on billboards; some experts suggest that billboard copy should be limited to no more than six words. In addition, the impact of billboards can vary dramatically depending on their location, and assessing locations is tedious and time-consuming. To assess locations, companies may have to send individuals to the site to see if the location is desirable. This activity, known in the industry as **riding the boards**, can be a major investment of time and money. Considering that billboards are constrained to short messages, often fade into the landscape, and are certainly not the primary focus of anyone's attention, their costs may be prohibitive for many advertisers.

Despite the cost issue, and frequent criticism by environmentalists that billboards represent a form of visual pollution, there are advocates for this medium who contend that important technological advances will make outdoor advertising an increasingly attractive alternative in the future. The first of these advances offers the prospect of changing what has largely been a static medium to a dynamic medium as we saw in the introduction to this chapter. Digital and wireless technologies have found their way to billboards with remarkable consequences. Both Google and Microsoft are experimenting with digital technology to make billboards a more targeted medium.[44] Coca-Cola has even purchased 14 foot by 48 foot LED screens in 27 markets so that they can run their own ads exclusively 24 hours a day.[45] Digital billboard displays let

43. Data on outdoor advertising categories obtained from Outdoor Advertising Association of America website, www.oaaa.org, accessed on August 4, 2007.

44. Andrew Hampp, "What Are Online Giants Doing in Out-of-Home?" *Advertising Age,* January 29, 2007, 30.

45. Natalie Zmuda, "Coca-Cola Gets Hands-on with Its Own Digital Billboards," *Advertising Age,* February 18, 2010, 12.

Exhibit 15.20 This wonderful old building has a big, flat backside, facing a major interstate freeway. No wonder the Gap wants to keep it in jeans. Does the Gap site (www.gap.com) show signs of integrated brand promotion?

Exhibit 15.21 Happy Berliners enjoy their Cokes at three degrees Celsius while waiting on the U-Bahn (subway).

advertisers rotate their messages on a board at different times during the day. This capability is especially appealing to local marketers—like television stations and food sellers—whose businesses are very time sensitive. For example, FreshDirect uses this technology to change the messaging for its food-delivery service—morning, noon, and night—on the billboard outside New York City's Queens Midtown Tunnel. Ultimately, billboard time may be sold in dayparts like radio or television, making them more appealing to time-sensitive advertisers.

Measuring the reach and impact of outdoor advertising has always been a challenge. Consumers view the billboard or poster message while they are, obviously, engaged in other important tasks—driving a car, sightseeing, or shopping. But, the Traffic Audit Bureau, the outdoor industry's measurement agency, has developed a system called "Eyes On," which is a sophisticated combination of traffic pattern studies, video monitoring, and travel surveys. The data provides advertisers with both demographic and ethnographic data on audiences "likely to see" an outdoor ad.[46] Another key development that also features technology to profile the people who see a billboard in any given day. For the past 70 years the only information available to assess the impact of billboard advertising came from raw traffic counts. Now, Nielsen Outdoor, part of the company known for rating television viewership, has developed a system using GPS satellites to track minute-by-minute movements in the "impact zone" of a billboard. Drivers in the Nielsen panel are paid a small stipend to have their latitude and longitude recorded by GPS every 20 seconds. Nielsen also knows the demographic characteristics of its panel so that they can advise advertisers about the characteristics of persons who viewed a billboard at any given time.

Out-of-Home Media Advertising: Transit, Aerial, Cinema.

A variety of support media are referred to as out-of-home media advertising. **Out-of-home media advertising** includes various advertising venues that reach primarily local audiences. **Transit advertising** is a close cousin to billboard advertising, and in many instances it is used in tandem with billboards. This is a popular advertising form around the world. As illustrated in Exhibits 15.20 and 15.21, transit ads can appear in many venues, including on backs of buildings, in subway tunnels, throughout sports stadiums, taxis, buses, and trucks. transit ads also appear as signage

46. Andrew Hampp, "Outdoor Ad Industry Finally Gets Its Improved Metrics, *Advertising Age,* March 30, 2010, 6.

Exhibit 15.22 The story is the same all around the world. Mass transit has become an advertising vehicle too. Can you identify this European city? www.converse.com

on terminal and station platforms, or actually envelop mass transit vehicles, as exemplified in Exhibit 15.22. One of the latest innovations in out-of-home media is digital signage that can deliver customized messages by neighborhood using wireless Internet technology. Such digital messages can be seen in retail settings (covered earlier in the chapter) or on taxi tops.[47] We've come a long way from the circus poster.

Transit advertising is especially valuable when an advertiser wishes to target adults who live and work in major metropolitan areas. The medium reaches people as they travel to and from work, and because it taps into daily routines repeated week after week, transit advertising offers an excellent means for repetitive message exposure. In large metro areas such as New York City—with its 200 miles of subways and 3 million subway riders—transit ads can reach large numbers of individuals in a cost-efficient manner. When working with this medium, an advertiser may find it most appropriate to buy space on just those train or bus lines that consistently haul people belonging to the demographic segment being targeted. This type of demographic matching of vehicle with target audience derives more value from limited ad budgets. Transit advertising can also be appealing to local merchants because their messages may reach a passenger as he or she is traveling to a store to shop.

Transit advertising works best for building or maintaining brand awareness. But, as with outdoor billboards, lengthy or complex messages simply cannot be worked into this medium. Also, transit ads can easily go unnoticed in the hustle and bustle of daily life. People traveling to and from work via a mass transit system are certainly one of the hardest audiences to engage with an advertising message. They can be bored, exhausted, absorbed by their thoughts about the day, or occupied by some other medium.

When advertisers can't break through on the ground or under the ground, they can always look to the sky. **Aerial advertising** can involve airplanes pulling signs or banners, skywriting, or those majestic blimps. For several decades, Goodyear had blimps all to itself; now, the availability of smaller, less-expensive blimps has made this medium more popular to advertisers. For example, Virgin Lightships has created a fleet of small blimps that can be rented for advertising purposes for around $200,000 per month that include huge, full-color 30 by 70-foot LED screens that can display brand images, advertising, and potentially live TV broadcast feeds.[48] Aerial billboards, pulled by small planes or jet helicopters equipped with screeching loudspeakers (bring back any spring break memories?), have also proliferated in recent years, as advertisers look for new ways to connect with consumers.

Cinema advertising includes those (somewhat annoying) ads that run in movie theaters before the film and other advertising appearing off-screen within a theater. Although consumers often claim that they are not particularly favorably inclined to watching advertising before a film they "paid" to see, research shows that 63 percent of movie goers surveyed actually don't mind the ads before the film and firms invest nearly $600 million in this form of out-of-home advertising.[49] Cinema advertising is not just on-screen. Off-screen ads advertising and promotion includes sampling, concession-based promotion (the ad on the side of your popcorn box), and lobby-based advertising.

47. Stephen Freitas, "Evolutionary Changes in the Great Outdoors," *Advertising Age,* June 9, 2003, C4.

48. Brad Bartz, "Face of Outdoor Advertising Changes with New Airship Design," SpaceDaily.com, May 15, 2006.

49. Research Brief, "Catch a Commercial at the Movies," Center for Media Research, www.mediapost.com, October 29, 2007; Jack Loechner, "After the Popcorn, Before the Show," Center for Media Research, www.mediapost.com June 18, 2010.

Directory Advertising.

Directory advertising includes all the local phone directory and local business advertising books published by a variety of firms—the most well known being the Yellow Book. The last time you reached for a phone directory to appraise the local options for Chinese or Mexican food, you probably didn't think about it as a traditional support medium. However, directory advertising plays an important role in the media mix for many types of organizations, as evidenced by the $16 billion spent in this medium annually.[50]

A phone directory can play a unique and important role in consumers' decision-making processes. Whereas most support media keep the brand name or key product information in front of a consumer, directory advertising helps people follow through on their decision to buy. By providing the information that consumers need to actually find a particular product or service, a directory can serve as the final link in a buying decision. Because of their availability and consumers' familiarity with this advertising tool, directories provide an excellent means to supplement awareness-building and interest-generating campaigns that an advertiser might be pursuing through other media.

On the downside, the proliferation and fragmentation of phone directories can make this a challenging medium to work in. Many metropolitan areas are covered by multiple directories, some of which are specialty directories designed to serve specific neighborhoods, ethnic groups, or interest groups. Selecting the right set of directories to get full coverage of large sections of the country can be a daunting task. Thus, of the $16 billion spent in this medium annually, less than $2 billion is from advertisers looking for national coverage.[51] In addition, working in this medium requires long lead times; and throughout the course of a year, information in a directory ad can easily become dated. There is also limited flexibility for creative execution in the traditional paper format.

Growth of the Internet was once viewed as a major threat to providers of paper directories. Many websites such as Switchboard (www.switchboard.com) and Superpages (www.superpages.com) provide online access to Yellow Pages–style databases that allow individualized searches at one's desktop. Other high-profile players such as Yahoo! and AOL have also developed online directories as components of their service offerings for Web surfers.

Packaging.

Why consider the brand package as an element of support media? It is not a "medium" in the classic sense, but it carries important brand information nonetheless, and that information carries a message. Classic quotes from consultants describe packaging as "the last five seconds of marketing" and "the first moment of truth."[52] Although the basic purpose of packaging seems fairly obvious, it can also make a strong positive contribution to the promotional effort. One of the best historical incidents of the power of packaging is when Dean Foods created the "Milk Chug," the first, stylish, single-serving milk package. Dean Foods officials noted that "One thing milk didn't have was the 'cool' factor like Pepsi and Coke."[53] Twelve months after introduction of the new package, sales of white milk increased 25 percent and chocolate and strawberry flavors saw increases as much as 50 percent. In addition, the Point-of-Purchase Advertising Institute has research to show that more than 70 percent of supermarket

50. 2007 Marketing Fact Book, *Marketing News,* July 15, 2007, 29.

51. Lisa Sanders, "Major Marketers Turn to Yellow Pages," *Advertising Age,* March 8, 2004, 4, 52.

52. Don Hootstein, "Standing Out in the Aisles," *Marketing at Retail,* June 2007, 22–24.

53. Catherine Arnold, "Way Outside the Box," *Marketing News,* June 23, 2003, 13–14.

Exhibit 15.23 An attractive, attention-grabbing package serves important IBP purposes. Crayons has developed a package for its all-natural fruit juice drink that reflects the quality and excitement of the brand.

purchases now result from in-store decisions.[54] In the simplest terms, **packaging** is the container or wrapping for a product. As Exhibit 15.23 demonstrates, packaging adds another strategic dimension and can serve an important role in IBP.

Promotional Benefits of Packaging to the Advertiser. Packaging provides several strategic benefits to the brand manufacturer. First, there is a general effect on IBP strategy. The package carries the brand name and logo and communicates the name and symbol to a consumer. In the myriad of products displayed at the retail level, a well-designed package can attract a buyer's attention and induce the shopper to more carefully examine the product. Several firms attribute renewed success of their brands to package design changes. Kraft Dairy Group believes that significant package changes helped its Breyer's ice cream brand make inroads in markets west of the Mississippi. A package consulting firm came up with a package with a black background, a radically different look for an ice cream product.

Additional value of packaging has to do with creating a perception of value for the product—remember that the "value" message is a key part of IBP communication. The formidable packaging surrounding computer software is made more substantial simply to add tangibility to an intangible product. Similarly, when consumers are buying image, the package must reflect the appropriate image. The color, design, and shape of a package have been found to affect consumer perceptions of a brand's quality, value, and image—and their willingness to pay a premium price over other brands.[55] Perrier, one of the most expensive bottled waters on the market, has an aesthetically pleasing bottle compared to the rigid plastic packages of it competitors. Perfume manufacturers often have greater packaging costs than product costs to ensure that the product projects the desired image.

54. *An Integrated Look at Integrated Marketing: Uncovering P.O.P's Role as the Last Three Feet in the Marketing Mix,* (Washington, DC: Point-of-Purchase Advertising Institute, 2000), 10.

55. Don Hootstein, "Standing Out in the Aisles," *Marketing at Retail,* June 2007, 24.

Summary

Explain the importance and growth of sales promotion.

Sales promotions use diverse incentives to motivate action on the part of consumers, members of the trade channel, and business buyers. They serve different purposes than mass media advertising does, and for some companies, sales promotions receive substantially more funding. The growing reliance on these promotions can be attributed to the heavy pressures placed on marketing managers to account for their spending and meet sales objectives in short time frames. Deal-prone shoppers, brand proliferation, the increasing power of large retailers, and media clutter have also contributed to the rising popularity of sales promotion.

Describe the main sales promotion techniques used in the consumer market.

Sales promotions directed at consumers can serve various goals. For example, they can be employed as means to stimulate trial, repeat, or large-quantity purchases. They are especially important tools for introducing new brands or for reacting to a competitor's advances. Coupons, price-off deals, phone and gift cards, and premiums provide obvious incentives for purchase. Contests and sweepstakes can be excellent devices for stimulating brand interest. A variety of sampling and trial offer techniques are available to get a product into the hands of the target audience with little or no risk to the consumer. Rebates and frequency (continuity) programs provide rewards for repeat purchase.

Describe the main sales promotion techniques used in the trade channel and business markets.

Sales promotions directed at the trade can also serve multiple objectives. They are a necessity in obtaining initial distribution of a new brand. For established brands, they can be a means to increase distributors' order quantities or obtain retailers' cooperation in implementing a consumer-directed promotion. Incentives and allowances can be offered to distributors to motivate support for a brand. Sales-training programs and cooperative advertising programs are additional devices for effecting retailer support. In the business market, professional buyers are attracted by various sales promotion techniques. Frequency (continuity) programs are very valuable in the travel industry and have spread to business-product advertisers. Trade shows are an efficient way to reach a large number of highly targeted business buyers. Gifts to business buyers are a form of sales promotion that is unique to this market. Finally, premiums, advertising specialties, and trial offers have proven to be successful in the business market.

4 Identify the risks to the brand of using sales promotion.

There are important risks associated with heavy reliance on sales promotion. Offering constant deals for a brand can erode brand equity and reputation and sales resulting from a promotion may simply be borrowing from future sales. Constant deals can also create a customer mindset that leads consumers to abandon a brand as soon as a deal is retracted. Sales promotions are expensive to administer and fraught with legal complications. Sales promotions yield their most positive results when carefully integrated with an overall advertising plan.

Understand the role and techniques of point-of-purchase advertising.

Point-of-purchase (P-O-P) advertising refers to materials used in the retail setting to attract shoppers' attention to a firm's brand, convey primary brand benefits, or highlight pricing information. The effect of P-O-P can be to reinforce a consumer's brand preference or change a consumer's brand choice in the retail setting. P-O-P displays may also feature price-off deals or other consumer and business sales promotions. A myriad of displays and presentations are available to marketers. P-O-P materials generally fall into two categories: short-term promotional displays, which are used for six months or less, and permanent long-term displays, which are intended to provide point-of-purchase presentation for more than six months. In trade and business markets, P-O-P displays encourage retailers to support one manufacturer's brand over another; they can also be used to gain preferred shelf space and exposure in a retail setting. Recently, new technologies have made P-O-P a mobile marketing devices as deals and offers can be sent to consumers via mobile devices like smartphones, iPods, and iPads.

Describe the role of support media in a comprehensive IBP plan.

The traditional support media include billboard, transit, aerial, cinema, and directory advertising. Billboards and transit advertising are excellent means for carrying simple messages into specific metropolitan markets. Street furniture is becoming increasingly popular as a placard for brand builders around the world. Aerial advertising can also be a great way to break through the clutter and target specific geographic markets in a timely manner. Directory advertising can be a sound investment because it helps a committed customer locate an advertiser's brand. Again, new technologies have allowed for digitization billboard, transit, and aerial ads. Cinema advertising is becoming more prevalent and despite consumer protests, most consumers are not vehemently opposed to ads in theaters. Finally, packaging can be considered in the support media category because the brand's package carries important information for consumer choice at the point of purchase, including the brand logo and "look and feel" of the brand.

Key Terms

sales promotion
consumer-market sales promotion
trade-market sales promotion
business-market sales promotion
coupon
price-off deal
premiums
free premium
self-liquidating premium
advertising specialties
contest
sweepstakes
sampling
in-store sampling
door-to-door sampling
mail sampling
newspaper sampling
on-package sampling
mobile sampling
trial offers
rebate
frequency programs
push strategy
push money
merchandise allowances
slotting fees
bill-back allowances
off-invoice allowances
cooperative advertising
trade shows
point-of-purchase (P-O-P) advertising
short-term promotional displays
permanent long-term displays
support media
riding the boards
out-of-home media advertising
transit advertising
aerial advertising
cinema advertising
directory advertising
packaging

Questions

1. Compare and contrast sales promotion and mass media advertising as promotional tools. In what ways do the strengths of one make up for the limitations of the other? What specific characteristics of sales promotions account for the high levels of expenditures that have been allocated to them in recent years?

2. What is brand proliferation and why is it occurring? Why do consumer sales promotions become more commonplace in the face of rampant brand proliferation? Why do trade sales promotions become more frequent when there is excessive brand proliferation?

3. What role does sales promotion play in the trade channel and in business markets?

4. Why are sales promotions considered "risky" as an IBP tool?

5. Consumers often rationalize their purchase of a new product with a statement such as, "I bought it because I had a 50-cent coupon and our grocery store was doubling all manufacturers' coupons this week." What are the prospects that such a consumer will emerge as a loyal user of the product? What must happen if he or she is to become loyal?

6. In the chapter, it was suggested that large retailers like Walmart are assuming greater power in today's marketplace. What factors contribute to retailers' increasing power? Explain the connection between merchandise allowances and slotting fees and the growth in retailer power.

7. What role does point-of-purchase advertising play as an IBP tool? In what ways can a firm ensure coordination of its P-O-P with other promotional efforts?

8. What advantages do billboards and transit advertising offer an advertiser as part of an IBP program?

9. A consumer can go to various websites to find local businesses and services. Is the Internet a threat to traditional directories like the Yellow Pages?

10. How does packaging function as a support medium? What sort of "message" does a consumer get from a brand package?

Experiential Exercises

1. The "Cash for Clunkers" program was one of the most talked about sales promotions of recent memory. As part of the government's $3 billion effort to jumpstart sales at slumping auto dealerships, owners of old gas-guzzling vehicles received a $4,500 rebate if they traded in their "clunkers" for new fuel-efficient vehicles. Research the Cash for Clunkers sales promotion and have an in-class debate on what impact, if any, the stimulus program had on short- and long-term auto sales. The class should also debate the environmental benefits of the program.

2. Billboard ad campaigns often make headline news as advertisers from fashion designers to political groups use this roadside support media to communicate splashy or controversial messages. Search recent news headlines about billboards and write a report on a hot billboard campaign that's making waves. Who is responsible for the ads? Does the billboard make its appeal primarily through visuals or through text? Are the billboard ads placed in locations that make strategic sense? Write an evaluation of the billboard campaign and provide detailed answers to these questions, drawing upon information discussed in the chapter.

3. Working in small teams, imagine that you have been hired by a major American automaker to design a sales promotion campaign to stimulate sales of its newly developed economy car, known as the Zoom. Identify which of the sales promotions techniques described in the chapter could be most effective and why. Your answer also should outline for the manufacturer what potential risks the firm takes in incorporating sales promotions into its broader IBP campaign.

4. Working in the same teams, imagine that you have been hired by the Gap to develop a support media campaign in Washington, D.C., intended to stimulate sales among young professionals ages 22 to 30. The clothing manufacturer is particularly interested in developing an edgy, out-of-home media campaign that can capture the attention of the large population of young professionals who work in the city and are frequent users of the Washington subway system. What would you develop, and why do you think it would be effective?

Chapter 16

Event Sponsorship, Product Placements, and Branded Entertainment

After reading and thinking about this chapter, you will be able to do the following:

1. Justify the growing popularity of event sponsorship as another means of brand promotion.
2. Summarize the uses and appeal of product placements in venues like TV, movies, and video games.
3. Explain the benefits and challenges of connecting with entertainment properties in building a brand.
4. Discuss the challenges presented by the ever-increasing variety of communication and branding tools for achieving integrated brand promotion.

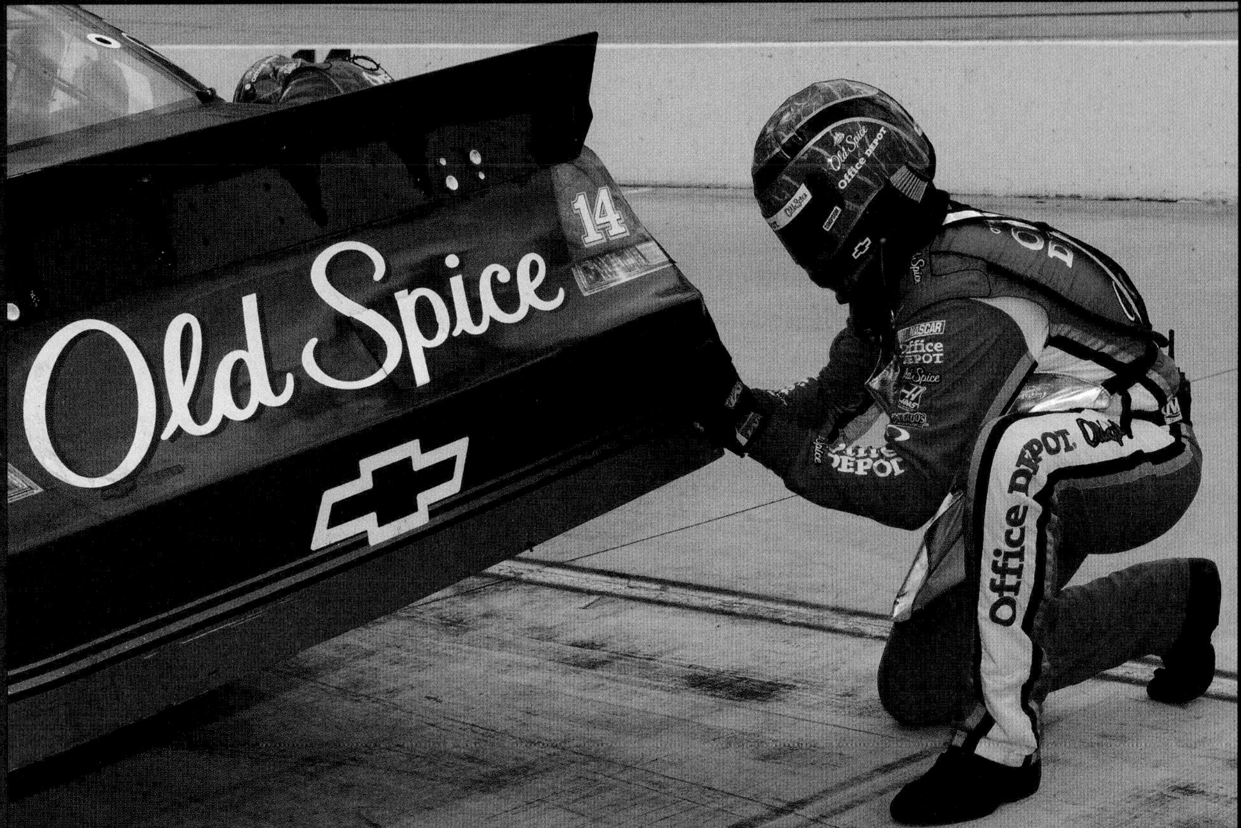

Old Spice
14
Office DEPOT

Introductory Scenario: Brand + Entertainment² = IBP!

The Healthy Choice brand was launched in 1988 as an innovation in prepared foods that brought healthy options to the freezer case. Today Healthy Choice competes with the likes of Lean Cuisine and Weight Watchers in kind of a convenient-but-healthy-eating product space. From their inception, the mantra of Healthy Choice has been to win through innovation to meet the needs of ever more demanding and time-starved consumers. A recent addition to their product portfolio is Healthy Choice *Fresh Mixers*—per Exhibit 16.1. *Fresh Mixers* are a "shelf-stable solution" that puts sauce and rice or pasta together in a single serving container to yield a wide array of flavor options like Sesame Teriyaki Chicken, and Szechwan Beef with Asian Style Noodles. Yum!

But as is the case for any new product the question arises: Who really needs it? For example, "shelf stable" is a nice feature because you just throw the package in your back pack, jostle it around all morning with no damage done, and heat and eat in any microwave at your convenience. However, "shelf stable" created an interesting marketing challenge—where do you find it in the grocery store? Since shoppers typically reach for their Lean Cuisine in the freezer section, they won't know where to reach for *Fresh Mixers*. Said another way, an early advertising challenge in this

Exhibit 16.1 Don't look for these in the freezer!

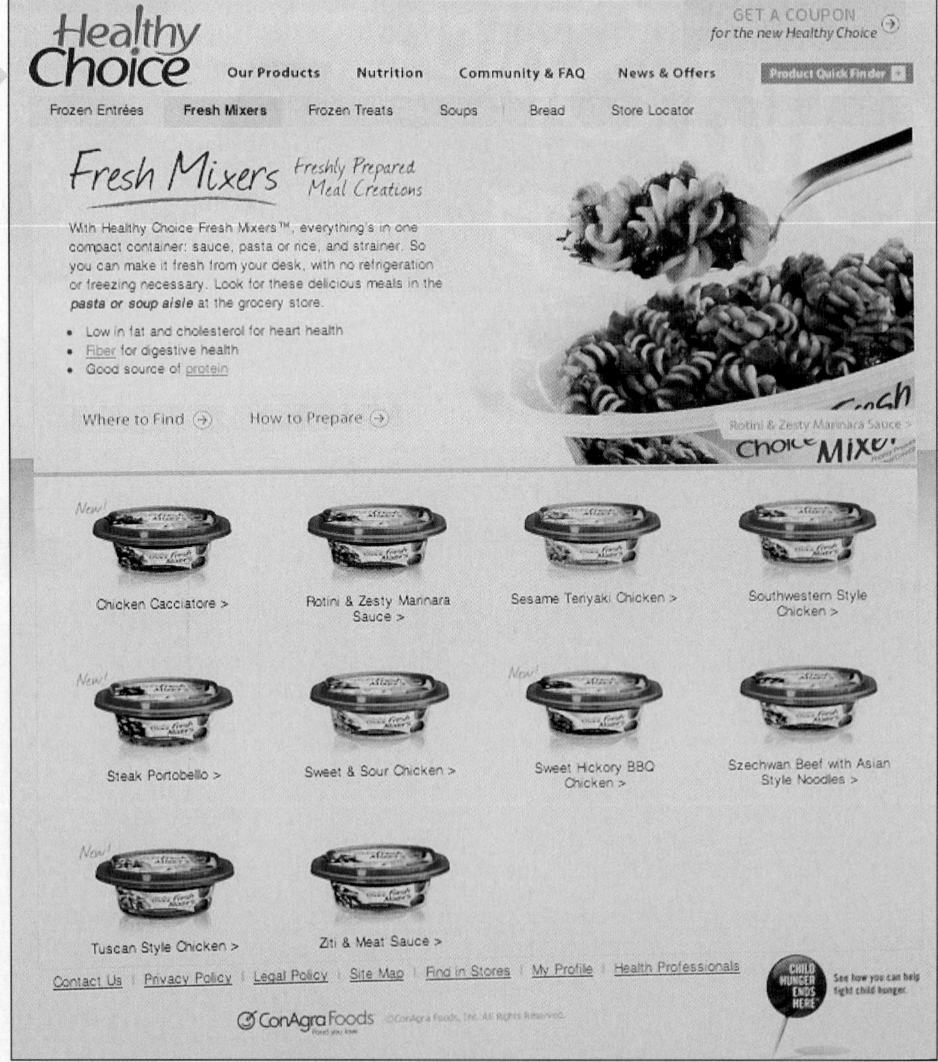

Courtesy, Susan Van Etten

brand's launch was to help consumers find it at the grocery store. If they can't find it, they can't buy it.

Turns out Healthy Choice marketers had great insights about their target audience, and as we emphasized back in Chapter 6, these insights involved identification and understanding of the target segment—which they described as young, health-conscious, working professionals seeking new options for lunch on the job. In addition, these insights, developed in partnership with the digital ad agency Bridge Worldwide, formed the basis for merging brand with entertainment to yield dynamic and integrated brand promotion.

Client and agency worked closely to get to know their target. The prime prospect for *Fresh Mixers* was 25–35 years old, so naturally they were heavy users of social networking sites and expected their workplace to embrace their need to stay connected. They find entertainment, news, and gossip online and like to share the good stuff. How is good stuff defined? Usually by humor... Think about it—when you find a video online that you think is really funny—you want to share it. Right? And one more thing about the prime prospect—they commonly eat lunch at their desk and multi-task. Of course, sometimes, the multi-tasking is really just goofing off....

Okay, you've got the big insights, so perhaps you can see where this is going. We need a way to reach young professionals in their cubicles at lunchtime that they'll find engaging while allowing Healthy Choice to put in a good word for *Fresh Mixers*. Not a problem if you have the right team; and Bridge Worldwide pulled a great team together on behalf of Healthy Choice. That team included Second City Communications, who just happen to be experts in humor and know how to package that humor on behalf of clients like IBM, Heineken, and Major League Baseball (see Exhibit 16.2). Second City's product is to make people laugh. Of course, to reach people in their cubicles, we need to pipe in the humor over the Internet. We'll thus need another partner to help get people to a website where we can make them laugh and promote *Fresh Mixers*. Driving people to the website takes an expert like MSN's Branded Entertainment and Experience Team (BEET).

So Bridge, the BEET Team, Second City Communications, and Healthy Choice, put it all together for *Fresh Mixers*. Thus was born Healthy Choice *Fresh Mixers Working Lunch*: live improv comedy at lunchtime across every U.S. time zone that spoofed tedious office meetings at a really wacky ad agency, where poor Hank had trouble keeping track of his pants. *Working Lunch* was the first ever live performance directed by a nationwide audience where improv actors adapted to audience polls in real time. Now of course the portal into *Working Lunch* featured *Fresh Mixers* as the perfect food to go with improv, along with simple messages like "Not in the Freezer

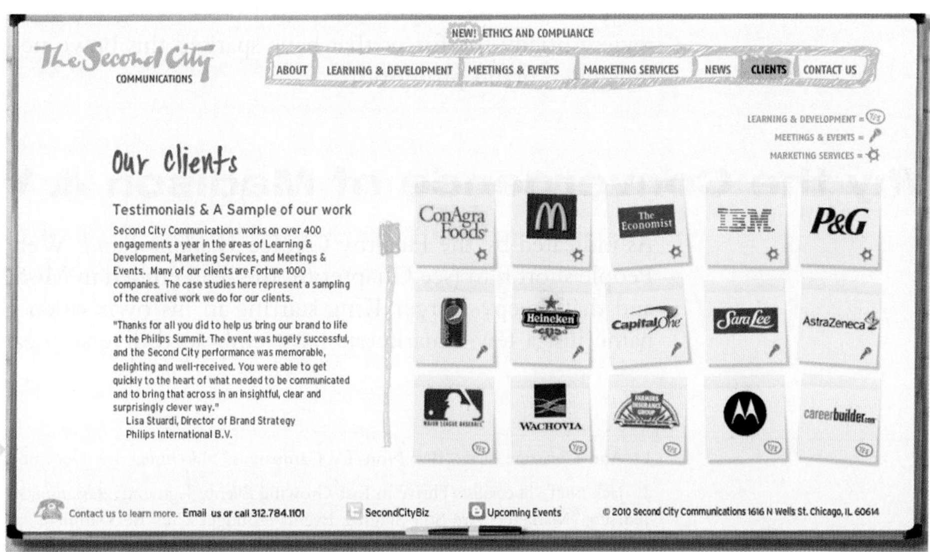

Exhibit 16.2 Second City in Chicago is one of the best-known comedy clubs in the world, and improv for them is both an art and a science. It's only natural that this remarkable capability would find many uses.

Courtesy, Susan Van Etten

Section." In addition, the improv players spent a lot of time at their office microwave—preparing to enjoy you know what. But they never did find Hank's pants....

Among other things, the *Working Lunch* Web series is a perfect example of branded entertainment. Importantly for Healthy Choice, it also built a lot of buzz for *Fresh Mixers*. From just 3½ weeks of live programming, more than 5 million prime prospects visited the site, with more than a million repeat visitors. Compared against a control population, those who visited *Working Lunch* naturally had much higher awareness of *Fresh Mixers*; they knew about features like 'easy to prepare' and 'doesn't need refrigeration'; and expressed more positive intent to purchase. Watching a little improv at lunchtime made it more likely that a person would go shopping for *Fresh Mixers*, knowing to not look for them in the freezer section. No small accomplishment.

The Healthy Choice *Fresh Mixers* example is also a perfect starter for this chapter because it exemplifies the creative and entertaining means that marketers are now using to make meaningful connections with consumers. In addition, it reminds us that the unconventional is becoming conventional, and that traditional mass media are no longer enough. As you no doubt have already recognized, advertisers are always on the lookout for new venues to advance their messages, and this can lead them to many different places. Often these efforts are directed at hard-to-reach niche markets, particularly in urban locations, where new market trends typically originate. Another example that may be familiar to you involves the beaches of South Florida where students and brand builders gather every March to celebrate in the sun. The youthful crowd that gathers in this setting is of great interest to brands like MTV, Maxim, Coke, Gillette, and Axe. Brand builders are always looking to be where the action is, whether that means Daytona Beach, New York City, or any town named Springfield (to launch "The Simpsons Movie").[1]

This chapter discusses an array of tools and tactics that marketers are now using to create unique experiences with consumers. The array is so wide that it is not always obvious what these innovations have in common. The dynamic nature of this subject matter also means that the rules for success are hard to pin down. But a new order does appear to be emerging from this dynamic environment, built around the central premise that the fields of advertising, branding, and entertainment are converging and collapsing on one another. More than ever before, brand builders want to be embedded in the entertainment that their target consumers enjoy.

This chapter assesses event sponsorship, one of marketers long time favorites.[2] Related to event sponsorship is the latest rage in advertising circles—branded entertainment. We'll examine this "new" form of brand building and assess what's new about it. When it comes to building brands—as with Healthy Choice *Fresh Mixers*—there are very few limits on what one can try, and quirky/edgy/off-the-wall may be just what the doctor ordered. Before we get to the specific applications, let's review briefly the forces that have sparked this brave new world of advertising and integrated brand promotion.

Why the Convergence of Madison & Vine?

As indicated by the Healthy Choice *Working Lunch* Web series, the Folgers Yellow People short film (see Chapter 6), the iPad embed in Modern Family (see Chapter 8), and that creepy Burger King starring in his own video games (see Chapter 9)—to name just a few—marketers have embraced diverse means for brand building, and

1. Ann-Christine Diaz, "Best Non-TV Campaigns," *Advertising Age,* December 14, 2009, 14.

2. Jack Neff, "Specialists Thrive in Fast-Growing Events Segment," *Advertising Age,* March 19, 2007, S-2, S-4; Richard Tedesco, "Marketers Are Still Staging Events—Budget Cuts Be Damned," promomagazine.com/eventmarketing, January 1, 2009.

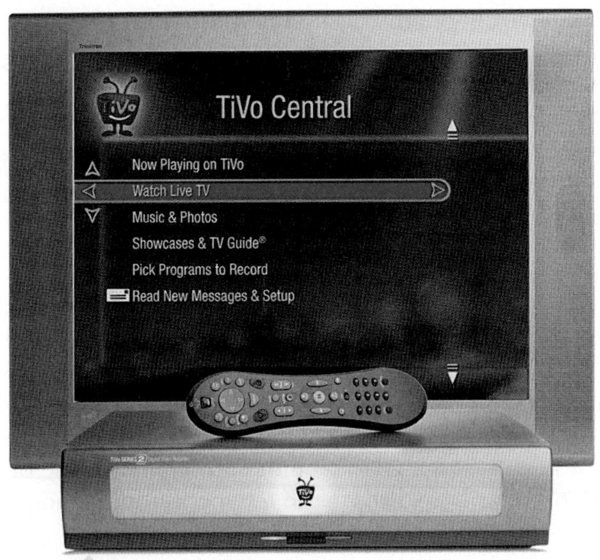

Exhibit 16.3 A TiVo DVR automatically finds and records your favorite shows without videotape and allows you to pause live TV, watch in slow motion, and create your own instant replays. You can also fast forward quickly through any pre-recorded content.

the list of options continues to grow.[3] Yet think about what all these examples have in common. Whether it's laughing at lunchtime, scanning videos on YouTube, watching a brand take center-stage in a TV show, or playing "Pocketbike Racer" with the Creepy King, in all cases we see brands coupled with entertainment. Advertising, branding, and entertainment are converging at an accelerating rate, and because of the advertising/entertainment linkage, this convergence is sometimes slotted under the heading of **Madison & Vine**, which of course refers to two renowned avenues representing the advertising and entertainment industries, respectively. Why the accelerating convergence? There are many reasons.

An important issue propelling this search for new ways to reach consumers is the erosion in effectiveness of traditional broadcast media. By now you have been sensitized to the many forces that are working to undermine "old school" media. One is simply a question of options. People have an ever-expanding set of options to fill their leisure time, from playing video games to surfing the Web to "always on" social networking. Does anyone under the age of 55 actually watch network television anymore? Even if they do, there is growing concern among advertisers that soon we will all have set-top technology that will make watching TV ads a thing of the past. As noted in Exhibit 16.3, TiVo Central offers an array of features, but in the minds of many, the best one is that it lets you skip commercials. With the integration of inexpensive DVR systems into cable set-top boxes, DVR penetration has accelerated. As you know, people are time shifting their viewing, often recording programming during the week, with catch-up scheduled for the weekends. This so-called "appointment viewing" is just not going to be advertiser friendly.[4]

In the "**Chaos Scenario**" predicted by *Advertising Age*'s Bob Garfield, a mass exodus from the traditional broadcast media is coming. Shifts happen. According to Garfield, it will work something like this: Advertisers' dollars stop flowing to traditional media because audience fragmentation and ad-avoidance hardware are undermining their value. With reduced funds available, the networks will have less to invest in the quality of their programs, leading to further reductions in the size of their audiences. This then causes even faster advertiser defections, and on and on in what Garfield calls an "inexorable death spiral" for traditional media.[5] He predicts a brave new world where "marketing—and even branding—are conducted without reliance on the 30-second [television] spot or the glossy [magazine] spread."[6] Nudged along by the recent recession, Garfield's Advertising Armageddon looks to be arriving ahead of schedule.[7]

With the old model collapsing, billions of advertising dollars will be freed up to move to other brand-building tools. As discussed in Chapter 14, digital and social media marketing in its many forms will continue to surge because of this new money. But according to a Trendwatch survey, the brand-building options preferred

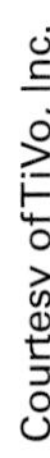

3. Kunur Patel, "All The World's a Game, and Brands Want to Play Along," *Advertising Age,* May 31, 2010, 4.
4. "How DVRs Are Changing the Television Landscape," blog.nielsen.com/nielsenwire, April 30, 2009.
5. Bob Garfield, "The Post Advertising Age," *Advertising Age,* March 26, 2007, 1, 12–14.
6. Ibid.
7. Bob Garfield, "Future May Be Brighter, but It's Apocalypse Now," *Advertising Age,* March 23, 2009, 1, 26–27.

by marketers as a replacement for old-school advertising comprise the brave new world of events and experiential marketing.[8]

Why events and experiential marketing? Well, the reasons are many, and this chapter will explain and celebrate those reasons. But it is important to stress that the collection of tools and tactics featured in this chapter are surging in popularity not just because advertisers *must* find new ways to connect with their consumers. Event sponsorship, product placements, and branded entertainment can work in numerous ways to assist with a brand-building agenda. In theory, these things can foster brand awareness and even liking through a process known as mere exposure.[9] In addition, the meaning-transfer process discussed in Chapter 5 can change people's perceptions of the brand. That is, the fun and excitement of Daytona Beach at spring break can become part of your feelings about the brands that were there with you. The brand evokes that pleasant memory. Similarly, consumers' sense of self may be influenced by the events they attend (as in a NASCAR race or a sporting event), and brands associated with such venues may assist in embellishing and communicating that sense of self.[10] But enough with the justifications for now. Let's get to the specific applications.

1 Event Sponsorship.

One of the time-tested and increasingly popular means for reaching targeted groups of consumers on their terms is event sponsorship. **Event sponsorship** involves a marketer providing financial support to help fund an event, such as a rock concert, tennis tournament, or hot-dog-eating contest. In return, that marketer acquires the rights to display a brand name, logo, or advertising message on-site at the event. If the event is covered on TV, the marketer's brand and logo will most likely receive exposure with the television audience as well. As you might suspect, sports sponsorships draw the biggest share of advertising dollars when it comes to events. After a long growth surge, spending on events by North American companies has stagnated in recent years with the economic downturn, but around the world event spending has continued to grow even in the face of recession, approaching the $50 billion level as an aggregate worldwide.[11]

Even in the face of bankruptcy, recession, and retrenchment, the Big Three automakers in the United States remain aggressive with their event sponsorship. General Motors, one of the world's foremost old-school ad spenders, typifies this commitment to events. GM has experimented with a number of ways to "get closer" to its prospective customers. Most entail sponsoring events that get consumers in direct contact with its vehicles, or events that associate the GM name with causes or activities that are of interest to its target customers. For example, GM has sponsored a traveling slave-ship exhibition, a scholarship program for the Future Farmers of America, the Woodward Dream Cruise hot-rod show, and a week of fashion shows in New York City. GM has also launched a movie theater on wheels that travels to state fairs, fishing contests, and auto races to show its 15-minute film about the Silverado pickup truck. Like many marketers large and small, GM has been shifting more and more of its budget out of the measured media and into events and the Web.[12]

8. Dan Lippe, "Events Trail Only Ads in Alignment with Brands," *Advertising Age,* March 19, 2007, S-2.

9. Bettina Cornwell, Clinton Weeks, and Donald Roy, "Sponsor-Linked Marketing: Opening the Black Box," *Journal of Advertising,* Summer 2005, 21–42.

10. Chris Allen, Susan Fournier, and Felicia Miller, "Brands and Their Meaning Makers," in *Handbook of Consumer Psychology* (Hillsdale, NJ: LEA Publishing, 2008) Chapter 31.

11. Patricia Odell, "Sponsorship Spending Struggles to Recover," promomagazine.com/news/sponsorship, January 28, 2010.

12. Emily Steel, "Measured Media Lose in Spending Cuts," *The Wall Street Journal,* March 14, 2007, B3; Mike Spector and Gina Chon, "The Great Texas Truck Fair," *The Wall Street Journal,* October 20, 2006, B1, B10.

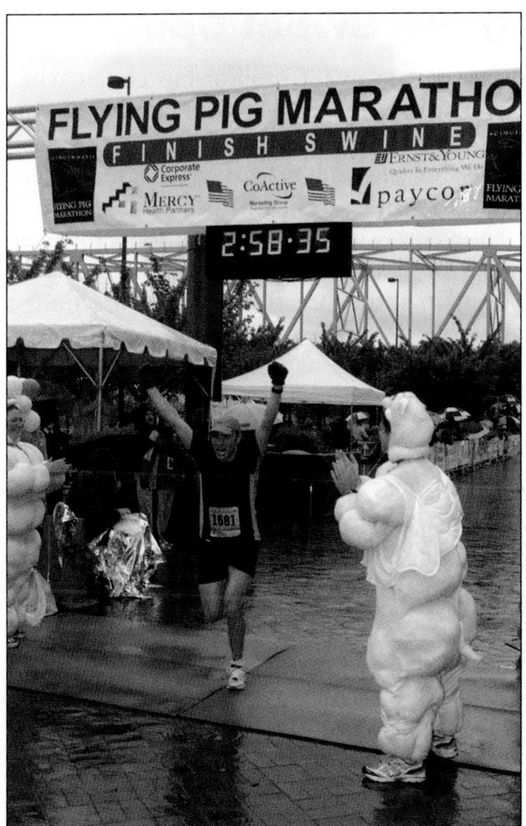

Exhibit 16.4 Although there are no gold medals at the Flying Pig Marathon in Cincinnati (a.k.a. Porkopolis), crossing the "finish swine" at the head of the pack is still cause for a bit of snorting.

Courtesy, Cincinnati Flying Pig Marathon; Photographer: Mark Bowen

Who Else Uses Event Sponsorship?

Event sponsorship can take varied forms. The events can be international in scope, as in the 2010 FIFA World Cup with big-name sponsors like Adidas, McDonald's, Coke, Sony, Hyundai, and Visa. Or they may have a distinctive local flavor, like the Smucker's Stars on Ice tour or the Flying Pig Marathon. As shown in Exhibit 16.4, local events provide sponsorship opportunities for organizations like Mercy Health Partners and a regional office of the accounting firm Ernst & Young. Events like the World Cup or the Flying Pig Marathon provide a captive audience, may receive radio and television coverage, and often are reported in the print media and covered online. Hence, event sponsorship can yield face-to-face contact with real consumers and receive simultaneous and follow-up publicity... all good things for a brand.

The list of companies participating in various forms of event sponsorships seems to grow every year. Jeep, Best Buy, Reebok, Atlantic Records, Revlon, Heineken, Citibank, and a host of other companies have sponsored tours and special appearances for recording artists such as Faith Hill, Tim McGraw, Jewel, Jay-Z, Sting, Sheryl Crow, Elton John, and 50 Cent. Soon after ESPN launched the X games to attract younger viewers, a host of sponsors signed on, including Taco Bell, Levi Strauss, Kellogg's, Gatorade, and Activision. Similarly, in an attempt to engage with young viewers, McDonald's, Coke, and Old Navy prowl for up and coming artists like IB Fokuz, DJ Kaskade, and Ingrid Michaelson.[13] These brand builders are looking for benefits through unique associations with something new and hip via a process that anthropologist Grant McCracken has labeled "the movement of meaning."[14]

And of course, the world is absolutely crazy about football—no, not that kind of football. English professional soccer has become one of the darlings of the sports business because of the valuable marketing opportunities it supports. For example, Manchester United of the English Premier Soccer League surpasses the New York Yankees in its ability to generate revenues. In this world of big-time sports, global companies like Pepsi, Nike, and Vodafone pay huge amounts to have their names linked to the top players and teams. Regarding the FIFA World Cup, Nike's marketing VP says simply—"It's the No. 1 event in all of sports."[15] Nike should know.

Sports sponsorships truly come in all shapes and sizes, including organizations like Professional Bull Riders and the World Hunting Association. Advertisers thus have diverse opportunities to associate their brands with the distinctive images of various participants, sports, and even nations.[16] For another example, examine Exhibit 16.5. What benefit might Puma be looking for as a proud sponsor of the Jamaican Athletics Federation?

13. Emily York, "McDonald's, Pepsi and Coca-Cola Troll for Up-and-Coming Artists," *Advertising Age*, June 7, 2010, 3, 38.

14. Grant McCracken, "Culture and Consumption: A Theoretical Account of the Structure and Movement of the Cultural Meaning of Consumer Goods," *Journal of Consumer Research,* June 1986, 71–84.

15. Jeremy Mullman, "World Cup Kicks Off International Marketing Games on Epic Scale," *Advertising Age*, May 17, 2010, 4.

16. Jim Hanas, "Going Pro: What's with All These Second-Tier Sports?" *Advertising Age,* January 29, 2007, S-3.

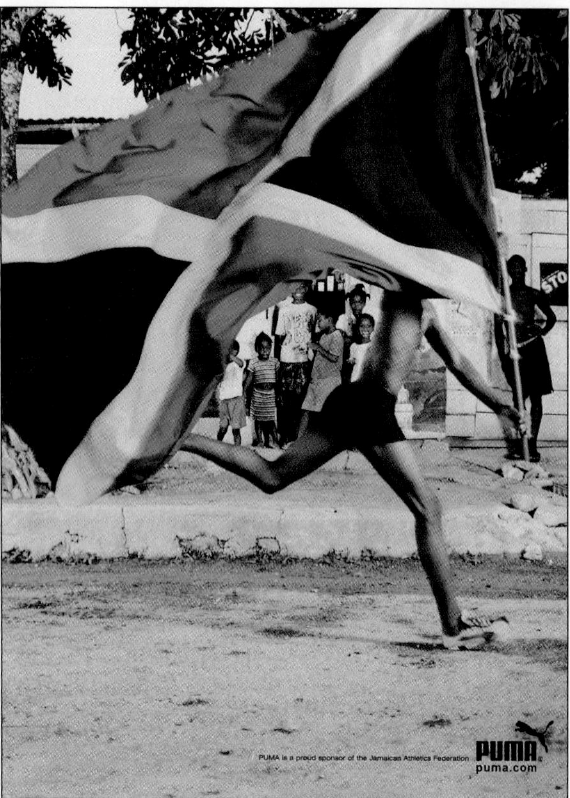

Exhibit 16.5 It's hard to compete with the Nikes and the Reeboks of the world when it comes to sports sponsorship. The dollars that get thrown around in this regard are simply prohibitive for some companies. But rather than abandoning sport, here we see Puma choose a different path. If all sports fans have a place in their hearts for the underdog, then perhaps it makes perfect sense to be on the sideline with teams from Jamaica.

Exhibit 16.6 Passionate event participants often become passionate brand advocates through their loyalty to an exclusive sponsor.

Finding the Sweet Spot.

A major sweet spot in event sponsorship comes when significant overlap is achieved between an event's participants and the marketer's target audience. If the event has big numbers of fans and/or participants, that's even better. Moreover, marketers stand to gain the most in supporting an event as its exclusive sponsor. However, exclusivity can be extremely pricey, if not cost prohibitive, except in those situations where one finds a small, neighborhood event with passionate supporters just waiting to be noticed. Consider, for example, the World Bunco Association (WBA), which was chartered in 1996. Bunco is a dice game, usually played in groups of 8, 12, or 16. It's especially popular with middle-aged women, sort of a ladies' version of "poker night." Bunco is a game of chance, so its leaves players with lots of time for eating, drinking, and intimate conversation about everything from a daughter's new baby to the recipe for yummy Snickers Salad (a concoction of Cool Whip, marshmallow crème, cream cheese, chopped Snickers bars, and just a touch of apple to make it good for you).

"So where is the sponsorship opportunity?" you ask. Consider a few facts: Approximately 14 million women in the United States have played Bunco and 4.6 million play regularly. Six out of 10 women say that recommendations from their Bunco group influence their buying decisions.[17] In addition, about a third of all regular Bunco players suffer from frequent heartburn and it just so happens that 70 percent of frequent heartburn suffers are women. Can you see where this is going now?

The makers of Prilosec OTC®, an over-the-counter heartburn medication, discovered Bunco and went to work learning about the women who play it regularly. They attended Bunco parties, listened to country music, camped in RVs, and watched a lot of NASCAR races. Naturally, they entered into a partnership with the World Bunco Association to sponsor the first Bunco World Championship. With a $50,000 first prize, associated fund-raising for the National Breast Cancer Foundation, and lots of favorable word-of-mouth from regional Bunco tournaments, the World Championships caught on fast. It wasn't long before cable TV caught Bunco fever and began covering the championship matches, where the Prilosec OTC purple tablecloths made it a branded experience. Per Exhibit 16.6, the Bunco World Tour packed plenty of excitement, and as shown in Exhibit 16.7, provided plenty of great photo ops for Prilosec OTC.

The Bunco World Championship is an opportunity for a brand like Prilosec OTC and illustrates an attractive scenario. Again, this is a scenario where there

17. Ellen Byron, "An Old Dice Game Catches On Again, Pushed by P&G," *The Wall Street Journal*, January 30, 2007, A1, A13.

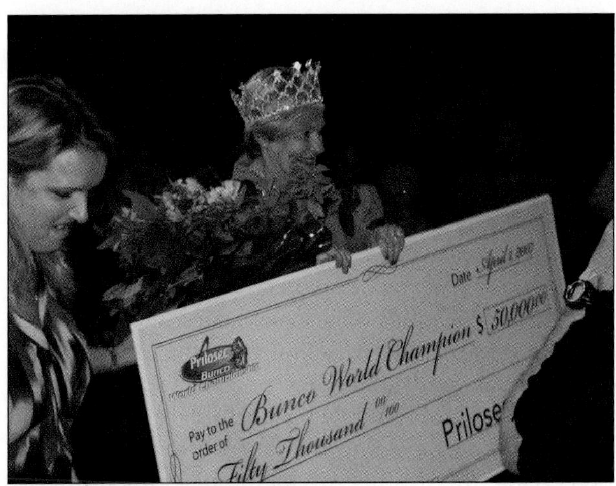

Exhibit 16.7 The look of a champion.

is excellent overlap between the lifestyles of event enthusiasts and benefits that your product can deliver. Supporting Bunco allowed Prilosec OTC to connect with its core customer in a fun and meaningful way, and the unique connection between Prilosec OTC and Bunco fostered brand loyalty and favorable word-of-mouth. There is much to be said for the sponsorship opportunity that your brand can uniquely own.

Assessing the Benefits of Event Sponsorship.

In the early days of event sponsorship, it often wasn't clear what an organization was receiving in return for its sponsor's fee. Even today many critics contend that sponsorships, especially those of the sporting kind, can be ego-driven and thus a waste of money.[18] Company presidents are human, and they like to associate with sports stars and celebrities. This is fine, but when sponsorship of a golf tournament, for example, is motivated mainly by a CEO's desire to play in the same foursome as Paul Azinger, Annika Sorenstam, or Phil Mickelson, the company is really just throwing money away.

One of the things fueling the growing interest in event sponsorship is that many companies have found ways to make a case for the effectiveness of their sponsorship dollars. Boston-based financial services company John Hancock has been a pioneer in developing detailed estimates of the advertising equivalencies of its sponsorships. John Hancock began sponsoring a college football bowl game in 1986 and soon after had a means to judge the value of its sponsor's fee. Hancock employees scoured magazine and newspaper articles about their bowl game to determine name exposure in print media. Next they'd factor in the number of times that the John Hancock name was mentioned in pre-game promos and during the television broadcast. Early on, Hancock executives estimated that they received the equivalent of $5.1 million in advertising exposure for their $1.6 million sponsorship fee. However, as the television audience for the John Hancock bowl dwindled in subsequent years, Hancock's estimates of the bowl's value also plunged. Subsequently, Hancock moved its sports sponsorship dollars into other events, like the Boston Marathon and Major League Baseball. The famous John Hancock signature is now a fixture at Dodger Stadium and Fenway Park.

Improving one's ability to gauge the effectiveness of dollars spent will generally drive more spending on any IBP tool.[19] Enter a familiar player—Nielsen Media Research—and its Sponsorship Scorecard. Nielsen developed this service to give advertisers a read on the impact of their signage in sports stadiums. In one assessment for Fleet Bank in Boston's Fenway Park, Nielsen calculated that Fleet signage received 84 impressions of at least five seconds each during a telecast of the Red Sox/Yankees game.[20] That's the rough equivalent of 14, 30-second TV spots. But don't get sold on Fenway—in a head-to-head comparison during the World Series, Coors Field delivered 2.4 billion gross impressions for its top five sponsors, versus a measly 791,000 for Fenway.[21] The Colorado Rockies didn't fare as well in their first-ever World Series.

18. Amy Hernandez, "Research Studies Gauge Sponsorship ROI," *Marketing News,* May 12, 2003, 16; Ian Mount, "Exploding the Myths of Stadium Naming," *Business 2.0,* April 2004, 82, 83.

19. Kate Fitzgerald, "Events No Longer Immune to Marketer Demand for ROI," *Advertising Age,* March 19, 2007, S-3.

20. Rich Thomaselli, "Nielsen to Measure Sports Sponsorship," *Advertising Age,* May 3, 2004, 14.

21. "Coors Field Serves 2.4B Total Ad Impressions during World Series," mediabuyerplanner.com/entry, November 20, 2007.

Exhibit 16.8 One of the best uses of events is in reaching well-defined audiences that may be hard to reach through other channels. JBL and Trek have teamed up to support events that reach a target segment that interests them both.

Courtesy, JBL Harman International

As we see illustrated in both the John Hancock and Fleet Bank examples, the practice of judging sponsorship spending through **media impressions** is a popular approach. The idea is to create a metric that lets a marketer judge sponsorship spending in a direct comparison to spending in the traditional measured media. But gross impressions only tell part of the story. Sponsorships provide a unique opportunity to foster brand loyalty. When marketers connect their brand with the potent emotional experiences often found at rock concerts, in soccer stadiums, at the Bunco table, or on Fort Lauderdale beaches, positive feelings may be attached to the sponsor's brand that linger well beyond the duration of the event. Judging whether your brand is receiving this loyalty dividend is another important aspect of sponsorship assessment. Getting a good read on the return from one's sponsorship dollars will require a mix of qualitative and quantitative approaches. This of course is true of most advertising expenditures.

Since various types of events attract well-defined target audiences, marketers should also monitor event participants to ensure they are reaching their desired target. Such is the case for the sponsors featured in Exhibit 16.8. Notice that JBL Electronics has teamed up with Trek Bikes to sponsor nationwide mountain biking events. These so-called "gravity" sports are particularly attractive to skeptical teens. Their support of these sports at least puts JBL and Trek on the radar screen for this demanding audience.

Leverage, Leverage, Leverage.

As noted above, one way to justify event sponsorship is to calculate the number of viewers who will be exposed to a brand either at the event or through media coverage of the event, and then assess whether the sponsorship provides a cost-effective way of reaching the target segment. This approach assesses sponsorship benefits in direct comparison with traditional advertising media. Some experts now maintain, however, that the benefits of sponsorship can be fundamentally different from anything that traditional media might provide. Finding ways to leverage the sponsorship is especially critical. Any collateral communication or activity reinforcing the link between a brand and an event is referred to as **leveraging** or activating a sponsorship.[22]

Events can be leveraged as ways to entertain important clients, recruit new customers, motivate the firm's salespeople, and generally enhance employee morale. Events provide unique opportunities for face-to-face contact with key customers. Marketers commonly use this point of contact to distribute specialty-advertising items so that attendees will have a branded memento to remind them of the rock concert or their New York City holiday. Marketers may also use this opportunity to sell premiums such as T-shirts and hats, administer consumer surveys as part of their marketing research efforts, or distribute product samples. A checklist of guidelines for selecting the right events and maximizing their benefits for the brand are outlined in Exhibit 16.9.

22. Cornwell, Weeks, and Roy, "Sponsor-Linked Marketing: Opening the Black Box."

Exhibit 16.9 Guidelines for event sponsorship.

Guidelines for Event Sponsorship

1. **Match the brand to the event.** Be sure that the event matches the brand personality. Stihl stages competitions at Mountain Man events featuring its lumbering equipment. Would the Stihl brand fare as well sponsoring a boat race or a triathalon? Probably not.

2. **Tightly define the target audience.** Closely related to point number one is the fact that the best event in the world won't create impact for a brand if it's the wrong target audience. Too often the only barometer of success is the number of bodies in attendance. Far more important is the fact that the brand is getting exposure to the right audience. This is what JBL and TREK accomplished with the mountain bike tour sponsorship.

3. **Stick to a few key messages.** Most events try to accomplish too much. People are there to experience the event and can accommodate only a limited amount of persuasion. Don't overwhelm them. Stick to a few key messages and repeat them often.

4. **Develop a plot line.** An event is most effective when it is like great theater or a great novel. Try to develop a beginning, a middle, and an exciting ending. Sporting events are naturals in this regard, which explains much of their popularity. In nonsporting events, the plot line needs to be developed and delivered in small increments so that the attendees can digest both the event and the brand information.

5. **Deliver exclusivity.** If you are staging a special event, make it by invitation only. Or, if you are a featured sponsor, invite only the most important customers, clients, or suppliers. The target audience wants to know that this event is special. The exclusivity provides a positive aura for the brand.

6. **Deliver relevance.** Events should build reputation, awareness, and relationships. Trying to judge the success of an event in terms of sales is misleading and shortsighted. Don't make the event product-centric; make it a brand-building experience for the attendees.

7. **Use the Internet.** The Internet is a great way to promote the event, maintain continuous communication with the target audience, and follow up with the audience after an event. Plus, it's a good way to reach all the people who can't attend the event in person. For golf fans, pga.com gets viewers involved with each event on the PGA tour and gives sponsors another chance to reach the target audience.

8. **Plan for the before and after.** Moving prospects from brand awareness to trial to brand loyalty doesn't happen overnight. The audience needs to see the event as part of a broad exposure to the brand. This is the synergy that needs to be part of the event-planning process. The event must be integrated with advertising, sales promotions, and advertising specialty items.

Source: Based on Laura Shuler, "Make Sure to Deliver When Staging Events," *Marketing News,* September 13, 1999, 12.

As you will see again in Chapter 18, a firm's event participation may also be the basis for public relations activities that then generate additional media coverage. A great example of this comes from the 2010 Winter Olympics where P&G, the maker of Pampers, partnered with Team USA to introduce a new line of Pampers Swaddlers and Cruiser Diapers. Olympic athletes like Chad Hedrick and Noelle Pikus-Pace competed in Vancouver with their families in the stands. They also received limited-edition, specially-branded Team USA diapers to keep their little one's dry. These athletes and their families then shared the sights and sounds of the Winter Olympics with everybody back home via photos and videos posted on Pampers.com. Babies, the Olympics, and a beautiful city like Vancouver make for a lot of great stories. It's the kind of story that news media are also eager to cover—much to the delight of Pampers' brand managers.

'Good PR' was also likely part of Coca-Cola's rationale for their zero-waste, carbon-neutral sponsorship at the Winter Olympics in Vancouver. Can Coca-Cola really be green? Read more about that possibility in the *Ethics* box that follows.

Ethics

Make Mine Carbon Neutral...

Bottled water has become ubiquitous. But it is also an expensive habit, on multiple levels. For example, 250,000 plastic water bottles are dumped in landfills every hour; they make up around 50 percent of the contents of any landfill. The bottle that takes 15 minutes to consume will take 700 years to decompose. And of course billions of barrels of oil are required annually to produce and haul those bottles to store shelves and then off to the landfill. You know the companies who are pushing this habit: Ice Mountain from Nestle, Aquafina from Pepsi, and Dasani from Coca-Cola are among the heavyweights in this multibillion dollar industry. Given their role in contributing to our landfills, these firms often attract criticism because of their water businesses.

It is natural then that a firm like Coca-Cola would want to counteract some of the negative press with positive stories about their commitment to sustainability. Coke went for the Gold at the 2010 Winter Olympics with a high-profile commitment to an eco-friendly, carbon neutral sponsorship. Obviously, big events like the Olympics will generate a mountain of trash. Coke, for their part, vowed to produce zero waste through multiple initiatives. For example, all staff uniforms were made from recycled bottles and every athlete received a T-shirt made from recycled bottles. Electric carts were used to deliver beverages to various Olympic venues and recycling bins were scattered throughout in an effort to stop the flow to the landfill. Menu boards were made of recycled materials and café tables were made from pine trees that had been destroyed by a beetle infestation in British Columbia's forests.

As events go, the Olympics have definitely been a proponent of sustainability, and Coca-Cola received the Vancouver Organizing Committee's "Sustainability Star" award in 2010. So which Coca-Cola does one want to embrace—the Dasani marketer filling our landfills, or the Sustainability Star protecting our landfills? Do more research. Develop your own point of view. You be the judge.

Sources: Emily York, "Nestle, Pepsi, and Coke Face Their Waterloo," *Advertising Age*, October 8, 2007, 1, 45; Michael Bush, "Sustainability and a Smile," *Advertising Age*, February 25, 2008, 1, 25; Natalie Zmuda, "Big Red Goes Completely Green at Olympics," *Advertising Age*, February 1, 2010; "Recycling Statistics and Facts," all-recycling-facts.com, June 23, 2010.

2 Product Placements.

As noted early in this chapter, the fields of advertising, branding, and entertainment are converging and collapsing on one another. Brand builders aspire to be embedded in any form of entertainment that their target consumers enjoy. And even though event sponsorship has been around for decades, brand builders are also looking elsewhere to help put on the show. Indeed, in today's world of advertising and integrated brand promotion, no show seems to be off limits. Brands can now be found whenever and wherever consumers are being entertained, whether at a sporting event, in a movie theatre, on the Internet, or in front of a TV set or video game console. If it entertains an audience, some brand will want to be there, on the inside.

Product placement is the practice of placing any branded product into the content and execution of an established entertainment vehicle. These placements are purposeful and paid for by the marketer to expose and/or promote a brand. Product placement has come a long way since E.T. nibbled on Reese's Pieces in the movie *E.T. the Extra-Terrestrial*. But that product (or brand) placement foreshadowed much that has followed. The genie, as they say, is now definitely out of the bottle.

In today's world, product-placement agencies work with marketers to build bridges to the entertainment industry. Working collaboratively, agents, marketers, producers, and writers find ways to incorporate the marketer's brand as part of the show. The show can be of almost any kind. Movies, short films on the Internet, and reality TV are great venues for product placements. Videogames, novels, and magazines (or mag-a-logs) offer great potential. There may be an opportunity for a brand to be involved any where and any time people are being entertained.

On Television.

Television viewers have become accustomed, maybe even numb, to product placements. Soap operas and reality shows have helped make product placements seem the norm: Vietnam Airlines saves the day with transportation to Cambodia for contestants on *The Amazing Race*, and text a vote for your favorite on *Dancing with the Stars* via AT&T. But the tactic has spread like wildfire. On Time Warner's WB network, a shiny orange Volkswagen Beetle convertible played an important role in the teen superhero drama *Smallville*. Ray Romano chased his wife around the grocery store, knocking over a display of Ragu products, in an episode of *Everybody Loves Raymond. Queer Eye for the Straight Guy,* on the Bravo network, has provided a bonanza of placement opportunities with brands like Amaretto, Redken, and Diesel. The final episode of NBC's long-running comedy *Frasier* included a special moment where Niles gave his brother a little gift to cheer him up. That gift? Pepperidge Farm Mint Milano cookies. Nothing says lovin' like Pepperidge Farm...

There's even a school of thought contending that product placements can be television's savior.[23] Recall Bob Garfield's Chaos Scenario discussed previously in this chapter, with its "inexorable death spiral" for the traditional media like TV. So, if consumers won't watch ads on TV, why not turn the programming itself into an ad vehicle? When Randy has a sip of Coke on *American Idol,* or when contestants get rewarded with a Pringles snack on an episode of *Survivor,* these brands are in effect receiving an implicit endorsement. No telling where this trend is headed; but it is, of course, hard to put the genie back into the bottle. Maybe TV will be saved.

At the Movies.

The "car chase" is a classic component of many action/adventure movies, and in recent years has been seized as a platform for launching new automotive brands.[24] If you'd like to immerse yourself in a superb example of branded entertainment, download *The Italian Job,* a movie starring the lovable Mini Cooper, like the one on display in Exhibit 16.10. The Mini proves to be the perfect getaway car, as it deftly maneuvers in and out of tight spots throughout the movie. BMW has been a pioneer in the product-placement genre, starting with its Z3 placement in the 1995 James Bond thriller *Goldeneye.* Toyota tried to rev up sales of its boxy Scion brand through a featured role in the made-for-the-Internet film *On the D.L.* And Audi touted its futuristic RSQ concept car in the science fiction feature film *I, Robot.* As they say, birds of a feather flock together.

Exhibit 16.10 The Mini Cooper launch campaign featured many innovative examples of integrated brand promotion, including a starring role in the film The Italian Job. Let's motor!

Of course it is not just automakers that have discovered product placements in movies and films. White Castle, American Express, Nokia, and the Weather Channel—to name just a few—have joined the party as well. *Talladega Nights: The Ballad of Ricky Bobby,* starring Will Ferrell, featured a cornucopia of product placements for everything from Applebee's to Old Spice.[25] All this activity is supported by research

23. Marc Graser, "TV's Savior?" *Advertising Age,* February 6, 2006, S-1, S-2.

24. Marc Graser, "Automakers: Every Car Needs a Movie," *Advertising Age,* December 11, 2006, 8.

25. Kate Kelly and Brian Steinberg, "Sony's 'Talladega Nights' Comedy Is Product-Plug Rally," *The Wall Street Journal,* July 28, 2006, A9, A12.

indicating that persons under 25 years old are most likely to notice product placements in films, and are also willing to try products they see in movies and films.[26] As we have emphasized throughout, young consumers are increasingly difficult to reach via traditional broadcast media. Although they are likely to soon get their fill of product placements at the movies, in the near term this looks like a good tactic for reaching an age cohort that can be hard to reach.

In Your Videogame.

Speaking of reaching the unreachable, consider these numbers: According to Forrester Research, 100 million U.S. households have at least some gaming capability.[27] Moreover, most analysts conclude that around 40 percent of the hard-core players are in the 18-to-34 age cohort—highly sought after by advertisers because of their discretionary spending but expensive to reach via conventional media. Now factor in that video games are not only an attractive entertainment option but also a form of entertainment where players rarely wander off during a commercial break. With all those focused eyeballs in play, is it any wonder that marketers want to be involved?

Billboard ads and virtual products have become standard fare in games like True Crime: Streets of L.A., starring Puma-wearing Nick Kang. In the Ubisoft game Splinter Cell: Chaos Theory, secret agents sneak past Diet Sprite vending machines as they track down terrorists. And Tony Hawk must be a Jeep fan, because Wranglers, Grand Cherokees, and Liberties are always on the scene in his games. Nielsen research has established that the majority of players see brand placements as adding to the quality of play, and because of the repetitive brand exposures in games, they affect purchase intent more than old-style media do. The next big thing for marketers is Web-enabled consoles that allow more dynamic ad placements and precise tracking of where and how often players pause to take a closer look.[28] Whether you call it "game-vertising" or "adver-gaming," you can expect to see more of brands like these in the virtual world: LG Mobile, Coca-Cola, BMW, Sony, Old Spice, Levi Strauss, Nokia, Callaway Golf, Ritz Bits, Target, Radio Shack, the U.S. Army, and oodles more.

What We Know About Product Placement.

The business of product placements has evolved at warp speed during the past decade. An activity that was once rare, haphazard, and opportunistic has become more systematic, and in many cases, even strategic. Even though product placement will never be as tidy as crafting and running a 30-second TV spot, numerous case histories make several things apparent about using this tool, both in terms of challenges and opportunities.[29]

First, product placements will add the greatest value when they are integrated with other elements of an advertising plan. No big surprise here; it's always about the synergy. As with event sponsorship, the idea is to leverage the placement. One should avoid isolated product placement opportunities and create connections to other elements of the advertising plan. For instance, a placement combined with a well-timed public relations campaign can yield synergy: novel product placements

26. Emma Hall, "Young Consumers Receptive to Movie Product Placements," *Advertising Age,* March 29, 2004, 8; Federico de Gregorio and Yongjun Sung, "Understanding Attitudes Toward and Behaviors in Response to Product Placement," *Journal of Advertising*, Spring 2010, 83–96.

27. David Kiley, "Rated M for Mad Ave," *BusinessWeek,* February 27, 2006, 76, 77.

28. John Gaudiosi, "In-Game Ads Reach the Next Level," *Business 2.0,* July 2007, 36, 37.

29. See also Cristel Russell and Michael Belch, "A Managerial Investigation into the Product Placement Industry," *Journal of Advertising Research,* March 2005, 73–92.

create great media buzz and that often translates into consumers picking up the buzz and sharing it with their peer group. Recent research suggests that brands stand to gain the most from product placements when consumers are engaged enough to make it a part of their daily conversation.[30] So if you want to get people talking about your brand, give them something to talk about! Favorable word-of-mouth is always a great asset for a brand and helps in building momentum. This can make product placements just the right thing to complement other advertising initiatives that attend the launch of a new product. We have seen this use on numerous occasions in the launch of new car models and brands.

Also, much like event sponsorship, product placements present marketers with major challenges in terms of measuring the success or return on investment of the activity. Here again the collective wisdom seems to be that calculating media impressions for placements does not tell the whole story regarding their value. Product placements can vary dramatically in the value they offer to the marketer. One key item to look for is the celebrity connection in the placement.[31] When Tom Cruise puts on Wayfarer shades in one of his movies, the implied endorsement drives sales of the product.[32] Astute users of product placements are always looking for plot connections that could be interpreted by the audience as an implied brand endorsement from the star of the show.

Another factor affecting the value of any placement has to do with the illusive concept of authenticity. **Authenticity** refers to the quality of being perceived as genuine and natural. As advertisers and their agents look for more and more chances to write their brands into the script of shows, it is to be expected that some of these placements will come off as phony. For example, when Eva Longoria plugs a new Buick at a shopping mall during an episode of *Desperate Housewives,* the scene looks phony and contrived. No way would Longoria or her character in this TV show ever stoop to such an unflattering activity. Conversely, when Kramer argues with a homeless man in the TV show *Seinfeld* about returning his Tupperware containers, the spoof is perfect and adds to the comedic moment. Brands want to be embedded in the entertainment, not detract from it. This is often a difficult goal to achieve.

But like so many other things in the advertising business, success with product placements is fostered through developing deep relationships with the key players in this dynamic business. You need to have the right people looking for the right opportunities that fit with the strategic objectives that have been established for the brand. This too is not a new idea for the business of advertising. As was emphasized in Chapter 8, advertising is a team sport and the best team wins most of its games. You want to be part of a team where the various members understand each other's goals and are working to support one another. Good teams take time to develop. They also move product placement from an opportunistic and haphazard endeavor to one that supports integrated brand promotion. That's always the right thing.

In the next section we will turn our attention to branded entertainment, another topic that is closely related to everything considered in this chapter thus far. To set the stage, one way to see branded entertainment is as a natural extension and outgrowth of product placement. Branded entertainment raises the stakes but also raises the potential payout. With product placement, the question is: "What shows are in development that we might fit our brand into?" With branded entertainment, advertisers create their own shows, so they never have to worry about finding a place for their brand. This of course guarantees that the brand will be one of the stars in the show.

30. Federico de Gregorio and Yongjun Sung, "Understanding Attitudes Toward and Behaviors in Response to Product Placement," *Journal of Advertising*, Spring 2010, 83–96.

31. James Karrah, Kathy McKee, and Carol Pardun, "Practitioners' Evolving Views on Product Placement Effectiveness," *Journal of Advertising Research,* June 2003, 138–149.

32. Christina Passariello, "Ray-Ban Hopes to Party Like It's 1983 by Re-launching Its Wayfarer Shades," *The Wall Street Journal,* October 27, 2006, B1, B4.

Branded Entertainment.

For a stock-car racing fan, there is nothing quite like being at the Lowe's Motor Speedway on the evening of the Coca-Cola 600. It's NASCAR's longest night. But being there live is a rare treat, and so the NASCAR Sprint Cup Series gets plenty of coverage on television, making it among the most popular televised sporting events in North America.[33] If you've never watched a NASCAR race, you owe it to yourself to do so, because even though NASCAR is all about the drivers and the race, every race is also a colossal celebration of brands. There are the cars themselves—as in Exhibit 16.11—carrying the logo large and small of something like 800 NASCAR sponsors. The announcers keep you informed throughout via the Old Spice Lap Leaders update and the Visa Race Break. We are told that Home Depot is the Official Home Improvement Warehouse of NASCAR and UPS is the Official Delivery Service of NASCAR. At commercial breaks there's the beer ads with Budweiser and Miller shouting at each other, and we rejoin the race to follow the Budweiser or Miller Lite car around the track. None of this comes as any surprise, because NASCAR openly and aggressively bills itself as the best marketing opportunity in sports. Said another way, a NASCAR race is a fantastic example of branded entertainment.

It's not hard to understand why Gillette or Budweiser would be willing to shell out millions of dollars to be a featured brand in the NASCAR Sprint Cup Series. Same could be said for the Old Spice team, leading the way there in Exhibit 16.12. Huge television audiences will yield hundreds of thousands of media impressions, especially for those cars (and brands) leading the race. A hundred thousand fans in the stands will make your brand a focal point, and many will visit a branded showcase before or after the race to meet car and driver. In addition, general industry research indicates that NASCAR fans are unusually loyal to the brands that sponsor cars and have absolutely no problem with marketers plastering their logos all over their cars and their drivers. Indeed, many NASCAR fans often wear those logos proudly. Moreover, the data say that race fans are three times more likely to purchase a product promoted by their favorite NASCAR driver, relative to the fans of all other sports.[34] One NASCAR marketing executive put it something like this: "Our teams and drivers have done a wonderful job communicating to fans that the more Old Spice they buy, the faster Tony Stewart is going to go." Obviously, this entails impressing and connecting with consumers in a most compelling way, making the Gillette car or the Bud car or the Viagra car or the Lowe's car all great icons of branded entertainment.

NASCAR is truly a unique brand-building "vehicle" with numerous marketing opportunities for brands large and small.[35] But we use it here as an exemplar of something bigger, something more pervasive, and something that is growing in popularity as a way to support and build brands. Although

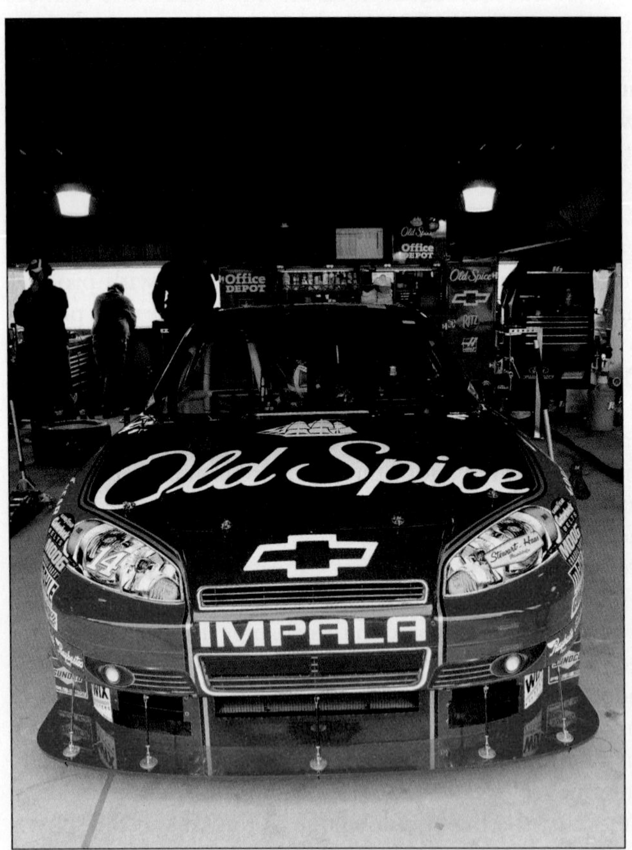

Exhibit 16.11 Brands are the stars of this show.

33. Tom Lowry, "The Prince of NASCAR," *BusinessWeek,* February 23, 2004, 91–98; Rich Thomaselli, "How NASCAR Plans to Get Back on the Fast Track," *Advertising Age,* February 12, 2007, 3, 26.

34. Rich Thomaselli, "Nextel Link Takes NASCAR to New Level," *Advertising Age,* October 27, 2003, S-7.

35. Rich Thomaselli, "Hitch a Ride with NASCAR for Under $5M," *Advertising Age,* November 6, 2006, 4, 80.

Exhibit 16.12 The stars—doing their thing.

it has been called many things, we have settled on the label branded entertainment. **Branded entertainment** entails the development and support of any entertainment property (e.g., TV show, theme park, short film, movie, or video game) where a primary objective is to feature one's brand or brands in an effort to impress and connect with consumers in a unique and compelling way.

What distinguishes branded entertainment from product placement is that in branded entertainment, the entertainment would not exist without the marketer's support, and in many instances, it is marketers themselves who create the entertainment property. BMW's efforts in product placement versus branded entertainment provide a perfect example. The appearance of the Z3 in the 1995 James Bond thriller *Goldeneye* is a nice example of product placement. But BMW did not stop there. In 2001, BMW and its ad agency Fallon Minneapolis decided it was time to make their own movies with BMW vehicles as the star of the show. The result was a series of original, Web-distributed short films like *Beat the Devil,* starring Clive Owen, James Brown, Marilyn Manson, and most especially, the BMW Z4. The success of these custom-made BMW films helped launch the new era of branded entertainment.

Many have followed BMW's lead in developing their own forms of entertainment as a means to feature brands.[36] Goen Group has developed a reality show, the *Million Dollar Makeover Challenge,* starring its diet pill Trimspa. Unilever helped produce two specials to promote its Axe body wash that ran on MTV and SpikeTV. *The Fairway Gourmet,* featured on PBS, promoted images of the good life, courtesy of the Hawaii Visitors & Convention Bureau. By creating shows themselves (often with their ad agencies), marketers seek to attract a specific target audience with a carefully tailored story that shows their brands at their best. This is something quite different from trying to find a special place for one's brand in an existing show. As others have suggested, "clients often enter the (general) realm of entertainment marketing via small product placements that eventually develop into larger promotional programs."[37]

36. Burt Helm, "Bet You Can't TiVo Past This," *BusinessWeek,* April 24, 2006, 38, 40; Louise Story, "Brands Produce Their Own Shows," *The New York Times,* available at www.nytimes.com, November 10, 2006.

37. Cristel Russell and Michael Belch, "A Managerial Investigation into the Product Placement Industry," *Journal of Advertising Research,* March 2005, 82, 83.

On the path of brand building, it is natural to evolve from the simple product placement to the more elaborate enterprise of branded entertainment.

Returning to the NASCAR example, today's NASCAR racing circuit could not exist without big brands like Gillette, Budweiser, Toyota, and Old Spice sponsoring racing teams and their drivers. Without the brands, there would be no NASCAR. As exemplified by a NASCAR race, in today's world of brand building, it is often impossible to disentangle the brand building from the entertainment. That's a great scenario for brand builders, because, among other things, it makes their efforts DVR-proof. You can't skip the brands in a NASCAR race.

Where Are Product Placement and Branded Entertainment Headed?

It is easy to understand the surging popularity of product placements and branded entertainment. Reaching the unreachable through a means that allows your brand to stand out and connect with the consumer can only mean more interest from marketers. But there are always complicating and countervailing forces. No one can really say how rapidly advertising dollars will flow into branded entertainment in the next decade. Several forces could work to undermine that flow.

One of the obvious countervailing forces is instant oversaturation. Like any other faddishly popular promotional tactic, if advertisers pile on too quickly, a jaded consumer and a cluttered environment will be the result.[38] Some will argue that creative collaboration can always yield new opportunities for branded entertainment (as in Healthy Choice's *Working Lunch*), but you have to acknowledge at some point that yet another motion picture featuring another hot automobile or even that Creepy King will start to feel a little stale. Indeed, we may already be there.

A related problem involves the processes and systems that currently exist for matching brands with entertainment properties. Traditional media provide a well-established path for reaching consumers. Marketers like that predictability. Branded entertainment is a new and often unpredictable path. As noted by a senior executive at Fallon Minneapolis, a pioneer in branded entertainment with BMW Films, "For every success you have several failures, because you're basically using a machete to cut through the jungle... with branded entertainment, every time out, it's new."[39] Lack of predictability causes the process to break down.

A soured relationship between General Motors and Warner Bros. over the promotion of the film *Matrix Reloaded* illustrates that marketers and filmmakers don't always appreciate the needs of the other. In this instance, GM's Cadillac division abandoned a big-budget TV campaign associated with the sequel when it couldn't get the talent cooperation or film footage it wanted. Samsung, Heineken, and Coke also complained in public about poor treatment from Warner Bros. These kinds of high-profile squabbles make big news and leave the people with the money to spend wondering whether the branded entertainment path is really worth all the aggravation.[40]

Finally, there is a concern about playing it straight with consumers. For example, Ralph Nader's Commercial Alert consumer advocacy group has charged that TV networks deceive the public by failing to disclose the details of product-placement deals. The group's basic argument seems to be that since many product placements are in fact "paid advertisements," consumers should be advised as such. It is conceivable that a federal agency will call for some form of disclosure when fees have been paid to place brands in U.S. TV shows, although now that the practice has become so prevalent, we expect that consumers already perceive that there is money changing hands behind the

38. Larry Dobrow, "Is It Time to Put an End to Brand Integration?" adage.com, May 21, 2009.

39. Kate MacArthur, "Branded Entertainment, Marketing Tradition Tussle," *Advertising Age,* May 10, 2004, 6.

40. T. L. Stanley, "Sponsors Flee Matrix Sequel," *Advertising Age,* October 13, 2003, 1, 71.

scenes. Consumers are generally pretty savvy about this sort of thing. On the global front, this can be one of those issues where you find great differences of opinion from country to country. For example, as described in the *Globalization* box, the Spanish approach product placements much like the United States, whereas the Brits, raised on watching the noncommercial BBC, see things quite a bit differently.

What's Old Is New Again.

Turns out marketers, media moguls, ad agencies, and entertainers have much in common. They do what they do for business reasons. And they have and will continue to do business together. That's reality. It has been reality for decades. Smart advertisers have always recognized this, and then go about their business of trying to reach

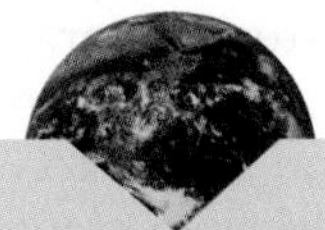

Globalization

Europeans Run Hot and Cold on Product Placements

H.J. Heinz will tell you that the world is a very complicated place when it comes to the use of product placements. All you need to know about the United Kingdom is that when reruns of *American Idol* ran there, the U.K.'s Independent Television Commission made producers disguise the Coca-Cola logo on those big red cups. And when Heinz launched a cooking show called *Dinner Doctors* in the U.K., they of course had in mind featuring many of their foods products as part of the show's normal fare. The regulator's response: no way. No products could be mentioned in any part of the programming. When one Heinz executive from the home office in Pittsburgh asked, "How many times is the product shown?" he was told bluntly by Heinz's general manager of corporate affairs in Europe, "It's not shown." Why bother with such programming? Heinz did get sponsorship mentions as part of the credits, and in Britain's sparse product placement environment, apparently that's enough to generate positive feedback from consumers. Perhaps this is just another example of the "law of advertising relativity." In a sparse environment, a little bit of credit can seem like a lot.

The situation for advertisers in Spain couldn't be more different. Turns out that Spain is an advertisers dream come true. But maybe that dream is just an illusion. There is so much advertising clutter on Spanish television that it is hard to argue that anyone can break through to engage the consumer. During prime time evening hours, commercial breaks can last up to 15 minutes with as many as 30 ads in a row. By the time the program resumes, many viewers can easily forget what show they were watching. A movie like *The Lord of the Rings* runs about three hours in the theatre, but check your program guide in Spain and you'll see it's scheduled for five hours. That's right; two hours of advertisements are embedded in a three-hour movie. Wonder how one says TiVo in Spanish?

How can an advertiser avoid the dreaded TiVo? Build your brand into the show itself. Again, not a problem in Spain. General Motors and McDonald's wanted to be part of Spain's top-rated TV show, *Aquí no hay quien viva* (*No One Can Live Here*). The show's writers were happy to oblige. During a wedding scene on the show the bride and groom had a special surprise for their guests: They drove to McDonald's in a Hummer and ordered Big Macs, McNuggets, and of course fries, for everyone. But the home-improvement show *Decogarden* sets the standard for product placements on Spanish TV. That would be 105 placements in just four episodes running in four consecutive weeks. As expressed by the head of one ad agency in Spain: "We are a paradise for product placement."

So how about the rest of Europe? Other European countries currently fall somewhere between the two extremes represented by Britain and Spain when it comes to product placement, but the trend is toward the Spanish model. New rules from the European Union are encouraging a more open advertising environment across Europe. But don't expect a quick conversion from the Brits. As one agency executive put it: "We Brits are cynical about clunky brand communications, and as practitioners we also kick against it." It's a good bet that serving McNuggets at a wedding reception would qualify as clunky in a lot of places.

Sources: Emma Hall, "Product Placement Faces a Wary Welcome in Britain," *Advertising Age*, January 8, 2007, 27; Aaron Patrick and Keith Johnson, "Spanish Television Reigns as King of Product Plugs," *The Wall Street Journal*, February 2, 2007, A1, A16; Laurel Wentz, "It's No Coincidence Everyone in This Spanish Soap Drives a Ford," *Advertising Age*, February 1, 2010, 3, 19; Emma Hall, "U.K. Tightens Rules on Newly Approved Product Placement," *Advertising Age*, February 15, 2010, 4, 22.

Exhibit 16.13 In the 1920s, P&G was an innovator in the new medium of radio, trying to reach consumers on behalf of brands like Crisco, Ivory, and Oxydol.

consumers with a positive message on behalf of their brands. No firm has managed this collaboration better throughout the years than Procter & Gamble, and to close this section, we take a then-and-now look at P&G initiatives to acknowledge that. Even though it is enjoying a huge surge of popularity recently, branded entertainment has been around for decades.

In 1923, P&G was on the cutting edge of branded entertainment in the then-new medium of radio. (Try if you dare to imagine a world without television or Facebook—how did people survive?) To promote their shortening product Crisco, they helped create a new radio program called *Crisco Cooking Talks.* This was a 15-minute program that featured recipes and advice to encourage cooks, like the one in Exhibit 16.13, to find more uses for Crisco. Although it was a good start, P&G's market research soon told them that listeners wanted something more entertaining than just a recipe show. So a new form of entertainment was created just for radio that would come to be known as the soap opera. These dramatic series used a storyline that encouraged listeners to tune in day after day. *Guiding Light,* P&G's most enduring "soap," was started on the radio in 1937. In 1952 *Guiding Light* made a successful transition to television. It thus holds the distinction of being the longest-running show in the history of electronic media.[41] One more thing—P&G has done all right selling soap (and today, many other products as well).

Fast forward to the new millennium. P&G's consumer has changed, and new forms of integrated brand promotion are necessary. Today P&G works with partners like NBC Digital Networks and Starcom MediaVest Group to ensure that its brands are embedded in the entertainment venues preferred by its targeted consumers. A great example is the integration of P&G's CoverGirl brand in the CW Network's *America's Next Top Model,* hosted by former CoverGirl Tyra Banks. In this CoverGirl/*Top Model* relationship, we see exemplified many best practices for branded entertainers.

An enduring relationship is clearly something to strive for. Long-term relationships beget trust, and when partners trust each other, they also look out for each other. So although P&G does not have direct control over the content of *Top Model,* it is able to ask for brand inserts and sometimes influence the show's content because of the relationship. However, P&G has learned to not push too hard to get its brand featured. That can detract from the entertainment value of the programming, which wouldn't help anyone. To maintain the right balance, the CoverGirl brand receives strong integration into the plot in just a few episodes per season.

Authenticity of the brand integration is always desirable, and CoverGirl definitely gets that on *Top Model.* For example, each season the finalists must prepare to be photographed for a magazine ad. This is after all what models get paid to do: appear in ads. So it's perfectly natural that this is part of the show, and it's perfectly natural that the magazine ad will be for CoverGirl, as this is a brand that stands for "enhancing your natural beauty." The content of the show and the essence of the brand

41. Davis Dyer, Frederick Dalzell, and Rowena Olegario, *Rising Tide: Lessons from 165 Years of Brand Building at Procter & Gamble* (Boston, MA: Harvard Business School Publishing, 2004); Jack Neff, "Last P&G Produced Soap Opera to End," adage.com, December 8, 2009.

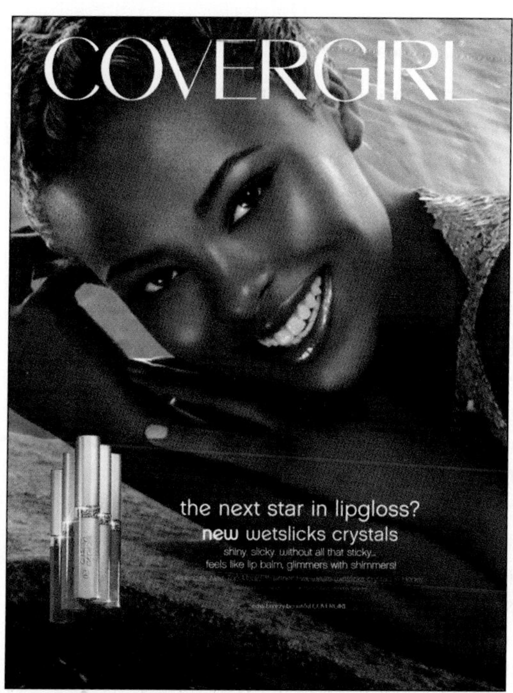

Exhibit 16.14 Every winner of the Top Model competition goes on to be a CoverGirl model for P&G, delivering an instant endorsement for the brand from this new celebrity.

become completely intertwined, with an implied endorsement from *America's Next Top Model,* like Eva in Exhibit 16.14. It doesn't get any better than that in the brave new world of brand building.

Like many other marketers, P&G Productions is also moving to the Internet to create original content. Per *Advertising Age*, this tracks with the trend of Madison & Vine moving to Silicon Valley.[42] One of P&G's recent "Webisodes" is the series *A Parent Is Born* (Exhibit 16.15). This series was an online documentary following Suzie and Steve on their emotional journey to parenthood. Each of its 12 episodes was about five minutes in length and tracked the experience for Suzie and Steve from finding out the sex of their baby through baby showers and childbirth class to the grand finale where the newborn (baby Leo) comes home. Now you're thinking—who'd be interested in watching this sort of thing? The obvious answer—expecting couples—who, oh by the way, will soon be prime prospects for Pampers. Therein lies the appeal of the Webisode—it is relatively inexpensive to produce and brands get total control in developing the content so as to meet their specific objectives and appeal to their specific target audience. And as we have seen over and over again, like with the *Working Lunch* example that began the chapter, marketers will always prefer the IBP tools that take them right to their target audience.

Exhibit 16.15 Episode 12: Cute baby comes home makes a great ending to any story.

42. Andrew Hampp, "How Madison & Vine Moved to Silicon Valley," *Advertising Age*, March 15, 2010, 4.

4 The Coordination Challenge.

The choices for delivering messages to a target audience continue to evolve. As you have seen, marketers and advertisers are constantly searching for new, cost-effective ways to break through the clutter and connect with consumers. Today, everything from advertising in restrooms to sponsoring a marathon to adver-gaming to producing short films for the Internet is part of the portfolio.

In concluding this chapter, a critical point about the explosion of advertising and IBP tools needs to be reinforced. Advertisers have a vast and ever-expanding array of options for delivering messages to their potential customers. From cable TV to national newspapers, from high-tech billboards to online contests and giveaways, the variety of options is staggering. The keys to success for any campaign are choosing the right set of options to engage a target segment and then coordinating the placement of messages to ensure coherent and timely communication.

Many factors work against coordination. As advertising and IBP have become more complex, organizations often become reliant on diverse functional specialists. For example, an organization might have separate managers for advertising, event sponsorship, branded entertainment, and digital development. Specialists, by definition, focus on their specialty and can lose sight of what others in the organization are doing.[43] Specialists also want their own budgets and typically argue for more funding for their particular area. This competition for budget dollars often yields rivalries and animosities that work against coordination. Never underestimate the power of competition for the budget. It is exceedingly rare to find anyone who will volunteer to take less of the budget so that someone else can have more.

Coordination is further complicated by the fact that there can be an incredible lack of alignment around who is responsible for achieving the integration.[44] Should the client accept this responsibility? Or should integration be the responsibility of a "lead" agency? Ad agencies often see themselves in this lead role, but have not played it to anyone's satisfaction.[45] One vision of how things should work has the lead agency playing the role of an architect and general contractor.[46] The campaign architect is charged with drawing up a plan that is media neutral and then hiring subcontractors to deliver those aspects of the project that the agency itself is ill suited to handle. The plan must also be profit-neutral. That is, the budget must go to the subcontractors who can deliver the work called for in the master plan. Here again the question becomes, Will the "architect/general contractor" really spread the wealth, if by doing so, it forfeits wealth? Life usually doesn't work that way. But one thing is for sure: When it is not clear who is accountable for delivering an integrated campaign, there is little chance that synergy or integration will be achieved.

Remember finally that the objective underlying the need for coordination is to achieve a synergistic effect. Individual media can work in isolation, but advertisers get more for their dollars if various media and IBP tools build on one another and work together. Even savvy marketers like American Express are challenged by the need for coordination, and especially so as they cut back on their use of the 30-second TV spot and venture into diverse IBP tools. For instance, to launch its Blue card, AmEx employed an innovative mix, starting with Blue-labeled water

43. Don E. Schultz, Stanley I. Tannenbaum, and Robert F. Lauterborn, *Integrated Marketing Communications* (Lincolnwood, IL: NTC Business Books, 1993); Daniel Klein, "Disintegrated Marketing," *Harvard Business Review*, March 2003, 18–19.

44. Laura Q. Hughes and Kate MacArthur, "Soft Boiled: Clients Want Integrated Marketing at Their Disposal, but Agencies Are (Still) Struggling to Put the Structure Together," *Advertising Age*, May 28, 2001, 3, 54; Claire Atkinson, "Integration Still a Pipe Dream for Many," *Advertising Age*, March 10, 2003, 1, 47; Burt Helm, "Struggles of a Mad Man: Saatchi & Saatchi CEO Kevin Roberts," *BusinessWeek*, December 3, 2007, 44–50.

45. Joe Cappo, *The Future of Advertising* (Chicago, IL: McGraw-Hill, 2003), Ch. 8.

46. Ibid, 153, 154.

bottles given away at health clubs and Blue ads printed on millions of popcorn bags. The company sponsored a Sheryl Crow concert in New York's Central Park and transformed L.A.'s House of Blues jazz club into the "House of Blue," with performances by Elvis Costello, Stevie Wonder, and Counting Crows. Print ads and TV have also been used to back the Blue, but AmEx's spending in these traditional media was down by more than 50 percent relative to previous campaigns. Making diverse components like these work together and speak to the targeted consumer with a "single voice" is the essence of advertising and integrated brand promotion. AmEx appears to have found a good formula: The Blue card was the most successful new-product launch in the company's history.[47]

The coordination challenge does not end here. Chapters that follow will add more layers of complexity to this challenge: Topics to come include direct marketing, personal selling, public relations, and corporate advertising. These activities entail additional contacts with a target audience that should reinforce the messages being delivered through broadcast, print, digital, and support media. Integrating these efforts to speak with one voice represents a marketer's best and maybe only hope for breaking through the clutter to engage with a target segment in today's crowded marketplace.

Summary

1 Justify the growing popularity of event sponsorship as another means of brand promotion.

The list of companies sponsoring events grows with each passing year, and the events include a wide variety of activities. Of these various activities, sports attract the most sponsorship dollars. Sponsorship can help in building brand familiarity; it can promote brand loyalty by connecting a brand with powerful emotional experiences; and in most instances it allows a marketer to reach a well-defined target audience. Events can also facilitate face-to-face contacts with key customers and present opportunities to distribute product samples, sell premiums, and conduct consumer surveys.

2 Summarize the uses and appeal of product placements in venues like TV, movies, and video games.

Product placements have surged in popularity during the past decade and there are many reasons to believe that advertisers will continue to commit more resources to this activity. Like any other advertising tactic, product placements offer the most value when they are connected to other elements of the advertising plan. One common use of the placement is to help create excitement for the launch of a new product. Implicit celebrity endorsements and authenticity are key issues to consider when judging placement opportunities. High-quality placements are most likely to result from great collaboration among marketers, agents, producers, and writers. As always, the best team wins.

3 Explain the benefits and challenges of connecting with entertainment properties in building a brand.

Brand builders want to connect with consumers, and to do so they are connecting with the entertainment business. Even though not everyone can afford a NASCAR sponsorship, in many ways NASCAR sets the standard for celebrating brands in an entertaining setting. Many marketers, such as BMW, P&G, and Unilever, are now developing their own entertainment properties to feature their brands. However, the rush to participate in branded entertainment ventures raises the risk of oversaturation and consumer backlash, or at least consumer apathy. As with any tool, while it is new and fresh, good things happen. When it gets old and stale, advertisers will turn to the next "big thing."

47. Suzanne Vranica, "For Big Marketers Like AmEx, TV Ads Lose Starring Role," *The Wall Street Journal,* May 17, 2004, B1, B3.

Discuss the challenges presented by the ever-increasing variety of communication and branding tools for achieving integrated brand promotion.

The tremendous variety of media options we have seen thus far represents a monumental challenge for an advertiser who wishes to speak to a customer with a single voice. Achieving this single voice is critical for breaking through the clutter of the modern advertising environment. However, the functional specialists required for working in the various media have their own biases and subgoals that can get in the way of integration. We will return to this issue in subsequent chapters as we explore other options available to marketers in their quest to win customers.

Key Terms

Madison & Vine
Chaos Scenario
event sponsorship
media impressions
leveraging
product placement
authenticity
branded entertainment

Questions

1. Read the opening section of this chapter and briefly describe the *Working Lunch* promotion. In what ways does it exemplify the latest trends in integrated brand promotion?

2. Who is Bob Garfield? Do you agree with his Chaos Scenario?

3. Present statistics to document the claim that the television viewing audience is becoming fragmented. What are the causes of this fragmentation? Develop an argument that links this fragmentation to the growing popularity of event sponsorship and branded entertainment.

4. Event sponsorship can be valuable for building brand loyalty. Search through your closets, drawers, or cupboards and find a premium or memento that you acquired at a sponsored event. Does this memento bring back fond memories? Would you consider yourself loyal to the brand that sponsored this event? If not, why not?

5. What lessons can we learn from Prilosec's sponsorship of the WBA regarding the things one should look for in judging sponsorship opportunities?

6. Why have video games attracted so much interest recently as a venue for product placements? What makes this venue even more appealing for advertisers as games and game players move to the Internet?

7. What is the role for celebrities in the business of product placement and branded entertainment? Describe a scene from a TV show or movie that illustrates the best way to involve a celebrity as part of a product placement.

8. Why is NASCAR a good affiliation for the Old Spice brand?

9. Using BMW as the example, explain the difference between product placements and branded entertainment.

10. Explain the need for functional specialists in developing IBP campaigns. Who are they and what skills do they offer? What problems do these functional specialists create for the achievement of integrated brand promotion?

Experiential Exercises

1. Walmart has a new logo, new stores, and a new green business model, and now the retail giant is working on a new way to advertise. Walmart's Family Moments campaign integrates the retailer's store brands into films and activities for the whole family. Write a report on Walmart's recent move to sponsor Friday night films at NBC, and explain how the films provide targeted advertising opportunities for the retailer. In your report, brainstorm a new idea for this Walmart campaign that makes use of product placement, branded entertainment, or event sponsorship.

2. Event sponsorship is becoming increasingly important to advertisers as the effectiveness of traditional media is eroded due to audience fragmentation. Event sponsorship can take many forms—it's even commonplace on college campuses. Select an example of event sponsorship at your school and describe the relationship between the advertiser and the event. What role does the advertiser perform during the event? Why would a company consider the event an effective method to reach its target audience?

3. Video-game maker Incredible Technologies Inc. has in recent years steadily expanded its corporate partnerships and product placements in its most popular game, the pub-based, Web-connected golfing game Golden Tee Live. Players can purchase Top-Flite branded virtual golfing equipment, and as they work through the course they spot Coca-Cola vending machines, billboards, and even groundhogs that pop up on the screen guzzling from a Coke can.

Working in small groups, brainstorm other possible product placement opportunities for the game and identify how they could be incorporated. Your answers should address specifically how the unique characteristics of a videogame, particularly one with a Web-linked console, support the product placement suggestions.

4. Working in the same teams, create a branded entertainment proposal for the coffee giant Starbucks. As discussed in the chapter, your proposal should identify a specific target audience and describe in detail a proposed storyline for a short film, television series, or other entertainment product that would effectively promote the brand and capture the attention of that market segment.

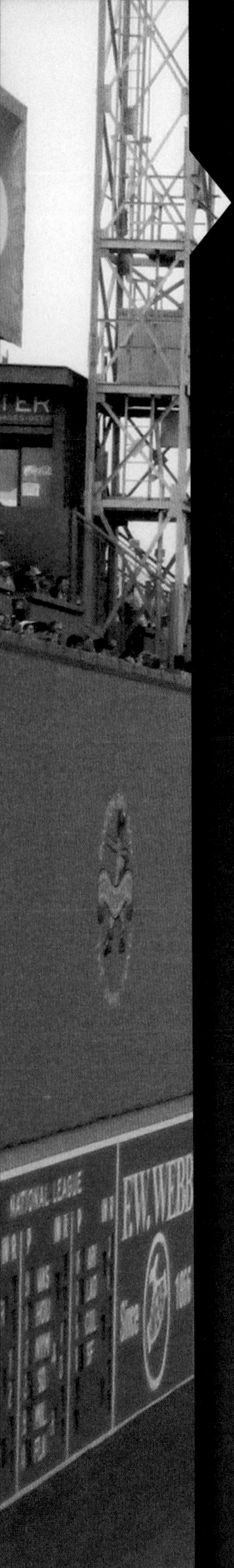

Chapter 17

Integrating Direct Marketing and Personal Selling

After reading and thinking about this chapter, you will be able to do the following:

1. Identify the three primary purposes served by direct marketing and explain its growing popularity.
2. Distinguish a mailing list from a marketing database and review the many applications of each.
3. Describe the prominent media used by direct marketers in delivering their messages to the consumer.
4. Explain the key role of direct marketing and personal selling in complementing other advertising activities.

http://www.llbean.com/customerService/aboutLLBean/guarantee.html

Customer Service 800-441-5713 Email Updates L.L.Bean® Visa® Card Log In My Account

L.L.Bean GUARANTEED You Have Our Word.

Search

L.L.BEAN VISA CARD FREE SHIPPING All Year Long Learn more See Terms and Conditions

Shopping Bag 0 items

Men's Women's Kids' Footwear Outdoor Gear - Hunt/Fish Luggage Home Sale Gift Cards

Customer Service
Contact Us
Live Help
100% Guaranteed
Order Tracking/History
Easy Returns
Your Privacy
About Security
Recall Notices
"Phishing" Scams
Site Map

Help Desk
Shopping Information
My Account
Shipping & Delivery
Tracking Your Order
Return & Exchange Information
Monogramming & Engraving
Catalog Requests & Information
International Help

Guaranteed
You Have Our Word®

Our products are guaranteed to give 100% satisfaction in every way. Return anything purchased from us at any time if it proves otherwise. We do not want you to have anything from L.L.Bean that is not completely satisfactory.

From kayaks to slippers, fly rods to sweaters, everything we sell at L.L.Bean is backed by the same rock-solid guarantee of satisfaction. It's been that way since our founder sold his very first pair of Bean Boots in 1912. Today we're proud to continue the tradition – by offering quality products and standing behind them.

L.L. Bean placed this notice on the wall of our Freeport store.

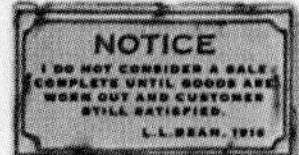

NOTICE
I DO NOT CONSIDER A SALE COMPLETE UNTIL GOODS ARE WORN OUT AND CUSTOMER STILL SATISFIED.
L.L.BEAN, 1916

Order Tracking | Visit a Store | Easy Returns | Shop Catalogs Online | Email Updates | Sign up

We Make Shopping Safe, Secure, Easy

Click for Live Chat
Call 800-441-5713
About Security | Your Privacy

MORE WAYS TO SHOP
Gift Cards
Shop Catalogs Online
Free Catalogs
Retail Stores
Outlets
Direct to Business
Product Videos

L.L.BEAN VISA CARD
Apply Now
Coupon Lookup
Store Your Card for Checkout

CUSTOMER SERVICE
Contact Us
FAQs & Helpful Links
Check Gift Card Balance
Shipping Information
International Help
Live Help
Site Map

EXPLORE THE OUTDOORS
Park Search
L.L.Bean Adventures
Customer Photos
Outdoor Heroes

ABOUT L.L.BEAN
Company Information
Employment
Social Responsibility
Conservation Partners
Outdoor Partners

CONNECT WITH L.L.BEAN
Join Us on Facebook
Follow Us on Twitter
Subscribe to Our YouTube Channel

Introductory Scenario: Don't Mess with Les.

In 1958 Lester Wunderman launched a new services firm to help clients with a different style of marketing—a style he would label "direct marketing." It turned out to be a potent style and his firm prospered, changed names, and today is part of WPP Group, the global ad-agency holding company based in London.[1] Throughout his career, Les Wunderman worked with numerous clients to help them grow their businesses. One of his success stories involved Columbia House Music Club, and a brief look back at Wunderman's work with Columbia provides instant insights regarding the unique style of the direct marketer.[2]

Wunderman had worked with Columbia for a number of years when executives at Columbia had a notion to hire another ad agency to help with the job. The other agency was McCann Erickson, renowned for its creativity and sophistication in ad development. To put it mildly, Les was not thrilled about sharing the account with McCann, but Columbia wanted something different. So Les proposed a test. He said, give me 13 cities to work in, give McCann a comparable 13 cities, and the two of us will develop and run new campaigns—winner take all. Everyone agreed a test was in order.

McCann took the classic approach of the traditional ad agency. They developed an awareness-building campaign featuring prime-time TV ads, designed to heighten familiarity with Columbia. Then, as consumers found Columbia House offers in *TV Guide* and *Parade* magazines (you know, Buy One and Get 12 FREE), the more-aware consumer was expected to jump at the offer.

Wunderman used a different approach. Rather than glitzy, prime-time TV ads, he went late night, where airtime is much less expensive (about one-quarter the cost of McCann's programming). However, the key to his plan was the "treasure hunt." In every magazine ad, Wunderman's designers incorporated a little gold box. Then, in his series of TV commercials, a critical theme was the invitation to solve the "Secret of the Gold Box" and win a prize. The gold box gave viewers a reason to look for the companion ads in *TV Guide* and *Parade* magazines. In Wunderman's words, "It made the readers/viewers part of an interactive advertising system. Viewers became participants."[3] The little gold box served to "integrate" the different components of the overall campaign. That's the magic word, so you can already guess who wins this competition.

Both the McCann and Wunderman approaches showed results. Spending four times as much on prime-time media, McCann produced nearly a 20 percent increase in the sign-up rate for Columbia's Music Club. But Wunderman and his, some might say, cheesy idea of the Secret of the Gold Box generated an 80 percent increase in sign-ups. Needless to say, Les preempted the splitting of Columbia's business, and the Gold Box tactic was unveiled as part of Columbia's national campaign.

Several aspects of this story illustrate the mind-set of the direct marketer. First is simply the idea of staging a test. Direct marketers always seek to be in a position to judge results. Clients want results, and the Les Wundermans of the world recommend first going to the marketplace to see what works, and then spending the big dollars after you know the winner. Testing "in-market" is a hallmark of the direct marketer. Second, we see in the Wunderman gold box tactic keen insight about how to initiate a dialogue with the consumer. Use a little bit of mystery and throw in the prospect of winning something and consumers get interested and send you back a response. This proclivity for promoting dialogue is another defining characteristic of the direct marketer's style. Getting in a dialogue with consumers leads

1. Catherine Arnold, "Up Close, Personal," *Marketing News*, February 15, 2005, 15, 16.

2. This account is adapted from Malcolm Gladwell, *The Tipping Point* (Boston: Little, Brown and Company, 2002), 93–95.

3. Ibid, 95.

to relationships that can mean multiple purchases over time (as in a CD/DVD club like Columbia's). And that's where the real gold lies—in those multiple purchases.

In this chapter we examine the growing field of direct marketing and explain how it may be used to both complement and supplant other forms of advertising. In addition, we conclude this chapter with a brief introduction to the field of personal selling. Personal selling brings the human element into the marketing process and shares many important features with direct marketing. For instance, as with direct marketing, an organization's sales personnel are looking to develop a dialogue with customers that can result in product sales in the short run, and repeat business over the long run. Trial purchases are a good thing, but a satisfied customer who comes back to purchase again and again (and encourages friends and family to do likewise) is the ultimate goal.

1 The Evolution of Direct Marketing.

This theme should be familiar to you by now. With the growing concern about fragmenting markets and the diminishing effectiveness of traditional media in reaching those markets, one can expect that more and more advertising dollars will be moved into other options, like direct marketing programs.[4] Before we examine the evolution of direct marketing and look deeper at the reasons for its growing popularity, we need a clear appreciation for what people mean when they use the term *direct marketing*. The "official" definition from the Direct Marketing Association (DMA) provides a starting point:

> ***Direct marketing*** *is an interactive system of marketing, which uses one or more advertising media to effect a measurable response and/or transaction at any location.*[5]

When examined piece by piece, this definition furnishes an excellent basis for understanding the scope of direct marketing.[6]

Direct marketing is interactive in that the marketer is attempting to develop an ongoing dialogue with the customer. Direct marketing programs are commonly planned with the notion that one contact will lead to another and then another so that the marketer's message can become more focused and refined with each interaction. The DMA's definition also notes that multiple media can be used in direct marketing programs. This is an important point for two reasons. First, we do not want to equate direct mail and direct marketing. Any medium can be used in executing direct marketing programs, not just the mail. Second, as we have noted before, a combination of media is likely to be more effective than any one medium alone.

Another key aspect of direct marketing programs is that they almost always are designed to produce some form of immediate, measurable response. Direct marketing programs are often designed to produce an immediate sale. The customer might be asked to return an order form with check or money order for $189 to get a stylish Klaus Kobec Couture Sports Watch, or to call an 800 number with credit card handy to get 22 timeless hits on a CD called *The Very Best of Tony Bennett*. Because of this emphasis on immediate response, direct marketers are in a position to judge the effectiveness of a particular program. As in the Wunderman example, this ability to gauge the immediate impact of a program has great appeal for the client.

The final phrase of the DMA's definition notes that a direct marketing transaction can take place anywhere. The key idea here is that customers do not have to make a trip to a retail store for a direct marketing program to work. Follow-ups can

4. Anthony Bianco, "The Vanishing Mass Market," *BusinessWeek*, July 12, 2004, 61–68.

5. Bob Stone, *Successful Direct Marketing Methods* (Lincolnwood, IL: NTC Business Books, 1994).

6. The discussion to follow builds on that of Stone, *Successful Direct Marketing Methods.*

be made by mail, over the telephone, or on the Internet. At one time the thinking was that Web-based direct marketers such as Amazon, pets.com, and eToys.com could ultimately provide so much convenience for shoppers that traditional retail stores might fall by the wayside. Not! It now seems clear that consumers like the option of contacting companies in many ways, and vice versa.[7] So smart retailers both large (see Exhibit 17.1) and small (see Exhibit 17.2) make themselves available in both the physical and virtual worlds.[8] Customers are then free to choose where and how they want to shop.

Direct Marketing—A Look Back.

From Johannes Gutenberg and Benjamin Franklin to Richard Sears, Alvah Roebuck, Les Wunderman, and Lillian Vernon, the evolution of direct marketing has involved some of the great pioneers in business. As Exhibit 17.3 shows, the practice of direct marketing today is shaped by the successes of many notable mail-order companies and catalog merchandisers.[9] Among them, none is more exemplary than L. L. Bean. Bean founded his company in 1912 on his integrity and $400. His first product was

Exhibit 17.1 Among other things, pure-play Internet retailers came to realize that when shoppers are dissatisfied with their purchases, many want a physical store where they can return the merchandise for a refund or a trade. In this ad, BestBuy.com has some fun with this issue in the context of online CD shopping. At Best Buy, if Folksongs from Rumania is not what you thought it would be, you can always return it to one of their retail stores.

Exhibit 17.2 How about a new moose rug or carved loon for your grandparents' cottage up north? Well, you could visit the Adirondack Country Store in upstate New York, call them at 1-800-LOON-ADK for the catalog, or go online to pick out something nice. Check out the call of the loon at www.adirondackcountrystore.com

7. Louise Lee, "Catalogs, Catalogs, Everywhere," *BusinessWeek*, December 4, 2006, 32–34; Elisabeth Sullivan, "Direct to Digital," *Marketing News*, November 5, 2009, 25.

8. Allanna Sullivan, "From a Call to a Click," *The Wall Street Journal*, July 17, 2000, R30.

9. See Edward Nash, "The Roots of Direct Marketing," *Direct Marketing Magazine*, February 1995, 38–40; Cara Beardi, "Lillian Vernon Sets Sights on Second Half-Century," *Advertising Age*, March 19, 2001, 22.

Exhibit 17.3 Direct marketing milestones.

c. 1450	Johannes Gutenberg invents movable type.
1667	The first gardening catalog is published by William Lucas, an English gardener.
1744	Benjamin Franklin publishes a catalog of books on science and industry and formulates the basic mail-order concept of customer satisfaction guaranteed.
1830s	A few mail-order companies began operating in New England, selling camping and fishing supplies.
1863	The introduction of penny postage facilitates direct mail.
1867	The invention of the typewriter gives a modern appearance to direct mail materials.
1872	Montgomery Ward publishes his first "catalog," selling 163 items on a single sheet of paper. By 1884 his catalog grows to 240 pages, with thousands of items and a money-back guarantee.
1886	Richard Sears enters the mail-order business by selling gold watches and makes $5,000 in his first six months. He partners with Alvah Roebuck in 1887, and by 1893 they are marketing a wide range of merchandise in a 196-page catalog.
1912	L. L. Bean founds one of today's most admired mail-order companies on the strength of his Maine Hunting Shoe and a guarantee of total satisfaction for the life of the shoe.
1917	The Direct Mail Advertising Association is founded. In 1973 it becomes the Direct Mail/Direct Marketing Association.
1928	Third-class bulk mail becomes a reality, offering economies for the direct mail industry.
1950	Credit cards first appear, led by the Diners' Club travel and entertainment card. American Express enters in 1958.
1951	Lillian Vernon places an ad for a monogrammed purse and belt and generates $16,000 in immediate business. She reinvests the money in what becomes the Lillian Vernon enterprise. Vernon recognizes early on that catalog shopping has great appeal to time-pressed consumers.
1953	Publishers Clearing House is founded and soon becomes a dominant force in magazine subscriptions.
1955	Columbia Record Club is established, and eventually becomes Columbia House—the music-marketing giant.
1967	The term *telemarketing* first appears in print, and AT&T introduces the first toll-free 800 service.
1983	The Direct Mail/Direct Marketing Association drops Direct Mail from its name to become the DMA, as a reflection of the multiple media being used by direct marketers.
1984	Apple introduces the Macintosh personal computer.
1992	The number of people who shop at home surpasses 100 million in the United States.
1998	The Direct Marketing Association, www.the-dma.org, eager to adapt its members' bulk mailing techniques for the Internet, announces it will merge with the Association for Interactive Media, www.interactivehq.org.
2003	U.S. consumers register more than 10 million phone numbers in the first four days of the national Do Not Call Registry.

Sources: Adapted from the DMA's "Grassroots Advocacy Guide for Direct Marketers" (1993). Reprinted with permission of the Direct Marketing Association, Inc.; Rebecca Quick, "Direct Marketing Association to Merge with Association of Interactive Media," *The Wall Street Journal,* October 12, 1998, B6.

a unique hunting shoe made from a leather top and rubber bottom sewn together. Other outdoor clothing and equipment soon followed in the Bean catalog.

A look at the L.L. Bean catalog of 1917 (black and white, just 12 pages) reveals the fundamental strategy underlying Bean's success. It featured the Maine Hunting Shoe and other outdoor clothing with descriptive copy that was informative, factual, and low-key. On the front page was Bean's commitment to quality. It read: "Maine Hunting Shoe—guarantee. We guarantee this pair of shoes to give perfect satisfaction in every way. If the rubber breaks or the tops grow hard, return them together with this guarantee tag and we will replace them, free of charge. Signed, L.L. Bean."[10] Bean realized that long-term relationships with customers must be based on trust, and his guarantee policy was aimed at developing and sustaining that trust.

As an astute direct marketer, Bean also showed a keen appreciation for the importance of building a good mailing list. For many years he used his profits to promote his free catalog via advertisements in hunting and fishing magazines. Those replying to the ads received a rapid response and typically became Bean customers. Bean's obsession with building mailing lists is nicely captured by this quote from his friend, Maine native John Gould: "If you drop in just to shake his hand, you get home to find his catalog in your mailbox."[11]

Today, L.L. Bean is still a family-operated business that emphasizes the basic philosophies of its founder, as illustrated in Exhibit 17.4. Quality products, understated advertising, and sophisticated customer-contact and distribution systems sustain the business. But Bean's 100-percent-satisfaction guarantee remains at the heart of the relationship between Bean and its customers.

Exhibit 17.4 A good guarantee never goes out of fashion.

Courtesy, Susan Van Etten

10. Allison Cosmedy, *A History of Direct Marketing* (New York: Direct Marketing Association, 1992), 6.

11. Ibid.

Direct Marketing Today.

Direct marketing today is rooted in the legacy of mail-order giants and catalog merchandisers such as L.L. Bean, Lillian Vernon, Publishers Clearing House, and JCPenney. Today, however, direct marketing has broken free from its mail-order heritage to become a tool used by all types of organizations throughout the world. Although many types of businesses and not-for-profit organizations are using direct marketing, it is common to find that such direct-marketing programs are not carefully integrated with an organization's other advertising efforts. Integration should be the goal for advertising and direct marketing (remember the Gold Box!). Again and again the evidence supports our thesis that integrated programs are more effective than the sum of their parts.[12]

Because the label "direct marketing" now encompasses many different types of activities, it is important to remember the defining characteristics spelled out in the DMA definition given earlier. Direct marketing involves an attempt to interact or create a dialogue with the customer; multiple media are often employed in the process, and direct marketing is characterized by the fact that a measurable response is immediately available for assessing a program's impact. With these defining features in mind, we can see that direct marketing programs are commonly used for three primary purposes.

Exhibit 17.5 Most people are not going to buy a major piece of exercise equipment based on this or any other magazine ad. That's not the intent of this ad. The purchase process could start here, however, with the simple act of ordering that free video.

Courtesy of Stairmaster Co., Kirkland, WA

As you might imagine, the most common use of direct marketing is as a tool to close the sale with a customer. This can be done as a stand-alone program, or it can be coordinated with a firm's other advertising. Telecommunications giants such as AT&T, Sprint, T-Mobile, and Verizon make extensive use of the advertising/direct marketing combination. High-profile mass media campaigns build awareness for their latest offer, followed by systematic direct marketing follow-ups to close the sale.

A second purpose for direct marketing programs is to identify prospects for future contacts and, at the same time, provide in-depth information to selected customers. Any time you respond to an offer for more information or for a free sample, you've identified yourself as a prospect and can expect follow-up sales pitches from a direct marketer. The StairMaster ad in Exhibit 17.5 is a marketer's attempt to initiate a dialogue with prospective customers. Ordering the free catalog and video, whether through the 800 number or on the website, begins the process of interactive marketing designed to ultimately produce the sale of another Free-Climber 4600.

Direct marketing programs are also initiated as a means to engage customers, seek their advice, furnish helpful information about using a product, reward customers for using a brand, and in general foster brand loyalty. For instance, the manufacturer of Valvoline motor oil seeks to build loyalty for its brand by encouraging young car owners to join the

12. Daniel Klein, "Disintegrated Marketing," *Harvard Business Review*, March 2003, 18, 19; Michael Fielding, "Spread the Word," *Marketing News*, February 15, 2005, 19, 20; Michael Fielding, "Direct Mail Still Has Its Place," *Marketing News*, November 1, 2006, 31, 33.

Valvoline Performance Team.[13] To join the team, young drivers just fill out a questionnaire that enters them into the Valvoline database. Team members receive posters, special offers on racing-team apparel, news about racing events that Valvoline has sponsored, and promotional reminders at regular intervals that reinforce the virtues of Valvoline for the driver's next oil change.

What's Driving the Growing Popularity of Direct Marketing?

The growth in popularity of direct marketing is due to a number of factors. Some of these have to do with changes in consumer lifestyles and technological developments that in effect create a climate more conducive to the practice of direct marketing. In addition, direct marketing programs offer unique advantages vis-à-vis conventional mass media advertising, leading many organizations to shift more of their marketing budgets to direct marketing activities.

From the consumer's standpoint, direct marketing's growing popularity might be summarized in a single word—*convenience*. Dramatic growth in the number of dual-income and single-person households has reduced the time people have to visit retail stores. Direct marketers provide consumers access to a growing range of products and services in their homes, thus saving many households' most precious resource—time.

More liberal attitudes about the use of credit and the accumulation of debt have also contributed to the growth of direct marketing. Credit cards are the primary means of payment in most direct marketing transactions. The widespread availability of credit cards makes it ever more convenient to shop from the comfort of one's home.

Exhibit 17.6 Finding that waterfall in Wyoming will take some planning, and Wyoming's Office of Travel & Tourism is happy to help. The adventure begins with a request for their vacation packet, and if the phone feels a little old fashioned, you know you can start the visit at www.wyomingtourism.org

Courtesy, Wyoming Travel & Tourism

Developments in telecommunications have also facilitated the direct marketing transaction. After getting off to a slow start in the late 1960s, toll-free telephone numbers have exploded in popularity to the point where one can hardly find a product or a catalog that does not include an 800 or 888 number for interacting with the seller. Whether one is requesting the StairMaster video, ordering a twill polo shirt from Eddie Bauer, or planning that adventure in Wyoming (see Exhibit 17.6), the preferred mode of access for many consumers has been the 800 number.

Another obvious development having a huge impact on the growth of direct marketing is the computer. The incredible diffusion of computer technology sweeping through all modern societies has been a tremendous boon to direct marketers. The computer now allows firms to track, keep records on, and interact with millions of customers with relative ease. As we will see in an upcoming discussion, the computer power now available for modest dollar amounts is fueling the growth of direct marketing's most potent tool—the marketing database.

And just as the computer has provided marketers with the tool they need to handle massive databases of customer information, it too has provided

13. Nash, "The Roots of Direct Marketing."

convenience-oriented consumers with the tool they need to comparison shop with a point and click. What could be more convenient than logging on to the Internet and pulling up a shopping agent like PriceScan.com or mySimon to check prices on everything from toaster ovens to snowboards? Why leave the apartment?

Direct marketing programs also offer some unique advantages that make them appealing compared with what might be described as conventional mass marketing. A general manager of marketing communications with AT&T's consumer services unit put it this way: "We want to segment our market more; we want to learn more about individual customers; we want to really serve our customers by giving them very specific products and services. Direct marketing is probably the most effective way in which we can reach customers and establish a relationship with them."[14] As you might expect, AT&T is one of those organizations that has shifted more and more of its marketing dollars into direct marketing programs.

The appeal of direct marketing is enhanced further by the persistent emphasis on producing measurable effects. For instance, in direct marketing, it is common to find calculations such as **cost per inquiry (CPI)** or **cost per order (CPO)** being featured in program evaluation. These calculations simply divide the number of responses to a program by that program's cost. When calculated for every program an organization conducts over time, CPI and CPO data tell an organization what works and what doesn't work in its competitive arena.

This emphasis on producing and monitoring measurable effects is realized most effectively through an approach called *database marketing*.[15] Working with a database, direct marketers can target specific customers, track their actual purchase behavior over time, and experiment with different programs for affecting the purchasing patterns of these customers. Obviously, those programs that produce the best outcomes become the candidates for increased funding in the future. Let's look into database marketing.

2 Database Marketing.

If any ambiguity remains about what makes direct marketing different from marketing in general, that ambiguity can be erased by the database. The one characteristic of direct marketing that distinguishes it from marketing more generally is its emphasis on database development. Knowing who the best customers are along with what and how often they buy is a direct marketer's secret weapon.[16] This knowledge accumulates in the form of a marketing database.

Databases used as the centerpieces in direct marketing campaigns take many forms and can contain many different layers of information about customers. At one extreme is the simple mailing list that contains nothing more than the names and contact information of possible customers; at the other extreme is the customized marketing database that augments names and contact info with various additional information about customers' characteristics, past purchases, and product preferences. Understanding this distinction between mailing lists and marketing databases is important in appreciating the scope of database marketing.

Mailing Lists.

A **mailing list** is simply a file of names and addresses that an organization might use for contacting prospective or prior customers. Mailing lists are plentiful, easy to access, and inexpensive. For example, CD-ROM phone directories available for a

14. Gary Levin, "AT&T Exec: Customer Access Goal of Integration," *Advertising Age*, October 10, 1994, S1.

15. Like many authors, Winer contends that direct marketing starts with the creation of a database. See Russell Winer, "A Framework for Customer Relationship Management," *California Management Review*, Summer 2001, 89–105.

16. Ibid.

few hundred dollars provide a cheap and easy way to generate mailing lists. More-targeted mailing lists are available from a variety of suppliers. The range of possibilities is mind-boggling, including groupings like 238,737 subscribers to *Mickey Mouse Magazine*; 102,961 kindergarten teachers; 4,145,194 physical fitness enthusiasts; 117,758 Lord & Taylor credit card purchasers, and a whopping 269 archaeologists.[17]

Each time you subscribe to a magazine, order from a catalog, register your automobile, fill out a warranty card, redeem a rebate offer, apply for credit, join a professional society, or log in at a website, the information you provided about yourself goes on another mailing list. These lists are freely bought and sold through many means, including over the Internet. Sites such as Worldata and InfoUSA allow one to buy names and addresses, or email address lists, for as little as 10 cents per record. What's out there is remarkable—as exemplified by Exhibit 17.7

Two broad categories of lists should be recognized: the internal, or house, list versus the external, or outside, list. **Internal lists** are simply an organization's records of its own customers, subscribers, donors, and inquirers. **External lists** are purchased from a list compiler or rented from a list broker. At the most basic level, internal and external lists facilitate the two fundamental activities of the direct marketer: Internal lists are the starting point for developing better relationships with current customers, whereas external lists help an organization cultivate new business.

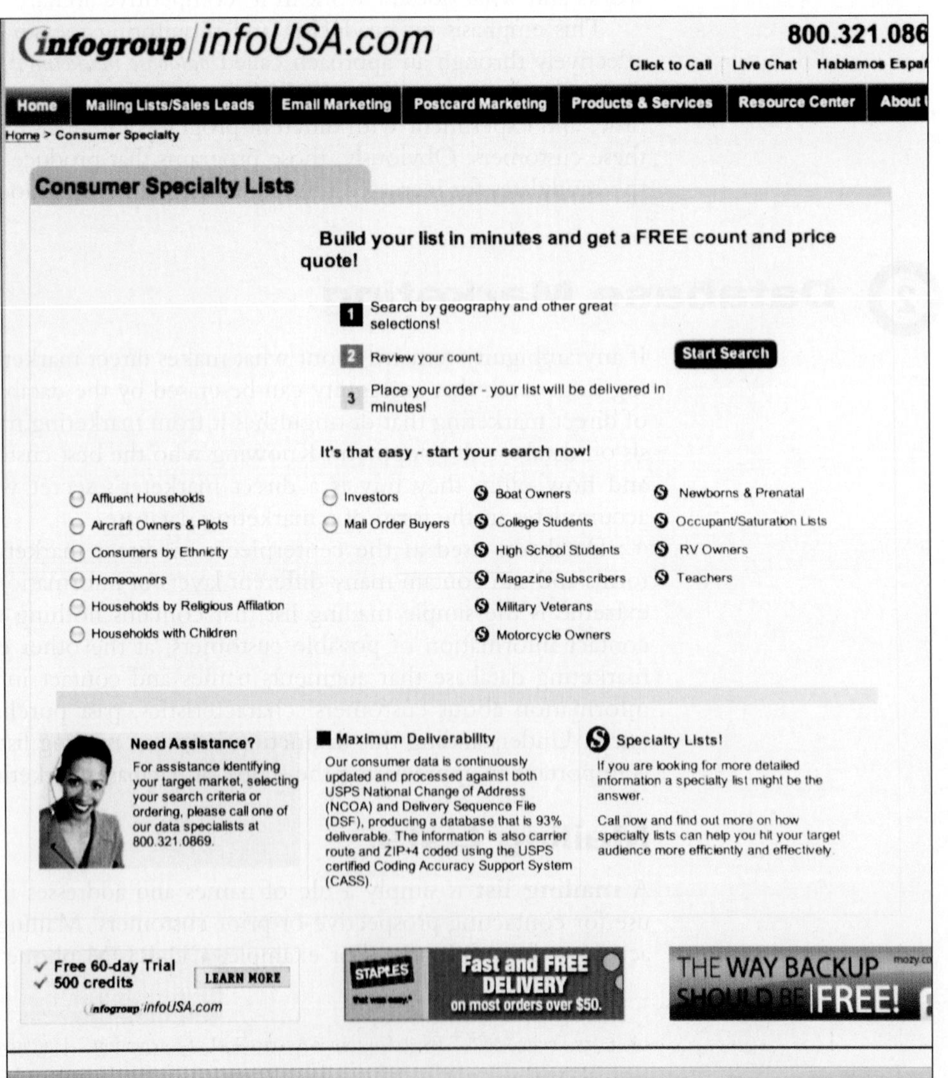

Exhibit 17.7 Start by defining the target, and then build your list!

Courtesy, Susan Van Etten

17. *The 2001 Mailing List Catalog* (New York: Hugo Dunhill Mailing Lists, 2001).

List Enhancement.

Name-and-address files, no matter what their source, are merely the starting point for database marketing. The next step in the evolution of a database is list enhancement. Typically this involves augmenting an internal list by combining it with other, externally supplied lists or databases. External lists can be appended or merged with a house list.

One of the most straightforward list enhancements entails simply adding or appending more names and addresses to an internal list. Proprietary name-and-address files may be purchased from other companies that operate in noncompetitive businesses. With today's computer capabilities, adding these additional households to an existing mailing list is simple. Many well-known companies such as Sharper Image, American Express, Bloomingdale's, and Hertz sell or rent their customer lists for this purpose.

A second type of list enhancement involves incorporating information from external databases into a house list. Here the number of names and addresses remains the same, but an organization ends up with a more complete description of who its customers are. Typically, this kind of enhancement includes any of four categories of information:

- ***Demographic data***—the basic descriptors of individuals and households available from the Census Bureau.
- ***Geo-demographic data***—information that reveals the characteristics of the neighborhood in which a person resides.
- ***Psychographic data***—data that allow for a more qualitative assessment of a customer's general lifestyle, interests, and opinions.
- ***Behavioral data***—information about other products and services a customer has purchased; prior purchases can help reveal a customer's preferences.

List enhancements that entail merging existing records with new information rely on software that allows the database manager to match records based on some piece of information the two lists share. For example, matches might be achieved by sorting on zip codes and street addresses. Many suppliers gather and maintain databases that can be used for list enhancement. One of the biggest is InfoUSA of Omaha, Nebraska. With 210 million people in its database, and literally dozens of pieces of information about each person, InfoUSA offers exceptional capabilities for list enhancement. Because of the massive size of the InfoUSA database, it has a high match rate (60 to 80 percent) when it is merged with clients' internal lists. A more common match rate between internal and external lists is around 50 percent.

The Marketing Database.

Mailing lists come in all shapes and sizes, and by enhancing internal lists they obviously can become rich sources of information about customers. But for a mailing list to qualify as a marketing database, one important additional type of information is required. Although a marketing database can be viewed as a natural extension of an internal mailing list, a **marketing database** also includes information collected directly from individual customers. Developing a marketing database involves pursuing dialogues with customers and learning about their individual preferences and behavioral patterns. This can be potent information for hatching marketing programs that will hit the mark with consumers.

Aided by the dramatic escalation in processing power that comes from every new generation of computer chip, marketers see the chance to gather and manage more information about every individual who buys, or could buy, from them. Their goal might be portrayed as an attempt to cultivate a kind of cybernetic intimacy with the customer. A marketing database represents an organization's collective memory, which allows the organization to make the kind of personalized offer that once was characteristic of the corner grocer in small-town America. For example, working in conjunction with The Ohio State University Alumni Association, Lands' End created a special autumn promotion to offer OSU football fans all their favorite gear just in time for the upcoming session. Print ads in the September issue of the OSU alumni magazine set the stage for a special catalog of merchandise mailed to Buckeye faithful. Of course, Lands' End had similar arrangements with other major universities to tap into fall football frenzy. Database marketing at its best puts an offer in the hands of the consumer that is both relevant and timely. That's cybernetic intimacy.

Database marketing can also yield important efficiencies that contribute to the marketer's bottom line. As suggested in Exhibits 17.8 and 17.9, like many other multichannel retailers, Cabela's finds it useful to create many targeted versions of its base or master catalogs, with seasonal points of emphasis. Why? The gender or age-specific versions run about 100 pages, versus more than 1,000 pages for some of its master catalogs. A customer or household receives the targeted versions based on its profile in Cabela's database and the time of year. These streamlined catalogs are a great way to make timely offerings to targeted households in a cost-effective manner. In a nutshell, that's what database marketing is all about.

A marketing database can have many valuable applications. Before we look at more applications, let's review the terminology introduced thus far. We now have seen that direct marketers use mailing lists, enhanced lists, and/or marketing databases as the starting points for developing many of their programs. The crucial distinction between a mailing list and a marketing database is that the latter includes direct input from customers. Building a marketing database entails pursuing an ongoing dialogue with customers while continually updating their records, and may also include attempts to engage a peer group to amplify the dialogue. Even though mailing lists can be rich sources of information for programming, a marketing database has a dynamic quality that sets it

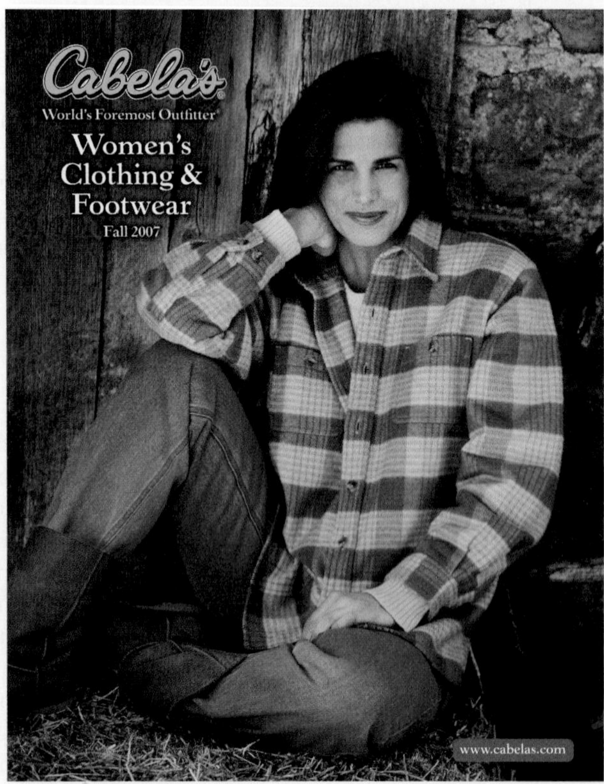

Exhibit 17.8 Cabela's for Women makes it easy to prepare for autumn's chill with style.

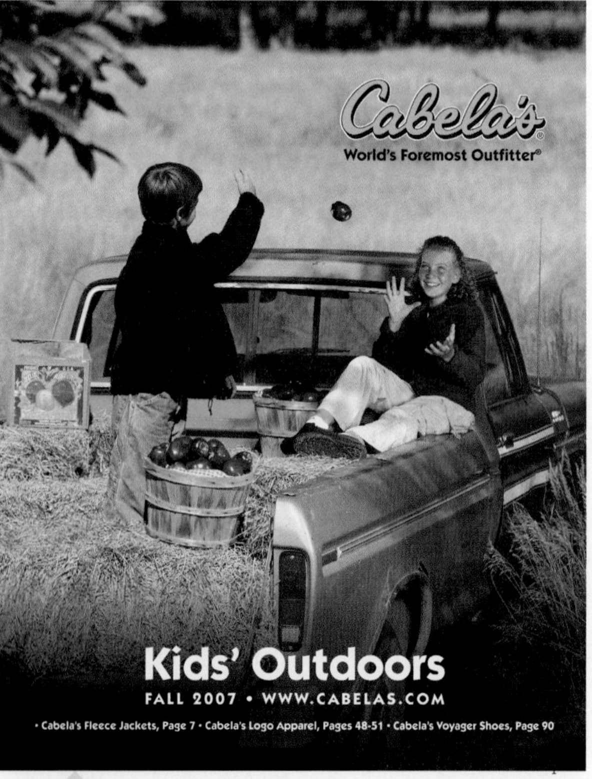

Exhibit 17.9 Cabela's for Kids is perfect for the shopper looking for those back-to-school bargains.

Social Media

Building Connections with NASCAR Fans

When Josh Linkler was young, he bought a lot of Cracker Jacks in hopes of finding decoder rings as his sticky surprise. Always intrigued by the decoder mystique, he used it as the big idea in launching a new marketing service. His company, ePrize, uses decoder contests to drive curious customers to the Web, where they can play games online and in the process provide information about themselves and their interests. Just like that, we have the makings of a marketing database.

In one program, Linkler worked with the Michigan International Speedway to build a database to unlock the secrets of NASCAR fans. It all starts with mass distribution of e-decoder game pieces, through ticket-order envelopes, movie theaters, and Pepsi retailers. The game pieces encourage NASCAR fans to go online to win prizes like a $10,000 garage makeover from Gladiator Garage Works (part of Whirlpool Corp. in Benton Harbor, Michigan). First-time players are required to give their name, address, email, age, and gender. With each return visit, more questions must be answered to go deeper into the game. Ultimately, the database gets enriched with answers to something like 150 demographic and lifestyle questions. There are also questions dealing with leisure-time pursuits like camping and fishing, and specific questions like "Do you shop at Cabela's?"

Detailed insights about NASCAR fans help advertisers to connect with them via personalized offers that are timely and relevant. For example, Cabela's, a huge outdoor sports retailer in Dundee, Michigan, can target just the right offers to hunters versus campers versus boaters versus fisherman in the ePrize database. But in this age of privacy concerns, why are these NASCAR fans so willing to divulge their personal information? Well, not all are willing, but Josh Linkler sees it simply as an issue of value. According to Linkler, "If you want consumers to speak to you and provide information, you have to give them something to get them to react." That's the essence of good "game mechanics," and apparently, the combination of a decoder game and a $10,000 Grand Prize can be pretty hard to resist.

Source: Kris Oser, "Speedway Effort Decodes NASCAR Fans," *Advertising Age,* May 17, 2004, 150; Kunel Patel, "All the World's a Game, and Brands Want to Play Along," *Advertising Age,* May 31, 2010, 4.

apart. The *Social Media* box above features a simple example of "game mechanics" to illustrate a proven tactic for fostering dialogue with focal customers.

Marketing Database Applications.

Many different types of customer-communication programs are driven by marketing databases. One of the greatest benefits of a database is that it allows an organization to quantify how much business the organization is actually doing with its current best customers. A good way to isolate the best customers is with a recency, frequency, and monetary (RFM) analysis. An **RFM analysis** asks how recently and how often a specific customer is buying from a company, and how much money he or she is spending per order and over time. With this transaction data, it is a simple matter to calculate the value of every customer to the organization and identify customers that have given the organization the most business in the past. Past behavior is an excellent predictor of future behavior, so yesterday's best customers are likely to be any organization's primary source of future business.

A marketing database can be a powerful tool for organizations that seek to create a genuine relationship with their best customers. The makers of Ben & Jerry's ice cream have used their database in two ways: to find out how customers react to potential new flavors and product ideas, and to involve their customers in social causes.[18] In one program, their goal was to find 100,000 people in their marketing database

18. Murray Raphel, "What's the Scoop on Ben & Jerry?" *Direct Marketing Magazine,* August 1994, 23, 24.

who would volunteer to work with Ben & Jerry's to support the Children's Defense Fund. Jerry Greenfield, cofounder of Ben & Jerry's, justified the program as follows: "We are not some nameless conglomerate that only looks at how much money we make every year. I think the opportunity to use our business and particularly the power of our business as a force for progressive social change is exciting."[19] Of course, when customers feel genuine involvement with a brand like Ben & Jerry's, they also turn out to be very loyal customers.

Reinforcing and recognizing your best customers is an essential application of the marketing database. This application may be nothing more than a simple follow-up letter that thanks customers for their business or reminds them of the positive features of the brand to reassure them that they made the right choice. Since date of birth is a common piece of information in a marketing database, it naturally follows that another great time to contact customers is on their birthday. Sunglass Hut International has used a birthday card mailing as part of its program to stay in a dialogue with its best customers. Of course, everyone likes a little birthday present too, so along with the card, Sunglass Hut includes a Customer Appreciation Check for $20 (shown in Exhibit 17.10) good at any Sunglass Hut store nationwide. Sunglass Hut executives maintain that this birthday card promotion, targeted to current best customers identified from their marketing database, is one of their best investments of advertising dollars.

To recognize and reinforce the behaviors of preferred customers, marketers in many fields are offering frequency-marketing programs that provide concrete rewards to frequent customers. **Frequency-marketing programs** have three basic elements: a *database*, which is the collective memory for the program; a *benefit package*, which is designed to attract and retain customers; and a *communication strategy*, which emphasizes a regular dialogue with the organization's best customers.

The casino industry is renowned for its application of frequency-marketing principles, and Harrah's Entertainment has set the standard for program innovation.[20] Harrah's "Total Rewards" program started out as a way for its 27 million members to accumulate points that could be cashed in for free meals and other

Exhibit 17.10 Think of your "best customer" as your most profitable customer. For most businesses, spending more advertising and promotional dollars to win more business from best customers is often money well spent. The real gold lies in not only one purchase but also in a continuous stream of purchases. Can a person ever have too many pairs of cool shades?

Courtesy, Sunglass Hut International

19. Murray Raphel, "What's the Scoop on Ben & Jerry?" *Direct Marketing Magazine*, August 1994, 23, 24.

20. Michael Bush, "Why Harrah's Loyalty Effort Is Industry's Gold Standard," *Advertising Age*, October 5, 2009, 8.

casino amenities. This is a good, simple approach, which was quickly copied by the competition. Harrah's subsequently upgraded its program on a number of dimensions. Now Harrah's has 10 million active members in its Total Rewards program, and they know a lot about each one. Things like—are you a golfer, do you like down pillows, do you prefer a room close to the elevator, and what games do you play—are all in the database. This information helps Harrah's tailor 250 million direct mail pieces per year and 8 million email messages per month to its Total Rewards members. This Total Rewards group generates $6.4 billion and 80 percent of Harrah's gaming revenue annually. That's why companies need to know their best customers.

Another common application for the marketing database is **cross-selling.** Since most organizations today have many different products or services they hope to sell, one of the best ways to build business is to identify customers who already purchase some of a firm's products and create marketing programs aimed at these customers but featuring other products. If they like our ice cream, perhaps we should also encourage them to try our frozen yogurt. If they have a checking account with us, can we interest them in a credit card? If customers dine in our restaurants on Fridays and Saturdays, with the proper incentives perhaps we can get them to dine with us midweek, when we really need the extra business. A marketing database can provide a myriad of opportunities for cross-selling.

A final application for the marketing database is a natural extension of cross-selling. Once an organization gets to know who its current customers are and what they like about various products, it is in a much stronger position to go out and seek new customers. Knowledge about current customers is especially valuable when an organization is considering purchasing external mailing lists to append to its marketing database. If a firm knows the demographic characteristics of current customers—knows what they like about products, knows where they live, and has insights about their lifestyles and general interests—then the selection of external lists will be much more efficient. The basic premise here is simply to try to find prospects who share many of the same characteristics and interests with current customers. And what's the best vehicle for coming to know the current, best customers? Marketing database development.

The Privacy Concern.

One large dark cloud looms on the horizon for database marketers: consumers' concerns about invasion of privacy. It is easy for marketers to gather a wide variety of information about consumers, and this is making the general public nervous. Many consumers are uneasy about the way their personal information is being gathered and exchanged by businesses and the government without their knowledge, participation, or consent. Of course, the Internet only amplifies these concerns because the Web makes it easier for all kinds of people and organizations to get access to personal information. In addition, there has been a recent surge in database development merging offline data like credit rating, savings levels, and home value with individuals' online search activities.[21] It's a pretty safe assumption these days that if you are online, some database somewhere is capturing your every click.

In response to public opinion, state and federal lawmakers have proposed and sometimes passed legislation to limit businesses' access to personal information. For instance, consumers' desire for privacy was clearly the motivation for the launch of the Federal Trade Commission's Do Not Call Registry. It proved to be a popular idea with consumers, but has many opponents in business, including the Direct Marketing Association.[22] The DMA estimated that the list would cost telemarketers on the order of $50 billion in lost sales. However, clever marketers have found ways to circumvent

21. Michael Learmonth, "Holy Grail of Targeting Is Fuel for Privacy Battle," *Advertising Age*, March 22, 2010, 1, 21.

22. Ira Teinowitz and Ken Wheaton, "Do Not Market," *Advertising Age*, March 12, 2007, 1, 44.

the "do not call" list with tactics like the lead card.[23] The lead card asks unsuspecting consumers to send in a postcard to receive free information about a product or service. By replying this way, consumers unknowingly forfeit their protection from telemarketers that "do not call" was supposed to provide.

As suggested by Exhibit 17.11, many in business are keenly aware of consumers' concerns about the privacy of their personal information. Companies can address customers' concerns about privacy if they remember two fundamental premises of database marketing. First, a primary goal for developing a marketing database is to get to know customers in such a way that an organization can offer them products and services that better meet their needs. The whole point of a marketing database is to keep junk mail to a minimum by targeting only exciting and relevant programs to customers. If customers are offered something they value, as with Harrah's Total Rewards members, they will welcome being in the database.

Second, developing a marketing database is about creating meaningful, long-term relationships with customers. If you want people's trust and loyalty, would you collect personal information from them and then sell it to a third party behind their back? We hope not! When collecting information from customers, an organization must help them understand why it wants the information and how it will use it. If the organization is planning on selling this information to a third party, it must get customers' permission. If the organization pledges that the information will remain confidential, it must honor that pledge. Integrity is fundamental to all meaningful relationships, including those involving direct marketers and their customers. Recall that it was his integrity as much as anything else that enabled L. L. Bean to launch his successful career as a direct marketer.

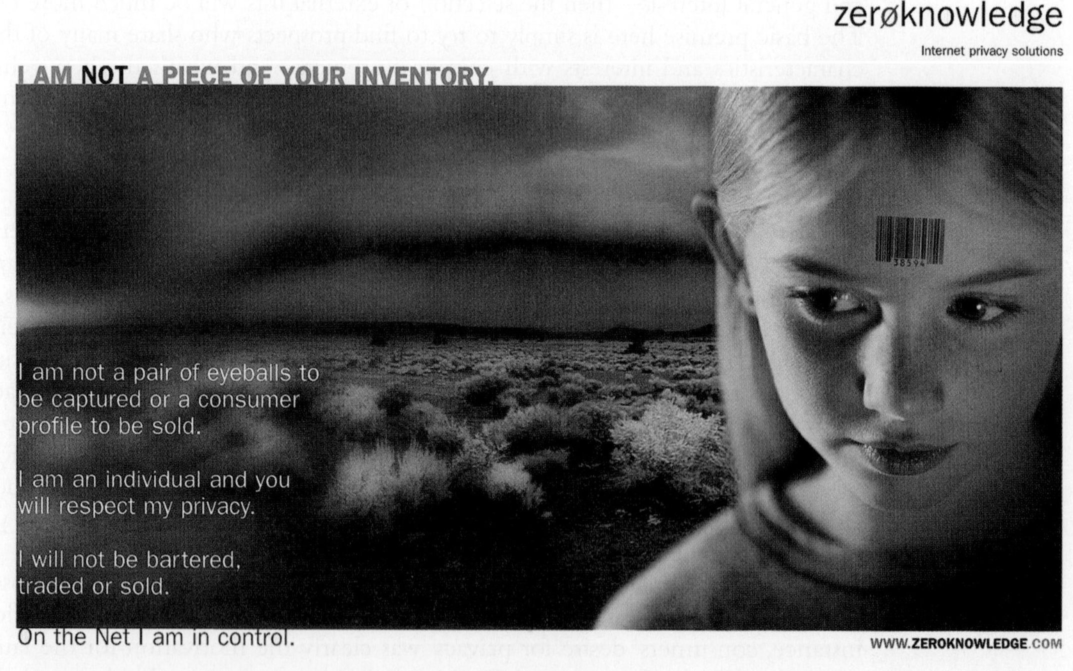

Exhibit 17.11 This Orwellian ad paints a dark picture of our future if database marketers go unchecked. There is definitely something about the Internet that has heightened people's concerns about who is in control of their personal information. Who controls your personal information? Does it matter to you?

Courtesy, Zero Knowledge Systems, Inc.

23. Jennifer Levitz and Kelly Greene, "Marketers Use Trickery to Evade No-Call Lists," *The Wall Street Journal*, October 26, 2007, A1, A14.

It will work for you too. Oh by the way, if you are one of those people who would like to do more to protect the privacy of your personal information, start with a visit to www.ftc.gov/privacy.

3 Media Applications in Direct Marketing.

Because mailing lists and marketing databases are the focal point for originating most direct marketing programs, information and arguments need to be communicated to customers in implementing these programs. As we saw in the definition of direct marketing offered earlier in this chapter, multiple media can be deployed in program implementation, and some form of immediate, measurable response is typically an overriding goal. The immediate response desired may be an actual order for services or merchandise, a request for more information, or the acceptance of a free trial offer. Because advertising conducted in direct marketing campaigns is typified by this emphasis on immediate response, it is commonly referred to as **direct response advertising.**

As you probably suspect, **direct mail** and **telemarketing** are the direct marketer's traditional media. However, all conventional media, such as magazines, radio, and television, can be used to deliver direct response advertising; nowadays, a wide array of companies are also deploying email as a most economical means of interacting with customers. In addition, a dramatic transformation of the television commercial—the infomercial—has become especially popular in direct marketing. Let's begin our examination of these media options by considering the advantages and disadvantages of the dominant devices—direct mail and telemarketing.

Exhibit 17.12 The U.S. Postal Service is saying, Use our services to drive consumers to your website. It's a great point: With millions of websites out there in cyberspace, you really must find economical ways to help people notice yours. For help reaching qualified visitors, the Postal Service suggests you visit—where else?—its website, www.usps.com/directmail/welcome.htm

Courtesy, United States Postal Service

Direct Mail.

Direct mail has some notable faults as an advertising medium, not the least of which is cost. It can cost 15 to 20 times more to reach a person with a direct mail piece than it would to reach that person with a television commercial or newspaper advertisement.[24] In addition, in a society where people are constantly on the move, mailing lists are commonly plagued by bad addresses. Each bad address represents advertising dollars wasted. And direct mail delivery dates, especially for bulk, third-class mailings, can be unpredictable. When precise timing of an advertising message is critical to its success, direct mail can be the wrong choice.

But as suggested by the ad from the U.S. Postal Service in Exhibit 17.12, there will be times when direct mail is the right choice. Direct mail's advantages stem from the selectivity of the medium. When an advertiser begins with a database of prospects, direct mail can be the perfect vehicle for reaching those prospects with little waste. Also, direct mail is a flexible medium that allows message adaptations on literally a household-by-household basis.

24. Stone, *Successful Direct Marketing Methods.*

Direct mail as a medium also lends itself to testing and experimentation. With direct mail it is common to test two or more different appeal letters using a modest budget and a small sample of households. The goal is to establish which version yields the largest response. When a winner is decided, that form of the letter is backed by big-budget dollars in launching the organization's primary campaign.

In addition, the array of formats an organization can send to customers is substantial with direct mail. It can mail large, expensive brochures, CDs, or DVDs. It can use pop-ups, foldouts, scratch-and-sniff strips, or a simple, attractive postcard, as in Exhibit 17.13. If a product can be described in a limited space with minimal graphics, there really is no need to get fancy with the direct mail piece.

Telemarketing.

Telemarketing is probably the direct marketer's most invasive tool. As with direct mail, contacts can be selectively targeted, the impact of programs is easy to track, and experimentation with different scripts and delivery formats is simple and practical. Because telemarketing involves real, live, person-to-person dialogue, no medium produces better response rates. On the other hand, telemarketing is expensive on a cost-per-contact basis. Further, telemarketing does not share direct mail's flexibility in terms of delivery options. When you reach people in their home or workplace, you have a limited amount of time to convey information and request some form of response.

You already know the biggest concern with telemarketing. It is a powerful yet highly intrusive medium that must be used with discretion. High-pressure telephone calls at inconvenient times can alienate customers. Telemarketing will give best results over the long run if it is used to maintain constructive dialogues with existing customers and qualified prospects.

Email.

Perhaps the most controversial tool deployed of late by direct marketers has been unsolicited or "bulk" email. Commonly referred to as spam, this junk email can get you in big trouble with consumers. In a worst-case scenario, careless use of the

Exhibit 17.13 This postcard for Fleece and Flannel announces the grand opening of its new store in Livingston, Montana. In that part of the world, it's perfectly natural to select a fly-fishing guide and guru to serve as your spokeswoman. Learn more at www.MontanaFleeceAndFlannel.com and www.visitmt.com

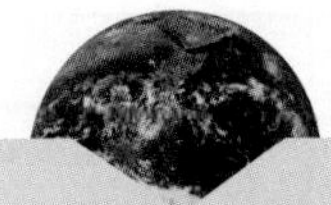

Globalization

USA Dominates in World Cup of SPAM

The results are in and USA is number 1 again. USA produces twice as much spam as any other country in the world. Here's your Top 5, with their percentage of spam generated in parentheses: USA (15.2 percent), India (7.7 percent), Brazil (5.5 percent), United Kingdom (4.6 percent), and S. Korea (4.2 percent). France, Germany, Italy, Russia, and Vietnam round out the Top 10.

Seems everybody hates spam, which raises the perplexing question, why is there more all the time? Well, it's probably not accurate to say that everybody hates spam. Laura Betterly prefers to call it commercial or bulk email, and she certainly doesn't hate it. After all, she makes her living by delivering bulk email, direct from her home office to you. The company that Betterly founded with three of her friends can send out as many as 60 million email messages a month.

Her crown jewel is a list of 100 million email addresses. Betterly assembled it from a number of sources, including Excite, About.com, and Ms. Cleo's psychic website. Like most spammers, she also makes money by selling email addresses to other bulk emailers, and she is always looking to add more names to her list, when the price is right. Although large companies too are in the business of sending unsolicited, bulk email, a large part of this industry is small entrepreneurs like Laura Betterly. There's nothing hard about it.

Now here's the secret as to why there is more spam all the time—it's a profitable business. According to Betterly, depending on the commission she negotiates, it is possible to make money on a bulk emailing when as few as 100 people respond out of a mailing of 10 million. No doubt spammers are able to survive with response rates that could never work for the paper-junk mailer. For "snail mail" the direct marketer is typically looking for a response of 2 percent or better to turn a profit on the program. For bulk email, profits kick in with a response rate of 0.001 percent. Sometimes you wonder how anyone would respond to the kinds of messages we all receive in our email boxes, but the point is, if 1 out of 1,000 responds, Betterly is making money, and helps keep USA number 1!

Sources: Mathew Schwartz, "U.S. Extends Spam Lead," www.informationweek.com, July 14, 2010; Mylene Mangalindan, "Web Vigilantes Give Spammers a Big Dose of Their Medicine," *The Wall Street Journal*, May 19, 2003, A1, A13; Mylene Mangalindan, "For Bulk Emailer, Pestering Millions Offers a Path to Profit," *The Wall Street Journal*, November 13, 2002, A1, A17.

email tool can earn one's company the label of a "spammer," and because of the community-oriented character of the Internet, can then be a continuing source of negative buzz. But is this discouraging companies from deploying this tool? Hardly. Recent studies document that 97 percent of all emails received by business email servers are essentially spam.[25] Better filtering tools are helping control this epidemic, but as suggested by the *Globalization* box, there is no end in sight for the worldwide scourge.

There is a school of thought that says some consumers are not averse to receiving targeted email advertisements, and that as the Internet continues to evolve as an increasingly commercial medium, those companies that observe proper etiquette on the Net (dare we say "Netiquette"?) will be rewarded through customer loyalty.[26] The key premise of netiquette is to get the consumer's permission to send information about specific products or services, or, to use the current buzzword, they must "opt in." This opt-in premise has spawned a number of e-marketing service providers who claim to have constructed email lists of consumers who have "opted in" for all manner of products and services. Exhibit 17.14 features a firm that works diligently to make email marketing a workable alternative for conscientious advertisers. They contend the future of direct marketing will be in reaching those people who have already said "Yes."

25. Mathew Schwartz, "U.S. Extends Spam Lead," www.informationweek.com, July 14, 2010.

26. Cara Beardi, "Opt-In Taken to Great Heights," *Advertising Age*, November 6, 2000, S54; Michael Battisto, "Preparation Yields Spam-Free Email Lists," *Marketing News*, February 17, 2003, 17.

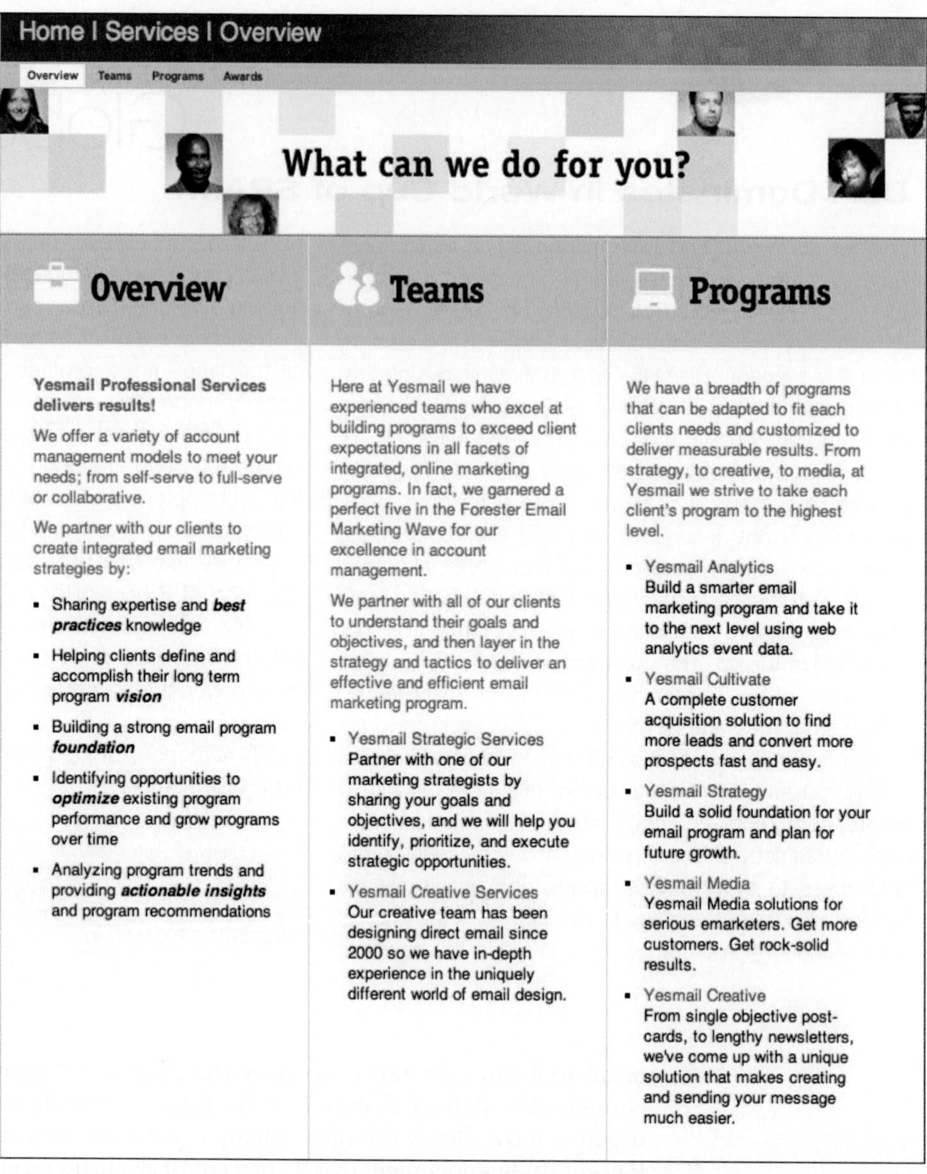

Exhibit 17.14 As always, be sure to engage with the right team.

Courtesy, Susan Van Etten

Our advice is to stay away from the low-cost temptations of bulk email. The quickest way to get flamed and damage your brand name is to start sending out bulk emails to people who do not want to hear from you. Instead, through database development, ask your customers for permission to contact them via email. Honor their requests. Don't abuse the privilege by selling their email addresses to other companies, and when you do contact them, have something important to say. Seth Godin, whose 1999 book *Permission Marketing* really launched the "opt-in" mindset, puts it this way: "The best way to make your [customer] list worthless is to sell it. The future is, this list is mine and it's a secret."[27] Isn't it funny—you can imagine L. L. Bean feeling exactly the same way about his customer list a century ago.

Direct Response Advertising in Other Media.

Direct marketers have experimented with many other methods in trying to convey their appeals for a customer response. In magazines, a popular device for executing

27. Jodi Mardesich, "Too Much of a Good Thing," *Industry Standard*, March 19, 2001, 85.

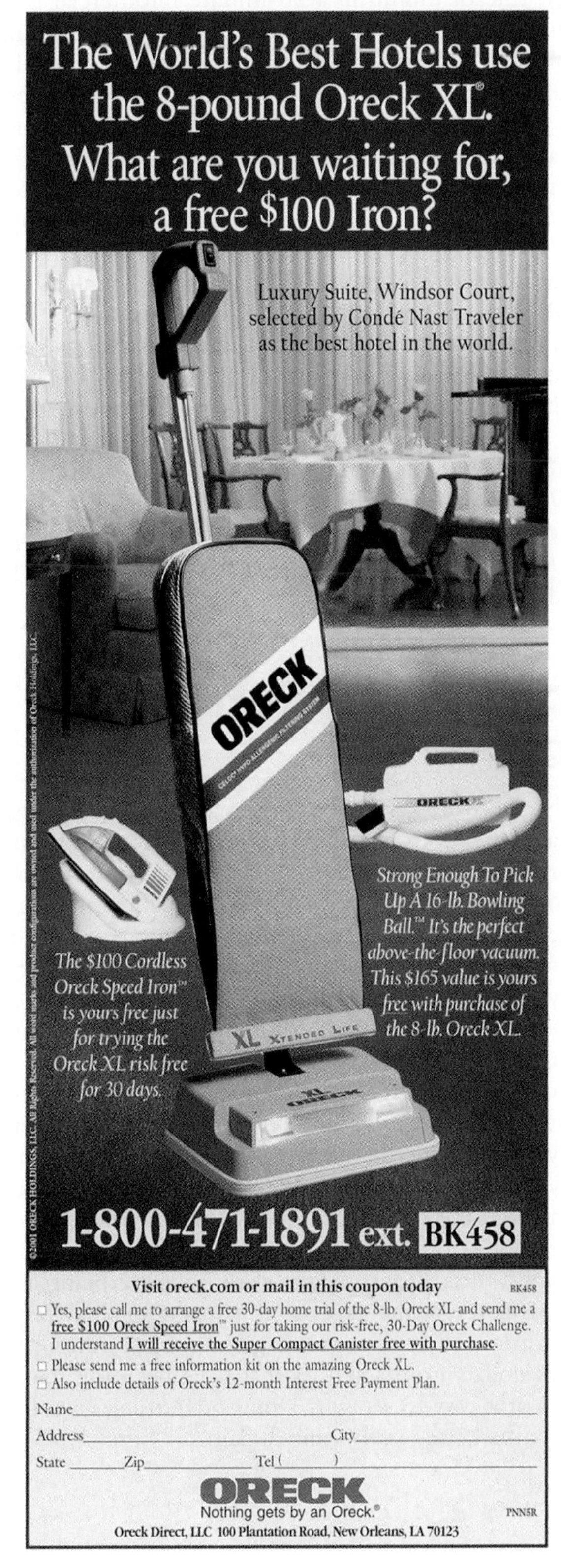

Exhibit 17.15 Nothing fancy here. Just good, sound, direct marketing.

Courtesy, Oreck Corporation

a direct marketer's agenda is the bind-in insert card. Thumb through a copy of any magazine and you will see how effective these light-cardboard inserts are at stopping the reader and calling attention to themselves. Insert cards not only promote their product but also provide tempting offers like $25 off your next order at Coldwater Creek, a free sample of Skoal smokeless tobacco, or 12 CDs for the price of one for new members of the BMG Music Club.

When AT&T introduced the first 800 number in 1967, it simply could not have known how important this service would become to direct marketing. Newspaper ads from *The Wall Street Journal* provide toll-free numbers for requesting everything from really cheap online trading services to leasing a Learjet. If you watch late-night TV, you may know the 800 number to call to order that Snuggie for you and your dog (sales to date: people—18 million; dogs—only 2 million).[28] Finally, magazine ads like the one shown in Exhibit 17.15 from *Bon Appetit* are commonly used to provide an 800 number to initiate contact with customers. As these diverse examples indicate, toll-free numbers make it possible to use nearly any medium for direct response purposes.

Infomercials.

The infomercial is a novel form of direct response advertising that merits special mention. An **infomercial** is fundamentally just a long television advertisement made possible by the lower cost of ad space on many cable and satellite channels. They range in length from 2 to 60 minutes, but the common length is 30 minutes. Although producing an infomercial is more like producing a television program than it is like producing a 30-second commercial, infomercials are all about selling. There appear to be several keys to successful use of this unique vehicle.[29]

A critical factor is testimonials from satisfied users. Celebrity testimonials can help catch a viewer as he or she is channel surfing past the program, but celebrities aren't necessary, and, of course, they add to the production costs. Whether testimonials are from celebrities or from folks just like us, without them your chances of producing a profitable infomercial diminish hugely.

Another key point to remember about infomercials is that viewers are not likely to stay tuned for the full 30 minutes. An infomercial is a 30-minute direct response sales pitch, not a classic episode of *South Park* or *The Simpsons*. The implication here is that the call to action should come not only at the end of the infomercial; most of the audience could be long gone by

28. Katherine Rosman, "As Seen on TV… and in Aisle 5," *The Wall Street Journal*, January 28, 2010, D1, D4.

29. Thomas Mucha, "Stronger Sales in Just 28 Minutes," *Business 2.0*, June 2005, 56–60; Elizabeth Holmes, "Golf-Club Designer Hopes to Repeat TV Success," *The Wall Street Journal*, January 30, 2007, B4.

minute 28 into the show. A good rule of thumb in a 30-minute infomercial is to divide the program into 10-minute increments and close three times. Each closing should feature the 800 number or Web address that allows the viewer to order the product or request more information. And an organization should not offer information to the customer unless it can deliver speedy follow-up; same-day response should be the goal in pursuing leads generated by an infomercial.

Many different types of products and services have been marketed using infomercials. CD players, self-help videos, home exercise equipment, kitchen appliances, and Annette Funicello Collectible Bears have all had success with the infomercial. Although it is easy to associate the infomercial with things such as the Ronco Showtime Rotisserie & BBQ (yours for just four easy payments of $39.95!), many familiar brands have experimented with this medium. Brand marketers such as Quaker State, Primestar, Lexus, Monster, Disney, Hoover, Kal Kan, and yes, Mercedes-Benz, have all used infomercials to help inform consumers about their offerings.[30]

How does one explain the growing appeal of the infomercial for all manner of marketers? Data generated by TiVo's StopWatch service are revealing.[31] They show that bare-bones, direct response ads for products like Perfect Pushup exercise equipment are among the least likely to be zapped. That kind of result will get lots of scrutiny from all corners of the advertising business.

4 Closing the Sale with Direct Marketing and/or Personal Selling.

As we have pointed out repeatedly, the wide variety of options available to marketers for reaching customers poses a tremendous challenge with respect to coordination and integration. Organizations are looking to achieve the synergy that can come when various options reach the consumer with a common and compelling message. However, to work in various media, functional specialists both inside and outside an organization need to be employed. It then becomes a very real problem to get the advertising manager, special events manager, sales promotion manager, and Web designer to work in harmony.[32] And now we must add to the list of functional specialists the direct marketing or database manager.

The evolution and growing popularity of direct marketing raise the challenge of achieving integrated communication to new heights. In particular, the development of a marketing database commonly leads to interdepartmental rivalries and can create major conflicts between a company and its advertising agency. The marketing database is a powerful source of information about the customer; those who do not have direct access to this information will be envious of those who do. In addition, the growing use of direct marketing campaigns must mean that someone else's budget is being cut. Typically, direct marketing programs come at the expense of conventional advertising campaigns that might have been run on television, in magazines, or in other mass media. Since direct marketing takes dollars from activities that have been the staples of the traditional ad agency business, it is easy to see why a pure advertising guru like Saatchi's Kevin Roberts views direct marketing with some disdain.[33]

30. Evantheia Schibsted, "Ab Rockers, Ginsu Knives, E320s," *Business 2.0*, May 29, 2001, 46–49; Jack Neff, "Wait, There's More! DRTV Is Gaining Mainstream Appeal," *Advertising Age*, March 23, 2009, 17.

31. Brian Steinberg, "How To Stop Them from Skipping: TiVo Tells All," *Advertising Age*, July 16, 2007, 1, 33.

32. Laura Q. Hughes and Kate MacArthur, "Soft Boiled," *Advertising Age*, May 28, 2001, 3, 54; Klein, "Disintegrated Marketing," 18, 19.

33. Alessandra Galloni, "Is Saatchi Helping Publicis' Bottom Line?" *The Wall Street Journal*, June 22, 2001, B6.

There are no simple solutions for achieving integrated communication, but one classic approach is the establishment of a marketing communications manager, or "marcom" manager for short.[34] A **marcom manager** plans an organization's overall communications program and oversees the various functional specialists inside and outside the organization to ensure that they are working together to deliver the desired message to the customer, which ultimately yields a product sale. Of course the pivotal role for direct marketing programs in this process is to establish dialogue with customers, and then close the sale.

The Critical Role of Personal Selling.

This brings us to the field of personal selling, yet another unique functional specialization in the business world. **Personal selling** is the face-to-face communications and persuasion process. Products that are higher priced, complicated to use, require demonstration, must be tailored to user needs, involve a trade-in, or are judged at the point of purchase are heavily dependent on personal selling. Household consumers and business buyers are frequently confronted with purchase decisions that are facilitated by interaction with a salesperson. In many decision contexts, only a qualified and well-trained salesperson can address the questions and concerns of a potential buyer. Fail to get the dialogue right at this critical stage of the purchase process and all other advertising efforts will end up being wasted.

There are many different types of sales jobs. A salesperson can be engaged in order taking, creative selling, or supportive communication. The discussion that follows demonstrates that the communication task for each type of selling varies dramatically.

The least complex type of personal selling is order taking. Its importance, however, should not be underestimated. **Order taking** involves accepting orders for merchandise or scheduling services. Order takers deal with existing customers who are lucrative to a business due the low cost of generating additional revenues from them. Order takers can also deal with new customers, which means that they need to be trained well enough to answer the basic questions a new customer might have about a product or service. Order takers are responsible for communicating with buyers in such a way that a quality relationship is maintained. This type of selling rarely involves communicating large amounts of information. However, a careless approach to this function can be a real turn-off for the loyal consumer, and can end up damaging the relationship.

Creative selling requires considerable effort and expertise. Situations where creative selling takes place range from retail stores through the selling of services to business and the sale of large industrial installations and component parts. **Creative selling** is the type of selling where customers rely heavily on the salesperson for technical information, advice, and service. In retail settings like those illustrated in Exhibits 17.16 and 17.17, stores selling higher-priced items and specialty goods must have a trained sales staff and emphasize customer and product knowledge. The services of an insurance agent, stockbroker, media representative, or real estate agent represent another type of creative selling. These salespeople provide services customized to the unique needs and circumstances of each buyer.

The most complex and demanding of the creative selling positions is in business-to-business markets. Many times these salespeople have advanced degrees in technical areas like chemical engineering, computer science, or any of the medical professions. Technical salespeople who deal in large-dollar purchases and complex corporate decisions for specialized component parts, medical equipment, or raw materials have tremendous demands placed on them. They are often called on to analyze the customer's product and production needs and carry this information

34. Don E. Schultz, Stanley I. Tannenbaum, and Robert F. Lauterborn, *Integrated Marketing Communications* (Lincolnwood, IL: NTC Business Books, 1993).

Exhibit 17.16 It's the salesperson's job to help the customer find the perfect gift.

Exhibit 17.17 Point of purchase is where the salesperson plays a critical role in determining the consumer's ultimate choice. The myriad of options available in today's markets for all sorts of cell phones amplifies the need for knowledgeable and well-trained sales personnel in this category.

back to the firm so that product design and supply schedules can be tailored for each customer.

Another noteworthy form of creative selling that has emerged in recent years is system selling. **System selling** entails selling a set of interrelated components that fulfill all or a majority of a customer's needs in a particular area. System selling has emerged because of the desire on the part of customers for "system solutions." Large industrial and government buyers, in particular, have come to seek out one or a small number of suppliers that can provide a full range of products and services needed in an area. Rather than dealing with multiple suppliers, these buyers then "system buy" from a single source. This trend in both buying and selling emphasizes the customer-relationship-management aspects of selling.

Creative selling tasks call for high levels of preparation, expertise, and contact with the customer and are primary to the process of relationship building. This doesn't happen by chance. Companies work hard to train their salespeople to be ready to address the needs of specific target markets. Take, for example, Honda and its launch of the Honda Fit.[35] This was an important launch for Honda because Fit represented the company's first true entry-level vehicle since the 1970s. But the buyers of entry-level vehicles have changed dramatically since the 1970s, and Honda was keen to bring its 7,500 U.S. sales associates up to speed on the profile of that new buyer. One key issue: This consumer is Internet savvy and likely will come to the showroom with lots of background research on the car. So step one for the salesperson: Find out what the customer already knows about the car. Don't rehash what she already knows. Surprise her and excite her with something new.

Finally, when a sales force is deployed for the purpose of supportive communication, it is not charged directly with closing the sale. Rather, the objective is to provide information to customers, offer services, and generally to foster goodwill. The **missionary salesperson** calls on accounts with the express purpose of monitoring the satisfaction of buyers and updating buyers' needs. They may provide product information after a purchase. Many firms also use direct marketing tools like telephone, fax, and email reminders to complement the efforts of the missionary salesperson in maintaining a dialogue with key customers.

Customer Relationship Management.

Salespeople can play a critical role as well in cultivating long-term relationships with customers—which often is referred to as a **customer relationship management (CRM)** program.[36] As an example, Merck spends 12 months training its sales representatives not only in knowledge of pharmaceuticals but also in trust-building techniques. Reps then are required to take regular refresher courses. Similarly, General Electric went so far as to station its own engineers full time at Praxair, Inc., a user of GE electrical equipment, to help the firm boost productivity. Furthermore, firms are discovering that CRM is a key strategy for gaining competitive advantage in many global markets.

Likewise, salespeople are also instrumental in ensuring customer satisfaction. Salespeople no longer simply approach customers with the intention of making a sale. Rather, they are problem solvers who work in partnership with customers. The salesperson is in the best position to analyze customer needs and propose the right solution on a case-by-case basis. By accepting this role, the sales force helps determine ways in which a firm can provide total customer satisfaction through its entire market offering. The great thing about satisfied consumers is they come back and buy again and again, which ultimately is the mechanism that sustains any business.

A Case in Point.

To wrap things up for this chapter, let's consider an example of what happens for a company when it strikes just the right balance among advertising, brand building, direct marketing, and personal selling. Let's start with a quiz. Who's number one in the specialty bedding business? No, it's not Crazy Larry's Mattress Barn or the House of Pillows. Think instead *The Sleep Number Bed* by Select Comfort.

The Select Comfort story represents a real metamorphosis from a tiny niche brand to a market leader.[37] For years, Select Comfort promoted its air mattresses with late-night infomercials along the lines of the Ronco Showtime Rotisserie & BBQ. Some consumers found value in the product as a good option to pull out of

35. Jacqueline Durett, "Road Warriors," *Sales & Marketing Management*, September 2006, 46–48.

36. Daniel Tynan, "The 10 Biggest CRM Mistakes," *Sales & Marketing Management*, December 2005, 30–33.

37. Willow Duttge, "Counting Sleep," *Advertising Age*, June 5, 2006, 4, 50.

the closet and blow up when friends dropped in for the night. But that's hardly a mainstream market, and Select Comfort was looking for more. Thus, the company invented a new brand, the Sleep Number bed, where the user can adjust the firmness of the mattress with a simple remote control using a numerical range from 1 to 100 (see the really big remote in Exhibit 17.18). But the company had a lot of work to do in building this brand. First, it had to overcome the perception that this is just a *very* expensive air mattress. Second, it had to shed the association with late-night cable TV to be accepted as a high-quality product found in upscale shopping malls across the United States.

A lot of things changed in building the Sleep Number brand. Although Select Comfort did not abandon its heritage as a direct marketer, new ad campaigns also included a healthy mix of newspaper advertising and local and prime-time TV spots. Often these ads would feature the first point of difference for the mattress: Couples sharing a bed could each adjust their side to just the right level of firmness (typically less than 50 for gals and more than 50 for guys). Patented technology in the remote control made this a sustainable point of difference.

Once basic awareness was established for the brand, Select Comfort next proceeded with the communication objective of associating the bed with deep, restorative sleep. And while all this brand building was taking place, targeted consumers continuously received direct mail pieces like the one in Exhibit 17.19 that were seeking to close the sale. A person typically doesn't buy a $1,000 mattress online or over the phone, but a visit to one of the company's 400 or so retail stores is another matter. There, well-trained sales personnel (often in their pajamas) patiently helped each customer find his or her sleep number, while reinforcing the importance of deep, restorative sleep. Of course, it is also the job of that salesperson to work to close the sale.

The Select Comfort example typifies a theme developed throughout this book. Each marketer must find the right balance of tools and tactics to get its points across to targeted consumers. Different tools and tactics play various roles in the process from building brand awareness to communicating key brand benefits, and ultimately closing the sale. If the various media and programs an organization employs are

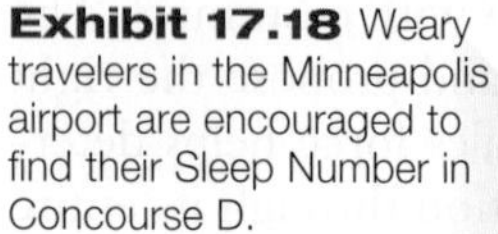

Exhibit 17.18 Weary travelers in the Minneapolis airport are encouraged to find their Sleep Number in Concourse D.

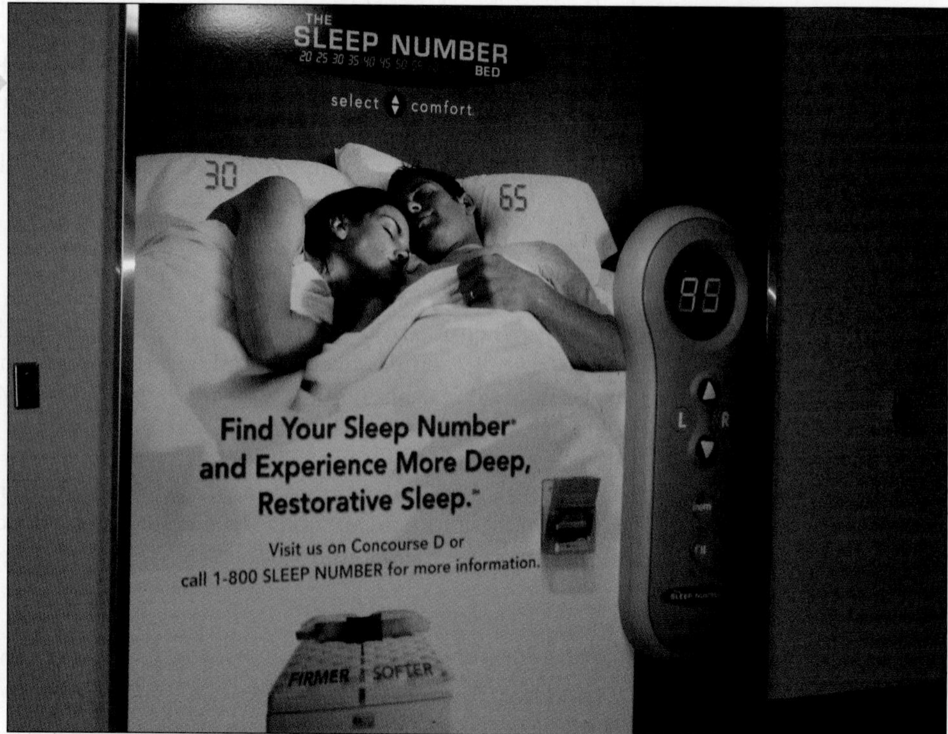

Exhibit 17.19
Hallmarks of the direct mail piece designed to help close the sale are an offer of special pricing, free accessories, encouragement to ACT NOW, and great financing arrangements if you ACT NOW.

sending different messages or mixed signals, the organization is only hurting itself. All the functional specialists who are part of the marketing and sales team must be working as a team. To achieve the synergy that will allow it to overcome the clutter of today's marketplace, and, for example, move to the top spot in the specialty bedding market, an organization has no choice but to pursue advertising and integrated brand promotion.

Summary

1 Identify the three primary purposes served by direct marketing and explain its growing popularity.

Many types of organizations are increasing their expenditures on direct marketing. These expenditures serve three primary purposes: direct marketing offers potent tools for closing sales with customers, for identifying prospects for future contacts, and for offering information and incentives that help foster loyalty. The growing popularity of direct marketing can be attributed to several factors. Direct marketers make consumption convenient: Credit cards, 800 numbers, and the Internet take the hassle out of shopping. In addition, today's computing power, which allows marketers to build and mine large customer information files, has enhanced direct marketing's impact. The emphasis on producing and tracking measurable outcomes is also well received by marketers in an era when everyone is trying to do more with less.

2 Distinguish a mailing list from a marketing database and review the many applications of each.

A mailing list is a file of names and addresses of current or potential customers, such as lists that might be generated by a credit card company or a catalog retailer. Internal lists are valuable for creating relationships with current customers, and external lists are useful in generating new customers. A marketing database is a natural extension of the internal list, but includes information about individual customers and their specific preferences and purchasing patterns. A marketing database allows organizations to identify and focus their efforts on their best customers. Recognizing and reinforcing preferred customers can be a potent strategy for building loyalty. Cross-selling opportunities also emerge once a database is in place. In addition, as one gains keener information about the motivations of current best customers, insights usually emerge about how to attract new customers.

3 Describe the prominent media used by direct marketers in delivering their messages to the customer.

Direct marketing programs emanate from mailing lists and databases, but there is still a need to deliver a message to the customer. Direct mail and telemarketing are common means used in executing direct marketing programs. Email has recently emerged as a low-cost alternative. Because the advertising done as part of direct marketing programs typically requests an immediate response from the customer, it is known as direct response advertising. Conventional media such as television, newspapers, magazines, and radio can also be used to request a direct response by offering an 800 number or a Web address to facilitate customer contact.

4 Explain the key role of direct marketing and personal selling in complementing other advertising activities.

Developing a marketing database, selecting a direct mail format, and producing an infomercial are some of the tasks attributable to direct marketing. These and other related tasks require more functional specialists, who further complicate the challenge of presenting a coordinated face to the customer. In addition, many products and services must be supported by well-trained sales personnel. Here again, the message consumers hear in advertising for any brand needs to be skillfully reinforced by the sales team. Fail to get the dialogue right at this final, critical stage of the purchase process and all other advertising efforts will end up being wasted. The sales force plays a critical role in the process because theirs is the job of closing the sale, while at the same time ensuring customer satisfaction.

Key Terms

direct marketing
cost per inquiry (CPI)
cost per order (CPO)
mailing list
internal lists
external lists
marketing database
RFM analysis
frequency-marketing programs
cross-selling
direct response advertising
direct mail
telemarketing
infomercial
marcom manager
personal selling
order taking
creative selling
system selling
missionary salesperson
customer relationship management (CRM)

Questions

1. Who is Lester Wunderman and in what ways does his historic campaign for Columbia House illustrate the mindset of direct marketing?

2. Direct marketing is defined as an interactive system of marketing. Explain the meaning of the term *interactive system* and give an example of a noninteractive system. How would an interactive system be helpful in the cultivation of brand loyalty?

3. Review the major forces that have promoted the growth in popularity of direct marketing. Can you come up with any reasons why its popularity might be peaking? What are the threats to its continuing popularity as a marketing approach?

4. Describe the various categories of information that a credit card company might use to enhance its internal mailing list. For each category, comment on the possible value of the information for improving the company's market segmentation strategy.

5. What is RFM analysis, and what is it generally used for? How would RFM analysis allow an organization to get more impact from a limited marketing budget? (Keep in mind that every organization views its marketing budget as too small to accomplish all that needs to be done.)

6. Compare and contrast frequency-marketing programs with the tools described in Chapter 15 as sales promotions directed at consumers. What common motivators do these two types of activities rely on? How are their purposes similar or different? What goal is a frequency-marketing program trying to achieve that would not be a prime concern with a sales promotion?

7. There's a paradox here, right? On the one hand, it is common to talk about building relationships and loyalty with the tools of direct marketing. On the other hand, direct marketing tools such as spam and telephone interruptions at home during dinner are constant irritants. How does one build relationships by using irritants? In your opinion, when is it realistic to think that the tools of direct marketing could be used to build long-term relationships with customers?

8. What is it about direct marketing that makes its growing popularity a threat to the traditional advertising agency?

9. Compare and contrast the purposes served by direct marketing versus personal selling.

10. Use the example of the Sleep Number bed to illustrate the importance of a balanced approach in executing advertising and integrated brand promotion.

Experiential Exercises

1. Since launching in 2004, Facebook has grown to more than 500 million users, many of whom frequent the site daily to interact with friends and join interest groups. Despite its popularity, Facebook has encountered ongoing privacy issues related to the capture and management of user data. Investigate a recent privacy controversy surrounding Facebook and answer the following questions: What data was captured without the consent of users? What might have been Facebook's purpose for capturing the data? Were third-party marketers involved in compromising user privacy? How might privacy concerns affect the relationship between Facebook and its customers?

2. Direct marketing is more than telemarketing and direct mail. The infomercial and direct response TV commercial are two forms of direct marketing that have proven wildly successful for Time Life Music, the Snuggie®, ShamWow®, and Slap Chop™. Break into groups and develop a direct marketing pitch that contains the key elements found in a popular infomercial or direct-response TV commercial. Present your product pitch to the class and hold a vote to determine which group delivered the most compelling direct response appeal.

3. Working in small teams, assess the direct marketing components at the website of Moosejaw, the athletic apparel retailer popular on college campuses. (See www.moosejaw.com.) For each direct marketing appeal that you can identify on the site, explain how the company would be able to measure the effectiveness of the appeal. As you evaluate the site, also identify any and all opportunities for the company to gather customer information that could enhance its database marketing efforts.

4. The chapter discusses how database marketing can be used not only as a tool to reach customers and close sales but also to aid product development. Working again in small teams, identify three distinct offerings that could be developed for well-known brands based on input and knowledge gleaned from customer and sales databases. As you propose the new products or services, identify specific types of database information that could influence the development process.

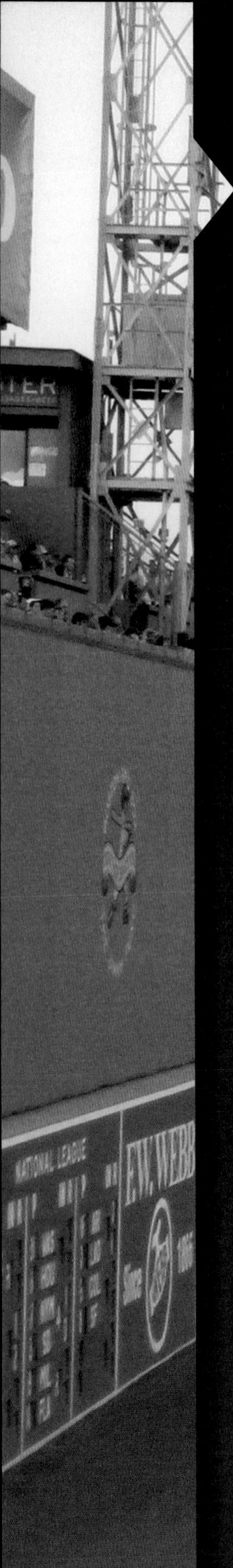

Chapter 18

Public Relations, Influencer Marketing, and Corporate Advertising

After reading and thinking about this chapter, you will be able to do the following:

1. Explain the role of public relations as part of an organization's overall advertising and IBP strategy.
2. Detail the objectives and tools of public relations.
3. Describe two basic strategies motivating an organization's public relations activities.
4. Illustrate the strategies and tactics used in influencer marketing programs.
5. Discuss the applications and objectives of corporate advertising.

Charmin
Restrooms!
enjoy the go
SEE THE FUTURE OF POWER
DURACELL
MARTPOWER LAB

Introductory Scenario: Bring on the Buzz.

When one has a hip or novel brand like Red Bull, Droid, Mini Cooper, iPad, or Lady Gaga, it's not hard to get consumers and the media buzzing. But in many ways those are the exceptions. Often it is the case that we are working with simple products and well-known brands where the excitement has faded long ago. The challenge faced by many marketers is creating interest, building buzz, motivating trial (or re-trial), and cultivating relevance for brands that are all too familiar. Take, for example, toilet paper.

Most people use it on a regular basis. Many don't recall the brand they last bought and believe that it's all pretty much the same stuff. It's a low-interest, hard-to-differentiate product category where brands like Charmin and Cottonelle have been around forever. "Mr. Whipple, please don't squeeze the Charmin!" was an ad slogan that created great buzz for the Charmin brand and made Mr. Whipple famous—40 years ago.

So how does one build buzz for a brand like Charmin? Well, it can be as simple as start with a good idea and build it over time. Ask yourself the question, where could we go to feature our brand that would delight the consumer and get people talking? Better yet, get lots of people talking and tweeting with lots of coverage by media of all kinds. Add in a little potty humor with a heavy dose of celebrity and you're really on to something. The Charmin people now refer to that something as their Enjoy the Go! Campaign hosted every year over the holiday season at the "Crossroads of the World" in Times Square in NYC. It's an ideal venue to offer thousands of holiday revelers a perfect Broadway experience, with Charmin as the star of the show (see Exhibits 18.1 and 18.2).

From its humble beginnings in 2000 as a campaign to provide clean restrooms at state fairs, Enjoy the Go! has emerged as a marketing juggernaut for Charmin, involving a dozen or more support agencies and the intensity of a new product launch, each time out. To reach its goal of a billion media impressions, the Charmin team used a multi-stage program in one of its most successful executions. The first stage (following months of planning) involved a national job search to create The Go

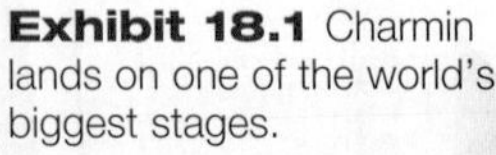

Exhibit 18.1 Charmin lands on one of the world's biggest stages.

Exhibit 18.2 The perfect potty on Broadway, brought to you by those lovable Charmin bears.

Team (TGT), who would serve as street ambassadors welcoming visitors to the Charmin restrooms. TGT members were also screened for social media skills, in that they would play a key role in activating social media from the front lines. The offer of $10,000 for five weeks of work generated hundreds of applicants and lots of enthusiasm, per Exhibit 18.3. An American Idol-like interviewing format caught the fancy of media outlets ranging from Fox News to The Huffington Post to NBC Nightly News. It was a genius idea that generated more than a billion media impressions, *before* the first flush.

Next up was the first flush with Charmin's King of the Throne Mario Lopez doing the honors, and lots more media attention from outlets like Yahoo! News and NPR. Grand openings are good, but you can't stop there if you want the buzz to endure. To get more media attention, it's always helpful to engage more celebrities, and they get excited when there's a chance to benefit their favorite causes. Mario Cantone, Mario Lopez, Sherri Sheppard, and Martina McBride, along with the TGT, designed fanciful toilet covers to draw donations for designated charities. It's a natural combination in the holiday season and brought the media back again and again after opening day.

So you're on Broadway—what else might motivate the media to write more, say more, blog more about an upscale potty experience? Seems like a no brainer to stage the first ever Broadway musical in a public restroom with the Charmin bears playing a support role. More celebrities, more cheeky

Exhibit 18.3 Potty madness in Times Square! A $10,000 salary for five weeks of work generated an enthusiastic response, per the tweet of corner 311… walked by 1000 people by the Sheraton auditioning to be a Charmin Ambassador.

humor, more YouTube videos, and naturally, more media coverage followed. *The New York Post*, The Daily Beast, CNN, The Today Show, *The Seattle Times*, The Street.com, Jay Leno—it would be impossible to list them all, but suffice it to say that the marketers of Charmin know how to create a big buzz for toilet paper. And they busted the doors off any of their previous programs with more than 3 billion conventional and social media impressions. That's a worthy outcome for Charmin, because media impressions translate into top-of-the-mind awareness, which is an important driver of brand choice for toilet tissue at the shelf. See you next season in Times Square!

The Charmin campaign in NYC is a great example to launch this final chapter. It brings to life the whole idea of buzz building that is increasingly popular in marketing today, and illustrates the synergies that obtain when all the pieces fit together, no matter what the product category. Activating social media, engaging mainstream media, selecting celebrity spokespersons, staging a branded experience, and orchestrating skillful teamwork among client, PR firm, digital, design, and talent agencies, just to name a few, is the ticket to blowing the doors off. As many have argued, there is a convergence taking place among the skill sets of marketers, advertisers, and public relations professionals.[1] In this chapter we will take you through the fundamentals of buzz building while adding public relations savvy to your IBP tool kit to fill out that skill set.

One can argue that we've entered an exciting new era for public relations. PR and buzz building have never been hotter. Public relations has moved well beyond its traditional role of simply managing goodwill or "relations" with a firm's many "publics," which can take the form of "damage control" in the face of negative publicity. The traditional functions are still important, but there's much more going on in PR circles today. Another major topic in this chapter—Influencer Marketing—will emphasize public relations activities as a dedicated brand-building agenda, reflecting the new emphasis in PR.

Last but not least, corporate advertising is also considered in this final chapter. Corporate advertising typically uses major media to communicate a unique, broad-based message that is distinct from more product-specific brand building. Corporate advertising contributes to the development of an overall image for a firm without touting specific products or services. Corporate advertising has a lot to do with the trustworthiness and reputation of a firm. As consumers are becoming increasingly informed and sophisticated, they are also demanding a higher standard of conduct from the companies they patronize. When a company has established trust and integrity, it is of course much easier to build productive relationships with consumers.

1 Public Relations.

The classic role of **public relations** is to foster goodwill between a firm and its many constituent groups. These constituent groups include customers, stockholders, suppliers, employees, government entities, citizen action groups, and the general public. The firm's public relations function seeks to highlight positive events like outstanding quarterly sales and profits (to stockholders), or noteworthy community service programs (to government entities and the general public). PR is also used strategically for "damage control" when adversity strikes. All organizations at some point face adversity. In addition, new techniques in public relations have fostered a bolder, more aggressive role for PR in many IBP campaigns.

1. Matthew Schwartz, "New Influence," *Advertising Age*, October 26, 2009, S4, S5; Michael Bush, "Growth of Social Media Shifts PR Chiefs Toward Center of Marketing Departments," *Advertising Age*, September 21, 2009, 7.

A New Era for Public Relations?

There are many forces at work that support a growing role for PR activities as part of the advertising and IBP campaigns for all sorts of products and services. Among these are familiar things like increasingly sophisticated and connected consumers who are talking to each other more and more about brands, online and off. As noted by Stephen Brown, a prolific and provocative writer on the subject of branding, we are living in a different world from the one that operated in the heyday of mass marketing.[2] As he notes, we have evolved to an intensely commercial world where TV shows feature stories about marketing and consumer psychology, stand-up comics perform skits about shopping routines and brand strategies, and documentaries like *Who Killed the Electric Car?* and *Beer Wars*, with General Motors and Budweiser playing the villains, make great anti-brand entertainment. Industry gossip, executive screw-ups, and product critiques are bloggers' standard fodder. It is a brand-obsessed world.

And as you already know, the consumer is increasingly in control in this brand-obsessed world, using tools like blogs, podcasts, YouTube, Twitter, and whatever will be invented next week to exert that control across the Internet.[3] It's a world where marketers must monitor the current buzz about their brands and become part of the dialogue in an effort to rescue or revive their brands. Of course, mass media advertising has never been about dialogue.

Consumers are spreading the word about brands as never before. Even though marketers have always believed that the most powerful influence in any consumer's decision is the recommendations of friends and family, they have never known exactly what to do about it. Some clues about what to do were provided by Malcolm Gladwell in his best-seller *The Tipping Point,* wherein he makes the case that "mavens" and "connectors" are critically important in fostering social epidemics. The key idea here is that these mavens and connectors can be located, and if you give them useful information or interesting stories about your brand, they may share it with their networks. Of course that sharing is a more robust phenomenon when there exists a medium like the Internet that allows one to spread the word to thousands of one's close, personal friends with a single click.

People talk about brands. The challenge is to give them interesting things to talk about, things that bring one's brand into the conversation in a positive way. Marketers are starting to get it. PR isn't just about managing goodwill; it can be about finding ways to get your brand into the day-to-day conversations of key consumers. Maytag is one among many companies that is learning how to use PR expertise in a proactive way to build its brand. Its nationwide contest to select the next Maytag Repairman generated 2,000 candidates and lots of buzz in the conventional media and across the Internet. Maytag's vice president of marketing described the effort as a $500,000 campaign that generated $10 million of value, and attributed its success to integrating PR expertise into the planning process for the brand early and often.[4] That's the right formula.

In today's dynamic marketplace, where we know there are lots of online and off-line conversations taking place about brands, a brand builder needs to take a proactive stance in influencing at least some of those conversations. As always, it takes a strong team effort to ensure integration, and it is becoming increasingly clear that PR expertise needs to be well represented as part of any marketing and advertising team.[5] Moreover, as evidenced by the *Social Media* box, when you give consumers something worth talking about, they surely will…

2. Stephen Brown, "Ambi-brand Culture," in *Brand Culture* (New York: Routledge, 2006), 50–66.

3. Frank Rose, "Let the Seller Beware," *The Wall Street Journal,* December 20, 2006, D10; Jack Neff, "Lever's CMO Throws Down the Social Media Gauntlet," *Advertising Age*, April 13, 2009, 1, 20.

4. Jeffrey Davidoff, "Want Great PR? Get Your Agencies to Share the Load," *Advertising Age,* August 13, 2007, 12–13.

5. Claire Stammerjohan, Charles M. Wood, Yuhmiin Chang, and Esther Thorson, "An Empirical Investigation of the Interaction Between Publicity, Advertising, and Previous Brand Attitudes and Knowledge," *Journal of Advertising,* Winter 2005, 55–67; Jonah Bloom, "With PR on the Rise, Here's a Refresher Course in the Basics," *Advertising Age*, May 11, 2009, 22.

Social Media

Join the Conversation

It shouldn't come as a big surprise. One of the primary content categories for chatter in the new media is what's on TV. That's right, old media still rule our lives—we just talk about it differently with the new tools. Betty White was a huge hit on Twitter after her appearance on *Saturday Night Live*. Justin Bieber went mega-viral after he appeared on Oprah. Glenn Beck and other news provocateurs know their message is getting out by tracking Twitter activity. The Disney Channel created pop stars Miley Cyrus and Jonas Brothers—who also garner their share of Tweets. Old media activates the new media.

Next question—what then is the largest source of content for online, word-of-mouth conversations about brands? Easy... it's television. Approximately 30 percent of all online buzz about brands is provoked by advertising. All forms of advertising play a role in provoking online conversations, but again, the number one stimulator is that old media stalwart, the TV ad.

Decades ago two communications researchers—Elihu Katz and Paul Lazarsfeld—did research on the connection between mass communications and word-of-mouth conversations. Their conclusion was that mass advertising works best when it stimulates conversations. Advertising messages get filtered through social networks and derive their potency from those social networks. That was 50 years ago but the implications haven't changed. We have always known that any form of advertising is working best when it stimulates a conversation. It just feels a little different in today's world because so many of those conversations are happening on Facebook and Twitter. You want to be in the conversation? Same as it ever was. Use the tools of advertising and integrated brand promotion and give your consumer something to talk about. They'll be tweeting before you know it....

Sources: Simon Dumenco, "In Praise of the Original Social Media: Good Ol' Television," *Advertising Age*, May 17, 2010, 30: Ed Keller, "All Media Are Social: The Unique Roles of TV, Print and Online in Driving Word of Mouth" MediaBizBloggers.com, July 15, 2010; Jack Neff, "Future of Advertising? Print, TV, Online Ads," *Advertising Age*, June 1, 2009, 3.

Public Relations and Damage Control. Public relations has always been an important and unique contributor in that PR serves a role that no other promotional tool can. Public relations is the one and only tool that can provide damage control from bad publicity. Such public relations problems can arise from either a firm's own activities or from external forces completely outside a firm's control. Let's consider a classic public relations debacle to illustrate the nature of damage control.

Intel is one of the great success stories of American industry. Intel has risen from relative techno-obscurity as an innovative computer technology company to one of the largest corporations in the world with one of the most visible brands (who doesn't know "Intel Inside"?). Sales have grown from $1.3 billion to around $40 billion annually in only 25 years. But all this success did not prepare Intel for the one serious public relations challenge that the firm encountered. In early 1994, Intel introduced its new-generation chip, the now-well-known Pentium, as the successor to the widely used line of X86 chips. But by November 1994, Pentium users were discovering a flaw in the chip. During certain floating-point operations, some Pentium chips were actually producing erroneous calculations—and even though the error showed up in only the fifth or sixth decimal place, power users in scientific laboratories require absolute precision and accuracy in their calculations.

Having a defect in a high-performance technology product such as the Pentium chip was one thing; how Intel handled the problem was another. Intel's initial "official" response was that the flaw in the chip was so insignificant that it would produce an error in calculations only once in 27,000 years. But then IBM, which had shipped thousands of PCs with Pentium chips, challenged the assertion that the flaw was

Exhibit 18.4 When Intel did not respond quickly and positively to problems with its Pentium chip, the press unloaded a barrage of negative publicity on the firm. Even Dilbert got into the act with this parody of Intel decision making.

insignificant, claiming that processing errors could occur as often as every 24 days. IBM announced that it would stop shipment of all Pentium-based PCs immediately.[6]

From this point on, the Pentium situation became a runaway public relations disaster. Every major newspaper, network newscast, and magazine carried the story of the flawed Pentium chip. Even the cartoon series *Dilbert* got in on the act, running a whole series of cartoon strips that spoofed the Intel controversy (see Exhibit 18.4). One observer characterized it this way: "From a public relations standpoint, the train has left the station and is barreling out of Intel's control."[7] For weeks Intel did nothing but publicly argue that the flaw would not affect the vast majority of users.

Finally Intel decided to provide a free replacement chip to any user who believed he or she was at risk. In announcing the $475 million program to replace customers' chips, Andy Grove, Intel's highly accomplished CEO, admitted publicly that "the Pentium processor divide problem has been a learning experience for Intel."[8]

Firms large and small encounter PR problems; that's not going to change. Indeed, as consumers become more informed and connected, the bad news just travels faster and lingers longer.[9] This "bad news" can take many forms. For Taco Bell it was an Internet video of rats running amok at its Greenwich Village restaurant.[10] You can close the restaurant, but that video is still out there. Johnson & Johnson walked into a PR firestorm by suing the Red Cross for logo infringement.[11] That's a hard case to win in the court of public opinion, but it's definitely a self-inflicted wound for J&J. And poor Colonel Sanders must be rolling over in his grave. Marketers at KFC have had great success dreaming up popular promotions, but do a poor job of coordinating with their store managers. When you offer a discount coupon but don't have product to back it up, everyone gets agitated. Everyone, that is, except Chick-Fil-A and Church's, whose sales are growing at KFC's expense.[12]

Companies need to learn how to handle the bad news. No company is immune. And even though many public relations episodes must be reactive, a firm can be prepared with public relations materials to conduct an orderly and positive relations-building campaign

6. Barbara Grady, "Chastened Intel Steps Carefully with Introduction of New Chip," *Computerlink,* February 14, 1995, 11.

7. James G. Kimball, "Can Intel Repair the Pentium PR?," *Advertising Age,* December 19, 1994, 35.

8. Grady, "Chastened Intel Steps Carefully with Introduction of New Chip."

9. Pete Blackshaw, *Satisfied Customers Tell Three Friends: Angry Customers Tell 3,000.* New York, NY: Doubleday, 2008.

10. Kate MacArthur, "Taco Hell: Rodent Video Signals New Era in PR Crises," *Advertising Age,* February 26, 2007, 1, 46.

11. Jack Neff, "J&J Targets Red Cross, Blunders into PR Firestorm," *Advertising Age,* August 13, 2007, 1, 22.

12. Emily York, "Grilled Chicken a Kentucky Fried Fiasco," *Advertising Age,* May 11, 2009, 1, 30.

with its constituents. To fully appreciate the potential of public relations, we will next consider the objectives and tools of public relations, and basic public relations strategies.

2 Objectives for Public Relations.

Even though reacting to a crisis is a necessity, it is always more desirable to take a proactive approach. The key is to have a structured approach to public relations, including a clear understanding of objectives for PR. Within the broad guidelines of image building, damage control, and establishing relationships with constituents, it is possible to identify six primary objectives of public relations:

- ***Promoting goodwill.*** This is an image-building function of public relations. Industry events or community activities that reflect favorably on a firm are highlighted. When Pepsi launched a program to support school music programs—programs hard-hit by funding decreases—the firm garnered widespread goodwill.
- ***Promoting a product or service.*** Press releases, events, or brand "news" that increase public awareness of a firm's brands can be pursued through public relations. Large pharmaceutical firms such as Merck and GlaxoSmithKline issue press releases when they discover new drugs or achieve FDA approval. Likewise, Starbucks champions sustainable production of its green coffee through its C.A.F.E. Practices, and encourages you to learn more, per Exhibit 18.5.
- ***Preparing internal communications.*** Disseminating information and correcting misinformation within a firm can reduce the impact of rumors and increase employee morale. For events such as reductions in the labor force or mergers of firms, internal communications can do much to dispel rumors circulating among employees and in the local community.
- ***Counteracting negative publicity.*** This is the damage-control function of public relations, as discussed earlier. The attempt here is not to cover up negative events but rather to prevent the negative publicity from damaging the image of a firm and its brands. When a lawsuit was filed against NEC alleging that one of its cellular phones had caused cancer, McCaw Cellular Communications used public relations activities to inform the public and especially cellular phone users of scientific knowledge that argued against the claims in the lawsuit. Also, one industry's public relations problems are another industry's golden opportunity, as the ad in Exhibit 18.6 shows.

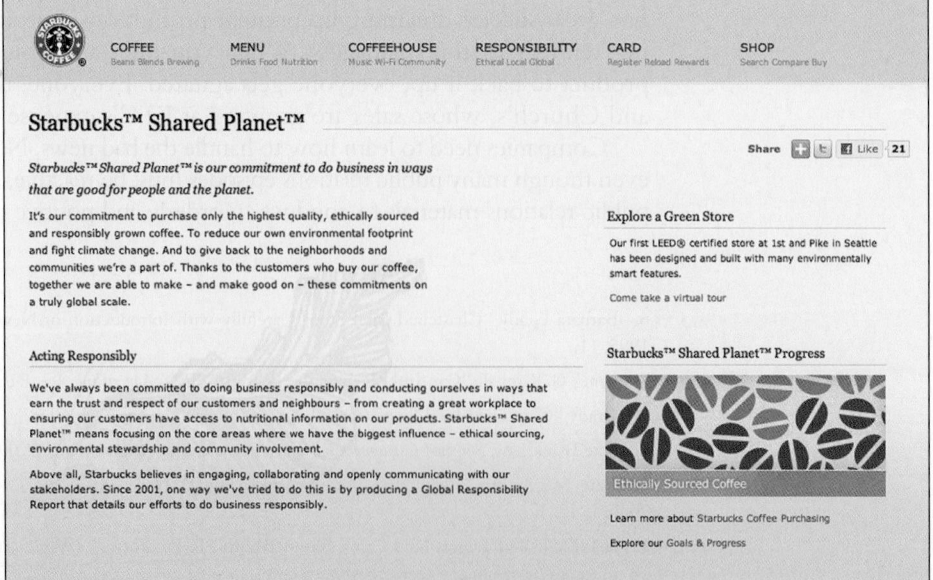

Exhibit 18.5 Starbucks actively promotes economic accountability and social responsibility as core brand values.

Courtesy, Susan Van Etten

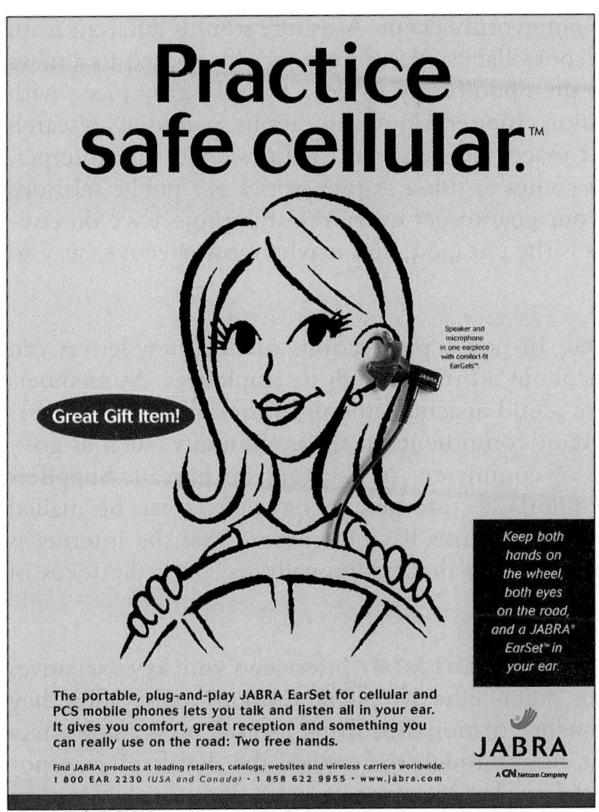

Practice safe cellular.™
Speaker and microphone in one earpiece with comfort-fit EarGels™.
Great Gift Item!
Keep both hands on the wheel, both eyes on the road, and a JABRA® EarSet™ in your ear.
The portable, plug-and-play JABRA EarSet for cellular and PCS mobile phones lets you talk and listen all in your ear. It gives you comfort, great reception and something you can really use on the road: Two free hands.
Find JABRA products at leading retailers, catalogs, websites and wireless carriers worldwide.
1 800 EAR 2230 (USA and Canada) · 1 858 622 9955 · www.jabra.com
JABRA
A GN Netcom Company

Exhibit 18.6 Public relations problems in one industry create opportunities in another. When medical research suggested that extensive cell phone use could be linked to brain tumors, firms developed cell phone accessories to address the issue. Here, Jabra is alluding to the negative publicity and the medical research as the basis for its brand appeal.

- ***Lobbying.*** The public relations function can assist a firm in dealing with government officials and pending legislation. Microsoft reportedly spent billions on such lobbying efforts when antitrust violations were leveled at the company. Industry groups also maintain active and aggressive lobbying efforts at both the state and federal levels. As an example, the beer and wine industry has lobbyists monitoring legislation that could restrict beer and wine advertising.
- ***Giving advice and counsel.*** Assisting management in determining what (if any) position to take on public issues, preparing employees for public appearances, and helping management anticipate public reactions are all part of the advice and counsel function of public relations.

The Tools of Public Relations.

There are several means by which a firm can pursue the objectives just cited. The goal is to gain as much control over the process as possible. By using the tools discussed in the following sections, a firm can integrate its public relations efforts with other brand communications.

Press Releases. One important tactical tool is the press release. Indeed, a narrow view of public relations envisions the PR department writing press releases and working with key contacts in the media to get them interested in the release, with the hope that a story of some kind will follow in that media outlet. Having a file of information that makes for good news stories puts one in a position to take advantage of press coverage. Some typical categories of information that make for a good story are:

- New products launches
- New scientific discoveries
- New personnel
- New corporate facilities
- Innovative corporate practices, such as energy-saving programs or employee benefit programs
- Annual shareholder meetings
- Charitable and community service activities

The only drawback to press releases is that a firm often doesn't know if or when the item will appear in the news. Also, journalists are free to edit or interpret a news release, which may alter its intended message. To help minimize unintended outcomes, it's key to develop working relationships with editors from publications the organization deems critical to its press release program. As with most communication endeavors, know your audience! Although public relations should not be defined by the press release ritual, this is still an important skill set. You can browse a wide variety of press releases at www.prnewswire.com/.

Feature Stories. Although a firm cannot write a feature story for a newspaper or any other medium, it can invite journalists to do an exclusive story on the firm when there is a particularly noteworthy event. A feature story is different from a press release in that it is more controllable. A feature story, as opposed to a news release, offers a single journalist the opportunity to do a fairly lengthy piece with exclusive rights to the information. Jupiter Communications, a leading research organization that tracks Internet usage and generates statistics about the Internet, has a simple philosophy when it comes to using feature stories as a public relations tool. Says Jupiter's CEO, "It is our goal to get every research project we do covered somewhere. We know this is the cheapest, and maybe most effective, way to market ourselves."[13]

Company Newsletters. In-house publications such as newsletters can disseminate positive information about a firm through its employees. As members of the community, employees are proud of achievements by their firm. Newsletters can also be distributed to important constituents in the community, such as government officials, the chamber of commerce, or the tourism bureau. Suppliers often enjoy reading about an important customer, so newsletters can be mailed to this group as well. As in other areas, firms have discovered that the Internet is an excellent way to distribute information that traditionally has been the focus of newsletters.

Interviews and Press Conferences. Interviews with key executives or staged press conferences can be highly effective public relations tools. Often they are warranted in a crisis management situation. But firms also call press conferences to announce important scientific breakthroughs or explain the details of a corporate expansion or a new product launch. Of course, no one does this better than Steve Jobs each and every time Apple has big news about a new product. The press conference has an air of credibility because it uses a news format to present salient information.

Sponsored Events. As was discussed in Chapter 16, sponsoring events can also serve as an important public relations tool. Sponsorships run the gamut from supporting community events to mega-events such as the Olympics. At the local level, prominent display of the corporate name and logo offers residents the chance to see that an organization is dedicated to supporting their community.

Another form of sponsorship is the fund-raiser. Fund-raisers for nonprofit organizations of all sorts give positive visibility to corporations. For many years, Chevrolet has sponsored college scholarships through the NCAA by choosing the best offensive and defensive player in televised football games. The scholarships are announced with much fanfare at the conclusion of the game. This sort of publicity for Chevrolet can also make a favorable impression.

Publicity. **Publicity** is essentially "free" media exposure about a firm's activities or brands. The public relations function seeks to monitor and manage publicity, but obviously can never actually control what the media chooses to say or report. This lack of control was demonstrated earlier in the chapter with the examples of Intel, Taco Bell, and KFC. As suggested by Exhibit 18.7, politics is another walk of life where the tone of one's publicity can be hard to manage. Organizations (or politicians) need to be prepared to take advantage of events that make for good publicity and to counter events that are potentially damaging to their reputation.

The appeal of publicity—when the information is positive—is that it tends to carry heightened credibility. Publicity that appears in news stories on television and radio and in newspapers and magazines assumes an air of believability because of the credibility of the media context. Not-for-profit organizations often use publicity

13. Andy Cohen, "The Jupiter Mission," *Sales and Marketing Management,* April 2000, 56.

Exhibit 18.7 Presidents get more than their fair share of publicity, usually slanted left or right.

in the form of news stories and public interest stories as ways to gain widespread visibility at little or no cost.

But publicity is not always completely out of the company's control. For instance, during the Academy Awards, a bracelet worn by actress Julia Roberts caused quite a stir. After Roberts won the award for best actress, she stood smiling (which we all know she does so well) and waving to the cameras, and suddenly the whole world wanted to know about the snowflake-design Van Cleef & Arpels bracelet that adorned her right (waving) wrist. What a lucky break for the designers! Not. The whole episode was carefully planned by Van Cleef's PR agency, Ted, Inc. The agency lobbied hard to convince Roberts that the bracelet and matching earrings were stunning with her dress, knowing that if she won the Oscar, she would be highly photographed waving that pretty bracelet.[14]

Stirring up a controversy is a sure way to get publicity, and many companies and their brands thrive on publicity. As suggested in Exhibit 18.8, Richard Branson was stirring up controversy even at age 15. In fact, there is an old saying in PR circles that goes something like, "There is no such thing as bad publicity." The point is that in most cases it is a good thing for your brand to be in the news—unless, of course, you are a big oil company.

3 Basic Public Relations Strategies.

Given the breadth of possibilities for using public relations as part of a firm's overall advertising and IBP effort, it's good to revisit the prospects in simple terms. Public relations strategies can be categorized as either proactive or reactive. **Proactive public relations strategy** is guided by marketing objectives, seeks to publicize a company and its brands, and should serve to build goodwill (and buzz) for the brand, as in the Charmin restroom example. **Reactive public relations strategy** focuses on problems to be solved rather than on opportunities, and requires a company to take defensive measures. Think BP.

Proactive Strategy. In developing a proactive PR strategy, a firm acknowledges opportunities to use public relations efforts to accomplish something positive. Companies often rely heavily on their public relations firms to help them put together a proactive strategy. The biotechnology industry, for instance, is subject of much controversy in the press regarding genetically altered food and seed products. A prime example is Monsanto, portrayed as the evil empire in the documentary *Food, Inc.* The advertisement in Exhibit 18.9 from the biotechnology industry attempts to take a proactive approach to dealing with the controversies by presenting a positive image and information.

In many firms, the positive aspects of employee achievements, corporate contributions to the community, and the organization's social and environmental programs go unnoticed by important constituents. To implement a proactive strategy, a firm

14. Beth Snyder Bulik, "Well-Heeled Heed the Need for PR," *Advertising Age*, June 11, 2001, S2.

Exhibit 18.8 "At age 15, his headmaster said he'd either wind up rich … or in prison … If his headmaster could only see him now." As the preceding quote from the body copy of this ad and its clever image demonstrate, even as a schoolboy Richard Branson was hard to control. Although he never really outgrew his naughty nature, he did put it to good use promoting all things Virgin.

Exhibit 18.9 The biotechnology industry is taking a proactive approach to the controversies surrounding the industry and its processes. See also www.whybiotech.com

needs to develop a comprehensive public relations program. The key components of such a program are as follows:

1. ***A public relations audit.*** A **public relations audit** identifies the characteristics of a firm or the aspects of the firm's activities that are positive and newsworthy. Information is gathered in much the same way as information related to advertising strategy is gathered. Corporate personnel and customers are questioned to provide information. This information may include descriptions of company products and services, market performance of brands, profitability, goals for products, market trends, new product introductions, important suppliers, important customers, employee programs and facilities, community programs, and charitable activities.
2. ***A public relations plan.*** Once the firm is armed with information from a public relations audit, the next step is a structured plan. A **public relations plan** identifies the objectives and activities related to the public relations communications issued by a firm. The components of a public relations plan include the following:
   a. ***Situation analysis.*** This section of the public relations plan summarizes the information obtained from the public relations audit. Information contained here is often broken down by category, such as product performance or community activity.
   b. ***Program objectives.*** Objectives for a proactive PR program stem from the current situation. Objectives should be set for both short-term and long-term

opportunities. Public relations objectives can be as diverse and complex as advertising objectives. The focal point is not sales or profits per se. Rather, factors such as the credibility of product performance (that is, placing products in verified, independent tests) or the stature of the firm's research and development efforts (highlighted in a prestigious trade publication article) are legitimate types of PR objectives.

c. ***Program rationale.*** In this section, it is critical to identify the role the public relations program will play relative to all the other communication efforts—particularly advertising—being undertaken by a firm. This is the area where an integrated brand promotion perspective is clearly articulated for the public relations effort.

d. ***Communications vehicles.*** This section of the plan specifies precisely what means will be used to implement the public relations plan. The tools discussed earlier in the chapter—press releases, interviews, newsletters—constitute the communications vehicles through which objectives can be implemented. There will likely be discussion of precisely how press releases, interviews, and company newsletters can be used.

e. ***Message content.*** Analysts suggest that public relations messages should be researched and developed in much the same way that advertising messages are researched and developed. Focus groups and in-depth interviews are being used to fine-tune PR communications. For example, a pharmaceutical firm learned that calling obesity a "disease" rather than a "condition" increased the overweight population's receptivity to the firm's press release messages regarding a new anti-obesity drug.[15]

A proactive public relations strategy has the potential for making an important supportive contribution to a firm's IBP effort. Carefully placing positive information targeted to potentially influential constituents—such as members of the community or stockholders—supports the overall goal of enhancing the image, reputation, and perception of a firm and its brands.

Reactive Strategy. A reactive PR strategy may seem like a contradiction in terms, but as stated earlier, firms must implement a reactive strategy when events outside the control of the firm create negative publicity. Coca-Cola was able to rein in negative publicity by acting swiftly after an unfortunate incident occurred in Europe. Seven days after a bottling problem caused teens in Belgium and France to become sick after drinking Coke, the firm acted quickly and pulled all Coca-Cola products from the market, with an apology from the CEO.[16] Coca-Cola's quick actions could not prevent negative consequences in terms of product sales. That would call for new marketing programs tailored to meet the needs of consumers on a country-by-country basis. The programs relied heavily on integrated brand promotion strategies, including free samples; dealer incentive programs; and beach parties featuring sound and light shows, DJs, and cocktail bars with free Cokes to win back the critical teen segment.[17] In the end it was a complete and integrated effort that restored consumers' trust and rebuilt the business across Europe.

It is difficult to organize for and provide structure around reactive PR. Since the events that trigger a reactive effort are unpredictable, a firm must simply be prepared to act quickly and thoughtfully. Two steps help firms implement a reactive public relations strategy:

1. ***The public relations audit.*** The public relations audit that was prepared for the proactive strategy helps a firm also prepare its reactive strategy. The information

15. Geri Mazur, "Good PR Starts with Good Research," *Marketing News,* September 15, 1997, 16.

16. Kathleen V. Schmidt, "Coke's Crisis," *Marketing News,* September 27, 1999, 1, 11.

17. Amie Smith, "Coke's European Resurgence," *Promo Magazine,* December 1999, 91.

provided by the audit gives a firm what it needs to issue public statements based on current and accurate data.

2. ***The identification of vulnerabilities.*** In addition to preparing current information, the other key step in a reactive strategy is to recognize areas where the firm has weaknesses in its operations or products that can negatively affect its relationships with important constituents. From a public relations standpoint, these weaknesses are called *vulnerabilities.* If aspects of a firm's operations are vulnerable to criticism, such as environmental issues related to manufacturing processes, then the public relations function should be prepared to discuss the issues in a broad range of forums with many different constituents. Leaders at Pepsi, Quaker Oats, and Philip Morris were taken somewhat by surprise when shareholders challenged the firms on their practices with respect to genetically modified foods. Even though the concern was among a minority of shareholders, there were enough concerned constituents to warrant a proxy vote on the issue of genetically modified foods.[18] Of course executives at these firms now understand that pursuing any form of genetically modified foods will always be one of their vulnerabilities.

A Final Word on Public Relations.

Public relations is a prime example of how a firm (or an individual) can identify and then manage aspects of communication in an integrated and synergistic manner to diverse audiences. Without recognizing public relations activities as a component of the firm's overall communication effort, misinformation or disinformation could compromise more mainstream communications such as advertising. The coordination of public relations into an integrated program is a matter of recognizing and identifying the process as critical to the overall IBP effort, and, as always, getting the right set of players on your IBP team. As an example of using public relations in a powerful and ideal way, consider how Guinness, the venerable Irish brewer, launched a PR effort that appealed to both long-time Guinness loyalists and a new generation of Guinness drinkers (see the *Globalization* box).

4 Influencer Marketing.

If public relations is the discipline devoted to monitoring and managing how people view us, then it can also be thought of as a discipline devoted to monitoring and managing what consumers are saying to one another about us. Moreover, as noted earlier in this chapter, consumers have become increasingly predisposed to talk about brands, both online and off-line. Since we know they are likely to talk about our brands anyway, it seems prudent to follow the advice of Bonnie Raitt from her album *Luck of the Draw.* As Bonnie says (and sings) in her 1990s blues-rock hit: "Let's give them something to talk about!"

That basic idea, "give 'em something to talk about," underlies the evolution of an important new communication discipline that we will represent under the general label of influencer marketing. As defined by Northlich, a leader in influencer marketing programming, **influencer marketing** refers to a series of personalized marketing techniques directed at individuals or groups who have the credibility and capability to drive positive word-of-mouth in a broader and salient segment of the population. The idea is to give the influencer something to talk about. In addition, it is useful to distinguish between professional and peer-to-peer influencer programs.

18. James Cox, "Shareholders Get to Put Bio-Engineered Foods to Vote," *USA Today,* June 6, 2000, 1B.

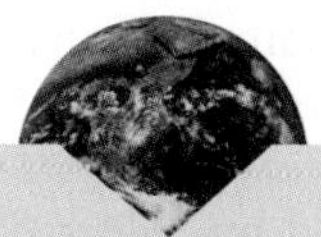

Globalization

Public Relations with Global Impact

Few brands generate as much cultural association as Guinness. The 250-year-old brand of stout beer has been attracting tourists to its St. James's Gate brewery in Dublin, Ireland, for more than a century. But executives at Guinness faced a tough challenge: The old reception area was totally inadequate to handle the thousands of tourists who flocked to the brewery each year. The task, however, was much larger than just building a new reception area. The brewery was the very pinnacle of the traditional image of the brand.

The task of building a new reception/visitor area was as much a public relations problem as it was a practical problem. The heritage of the brand had to be preserved while thousands of tourists had to be accommodated. Guinness strategists conceived the problem this way:

- How to accommodate the ever-growing flock of devotees who come to Dublin to connect with the brand's "spiritual home"
- How to modernize the conference and meeting room facilities for corporate use
- How to maintain its traditional relationships with Guinness loyalists while also appealing to younger consumers, many of whom have watched their fathers quaff many a pint of Guinness

The last point was of particular concern to marketing managers at Guinness. Stout beer has, during the past 10 years, been challenged in Ireland by a wide range of new, contemporary beers and other alcoholic drinks targeted to younger drinkers.

The solution chosen for all the public relations and promotion issues the firm felt it faced was a new seven-story structure called The Guinness Storehouse. The Storehouse preserved and incorporated the five-story Market Street Storehouse, which had served as a Guinness storage facility in the early 1900s. The solution was an expensive one, with a price tag of more than $45 million. But the investment seems to be paying off. Within two years of its opening, the visitor center attracted its millionth visitor and the Storehouse is now the number one fee-paying tourist spot in all of Ireland. Most importantly, the Storehouse aims to evoke in visitors an affinity with the brand. With 10 million glasses of Guinness consumed every day around the world, it would appear this PR effort is an appropriate testimony to the brand.

Source: Arundhati Parmar, "Guinness Intoxicates," *Marketing News*, November 10, 2003, 4, 6.

Both can provide one of the most valued assets for any brand builder—an advocacy message from a trusted source.[19]

Professional Influencer Programs.

If you're a pet owner, it's likely you've made many visits to the vet. And while visiting the vet, perhaps you asked a few questions about the best products to feed your puppy or kitten. Pet owners always want to do the right thing for their four-legged friends. If you've lived this scenario, you know what comes next. The vet is ready to talk about proper feeding, and not only that, he or she may be ready with product samples or informational brochures describing the benefits of a particular brand of pet food. Coincidence? Not at all. The makers of IAMS, Eukanuba, and Hill's Science Diet know that vets are key influencers in the decision about what to feed one's pet, especially for devoted pet owners who don't mind paying a little extra to get the best. These brands target vets with influencer marketing programs to try to earn their recommendation.

Many professionals are in this position where their advice about products is highly valued by consumers. Your doctor, dentist, neonatal nurse, auto mechanic, and hair stylist all have the credibility to influence product choices in their specific areas of expertise. Sometimes the opportunity is obvious, as with the example of vets and pet food. But more and more we are seeing creative programming that takes

19. Robert Berner, "I Sold It Through the Grapevine," *BusinessWeek*, May 29, 2006, 32–34.

influencer programming into new territory. An excellent example is that of Select Comfort, which targets many different types of health care professionals with an influencer program for its Sleep Number bed.

One particular group of health care professionals targeted by Select Comfort is Occupational Therapists (OTs). Persons in this field provide therapy to individuals with serious physical challenges, and they commonly receive promotional materials for things like the Moen bathtub grab bar, which makes it easier for persons with physical challenges to bathe safely. But are OTs experts on sleep? Doesn't matter. Many of their patients are likely to value their opinions, and all health care professionals commonly hear complaints from their patients about having trouble sleeping. So what advice can the OT provide to help a person sleep better?

Obviously, if you're Select Comfort, you'd like the OT to encourage patients to have a look at the Sleep Number bed. The first step is to get that OT to try and use the bed herself. Thus, Select Comfort offers special promotions to encourage OTs to purchase Sleep Number beds for their own bedrooms. Next, the OT needs tools to follow through on their potential advocacy. No problem. Like most professionals, OTs belong to associations and subscribe to journals. Name and address files from such sources allow a company to start building an OT marketing database. Once an OT expresses any kind of interest in the Sleep Number bed, she is sent an advocacy kit. Some key elements of that kit are displayed in Exhibit 18.10. Marketers at Select Comfort cannot control what the OT says to her patient about the Sleep Number bed. But they can put materials in her hands that will make it easy for her to become an advocate, if she believes such advocacy is justified. That's the nature of influencer marketing.

Think of influencer marketing as systematic seeding of conversations involving a consumer, an influencer, and a brand. Professionals in any field of endeavor take their role very seriously, so influencer programs directed to them must be handled with great care. Several points of emphasis should be kept in mind when developing programs for professionals. First, their time is money, so any program that wastes their time will be a waste of money. However, tactics designed to encourage professionals to try the product themselves can be very valuable. Also, messaging with professionals needs to provide intellectual currency and help the professional learn important benefits of the brand. For example, health care professionals' concerns will be better addressed

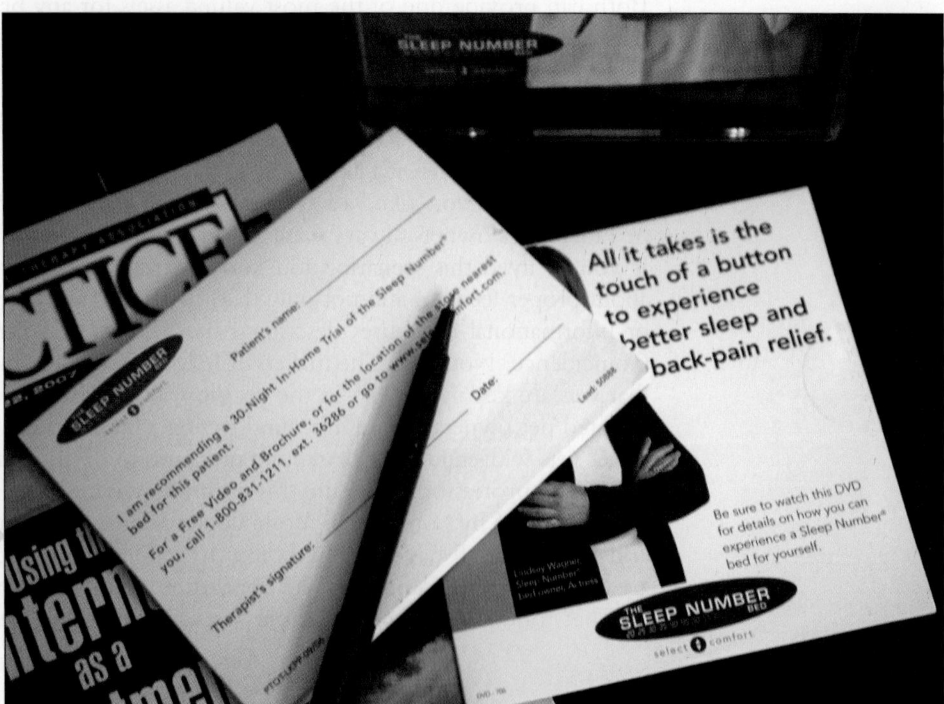

Exhibit 18.10 The information kit that Select Comfort provides to health care professionals includes a DVD and brochures that carefully document the benefits of the Sleep Number bed. The prescription pad allows the therapist to put his or her recommendation in writing.

through clinical studies than celebrity endorsements. Additionally, programs directed at professionals require a long-term commitment. For them to be advocates, trust first must develop, and any marketer must show patience and persistence to earn that trust.

Peer-to-Peer Programs.

Peer-to-peer programs typically have a very different tone than programs for professionals. In peer-to-peer programs, the idea is to give influencers something fun or provocative to talk about. Think of it as an emphasis on "social currency" for peer-to-peer versus "intellectual currency" for professionals. A great guiding principle for peer-to-peer programs is "Do something remarkable" to get people talking about your brand.[20] To promote Virgin Mobile's "Nothing to Hide" campaign, Richard Branson descended into Time Square on a giant cell phone while performing a strip-tease act. Pretty remarkable. To promote a book launch German publisher Eichborn attached tiny banners to 200 flies and let them buzz around at a book fair.[21] Pretty odd, but pretty remarkable. Just follow that advice from Bonnie Raitt: Give 'em something to talk about is always a good starting point.

Buzz and Viral Marketing. Two hot concepts in this area of peer-to-peer influence are buzz and viral marketing. Essentially, both of these refer to efforts to stimulate word-of-mouth involving key targets that might otherwise be impervious to more traditional advertising and promotional tools. **Buzz marketing** can be defined as creating an event or experience that yields conversations that include the brand. **Viral marketing** is the process of consumers marketing to consumers via the Web (e.g., via blogs or forwarding YouTube links) or through personal contact stimulated by a firm marketing a brand. The idea behind both buzz and viral marketing strategies is to target a handful of carefully chosen trendsetters or connectors as your influencers, and let them spread the word.[22]

So it is often the case that buzz marketing programs are fielded in cities like New York, London, and Los Angeles, because that's where you find these trendsetters. Consider this scene at the cafés on Third Street Promenade in and around Los Angeles. A gang of sleek, impossibly attractive bikers pulls up and, guess what, they seem *genuinely* interested in getting to know you over an iced latte—their treat, no less! Sooner or later the conversation turns to their Vespa scooters glinting in the sun, and they eagerly pull out a pad and jot down an address and phone number—for the nearest Vespa dealer. The scooter-riding, latte-drinking models are on the Vespa payroll, and they're paid to create buzz about the scooters by engaging hip café dwellers in conversation and camaraderie.[23]

Taking Buzz to the Next Level. Publicity stunts can be thought of as buzz builders, and there is nothing new about them. In 1863 P. T. Barnum orchestrated a wedding between two of his circus stars to boost attendance at the circus. The remarkable thing about this circus wedding was that bride and groom were both just 3 feet tall. P. T. Barnum knew how to create a buzz; he just didn't call it that.

But as you might expect, there is a lot that separates old-school publicity stunts from today's practice of influencer marketing. For one thing, there is the level of experience and sophistication of organizations like Northlich and Keller Fay Group when it comes to assisting clients with influencer programming. For instance, Keller Fay has developed a tracking system that can estimate the number of word-of-mouth

20. Michael Krauss, "To Generate Buzz, Do Remarkable Things," *Marketing News,* December 15, 2006, 6.

21. "Pretty Fly Campaign," *adage.com*, October 29, 2009.

22. Gerry Khermouch and Jeff Green, "Buzz-z-z Marketing," *BusinessWeek,* July 30, 2001, 50–56.

23. Ibid.

conversations taking place on a daily basis. Another familiar name and key supplier in this space is Nielsen BuzzMetrics. BuzzMetrics provides services to clients for tracking word-of-mouth activity across the Internet. And the Word of Mouth Marketing Association (WOMMA) founded by Andy Sernovitz is a great resource for learning about the art and science of buzz building. The WOMMA website is a fantastic resource for learning more about all the topics in this section, and Andy's five keys for success with influencer marketing are featured in Exhibit 18.11.

The point is, it's no longer just about the publicity stunt (but don't tell that to Richard Branson), and with billions of brand conversations happening every day, lots of brand builders, from Kodak to Kashi, want to be involved.[24]

Cultivating Connectors. One specific area where we see dramatic advancements in peer-to-peer marketing is in the activity of identifying and cultivating connectors. Meet Donna Wetherell. Donna is an outgoing mom and works at a customer-service call center where she knows about 300 coworkers by name. She likes to talk about shopping and lots of different brands. She always seems to have lots of extra coupons for the brands she likes, so much so that her coworkers call her the coupon lady. Donna is a connector, one of 600,000 that P&G has enrolled for its influencer program called Vocalpoint.[25]

That's right, your chatty next-door neighbor, who seems to know everyone and loves to talk about her favorite brands, could be one of these highly coveted connectors. For its connector database P&G focuses on women who have large social networks. They search for them over the Internet at sites like iVillage.com, and

Exhibit 18.11 To Generate Buzz, Five Ts Are the Keys.

Talkers. Much like our point about connectors, Andy Sernovitz asserts that you have to find the people who are predisposed to talk about brands in general, and/or your brand in particular. Often you need to be on the Internet to find these people. Find them and get to know them.

Topics. Next, of course, you have to give them something to talk about. This can't be a marketing message or a mission statement. There needs to be a mystery or a cool story or some breaking news that you are sharing to get people talking. Maybe the best at doing this is Steve Jobs at Apple. He definitely has a knack for stirring up interest and conversation with his suspenseful product announcements and his implied promise that our next great thing is just around the corner.

Tools. Make good use of the tools that promote a viral conversation. You can post a story on a Web page and some will find it there, but in the end it just sits there. You put the exact same story on a blog and it's linkable, portable, built to travel across the Internet. Suddenly lots of people are sharing the story.

Taking Part. Stop thinking in terms of one-way communication; start thinking in terms of dialogue. If you want favorable word-of-mouth, you need to be part of the conversation, not ignore it. Dell was slow to take part in a conversation about problems consumers had getting service. Basically, they ignored the conversation. When blogger Jeff Jarvis had big problems with his Dell and couldn't get the company's attention he coined the phrase "Dell Hell," which became a lightning rod for conversation about Dell on the Internet. You've got to be tuned in if you ever want to join the conversation.

Tracking. Word-of-mouth on the Internet is very measurable. With blogs, people write things down in full view. This is an opportunity for any company to know what people are saying about their brands and why they are saying it. Lots of companies are paying close attention to what consumers are saying about their brands. Even Dell is now among them.

Sources: Andy Sernovitz, *Word of Mouth Marketing: How Smart Companies Get People Talking,* Chicago, IL: Kaplan Publishing, 2006; Piet Levy, "Tease, Please," *Marketing News*, April 30, 2009, 6.

24. Michael Bush, "How Marketers Use Online Influencers to Boost Branding Efforts," *adage.com*, December 21, 2009.

25. Berner, "I Sold It Through the Grapevine."

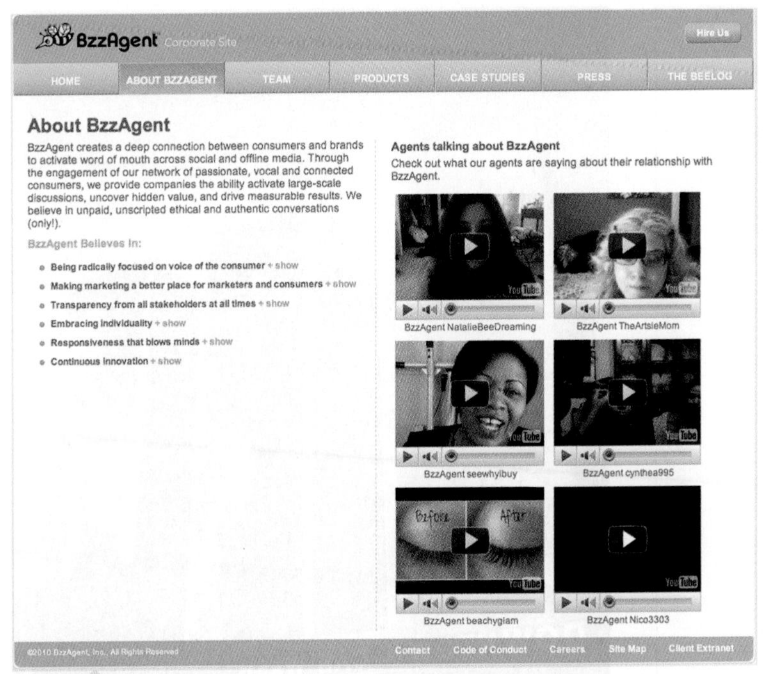

Exhibit 18.12 Clients ranging from Dunkin' Donuts to Mrs. Dash have bought into the buzz building mantra, with BzzAgent as their guide.

Courtesy, Susan Van Etten

are always looking for referrals (if you'd like to nominate your chatty neighbor). It seems connectors like the idea of being the first to receive new product samples and to feel that their voice is being heard by a big company.

Once the connector database is developed, it again becomes a matter of giving your connectors something to talk about. That's the part they enjoy. But in the end it's not always a simple thing to get consumers talking about a product like dishwashing detergent, so here again P&G execs assert that "We do tremendous research behind it to give them a reason to care."[26] Just as with professional programs, you can't force someone to be an advocate for your brand. You can identify people who have big social networks, but they're not going to compromise their relationships with others by sharing dull stories or phony information. You must give them something interesting to talk about.

Developing connector databases, finding the conversation starters, tracking the buzz online and off, that's the new era of influencer marketing. And it doesn't hurt to have a little of the P. T. Barnum flair as part of the process either. An area that once was very mysterious, that is, word-of-mouth marketing, is becoming increasingly demystified and in some ways made more scientific. Firms like BzzAgent of Boston, Mass., are a logical outgrowth of this movement. Per Exhibit 18.12, their 650,000 agent are ready to go to work buzzing for your brand. Or, you too could become a Bzz Agent!

5 Corporate Advertising.

Corporate advertising is not designed to promote the benefits of a specific brand, but instead is intended to establish a favorable attitude toward a company as a whole. A variety of highly regarded and successful firms use corporate advertising to enhance the image of the firm and affect consumers' attitudes. This perspective on corporate advertising is gaining favor worldwide. Firms with the stature of General Electric, Toyota, and Hewlett-Packard are investing in corporate ad campaigns. Exhibit 18.13 shows a corporate campaign for Elkay, a high-end manufacturer of sinks and other plumbing fixtures.

The Scope and Objectives of Corporate Advertising.

Corporate advertising is a significant force in the overall advertising carried out by organizations around the world. Billions of dollars are invested annually in media for corporate campaigns. Interestingly, most corporate campaigns run by consumer-goods manufacturers are undertaken by firms in the shopping-goods category, such as appliance and auto marketers. Studies have also found that larger firms are much more prevalent

26. Berner, "I Sold It Through the Grapevine," 34.

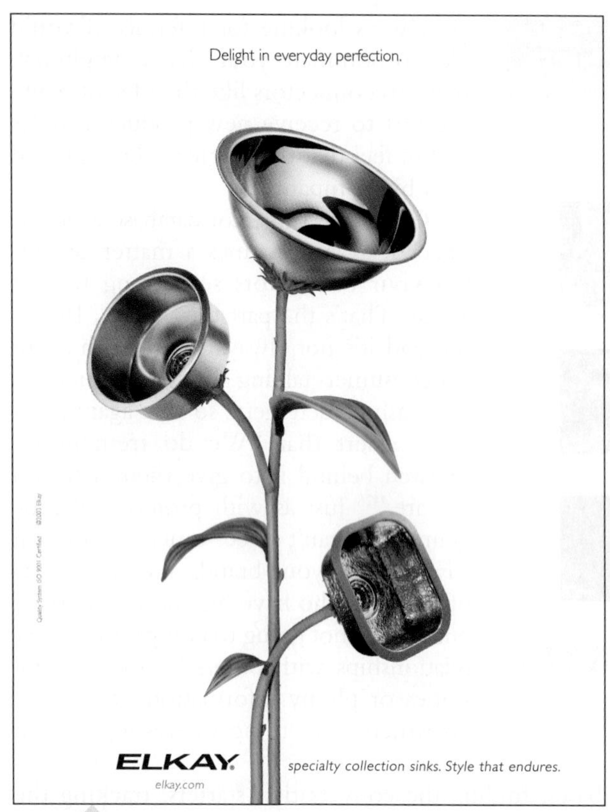

Exhibit 18.13 Firms often use corporate advertising as a way to generate name recognition and a positive image for the firm as a whole rather than for any one of its brands. Here, Elkay touts the company name rather than any specific features of a brand.

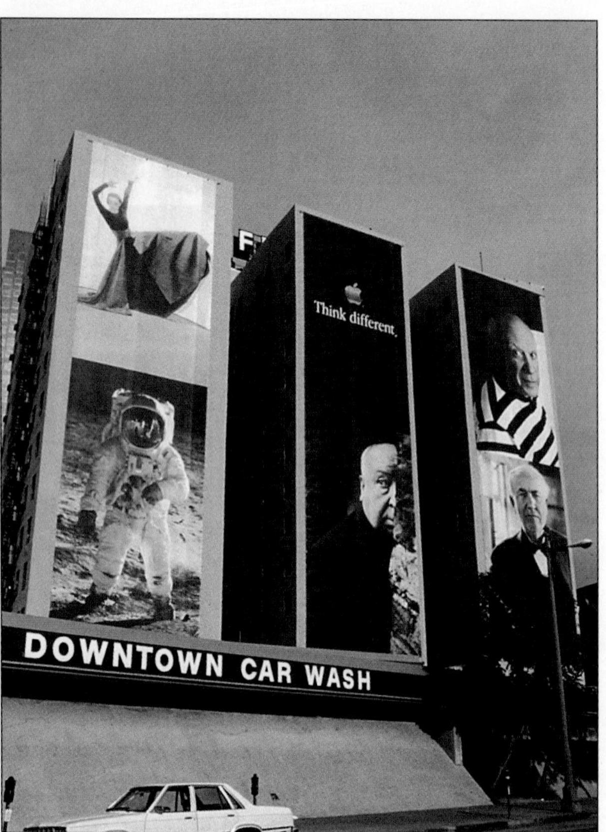

Exhibit 18.14 Corporate image advertising is meant to build a broad image for the company as a whole rather than tout the features of a brand. Does this ad qualify as a corporate image ad?

users of corporate advertising than smaller firms are. Presumably, these larger firms have broader communications programs and more money to invest in advertising, which allows the use of corporate campaigns. Apple is another company that has historically relied on corporate campaigns (see Exhibit 18.14) to support its numerous sub-brands.

Magazines and television are well suited to corporate advertising. Corporate advertising appearing in magazines has the advantage of being able to target particular constituent groups with image- or issue-related messages. Magazines also provide the space for lengthy copy, which is often needed to achieve corporate advertising objectives. Television is a popular choice for corporate campaigns because the creative opportunities provided by television can deliver a powerful, emotional message. Hewlett-Packard chose to use both television and magazine ads (see Exhibit 18.15) in a corporate campaign designed to reaffirm its image as an innovator.

The objectives for corporate advertising should be focused. In fact, corporate advertising shares similar purposes with proactive public relations when it comes to what companies hope to accomplish. Here are some of the possibilities for a corporate campaign:

- To build the image of the firm among customers, shareholders, the financial community, and/or the general public
- To boost employee morale or attract new employees
- To communicate an organization's views on social, political, or environmental issues
- To better position the firm's products against competition, particularly foreign competition
- To play a role in the overall advertising and IBP strategy of an organization, providing a platform for more brand-specific campaigns

The DNA of Silicon Valley.
The original company of inventors started here. 367 Addison Avenue, the garage out back.
Two young inventors, radicals really, with a few simple tools and a passion to invent. In this garage more than a company was born. The spirit that has launched hundreds of companies was born.
Today, this garage is still the workshop of the world's inventors, and it will be for years to come.
www.hp.com
hp
invent

Exhibit 18.15 Hewlett-Packard felt the company's image had become fragmented. This is one of the ads in a corporate image campaign designed to unify the image of the firm, harkening back to the roots of the company.

Notice that corporate advertising is not always targeted at the consumer. A broad range of constituents can be targeted with a corporate advertising effort. For example, when GlaxoWellcome and SmithKline Beecham merged to form a multibillion dollar pharmaceutical behemoth, the newly created firm, known as GlaxoSmithKline, launched an international print campaign aimed at investors who had doubts about the viability of the new corporate structure. The campaign was all about image and led with the theme: "Disease does not wait. Neither will we."[27]

Types of Corporate Advertising.

Three basic types of corporate advertising dominate the campaigns run by organizations: image advertising, advocacy advertising, and cause-related advertising. Each is discussed in the following sections. We then consider green marketing, which can be considered as a special case of any of these first three.

Corporate Image Advertising. The majority of corporate advertising efforts focus on enhancing the overall image of a firm among important constituents—typically customers, employees, and the general public. When IBM promotes itself as the firm providing "Solutions for a small planet" or when General Mills advances its motto "Nourishing Lives," the goal is to enhance the overall image of the firm.

Bolstering a firm's image may not result in immediate effects on sales, but as we saw in Chapter 5, attitude can play an important directive force in consumer decision making. When a firm can enhance its overall image, it may well affect consumer predisposition in brand choice.[28] Exhibit 18.16 is an example of an image-oriented corporate ad. In this ad Bristol-Myers Squibb is touting the life-saving impact of its high-technology line of pharmaceuticals.

Similarly, energy giant Shell Oil developed a series of television, print, online, and outdoor ads to tout their efforts to "unlock" cleaner sources of energy and let the world know that Shell is "ready to help tackle the challenge of the new energy future."[29] Launched in Spring 2010, just as BP oil was gushing into the waters of the Gulf of Mexico, the campaign also seemed to be saying that where BP has failed (remember "Beyond Petroleum?), Shell plans to succeed. It's a bold promise. Only time will tell if Shell delivers on the promise.

Advocacy Advertising. **Advocacy advertising** attempts to establish an organization's position on important social or political issues. Advocacy advertising attempts to influence public opinion on issues of concern to a firm. Typically, the issue featured in an advocacy campaign is directly relevant to the business operations

27. David Goetzl, "GlaxoSmithKline Launches Print Ads," *Advertising Age,* January 8, 2001, 30.

28. For an exhaustive assessment of the benefits of corporate advertising, see David M. Bender, Peter H. Farquhar, and Sanford C. Schulert, "Growing from the Top," *Marketing Management* (Winter–Spring 1996), 10–19, 24.

29. Michael Bush, "Shell Breaks Industry Silence with Aggressive Campaign," *Advertising Age,* June 28, 2010, 10.

Lance and Luke Armstrong
Two miracles. Three Bristol-Myers Squibb medicines.
And one very happy ending.
The little miracle above is Luke David Armstrong. The big one is his dad, Lance. Winner of the 1999 and 2000 Tours de France. And of an even more grueling battle — against testicular cancer. Using three Bristol-Myers Squibb cancer drugs, doctors worked with Lance to beat his illness. For over three decades, Bristol-Myers Squibb has been at the forefront of developing cancer medicines. Now, we're working with Lance to spread the word about early detection, treatment, hope, and triumph. Learn more by visiting our Web site: www.bms.com.
Bristol-Myers Squibb Company
Hope, Triumph, and the Miracle of Medicine

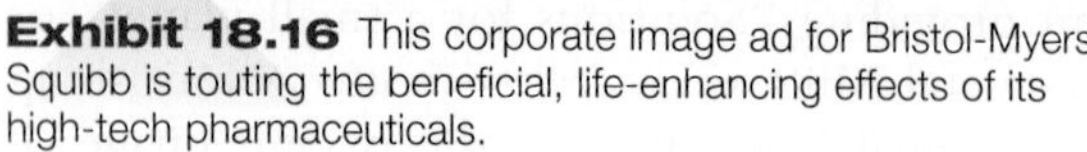

Exhibit 18.16 This corporate image ad for Bristol-Myers Squibb is touting the beneficial, life-enhancing effects of its high-tech pharmaceuticals.

Exhibit 18.17 In this cause-related corporate campaign, Anheuser-Busch is promoting the control of teenage drinking. This campaign helps establish the firm as a responsible marketer of alcoholic beverages. See also AB's programs at www.beeresponsible.com

of the organization. For example, Burt's Bees advocacy for a Natural Standard for Personal Care Products is perfectly aligned with its business model: No other company features natural ingredients in their products like Burt's Bees.

Cause-Related Advertising. **Cause-related advertising** features a firm's affiliation with an important social or societal cause—examples are reducing poverty, increasing literacy, conserving energy, protecting the environment, and curbing drug abuse—and takes place as part of the cause-related marketing efforts undertaken by a firm. The goal of cause-related advertising can be to enhance the image of the firm by associating it with important social issues; this tends to work best when the firm confronts an issue that truly connects to its business. The ad in Exhibit 18.17, in which Anheuser-Busch is promoting the control of teenage drinking, is a good example. This campaign helps establish the firm as a responsible marketer of alcoholic beverages, while also helping society deal with an important problem.

Cause-related advertising often features philanthropic activities that are funded by a company. Each year, *Promo Magazine* provides an extensive list of charitable, philanthropic, and environmental organizations that have formal programs in which corporations may participate. Most of the programs suggest a minimum donation for corporate sponsorship and specify how the organization's resources will be mobilized in conjunction with the sponsor's other resources.

Cause-related marketing is becoming increasingly common. There are several reasons for this. First, research supports the wisdom of such expenditures. In a consumer survey conducted by Cone, a Boston-based brand strategy firm, 91 percent of respondents said they have a more favorable impression of companies that support good causes, and also said they believed that the causes a company supports can be a valid reason for switching brands.[30] Other studies indicate that support of good causes can translate into brand preference with the important qualifier that consumers will judge a firm's motives.[31] If the firm's support is perceived as disingenuous, cause-related expenditures are largely wasted.

One would also like to think that the trend toward greater social responsibility by businesses is simply a matter of people wanting to do the right thing. For instance, Whirlpool Corporation is a Habitat Cornerstone Partner and assisted in the massive rebuilding effort needed in the wake of Hurricane Katrina. Jeff Terry, who manages the program of donations and volunteering on behalf of Whirlpool, says of the experience: "The first time you do this work it will change your life."[32] Sure, Whirlpool's participation in this program brings the company a lot of favorable publicity, but its people's hearts also appear to be in the right place. That makes the program a win–win activity for everyone involved.

The range of firms participating in cause-related marketing programs continues to grow. Pedigree has built its dog food brand through a commitment to finding homes for orphan animals, with free food and grant support for rescue shelters.[33] Campbell's Soup, Avon, and Yoplait have ongoing programs that generate funding to support research for a breast cancer cure. Home Depot promotes water conservation in areas of desperate need through its "Use Water Wisely" campaign; Nick at Nite funds an initiative called "National Family Dinner Day."[34] To advance the cause of families spending more time together, Nick at Nite networks shut off for the dinner hour on Family Day to help make their point. These examples illustrate the wide variety of programs that can be launched to support a cause.

Green Marketing. It is heartening to observe that numerous companies have sparked to the idea of supporting any number of causes. One area in particular seems to offer special opportunities in the years ahead. Like so many things, this one has numerous labels, but "green marketing" is probably the most popular. **Green marketing** refers to corporate efforts that embrace a cause or a program in support of the environment. Such efforts include shoe boxes made out of 100 percent recycled materials at Timberland and the "Dawn Saves Wildlife" program sponsored by Procter & Gamble. General Electric and its "Ecomagination" campaign is another high-profile exemplar of this movement. In funding this corporate campaign, GE has taken the stance that it is simply a good business strategy to seek real solutions to problems like air pollution and fossil-fuel dependency.[35] They are demonstrating that going green can really be a great business strategy.[36]

The green marketing movement has been on again and off again, especially in the United States. For example, in the early 1990s, Jacquelyn Ottman's book *Green Marketing* predicted that going green would be a marketing revolution. It didn't

30. Stephanie Thompson, "Raising Awareness, Doubling Sales," *Advertising Age,* October 2, 2006, 4.

31. Michael J. Barone, Anthony D. Miyazaki, and Kimberly A. Taylor, "The Influence of Cause-Related Marketing on Consumer Choice," *Journal of the Academy of Marketing Science,* vol. 28, no. 2, 2000, 248–262.

32. James Tenser, "The New Samaritans," *Advertising Age,* June 12, 2006, S-1, S-6.

33. Bob Liodice, "Ten Companies with Social Responsibility at the Core," *Advertising Age,* April 19, 2010, 88.

34. Tenser, "The New Samaritans;" Natalie Zmuda and Emily York, "Cause Effect: Brands Rush to Save World One Good Deed at a Time," *Advertising Age,* March 1, 2010, 1, 22.

35. Kathryn Kranhold, "GE's Environment Push Hits Business Realities," *The Wall Street Journal,* September 14, 2007, A1, A10.

36. Liodice, "Ten Companies with Social Responsibility at the Core."

come to pass, at least not in the United States. However, many signs now point to the prospect that this time around, green marketing really will take hold as a major source of opportunity for businesses, maybe just in time to save our planet. Most informed people now accept the inconvenient truth that our addiction to fossil fuels is putting the planet at risk. Surveys show that environmental issues are of major concern to consumers, and a formidable segment is acting on this concern.[37] The green movement looks sustainable this time around.

In addition, the Internet once again is changing the game. It is no longer possible for companies to pay lip service to environmental causes but hide their true motives. "Green sites" like Green Seal and EnviroLink can assist in determining who is really doing what to protect the environment. Or just google greenwashing and you'll find 2 million more sites to explore. Some of the "green claims" out there (see the Eco-Smart Hummer and Eco-Conscious Barbie) are so absurd they are almost funny. Motivated and well-informed consumers are hard to fool. Hopefully, companies will realize that it doesn't pay to make token gestures on behalf of the planet. Firms really only need to follow the one immutable law of branding to get it right when it comes to green marketing: Underpromise and overdeliver. Here's hoping that you too are getting on board the green bandwagon.

Happy trails.

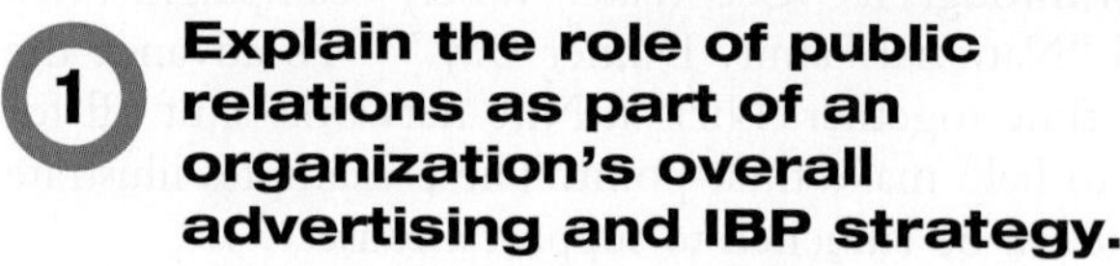

Summary

1 Explain the role of public relations as part of an organization's overall advertising and IBP strategy.

Public relations focuses on communications that can foster goodwill between a firm and constituent groups such as customers, stockholders, employees, government entities, and the general public. Businesses utilize public relations activities to highlight positive events associated with the organization; PR strategies are also employed for "damage control" when adversity strikes. Public relations has entered a new era, as changing corporate demands and new techniques have fostered a bolder, more aggressive role for PR in IBP campaigns.

2 Detail the objectives and tools of public relations.

An active public relations effort can serve many objectives, such as building goodwill and counteracting negative publicity. Public relations activities may also be orchestrated to support the launch of new products or communicate with employees on matters of interest to them. The public relations function may also be instrumental to the firm's lobbying efforts and in preparing executives to meet with the press. The primary tools of public relations experts are press releases, feature stories, company newsletters, interviews and press conferences, and participation in the firm's event sponsorship decisions and programs.

3 Describe two basic strategies motivating an organization's public relations activities.

When companies perceive public relations as a source of opportunity for shaping public opinion, they are likely to pursue a proactive public relations strategy. With a proactive strategy, a firm strives to build goodwill with key constituents via aggressive programs. The foundation for these proactive programs is a rigorous public relations audit and a comprehensive public relations plan. The plan should include an explicit statement of objectives to guide the overall effort. In many instances, however, public relations activities take the form of damage control. In these instances the firm is obviously in a reactive mode. Although a reactive strategy may seem a contradiction in terms, it certainly is the case that organizations can be prepared to react to bad news. Organizations that understand their inherent vulnerabilities in the eyes of important constituents will be able to react quickly and effectively in the face of hostile publicity.

37. Mya Frazier, "Going Green? Plant Deep Roots," *Advertising Age,* April 30, 2007, 1, 54–55; Jack Neff, "Green-Marketing Revolution Defies Economic Downturn," *Advertising Age,* April 20, 2009, 1, 23.

4 Illustrate the strategies and tactics used in influencer marketing programs.

We know that consumers are predisposed to talk about brands, and what they have to say is vital to the health and well-being of those brands. Hence it is no surprise that marketers are pursuing strategies to proactively influence the conversation. Influencer marketing refers to tools and techniques that are directed at driving positive word-of-mouth about a brand. In professional programs, important gatekeepers like veterinarians or any type of health care professional may be a focal point. In peer-to-peer programs, the new mantra has become finding the connectors. But whether it's professional or peer-to-peer, the marketer is always challenged to give the influencers something meaningful or provocative that they will want to talk about.

Discuss the applications and objectives of corporate advertising.

Corporate advertising is not undertaken to support an organization's specific brands but rather to build the general reputation of the organization in the eyes of key constituents. This form of advertising serves goals such as enhancing the firm's image and building fundamental credibility for its line of products. Corporate advertising may also serve diverse objectives, such as improving employee morale, building shareholder confidence, or denouncing competitors. Corporate ad campaigns generally fall into one of three categories: image advertising, advocacy advertising, or cause-related advertising. Corporate advertising may also be orchestrated in such a way to be very newsworthy, and thus it needs to be carefully coordinated with the organization's ongoing public relations programs.

Key Terms

public relations
publicity
proactive public relations strategy
reactive public relations strategy
public relations audit
public relations plan
influencer marketing
buzz marketing
viral marketing
corporate advertising
advocacy advertising
cause-related advertising
green marketing

Questions

1. Review the Charmin restrooms example and identify three of its elements that made it a record-setting buzz builder for Procter & Gamble.

2. Do you agree with our premise that consumers today are spreading the word about brands like never before? Does that assessment apply to you and the people in your network?

3. Obviously, some events will have more potential for generating favorable publicity than others. What particular criteria should be emphasized in event selection when a firm has the goal of gaining publicity that will build goodwill? How might the benefits of sponsorship be similar or different if that sponsorship involves a sporting event versus a noble cause?

4. Would it be appropriate to conclude that the entire point of public relations activity is to generate favorable publicity and stifle unfavorable publicity? What is it about publicity that makes it such an opportunity and threat?

5. There is an old saying to the effect that "there is no such thing as bad publicity." Can you think of a situation in which bad publicity would actually be good publicity? How is that possible?

6. Most organizations have vulnerabilities they should be aware of to help them anticipate and prepare for unfavorable publicity. What vulnerabilities would you associate with each of the following companies?

- R. J. Reynolds, makers of Camel cigarettes
- Procter & Gamble, makers of Pampers disposable diapers
- Kellogg's, makers of Kellogg's Frosted Flakes
- ExxonMobil, worldwide fossil-fuel company
- McDonald's, worldwide restaurateur

7. What key points need to be managed in creating successful influencer programs with medical professionals?

8. Imagine yourself as a connector. In that role, what kind of inside information would you find interesting enough to tell your friends about a new movie or TV show? What would it take for you to start that conversation?

9. Review the different forms of corporate advertising and discuss how useful each would be as a device for boosting a firm's image. Is corporate advertising always an effective image builder?

10. Do you ever select a brand based on the company's environmental track record? Investigate one of your favorite brands at the EnviroLink site. Did you find anything that changes your feelings about this brand?

Experiential Exercises

1. Texting while driving is a serious public safety concern, and the U.K.'s South Wales Police Department achieved international buzz recently by sending out a message that texting kills. The organization's graphic Hollywood-styled video featured three teenage girls on a joy ride when they text-and-drive their way into a head-on collision with another vehicle. The video went viral and left international viewers shocked and in tears; some complained the PSA was too terrifyingly realistic to air on television. What companies could benefit from making texting-and-driving a focus for ongoing cause-related advertising? Make your case by identifying companies that have successfully used cause-related advertising for similar causes.

2. Celebrity endorsements present opportunities and threats to top sports brands. Golf great Tiger Woods was leading the world in product endorsements until personal revelations stunned the public and damaged the golfer's pristine image. Write a report on the role public relations played in responding to the negative publicity, and be sure to answer the following questions: How did top brands react to the bad news? What public relations tools did management teams use to conduct damage control? Was the golfer's public relations strategy proactive or reactive? What was the primary public relations objective? What else might the golfer have done to rehabilitate his image and the brands with which he was associated?

3. To better position itself in the competitive college admissions field, your college or university is planning to launch a public relations campaign to encourage more highly qualified high school seniors to apply for admission. Working in small teams, identify what steps you would take to create a proactive public relations strategy for the school's admissions office. Your proposal should clearly identify the plan's objectives and rationale, what steps should be taken prior to the campaign's launch, and what communication methods and content would be most effective.

4. Working in the same teams, propose what steps you would take to launch an effective peer-to-peer marketing campaign as part of the effort to raise awareness of the college and increase applications to the school. In your answer, identify what types of individuals would make the most influential connectors to generate buzz about the school and explain what types of virtual and real-world tools could be developed to help those connectors have a compelling story about the college to share with others.

Project One: Understanding the Process of Advertising and Integrated Brand Promotions

For this project, groups will select a particular brand of eco-friendly reel mowers, electric mowers, or garden tools and develop an historical understanding of that product category as well as brands within that category. In addition, the group will provide an integrated brand promotions proposal to that brand in order to demonstrate the group's knowledge of that brand and its ability to promote that brand. Potential brands include, but are certainly not limited to, the following:

- Fiskars
- NaturCut
- RazorCut
- Scott
- American Deluxe
- Earthwise
- Neuton
- Solaris

A good starting point to find information about these brands can be found at www.ecomowers .com and www.american-lawns.com. In addition, you may find a brand of eco-friendly lawn mower or garden tools that are not mentioned here and are welcome to do so. Ultimately, the completed project will include a paper and/or presentation that demonstrates your understanding and integration of the concepts outlined in Part 1 of this text.

The Scenario

Your advertising agency has been contacted by a brand of eco-friendly lawn-care equipment that is attempting to develop a new advertising campaign that will promote the purchase and usage of reel mowers, electric mowers, and/or electric garden tools in contrast to the traditional gas-powered lawnmowers. They have the funds and the management in place to mount a full-scale advertising campaign that utilizes the principles and tools of integrated brand promotion, yet they want to make sure that the agency they contract with has an in-depth knowledge of the product category and the major brands within that category before moving forward. As such, your company has been asked to provide an introductory proposal that will demonstrate your understanding of the product and its industry, the brands that supply that product to customers, as well as an understanding of the ethical and social issues associated with the product and how it has been advertised. Furthermore, the introductory proposal must offer an understanding of the brand and what it is attempting to accomplish and conclude with an assessment of what your company can do for the brand.

Your group has been brought together to complete this introductory proposal, which has been broken down into several distinct parts.

- Introduction
- Product Category Analysis
- Major Brand Analysis
- Client Analysis
- Self-Analysis
- Conclusion

The final product should not only contain these components, but it should also demonstrate the quality of your company's professionalism and marketing savvy. In other words, your group has not only been tasked with demonstrating your understanding of the product category but with your ability to market the company within the context of this proposal.

Introduction

An introduction is simply where you introduce your company, state the purpose of the proposal, and provide an overview of the paper that your audience will read. You might start off with some secondary data or a vignette that begins the discussion of the product category that you are analyzing. Then, clearly express the purpose of the paper and provide a brief summary of what will be covered in the paper. You will begin your purpose in a manner such as this: "The purpose of this analysis is to…" and then state what it is you are doing. Any introduction should be designed to capture your reader's attention and make them want to read further.

The introduction should also be directed at a particular audience. Remember, your group will address a company that will decide whether to contract with your advertising agency. You may pick one of the brands mentioned earlier or find a brand of eco-friendly lawn equipment not mentioned here. Either way, you will need to address the brand as your audience. You will also want to transition into the next section as cleanly as you can.

Product Category Analysis

To complete the proposal, you will need to demonstrate your grasp of the history of the lawn-care product category as well as its current standing in the marketplace. This analysis can be broken into three parts: the product history, the current product state, and the ethical and social issues associated with the product.

Product History: You will need to build an introductory understanding of the product's history beginning from when the product first hit the market, under what circumstances it was introduced, and its evolution throughout the years. This evolution may include any major technological changes associated with the product, an overview of the major brands or companies that have succeeded and/or failed in the lawn-care product category, how the size of the market has fluctuated throughout the years, and anything else that is relevant in understanding lawn-care's history.

Current Product State: You will also construct an understanding of the product category's current standing in the marketplace. This should include a description of what the product category is, the size of the market, who the major brands or companies producing the product are, and the current target markets those companies are attempting to reach. Keep in mind that the current product state should not only include the state of eco-friendly lawn-care products but their major competitors (i.e. gas-powered mowers) as well. In addition, you may include an overview of the various IBF tools that are used to market the product.

Ethical and Social Issues: Finally, you will provide an overview of the various ethical and social issues associated with the lawn-care product category. These issues may range from the effect the product has on the environment to how it targets a particular audience or who that audience is to begin with. In addition, you will discuss any regulatory issues that govern the product category and how it may be advertised. In short, here is where you begin the process of demonstrating your understanding of why the brand you've chosen may be seeking your help.

Major Brand Analysis

Once you have completed your analysis of the product category, then you will find three major brands that market the lawn mowers and/or garden tools. You may choose three brands of gas-powered mowers in order to contrast the benefits of the eco-friendly versus gas-powered lawn care; you may choose three brands of eco-friendly mowers in order to contrast them with your brand as more direct competitors; or you may choose a combination of the two. The idea here is to select the brands that have essentially achieved top-of-mind awareness in the marketplace. This may involve a small, informal survey where you ask a number of people to name three brands in the product category.

Brand History: Once you have the three brands, you will provide a brief history of each brand, determine best as you can their current market share and/or sales in that product category, and their past and current advertising efforts. You should also collect at least 15 promotional efforts for each brand that you will analyze for their meaning. These efforts should be relatively current efforts (no more than five years old) and should come from several different media formats and incorporate a variety of IBP tools.

Brand Meaning: When you analyze the meaning of the advertisements, you will be looking for how these ads "speak with a single voice" or, in other words, what story is told across the various ads. For instance, in the famous "Got Milk?" campaign, various popular culture figures are pictured with a milk mustache. These figures include entertainment, sports, and other celebrities as well as fictional characters that have gained notoriety with the public. The campaign as a whole tells a story of success. The meaning underlying the campaign appears to be that in order to achieve the success these pop culture icons have achieved, one must drink milk. You will look for the story that is told in the ads you've selected for each brand.

Product Meaning: Once your analysis of each brand is completed, you will then compare and contrast the meanings you found for each brand. This should give you a basic understanding of the central meaning associated with the product itself. In addition, you will provide an overview of the ethical and social issues associated with the meanings you have located and how they may impact the target audience that is being addressed. Be sure to focus on issues that are important to the brand you have selected for this project.

Client Analysis

Now that you have demonstrated your understanding of the lawn-care product category and the major players in that category, you will demonstrate your understanding of the eco-friendly brand and the goals it is attempting to achieve with a new advertising campaign. You will provide a brief history of the organization, explore its mission, and make a few basic recommendations about how it might promote the product in question.

Company History and Mission: For the historical analysis of the company and its brand, you will need to provide a history that includes when and under what circumstances the organization was founded, what it has achieved since its founding, and what its basic mission is. Keep in mind that a brand like Fiskars is not necessarily a lawn-care company but a precision-blade company that makes, among other things, scissors, so don't be trapped by marketing myopia if it comes up. In addition, you will want to provide your understanding of what the company is trying to accomplish by hiring your agency.

Recommendations: Now that you have an understanding of the history and IBP efforts of the product and several brands within that product category, you are in a position to offer a few basic recommendations to the organization. These recommendations may include a story the brand can tell to counter both the story told by individual brands of gas-powered mowers as well as the product category as a whole, the IBP tools the brand can utilize to promote its message, and various advertising and/or industry regulations it may need to contend with. Ultimately, you will make a recommendation how advertising and IBP will help the organization to achieve its goals.

Self-Analysis

Here is your opportunity to sell your advertising agency to the organization. In short, you will describe what type of agency you are, how you address current trends in advertising and IBP, and what type of services you can offer to the company. In addition, you may provide the fee structure your company utilizes, the skills and makeup of the project team, and any additional information you feel is pertinent to the brand's decision-making process. Be creative and come up with a name, mission statement, and history for your own organization. You may even discuss other projects you have worked on that demonstrate your ability to meet the needs of the brand.

Conclusion

The conclusion provides you with an opportunity to give your closing thoughts on this introductory proposal, providing the reader with a brief summary of what you have uncovered with the research you have completed concerning the product category and the brands you have covered. It also provides you with the opportunity to give an overview of why you believe your group is the best choice to handle the account with the brand-soliciting help. In other words, here is your final opportunity to sell the idea that you are the best choice the company can make when it comes to developing its advertising and IBP plans for the future.

Final Paper

Again, you will want the final product to address the appropriate audience as outlined here. You will also want to construct the paper in a way that markets your advertising agency by demonstrating both the breadth of your knowledge on the material and your ability to wield the tools available to you. Include any actual advertisements, charts and graphs, or other images that are pertinent to your work in a neat and organized fashion. Use appropriate headings, font, margin sizes, etc. Make sure you include an executive summary, a table of contents, and appendices as well as any other sections deemed necessary. In short, make the paper look professional and ready to submit to the client who has requested this proposal.

Final Presentation

The client may have also requested a presentation of your work. You will want to discuss the high points of your work, focusing on what will distinguish your advertising agency as the most suitable to the brand's needs. As with the final paper, you will want to create a presentation that showcases not only what you know but also how you present what you know. Remember, ice skaters and gymnasts are not simply judged on technical skill but on artistry as well. Here is your opportunity to demonstrate your artistry in motion.

Project Two: Understanding the Role of Analyzing Advertising and IBP Environments in Planning

For this project, groups will create an advertising plan for General Motors (GM), a company that is resuscitating and rebuilding its image in the wake of bankruptcy and a controversial government loan. In order to complete this project, the group will have to demonstrate an understanding of the consumer's perspective of GM and, perhaps, of the modern automobile industry in general, divide the potential market into segments to be targeted, and develop a positioning statement that will allow GM to restore its standing, to some extent, with that particular target market or markets.

You may need to think about the various approaches to advertising that GM can take with this particular endeavor as well as the different audiences that are involved. For instance, GM may need to address the farmers and construction workers in a way that is different than they would address environmentalists or a general audience. Furthermore, they might address the main issue directly or they might simply go about the business of extolling the benefits of GM and its products. Regardless, the completed project will include a paper and/or a presentation that demonstrates your understanding and integration of the material as outlined in Part 2 of this text.

This project is designed to help you learn the basics of an advertising plan, particularly as it pertains to developing a sophisticated situation analysis and your recommendations based upon that analysis. This project is also designed to help you develop your research skills as well as your ability to make and justify recommendations for budgeting, strategy, and promotions implementation.

The Scenario

In the wake of the economic downturn and the collapse of the American auto industry, GM is looking to restore its image with the American public. Congratulations, your advertising agency has been selected by GM to develop an advertising plan that will assist in the clarification of the organization's objectives and the strategy by which it will meet those objectives. The organization has the funds and management in place to mount an advertising campaign that they hope will counter the bad press and unfortunate circumstances that has befallen the company. Your goal is to help GM formalize their value proposition in the wake of the disaster and extend that into an advertising plan that they can then use to develop the advertising campaign itself.

In order to do this, you will need to conduct research into how consumers feel about the company and the product it sells. You will also need to investigate the situation surrounding the need for this particular advertising push from GM in order to understand the market it faces as well as the various segments the company may need to address in order to effectively counter negative press, anti-GM sentiment, and the "conventional wisdom" that GM built too many trucks and SUVs. Due to the pressing need of this advertising in the wake of its bankruptcy and of falling profits, GM has set aside an operating budget of $10,000,000 with which to conduct an advertising campaign during the coming year. This includes paying for your company's services as well as the media formats selected for this campaign, so you will have to be conscious of the overall budget.

Your group has been brought together to complete the advertising plan, which has been broken into several distinct parts.

- Introduction
- Situation Analysis
- Objectives

- Budgeting
- Strategy
- Execution
- Evaluation

The final plan should not only contain these components, but it should also demonstrate the quality of your company's professionalism and marketing skills. In other words, your group has not only been tasked with demonstrating your understanding of how to build an advertising plan but with your ability to market the company within the context of this advertising plan so that you could use it as an example for future clients.

Introduction

For the introduction, you will provide a brief encapsulation of the entire advertising plan in no more than two or three pages. This will include the executive summary, which is intended for executive review, and should contain all of the most important information you cover in the paper, including—but not limited to—summaries of the advertising objectives, the advertising strategy, and budget.

You will also provide an overview of the paper that provides the purpose for writing the advertising plan as well as an overview of the structure of the advertising plan. The purpose statement should be clear and concise, beginning in the following fashion: "The purpose of this advertising plan is to..." followed by the reason this advertising plan is being constructed.

The introduction should also be directed at a particular audience. Remember, your group will address the company (GM) that will be implementing this plan. Given this, you will need to address GM and its executives as your audience. You may also need to determine exactly who will be reading this document, which may require finding a copy of the annual report online at www.gm.com.

Situation Analysis

The situation analysis provides a condensed review of all the pertinent contextual elements that will guide the development of any advertising plan. This includes the historical situation in which GM finds itself, an analysis of the industry and how it has dealt with recessions or negative press in the past (i.e., the Chrysler loan in the 1980s, Toyota's recent recall, the backlash against trucks and SUVs, etc.), an analysis of the market for this product, and a competitor analysis. The group will need to conduct the necessary research that will provide the information that will enable it to accomplish this portion of the advertising plan.

As the authors of this textbook explain, there is no exhaustive list of situational factors that go into the creation of a situation analysis. With this in mind, the following components of the situation analysis are suggested; however, the group should feel empowered to provide additional components or subtract from this list as deemed necessary. Regardless, the group should conduct the appropriate developmental research, drawing from both primary and secondary data to provide as clear a picture of the environment as possible.

Historical Context: advertising campaigns are not created in a vacuum. This section demonstrates that the group understands the historical context of the advertising campaign to be planned. This may include such items as GM's history, the basic history of their bankruptcy, the cultural context of the bankruptcy in terms of the "Great Recession" in American and other Western countries, a timeline of GM's collapse and bankruptcy itself, and any other historical nuances that may be deemed necessary.

Product Analysis: An analysis of the product that GM offers may also be useful to the development of the advertising campaign. Here, the group may focus on the attributes and benefits that make up the value proposition of the product as well as the physical description of the product and its components. It is also useful to understand how consumers use the product in question and their perception of the product, so conducting research via focus groups, real usage techniques, projective techniques, and field work would also be useful. In addition, the group may explore the various ethical and social issues that surround the product in its current state, and it may provide and explain any regulations that control the development, sale, and usage of the product. In short, the group wants to demonstrate that it understands the product and the issues surrounding the product. Furthermore, the group should not fall victim to marketing myopia when it comes to determining what GM's product is.

Industry Analysis: In this section, the group will focus on the industry itself, answering several basic questions. First, what is the size and makeup of the industry? Second, what are some of the important trends in that industry? For instance, anyone examining the auto industry would be interested in understanding the effects of the "Green Revolution" and the "Great Recession" on other players in the industry and what kind of regulations may befall the industry in the aftermath of the government bailout of the auto industry. In addition, the group may need to explore the direction the industry is heading as other issues such as peak oil, resource depletion, and others arise.

Market Analysis: As the authors of this text point out, the market analysis discusses the demand side of the equation, focusing on who is using the product and why. As such, it is important to understand the size of the market, how it is segmented, and what target groups are focused on within the industry. In short, it allows the group to uncover who GM should be targeting with this advertising campaign and potentially how it should position itself within that segment. The group may also explore where the product is sold, how consumers acquire knowledge about the product, and any other market information that may be important for the development of the advertising campaign.

Competitor Analysis: The competitor analysis for this project provides an interesting opportunity for the group because there are essentially two types of competitors in this situation. First, there are those competitors that are actively advertising the consumption of the same or similar product that GM also is selling. In other words, there are other auto companies out there that may be taking advantage of GM's missteps in recent years. Second, there are a number of ecologically minded organizations that are attempting to reduce consumption of the product and lambast GM as an environmental killer and a resource waster that should have been completely dismantled before being bailed out. Understanding both is important in the development of this advertising campaign. In the former, the group will develop an understanding of what GM is working against in terms of direct competitors. In the latter, the group will develop an understanding of what GM is working against in terms of direct naysayers. Ultimately, the competitor analysis discusses the strengths and weaknesses of the GM's competitors, culminating in an understanding of the opportunities and threats that may be exploited by not only GM but by those individuals actively working against GM and the automobile industry.

Company Analysis: Finally, it would be beneficial to all involved to understand the strengths and weaknesses of GM itself. It would also benefit the group to understand potential issues that GM faces by going forward with this advertising campaign. For example, Oprah Winfrey famously spoke out against the beef industry, which attempted to sue the talk show host. They eventually lost; however, in defending herself, Ms. Winfrey spent a great deal of time, effort, and money. In another example, Exxon is still dealing with issues related to the Exxon Valdez spill that occurred more than 20 years ago both as a public relations issue as well as a litigation issue. In other words, it is important to understand the potential ramifications of mounting a campaign to support a company that has directly affected the livelihood of American workers who have been laid off, of communities that have been decimated as a result of the collapse, and even the American taxpayer who has footed the bill for GM's resurrection.

Objectives

The group will provide an analysis and statement of what the advertising and other communication efforts are expected to accomplish. In a nutshell, this is the heart of the advertising plan in that it outlines what GM wants to do, and it extends from a sound situational analysis. For each objective discussed here, the group will provide a quantitative benchmark, measurement methods, criteria for success, and a timeframe for success as necessary. Be sure to be realistic with the objectives. An advertising campaign with the expressed goal of informing the public that GM is giving away 10,000 free cars and devoting all resources to developing a solar-powered automobile is most likely an unrealistic (and unbelievable) objective. On the other hand, an advertising campaign that is designed to increase awareness of ecologically related issues and GM's involvement with them during the course of the coming year is something that may be a bit more realistic.

Budgeting

As stated previously, GM has set aside $10,000,000 to mount this advertising campaign, which will be used to develop, implement, and measure the campaign in total. The group will need to discuss the method for budgeting, the amounts to be used in particular areas (including how much the advertising agency should be paid) as well as a justification for those amounts. If the overall budget that the group proposes is greater than the $10,000,000, then the group will need to justify the overage and attempt to convince GM that the advertising campaign requires more money.

Strategy

The group will then develop the intended blend of the creative mix for the campaign as a whole. In other words, the group will provide an overview of the strategic communications efforts that will be used to meet the objectives previously set forth. Remember that the resources the group has available to it may limit what it can implement within the time allotted. In addition, the plan should outline the positioning of the product to be achieved by the advertising campaign, and it should provide a detailed description of the target audience to be address.

Execution

In this section, the group will discuss how the advertising message or messages will be set into motion as well as the media strategy that will be used to get those messages to the target audience. The advertising message strategy will include what the company wants to say and how it wants to say it, both verbally and nonverbally; and the communications media strategy will include the justification for selecting the various media vehicles that will communicate the advertising message. The group may also want to include examples of the message that may include—but are certainly not limited to—printed ad design, storyboards, radio scripts, etc.

Evaluation

Finally, the group must provide an overview of how the effectiveness of the communications efforts will be tested. This will include the criteria and the methods that will be used to measure the effectiveness of the plan as well as an overview of the consequences and contingencies of how the plan measures up to the objectives that have been established. Be sure to mention the starting point for whatever variables you are seeking to measure. In other words, if you are selecting a measure of GM's brand image favorability with the public, what is it at this point and how do you expect it to change during the course of the campaign?

Final Paper

Again, you will want the final product to address the appropriate audience as outlined here. You will also want to construct the advertising plan in a way that markets your advertising agency by demonstrating both the breadth of your knowledge on the material and your ability to wield the tools available to you. Include any actual advertisements, charts and graphs, or other images that are pertinent to your work in a neat and organized fashion. Use appropriate headings, font, margin sizes, etc. Make sure you include an executive summary, a table of contents, and appendices as well as any other sections deemed necessary. In short, make the paper look professional and ready to submit to the client who has requested this proposal.

Final Presentation

The client may have also requested a presentation of your work. You will want to discuss the high points of your work, focusing on what will distinguish your advertising agency as the most suitable to GM's needs. As with the final paper, you will want to create a presentation that showcases not only what you know but also how you present what you know. Remember, ice skaters and gymnasts are not simply judged on technical skill but on artistry as well. Here is your opportunity to demonstrate your artistry in motion.

Project Three: Planning the Creative

Trader Joe's has decided to open a store in your area and has contacted your advertising agency to develop their advertising for the local market. For those groups that already have a Trader Joe's within a 50-mile radius of the local university, the company is seeking to introduce a new store in a different location within that radius. For the project, groups will demonstrate their understanding of how advertising messages are created and implemented through the development of a creative brief and the subsequent development of both the message strategy that responds to that brief and the advertising art and copy that flows from the message strategy. In other words, this is a three-part project from which the groups will develop a portfolio of information rather than a simple paper or presentation.

You will need to think about this project from a perspective that will address three distinct target audiences while honoring the mission and integrity of the company. You will also need to think about how the message strategy may change over a period of time and, as such, how the advertising art and copy will change while keeping the same message. In addition, you will want to perform as much research into the Trader Joe's brand as you can in order to be able to fully address their needs and maintain their values. Information concerning Trader Joe's can be found at www.traderjoes.com and www.trackingtraderjoes.com as well as in a number of magazines and newspaper articles.

The Scenario

Originally named Pronto Markets, Trader Joe's has been in business since the 1950's where it began as a small chain of convenience stores. It has since evolved into an "alternative" grocery store, in the vein of Whole Foods, that offers value and a reasonable cost to its customers while supporting the local economy and promoting joy and healthy living. Along the way, they have provided innovative methods for not only promoting consumer value but also for promoting an environmentally and physically healthy lifestyle. Long before the move towards sustainability, Trader Joe's developed a canvas grocery bag in 1977 that they'd like to think is still being used and has always been a leader in stocking organically developed foods. In addition, they recently made a commitment to ensure the removal of all added trans fats from their private label brands and took the lead in introducing appropriate symbols on packaging so that customers could make more appropriate choices.[1]

In short, Trader Joe's is committed to not only their own profit but also to the health of their customers and of the environment in general. And now they are coming to your town and would like to develop an advertising strategy that expands upon their current advertising efforts while addressing the needs of your community. Traditionally, Trader Joe's has simply advertised through radio advertisements and a customer newsletter; however, they are open to new opportunities that will address both the customers they are looking to target while still maintaining the charm and charisma of their brand. Your job is to help them develop just such an advertising campaign.

To do so, you will need to develop a creative brief that will allow you to set the goals and determine the strategy for the advertising to come. Based on this brief, you will then set about developing the message strategy that will be used to address each of three target audiences that Trader Joe's hopes to reach during the course of a year. And finally, you will develop the advertising copy and art that emerges from

1. www.traderjoes.com

the message strategy that you develop. Your work will culminate in a portfolio that you will present to your client.

The Creative Brief

The creative brief is a document that ensures good communication between all parties involved in the creative process and demonstrates an understanding of the client's needs as well as any customer insights that your group has developed. The authors have provided a basic template for the creative brief on page 381 of this text, and this template can essentially be broken down into three distinct parts: the client overview, the target audience overview, and the message overview.

Client Overview.

Here, you will briefly discuss who your client is, showing that you are familiar with the client and the products that they offer. In other words, you are answering two very basic questions: who is Trader Joe's and what products and/or services do they offer? In addition, you may want to provide an overview of what the company is attempting to accomplish with the advertising campaign. In other words, what is their overall strategy? Furthermore, you will most likely need to determine who their competition in the area will be. Draw from the pool of direct and indirect competitors in your area in order to develop an understanding of just who Trader Joe's will need to differentiate itself from. As the authors of this text state, here is where you will provide a "snapshot of the brand situation" that Trader Joe's is facing as they enter into your market.

Target Overview.

The target overview answers three basic questions: who is the target, what consumer needs or problems are we addressing, and what do the consumers currently think about the company. Trader Joe's has come to you with three specific local segments that they wish to address with their advertising, and you will need to show an understanding of each. These segments include college students, single consumers who live alone, and soccer moms. You will need to demonstrate knowledge of each of these segments within your community, including their needs and what they think of Trader Joe's.

You will also need to show how Trader Joe's can fulfill the basic unmet needs for each of these segments. For instance, single consumers who live alone often find themselves wasting packaged food because much of it is designed for multiple-person families. Trader Joe's has, in some ways, addressed this issue, a fact that can play out in the advertising. Ultimately, each of the three segments has different needs to be addressed, but keep in mind that all three have many of the same needs and problems that Trader Joe's can address.

Finally, you will need to develop a basic understanding of what the consumer currently thinks of Trader Joe's. For this, you may need to develop research that taps into the attitudes and behaviors the targeted segments carry with them about the product category as well as about the Trader Joe's brand. Such insight will help you to understand your starting point in terms of addressing these segments in your area.

Message Overview.

The message overview provides an understanding of what your message needs will be. Based on the insights you have just developed about the company and about the segments to be targeted, you will again answer three basic questions. The first involves the one thing that you want your customers to believe about Trader Joe's. Although you want to be as single-minded as possible, you will also need to make sure that this one thing will hold true with each targeted segment. In other words, if you want customers to believe that Trader Joe's has everything one needs to enjoy the single life, this may not work for one of the segments you've been challenged to address.

You will then need to determine what it is you can tell the customers that will help them to believe what it is you want them to believe. In other words, here is where you really start thinking about the advertising and how you can use words and images to convey the ideas you hope to get across to the consumer. Here is also where you begin to develop an answer to the question concerning the advertising tonality. In short, think about the personality of the advertisements and how they should come across.

The Message Strategy

Once the creative brief is complete, the group will then move into the development of the message strategy. There is a veritable menu of potential strategies for your group to choose, but there are several considerations to keep in mind as you move forward. First of all, one or more message strategies may overlap in a variety of ways. You will need to make sure to choose the strategy (or strategies) that best fits with the creative brief that you've developed and ultimately meets both the needs of Trader Joe's and the needs of their potential customers.

Second, you will need to make sure that the message strategy and the method of conveying that strategy fits well with the three distinct segments that you are addressing. This may mean that you develop an advertising campaign that adopts a different strategy and multiple methods for each of the segments. In other words, you may choose an Instill Brand Preference strategy but suggest a feel good ad for the soccer moms, humor ads for college students, and sexual-appeal ads for the single customer who lives alone. Here is where the insight into the individual segments you developed while constructing the creative brief comes into play.

Finally, you will also need to consider how the message strategy you've chosen might evolve over time. Trader Joe's is looking for a plan that will carry them through the first two years of business in your area. They would like you to make sure you develop a plan, and advertising messages, that will address their needs on day one, at the one-year mark, and again at the two-year mark. Here, you are basically answering the question, how will the message strategy change as Trader Joe's becomes more established in its location and within the minds of its targeted segments.

The Art and Copy

And now for the fun part. Based upon the creative brief and your development of the message strategy, the group will now develop the creative plan for the advertising campaign as well as several advertisements that are the culmination of the work conducted thus far. The creative plan is the guideline to be used throughout the development of your advertisements. It contains the various message elements that will help you to coordinate the copy you will write as well as the art and production to be utilized in the advertisements. These elements include the types of media you will be using, the main product claims to be made in the advertisements, creative devices within those advertisements, and any other important elements that the creative people need to know in order to develop copy and art for the campaign.

Your group will then create at least nine advertisements, one for each target segment at each stage of the campaign. In other words, you will develop at least three advertisements that address the college student segment, one for the day-one stage of the campaign, one for the year-one stage of the campaign, and one for the year-two stage of the campaign. You will then do the same for the single-person household segment and the soccer mom segment. For these advertisements, you will need to show your awareness of the copywriting aspect and the art aspect for each advertisement.

Copywriting consists of the written and/or verbal descriptions contained within the advertisements themselves. How copy is constructed is very much dependent on the type of media you will be using, particularly as it pertains to print or broadcast advertising. As such, you will need to be cognizant of exactly which media will be used for the different segments as well as the different copywriting elements associated with each media.

In addition, your group will also create mock-ups of the art to accompany the copy you have written. These mock-ups may be as simple as basic "stick-figure" sketches for a print ad or a storyboard for a television commercial to something as complex and polished as actual photographs, art, or video to closely approximate the visual look of the advertisements you are proposing. Whichever route you choose to take, you will need to make sure that the copy and the art fit seamlessly together and fulfill the elements of the creative plan as well as address the needs of the creative brief.

Final Portfolio

You will want the final portfolio to address the appropriate audience as outlined here. That audience will be Trader Joe's. You will also want to organize the contents of the portfolio in such a way that markets your advertising agencies professionalism and expertise. Be sure to include any actual advertisements, charts and graphs, and other images that are pertinent to your work in a neat and organized fashion. Use appropriate headings, font, margin sizes, etc. Make sure you include an executive summary, a table of contents, and appendices as well as any other sections deemed necessary. In short, make the portfolio look professional and ready to submit to the client who has requested this proposal.

Final Presentation

The client may have also requested a presentation of your work. You will want to discuss the high points of your work, focusing on what will distinguish your advertising agency as the most suitable to the needs of Trader Joe's. As with the final portfolio, you will want to create a presentation that showcases not only what you know but also how you present what you know as well. Remember, ice skaters and gymnasts are not simply judged on technical skill but on artistry as well. Here is your opportunity to demonstrate your artistry in motion.

Project Four: Planning the Media.

A local microbrewery has decided to expand its operations a bit, bottling and selling its critically acclaimed ales within your state, starting with your city. During the course of determining their advertising plan, the owners of the microbrewery discovered that they knew very little about local media opportunities through which to conduct their advertising. For this project, groups will develop a media plan and analysis for the microbrewery, demonstrating that they have an understanding of their local media market as well as how the type of media selected for an advertising campaign can impact that campaign. Furthermore, groups will also need to think about media in relation to the targeted audiences.

You will need to approach this project as if you are the media experts for your area. To do so, you will also need to work within the constraints provided by the company. Those constraints include the groups they wish to target, the budget set aside for media buys, and the basic advertising message and approach they have already developed. All of this will culminate in a media plan that contains an analysis of the targeted audiences and the media that they pay attention to, the pros and cons of the various advertising media outlets available in your area, and your recommendations for which media to use and how to tailor the central message they wish to utilize within those different media selections.

The Scenario.

Mystic Microbrewery is a locally owned and operated brew-pub that has recently decided to expand its brewery operations to include a bottling plant. They have decided to start bottling and selling their various ales to the public much like the Sam Adams' and Fat Tires of the world. In fact, Mystic considers both the Sam Adams and Fat Tire brands to be direct competitors. However, they wish to start off in a smaller market than the national market those two brands possess, starting with your city in the first year before moving to a statewide distribution process. They have already begun the process of developing an advertising plan that will feature the brand name, Mystic Ales, and their three most popular flavors: Indian pale ale, orange wheat, and golden wheat. Before completing the advertising plan, however, they would like to gain a better understanding of the local media market so that they can better develop their advertising to fit the available media.

Your advertising firm has been contacted to develop a media plan for Mystic Microbrewery that will include an analysis of the local media market, an understanding of the market segments that they target and how they align with Mystic's desired segments, and recommendations for which media Mystic should choose as well as how the different media will affect their proposed advertising. Mystic wants to use the slogan "Sail Into the Mystic" in all of its advertising and has already contracted with recording artist Van Morrison to use the song "Into the Mystic" as well as his likeness in any advertising they decide upon. They believe that he will help them to reach the market segments they wish to target: educated baby boomers with discerning tastes and a sophisticated lifestyle, college students who listen to alternative music and aspire to a Bohemian lifestyle, and young urban professionals in your area who enjoy a good Irish pub.

The company also wants to emphasize a few things in the advertising that the media will also have to convey in some way. The company wants to emphasize that it is completely a local company, buying only local grains and hops for its ales, contracting with a local company to make the bottles it will use, and favoring locally owned stores where available. Mystic also wants to emphasize that they are a green company much in the vein of the Fat Tire brewery and that they promote the recycling of their bottles and other goods. Finally, the company would like the media they use to reflect these elements: be locally owned as best as possible and be environmentally friendly.

In addition, Mystic has set aside a budget of $75,000 to purchase space and time on various media with the possibility of accessing another $25,000 if the extra is justified in some manner. Your job is to analyze your local media markets (traditional, digital, and alternative) for the best opportunities available to Mystic and provide the company with your recommendations for which media to use, how and for how long to use those media, and how to develop their advertising in relation to the media they use.

Media Strategy.

Any media plan will start with a basic understanding of the strategic considerations the company will make with its media selections. This media plan is no different; however, you will also want to demonstrate an understanding of Mystic Microbrewery and its brand. You will also investigate the competitor media strategy within your area.

The Mystic Brand.

Based on the information provided, the group should be able to infer much about the brand personality the company is attempting to convey through the media it will eventually choose. In other words, this is the only information the company has provided you. Your job is to develop a description of the brand personality and demonstrate that you understand who this company is. In addition, you may provide an overview of what the company is attempting to accomplish on a long-term basis.

Mystic Media Strategy.

Your media plan will also demonstrate an understanding of the media strategy that Mystic Microbrewery is attempting to implement. In short, the media strategy provides an overview of what the company is trying to do with the media that it selects. Based on the information provided above, your goal is to flesh out this strategy by listing and explaining the objectives that Mystic Microbrewery hopes to accomplish in the first year of the bottling enterprise. Although these objectives should be based on the information provided in the scenario section, feel free to expand on those objectives, keeping in mind that the individuals developing the advertising plan do not necessarily know what various media can do for them.

Competitor Media Strategy.

Since Mystic considers both Sam Adams and Fat Tire to be competitors, it would behoove you to understand, as best you can, the media strategy of both within the market you are pursuing. In other words, conduct some research into the media that both entities utilize to get their brand messages across in your areas. From this research, infer certain basic objectives that the two brands are attempting to meet. Finally, you will want to compare and contrast Mystic's objectives with those of Sam Adams and Fat Tire before moving on to the media analysis.

Media Analysis.

For the media analysis, the group will provide an overview of all the media options available in your area, focusing as much as possible on the locally owned options as per Mystic's request. For each available media outlet in your area, you will need to provide an overview of the media type; an analysis of what each medium will offer Mystic in terms of reach, weight, etc.; and an analysis of the advantages and disadvantages of using that particular medium in relation to the media strategy outlined in the previous section.

Media Overview.

For the media overview, groups will explore the options available in each media type covering traditional media, Internet and digital media, and alternative media formats. For instance, a group that looks at the radio as a possible media may be dealing with several different radio channels in a given local market, so the group must be cognizant of both the medium as well as the potential vehicles that are at play in the area. In this section, you may want to read ahead a bit, particularly to Chapter 17, so that you can potentially explore some other media types besides the print, broadcasting, and Internet media presented in this section.

Traditional Media. Traditional media opportunities include print and broadcasting formats. Mystic would definitely like to take advantage of any traditional opportunities available in their area, but they certainly do not want to focus solely on traditional media. That being said, they want their traditional media outlets to be local in nature.

Internet, Digital, and Interactive Media. Mystic also understands that marketing communications efforts in the 21st century require the use of the Internet and other interactive media formats such as games, social networking, and other formats. Any media overview must outline the opportunities available to them in terms of their Internet presence and digital formats.

Alternative Media. In addition to the media formats already mentioned, Mystic would also like a better understanding of other media formats that are available to them such as point-of-purchase displays, billboards, etc. Feel free to be creative in determining what alternative media are available in your area.

Media Analysis.

Once you have an overview of the specific media type, you will need to analyze the various elements of that media type in relation to the various targeted segments in your market. In other words, you will need to conduct research into the reach, weight, geographic scope, frequency, and any other characteristics of the media pertinent to Mystic and their media strategy. In addition, you will want to discuss the cost elements associated with the medium in question. Here is where you can answer the question, what can the various media in the area do for Mystic?

Advantages and Disadvantages.

Finally, you will want to discuss the advantages and disadvantages of using the media in relation to Mystic's various objectives. Some of these advantages and disadvantages may be found in the textbook, but you will also develop an understanding of advantages and disadvantages associated with the local market, the media objectives Mystic has, and the market segments Mystic wishes to reach. Regardless of whether or not you will recommend the use of the media in question, you need to list their advantages and disadvantages so that Mystic can make the most informed decision it can make.

Media and Advertising Recommendations.

Finally, you will provide Mystic with your recommendations for how to proceed with their media plan. This section should include your recommendations for the media to be used as well as your recommendations for how they can use that media to convey the message they are trying to convey. This will require some creative thinking on your part.

Media Recommendations.

Your media recommendations should include an overview of all media that you would recommend for Mystic. Since Mystic is looking to take advantage of a variety of different avenues, it is best to recommend media from each of the traditional media, Internet and digital media, and alternative media formats you discussed during the Media Overview section. In addition, you will want to recommend specific vehicles within the medium or media that you choose and the length of time to use the media and the continuity associated with the media. Remember, there is a budget to consider and your recommendations will have to fit into that budget.

Advertising Recommendations.

Mystic has a very clear advertising message that they would like to convey to their targeted customers: "Sail Into the Mystic." How this message is conveyed will differ with each type of media. After making your recommendations for specific media and vehicles, you will also make suggestions concerning how Mystic Microbrewery can alter their advertisements accordingly. Keep in mind that they have permission to use the song "Into the Mystic" by Van Morrison as well as his likeness in advertisements. How these are used will change depending on the media. Provide specific examples of what Mystic can do with the advertising as well as how what they do fits with the specific media you have recommended.

Conclusion.

Finally, you will want to provide an overview of your services in executing the media plan. Describe what your organization can do for Mystic in terms of media buying processes, adapting the advertising to different media and vehicles, and other such activities. In essence, here is your opportunity to sell your experience and expertise to Mystic in helping them shape and execute their media strategy both now and in the future. Remember, Mystic is only beginning to roll out their product in your city throughout the course of the first year. Perhaps you can prepare them for what will happen as they expand to the rest of your state.

Final Paper.

As with all projects within this textbook, you will want the final product to address the appropriate audience as outlined here. You will also want to construct the media plan in a way that markets your advertising agency by demonstrating both the breadth of your knowledge on the material and your ability to wield the tools available to you. Include any actual advertisements, charts and graphs, or other images that are pertinent to your work in a neat and organized fashion. Use appropriate headings, font, margin sizes, etc. Make sure you include an executive summary, a table of contents, and appendices as well as any other sections deemed necessary. In short, make the paper look professional and ready to submit to the client who has requested this proposal.

Final Presentation.

The client may have also requested a presentation of your work. You will want to discuss the high points of your work, focusing on what will distinguish your advertising agency as the most suitable to the needs of Mystic Microbrewery. As with the final paper, you will want to create a presentation that showcases not only what you know but also how you present what you know as well. Remember, ice skaters and gymnasts are not simply judged on technical skill but on artistry as well. Here is your opportunity to demonstrate your artistry in motion.

Project Five: Planning Integrated Brand Promotion.

For this project, the groups are given the task of developing an IBP plan that encompasses the creation and promotion of a branded entertainment venue for Victoria's Secret. Not only will groups have the opportunity to build a branded event, but they will also determine what additional sponsors will be pursued to help provide financial or logistic support for the event, decide what sales promotion and direct marketing efforts will be used to support the event and—more importantly—sell tickets to the event, and discuss how public relations will be used to promote the event and what it stands for.

This project is designed to give you an opportunity to explore the promotional side of advertising and promotions, setting the advertising element aside for the time being. Although advertising does play a part in any IBP effort, this project is simply not about the advertising. Instead, students will focus on other opportunities for promoting a company, its products, and even the message it is trying to convey to an audience. In this case, students will focus on several audiences. The first is the consumer audience, answering the question: how do we attract consumer attendance at our event using methods other than advertising? The second is the corporate audience, determining how we can attract corporate sponsorship of our event.

The Scenario.

Victoria's Secret has decided to make a concerted effort to raise money for Breast Cancer research. As part of this effort, they have decided to put together an event that connects their brand with the consumer and with the cause in a "unique and compelling" way. Given the success of the annual fashion show that is televised on CBS, Victoria's Secret has decided to take the show on the road. Starting this year, Victoria's Secret is putting together a music festival that will feature a number of popular bands, several fashion shows, including all the Victoria's Secret models, and other attractions that lend themselves to a traveling festival of this sort. At its heart, however, the company wants the event to help raise awareness for their cause as well as the money that they believe will help find the cure.

Your group has been hired to help develop this event, plan the promotional efforts for the event, and determine what other brands will be pursued as sponsors for this event. As such, you have been given relative carte blanche in building this event from the ground up. In other words, the only direction the company has given you in terms of building the event is that they want you to build a music festival that fits with and is an extension of the Victoria's Secret brand and is as completely an immersive experience as can be managed.

To that end, you will produce an event proposal that provides an overall blueprint of the festival and all that it entails. Included in this proposal will be a description of the event itself, a discussion of the sales promotional and direct marketing efforts that will attract consumers to the event, an overview of the proposed sponsorships and how to attract those sponsors, and, finally, an outline of the public relations efforts that will not only promote the event but also the cause the event is designed to support. Your final proposal should not only contain these components, but it should also demonstrate the quality of your company's professionalism and marketing skills. In other words, your group has not only been tasked with demonstrating your understanding of how to build an event of this nature but also with your ability to market your consulting company within the context of this plan so that you could use it as an example for future clients.

Event Analysis.

This section provides an overview of the event that you have designed for this project. In it, you will describe, in detail, the event that your group has designed, making sure to discuss how the event fits with the Victoria's Secret brand. You will begin this analysis with a discussion of what your assessment of the Victoria's Secret brand is and what it is hoping to accomplish with this branded entertainment event. Then, you will want to discuss the audience for this event as well as the music and the bands or artists that will be pursued for this event (making sure to think about alternatives in case the artists you've chosen don't have the time or inclination to join this particular music festival). Finally, you will want to discuss the other activities and event details that will be a part of the festival.

Brand Analysis.

For the brand analysis, you will want to demonstrate the breadth and depth of your knowledge of the Victoria's Secret brand, which will require some research on your part. You can find much of the information you need at www.victoriassecret.com or through a Google search. You might also explore the Limited Brands annual report for additional information concerning the brand. Ultimately, you will want to define the essence of the brand in order to match appropriate bands, activities, and sponsors to the Victoria's Secret brand.

Audience Analysis.

In this section, you will answer a very basic question: who will be coming to the event? In other words, what market segments will most likely attend a Victoria's Secret branded event and who would Victoria's Secret like to come to the event. Understanding the audience the event should attract will provide your group with insight into what bands should be invited to the festival as well as what other activities will be held. In short, you will determine where the audience will come from and why they will come to your event when there are so many others that they could attend.

Band Analysis.

Once the brand and the audience have been analyzed, the group can start to put together a list of musical artists that will fit with both. Feel free to use your imagination and think big, but also keep an eye towards the brand and the audience. Although very popular bands in their own right, it is unlikely that Slayer and Metallica will fit with the Victoria's Secret brand. An artist like Bob Dylan, on the other hand, might fit because he's done commercial work for Victoria's Secret in the past. In addition, keep the cause in mind. An artist like Kylie Minogue, a breast cancer survivor, might be a perfect fit for the festival.

Event Details.

Finally, the group will want to put together other important details of the event. What other activities will take place during the course of the festival (e.g., fashion shows, contests, makeovers), how many days will the festival last in any given city, how many cities will it visit during the course of its run, and even when will it run? Again, feel free to use your imagination and think big, but make sure you keep the brand and its cause in mind as you go forward.

Sponsorship Analysis.

Once you have the event itself planned, you can then move forward with an analysis of potential sponsors for the event. Each group will assess the sponsorship potential of at least eight possible sponsors for the event. You will need to choose four nationally and/or internationally recognized brands as well as four local industries to approach for sponsorship possibilities. Again, your group must keep in mind the brand and cause when going forward with the sponsorship analysis.

National Brands as Sponsors.

For each national or international sponsor, you will need to provide a quick description of their brand and how it could fit with the festival and its overall branded feeling. You will describe why and how that brand will fit with the event, what benefits the brand may receive from the audience gathered at the event, and the sponsorship requirements expected from each brand (e.g. money, space, advertising, etc.). Ultimately, you need to be able to show how the event, audience, and sponsors match up.

Local Industries as Sponsors.

Local sponsors can provide a great deal of logistical support for a festival of this sort. Although you may not, at this point, know all the different brands available in any given location, you can at least determine what industries contain potential sponsors in different locations that fit with the event. In other words, you could potentially select OB-GYN doctors as a potential sponsor, which would then require research into the doctors available in different areas. Again, you will want to discuss how the sponsorship will benefit both parties involved and show how the event, audience, and sponsors match up.

Selling Sponsorships.

Finally, once you have an idea of what companies potentially fit with the event as sponsors, you will need to discuss how to approach those companies. This will require a bit of discussion concerning direct marketing and other sales efforts. Your goal here is to determine how best to sell sponsorships to the event both to national brands as well as the local brands you've chosen.

Promotional Efforts.

In addition, you will want to discuss the various sales promotion efforts that will bring people to the event. Victoria's Secret is taking care of the advertising on the large scale, so your task is to determine how best to support that advertising through the use of point-of-purchase advertising, sales promotion techniques, social networking opportunities, and support media. Keep in mind that you will want these efforts to fit with the overall theme of the event as well as with the Victoria's Secret brand and other brands that have been selected as sponsors. You may also want to discuss direct marketing and personal selling efforts that are designed to bring larger groups into the event or even corporate groups.

Public Relations Efforts.

Finally, Victoria's Secret will want to launch a full-blown public relations effort to promote the event and the cause that it supports. Here, your task is to design both a proactive strategy for promoting the company, its cause, and the event and a reactive strategy that analyzes potential problems that could arise during the course of the festival.

Proactive Strategy.

With a proactive strategy, the public relations efforts are related to the marketing objectives associated with the branded entertainment event. The idea is to develop a plan for communicating the *raison d'être* for the event, including how and through what avenues the event will be communicated. Again, feel free to think big and be imaginative. Sending Heidi Klum to *Late Night with David Letterman* is most likely a very manageable (and very lucrative) part of the public relations plan. However, you also want to keep in mind some of the "smaller" opportunities open to you such as that provided by social networking avenues.

Reactive Strategy.

The job of the reactive strategy is to anticipate potential problems and work out how to solve them before they even come to pass. For instance, a festival of this size is bound to produce a rather large carbon footprint… or at the very least, the perception of a large carbon footprint. What happens if a number of people and organizations call for a boycott of the festival as a result of the perception of its carbon footprint? It serves the event and Victoria's Secret well if they have a response to the outcry even before there is an outcry.

Final Paper.

Again, you will want the final product to address the appropriate audience as outlined here. You will also want to construct the branded event plan in a way that markets your consulting agency by demonstrating both the breadth of your knowledge on the material and your ability to wield the tools available to you. Include any actual promotions, charts and graphs, or other images that are pertinent to your work in a neat and organized fashion. Use appropriate headings, font, margin sizes, etc. Make sure you include an executive summary, a table of contents, and appendices as well as any other sections deemed necessary. In short, make the paper look professional and ready to submit to the client who has requested this proposal.

Final Presentation.

Victoria's Secret may have also requested a presentation of your work. You will want to discuss the high points of your work, focusing on what will distinguish your consulting agency as the most suitable to Victoria's Secret's needs. As with the final paper, you will want to create a presentation that showcases not only what you know but also how you present what you know as well. Remember, ice skaters and gymnasts are not simply judged on technical skill but on artistry as well. Here is your opportunity to demonstrate your artistry in motion.

Glossary

3P's creativity framework Indicates creativity is fostered by 3 inputs: people, process and place.

A

above-the-line promotion Traditional measured media advertising: any message broadcast to the public through conventional means such as television, the Internet, radio, and magazines.

account executive The liaison between an advertising agency and its clients; the nature of the account executive's job requires excellent persuasion, negotiation, and judgment skills in order to both successfully alleviate client discomfort and sell highly effective, groundbreaking ideas.

account planning A system by which, in contrast to traditional advertising research methods, an agency assigns a coequal account planner to work alongside the account executive and analyze research data. This method requires the account planner to stay with the same projects on a continuous basis.

account team A group of people comprising many different facets of the advertising industry (direct marketing, public relations, graphic design, etc.) who work together under the guidance of a team leader to both interface with other members of the account team and team members of their own respective specialties.

Action for Children's Television (ACT) A group formed during the 1970s to lobby the government to limit the amount and content of advertising directed at children.

advertisement A specific message that an organization has placed to persuade an audience.

advertising A paid, mass-mediated attempt to persuade.

advertising campaign A series of coordinated advertisements and other promotional efforts that communicate a single theme or idea.

advertising clutter An obstacle to advertising resulting from the large volume of similar ads for most products and services.

advertising plan A plan that specifies the thinking and tasks needed to conceive and implement an effective advertising effort.

advertising response function A mathematical relationship based on marginal analysis that associates dollars spent on advertising and sales generated; sometimes used to help establish an advertising budget.

advertising specialties A sales promotion having three key elements: a message, placed on a useful item, given to consumers with no obligation.

advertising substantiation program An FTC program initiated in 1971 to ensure that advertisers make available to consumers supporting evidence for claims made in ads.

advocacy advertising Advertising that attempts to influence public opinion on important social, political, or environmental issues of concern to the sponsoring organization.

aerial advertising Advertising that involves airplanes (pulling signs or banners), skywriting, or blimps.

affirmative disclosure An FTC action requiring that important material determined to be absent from prior ads must be included in subsequent advertisements.

agency of record The advertising agency chosen by the advertiser to purchase media time and space.

appropriation The use of pictures or images owned by someone else without permission.

attitude An overall evaluation of any object, person, or issue that varies along a continuum, such as favorable to unfavorable or positive to negative.

attitude study A method of obtaining customer feedback that measures target markets' feelings and opinions about a company's product, as well as that of the competing brand.

audience A group of individuals who may receive and interpret messages sent from advertisers through mass media.

authenticity The quality of genuineness inherent in something. Advertisers value product placement with a high degree of apparent authenticity, as more blatant approaches are easily detected by consumers, resulting in possible disgust or irritation and achieving the opposite of the advertiser's aim.

average quarter-hour persons The average number of listeners tuned to a radio station during a specified 15-minute segment of a daypart.

average quarter-hour rating The radio audience during a quarter-hour daypart expressed as a percentage of the population of the measurement area.

average quarter-hour share The percentage of the total radio audience that was listening to a radio station during a specified quarter-hour daypart.

axis A line, real or imagined, that runs through an advertisement and from which the elements in the ad flare out.

B

balance An orderliness and compatibility of presentation in an advertisement.

barter syndication A form of television syndication that takes both off-network and first-run syndication shows and offers them free or at a reduced rate to local television stations, with some national advertising presold within the programs.

behavioral targeting The process of database development made possible by online tracking markers that advertisers place on a Web surfer's hard drive to track that person's online surfing and shopping behavior.

beliefs The knowledge and feelings a person has accumulated about an object or issue.

below-the-line promotion A promotional effort that includes in-store promotions, coupons, dealer discounts, and product placement.

benefit positioning A positioning option that features a distinctive customer benefit.

benefit segmentation A type of market segmenting in which target segments are delineated by the various benefit packages that different consumers want from the same product category.

between-vehicle duplication Exposure to the same advertisement in different media.

bill-back allowances A monetary incentive provided to retailers for featuring a marketer's brand in either advertising or in-store displays.

blackletter A style patterned after monastic hand-drawn letters characterized by the ornate design of the letters. Also called *gothic.*

bleed page A magazine page on which the background color of an ad runs to the edge of the page, replacing the standard white border.

blog (short for Weblog) A personal journal on a website that is frequently updated and intended for public access. Such sites are emerging as new and sophisticated sources of product and brand information.

blogger The author of a blog.

brainstorming An organized approach to idea generation; for effective brainstorming, it is necessary to learn about the material in question beforehand, foster a safe environment free of destructive criticism, and openly discuss disagreements that may arise.

brand A name, term, sign, symbol, or any other feature that identifies one seller's good or service as distinct from those of other sellers.

brand advertising Advertising that communicates the specific features, values, and benefits of a particular brand offered for sale by a particular organization.

brand attitudes Summary evaluations that reflect preferences for various products and brands.

brand awareness An indicator of consumer knowledge about the existence of the brand and how easily that knowledge can be retrieved from memory.

brand communities Groups of consumers who feel a commonality and a shared purpose grounded or attached to a consumer good or service.

branded entertainment Embedding one's brand or brand icons as part of any entertainment property (e.g., a sporting event) in an effort to impress and connect with consumers in a unique and compelling way.

brand equity Developed by a firm that creates and maintains positive associations with the brand in the mind of consumers.

brand extension An adaptation of an existing brand to a new product area.

branding The strategy of developing brand names so that manufacturers can focus consumer attention on a clearly identified item.

brand loyalty A decision-making mode in which consumers repeatedly buy the same brand of a product as their choice to fulfill a specific need.

brand-loyal users A market segment made up of consumers who repeatedly buy the same brand of a product.

brandscape An environment, typically retail or entertainment, that is used as a living brand promotion: NIKETOWN is the perfect example.

brand switching An advertising objective in which a campaign is designed to encourage customers to switch from their established brand.

build-up analysis A method of building up the expenditure levels of various tasks to help establish an advertising budget.

business-market sales promotion Promotion designed to cultivate buyers from large corporations who are making purchase decisions.

business markets The institutional buyers who purchase items to be used in other products and services or to be resold to other businesses or households.

buzz marketing The process of creating events or experiences that yield conversations that include the brand or product advertisers are trying to sell.

C

cable television A type of television that transmits a wide range of programming to subscribers through wires rather than over airwaves.

cause-related advertising Advertising that identifies corporate sponsorship of philanthropic activities.

cease-and-desist order An FTC action requiring an advertiser to stop running an ad within 30 days so a hearing can be held to determine whether the advertising in question is deceptive or unfair.

celebrity A unique sociological category that matters a great deal to advertisers.

celebrity endorsements Advertisements that use an expert or celebrity as a spokesperson to endorse the use of a product or service.

channel grazing Using a television remote control to monitor programming on other channels while an advertisement is being broadcast.

Chaos Scenario As predicted by Bob Garfield, the mass exodus of advertising revenue from traditional broadcast media due to audience fragmentation and ad-avoidance hardware, which in turn reduces funding for the affected media and serves to limit their product quality, reducing audience size. This of course accelerates diversion of advertising dollars even further until there is little reliance on these media at all for marketing.

cinema advertising Includes ads that run in movie theaters before the film and other advertising appearing off-screen within a theater.

circulation The number of newspapers distributed each day (for daily newspapers) or each week (for weekly publications).

classified advertising Newspaper advertising that appears as all-copy messages under categories such as sporting goods, employment, and automobiles.

click fraud The act of clicking on Internet advertising links solely to generate illegitimate revenue for the website carrying the ad; can occur by persons paid to do so or by computer programs designed to imitate people.

click-throughs When Web users click on advertisements that take them to the home pages of those advertisers.

closing date The date when production-ready advertising materials must be delivered to a publisher for an ad to make a newspaper or magazine issue.

cognitive consistency The maintenance of a system of beliefs and attitudes over time; consumers' desire for cognitive consistency is an obstacle to advertising.

cognitive dissonance The anxiety or regret that lingers after a difficult decision.

cognitive responses The thoughts that occur to individuals at that exact moment in time when their beliefs and attitudes are being challenged by some form of persuasive communication.

cognitive style The unique preference of each person for thinking about and solving a problem. Cognitive style pioneer Carl Jung proposed three different dimensions in which thinking differs: Sensing versus Intuiting, Thinking versus Feeling, and Extraverted versus Introverted.

column inch A unit of advertising space in a newspaper, equal to one inch deep by one column wide.

communication tests A type of pretest message research that simply seeks to see if a message is communicating something close to what is desired.

community A group of people loosely joined by some common characteristic or interest.

comp A polished version of an ad.

comparison advertisements Advertisements in which an advertiser makes a comparison between the firm's brand and competitors' brands.

competitive field The companies that compete for a segment's business.

competitive positioning A positioning option that uses an explicit reference to an existing competitor to help define precisely what the advertised brand can do.

competitor analysis In an advertising plan, the section that discusses who the competitors are, outlining their strengths, weaknesses, tendencies, and any threats they pose.

concept test A type of developmental research that seeks feedback designed to screen the quality of a new idea, using consumers as the final judge and jury.

consent order An FTC action asking an advertiser accused of running deceptive or unfair advertising to stop running the advertisement in question, without admitting guilt.

consideration set The subset of brands from a particular product category that becomes the focal point of a consumer's evaluation.

consultants Individuals who specialize in areas related to the promotional process.

consumer behavior Those activities directly involved in obtaining, consuming, and disposing of products and services, including the decision processes that precede and follow these actions.

consumer culture A way of life centered around consumption.

consumerism The actions of individual consumers to exert power over the marketplace activities of organizations.

consumer-generated content (CGC) Advertisements for products produced either in part or completely by their end users. The recent explosion of consumer-generated content is largely due to the advent of content-sharing Internet websites (like YouTube) that essentially enable anyone to post (and view) video content.

consumer markets The markets for products and services purchased by individuals or households to satisfy their specific needs.

consumer-market sales promotion A type of sales promotion designed to induce household consumers to purchase a firm's brand rather than a competitor's brand.

contest A sales promotion that has consumers compete for prizes based on skill or ability.

context effects How the context of the media through which an ad is presented affects consumers' impressions of the ad.

continuity The pattern of placement of advertisements in a media schedule.

continuous scheduling A pattern of placing ads at a steady rate over a period of time.

controlled circulation The number of copies of a newspaper that are given away free.

co-op advertising *See* **cooperative advertising**.

cooperative advertising The sharing of advertising expenses between national advertisers and local merchants. Also called *co-op advertising*.

copywriting The process of expressing the value and benefits a brand has to offer, via written or verbal descriptions.

corporate advertising Advertising intended to establish a favorable attitude toward a company as a whole, not just toward a specific brand.

corporate home page A site on the World Wide Web that focuses on a corporation and its products.

corrective advertising An FTC action requiring an advertiser to run additional advertisements to dispel false beliefs created by deceptive advertising.

cost per inquiry (CPI) The number of inquiries generated by a direct-marketing program divided by that program's cost.

cost per order (CPO) The number of orders generated by a direct-marketing program divided by that program's cost.

cost per rating point (CPRP) The cost of a spot on television divided by the program's rating; the resulting dollar figure can be used to compare the efficiency of advertising on various programs.

cost per thousand (CPM) The dollar cost of reaching 1,000 members of an audience using a particular medium.

cost per thousand–target market (CPM–TM) The cost per thousand for a particular segment of an audience.

coupon A type of sales promotion that entitles a buyer to a designated reduction in price for a product or service.

cover date The date of publication appearing on a magazine.

creative abrasion The clash of ideas, abstracted from the people who propose them, from which new ideas and breakthroughs can evolve. *Compare* **interpersonal abrasion**.

creative brief A document that outlines and channels an essential creative idea and objective.

creative revolution A revolution in the advertising industry during the 1960s, characterized by the "creatives" (art directors and copywriters) having a bigger say in the management of their agencies.

creative selling The act of assisting and persuading customers regarding purchasing decisions; creative selling typically involves products in which customers require extensive knowledge about the product before buying, such as specialty goods or higher-priced items (for example, sports equipment, cookware, insurance, or real estate).

creative team The copywriters and art directors responsible for coming up with the creative concept for an advertising campaign.

creativity The ability to consider and hold together seemingly inconsistent elements and forces, making a new connection; creativity is essential in the advertising world because successful marketing demands a constant seamless synthesis of the product and entirely different ideas or concepts.

cross-selling Marketing programs aimed at customers that already purchase other products.

crowdsourcing The online distribution of certain tasks to groups (crowds) of experts, enthusiasts, or even consumers.

culture What a people do—the way they eat, groom themselves, celebrate, mark their space and social position, and so forth.

cume The cumulative radio audience, which is the total number of different people who listen to a station for at least five minutes in a quarter-hour period within a specified daypart.

customer relationship management (CRM) The continual effort toward cultivating and maintaining long-term relationships with customers; many companies have recognized trust and rapport are key elements to repeated sales and thus train their sales teams to emphasize each particular customer's needs rather than the bottom line.

customer satisfaction Good feelings that come from a favorable postpurchase experience.

D

dailies Newspapers published every weekday; also, in television ad production, the scenes shot during the previous day's production.

dayparts Segments of time during a television broadcast day.

deal-proneness The ease with which a consumer can get a deal, know what a good deal is, operate with knowledge of what a good price would be, and know a seller's cost.

deception Making false or misleading statements in an advertisement.

defamation When a communication occurs that damages the reputation of an individual because the information was untrue.

delayed response advertising Advertising that relies on imagery and message themes to emphasize the benefits and satisfying characteristics of a brand.

demographic segmentation Market segmenting based on basic descriptors like age, gender, race, marital status, income, education, and occupation.

design The structure (and the plan behind the structure) for the aesthetic and stylistic aspects of a print advertisement.

developmental copy research A type of copy research that helps copywriters at the early stages of copy development by providing audience interpretations and reactions to the proposed copy.

dialogue Advertising copy that delivers the selling points of a message to the audience through a character or characters in the ad.

dialogue balloons A type of projective technique that offers consumers the chance to fill in the dialogue of cartoonlike stories, as a way of indirectly gathering brand information.

differentiation The process of creating a perceived difference, in the mind of the consumer, between an organization's brand and the competition's.

digital video recorder (DVR) A computer-like hard drive that can store up to 140 hours of television programming.

direct broadcast by satellite (DBS) A program delivery system whereby television (and radio) programs are sent directly from a satellite to homes equipped with small receiving dishes.

direct mail A direct-marketing medium that involves using the postal service to deliver marketing materials.

direct marketing According to the Direct Marketing Association, "An interactive system of marketing which uses one or more advertising media to affect a measurable response and/or transaction at any location."

direct response Copy research method measuring actual behavior of consumers.

direct response advertising Advertising that asks the receiver of the message to act immediately.

direct response agency Also called direct marketing agency.

direct response copy Advertising copy that highlights the urgency of acting immediately.

directory advertising Includes all the local phone directory and local business advertising books published by a variety of firms.

display advertising A newspaper ad that includes the standard components of a print ad—headline, body copy, and often an illustration—to set it off from the news content of the paper.

display/banner ads Advertisements placed on World Wide websites that contain editorial material.

door-to-door sampling A type of sampling in which samples are brought directly to the homes of a target segment in a well-defined geographic area.

double-page spreads Advertisements that bridge two facing pages.

E

e-business A form of e-advertising and/or promotion in which companies selling to business customers rely on the Internet to send messages and close sales.

E-commerce The process of selling goods and services over the Web, including transactions conducted using a computer or smart device.

economies of scale The ability of a firm to lower the cost of each item produced because of high-volume production.

effective frequency The number of times a target audience needs to be exposed to a message before the objectives of the advertiser are met.

effective reach The number or percentage of consumers in the target audience that are exposed to an ad some minimum number of times.

elaboration likelihood model (ELM) A model that pertains to any situation where a persuasive communication is being sent and received.

embedded Tightly connected to a context.

emergent consumers A market segment made up of the gradual but constant influx of first-time buyers.

emotional benefits Those benefits not typically found in some tangible feature or objective characteristic of a product or service.

ethics Moral standards and principles against which behavior is judged.

ethnocentrism The tendency to view and value things from the perspective of one's own culture.

evaluative copy research A type of copy research used to judge an advertisement after the fact—the audience expresses its approval or disapproval of the copy used in the ad.

evaluative criteria The product attributes or performance characteristics on which consumers base their product evaluations.

event sponsorship Providing financial support to help fund an event, in return for the right to display a brand name, logo, or advertising message on-site at the event.

extended problem solving A decision-making mode in which consumers are inexperienced in a particular consumption setting but find the setting highly involving.

external facilitator An organization or individual that provides specialized services to advertisers and agencies.

external lists Mailing lists purchased from a list compiler or rented from a list broker and used to help an organization cultivate new business.

external position The competitive niche a brand pursues.

external search A search for product information that involves visiting retail stores to examine alternatives, seeking input from friends and relatives about their experiences with the products in question, or perusing professional product evaluations.

eye-tracking systems A type of physiological measure that monitors eye movements across print ads.

F

fact sheet radio ad A listing of important selling points that a radio announcer can use to ad-lib a radio spot.

Federal Trade Commission (FTC) The government regulatory agency that has the most power and is most directly involved in overseeing the advertising industry.

field work Research conducted outside the agency, usually in the home or site of consumption.

first cover page The front cover of a magazine.

first-run syndication Television programs developed specifically for sale to individual stations.

flighting A media-scheduling pattern of heavy advertising for a period of time, usually two weeks, followed by no advertising for a period, followed by another period of heavy advertising.

focus group A brainstorming session with a small group of target consumers and a professional moderator, used to gain new insights about consumer response to a brand.

"forgetting function" Idea that people's forgetting is fairly predictable and seems to obey a mathematical function.

formal balance A symmetrical presentation in an ad—every component on one side of an imaginary vertical line is repeated in approximate size and shape on the other side of the imaginary line.

fourth cover page The back cover of a magazine.

frame-by-frame test Copy research method that works by getting consumers to turn dials (like/dislike) while viewing television commercials in a theater setting.

free premium A sales promotion that provides consumers with an item at no cost; the item is either included in the package of a purchased item or mailed to the consumer after proof of purchase is verified.

free-standing insert (FSI) A newspaper insert ad that contains cents-off coupons for a variety of products and is typically delivered with Sunday newspapers.

frequency The average number of times an individual or household within a target audience is exposed to a media vehicle in a given period of time.

frequency-marketing programs Direct-marketing programs that provide concrete rewards to frequent customers.

frequency programs A type of sales promotion that offers consumers discounts or free product rewards for repeat purchase or patronage of the same brand or company.

full position A basis of buying newspaper ad space, in which the ad is placed near the top of a page or in the middle of editorial material.

functional benefits Those benefits that come from the objective performance characteristics of a product or service.

G

gatefold ads Advertisements that fold out of a magazine to display an extra-wide ad.

gender The social expression of sexual biology or choice.

geodemographic segmentation A form of market segmentation that identifies neighborhoods around the country that share common demographic characteristics.

geographic scope Scope of the geographic area to be covered by advertising media.

geo-targeting The placement of ads in geographic regions where higher purchase tendencies for a brand are evident.

global advertising Developing and placing advertisements with a common theme and presentation in all markets around the world where the firm's brands are sold.

government officials and employees One of the five types of audiences for advertising; includes employees of government organizations, such as schools and road maintenance operations, at the federal, state, and local levels.

Great Depression A period (1929–1941 for the United States) in which the vast majority of people in many countries suffered from a severe economic decline.

Great Recession Refers to the U.S. recession of the late 2000s.

green marketing Corporate efforts that embrace a cause or program in support of the environment. Green marketing is currently of particular importance, as the public is becoming increasingly aware and concerned about the urgency of environmental issues.

gross domestic product (GDP) A measure of the total value of goods and services produced within an economic system.

gross impressions The sum of exposures to all the media placement in a media plan.

guaranteed circulation A stated minimum number of copies of a particular issue of a magazine that will be delivered to readers.

H

habit A decision-making mode in which consumers buy a single brand repeatedly as a solution to a simple consumption problem.

headline The leading sentence or sentences, usually at the top or bottom of an ad, that attract attention, communicate a key selling point, or achieve brand identification.

heavy users Consumers who purchase a product or service much more frequently than others.

hits The number of pages and graphical images requested from a website.

household consumers The most conspicuous of the five types of audiences for advertising; most mass media advertising is directed at them.

households using television (HUT) A measure of the number of households tuned to a television program during a particular time period.

hyperlocalism The process where people will get their global and national news from the Web, but turn to local newspapers for items on sale at local stores.

I

illustration In the context of advertising, the drawing, painting, photography, or computer-generated art that forms the picture in an advertisement.

illustration format The way the product is displayed in a print advertisement.

implicit memory measures Techniques used to obtain feedback that determines consumers' recognition of products (and thus marketing success), characterized by questions or tasks that do not explicitly make reference to the advertisement in question. The perceived advantage of this type of test is a more subconscious, unadulterated response.

Industrial Revolution A major change in Western society beginning in the mid-eighteenth century and marked by a rapid change from an agricultural to an industrial economy.

industry analysis In an advertising plan, the section that focuses on developments and trends within an industry and on any other factors that may make a difference in how an advertiser proceeds with an advertising plan.

inelasticity of demand Strong loyalty to a product, resulting in consumers being less sensitive to price increases.

influencer marketing A series of personalized marketing techniques directed at individuals or groups who have the credibility and capability to drive positive word of mouth in a broader and salient segment of the population.

informal balance An asymmetrical presentation in an ad—nonsimilar sizes and shapes are optically weighed.

inquiry/direct response measures A type of posttest message tracking in which a print or broadcast advertisement offers the audience the opportunity to place an inquiry or respond directly through a reply card or toll-free number.

in-store sampling A type of sampling that occurs at the point of purchase and is popular for food products and cosmetics.

institutional advertising Corporate advertising that takes place in the trade channel. This form of advertising is used most prominently by retailers.

integrated brand promotion (IBP) The use of various promotional tools, including advertising, in a coordinated manner to build and maintain brand awareness, identity, and preference.

integrated marketing communications (IMC) The process of using promotional tools in a unified way so that a synergistic communications effect is created.

interactive agencies Advertising agencies that help advertisers prepare communications for new media like the Internet, interactive kiosks, CD-ROMS, and interactive television.

interactive media Media that allow consumers to call up games, entertainment, shopping opportunities, and educational programs on a subscription or pay-per-view basis.

intergenerational effect When people choose products based on what was used in their childhood household.

internal lists An organization's records of its customers, subscribers, donors, and inquirers, used to develop better relationships with current customers.

internal position The niche a brand achieves with regard to the other similar brands a firm markets.

internal search A search for product information that draws on personal experience and prior knowledge.

international advertising The preparation and placement of advertising in different national and cultural markets.

interpersonal abrasion The clash of people, often resulting from an inability to regard idea feedback as separate from personal feedback, from which communication shuts down and new ideas get slaughtered. *Compare* **creative abrasion**.

involvement The degree of perceived relevance and personal importance accompanying the choice of a certain product or service within a particular context.

IRI Behavior Scan Supplier of single-source data testing.

J, K, L

layout A drawing of a proposed print advertisement, showing where all the elements in the ad are positioned.

leveraging Any collateral communication or activity reinforcing the link between a brand and an event.

libel Defamation that occurs in print and would relate to magazine, newspaper, direct mail, or Internet reports.

life-stage A circumstantial variable, such as when a family's youngest child moves away from home, which changes the consumption patterns of the family.

lifestyle segmentation A form of market segmenting that focuses on consumers' activities, interests, and opinions.

limited problem solving A decision-making mode in which consumers' experience and involvement are both low.

live script radio ad A detailed script read by an on-air radio personality.

local advertising Advertising directed at an audience in a single trading area, either a city or state.

local spot radio advertising Radio advertising placed directly with individual stations rather than with a network or syndicate.

local television Television programming other than the network broadcast that independent stations and network affiliates offer local audiences.

long copy email Copy written for an email message designed to offer the receiver incentives to buy the product and usually offers a link to a short copy landing page.

long-copy landing page Website copy designed to sell a product directly; the copy might equal the equivalent of a four to eight-page letter to a potential customer

M

Madison & Vine A reference to continually converging advertising and entertainment, coined from the names of two renowned avenues that represent the two industries, respectively.

mailing list A file of names and addresses that an organization might use for contacting prospective or prior customers.

mail sampling A type of sampling in which samples are delivered through the postal service.

marcom manager A marketing-communications manager who plans an organization's overall communications program and oversees the various functional specialists inside and outside the organization to ensure that they are working together to deliver the desired message to the customer.

market analysis Complements the industry analysis, emphasizing the demand side of the equation, where an advertiser examines the factors that drive and determine the market for the firm's product or service.

marketing The process of conceiving, pricing, promoting, and distributing ideas, goods, and services to create exchanges that benefit consumers and organizations.

marketing database A mailing list that also includes information collected directly from individual customers.

marketing mix The blend of the four responsibilities of marketing—conception, pricing, promotion, and distribution—used for a particular idea, product, or service.

market niche A relatively small group of consumers who have a unique set of needs and who typically are willing to pay a premium price to a firm that specializes in meeting those needs.

market segmentation The breaking down of a large, heterogeneous market into submarkets or segments that are more homogeneous.

mash-up A combination of one or more websites into a single site for purposes of analyzing or comparing information side-by-side.

meaning What an advertisement intends or conveys.

measured media Media that are closely measured to determine advertising costs and effectiveness: television, radio, newspapers, magazines, and outdoor media.

media buying Securing the electronic media time and print media space specified in a given account's schedule.

media-buying service An independent organization that specializes in buying media time and space, particularly on radio and television, as a service to advertising agencies and advertisers.

media class A broad category of media, such as television, radio, or newspapers.

media impressions Instances in which a product or brand is exposed to potential consumers by direct newspaper, television, radio, or magazine coverage (rather than the payment of these media as venues in which to advertise). The effectiveness of sponsorship spending is often judged by the comparison of media impressions to traditional media advertising, such as commercials.

media mix The blend of different media that will be used to effectively reach the target audience.

media plan A plan specifying the media in which advertising messages will be placed to reach the desired target audience.

media planner An advertising agency (although on occasion an in-house person) with expertise in buying and scheduling media for ad placements.

media vehicle A particular option for placement within a media class (e.g., *Newsweek* is a media vehicle within the magazine media class).

medium The means by which an illustration in a print advertisement is rendered: either drawing, photography, or computer graphics.

members of business organizations One of the five types of audiences for advertising; the focus of advertising for firms that produce business and industrial goods and services.

members of a trade channel One of the five types of audiences for advertising; the retailers, wholesalers, and distributors targeted by producers of both household and business goods and services.

merchandise allowances A type of trade-market sales promotion in which free products are packed with regular shipments as payment to the trade for setting up and maintaining displays.

message weight A sum of the total audience size of all the media specified in a media plan.

missionary salesperson A person who proactively contacts customers after a purchase has been made, in order to ensure customer satisfaction and foster goodwill, by asking if the customer has questions about the product, providing additional information, and checking to see if the customer's current needs have changed (and may present an opportunity for further sales).

miscellaneous In regard to font styles, a category that includes display fonts that are used not for their legibility, but for their ability to attract attention. Fonts like garage and novelty display belong in this category.

mobile marketing Directing advertising and IBP campaigns to consumers' mobile devices—smartphones, iPods, and e-readers.

Mobile-Fi Wireless Internet technology having multi-mile access and the capability of accessing the Net while the user is moving in a car or train.

mobile sampling A type of sampling carried out by logo-emblazoned vehicles that dispense samples, coupons, and premiums to consumers at malls, shopping centers, fairgrounds, and recreational areas.

monopoly power The ability of a firm to make it impossible for rival firms to compete with it, either through advertising or in some other way.

multi-attribute attitude models (MAAMS) A framework and set of procedures for collecting information from consumers to assess their salient beliefs and attitudes about competitive brands.

N

narrative Advertising copy that simply displays a series of statements about a brand.

narrowcasting The development and delivery of specialized television programming to well-defined audiences.

national advertising Advertising that reaches all geographic areas of one nation.

National Advertising Review Board A body formed by the advertising industry to oversee its practice.

national spot radio advertising Radio advertising placed in nationally syndicated radio programming.

need state A psychological state arising when one's desired state of affairs differs from one's actual state of affairs.

net promoter scores Number of recommendations for a brand.

network radio advertising Radio advertising placed within national network programs.

network television A type of television that broadcasts programming over airwaves to affiliate stations across the United States under a contract agreement.

newspaper sampling Samples distributed in newspapers to allow very specific geographic and geodemographic targeting.

nonusers A market segment made up of consumers who do not use a particular product or service.

normative test scores Scores that are determined by testing an ad and then comparing the scores to those of previously tested, average commercials of its type.

O

objective-and-task approach A method of advertising budgeting that focuses on the relationship between spending and advertising objectives by identifying the specific tasks necessary to achieve different aspects of the advertising objectives.

off-invoice allowance A program allowing wholesalers and retailers to deduct a set amount from the invoice they receive for merchandise.

off-network syndication Television programs that were previously run in network prime time.

on-package sampling A type of sampling in which a sample item is attached to another product package.

on-sale date The date on which a magazine is issued to subscribers and for newsstand distribution.

opt-in email A list of website visitors who have given their permission to receive commercial email about topics and products that interest them.

order The visual elements in an ad that affect the reader's "gaze motion" through the ad.

order taking The practice of accepting and processing needed customer information for pre-arranged merchandise purchase, or scheduling services that a consumer will purchase once rendered. While their role in the transaction process rarely involves communicating large amounts of information, order takers must be able to answer customer questions and be accommodating and considerate.

out-of-home media The combination of transit and billboard advertising.

P

packaging The container or wrapping for a product; packaging serves as an important vessel for product information and user appeal, as it is often viewed by the customer in a potential buying situation.

page views The record of the pages (as indicated by the request for the HTML files that comprise them) that have been sent to a user's computer. Page views provide somewhat inaccurate user documentation because they do not distinguish between repeat and initial visitors, or track whether a user has viewed more than one screen of the page if it takes up several screens.

paid circulation The number of copies of a newspaper sold through subscriptions and newsstand distribution.

paid search Process by which companies pay Web search engines and portals to place ads in or near relevant search results.

parallel layout structure A print ad design that employs art on the right-hand side of the page and repeats the art on the left-hand side.

participation A way of buying television advertising time in which several different advertisers buy commercial time during a specific television program.

pass-along readership An additional number of people, other than the original readers, who may see a magazine.

pay-for-inquiry advertising model A payment scheme in which a media company gets paid by advertisers based solely on the inquiries an advertiser receives in response to an ad.

percentage-of-sales approach An advertising budgeting approach that calculates the advertising budget based on a percentage of the prior year's sales or the projected year's sales.

peripheral cues The features of an ad other than the actual arguments about the brand's performance.

permanent long-term displays P-O-P materials intended for presentation for more than six months.

permission marketing Web users agree to receive emails from organizations.

personal selling The face-to-face communications and persuasions process, often used with products that are higher-priced, complicated to use, must be tailored to individual user needs, involve a trade-in, or are judged at the point of purchase.

phishing A form of email spam with which spammers try to entice web users to enter personal information on fake websites that are forged to look like authentic sites such as a bank, the IRS or other organization that will get the email users attention.

physiological assessment The interpretation of certain biological feedback generated from viewers who are exposed to an ad. Although physiological assessment has advanced with devices such as MRIs and PT scans, its overall value is still questionable.

pica A measure of the width or depth of lines of type.

pilot testing A form of message evaluation consisting of experimentation in the marketplace.

point A measure of the size of type in height.

point-of-entry marketing Advertising strategies designed to win the loyalty of consumers whose brand preferences are still under development in hopes of gaining their loyalty.

point-of-purchase (P-O-P) advertising Advertising that appears at the point of purchase.

pop-up/pop-under ad An Internet advertisement that appears as a website page is loading or after a page has loaded.

pop-up/pop-under copy Copy to accompany pop-up/pop-under digital/interactive ads.

portal A starting point for Web access and search.

positioning The process of designing a product or service so that it can occupy a distinct and valued place in the target consumer's mind, and then communicating this distinctiveness through advertising.

positioning strategy The key themes or concepts an organization features for communicating the distinctiveness of its product or service to the target segment.

preferred position A basis of buying newspaper ad space, in which the ad is placed in a specific section of the paper.

premiums Items that feature the logo of a sponsor and that are offered free, or at a reduced price, with the purchase of another item.

preprinted insert An advertisement delivered to a newspaper fully printed and ready for insertion into the newspaper.

preproduction The stage in the television production process in which the advertiser and advertising agency (or in-house agency staff) carefully work out the precise details of how the creative planning behind an ad can best be brought to life with the opportunities offered by television.

price/cost transparency Ease with which consumers can find out the price of a product and the seller's cost.

price-off deal A type of sales promotion that offers a consumer cents or even dollars off merchandise at the point of purchase through specially marked packages.

primary demand The demand for an entire product category.

primary demand stimulation Using advertising to create demand for a product category in general.

principle of limited liability An economic principle that allows an investor to risk only his or her shares of a corporation, rather than personal wealth, in business ventures.

principles of design General rules governing the elements within a print advertisement and the arrangement of and relationship between these elements.

proactive public relations strategy A public relations strategy that is dictated by marketing objectives, seeks to publicize a company and its brands, and is offensive in spirit rather than defensive.

production facilitator An organization that offers essential services both during and after the production process.

production stage The point at which the storyboard and script for a television ad come to life and are filmed. Also called the *shoot*.

production timetable A realistic schedule for all the preproduction, production, and postproduction activities involved with making a television commercial.

product placement The sales promotion technique of getting a marketer's product featured in movies and television shows.

professionals One of the five types of audiences for advertising, defined as doctors, lawyers, accountants, teachers, or any other professionals who require special training or certification.

program rating The percentage of television households that are in a market and are tuned to a specific program during a specific time period.

projective techniques A type of developmental research designed to allow consumers to project thoughts and feelings (conscious or unconscious) in an indirect and unobtrusive way onto a theoretically neutral stimulus.

proportion The size and tonal relationships between different elements in an advertisement.

psychographics A form of market research that emphasizes the understanding of consumers' activities, interests, and opinions.

publicity Unpaid-for media exposure about a firm's activities or its products and services.

public relations A marketing and management function that focuses on communications that foster goodwill between a firm and its many constituent groups.

public relations audit An internal study that identifies the characteristics of a firm or the aspects of the firm's activities that are positive and newsworthy.

public relations plan A plan that identifies the objectives and activities related to the public relations communications issued by a firm.

puffery The use of absolute superlatives like "Number One" and "Best in the World" in advertisements.

pulsing A media-scheduling strategy that combines elements from continuous and flighting techniques; advertisements are scheduled continuously in media over a period of time, but with periods of much heavier scheduling.

purchase intent A measure of whether or not a consumer intends to buy a product or service in the near future.

Pure Food and Drug Act A 1906 act of Congress requiring manufacturers to list the active ingredients of their products on their labels.

push money A form of trade incentive in which retail salespeople are offered monetary reward for featuring a marketer's brand with shoppers.

push strategy A sales promotion strategy in which marketers devise incentives to encourage purchases by members of the trade to help push a product into the distribution channel.

Q, R

RADAR (Radio's All Dimension Audience Research) A radio audience measure process in which radio audience listening characteristics are collected twice a year based on interviews with radio listeners.

radio networks A type of radio that delivers programming via satellite to affiliate stations across the United States.

radio syndication A type of radio that provides complete programs to stations on a contract basis.

rate card A form given to advertisers by a newspaper and containing information on costs, closing times, specifications for submitting an ad, and special pages or features available in the newspaper.

ratings point A measure indicating that 1 percent of all the television households in an area were tuned to the program measured.

reach The number of people or households in a target audience that will be exposed to a media vehicle or schedule at least one time during a given period of time. It is often expressed as a percentage.

reactive public relations strategy A public relations strategy that is dictated by influences outside the control of a company, focuses on problems to be solved rather than opportunities, and requires defensive rather than offensive measures.

readership A measure of a newspaper's circulation multiplied by the number of readers of a copy.

rebate A money-back offer requiring a buyer to mail in a form requesting the money back from the manufacturer.

recall tests Tests of how much the viewer of an ad remembers of the message; they are used to measure the cognitive residue of the ad. These are the most commonly employed tests in advertising.

recognition In a test, when the audience members indicate that they have seen an ad before.

recognition tests Tests in which audience members are asked if they recognize an ad or something in an ad. These are the standard cognitive residue test for print ads and promotion.

regional advertising Advertising carried out by producers, wholesalers, distributors, and retailers that concentrate their efforts in a particular geographic region.

repeat purchase A second purchase of a new product after trying it for the first time.

repositioning Returning to the process of segmenting, targeting, and positioning a product or service to arrive at a revised positioning strategy.

resonance test A type of message assessment in which the goal is to determine to what extent the message resonates or rings true with target audience members.

RFM analysis An analysis of how recently and how frequently a customer is buying from an organization, and of how much that customer is spending per order and over time.

rich media/video and audio The process in which a Web ad uses advanced technology like streaming video or audio that interacts with the user when the user's mouse passes over the ad.

riding the boards Assessing possible locations for billboard advertising.

rituals Repeated behaviors that affirm, express, and maintain cultural values.

roman The most popular category of type because of its legibility.

rough layout The second stage of the ad layout process, in which the headline is lettered in and the elements of the ad are further refined.

RSS (Really Simple Syndication) A channel or feed (often commercial in nature) that a computer user is linked to from visited blogs, podcasts, or other content on the Internet.

run-of-paper or **run-of-press (ROP)** A basis of buying newspaper or magazine ad space, in which an ad may appear anywhere, on any page in the paper or magazine.

S

sales promotion The use of incentive techniques that create a perception of greater brand value among consumers or distributors.

salient beliefs A small number of beliefs that are the critical determinants of an attitude.

sampling A sales promotion technique designed to provide a consumer with a trial opportunity.

sans serif A category of type that includes typefaces with no small lines crossing the ends of the main strokes.

satellite and closed-circuit A method of transmitting programming to highly segmented audiences.

script (television) The written version of an ad; it specifies the coordination of the copy elements with the video scenes.

script (typeface) A style of print in which letters connect to one another, resembling handwriting; often used for occasions in which elegance or particularly high quality is appropriate (wedding invitations, etc).

search engine A software tool used to find websites on the Internet by searching for keywords typed in by the user.

search engine optimization (SEO) Utilizing a search engine to a company's best advantage.

secondary data Information obtained from existing sources.

second cover page The inside front cover of a magazine.

Second Life The most prominent network of the virtual world phenomenon, in which participants log into a space as an avatar (alternate identity/character), then use their mouse and keyboard to perform a variety of activities that simulate how those people perform in the real world. Often the line between the real world and the virtual one can become blurred, and users may indeed do "real" activities (such as conducting business) in a virtual setting.

selective attention The processing of only a few advertisements among the many encountered.

selective demand stimulation Using advertising to stimulate demand for a specific brand within a product category.

self-liquidating premium A sales promotion that requires a consumer to pay most of the cost of the item received as a premium.

self-regulation The advertising industry's attempt to police itself.

sentence and picture completion A type of projective technique in which a researcher presents consumers with part of a picture or a sentence with words deleted and then asks that the stimulus be completed; the picture or sentence relates to one or several brands.

serif The small lines that cross the ends of the main strokes in type; also the name for the category of type that has this characteristic.

share of audience A measure of the proportion of households that are using television during a specific time period and are tuned to a particular program.

share of voice Percent of the total advertising in a category (e.g. Autos) spent by one brand (e.g. Ford).

shoot The process of recording (shooting) a television advertisement using film or digital recording.

short-copy landing page Digital/interactive copy, a brand offer that may be accessed by a consumer through key word search and has the length and look of a magazine ad.

short-term promotional displays P-O-P materials that are used for six months or less.

single-source data Information provided from individual households about brand purchases, coupon use, and television advertising exposure by combining grocery store scanner data with TV-viewing data from monitoring devices attached to the households' televisions.

single-source tracking services Services that provide data on media exposure, sales, customer demographics, and other related information in one source.

situation analysis In an advertising plan, the section in which the advertiser lays out the most important factors that define the situation, and then explains the importance of each factor.

slander Oral defamation that in the context of promotion would occur during television or radio broadcast of an event involving a company and its employees.

slogan A short phrase used in part to help establish an image, identity, or position for a brand or an organization, but mostly used to increase memorability.

slotting fees A type of trade-market sales promotion in which manufacturers make direct cash payments to retailers to ensure shelf space.

social meaning What a product or service means in a societal context.

social media Highly accessible web-based media that allow the sharing of information between individuals and between individuals and groups. Prominent examples are Facebook, Twitter, and LinkedIn.

social media copy Language in social media communications that highlights a brand name or brand features.

space contract A contract that establishes a rate for all advertising placed in a magazine by an advertiser over a specified period.

space order A commitment by an advertiser to advertising space in a particular issue of a magazine. Also called an *insertion order.*

spam To post messages to many unrelated newsgroups on Usenet.

splash screen A subcategory of a pop-up ads know as an *interstitial,* this form of pop-up ad appears on a website after a page has been requested but before it has loaded, and stays onscreen long enough for the message to be registered by the website user.

split-transmission A type of pilot testing in which two different broadcast signals (which become advertisements when viewed on television) are simultaneously sent to two groups of households for reaction comparison.

sponsorship A way of buying television advertising time in which an advertiser agrees to pay for the production of a television program and for most (and often all) of the advertising that appears in the program.

spot advertising A way of buying television advertising time in which airtime is purchased through local television stations.

square root law The recognition of print ads increases with the square of the illustration.

standard advertising unit (SAU) One of 57 defined sizes of newspaper advertisements.

Starch Readership Services An example of a company that performs recognition tests.

storyboard A frame-by-frame sketch or photo sequence depicting, in sequence, the visual scenes and copy that will be used in an advertisement.

story construction A type of projective technique that asks consumers to tell a story about people depicted in a scene or picture, as a way of gathering information about a brand.

STP marketing (**s**egmenting, **t**argeting, **p**ositioning) A marketing strategy employed when advertisers focus their efforts on one subgroup of a product's total market.

straight-line copy Advertising copy that explains in straightforward terms why a reader will benefit from use of a product or service.

stratification (social class) A person's relative standing in a social system as produced by systematic inequalities in things such as wealth, income, education, power, and status. Also referred to as *social class.*

subhead In an advertisement, a few words or a short sentence that usually appears above or below the headline and includes important brand information not included in the headline.

subliminal advertising Advertising alleged to work on a subconscious level.

support media Media used to reinforce a message being delivered via some other media vehicle.

surfing Gliding from website to website using a search engine, direct links, or word of mouth.

surveys A method of soliciting customer feedback through questions related to a viewed ad; surveys are administered in various ways, such as over the telephone or on the Internet, as well as at different lengths of time after the viewing takes place.

sweepstakes A sales promotion in which winners are determined purely by chance.

switchers A market segment made up of consumers who often buy what is on sale or choose brands that offer discount coupons or other price incentives. Also called *variety seekers.*

symbolic value What a product or service means to consumers in a nonliteral way.

system selling Selling a set of interrelated components that fulfills all or a majority of a customer's needs in a particular area.

T

target audience A particular group of consumers singled out for an advertisement or advertising campaign.

target segment The subgroup (of the larger market) chosen as the focal point for the marketing program and advertising campaign.

taste A generalized set or orientation to consumer preferences.

teaser email Copy written for an email message that is a short message designed to drive readers to a long copy landing page where they can order the brand directly.

telemarketing A direct-marketing medium that involves using the telephone to deliver a spoken appeal.

television households An estimate of the number of households that are in a market and own a television.

testimonial An advertisement in which an advocacy position is taken by a spokesperson.

third cover page The inside back cover of a magazine.

thought listing A type of pretest message research that tries to identify specific thoughts that may be generated by an advertisement.

three-point layout structure A print ad design that establishes three elements in an ad as dominant forces.

thumbnails, or **thumbnail sketches** The rough first drafts of an ad layout, about one-quarter the size of the finished ad.

top-of-the-mind awareness Keen consumer awareness of a certain brand, indicated by listing that brand first when asked to name a number of brands.

tracking studies Studies that document the apparent effect of advertising over time, assessing attitude change, knowledge, behavioral intent, and self-reported behavior. They are one of the most commonly used advertising and promotion research methods.

trade journals Magazines published specifically for members of a trade that carry highly technical articles.

trade shows Events where several related products from many manufacturers are displayed and demonstrated to members of the trade.

transit advertising Advertising that appears as both interior and exterior displays on mass transit vehicles and at terminal and station platforms.

trial offers A type of sales promotion in which expensive items are offered on a trial basis to induce consumer trial of a brand.

trial usage An advertising objective to get consumers to use a product new to them on a trial basis.

type font A basic set of typeface letters.

U

ultrabroadband Wireless Internet technology allowing people to move extremely large files quickly over short distances.

unfair advertising Defined by Congress as "acts or practices that cause or are likely to cause substantial injury to consumers, which is not reasonably avoidable by consumers themselves and not outweighed by the countervailing benefits to consumers or competition."

unique selling proposition (USP) A promise contained in an advertisement in which the advertised brand offers a specific, unique, and relevant benefit to the consumer.

unique visitors The name used to describe different "people" who visit a website (determined from the user's registration with the site). Because unique visitors are also sometimes distinguished by the different IP numbers used by Internet services that connect users, and these services often use changing IP numbers, the record of unique visitors may reflect the same user as many different users.

unity The creation of harmony among the diverse components of an advertisement: headline, subhead, body copy, and illustration.

unmeasured media Media less formally measured for advertising costs and effectiveness (as compared to the measured media): direct mail, catalogs, special events, and other ways to reach business and household consumers.

upfronts A period of media buying in which advertisers purchase time on network television a few months before (May) the new season of shows begin (September). They are thus bought "up-front."

user positioning A positioning option that focuses on a specific profile of the target user.

V

value A perception by consumers that a product or service provides satisfaction beyond the cost incurred to acquire the product or service.

value proposition A statement of the functional, emotional, and self-expressive benefits delivered by the brand, which provide value to customers in the target segment.

values The defining expressions of culture, demonstrating in words and deeds what is important to a culture.

variety seekers *See* **switchers**.

variety seeking A decision-making mode in which consumers switch their selection among various brands in a given category in a random pattern.

V-chip A device that can block television programming based on the program rating system.

vertical cooperative advertising An advertising technique whereby a manufacturer and dealer (either a wholesaler or retailer) share the expense of advertising.

video on demand (VOD) A cable television service that enables subscribers to select and watch a selection of videos at any time.

viral marketing The process of consumers marketing to consumers over the Internet through word of mouth transmitted through emails and electronic mailing lists.

virtual mall A gateway to a group of Internet storefronts that provides access to mall sites by simply clicking on a storefront.

visits The number of occasions on which a user X looked up Y website during Z period of time.

W

Web analytic software Measurement software that not only provides information on hits, pages, visits, and users, but also allows a site to track audience traffic within itself. Web analytic software can detect which pages are more popular, when they are viewed, how long they are viewed, etc.

website A collection of Web pages, images, videos, and other digital content that is hosted on a Web server.

widget A software module that people can drag and drop onto their personal Web page of their social network (for example, Facebook) or onto a blog. For a fee (per click), advertisers can create widgets that feature their brands or that direct the user to an e-commerce site.

WiFi Wireless technology allowing Internet access connections to reach out about 300 feet.

WiMax A wireless Internet technology similar to WiFi but capable of creating a hot spot with a range of 25-30 miles.

within-vehicle duplication Exposure to the same advertisement in the same media at different times.

World Wide Web (WWW) A universal database of information available to Internet users; its graphical environment makes navigation simple and exciting.

X, Y, Z

Zaltman Metaphor Elicitation Technique (ZMET) A research technique to draw out people's buried thoughts and feelings about products and brands by encouraging participants to think in terms of metaphors.

Name/Brand/Company Index

C

G

H

I

J

N

S

T

U

Subject Index

D

Y

Z